Encyclopedia of American Business History and Biography

The Airline Industry

Edited by

William M. Leary
University of Georgia

A Bruccoli Clark Layman Book

Facts On File
New York · Oxford

Encyclopedia of American Business History and Biography: The Airline Industry

Copyright © 1992 by Bruccoli Clark Layman, Inc., and Facts On File, Inc.

Facts On File, Inc.
460 Park Avenue South
New York NY 10016
USA

Facts On File Limited
c/o Roundhouse Publishing Ltd.
P. O. Box 140
Oxford OX2 7SF
United Kingdom

Library of Congress Cataloging-in-Publication Data

Encyclopedia of American business history and biography : the airline
   industry / edited by William M. Leary.
      p.   cm. — (Encyclopedia of American business history and
biography)
   "A Bruccoli Clark Layman book."
   Includes bibliographical references and index.
   ISBN 0-8160-2675-0
   1. Aeronautics, Commercial—United States—Encyclopedias.
2. Airlines—United States—Encyclopedias. 3. Aircraft industry-
-United States—Encyclopedias. I. Leary, William M. (William
Matthew). II. Series.
TL509.E54 1992
387.7'0973—dc20   92-17993

A British CIP catalogue record for this book is available from the British Library.

Facts On File books are available at special discounts when purchased in bulk quantities for businesses, associations, institutions or sales promotions. Please call our Special Sales Department in New York at 212/683-2244 (dial 800/322-8755 except in NY, AK or HI) or in Oxford at 865/728399.

Manufactured by the Maple-Vail Book Manufacturing Group
Printed in the United States of America

10 9 8 7 6 5 4 3 2 1

To Margaret

Encyclopedia of American Business History

Railroads in the Age of Regulation, 1900-1980, edited by Keith Bryant (1988)

Railroads in the Nineteenth Century, edited by Robert L. Frey (1988)

Iron and Steel in the Nineteenth Century, edited by Paul F. Paskoff (1989)

The Automobile Industry, 1920-1980, edited by George S. May (1989)

Banking and Finance to 1913, edited by Larry Schweikart (1990)

The Automobile Industry, 1896-1920, edited by George S. May (1990)

Banking and Finance, 1913-1989, edited by Larry Schweikart (1990)

The Airline Industry, edited by William M. Leary (1992)

Contents

Contents

Foreword

The Encyclopedia of American Business History and Biography chronicles America's material civilization through its business figures and businesses. It is a record of American aspirations—of success and of failure. It is a history of the impact of business on American life. The volumes have been planned to serve a cross section of users: students, teachers, scholars, researchers, and government and corporate officials. Individual volumes or groups of volumes cover a particular industry during a defined period; thus each *EABH&B* volume is freestanding, providing a history expressed through biographies and buttressed by a wide range of supporting entries. In many cases a single volume is sufficient to treat an industry, but certain industries require two or more volumes. When completed, the *EABH&B* will provide the fullest available history of American enterprise.

The editorial direction of *EABH&B* is provided by the general editor and the editorial board. The general editor appoints volume editors whose duties are to prepare, in consultation with the editorial board, the list of entries for each volume, to assign the entries to contributors, to vet the submitted entries, and to work in close cooperation with the Bruccoli Clark Layman editorial staff so as to maintain consistency of treatment. All entries are written by specialists in their fields, not by staff writers. Volume editors are experienced scholars.

The publishers and editors of *EABH&B* are convinced that timing is crucial to notable careers. Therefore, the biographical entries in each volume of the series place businesses and their leaders in the social, political, and economic contexts of their times. Supplementary background rubrics on companies, inventions, legal decisions, marketing innovations, and other topics are integrated with the biographical entries in alphabetical order.

The general editor and the volume editors determine the space to be allotted to biographies as major entries, standard entries, and short entries. Major entries, reserved for giants of business and industry (e.g., Henry Ford, J. P. Morgan, Andrew Carnegie, James J. Hill), require approximately 10,000 words. Standard biographical entries are in the range of 3,500-5,000 words. Short entries are reserved for lesser figures who require inclusion and for significant figures about whom little information is available. When appropriate, the biographical entries stress their subjects' roles in shaping the national experience, showing how their activities influenced the way Americans lived. Unattractive or damaging aspects of character and conduct are not suppressed. All biographical entries conform to a basic format.

A significant part of each volume is devoted to concise background entries supporting and elucidating the biographies. These nonbiographical entries provide basic information about the industry or field covered in the volume. Histories of companies are necessarily brief and limited to key events. To establish a context for all entries, each volume includes an overview of the industry treated. These historical introductions are normally written by the volume editors.

We have set for ourselves large tasks and important goals. We aspire to provide a body of work that will help reduce the imbalance in the writing of American history, the study of which too often slights business. Our hope is also to stimulate interest in business leaders, enterprises, and industries that have not been given the scholarly attention they deserve. By setting high standards for accuracy, balanced treatment, original research, and clear writing, we have tried to ensure that these works will commend themselves to those who seek a full account of the development of America.

—*William H. Becker*
General Editor

Acknowledgments

This book was produced by Bruccoli Clark Layman, Inc. James W. Hipp is series editor for the *Encyclopedia of American Business History and Biography Series*. Michael D. Senecal was the in-house editor.

Projects manager is Charles D. Brower. Photography editors are Edward Scott and Timothy C. Lundy. Layout and graphics supervisor is Penney L. Haughton. Copyediting supervisor is Bill Adams. Typesetting supervisor is Kathleen M. Flanagan. Systems manager is George F. Dodge. The production staff includes Rowena Betts, Teresa Chaney, Patricia Coate, Janet Connor, Gail Crouch, Henry Cuningham, Margaret McGinty Cureton, Bonita Dingle, Mary Scott Dye, Denise Edwards, Sarah A. Estes, Robert Fowler, Avril E. Gregory, Ellen McCracken, Kathy Lawler Merlette, John Myrick, Pamela D. Norton, Jean W. Ross, Thomasina Singleton, Maxine K. Smalls, Jennifer C. J. Turley, and Betsy L. Weinberg.

Walter W. Ross and Dennis Lynch did library research. They were assisted by the following librarians at the Thomas Cooper Library of the University of South Carolina: Jens Holley and the interlibrary-loan staff; reference librarians Gwen Baxter, Daniel Boice, Faye Chadwell, Jo Cottingham, Cathy Eckman, Rhonda Felder, Gary Geer, Jackie Kinder, Laurie Preston, Jean Rhyne, Carol Tobin, Virginia Weathers, and Connie Widney; circulation-department head Thomas Marcil; and acquisitions-searching supervisor David Haggard.

Compiling a list of historically significant entries for an industry that grew up in the 20th century proved a challenging task. Early in the project a decision was made to devote this volume to the airline industry and not the aerospace industry. This distinction became difficult for the early period, when many figures were involved with both manufacturing and transport. I compiled a preliminary list of entries for this volume, which I then sent to several scholars and writers for comment. Thanks to their efforts, a much better list emerged. A review by the editorial board of the *Encyclopedia of American Business History and Biography* further refined the list. I should emphasize that final responsibility for selection belongs to me.

Had it not been for the enthusiastic and generous response of numerous aviation historians, this volume would not have appeared. Many individuals took time from their busy schedules to contribute essays for this work, and I am grateful to them. In addition, Roger E. Bilstein, R. E. G. Davies, and John Wegg made helpful comments on a draft of my introduction.

I know that I speak for all the contributors when I express the hope that everyone interested in the development of the airline industry in the United States will find this volume a useful reference tool.

—W.M.L.

Introduction

Pride of place as the first airline in the United States goes to the St. Petersburg-Tampa Airboat Line. In 1913 Percival E. Fansler, a sometime electrician, road machinery salesman, and motorboat racer, came up with the idea of starting "a real commercial line running from somewhere to somewhere else." First, he sold the notion to Thomas W. Benoist, a pioneer St. Louis aircraft manufacturer. Benoist agreed to provide two flying boats and pilots if the operating details could be worked out. Familiar with the west coast resort areas of Florida, Fansler believed that an air service between St. Petersburg and Tampa offered the best commercial possibilities. He knew about the difficulties of reaching St. Petersburg, then a city of 9,000 people that depended upon winter tourists for its economic survival. Visitors arrived in Tampa by train. To reach St. Petersburg, they had a choice of a two-hour steamer trip across Tampa Bay, a 12-hour train ride, or a day-long automobile trek over dirt roads. An airline route of 23 miles—15 along the shore of Tampa Bay and eight over open water—would cut this travel time to 20 minutes.

Fansler offered the scheme to the city fathers of Tampa, but they were not interested. The business and civic leaders of St. Petersburg, however, responded with enthusiasm. They promptly raised $1,500 to guarantee the air service against loss. Summoned by Fansler, Benoist came to St. Petersburg and on December 17, 1913, signed the first airline contract in U.S. history. Operations would begin on January 1, 1914, and last for three months. Benoist pledged to operate twice-daily, scheduled service, six days a week. The city guaranteed him $40 a day during January, and $25 a day for February and March.

Benoist planned to use two Type XIV flying boats. An advanced machine for its day, the Type XIV weighed 1,250 pounds empty and could carry a pilot and a passenger. Twenty-six feet long, the biplane was powered by a 75 horsepower Roberts engine and had a top speed of 64 miles per hour. The

first machine, shipped by rail to St. Petersburg, arrived just in time to begin operations on schedule.

January 1 proved to be a gala occasion. Thousands of people turned out for a downtown parade, while thousands more crowded around the 2nd Avenue pier. A. C. Pheil, former mayor of the city, won a lively bidding war and for $400 became the airline's first passenger. Fansler made a short speech. "What was impossible yesterday is an accomplishment today," he said, "while tomorrow heralds the unbelievable." Pilot Antony H. Jannus then taxied out toward the harbor entrance, increased speed, and lifted off the water—and into history.

The St. Petersburg-Tampa Airboat Line did a lively business during its three months in operation. The airline charged $5 for a one-way flight (5 cents per pound extra for passengers who weighed over 200 pounds), and earned about 25 cents per passenger-mile. In all, it carried 1,205 passengers without accident or injury. There was even talk about raising $50,000 to maintain the service. The departure of winter visitors, however, brought an end to these visionary schemes.

This first U.S. airline had no immediate successors. Despite the Airboat Line's impressive record, aeronautical technology had not yet reached the point where passengers could be carried with regularity, safety, and profit. The groundwork for the development of commercial aviation came not from the efforts of private enterprise, which was reluctant to risk capital on ventures of such dubious economic merit, but from the vision and determination of the U.S. Post Office.

Postal officials first become interested in using airplanes to expedite the mails in 1911. Postmaster General Frank H. Hitchcock, believing that aviation had reached the stage where it could be employed to carry mail in remote areas of the country, asked Congress for $50,000 to conduct experimental contract operations. The legislature turned down his request on the grounds of economy and impracticality. Not until 1916 did Congress decide to make funds available for airmail experiments.

On February 12, 1916, the Post Office advertised for bids to carry airmail on seven routes in Alaska and one in Massachusetts. Unfortunately, no responsible bidders came forward. After attempts to promote a New York-Chicago overnight mail route also failed, the Post Office turned for advice to the National Advisory Committee for Aeronautics (NACA), the government's expert body on aviation. NACA knew that unreliable engines and the inability of pilots to fly in bad weather would make it impossible for the Post Office to locate responsible private companies to maintain even a semblance of a regularly scheduled service. Instead, NACA recommended that the Post Office itself operate an experimental route between Washington and New York.

Early in 1918 Postmaster General Albert S. Burleson decided to act on NACA's recommendation. He instructed Otto Praeger, second assistant postmaster general in charge of all mail transportation, to find out if airplanes could be operated on a regular schedule in all kinds of weather. If so, they would become a permanent part of the postal service. However, Burleson warned Praeger that he did not want to start an airmail service and then be forced to abandon it.

In many ways, Otto Praeger was the ideal man for the job. A former newspaper reporter, he had won Burleson's admiration by modernizing Washington's antiquated postal system following his appointment as the city's postmaster in 1914. Determined and stubborn, Praeger's lack of aeronautical experience probably was more of an advantage, albeit ruthlessly applied, than a disadvantage. Not knowing the bounds of existing technology, he would push men and equipment to new limits. The result would be enormous progress; the cost would be measured in lives lost while carrying the mail.

In February 1918 Praeger called for bids to construct five airplanes for a Post Office operated Washington-New York airmail route. But before he even had a chance to open the bids, the Army Air Service volunteered to fly the route as part of its wartime training program. Although Praeger was concerned that the military would not allocate adequate resources to the airmail line, he had no choice except to agree.

The army inaugurated the nation's first scheduled airmail service on May 15, 1918. Over the next three months, military pilots made 270 flights between Washington and New York via Philadel-

phia. Given the embryonic state of aeronautical technology, the young fliers compiled an impressive record, carrying 40,500 pounds of mail. Praeger, however, remained dissatisfied, especially with the military's tendency to cancel flights because of bad weather. As Air Service officials lost their enthusiasm for the experiment, Praeger had little trouble convincing Postmaster Burleson that the Post Office should go back to his original scheme and operate its own airmail service.

The civilian-operated U.S. Air Mail Service began flying the Washington-New York route on August 12. Pleased with the new arrangements, Praeger soon turned to plans for expansion. The Washington-New York route, he knew, saved little time over rail transportation. To demonstrate the advantages of the airplane, a longer route would be necessary. Late in August, Praeger announced his intention of developing an airway from New York to Chicago as part of an eventual transcontinental airmail service.

Executing Praeger's grand design proved difficult. Although a survey flight was made in September, regular service from New York to Chicago did not begin until July 1, 1919. Nonetheless, the New York-Chicago route, 755 miles in length, represented a monumental undertaking by the Post Office. As the National Advisory Committee for Aeronautics pointed out in its annual report for 1919, by attempting to operate a scheduled air service over such a distance the Post Office was making "a substantial contribution in the practical development of commercial aviation."

Next came the even more daunting task of building an airway from Chicago to San Francisco across 1,900 miles of prairies, deserts, and towering mountains. The Post Office had to persuade local communities to provide adequate airfields and hangars (at their own expense), establish a point-to-point radio network along the route, requisition and ship spare parts, and look after the numerous minor items that so often spell the difference between success and failure.

Praeger also had to search for better airplanes than the de Havilland DH-4Bs that were being used on the New York-Chicago route. The most promising new machine came from Germany. Hugo Junkers, a pioneer in all-metal construction, had produced a cabin monoplane that was far ahead of its time in structural and aerodynamic design. Known as the Junkers-F13 in Europe, it was marketed in the United States by John M. Larsen as the JL-6.

Impressed with the performance of this all-metal monoplane, Praeger ordered eight JL-6s for use on the western portion of the transcontinental route. Unfortunately, the airplane had a design flaw in its fuel system. Seven postal airmen would die before the JL-6s were taken out of service. These accidents—and others—undermined public confidence in the Air Mail Service and provided ammunition for the critics of Burleson and Praeger.

Despite the failure to find a replacement for the DH-4B, the Post Office pushed ahead with its plans for a coast-to-coast airmail route. Finally, on September 8, 1920, pilot Randolph Page left New York for the West Coast with 400 pounds of mail. Operating like an airborne Pony Express, relays of pilots and planes carried the mail to Iowa City by nightfall. The next day, another group of airmen flew the mail to Cheyenne. On September 10, postal pilots crossed the Rocky Mountains, reaching Reno just before sunset. Edison F. Mouton completed the epoch-making aerial journey on September 11 when he landed at San Francisco's Marino Field at 2:33 P.M.

While aviation interests celebrated the path-breaking efforts of the Post Office, growing political opposition to the Air Mail Service threatened to end the government's aeronautical experiments. Many Republicans—and some Democrats—complained that the high cost of flying the mail far outweighed any benefits derived from the service. After all, trains not only were more reliable but they also moved the mail nearly as expeditiously. Even the new transcontinental service did not offer much in the way of speed, as trains made up the airplane's daytime advantage at night. And there was the growing human price; in 1920 alone, 12 postal airmen were killed.

Aware that the new Republican administration, due to take office in March 1921, might well terminate his beloved Air Mail Service, Praeger decided to stage a convincing demonstration of the potential of airmail. On February 22-23, 1921, airmail pilots made a dramatic day-and-night transcontinental crossing in 33 hours and 20 minutes. This shattered the previous best coast-to-coast mail record of 72 hours by airplane and four and a half days by train. "There are critics who think that the Post Office Department's air mail service is dangerous and costly," the *New York Times* observed,

"but nothing ventured, nothing gained. The modern world demands efficiency and speed; aviation is international and competitive. The United States has distanced all countries in transportation of mails through the air."

The incoming administration of President Warren G. Harding was not impressed. Postmaster General Will H. Hays believed that the government should get out of the airmail business and allow private enterprise to take over. It soon became apparent, however, that private interests would need a financial incentive to do the job. Opposed to governmental subsidies on economic and ideological grounds, Hays decided to continue with the postal airmail service while waiting for commercial airlines to emerge.

It turned out to be a long wait. As European nations were discovering during the 1920s, commercial airlines required a subsidy to survive. This was confirmed in the United States by the sad fate of Aeromarine Airways. Between 1919 and 1923, Inglis M. Uppercu, a wealthy Cadillac distributor and aircraft manufacturer, made a valiant effort to operate an airline without government support. Flying between Key West and Havana during the winter, and offering air service in the New York and Great Lakes areas during the summer, Aeromarine compiled an outstanding operational record. The airline carried 30,000 passengers and flew more than one million passenger-miles with only one serious accident in three and a half years. It had intelligent and imaginative management, generous financing, excellent equipment, and superb pilots. But it never turned a profit. Aeromarine's failure to survive emphasized, in a dramatic manner, the limitations of private enterprise at this formative stage of the air transportation industry.

Meanwhile, the U.S. Air Mail Service soldiered on as the unwanted burden of the Post Office. Edward H. Shaughnessy, postal official in charge of the airmail, took steps to insure that the service would be operated economically and safely. He abandoned the original Washington-New York route. He also cut the transcontinental branch routes that Praeger had started from Chicago southward to St. Louis and northward to Minneapolis. As a result of his efforts, costs went down, efficiency increased, and the accident rate improved dramatically.

Paul Henderson, who took over the Air Mail Service following Shaughnessy's death in 1922, also favored private operation of the airmail, but he did not want the government-run service to stagnate while waiting for responsible companies to appear. He believed that the government should lead the way in developing night flying. Under his able direction, remarkable progress was made. The Post Office built a marvelous lighted airway to mark the route from New York to San Francisco, permitting the kind of day-and-night operations that Praeger had envisioned. Pilots could follow a series of rotating and flashing beacons as they crossed the country. Giant 36-inch electric arc beacons, the most powerful artificial light ever created by man, projected a rotating beacon of light equivalent to 450 million candlepower that guided airmen to their primary landing fields. Aviation entered a new era when regular service along the world's first lighted airway began on July 1, 1924.

The mid 1920s finally saw the federal government take action to lay the economic foundations for the American airline industry. After considerable wrangling, Congress passed the Air Mail (Kelly) Act of 1925. This landmark piece of legislation authorized the postmaster general to contract for the transport of mail by air at a rate not to exceed four-fifths of the postage charged for letters. Although it was based on a somewhat impractical formula for payment that had to be changed in 1926 to a poundage rate, the Kelly Act drew influential businessmen and financiers into aviation and led to the formation of new air transportation companies. Increased commercial activity, in turn, forced the government to take regulatory action.

Although both President Harding and his successor Calvin Coolidge had voiced their support for federal regulation of aviation, they had failed to provide legislative leadership. As a result, Congress had become bogged down in sterile debates over states' rights. In 1925, however, the important businessmen who had become interested in aviation following passage of the Kelly Act began to pressure Coolidge for action. Matters came to a head in September after air enthusiast Gen. Billy Mitchell created a storm of public controversy by blaming the crash of the U.S. Navy airship *Shenandoah* on the "incompetency, criminal negligence, and almost treasonable administration" of the War and Navy departments.

Coolidge responded by appointing a special board, headed by Dwight W. Morrow, to look into the nation's aeronautical requirements. With respect to civil aviation, the board recommended the creation of a bureau of air navigation in the Department of Commerce, extension of airmail routes, and federal support for airways, weather forecasting, and air navigation facilities. With Coolidge's blessing, Secretary of Commerce Herbert Hoover took the lead in shaping the necessary legislation. The Air Commerce Act of 1926 instructed the secretary of commerce to foster air commerce, designate and establish airways, operate and maintain aids to air navigation, license pilots and aircraft, and investigate accidents. Hailed by the National Advisory Committee for Aeronautics as the "legislative cornerstone for the development of civil and commercial aviation in America," the new law gave private enterprise the legal foundations necessary to build an airline industry.

Although the Kelly Act had become law in February 1925, the postmaster general waited until he was assured that the Air Commerce Act would pass Congress before accepting bids for airmail routes. In October 1925 he awarded the first contracts to National Air Transport, Robertson Aircraft Corporation, Colonial Airlines, Western Air Express, and Varney Air Lines. Operations got under way on February 15, 1926, when Ford Air Transport, a later bidder, began to carry mail between Detroit and Cleveland on its corporate courier service already in operation. By the end of the year, 11 airlines were providing feeder services for the transcontinental route, which the U.S. Air Mail Service continued to fly.

Henry Ford's entry into aviation attracted the most attention. "People said that if Ford had faith in aircraft," reporter Howard Mingos wrote in the *New York Times*, "then flying must be practical." In April 1925 Ford had started an air freight service between Detroit and Chicago; it was expanded to Cleveland in July. At the same time, he had developed plans to build a trimotored airplane. Although initially based on a design by aircraft entrepreneur William B. Stout, the resulting Ford Trimotor, which first flew in June 1926, owed more to the work of aeronautical engineers Tom Towle and John G. Lee.

As it turned out, Ford's aeronautical ventures failed to prosper. The airmail contract for service between Detroit, Chicago, and Cleveland never lived up to expectations. By the summer of 1927, revenue on the routes amounted to less than $1,300 a month. Ford gave up the contract in July 1928.

The aircraft manufacturing business proved an even greater disappointment. Although the all-metal eight-passenger (later increased to twelve-passenger) Ford Trimotor was the premier airliner in the United States between 1926 and 1932, sales dried up during the Depression. Having lost an estimated $5.6 million on his aviation enterprises, Ford called it quits in 1932.

While Ford's interests lay more in manufacturing than operating airplanes, National Air Transport (NAT) was in the airline business. The most impressive of the new companies that were organized in the wake of the Kelly Act and the only one whose capital was measured in millions of dollars, NAT benefited from generous financial and expert management. Clement M. Keys, president of the Curtiss Aeroplane and Motor Company, supplied the financial acumen for the company, while former postal official Paul Henderson took charge of operations. With high hopes for the future, NAT began contract service on the attractive route from Chicago to Dallas in May 1926.

By 1927 the Post Office was ready to give up the transcontinental route. The San Francisco–Chicago portion of the airway went to Boeing Air Transport, the creation of Seattle aircraft manufacturing William E. Boeing. Operations began on July 1, 1927, with 24 new Boeing 40A mail planes, many flown by former pilots of the U.S. Air Mail Service. Two months later, the powerful National Air Transport took over most of the remaining airplanes and personnel of the service and inaugurated contract operations between New York and Chicago.

The aviation industry seemed poised for rapid growth by 1927. The Air Commerce Act of 1926 had laid the regulatory foundations for commercial air transportation, while the Kelly Act, as amended, held out at least the possibility of profit. At the same time, the Coolidge administration's decision to reequip the nation's military air forces revitalized a flagging aircraft industry. Added to this was the dramatic transatlantic solo flight of Charles A. Lindbergh on May 20-21, 1927. No other single event so captured the imagination of the American people during the 1920s. Overnight, the nation became "air minded." Among other things, this new public enthusiasm for aviation produced a flood of speculative capital—a frenzy to get in on the ground floor of the glamorous new industry. The boom times had arrived.

During 1928 and 1929 the airline industry grew at a frenetic rate as new companies began service on routes that too often made little economic sense. This unwise growth was encouraged when the Post Office lowered airmail postage from 10 cents to 5 cents an ounce on August 1, 1928. Mail volume shot up as a consequence. So did airline income, which doubled within a year. The Post Office, for the first time, began to lose money on the transport of mail by air.

In a pattern of events reminiscent of railroad experience during the 1890s, the competing companies of the aviation industry soon combined into a small number of giant corporations. One of the first of the large enterprises to emerge was the United Aircraft and Transportation Company, formed on February 1, 1929, by William Boeing and Frederick B. Rentschler, head of Pratt & Whitney, a prominent manufacturer of aircraft engines. In 1930, following a bitter proxy fight, the company acquired National Air Transport. It later combined NAT with Boeing Air Transport and other airline holdings to form United Air Lines.

The North American Aviation Corporation, put together by Clement Keys of the Curtiss-Wright Corporation (successor to Curtiss Aeroplane and Motor), and later backed by the General Motors Corporation, bought up aviation properties of all types during the late 1920s. Its airline holdings included the innovative Transcontinental Air Transport (TAT), which inaugurated the first scheduled coast-to-coast air and rail passenger service on July 7, 1929. Passengers could travel between New York and Los Angeles in 48 hours flying on Ford Trimotors during the day and going by train at night. Well funded and well run, TAT lost $2,750,000, however, in its first 18 months of operations. Aircraft simply were too expensive to buy, operate, and maintain; they could not generate enough revenue from an elite traveling public to cover costs. TAT again proved (as had Aeromarine Airways earlier in the decade) that an airmail subsidy was needed to survive.

The third aviation complex to emerge during the years of consolidation was the Aviation Corporation (AVCO). Late on the scene, AVCO picked up the pieces that had been left behind by United and North American. Its varied holdings included airports, aircraft factories, instrument companies, and airlines throughout the country. On January 25, 1930, AVCO put together its transportation enterprises in a single subsidiary called American Airways.

The stock market crash of 1929 and the economic disaster that followed raised major questions about the federal government's ability to continue its subsidy of the airline industry. In 1929 the government lost approximately $7 million on the airmail, and 1930 promised no improvement. Determined to ease the financial burden on the federal treasury, President Herbert Hoover instructed Postmaster General Walter Folger Brown to take steps to regulate—for the first time—the economic side of the industry.

A Toledo attorney who had been active in Republican politics, Brown made a thorough survey of the airline industry and came away convinced that it "was going into a tailspin." Immediate action was required to prevent disaster. He decided that two major steps had to be taken. First, the government had to encourage airlines to carry passengers as a way to reduce their dependence on airmail revenue. Second, Washington had to insure that a rational route structure replaced the current chaotic situation so that the airlines could function in the most efficient manner possible.

The Air Mail (Watres) Act of April 29, 1930, gave Brown the authority to impose his vision on the industry. Granting the postmaster general wide authority to award contracts, the new law substituted a space formula for weight in airmail payments. Top pay would go to airlines that used large, multiengine cabin planes equipped with two-way radios and the latest radio aids to navigation. In short, the Post Office would reward companies that flew airplanes designed to carry passengers.

Two weeks after the passage of the Watres Act, Brown called together the leading air transport companies for a series of meetings that later were labeled "spoils conferences." The postmaster general wanted an efficient nationwide airways system, with three transcontinental routes at its heart. When the airline operators could not agree, Brown imposed his wishes on the group. After United Air Lines was confirmed on the old Air Mail Service route from New York to San Francisco, Brown forced the merger of TAT with Western Air Express to form Transcontinental and Western Air (TWA), the second coast-to-coast air carrier. Finally, a series of complex maneuvers led to an award of the southern transcontinental route to a restructured American Airways.

As aviation historian Henry Ladd Smith has pointed out, by the time Brown left office in March 1933 "he had brought order to a chaotic industry." Passenger traffic increased from 84 million passenger-miles in 1930 to 127 million in 1932, while the average per mile rate for airmail declined from $1.09 to $0.54. At the same time, Brown's actions had created great bitterness, especially among those independent airline operators, like Thomas E. Braniff, who had fared poorly under the reorganization scheme. To their minds, a great injustice had been done, and they were determined to see the wrong righted.

While Brown encouraged passenger traffic, other officials in the Hoover administration (especially Department of Commerce chief air regulator Clarence M. Young) worked to ensure that the airlines would operate with regularity and safety. Despite the severe financial constraints imposed by the Depression, the Department of Commerce went ahead with plans to equip the nation's airways with low-frequency radio range beacons that guided pilots by means of aural signals. It also promoted experiments on a wide range of en route radio aids to navigation, instrument landing systems, and two-way radio voice communication. In 1932 it ended a lengthy debate over the value of instrument flying by requiring pilots on interstate air carriers to possess the rating of airline transport pilot, which involved a stiff examination on instrument navigation.

The policies of Franklin D. Roosevelt, at least at first, contrasted sharply with those of Herbert Hoover. For example, a drastic economy move in 1933 forced a sharp reduction in the staff of the National Bureau of Standards' radio section, the center of aeronautical research. This led to the end of its highly successful development program with the Department of Commerce's Aeronautical Branch. At the same time, the Roosevelt administration slashed the budget of the Aeronautics Branch itself, causing it to reduce its regulatory and inspection activities severely. And these moves proved only preliminary to a full scale disruption of the airline industry in 1934.

Reporter Fulton Lewis, Jr., a journalist employed by the Hearst press, had looked into Postmaster General Brown's efforts to rationalize the airline industry and concluded that he had acted improperly. Although William Randolph Hearst declined to publish the story, lest it embarrass the Republican party, the information found its way to a special senatorial committee that had been established in September 1933 to investigate the award of airmail and ocean mail contracts. Putting the worst possible interpretation on Brown's activities, committee chairman Senator Hugo L. Black of Alabama used the hearings to berate the Hoover administration and all its works. Following a report that existing airmail contracts had been awarded as the result of collusion, President Roosevelt on February 9, 1934, canceled them, effective February 19, and ordered the Army Air Corps to fly the mail.

Although assured by Maj. Gen. Benjamin D. Foulois, Chief of the Air Corps, that his men were fully capable of doing the job, Roosevelt soon had cause to regret his decision. Military operations began on February 20. Unfortunately, most army pilots lacked training in instrument flying. Encountering terrible weather, they substituted courage for skill—and it proved disastrous. By the end of February, five army pilots had been killed and six seriously injured. In the face of a storm of adverse publicity, much of it generated by the airlines who wanted their subsidy back, Roosevelt suspended operations on March 10 and announced that the airmail would be returned to private contractors as soon as possible. The Air Corps resumed flying on a restricted basis on March 19 and continued until June 1, compiling a creditable record and strongly suggesting that allegations of incompetence had been grossly exaggerated.

On April 20 and 27 Postmaster General James A. Farley awarded new airmail contracts. Although initially valid only for three months, the contracts were later confirmed as permanent. Farley decreed that no company or person who had been involved in the "spoils conferences" of 1930 would be eligible for an award, a stipulation that had more impact on innocent individual participants than on the companies which cynically circumvented the law by minor changes in corporate names. Also, under pending legislation (passed by Congress on June 12 as the Air Mail Act of 1934), airlines had to be separated from aircraft manufacturers. This latter provision meant the end of the giant holding companies.

The striking thing about the resulting airline structure was how little had changed. Although several new companies—Braniff Airways foremost among them—secured mail contracts, the major awards went to the same companies that had held

them before cancellation. United, TWA, and American Airlines (formerly American Airways) were confirmed on their transcontinental routes. Also securing an important contract for north-south routes on the east coast of the United States was Eastern Air Lines (formerly Eastern Air Transport). Over the next 40 years, these "Big Four" companies would dominate the domestic airline industry.

The mid 1930s saw the culmination of major technological developments in aeronautics that led to the appearance of a new generation of airliners. Airframes benefited from German designer Adolph Rohrbach's work with stressed-skin wings and fuselages and box-spar wing construction. At the same time, improved design of cylinder heads and pistons, plus better fuel, resulted in engines that were more efficient, reliable, and powerful. The first modern passenger transport to appear was the Boeing 247, which went into service with United Air Lines in March 1933. A streamlined, all-metal stressed-skin plane powered by two 550-horsepower Pratt & Whitney Wasp engines mounted into nacelles on the wing, the 247 could carry ten passengers at a cruising speed of approximately 160 miles per hour. A modified version, the 247D, featured the first hydraulically controlled variable pitch propellers, which significantly improved its already impressive performance.

Not far behind the 247 was the Douglas Aircraft Company's competing DC-2. This transport, destined to evolve into the classic DC-3, traces its origin to TWA's need for a replacement for its wooden Fokker trimotors. In 1931 a crash of a TWA Fokker killed Notre Dame football coach Knute Rockne and created a public furor. The government at first grounded all Fokkers, then restricted them to mail carrying only. TWA looked with interest on the evolving 247 as a replacement, but United had tied up Boeing's production line with its order for 59 airplanes. On August 2, 1932, TWA vice-president Jack Frye called for bids from various aircraft manufacturers for a new trimotor that would carry 12 passengers at 150 miles per hour. Only Donald Douglas responded, and his proposal envisioned a twin-engine, stressed-skin monoplane that was similar to the 247 but would incorporate new design features. TWA's technical director, Charles Lindbergh, accepted the DC-2 after stringent performance tests.

The prototype, designated the DC-1, first flew in July 1933, while an improved production model, the 14-passenger DC-2, entered service with TWA in May 1934. It soon proved superior to the Boeing 247, breaking the Newark-Chicago speed record four times in eight days. At the urging of President C. R. Smith of American Airlines, Douglas later widened and lengthened the fuselage of its popular transport, creating the 21-passenger DC-3 (or DST—Douglas Sleeper Transport—when configured with 14 berths). The DC-3/DST began flying for American in June 1936. Within three years, the new transport was carrying approximately 80 percent of all U.S. airline passengers. As historian R. E. G. Davies has pointed out, the appearance of the DC-3 "marked the beginning of the end of profitless air transport operations and a real chance to escape from dependence on mail payments to make up the difference between operating costs and passenger revenue."

Despite the new equipment, passenger traffic increased slowly during the mid 1930s. In 1934 the airlines carried fewer passengers (475,000) than they did in 1933 (502,000). Boardings climbed thereafter, but not until 1938 did the airlines cross the one million mark. A variety of factors accounted for this limited progress, but, as Henry Ladd Smith has emphasized, "the greatest deterrent to air travel has been *fear*."

In 1930 passenger fatalities occurred at the rate of 28.2 per 100 million passenger-miles. Applied to 1980, the last year that the government used the formula of fatalities per 100 million passenger-miles, that rate would have resulted in the deaths of more than 59,000 passengers. The rate improved to 14.9 in 1932; however, a $5,000 insurance policy for travel by airplane still cost $2, compared to $0.25 for rail travel.

Even during a comparatively good year, a single accident could generate adverse publicity for the entire industry. This happened in 1935, when a TWA DC-2 crashed near Kirkville, Missouri, in bad weather. Five people were killed in the accident, including Senator Bronson Cutting of New Mexico, a leading progressive and popular member of Congress. In the short term, the Cutting accident generated hundreds of stories about the perils of air travel. In the long term it led to significant changes in the government's policy toward aviation.

The Senate responded to the death of one of its own by launching an investigation into the cause of the accident. Led by Democratic senator Royal S. Copeland (whose devotion to aviation safety, histo-

rian Nick A. Komons has observed, "was on a par with, if not exceeded by, his antipathy to the New Deal"), the investigating committee soon broadened its inquiry to encompass the entire policy of the Roosevelt administration toward aviation. Revealing the sharp decline in the government's regulatory activities since 1933, the Copeland committee helped to force a reversal in policy. The budget of the Bureau of Air Commerce, which had been declining since the Republicans left office, increased by 59 percent to $10.8 million for fiscal 1938. The government expanded its regulatory activities, taking over in July 1936 the three air traffic control centers that had been established by the airlines six months earlier. Also, a much needed program of airways modernization got under way; Congress would appropriate $21.7 million for the program during Roosevelt's second term.

The high point of this flurry of federal activity came with the passage of the Air Commerce Act of 1938. This landmark piece of legislation established a framework for governmental policy toward aviation that would last for the next 20 years. It created a five-member Civil Aeronautics Authority with wide powers to regulate the economic aspects of aviation. Within the authority, a three-member Air Safety Board was charged with investigating aircraft accidents and making recommendations for their prevention. An office of administrator would be responsible for the operational functions of the agency, such as certification of aircraft and airmen, establishment and maintenance of civil airways, and other tasks that previously had been assigned to the Bureau of Air Commerce. In 1940 President Roosevelt renamed the five-man Authority the Civil Aeronautics Board (CAB) and assigned it to the Department of Commerce. At the same time, he abolished the Air Safety Board, transferring its accident-investigating function to the new CAB. The office of administrator also went to Commerce, where it was renamed the Civil Aeronautics Administration.

The government's new policy had a salutary effect on the airline industry. So, too, did an outstanding safety record: during the period from January 1939 to August 1940, the scheduled airlines did not suffer a single passenger fatality. Passenger traffic, which had been increasing at an annual rate of less than 20 percent during the mid 1930s, began to register increases in excess of 50 percent. In 1939 the airlines carried 1.5 million passengers, most of them in the 21-passenger DC-3. This number shot up to 2.5 million in 1940 and 3.4 million in 1941. By the time of American entry into World War II in December 1941, the increasingly robust airline industry had become a major factor in the nation's transport system.

The United States also made important strides in international aviation during the 1930s, thanks in large measure to a de facto partnership between Pan American World Airways and the Post Office. Pan American began operations between Key West and Havana on October 28, 1927. It grew slowly over the next year, with only 261 miles of routes by the end of 1928. The airline, however, was poised for rapid expansion. Postmaster General Brown, with the full backing of the departments of War and State, selected Pan American as the "chosen instrument" to carry the American flag to foreign countries—the equivalent of a national airline. A pattern of expansion quickly emerged. Under the able leadership of Juan T. Trippe, Pan American secured landing rights and other concessions from a foreign government. The Post Office then called for bids on the route, and followed by awarding the airmail contract to Pan American. And the mail contract was lucrative. Under the Foreign Air Mail Act of 1928, Brown could compensate international carriers at a maximum rate of $2 per mile. This compared to a maximum of $1.25 for domestic routes. Whereas domestic airlines by 1933 averaged $.54 a mile, Pan American, with no competition to worry about, received $2 for all of its routes.

Brown used the award of mail contracts to discourage unwanted competition, which he believed would cost the government more in the long run. The fate of the New York, Rio & Buenos Aires Line (NYRBA) served as an example to other potential rivals of the government's favored carrier. Well funded and expertly managed, NYRBA pioneered air routes from Miami, down the east coast of South America, to Buenos Aires. On February 18, 1930, it began scheduled passenger operations with elegant Consolidated Commodore flying boats. Postmaster General Brown, however, made it clear that only Pan American would receive a mail contract from the U.S. government on the route, even though NYRBA's experience and demonstrated technical resources were greater. As a result, NYRBA's financially strapped owners had to sell out to Juan Trippe at a bargain price.

By the early 1930s Pan American had nearly 20,000 miles of routes throughout the Caribbean, Mexico, and Central and South America. Even the change of administration failed to slow the airline's growth. Pan American was the only carrier to escape punishment in 1934, despite the fact that Postmaster Brown's policy of favoritism toward the airline was abundantly clear. Pan American had become a part of Roosevelt's Good Neighbor policy. It provided important economic links to Latin America. Also, its routes had significant diplomacy and military implications for the United States. As historian Henry Ladd Smith has concluded, "Pan American Airways was just too big to be treated as ruthlessly as were the domestic carriers."

The airline expanded across the Pacific Ocean in the mid 1930s. After careful preparations, a four-engine Martin M-130 flying boat—the "China Clipper"—left San Francisco on November 22, 1935, for Manila, inaugurating scheduled transpacific service. The transatlantic route took longer to achieve, largely because of political problems, mainly with the British. On May 20, 1939, the "Yankee Clipper," a larger four-engine Boeing 314 flying boat, inaugurated scheduled transatlantic service between New York and Marseilles via the Azores and Lisbon. The following month, Pan American started flying from New York to Southampton.

Pan American accomplished a great deal during the 1930s. Superbly run, it pioneered long distance routes over two oceans, built air bases across the Pacific, developed long-range radio direction-finding equipment, and sponsored a series of impressive flying boats, culminating in the Boeing 314. The developmental expenses for all this were underwritten by the government in the form of postal subsidies. Between 1929 and 1940 Pan American received $47.2 million in mail payments, compared to the $59.8 million received by *all* domestic airlines. This generous funding enabled Pan American not only to expand throughout the world but also to turn a modest profit. Many who observed Pan Am's acquired role as unofficial ambassador for the United States, worldwide, considered the money well spent.

American entry into World War II in December 1941 brought an end, at least temporarily, to the rapid growth that the domestic airline industry had been experiencing since 1938. Thanks largely to the efforts of Edgar S. Gorrell, president of the Air Transport Association (the airline industry's trade organization), mobilization of the airlines personnel and equipment proceeded rapidly in an orderly fashion. Within months of the new year, the army had requisitioned 200 airplanes out of the industry's total fleet of 360.

The war years saw a dramatic increase in aircraft utilization as the airlines struggled to meet the demand for priority air travel. Despite the sharp reduction in equipment, the airlines carried nearly as many passengers in 1942 and 1943 as they had in 1941. With load factors averaging 89 percent, the industry's problem was not sales but ensuring that seats were allocated fairly. They established a three-tier priority system that was rigorously enforced. In one well-publicized incident, First Lady Eleanor Roosevelt, who was traveling on a low priority ticket, had to give up her seat to a higher priority army pilot. Her cheerful acceptance of the situation gave the priority system a good deal of credibility.

Pan American Airways not only continued to fly many of its international routes during the war but also became especially active in the growing worldwide military air transport network. Even before the Japanese attack on Pearl Harbor, the army had called upon Pan American to establish a route across the South Atlantic to Cairo. The airline accomplished the task in two months during the summer of 1941, building a chain of airfields across Africa. Other crucial assignments followed. One of the most important took place in 1942 when a Pan American subsidiary, the China National Aviation Corporation, pioneered the air route over the towering mountains between India and China—soon to become known as the Hump.

At the same time, requisitioned crews and equipment from the domestic airlines were gaining a good deal of experience on far-flung air routes. Northeast Airlines, a small company that had never flown beyond Montreal, began a scheduled passenger and cargo service in the North Atlantic region that eventually reached the British Isles. TWA also flew across the Atlantic, making more than 10,000 crossings during the war, while Eastern ferried C-46s across the South Atlantic and on to India. Northwest Airlines and Western Air Lines opened routes to Alaska, and the former became the leading carrier to serve that strategically important area. United Air Lines was especially active in the Pacific; between September 1942 and March 1945, it made 1,700 trips across the ocean. American Airlines had a varied wartime experience, flying across

both the North and South Atlantic, reaching to Alaska, and even making more than 1,000 trips across the Hump. Needless to say, the war years expanded the horizons of all these airlines, giving Pan American cause to fear for the continuation of its monopoly of international air routes in the postwar period.

The airlines expected good times following the war, and for one brief period it seemed as if their high expectations might come true. As American industrial production reached a peak, the scheduled airlines increased their fleet from 204 airplanes in 1943 to 288 in 1944. This number rose to 421 in 1945, then to 674 in the immediate postwar boom year of 1946. Passenger traffic increased with capacity, from 4 million in 1943 to 6.5 million in 1945, and a breathtaking 12.3 million in 1946. Profits, however, proved elusive. Although operating revenues rose to an all-time high of $316.2 million in 1946, operating expenses soared to $322.2 million, giving the industry its first net loss since 1938.

In 1947 it became clear that there would be no boom times. Suffering five major accidents and 199 passenger fatalities, the domestic airline industry experienced its poorest year in history. The worst accident came on October 24, when a United Air Lines DC-6 crashed near Bryce Canyon, Utah, killing all 52 people on board. Developed by the Douglas Aircraft Company from the unpressurized wartime C-54 cargo transport to compete with TWA's pressurized Lockheed Constellation, which had been placed into regular service by TWA on its transcontinental route in March 1946, the pressurized DC-6 had joined the fleets of United and American in the spring of 1947. Its debut had been a spectacular success. Carrying 52 passengers, it could fly across the country, from west to east, in ten hours. However, less than three weeks after the Bryce Canyon disaster, another DC-6 caught fire over Gallup, New Mexico. This time, the smoke-blinded pilot managed to land safely. The Civil Aeronautics Administration promptly grounded all DC-6s. Investigators discovered that the fires had been caused by gasoline leaking into cabin heaters during fuel transfer. Modifying the aircraft kept them out of service until March 1948.

Passenger traffic stagnated in 1947, rising only 6 percent over 1946. As industry losses reached an all-time high of $21.3 million, airline executives began to search for new ways to attract air travelers. The answer to their problem came with an expansion of the market. Traditionally, airlines had catered primarily to businessmen, who provided the bulk of their passengers. Now, they had to appeal to leisure travelers, who might consider flying as a speedy alternative to the train. The key to this market was price.

United Air Lines had experimented with low fares prior to World War II. In April 1940 it started the first air coach service, carrying passengers between San Francisco and Los Angeles (with stops) in Boeing 247s. United charged $13.90 for the trip, or 3.5 cents a mile. This innovative marketing strategy ended with the Japanese attack on Pearl Harbor. After the war, there was an explosive growth of charter, or nonscheduled, air carriers. In fact, the Civil Aeronautics Board estimated that 2,720 "airlines" were started in 1945. Requiring no operating certificate for their contract service, most were tiny companies that soon faded from view. Notable among those that survived was Stanley Weiss's North American Airlines. Emphasizing no-frills service and charging $99 for one way and $160 for a round-trip across the country, North American resisted the combined legal efforts of the established industry to dislodge it.

Capital Airlines, a small trunk carrier with ambitions to join the ranks of the industry's Big Four, was the first to introduce coach class, low-fare service on a certified route. In November 1948 it began "Nighthawk" flights between New York and Chicago. Using high-density seating in its DC-4s (60 passengers), flying during the night only, and offering minimal cabin service, it charged $33.30 for a one-way fare. This translated into 4 cents a mile on the route instead of the standard 6 cents.

Although reluctant to embrace the idea, the major carriers were forced to follow suit. In December 1949 TWA and American began transcontinental coach service with 60-passenger DC-4s, charging $110. As traffic and profits increased during the early 1950s, restrictions on coach class diminished, finally reaching a stage where the difference in comfort and amenities between coach and first class were ones of detail rather than substance.

The domestic airline industry experienced another period of growth during the 1950s, reflecting partly the vibrant nature of the American economy. Passenger boardings, which had increased slowly following the war, shot up dramatically, rising from 17.3 million in 1950 to 38 million in 1955, the year in which airlines for the first time carried

more passengers than did railroads. During this same period, operating revenues exceeded expenses by an average of $96.1 million a year.

The Big Four—United, American, TWA, and Eastern—continued their domination, accounting for more than half the seat-mile productivity of the entire industry. The other 11 trunk carriers were reduced to eight during the decade, as Mid-Continent merged with Braniff Airways (1950), Chicago & Southern with Delta (1953), and Colonial with Eastern (1956). Although the Civil Aeronautics Board made several significant awards to the smaller trunk airlines, allowing them to compete with the Big Four on several high density routes, it was difficult for them to mount an effective challenge. As the CAB effectively controlled fares, the smaller carriers could compete for a greater market share only by offering better service.

The most determined challenge to the Big Four during the 1950s came again from Capital Airlines, which earlier had disturbed the status quo by pioneering coach fares. This time Capital stole a march on the industry's giants by ordering a fleet of 60 Vickers Viscounts. The first of these British-built turboprop airliners went into service on the highly competitive New York-Chicago route in July 1955. Blatantly advertised as "Rolls-Royce Jets," they proved an immediate success. Passengers enjoyed traveling on the speedy, vibrationless airplane, and Capital's market share jumped. Buoyed by the Viscount's initial success, Capital ordered 15 more turboprops, and began negotiations for 14 all-jet de Havilland Comets. Unfortunately for Capital, the bubble burst in 1956-1957. Heavy debt payments combined with Capital's high-cost short-haul routes forced the cancellation of the new order. The CAB's foot-dragging on granting new routes, a series of accidents with the Viscounts, and the appearance of the Lockheed Electra turboprop in 1959 led to the demise of the airline. In June 1961 United absorbed it in the largest merger in the industry's history.

Competition also developed on international air routes following World War II. Indeed, the assault on Pan American's monopoly had begun even earlier. In July 1940 President Roosevelt had granted seven-year temporary authority to American Export Airlines to operate a transatlantic service. Although intense lobbying by Pan American prevented American Export from receiving a mail contract, the rival carrier began operating Vought-

Sikorsky VS-44 flying boats from New York to Foynes, Ireland, in June 1942.

As the domestic airlines gained experience on overseas routes during the war, thanks to their service with the Air Transport Command, Pan American worked with its allies in Congress to create a postwar all-American flag carrier. This equivalent of a national flag carrier obviously would be dominated by Pan American. But Juan Trippe failed to persuade a majority of Congress—and the Civil Aeronautics Board—that monopoly would be preferable to competition.

In June 1945 the CAB granted TWA and American Export—soon to be acquired by American Airlines and renamed American Overseas Airlines—seven-year authorization to fly the North Atlantic. Although Pan American took over American Overseas by merger in 1950, TWA remained to challenge its dominance of the North Atlantic routes. In the Pacific, Northwest Airlines became Pan American's chief rival. In August 1946 the CAB authorized Northwest to fly to the Orient via the Great Circle route. It began service to Anchorage in September, then reached Manila, via Tokyo, in July 1947. Braniff Airways provided the main competition in Latin America. Securing 7,700 miles of routes in Central and South America, Braniff inaugurated service to Lima in June 1948, Rio in March 1949, and Buenos Aires in May 1950. President Harry Truman quickly gave his approval to this far-reaching series of international route awards, ignoring the frantic lobbying efforts of Pan American.

The international carriers, which had carried only 229,000 passengers in 1941, flew over one million people in 1946. Traffic reached two million in 1951 and nearly three million in 1954, when international coach class was introduced. The mid 1950s recorded more rapid growth. In 1956—a year that saw Pan American taken off subsidy—the international airlines carried nearly four million passengers and posted a record net operating profit of $34.9 million. Two years later an air transport milestone was reached when, for the first time, more people traveled to Europe by air than by ship.

On October 13, 1955, Pan American's Juan Trippe led the American airline industry into the jet age when he ordered 20 Boeing 707s and 25 Douglas DC-8s. The appearance of these new jet transports would bring about revolutionary changes in the nation's transport system. But even before the first jet went into service, the rapid growth of avi-

ation during the 1950s was creating an intolerable strain on an airways and air traffic system that had been designed for DC-3s.

The federal government had at first responded slowly to the new demands. With military and civil aviation competing for control of airspace and unable to agree on the most appropriate radio aids to navigation, President Dwight D. Eisenhower ordered studies to consider the needs of aviation. It took a major air tragedy, as it often does, to accelerate the glacial pace of change. On June 30, 1956, a TWA Constellation and United Air Lines DC-7 collided over the Grand Canyon, killing 128 people. Both pilots were operating by Visual Flight Rules and were responsible for avoiding other aircraft. However, the speeds at which these aircraft traveled made such regulations archaic. Congress immediately opened an investigation into the air traffic control system.

While the legislature exposed the deficiencies of the nation's antiquated air traffic control system. Eisenhower's special assistant for aviation facilities planning, Edward P. Curtiss, prepared a report on what could be done to solve the problem. In May 1957 Curtiss submitted a study that warned of "a crisis in the making." The growing congestion in the skies, a situation likely to grow far worse when the jets arrived, required both technical and administrative responses on the part of the government. His central recommendation called for the creation of an independent Federal Aviation Agency.

Fifteen months later, after two midair collisions between military aircraft and commercial transports, the necessary legislation was ready for Eisenhower's approval. The Federal Aviation Act, signed in August 1958, created two independent agencies. The Federal Aviation Agency, which took over the organization and functions of the Civil Aeronautics Administration, was given broad powers to insure safety in the air. The CAB remained responsible for the economic regulation of the airline industry and for determining the probable cause of aircraft accidents; but most of its authority over safety regulation and enforcement was transferred to the FAA.

The creation of the new federal regulatory structure came none too soon. In October 1958 the first jet transport went into service with Pan American. The early Boeing 707-120, even though it was soon superseded by models with better engines that provided longer range and superior economy, was an immediate economic success. Passengers loved the speed and comfort of the sleek Boeing. During the first three months of 1959, Pan American carried 33,400 passengers in its growing fleet of jet transports, recording an extraordinary 90.8 percent seat occupancy. And this was only the beginning. Overseas traffic doubled over the next five years, and Pan American reaped the competitive rewards for introducing the new airplanes. In 1963, for example, the company recorded an after-tax profit of $33.5 million.

Jet aircraft had an equally dramatic impact on the domestic airlines. National Airlines surprised rival Eastern by introducing Boeing 707s leased from Pan American on the highly competitive (and profitable) New York-Miami run in December 1958. American Airlines was the first of the Big Four to bring jets into service, placing Boeings on its transcontinental route in January 1959. Before the end of the year, TWA and United (with DC-8s) were also flying jets across the country.

Piston engined and turboprop equipment quickly gave way to a variety of jet transports, as all major and many minor airlines committed millions of dollars to purchase the marvelous and far more efficient new airplanes. In July 1960 United and American introduced the Boeing 720, a shortened version of the 707, on their New York-Chicago routes. The three-engine Boeing 727, destined to become the most economical and widely used of the smaller jet transports, made its debut in 1964 with Eastern, American, and TWA. The following year saw Delta begin operating DC-9s, while Braniff and Mohawk Airlines acquired British-built BAC One-elevens.

Several innovations contributed to increased air travel during a decade of prosperity. In April 1961 Eastern Air Lines began a "shuttle" service on the heavily traveled Boston-New York-Washington route. Passengers did not need to make reservations; they had only to show up at the airport for the hourly flights. They were guaranteed a seat by the immediate addition of extra sections when aircraft filled up. On June 12 Eastern had to fly a second section of the shuttle for a single passenger. The enormous publicity given to this event far overshadowed the operational loss. Eastern needed only 13 and a half months to carry one million passengers. By the end of 1965, the Air Shuttle had transported ten million people.

In other areas, American Airlines led the way. In 1960 it introduced SABRE (for Semi-Automated Business Research Environment), a computerized reservation system. Developed in partnership with IBM, SABRE revolutionized data processing in the airline industry, enabling American to process reservations in three seconds instead of the usual 45 minutes. The user fees from other airlines and travel agents would become a significant source of profit for American. The airline also pioneered a low-cost youth fare, inaugurated in 1966. In many ways this was a sign of the times. By the mid 1960s, some 50 percent of airline passengers were traveling for reasons of vacation and pleasure rather than business.

The booming air travel market was reflected in the growth of feeder or local service airlines. The Civil Aeronautics Board had established this new category of airline in July 1944, issuing temporary operating certificates to companies that were designed to serve smaller communities throughout the nation. In May 1955 President Eisenhower authorized permanent certificates for the 13 surviving companies out of the original 26. Throughout most of the 1950s, the local service airlines relied on DC-3s (with Fokker-Fairchild F-27s appearing toward the end of the decade) to provide air service to communities that were not large enough to attract the attention of the trunk carriers.

During the 1960s the local service airlines modernized their fleets and began to compete directly with trunk carriers on shorter routes. Mohawk Airlines, under the aggressive leadership of Robert F. Peach, became the first small airline to operate jets, beginning service with BAC One-elevens in July 1965. This move enabled Mohawk to challenge American Airlines for a market share on such important routes as New York-Syracuse. Other local service carriers followed Mohawk's lead, ordering DC-9s, Boeing 727s, and Boeing 737s. By the end of the decade, mergers had reduced the number of local service carriers from 13 to nine, including such strong regional airlines as Mohawk, Allegheny, Piedmont, Ozark, Frontier, and North Central.

As the local service carriers took on the character of regional airlines and pressed for entry into the ranks of the trunks, a new type of company grew up to tap the smaller markets that the local service airlines began to neglect. Granted an exemption from CAB jurisdiction, provided that they did not operate aircraft heavier than 12,500 pounds, the scheduled air taxi or third level carriers grew from 12 companies in 1964 to more than 200 by the end of 1968. As airline historian R. E. G. Davies remarked at the time, "This rate of expansion has been a phenomenon unparalleled in modern air transport history."

Another category of airline that prospered during the decade was the intrastate carrier, especially those companies that operated in California and Texas. Not covered by CAB rules and regulations, the intrastate airlines may have lacked subsidy, but they had a competitive freedom that was denied the certificated airlines. The preeminent intrastate carrier was Pacific Southwest Airlines (PSA). Featuring low fares and high frequency of service, PSA could challenge all competition on the rich market from San Francisco to Los Angeles. Nor did it operate inferior equipment. In 1959 PSA introduced Lockheed Electra turboprops into service on its routes. Six years later, the innovative carrier added five Boeing 727s to its fleet. So successful were the intrastate carriers that they later were used as examples of the virtues to be found in a deregulated environment.

The 1960s are recalled as a turbulent decade in American history. It was a time of civil rights struggles, youth rebellion, assassination of political leaders, and deep and bitter controversy over the war in Vietnam. However, these years also were part of an era of unprecedented economic growth. During the 30 years after 1940, for example, per capita disposable income doubled, while the gross national product increased from $355 billion to $727 billion. The airline industry reflected the general state of the economy. Between 1960 and 1969 travel on scheduled airlines rose from 56.3 million to 158.4 million passengers. During this same period, the net operating income of domestic airlines averaged $255.4 million a year, while international airlines averaged $139.4 million.

The good times came to an end in 1970. For the first time in 12 years, domestic passenger traffic dropped—by 5 million boardings. The airlines posted their first net operating loss since 1947. And things were not much better in 1971. At the time, many analysts blamed the industry's ills on overcapacity. In 1966, in the midst of prosperity, Juan Trippe of Pan American had persuaded the Boeing company to build the first "jumbo jet." The 350-ton Boeing 747 went into service with Pan American in January 1970. The next month, TWA began using the giant transport on its New York-

Los Angeles route. The three-engine wide-bodied Douglas DC-10 appeared in August 1971, joining the fleets of American and United, while the Lockheed L-1011 Tristar began flying on Eastern's routes the following April.

It would be a grave oversimplification, however, to blame the economic ills of the airlines on the appearance of the wide-bodied airliners. Without these aircraft, the nation's air traffic control system and airport infrastructure could not have coped with the later growth in air travel. More significant than the temporary overcapacity and sluggish growth in passenger traffic during the early 1970s was the impact of the first "oil shock." During the winter of 1973-1974, oil prices quadrupled. The actions of the OPEC oil cartel signaled the end of an era of cheap energy. In the short run, this helped to produce one of the most sustained price increases in American history. Nor was this all. Late 1974 marked the beginning of the worst recession of the postwar period, producing a phenomenon that the press labeled "stagflation."

As the airlines struggled to cope with rapidly rising costs, the federal government prepared to abandon the economic regulatory structure that had existed since 1938. The old system of controlled routes and prices had been showing signs of increasing wear and tear, as the airlines tried to cope with the hostile economic environment of the 1970s. For example, the CAB had permitted a price war in 1977, beginning with Texas International's "Peanut" fares, followed by American Airlines' deeply discounted "Super Saver" fares. Also, the entire idea of federal economic regulation was falling into disfavor. Advocates of the "free market system" had only to point to California, where unregulated intrastate airlines flourished.

In October 1978 Congress passed and President Jimmy Carter signed the landmark Airline Deregulation Act. Under its provisions, during a four-year transition period, the CAB gave up its control over routes and prices. The airlines were free to come and go as market conditions dictated, and to charge whatever fares they pleased.

The new system could not have come at a worse time. Another round of price increases occurred in 1979 and 1980, together with a deep recession that lasted into 1982. In the midst of these economic woes, the Professional Air Traffic Controllers Organization went out on an illegal strike, crippling the nation's air traffic system. President

Ronald Reagan fired 11,000 strikers, breaking both the strike and the union, and several years were to pass before the air traffic system reached its prestrike capacity.

New airlines seemed to spring up daily in the unregulated environment, increasing from 36 in 1978 to 96 in 1983 (although only two were fated to survive the decade). At the same time, the industry saw its costs double. After a good year in 1978, profits tumbled in 1979 as the airlines fought a vicious price war. Between 1980 and 1983 the domestic airline industry suffered a staggering net loss of $1.2 billion, placing several respected companies at risk.

To survive in the turbulent postderegulation era airlines had to cut costs. One way to effect savings was to employ nonunion labor at wages well below the industry average. Frank Lorenzo of Texas Air led the way in this direction. Another option was to negotiate with the unions a two-tier wage system, bringing in new employees at lower salaries. Robert Crandall of American selected this course of action. Failure to reduce costs meant disaster. Braniff Airways stood as the prime example of an airline unable to cope with the new environment. In May 1982 the once-proud Texas-based carrier went bankrupt with a debt of $733 million.

Another sign of the times was the wave of mergers that took place during the latter part of the 1980s. Only larger companies stood a chance of surviving. Northeast (to Delta) and National (to Pan American) had already disappeared. In 1986 TWA acquired Ozark Airlines, Northwest bought Republic, and Texas Air/Continental took over People Express and Eastern. The next year Delta acquired Western. USAir (formerly Allegheny) bought Pacific Southwest in 1986 and Piedmont in 1989.

The early 1990s saw only a continuation of previous trends. In January 1991 the giant Eastern Air Lines stopped flying after a two-year struggle to emerge from Chapter 11 bankruptcy. Continental, America West, and Pan American entered Chapter 11 during 1990-1991, while heavily leveraged TWA struggled to survive. With Northwest also deeply in debt and USAir awash in red ink (it suffered a record net loss of $454.4 million in 1990), only three carriers seemed assured of longterm survival: American, Delta, and United.

As the airline industry makes the transition to what economist Alfred H. Kahn (once the leading advocate of deregulation) has termed an "uncomfortably tight oligopoly," there are increasing predictions that some form of re-regulation will occur before the end of the century. While a return to the old system of tight control seems unlikely, an alternative structure might well be instituted—perhaps something along the lines of the independent Federal Transportation Commission that has been proposed by Professor Paul Stephen Dempsey in his critical study of the current state of the industry, *Flying Blind: The Failure of Airline Deregulation* (1990). Whatever the future holds in the way of regulation, the airline industry will require creative leadership of the highest order to meet the challenges of transporting with safety and reasonable convenience the 750 million passengers that are expected to travel by air in the year 2000.

—*William M. Leary*
University of Georgia

Encyclopedia of American Business History and Biography

The Airline Industry

C. Edward Acker

(April 9, 1929 -   )

by Joseph F. Ross

Prachuap Khiri Khan, Thailand

CAREER: Vice-president, president and chief operating officer, Braniff Airways (1965-1975); president, Transway International Corporation (1975-1976); president, Gulf United Corporation (1976-1977); chairman and chief executive officer, Air Florida (1977-1981); chairman and chief executive officer, Pan American World Airways (1981-1988); director and chairman, Pan Am Corporation (1982-1988).

C. Edward Acker presided over the nation's most sedate and then its most flamboyant airline at a time when risk and opportunity were given the same face by the Airline Deregulation Act of 1978. Schooled in economics and psychology, Acker met the challenge of unregulated fares and unfettered access to routes boldly and creatively, but with mixed results. Two Acker-managed carriers prospered only to pass from existence shortly after his departure, while his effort to resuscitate a third amounted to no more than a holding action. Still, since airlines were no longer protected from the caprices of chance after 1978, the fate of some ventures was decided by such unpredictable or ill-timed events as soaring inflation and interest rates, the unprecedented volatility of fuel prices, the firing of 13,000 air traffic controllers, and the rise of terrorist acts aimed at commercial aircraft and passengers.

Born on April 9, 1929, in Dallas, Texas, Acker received his B.A. degree in economics and psychology at Southern Methodist University in 1950. Barely 15 years later, at the age of thirty-six, he became a senior vice-president of Braniff Airways. Earlier, as finance officer for Greatamerica Corporation, a holding company, Acker had made a study of Braniff's potential and recommended that Greatamerica acquire a controlling interest in the airline. Asked to head the airline after its purchase in 1964, Acker—aware of his scant knowledge of commercial aviation—had recommended that Harding

C. Edward Acker

L. Lawrence, a forty-five-year-old executive vice-president of Continental Airlines, be named president instead. Working side-by-side, the two raised Braniff's revenues from $134 million to nearly $600 million in less than a decade.

A visionary, aggressive and autocratic, Lawrence came to Braniff in 1965 with the determination to double its size in five years. Anxious to rid the airline of its prop-driven Electras, in the first week Lawrence confirmed a previous order for 18 jets, and at the same time put in motion applications for new routes. While Acker was bringing computerization and control of finances up to industry standards, Lawrence drastically altered Braniff's public image by launching a fleet of garishly painted aircraft (dubbed "Easter Eggs") so eye-catching as to multiply their number in the public's mind. With wildly colored flight-attendant uniforms and aircraft interiors, Braniff was announcing "the end of the plain plane," and the end of stodgy airline management.

Braniff's stock soared, from $24 a share in April of 1965 to $124 and climbing by mid 1966. Operating revenues kept pace: from $134 million in 1965 to $194 million in 1966. However much might have been due to Braniff's new look, Acker and Lawrence had not neglected marketing, operations, or expansion. In 1966, for example, Braniff's modest operation in South America was turned into a major one by negotiating the purchase of Panagra (Pan American Grace), a well-established South American airline owned by W. R. Grace and Company and Pan American World Airways. After approval by the Civil Aeronautics Board (CAB), the two airlines were merged, and by early 1967 the entire acquisition cost had been recouped through the sale of surplus aircraft and the consolidation of tax credits.

Meanwhile, Greatamerica—and its 80 percent control of Braniff—had been absorbed by LTV (Ling-Tempco-Vought) Corporation. By 1970 LTV was both ailing and defending itself from an antitrust suit brought by the Securities Exchange Commission. Acker, by then president of Braniff under chairman Lawrence, joined LTV's board and thus became party to an eventual settlement that required LTV to divest itself of Braniff Airways (and one other entity). Although Acker was considered for the presidency of LTV, it could not have escaped him that Braniff henceforth would control its own destiny and that he could be party to that also.

In early 1972, driven less by political conviction than by a concern for route awards, Acker and Lawrence each made a $5,000 contribution to Richard M. Nixon's presidential reelection campaign. When fund-raiser Maurice Stans pointedly let it be known that donations usually were in the hundreds of thousands, the two embarrassed executives decided that *Braniff* would contribute $50,000. In the wake of the Watergate scandal, the disclosure of that illegal contribution led to an investigation and findings that cast a cloud over Acker.

As detailed by John J. Nance in his 1984 book *Splash of Colors*, what came to light was a scandalous picture of Braniff adopting "a system of off-the-books tickets ... sold to [pay] ... South American travel agents" for steering business away from the competition and to Braniff. The plan, according to Nance, had been approved by Acker in mid 1969. The CAB brought an action against Braniff in 1975, charging the airline with widespread violations and with falsification of CAB reports. Several months later, in what was rumored to be (quoting Nance) "a sacrifice to the CAB," Acker resigned from Braniff, and shortly thereafter the issue was settled when Braniff paid a $300,000 fine.

In mid 1977, after brief stays as president of Transway International Corporation and Gulf United Corp., Acker joined Air Florida, a small and debt-ridden intrastate carrier founded in 1972 by Miami entrepreneur Eli Timoner. Bringing with him a transfusion of $2 million in capital provided by private investor Carl Lindner, plus a decade of experience at Braniff, Acker ran the airline as chairman and chief executive officer while owner-president Timoner handled finance. Starting with a fleet of three prop-driven Electras serving four cities, the pair opened an era of expansion and financial maneuvering that was meteoric in every way—including its brilliant but fleeting existence.

With interest rates in double digits, Acker turned to leasing as the quickest means of acquiring the jet aircraft needed to expand Air Florida's meager intrastate network. In the fiscal year before Acker's arrival the company lost $2.1 million. In fiscal year 1978, with five planes (sporting new green-and-blue livery and a distinctive swirling logo) serving 17 cities, the losses slowed to a mere $160,000. In October 1978 came deregulation, and by year's end Air Florida was an interstate carrier flying scheduled service between Washington, D.C., and Miami.

Along with offering charters and adding routes to New York City, Philadelphia, and the Caribbean in 1979, Air Florida suddenly became an international carrier when, to the industry's surprise and shock, the CAB awarded the airline the coveted Miami-London route. Serving 24 cities with 15 planes and carrying over one million passengers, Air Florida more than doubled its operating revenues that year to $44.2 million, a performance that undoubtedly helped Acker to establish a line of credit with InterFirst Bank Dallas. With that loan and the year's $2.4 million profit in hand, Acker could order the latest Boeing 737s and acquire a stake in Piedmont Aviation that later would earn $2.2 million in profit.

By spring of 1980 Air Florida was established as an interstate, intrastate, and international scheduled and charter airline. Encouraged by bookings for 100 European charters worth $60 million, Acker planned to exercise scheduled rights to Amsterdam, Brussels, Zurich, Honduras, the Dominican Republic, and Jamaica. Taking advantage of a Federal Aviation Administration program that guaranteed 90 percent of principal and 100 percent of interest for aircraft purchases made by small carriers, Acker gained access to $82.5 million, enabling him to build a fleet of 18 B-737s, three DC-9s, and a DC-10. Air Florida posted a profit of $5.1 million on revenues of $114.3 million in 1980, and an accumulated debt that once stood at $3.9 million was turned into a $667,000 profit. During that time major domestic carriers were experiencing record losses and near zero growth.

There were no secrets underlying Air Florida's success. Most important was Acker's willingness to plunge headlong into the murky deep of deregulation while others tested the waters. Furthermore, Air Florida boasted a lean management team and a roster of highly motivated nonunion flight crews (whose 74 monthly hours of actual flying time dwarfed the industry's best of 54). Finally, the airline had ready access to capital, high load-factors made possible by offering reduced fares and serving cold food, fuel efficient aircraft, and shrewd financial dealings—the last being an investment in Air California that eventually realized a profit of $10 million.

Following a successful $40 million public offering of Air Florida stock in May 1981, Carl Lindner (who in 1977 had invested $2 million at $3 a share) sold his holdings as the stock was on its way to an all-time high of nearly $18. By late 1981 the company had 30 planes, half of them leased, and 11 more on order. As of June, however, Air Florida was a precariously leveraged airline. Its debt of $188 million was 3.7 times its equity of $50 million. Past success notwithstanding, at a time when recession was setting in, when interest rates were hovering around 20 percent, and when low-overhead entrants were rushing into the booming air-

line business, Air Florida was all but totally dependent on cash flow to survive.

In September 1981, Acker stunned industry watchers by leaving Air Florida to become chairman of deeply troubled Pan American World Airways. Acker inherited an airline with an illustrious reputation for having pioneered world travel with its fabled China Clippers, and little else to commend it. Still serving 72 cities in 38 countries on six continents, Pan Am was losing $1 million a day. Having had its $470 million in revolving credit canceled, Pan Am's board lured Acker to the chairmanship (along with undisclosed incentive arrangements) by selling its Intercontinental Hotels chain for $500 million, most of which would go to service $900 million in long-term debt.

Not the least of Pan Am's debits was its disaffected work force, which had grown unhappy, during the years spent merging National Airlines (purchased for $400 million on the eve of its routes becoming free for the asking) with Pan Am. Burdened with some of the highest overhead costs in the industry, Acker nevertheless was able to persuade employees to accept a 10 percent wage cut and temporary freeze. Along with trimming the work force by 10 percent, Acker sold two B-747 freighters and the company's low-rent lease on 340,000 square feet of office space in the high-rent Pan Am Building in New York City. Pan Am's difficulties in 1981 were such that, with its stock mired at $3, the company, with $4 billion in sales, could have been purchased on the open market for about $250 million.

The new Pan Am chairman took a radical approach in solving his company's problems. Reversing his predecessor's decision to retrench, Acker not only announced plans to take delivery of eight B-727-200s and ten Lockheed L-1011s, but he also slashed fares by as much as 67 percent on prime routes to Miami, London, and Frankfurt. Acker was accused of "suicidal marketing" by England's low-fare advocate Sir Freddie Laker, but his deep fare cuts, ironically, hit hardest at Air Florida, where Eli Timoner, had taken over from Acker.

Burdened by Pan Am's fare cuts, Air Florida suddenly needed to fill 72 percent of its seats to turn a profit instead of the previous 57 percent. Despite tax credits and $303 million in revenues, Air Florida lost $5.9 million in 1981. In January of 1982 an Air Florida B-737 plunged into the Potomac River, killing 78. The sight of Air Florida's distinctive logo jutting out of the Potomac generated intense publicity and focused attention on the airline's weak financial position. With its management diverted for months by the effects of the crash, in 1982 Air Florida suffered a loss of $93.4 million, a blow from which it never recovered.

Meanwhile Acker's radical fix had begun to work wonders at Pan Am. The third quarter of 1982 saw the airline post a profit of $7.1 million (which reduced the forecast loss for that year to $200 million). Acker's intent was to fly the airline out of trouble by reducing costs, increasing productivity, and expanding to more profitable routes. Criticized for not retrenching, Acker responded by saying, "I don't want to dump 75 percent of our employees. But if . . . proven wrong I'm not going to let the stockholder's equity go down the drain."

As a result of restructuring domestic routes to feed Pan Am's international hubs, in 1983 Acker could celebrate both a third-quarter operating profit of $76.3 million, and a relatively modest $51 million loss for the year. The joy was short-lived, however. A strong U.S. dollar in 1984 brought higher operating expenses, lower international traffic, and a $29 million loss in foreign currency exchange. Added to the expiration of wage concessions worth $61 million, 1984's loss totaled $206 million.

The Transport Workers Union erased any chance of a profit in 1985 by staging a 28-day strike early in the year. Having sold most of the company's nonflying assets (including the prestigious Pan Am Building), Acker brought gasps from the industry be selling the jewel in Pan Am's crown— its storied Pacific Division—to United Airlines for $750 million.

The sale, which vaulted working capital to nearly $1 billion, would enable Pan Am "to concentrate [its] resources and efforts in one geographic area," said Acker. Using 43 high-density B-747s and 16 Airbus jetliners (leased while awaiting delivery of Airbus 300s and 320s), Acker intended to make Pan Am *the* major transatlantic carrier by offering 175 transatlantic flights a week to 40 cities. Brightening the prospects for 1986, four of the company's five major unions signed contracts with reduced crew size requirements, work-rule changes, or other concessions. Not surprisingly, rumors of merger or takeover abounded, raising Pan Am's stock from $4 to $9 a share.

Acker's plans for 1986 came to nought, however, largely as a result of a factor beyond Pan Am's control. A campaign of random terrorism, aimed mainly at Americans in Europe, hurt the entire airline business. The campaign began in early February with the bombing of a fashion shop in Paris. On April 2 a bomb exploded aboard a Trans World Airlines plane en route to Athens, and three days later a Berlin nightclub frequented by American soldiers was bombed. On April 14 the United States responded with an aerial attack against Libya. Further terrorist activity in May, June, and July led to a climax on September 2. Gunmen forced their way aboard a Pan Am B-747 on the ground in Karachi, Pakistan, and began shooting and lobbing grenades into the already loaded passenger cabin.

Long before then, however, cancellation of reservations showed that Americans had decided either to spend their vacations at home or to head for Pacific destinations. Rumors of a Pan Am merger or takeover faded, sending the company's stock back to $4. The year ended with a staggering loss of $462 million, and the new year began with a first-quarter loss of $96 million.

On May 25, 1987, *Business Week* reported a Pan Am shareholder revolt that placed Acker's position with the airline in jeopardy. Led by Jeffrey Epstein, chairman of Intercontinental Assets, and backed by 40 percent of voting power, the group demanded control over Pan Am's management. Acker resisted and again turned to the unions, asking for $180 million in annual wage concessions. In the midst of the external battle for control of management, and an internal argument over whether or not to sell the airline or seek new financing, the unions agreed to concessions—provided that Acker was replaced. The company's board of directors complied. In a proxy statement, Pan Am Corporation announced that Acker would be paid $1 million "in connection with [his] termination" on January 21, 1988. Having failed to work a miracle, Acker took his "golden parachute" and retired from the airline wars. Whether this move was temporary or permanent remained to be seen.

References:

"Behind the Rise and Fall of Air Florida," *Business Week* (July 23, 1984): 122-123, 125;

J. A. Donoghue, "Air Florida is on the Prowl . . . and No Market is Safe from its Competition," *Air Transport World*, 17 (May 1981): 32-36;

Louis Kraar, "Putting Pan Am Back Together Again," *Fortune*, 104 (December 28, 1981): 42-47;

Gene G. Marcial, "Sure, Pan Am could be Sold—But Not 'As Is,'" *Business Week* (September 21, 1987): 108;

Marcial, "This Shareholder Uprising May Give Pan Am a Tailwind," *Business Week* (May 25, 1987): 130;

Joseph F. Murphy, "Air Florida's Fortunes Soar in Six Markets," *Airline Executive*, 4 (May 1980): 11-14;

John J. Nance, *Splash of Colors: The Self-Destruction of Braniff International* (New York: Morrow, 1984);

"Pan Am Paid $1 Million to Acker as Departure Fee," *Wall Street Journal*, April 19, 1988, p. 43;

Anita Schrodt, "Acker's Pan Am Comeback," *Airline Executive*, 7 (December 1983): 22-25;

Shawn Tully, "Pan Am's $200-Million Tranquilizer," *Fortune*, 106 (November 29, 1982): 110-112.

Aeromarine Airways

by William M. Leary

University of Georgia

Aeromarine Airways, one of the nation's earliest airlines, traces its beginnings to the efforts of a group of ex-servicemen to capitalize on U.S. Prohibition by flying Americans from Key West, Florida, to Havana, Cuba, where alcohol remained legal. In November 1919 the group incorporated Florida-West Indies Airways under Cuban law and began to search for investors. Although the company secured the first-ever U.S. airmail contract from the Post Office ($20,000 for a daily, except Sunday, trip from Key West to Havana with up to 500 pounds of regular mail), it was unable to raise sufficient funds to begin operations. The owners had no choice but to sell a controlling interest in the airline to Inglis M. Uppercu, president of the Aeromarine Plane and Motor Company, a chief supplier of seaplanes to the U.S. Navy during World War I.

In October 1920 Uppercu formed Aeromarine-West Indies Airways and set out to demonstrate the profitability of commercial air service as a way to promote sales for military aircraft that he was modifying for commercial use at his factory. Twice-daily flights between Key West and Havana began on November 1, 1920, using Curtiss F-5L flying boats that Uppercu had converted into plush commercial airliners. During the first six months of operation the airline carried 1,100 passengers and 34,495 pounds of mail.

In the spring of 1921, with business falling off, Uppercu surrendered the mail contract and transferred his base of operations to New York City. He spent the summer flying charters through the Northeast. He also replaced the old management of the company, which he renamed Aeromarine Airways.

Aeromarine returned to Florida for the winter season of 1921-1922. Although the Post Office did not renew the one-year mail contract, passenger traffic increased by more than 100 percent. The airline made 744 flights between Key West and Havana, carrying 2,399 customers.

During the summer of 1922 Aeromarine not only continued charter operations from New York but also operated a new Great Lakes division. On July 17 daily service began between Cleveland and Detroit. In two months 4,388 passengers traveled by air between the two lakeside cities.

Aeromarine planned to expand service throughout the Caribbean in 1922-1923, but its first fatal accident on January 13, 1923 (in which four passengers drowned following a forced landing in the Straits of Florida), threatened the airline's already-shaky financial base. Only Uppercu's generous subsidy had kept the enterprise economically viable.

Although the Great Lakes division continued to fly throughout the summer of 1923, carrying more than 5,000 passengers between Cleveland and Detroit, Uppercu decided that he could no longer tolerate the airline's financial losses. Having spent $500,000 in promoting commercial aviation, Uppercu gave up and sold the company to the Florida Railroad and Steamship Company. The new owners operated a few charter flights before suspending all service early in 1924.

While not a financial success, Aeromarine Airways compiled an outstanding operational record.

Aeromarine Curtiss F-5L (courtesy of the National Air and Space Museum)

During three and a half years, it flew more than one million passenger-miles and carried over 30,000 passengers with only one serious accident. As historian Edward P. Warner has pointed out, Aeromarine stands as "a landmark in the record of commercial progress." Its inability to survive emphasized the limitations of private enterprise and the need for federal subsidy during the formative years of commercial aviation in the United States.

References:

William M. Leary, *Aerial Pioneers: The U.S. Air Mail Service, 1918-1927* (Washington, D.C.: Smithsonian Institution, 1985);

Leary, "At the Dawn of Commercial Aviation: Inglis M. Uppercu and Aeromarine Airways," *Business History Review*, 53 (Summer 1979): 180-193;

Edward P. Warner, *The Early History of Air Transportation* (York, Penn.: Maple Press, 1938).

African Americans in the Airline Industry

by Theodore W. Robinson

Silver Spring, Maryland

African Americans were completely excluded from the professional and craft ranks of the American airline industry during the first half century of its development. Even in largely blue-collar ground-service positions—"sky caps" in airport terminals or janitors, for example—African Americans occupied a disproportionately small number of positions for much of the early history of the industry. This policy of exclusion in part reflected the practices of established transportation industries: during the same period few blacks were employed as railroad engineers or conductors, ship captains or mates, bus drivers, or truck drivers. But the situation was undoubtedly intensified in the air industry because airline jobs carried with them an even higher amount of prestige—and pay—than other transport jobs.

The first sustained use of air transport began in 1918, when the U.S. Post Office arranged to fly airmail routes using military pilots. Since the military barred African Americans from training to become pilots or flight mechanics, none were available to fly the mail. The civilian flight-training and mechanics' schools that sprouted after commercial companies began flying the mail in 1926 generally followed the existing policy of exclusion, as did the pilots' and mechanics' unions. In spite of all the obstacles, by 1937 four African Americans had managed to earn the Transport License, the highest-level commercial pilots' license; and three—including two of the four Transport License holders—had earned mechanics' licenses. None of those individuals ever found employment in the industry.

In 1939, with war on the horizon, the U.S. Army Air Corps established the Civilian Pilot Training Program, and with that came the first opportunity for African Americans to participate in government-sponsored aviation training. Segregated military training of pilots and mechanics took place at the newly established Tuskegee Army Air Field at

Tuskegee Institute in Alabama, and black pilots and mechanics saw action during World War II as the 99th Fighter Squadron in North Africa and the 332d Fighter Group in Europe. During the war the Air Corps trained a total of 990 black pilots, about 900 of whom survived the fighting and reentered civilian life qualified to work for the commercial airlines. Nevertheless, in the immediate postwar years no African American found work as a pilot for an American airline.

Even though by the end of World War II the air industry unions had removed racially restrictive clauses from their bylaws, the unions—the Air Line Pilots Association, the International Association of Machinists, and the Brotherhood of Railroad and Airline Clerks—continued to practice a de facto policy of segregation. Typically, African Americans who applied for flying jobs were told that their applications could not be accepted because they were not union members. Upon applying to the unions they were told that since they were not working for the airlines they were not eligible to join.

During the 1950s African Americans made the first significant progress in attaining airline industry jobs, largely through the work of state human relations commissions in Massachusetts, New Jersey, and, especially, New York. In response to complaints directed to the New York commission, Colonial Airlines hired a black ticket seller in Manhattan in 1951, and American Airlines hired a black reservations clerk in Buffalo in 1952. By 1960 African Americans had attained nearly proportionate representation in airline office and clerical employment in New York. In 1957 Mohawk Airlines hired a black airline stewardess, and by 1960 Trans World and Capital had done likewise. Interestingly, in a 1931 article in the trade journal *Aviation*, C. B. Allen reported that during the summer of 1930 New England and Western Air hired a group of "negro Pullman Porters as cabin attend-

*Marlon Green, who in 1963 became the first African American hired as a pilot by a commercial passenger
airline (courtesy of J. S. Flipper Learning Resource Center, Allen University, Columbia, S.C.)*

ants with very good results." Allen went on to say that "the porters, once they overcame their nervousness about flying, were tremendously proud of their jobs and, of course, had the necessary training and background to render the right sort of service. From the novice passenger's point of view the experiment was very reassuring, for it supplied the familiar atmosphere of the Pullman car and made flying seem a lot less strange."

African American pilots found it more difficult to break into the ranks of the commercial airlines. In 1955 the cargo carrier World Airways hired August Martin, who later became the first African American to qualify as a captain on a commercial jet aircraft. In 1956 the helicopter airline New York Airways hired Perry Young, a former Army Air Corps pilot trained at Tuskegee Air Field who then found work as a civilian instructor at Tuskegee.

A major breakthrough occurred in 1963, when former air force captain Marlon Green, an African American who applied for a pilot's position at Continental Airlines in 1957, won a discrimina-

tion case before the U.S. Supreme Court. The Court ordered Continental to hire Green and grant him back pay dating from the time of his first interviews for the job. Green had been invited for an interview because he left blank the space on the Continental application asking for racial identity, but, rather than hire a black, Continental hired five whites with less flight time than Green. As he pursued his case through the courts Green had been turned down by no less than ten other commercial airlines.

The hiring of Green by Continental in 1963 took place during a time of great change in American race relations. In the South protesters, black and white alike, were destroying the barriers of racial segregation. The federal government became increasingly involved in civil rights issues. In 1961 President John F. Kennedy issued Executive Order 10925, introducing the concept of "affirmative action" as a way to achieve equal employment of blacks in federal organizations and businesses engaged in interstate commerce. The passage of the Civil Rights Act of 1964 gave further impetus to the drive to give all members of American society an equal opportunity for success.

In responses to federal pressure, the airline industry reluctantly changed its policies. Many airlines inaugurated policies designed to attract qualified African American clerks, office personnel, mechanics, stewardesses, and pilots. Blacks rapidly approached parity in ground jobs and made inroads in the managerial echelon. Although the airlines found that the public readily accepted black stewardesses, in 1969 only .25 percent of the total commercial pilot population of 33,000 was black. By 1978 that figure dropped to only .2 percent out of a total of 53,000. This decline contrasted sharply with the situation among female pilots, the overwhelming majority of which are white. Female pilots were not hired by the airlines in significant numbers until 1972, when the U.S. Army began training women to fly. By 1992 female pilots outnumbered black pilots by a ratio of 4 to 1.

In 1988 a subcommittee of the U.S. House Committee on Government Operations reported that the promise of the 1960s had failed to come to fruition. African Americans occupied fully 30 percent of the unskilled jobs in the airline industry, 14 percent of the semiskilled jobs, and less than 2 percent of the professional positions. Several airlines, including Trans World and United, had been forced by court order to improve minority hiring practices for pilots, managers, and stewardesses.

While African Americans struggled to overcome a tradition of exclusion from employment in the commercial airline industry, a few individuals struck out on their own and founded black-owned airlines. Warren Wheeler, who in 1966 became the first African American hired as a pilot by Piedmont Airlines, founded a flying school that developed in the mid 1970s into Wheeler Airlines, a scheduled service that at its peak in the early 1980s flew five Beechcraft twin-engine turboprops and a 50-seat Fairchild F-27. The pressures of deregulation in 1978 forced Wheeler Airlines to declare bankruptcy in 1986, however, and Wheeler has since reorganized his company on a reduced scale.

In 1981 African American attorney Michael Hollis took advantage of the freedom deregulation brought to the air industry to organize Air Atlanta, which targeted the business traveler using Boeing 727 aircraft carrying reduced numbers of passengers. Air Atlanta also followed such deregulation pioneers as People Express in training employees to perform "collateral" duties: stewardesses worked as reservation clerks, and pilots as public relations officials, for example. The airline operated for three years beginning in 1984 before failing due to inadequate passenger loads.

Future prospects for African Americans as employees and entrepreneurs in the airline industry largely depend on whether American society will accept them as equal members. The question is one of access to the opportunity that already exists. African Americans have proven that they can acquire the skills needed to function at all levels of industry. What seems more difficult is gaining the acknowledgement of industry that this is a sustainable truth, along with a commitment on the part of government to the ideal of equal opportunity for all of the nation's citizens.

References:

C. B. Allen, "The Airline Attendant's Job," *Aviation*, 30 (April 1931): 244-245;

"Black Pilots," *Ebony* (January 1978): 58-66;

Janet L. Fix, "Twelve O'Clock Low," *Forbes*, 137 (June 16, 1986): 58;

Herbert R. Northrup, Armand J. Thieblot, Jr., and William N. Chernish, *The Negro in the Air Transport Industry*, Racial Policies of American Industry Report No. 23 (Philadelphia: University of Pennsylvania, Wharton School of Finance and Commerce, 1971);

Robert J. Serling, *Eagle: The Story of American Airlines* (New York: St. Martin's Press/Marek, 1985);

Henry Ladd Smith, *Airways: The History of Commercial Aviation in the United States* (New York: Knopf, 1942);

United States Congress, House Committee on Government Operations, *Slow Progress Regarding Affirmative Action in the Airline Industry*, 100th Congress, 2d Session, 56th Report, July 19, 1988 (Washington, D.C.: U.S. Government Printing Office, 1988).

Air California

by Myron J. Smith, Jr.

Tusculum College

Launched in mid December 1965 and granted a California certificate in 1966, Air California began service between Los Angeles and San Francisco with Lockheed Electras in January 1967. With 650,000 passenger boardings during its first year of operations, the airline became one of the quickest starters in pre-deregulation U.S. commercial aviation history.

Air California expanded operations to Oakland and San Jose in 1968, ordering DC-9s and Boeing 737s. Passenger traffic and revenues continued to increase, and the company recorded its first real profit in 1972. Westgate-California Corporation obtained a controlling interest in the airline in June 1970 and full ownership in October 1977.

In 1978, following passage of the Airline Deregulation Act, Air California broke into the ranks of the interstate carriers when it extended service to Reno, Nevada. The following year, during which it inaugurated a route to Las Vegas, passenger boardings rose 20.1 percent. At the same time, the fleet's last three Electras were phased out, making the airline an all-jet carrier. Service to Portland, Oregon, was begun in 1980, and traffic accelerated by 4.8 percent for the year. Following adoption of a new Civil Aeronautics Board (CAB) classification scheme, Air California was rerated a national carrier, based upon its income of $159 million and net profit of $9.8 million.

A bidding war with Air Florida was resolved in May 1981 when William Lyon and George L. Argyros purchased the company from Westgate Corporation for $61.5 million. The new owners immediately changed the name of their prize to AirCal and adopted a new corporate identification program. Meanwhile, Phoenix and Seattle were added to the route system, new DC-9s were acquired, and passenger boardings rose 16.7 percent from 1980 to 1981. Despite an operating loss of $1.3 million,

due in part to the effects of the PATCO air traffic controllers strike, the airline posted a net profit of $5.6 million.

Financial difficulties in 1982 forced AirCal to drop its Phoenix, Fresno, Monterey, and Las Vegas service as traffic dipped 1.2 percent. Although the airline eliminated four Boeing 737s and acquired two DC-9-80s, it reported to the CAB that expenses exceeded income. AirCal recorded revenues of $214.7 million, but expenses of $235.4 million caused a net loss of $35.6 million.

After adjusting its route structure, streamlining its cost management, and accelerating its marketing, AirCal experienced a remarkable turnaround in 1983. Redeploying many of its 16 Boeing 737s and 7 McDonnell-Douglas MD-80s into California's north-south corridor and increasing scheduling, it enplaned a record 3.5 million passengers and increased revenues by 11.3 percent. Coupled with a 5.8 percent decline in expenses, the amount of net loss improved as red ink fell to only $2.9 million. With continued aggressive marketing, AirCal's economic health made even more rapid progress in 1984. Traffic rose 11.9 percent to $304 million, and expenses, though rising 26 percent to $279.5 million, were sufficiently under control to allow a net profit of $8.5 million. As new Boeing 737-300s were added in 1985, AirCal became an international carrier in June when it began scheduled flights to Vancouver, British Columbia. Again, increased traffic offset rising expenses to produce a net profit of $9.2 million.

On November 17, 1986, American Airlines announced plans to purchase AirCal, which had lost $6.2 million during the first nine months of the year, for $225 million. The Department of Transportation approved the agreement in March 1987, commenting that there was no evidence that the merger would harm competition.

References:
R. E. G. Davies, *Airlines of the United States since 1914*, revised edition (Washington, D.C.: Smithsonian Institution, 1982);
Scott Hamilton, "All's Quiet on the West Coast Front ... For Now," *Airline Executive*, 10 (December 1986): 32-37;

Danna K. Henderson, "AirCal Moves in Right Direction," *Air Transport World*, 21 (September 1984): 70-72;
Henry Lefer, "AirCal Builds New Niche in Tough California Corridor," *Air Transport World*, 21 (February 1984): 60-61.

Air Commerce Act of 1926

by William M. Leary

University of Georgia

The Air Commerce Act of 1926 provided the essential regulatory structure for the early development of commercial aviation in the United States. Long in gestation, it placed responsibility squarely on the federal government for establishing and maintaining airways and aids to navigation, licensing aircraft and airmen, and in general overseeing the development and safe operation of a national system of air transportation.

In 1919 the National Advisory Committee for Aeronautics formulated a policy for federal regulation of civil aviation. President Woodrow Wilson approved the legislative draft of the government's expert body on aeronautical matters, but Congress failed to take action on the proposal. Similar regulatory schemes were discussed on Capitol Hill over the following six years, but none came to fruition. Debates over legislative action focused less on the need for federal regulation than on its form. In the absence of effective executive leadership and significant public pressure, Congress embarked on a seemingly interminable series of investigations while pleas from the aviation community for action went unanswered.

The impetus for legislative action finally came in 1925. In February, President Calvin Coolidge approved the Air Mail Act of 1925, setting the stage for a flurry of commercial aviation activity. As historian Thomas Worth Walterman has pointed out, this increased business interest in civil aviation "made eventual regulation by the federal government inevitable."

Later in the year, in the wake of Gen. William "Billy" Mitchell's charges of incompetence and criminal negligence in the conduct of aeronautical activities by the War and Navy Departments, President Coolidge appointed a prestigious special board, headed by Dwight W. Morrow, to look into and make recommendations about a national aviation policy. In December the Morrow Board proposed, with respect to civil aviation, that the government regulate commercial activity through the Department of Commerce. Secretary of Commerce Herbert Hoover, with Coolidge's warm approval, took the lead in shaping the specifics of the new national aviation policy. The result was the Air Commerce Act of 1926, signed into law on May 20. Hoover quickly created a Bureau of Aeronautics to administer the law and appointed William P. MacCracken, Jr., as the first assistant secretary of commerce for aeronautics. By the end of the year, private enterprise had the legal foundations and regulatory structure necessary to build an airline industry.

References:
Nick A. Komons, *Bonfires to Beacons: Federal Civil Aviation Policy under the Air Commerce Act, 1926-1938* (Washington, D.C.: U.S. Department of Transportation, 1978);
David D. Lee, "Herbert Hoover and the Golden Age of Aviation," in *Aviation's Golden Age*, edited by William M. Leary (Iowa City: University of Iowa Press, 1989), pp. 127-148;
Henry Ladd Smith, *Airways: The History of Commercial Aviation in the United States* (New York: Knopf, 1942);
Thomas Worth Walterman, "Airpower and Private Enterprise: Federal-Industrial Relations in the Aeronautics Field, 1918-1926," dissertation, Washington University, 1970;
Donald R. Whitnah, *Safer Skyways: Federal Control of Aviation* (Ames: Iowa State University Press, 1966).

Air Florida

by William M. Leary

University of Georgia

Founded in 1972 by Miami entrepreneur Eli Timoner, Air Florida had an unpromising beginning as a struggling intrastate airline. By 1976 it was using three Lockheed Electra turboprops to serve four cities. Air Florida carried 191,600 passengers during that year and lost $748,000. In 1977, however, Texas financial expert C. Edward Acker joined the airline, bringing with him $2 million in new capital that had been provided by Carl Lindner, a Cincinnati private investor. Although Timoner remained as president, operational control of the company passed to Acker, former head of Braniff Airways.

Following passage of the Airline Deregulation Act of 1978, Air Florida embarked upon a policy of rapid expansion. Acker took over Air Sunshine, a Key West-based commuter line, acquired Boeing 737-200 jet transports, and opened service from Miami to Washington, D.C., and the Bahamas. In 1979, with new routes to Philadelphia, New York City, and the Caribbean, Air Florida transported over one million passengers and posted a profit of $2.4 million. The airline's best year came in 1980. Flying regular service between Miami and London with DC-10s, operating more than 100 charter flights to England and Switzerland, and starting new routes to Central America, Air Florida recorded net earnings of $5.1 million.

Many observers came to regard Air Florida as a shining example of the beneficent effects of deregulation. "The little airline that could" seemed destined to join the giants of the industry. With low labor costs, thanks in large part to high utilization of its nonunion flight crews, and minimum service (no hot meals), Air Florida could charge lower fares than its competitors and still make money. Its stock, which sold for $3 a share in 1977, rose to over $17 in mid 1981, attesting to the airline's performance—and future prospects.

Following a successful $40 million public stock offering in May 1981, investor Lindner sold out. In September, chairman Acker left Air Florida to become head of Pan American World Airways. The following month, as the market value of Air Florida began to plummet, Acker sold the balance of his 450,000 shares of stock in the company at $9.75. Air Florida recorded a loss of $5.9 million for the year.

Disaster followed in 1982. On January 13 one of the airline's Boeing 737s plunged into the Potomac River while attempting to take off from Washington's National Airport. The accident received wide publicity, focusing attention on the airline and exposing its underlying weakness. Air Florida was highly leveraged, with a debt that was 3.7 times the airline's equity. It owned few of its airplanes, flying mostly leased equipment. It never made money on its scheduled passenger service, its profit coming from aircraft sales, financial deals, and charter flights. In 1982 the charter business fell off. Furthermore, Acker at Pan American launched a fare war in Florida against his former company. By May, Air Florida's stock was down to $1 a share. The airline posted a staggering $93.4 million loss at the end of the year.

Air Florida tried to retrench in 1983, reducing the size of its staff by one-third and emphasizing interstate service. But the red ink continued to flow, and the airline recorded a $39.2 million loss for the year. As creditors began to seize the airline's limited assets, Air Florida filed for protection under chapter 11 of the bankruptcy laws. With a negative net worth of $81 million, the once-promising air carrier had become a case study in the pitfalls of deregulation.

References:

"Behind the Rise and Fall of Air Florida," *Business Week* (July 23, 1984): 122-123, 125;

J. A. Donoghue, "Air Florida is on the Prowl . . . and No Market is Safe from its Competition," *Air Transport World*, 17 (May 1981): 32-36;

Joseph S. Murphy, "Air Florida's Fortunes Soar in Six Mar-

ket Areas," *Airline Executive*, 4 (May 1980): 11-14; John J. Nance, *Blind Trust: The Human Crisis in Airline Safety* (New York: Morrow, 1986).

Airline Deregulation Act of 1978

by Donald R. Whitnah

University of Northern Iowa

Passage of the Airline Deregulation Act in October 1978 marked a retreat by the federal government from a policy of strict economic control over the commercial airline industry that had begun with the enactment of the Civil Aeronautics Act of 1938. The earlier law had charged a five-member Civil Aeronautics Authority—later, Civil Aeronautics Board (CAB)—with responsibility for promoting an "adequate, economical, and efficient" airline system that would provide service at a "reasonable charge" to the traveling public. Competition would be permitted "to the extent necessary to assure the sound development of an air transportation system." Over the next four decades the federal regulatory agency sought to fulfill its legislative mandate through control of entry, routes, and rates. For the most part it succeeded: the nation's scheduled airlines grew to maturity under the government's paternalistic guidance, providing the American traveler with the world's finest airline system.

A series of economic shocks in the early 1970s, however, revealed the flaws in the regulatory structure. The hard times began in 1970. Just as the airlines introduced a new series of wide-bodied jets (Boeing 747s, McDonnell Douglas DC-10s, and Lockheed L-1011s), an economic recession slowed demand for air travel. The resulting excess capacity led to a staggering loss of $100 million for the nation's 11 domestic trunk carriers.

The situation only grew worse as the American economy wrestled with the twin ills of recession and inflation. The hardest blow to the airline industry came late in 1973 when the oil crisis sent fuel prices skyrocketing. Until this time the cost of fuel contributed about 10 percent to airline direct operating costs; almost overnight the figure rose to over 20 percent.

The airlines cried out for higher fares. In December 1973 the CAB responded with a 5 percent increase. This helped, but it left the airlines far from satisfied. Unless additional increases were soon forthcoming, a Pan American official warned, it might be necessary to seek a subsidy. Other airline executives painted a grim scenario that saw the airlines going the way of the railroads, with subsidy leading to an eventual takeover by the government.

As the economic fortunes of the nation's airlines declined, the federal regulatory structure came under increasing attack from both the political right and left. On the one hand, advocates of a free market economy on President Gerald R. Ford's Council of Economic Advisers, officials in the Office of Management and Budget, members of other executive agencies, and influential congressmen, all agreed that federal regulation fostered inefficiency. The less government interference with business, the better, they felt. At the same time, consumer advocates both in and out of Congress reached a similar conclusion: government regulation was protecting an inefficient industry and leading to higher airfares.

In February 1974 officials in the Ford administration announced that legislation would be proposed later in the year to deregulate the airline industry. Under the new scheme airlines would be given greater freedom to set their own fares and select their own routes. Also, new companies would be allowed to enter and compete against the CAB-protected airlines.

While the administration was developing its plans to deregulate the industry, Senator Edward M. Kennedy was conducting an investigation of the CAB. Kennedy's Subcommittee on Administrative Practice and Procedure held hearings in February and March, examining witnesses from the airlines, unions, federal agencies, and other interested parties. The hearings documented the inefficiency of the regulated airlines, contrasting them unfavorably with the more efficient intrastate airlines in California and Texas. The regulated airlines, it was pointed out, had no incentives to reduce costs, which would be passed along to the consumer by a compliant CAB. For example, between 1968 and 1972 average pay for airline employees rose by 51 percent at a time when average pay for all U.S. workers rose by only 28 percent. In all too many cases, the subcommittee concluded, the CAB "has chosen to protect the industry at the expense of the consumer." Deregulation, the report continued, would lead to lower prices for the consumer while enhancing airline productivity and efficiency.

Even the CAB saw the handwriting on the wall. In July a CAB task force issued a report that supported deregulation. It proposed a relaxation of control over exit and entry and an easing of rate regulation. These reforms would take place over a period of three to five years.

The only opposition to the tidal wave of sentiment for deregulation came from the regulated carriers and their unions. The Air Transport Association (ATA), the industry trade organization, took the lead in arguing against deregulation. "It would adversely affect millions of passengers and shippers," the ATA claimed, "thousands of businesses in hundreds of communities, the reliable transportation of the mail, the welfare of 300,000 airline employees, millions of shareholders, investors holding billions of dollars of airline debt, aircraft manufacturers and suppliers and will endanger the financial integrity of the nation's vital airport system."

While Congress considered legislation to deregulate the industry, the CAB experimented with fare competition. During the Ford years the CAB approved deeply discounted fares by Texas International ("Peanut Fares") and American Airlines ("Super Savers"). This trend accelerated after President Jimmy Carter appointed Alfred E. Kahn to head the CAB in 1977. Initial results of the new policy seemed promising, as fares went down and airline profits rose.

On April 19, 1978, the Senate passed its version of the deregulation legislation by the wide nonpartisan margin of 83 to 9. The House acted on September 21, voting 363 to 8 for a measure that not only would deregulate the industry but also abolish the CAB. The Senate accepted the House version, which was signed into law by President Carter on October 28.

The Airline Deregulation Act placed "maximum reliance on competitive market forces" to determine the course of the airline industry. It mandated a gradual relaxation of CAB regulation. The CAB's authority over routes would lapse on January 1, 1981; its control of fares would end on January 1, 1983; and the board itself would cease operations by January 1, 1985.

In practice the transition to deregulation happened with much greater speed than the law envisioned. By spring 1980 airlines had almost total freedom to determine routes and fares.

The first years of deregulation saw intense competition, with wild fare discounting and with new airlines appearing almost daily. As it happened the transition to the new system could not have come at a worse time. An economic recession caused passenger traffic to slump. At the same time, another oil crisis caused the price of jet fuel to double. The result of these factors could be measured by the airlines in red ink.

After the initial shock of deregulation had worn off, the major airlines responded to the new competitive environment with an emphasis on hub-and-spoke route structures. Several large carriers, with American Airlines in the lead, acquired fuel efficient aircraft, developed efficient route structures, and made do with smaller and more productive work forces. Weaker carriers soon went under, either disappearing into bankruptcy or merging with stronger companies. By the early 1990s all the airlines that had entered the industry since deregulation had disappeared, with the exception of America West (which was operating under Chapter 11 of the bankruptcy laws). As a few giant carriers came to dominate the industry, competition faded, fares increased, service deteriorated, and profits remained elusive, the virtues of deregulation seemed less clear in the 1990s than they had been in the 1970s.

References:

Anthony E. Brown, *The Politics of Airline Deregulation* (Knoxville: University of Tennessee Press, 1987);

Paul Stephen Dempsey, *Flying Blind: The Failure of Airline Deregulation* (Washington, D.C.: Economic Policy Institute, 1990);

Steven A. Morrison, *The Economic Effects of Airline Deregulation* (Washington, D.C.: Brookings Institution, 1986);

Louis Uchitelle, "Off Course," *New York Times Magazine*, September 1, 1991, pp. 12, 14-17, 25-27; Richard H. K. Vietor, "Contrived Competition: Airline Regulation and Deregulation, 1925-1988," *Business History Review*, 64 (Spring 1990): 61-108.

Air Line Pilots Association

by George E. Hopkins

Western Illinois University

The Air Line Pilots Association (ALPA) is a labor union which represents most of the professional airline pilots in the United States. The origins of the ALPA lie in the peculiar working conditions of the first generation of professional airline pilots during the late 1920s.

The Post Office Department's Air Mail Service (AMS) offered the first significant employment for pilots. Early experiments using army pilots to fly the mail proved successful, so the Post Office began a civilian service devoted to high priority mail and freight. By the early 1920s, AMS pilots were spanning the continent in open cockpit aircraft, night and day, over a system of lighted federal airways. The AMS was dangerous work—a pilot who flew during the entire period of postal operations, from 1918 to 1928, stood one chance in four of being killed. Still, it was a glamorous and well-paying position. Counting all forms of compensation, an AMS pilot could earn as much as $1,000 per month.

Congress clearly saw the AMS as a developmental project to prepare the way for private contractors. The Air Mail Act of 1925 and the Air Commerce Act of 1926 created a system of privately operated airmail routes under government regulation. Between 1926 and 1928, as the successful bidders began flying the postal routes, former AMS pilots found themselves either without jobs or forced to work for private contractors. While labor relations between the Post Office and its pilots had not always been smooth (there had been a formal strike of airmail pilots over safety in 1919), discontent with the policies of the new airmail contractors spread rapidly among pilots, particularly those who had flown for the Post Office. Generally the new airmail contractors continued paying pilots the old AMS scale, but they clearly intended to change their pilots' wages and working conditions.

The leader of the effort to form a union of professional airline pilots was David L. Behncke, a United Air Lines pilot based in Chicago. Although many pilots were wary of the connection with organized labor, Behncke persuaded a core constituency to affiliate with the American Federation of Labor (AFL). On July 27, 1931, after an intense period of secret organization, a convention of "Key Men" (organizers who had persuaded the pilots of their respective airlines to sign an undated letter of resignation and contribute $50 in "escrow") met at the Morrison Hotel in Chicago to ratify the formal affiliation with the AFL. On August 10, 1931, the AFL formally granted a charter to Behncke's group, naming it the sole agent empowered to represent the "craft of airline pilot."

During the first decade of its existence, ALPA avoided direct bargaining with employers. Instead the pilots sought protection of their wages and working conditions through federal legislation. Since former airmail pilots made up the core of ALPA, the wages and working conditions they favored closely resembled the Post Office pay system, which consisted of base pay, per diem, increments for day and night flying, and a mileage increment for difficult terrain.

One striking fact about the period of ALPA's formation is that only a few pilots actually had their wages cut or their work load increased. It was the fear of changes, rather than the fact of them, which motivated pilots. Owing to the deflationary cycle which followed the onset of the depression of 1929, most pilots' relative economic condition actually improved, since their wages remained stable. But there was widespread fear among pilots that their status as professionals was eroding. The pilots saw themselves as the only guarantors of air safety, and they believed that increased hours of flying, which their new employers wanted, would lead to more accidents. These fears were not without foundation.

Most of the established operators continued the pay practices of the Post Office, but they were vulnerable to those who did not. Several aspiring airmail contractors, such as E. L. Cord, saw that by taking advantage of the large pool of qualified pilots, many of whom were willing to work for practically nothing, airmail operations could be immensely profitable. Cord and other potential airline operators hoped to underbid the existing contractors, but President Herbert Hoover's postmaster general, Walter Folger Brown (the de facto czar of the airlines owing to his control of the airmail subsidy system), prevented people like Cord from obtaining contracts during the airmail bidding of 1930. Brown wanted the new airlines to operate with substantial financial reserves, which only large corporations could provide. Brown was justifiably suspicious of small operators, but his actions would lead, in 1934, to President Roosevelt's cancellation of the contracts of 1930. ALPA, almost alone among industry insiders, sided with Roosevelt during this controversy, thus demonstrating political loyalty and gaining credit for future battles.

Shortly after the airmail contracts of 1930 were let, Cord began Century Airlines, a passenger service whose purpose was to demonstrate to an economy-minded Congress the efficiencies of a low-wage operation. The Century pilots rebelled at Cord's labor strategies and sought affiliation with ALPA, whereupon Cord locked them out and hired replacements. The "Century Strike," which began in February 1932, offered ALPA the opportunity to build political alliances in Congress. Cord was unpopular with many liberal politicians because of his antiunionism, so supporting ALPA was for them an easy way to curry favor with organized labor. During 1932 ALPA built a coalition in Congress which denied Cord a mail contract, gained favorable national publicity, and established good relations with powerful politicians, most notably Representative Fiorello H. La Guardia, who criticized Cord for paying pilots "less than a union truck driver gets in New York."

These connections proved crucial in establishing Decision 83 during the early New Deal. The National Industrial Recovery Act was the most radical New Deal program. It created the National Recovery Administration (NRA), under which each industry was encouraged to draw up a code of Fair Competition designed to make cooperation rather than competition the basis for economic recovery. Each code specified wages and working conditions for labor. The Air Transport Code offered management an ideal way to change pilot wages and working conditions. ALPA resisted these proposals, threatened a nationwide strike in 1933 when management sought to implement changes unilaterally, and secured a special "Fact Finding Committee" from the National Labor Board (NLB), an NRA agency. The committee, chaired by retired New York jurist Bernard L. Shientag, exempted the pilots from regulation by the Air Transport Code, thus leaving intact the existing pay system. Subsequently this finding was formalized as Decision 83 of the NLB. Through intense lobbying, ALPA incorporated the substance of Decision 83 in subsequent federal aviation legislation, including the Civil Aeronautics Act of 1938. ALPA had thus secured for airline pilots a unique position as wards of the federal government, with their wages and working conditions legislatively protected. In 1936 ALPA won a pilots' amendment to the Railway Labor Act, which provided a means of grievance resolution.

Shortly before World War II, ALPA began negotiating contracts with each airline. By avoiding industrywide bargaining, using the technique of "jacking up the house one corner at a time," ALPA made its members affluent. It won a strike against National Airlines in 1948 and secured incremental gains as new, multiengine aircraft entered service.

Behncke himself failed to keep pace with changes in the industry and was ousted from office in 1952. His replacement was Clarence N. Sayen, a former Braniff pilot who had been Behncke's administrative assistant. Sayen proved an astute bargainer who won truly impressive wage gains for pilots during the jet era. This progress was not achieved without strife, but the pilots proved adept at "job actions" (strikes) during the 1950s. Under Sayen, ALPA became more involved in technical matters, particularly safety and crew complement. The latter of these issues involved ALPA in a bitter jurisdictional dispute with the flight engineers' union. ALPA insisted that all flight deck crew members be qualified as pilots. By negotiating contracts which required employers to pay for the flight training of engineers, ALPA sapped support for the flight engineers' union. Few professional flight engineers could resist the opportunity to improve their own fortunes in ALPA at the expense of their former union.

Despite his success, Sayen's acerbic, professorial manner irritated many pilots. He faced considerable internal opposition throughout his career, much of it stemming from the fact that he had never been a captain and had no intention of returning to flying. In 1962, beleaguered by the long strike on Southern Airways (which ALPA eventually won) and a running dispute with detractors on American Airlines, Sayen resigned in midterm.

Sayen's successor, Charles H. Ruby, weathered the worst crisis in ALPA's history to that date when he held the union together following the defection of the American Airlines pilots. ALPA stood a real chance of disintegrating owing to the declining sense of unionism which characterized pilot opinion during the period of strict government regulation. Most pilots took their protected position for granted and became increasingly conservative politically, unaware that free market forces would have a profound impact upon them. Ruby, who was quite conservative himself, distanced ALPA from the mainstream of organized labor during the 1960s. His era saw ALPA move its national headquarters from Chicago to Washington, D.C., and assume a prominent role in the fight against air piracy. Many pilots disapproved of his stewardship, but he survived two full terms in office, finally retiring in 1970.

Ruby's successor was John J. O'Donnell, an Eastern Air Lines captain with a long history of union activism. During his tenure O'Donnell repaired the breach with organized labor and confronted the most serious crisis in ALPA's history since the 1963 American Airlines defection—airline deregulation. The Airline Deregulation Act of 1978 subjected airline pilots to the vagaries of the free market for the first time since the 1920s.

Deregulation's impact proved devastating. Literally thousands of professional airline pilots lost their jobs as long-established carriers like Braniff and Continental either failed or won disputes with ALPA. During the 1980s, airline pilots as a group saw their wages and working conditions erode as they sought to assist their employers through concessions. Ruthless cost cutting by employers such as Frank Lorenzo, stiff competition from nonunion carriers, and several lost strikes further damaged ALPA. A significant success during a strike against United in 1985 leavened the gloom somewhat, but overall, J. J. O'Donnell's successor, Henry A. Duffy, who assumed office in 1983, has confronted crises his successors never envisioned. Despite the antilabor atmosphere of the recent past, ALPA remains the most important institutional voice for professional pilots. It represents 32,000 active airline pilots and holds bargaining rights for an additional 8,000 apprentices and inactive members.

References:

George E. Hopkins, *The Airline Pilots: A Study in Elite Unionization* (Cambridge, Mass.: Harvard University Press, 1971);

Hopkins, "The Century Strike—1932," *Air Line Pilot,* 44 (March 1975): 30-33, 51;

Hopkins, *Flying the Line: The First Half Century of the Air Line Pilots Association* (Washington, D.C.: Air Line Pilots Association, 1982).

Archives:

Records of the Air Line Pilots Association are housed at the Walter P. Reuther Library, Wayne State University, Detroit, Michigan.

Air Mail Act of 1925

by Donald R. Whitnah

University of Northern Iowa

Mail was first carried by plane in the United States on September 23, 1911, but it was thirteen and a half years before Congress enacted a law regulating airmail service. Meanwhile, using planes, pilots, and mechanics supplied by the U.S. Army, the Post Office inaugurated regular airmail service between Washington, D.C., and New York City in May 1918. After the Republican administration of President Warren G. Harding assumed office in 1921, debate began over the role airline companies might play in expanding the service. Several ensuing attempts to pass legislation granting private enterprise a place in the airmail business failed, largely because congressmen and the business community could not agree on the amount of subsidy the government should award for performing the service. Finally, however, a bill introduced by Representative M. Clyde Kelly passed Congress and was signed into law by President Calvin Coolidge as the Air Mail Act of 1925.

The Air Mail Act of 1925 gave the U.S. postmaster general the authority to award contracts to commercial aviation firms to deliver the mail at rates not to exceed 80 percent of the revenue the Post Office could generate from a charge of 10 cents per ounce of airmail. In addition, the act allowed contractors to carry first class mail, earning 80 percent of the revenue thereof, until the airmail business expanded sufficiently to furnish consistent full loads at the 10 percent rate.

As had been predicted, the act proved a boon to the commercial air industry. William M. Leary reports that it "drew highly influential businessmen and financiers into aeronautics and led to the rapid growth of new companies." Soon after its passage in February 1925, the Ford Motor Company started a private air freight service to carry company cargo, and Henry Ford announced his intention to increase his firm's involvement in aviation. In May automotive entrepreneur Howard E. Coffin

declared his intention to bid for the Post Office business with the formation of National Air Transport, capitalized at $10 million. By late August some 50 aviation concerns were at some stage of formation, and the Post Office began the process of evaluating the many applications it received for contract airmail service. In October the first five contractors were announced: Colonial Air Transport would fly the Boston-New York route; Robertson Aircraft Corporation the Chicago-St. Louis route; National Air Transport the Chicago-Dallas route; Western Air Express the Salt Lake City-Los Angeles route; and Varney Air Transport the route from Elko, Nevada, to Pasco, Washington. Coffin's company led the effort to spur the federal government to pass aviation regulatory legislation in order to safeguard the expected expansion in commercial aviation, and the resulting Air Commerce Act of 1926 gave the government the responsibility of establishing airways and air-navigation aids and licensing methods for pilots and aircraft.

Though it intended to remove itself from the aviation business as soon as it could do so, the Post Office continued to operate the backbone of its airmail system, the New York-San Francisco transcontinental route, while it evaluated the companies it charged with operating the service. In early 1926 Henry Ford received a contract to carry the mail from Detroit to Cleveland and Chicago, and Ford airplanes became the first actually to begin operations under the Post Office contracts. Between February 1926 and April 1927, monthly contract mileage rose from 328 to 4,713. Rates were changed, eventually to a flat rate of 10 cents per half-ounce of mail in February 1927, and mail loads steadily increased. The Post Office awarded the Chicago-San Francisco section of the transcontinental route to Boeing Air Transport in January 1927, and in April it awarded the New York-Chicago route to National Air Transport. Post Office planes ceased flying the mail on September 1, 1927.

References:
William M. Leary, *Aerial Pioneers: The U.S. Air Mail Ser-*

vice, 1918-1927 (Washington, D.C.: Smithsonian Institution, 1985);
Carl H. Scheele, *A Short History of the Mail Service* (Washington, D.C.: Smithsonian Institution, 1970).

Air Mail Act of 1930

by David D. Lee

Western Kentucky University

The Air Mail Act of 1930, also known as the Watres Act, attempted to rationalize the fledgling commercial aviation industry and to rescue it from the impact of the Great Depression. Previous airmail legislation created no incentive for contractors to carry passengers nor did it provide extra pay for contractors who flew difficult routes or purchased better equipment. The chief architect of Hoover administration aviation policy, Postmaster General Walter Folger Brown, wanted a compensation formula which would encourage operators to buy larger, better-equipped planes and to establish regularly scheduled passenger flights. Dubious about the value of competitive bidding on airmail contracts, Brown intended to award them by negotiation as a subsidy for the larger, well-financed operators who could provide efficient and dependable service. Instead of compensating carriers on a weight formula, he preferred a space per mile system which would encourage the operators to carry passengers and freight as well as mail. He also wanted them to use multimotored cabin aircraft equipped with two-way radio communication. Airmail contracts would support the industry until a sufficient market developed in the private sector.

William P. MacCracken, Paul Henderson, and Mabel Walker Willebrandt, people with considerable aviation experience in government and business, joined Brown and his assistant W. Irving Glover in drafting a new airmail bill. The proposed legislation would authorize any airmail contractor with two years of operating experience to exchange his contract for a ten-year route certificate. While a route certificate would give the contractor a sense of permanence and an incentive to invest, it would also permit the postmaster general to reduce payments through negotiation. The bill changed the

method of compensation to a space-mile formula, eliminated competitive bidding, and permitted the postmaster general to extend and consolidate mail routes in the public interest.

Brown's proposal received a hostile reception on Capitol Hill. Convinced that the bill gave the postmaster general too much power, Representative M. Clyde Kelly and others insisted Congress should not compromise the principle of competitive bidding. Comptroller General John McCarl also vigorously supported competitive bidding. When Kelly's influence with the House leadership prevented the bill from reaching the floor, MacCracken engineered a compromise which eliminated the provisions giving Brown the power to evade competitive bidding. Airmail subcommittee chairman Representative Laurence Watres then introduced the revised bill.

Although it was quickly approved, the final version of the bill disappointed Brown. Still committed to his original plans for the industry, he called a meeting of the airmail contractors, a session later denounced as a "spoils conference." The Watres Act authorized the postmaster general to use the airmail contracts as an instrument of industrial rationalization, and Brown was inviting the airmail contractors to join him in the process. The subsequent charges of collusion seem to have been tangential to the real purpose of the meetings, namely to formulate a coordinated response to economic trauma created by the needs of a new industry and compounded by the Depression. In that sense, the spoils conferences were not only typical of the recovery mechanisms devised by the Hoover administration, but also they anticipated the industrywide conferences arranged during the New Deal under the National Industrial Recovery Act.

Crucial to Brown's regulatory strategy was the achieving of consensus by the industry on an appropriate solution for its problems. Aware of how deeply the operators distrusted each other, he anticipated that they would ask him to referee their disputes. When they ultimately did so, Brown forcefully imposed his own solutions. Initially he extended the routes of existing contractors, thereby molding the air network to his model while avoiding competitive bidding. However, Comptroller General McCarl ruled that such extensions must be modest and not major additions to the original route, so Brown used another strategy to avoid competitive bidding. He adopted a suggestion from MacCracken that bidders be required to have at least six months of night-flying experience over routes of at least 250 miles. Because only mail carriers had such experience, the provision effectively excluded the independents from bidding.

Brown now proceeded to dominate the field, ruthlessly managing the contracts to nurture the strong companies and to eliminate the weak. He functioned almost as a public utility commission might, determining routes, setting bidding conditions, and establishing rates. The results were dramatic. By 1933 the nation was bound together by eight north-south lines as well as the three transcontinental routes. Passenger-carrying lines were prospering in the midst of the nation's worst depression, and mail rates per mile had fallen from $1.09 to 54 cents. Nevertheless, Brown's highhanded approach and expansive interpretation of the Watres Act created many enemies for his system. The process of awarding contracts seemed tainted by collusion, and company profits seemed excessive to a depression-battered public suspicious of the business community. The Black committee investigation of 1934 discredited and overturned much of the work of the Brown years.

References:

Paul David, *The Economics of Air Mail Transportation* (Washington, D.C.: Brookings Institution, 1934);

Nick A. Komons, *Bonfires to Beacons: Federal Civil Aviation Policy under the Air Commerce Act, 1926-1938* (Washington, D.C.: U.S. Department of Transportation, 1978);

Henry Ladd Smith, *Airways: The History of Commercial Aviation in the United States* (New York: Knopf, 1942);

Francis A. Spencer, *Air Mail Payment and the Government* (Washington, D.C.: Brookings Institution, 1941).

Air Mail Act of 1934

by David D. Lee

Western Kentucky University

The Air Mail Act of 1934, also known as the Black-McKellar Act, grew out of Senator Hugo Black's investigation of airmail contracts awarded by Postmaster General Walter Folger Brown during the Hoover administration. Forged in a politically charged atmosphere, the law addressed perceived abuses of the Brown years without developing a comprehensive plan for commercial aviation. Under its provisions, three government agencies administered an awkward and unwieldy airmail system. The Post Office Department awarded contracts based on competitive bidding at rates substantially lower than those of the Brown years. Once contracts were let, the Interstate Commerce Commission (ICC) could lower rates it believed resulted in excess profits. Finally the Commerce Department continued to license pilots and assure the safety of equipment and procedures.

The act also sought to decentralize the industry and to restrict the profits of individuals. It outlawed interlocking directorates between contractors and other aviation interests, prohibited mergers between competing companies, and capped the salaries of company officials at $17,500 per year. As a check against excess profits, it required companies to list those who held over 5 percent of their stock and the original amounts paid for it. No contractor could employ any of the participants in the 1930 "spoils conference" convened by Brown, a requirement which ended the careers of some 30 leading figures in the industry. Finally, the law created the Federal Aviation Commission to study the problems of air transport and make recommendations, a provision which suggested the temporary nature of the Black-McKellar Act itself.

Companies hoped that the bidding conducted in March 1934, shortly before the Black-McKellar Act passed, would result in only short-term contracts, so many made painfully low bids to assure themselves of getting the routes they sought. However, the act extended those original 90-day contracts to a year and authorized the Post Office Department to extend them indefinitely. Moreover, the ICC concluded that while it had the power to lower rates, the act did not authorize the agency to raise them. The situation forced companies to compete, often in destructive ways, for passengers in order to earn badly needed revenue. To ameliorate these problems, Congress passed the Mead-McKellar Amendment in 1935. Incorporating changes recommended by the Federal Aviation Commission, the amendment permitted the ICC to raise rates and limited competition for passenger and express service.

A victory for advocates of small business and enforced competition, the Black-McKellar Act, un-like most 1930s transportation laws, tried to restore competition rather then eliminate it. Unfortunately the law dealt only with airmail while ignoring the broader problem of commercial aviation in general. The carriers lost money and many provided inferior service. The blacklisting of the spoils conference participants raised civil liberties questions. The divided responsibility for setting rates created considerable friction between the Post Office Department and the ICC. The Civil Aeronautics Act of 1938, influenced by the recommendations of the Federal Aviation Commission, largely superseded it and returned the industry to the more regulated environment of the early 1930s.

References:
R. E. G. Davies, *Airlines of the United States since 1914* (London: Putnam's, 1972);

Nick A. Komons, *Bonfires to Beacons: Federal Civil Aviation Policy under the Air Commerce Act, 1926-1938* (Washington, D.C.: U.S. Department of Transportation, 1978);

Henry Ladd Smith, *Airways: The History of Commercial Aviation in the United States* (New York: Knopf, 1942);

Francis A. Spencer, *Air Mail Payment and the Government* (Washington, D.C.: Brookings Institution, 1941).

Air Mail Episode of 1934

by David D. Lee

Western Kentucky University

As postmaster general during the Hoover administration, Walter Folger Brown used airmail contracts to shape the commercial aviation industry in the United States. Determined to restrict admittance to the industry and to limit competition, Brown saw the contracts as a temporary government subsidy which would support firms until they could develop adequate passenger traffic. Accordingly, he stretched the provisions of the Air Mail Act of 1930 to their limits as he sponsored the growth of well-established firms and squeezed out the others. When the Democrats defeated Hoover and came to power in 1933, Brown's opponents seized the opportunity to challenge his actions.

Ironically, the initial salvo against Brown came from two executives whose companies had profited from his actions. Al Franks of National Parks Airways and Paul Henderson of United Air Lines visited Capitol Hill to complain about Brown's extension of mail routes. Alabama senator Hugo Black found their story to be "almost beyond belief" and launched a major investigation of airmail contracts. Democrats William King of Utah and Patrick McCarran of Nevada joined Black on

Loading mail on an Army Air Corps Curtiss B-2 bomber (courtesy of the U.S. Air Force)

the committee as did Republicans Wallace White, Jr., of Maine and Warren Austin of Vermont. Black named an old friend from Alabama, Andrew G. Patterson, as the committee's chief investigator. A former probate judge, Patterson had once headed the Alabama Public Service Commission and had run for governor in 1926. Black believed the committee needed "an investigator who will take in the vast details of the probe," and Patterson's appointment gave Black a trusted confidant in a vital role.

The investigators had barely begun their work when a treasure trove of valuable material fell into their laps. A Hearst newspaper reporter, Fulton Lewis, Jr., had conducted an extensive investigation of the airmail contracts and prepared a lengthy report on his findings. Weeks of work in late 1931 resulted in a 200-page manuscript that he dispatched directly to William Randolph Hearst himself, but Lewis never heard anything from his boss. The frustrated reporter then sought an audience in Congress where he found Hugo Black and Andrew Patterson to be eager listeners. Armed with the outline of events provided by Lewis, committee investigators

moved to secure evidence supporting his charges. Early one October morning in 1933, their watches synchronized to Western Union time, investigators abruptly raided airline company offices across the country, seizing documents on the inner workings of the industry.

Senator Black convened the airmail hearings on the morning of January 9, 1934, and promptly arranged the first in a long series of sensational disclosures. The opening witnesses testified that important Post Office Department files were missing and that Brown had ordered the destruction of documents pertaining to air and ocean mail contracts. United's Paul Henderson then testified that Brown's actions were rooted in obvious collusion and denounced his policy of extending routes as "so contrary to the spirit of the law ... that I personally took the thing as a joke." Other witnesses described how Brown had squeezed the small operators out of the process of awarding airmail contracts. Black was especially effective in his interrogation of such major industry leaders as Frederick Rentschler of United Aircraft Corporation.

The senator established that between 1927 and 1933, inclusive, Rentschler had received approximately $1.6 million in salary, bonuses, and director's fees, while during that same period, United Aircraft had drawn some $40 million in subsidies from the government. Almost simultaneously the value of Rentschler's stock in Pratt and Whitney, a United subsidiary, had risen from $253,000 to $35 million before settling back to a Depression low of roughly $7 million.

Black's efforts to prove dishonesty in aviation transactions received an unexpected boost from two egregious Republican blunders. After Brown's vigorous denial that he had tampered with Post Office Department records, he suddenly discovered two large files on air and ocean mail contracts among personal papers stored at his hotel. He immediately delivered the papers by hand to Postmaster General James Farley, but his "discovery" seemed to indicate to the public that he really was concealing potentially incriminating information.

That impression was underscored over the next few weeks by the actions of William P. MacCracken, an experienced Washington lawyer usually noted for considerable political shrewdness. When the Black committee subpoenaed his files, MacCracken asked the committee to allow him to contact each of his clients requesting permission to release their files. Black countered that MacCracken's work as a lobbyist was not the sort of lawyer-client relationship which merited confidentiality, but he reluctantly permitted MacCracken to delay complying with the subpoena. With the files still under subpoena, MacCracken and two associates removed material later revealed to pertain to airmail issues. An outraged Hugo Black called on his Senate colleagues to try MacCracken and the others on contempt charges.

MacCracken compounded the gaffe by acting on his contention that while the Senate could cite him for contempt, only a court could try him. He went into hiding, and his attorney announced that the accused would surrender himself only in the presence of a judge. Clearly MacCracken would then ask immediately for a writ of habeas corpus. MacCracken and the Senate sergeant-at-arms played a bizarre game of hide-and-seek, but the Senate ultimately convicted MacCracken and Northwest Airways executive L. H. Brittin of contempt. They were sentenced to ten days in the District of Columbia jail. Brittin promptly served his sen-

tence, but MacCracken appealed the action. Ultimately the U.S. Supreme Court unanimously rejected MacCracken's plea, forcing him to serve his sentence. Many legislators and journalists dismissed the incident as an "opera bouffe," yet *Jurney* v. *MacCracken* was, as one scholar has noted, "of considerable import to investigating committees." A verdict in favor of MacCracken would have seriously curbed the power of congressional committees to subpoena materials because Congress would be unable to punish those who failed to comply with its summons. According to M. Nelson McGeary, a leading student of congressional investigations, "The opinion . . . in effect strengthened the investigatory power of the Senate and the House."

While the Senate was pursuing its elusive quarry, the Roosevelt administration announced through Postmaster General Farley that existing domestic airmail agreements were rooted in fraud and collusion and would be canceled on February 19, 1934. The president ordered the Army Air Corps to fly the mail until new contracts with private companies could be negotiated. The system Brown had established was swept aside, and the New Deal now set about constructing a different model. The announcement represented the zenith of the Black investigation; its findings had widely discredited the architects of the existing airmail structure and prompted the administration to embrace a new policy which largely reflected the assumptions undergirding the investigation.

Although public opinion polls initially showed wide public support for Roosevelt's actions, the cancellation also provoked considerable criticism. Industry representatives charged that they had been denied due process. Popular aviator Charles A. Lindbergh, a Transcontinental and Western Air (TWA) consultant, telegraphed Roosevelt that his action "condemns the largest portion of our commercial aviation without just trial." Aviation enthusiast Will Rogers hoped the president would not halt every industry where he found crookedness at the top.

The barrage of criticism intensified as it became obvious that the Army Air Corps was completely unprepared to take responsibility for the airmail. Air Corps chief Benjamin Foulois, eager to win budget support for the sparsely funded military aviation wing, had assured Second Assistant Postmaster General Harllee Branch that the Air Corps could handle the task, but General Foulois was tragically mistaken. Its equipment inappropriate to the requirements of a civilian assignment and lacking night flying experience, the Air Corps was unready to fly the nation's civilian airways.

To make matters worse, on February 19, the day the army took over, a major winter storm blanketed much of the nation. The last civilian mail plane, piloted by Jack Frye of TWA and Eddie Rickenbacker of Eastern, set a new speed record on the Los Angeles-to-Newark run, racing past the storm in the process, but the weather meant disaster for the army. Three fliers died while training for the assignment and three more died during the first week of operations. An additional six suffered critical injuries, and eight aircraft were lost. Moreover, the military was flying less than two-thirds of the routes handled by the civilian pilots. Within a month of Farley's cancellation order, ten men died as a consequence of the army's attempt to fly the mail.

The incident angered and embarrassed President Roosevelt. Finding himself on the defensive for the first time since taking office, the president summoned Foulois to the White House for what the general recalled as the harshest tongue-lashing of his military career. The administration suspended airmail flights completely on March 12 and resumed a drastically reduced schedule a week later. Finally, on May 8, private companies holding 90-day contracts resumed temporary service, and the army flew its last mail pouch on June 1. The Air Mail (Black-McKellar) Act of 1934 establishing a new airmail system became law on June 12, 1934. In less than four months of flying the mail, the Army Air Corps suffered 12 fatalities in 66 accidents.

The last act of the cancellation drama was played out in the courts. Several of the lines that saw their contracts canceled on February 19 sued the government for the payment of withheld mail fees accrued prior to February 19, the return of performance bonds, and damages. All but United settled out of court with the government returning their bonds and making back payments. United pressed the suit to its conclusion despite the delaying tactics of government attorneys. Finally, in 1942, a U.S. Court of Claims three-judge panel returned an ambiguous verdict by a 2 to 1 vote. The majority found that the contractors were indeed guilty of collusion and that the administration had acted properly in suspending the agreements. How-

ever, the court also ordered the government to pay United $364,000 it earned while flying the airmail under the terms of those apparently tainted contracts during January and February 1934.

The fallout from the airmail cancellation episode was extensive. The cancellation itself completely disrupted the nation's airmail system and delivered the first sharp blow to public confidence in the Roosevelt administration. The findings of the Black committee precipitated a dramatic restructuring of the government's relationship with civilian air transport. Black coauthored a bill with Tennessee senator Kenneth McKellar which replaced the Air Mail (Watres) Act of 1930 with legislation encouraging competition among small firms for airmail contracts. The hearings also made Black a national figure and brought him closer to the Supreme Court appointment he received in 1937. Finally, because the Air Mail Act of 1934 blacklisted those who had participated in the awarding of contracts during the Hoover administration, the Air Mail Episode of 1934 ended the aviation careers of many industry leaders. In addition to men such as MacCracken and Brittin, the blacklist included, ironically, Al Franks and Paul Henderson, the men whose complaints had sparked the Black investigation in the first place.

References:

R. E. G. Davies, *Airlines of the United States since 1914* (London: Putnam's, 1972);

Nick A. Komons, *Bonfires to Beacons; Federal Civil Aviation Policy under the Air Commerce Act, 1926-1938* (Washington, D. C.: U.S. Department of Transportation, 1978);

M. Nelson McGeary, *The Development of Congressional Investigating Power* (New York: Columbia University Press / London: P. S. King, 1940);

Henry Ladd Smith, *Airways: The History of Commercial Aviation in the United States* (New York: Knopf, 1942);

Virginia Van der Veer Hamilton, "Barnstorming the U.S. Mail," *American Heritage*, 25 (August 1974): 32-36, 86-88.

Archives:

For the work of the Black Committee, see U. S. Senate, *Investigation of Air Mail and Ocean Mail Contracts, Hearing Before a Special Committee* (73rd Congress, 2d session). Committee records are housed in Record Group 46, National Archives, Washington, D.C.

Air Midwest

by William M. Leary

University of Georgia

Acclaimed by I. E. Quastler as the "pioneer of the third level," Air Midwest had a somewhat curious beginning. On May 7, 1965, Gary M. Adamson founded Aviation Services, Inc. (ASI), in Wichita, Kansas. With an initial capitalization of $6,000, the company purchased a Cessna 206 with the idea of making money by transporting human remains for mortuaries. That scheme was not profitable, and Adamson started carrying stretcher-confined patients. The flying ambulance, however, soon gave way to general charter work. Eventually, in April 1967, ASI began a scheduled passenger service between Wichita and Salina.

In 1968-1969, under a new program developed by the Civil Aeronautics Board (CAB), ASI began replacing Frontier Airlines on routes to smaller communities in western Kansas and eastern Colorado. On May 19, 1969, the company changed its name to Air Midwest. Later in the year it purchased a turboprop Beech 99A. In an effort to attract customers, it hired stewardesses (who had to be under four feet eleven inches tall because of limited headroom) for the Beech.

In 1974 Air Midwest won a lengthy battle to earn a subsidy when the CAB approved "flow-through" payments to the airline that reached the company via Frontier Airlines. Thanks to $97,952 in federal funds, the airline turned its first net profit in that year, posting earnings of $131,854. In 1975 the airline took a further step toward respectability and permanence when it gained certification as a "regional feeder," with routes from Kansas City to Denver.

With the acquisition of Fairchild-Swearingen Metros in 1977, Air Midwest embarked on a period of rapid growth. Operating revenues jumped from $1.2 million in 1976 to $4.1 million in 1977, while revenue passenger-miles climbed from 6.3 million to 18.4 million. Deregulation in 1978 enabled the airline to expand into Texas, Oklahoma, Ne-

braska, Iowa, and New Mexico. Between 1979 and 1983 it quadrupled in size.

The year 1984 marked the high point in Air Midwest's progress. It was the nation's leading regional feeder and posted a record operating profit of $4.3 million on operating revenues of $58.5 million. Serving 51 cities with 42 aircraft, it carried more than 700,000 passengers and flew 137.6 million revenue passenger-miles. Buoyed by the company's success, President Adamson purchased two 30-seat SAAB 340s and acquired through merger Scheduled Skyways of Fayetteville, Arkansas.

The new acquisition, Adamson later admitted, was "our big mistake." The merger seemed like a good idea at the time because the two lines had adjoining route systems and compatible equipment. However, Scheduled Skyways's 14 Fairchild Metros turned out to have been poorly maintained and required extensive repairs. Air Midwest also ran into problems when code-sharing agreements with Ozark Airlines at Kansas City and with American Airlines at Nashville failed to generate the expected traffic. From 1985 to 1987 the airline suffered three straight operating losses that totaled nearly $9 million.

In January 1988 Robert L. Priddy, who owned 12 percent of the company's stock, replaced founder Adamson as president and chief executive officer. Priddy launched an economy drive, laying off 7 percent of the airline's 1,050 employees. He also won agreement from the machinists' and pilots' unions for minimal wage increases over the life of a four-year contract. Emphasizing a hub-and-spoke system, Air Midwest concentrated on interchanging passengers with Eastern Air Lines at Kansas City and TWA at St. Louis. Despite Priddy's efforts, the airline posted a net loss of $1.4 million for the year, due in large part to Eastern's sudden decision to close its Kansas City hub at the end of August.

Losses continued in 1989, totaling $5.1 million for the year. In 1990 Air Midwest sold its feeder operation at Kansas City (TWExpress) to Trans States Airlines for $12 million. At the same time, under the name USAir Express, it began serving as a feeder for USAir at Kansas City. While on the way to a net profit of $4 million for the year, the airline was acquired, for $27 million in cash and stock, by Mesa Airlines, a New Mexico-based regional carrier. Mesa announced that it would continue to operate Air Midwest as a subsidiary.

References:
Danna K. Henderson, "Robert Priddy's $1 Million Midwest Gamble," *Air Transport World*, 26 (May 1989): 98-100, 104, 106-107;
Len Morgan, "Heartland Express," *Flying*, 115 (September 1988): 64-71;
I. E. Quastler, *Air Midwest: The First Twenty Years* (San Diego: Airline Press of California, 1985).

Air Transport Association

by Robert Burkhardt

Lewes, Delaware

Founded on January 3, 1936, as the trade organization for the airline industry, the Air Transport Association of America (ATA) has several features not common to trade associations. While the ATA has in the past become involved in areas that other associations have made a point of avoiding, it has not done things that many trade organizations consider a normal part of trade promotion. For example, it has not held annual conventions where suppliers to the industry take booths to display their wares and where industry leaders make speeches and hold grand banquets to honor people in government— and elsewhere—who have rendered service to the industry.

Like most trade associations, the ATA has been an active persuader in behalf of its members. Its lobbying efforts mainly have been directed at federal regulatory agencies and Congress. Although the ATA routinely has registered under the lobbying registration laws, it does not want to be known merely as a "lobbying" organization because it believes that its work on behalf of its members is more broadly based than simply trying to influence federal regulation. However, there is no question that the ATA has exerted such influence. Indeed, the organization helped to draft the Civil Aeronautics Act of 1938, which led to the establishment of the Civil Aeronautics Board (CAB). It was closely involved in the development and passage of the Federal Aviation Act of 1958. It also has been concerned with the airports and airways modernization trust fund, financed by direct taxes on passen-

ger tickets and cargo waybills. After the CAB was abolished its focus shifted to the Department of Transportation (DOT), which took over most of the CAB's regulatory functions, particularly the awarding of international air routes.

Whether working with the CAB or DOT, the ATA has stayed as far away as possible from the consumer complaint activities of both agencies. One reason for this long-standing refusal to have direct contact with dissatisfied air travelers—except in the theoretical arguments about airline deregulation and its effect on airline service and ticket prices—is that the ATA early learned to stay out of the competitive battles among its members. Such consumer-sensitive subjects as on-time performance of the individual airlines and the level of consumer complaints received by the DOT about each airline thus remain the exclusive province of the government.

In the awarding of air routes for overseas services, the ATA gets more closely involved in the negotiations with foreign governments which are being pressured to adopt a more "open skies" approach to service by U.S. flag carriers to their cities. It functions mostly as an observer and limited representative for those domestic airlines that will be affected by the routes obtained, particularly by the routes to be opened up by the United States to foreign airlines as part of the quid pro quo of international route bargaining.

The ATA also takes an active role in what the airlines call "facilitation." This includes all of the government regulations that have the effect of slowing down and even stopping the movement of passengers and cargo across borders. In the opinion of many international air travelers, the U.S. Customs Service is one of the worst offenders in causing delays at border crossings. In trying to promote "preclearance"—the stationing of customs officials at foreign airports, such as Bermuda, to clear travelers to the United States before they leave foreign soil— the ATA speaks with the voice of all the U.S. airlines. It also is active in trying to minimize delays caused by security screening intended to catch weapons and explosive devices before they can make their way aboard U.S. aircraft. Efforts to detect the smuggling of drugs also can cause delays, and the ATA works closely with the appropriate authorities to make the procedures as easy as possible on innocent passengers.

Some other interesting ways the ATA serves it members include the operation, through a subsidiary, of a ticket clearinghouse which makes it possible for a passenger to buy a ticket to any scheduled destination for any associated airline. Several other service organizations, such as Air Cargo, Inc., and Aeronautical Radio, Inc., which provides air-to-ground communication services for all airlines, are wholly owned by the airlines, but ATA usually has a seat on the service company's board of directors for informal coordination purposes.

The ATA takes special pride in its contributions to air safety. The organization serves as a clearinghouse for the exchange of ideas among airlines on matters relating to safety, including technical developments and operational experiences. In 1939 the ATA received the prestigious Collier Trophy for its "high record of safety."

References:

Air Transport Association of America, *Air Transport Association: 50th Anniversary* (Washington, D.C.: Air Transport Association, 1986);

Robert Burkhardt, *CAB—The Civil Aeronautics Board* (Dulles International Airport, Va.: Green Hills Publishing Co., 1974).

Air Wisconsin

by William M. Leary

University of Georgia

Incorporated by business leaders of Appleton, Wisconsin, on December 2, 1963, Fox Cities Airlines was intended to provide air service to cities bordering the Fox River of east central Wisconsin that were being abandoned by North Central Airlines. After changing the name of the company to Air Wisconsin, the airline's promoters sold 50,000 shares of stock at $5 each, mainly to local citizens. Operations got underway on August 23, 1965, with two nine-seat de Havilland Doves flying between Appleton and Chicago's O'Hare Airport. Two years later, Air Wisconsin introduced the first of four de Havilland DHC-6 Twin Otter turboprops on its routes, which now included Milwaukee, Minneapolis, and several smaller communities. The company turned its first net profit in 1971, marking the beginning of nearly two decades of profitability.

The 1970s were years of careful expansion for this well-managed regional airline. Beginning in 1973, the company acquired 13 Fairchild-

Swearingen Metros, becoming the first major operator of this 16-seat, twin-engine, turboprop airliner. With traffic increasing over an expanding route system that included cities in Nebraska, Ohio, North Dakota, and Pennsylvania, Air Wisconsin introduced in 1979 the 50-passenger de Havilland DHC-7 (known as the Dash 7). In 1980 the airline carried 667,000 passengers in its 13 Metros and five Dash 7s, recording a net profit of $8.8 million.

By the beginning of the 1980s, Air Wisconsin had become "the strongest and fastest-growing large regional airline in the country." In 1983 the company acquired three British Aerospace BAe 146s, a 100-passenger, four-engine, pure jet transport that was specifically designed for the short-haul market. The airline was able to finance the purchase of these fast, quiet, fuel-efficient aircraft on favorable terms, thanks to the low-interest loan from the Export Credit Guarantee Department of England. In 1984 Air Wisconsin obtained two additional BAe 146s, carried more than a million passengers for the first time (some 79 percent of them business travelers), and posted its fourth straight profit of over $4 million.

In 1985 Air Wisconsin moved into the ranks of the national carriers (those with over $75 million in revenue) when it merged with Mississippi Valley Airlines, a Moline-based commuter line that had carried 75,000 passengers in 1984. Deciding that a single large carrier would be in the best interests of both companies, the management of Air Wisconsin and Mississippi Valley agreed on an exchange of stock that cost Air Wisconsin $10 million. Serving 31 cities in eight states, the strengthened air carrier further improved its marketing position by signing an agreement with United Air Lines for participation in its Apollo central reservations system. In 1986 the connection with United became even closer when Air Wisconsin changed its name to United Express and dedicated its fleet to operating feeder routes from Chicago (O'Hare) and Washington (Dulles).

Air Wisconsin initially prospered under the arrangement with United, posting a record net profit of $17.9 million in 1988. A sharp drop in profits in 1989 (to $400,000), however, caused airline officials to question a continuation of the marketing agreement with United Air Lines. Following prolonged negotiations, a new—and more favorable—agreement was reached with United in 1990. This contributed to a net profit of $1.9 million for the year, despite a loss of $1.1 million by a new acquisition, Aspen Airways. Industry observers continue to regard the airline as one of the best examples of what can be achieved by astute management in a deregulated environment.

References:

"Air Wisconsin Survives the CRS Blues," *Air Transport World,* 22 (September 1985): 32-36;

Jan W. Steenblik, "Air Wisconsin: A Short-Haul Success Story," *Air Line Pilot,* 52 (April 1983): 8-11, 40-41;

James P. Woolsey, "Air Wisconsin Girds for Coming Competitive Struggles," *Air Transport World,* 19 (September 1982): 78-79, 81-82.

Alaska Airlines

by Claus-M. Naske

University of Alaska Fairbanks

The Sunday edition of the *Anchorage Daily News* on November 20, 1983, carried a story headlined, "Alaska Airlines Avoid Industry Nosedive: Most Carriers Falter; Alaska Pumps Out Profits." In the wake of deregulation, the newspaper observed, airlines had found profits as elusive as sunny skies over the North Pacific. Yet Seattle-based Alaska Airlines had been profitable since 1972, expanding its market sufficiently "to draw not only the envy and admiration of the nation's largest airlines, but also a renewed competitive assault from them."

It had not always been that way. Like so many other successful companies, Alaska Airlines had modest beginnings. In 1929 Linious McGee, a California miner who had less than a dollar in his pocket and little idea of what to do next, stowed away on a steamer bound for Alaska. Arriving in Anchorage, he soon found a job as a truck driver. Later, he became a fur buyer. McGee did a lot of fly-

ing in his new occupation, but because he disliked the high charter rates, he got together with pilot Harvey W. Barnhill and purchased a Stinson monoplane. By late 1932, Barnhill had departed, McGee had learned to fly and had acquired a second aircraft, and McGee Airways had begun charter flights.

McGee was an efficient operator. He hated empty airplanes. If there were not enough passengers, he would load foodstuffs, which the pilots—who were paid commissions instead of salaries—were expected to peddle along the way. Despite the economies, McGee Airways chronically stood on the edge of financial ruin.

During the winter of 1934-1935, McGee Airways combined with Star Air Service, another struggling charter operator. McGee managed Star Air Service until 1937, when he left to open a liquor store. That same year, Donald Goodman purchased

Alaska Airlines Douglas DC 9-80 (courtesy of the John Wegg Collection)

Star Air Service, which he renamed Star Air Lines, and began regular flights between Anchorage and Fairbanks. By 1942 Star had become Alaska's largest airline, with 15 airplanes and a network of radio stations scattered across the Kuskokwim and Yukon deltas all the way to Bristol Bay.

The war years brought changes to the airline. In late 1942 the company, by then known as Alaska Star Airlines, received temporary certification from the Civil Aeronautics Board (CAB) for mail routes from Anchorage to McGrath, Seward, Fairbanks, and other points in the territory. In late 1943 it acquired three small companies: Lavery Airways, Pollack Flying Service, and Mirow Air Service. In 1944 it changed its name again, to Alaska Airlines.

During this time, management of the airline fell under the control of Raymond W. Marshall, an exceptionally successful New York junk dealer. Between 1942 and 1974, the airline suffered from poor leadership and inadequate financing. The situation improved somewhat when Marshall signed a management contract with James A. Wooten in June 1947. Under Wooten's guidance the airline greatly expanded its charter business and also finally secured entry into the "Lower 48." On August 17, 1951, Alaska Airlines began scheduled DC-4 service between Fairbanks and Seattle.

In 1957 Marshall sold most of his stock to Charles F. Willis, Jr., a much-decorated navy veteran. Willis tackled his new job as head of the airline with enthusiasm and energy. He sponsored maintenance and marketing innovations and presided over route expansions. In 1960 the CAB awarded Alaska Airlines' bush routes to Wien Alaska Airways, enabling it to serve its trunk routes more efficiently. Four years later, Alaska Airlines finally received authority to fly between Seattle and Anchorage. In 1968 it acquired, through merger, Alaska Coastal-Ellis Airlines, giving it virtual control of the commercial traffic between Ketchikan and Anchorage. At the same time, Alaska Airlines also acquired Cordova Airlines, another regional carrier.

By the late 1960s, Alaska Airlines had established many firsts. It was the first commercial airline to fly over the North Pole, the first to fly charter routes from Alaska to Hawaii and from the United States to the Soviet Union, the first to land Boeing 727s on gravel runways, the first to use

DC-3s mounted on skis, and the first to put C-130s to work hauling oil drilling equipment to the Arctic and to South America. It was also the first Alaskan air carrier to use helicopters.

Despite the airline's many accomplishments, profits remained elusive under Willis. Also, on September 4, 1971, an Alaska Airlines' jet en route from Anchorage to Juneau slammed into the side of a mountain, killing all 104 passengers and seven crew in the worst single-plane domestic air disaster up to that time.

The company's fortunes began to improve in 1972. In February the CAB awarded the airline exclusive authority to serve southeast Alaska. Also, later in the year, the airline's management changed. Two young graduates of the University of Alaska, Ronald F. Cosgrave and Bruce Kennedy, who were owners of Alaska Continental Development Company (ALCO), a successful real estate and construction firm, traded just over $400,000 of their company's properties for 58,000 shares of Alaska Airline stock, making them the airline's second-largest stockholder and giving Cosgrave a seat on the board of directors. Cosgrave found a dismal financial picture. The airline owned a variety of properties, including tourist resorts, newspapers, and even a print shop in Fairbanks—and all were losing money. He put in another $3 million of ALCO's as-

sets, bringing the Cosgrave-Kennedy holdings to 700,000 shares, or 23 percent of the company. That enabled him to force Willis out of office on May 12, 1972.

Cosgrave took over management of the airline at a time when it had a negative net worth and had lost $2.5 million during the first six months of 1972. Over the next six months, however, he stopped the flow of red ink. Between 1973 and 1975, the company earned $6.4 million.

In 1978 Kennedy replaced Cosgrave as head of the airline. During the following three years, the company added four Boeing 727-200s and three Boeing 737-200s to its fleet and extended its route system to include Portland and San Francisco. In 1981 Alaska Airlines posted a record net profit of $8 million. During the remainder of the decade, the airline purchased new airplanes, expanded into new markets (including Los Angeles, Las Vegas, and Phoenix), and continued to earn record profits.

References:

R. E. G. Davies, *Airlines of the United States since 1914,* revised edition (Washington, D.C.: Smithsonian Institution, 1982);

Bruce Johnson, "Alaska Airlines: Hot Item in the 'Upper 1,'" *Airline Executive,* 8 (December 1984): 9-40;

Archie Satterfield, *The Alaska Airlines Story* (Anchorage: Alaska Northwest Publishing Co., 1981).

All American Aviation

by W. David Lewis

Auburn University

and

William F. Trimble

Auburn University

Chartered on March 5, 1937, All American Aviation was formed to hold patents and issue licenses for a nonstop airmail pickup and delivery system invented by Lytle S. Adams. Born in Kentucky, Adams, who had a degree in dental surgery, moved to Illinois and Kansas before settling in southern California, where he became friends with aircraft designer and builder Glenn L. Martin. Adams left California for Seattle in 1923. There he conceived

the idea for a system that would enable an airplane to pick up and deliver mail or other goods without landing. The Adams system consisted of a cable trailing below and behind the airplane. At the end of the cable was a steel ball. The ball passed through a V-shaped ground apparatus and into a slotted thimble at the end of the V, thus effecting the transfer of the mail bag or other package. Later Adams simplified the system by using a delivery rope hung between two vertical posts. The low-flying airplane engaged the rope with a cable and grappling hook, carrying aloft the attached package while simultaneously dropping the incoming cargo. Adams surmised that his pickup and delivery system would maximize the speed potential of the airplane and bring the benefits of airmail to remote towns and villages that did not have airfields.

All American Aviation remained dormant until a financial agreement was reached between Adams and Richard C. du Pont, a former national gliding champion, in 1938. Transformed into an operating airline with du Pont as president and Adams as vice-president, All American received an experimental airmail contract in late 1938, buying and modifying Stinson Reliant aircraft to begin the service. After numerous tests and improvements to the equipment, the company inaugurated flights on May 12 and 14, 1939, out of Pittsburgh over two routes encompassing cities and towns in Pennsylvania and West Virginia.

During its first 12 months of operation, All American achieved an outstanding record of reliability and on-time performance, only to see the pickup service suspended in May 1940, upon termination of its experimental certificate. Not until the newly formed Civil Aeronautics Board (CAB) issued a permanent certificate to All American on July 22, 1940, was the airline able to resume operations, under the terms of a special enabling act passed a few weeks earlier. By that time, Adams had left the company and du Pont had taken over complete financial and managerial control.

Operations during World War II brought triumph and tragedy to All American. The airline flew increasingly greater volumes of mail, added new points to its four routes in Pennsylvania, West Virginia, New York, and Delaware, signed a contract to fly cargo for the army, and, through its manufacturing and development division, provided the Army Air Forces with equipment for picking up and towing assault gliders. All American also experienced its first accidents, two of which in 1944 and 1945 resulted in fatalities. Compounding these losses was the death of du Pont in an army glider crash in September 1943.

Under du Pont's successor, Halsey R. Bazley, All American entered the uncertain postwar era pre-

pared to expand its route system and to foster the extension of the pickup system by other airlines to new areas of the country. These ambitious schemes fell prey to economic reality. All American's mail volume fell off precipitously, revenues declined, and the CAB rejected the company's plans for a combination passenger-pickup system on the grounds that it was potentially unsafe. Making the airline's position even less tenable, the CAB turned down applications for new routes and refused to subsidize the pickup system indefinitely.

With few options left, All American took steps to abandon the pickup and become a passenger-carrying feeder line. The critical change in the company's fortunes came with the appointment of Robert M. Love as president in 1946. Committed to passenger carrying and having no sentimental ties to the pickup, Love first changed the name of the firm to All American Airways, Inc., in 1948. Following this, he forced All American into the passenger business with the acquisition of converted C-47s and the inauguration of passenger routes in March 1949. In accordance with the CAB's stipulations in granting All American its certificate, pickup operations ended on June 30, 1949. On January 1, 1953, All American split into two companies: the air transport operations became Allegheny Airlines; and the engineering and development division became All American Engineering and Research Corporation.

References:

W. David Lewis and William F. Trimble, *The Airway to Everywhere: A History of All American Aviation, 1937-1953* (Pittsburgh: University of Pittsburgh Press, 1988);

Page Shamburger, "All American Aviation," *American Aviation Historical Society Journal,* 9 (Fall 1964): 198-206;

Harry R. Stringer, ed., *A Headline History of the Air Pickup, 1939-1942, As Told in Selected Press and Magazine Articles and Photographs, Newspaper Captions and Public Documents* (Wilmington, Del. & Pittsburgh: All American Aviation, n.d.);

William F. Trimble, *High Frontier: A History of Aeronautics in Pennsylvania* (Pittsburgh: University of Pittsburgh Press, 1982).

Allegheny Airlines

by William F. Trimble

Auburn University

Known as All American Airways before 1953, Allegheny Airlines grew from a feeder line serving Pennsylvania and adjacent states into one of the nation's major passenger carriers. Under its first president, Leslie O. Barnes, Allegheny during the 1950s moved from a local-service carrier to regional status, replacing its aging fleet of DC-3s with highly efficient Convair 340/440s. It also inaugurated reduced fares and service without reservations between Pittsburgh and Philadelphia in 1959, placing it in direct competition with Trans World Airlines and other carriers on that lucrative, high-volume route.

Allegheny steadily expanded during the 1960s. In 1961 it moved its maintenance and operations base from Washington National Airport into larger and more modern quarters at Greater Pittsburgh Airport. Thenceforth Pittsburgh became the major hub of Allegheny and its successor, USAir, while Washington, D.C., remained corporate headquarters. Allegheny bought Indianapolis-based Lake Central Airlines in 1967, the acquisition receiving the approval of the Civil Aeronautics Board (CAB) the following year. Although the Lake Central purchase provided access to major markets in the Midwest, it also resulted in short-term losses for the airline.

During the 1960s, Allegheny also moved into the jet era. Convair 580 turboprops replaced Martin 2-0-2s and some of the older Convairliners. In 1966 Allegheny placed its first Douglas DC-9 fanjet in service between Pittsburgh and Philadelphia. By the end of the decade, it had 35 of the new airliners.

Allegheny provided an innovative solution to the problem of maintaining service over shorter, less profitable routes. In 1967 the company began the Allegheny Commuter System by contracting with local-service airlines to provide connections from smaller population centers to major cities, reasoning that this would add passenger volume on longer routes. Though they remained independent, the small airlines used Allegheny's reservations network and guaranteed a specified level of service in return for a minimum monthly payment.

During the early 1970s Allegheny underwent further change. Though much larger than most regional carriers, Allegheny early in the 1970s had many of the characteristics of a small trunk line. Nearly every major city in the Northeast and many in the Midwest were part of its route structure. President Barnes brought Mohawk Airlines—a highly respected and profitable regional carrier based in upstate New York—into the Allegheny structure in 1972. That acquisition significantly expanded Allegheny's jet fleet, tied into the carrier's route map nearly every city in New York and New England, and made the airline the sixth largest in the country. Three years after the Mohawk merger, Barnes retired, turning over Allegheny's presidency to Edwin I. Colodny.

Colodny took over the company under less than optimum circumstances. A general downturn in the economy, higher fuel costs, and cash flow problems led to deficits at Allegheny. Under Colodny the airline began a cautious growth that paid off after deregulation in 1978. Freed from the CAB's route-granting authority, many airlines precipitously moved into new markets, where they tried to compete with loss-leading cut-rate fares. Allegheny instead built upon its already nearly impregnable base in the Northeast, adding nonstop service to select cities in Florida, Texas, and Arizona in 1978 and 1979. Despite the costly addition of new DC-9s and Boeing 727s, the airline returned to profitability by the end of the decade.

On October 28, 1979, Allegheny changed its name to USAir. Though undertaken primarily for short-term market reasons, the change reflected nearly three decades of growth and marked Allegheny's rite of passage from a regional carrier to an airline that was poised to compete on a national scale.

References:
Helen Foster, "Allegheny Airlines, 1939-1966," *Greater Pittsburgh*, 46 (October 1966): 84, 86;
W. David Lewis and William F. Trimble, *The Airway to Everywhere: A History of All American Aviation,*

1937-1953 (Pittsburgh: University of Pittsburgh Press, 1988);
"The Sky's the Limit for Allegheny," *Business Week* (April 17, 1971): 118-119;
Preble Staver, "Allegheny's Expansion Program," *Aviation Week*, 62 (May 30, 1955): 94;
William F. Trimble, *High Frontier: A History of Aeronautics in Pennsylvania* (Pittsburgh: University of Pittsburgh Press, 1982).

Aloha Airlines

by William M. Leary

University of Georgia

Trans-Pacific Airlines (TPA), the original name of Aloha Airlines, first appeared after World War II; it was one of several companies that hoped to challenge Hawaiian Airlines' monopoly of interisland air routes. Incorporated in the territory of Hawaii on June 9, 1946, TPA began nonscheduled operations with a single war-surplus DC-3 on July 26. By the end of the year it had four DC-3s in service and was carrying 4,000 passengers a month. In the fall of 1947, however, it had to suspend operations after Hawaiian Airlines secured a court injunction on the grounds that TPA was flying a scheduled service without proper authorization from the Civil Aeronautics Board (CAB).

In 1948 the CAB recommended a five-year temporary certificate for TPA, a decision approved by President Harry S. Truman on February 17, 1949. The airline began flying scheduled service on June 6. However, this came in the midst of a longshoremen's strike that caused a general decline in interisland traffic. As a result, TPA lost over $300,000 by the end of the year. In June 1951 the CAB granted the airline's request for a postal subsidy.

TPA made steady progress during the 1950s. Calling itself the "poor man's airline," it attracted traffic for its high-density (28-passenger) DC-3s by increasing its schedules, introducing family fares, and sponsoring various promotional activities. TPA's share of interisland passenger traffic rose from 18.7 percent in 1950 to over 40 percent by the end of the decade.

On February 11, 1959, six months before the territory of Hawaii received statehood, TPA changed its name to Aloha Airlines. Later that year, it introduced the turboprop Fairchild F-27 on its interisland routes. By 1961 it had six F-27s in service, replacing its DC-3 fleet.

The 1960s saw intense competition with Hawaiian Airlines, as both carriers introduced new equipment in an effort to secure a competitive advantage. Aloha brought in Vickers Viscounts in 1963, followed by pure jet British Aircraft Corporation BAC One-Elevens in 1966 and Boeing 737s in 1969. The rivalry between the two carriers eventually proved destructive, with Aloha losing more than $6 million between 1968 and 1971. In January 1970 Aloha and Hawaiian announced plans to merge. However, a satisfactory agreement proved impossible to reach, and talks were broken off in April 1971.

Aloha posted a profit in 1972, marking the beginning of ten prosperous years. But the tide began to turn in 1981 with the appearance of Mid-Pacific Airlines, a low-cost carrier that took advantage of the opportunities afforded by the Airline Deregulation Act of 1978 to mount a challenge to the established airlines. Aloha's interisland market share dropped by 10 percent in 1982, turning a 1981 profit of $2.6 million into a loss of $324,000.

Aloha responded to the new competitive environment by obtaining wage concessions from its employees and instituting cost-cutting measures. In 1984 the former "poor man's airline" sought to improve its market position by inaugurating first-class service on its interisland routes. In May it began to fly from Honolulu to Taipei via Guam with a DC-10-30 leased (later purchased) from Philippine Airlines. The international experiment, however, proved unprofitable. After suffering $5 million in losses, Aloha abandoned it in January 1985.

Aloha's situation brightened during the second half of the decade. In 1985 it carried 2.5 million passengers, a 7.9 percent increase over 1984, and flew 335 million revenue passenger-miles. It recorded a net profit of $2.9 million on revenues of $95 million. By 1988 revenue passenger-miles had increased to 451 million, while profits rose to $10.2 million on revenues of $134.2 million. Although net profits declined to $2.2 million in 1989 and

$1.5 million in 1990, the airline stood as one of the few carriers to record any profit at all during a time of financial trouble in the industry. As such, its prospects for the remainder of the 1990s seemed reasonably bright.

References:
David L. Brown "Aloha Girds for Battle," *Airline Executive,* 9 (July 1985): 21-23;

C. V. Glines, "Aloha," *Air Line Pilot,* 54 (January 1985): 20-25;

Vernon A. Mund, *Competition and Regulation of Air Transportation in Hawaii* (Honolulu: University of Hawaii Press, 1965);

James P. Woolsey and Lisa A. Henderson, "Aloha Takes the High Road," *Air Transport World,* 21 (July 1984): 52-53, 57.

American Airlines

by Lloyd H. Cornett, Jr.

Montgomery, Alabama

American Airlines (originally known as American Airways) arrived on the aviation scene on January 25, 1930. It combined a diverse group of aviation concerns held together by the slenderest common thread—the desire to profit from airmail subsidy and passenger service. Before its consolidation, the loose confederation had operated as separate entities under a holding company called the Aviation Corporation (AVCO), which was chartered in Delaware on March 3, 1929.

AVCO had its origins in the Embry-Riddle Company of Cincinnati, Ohio, which was formed in 1925 and bid on Contract Air Mail (CAM) route 24, from Cincinnati to Chicago. Service began on December 17, 1927. The company soon found that its initial capitalization of $10,000 was inadequate. Hence, the partners, John P. Riddle and T. Higbee Embry, agents for the Fairchild Aviation Corporation, sought financial assistance from that firm. Meanwhile another aviation concern, Curtiss Aeroplane and Motor Company, evinced an interest that was quickly short-circuited by Fairchild, whose board had decided the time was right to make a major investment in air transport. The result was AVCO.

With Embry-Riddle in place as the holding company's first operating concern, AVCO embarked on a purchasing spree that by September 1929 netted nine airlines—themselves parts of two holding companies, Colonial Airways Corporation and Universal Air Lines System.

The first of the three airlines that made up Colonial Airways Corporation was Colonial Air Transport, which began mail and passenger service on CAM-1 from Boston to New York on June 18, 1926. Colonial went on to acquire two more airlines, Colonial Western Airways, which operated the Mohawk Valley mail route, CAM-20, and Canadian Colonial Airways, holder of Foreign Air Mail (FAM) route 1 from New York to Montreal via Albany. Those three had formed Colonial Airways Corporation early in 1929, and that corporation became part of AVCO in May 1929.

The first of the companies that formed Universal Air Lines, Universal Aviation Corporation, flew a passenger route between Chicago and Cleveland beginning on September 15, 1928. On December 31 the company purchased Northern Air Lines and Robertson Aircraft Corporation and formed a holding company known as Universal Air Lines System for

American Airlines Curtiss Condor (courtesy of the National Air and Space Musuem)

all three operators. Robertson had begun service on CAM-2 between St. Louis and Chicago on April 15, 1926. Universal then claimed another CAM holder, Continental Airlines, which held CAM-16 from Cleveland to Louisville. Braniff Air Lines and Central Airlines followed Continental into the Universal fold. Shortly thereafter, Universal became part of AVCO.

AVCO was by no means finished expanding. In January 1930 it absorbed Southern Air Transport System, a combination of two airlines and holder of CAM routes 21, 22, 23, and 29. Soon after, it purchased Interstate Airlines, holder of CAM-30 from Atlanta to Chicago.

The acquisition of Interstate gave AVCO 13 subsidiary airlines and 11 contract airmail routes. Not surprisingly, the system was so disorganized that it could not operate efficiently. The lack of connecting routes and integrated scheduling made it difficult for passengers to utilize the extensive system fully. Moreover, AVCO's fleet contained examples of nearly every commercial aircraft then in existence, adding expense and unpredictability to maintenance. As aviation historian Robert J. Serling has remarked, running AVCO was like "presiding over a Chinese fire drill." From the time it began acquir-

ing other airlines, the company lost $1.4 million. To remedy the situation, AVCO's directors formed another subsidiary, American Airways, and offered to purchase the stock of the 13 existing companies in return for a proportionate amount of American stock. All the companies except Embry-Riddle accepted.

Frederick G. Coburn was named president of both AVCO and American when the new arrangement took effect on January 25, 1930. Coburn coordinated American's routes and schedules and began the process of standardizing the company's aircraft, securing a newly designed, single-engine monoplane—the Pilgrim—an aircraft capable of carrying both mail (accounting for 75 percent of its revenue), and nine passengers.

American's lucrative airmail arrangement changed after Postmaster General Walter Folger Brown, who assumed office in 1929, decided to rationalize the nation's airmail system. Brown envisioned a system in which three airlines operated transcontinental airmail routes, which he believed would improve mail service and lead to better passenger service. In addition to the northern route from New York to San Francisco operated by National Air Transport and Boeing Air Transport (later

United Air Lines), he believed the country needed a central route from New York to Los Angeles via Pittsburgh and St. Louis, and a southern route from New York to Los Angeles via Atlanta and Dallas. Armed with the authority of the Air Mail (Watres) Act of 1930, Brown set about his task, calling a 12-day conference in Washington, D.C., from May 15 to June 9, 1930, with representatives of the six major aviation corporations.

At the 12-day series of meetings, which later came to be known as the "spoils conferences," Brown implemented his plan. He organized the central route by forcing a merger of Transcontinental Air Transport and Western Air Express into a renamed Transcontinental and Western Air (TWA). American wanted the southern route but found itself blocked by a Tulsa, Oklahoma, firm, Southwest Air Fast Express (SAFE), which had been formed by Erle P. Haliburton. American's only solution lay in buying out Haliburton, which was the course the company took. It paid $1.4 million, about double what SAFE was probably worth.

Brown favored American with various extensions that forged a route from New York to Los Angeles by way of Nashville and Dallas, adding almost 1,800 miles to the airline's route system. American assisted by purchasing Standard Airlines (a subsidiary of Western Air Express), which operated between Los Angeles and Dallas through Phoenix, Tucson, and El Paso. Brown also found the means to add extensions from Jackson, Mississippi, to Memphis, Tennessee, and from Jackson to New Orleans. Topping this was Brown's extension of American's route from Chicago through St. Louis to New Orleans. Still, the addition of mileage did not solve American's basic problem of meager revenues.

In the three years Coburn served as president of American, the company lost some $38 million. Coburn resigned by request, and Lamotte T. Cohu replaced him in March 1932. Cohu then purchased two airlines from Errett L. Cord: Century Airlines, operating between Chicago and St. Louis and Detroit and Cleveland; and Century Pacific Lines, serving the route from San Francisco to San Diego via Oakland, Fresno, Bakersfield, and Los Angeles. Cord accepted stock and a seat on AVCO's board in April 1932, and Cord and Cohu began an internal struggle over managerial policies. Cohu lost and left the firm in December 1932. His lone accomplishment consisted of paring the four former divisions

of American into two: Southern, headquartered in Ft. Worth, and Eastern, in New York.

Cord obtained the appointment of Lester D. Seymour as American's president, effective December 25, 1932. Seymour set about fashioning a less circuitous route system, and to accomplish this he purchased Thompson Aeronautical Corporation, which held the airmail contract between Bay City, Michigan, and Chicago (CAM-27). American thus secured a through route from Buffalo to Chicago. To obtain a remaining link—New York to Chicago—American had to take over Martz Airlines, a step accomplished at the end of 1932. This acquisition meant that American could fly from Newark (then the New York air terminus) to Chicago, enabling it to bypass its former path to Albany and compete better with TWA and United, both of which had more direct routes.

The Democratic administration that swept into office in March 1933 threatened American's cozy relationship with the U.S. Post Office. Brown was replaced by James A. Farley, who landed in the middle of a heated controversy over airmail practices. When the Ludington Line questioned why Eastern had been given a contract when the former's bid had been 64 cents cheaper, a special committee headed by Senator Hugo L. Black of Alabama delved into the airmail subsidy mystery. Charges of fraud, conspiracy, and outright favoritism were bandied about, and the result was an executive order by President Franklin D. Roosevelt on February 9, 1934, canceling the contracts. The mail still needed to reach its destination, and Roosevelt made an ill-advised decision to allow the Army Air Corps to carry it. Army service commenced February 20, but inclement weather, lack of adequate training, and inadequate equipment all combined to turn the assignment into a fiasco. Because of numerous fatal accidents and poor press, the president had to terminate the army service also. The last scheduled army mail flight took place on June 1.

Meanwhile, on March 30, 1934, the federal government readvertised for bids for commercial airmail service, with certain restrictions. One central condition was that companies that had participated in Brown's so-called spoils conferences were ineligible for new route awards. Legislation also stipulated that no airline transport operation could have an association with an aircraft manufacturer, ending the holding company monopoly. On April 20 and 27, 1934, representatives of 45 airlines gath-

American Douglas DC-3 (courtesy of the National Air and Space Musuem)

ered in Farley's office to learn which would obtain the revised contracts. AVCO had distributed American's stock to subholders and left the airmail scene. American, by the simple expedient of changing its name from American Airways to American Airlines, effective April 11, 1934, became eligible to compete. The company secured eight of the 32 new airmail routes.

Putting American's corporate house in order fell to Cyrus R. Smith, appointed president on May 13, 1934. As an initial step he sold over 50 of the miscellaneous aircraft that American had acquired over its brief history. American placed the DC-2, the first successful, truly modern airliner, on its New York-Chicago route starting in December 1934. For longer routes, Smith acquired Curtiss Condors. Desiring faster transports that would allow passengers to sleep on transcontinental flights, Smith pressured Douglas into modifying the DC-2. The resulting DC-3, a stretched version of the DC-2, would dominate the airline scene for years to come. Smith ordered 12 21-passenger DC-3s and eight Douglas

Sleeper Transports (DST), the sleeper version of the DC-3.

American started DST service from New York to Chicago on June 25, 1936. The first DC-3 arrived on August 18, releasing the DSTs to perform their intended transcontinental missions beginning on September 18. The economical DC-3 could carry enough passengers to make money for American without mail revenues. Total passenger miles rose from 20 million in 1934 to 141 million in 1938, the airline's first profitable year. Prior to 1938, American had been losing an average of $758,000 annually.

American had its hands full attracting passenger traffic. One of the airline's more controversial public relations efforts was a campaign labeled "Afraid to Fly," started in 1937 to overcome the public's fear of flying. Two years before, the airline had established its own flight control system, which followed every American Airlines flight approaching within 100 miles of Chicago. Later the system was extended to Newark and Cleveland, and other airlines began using it. Eventually the federal government adopted the system, improved it, and extended it nationwide.

In 1939 American decided to move its headquarters from Chicago to New York City, to take advantage of the opening of La Guardia Airport in December. At La Guardia, Smith organized the first American Admirals Club, which proved a welcome haven for tired VIP travelers. Soon American expanded its VIP service to other airports, and other airlines followed American's lead. American was the second airline, after United, to introduce DC-3s equipped with in-flight kitchens. In 1940, the first year of operation, American's kitchen service lost money, but hot meals soon became a financial success. In 1942 the airline formed a subsidiary, Sky Chefs, to operate its in-flight meal service. Between 1939 and 1941 American greatly increased the size of its work force, from 2,795 to more than 4,000.

The coming of World War II saw the nation's airlines direct their efforts to military-related tasks. American's first wartime mission, levied by Gen. Henry H. "Hap" Arnold, involved ferrying communications troops and equipment to Natal, Brazil. By February 1942 the War Department had requisitioned 200 of the 360 aircraft in the civil fleet (including 38 of American's 79). American's role after the Natal mission proved its versatility. In May 1942 the airline joined Northeast Airlines to fly servicemen to strategic sites in Labrador, South Baffin Island, Greenland, and Iceland. In June, American flew 200 flights from Edmonton, Alberta, to Alaska. Routine flights across the North Atlantic began in October 1942, and similar service across the South Atlantic began in December. By early 1943 American was flying regularly to India. That year the airline achieved an average of 150 transatlantic trips a month. American's most dramatic (and dangerous) assignment involved flying the "Hump" from India to China in C-87 Liberators. Starting in 1943 and lasting four months, this operation saw American crews make over 1,000 flights and carry 2,500 tons of vital cargo.

Although American's last war-related flights did not take place until January 1946, the airline had been receiving planes back from the ATA since 1944. They required massive overhauls before they could be used again as commercial vehicles. Still, civilian reconversion was rapidly achieved. By the end of the war, American operated 93 DC-3s and employed 11,450 workers.

Even before the war ended, American had made inroads in the international market, first to Mexico in 1942. Service began in September 1942 but had to be suspended in 1946 until the U.S. and Mexican governments could reach an agreement on air transport. This was not forthcoming until 1957, and American reentered the Mexican market by the end of that year.

American's second foray into international skies came with its acquisition of American Export Airlines. Amex, which had been granted authority by the Civil Aeronautics Board (CAB) to serve all of northern Europe, feared a hostile takeover by Pan American and countered by discussing a merger with American. On July 5, 1945, the CAB approved American's offer of $3 million for 51.4 percent of Amex's stock. American renamed the airline American Overseas Airlines and started service to Great Britain, Scandinavia, the Netherlands, and Germany, using Douglas DC-4s, on October 23. Ironically, American sold American Overseas to Pan American in September 1950.

American introduced Douglas DC-6s in transcontinental service on March 7, 1946. Unfortunately, the aircraft had a fuel transfer problem that led to fires, and they had to be grounded from November 1947 to March 1948. The reconfigured aircraft—known as the DC-6B—started on a route (awarded by the CAB in 1947) from New York to Chicago to Los Angeles on April 29, 1951. This placed American in direct competition with United. Competition with TWA over a direct New York-to-California route started with DC-7s (ordered in December 1951) on November 29, 1953.

In the Denver Service Case, the CAB awarded American a direct route from Chicago to San Francisco effective January 13, 1956. Where route awards were not forthcoming, the airlines initiated service through an ingenious system known as interchange service, which allowed a carrier to pair with another and take turns operating aircraft for agreed periods over each others' sections of interchange routes. American paired with Delta starting on September 22, 1949, over a route from Detroit to Cincinnati to Atlanta; with Continental beginning on July 26, 1951, over a route from Houston to San Antonio to El Paso to Los Angeles; and with National and Delta beginning on May 1, 1951, over a route from Miami to Tampa to New Orleans to Dallas to Los Angeles. All three interchange routes became unnecessary when the CAB made the Southern Transcontinental Route awards on June 11, 1961.

American constantly worked to upgrade its equipment. Throughout the early 1940s the DC-3 was American's workhorse; the airline owned a fleet of 74 DC-3s in 1942 and retained the planes in its fleet until April 1949. By 1946 American's management had become enamored of the Convair CV-240 and ordered one hundred of these pressurized twin-engine planes on December 26, 1946, at a price of $18 million. The Convair order was followed by orders for 50 DC-6s, 20 Republic Rainbows (which never flew), and 50 DC-4s. In 1951 American ordered 25 DC-7s at $1.25 million each. Nothwithstanding American's improvement expenses, the airline managed to make profits. From 1949 through 1951 the firm made $27.4 million, and in 1952 it made another $12.5 million.

Striving to forge further ahead, American entered the jet era with a November 1955 order for 30 Boeing 707s, which started service over the New York-to-Los Angeles route on January 25, 1959. In August 1958 American ordered 25 Convair 990s. The plane failed to live up to expectations and was not placed in service until March 18, 1962, on the Chicago-to-New York route. Meanwhile a shortened version of the 707—the 720 medium jet—started service on the Chicago-Denver-Los Angeles route on July 31, 1960. When Boeing introduced the three-engine 727 in early 1963, American turned to the British Aircraft Corporation (BAC) for a new product, the BAC-One-eleven. That aircraft started service on March 6, 1966. American used the BAC to compete with Eastern's shuttle service in the commuter market of the Northeast corridor, inaugurating JET EXPRESS service on February 12, 1967, over the New York-to-Boston route. It also introduced Douglas DC-10s over the Los Angeles-to-Chicago route on August 5, 1971.

On July 22, 1969, American received CAB authority to serve Australia, New Zealand, Fiji, and American Samoa from four East Coast points. It also obtained limited authority to serve Hawaii. The company also attempted to secure further markets by acquiring through merger Trans Caribbean Airways (TCA). American took over TCA's routes and began service March 2, 1971. It soon became a dominant force in the New York-San Juan sector. It also served the Virgin Islands, Haiti, Curaçao, and Aruba.

American suspended service on the former TCA routes in March 1974 because government restrictions made the market unprofitable. To compensate for the loss, American asked for permission to exchange routes with Pan Am: American would give up its Pacific routes except to Honolulu for Pan Am's routes to Bermuda, the Dominican Republic, and Barbados. Approval came in June 1975, and American began service that same fall. Less than three years later, American received permission to suspend its nonstop service from Boston to Honolulu via St. Louis. The airline began nonstop service between Los Angeles and Honolulu on December 17, 1980, and added nonstop routes from Dallas-Ft. Worth to Honolulu in June 1981 and from Chicago to Honolulu in May 1985. Meanwhile in early 1976 and 1977 service began to Montreal, Jamaica, Guadeloupe, and Martinique.

After the passage of the Airline Deregulation Act in 1978, American entered the race for new routes with its largest domestic expansion in years, beginning service on January 20, 1979, to 19 new routes at eight new destinations: Albuquerque, Las Vegas, Miami, Minneapolis-St. Paul, New Orleans, Reno, Tampa-St. Petersburg, and St. Martin in the Caribbean. The following February, American added Nassau and, later in 1979, Guadalajara and Puerto Vallarta, Mexico. In 1978 corporate headquarters were moved from New York City to Dallas-Ft. Worth, which had opened Dallas-Ft. Worth Airport in 1974. American could save money in leases, taxes, wage scales, and increase productivity with a longer work week (40 hours in Texas, 35 in New York). The move started in the summer of 1979, and initially the headquarters stood in Grand Prairie, Texas, until a new facility was completed at the Dallas site in January 1983.

Meanwhile, on June 11, 1981, American added 11 more cities in Texas, Mississippi, Alabama, Oregon, and Florida along seven new routes, and then that fall added service to Denver, Kansas City, and the Yucatán Peninsula of Mexico. The following year American entered Alaska with an interchange agreement with Alaska Airlines, linking Anchorage and Fairbanks with Houston and Dallas-Ft. Worth via Seattle. American also secured a Dallas-to-London nonstop service from the bankrupt Braniff beginning on May 19. Further European service came in May 1985 to include nonstop service between Dallas and Paris, Dallas and Frankfurt, and Chicago and Frankfurt. Two years later, in May

American DC-6 (courtesy of the National Air and Space Museum)

1987, nonstop Dallas-to-Tokyo flights were added. May 1988 saw further expansion with flights from New York to Zurich, Dallas to Madrid, and Raleigh-Durham to Paris.

All of this was not accomplished without problems. A new president, Albert V. Casey, took over the reins of American from Smith in February 1974. In Casey's first year American showed a $20.4 million profit. But 1975 brought a $20 million loss. Merger discussions were rampant, but none panned out. American's hotel chain, which had been started in 1963 as Flagship Inns but in 1972 became the Americana chain, was losing $12 million annually. Casey sold it. By 1976 American's profit was $76.3 million. Profits jumped to $81 million the next year, reached $134.4 million in 1978, and $87.4 million in 1979.

Part of the profit came from American's Super Saver fares. Travelers had to purchase tickets in advance and agree to stay at their destination at least 14 days. Such restrictions discouraged full-fare customers, yet attracted those who might not normally fly. Introduced in the transcontinental market in 1977, Super Saver covered all of American's system

in 1978. Another saving came with the sale of American's Boeing 747s. While the 747 proved to be an excellent aircraft, it operated best in high-density markets, and the DC-10 could do the same thing more cheaply. Then deregulation hit with its flood of new, low-cost airlines, injurious fare wars, and soaring fuel prices. Moreover, American felt it was handicapped by a fleet that averaged nearly ten years of age.

The year 1980 saw a loss of $76 million. It also brought a new president, Robert L. Crandall. Crandall's first steps included selling American's 63 Boeing 707s, which guzzled fuel yet represented 21 percent of the carrier's passenger capacity. The remaining fleet was focused at the Dallas-Ft. Worth hub, the company pulled out of unprofitable routes in the northeast, and all aircraft were reconfigured to accommodate more seats. Moreover, American developed the AAdvantage program, a frequent-flyer plan. It was, the airline explained, a discount in exchange for loyalty—which meant one flew with American. It went into effect in 1981 and gave American a head start on the other airlines. How much AAdvantage contributed to the $47.4 million profit in 1981 may never be known. However, reality set in again in 1982 with a loss of $19.6 million. American management reassessed the problem.

There were, Crandall believed, many causes for the 1982 loss. Recession had hit the nation once again. Passenger loads had plummeted, and it appeared that many of those that did fly flew on discounted fares. Labor costs had reached unprecedented heights, and it was this final factor that American sought to control. Crandall and his management staff proposed a two-tier wage program. In essence, American proposed to lower starting salaries, in some cases 50 percent lower than wage scales in existing union contracts. Negotiating with the unions, Crandall offered to give up the right to furlough people and not to cut wages or benefits of those then employed, but they had to agree to change their work rules to provide more productivity. Further, they had to agree to let American bring in new labor at lower starting salaries. Crandall also promised to buy newer equipment (including aircraft) and institute a profit-sharing plan. The unions somewhat reluctantly agreed to these terms.

Promises were kept. American negotiated with McDonnell Douglas to lease 20 DC-9 Super 80s (a stretched version of the DC-9) with a five-year return clause if not satisfied. But the fuel efficient bypass engines and aerodynamically designed wings proved so successful that American leased 13 more, and still later ordered an additional 67 with an option for 100 more. The DC-9 Super 80 began service in May 1983. It was quiet and cost less to operate; it not only used less fuel but carried a two- instead of a three-person crew, lowering labor bills.

During 1982, according to American's statistics, the carrier boarded its 500 millionth passenger. On May 19 stockholders approved a reorganization plan that formed a new holding company, AMR Corporation, which aimed to provide better flexibility for financing and investment. The carrier had come full circle. In 1982 American introduced the first of 30 fuel-efficient Boeing 767s, which were needed to accommodate passengers attracted by the three-tier discount fare structure planned for 1985. While retaining restrictions, the new fares allowed discounts as high as 70 percent.

These steps culminated in the ultimate goal—

profit. In 1984 American had a $233.9 million profit (up from $34.4 million in 1983) and ranked seventh among American transportation companies. The airline climbed to third a year later and continued to expand. In 1984 it began the Eagle program, a commuter feeder network that consisted of seven smaller carriers (five of which became AMR subsidiaries under AMR Eagle, Inc., in 1988) serving 103 points. Construction started in 1985 on new hubs at Nashville, Raleigh-Durham, and San Juan.

Further expansion included more new hubs (San Jose, California, and Miami, Florida), raising the total to seven; another airline was taken over—AirCal, a successful West Coast regional carrier. American purchased it for $225 million in July 1987, merged the routes into its own by October 1988, and announced the development of a hub at San Jose. The carrier continued modernizing the fleet with orders for 286 aircraft, with options on 308 more. In November 1989, the active fleet consisted of 487 aircraft. That fleet flew more than 61 billion passenger miles in 1988 and over 72 billion in 1989. The passenger load factor (seats filled) hovered around 63 percent. The airline served 162 points, 112 in the United States and 50 outside the U.S. mainland.

American's history spans more than half a century. It started under a holding company as a full-fledged carrier and by the 1980s had returned to yet another holding company. Over the years the airline grew from a disorganized amalgam to an efficient, profitable business and one of the largest transportation companies in the world, with operating revenues in the billions of dollars and 75,470 employees.

References:

George W. Cearley, Jr., *American Airlines: An Illustrated History* (Dallas: American Airlines, 1981);

R. E. G. Davies, *Airlines of the United States since 1914* (Washington, D.C.: Smithsonian Institution, 1982);

Davies, *A History of the World's Airlines* (New York: Oxford University Press, 1983);

L. J. Davis, "And Now, Can Bob Crandall Have It All?," *New York Times Magazine*, September 23, 1990, pp. 25, 42, 44, 46;

Robert J. Serling, *Eagle: The Story of American Airlines* (New York: St Martin's Press/Marek, 1985).

American Overseas Airlines

by William M. Leary

University of Georgia

American Overseas Airlines traces its origins to April 1937, when American Export Lines, a shipping company, incorporated American Export Airlines (Amex) as an aviation subsidiary. The shipping company, which operated a fleet of 24 steamships between the Atlantic coast of the United States and ports in the Mediterranean and Black seas, had decided that transatlantic passenger traffic could be handled more economically by air than by building and operating superliners in competion with British and French companies. By the summer of 1939, Amex had conducted three round-trip transatlantic survey flights with a Consolidated PBY-5 am-

phibian and had applied to the Civil Aeronautics Board (CAB) for permission to serve England and France.

Although supported by the Department of State, the Post Office, and the U.S. Navy, Amex encountered strong opposition from Pan American Airways and its political allies. On July 15, 1940, President Franklin D. Roosevelt approved the CAB's decision to grant Amex a seven-year authority to fly to Europe. However, Pan American managed to delay Amex's inauguration of service by challenging the legality of a steamship company's ownership of an airline. The courts eventually

Consolidated PBY-5 of American Export Airlines, predecessor to American Overseas Airlines
(courtesy of the National Air and Space Museum)

agreed with Pan American, and Amex had to separate from its maritime parent. At the same time, Pan American's congressional supporters successfully denied Amex a mail subsidy.

American entry into World War II in December 1941 brought a temporary end to Pan American's struggle to maintain its monopoly on international air routes. On January 12, 1942, after having acquired three long-range Vought-Sikorsky VS-44 flying boats, Amex signed a contract with the Naval Air Transport Service to fly the Atlantic. Operations between New York and Foynes, Ireland, began in June 1942 and continued until the end of 1944.

In June 1945 the CAB adopted a policy of competition in international air routes and awarded seven-year certificates for transatlantic service to Amex and Transcontinental and Western Air Lines. The CAB also approved the merger of Amex with American Airlines. On October 24, 1945, Amex began DC-4 service between New York and London. The following month, the company changed its name to American Overseas Airlines (AOA).

Serving England and northern Europe, AOA offered strong competition to Pan American. Known for its safety and superior service, the airline recorded over 15,500 transatlantic crossings by the end of 1947 and received the National Safety Council Award for flying 206,385,000 passenger-miles

without a fatality. Pressed into duty during the Berlin Airlift of 1948-1949, it carried more than 13 million pounds of cargo and over 28,000 passengers between Frankfurt and Berlin.

Despite the operational success of AOA, American Airlines' president C. R. Smith decided that the company's financial losses were unacceptable. In December 1948, he reached a tentative agreement with Pan American head Juan T. Trippe to sell AOA to its arch rival. Although the CAB rejected the merger application, President Harry S. Truman overruled the board on September 25, 1950.

When later questioned about the wisdom of selling AOA (for $17,450,000) to Pan American, C. R. Smith responded: "On the basis of the situation at the time of the decision, we did right, I believe. On the basis of the situation many years later, the decision is debatable."

References:

Marylin Bender and Selig Altschul, *The Chosen Instrument* (New York: Simon & Schuster, 1982);

Charles F. Blair, *Red Ball in the Sky* (New York: Random House, 1969);

R. E. G. Davies, *Airlines of the United States since 1914*, revised edition (Washington, D.C.: Smithsonian Institution, 1982);

Henry Ladd Smith, *Airways Abroad* (Madison: University of Wisconsin Press, 1950);

Robert J. Serling, *Eagle: The Story of American Airlines* (New York: St. Martin's Press/Marek, 1985).

America West

by William M. Leary

University of Georgia

America West, often hailed during the 1980s as the strongest of the post-deregulation airlines, was founded by Edward R. Beauvais and seven associates in September 1981. With faith in the potential of Phoenix as a gateway to California, the group spent two years planning and raising the necessary $20 million to begin operations. On August 1, 1983, America West inaugurated service to five cities from its Phoenix base, using three Boeing 737s. By year's end it was flying ten Boeing 737s to 13 cit-

ies. The airline carried 304,000 passengers and lost $9.9 million.

America West had all the hallmarks of a post-deregulation carrier as it grew in size. The airline emphasized a hub-and-spoke system, with low fares and frequent departures to attract business travelers. "We want a passenger to be able to go from our cities east of the hub to anywhere in California," Beauvais pointed out, "for about half of what he was paying before." It also featured low labor costs. As compensation for low salaries, employees participated in stock ownership and profit-sharing programs. During 1984 America West became the second largest (after People Express) post-deregulation airline, carrying 2.3 million passengers and losing $15.4 million.

The airline finally became profitable in 1985 and 1986 as it expanded into new markets. By the end of 1985 it served 32 cities with 46 airplanes and made $11.3 million. The following year America West added de Havilland Dash 8s to its growing fleet and began operating feeder routes from Phoenix. It also inaugurated a popular "Nite Flite" passenger-cargo service from Las Vegas. Passenger enplanements rose from 5.1 million in 1985 to 7.1 million in 1986, and the airline posted a profit of $3 million.

The pace of expansion quickened in 1987. Chairman Beauvais acquired six Boeing 757s, which he used to open routes to Chicago, New York, and Baltimore. The airline, however, found it difficult to become established in East Coast markets and suffered heavy losses. Although passenger boardings increased to 11.2 million during the year, America West posted a staggering net loss of $45.6 million. That same year, an affiliate of Australia's Ansett Airlines acquired a 20 percent interest in the company for $32 million.

America West's growth slowed in 1988 as Beauvais sought to return the airline to profitability. By reducing capacity by 10 percent, dropping service to unprofitable cities, lowering the frequency of flights on certain routes, and laying off part-time employees, the company made an impressive recovery, registering a net profit of $9.3 million. The next year proved even better. Recording operating revenues in excess of $1 billion—and a net profit of $20 million—it entered the ranks of the major airlines as the 11th largest air carrier in the country.

In 1990 disaster struck America West. The year began with high optimism, as the airline expanded its routes across the Pacific to Honolulu and Nagoya, Japan. Later in the year, however, rising fuel costs following Iraq's invasion of Kuwait contributed to crippling losses. The airline posted a net loss of $74.7 million for 1990. On June 27, 1991, the heavily leveraged carrier filed for protection under Chapter 11 of the U.S. Bankruptcy Code. Although Chairman Beauvais remained optimistic that America West would be able to recover from its financial woes, many industry observers predicted that the airline would be swallowed up by a larger—and more fiscally healthy—rival.

References:

Danna K. Henderson, "America West Gambled and Won," *Air Transport World,* 21 (June 1984): 60-62, 64;

Henderson, "Rolling the Dice in the Desert," *Air Transport World,* 26 (December 1989): 22-24, 27-30;

Paul Seidenman and David J. Spanovich, "America West's Ed Beauvais: Finding Success in Phoenix," *Airline Executive,* 10 (July 1986): 20-24;

John Wegg, "Cactus Flower: America West—Darling of Deregulation?" *Airliners,* 1 (Winter 1988): 8-13.

George T. Baker

(December 21, 1900 - November 4, 1963)

by George E. Hopkins

Western Illinois University

CAREER: Partner, Bower & Baker (1919-1934); president, National Airlines Taxi System (1929-1934); distributor, Eastman Flying Boats (1930-1934); president, National Airlines (1934-1962).

George Theodore "Ted" Baker was the founder of National Airlines, which began operating following the airmail contract cancellation crisis of 1934. Alone among the "new entry" postcancellation airlines, National survived to become a trunk carrier. Most observers credit Baker's steely will as the key ingredient in National's success. Like Edward V. Rickenbacker of Eastern Airlines and W. A. "Pat" Patterson of United, Baker ranks as one of the pioneers of commercial airline service in the United States. Unlike his contemporaries Rickenbacker and Patterson, however, Baker entered the airline business belatedly and with little capital.

Born in Chicago on December 21, 1900, the son of a Chicago newspaperman, Baker was fascinated with automobiles. Following a brief army service during World War I, Baker became a founding partner in Bower & Baker, a Chicago auto financing business, which was later extended to boats and airplanes. In 1930 he acquired the Eastman Flying Boat franchise in Chicago, but his dubious business practices forced the company to withdraw his dealership: his habit of accepting new flying boats "on consignment" and then using them for charter work was considered unethical. Although Baker loyalists admit that "sharp" business practices often characterized his operation of National Airlines, they insist that he had no alternative, given the stern competition he faced from Eastern's hard-eyed Rickenbacker in the early days.

Charges of unethical behavior, often buttressed with ample documentation, dogged Baker to

George T. Baker

the end of his days. Perhaps one of his most egregious transgressions of the moral code was his willingness to permit wealthy friends' sons to become "airline pilots" (in name only) during World War II, thus evading the draft owing to the exemption pilots enjoyed. Veteran National pilots observed that Baker hired wealthy young socialites who flew briefly and then disappeared from the flight line while still being carried on National's roster.

Although he earned a pilot's license in the late 1920s, Baker was never smitten with the romance of aviation. To him an airplane was simply a device from which he might profit. While he often spent money on expensive cars and boats, he never owned an airplane for recreation. The flights he made during his career with National were infrequent and for publicity. For example, in November 1940 Baker took credit for setting a transcontinental speed record from California to Florida in transporting a new Lockheed Lodestar aircraft from its Burbank factory, but someone else actually flew the plane. He was again "at the controls" for National's maiden flight from Miami to New York in 1944, but only nominally so. Baker saw nothing wrong with these spurious "celebrity" flights, because his rival Rickenbacker did the same thing. Rickenbacker, a celebrated World War I fighter pilot, never held a civil license.

Many details of Baker's early life remain unclear because he chose to keep them so. He enjoyed cultivating a "Jay Gatsby" image of mystery and glamour. He deliberately misstated his educational achievements (claiming to have attended the Montana School of Mines as a youth), his wartime service (claiming to have commanded a tank unit), and his employment history prior to 1929. For Ted Baker, truth was a relative thing. He married a movie starlet after divorcing his first wife. He seemed to relish the possibility that people would think he skirted the law when it was to his advantage to appear to have done so.

The profit potential of aviation lured Baker into dabbling in it in the 1920s. Since obtaining a mail contract was the only sure means of making money from airplanes, Baker set his mind on securing one. Like much in Baker's life during this period, there is considerable confusion about the process. His possession of three decrepit single-engine airplanes (two of them Ryan monoplanes similar to the one in which Charles Lindbergh flew the Atlantic in 1927) gave him minimal qualification to bid on a mail contract following the February 1934 airmail cancellations. Baker seems to have acquired these airplanes for the specific purpose of securing a mail contract, although from 1929 to 1934 he was only able to use them unprofitably. Detractors claimed the only money Baker made during the years he operated his rather grandiosely named National Airlines Taxi System was by flying bootleg whiskey in from Canada—a charge Baker always denied.

Owing to alleged fraud and malfeasance in the letting of airmail contracts by the Hoover administration in 1930, President Franklin D. Roosevelt ordered his postmaster general, James A. Farley, to seek new bids. Shortly after the new bids were announced, Baker met with Farley on a yacht moored in the Chicago boat basin. Baker wanted the mail run from Nashville to Cleveland, but he informed Farley that he would take the short St. Petersburg-Daytona Beach route in Florida. Either through luck or political influence, Baker was the successful bidder on the Florida route, which Eastern Air Lines ignored. At 17 cents per mile, Baker's bid would pay only about $50 per trip each way. His airliners were barely sufficient to service the route, but with chewing gum, bailing wire, and sharp business practices Baker managed to satisfy the Post Office.

During the first decade of its existence, National remained essentially an intrastate airline, expanding its routes gradually to service Florida cities. Baker's managerial style, which can only be described as unorthodox, either hampered National's growth or accounted for its success, depending upon one's viewpoint. Perhaps Baker's most singular managerial trait was his excessive parsimony. While his airline expanded to serve Gulf Coast cities in the late 1930s, and northward to New York after 1944, Baker persisted in treating the business as if it were still a one-route operation. His feuds with oil companies were notorious, mostly owing to his refusal to pay bills on time. Documented cases exist in which pilots actually paid for fuel with their own credit cards because National's credit had been cut off. Characteristically, Baker would delay for months before reimbursing his pilots. In short, his operation of the mature National Airlines continued to exhibit many of the petty acts of chicanery which had led the Eastman Flying Boat Company to fire him in 1934.

Baker's most enduring claim to fame in the history of commercial aviation lies in his attempt to popularize air travel as a low-cost alternative to surface travel between New York and Florida. In the beginning, owing to the low bid he submitted to the Post Office to carry the mail from St. Petersburg to Daytona Beach, passengers were the difference between success and failure. During the first year of its operation, National carried 400 passengers. By 1935, keenly aware of passenger revenue potential, Baker expanded his fleet, adding secondhand Stinson Trimotor transports. As his little airline grew, Baker attracted the enmity of his principal rival, "Captain Eddie" Rickenbacker. By hauling passengers from Ft. Myers to Sarasota, and between St. Petersburg and Miami, Baker actually opened new markets which Eastern had ignored. In time,

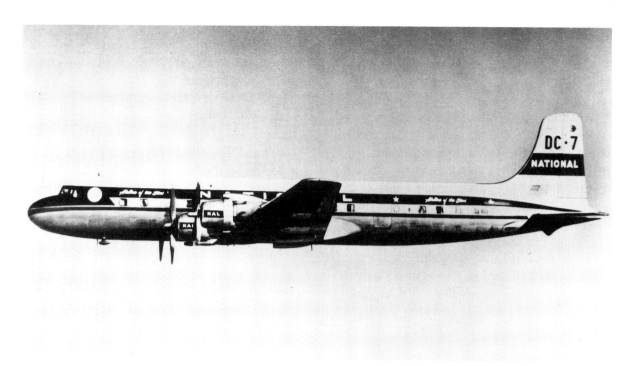

National Airlines Douglas DC-7 (courtesy of the National Air and Space Museum)

Baker's success generated an enmity with Rickenbacker which became personal as well as professional.

The rivalry between Baker, Rickenbacker, and their two airlines neatly encompasses much of the technological history of commercial aviation during the era. In 1944, when federal authorities opened the East Coast route between New York and Miami to direct competition between Eastern and National, Baker's airline was at a technological disadvantage. At first, Baker expanded his fleet from the poor Ryan single-engine monoplanes he began with to include a variety of secondhand aircraft (again reflecting his parsimoniousness). But in 1940 Baker acquired the first new aircraft National had ever purchased direct from the factory. These planes were Lockheed Lodestars, 17-passenger aircraft which were perfect for National's short Florida and Gulf Coast routes, but uncompetitive with the larger Douglas DC-3s flown by Eastern on the New York–Miami run.

Baker inaugurated service on the New York–Miami route in 1944 using his Lodestars, even though they had to stop for fuel en route. During World War II, these en route stops were no handicap, owing to the heavy demand for air transportation between the two cities. But with the coming of peace, the business climate changed. Baker, desperate to buy aircraft which would give him a competitive edge over Eastern, was unable to get postwar delivery dates from any manufacturer on the new four-engine transports which had been developed during World War II. But in an inspired act of innovation, Baker persuaded Douglas Aircraft to sell him several uncompleted surplus military versions of the DC-4. These aircraft were never intended for civil use, and they were, by all accounts of the pilots who flew them, quite spartan. But despite their shortcomings, Baker's jerry-rigged military conversion DC-4s were superior to the Douglas DC-3s Rickenbacker had used to dominate the East Coast route. But National's advantage was only temporary. Very shortly, Eastern began service with Lockheed Constellation aircraft, which eclipsed the DC-4. Thus began a long technological rivalry between Eastern and National, as Baker shortly countered Rickenbacker's Connies with the new, pressurized version of the DC-4, the DC-6. Further upgrades featured Eastern's Super Constellations against National's DC-7s and the introduction of Lockheed's turboprop Electra in 1954. This competition continued through the jet age, and East Coast travelers were the beneficiaries.

In one area of the Eastern-National competition, passenger amenities, Baker clearly began to hurt his competitor. Largely owing to Rickenbacker, Eastern lagged behind other carriers in such things as in-flight meals and creature comforts.

Baker himself had qualms about introducing luxury service, but after hiring away several Eastern executives (who understood fully the weaknesses of Rickenbacker's approach to the airline business), National began to advertise itself as "The Airline of the Stars." This trendy and elitist attempt to depict National as the airline of Broadway celebrities, while tacitly depicting Eastern as stodgy and unimaginative, benefited from National's status. In 1945 Baker (who loved to gamble) secured the permission of the Civil Aeronautics Board (CAB) to expand his service to Cuba, where the principal attractions for American tourists were the fleshpots and casinos of the pre-Castro regime.

By 1948 Baker stood at a peak of achievement, and the future looked bright for his airline. Then, in a crisis largely of his own making, he nearly lost everything. The issue was labor unions—which Baker hated.

The Air Line Pilots Association (ALPA) was, like National, headed by a strong-willed Chicagoan. His name was David L. Behncke, and as a United pilot during the period from 1928 to 1935 (when he quit flying the line to become ALPA's full-time president), he had developed a union which was unique in the American labor movement, a prototype for white-collar workers to emulate. Behncke hated what he regarded as "chiselers," and in his opinion, Baker was first among equals in that category. National's pilots had unionized through ALPA, and on December 9, 1941 (just two days after the Japanese bombing of Pearl Harbor), Baker agreed to their collective bargaining contract. But he was not happy about it, as his summary firing of two previous negotiators had proven. In the unanimous opinion of those who knew him, Baker was a "pilot hater." Any infraction, no matter how trivial, was sufficient to rouse Baker's ire. The fact that the rest of his workers soon followed the pilots into unionism stirred deep animosity in him.

He moved to break the mechanics union first, shortly after World War II. The pilots had a long list of grievances against him. Behncke, from his headquarters in far-off Chicago, saw Baker as the most antiunion airline president ALPA had to deal with—even worse than Rickenbacker (who had once tried to punch Behncke out). The pilots watched with dismay as Baker succeeded in breaking the mechanics' strike and fully replacing them with scabs. Baker's increasing intransigence on a variety of issues led many pilots to believe that they

had no alternative to a strike. In addition, the pilots were seriously worried about the quality of the maintenance work being done on their aircraft by replacement mechanics.

Charles Ruby, the leader of ALPA pilots at National, who had been with the airline since 1935, put it this way: "Baker had a bunch of typewriter mechanics out there masquerading as airplane mechanics and our airplanes were just accidents waiting to happen."

The ostensible cause of the pilots' walkout was the firing of a pilot after a trivial accident. Baker's refusal to negotiate even the possibility of the pilot's reinstatement precipitated the strike. Although the decision to strike was a purely local one, based on friction of long duration between Baker and his pilots, ALPA president Behncke approved. He believed that a short strike would prove therapeutic and lead to improved relations at National. He could not have been more wrong.

The longest pilot strike in airline history up to that point began on February 3, 1948. Baker, whose charm was the flip side of his ruthlessness, set out to destroy his pilots' union. He easily recruited qualified pilots from among the surplus of World War II military pilots who had been unable to find airline jobs. He also changed the color of his pilots' uniforms—a token of his pledge of permanency for the scab pilots. Ultimately, Baker would have succeeded in breaking the pilots in purely economic terms. Despite the pilots' well-organized campaign of picketing and public relations, Baker's airline was flying a full schedule by midsummer. The ultimate disposition of the strike would come not by dint of economic muscle, but through political intervention. By coincidence, 1948 was a presidential election year. Had Republican Thomas E. Dewey won the election instead of Democrat Harry S. Truman, Baker would have won. But because the Democrats won with heavy support from organized labor, Baker lost. Confronted with a dismemberment hearing which would have divided National among its competitors, and having formally been found guilty of unfair labor practices as defined by federal law, Baker surrendered. Although he continued to make life difficult for unionized workers, he ended the strike on terms favorable to the pilots.

None of this came as a surprise to his pilots, who were well acquainted with Baker's quirks. With the passage of years, many of them even came to regard his cranky way of managing National with something approaching affection. In a 1979 interview Sid Wilson, a retired National pilot who went through the strike, reminisced, "If Ted Baker were here tonight, he'd charm the socks off everybody, buy drinks, waltz the ladies, you'd think he was the greatest guy in the world. He'd have everybody eating out of his hand. Tomorrow, he'd cut your throat in a second!"

One curious aspect of the 1948 pilots' strike was Baker's embrace of Dr. Frank Buchman's "Moral Re-Armament" crusade. Buchman's curious blending of Christianity and business management principles appealed to many executives. The genuineness of Baker's conversion has always been suspect. Rather than admit political defeat, many observers believe Baker's crediting of Buchman's influence as the source of his settlement with his pilots was a face-saving device.

By 1962, as the jet age dawned, Ted Baker began to weaken physically. He had seen National become a transcontinental airline via CAB route awards in March 1961, and he had engineered the interchange agreement with Pan American which had made National the first to fly turbojets in the United States. But his health, always precarious, was worsening due to heart trouble. His weaknesses as an executive and his failure to secure a merger which would strengthen National's route structure made his airline an obvious candidate for new, more modern management. In November 1961 Baker retired in favor of his nephew, Robert Weiland. But this titular change was deceptive—Baker remained in control. The clear implication was that Baker intended to retire from active management in favor of someone who could afford to buy him out. Premonitions of mortality undoubtedly hastened his decision. Eventually, after complicated legal and business transactions which lasted for nearly a year, Baker sold National to Lewis B.

"Bud" Maytag, who had formerly owned Frontier Airlines. After second thoughts which triggered a lawsuit against Maytag, and a brief time during which he tried to influence events through his position on the Board of Directors, Baker let go, deciding that the $6.5 million he had accepted from Maytag in April 1962 was enough.

Ted Baker was an autocrat who ruled his airline in a quirky, personal way. He had a genius for precipitating crises, and he seemed unhappy unless he had an enemy. Ironically, he needed an enemy in order to function at peak efficiency. Throughout his long career he sought confrontation with many foes—pilots, Rickenbacker, politicians. His downfall, hastened by failing health, came when he found an enemy who would not fight him—Bud Maytag. Maytag's style of management was nonconfrontational, and he knew how to turn away wrath with a soft answer. Apparently nobody had ever tried that on Baker before. Baker's final attempt to retain control of National, during the months he dawdled before finally surrendering control of the airline he had already technically sold, was one of the most frustrating of his life.

Shortly after exiting from the picture on National, Ted Baker took his wife, the former Hollywood starlet Irma Wilson, whom he had married in 1941, on an extended trip to Europe. On November 4, 1963, while visiting Vienna, Baker died of a heart attack.

References:

R. E. G. Davies, *Airlines of the United States since 1914*, revised edition (Washington, D.C.: Smithsonian Institution, 1982);

George E. Hopkins, *Flying the Line: The First Half Century of the Air Line Pilots Association* (Washington, D.C.: Air Line Pilots Association, 1982);

Brad Williams, *The Anatomy of an Airline* (Garden City, N.Y.: Doubleday, 1970).

David L. Behncke

(May 1, 1897 - April 14, 1953)

by George E. Hopkins

Western Illinois University

CAREER: U.S. Army (1915-1919, 1927-1928); aviation entrepreneur (1920-1926); pilot, Northwest Airways (1926-1927), Boeing Air Transport/United Air Lines (1928-1934); president, Air Line Pilots Association (1931-1951).

David L. Behncke was the founder of the Air Line Pilots Association (ALPA), International (AFL-CIO), a union which represents most of the professional airline pilots in the United States. In 1931, following a period of secret organizational activity dating back to early 1930, Behncke, a Chicago-based pilot for United Air Lines, secured a charter from the American Federation of Labor (AFL) to organize his fellow airline pilots. At a meeting Behncke organized on July 27, 1931, at the Morrison Hotel in Chicago, 13 pilots representing several airlines ratified the organizational affiliation with the AFL and elected him president of the fledgling union. On August 10, 1931, the AFL accepted ALPA as the sole affiliate empowered to represent the craft of commercial airline pilot. Behncke served continuously as president of ALPA until July 16, 1951, when the union's board of directors fired him. From 1931 until his ouster, Behncke dominated the union and attained national stature as a labor leader.

Behncke was born on May 1, 1897, on a hardscrabble dairy farm near Cambria, Wisconsin, to parents of German ancestry. His youth was austere and his formal education ended with grade school. Sometime during his early adolescence, Behncke attended a county fair which featured a flying exhibition. He was enthralled. Aviation offered him a tangible glimpse of freedom from the unremitting drudgery of farm work. But his father disapproved of such foolishness, and Behncke had no money of his own for flying lessons. Only the U.S. Army Signal Corps, which flew airplanes, offered

David L. Behncke (courtesy of the Archives of Labor and Urban Affairs, Wayne State University)

him the possibility of a career in aviation. So in 1913, at the age of sixteen, he ran away from home to join the army. Army recruiters in Milwaukee rejected the underage Behncke's claim to be eighteen. Fearful of his father's wrath, he remained away from home. He found a dairy job, taking advantage of the only skill he possessed, contracted tuberculosis after six months, and went home to die.

In 1915 Behncke miraculously recovered from his illness and secured his father's blessing to join the army. Owing to his lack of education, he at first got no closer to flying than peeling potatoes in an aviation unit. He served in Mexico during General Pershing's fruitless pursuit of Pancho Villa in 1916, impressing superiors with his diligence and native intelligence. After the Pershing expedition he was promoted to corporal and sent to flight training at San Diego, where he won enlisted pilot's wings. In 1917, owing to the expanded opportunities of wartime, he served as a flight instructor and earned a commission.

After demobilization in 1919, Behncke, like thousands of other young Americans, sought to earn his living in aviation. During the 1920s he was, by turn, a barnstormer, aviation entrepreneur, a promoter of flying circuses, and finally, an airline pilot. In September 1921 he won the Chicago Air Derby, which attracted national attention. As an independent businessman he managed Chicago's Checkerboard Field. He barnstormed through several midwestern cities on a regular basis with "Behncke's Flying Circus," which featured wing-walking and other acts of aerial derring-do. Practicing medicine without a license, he advertised a cure for deafness which involved taking a passenger up to 5,000 feet and then spinning down rapidly to the surface. He took out patents on several aviation inventions and published an article in the May 1927 issue of *Aviation,* the industry's most prestigious magazine. When Northwest Airways picked up its new Stinson Detroiter Aircraft at the factory in 1926, Behncke was one of the pilots. He joked that he engaged in every form of 1920s aeronautical exotica except the one that paid best—rum running. He was, in the unanimous opinion of those who knew him, a puritanical man, particularly where women and alcohol were concerned. Furthermore, he coveted a military career, and he wanted no brush with the law which might jeopardize his reserve commission.

As an airline pilot Behncke chafed at what he regarded as management's exploitation of pilots. He also believed that the majority of airline operators cared little for the safety of their pilots. Unhappiness over management's safety policies offered him a natural issue in recruiting pilots to the idea of a union, since most of them shared his jaundiced view.

In 1926 Behncke began flying for newly organized Northwest Airways (NWA). NWA flew the Chicago-Minneapolis route pioneered by Charles Dickenson, a Minneapolis entrepreneur. In terms of seniority, NWA ranks second oldest among continuously operating U.S. airlines. Thus, ALPA's founder was present at the creation of commercial aviation. On February 1, 1927, Behncke carried the first paying passengers in NWA's history (there had been earlier nonpassenger flights).

NWA began operations with three pilots, one of whom was Charles W. "Speed" Holman, a celebrated stunt flyer and daredevil. Management at NWA, headed by St. Paul businessman Col. Lewis H. Brittin, designated Holman "First Pilot," giving him authority over Behncke. A long-simmering feud with Holman over safety continued when, shortly before Behncke was scheduled to fly one of NWA's Stinsons with passengers aboard, Holman took it up for acrobatic practice. After Holman landed, Behncke refused to fly the aircraft until mechanics checked it for damage. In the dispute which followed, Behncke was fired. This incident kindled in Behncke a resentment of management which goes far toward explaining why he became a union leader. (Holman was killed while piloting an aircraft at an Omaha air show the following year.)

In 1928, after brief active duty as an army pilot, Behncke went to work for Boeing Air Transport, which later became part of United Air Lines. Having worked for two airlines, he realized that airline pilots, regardless of the company they worked for, shared common goals and concerns.

With an eye to improving airline pilots' working conditions, Behncke became active in the National Air Pilots Association (NAPA). In 1928 he won election as governor of the Central District of the NAPA. Although the NAPA's charter allowed for union activities, Behncke complained that its primary function was as a "semi-social flying club." He soon became discouraged with the organization. By 1930 he was furiously but secretly using his position inside the NAPA to organize a splinter organization limited strictly to commercial airline pilots who were actively working in the profession. The NAPA had a division open only to airline pilots, but the rules were so loosely interpreted that pilots working for crop-dusting outfits could join.

By 1930 Behncke had built a network of "Key Men," whose identities were secret, pledged to organize the pilots on their respective airlines. The tech-

Air Line Pilots Association staffers watching Behncke breaking ground for a new union headquarters building, Chicago, Illinois, April 28, 1949

nique was similar for each airline. Once the key man had persuaded a majority of his fellow pilots to act collectively (through the device of signing an undated letter of resignation and paying $50 "escrow money"), Behncke would add them to the roster of pilots committed to unionization. From his base in Chicago, which was the nation's air hub, he was ideally located to coordinate these surreptitious activities. He insisted on secrecy because he suspected that management would retaliate against any pilot who could be identified as a union activist.

By early 1931 the covert organizational activity, centered at Behncke's Chicago home, had succeeded to the point that the pilots were ready to seek formal affiliation with organized labor. Behncke wanted to join the AFL, but many pilots, fearing the opprobrium associated with unionism in the 1920s, favored affiliation with the Railroad Brotherhood. Citing the similarities between airline piloting and craft unions which were already part of the AFL, such as the Great Lakes Pilots Association, Behncke persuaded his fellow pilots that the AFL was the better choice.

One key to understanding Behncke's emergence as a labor leader is his anger at the establishment. Despite excellent performance during his tours of active duty, Behncke failed to gain the coveted regular commission which would have allowed

him to make the army a career. During his year of active duty at Langley Field, he won promotion to first lieutenant, served as executive officer of the newly formed Second Bombardment Group, and won a commendation for destroying the Pee Dee River Bridge (which the artillery had failed to do) during war games in late 1927. But Behncke lacked the formal education which the army required of career officers, and his aviation specialty was viewed with distrust by the "old" army. His rejection by the army and his unhappy experience at NWA caused Behncke profound disillusionment. It seemed that no matter how well he performed or how much he achieved, the plums would always go to educated patricians who possessed the proper paper qualifications. In 1928, after the army released him from active duty, Boeing Air Transport had no way of knowing that it was hiring a man who had all the prerequisites of a successful labor leader—drive, suspicion, intelligence, and a grudge.

Under Behncke's leadership, ALPA expanded its membership and established itself as a major factor in the industry. From ALPA's inception until the passage of the Civil Aeronautics Act in 1938, Behncke concentrated on securing federal legislation protecting airline pilots' wages and working conditions. He was a strong supporter of President Franklin D. Roosevelt and the New Deal, but re-

mained suspicious of all politicians and would culti-
vate anyone who might prove useful. Republicans
such as Mayor Fiorello H. La Guardia of New
York, an army pilot during World War I, championed ALPA's cause. "It doesn't matter where the
coal comes from, so long as it gets on the fire,"
Behncke often said.

Behncke proved adept at the game of public relations, capitalizing on the glamour of the pilot's
image as he maneuvered ALPA through its early
years. His frank, coolheaded use of public opinion resulted in a string of significant legislative victories
for ALPA.

Behncke first attracted attention as a labor
leader during the 1932 Century Airlines strike. Century was one of E. L. Cord's many entrepreneurial
ventures. By paying substandard wages to pilots,
Cord hoped to demonstrate to Congress that he
could fly mail more cheaply than the established operators. His pilots rebelled at their low wages and
turned to Behncke and the newly formed ALPA for
help. Based in Chicago, Cord's airline quickly replaced the pilots (who were actually locked out)
and resumed operation. Behncke orchestrated the
public relations campaign against Cord, both in Congress and locally in Chicago. Striking Century pilots flew airplanes painted "Century Unfair to
Pilots" alongside Cord's Stinson Trimotor aircraft
as they arrived and departed Chicago. Assessing
every ALPA member $25 per month, Behncke of-
fered a stipend to the Century pilots while they pick-
eted, appeared at public forums, broadcast imaginary flights over WCFL radio in Chicago, and lobbied the Chicago City Council. He carried the fight
to Washington himself, mobilizing congressional
opinion against Cord's hopes for an airmail contract. By the time the Century strike ended (with
Cord's decision to fold the airline), Behncke had
achieved favorable standing in Washington.

Behncke's prominence paid off the following
year. In 1933 he led a successful fight to exempt pilots from the provisions of the National Recovery Administration's Code of Fair Competition. The codes
specified maximum hours and minimum wages for
workers. Airline management saw the airline code
as an opportunity to reduce pilot wages and increase the number of flying hours per month.
Again, through adroit use of congressional friends
to manipulate the process, Behncke not only prevented the operators from achieving their goals, but
also stabilized pilots' wages and working conditions

at the existing level. By bluffing a national strike
(which almost surely would have failed and destroyed ALPA in the process), Behncke got the pilots' part of the code a hearing before the National
Labor Board, which rendered Decision 83 stabiliz-
ing pilots' wages and working conditions. Decision
83 was written into all subsequent airmail legislation and the Civil Aeronautics Act of 1938. It fixed
a floor under pilot pay and a ceiling on the number
of hours a pilot could fly each month. Subsequently, Behncke negotiated collective bargaining
agreements with each airline, using Decision 83 as
the base.

In 1934 Behncke again demonstrated his political savvy by supporting the Roosevelt administration's decision to cancel the airmail contracts of
1930. Following a Senate investigation into possible
fraud, Roosevelt canceled the contracts in February
1934 and ordered the army to fly the mail. Although the cancellations put many of his pilots out
of work, Behncke persuaded them that it would
only be temporary, and that as Roosevelt loyalists
(when every other prominent aviation industry interest was denouncing the cancellations) they would
reap rewards in the future.

Behncke proved correct. When Congress
drafted legislation to reform the airmail bidding
process, Roosevelt insisted that it contain the substance of Decision 83. Furthermore, when the cap-
stone Civil Aeronautics Act of 1938 was passed,
Behncke used his credit with the administration to secure incorporation of the Air Safety Board (ASB),
to investigate airline accidents. The ASB had to include at least one "active airline pilot" among its
three members. Pilots had long chafed at what they
regarded as a rigged system of accident investigation, which tended always to blame the dead pilot instead of management or government. The new
ASB's airline pilot member was Tom Hardin,
ALPA's first vice-president, second in command to
Behncke. By 1938 his achievements included de
facto power to name the pilot member of the ASB.

During World War II Behncke fought a stubborn rearguard action against attempts by both management and government to whittle away at his
pilots' wages and working conditions. Always a flag-
waving patriot, this opposition did not come easily,
but he felt compelled by events to oppose the government. In 1934 he survived a crash of his Boeing
247 near Chicago. He never flew again as an airline pilot, retiring to become full-time president of

ALPA in 1935, but he retained his Army Air Corps Reserve commission. Upon the outbreak of World War II, Behncke expected to be offered a promotion and high rank in the newly formed Air Transport Command (ATC). He even began flying again in the army reserves in order to be fully qualified. His orders to active duty were a bitter disappointment. While desk-bound executives such as C. R. Smith of American Airlines received direct promotions to colonel and important posts in the ATC Behncke received only a measly promotion to captain and orders to a flight instructor's billet in Texas. His outrage was such that he used his political influence to have the orders canceled. He blamed these events on the vengeance of airline executives whom he had opposed, and seemed to understand that Roosevelt's hands were tied. Hence Behncke was particularly vigilant in protecting airline pilots from what he called "war hysteria to tear down our hard-won gains." At one wartime meeting in Washington, D.C., Eastern's Edward V. Rickenbacker had to be restrained from striking Behncke over his "unpatriotic" objection to increased hours of flying for ATC crews.

In the late 1940s Behncke reached his apogee of political and personal prominence. In 1946 he led Transcontinental and Western Air Lines pilots to a successful resolution of the first true nationwide strike in ALPA's history. In 1947 he was the subject of a feature article, "Labor's Biggest Wind," in the *Saturday Evening Post*. In 1948 his political connections with the Harry S. Truman administration proved vital in winning a strike against National Airlines. Behncke's high public profile made him the target of several unflattering news stories, such as *Time*'s sneering 1946 article "Golden Boys." But so long as he was winning, Behncke's hold on his union seemed secure. There was trouble beneath the surface, however.

By 1950 Behncke's control of ALPA had weakened. The "Old Man," as everybody in ALPA called him, was visibly failing to keep pace with the changes in the industry. In 1947 he faced opposition from American Airlines' captain Willis H. Proctor, the first contested election in ALPA's history. Partly to remedy what ALPA members saw as Behncke's administrative deficiencies, in 1947 they mandated a new office, executive vice-president, to take over the paperwork. Behncke saw this action by the 1947 Board of Directors Convention as a threat to his leadership, and he resisted filling the of-

fice for over a year. This kind of procrastination had become an increasing problem with Behncke, who habitually delayed important decisions and missed deadlines. Coupled with a visible decline in his health owing to heart trouble, these deficiencies led to widespread dissatisfaction with his leadership by early 1951. There was particular concern over finances, owing to Behncke's erratic spending. The building of ALPA's new headquarters on the edge of Chicago's Midway Airport was a particular problem. Behncke, who had long dreamed of the building as a monument to his leadership, insisted on "aircraft specifications" in its construction. As a consequence, costs soared out of control while Behncke neglected administrative duties in favor of sidewalk supervising at the construction site.

All these discontents with Behncke's leadership were surfacing at a time when a new generation of airline pilots, many of them with university educations, were entering the profession and becoming active in ALPA affairs. To them, Behncke was a relic from a bygone era who seemed unable to adapt to new circumstances. This problem was particularly noticeable in the negotiations for a new "four-engine" contract.

Behncke, still clinging to the pay formula which was embodied in Decision 83 of 1933, insisted that the new contracts contain something he called "mileage increase determination." Put simply, this meant that ALPA favored a contract which would treat pilot productivity on the twin engine DC-3 as the industry standard. That is, while a pilot might fly more passengers at greater speed over greater distances on one of the new four-engine aircraft, Behncke insisted that compensation levels ought to be geared to the old standard. His approach was a crude attempt to cope with the problem of technological unemployment, and it struck many observers as rank featherbedding. There was no chance that any airline would agree to this approach, so by 1951 every pilot group in the country was at a deadlock in negotiations. Many pilots believed that Behncke had to be removed from office. In unauthorized negotiations with management, several pilot groups had already achieved tentative agreement on favorable contracts which included gross weight pay, a minimum monthly guarantee, landing pay, deadhead pay (for pilots being ferried to work), and even the long-sought new method of computing copilot pay. But Behncke would not budge.

Finally, following Behncke's sabotage of a Federal Emergency Board hearing in New York on April 1951, a revolution broke out. The catalyst in Behncke's downfall was the ALPA professional staff. Over the years he had recruited an able staff of professional engineers, technicians, and lawyers to serve the multiple needs of ALPA's 7,000 members. He behaved autocratically and arbitrarily with these employees. Frustrated with the working conditions, ALPA's staffers formed their own union, The ALPA Professional Employees Association, and approached senior pilots on one of the union's governing bodies, the "Executive Board." Four Eastern Air Lines captains, Jerry Wood (first vice-president and second in command to Behncke), Vern Peterson, John P. Talton, and W. T. "Slim" Babbitt, each of whom was known for probity and long service to ALPA, investigated the professional staff's complaints and brought the problem to the attention of pilots from other airlines.

At the time many pilots thought Behncke was suffering from some form of mental illness. Although a consensus was emerging that the "Old Man" had to go, nobody knew exactly how to do it. Behncke was in midterm, duly elected, and in command of the union's administrative machinery. The revolutionaries hoped that Behncke would see reason, accept a "President Emeritus" position at full salary for life, and quietly retire. Behncke refused all compromises.

On July 16, 1951, a specially constituted executive board removed Behncke from office and named his executive vice-president, Clarence N. Sayen, to replace him. Although the pilots found it necessary to fire Behncke, they still had great respect for him. In a moving summary of his career, Pan American captain A. J. "Tony" O'Donnell persuaded the delegates to continue paying Behncke's salary for life,

and even give him a raise. Karl Ruppenthal, one of the leading revolutionaries against Behncke, noted that there were few dry eyes in the house after O'Donnell's speech. "Better watch out," noted one observer, "or he'll have them reelecting the guy!"

But Behncke refused all compromise and fought on. After a costly and confusing series of legal battles, a federal court confirmed Behncke's ouster on July 31, 1952. Behncke still refused to surrender ALPA's property. Finally, on August 15, 1952, a federal appellate court found Behncke in contempt. In barely a month, ALPA's regular convention would meet, and the delegates certainly would not sustain him. He had used up his credit with the pilots to whom he had given his life. So he did something he had never in his entire life done before— he quit. He was old, tired, and sick. And he was beaten.

Dave Behncke lived only another few months. On April 14, 1953, following a light exercise session and massage at a Chicago YMCA, he died of a heart attack. At his own request he was cremated and his ashes were scattered along the old airmail route he had flown for Boeing Air Transport in 1928. Today the circumstances of his ouster have been largely forgotten, and he is uniformly revered by professional airline pilots as the founder of their union.

References:

"Golden Boys," *Time,* 47 (February 4, 1946): 22;

George E. Hopkins, *The Airline Pilots: A Study in Elite Unionization* (Cambridge, Mass.: Harvard University Press, 1971);

Hopkins, *Flying the Line: The First Half Century of the Air Line Pilots Assocciation* (Washington, D.C.: Air Line Pilots Association, 1982);

Wesley Price, "Labor's Biggest Wind," *Saturday Evening Post,* 220 (August 2, 1947): 117-118.

Black Committee

by Wesley Phillips Newton

Auburn University

A month before Franklin D. Roosevelt took office in 1933, Senator Hugo L. Black, Democrat of Alabama, was empowered to head a special committee to investigate the award of ocean mail contracts by the Hoover administration. Black had populist tendencies and, having once served as a police court judge and county prosecutor, knew how to conduct a hearing and cross-examine. During the last six months of 1933 the Black committee examined the ocean mail situation, uncovering administrative favoritism and some fast and loose spending, but none of this generated public indignation or media attention.

Meanwhile, newspaper writer Fulton Lewis, Jr., of the Hearst chain, approached Black and suggested that the committee redirect its attention to the award of airmail contracts by Herbert Hoover's postmaster general, Walter Folger Brown. Lewis had become suspicious of these awards after learning that the Ludington Line had failed to win a New York-Washington contract despite the fact that its bid was far lower than that of the winner, Eastern Air Transport. Eastern subsequently gobbled up Ludington. Lewis dug into the circumstances of all the Brown awards, initially with the approval of his publisher, William Randolph Hearst, and the deeper he dug the more scandal he seemed to uncover. When he brought his findings to Hearst, the media lord decided the material was too embarrassing to the Hoover administration to publish.

Black received the cooperation of the Post Office solicitor, who sent his inspectors to search postal and other files. He met with Roosevelt early in 1934 and briefed the president about what the Lewis files seemed to indicate. Roosevelt gave him the green light to proceed with vigor. The senator took him at his word. As Marylin Bender and Selig Altschul describe it: "Courteously, he led the witnesses to the question trough. When they shied, he

took them down another lane, and when their attention was thus diverted, he led them back again." Black "made them all tell their stories, the high and not-so-mighty men of aviation; who had bent their knees to the Great God Brown and benefited from his favors."

At one point William E. Boeing was on the stand. Black confronted him with a letter of December 5, 1929, written to Boeing by Frederick B. Rentschler (how some of these documents were obtained by the Black committee later raised questions about legal procedure on the part of a man who was to become a Supreme Court justice celebrated for his defense of constitutional rights). The letter described how Richard F. Hoyt, chairman of the board of the Aviation Corporation of the Americas (ACOTA), offered Boeing and Rentschler the opportunity to purchase a large amount of ACOTA stock, part of which they were to retain until Hoyt could convince his board to buy back a partial amount at the total purchase price, with some of the stock to go into Hoyt's personal holdings. When asked by Black if the transaction went through, Boeing could not remember. Neither could Rentschler in later testimony, but Hoyt had announced at the time that the Boeing Airplane-United Aircraft combine (Rentschler's affiliation) had purchased 50,000 shares of ACOTA stock. The main purpose of this financial crossbreeding, which on the surface was not illegal, was so Hoyt could fatten his and his associates' stock portfolios and so Boeing-United Aircraft could gain an advantage in selling equipment to Pan American Airways, ACOTA's operating company. Rentschler soon became a member of the ACOTA board. Black committee revelations of such collusion between airlines and airline manufacturers contributed to the separation of ownership as well as board membership in those enterprises.

Army Air Corps pilot preparing to leave March Field, California, with mail in a Boeing P-12 pursuit, February 15, 1934 (courtesy of the U.S. Air Force)

Another witness to appear before the Black committee was C. E. Woolman, an airline official of a small company that had lost in the parceling out of airmail contracts by Brown to the "Big Four"—Eastern, American, United, and TWA. Black asked Woolman, whose company, Delta, had failed to obtain a contract for the route from Dallas to Atlanta, which it had developed but lost to American, if he had sold his interest in the route to American willingly. Woolman replied that he had sold out because, having lost the chance to carry mail, his line could not compete with American, the winner of the contract, because Woolman's experience had shown him that the carriage of passengers alone, even in the absence of competition, was a losing proposition.

Other witnesses, such as the Braniff brothers, Tom and Paul, told the committee essentially the same sad tale. From their perspective it was a matter of discrimination: routes had been developed under arduous conditions at considerable expense by struggling organizations, then awarded to other organizations that had little or nothing to do with these pioneer endeavors. Brown and the Big Four wanted an orderly system run by a few well-

financed airlines. The same, from Brown's standpoint, was true of the international mail routes, where one line, Pan American Airways, had demonstrated the ability as well as determination to survive under trying conditions.

From Chairman Black's viewpoint, the controversy pitted greedy barons of Republican-favored capitalism against little guys struggling to earn a living. Brown, the committee's natural main target, agreed to come out of retirement to defend himself. The committee had already received testimony from a postal clerk that Brown had ordered him to burn documents having to do with airmail contracts. Brown denied that his motive was sinister, claiming he had merely cleaned out miscellaneous papers in order to leave his successor uncluttered files. But he soon showed up in Postmaster General James Farley's office with some documents relating to contracts, which he said he had discovered recently among his personal effects. Someone, he speculated, must have planted them there.

When pressed in his testimony to explain why he had discriminated against small carriers in favor of big ones, Brown insisted that he had done so only to create a stable airline system that could generate enough profits to permit the design and manufacture of larger and safer aircraft and to maintain U.S. leadership in commercial aviation. Why, asked Black, did you not permit the New York, Rio & Buenos Aires Line (NYRBA) to bid on a mail contract after it had established a route ahead of Pan American Airways on the east coast of South America? Brown at first seemed vague about the situation, and Black shifted to another topic. At the next session, however, he went back to NYRBA. This time Brown was not vague. Competition between American carriers overseas would lower their rates for foreign mail bound for the United States, and the Post Office would thus not recoup its subsidy granted the contractor bearing U.S. bound mail. By implication, the competitors would both be weakened. It was best that there be one strong, subsidized airline. Brown could not be shaken from his position that he had acted in the best interest of the U.S. government and, at the same time, American entrepreneurship.

Brown, like Black, was a politician, steeped in the tradition of divide and conquer. He suggested to the cigar-chomping committee head that Postmaster General Farley had been critical of Black's investigation. The chairman reacted vigorously, demanding to know the nature of the criticism and threatening to have Farley subpoenaed to confront Brown. The witness at first refused to reveal the nature of the alleged remarks but then asserted that Farley termed the investigation political and Black a publicity seeker. Black's reaction was tension-easing laughter, and Farley's response was to deny making the remarks.

Farley had cautioned Roosevelt that the Black committee findings might prove embarrassing, for during the ocean mail phase of the investigation some of the questionable actors were personal friends or political allies of Roosevelt. This information had not deterred the president from authorizing Black to charge ahead. Farley had gotten in on the spirit of the proceedings by publicly casting aspersions on Brown's actions in the award of the airmail contracts.

The hearings took a bizarre turn when Black attempted to subpoena the files of William P. MacCracken, Jr., Washington attorney and lobbyist for the airlines and former assistant secretary of commerce for aeronautics. At first MacCracken refused to yield his files, claiming attorney-client privilege; but he relented when when Black gave him permis-

sion to seek the consent of the various airline executives for the release of each one's individual correspondence. All but two of the executives agreed to the release of their correspondence; those two wanted to examine their papers before release, and MacCracken and his law partner permitted it. One of the executives took some of his papers with him and shredded certain letters into the trash outside his office building.

Black had gotten wind of these doings, and postal agents were sent to search the trash. With the pieced-together letters, Black confronted MacCracken and the two executives, as well as the secretary of one of the latter who had done some searching in the MacCracken files. Refusing to accept their various explanations, Black appeared before the Senate charging contempt of that body. The Senate issued a show-cause order, and there then ensued a game of hide-and-seek in which Senate sergeant-at-arms C. W. Jurney, garbed in such strange apparel as a cowboy hat, black coat, and gray-striped trousers, pursued MacCracken to arrest him, and MacCracken, after an initial evasion, sought to be arrested and taken to court, instead of the Senate, so he might serve a writ of habeas corpus on Jurney. Jurney finally won the contest, and MacCracken and his codefendants, with Black serving as prosecutor, were tried before the Senate. MacCracken was found guilty of contempt and sentenced to ten days in jail. On appeal MacCracken denied the right of the Senate to try him, but the Supreme Court in 1935 upheld that right.

The vaudeville aspect of MacCracken's relationship with the Black committee tended for a time to obscure the more serious charges emerging from the testimony and evidence. The charges, which the solicitor general summarized for Farley and Roosevelt, were: 1) airmail revenue went to a few favored companies, whose officials often used the funds to engage in self-promoting stock speculation; 2) the five original airmail contracts, due to expire on November 7, 1929, were extended by the postmaster general so that those favored few could fall under the jurisdiction of the Air Mail (Watres) Act passed in 1930, which authorized the postmaster general to select the lowest, most responsible bidder; 3) Brown held a secret "spoils conference" in 1930 to divide the airline routes among the favored few; 4) thousands of miles of airline routes had been awarded without competitive bidding; 5) airline and postal executives had destroyed or withheld incriminating evidence; 6) American Airways had bought out Delta's rights to part of the southern transcontinental route when C. E. Woolman learned he was frozen out from winning a contract, and American was the lone bidder for that route; 7) the central transcontinental route had gone to the highest bidder, resulting in a considerable loss of revenue to the government; 8) the Post Office Department had greatly overpaid its contractors; and 9) the airmail contracts, having been obtained by collusion, were illegal.

Black, the solicitor general, Farley, and the president met early in February 1934 to consider the charges. At a previous meeting Black pointed out to Roosevelt that the president had legislative authority to cancel airmail contracts when fraud was involved. Now Roosevelt decided that was precisely the action to take in the face of the evidence Black's committee had gathered. Farley tried to prevent cancellation, advocating instead that the contracts continue in force until new ones could be negotiated. The president felt that this move would not inspire the obvious reforms the charges called for. On February 9, 1934, Roosevelt ordered the existing airmail contracts canceled and instructed the air corps to fly the mail.

Maj. Gen. Benjamin Foulois, chief of the air corps, had been reminded that the army had been the first to carry U.S. airmail, in 1918. On February 16, 1934, he told the House Post Office Committee that veteran pilots would fly the mail, men with experience in all conditions. As if to mock his assurances, three air corps pilots crashed to their deaths on the way to airmail assignments on the night of February 16. Two days later, on the eve of air corps mail operations, the airlines decided on a dramatic gesture—part a thumbing of the nose, part a flaunting of technological superiority. Jack Frye of TWA and Edward Rickenbacker of Eastern Air Transport flew a new airliner, the DC-1, between California and New Jersey, with stops at Kansas City and Columbus, Ohio, in the record time of 13 hours, four minutes. Prior to takeoff Rickenbacker had called the deaths of the air corps pilots "legalized murder."

With obsolete, mainly fighter planes with small load capacities, the Army Air Corps inaugurated its airmail service on February 19. A major snowstorm began across the northern United States the same day. On February 22 the first operational

death occurred, along with the fourth fatality of a pilot flying to his assignment.

Senator Black had defended the cancellation of the contracts stoutly. In answer to such attacks as those by Charles A. Lindbergh and humorist and aviation advocate Will Rogers that the airlines had not been given due process, Black pointed out that such criticism would be valid if the administration had proceeded as if the airlines were accused of criminal acts; instead, it had proceeded properly in what was a civil matter, in which the government was compelled to take swift corrective action. The senator also spoke to the sentiments of economically depressed times. The public had no intention of seeing public money diverted into the pockets of a select few by collusion and fraud. Billy Mitchell repeated more or less the same theme before a House committee. The more liberal in the media played a background chorus. But the mainstream of the nation's newspapers were Republican and hence pro-airline and anticancellation. As accidents, injuries, and deaths mounted, the administration was subjected to withering editorial and congressional fire. The roll call of the names of the dead—Grenier, White, Eastham, Lowry, Patrick—received additions: Lt. George F. McDermott on February 23 off Long Island; Otto Wienecke in a snowstorm on March 9 in Ohio. The last and 12th fatality was Lt. Thurman A. Wood, who went down on a farm in Iowa on March 31. Of the 12 dead, four were killed while actually flying mail. But to the public it was all the same.

Meantime, a shaken Roosevelt knew he had made a serious political mistake. The howling winds of controversy were detracting from the effort to win support for his New Deal programs. The president called in army chief of staff Douglas MacArthur and Foulois and raked them over the coals. They were his scapegoats, not Farley or Black. Mail carrying by the air corps, he ordered, was to be carried out only under the most favorable conditions. Foulois then suspended mail operations for ten days to make adjustments. It was a generally welcomed respite. When operations were resumed, there was only one fatality, on March 31. With better and newer equipment (the Martin B-10 bomber), a reduced schedule, and improving weather, the air corps compiled an improved safety record that gave indication of what it might have been capable of doing if proper planning and equipment had been present at the outset. The air corps flew its last mail early in May. Its final flight was in a sense a response to the Frye-Rickenbacker flight of February 18: a group of newer air corps planes carried the mail from California to New Jersey in a little over 14 hours. One important result of the air corps' somewhat tragic participation in the airmail crisis was the formation of a blue-ribbon committee known as the Baker committee that marked the beginning of a slow but ultimately enlarged effort to strengthen an obviously neglected army air arm.

Roosevelt felt pressure to turn the airmail back to civil carriers sooner than he had planned. On April 20, 1934, Farley opened bids for temporary contracts. A condition of bidding was that a company could not have been represented at the "spoils conference" of 1930. Farley himself suggested to operators of the affected companies that they change their names and that he would wink at the subterfuge. American Airways became American Airlines; Eastern Air Transport became Eastern Air Lines; TWA became TWA, Inc. United did not bother to change its name. Another condition was that the executives who had participated in the 1930 meeting to be purged. The new awards did not profoundly change the route network, but some new players got into the game, such as Delta, which won a considerable chunk of the southern transcontinental route, much of which it had pioneered. Out of Fulton Lewis, Jr.,'s muckraking and the Black committee's relentless probing also emerged legislation that profoundly affected the airline and aircraft manufacturing industries: the Air Mail Act of 1934 and the Civil Aeronautics Act of 1938.

References:

Marylin Bender and Selig Altschul, *The Chosen Instrument* (New York: Simon & Schuster, 1982);

Virginia Van der Ver Hamilton, *Hugo Black: The Alabama Years* (Baton Rouge: Louisiana State University Press, 1972);

Nick A. Komons, *Bonfires to Beacons: Federal Civil Aviation Policy under the Air Commerce Act, 1926-1938* (Washington, D.C.: Smithsonian Institution, 1989);

Maurer Maurer, *Aviation in the U.S. Army, 1919-1939* (Washington, D.C.: Office of Air Force History, 1987);

Wesley Phillips Newton, *The Perilous Sky: U.S. Aviation Diplomacy and Latin America, 1919-1931* (Miami, Fla.: University of Miami Press, 1978).

Frank Borman

(March 14, 1928 -   )

by W. David Lewis

Auburn University

CAREER: Fighter pilot and instructor, U.S. Air Force (1950-1962); astronaut, Gemini and Apollo projects, National Aeronautics and Space Administration (1962-1970); vice-president for operations (1970-1974), executive vice-president, general operations manager (1974-1975), president (1975-1985), chief executive officer (1975-1986), chairman, Eastern Air Lines (1985-1986); vice-chairman and director, Texas Air Corporation (1986-   ).

Frank Borman, who won fame as an astronaut and became the most significant chief executive of Eastern Air Lines after Edward V. Rickenbacker, was born on March 14, 1928, in Gary, Indiana, the son of Edwin Borman, a garage and fill-ing station operator, and Marjorie Borman. Named Frank Frederick Borman II in honor of his paternal grandfather, the son of a German musician who had immigrated to the United States shortly before the Civil War, he was an only child. Because he suffered from sinus trouble and other chronic illnesses as a youth, his parents moved to Tucson, Arizona, when he was six years old. Growing up there, he excelled in academic subjects and was also highly proficient in sports despite his relatively small build, becoming quarterback of his high school football team in 1945. Then, as later in his career, sheer determination compensated for a lack of other endowments; although he had a weak arm and did not complete a single forward pass, his team went undefeated and won the state championship.

Frank Borman

Borman's interest in flight began early. Through his father's influence, he became a model airplane builder, which remained a lifelong hobby. He learned to fly when he was fifteen years old, soloed after eight hours of lessons, won a student license, and joined a Tucson flying club. Determined to become a military pilot, he secured an appointment to the U.S. Military Academy at West Point in 1946 with the help of a judge whose son he had taught to build model aircraft.

Borman's training at West Point left an enduring stamp on his life and career; the conviction that "the mission is everything," which he carried with him from then on, became embedded in the depths of his being at the Academy. Committing himself unreservedly to its discipline and traditions, he rose steadily to become a company commander and cadet captain in his final year and graduated eighth among 670 members of his class in 1950. Returning to Tucson prior to his first assignment at Perrin Air Force Base in Texas, he married his high school sweetheart, Susan Bugbee, on July 20, 1950. They had two sons, Frederick, born October 4, 1951, and Edwin, born July 20, 1953.

From the beginning of his air force career, Borman exhibited the qualities of intense ambition and ceaseless drive that ultimately won him fame as an astronaut and corporate leader. After receiving his initial flight training in T-6 aircraft at Perrin, he chose to become a fighter pilot and was assigned to Williams Air Force Base in Arizona, where he graduated from T-28 trainers to his first jet, the Lockheed F-80, and eagerly embraced the motto of the installation: "Every Man a Tiger." Combat flying instruction came next at Nellis Air Force Base, where his previously smooth progress toward his professional objectives received a severe setback. Practicing dive bombing while suffering from a head cold, he incurred a badly ruptured eardrum that nearly ended his flying career. Thus began a series of frustrations that dogged him for nearly a decade.

Posted to the Philippines with the 44th Fighter/Bomber Squadron at Clark Field, Borman was grounded because of his ear impairment and never saw combat despite his intense desire to take part in the ongoing Korean War. He did, however, gain valuable administrative experience by being placed in charge of approximately 1,500 military and civilian personnel who were responsible for maintaining the base. Determined to get back into the air despite his damaged ear, he took experimental radium treatments and secured reinstatement as a pilot in September 1952. Still denied assignment to Korea, he ferried reconditioned aircraft from Japan to the Philippines and was ultimately posted to Moody Air Force Base in Valdosta, Georgia, at the end of his tour.

At Moody, Borman taught instrument flying in jet aircraft and got his first taste of test operations when he was assigned to put a modified T-33 into a deliberate spin. Still hoping to revert to combat status and disliking the social climate in Valdosta, he won transfer to Luke Air Force Base in Arizona, but he was disappointed to be continued as an instrument instructor despite wanting to become involved in fighter weapons training. He next received an unwanted assignment to teach aerodynamics and fluid mechanics at West Point, requiring him to earn a master's degree in aeronautical engineering at the California Institute of Technology (Caltech); while there, he satisfied his craving for actual flying by going aloft on weekends in any plane he could find at nearby airfields, even going to the extent of deserting his family at Thanksgiving in 1956 in order to take a friend to Washington, D.C., in a borrowed T-33.

After receiving his master's degree at Caltech in 1957, Borman enjoyed teaching at West Point but was still desperate to return to the role of a fighter pilot. Volunteering for any assignment that might help him regain this status, he spent one summer enduring the rigors of the Air Force Survival School, submitting to tortures designed to enable pilots to undergo severe mistreatment if captured behind enemy lines. Gradually, however, he reconsidered his career path. Although it did not immediately incline him toward becoming an astronaut, the outburst of national anxiety that followed the successful Soviet launching of Sputnik I in 1957 helped refocus his thinking. Realizing that his academic training and experience as a flight instructor could open the way to becoming a test pilot, he succeeded in negotiating the highly selective process of gaining assignment to an exclusive training program at Edwards Air Force Base in California. Among his classmates were Michael Collins, James Irwin, and Thomas Stafford, all of whom would later join him in the National Aeronautics and Space Administration (NASA) Apollo project.

Working with fierce determination—Collins wrote that he "raced through the academic curriculum with slide rule practically smoking"—Borman graduated at the head of his class scholastically, finished second in flying, and was voted the best overall student in the entire group. Spurning the opportunity to return to fighter pilot status that was now within his grasp, he elected instead to capitalize upon his educational and instructional experience by enrolling in the pioneering Aerospace Research Pilot School that the air force had established to prepare its personnel for participation in the space program. After studying orbital mechanics at the University of Michigan and enduring parabolic flights in the famed "Vomit Comets" at Wright-Patterson Air Force Base, he volunteered for the even more stressful research program being conducted at Johnsville Naval Air Station near Philadelphia to test the ability of human subjects to withstand severe gravity forces in a large centrifuge. Back at Edwards he performed extremely demanding maneuvers at high altitudes under the command of Brig. Gen. Charles ("Chuck") Yeager; in one test he received an award for refusing to bail out and bringing a crippled F-104 safely back to base after successfully restarting a J-79 engine that had exploded from excessive heat.

In 1961 Borman reached the crossroads of his career when NASA began seeking air force and navy recruits for the Gemini and Apollo programs. Reassured by a trip to Washington, where the fa-

bled Curtis LeMay counseled air force personnel not to fear the career risks involved in transferring to NASA, Borman underwent stringent testing for NASA at Brooks Air Force Base in San Antonio, Texas. Despite his still severely damaged eardrum, he was one of nine persons to qualify for Gemini. Moving to Houston, he specialized in the study of booster rockets, particularly the Titan II, and he also became an expert in launch abort and safety techniques, working closely with NASA rocket scientist Wernher von Braun. Experience gained as backup commander of Gemini IV prepared him to lead the crew of Gemini VII, the longest mission thus far scheduled in the development of the American space program.

Borman's responsibilities became even greater when the disintegration of the Atlas-Agena vehicle, with which the crew of Gemini VI was supposed to rendezvous in October 1965, led to a decision to reconceive the next flight as a joint mission in which the Gemini VI and Gemini VII crews were to effect rendezvous. His capacity for intense and highly disciplined work had much to do with the success of the venture, in which the two spacecraft maneuvered to within one foot of each other and Borman's vehicle remained aloft for a record 206 orbits, encompassing approximately 14 days. Upon returning from this grueling mission, Borman, who had become a lieutenant colonel just prior to the flight, was elevated to a full colonelcy, making him at age thirty-seven the youngest officer of that rank in the air force.

Along with Stafford and James McDivitt, Borman was one of the three leading astronauts in the Gemini group. "He seemed to glow," one of his peers wrote about him. "He wore the smug look of one who knows he will be the anointed one to do 'it,' whatever 'it' may be." The impression he had made upon top NASA administrators was revealed in late January 1967 when he was appointed to a high-level committee to investigate the causes of a tragic accident in which three Apollo astronauts—Roger Chaffee, Virgil ("Gus") Grissom, and Edward H. White II—were killed in a fire that broke out in their capsule while they were performing a supposedly routine test on the ground. Normally a loner, Borman had formed an unusually close friendship with White, and pursued his duties with relentless determination to uncover the truth. After conducting a four-month probe, the committee failed to determine conclusively the exact cause of the disaster, but did make many recommendations to increase the safety of such tests and of the Apollo vehicles. Borman played a key role in implementing the recommendations by being placed in charge of a NASA team that oversaw the Apollo modification process at the North American Aviation Corporation plant in Downey, California.

This assignment prevented Borman from leading the backup crew of Apollo VII, the first manned venture in the series of missions that was to culminate in the lunar landing of 1969. Instead, he received a much more important role by being selected to command the crew of Apollo VIII, which was to travel for the first time outside the Earth's gravitational field and go into orbit around the moon. Borman's well-honed expertise in rocket boosters was an asset in preparations for this flight, the first to utilize the enormous new Saturn V launch vehicle. Blasting off from Kennedy Space Center on December 21, 1968, the crew became "the first humans to see the world in its majestic totality," as Borman later described the experience, and achieved lunar orbit on December 24 as an estimated one billion viewers watched their television sets. Focusing a camera on the home planet, Borman took one of the most famous pictures in the history of photography, showing the earth shining brightly against the darkness of outer space. Then, just prior to setting out on the return flight, he and his companions read aloud to the world a Christmas message from the first chapter of Genesis.

After the successful splashdown in the Pacific on December 27, Borman was a world figure. Addressing a joint session of Congress, he urged the members not to retreat from the nation's commitment to space exploration. Not long after, he and his wife were prominently seated near Richard M. Nixon at Nixon's inauguration as president. Admiring Borman as an ideal specimen of American manhood, Nixon soon sent the astronaut and his wife on a European goodwill tour in which they were received by the kings and queens of Great Britain and other countries, and by president Charles de Gaulle of France, who asked Borman how he had maintained order on the flight of Apollo VIII. Much to de Gaulle's satisfaction, Borman replied, "Mr. President, there were three men but only one commander—*me*." Later, in Rome, Borman had an audience with Pope Paul VI and spoke to the College of Cardinals, taking pride in delivering his remarks

"from the very spot where in 1616 Galileo . . . had been tried and found guilty of heresy for supporting Copernicus's theory that the earth revolved around the sun and not the opposite."

Further evidence of Borman's dramatically enhanced stature followed his return to the United States when NASA appointed him a special liaison to the White House to counsel the Nixon administration on how to handle publicity growing out of the upcoming flight of Apollo XI, in which Neil Armstrong and Edwin ("Buzz") Aldrin were to become the first human beings to set foot on the moon. Working with such presidential advisers as William Safire, he helped compose what he later characterized as "the most historic telephone call ever made," transmitted by Nixon to the astronauts after their successful landing. At Nixon's request, he also toured college and university campuses that were seething with unrest during the heyday of the New Left, and came away dismayed by "the uncertainty, the absolute ineffectiveness, of . . . faculty and administrators in dealing with sheer anarchy." Much more enjoyable was a subsequent trip that he and his family made to the Soviet Union, where they were cordially received by such cosmonauts as Georgi Beregovoi and Gherman Titov, visited the Soviet aerospace complex at Star City, and, with difficulty, secured permission to inspect the ill-fated Soviet supersonic transport, the TU-144. This mission not only paved the way for a subsequent visit to the United States by Soviet cosmonauts, but also helped Borman take some credit for laying the groundwork for the Apollo-Soyuz mission of July 1975.

Borman had already decided to leave NASA, but was not yet sure which of several possible civilian career alternatives to pursue. After turning down an opportunity to remain on the White House staff under chief of staff Robert Haldeman and declining several business offers because of a feeling that by accepting them he might become "a dancing bear, living off my astronaut fame for the rest of my life," he accepted an invitation by Floyd Hall, chairman of the board and chief executive officer of Eastern Air Lines, to become a technical consultant to that carrier. Soon after, Hall prevailed upon him to become vice-president for operations, indicating that he was looking upon Borman as a likely successor. Despite knowing that Eastern was "a sick airline, torn by internal feuding," Borman accepted, joining the company on July 1, 1970.

With Hall's consent, Borman undertook one final mission for the White House: an unsuccessful effort to gain support among world leaders for putting pressure on the government of North Vietnam to provide more humane treatment to American prisoners of war. After returning from this "bitter lesson in international politics," in which only Great Britain and West Germany promised full cooperation, he plunged into his new duties at Eastern with the same fierce intensity that he had exhibited throughout his previous career. A 13-week crash course in management at Harvard Business School helped prepare him for his responsibilities but did not prevent him from blundering in his first assignment, that of negotiating a new contract with the company's pilots, who were conducting a slowdown of operations in an effort to force a favorable settlement. Ill-informed about the history of recent labor disputes and naively believing that the pilots were "fellow birdmen" who would be "as concerned with Eastern's welfare as any fighter pilot would be with his squadron's," he was lured into a settlement even more damaging to the company than a previous contract that had already "saddled Eastern with the lowest pilot utilization in the industry." Like his recent campus tour and his unsuccessful diplomatic mission on behalf of the POWs, it was another rude awakening to the realities of a world far different from the restricted environment with which he was familiar.

Spared by Hall from punitive action that Eastern's president and chief operating officer, Sam Higginbottom, would have taken, Borman studied his new environment and discovered that, from his military perspective, Eastern was even sicker than he had realized. Instead of a well-defined chain of command, it had two conflicting centers of authority, New York and Miami, and two heads, Hall and Higginbottom, each with his own coterie of supporters. The company's bloated and flabby administrative hierarchy excelled in buck-passing and was constantly engaged in vicious internecine warfare. Enjoying all sorts of costly perquisites, its pampered executives flew here and there in a luxurious Lockheed JetStar and drove flashy rental cars at company expense. Meanwhile, its employees, whom Borman interviewed extensively in trips around the system, lacked any sense of identification with the firm's well-being and pursued their own selfish ends, as Eastern's pilots had done in staging slowdowns.

Such behavior contrasted starkly with Borman's values; so far as he was concerned, for example, the pilots had been guilty of "stealing from the company" when they staged their slowdowns. During his previous career, he had willingly endured all sorts of privations without thought of material reward and devoted himself to his responsibilities so unstintingly that he had grossly neglected his wife and family. Once, while overseeing modifications of the Apollo space capsule at Downey, he had not even been present when his wife had undergone a hysterectomy. Coming from such a background, he deeply resented civilian behavior that would have seemed normal to less heavily indoctrinated observers. With every fiber of his being, he was shocked and sickened by what he saw at Eastern.

Realizing that he as yet had no real power despite his high-sounding position, and disparagingly referred to as "Moon Man" by associates who scoffed at his "Boy Scout morality," Borman waited impatiently for a chance to impose his will upon the enterprise. During his first few years with Eastern, he took heart from only one episode, when a company L-1011 jetliner, approaching Miami on a flight from New York, crashed into the Everglades after one of the cockpit crew had accidentally disengaged the autopilot. Taking a helicopter to the scene and doing what he could to comfort the injured and dying, Borman was deeply moved by the way employees helped the survivors of the tragedy. In the days that followed, he saw Eastern functioning at its best to minimize the impact of the disaster upon its victims, striving in an unselfish way to meet their needs and making generous voluntary settlements to resolve pressing claims. "For the first time I felt encouraged and believed that this airline, even riddled with inept management and uncaring unions, deserved to be saved," he later stated. "Out of tragedy had come a deep love for Eastern, not as an inanimate corporation, but as a living entity made up of a gallant, spirited army of human beings."

For the most part, however, Borman was appalled by the magnitude of the company's problems. Despite recent efforts to improve its fleet, which was largely obsolete due to a series of poor decisions made in the transition to the jet age by its longtime chief executive, Edward V. Rickenbacker, it remained technologically behind other major carriers, particularly its chief competitor, Delta. Even many of its newer aircraft, such as a special model of the Boeing 727 that had been designed for quick conversion from cargo to passenger operations, were excessively costly to operate, and the engines of its Lockheed L-1011 jumbo jets were so undependable, due to forged fan discs that could not withstand extreme heat, that the planes were out of service much of the time, with resulting heavy financial losses. Ground facilities were in poor condition, and deliveries of new equipment, such as jetways needed to improve passenger service, were running as much as 18 months behind schedule on account of poor management. The company's route structure was characterized by an excess of relatively short flights and a shortage of long, nonstop flights from which money could be made. In addition, the firm was overdependent on the seasonal vacation trade, unbalancing its cash flow. Once the most profitable carrier in the industry, it was reeling under annual deficits that mounted to $50 million in 1973. As the situation deteriorated, Higginbottom resigned as president and Hall assumed full control, but his health was deteriorating and he could not provide the leadership so desperately needed by the floundering enterprise.

In 1975, after Eastern's dominant stockholder, Laurance Rockefeller, had initiated an investigation of the company's condition and received a dismaying report by his chief representative on its board, Walter Hitesman, the directors finally put Borman in charge as president and chief executive officer. Forcing Hall into early retirement and centralizing all aspects of the company's management at the Miami operational base, the ex-astronaut launched the sweeping program of change that he had been contemplating throughout five years of impatient watching and waiting. From the beginning, he imposed a stern discipline befitting his military background. Walter Cunningham, a fellow astronaut who wrote admiringly about Borman, nevertheless indicated that the latter could "be an imperious martinet to those who work for him." This was an accurate assessment. In his own autobiography Borman summed up his intentions by stating that, under his rule, Eastern would soon be "going down a one-way street with everyone marching in the same direction, management and workers alike, and anyone doing an about-face was going to get stepped on."

The pace of Borman's own activities emphasized what he expected of those around him. "Frank doesn't walk," said one Eastern executive.

"He bolts." Having no patience with what he once called "committees and claptrap," he cut short anybody who came to a conference with him unprepared to get directly to the point. "Even when Col. Borman and his wife ... go hiking on rare occasions in such places as the Grand Tetons in Wyoming," one writer declared, "he hikes fast." His personal example was also important when he banned drinking at lunch among Eastern employees, including executives long accustomed to downing midday martinis. Not surprisingly, considering his other straitlaced tendencies, he neither smoked nor used alcohol.

Because of existing labor contracts which he could not immediately abrogate, most of Borman's early moves involved disciplining the managerial ranks. Taking an axe to executive deadwood, he sacked no less than 24 vice-presidents within one year, and insisted that those who remained conduct their own purges despite the human costs involved. "Sometimes butts have to be kicked even when you feel the pain yourself," he observed after forcing a more softhearted executive to fire a subordinate with personal problems. "If a patient requires surgery, you have no choice but to start cutting," he remarked on another occasion. Reportedly, no less than 3,000 people had been fired from Eastern by November 1977.

Setting a Spartan example by driving a secondhand Chevrolet Camaro to work, Borman abruptly canceled costly managerial perquisites. In one muchpublicized episode, he forced senior vice-presidents to load baggage at Miami International Airport, rolling up his own shirtsleeves and working straight through an entire shift without pausing for lunch. For those who protested that he was "tough and unfeeling," he responded with the same hard-bitten attitude that had characterized him throughout his previous career. "If you don't like what I'm doing," he once stated, "just get the hell out of the way because it has to be done."

In 1976, labor, too, began to feel the impact of Borman's program. After going to nearly every station in the system to talk to union members and their leaders about the desperateness of the company's plight, he implemented a wage freeze—the first to occur in the industry—to reduce labor costs. As a quid pro quo, he instituted a relatively simple profit-sharing plan that gave employees the choice of receiving a percentage of company earnings or securing options to buy stock at a stipulated

Eastern Air Lines Lockheed L-1011 (courtesy of the John Wegg Collection)

price. Soon, however, Borman came up with a more complicated five-year arrangement that involved sharing deficits as well as profits. Known as the Variable Earnings Plan (VEP), it involved withholding a small percentage from paychecks that would be used to augment company earnings if they fell below a stipulated level, in exchange for the right to share to a limited degree in any profits that went above it. After a strenuous campaign involving tough negotiations with national labor leaders and meetings with worker groups throughout the Eastern system, Borman succeeded in getting the proposal ratified in a vote by members of the company's most stubborn union, the International Association of Machinists and Aerospace Workers (IAM). Securing the consent of the other workers was much easier, and the plan went into effect.

Borman moved with equal decisiveness to upgrade Eastern's fleet. Searching for fuel economy and a seating capacity that would be more appropriate for Eastern's route structure than that of the excessively large L-1011s, he could not find an American jetliner that met his specifications or would be available soon enough to meet the company's needs. In a daring move, he responded fa-

vorably to a presentation made in March 1977 by Roger Beteille of Western Europe's Airbus Industrie, which had gone through a 16-month dry spell and was desperate to find markets for its A-300 airliner in the wake of a failed deal with Western Airlines. Although the A-300 had 250 seats and Borman wanted only 170, Beteille offered to charge Eastern a price corresponding to the capacity it wanted until it could actually use the extra seats.

Stressing the need to familiarize Eastern's employees with the European plane and the past reluctance of American passengers to accept foreign airliners, Borman demanded an arrangement under which Eastern would lease four of the new planes on a trial basis for six months at no cost. These were extremely unusual terms, but Airbus accepted. After the A-300s proved highly successful on Eastern's main routes, Borman and his chief financial adviser, Charles Simons, worked out a complex financing scheme with Airbus and General Electric, which supplied the engines, enabling Eastern to acquire 23 of the aircraft on terms the company could afford. Soon after, in a move that was to have fateful repercussions in the 1980s when union leaders effectively exploited it as an example of his alleged extravagance, Borman signed an order for 21 Boeing 757s and secured a commitment from British prime minister James Callahan to guarantee the Rolls-Royce RB-211-535 engines with which Eastern decided to equip it. All in all, Eastern's fleet modernization program cost approximately $1.4 billion.

Seeking to build a progressive new image for Eastern, Borman reluctantly agreed to innovate by playing the starring role in a series of television commercials. Utilizing a new slogan, "We Have to Earn Our Wings Every Day," the commercials became extremely popular and gained him public exposure rivaling that which he had received as an astronaut.

Under Borman's hard-driving leadership, Eastern enjoyed four profitable years, achieving total net earnings of nearly $200 million from 1976 through 1979. The $67.2 million profit garnered in 1978 was the highest in the company's history. That same year, however, passage of the Airline Deregulation Act brought about changes for which Eastern was ill-prepared. Fearing unrestricted competition with such carriers as People Express, which had much lower operating costs, Borman opposed the legislation in congressional hearings and debated its merits with Massachusetts senator Edward M. Kennedy on television, but to no avail. Seeing trouble ahead, Borman tried to acquire National Airlines, which was also a merger target of Pan American and Texas Air, to give Eastern greater critical mass in facing the new order. When this failed, he tried to negotiate a merger with Northwest, but that carrier's chief executive, Donald Nyrop, shrank from embracing Eastern's high labor costs. Still apprehensive about surviving deregulation, Borman pursued corporate mergers with Braniff and Trans World, but these overtures also came to nothing.

Forced to deal with deregulation alone, Eastern plunged into increasing turmoil in the early 1980s. As Borman had feared, the new legislative order led to frequent rate cutting; in addition, Eastern had to deal with intensified competition on the crucial New York-to-Miami run, particularly after Pan American Airways won its merger battle with Texas Air and absorbed National. Meanwhile, despite expectations to the contrary, markets softened under the impact of a recession. Abruptly, Eastern's four-year run of profits ceased. In 1980, it lost $17.3 million; in 1981, $66 million; and in 1982, nearly $75 million.

Relations with Eastern's unions, particularly the IAM, also became increasingly sour. Early in its utilization, the VEP had worked to the benefit of employees, yielding a 98 percent return on their contribution in 1978. But, as Borman had intended, it was also a deficit-sharing plan; when profits disappeared after 1979, it became unpopular. Furthermore, Borman's problems were compounded after October 1980 when Charles Bryan, an aggressive West Virginian who had staked his leadership on ending the VEP, was elected president of Eastern's District 100 of the IAM. From this point on, Borman's relations with employees belonging to that union became increasingly adversarial.

Taking advantage of a legal technicality, Borman managed for a short time to extend the VEP beyond its original five-year term, but this only intensified ill feeling among employees, who felt that they had been cheated. By the end of 1982, Bryan had forced Borman to abandon the VEP, which was replaced by an Employee Investment Program (EIP) under which the company continued to withhold earnings as a hedge against losses but agreed to pay the workers back with interest within a stipulated time. This victory emboldened Bryan in future clashes with Borman.

In 1983 Eastern's losses mounted sharply in each quarter and finally reached more than $183 million for the year, a company record. Against this menacing backdrop Borman tried to reach a new wage accord with the IAM, replacing a previous contract that had already expired. Insisting on a substantial retroactive hike, and threatening a strike if it were not granted, Bryan laid much of the blame for the company's troubles on Borman's ongoing acquisition of new Boeing 757s, which the union leader branded as extravagant. Emphasizing the bargain prices under which the company had acquired the planes, Borman responded by arguing that the need to cut fuel costs and eliminate antiquated equipment under deregulated conditions gave him no choice but to continue the program, particularly because Delta was constantly upgrading its already significantly younger fleet. "In a free market," he declared, "the only way to survive is from a position of leadership."

Even probusiness *Fortune* magazine, however, did not find Borman's position convincing, pointing out that he had added approximately 150 percent more seats to Eastern's fleet than had been planned five years earlier; that the increasingly weak market had been unable to sustain such an ambitious expansion; and that more and more of the company's planes were flying with large numbers of empty seats while its debts had grown to approximately $2 billion. Noting that Borman's credibility had become "terribly tattered" because of his highhanded methods and further undermined by erratic forecasts issued under his management, the same periodical reminded Borman that there was a limit to how often he could use predictions of impending corporate bankruptcy as a weapon in winning concessions from labor, likening him to the legendary boy who kept shouting "Wolf!" until his warnings ceased to have any effect.

Unfortunately, Borman found that the same legend applied to his relationships with credit institutions, which had been listening to similar predictions for years and now refused at a critical juncture to authorize emergency loans to tide the company over in the event of a strike by the IAM. Without such support, Borman, who had already been assured of cooperation by other major employee constituencies if the IAM conducted a walkout, committed a major blunder by abruptly turning an about-face and granting that union's demands. Stating publicly that the company had been "raped" and "mugged," he took this sudden step in full knowledge that he would soon be asking the IAM to give back much of what it had gained.

Not surprisingly, this sudden reversal of Borman's previous promises to stand firm against Bryan turned out disastrously. As Borman later acknowledged in his autobiography, his submission to the IAM cost him much of whatever credibility he had earlier enjoyed among pilots, flight attendants, and noncontract employees, who felt betrayed. In the future they would be far more militant. Borman defended his move by stating that a strike of practically any duration would have led to bankruptcy, which he could not face. Actually, his previous military training may have come back to haunt him at this critical juncture in his career. To a person with his intense dedication to completing any assignment he was given, risking bankruptcy was unthinkable because it would have represented a failure to achieve what he had set out to do. In a moment of extreme crisis, the deeply ingrained mission orientation that had guided him ever since his days as a cadet at West Point had led to his worst mistake.

As Borman had foreseen, the strike settlement of 1983 imposed insupportable burdens upon the company. As its plight worsened, Borman demanded that the IAM give back some of the benefits it had won, leading to yet another crisis. Recognizing how badly his credibility had been impaired, Borman hired William Usery, a veteran union member who had been secretary of labor in President Gerald R. Ford's cabinet, to serve as "sort of a permanent arbitrator or mediator" in disputes between Eastern and its workers. After obtaining two separate audits that demonstrated how desperate Eastern's problems were becoming, Usery won a one-year cutback in wages in exchange for company stock that gave employees one quarter of the firm's outstanding shares, and gained a further commitment on the part of Eastern's unions to lessen costs through productivity gains. As a result of the deal, labor secured four seats on the board of directors. Being inside the tent, however, only increased its capacity to be a thorn in Borman's side. Meanwhile, executives of other airlines and important Wall Street financiers alike blamed Borman for having given away too much.

In his autobiography Borman belittled the productivity gains achieved by the company through the settlement Usery had negotiated and charged that most of those that did occur were due to action on the part of the pilots, not the machinists. Actually, the latter did achieve considerable savings for Eastern by designing new tools to expedite engine repair, recycling salvageable engine components, performing jobs in-house that had previously been done at higher cost by outside contractors, and detecting instances in which the company had been overcharged by suppliers. Although estimates of the money saved in these ways were undoubtedly padded, the savings were not inconsiderable. Predictably, however, Usery's settlement did nothing to solve the company's fundamental problems. Although its financial performance did improve considerably in 1984, it still incurred a loss of $38 million, and Borman demanded an extension of the new wage cut. When the unions failed to respond as he wished, he arbitrarily continued to impose it without their consent after the beginning of 1985. After Eastern actually went into default on its debts, Bryan relented and the extension continued in effect.

Later in the year Borman promoted Joseph Leonard, who had left American Airlines to join the company in 1984 as head of maintenance, to the rank of president and chief operating officer.

Borman (fourth from left) discussing the Eastern Air Lines Variable Earnings profit-sharing plan with mechanics at Newark International Airport

Moving up to chairman of the board, Borman remained Eastern's chief executive. Thanks in part to an imaginative nighttime passenger and cargo operation known as the "Moonlight Special," and partly also because of a temporary lull in the fare cutting that had continued to be widespread throughout the industry, the company began to operate in the black, achieving a net yield of $73.8 million in the first three quarters of 1985. Although most of this was erased in a last-quarter downturn, the company eked out a profit of $6.3 million for the year as a whole.

Eastern was dipping liberally into employee withholdings under the EIP as 1985 came to a close, and Borman could foresee trouble ahead as the year-end slump continued into 1986. In a bold attempt to win fresh concessions from all of the company's unions, including the machinists, despite the fact that their existing contract still had two more years to run, Borman demanded an across-the-board cut of 20 percent, coupling this with his customary predictions of doom for the company if the employees did not concede. Reasoning that none of the unions would be willing to see the firm go bankrupt or be sold to another firm, particularly Frank

Lorenzo's Texas Air Corporation, he reinstituted merger talks with potential buyers and declared that Eastern was faced with three alternatives: "Fix it, sell it, or tank it." By taking such added steps as persuading federal authorities to release the company and its weakest union, that of the flight attendants, from further mediation efforts and to declare a 30-day cooling off period at the conclusion of which management would be free to impose its own terms, Borman deliberately set up a crisis early in 1986, confident that he could force a settlement favorable to himself in such an atmosphere.

TWA and USAir were uninterested in discussing merger with Eastern, and brief discussions with Donald Burr of People Express also came to nothing. Key leaders in the aviation industry and Wall Street financiers alike were not convinced that Borman was sincere in entertaining merger possibilities, believing that he was merely using these as a club to bring his unions to heel. Lorenzo, however, was not only receptive but in fact eager to acquire Eastern. Having already dealt forcefully with labor problems at Continental by taking that carrier into Chapter 11 bankruptcy five days after assuming control in a recent merger, he was willing to gamble that he could handle Eastern's troubles just as effectively. Testing Borman's sincerity, he responded to initial overtures by stating that he was unwilling to make a bid for Eastern unless Borman personally supported it. When Borman refused to go that far, a compromise was proposed by financial intermediaries under which Borman would consent to have a proposal from Lorenzo submitted to Eastern's board of directors, with or without his approval. Perhaps not realizing that some of his ostensible backers had actually lost faith in his ability to save Eastern and had already assured Lorenzo that they would not allow Borman to use him as a chess piece in his battle to checkmate Bryan and other union leaders, Borman agreed to the idea and thereby lost control of the situation.

The stage was thus set for a climactic showdown with Eastern's union leaders that took place in the last week of February 1986. Finally entering the negotiating arena in person after earlier allowing subordinates to parley with the unions, Borman hoped that his influence with such national IAM leaders as John Peterpaul and William Winpisinger, both of whom had previously seemed sympathetic to his arguments, would help him bring Bryan to heel. If this succeeded, the pilots had already agreed to allow the chairman of their negotiating group to accept whatever cuts Bryan might agree to, and the battle would be won. Borman, however, was mistaken in all of his critical assumptions. At the last moment, neither Peterpaul nor Winpisinger came to his rescue. Furthermore, Bryan, who believed that he could deal successfully with Lorenzo, turned a deaf ear to Borman's predictions of doom if the company were sold and refused to be moved by statements that the blame would rest on his shoulders should this be done.

At the final frenzied sessions, which took place during the night of February 23-24, Bryan offered to accept a 15 percent cut if Borman resigned, but the latter was willing to do so only if the IAM agreed to the full 20 percent cut he was demanding. Too inflexible in their hatred of one another to yield, neither man would concede. Meanwhile, having already negotiated the terms of a potential merger agreement with Lorenzo and his top advisers at a meeting in Houston, the investment bankers upon whose approval most of the directors were waiting turned the board free to decide as its members saw fit. When the impasse could not be resolved, a majority of the directors voted to sell the company to Lorenzo. Borman's grand strategy for imposing a settlement on his own terms had backfired.

As the transition to new ownership got underway, Borman remained temporarily in charge of Eastern, spending much of his time fighting a record $9.5 million fine that the Federal Aviation Administration had levied on the company for alleged maintenance violations. The episode only added to his bitterness; in his autobiography he later charged that Secretary of Transportation Elizabeth Dole, then under public criticism because of mounting concern about air safety, had made Eastern a scapegoat for political ends. Finally, on July 1, 1986, he resigned. Moving to Los Cruces, New Mexico, he became an aviation consultant. As vice-chairman and director of Texas Air Corporation, he also, at least temporarily, retained a role in Lorenzo's greatly expanded aviation empire.

As Borman launched this new phase of his career, Lorenzo fought bitterly with the same unions that had opposed the ousted Eastern president. Lacking Borman's intense mission orientation, however, he did not hesitate to take the company into Chapter 11 bankruptcy in 1989 when Bryan and his fellow mechanics carried out the strike that Borman had gone to such lengths to avoid. Within a year, having sold off many of its most valuable assets, Eastern faced potential oblivion, and Lorenzo was no longer in charge after federal bankruptcy judge Burton Lifland lost patience with his increasingly hollow promises to reach a reasonable settlement with the company's creditors.

In 1981 a veteran Delta employee spoke disparagingly about "Eastern's habit of choosing military heroes to solve its problems." His remarks reflected the long-standing animosity that existed between Delta and Eastern. Certainly, high achievements in the armed services do not disqualify a person for subsequent accomplishments of a similar nature in the corporate world. Nevertheless, Eastern's experience under both Edward V. Rickenbacker and Frank Borman would be an extremely poor source of evidence for any effort to demonstrate the wisdom of appointing former military officers to head civilian enterprises. There can be no mistaking the courage and determination that Borman brought to the task of saving a company that was already in desperate straits before he first became associated with it in 1970. On the other hand, evidence abounds, even in Borman's own autobiography, that his authoritarian style of leadership was badly miscast in the intensifying crisis that engulfed the company after the onset of deregulation. Sooner or later his dictatorial approach and his penchant for manipulation were bound to expose him to a nemesis that he lacked the sensitivity or experience to avoid. Ironically, Borman's intense mission orientation worked to his disadvantage in his efforts to deal with such persons as Bryan, who was equally bent on domination. In 1983 Bryan took advantage of this Achilles' heel with great effectiveness. In 1986 Borman's own miscalculations did the rest.

Despite his temporary success in his first few years as chief executive of Eastern, Borman would have been better off remaining in the military and quasi-military activities for which he was so ideally suited. It is not surprising, given his determination to command at any cost and his distaste for the give-and-take of civilian relationships, that this modern-day samurai ultimately failed to master the strange new circumstances into which he was thrust after Apollo VIII had taken him where no man had ever gone before.

Publication:
Countdown: An Autobiography, by Borman with Robert J. Serling (New York: Morrow, 1988).

References:
Aaron Bernstein, *Grounded: Frank Lorenzo and the Destruction of Eastern Airlines* (New York: Simon & Schuster, 1990);

Michael Collins, *Carrying the Fire: An Astronaut's Journeys* (New York: Ballantine, 1975);

James Conaway, "Borman to the Rescue," *New York Times Magazine,* May 9, 1976, pp. 37-41;

Walter Cunningham, *The All-American Boys* (New York: Macmillan, 1977);

"Eastern's Astronaut," *Time,* 104 (November 18, 1974): 65;

"Eastern's New Pilot," *Newsweek,* 86 (November 3, 1975): 74;

"Moon Man Turns Eastern Around," *Time,* 109 (February 7, 1977): 53;

Robert J. Serling, *From the Captain to the Colonel: An Informal History of Eastern Air Lines* (New York: Dial, 1980);

Stratford P. Sherman, "Eastern Air Lines on the Brink," *Fortune,* 108 (October 17, 1983): 102-109;

Sterling G. Slappey, "The Astronaut Who Flies Eastern," *Nation's Business,* 66 (September 1978): 63-67.

Thomas E. Braniff
(December 6, 1883 - January 10, 1954)

by Roger E. Bilstein

University of Houston—Clear Lake

CAREER: Partner in insurance business (1902-1919); president, T. E. Braniff Company (1919-1954); partner, Paul R. Braniff, Inc. (1928-1929); president, Braniff Airways (1930-1948), Braniff International Airways (1948-1954).

In the years before World War II, several aspiring airlines in America took off with their founders' names emblazoned on the planes' fuselages. By the 1950s, only one major airline still soldiered on with the owner's name intact—Braniff. Braniff's success owed much to the peculiarities of its southwestern market, where shrewdly chosen routes tapped a travel-conscious clientele. At the same time, Thomas Elmer "Tom" Braniff himself deserved considerable credit. He was a successful businessman long before he entered the airline industry. Moreover, his personal commitments built a public

image that set him apart from other airline entrepreneurs of his day. Braniff was a civic leader whose associations ranged from the Boy Scouts to grand opera, and he played a key role in international groups such as the World Council of Christians and Jews. As a result, he was seen not only as an industry executive but also as a caring person whose work intimately touched the lives of thousands of individuals who considered themselves friends and acquaintances.

Braniff was proud to be a Catholic in a region of the country where most Protestants still viewed the pope as a grave threat to "that old-time religion." Irish-born ancestors settled first in Pennsylvania before moving on to Salina, Kansas, where Braniff was born on December 6, 1883, to J. A. and Mary Catherine (Baker) Braniff. The family also lived in Kansas City, Missouri, where Tom and

Thomas E. Braniff (courtesy of the National Air and Space Museum)

his younger brother, Paul, enrolled in public school. Around the turn of the century, the Braniffs left for the Southwest when the Oklahoma Territory opened up under the Homestead Act. Braniff's father started an insurance business, with rural homesteaders as his clients. As a teenager, Tom hit the road for his father, driving a buckboard through the dusty trails of western Oklahoma's "Indian Country" while hawking tornado and fire insurance to settlers.

Young Braniff did well as an insurance salesman. By 1902, in partnership with Frank Merrill, he opened his own insurance business in Oklahoma City. He was married in 1912 to Bess Thurman, daughter of a Missouri judge. The Braniffs had two children.

When Merrill, who was two decades older than Braniff, decided to retire in 1919, Braniff bought him out. The T. E. Braniff Company expanded rapidly, fielding dozens of agents, riding the crest of the southwest region's oil boom. Within five years the Braniff Building in the heart of Oklahoma City went up as one of the state's first skyscrapers, and Braniff had already made a sizable fortune. Even though airline development eventually ab-

sorbed much of his energies, he continued as president of the T. E. Braniff Company, which wrote $1.5 million in premiums per year in the early 1950s. In addition, he played a role in the banking and insurance industries, with directorships in the Republican National Bank of Dallas and the Kansas City Fire and Marine Insurance Company; he was also board chairman of the Prudential Fire Insurance Company of Oklahoma.

Described as pink-cheeked and affable, Braniff enjoyed golf and developed a special interest in hunting, a pastime he never relinquished no matter how pressing his executive duties. From his early years as a salesman, he maintained a close personal touch with customers and acquaintances, a habit that remained with him through his entire life and which colored his role in Braniff Airways as well.

Tom first developed an interest in aviation during the 1920s. After he bought a share in a single-engine Stinson in 1928, his younger brother, Paul—who had been a pilot in World War I—convinced him to utilize it on a 116-mile passenger run between Oklahoma City and Tulsa, two towns joined only by a weather-beaten, unpaved road and a painfully slow passenger train. With backing from two oil companies, Paul R. Braniff, Inc., was organized by the two brothers, with Paul as chief pilot. The operation grew at a surprising speed, acquiring three more six-place Stinsons and carrying a remarkable 3,000 passengers during the first year. By early 1929, the route expanded to include Dallas and Ft. Worth.

The terrain and climate of that part of the Southwest favored aviation, with no threatening mountains and year-round good flying weather. Moreover, rapid transportation in the region represented a valuable commodity. The clientele for Braniff and others came primarily from the thriving petroleum business. From Wichita, Kansas, down through Oklahoma and across Texas, a rapidly expanding economy based on oil created a new transportation market. Along this axis, from the Midwest to the Gulf Coast, lay many cities that had been bypassed during the nineteenth-century railway construction boom. Existing roads were frequently no more than dirt tracks: perilously potholed in dry seasons and impassable mud holes in wet seasons. Lacking convenient, traditional transportation and communication links, communities throughout the oil boom region turned to air travel.

Braniff Convair 340 (courtesy of the National Air and Space Museum)

In 1929 the Braniffs sold out to a larger conglomerate, Universal Aviation Corporation, which eventually became the Aviation Corporation and ended up as American Airlines. Meanwhile, the Braniff brothers had so enjoyed their early experience in the aviation business that they started a new company named Braniff Airways late in 1930, on a route that included Tulsa, Oklahoma City, and Wichita Falls.

Braniff wooed its passengers with appealing schedules and fast airplanes. The new equipment constituted a pair of single-engine Lockheed Vegas with room for six passengers. Not as big as the trimotored Fords and Fokkers of competitors, the Vegas had a reputation for speed that appealed to wildcatters and petroleum executives in a hurry to close a deal or scout new territory. The company added service to St. Louis and Chicago in 1931. In 1934 Braniff obtained its first mail route, from Chicago to Dallas; Houston came soon after. The demise of Bowen Airlines permitted Braniff's expansion to the border town of Brownsville and elsewhere in Texas; acquisition of Long and

Harmon Airlines added to the Texas market and brought in bigger planes such as Ford Trimotors. Braniff broke even in 1934 and reported its first profit of $28,000 in 1938.

Braniff proudly promoted itself as the "Great Lakes to the Gulf" airline and shed its outdated Fords for Lockheed Electras. By 1941 Tom Braniff, president of the line, could boast of a modern fleet that included five DC-2s and a quartet of DC-3s.

Braniff ran his growing company as a paternalistic enterprise. When he spoke of the "Braniff family" he was not mouthing a slogan but expressing a genuine personal outlook. He knew his folksy operation could be an easy target for a bigger rival, so he took the lead, in 1931, in creating the Independent Scheduled Air Transport Operators' Association for the smaller airlines in the region. The organization offered an arena to help stave off intramural squabbles over each others' routes, and, more important, gave them an attorney in Washington who would look after their interests, especially the contract mail routes.

When World War II broke out, Braniff joined other carriers in surrendering half its planes to the government. The war brought significant changes for the carrier. The company had already concentrated its maintenance operations at Dallas in 1936, and Braniff decided to shift its headquarters there in 1942, taking advantage of the city's growing role as a transportation hub and corporate center. Under contract to the Air Transport Command, Braniff not only flew domestic routes, but also got its first international exposure. The company's Cargo Air Contract Division operated a route through Central America to Panama. As a result, the company picked up invaluable experience for future operations beyond U.S. boundaries. Braniff successfully petitioned the Civil Aeronautics Board (CAB) for a Mexican route in 1943 but postponed its activation until after the war.

In the postwar era, the Dallas-Ft. Worth area boomed. The war had brought a new industrial base, adding to the city's existing petroleum and banking activities. Low taxes, surplus labor, and good airline connections became synergistic forces that rapidly advanced the pace of the region's economy, and Braniff shared in it.

Tom Braniff kept his Douglas DC-3s, bought some new ones (the last one was retired in 1960), and decided to go shopping with some of the millions of dollars in profits the company accumulated during the last two months of the war. He bought several war-surplus C-54 four-engine cargo planes, refurbished them as airliners, and introduced them as DC-4 transports on the Dallas-Kansas City-Chicago run in the spring of 1946. Realizing that he would need even more modern planes to keep up with competitors, he introduced pressurized DC-6 service on the same route by the end of the year. Although expansion of domestic routes through the mid 1950s was modest, Braniff paid careful attention to equipment in an increasingly competitive environment. In 1952 the company acquired Mid-Continent Airlines, which brought 26 new cities into its route structure. With foresight, Braniff had already placed orders for the Convair CV-340, becoming the first operator to put this twin-engine transport into service to many of these new markets. Braniff's biggest decisions, however, had to do with his airline's audacious penetration into Latin America, long the special preserve of Pan Am.

In the 1980s the meteoric rise and fall of Braniff International as an airline seems to have ob-scured the trail-breaking role of Braniff's Latin-American venture. The airline's wartime cargo runs to Panama and route authority to Mexico City provided a beachhead from which to challenge Pan Am. Tom Braniff created a Mexican company, Aerovias Braniff, S.A., to connect with Braniff's U.S. routes. From Nuevo Laredo on the Rio Grande, a trio of DC-3 transports were assigned the route to Mexico City, and flights began in April 1945. Pan Am's own subsidiary in Mexico immediately raised a ruckus, challenging schedules, questioning landing rights, and raising various legal issues; traditional operational assistance was denied Braniff at Mexican airfields. Braniff finally pulled out after two years of frustration, and Tom Braniff's bitterness at Pan Am's posture simmered for years.

At the same time, CAB actions in 1946 opened the door to South America by other routes. Braniff won authority to fly to Rio de Janeiro and Buenos Aires, and to serve several South American countries en route. Pan Am belligerently refused to grant joint use of its airfield facilities throughout the continent. Determined to succeed, Braniff built its own radio station in Ecuador and arranged for passenger facilities in Lima, Peru, and La Paz, Bolivia. Service to these cities got underway by 1948 and 1949, respectively, preparing the way for a major leap across the 20,000-foot Andes to Rio de Janeiro and Buenos Aires, where the first Braniff DC-6 arrived in 1950. Tom Braniff was aboard to meet a welcoming committee of Juan and Eva Perón. An admiring journalist from *Newsweek* called the flight "a victory over climate conditions, hostile foreign governments, and competing Pan American Airways." Other South American cities appeared on Braniff's route maps, underscoring the company's 1948 name change to Braniff International Airways.

Throughout his career, Tom Braniff had been a formidable force in an impressive range of public and private organizations. There were the usual industry groups, such as the Air Transport Association, but others were more indicative of special concerns. Due largely to the company's Latin-American interests, he also served on several inter-American boards and committees, such as the U.S. Council of the International Chamber of Commerce. But his international interests extended beyond business. In 1946 Braniff was elected Catholic cochairman of the National Conference of Chris-

Braniff Lockheed Vega (courtesy of the National Air and Space Museum)

tians and Jews, a post he held in 1952 as well. He was deeply concerned about sectarianism, an issue that made him part of a small group associated with Charles Evans Hughes and led to the founding of the World Council of Christians and Jews in 1947. The goal of religious tolerance took him to Europe in 1950 to help inaugurate the World Brotherhood Organization.

In addition, Braniff took an active role in the civic affairs of both Oklahoma City and his adopted hometown of Dallas. He worked with the American Cancer Society, Boy Scouts, colleges and universities, deaf people, Dallas Grand Opera, and other educational and philanthropic groups. In 1944 he and his wife set up the Braniff Foundation to support religious, educational, and scientific projects. At ceremonies in Rome in 1944, he received the Knight Commander of the Order of St. Gregory, the highest honor the pope can bestow on a lay person, in recognition of his humanitarian leadership. Among his peers, few could compare in stat-

ure with Braniff for voluntary service to society and international understanding.

Braniff never gave up his keen interest in hunting. Not long after the New Year celebrations for 1954 were over, he joined a group of ten prominent businessmen for some duck hunting in Louisiana. Returning home on January 10, 1954, the Grumman Mallard amphibian carrying the hunters ran into severe icing conditions near Shreveport. The pilot tried to land the plane on a lake, but icing forced it down short of its goal, and the pilot, copilot, and all ten passengers were killed. Tom Braniff died at the age of seventy-one.

References:

Charles E. Beard, *Thomas E. Braniff: Southwest Pioneer in Air Transportation* (New York: Newcomen Society in North America, 1955);

R. E. G. Davies, *Airlines of the United States since 1914*, revised edition (Washington, D.C.: Smithsonian Institution, 1982);

John J. Nance, *Splash of Colors: The Self-Destruction of Braniff International* (New York: Morrow, 1984).

Archives:
A large, uncatalogued collection of materials relat-

ing to Braniff Airways is housed in the Aviation Collection at the University of Texas at Dallas.

Braniff Airways

by Linda Bilstein

University of Houston—Clear Lake

and

Roger E. Bilstein

University of Houston—Clear Lake

In 1928 the Braniff brothers, Thomas and Paul, along with several other partners ventured into commercial aviation. Paul R. Braniff, Inc., began operations between Tulsa and Oklahoma City (and later Wichita Falls) with a six-seat Stinson Detroiter. These same routes were continued when the Braniff brothers incorporated Braniff Airways in 1930. At this time the first Braniff flight attendants were hired. These unmarried women had to have at least two years of college, meet specific physical and age requirements, and be able to speak Spanish.

By 1937 Braniff had secured airmail contracts and improved its equipment, which included two Ford Trimotors (retired in 1936), seven Lockheed Electras, and an order for five Douglas DC-2s. In 1940 the first of four 21-passenger DC-3s appeared on the Dallas-Amarillo run, and Braniff retired the smaller Electras the same year. Between 1942 and 1945, more than 50 percent of the Braniff fleet was used by the U.S. government for war service, with the remainder contracted to fly to Panama and on domestic runs for the Army Air Transport Command. In 1942 Braniff Airways moved its headquarters from Oklahoma City to Dallas's Love Field.

Braniff expanded rapidly at the close of World War II, employing more than 1,300 people by 1946. Tom Braniff's enthusiasm for the Caribbean and Latin America was rewarded when the Civil Aeronautics Board (CAB) awarded the airline 7,700 miles of routes in Latin America and the right to extend service to Panama, Colombia, Ecuador, Brazil, Argentina, Mexico, and other countries. On June 4, 1948, two years after purchasing six Douglas DC-6s to meet these new demands, Braniff inaugurated DC-6 flights from Houston to Lima, Peru. On the same day it inaugurated the Lima service,

Braniff Airways became Braniff International Airways. The next 12 years saw flights to seven other South American cities, as Braniff realized his dream of operating an international carrier.

While Tom Braniff was putting his own money into developing a communications and navigation system across South America, he also led the airline into a decade of continued domestic expansion. In 1952 Braniff International acquired Mid-Continent Airlines, increasing its cities served by 26. A few months later, the airline became the first in the world to use the Convair CV-340 for scheduled flights. Unfortunately, Braniff did not live to see the continuation of this dramatic growth into the decade of the 1960s. In 1954 he died in the crash of a corporate plane in Louisiana. Within a few days, Fred Jones was selected to replace him as board chairman, and Charles E. Beard took over as president. Looking toward the Atlantic seaboard market, Braniff soon joined Eastern in opening an equipment interchange at Miami. By mid 1956, the carrier had begun service over a 1,050-mile route segment between Texas, the midsouth, Washington, and New York. Later that same year, Braniff added the Douglas DC-7 to its fleet and, in 1959, the Lockheed L-188 Electra. Then, in the final month of 1959, the airline achieved jet service when it introduced the Boeing 707.

During the 1960s, Braniff International underwent a dramatic transformation. In 1965 Great-America Corporation purchased the 37-year-old Braniff Airways and hired Harding Lawrence from Continental Airlines as president. Lawrence promised to double Braniff's size within five years while changing its image from a quiet, conservative airline into a dynamic industry trendsetter. One of his

Braniff Lockheed L-10A Electra (courtesy of the National Air and Space Museum)

first actions as president was to order 18 Boeing 727 jets. In addition, the new president redesigned everything from advertising to employee uniforms. Along with remodeled waiting rooms and aircraft interiors, the new Easter-egg-colored aircraft caught the attention and imagination of the American public as Braniff rapidly expanded its domestic and international routes. In early 1967, under Lawrence's guidance, the airline acquired Pan American-Grace Airways (PANAGRA), giving the company control of half the U.S. international routes in the Latin-American market.

The Lawrence regime brought dizzying growth. By 1978 Braniff reached into the Pacific with a new route to Hawaii and across the Atlantic to Great Britain. When Dallas-Ft. Worth International Airport opened in 1973, Braniff became a major tenant and built a huge headquarters complex on the site. Braniff also entered into a cooperative agreement with British Airways and Air France to operate the supersonic Concorde on flights from Texas to Washington, D.C., during 1978. As the Airline Deregulation Act went into effect, Lawrence filed for some 700 new routes. Not all were granted, but Braniff scrambled to add dozens of non-

stop segments and many new cities to its growing empire. Passenger boardings surged ahead nearly 18 percent, operating revenues jumped 23 percent to $966 million, and net profits hit $45 million, a 34 percent rise.

On the surface things looked bright indeed. Braniff added more cities in Europe, announced new service to Seoul, Hong Kong, and Singapore on the Asian mainland, and continued to build its domestic network. In 1980 revenues reached a record $1.45 billion dollars. But the airline had outstripped its management, and operational troubles began to mount with a consequent loss of passenger boardings. The hurried addition of new equipment and route maintenance costs added to growing financial burdens, so that Braniff's losses came to $38 million in 1979 and $128 million in 1980.

Lawrence was forced into retirement in 1981, and Howard Putnam, a Southwest Airlines executive, became Braniff's new president. Putnam tried to keep the airline afloat by eliminating first-class service and imposing harsh economy measures, including elimination of many routes. But it was too late. With debts of $733 million, Braniff filed for

Chapter 11 bankruptcy in May 1982. This was a brutal move, carried out in secret, that not only left thousands of stranded passengers but also canceled paychecks and benefits for thousands of Braniff employees trying to hold the airline together.

Over the next several months, Braniff's South American routes were sold to Eastern, along with most of its domestic slots. The company was recapitalized in 1983 and began service the following year with 30 leased Boeing 727 jets. As Braniff Inc., the company operated as a low-fare, no-frills carrier, although consistent profits seemed elusive. Kansas City became the major hub. Chicago investor Jay Pritzker, who had financed the "New Braniff," sold out in 1988 to BIA-COR Holdings, which moved its headquarters to Orlando, Florida, a year later. A major order for Airbus A-320 transports appeared to mark renewed vigor, but Braniff declared Chapter 11 bankruptcy again in the autumn of 1989, from which it seemed unlikely to emerge.

References:

Stanley H. Brown, "The Golden Castles of Troy V. Post," *Fortune*, 71 (January 1965): 154-159;

Len Morgan, *The View from the Cockpit* (Manhattan, Kans.: Sunflower Press, 1985);

John J. Nance, *Splash of Colors: The Self-Destruction of Braniff International* (New York: Morrow, 1984);

Arthur Norman, "Braniff International Airways," *Flight International*, 87 (April 22, 1965): 636-669;

Arthur Stuart, "Braniff's Dizzying Takeoff Into Deregulated Skies," *Fortune*, 99 (March 26, 1979): 52-56.

L. H. Brittin

(February 8, 1877 - September 4, 1952)

by Patricia A. Michaelis

Kansas State Historical Society

CAREER: Engineer, Newhall Engineering Co., Sierra Madre Land & Lumber Co.; manager, National Lamp Division of General Electric Co.; vice-president and general manager, Northwestern Terminal, Minneapolis, Minnesota; founder, vice-president, and general manager, Northwest Airways (1926-1934); director, Air Freight Association (1934-1950).

Lewis Hotchkiss Brittin was an engineer and industrialist in the Minneapolis-St. Paul area who became a central figure in early development of commercial aviation in the region. Founder, vice-president, and general manager of Northwest Airways, Brittin also served in several aviation organizations, including on the board of directors of the Aeronautical Chamber of Commerce, as president of the National Association of State Aviation Officials, and as chairman of the Minnesota Aeronautics Commission.

Brittin was born in Derby, Connecticut, on February 8, 1877, the son of Edwin and Mary Hotchkiss Brittin. Orphaned as a child, he spent his boyhood in boarding schools in Connecticut. A student at Harvard University from 1897 to 1899, he left school to serve as a corporal in Battery A of the 1st Massachusetts Volunteers during the Spanish-American War. He returned to military service during World War I, this time as a lieutenant colonel in the Quartermaster Corps. Thereafter, he was commonly referred to as Colonel Brittin.

Following his service in the Spanish-American War, Brittin worked as an industrial engineer. He spent five years in Mexico building factories. Later he managed the National Lamp Division of the General Electric Company and the Northwestern Terminal, a multimillion-dollar industrial district for the Minneapolis-St. Paul area.

Brittin's involvement in the aviation industry began in 1926 when he was serving as vice-president of the St. Paul Association of Public and Business Affairs. While Charles M. Dickinson prepared to inaugurate a contract airmail line between the Twin Cities and Chicago, Brittin campaigned for passage of a bond issue to construct an airport in St. Paul. The airmail operation began on June 7, 1926, but several accidents, combined with inadequate financing, forced Dickinson to abandon the contract before the end of the summer.

L. H. Brittin (courtesy of Northwest Airlines)

Determined that the Twin Cities should have air service, Brittin persuaded several business contacts in Detroit to join him in organizing Northwest Airways on August 1. The new company promptly received a contract from the Post Office to carry airmail between Chicago and Minneapolis-St. Paul, stipulating the service would begin on October 1. This left Brittin only seven weeks to organize an airline. He ordered three Stinson Detroiters for the route. While awaiting their delivery, he inaugurated service on time with two rented open-cockpit biplanes. Fortunately, the Stinsons arrived in early November. They were needed to maintain schedules during the harsh winter flying conditions of the region.

As general manager of Northwest Airways, Brittin was actively involved in all aspects of the company's operations. "In this industry," he said in 1928, "rigid economy in operating costs is absolutely essential." He practiced what he preached: Northwest had the second-best operating efficiency among the 20 contract airmail lines.

Brittin also was an innovator. He was responsible for the first ever air-rail service. Six railroads participated in the arrangement. Beginning on September 1, 1928, a passenger could travel by rail during the night from Fargo, North Dakota, to Minneapolis, then board a Northwest Ford Trimotor for a flight to Chicago and a rail connection for the East Coast. Using this system, it was possible to save up to eight hours on a trip between the Midwest and New York.

Northwest grew slowly and steadily under Brittin's careful guidance. By 1929 it was making two daily round trips between Chicago and the Twin Cities, carrying 9,000 pounds of mail per month. During the year it transported more than 6,000 passengers.

Brittin had his sights set on a northern transcontinental route. Postmaster Walter Folger Brown, however, had a different idea. He supported only central and southern routes (by United and American), and he used his power to award mail contracts to insure that his plans were followed. In 1930, when Brown called airline operators to Washington to discuss the new route structure, Northwest was not invited.

Beginning in 1931, Brittin began spending a great deal of time in Washington, lobbying for a westward extension of Northwest's routes. In 1933 Croil Hunter took over as general manager of the airline, enabling Brittin to devote his full time to looking after Northwest's interests in the nation's capital. Largely due to his efforts, Northwest finally reached Seattle in December 1933.

Brittin had little time to enjoy his victory. Early in the new year, a Senate investigating committee chaired by Hugo Black that was looking into irregularities in the awarding of airmail contracts during the presidency of Herbert Hoover, subpoenaed the files of William P. MacCracken, Jr. An assistant secretary of commerce in the previous Republican administration, MacCracken had opened a law practice in Washington that catered to the airlines. Among his clients was Brittin, who kept his personal files in MacCracken's office to save money. As Julian Baird, secretary of Northwest, observed, "The Colonel put *everything* down in writing, including gossipy little facts about the idiosyncrasies and weaknesses of the senators and congressmen he met." Also, according to historian Henry Ladd Smith, the files contained material of "a little domestic trouble" that Brittin wished to keep confidential. In any event, Brittin went to MacCracken's office and tore up many of the documents. Investigators learned about Brittin's action, collected MacCracken's trash, and pieced together the torn papers. Although the documents did not show any illegal activities on Brittin's part, he was tried and convicted of contempt by the Senate. He spent ten days in jail, the only airline executive to receive a prison sentence during the airmail investigations and, according to most observers, the least deserving.

To spare Northwest embarrassment, Brittin had resigned from the airline during his trial. "You will appreciate that this resignation is a very serious matter to me," he had written, "as my life has been entirely wrapped up in the development of Northwest Airways."

Brittin subsequently remained on the fringes of the airline business for some years, associated with companies involved in the shipment of air and rail freight. He served as a director of the Air Freight Association until he retired in 1950. He died on September 4, 1952.

References:

H. A. Lindbergh, "Conservatism—the Dominating Characteristic of Northwest Airways," *Airway Age*, 11 (June 1930): 801-803;

"The Northwest Airways—Notable Record of Efficiency and Safety in Operation—Established First Air-rail Passenger Service," *Airway Age*, 10 (January 1929): 19-21;

Kenneth D. Ruble, *Flight to the Top* (New York: Viking, 1986);

Henry Ladd Smith, *Airways: The History of Commercial Aviation in the United States* (New York: Knopf, 1942).

Archives:

The Lewis H. Brittin Papers are housed in the Archives and Manuscripts Division, Minnesota Historical Society, St. Paul, Minnesota.

Walter Folger Brown

(May 31, 1869 - January 26, 1961)

by David D. Lee

Western Kentucky University

CAREER: Attorney, Toledo, Ohio (1894-1905); partner, Brown, Hahn & Sanger (1905-1927); chairman, Joint Congressional Committee on Reorganization (1921-1924); assistant secretary of commerce (1927-1929); postmaster general (1929-1933); chairman, Hudson & Manhattan Railroad (1933-1946).

A major figure in the history of American commercial aviation, Walter Folger Brown served as postmaster general in the Herbert Hoover administration from 1929 to 1933 and played an important role in structuring the nascent air transport industry. Brown's appointment as postmaster general capped a long and successful political career built largely around his considerable administrative ability. The son of an attorney and Republican party activist, he was born in Massillon, Ohio, on May 31, 1869, but his family soon moved to Toledo. He earned a degree from Harvard in 1892 and spent two years at Harvard Law School before gaining admission to the Ohio Bar and joining his father's law firm.

Brown's real interest was politics, however, and he threw himself into local and statewide political campaigns. Starting as a precinct worker, he rose to the chairmanship of the Toledo Republican Central Committee in 1897. Within a few years his organization dominated Toledo politics. Brown cemented his position by serving as attorney for the local traction company, utilities firms, and other businesses linked to local government. In 1899 he became a member of the Ohio Republican Central Committee, and he chaired the group between 1906 and 1912.

Despite his reputation as a political operative, Brown occasionally supported such prominent progressives as Toledo's Samuel "Golden Rule" Jones (although he and Jones eventually broke with each other), but in 1912 Brown moved dramatically to the progressive side when Theodore Roosevelt chal-

Walter Folger Brown (courtesy of the U.S. Postal Service)

lenged the renomination of President William Howard Taft. The president's failure to consult Brown on local appointments and his refusal to assist a Brown client facing an antitrust indictment contributed to the Toledoan's disenchantment with Taft. Despite the president's Buckeye State connections, Brown delivered 34 of Ohio's 42 convention votes to Theodore Roosevelt at the Republican National Convention.

When Taft won the nomination, Brown followed Roosevelt into the Progressive "Bull Moose" party. Roosevelt especially valued Brown's organizing talents and assigned him the task of creating a structure for the new party. Returning to the Republican fold after the Bull Moose debacle, Brown was prepared to support Roosevelt for president again in 1920, but after the Rough Rider's sudden death he switched to fellow Ohioan Warren G. Harding and worked as Harding's floor manager at the tumultuous Republican convention in Chicago. Harding easily defeated James Cox in the fall campaign and launched a 12-year Republican tenure in the White House.

Brown's administrative talent continued to boost his career throughout the Republican-

dominated 1920s. In his only bid for elective office, he ran for Harding's vacant Senate seat but lost the Republican primary to Frank Willis. The president then offered to name Brown ambassador to Japan, but he chose instead to become Harding's representative on the Joint Congressional Committee on Reorganization of the Executive Departments. Created by Congress in 1921, it was composed of three senators, three congressmen, and Brown, who served as chairman. Under his leadership the group prepared an insightful report which foreshadowed future government restructuring. Among other things, it suggested consolidating the War Department and the Navy Department into a Defense Department and combining a cluster of other agencies into a cabinet-level Department of Health and Education. Brown insisted that such changes could save the executive branch millions of dollars annually.

Although the report was considered controversial and was eventually shelved, Brown's work brought him to the attention of another student of government reorganization, Secretary of Commerce Herbert Hoover, who made Brown an assistant secretary in 1927. The pairing of Hoover and Brown marked the beginning of a fruitful collaboration. In personal terms, both were distant, rather austere men with great intelligence and a zeal for administration. Each had supported Roosevelt in 1912 and remained committed to applying progressive principles to the problems of the 1920s. Moreover, Brown, as a widely known party professional, could link Hoover with the Republican leaders who would be so important to his impending presidential bid. After a brief tenure, Brown left the Department of Commerce to manage Hoover's successful campaign, and the president-elect ultimately named him postmaster general.

Among the assigned duties of the postmaster general was "encouraging commercial aviation," a rather vague charge to sponsor an enterprise Brown knew little about when he took office. He quickly discovered aviation was a delicate industry in danger of collapse. The October stock market crash choked off the fragile prosperity of the late 1920s. Stocks which had once ranged between $150 and $200 per share sold for less than $30. As the Depression settled in, the passenger airline companies, still striving to create a market, were particularly hard hit.

The stock market crash roughly coincided with another worrisome problem, the expiration of airmail contracts with the government. At a time when carrying passengers and freight was simply not profitable, the lucrative airmail contracts in effect functioned as a government subsidy. Operators blessed with contracts generally prospered while those left to build their businesses solely from the private sector teetered on the edge of bankruptcy. As important as these contracts were to the industry, they were creating an enormous financial headache for the Post Office Department because the revenue from the postal rate lagged far behind the weight-based compensation the department was paying to its carriers. By 1929 the government was losing roughly $7 million a year on its airmail operations, a situation Brown considered intolerable. With the contracts due to expire in October 1929, Brown had announced his intention the previous May to revise them substantially. Postal officials and industry leaders were still haggling over the terms of this proposed revision when the stock market collapsed.

Almost simultaneously, Brown reached some definite conclusions about the industry he was assigned to nurture. For one thing, he decided strong commercial aviation was central to the national defense. If commercial flying prospered, he said, "we need have no anxiety about being able to defend ourselves in the air if the occasion should ever arise." Prosperous commercial aviation "will keep our country abreast of the flying" and would guarantee that equipment and personnel would be available in case of a national emergency. He made the link between civilian and military flying explicit in a 1931 speech to the New York City Bond Club: "The design of the large plane that flies several times a day between Washington and New York is that of an army bomber," Brown told the financiers. "It would be a matter of a very few weeks for the factory that turns out that plane to be turning out the finest bombers that have yet been produced." A thriving aviation industry would thus serve as a defense auxiliary and reduce the cost of a military air branch.

Brown also decided that America's rickety aviation industry could not hope to provide such a defense auxiliary. In the future, the United States would need "air lines which will carry not only the fast mail but express and passengers as well, to establish a comprehensive air transport system." For Brown, this meant an emphasis on large, well-financed, well-equipped companies flying the latest equipment over long routes linking major cities,

routes that "have been travelled by ox team, pony express, railroad, automobile, and airplane . . . since white men have inhabited North America."

Brown also concluded that the government's method of awarding airmail contracts actually exacerbated some of the problems facing the industry. Would-be contractors filed compensation-per-pound bids with the Post Office Department, and authorities then gave the route to the lowest bidder. Distance was a factor only if the route was over a thousand miles, and the department completely ignored such considerations as weather, terrain, or type of aircraft. As a result, the airmail contractors were compensated in a very irregular fashion. Obviously contractors flying short, relatively safe routes with a heavy mail volume made a substantial profit, while those flying more challenging routes or perhaps carrying little mail were barely surviving.

Even more pressing for Brown was the need "to induce air mail contractors to create nonpostal revenues to relieve the Post Office Department of a burden that was becoming more intolerable." The weight-based method of payment made companies reluctant to seek other customers as Brown wanted them to do. While a coast-to-coast ticket for a 200-pound man would cost about $300, 200 pounds of mail at the maximum rate meant $1,800 from the Post Office Department. Companies occasionally bumped ticketed passengers to make room for larger mail shipments. Moreover, carrying passengers involved extra expenses such as hiring ticket agents, purchasing larger planes, and providing creature comforts, all features which sacks of mail did not require. Consequently, much to Brown's chagrin, the contractors concentrated on airmail and avoided human cargo.

In late 1929 Brown unveiled his strategy for managing the situation. "In our judgment," he said, "the method of determining the compensation of air mail contractors must be revolutionized" in order to permit "the dispatch of air mail on regularly scheduled passenger flights." To do this, he proposed to junk the weight-based formula in favor of paying a fixed rate per mile for space in the aircraft. Furthermore the department would pay extra for night flying, for flying mountainous or fog-enshrouded routes, and for carrying passengers.

Brown believed his plan would work only if he could drastically curtail competition in the industry and guarantee the contractor that his invest-

Brown (right) and President Herbert Hoover at the cornerstone ceremony for the new Post Office building, Washington, D.C., September 26, 1932 (courtesy of the Herbert Hoover Presidential Library)

ment in passenger-related planes and equipment would be protected. He also feared bids from companies with too little flying experience or firms not interested in becoming passenger carriers. Such companies did not fit Brown's vision of a flourishing, responsible industry, and he wanted to make sure these companies could not obtain a government contract. Therefore, he wanted to end competitive bidding for contracts and negotiate terms with firms of "good character and financial responsibility."

Such a plan required revision of the existing air-mail laws, so in November 1929 Brown assembled a committee of three aviation experts from the private sector and put them to work preparing new legislation based on his ideas. The three were William P. MacCracken, Jr., Paul Henderson, and Mabel Walker Willebrandt, all people with prior experience in both government and aviation. They were joined in their deliberations by Second Assistant Postmaster General Warren Irving Glover and Brown himself. Neither the small operators nor the

nonmail operators played any role in the drafting process. These sessions were illustrative of Brown's attitude toward government regulation of the industry. He preferred to deal with "industrial statesmen," business leaders who supposedly were aware of the public dimension of their enterprises, in preparing a regulatory system based on cooperative rather than adversarial proceedings. Within a few weeks the group had drafted a bill changing the method of compensation for air mail carriers to a space-mile formula, giving the postmaster general authority to negotiate terms of the contracts and permitting him to extend and consolidate routes in the public interest.

The proposal, cosponsored by Senator Charles P. McNary of Oregon and Representative Laurence H. Watres of Pennsylvania, received a hostile reception on Capitol Hill largely due to the opposition of M. Clyde Kelly. A Republican congressman from Pennsylvania, Kelly was known as the "father of the air mail" because he had introduced the Air Mail Act of 1925, which turned the system over to private contractors. A mutual antipathy existed between Brown and Kelly, and the latter believed the McNary-Watres bill would give the postmaster too much power with regard to airmail contracts. He especially opposed the provision that would eliminate competitive bidding, a point of view shared by Comptroller General John McCarl. Although the bill passed the House Committee, Kelly used his influence with the House leadership to keep it from coming to the floor. Frustrated, Brown met with Kelly, Watres, and a few others in a six-hour session which resulted in H. B. 11704, a revised bill which Watres introduced in mid April. The new measure eliminated the provisions which would have given Brown the power to evade competitive bidding. Kelly then withdrew his opposition, and the bill quickly passed both houses of Congress. It became law on April 29, 1930, a few days before the old airmail contracts would have started to expire.

Although the final version of the Watres Act disappointed Brown, he still intended to carry out his plans for the industry. In accord with his usual practice, he began by calling a meeting, the first of the so-called "spoils conferences." Brown opened the May 19 meeting by outlining his plans for the future of commercial aviation. Gesturing toward a map of the nation's airways, he announced his determination to consolidate and rationalize the system while integrating the mail and passenger lines. The economics of air travel dictated long routes, yet many routes stretched merely a few hundred miles. Only United Air Lines had established transcontinental service, and Brown was determined no single company would have such a monopoly. Instead, he wanted two additional competitive routes with all three supplemented by a system of north-south feeders. Simultaneously, Brown wanted to protect the pioneering investments of both mail operators and independents, so he invited members of the council to negotiate among themselves how the airmail pie would be divided. Only by agreeing on trades and consolidations of routes could the conferees hope to avoid competitive bidding. With that admonition, Brown withdrew to let the companies deliberate.

Crucial to Brown's regulatory strategy was the achieving of consensus by the industry on an appropriate solution for its problems. Acutely aware of how deeply the operators distrusted each other, he did not really expect them to agree among themselves, but he did expect them to agree that he

should serve as a referee for their disputes. The conference participants chose MacCracken as their chairman and convened almost daily for the next two weeks, but to little avail. Of the 12 routes Brown outlined on the map, the committee could agree on contractors for only seven. The five remaining included the two new transcontinental routes Brown intended to establish. The operators agreed to submit their differences to the postmaster general for his resolution.

Brown now moved forcefully to impose his own solutions. His initial approach was simply to extend the routes of existing contractors, thereby molding the air network to his model while avoiding competitive bidding. This strategy, however, raised the possibility that Comptroller General McCarl might disallow the transaction. McCarl, who had testified against the original McNary-Watres bill, took a narrow view of Brown's power to grant extensions. In early June the postmaster general tested his attitude by extending the Chicago-Minneapolis route held by Northwest Airways all the way to Winnipeg, Manitoba, an action that roughly doubled the original route. Within a week McCarl rejected the change. He claimed Brown had exceeded his authority and further asserted that extensions must be fairly modest and not major additions to the original route.

The McCarl ruling meant Brown would have to award the contracts on the basis of competitive bidding, but the resourceful Brown now moved to eliminate the competition. Predictably, he first called an industry conference to consider the possible options. After considerable deliberation MacCracken hit upon the device of requiring bidders to have at least six months of experience in flying night schedules over routes of at least 250 miles. Because only mail carriers had such experience, the provision effectively excluded the independents from bidding.

Brown now proceeded to dominate the field through a judicious blending of the carrot and the stick. His plan to award the central transcontinental route to Transcontinental and Western Air (TWA), a firm being created by the merger of Transcontinental Air Transport and Western Air Express, was challenged by a new firm, United Aviation (UA), an amalgamation of three small lines, the most important of which was N. A. Letson's United States Airways. United Aviation was precisely the kind of firm Brown wanted to exclude from his network. Underfinanced and hastily assembled, the business existed only on paper and was primarily a vehicle for bidding on the lucrative mail contract. Although UA substantially underbid TWA, Brown disallowed its submission because it had no night flying experience. TWA received the contract, but Letson appealed to Comptroller General McCarl, arguing the night flying provision was not part of the Watres Act and therefore illegal. Anxious to forestall another unfavorable ruling, Brown quietly promised part of the southern route would be sublet to Letson if he withdrew his appeal. Letson complied and received his route the next spring.

Brown also moved boldly to guarantee that American Airways would receive the southern transcontinental route. Although five other lines were interested in the contract, the postmaster general removed each one from the picture before bids were let. In a complicated series of transactions, Brown arranged for American to buy out three of its rivals, none of which met the night flying requirement. One of these operators, Erle Halliburton of Southwest Air Fast Express, received an especially good price when he threatened to reopen the night flying question. A fourth contender, Eastern, withdrew when Brown threatened to exclude the company entirely if it challenged his plans. Wedell-Williams, a small New Orleans-based carrier already in dire financial straits, simply went out of business. As Brown intended, American was the only bidder on the southern route.

Over the next three years, Brown steadily perfected his design for America's airways through his route extension powers. By 1933 the nation was bound together by eight north-south routes as well as the three transcontinental routes, while in the far north Northwest Airways aspired to establish a fourth transcontinental route. Perhaps most strikingly, the once frail passenger-carrying lines were prospering in the midst of the nation's worst depression. Between 1930 and 1932, the latter being Brown's last full year in office, the number of passenger miles flown rose from 84 million to 127 million. Scheduled aircraft miles during the same period went from 16.2 million to 34.5 million. Simultaneously, Brown cut the rates the government paid to the haulers through periodic renegotiation of the contracts. The average rate per mile had been $1.09 when he took office, but the Post Office Department was paying only 54 cents per mile in

March 1933. Clearly Brown's efforts mark one of the most important achievements of the Hoover administration.

Even before Brown left office, however, opponents of his grand design were positioning themselves to overturn it. Much of this opposition centered on the independents Brown had deliberately excluded from his network. Led by Tom and Paul Braniff of Braniff Airways, they charged that Brown had perverted the intent of the Watres Act and paid inflated rates to a few favored carriers. Given the opportunity to bid on contracts, they would demonstrate to the public how cheaply the mail could be carried with no reduction in the quality of service. The Braniffs also shrewdly tarred their rivals with the brush of Wall Street. Such rhetoric struck a responsive chord in a nation in the midst of an economic collapse which many blamed on the greed of rapacious plutocrats.

Brown's numerous personal and political enemies made up another element in the growing coalition against him. As the Democrats gained in the elections of 1930 and 1932, some party leaders saw the airmail dispute as a potential scandal which would further embarrass and discredit the Republicans. Moreover, many independents had affiliations with the Democratic party, and they charged that the contractors were mostly Republicans who enjoyed their favored status because of past support for the Republicans.

The building opposition to Brown climaxed in the creation of the Special Committee to Investigate Foreign and Domestic, Ocean, and Air Mail Contracts chaired by Senator Hugo Black of Alabama. Joining Black on the committee were William H. King (D., Utah), Patrick McCarran (D., Nev.), Warren Austin (R., Vt.), and Wallace H. White, Jr. (R., Maine). Formed on February 25, 1933, the committee spent several months in background investigation and then began hearings on the ocean mail contracts. Not until January 9, 1934, did the members begin public hearings on airmail.

From the moment the Senate investigation began to gather steam, Brown repeatedly asserted his willingness to testify in his own defense. His efforts to vindicate himself, however, were at least partially undercut by charges he had ordered the destruction of pertinent documents during the last days of his tenure as postmaster general. James Maher, a department stenographer, indicated to postal authorities that he had burned the contents of several filing cabinets on orders from Brown. Brown and other members of his office staff vigorously denied that anything of substance was destroyed, and Maher himself became increasingly equivocal as time passed. Indeed, Brown later insisted that Maher had told him his questioners had put words in his mouth.

In light of these accusations, Brown was deeply embarrassed when he suddenly discovered two large files on ocean and airmail contracts among personal papers stored at his hotel. He immediately delivered the papers by hand to Postmaster General James Farley, claiming that "the material was surreptitiously placed among my personal papers at the instigation of someone who was engaged in a conspiracy of character assassination." He sarcastically presented the files to Farley "unscathed by their fantastic experience in the fiery furnace, as were Shadrach and his companions of old." Nevertheless, Brown's "discovery" seemed to indicate to the public that he really was a man with something to hide.

If anything, the incident made Brown even more determined to testify before the committee. Writing Ohio senator Simeon D. Fess, he asked Fess to convey to the committee "my urgent request to be heard at the date convenient." He told Fess "that I will appear voluntarily, that my testimony will be given without compulsion, and that anything I say may be used against me in any court in the land." Finally, on February 19, 1934, Brown began four days of testimony and cross-examination. Opening with a lengthy statement, Brown vigorously defended his airmail policies. "The major purpose," he declared, ". . . was not to transport the mails at the lowest possible cost to the Government, but to foster the . . . aeronautical industr[y]. . . ." Far from representing collusion, the spoils conferences of May and June 1930 resulted in a "tentative suggestion" which was "impracticable and unsound." Indeed Brown declared that he had suspected such a result and had convened the meeting so the competing firms would thereby be forced to acknowledge their conflicting claims. The way would then be open for Brown to step in and structure the various routes.

Brown also defended his reliance on the large firms at the expense of the small operators. In his opinion, "there was no justification in sound business practices" for supporting firms operating short lines. From the history of railroad development,

Brown said, "We had discovered that all short lines were absorbed by the larger lines, . . . and I could see nothing to be gained by covering the map over with . . . little, disjointed services." Very properly then, the Post Office Department "exerted every proper influence to consolidate the short, detached, and failing lines into well-financed and well-managed systems." All such consolidations "authorized by me were in the public interest," Brown declared, and "resulted in improved public service and ultimately in lower flying costs."

Questioning the witness sharply, Black maneuvered to destroy Brown's position. His approach generally followed the pattern suggested by postal inspector James Doran, who dispatched a memo to Patterson the day before Brown was to testify. Black began by examining Brown extensively about the background of the Watres Act, a piece of legislation which the latter admitted he "probably had as much to do with it as anybody." Prodded by the chairman, Brown read from his own testimony at a 1930 House hearing in which he had described competitive bidding on airmail contracts as being "of doubtful value and more or less of a myth" because there was "little real substantial bidding." Black then pointed out that although the bill as originally drawn had permitted negotiated contracts, Congress had not passed the bill until it had been rewritten specifically to include competitive bidding.

In accord with the strategy proposed by Doran, Black next raised the question of the spoils conferences, asking, "Was not the object and purpose of the proceeding . . . for the operators to attempt to decide among themselves as to which ones should have which lines?" He then read into the record a letter written by L. H. Brittin of Northwest Airways in which Brittin stated that Brown had "called the operators together, handed them this map and instructed them to settle among themselves the distribution of these routes." As further evidence Black referred to testimony by Hainer Hinshaw of American Airlines to the effect that the operators had no choice but to accept the division of routes which the postmaster general intended to make, regardless of competitive bidding. If such evidence were true, Black demanded, would the contracts awarded under such circumstances be illegal? Brown refused to answer, saying the question was hypothetical: "I am not going to answer a question as foolish as that."

Black also assailed Brown's reliance on the four major aviation holding companies in constructing his air network. He repeatedly demonstrated, for example, how Brown had disregarded equities in awarding mail contracts to large operators at the expense of smaller ones. Using C. E. Woolman's Delta Air Service as an example, Black pointed out that Woolman was the "first man and the only man" to fly between Birmingham and Dallas. However, the mail contract went to the giant Aviation Corporation, with the result that "the man who had pioneered the route, the only man who had ever flown over it on any schedule of any kind or type and who was flying on it at that time was compelled to sell out because he could not operate in competition with mail contractors." Brown countered that "a short line could not pay the expense of maintaining a ground force and the supervisory force that would be necessary." Woolman needed a line that "started some place and got some place"; in other words, he needed to fly on to Los Angeles, something Woolman was unwilling to do.

Increasingly the hearings became a bitter personal clash between prosecutor and witness. Black repeatedly interrupted answers he considered irrelevant by telling the clerk to read the question to Brown. Finally the exasperated Brown snapped, "Let me finish." "Answer these questions," the chairman responded. "If you don't care to listen to me, I won't answer any more questions." "I don't want any more speeches." "You want to make the speeches." This personal antipathy reached something of an anticlimax late in the hearings when Brown, describing a conversation with Postmaster General Farley, referred to a personal remark Farley allegedly made about Black. Brown refused to repeat the remark without Farley's approval, so the committee summoned him to a Saturday afternoon session to release Brown publicly from his pledge of discretion. Brown then quoted Farley as saying of Black, "He is just a publicity hound but don't tell anybody I said so, because I have to get along with him." The hearing room exploded in laughter although Farley diplomatically denied making the remark. The hostility between Brown and Black was not so easily expunged, however; nearly a decade later Brown was still referring to "that Ku Kluxer Black" in his private correspondence.

Largely as a result of the Black committee investigations, Brown's system for encouraging commercial aviation was overturned. Even before Brown's testimony, Postmaster General Farley had canceled all existing airmail contracts, and President Roosevelt had ordered the Army Air Corps to begin flying the mail. A few months later, Congress approved the Black-McKellar Act, which embodied the Democratic alternative to Brown's policy. Litigation between the carriers and the government over the cancellation continued until 1942, and Brown was occasionally called upon to testify as part of the proceedings. His direct involvement with aviation, however, ended completely when he left the government in 1933.

As a private citizen, Brown became chairman of the board of the Hudson & Manhattan Railroad in New York and struggled vainly to rehabilitate the rapid transit line operating between New York and New Jersey. He retired from the company in 1946. Brown continued to be active in Republican party circles. He served as national committeeman from Ohio between 1932 and 1947 and worked to further the national ambitions of his fellow Ohioans Robert Taft and John Bricker. His political career ended in 1948 when a political novice defeated him in a contest to choose delegates to the Republican National Convention. Also known for his civic and charitable work, Brown spent 51 years as chairman of the Toledo Humane Society and 48 years as a member of the Lucas County Children's Home Board (later the Child Welfare Board). Brown died in Toledo on January 26, 1961.

References:
Nick A. Komons, *Bonfires to Beacons: Federal Civil Aviation Policy under the Air Commerce Act, 1926-1938* (Washington, D.C.: U.S. Department of Transportation, 1978);
Henry Ladd Smith, *Airways: The History of Commercial Aviation in the United States* (New York: Knopf, 1942).

Archives:
The Walter Folger Brown Papers are at the Ohio Historical Society, Columbus, Ohio. Post Office Department records and Black committee records are available at the National Archives, Washington, D.C.

Donald C. Burr

(May 8, 1941 -   )

by William M. Leary

University of Georgia

CAREER: Securities analyst to president, National Aviation Corporation (1965-1973); corporate executive to president, Texas International Airlines (1973-1980); chief executive officer, People Express (1980-1987); executive vice-president, Texas Air Corporation (1987).

Donald Calvin Burr had a brief but illustrious career as the main force behind People Express, once hailed as the airline of the future. A post-deregulation, low-cost, no-frills carrier, People Express tapped a new market by attracting bus and auto travelers. Air traffic between Boston and New York, for example, tripled in four years, with People Express accounting for most of the increase. Eventually, overexpansion and competition from the major carriers proved fatal to the company.

But People Express was more than a briefly successful airline. Burr often said that his goal was "to make a better world." His emphasis was on the development of individual potential. As Steven Prokesch has pointed out, People Express was "one of the most radical experiments ever attempted in participative management." Burr built a company in which employees shared ownership and actively took part in the decision-making process that usually was reserved for management. For a time, the airline became the model for industrial relations in a new era of worldwide competition, while Burr was hailed as a business pioneer who belonged to a select group of entrepreneurs that represented, according to *Time* magazine, "the best American tradition: inventive, bold, resolute, eager to overcome the challenges that confront them."

Burr was born in South Windsor, Connecticut, on May 8, 1941. His father was an electrical engineer, and his mother for a time was a local assistant postmaster. Both parents were active in the Congregational church. Burr attended public

Donald C. Burr (courtesy of the National Air and Space Museum)

schools, directed a youth group at his church, played saxophone in the school band, and enjoyed sports. For a time, he thought about becoming a minister.

Following his graduation from Ellsworth High School, he entered Bowdoin College in Brunswick, Maine. After one year, however, he transferred to Stanford University. Initially an English major, Burr soon found business more interesting than literature, and he shifted his concentration to economics. Also, fascinated by aviation ever since his parents had taken him as a boy to a local airport to watch airplanes land and take off, he joined and later became president of the Stanford Flying Club. In

1961, while a student, he married his childhood sweetheart, Brigit Rupner. They had four children.

Graduating from Stanford in 1963 with a B.A. in economics, Burr matriculated to Harvard University's Graduate School of Business. He received his M.B.A. in 1965, then joined the National Aviation Corporation as a securities analyst. Burr rose rapidly in the executive ranks at National, a small New York investment firm that specialized in aerospace securities, becoming president of the company in 1971. Two years later, he left National for a job with Texas International Airlines.

At Texas International, Burr became a part of a team that new owner Frank A. Lorenzo was putting together in an effort to save the struggling regional carrier. By 1978, when Burr took over as chief operating officer, the airline was well on its way to recovery, posting a profit of $3.2 million on revenues of $120 million. The following year, Burr implemented a new low-fare strategy that was based on the experiences of Pacific Southwest Airlines, an intrastate carrier that he had studied and admired while working as a securities analyst. Texas International's "Peanut Fares," deeply discounted fares for off-peak hours, brought the company both notoriety and profit. As aviation historian R. E. G. Davies has commented, the new fare represented "a watershed in air passenger tariffs."

Texas International flourished as the industry's leader in discount fares, recording a profit of $13.2 million in 1978. In 1979, the year Burr became president of the airline, Texas International's earnings soared to $41.4 million. Despite the evident success, however, Burr was not happy with the Houston-based carrier. His relationship with Lorenzo had soured. Also, he later said, the pursuit of profit to the exclusion of all else left him uncomfortable. Texas International "had no vision, no excitement." Intent on finding a new challenge, he resigned as president in January 1980.

Working with Gerald L. Gitner, who gave up his position as senior vice-president of planning and marketing at Texas International, Burr drew up plans for a new, low-fare airline. By selling his car, house, and airline stock, he managed to raise $350,000 to invest in the enterprise. Gitner contributed $175,000. On April 7, 1980, they incorporated People Express.

The next 12 months brought moments of excitement and anxiety as Burr struggled with the many problems involved in creating a new airline.

In July 1980 People Express became the first company since the passage of the Airline Deregulation Act of 1978 to seek permission from the Civil Aeronautics Board (CAB) to operate a scheduled passenger service. While waiting for the board to act, Burr made a bold decision to raise start-up funds by taking the company public. Hambrecht & Quist, a San Francisco investment firm, agreed to underwrite the stock issue. On October 24 the CAB granted the necessary operating authority. The following month, People Express received $24 million from the sale of three million shares of stock.

The good fortune that so often is a part of successful enterprise came Burr's way when he read in a trade journal that Germany's Lufthansa airline wanted to sell its fleet of Boeing 737s. People Express purchased 17 of the well-maintained, fuel-efficient transports for the bargain price of $3.7 million each. Lufthansa agreed to reconfigure the airplanes from 90 to 118 seats. (Later models of People Express-operated Boeing 737s featured 130 seats.)

Meanwhile, Burr and Gitner were developing plans for a hub-and-spoke route system that would be based at Newark Airport in New Jersey. Realizing that underused Newark could be the key to tapping the great New York metropolitan market, People Express leased the airport's North Terminal, which had been vacant since 1973. "It was a ghost town," Burr observed. "What didn't fall on your head bit you in the ankle." But it was cheap: $6 per square foot, compared to $50 in Manhattan's Pan Am Building.

People Express launched service from Newark with three Boeing 737s on April 30, 1981, flying to Columbus, Ohio; Buffalo, New York; and Norfolk, Virginia. The airline charged rock-bottom fares, seeking to lure travelers from buses and automobiles. There were no frills on People Express. Passengers did not receive hot meals; they could purchase snacks or coffee (for 50 cents a cup). They were allowed two suitcases on board the aircraft; checked bags, which were transferred, cost $3 each. Space but not individual seats could be reserved, if one was fortunate enough to get through to the airline's reservation office. Tickets could be purchased only on board flights. The airline's passengers quickly acquired a reputation as "a hearty breed." As one of their number explained: "I could take anything for the price."

Burr could charge the lowest prices in the industry because he had the lowest costs. At first, People Express had an impressive seat-mile cost of $0.065, which was substantially below the competition. This soon decreased even further, to little more than 5 cents. The absence of frills helped to hold down expenses, but the major portion of savings came from increased employee productivity and high aircraft utilization. By the end of 1981, People Express had 800 employees, or 57 per aircraft. This compared to an industry average of 149. Furthermore, People's nonunion employees worked longer hours for lower wages than other airline employees.

Burr brought to People Express a managerial philosophy seldom seen in the American workplace. The airline, he said, represented "an attempt to create an environment in which the usual distinctions between the company and the employees are no longer relevant, because the two have become one." New employees were required to purchase 100 shares of stock in the company (at a discount of 60 percent). Thereafter, they had the opportunity to participate in profit-sharing programs. Burr wanted employees to become owners, sharing the profits and risks of such status.

At the same time, the employee-owner also would share decision-making responsibility. There were only three categories of employees: flight managers (pilots), maintenance managers, and customer service managers. Burr emphasized "cross-utilization" of individuals in all categories, with employees rotating into various jobs on the airline. "We asked them to work in both line and staff functions," he explained, "to work in teams and to share responsibility for implementing the [company's] objectives."

Burr preached his managerial doctrine with the fervor of an evangelist. He was a man with a vision. He wanted to create a new industrial environment, one which would "enable and empower employees to release their creative energies." The airline's employees, for their part, responded with such enthusiasm that, as *New York Times* reporter Steven Prokesch observed, People Express "seemed more cult than company." As they watched the daily increase in the price of People Express shares, they became convinced that the success of the company and their personal success were synonymous. They felt part of something new and special, exactly what Burr intended.

People Express encountered its first major crisis in August 1981, when the Professional Air Traffic Controllers went out on strike. The Federal Aviation Agency promptly instituted traffic restrictions, cutting People's 35 daily departures from Newark by 35 percent. "We were bleeding at a terrific rate," Burr recalled. In order to survive "we had to create a whole new airline and we had to do it overnight."

Burr and planning expert Gitner abandoned the airline's hub-and-spoke system. Early each morning, before departure restrictions went into effect, they dispatched the airline's transports to Buffalo, Columbus, and Baltimore. From these points, the airplanes flew back and forth to Sarasota and West Palm Beach. Burr and Gitner were gambling that inexpensive fares would lure northern vacationers to Florida during the winter. The gamble worked. People Express lost $9 million on revenues of $38 million, but it managed to survive the winter. As traffic restrictions eased, the airline returned to its original plan of operations.

Over the next two years, People Express became "the fastest growing airline in the history of aviation." In 1982, with additional transports coming into service, the company earned $1 million on revenues of $138.7 million. By the end of the following year, the "McDonald's of the air" operated 22 Boeing 737s, 10 Boeing 727s, and 1 Boeing 747. It flew to 19 domestic destinations, all for under $100. It also opened (on May 26, 1983) a Newark-London route, charging $149 for a one-way ticket. In July 1983 People Express recorded a phenomenal load factor of 83.6 percent (compared to an industry average of 60 percent), with an average aircraft utilization of 10.4 hours (versus an industry average of 7.12 hours). The airline's stock rose to $25.87 during the month, to the joy of the company's 3,000 employee-owners who held approximately one-third of the 4.5 million outstanding shares.

With the success of People Express, Burr became a national celebrity. *Newsweek* hailed him as "the American Samurai" whose innovative managerial philosophy had brought the benefits of the Japanese system to an ailing domestic economy. Alfred E. Kahn, considered by many to be the foremost advocate of deregulation, termed Burr "a public benefactor" who had opened up air travel to millions of first-time fliers. Harvard's School of Business used People Express as a case study in its advanced management course. As one professor commented, "Anyone who isn't studying People Express and the way they're managing people is out of their [sic] minds."

In 1983 the airline posted a profit of $10 million on revenues of $278 million. "We've designed a product which is so popular," Burr chortled, "we can't satisfy the demand for it."

People Express continued to grow as it struggled to meet the appetite of a traveling public that pursued low-cost airfares with undiminished determination. By the summer of 1985, the airline was using 71 airplanes to carry 1 million passengers a month to 39 U.S. cities and London. In October, Burr outmaneuvered Frank Lorenzo and purchased Denver-based Frontier Airlines for $307 million. People Express now ranked as the nation's fifth largest air carrier.

But all was not well with Burr's rapidly expanding air transport enterprise. In January 1985 American Airlines had announced an "Ultimate Super-Saver" fare which matched or undercut People's prices on competing routes while continuing to offer passengers the amenities commonly associated with air travel. Other established carriers soon followed American's lead. Although the increased competition was unsettling, problems with Frontier Airlines proved even more vexing. Burr's attempt to turn the airline into a no-frills carrier only drove away the business travelers upon whom Frontier had depended. Also, Frontier's unionized employees did not share Burr's managerial vision, and service on the airline deteriorated badly. With Frontier losing $10 million a month, People Express recorded a loss of $32.2 million during the fourth quarter of 1985. For the year, it lost $27.5 million on revenues of nearly a billion dollars.

The situation only became worse in 1986. With flights running only half full, People Express posted a first-quarter loss of $58 million. As the airline's stock sunk to $5.50 a share, employee morale sagged. No longer the darling of the business press, Burr was now viewed as an autocrat whose unilateral decisions—such as the purchase of two commuter lines during the winter of 1985-1986—were only making a bad situation worse. His "airline of the future" had become "People Distress."

In a desperate move, Burr tried to transform People Express into a traditional air carrier. The purchase of the two commuter lines—Britt Airways and Provincetown-Boston Airlines—had been part

of a new plan to attract business travelers. People Express also began offering first-class seats and a frequent-flier program. However, businessmen were not interested in an airline with a reputation for overbooked and delayed (or canceled) flights and lost baggage. Losing money in the West, Burr had to raise fares in the East. This only deepened the downward spiral.

On June 23, 1986, Burr announced that it might become necessary to sell all or part of the airline due to its deteriorating economic condition. With a loss of $74.4 million in the second quarter, the possibility of a sale became a certainty. In July, Burr rejected an offer from Lorenzo for the entire company and instead struck a deal with United Air Lines to unload the albatross of Frontier for $146 million. However, United's pilots could not agree on terms to absorb their fellow airmen on Frontier, and the agreement fell through. The next day, August 28, Frontier filed for protection under the Bankruptcy Code.

On September 15 Frank Lorenzo announced that Texas Air Corporation would acquire People Express in a stock deal worth an estimated $125 million. Texas Air also would acquire Frontier for $176 million, involving $25 million in cash and the balance in notes and assumption of debts. As Edward J. Starkman of Paine Webber observed, "That's a real good deal for them."

At the time, Burr blamed the demise of People Express on the acquisition of Frontier. "Frontier blew up in our faces," he said, "so we tried to get rid of it as soon as possible, but we couldn't." Later, he emphasized the use of sophisticated computer programs by the major carriers, enabling them immediately to match or undercut People Express fares. Also, he acknowledged charges of inexpert top-level management. "If I were doing it over," he reflected in 1989, "I would hire from outside and amend our compensation terms to attract good people."

Critics placed a large measure of responsibility for the airline's failures on Burr's own shortcomings. Caught up in the company's success, he overreached himself when he acquired Frontier, a unionized carrier that competed directly with both Continental and United out of Denver. Furthermore, Burr's talent was motivation; he was not able to develop the operating system that large companies require for success. Finally, as cofounder Gerald Gitner observed, Burr's innovative managerial philosophy tended to become an end in itself; he lost sight of the fact that participant management was only the means to a profitable company.

Burr remained with People Express while it operated independently following its sale to Texas Air. In January 1987, as it merged with Continental Airlines, he became an executive vice-president with Texas Air. In April, Texas Air announced that he had resigned "to pursue independent business interests." Since then, he has been giving speeches (for a fee of $10,000), writing a book about his experiences with People Express, and exploring opportunities in the airline industry.

References:

"Bitter Victories," *Inc.*, 7 (August 1985): 25-29, 31-35;

John A. Byrne, "Up, Up, and Away: Expansion is Threatening the 'Humane' Culture at People Express," *Business Week* (November 25, 1985): 80-83, 86, 90-91, 94;

R. E. G. Davies, *Rebels and Reformers of the Airways* (Washington, D.C.: Smithsonian Institution Press, 1987);

Peter Nulty, "A Champ of Cheap Airlines," *Fortune*, 105 (March 22, 1982): 127-128, 130, 134;

Steven Prokesch, "Behind People Express's Fall: An Offbeat Managerial Style," *New York Times*, September 23, 1986, section 1, p. 1; section 4, p. 8;

Prokesch, "Can Don Burr Go Back to the Future?," *New York Times*, July 6, 1986, section 3, pp. 1, 7;

Douglas K. Ramsey, *The Corporate Warriors: Six Classic Cases in American Business* (Boston: Houghton Mifflin, 1987);

Lucien Rhodes, "That Daring Young Man and His Flying Machines," *Inc.*, 6 (January 1984): 42, 44-46, 48, 50-52;

Sara Rimer, "The Airline That Shook the World," *New York Times Magazine*, December 23, 1984, pp. 18-19, 24, 28-30.

Capital Airlines

by Myron J. Smith, Jr.

Tusculum College

Capital Airlines traces its origins to an intense competition in the skies over the northeastern United States between Central Airlines and Pennsylvania Airlines. On November 1, 1936, the rival carriers merged to form Pennsylvania-Central Airlines. This small trunk airline proceeded to consolidate a route system west and south of the District of Columbia, with slots in cities from Baltimore and Buffalo to Chicago and Birmingham. Equipment employed included Boeing 247Ds and, after January 1940, DC-3s.

In late December 1941, following the Japanese attack on Pearl Harbor, U.S. military authorities took over two-thirds of the carrier's fleet, allowing the remainder to be employed (after March 1942) in the first domestic scheduled military cargo service. This Air Transport Command contract saw Penn-Central's planes delivering men and matériel initially between Chicago and Washington, and then between Harrisburg and San Francisco. In December 1944, the Civil Aeronautics Board (CAB) awarded the company civilian access to New York, a service begun in July 1945. James H. Carmichael,

a longtime executive with the company, became president of PCA in 1947.

On April 21, 1948, Penn-Central was rechristened Capital Airlines. Beginning on November 4 of that year, Capital made passenger airline history by offering a $33.30 one-way fare between New York and Chicago—the first American trunk to offer coach-class, low-fare service.

The early 1950s brought route expansion as the CAB often used the carrier as a counterweight to the domination of the Big Four airlines: American, United, Eastern, and TWA. Capital secured nonstop authority between New York and Pittsburgh, Detroit, Chicago, and other eastern cities. It also expanded southward to Atlanta and New Orleans.

Award of these new routes meant that new aircraft had to be financed and employed. Capital took a bold step to meet the challenge. It elected to become the first American operator of the Vickers Viscount, the world's first propeller-turbine (turboprop) passenger transport. Viscount service began on Capital's Washington-Chicago route on July 26, 1955. It proved a huge success. Everywhere the British airliner flew (to New York, New Orleans, Detroit, Pittsburgh, and elsewhere), the carrier's traffic grew. As the boarding level jumped, Capital ordered more Viscounts—75 in all by July 1956.

In 1956 the airline encountered economic difficulties as the expense of fleet improvement overshadowed profits. After Vickers threatened to foreclose due to late payments, Capital secured federal support in the form of $12.2 million in subsidies, plus longer nonstop routes. Despite this, fate and competition combined to doom the airline. Aircraft accidents in 1958 and 1959 hurt Capital's public image, and at the same time rivals introduced new jetliners and Lockheed Electra turboprops, stealing the carrier's traffic. By June 1960 Capital was in severe financial difficulty, having lost over $5 million in the year's first quarter. Meanwhile, its debt to Vickers stood at $33 million. Company officials faced the prospect of shutting down operations or merging with a stronger carrier. On January 6,

1961, following lengthy negotiations and after securing the CAB's approval, United Air Lines took over the ailing Capital, marking the largest (to that date) acquisition in the history of the U.S. passenger airline industry.

References:

Charles Baptie, *Capital Airlines: A Nostalgic Flight Into the Past* (Annandale, Va.: Charles Baptie Studios, 1986);

James H. Carmichael, *A Distinguished Briton in American Skies! The Viscounts: "Capital Airlines"* (New York: Newcomen Society in North America, 1957);

George W. Cearley, "Capital Airlines," *Airliners*, 1 (Winter 1988): 18-19;

R. E. G. Davies, *Airlines of the United States since 1914*, revised edition (Washington, D.C.: Smithsonian Institution, 1982);

William Price, "He Wants to Make Money on an Airline," *Saturday Evening Post*, 222 (September 3, 1949): 22-23, 48, 50.

James H. Carmichael

(April 2, 1907 - December 1, 1983)

by Lloyd H. Cornett, Jr.

Montgomery, Alabama

CAREER: Chief pilot, Central Airlines (1934-1936); chief pilot (1936-1938), operations manager (1938-1940), vice president for operations (1940-1945), executive vice-president (1945-1947), president (1947-1957), chairman, Pennsylvania Central/Capital Airlines (1957-1958); vice-president for commercial transportation (1958), president, Fairchild Engine and Airplane Corporation (1958-1960); president, J. H. Carmichael and Associates (1960-1970); chairman, Riddel Airlines/Airlift International (1960-1978).

James Henry Carmichael, Jr., a pioneer in the development of the airline industry, was born on April 2, 1907, in Newark, New Jersey, to James Henry and Margaret Miner Carmichael. His father soon thereafter moved the family to Riverside, California, the beginning of what James, Junior, later termed a "nomadic" existence. His early life was a series of moves from coast to coast and once to Europe as his father tried his hand as a salesman, a

farmer, and a rancher. While fairly successful at his many occupations, the optimistic Irishman had a penchant for spending more than he earned. James, Junior, ended up at a Connecticut military academy (Suffield), from which he graduated at age seventeen in 1924.

James, Junior, then returned to Riverside and tried his hand at raising oranges. When this failed to excite his interest, he moved to Reno, Nevada, for two and a half years, where he attended the University of Nevada for part of one semester. This constituted his formal education except for occasional technical courses which furthered his aviation skills.

James, Senior, reentered the boy's life at this point, offering to go halves on a farm if Junior would work it. They purchased an 80-acre truck farm in Bangor, Maine, but after laboring on the farm for two years with scant success, James, Junior, decided that aviation might offer better prospects. As he put it, "[I] had always had the desire to fly but optimistically looked forward to flying

James H. Carmichael (courtesy of Charles Baptie Studio)

purely for sport after having made my fortune as a gentleman farmer. While killing time one day it occured [*sic*] to me that it might be possible to earn a living at it."

Carmichael sold his interest in the farm to his father—possibly the only person he could sell to—and struck out for Chicago. The one consolation for his years in Bangor was a chance encounter with a young lady named Jessie Northrop whom he returned to marry on July 4, 1930. They would have two children: Joan, born in 1934, and Judith, born in 1937.

Carmichael, not yet twenty years old when he arrived in Chicago, sought out flying instructors Gus Palquist and Elmer Kane to teach him the intricacies of getting airborne and landing without crashing. Flying a Laird Swallow, he learned quickly, and after six to eight hours of instruction, he soloed successfully. It was at this time that he earned a nickname that was to follow him for the rest of his life. Standing 6 feet 3 inches tall and weighing 190 pounds, Carmichael was described in a newspa-

per article as "gaunt and undernourished." His peers translated this to "Slim," an appellation that remained with him despite the fact that in later years he would carry 235 pounds on a firm frame. Carmichael once described himself as a man with brown hair and eyes, and with big teeth and ears.

After Carmichael soloed in 1926, he started work at the Chicago Municipal Airport, carrying passengers and instructing others in the art of flying. He also added to his income, as did many other pilots of that era, by barnstorming throughout the Midwest (offering rides at $5), flying in aerial circuses, and crop dusting. This lasted until December 1929, when he returned to his birthplace and went to work for Newark Air Service as a charter pilot and night flying instructor. Periodically, Carmichael tried his skill with other companies. For example, in 1931 he spent nine months with Pittsburgh Airways, flying between New York and Pittsburgh. During 1932 and 1933 he flew part-time in a Loening for Albert C. Kluge, a clothing label manufacturer, making commuter trips to Lake Sunapee, New Hampshire, and New Brunswick, Canada.

The year 1934 marked a turning point in Carmichael's life. It began when the United States went through the so-called Air Mail Scandal. At the time, airmail was carried by various airlines under contract to the U.S. Post Office, receiving liberal payments for their efforts. Critics charged that the contracts had been granted unfairly, resulting in a special congressional investigation. On February 19, 1934, President Franklin D. Roosevelt canceled all contracts and turned the airmail routes over to Army Air Corps pilots. The military airmen proved ill-equipped and inexperienced, and accident followed accident. The government finally acknowledged its mistake and returned to the civilian contract system. When the Post Office advertised for new bids on the airmail routes, Central Airlines (formerly Pittsburgh Airways) won a contract covering Detroit-Cleveland-Pittsburgh-Washington, D.C. "With the formation of Central Airlines," Carmichael later recalled, "I became the first pilot hired by them."

Carmichael soon found life as a pilot flying Stinson and Ford Trimotors anything but boring. On Easter night, April 21, 1935, he departed Washington's Hoover Airport for Pittsburgh. After 85 miles en route, the outboard engine of his Ford Trimotor tore loose, shearing some electrical circuits as it fell off. Carmichael fought for control as

Capital Vickers Viscount (courtesy of the National Air and Space Museum)

the aircraft spun downward. Meanwhile, his copilot struggled in the now darkened cabin to restart a second engine that had shut down. After some harrowing moments, both were successful. Carmichael then returned to Washington's Bolling Field, which had excellent emergency facilities, and brought the plane down to a perfect landing. For this feat, he received the Congressional Air Mail Fliers Medal of Honor.

Six months later, Carmichael had another exciting experience when he lost all engines on a Stinson Trimotor during takeoff at Pittsburgh. He managed to stop the plane at the end of the runway but not quickly enough to prevent it from toppling over a steep embankment. Two other incidents, also potentially dangerous, caused emergency descents that culminated in normal landings. Such was life in the fledgling airline industry.

While Carmichael flew the line, Central waged a fierce battle for customers with Pennsylvania Airlines and Transport Company, which was flying over the same routes but without the benefits of

a mail contract. They were, as one writer said, duplicating timetables in a bankruptcy race. The rivalry eventually led to a merger on November 1, 1936. C. Bedell Monro became president of the new Pennsylvania-Central Airlines (PCA), while Carmichael took over as its chief pilot.

Carmichael began a steady if unspectacular climb up PCA's corporate ladder. He became operations manager in October 1938 and vice-president for operations in April 1940. Meanwhile, PCA was expanding its routes to include a Washington-Buffalo service and branches to Norfolk, Chicago, Pittsburgh, and Buffalo. As routes multiplied, the need for better and faster aircraft grew urgent. This led to the introduction of DC-3s, with Carmichael delivering the first one from the Douglas plant in California to Pittsburgh at the end of 1939. DC-3 service between Washington and Detroit began on January 2, 1940. In all, PCA purchased six DC-3s to augment its fleet of 13 Boeing 247Ds that had been acquired from United Air Lines in 1937.

PCA continued expanding, reaching out in 1939 to such southern states as Tennessee and Alabama. Progress continued unabated into 1941, the year that the company moved its headquarters from Pittsburgh to Washington, D.C. Then World War II intervened, and all but seven of PCA's planes were assigned to military operations. Carmichael kept as many schedules as these limited resources allowed, but the company had to suspend service on several routes. Meanwhile, PCA's military component flew special missions to Alaska and Greenland and set up pilot navigation and radio schools in Washington, D.C., and Roanoke, Virginia. By 1943 the company's military operations had become twice as large as its commercial business.

Although the government's regulatory agency, the Civil Aeronautics Board (CAB), began approving additional routes for PCA in the postwar period, the first awards involved lines that were too short and too costly to operate. Carmichael labeled these truncated routes the "curse" of PCA. While traffic was heavy on the short hauls, they did not produce enough revenue to ensure the airline's financial health. While the CAB granted some relief in the form of route extensions and nonstop authority, losses continued to mount. On October 1, 1947, PCA's directors moved Monro up to chairman of the board and appointed Carmichael as president with instructions to pull the airline out of the red.

Carmichael attacked the company's financial problems by cutting operational costs. With $3.5 million in losses over the past 20 months, he realized that PCA needed drastic reductions if it was going to survive. He laid off 1,500 employees, wiping out entire sections. Searching for ways to reduce expenses, he instituted numerous cost-cutting procedures, including a reduction in long-distance telephone calls. At the same time, he found additional business, especially in air freight. And while he hated subsidy, labeling it a dole that he hoped to see vanish someday, PCA took all the government largess it could get.

Carmichael also sought to give the airline a new image. With board approval, he changed its name to Capital Airlines, effective May 12, 1948. The new name not only called attention to its operations from the nation's capital but also that it served the "capitals" of industry.

The company's financial picture brightened in 1948. The airline secured important new routes to New Orleans and Atlanta. Even more important was the introduction of the so-called Nighthawk or Skycoach flights on November 4, 1948. By offering discounted service at night, Capital used otherwise idle aircraft to earn dollars. The schedules were inconvenient and the service was austere, but it was cheap. The fare between New York and Chicago (where the service was first offered) cost only $29.60 compared to a daytime fare of $44.10. Railroad coach fares remained lower, but the flying passenger saved 12 to 13 hours in travel time while paying approximately 4 cents a mile.

While Carmichael's efforts increased Capital's profits, other airlines saw what low fares could accomplish and also turned to cheap air travel. Slowly, they began cutting into Capital's earnings. Carmichael came to believe that the best long-term solution for Capital's problems lay in securing a better route structure through merger. Although he attempted to reach an agreement with at least two other airlines, his efforts fell through.

By the early 1950s, Capital ranked fifth among the nation's airlines. Forced to compete against financially stronger companies, Carmichael stunned the industry by ordering 75 British-made Vickers Viscount turboprop airliners. Capital introduced American passengers to jet-prop service on July 26, 1955. It proved an immediate success, enabling air travelers to fly above the weather without noise or vibration. The enormously popular Viscounts gave Capital a distinct advantage over its piston-engine competitors.

The good times did not last long. Capital's route structure prevented Carmichael from using the new equipment in the most efficient way. Also, the huge debt that had been incurred to acquire the aircraft soon began to drag revenues into the red. Carmichael was forced to defer an order for 14 deHavilland Comet IV jet aircraft and to extend the Viscount mortgage not once but three times. Finally, in a not unexpected move, Capital's directors moved Carmichael upstairs to chairman of the board on July 24, 1957. Maj. Gen. David H. Baker (USAF, retired) was brought in to become the airline's president and chief executive officer.

Reorganization failed to help Capital. Nor did the news that the CAB had awarded the airline a long-desired Florida route. On July 23, 1958, Carmichael resigned his position after vainly attempting to engineer yet another merger. The 29-year honeymoon had come to an end.

Carmichael soon found new employment. On September 9 he joined the Fairchild Engine and Airplane Corporation as vice-president for commercial transportation. Fairchild counted on his ability to market a twin turboprop that it had under development. The company hoped to sell over 1,000 of the new F-27s over the next ten years. It needed to market at least 300 to reach a break-even point for development.

Elevated to president on December 19, Carmichael worked hard to sell the airplanes, but the task proved impossible. With slow sales causing a financial loss, Carmichael urged the directors to diversify. Instead, they decided to get rid of Carmichael. In December 1960 Sherman M. Fairchild replaced him as president and chief executive officer.

Carmichael then started his own consulting firm in the nation's capital—J. H. Carmichael and Associates. He also served as chairman of the board for Airlift International (formerly Riddel Airlines). He went on to join the Federal Aviation Administration's International Division, remaining there until he retired to Florida in 1978 because of his wife's illness. Carmichael died at age seventy-six on December 1, 1983.

Thus passed into history a legend in the avia-tion industry, the man responsible for introducing turbo-powered aircraft to American aviation and initiating the airline industry's first scheduled coach-class service. Former Capital employees still gather at an annual meeting to wine and dine and recall the memory of the man who led their airline during a time of innovation and excitement.

Publication:

A Distinguished Briton in American Skies! The Viscounts: "Capital Airlines" (New York: Newcomen Society in North America, 1957).

References:

Charles Baptie, *Capital Airlines: A Nostalgic Flight Into the Past* (Annandale, Va.: Charles Baptie Studios, 1986);

Henry Beecken and Associates, *Financial Study of the Domestic Airlines Industry and of American Airlines, Inc., and Capital Airlines, Inc.* (Washington, D.C.: Henry Beecken and Associates, 1954);

R. E. G. Davies, *Airlines of the United States since 1914*, revised edition (Washington, D.C.: Smithsonian Institution, 1982);

Davies, *Rebels and Reformers of the Airways* (Washington, D.C.: Smithsonian Institution, 1987);

William Price, "He Wants to Make Money on an Airline," *Saturday Evening Post*, 222 (September 3, 1949): 22-23.

Chicago and Southern Airlines

by W. David Lewis

Auburn University

and

Wesley Phillips Newton

Auburn University

In 1933 Carleton Putnam, a young New Yorker with a distinguished family background, started an airline called Pacific Seaboard to provide passenger and express service between San Francisco and Los Angeles by way of several intermediate points. Putnam had only two secondhand five-passenger Bellanca aircraft in the beginning, and they switched back and forth between the Bay Area and several intermediate places before being able to carry passengers, mainly businessmen, and cargo, mainly newspapers, all the way to Los Angeles. Pacific Seaboard and similar lines served a worthy purpose in those relatively early days of airlines, for the small- and medium-sized communities they flew in and out of were often the hubs of a fairly populated surrounding area that was a mixture of urban and rural, which the larger airlines saw no profit in serving. These smaller airlines were the ancestors of the commuter lines of the 1990s.

Putnam hoped his airline would eventually

make money without resorting to government subsidy. He used his own resources to cover the rising deficits in meeting expenses such as salaries, including that of Erma Murray, who as auditor was one of the pioneer female airline officials. Eventually it became apparent that it had to be subsidy or failure. Given the opportunity to bid on an airmail contract by the turmoil that resulted from the Black committee hearings in 1934, Putnam chose Route 8, Chicago-St. Louis-Memphis-Jackson, Mississippi-New Orleans. His bid was successful in May 1934, and the renamed Chicago and Southern (C&S) Airlines moved to corporate headquarters in Memphis.

The story of C&S Airlines in the bleak 1930s is somewhat similar to that of other midsized regional lines, including Delta. While Delta's region was across the Southeast into Texas, C&S's was much of the Mississippi Valley, from Chicago to the Gulf of Mexico. Both lines struggled to stay alive even after securing airmail contracts. For several years Delta had significant revenue from crop dusting, while C&S had to turn to investment from people with capital. In order to have the funds to purchase the multiengine aircraft required by law, Putnam gained the support of St. Louis capitalists, with Shell's Jimmy Doolittle acting as intermediary. These aircraft, Stinson-As, were replaced beginning in 1936 by Lockheed Electras, for, as in Delta's case, C&S could not afford the larger DC-2s. The Electras and their successors, the great DC-3s beginning in 1939, were financed through stock sales and bank loans. C&S began to show economic respectability, turning its first profit in 1936, the year the company moved its headquarters to St. Louis. (It returned to Memphis in 1941.) At the same time Putnam received control over all common stock in

a "voting trust" to insure continuity of management. C&S's safety record was respectable through the end of World War II, with only two fatal crashes.

C&S, like Delta, began to receive additional routes—to Houston in 1940, into the Caribbean and to Detroit at the end of the war. It had the same general wartime experience as other lines—early loss of equipment and personnel, military business on contract, gradual return of equipment and personnel, plans for a prosperous postwar era. More than Delta, C&S overexpanded in that era but gradually recouped. Its postwar equipment was principally DC-4s along with the DC-3s, and Lockheed Constellations. Despite the returning prosperity of the early 1950s, Putnam and his associates decided, with the looming jet age, that a merger with another logical regional line was the path to take. In 1951 he began talks with the chief executive officer of the most logical line, Delta. There were problems, such as the fact that C&S was a thoroughly unionized line and only Delta's pilots were unionized; but gradually differences were worked out to the satisfaction of Putnam and C. E. Woolman of Delta, their boards, lawyers, stockholders, personnel, and finally the Civil Aeronautics Board. In 1953 a new major airline arose from the merger, at first called Delta-C&S but in a few years known only as Delta.

References:

W. David Lewis and Wesley Phillips Newton, *Delta: the History of an Airline* (Athens: University of Georgia Press, 1979);

Carleton Putnam, *High Journey: A Decade in the Pilgrimage of an Air Line Pioneer* (New York: Scribners, 1945).

Civil Aeronautics Administration

by Nick A. Komons

Federal Aviation Administration

The Civil Aeronautics Administration (CAA) was established by President Franklin D. Roosevelt on June 30, 1940, under Reorganization Plans III and IV, which split the Civil Aeronautics Authority into two organizations.

The authority had been created as an independent agency two years earlier by the Civil Aeronautics Act of 1938. It was a tripartite organization made up of (1) a five-member board responsible for safety and economic rule making, (2) a three-member board responsible for accident investigation and the determination of probable cause, and (3) an administrator responsible for enforcing the safety rules of the five-member board, fostering air commerce, establishing and maintaining airways, and controlling air traffic. The complex organizational structure of the authority did not work to the president's satisfaction. When Congress granted him the power to reorganize certain sectors of the executive branch, Roosevelt acted. He took the rule-making powers of the five-member board and the accident investigation functions of the three-member board and fashioned them into a new agency, the Civil Aeronautics Board (CAB), which he lodged in the Department of Commerce. The CAB, however, exercised its quasi-legislative and quasi-judicial functions independently of the secretary of commerce. Roosevelt also transferred to the Department of Commerce the executive functions of the administrator; he renamed him administrator of civil aeronautics, and put him at the head of a new executive agency, the Civil Aeronautics Administration. The CAA administrator initially operated under the direction of the secretary of commerce.

The CAA presided over the nation's airways for the next 18 years—years that saw U.S. entry into World War II, the start of the cold war, the Korean conflict, the dramatic expansion of aviation on a global scale, and the introduction of jet trans-

ports in civil aviation. The CAA played a crucial role in all of these events.

Even before the Japanese bombing of Pearl Harbor, the CAA's air traffic control (ATC) responsibilities took a quantum leap with the takeover of air traffic control towers at airports essential to the national defense. Up to the eve of U.S. entry into the war, the CAA controlled only en route traffic; terminal traffic was the responsibility of the airport operator. As early as 1940, the War Department expressed concern over the lack of uniform terminal control and the problems that divided ATC authority might bring in wartime. In August, Congress responded by empowering the CAA to assume responsibility for the operation of towers at airports certified either by the secretary of war or the secretary of the navy as essential to the national defense. On October 17, 1941, Secretary of War Henry L. Stimson certified the first list of airports; on November 15 the CAA took over 15 towers— and 100 more by May 1944. A few low-activity facilities were returned to airport operators at war's end, but the terminal control function remained primarily a federal responsibility.

Wartime necessity also involved the CAA in airport development. In October 1940 the CAA received an appropriation of $40 million for the construction, improvement, and repair of up to 250 public airports determined by the War, Navy, and Commerce Departments to be necessary for the national defense. This was the first time Congress appropriated airport development funds directly to the federal government's civil aviation agency. The total wartime expenditures for this program— Development of Landing Areas for National Defense (DLAND)—came to more than $383 million for 535 airport projects in the contiguous 48 states, Alaska, Hawaii, and other possessions. Congress appropriated an additional $9.5 million to the CAA to be spent under another program, the Development of Civil Landing Areas (DCLA). The authorizations for both DLAND and DCLA expired at war's end, but CAA participation in airport development was continued by the Congress with the passage of the Federal Airport Act of 1946. The agency became the largest single source of civil airport development funds in the postwar period.

Pilot training was another area engaged in by the CAA that aided the war effort. The agency had been running the Civilian Pilot Training Program (CPTP) since 1939. Conducted primarily through educational institutions, the objective of CPTP was to provide students with sufficient training to qualify for a private pilot certificate. With the war, however, came changes that geared the program more closely to the needs of the armed services. Beginning in July 1942, training was given only to members of the inactive reserves. Before the end of the year, the navy placed its CPTP trainees on active duty; the army did the same the following summer. On the first anniversary of Pearl Harbor the CPTP was redesignated the War Training Service, a name change that recognized the shift in emphasis. In all, the CAA trained some 300,000 pilots under the wartime phase of the program before it was discontinued in August 1944.

Perhaps the civilian aviation agency's most crucial wartime activity was assistance to the U.S. Army Signal Corps, beginning in 1942, in stepped-up efforts to establish worldwide airways for the Air Transport Command. The air forces initially assigned high priority to extending the Northeast Airway and establishing the Crimson Airway to guide the mounting flow of military aircraft to the British Isles. Before the invasion of Africa, CAA engineers installed radio communications and air navigation facilities at nine large air bases in South America and Africa on the Southeast Airway. CAA-installed radio ranges and other facilities also carried military airway services to Pacific battlefields—north from Seattle to Attu and southwest to Australia. By the end of 1945, the CAA had established at army and navy requests airway facilities at some 200 locations outside the United States.

The war over, the CAA turned to modernizing the nation's air traffic control and air navigation systems. The first-generation air traffic control system, which had been introduced in the mid 1930s, was a manually operated system that relied heavily on the ability of controllers to visualize in their minds the movement of aircraft in three-dimensional space.

The system depended more on technique than technology. Outside of radios, telephones, and teletype machines, the first-generation system was actually oblivious to technology. Radar, which was first put to civil use in the immediate postwar period, changed the system profoundly. It permitted controllers to track the traffic they were controlling. Radar launched the second-generation system.

The CAA adapted radar to three ATC uses: (1) airport surveillance, (2) en route control, and (3) airport surface detection. The CAA's learning curve in putting radar to the service of ATC was considerably shortened by events in Europe. On June 24, 1948, when the Soviet Union stopped rail and road traffic between Berlin and West Germany, the Western powers began airlifting vital supplies to the beleaguered city. In August, at the request of the U.S. Air Force, the CAA dispatched an initial group of 20 volunteer air traffic controllers for duty in the airlift operation at Frankfurt and Berlin. More controllers—and CAA air navigation aids— followed until the blockade was lifted on May 12, 1949. The world had never seen anything like the scale of air operations during the airlift. More than two million people in the blockaded areas were supplied entirely by air over a period of 321 days. Radar played no small role in the success of this operation; with it controllers delivered airplanes to runways at a rate never before contemplated—one every three minutes, 24 hours a day. That rate was matched in the 1980s only at the busiest aviation hubs. The experience was an eye-opener for the CAA. Radar could increase enormously the capacity and efficiency of any air traffic control system.

Airway capacity and efficiency—and, indeed, safety—received an additional boost from two other facilities that were installed on the airways in the postwar era: the very high frequency omnidirectional range (VOR) and the Instrument Landing System (ILS). The principal radio navigation facility on the U.S. airways prior to the appearance of the VOR was the four-course radio range. The facility emitted radio beams in four directions, any one of which a pilot flying an airplane equipped with an appropriate receiver could follow to his destination. But as aviation grew, more than four aerial paths were needed to handle traffic efficiently. The answer was the VOR. The radiation from this facility resembles a huge radio wheel, with the station at the center and 360 spokes radiating out from the hub. Each of the 360 spokes or radials is a radio course that a pilot can fly. While the VOR permits a pilot to guide his airplane through three-dimensional space, the pilot must eventually bring his craft down with precision on an airport runway. The facility favored by the CAA to assist the pilot in making safe approaches, particularly under poor weather conditions, was the ILS. This facility sends out two radio beams to approaching aircraft. One beam, the localizer, gives the pilot left-right guidance; the other, the glide slope, gives the pilot the correct angle of descent to the runway.

The technology was at hand to modernize and expand the capacity of the airways in the postwar period. The CAA, however, made only halting progress. It had estimated in 1948 that about 400 VORs would be required to blanket the country. As of June 30, 1950, the CAA had commissioned 270. These facilities were complemented by 94 ILSs at important airports. It was at this point that the Korean emergency supervened on the national scene. When the North Koreans crossed the line into South Korea on June 25, 1950, they set in motion a chain of events affecting, among other things, the development of the U.S. airways. Programs deemed more vital to the U.S. military effort received priority—and the necessary funding—in the years immediately following. The Truman administration made sharp cuts in CAA airway programs, and the first Eisenhower administration, motivated by economic philosophy as well as the military emergency, cut even deeper. In fiscal year 1950, the CAA commanded a budget of $187.1 million. Its budget went into a steady four-year decline, falling to $115.9 million in fiscal year 1954.

Airway development hit another impediment: the CAA and the Defense Department were unable to agree on how to equip the airways. "The toughest problems are not technical or scientific or mathematical," said one observer of the aviation scene, "[but] a maze of unresolved differences [between civil and military interests] on operational philosophy." The landing and navigational systems were particular points of contention. The CAA held out for the ILS, which had been developed at its technical center in Indianapolis, and the VOR. The military favored a landing system invented by Nobel laureate Luis W. Alvarez, Ground Controlled Approach (GCA), and a navigational system known as tactical air navigation (TACAN).

The CAA was never in a position to impose its will on the Pentagon. Nor could the Pentagon,

all its money and prestige notwithstanding, have its way, particularly during peacetime. Authority and responsibility within the federal structure were so diffused among civilian and military interests that differences could not be resolved. "A lack of central authority is at the 'root of the evil,'" noted another contemporary observer. "The CAA, intended to be the operating agency, has had neither the leadership nor the clear-cut authority to act decisively." The result was stalemate whenever civil and military interests failed to agree on policy—and that is where policymakers usually were on such important questions as the nature of the airway system and airspace allocation.

Precious time and effort were wasted before the CAA and the Pentagon agreed to adopt separate landing systems—the civil agency staying with ILS, the military with GCA. The navigational system proved more difficult to resolve. The international aviation community, as represented by the United Nations International Civil Aviation Organization, had already selected VOR, along with DME, the CAA's choice for distance-measuring equipment; yet the U.S. aviation community was still squabbling over which system to select. In 1956 the competing interests finally compromised. DME would be dropped, and VOR and TACAN would be combined to form a hybrid navigational facility, VORTAC.

By this time, the airways had fallen behind the growth curve. Long-range and secondary radar, both absolutely essential if air traffic control was to segregate fast-moving airliners from single-engine general aviation aircraft, were scarcely in evidence on the airways. Even certificated route air carriers were not required to fly on airways under the control of air route traffic control centers because the capacity did not exist to accommodate all such traffic. "Every time anyone of us either flies his own airplane or gets on an airplane, he is going into an air situation that is inefficiently instrumented and controlled," aviation expert Najeeb E. Halaby told a congressional hearing. Modern airliners and military aircraft traveled so fast, Halaby explained, that even if they saw each other as much as a mile away and realized they were on a collision course, it was not physically possible to avoid each other.

On June 30, 1956, a TWA Super Constellation and a United Air Lines DC-7 were flying "off airways" over the Grand Canyon when they collided in midair. It was a clear, sunny day and no other traffic was within miles of them. Each crew—not CAA controllers—was responsible for keeping its aircraft separated from other traffic. All 128 occupants of the two aircraft died in the collision.

The Grand Canyon midair collision proved a powerful catalyst for change. Critics of the Eisenhower administration's aviation policy, particularly Senator A. S. Mike Monroney, called for airway reform—even for replacing the CAA with a new aviation agency. People within Eisenhower's circle picked up the same theme. Edward P. Curtis, a former Army Air Forces major general who had been selected by Eisenhower in February 1956 to conduct a study of the nation's airway needs, warned in May 1957 that "a crisis was in the making" because of the inability of the national airspace system to cope with the complex patterns of civil and military traffic. Curtis concluded that the present governmental structure, with the CAA and the military sharing responsibility for managing the nation's airspace, was incapable of keeping pace with aviation growth. He recommended the establishment of an independent federal aviation agency "into which are consolidated all the essential management functions necessary to support the common needs of the military and civil aviation of the United States."

Curtis's recommendations, having received wide support in the Congress and in the aviation community, picked up more boosters in the spring of 1958 when two midair collisions occurred between military and civil aircraft. These disasters appeared as further proof that the Civil Aeronautics Administration was not up to the task of taking the United States into the coming jet age. Helping seal the CAA's fate was a widely held perception that the 18-year-old air agency had become soft and feckless and that laxness permeated its regulatory practices.

On August 13, 1958, Congress passed the Federal Aviation Act; in signing the measure ten days later President Eisenhower liberated civil-military policy from the trammels of divided authority and provided the nation's airways with a firmer hand at the controls. Among other things, the act repealed the Civil Aeronautics Act of 1938 and, as Curtis had recommended, established the independent Federal Aviation Agency (FAA) and gave it the authority to control "both civil and military operations" in the navigable airspace of the United States. On December 31, 1958, the FAA inherited as a nucleus the organization and functions of the CAA and the safety rule making functions of the Civil Aeronautics Board. That same day the CAA officially went out of existence.

References:

Arnold E. Briddon, Ellmore A. Champie, and Peter A. Marraine, *FAA Historical Fact Book: A Chronology, 1926-1971* (Washington, D.C.: U.S. Department of Transportation, 1974);

Stuart R. Rochester, *Takeoff at Mid-Century: Federal Civil Aviation Policy in the Eisenhower Years, 1953-1961* (Washington, D.C.: U.S. Department of Transportation, 1976);

Donald R. Whitnah, *Safer Skyways: Federal Control of Aviation, 1926-1966* (Ames: University of Iowa Press, 1966);

John R. M. Wilson, *Turbulence Aloft: The Civil Aeronautics Administration Amid Wars and Rumors of Wars, 1938-1953* (Washington, D.C.: U.S. Department of Transportation, 1979).

Archives:

The two most valuable manuscript collections dealing with the Civil Aeronautics Administration are Record Group 237, the Civil Aeronautics Administration Files, at the National Archives in Washington, D.C., and the Federal Aviation Administration History Files, at the FAA Headquarters Building in Washington, D.C. The FAA Library also has a valuable collection of CAA materials, particularly in the regulatory area, and an unpublished manuscript by Ben Stern, "Wartime History of the Civil Aeronautics Administration."

Civil Aeronautics Board

by Donald R. Whitnah

University of Northern Iowa

The Civil Aeronautics Board (CAB) played a major role in shaping commercial aviation policy in the United States for over 40 years. Born in the midst of depression, it presided over an airline industry that grew from 22 airlines with total operating revenues of $58 in 1938 to 50 airlines with total operating revenues of $19.7 billion in 1978. After surviving numerous political storms, the CAB finally succumbed to demands for deregulation in an era of free-market economics.

The movement that led to the establishment of the CAB began in the wake of the airmail scandal of 1934. Widely criticized for his handling of the controversial episode, President Franklin D. Roosevelt established a federal commission with a mandate to formulate a new civil aviation policy. After due deliberations, the commission recommended that the federal government undertake responsibility for economic regulation of the struggling airline industry. As the Interstate Commerce Commission (ICC) already was overburdened with regulatory duties, it wanted a separate independent body to be set up with the power to issue certificates of convenience and necessity for air carriers that were meeting the needs of the public.

The airline industry enthusiastically supported the commission's recommendations. President Roosevelt, however, was reluctant to create another federal agency that would be independent of executive control. Without his support, congressional action on the commission's findings came to naught.

By 1937 the deteriorating economic status of the airline industry forced Roosevelt to act. In the three years from 1933 to 1936, 13 of the nation's 19 domestic air carriers lost a total of $3.5 million, while the 6 profitable lines showed a combined return of only $134,000. Faced with this reality, Roosevelt in September 1937 appointed an Interdepartment Committee on Civil Aviation Regulation to review the dozens of bills that had been pro-

posed to regulate the airlines. The committee's recommendation—introduced in the Senate by Patrick A. McCarran of Nevada and in the House by Clarence F. Lea of California—survived the legislative process and was signed into law by President Roosevelt on June 23, 1938.

The Civil Aeronautics Act of 1938—hailed in 1942 by aviation historian Henry Ladd Smith as "the most important piece of air legislation ever passed by Congress"—created a new type of federal agency with quasi-legislative and quasi-judicial powers. The tripartite organization included an administrator who had responsibility for establishing and maintaining airways, controlling air traffic, and other executive functions; a three-member Air Safety Board with quasi-judicial powers for investigating accidents, determining probable cause, and making safety recommendations; and a five-member Civil Aeronautics Authority (CAA) that was given broad regulatory powers over fares and routes. Although the president appointed the administrator and members of the Safety Board and CAA, only the administrator served at his pleasure; individuals on the Safety Board and CAA (who served six-year terms) could be removed only for cause.

The first 18 months under the new law brought unprecedented prosperity for the nation's airline operators. It was "the happiest period in the history of air transportation," Henry Ladd Smith observed. The authority issued certificates of convenience and necessity to 22 airlines, giving them permanent route authority. This stabilized the industry and encouraged investment in new planes and equipment. At the same time, the airlines compiled a distinguished safety record. Increases in mail and passenger traffic brought record profits. However, all was not happy within the regulatory agency. The awkward tripartite structure of the organization caused administrative problems that were compounded by a bitter personal feud between Administrator Clinton M. Hester and CAA chairman Robert M. Hinckley.

In December 1939 President Roosevelt ordered the Bureau of the Budget to inquire into the status of the factious regulatory agency. The bureau ended up by pointing out the need to redefine the responsibilities of the administrator and CAA and recommending that the administrator be transferred to the Department of Commerce. Also, it called for the Safety Board to be combined into the CAA, which would be renamed the Civil Aeronautics Board. Roosevelt endorsed the bureau's proposals. Following some political skirmishing, the Senate gave its approval to the reorganization plan.

On July 1, 1940, the Civil Aeronautics Board assumed the duties of the CAA. It had the power to prescribe rates, decide routes, issue certificates of convenience and necessity, authorize antitrust exemptions for intercarrier discussions and agreements, pay subsidies, approve mergers, and maintain standards of safety. A Bureau of Air Safety within the CAB would investigate accidents and determine probable cause, but safety regulations were the province of the board.

The subsequent history of the CAB might conveniently be divided into three major phases. The first period, lasting until 1947, saw the board establish its role as arbitrator and protector of the economic fortunes of the airline industry, respond to the problems of world war, and decide the issue of postwar international air routes. The second phase, from 1948 to 1968, was a time of healthy national economic growth and low inflation; the CAB strengthened the linear point-to-point route system of the major airlines, resolved the problem of irregular carriers, supported local service lines, and lost control over safety matters. The final period lasted until 1978 and was a time of economic crises that saw the decline, and ultimate demise, of the CAB's economic control over the airline industry.

The controversy over international air routes occupied an inordinate amount of the CAB's time and attention throughout its existence. It first began in May 1939, when American Export Airlines (Amex) filed an application to fly the North Atlantic in competition with Pan American Airways. This challenge to Pan Am's international monopoly placed the CAB at the center of a monumental political battle. Following extensive hearings that produced over 4,000 typescript pages of testimony (an

omen of the future!), the CAB found that Pan Am's monopoly of the North Atlantic was not in the public interest. Preferring regulated competition to a single international line, the board in July 1940 granted Amex a temporary certificate to fly the route. Congress, however, responded to Pan Am's vigorous lobbying effort and denied Amex a mail contract.

American entry into World War II in December 1941 brought a truce in the struggle over international air routes. The CAB focused its attention on domestic matters. It suspended the route certification process, authorized special air service where necessary to meet wartime requirements, restricted nonessential traffic, and developed a system of priorities. At the same time the Air Transport Command pressed several domestic airlines into overseas service in support of military activities.

As a result, not until July 5, 1945, did the CAB announce a decision on the North Atlantic Route Case. Again supporting competition over monopoly, the board rejected Pan Am's arguments for a single U.S.-flag line and awarded transatlantic routes to American Overseas Airlines (the result of a merger between Amex and American Airlines) and TWA. The following year the CAB broke Pan Am's domination of Latin American and Pacific routes, with Braniff Airways and Northwest Airlines the main beneficiaries.

Having settled the immediate problem of allocating postwar international air routes, the CAB turned its attention to fostering the rapid growth of domestic airlines, primarily through its control over routes. The "Big Four"—United, American, TWA, and Eastern—continued to dominate the industry, although their share of revenue-passenger miles declined from 82 percent in 1938 to 71 percent in 1954. Still, at a time when total revenue-passenger miles increased from slightly less than 480 million to 16.7 billion, they had little cause to complain.

Smaller trunk carriers, such as Braniff, Delta, National, Western, and Continental, also benefited from CAB awards of new routes, although the regulatory process was often lengthy and acrimonious, with the board's decisions producing both joy and disappointment.

In addition to supporting the trunk carriers on major routes, the board sought to bring air service within the reach of all Americans by nurturing the growth of feeder or local service carriers. In July 1944 the board created the new classification of feeder (later, local service) airline to service smaller communities throughout the country. Initially 26 companies received authorization to fly various routes. In May 1955 the 13 surviving carriers were granted permanent certificates. Although the CAB later permitted the local service airlines to expand into regional trunks, the cost of serving marginal markets remained high, peaking during fiscal 1963 with a subsidy of $67.7 million.

Nonscheduled air carriers (nonskeds) that attempted to penetrate the ranks of the privileged few fared less well at the hands of the protective CAB. In an attempt to control the postwar proliferation of small airline operations, many of which consisted of a single C-47, the CAB in May 1946 required operators of large aircraft to obtain a Letter of Registration. Over the next 27 months the board issued 142 such letters. The few nonskeds that managed to survive into the 1950s found only limited sympathy from a CAB that placed emphasis on supporting and protecting the scheduled airlines. In January 1959 the 23 remaining nonskeds—by then known as Supplemental Airlines—attained a measure of respectability when the CAB issued them interstate certificates. Three years later, armed with new legislative authority, the CAB granted permanent certificates to the 15 surviving nonskeds. Although airline historian R. E. G. Davies believes that the CAB "acted fairly throughout the complicated history of the Nonskeds," several operators—most notably Orvis M. Nelson of Transocean Airlines—likely would disagree.

The CAB's record may be mixed in some areas, but without question the nation's scheduled airlines prospered under its paternalistic guidance. When new equipment was required, the board stood ready (after some initial hesitation) to provide the necessary funds. For example, in 1958 the CAB authorized a 10 percent fare increase. Two years later it granted an additional 5 percent. Its guideline for these increases was a rate of return on investment of 10.25 percent.

The results of the board's actions spoke for themselves. In 1938 the industry operated 260 aircraft over 34,879 miles of routes and carried over 1 million passengers. Twenty years later it operated 1,494 aircraft over 88,325 miles of routes and carried 48.4 million passengers.

The CAB took special pride in the safety record of the airlines under its charge. In 1957 the passenger fatality rate stood at 2.2 percent of the 1938 rate; domestic air travel was 13 times safer than automobile travel. Nonetheless, the board's responsibility for safety soon fell victim to the Eisenhower administration's reorganization schemes. The Federal Aviation Act, signed by President Eisenhower on August 23, 1958, placed responsibility for safety regulation and enforcement with the new Federal Aviation Agency. The CAB continued to investigate accidents and determine probable cause. Also, FAA orders to suspend or revoke a certificate due to safety violations could be appealed to the CAB. Eight years later, however, these remaining safety functions were lost to the newly created National Transportation Safety Board.

Erosion of the CAB's safety role coincided with national economic problems that placed the airline industry under increasing strain. Between 1969 and 1978 prices for jet fuel increased by 222 percent. At the same time industry labor costs rose by 135 percent. With declining load factors on their new wide-body jets, airline operators sought relief through fare increases. Although the CAB complied, earnings remained weak.

The 1970s saw increasing complaints about the CAB's regulatory role. Federal regulations, its critics charged, had produced high operating costs and an inefficient point-to-point route structure. In contrast, unregulated intrastate carriers in California and Texas seemed models of well-run, prosperous companies. At a time when the notion of deregulation found great favor in both political and academic circles, the CAB found few defenders—apart from the scheduled airline operators who feared a deregulated future.

The Airline Deregulation Act of 1978 marked the end of the regulatory era for the airline industry. The CAB slowly faded away, losing control over domestic routes and fares. Finally, the board petitioned to end its existence on October 1, 1983.

References:

Robert Burkhardt, *CAB—The Civil Aeronautics Board* (Dulles International Airport, Va.: Green Hills Publishing Co., 1974);

R. E. G. Davies, *Airlines of the United States since 1914*, revised edition (Washington, D.C.: Smithsonian Institution, 1982);

William A. Jordan, *Airline Regulation in America: Effects and Imperfections* (Baltimore: Johns Hopkins University Press, 1970);

Jordan, "Civil Aeronautics Board," in *Government Agencies*, edited by Donald R. Whitnah (Westport, Conn.: Greenwood Press, 1983), pp. 61-68;

Richard J. Kent, Jr., *Safe, Separated and Soaring: A History of Federal Civil Aviation Policy, 1961-1972* (Washington, D.C.: U.S. Department of Transportation, 1980);

Nick A. Komons, *Bonfires to Beacons. Federal Civil Aviation Policy under the Air Commerce Act, 1926-1938* (Washington, D.C.: U.S. Department of Transportation, 1978);

Stuart I. Rochester, *Takeoff at Mid-Century: Federal Civil Aviation Policy in the Eisenhower Years, 1953-1961* (Washington, D.C.: U.S. Department of Transportation, 1976);

Henry Ladd Smith, *Airways: The History of Commercial Aviation in the United States* (New York: Knopf, 1942);

Richard H. K. Vietor, "Contrived Competition: Airline Regulation and Deregulation, 1925-1988," *Business History Review*, 64 (1990): 61-108;

Donald R. Whitnah, *Safer Skyways: Federal Control of Aviation, 1926-1966* (Ames: Iowa State University Press, 1967);

John R. M. Wilson, *Turbulence Aloft: The Civil Aeronautics Administration Amid Wars and Rumors of Wars, 1938-1953* (Washington, D.C.: U.S. Department of Transportation, 1979).

Edwin I. Colodny

(June 7, 1926 -   )

by William F. Trimble

Auburn University

CAREER: Trial attorney, Civil Aeronautics Board (1954-1957); executive positions (1957-1969), executive vice-president for marketing and legal affairs (1969-1975), president and chief executive officer (1975-1978), chairman, Allegheny Airlines/USAir (1978-1991).

The 1970s and 1980s saw a new generation of air transport executives emerge. Unlike the pioneers and founders who had established the industry, the newcomers had experience in marketing, legal affairs, and finance. They were expressively brash, fresh from some of the nation's best business schools, and many of them aggressively recast airlines in the permissive atmosphere of economic deregulation. Their companies initiated massive route expansion, financed new equipment, and lured passengers from competitors with glitzy advertising campaigns and cut-rate fares. People Express and Air Florida were the most visible newcomers representing this trend; Braniff and Continental were established companies that embraced the new strategy. Following initial success, all four airlines encountered major financial difficulties and were forced into bankruptcy. These experiences, coupled with weak profits and marginal performance by more conservative airlines, led to doubts about deregulation and concerns about the stability of commercial aviation in the 1980s.

Edwin I. Colodny (courtesy of USAir)

In sharp contrast to most American airlines during the decade was the consistent performance and profitability of USAir, led by its president and chief executive officer, Edwin I. Colodny. Colodny adopted a more cautious approach for his company, and for the most part it paid off handsomely. Rather than plunging headlong into expansion after passage of the Airline Deregulation Act of 1978, Colodny pursued a conservative policy that built on the airline's traditional strengths in the Northeast and Middle Atlantic regions. USAir's corporate strategy mirrored the personality of Colodny, who, although representative of the second generation of airline executives and far removed from the company's roots in the airmail pickup days of the 1940s, was more the hands-on "organization man" than his flamboyant young counterparts at other airlines. Although he faced vexing problems associated with mergers and acquisitions in the late 1980s, Colodny ranks as one of the most uniformly successful airline executives of the postwar era.

Colodny was born on June 7, 1926, the son of Myer and Lena Colodny, who owned a grocery business in Burlington, Vermont. A skilled violinist, he attended the Eastman School of Music at the University of Rochester, but received his bachelor's degree in political science upon graduation in 1948. He earned a doctorate from Harvard Law School in 1951 and served as a first lieutenant in the office of the judge advocate general until 1954. He was a trial attorney with the Civil Aeronautics Board from 1954 to 1957, when he joined Allegheny Airlines, USAir's predecessor. Colodny's first position at Allegheny was assistant to President Leslie O. Barnes. From 1969 to 1975 Colodny served as the airline's executive vice-president for marketing and legal affairs.

During the late 1960s Allegheny expanded from a strictly local-service airline into a regional carrier that in some ways emulated the larger trunk lines. In part this expansion was the result of the acquisitions of Lake Central Airlines in 1967 and Mohawk Airlines in 1972, which gave Allegheny profitable new routes in the Midwest, New York, and New England. Allegheny also underwent a major transition with the purchase of jet equipment, starting with Douglas DC-9s in 1966. Finally, the airline pioneered cooperative arrangements in the 1960s with small local-service carriers which shared Allegheny's reservations network

and funneled passengers into Allegheny's route system.

Colodny became president and chief executive officer of Allegheny when Barnes stepped down in 1975. Although some members of the board of directors had doubts about Colodny because of his lack of experience in operations, they were soon allayed by the firm hand he took in the company's affairs. Allegheny was not prospering when Colodny took over. No longer receiving a federal subsidy, assaulted by soaring fuel costs, and facing possible cash flow restrictions, it lost nearly $10 million during the first year of Colodny's leadership. Colodny took drastic measures to stem the flow of red ink, including reductions in flights, seating capacity, and employee layoffs. He raised money by issuing new stock and reversed the firm's unfavorable debt-equity ratio. After taking over as chairman of the board of directors in 1978, Colodny concentrated on turning Allegheny's regional public image into that of a national carrier, and he pushed through the change of the company's name to USAir on October 28, 1979.

Although at first opposed to deregulation, Colodny soon found that by pursuing what he called "controlled growth," he could use the new competitive environment to the benefit of his company. His first goal was to make long-range plans for the purchase of new airplanes. While some airlines plunged into the wide-body market, USAir stayed with narrow-body aircraft that more closely fitted its short-to-medium-range routes. In 1979 the company placed orders for ten McDonnell Douglas DC-9-30s and three Boeing 727-200s; two years later, USAir ordered 15 Boeing 737-200s and ten of the new Boeing model 737-300, featuring more fuel-efficient engines and computerized avionics and flight-deck displays.

Expansion also included new routes and additions to the company's maintenance and operations facilities at its principal hub, Greater Pittsburgh International Airport. In late 1978 and early 1979 the airline opened routes from Pittsburgh and Philadelphia to Tampa, Orlando, and West Palm Beach, Florida. Later in 1979 USAir moved into the Southwest, adding New Orleans, Houston, and Phoenix to its list of destinations. Connections to the West Coast came in 1983, with the addition of routes from Pittsburgh to Los Angeles and San Francisco. A $16 million expansion of the South Dock at Pittsburgh added ten new boarding gates in 1981. Following this were a $40 million flight training center, a $16 million maintenance and overhaul facility, and a $5 million jet engine assembly building, all three of which opened at Pittsburgh in 1982.

Under Colodny, USAir could seemingly do no wrong through the first half of the 1980s. From profits of $33.4 million in 1979, earnings nearly doubled to $60.3 million in 1980, and reached a remarkable $121.6 million in 1984. In contrast, the American airline industry as a whole lost more than $150 million in 1980, and $580 million in 1983. Reorganized as the operating subsidiary of a holding company, USAir Group, Inc., on February 1, 1983, USAir flew 16.2 million passengers that year, nearly 11 percent more than in 1982; in 1984 the airline enplaned more than 17 million travelers. By 1985 USAir was flying more than 70 percent of the passengers who came through Greater Pittsburgh International.

In March 1984 Colodny analyzed his company's achievements in a speech before the Pittsburgh Chapter of the National Association of Accountants. In the age of deregulation, USAir faced challenges on two fronts: new low-fare, "no frills" airlines, which competed with the older companies on their more profitable, established routes; and intense fare cutting among all airlines as they tried to deal with excess capacity. Colodny emphasized that his company's response to the competition had been "niching," or retaining its basic services, focusing heavily on business fliers in the Northeast and Midwest, and slowly expanding into new markets with carefully chosen equipment and scheduling. Colodny foresaw difficulties over employee wages and benefits, productivity, growing federal involvement in consumer protection, and the tremendous costs of buying new equipment. He remained confident, however, of USAir's financial security and its ability to meet the uncertainties of the future.

Ironically, within two years USAir faced unexpected problems that strained Colodny's leadership capacity to its limits. The first of these concerned the airline's Pittsburgh hub. When Allegheny County, the airport's operator, approached USAir in May 1984 to work out a financial arrangement for a new $600 million midfield terminal building, it met opposition from Colodny, who was unwilling to commit his company to the major expense of a new terminal when gates at the present one had not yet reached capacity. Colodny refused to compromise until an independent analysis concluded that

renovation and expansion of USAir's gates at the existing terminal would be too costly. Only then did the airline enter into serious negotiations with the county, ending in a long-term lease agreement in June 1988. Under the terms of the understanding, USAir would have to pay $30 million in rent and landing fees annually starting when the new airport opened in 1993.

The airport agreement forced changes in Colodny's deliberate approach to expansion, but it did guarantee USAir's Pittsburgh hub until well into the next century. Far less certainty came from Colodny's handling of USAir's December 1986 acquisition of Pacific Southwest Airlines and its March 1987 purchase of Piedmont Aviation, Inc. Although Colodny tried to plan the mergers so that there would be a minimum of disruption, his carefully orchestrated program went awry. There were greater than anticipated costs involved in the introduction of first-class service, the need to add trained personnel at key points on the expanded route system, and the expense of bringing the salaries of former Pacific Southwest and Piedmont employees up to USAir's levels. Hurricane Hugo in September 1989 and an earthquake in San Francisco the next month forced the cancellation of hundreds of USAir flights and cost the airline tens of millions of dollars. The result of these and other difficulties was a loss of $63 million in 1989.

Colodny remained optimistic that USAir would overcome these obstacles and committed himself to seeing the company return to profitability. He retired in June 1991 after working to ensure that his successors were fully prepared to cope with the kinds of unforeseen problems that marred his last few years in office.

References:

Mark Belko, "County, USAir Sign Airport Agreement," *Pittsburgh Post-Gazette,* June 10, 1988;

Joan M. Feldman, "Blending the Elements of a Major Empire," *Air Transport World,* 25 (June 1988): 28-41;

Noreen Hickman, "USAir Coasts over Rocky Airline Industry," *Pittsburgh Press,* March 13, 1983;

W. David Lewis and William F. Trimble, *The Airway to Everywhere: A History of All American Aviation, 1937-1953* (Pittsburgh: University of Pittsburgh Press, 1988);

"USAir: Fifty Years of Flying High," *USAir,* 11 (May 1989): 71-92;

Chet Wade, "USAir Chief Flies Clear of Risks," *Pittsburgh Post-Gazette,* June 18, 1984;

William H. Wylie, "As Allegheny Airlines Grows, So Do Operations Here," *Pittsburgh Press,* May 27, 1979.

Commuter Airlines

by I. E. Quastler

San Diego State University

Commuter airlines, sometimes called regional airlines, provide scheduled services with small aircraft over relatively short distances. Their main function, traditionally, has been to link smaller cities with the nearest metropolitan centers, where most passengers connect with major airline flights. Originally, commuter airlines were called scheduled air taxis, for many evolved from air taxi operations, where a steady demand for flights sometimes led to the establishment of scheduled services. A few had existed in the United States since at least the 1940s, but a commuter airline industry did not emerge until the 1960s.

Unless they operated wholly within one state, early air taxis needed authorization from the Civil Aeronautics Board (CAB), the federal agency charged with the economic regulation of the airlines, to perform scheduled services. On October 5, 1949, however, the board announced an experiment: in the future, scheduled air taxis would be exempt from CAB regulations, provided that they used only small equipment. Small aircraft were defined as those with a certified gross takeoff weight (the maximum weight allowed for the aircraft and its contents, including fuel) of 12,500 pounds or less. This ruling laid the foundation for the eventual development of the U.S. commuter airline industry.

Thereafter, scheduled air taxis could enter and leave the industry without CAB approval, add and drop markets freely, fly any route (except those flown by the CAB-certificated airlines), and charge fares as they saw fit. In short, long before the Airline Deregulation Act of 1978, this segment of the industry was largely deregulated. In contrast, the CAB-certificated trunk and local service airlines, specializing in serving the largest cities and smaller cities, respectively, were strictly regulated as to entry, fares, routes, and business practices. In 1952 the

CAB provisionally adopted this experimental exemption as Part 298 of its economic regulations.

Despite this decision, there was no rush to establish scheduled air taxis during the 1950s. Perhaps the main reason was the inadequacy of the available piston-engined equipment. The most widely used aircraft within the 12,500-pound limit was the twin-engined Beech 18, a 1937 design. It could carry seven or eight passengers, but was costly to maintain and was regarded as outmoded. The more modern British de Havilland Dove could carry about ten passengers, but also was expensive to maintain. These airplanes were supplemented by a variety of other twin- and single-engined types.

Another reason for slow growth was the expansion of subsidized local service airlines, which preempted many of the more promising markets. At the same time, most people still could not afford airfares, and many were afraid to fly, especially in small aircraft.

Among the early pioneers was Provincetown-Boston Airlines (PBA), which began scheduled service on November 30, 1949, with a single-engined aircraft. By flying over Massachusetts Bay between Boston and Provincetown, on the tip of Cape Cod, PBA saved customers several hours versus the circuitous land route. It was the outgrowth of a successful air taxi operation between the same cities. Scheduled Skyways started in September 1953, with single-engined equipment, linking the university town of Fayetteville, Arkansas, with the state capital, Little Rock. An outgrowth of an FBO (fixed base operator, involving aircraft sales, maintenance, charters, and flying lessons), Scheduled Skyways' early passengers were mostly professors flying to Little Rock to teach extension courses. Aspen Airways began scheduled service in 1955 using Twin Beechcraft, two years after its founding as an air taxi to connect Denver to the ski resort of Aspen.

Air Midwest SAAB 340 (courtesy of SAAB Aircraft)

By the early 1960s the term commuter airline began to be applied to the industry. "Air commuting" had often been used to refer to business round-trips that were accomplished in a single day, and such trips were facilitated by the scheduled air taxis. The term *commuter* was eagerly promoted by the emerging industry and was widely adopted by the media. Soon the Association of Commuter Airlines began to represent the industry's interests.

Commuter airlines experienced explosive growth between 1965 and 1968. The number of companies listed by the Federal Aviation Agency (FAA) increased from 15 on July 1, 1964, to 228 on November 1, 1968. Between 1965 and 1968 the number of aircraft operated increased from 83 to 1,272. Based on estimates by *Time* magazine, commuter traffic increased from about one million boardings in 1966 to three million in 1968.

At first the boom was unevenly distributed, with a high concentration of routes in the northeastern seaboard and in California, but few elsewhere. Three years later most metropolitan areas were served by a radiating network of routes, although some carried only mail.

Among the major causes of the boom was the appearance of several efficient twin-engined aircraft that fit under the 12,500-pound limit. Leading piston types were the Cessna 402 and the Piper Navajo, both with about eight passenger seats. They soon constituted the backbone of the industry's fleet. Two important new turboprop twins were the 19-passenger de Havilland of Canada Twin Otter and the 15-passenger Beech 99; their lightweight turbine engines made possible much larger payloads. The Twin Otter, which appeared in 1966, had been designed for Canadian bush flights, but proved well suited to commuters. The Beech 99, a modified corporate aircraft, entered service in 1968.

Several other developments also contributed to the boom. In 1965 the CAB made permanent its Part 298 regulations and began to permit commuters to operate over routes flown by the certificated airlines. In 1967 the board began to allow the latter to suspend service to unprofitable small cities and to authorize substitute service by commuter airlines. These agreements were motivated, in part, by the phasing out of smaller aircraft by the local service airlines, a development that made them unsuited to flying to the very cities they had been established to serve. Such "suspension-substitution" agreements often provided excellent markets for the commuters.

Allegheny Airlines, a local service company, was especially active in pursuing suspension-substitution agreements. In the process it established a CAB-approved cooperative program whereby the commuters worked closely with Allegheny, under Allegheny Commuter titles, and acted primarily as traffic feeders to it. Eventually such partnerships allowed Allegheny to drop most of its money-losing cities without losing their feeder value.

Although the boom was impressive, it was not accompanied by increased profits. At this time only about 5 percent of commuter airlines were consistently making money, and companies were constantly going out of business.

How could such an unprofitable industry continue to attract so many newcomers? The main factor was a great optimism about the prospects for future profits, frequently based on unrealistic traffic projections. The lack of accurate financial information about an industry that contained few publicly held corporations (which have to reveal their financial status) also made it possible for entrepreneurs to imagine all kinds of successes.

In 1969 harsh economic facts caught up with the commuters. For the first time, the number of companies leaving the industry considerably exceeded the newcomers. Because of continued losses, many weak firms left the industry, some voluntarily or via merger, but many through bankruptcy. According to the FAA, between November 1968 and September 1969, the number of commuter airlines declined from 240 to 138. Most of those leaving the business were small.

Despite the sharp decrease in the number of firms, passengers actually increased from three million in 1968 to about four million in 1969. This reflected a major change in the industry, as fewer, larger companies often replaced many small ones. During the last half of 1969 the 50 largest airlines generated about 90 percent of the industry's available seat-miles, and the top ten accounted for 53 percent.

Between 1968 and 1972 the number of route-miles in the contiguous United States served by the most important commuter airlines, those listed in the *Official Airline Guide* (OAG), increased from 33,000 to about 44,000. In 1972 the routes were es-

pecially dense in the Northeast, with additional concentrations around Chicago, in California, and in Florida.

According to an FAA-sponsored report, covering the period from 1969 to 1970, most of the 56 passenger-carrying airlines studied had average route lengths of less than 100 miles, while 11 averaged less than 50 miles, and the average passenger on the 50 largest companies flew 91 miles. In 1969 the industry's load factor (the percent of seats occupied by revenue passengers) was only 32 percent, while 47 percent was required just to break even. This led to an operating loss of about $28 million. The report noted that 32 commuter airlines carried only cargo or mail.

In 1969 the CAB, reacting to airline industry pressure, began to regulate some aspects of the industry. The scheduled air taxis now were officially renamed "commuter air carriers." They were required to register with the CAB by July 1, 1969 (and annually thereafter), to carry liability insurance, and to file quarterly traffic reports. The new regulations led to 177 registrations.

Because of questions about commuter airline safety, in 1969 the FAA changed its Part 135 regulations (for operators of small aircraft), bringing the operating and maintenance standards closer to those for certificated airlines. For example, two pilots were now mandatory on all aircraft with a passenger capacity of ten or more and a flight attendant was required on airplanes with more than 19 passenger seats. The companies also had to prepare FAA-approved manuals that described their maintenance and operating procedures.

In 1969 Allegheny Airlines withdrew from the short-haul Washington-Philadelphia route in favor of Ransome Airlines, an Allegheny Commuter. This was the first important role for a commuter airline in serving a market connecting major cities. Thereafter the industry was operating the five main types of routes that it has served to the present. The four other types connect 1) smaller cities to nearby metropolitan airports (the most important function); 2) suburban airfields to the main airports of a region (such as in the New York and Los Angeles regions); 3) points already served by larger airlines, but at times when the latter do not fly ("filling the holes in the schedules"); and 4) downtown airports in a few large cities with regional centers or to other downtown airports (such as Detroit-City to Cleveland-Lakefront).

In July 1972 the CAB amended its Part 298 economic regulations to allow larger aircraft. Thereafter commuter airliners could seat up to 30 passengers or carry a freight payload of 7,500 pounds. In contrast to the 12,500-pound rule, the new capacity regulations allowed aircraft to be built with such items as pressurization, lavatories, and larger cabins without the need to sacrifice payload. The 30-passenger limit was meant to fit between the 19 seats available on the largest aircraft within the 12,500-pound rule and the 40 seats of the smallest local service airliners; the CAB thought it would improve the economic viability of the commuters without seriously affecting the certificated airlines.

Between 1973 and 1978 the commuter airlines continued to grow rapidly. Passengers increased from 5.7 million to 11 million, while cargo traffic increased even more rapidly; the number of contiguous U.S. route-miles flown by *OAG*-listed companies increased from 44,000 to 83,000. The Northeast, California, and Florida continued to be served intensively, and substantial passenger feeder networks had developed around most large cities.

In response to this growth and to the 30-passenger limit, several new aircraft were placed in service. One was the pressurized 19-passenger Swearingen (later Fairchild) Metroliner, a twin turboprop built in San Antonio that entered service in March 1973. The much improved Metro II, introduced in 1974, cruised at close to 300 mph; it soon became the best-selling turboprop in the industry. Other aircraft that could now be used by the commuter airlines included the pressurized, 26-passenger French Nord 262, dating from the 1960s, and the venerable 28-passenger DC-3.

Only one aircraft, Northern Ireland's Shorts SD3-30, was built to the CAB's new capacity limits. This boxlike, twin-turboprop, 30-passenger aircraft entered U.S. service in October 1976. Although not pressurized, it had stand-up headroom and a lavatory, and sold fairly well.

From the early 1970s there had been discussions about subsidies for commuter airlines. Under the law, however, only certificated airlines were eligible for subsidies, and the CAB generally opposed commuter certification. This topic was especially relevant at isolated small cities, where even commuters often could not be profitable; yet, the service seemed justified on social grounds. In 1973 Air Midwest became the first federally subsidized commuter, although indirectly, when its "flow through" proposal was approved by the CAB. Under it Frontier Airlines transferred its subsidy funds for three cities in western Kansas to its substitute carrier, Air Midwest.

This concept was challenged in the courts and was ruled illegal. Therefore, Air Midwest applied to become the first certificated commuter airline. This application was successful, and in 1977 the company began subsidized service to eight points in Kansas and Colorado. Soon two other commuters, Cochise and SkyWest, received similar certificates.

A landmark piece of legislation, the Airline Deregulation Act (ADA) of 1978, was passed late that year. Under this law the commuter aircraft size limit was further liberalized to a maximum of 55 seats (later increased to 60), and the payload limit was increased to 18,000 pounds. The Essential Air Service (EAS) provision stated that all cities that were currently on the certificated airline network were guaranteed air service for the next ten years, if necessary with subsidy. This section resulted from pressure from smaller communities that feared deregulation, which made it easier for the certificated airlines to delete cities, would mean the end of their air service.

The CAB then investigated those 555 cities that might be abandoned by the certificated airlines, and determined the minimum amount of service (the EAS, essential air service) to be guaranteed to them. This was usually expressed as a certain number of seats to be offered daily to the nearest air hub.

Under the ADA, certification was no longer required to qualify for subsidies; that is, even noncertificated commuter airlines were eligible. Such payments were to be awarded after competitive bids, with the company offering to provide the essential service at the lowest cost normally chosen. It was correctly assumed, however, that most EAS cities would be served voluntarily at the essential level without subsidies.

As predicted, after deregulation certificated airlines left small cities at an unprecedented rate. In the first year 46 places were deleted, compared to 172 in the 14 years before deregulation. In virtually every case commuters provided the new service. By mid 1982 commuter airlines were being subsidized at about 80 cities.

Given the many new opportunities, a second commuter air carrier boom began. Its impact was re-

AirOregon Metro II (courtesy of AirOregon)

inforced by the fuel crisis of 1979, as major airlines abandoned or curtailed many services, and commuters moved in to fill the vacuum. According to the Regional Airline Association (RAA), the number of passengers enplaned by commuter airlines increased from 11 million in 1978 to about 15 million in 1980 and to almost 23 million in 1983. In 1980 turbine-powered aircraft constituted 40 percent of the commuter fleet, and contained 70 percent of the seats.

After deregulation Fairchild produced the Metro III, which featured more powerful engines than the Metro II. In 1982 14.3 percent of the commuter industry's seats were accounted for by various versions of the Metro. Piper reentered the market with two eight-passenger models, the piston-powered T-1020 and the turbine-powered T-1040. These did not sell well, probably because they were too small for the postderegulation commuters. Two new unpressurized aircraft were Brazil's 19-passenger Embraer Bandeirante and the Shorts SD3-60, a 36-passenger development of the earlier

SD3-30. The 19-passenger British Aerospace Jetstream 31, introduced in 1983, became a best-seller because it was the only 19-seater with stand-up headroom and because the builder offered generous financial terms.

In October 1980 the CAB changed the way it classified U.S. airlines. The old classification of trunk, local service, and commuter airlines had been based on their functions, as reflected in the size of equipment. The new classification of major, national, and regional airlines was based strictly on yearly gross revenues. The majors were defined as those airlines grossing $1 billion or more per year, while nationals grossed between $75 million and $1 billion. Regionals grossed less than $75 million per year, and consisted mostly of commuter air carriers, but also included an assortment of small jet operators. The term *commuter airlines* was still commonly used to refer to the regionals running small aircraft.

Throughout the 1980s commuter lines grew impressively. In 1986, for example, they served about

155,000 contiguous U.S. route-miles, compared to 83,000 at the time of deregulation. Passenger traffic increased from 26 million in 1984 to 38 million in 1989; by the latter year, about 10 percent of major airline passengers connected to or from the commuters. However, during the same period the number of firms declined from 203 to 159. In 1988 the 50 largest companies handled 95 percent of commuter industry traffic, while the 63 smallest had a mere one percent. In 1990 commuters served almost 850 cities, far more than the other two categories of scheduled airlines combined.

Traffic growth was facilitated by the introduction of several advanced twin turboprop airliners with between 30 and 42 seats. In contrast to most of their predecessors, which were based on corporate aircraft designs, they were constructed specifically for the commuter market. Because of their high payload capacities, reliability, and speeds, and with many passenger amenities, they contributed greatly to the industry's growth and to its improved image.

The first newcomer was the 35-seat, 280 mph Swedish SAAB 340, which began U.S. service in October 1984. This was followed by the 36-passenger, 310 mph de Havilland of Canada Dash 8, first placed into U.S. service in April 1985. The fastest was the Embraer Brasilia, with a cruising speed of 330 mph and room for 30 passengers. The largest was the French-Italian 42-passenger ATR-42, which first went into service in 1986.

The diffusion of code sharing had a greater impact on the industry than the new airliners. Superficially, code sharing simply is an agreement whereby commuter airline flights are allowed to be listed in computer reservations systems (CRS) and in the *OAG* under the two-letter code of a large airline, such as the AA code of American Airlines. Because of favorable listings for code-sharers in computer systems and in the *OAG*, and because of other advantages, explained below, this practice made it almost impossible for independent commuter airlines to compete.

Code sharing involves many additional agreements between the major airline and its affiliate. At the hub airport, the latter normally shares the major airline's gates, ticket counters, and baggage-handling system, greatly facilitating passenger connections. The commuter also benefits from joint fares, joint advertising and marketing, and participation in frequent flyer programs, and it may receive management assistance in such areas as scheduling and employee training. Among the greatest advantages are the name recognition that comes with the adoption, in most cases, of the larger firm's name (such as United Express and American Eagle) and in having access to its CRS. Because of such benefits, upon implementation the commuter's traffic usually surged. For the major airlines, code sharing is a powerful way to reinforce their "fortresses," the connecting hubs, as their affiliates feed traffic to and from surrounding small- and medium-sized cities.

To a limited extent, code sharing had been practiced for many years. The first code sharers, from 1967, were the Allegheny Commuters. In the early 1980s Air Florida also allowed some commuter airlines to use its code while they provided substitute service. Then, in 1984 and 1985, this practice spread throughout the country.

Code sharing, in what may be called the current pattern, started around Houston late in 1983 when Continental and Eastern airlines each began to work closely with a commuter. These examples were soon followed by a steady stream of new ones; for example, in April 1984 "Eastern Metro Express" began to operate at Atlanta, and in the following month Atlantic Southeast Airlines became a "Delta Connection" carrier.

United Airlines and many independent commuters objected strongly to such agreements. United even threatened to remove code-sharing connections from its powerful Apollo CRS, saying that such listings claimed single-carrier (on-line) connections which did not exist. At about the same time 13 independent commuters petitioned the CAB to stop this "biased and deceptive" practice, which was seen as a threat to their existence. The CAB said that it would study the matter, but took no action.

As the advantages of code sharing became clear, it spread rapidly. In October 1984 three major airlines (American, Northwest, Orient, and Republic) announced they would soon implement such agreements. The first American Eagle operation, at Dallas-Ft. Worth, started on November 1, while Mesaba Airlines became the first Northwest Orient Airlink partner on December 1, 1984. Republic Express began operating at Memphis on May 31, 1985.

The power of code sharing was greatly reinforced, though not by design, by a CAB decision effective November 14, 1984. In response to many complaints about unfair CRS practices, the board ruled that in the future a nondiscriminatory, uniform way of listing flights had to be followed: all nonstops and direct services between cities should be listed first, followed by on-line connections and then by interline (involving two carriers) flights. Since code-sharing connections are classified as on-line, these services now had to be listed before the connections of the independent commuters. In practical terms, on-line connections appeared on the first computer screen, while interline connections did not appear until later screens. Because about 80 percent of travel agency reservations (which account for most reservations) are made from the first screen, the code-sharing commuter airlines had an enc ₁ous competitive advantage.

On June 1, 1985, United Airlines, the most important holdout, began to allow three commuter airlines to use its UA code. By that fall all 12 major airlines, and one national, had one or more partners. In 1987, 45 of the 50 largest commuter airlines were code sharers.

Before code sharing, direct competition between commuters had been unusual. Now, at large metropolitan centers where two or more major airlines had hubs, the common new pattern was for each commuter affiliate to serve generally the same outlying markets. Thus, direct competition between commuter airlines (which were now acting essentially as surrogates for the major airlines) became common. At those airports used as a hub by only one company, the affiliates now had a near monopoly on feeder traffic.

Perhaps most significantly, because of increased load factors and other advantages, code sharing brought profits and stability to an industry with a long history of financial instability. By 1985 the RAA estimated that all but 7 of the 50 largest commuter airlines were profitable.

In 1983 the largest airlines began to buy full or partial ownership of their affiliates. This gave total control over the commuter, and protected the major's feeder network from purchase by rivals. The first case was Piedmont's purchase, in 1983, of Henson Airlines, the original Allegheny Commuter; Henson's network was then reoriented to feed Piedmont hubs. Pan American, American and USAir were among the other major airlines that bought their partners in the following years. By early 1990, 20 large commuter airlines were owned by major and national carriers.

From the commuter's point of view, one great disadvantage of code sharing was the loss of managerial independence and of its separate identity. In addition, the affiliate's fate was now closely tied to that of its partner; thus, Eastern Air Lines' long strike in the late 1980s and its eventual demise were major blows to its affiliates. Costs also could increase substantially, notably when the commuter was told to adopt larger aircraft so as to minimize the discomfort to passengers who were transferring from jet flights.

Two types of the commuter airlines have remained independent. Some fly to medium or small metropolitan areas that have not been chosen as major airline connecting hubs, and others operate to cities too small to be of interest to the code sharers. By the late 1980s independents only accounted for 15 to 20 percent of the industry's traffic.

In the 1980s the essential air service program began coming under increasing attack. As early as 1985 the Reagan administration had proposed its elimination, but political support for continuation was too strong. Supporters stressed that the program had helped reduce subsidies from about $72 million in 1978 to $40 million in 1984, as commuter airlines replaced the larger companies at the subsidized points. There were many critics, however, who questioned the logic of giving federal subsidies to support local economies and felt that the minimal service offered was hardly worth the price.

In 1988 Congress extended EAS by ten years. The criteria were tightened somewhat; now a city had to be at least 45 miles from a large or medium hub to qualify for subsidies. However, the law also made it possible for communities to receive new or improved air service if they were willing to subsidize the additional cost. Pressurized aircraft were now normally required, and the minimum allowable level of weekly service was increased.

Despite this extension, Congress soon reduced funding so that the qualifications for subsidy had to be tightened further. In October 1989 a maximum subsidy of $300 per passenger was implemented, and 6 cities were eliminated. Because of meager 1990 appropriations, 20 more cities were dropped from the program, including 6 that exceeded the new $200 subsidy cap. After this change, 90 cities in the contiguous United States and 40 in Alaska were still subsidized.

The commuter airline industry of the early 1990s had three significant problems. One was the highly publicized topic of the industry's allegedly poor safety record. To the extent that this was a problem, it was largely confined to the smaller companies. Another concern was a high pilot turnover rate, which led to considerable training costs for replacements. Most pilots left for the major airlines, where pay scales were higher. Finally, there was the poor image of the industry's propeller-driven aircraft; no matter how modern, the public tended to view them as outmoded relics.

A few comments can be made about some likely short-term directions of the commuter airline industry. The FAA forecasts that the number of passengers will more than triple between 1989 and 2001, with an average annual growth rate of 6.9 percent. During the same period, the commuter fleet is projected to increase from 1,791 to 2,220 aircraft.

Since many future aircraft are already in the planning or prototype stages, short-range forecasts about them are fairly safe to make. Most new aircraft will be relatively fast and large; the typical new commuter airplane of the 1990s is expected to have between 30 and 60 seats, to cruise at about 350 mph, and to include many of the amenities found on larger jets.

Two 19-passenger turboprop twins may well be the first new aircraft to enter service in the 1990s. Beech is producing the 1900D, a Beech 1900 modified to have stand-up headroom. Brazil and Argentina jointly are producing the CBA-123, a 400 mph pressurized aircraft with rear-mounted pusher type engines.

Larger planned turboprops include Germany's 30-to-33 seat Dornier 328, a high-winged aircraft that will cruise at 400 mph, and the 50-passenger SAAB 2000 that will cruise at 425 mph; the latter is expected to enter service in 1993. A major question is whether it is cost-effective to push a turboprop to such high speeds, as it takes about twice as much power to operate at 400 mph as it does at 320 mph.

Much interest has been generated by two proposals for twin-engined 400 mph commuter jets, the 50-passenger Canadair RJ and the 45- to 48-seat Embraer EMB-145 from Brazil. Such aircraft would certainly improve the code sharers' images and would constitute a giant step toward the ideal type of feeder service desired by the majors. On the other hand, there are substantial questions about the economics of small jets, especially over the fairly short routes operated by commuter airlines. They may, however, be well suited to providing proposed longer-range nonstop services between important spoke cities, which would avoid congested hub airports.

Is it possible that independent commuter airlines will make a comeback in the future? By 1990 code sharers had pushed them into minor roles, but there were signs that this trend might be reversed. As the major partners have forced the adoption of larger aircraft, the code sharers' costs have been rising rapidly. In the future, 30-passenger aircraft may well be the smallest that are acceptable to the majors. If the code sharers standardize on such types and if their costs continue otherwise to increase, they will eventually have to delete many markets that are economical only for aircraft with 19 or fewer seats. If this happens, will there then be room for a new set of hardy pioneers to create another independent commuter airline industry?

References:

R. E. G. Davies and I. E. Quastler, *Commuter Airlines of the United States* (Washington, D.C.: Smithsonian Institution, forthcoming, 1992);

Daniel M. Kasper, *The U.S. Regional Airline Industry to 1996* (London: Economist Publications, 1987);

James F. Molloy, Jr., *The U.S. Commuter Airline Industry: Policy Alternatives* (Lexington, Mass.: Lexington Books, 1985);

Regional Airline Association, *Annual Report of the Regional/Commuter Airline Industry* (Washington, D.C.: Regional Airline Association).

Continental Airlines

by Lloyd H. Cornett, Jr.

Montgomery, Alabama

Continental Airlines began as the Southwestern Division of Varney Speed Lines, a company founded by Walter T. Varney, who supplied the name, and his longtime friend and partner, Louis H. Mueller, who was responsible for the finances. Varney and Mueller had submitted the winning bid for Contract Air Mail (CAM) route 29, a 530-mile stretch that extended from Pueblo, Colorado, to El Paso, Texas. They opened service from Denver to El Paso on July 15, 1934, flying the Denver-Pueblo portion of the route without benefit of a subsidy. Their initial fleet consisted of four Lockheed Vegas. In December, after Varney left the company to pursue business interests in Mexico, Mueller reorganized it as Varney Air Transport.

The next two years saw minor route additions: Trinidad, Colorado, was added in 1935, and Raton, New Mexico, the next year. On July 5, 1936, Robert Six purchased 40 percent of the airline, beginning an association that would last for 44 years.

When government regulations were changed in 1937 to require all scheduled airlines to use two-engine aircraft and carry two-way radios, the airline selected the Lockheed Model 12, a twin-engine transport with seating for eight passengers. The new airplanes were introduced on July 1, 1937. Simultaneously, the carrier changed its name to Continental Airlines. Also, it abandoned the promotional theme of "The Trail of the Conquistadors" (with a Spanish conquistador painted on the aircraft), in favor of the new slogan: "Fly the Old Sante Fe Trail."

Six became president of the airline on February 3, 1938, having assisted in moving its headquarters to Denver the previous October. Realizing the need to expand, he struggled to secure additional routes, but with little success at first. He did increase the frequency of trips between Denver and Albuquerque on February 15, 1938. He also insured

that Continental received its permanent route certificate ("Grandfather Rights") following passage of the Civil Aeronautics Act of 1938.

To bolster the line's finances, Six went public with a stock offering of $280,000. At the same time, he bid on an open route between Pueblo and Wichita, Kansas, by way of Garden City. Although litigation ensued, on July 5, 1939, Continental received the award, CAM-43. With additional funds, Six was able to purchase two ten-seat Lockheed 14s, which were placed into service on the Denver-El Paso route at the end of 1939.

Following minor route additions in New Mexico, Colorado, and Kansas, Six acquired additional aircraft for his growing company. In August 1940 he bought three Lockheed Lodestars. He added three more in 1941, while disposing of the Lockheed 14s. All in all, fiscal year 1941 was a successful one. From an average of five passengers a week in 1934, in fiscal year 1941 the airline transported 17,232 passengers, earning $218,000 plus another $419,000 in mail payments.

Continental secured one additional route extension before World War II. On June 21, 1941, the Civil Aeronautics Board (CAB) approved extending the Pueblo-Wichita line into Tulsa. Earlier that year Continental secured additional funds by another public stock offering of $170,000 and a loan of $425,000. Also, the traditional insignia changed again, this time on April 21, 1941, to a thunderbird design—just as the Pueblo Indian head had replaced the conquistador image in 1938.

Following American entry into World War II, Six joined the Air Transport Command, leaving Continental in the care of interim president Terrell C. Drinkwater. The airline surrendered half its Lodestar fleet to the military. At the same time, the company obtained a contract to modify bombers. Continental first leased a United Air Lines hangar in Denver, later replacing it with a $5 million facil-

Continental vice-president O. R. "Ted" Haueter in front of a Lockheed Lodestar, 1941
(courtesy of the National Air and Space Museum)

ity of its own. From 1942 to 1945, Continental workers modified over 1,000 B-17s, adding long-range tanks to the Flying Fortresses. Also, in 1944, it took on the chore of modifying standard B-29s into photo-reconnaissance planes.

Although Continental lost half its fleet, the airline saw mail rates raised from 38 cents to 48.5 cents per mile. Moreover, the CAB approved a new route between Denver and Kansas City on December 11, 1941. Barely able to serve its existing routes, let alone a new one, Continental had to forego inauguration of the addition. The airline welcomed the release by Air Transport Command of one Lodestar in December 1943, enabling it to begin service on the Kansas City route.

By 1944 Continental had major entry points for south Texas at San Antonio, the Rocky Mountain area at Denver, and the Midwest at Kansas City. In fiscal year 1944 the airline carried 51,800 passengers, up from 11,400 four years earlier, and 885,000 pounds of mail, up from 209,000 in 1940.

When C-47/DC-3s became available toward the end of the war, Continental was able to initiate nonstop service between Denver and Kansas City. In 1946 the airline used its growing fleet of DC-3s to begin through service from El Paso to Tulsa, and from Oklahoma City to Denver. During fiscal year 1946, Continental carried 167,000 passengers in its fleet of 11 DC-3s, earning $3.2 million. It also flew 486 tons of mail, worth another $637,000.

With business increasing, Continental placed five pressurized Convair 240s, equipped with the latest navigational equipment, into service at the end of 1948. In order to compete against Eastern's Constellations and American's DC-6s, the airline—now carrying the slogan of "The Blue Skyway"—introduced coach fare on July 15, 1949. A passenger now could fly on a Continental Convair from Denver to Kansas City for $22.10.

The early 1950s saw Continental expand its route system, both directly and indirectly. In 1951 the CAB granted an extension from San Antonio to Houston. Two years later Continental was able to add a Tulsa-Kansas City link. Expansion also took place through the device of a joint venture between paired airlines called interchange service. This allowed a carrier to pair with another airline and take turns operating aircraft for agreed periods over each other's sections of interchange routes. Continental paired with American over a Houston-San Antonio-El Paso-California route that began on July 26, 1951, and lasted for ten years. It also paired with Mid-Continent (Frontier) and United. These interchanges allowed the company to break free of its regional identification for the first time.

While reaching beyond the boundaries of the Southwest, Continental also strengthened its hold on the state of Texas. In 1954 it acquired by merger Pioneer Air Lines, a local service carrier with extensive routes in Texas and New Mexico. As a result, Continental then served every city in Texas with a population over 100,000.

An even more important development took place in 1955. On November 14, the CAB awarded Continental a direct route from Chicago to Los Angeles via Kansas City and Denver and gave the airline nonstop authority between all city pairs, including Chicago-Los Angeles. President Six recognized the futility of trying to service the route structure with his existing fleet of four DC-6Bs, seven Convairs, and nine DC-3s. After raising money through the sale of stock, he ordered four Boeing 707s, 15 Vickers Viscounts, and five DC-7Bs. The DC-7Bs were acquired as interim airplanes; the turboprop Viscounts could not be delivered until 1958, and the turbojet 707s until the following year.

Continental inaugurated service between Los Angeles and Chicago on April 28, 1957. By 1959 the airline's Boeing 707 "Golden Jets" carried half the traffic between the two cities. The airline's operating profit during that year stood at $4 million.

On March 13, 1961, the CAB announced its decision on the important Southern Transcontinental Service Case. Continental gained a route between Houston and Los Angeles via San Antonio, El Paso, Tucson, and Phoenix, with nonstop authority between all points. Within a short time, Continental became the dominant airline in the California-Arizona-Texas market, transferring its authority to serve smaller communities to local service carriers and concentrating on its trunk routes.

Anxious to expand across the Pacific, Six contracted with Military Airlift Command in May 1964 to transport men and equipment to Vietnam.

Beginning in September, Continental used two Boeing 707-320Cs on a route from Travis Air Force Base in California to Vietnam via Anchorage, Honolulu, and various points in the western Pacific. This profitable contract lasted until 1973.

Continental also operated a wholly owned subsidiary, Continental Air Services (CAS), in Southeast Asia between 1965 and 1975. Based in Vientiane, Laos, CAS flew everything from single-engine Pilatus Porters to four-engine C-130s, averaging 4,000 hours, 20,000 passengers, and 6,000 cargo tons a month.

Continental gained Pacific experience by taking over from Transocean Airlines interisland service in Micronesia. Air Micronesia, formed with Aloha Airlines, signed a five-year contract with the Trust Territory government on May 16, 1968. Air Mike, as the company was known, flew from its base on Saipan to such diverse points as Honolulu, Guam, Yap, Truk, Johnson Island, Naura, and Pohnpei. Continental also built and operated hotels on the major islands in Micronesia.

In 1971 the CAB awarded the Micronesian routes to Continental on a permanent basis. Six years later, following extended negotiations, Air Mike gained entry into Japan. Service between Tokyo and Saipan began on October 1, 1977, with a Boeing 707-100 leased from the parent company. By 1983 Air Mike was using four Boeing 727s on the route.

Continental finally secured transpacific authority in 1969. Service to Hawaii, with connections to Micronesia, began in September. This was followed in 1977 by authorization to fly between Los Angeles and New Zealand and Australia via Hawaii, American Samoa, and Fiji. Two years later, Continental opened service between Los Angeles and Taipei, Taiwan, its longest route ever.

The 1970s were a time of rapid growth. Not only did Continental expand into the Pacific, but it also secured a route from Houston to Miami, marking its first entry to the east coast of the United States. Nonetheless, by the end of the decade the airline had begun to show the effects of the numerous changes. In 1979 the company recorded a net loss of $13 million.

On February 1, 1980, in the wake of the Airline Deregulation Act of 1978, A. L. Friedman took over as Continental's president and set about restructuring the company's domestic route network. He concentrated on developing a hub-and-spoke system, centering on Houston and Denver. Yet the net loss for 1980 was over $20 million, and this despite the sale of the Micronesian hotel chain and three DC-10s. The situation only grew worse; in 1981 Continental lost a staggering $60 million.

While Continental was suffering financial woes, Texas Air's Frank Lorenzo was buying the airline's stock. By the end of 1981, he had acquired a controlling interest in the company. Continental resisted his takeover bid, with the airline's pilots forming the Continental Employees Association to fight the battle. The employees attempted to purchase the company through the so-called Employee Stock Ownership Plan, but the scheme fell through when the necessary financing could not be obtained. Lorenzo finally emerged victorious, following a bitter struggle. On July 13, 1982, stockholders of Continental and Texas Air voted to approve the merger of Texas International Airlines and Continental.

Despite cost-cutting measures, Continental continued to suffer massive losses that reached $218.5 million in 1983. Unable to secure further concessions from his employees, Lorenzo filed for bankruptcy under Chapter 11 of the Federal Bankruptcy Act on September 24, 1983.

The airline resumed limited operations as a nonunion carrier on September 27. By the end of the first week, it was serving almost 40 percent of its former passenger miles with 400 pilots (down from 1,400). By mid November Continental announced that it was serving half its former capacity. This figure climbed to 64 percent by February 1, 1984. Between April and December, the airline recorded a net profit of $10.4 million, its highest in five years.

In February 1987 Lorenzo added two recently purchased low-fare airlines, People Express and New York Air, to Continental. The enlarged carrier, now the industry's pacesetter on fares, had a fleet of 312 aircraft that made over 1,500 flights daily from 109 U.S. and 32 international airports. In the two years following this consolidation, Continental went on to lose more than $500 million. Furthermore, with a debt of $2.3 billion, future prospects for the nation's fourth largest airline (measured by passengers carried and miles traveled) remain far from bright.

References:

R. E. G. Davies, *Airlines of the United States since 1914*, revised edition (Washington, D.C.: Smithsonian Institution, 1982);

Davies, *Continental Airlines: The First Fifty Years* (The Woodlands, Tex.: Pioneer Publications, 1984);

Davies, *Rebels and Reformers of the Airways* (Washington, D.C.: Smithsonian Institution, 1987);

Thomas K. McCraw, *Prophets of Regulation* (Cambridge, Mass.: Harvard University Press, 1984);

Michael Murphy, *The Airline That Pride Almost Bought* (New York: Watts, 1986);

Robert J. Serling, *Maverick: The Story of Robert Six and Continental Airlines* (Garden City, N.Y.: Doubleday, 1974);

Robert F. Six, *Continental Airlines: A Story of Growth* (New York: Newcomen Society in North America, 1959).

E. L. Cord

(July 20, 1894 - January 2, 1974)

by George E. Hopkins

Western Illinois University

CAREER: Various automotive business activities (1912-1924); general manager (1924-1926), president (1926-1933), chairman, Auburn Automobile Company (1933-1937); president (1929-1933), chairman, Cord Corporation (1933-1937); president, Century Airlines (1931-1932); president, Century Pacific Airlines (1931-1932); chairman, Aviation Corporation (1933-1936); various business and political activities (1937-1974).

Errett Lobban Cord achieved fame in the related fields of automobiles and aircraft during the 1920s and 1930s. He was known for aggressive financial manipulation and deal making, which brought him control of several businesses in both industries. Cord was also the bane of organized labor, known for his firm adherence to the "iron law of wages," which postulates that an employee who will work for a lower salary is overpaid. During the Depression, Cord's labor relations policies led to notoriety and congressional denunciations. Many workers, particularly airline pilots, saw Cord as brutal and avaricious. In fact, Cord was a fairly typical 1920s entrepreneur, neither better nor worse than others.

Cord had a passion for anonymity and secrecy which gave him an aura of mystery. But in bold outline his career in corporate finance and entrepreneurial ventures is fairly straightforward. Born on July 20, 1894, on a farm in Warrensburg, Missouri, Cord migrated with his parents to California, where he completed high school in Los Angeles. He was a race car mechanic and driver during the first great spurt of interest in the sport just prior to World War I. He parlayed his racing connections into a successful auto repair business in California, from which he branched out into trucking, car rentals, used and new car sales, and virtually any other business which touched upon automobiles in some way. Eventually Cord became interested in

E. L. Cord

manufacturing, formed the Cord Corporation in Chicago, and in 1925 acquired the Auburn Automobile Company in Auburn, Indiana.

Cord achieved a nearly legendary status shortly thereafter, when he began marketing an automobile bearing his name. By 1932 his Cord 810, a sleek model which ranks as an American classic, was at the very pinnacle of chic design. Unlike other businessmen, hard times seemed to act as a stimulant for Cord, who rode easily through the financial chaos around him, profiting from it while others failed. His flagship line of Cord automobiles sold for nearly half again as much as comparably equipped Cadillacs, and his production facilities hummed with activity. Despite the general economic retrenchment of the post-1929 era, Cord's empire grew as he bought the manufacturing plants of Checker Cab, Yellow Cab, Duesenberg, and branched into aviation, acquiring both Lycoming (an engine manufacturer), and Stinson (an airframe maker). Critics charged that much of Cord's success rested on low wages and harsh working conditions in his plants.

Cord initially saw aviation as an extension of his automobile empire. He planned to market "personal" vehicles and popularize flying for the mass market with a "flivver" aircraft. However, the chance acquisition of an airliner, the Corman 3000, turned Cord toward the air transport business. Reequipped with three Lycoming engines, the Corman became the Stinson SM 6000B, commonly referred to as the model "T" or "U" depending upon modifications. It was a high-wing aircraft at first, although subsequent redesign converted it into a low-wing plane. Carrying ten passengers and requiring only one pilot (so Cord claimed), the new airliner sold for $25,000, thus enjoying a competitive advantage over the Bach Trimotor, which also carried ten passengers, but sold for $30,000. Ford Trimotors sold for $40,000 and carried only four more passengers. So Cord expected the new Stinson to be profitable. But he reckoned without taking into account the effects of the Depression, which cut demand for new airliners and left Cord with an unsold inventory of planes. Ever resourceful, Cord decided to enter the airline business directly. He had everything he needed except pilots.

In March 1931 Cord began serving several midwestern cities with his Chicago-based Century Airlines. True to form, Cord paid his pilots about half the going wage, but, owing to the hard times, found a surprisingly large pool of unemployed pilots willing to work for the $350 per month he offered. Intrigued with the success of his Chicago operation, Cord inaugurated Century Pacific Airlines on the West Coast in July 1931. It had been so easy to hire pilots at $350 per month, that on his new airline Cord offered only $150 per month— and found plenty of takers. Since Cord did not have an airmail contract, he was not bound by the pay rules which the existing airlines had inherited

from the old Post Office Air Mail Service of the 1920s. The result of his rigorous cost cutting was an efficient, low-overhead operation which would be lucrative if Cord could secure an airmail contract. Accordingly, Cord set out to persuade Congress that reopening the airmail contracts (which had been controversial ever since they were let in 1930) would result in great savings to the taxpayer.

Trouble between Cord and his pilots was inevitable. In 1929 Cord had learned to fly his own Stinson "Detroiter," and he was not impressed. He saw piloting as a fairly simple skill that did not require a high salary. In 1930 Cord declared: "I feel that 'aviators' have fostered an erroneous conception of flying. There was a time when I was no different from any other person who looks upon flying as something for especially gifted 'birdmen.' It is my conviction that any normal person can safely and easily handle an airplane." In short, Cord scorned the "pilot mystique," which held that fliers were supermen, and he saw the cult of scarf and goggle as an affectation he would not tolerate.

In February 1932 Cord's pilots in Chicago resisted his demand that they accept a cut in pay to equal the salaries he paid on Century Pacific. Having recently joined the new Air Line Pilots Association (ALPA), the Century pilots turned for help to David L. Behncke, the United Air Lines pilot who had founded the union. Behncke tried to negotiate with Cord but got nowhere. Instead, Cord promptly locked out his pilots, hired replacements, and resumed operations. Behncke then carried his fight against Cord to Congress, with the intention of denying him a mail contract, which was then under serious consideration.

Thus the highly unusual spectacle of a strike of airline pilots came at a bad time for Cord. The pilots had friends in Congress who rallied to their cause, and ALPA proved adept at mobilizing public opinion. Unemployed Century pilots, financially supported by their union, appeared on radio shows to describe imaginary flights and performed aerial picketing by flying alongside Cord's airliners in small planes painted "Century Unfair to Pilots." Important congressmen such as Fiorello H. La Guardia (an army pilot during World War I) denounced Cord as an exploiter of labor who was undeserving of a mail contract.

Cord, apparently somewhat bemused by the hornet's nest he had stirred up, rather stupidly counterattacked by labeling ALPA "Communistic."

Behncke, who was developing into a talented polemicist, responded by pointing out Cord's lack of military service in World War I. La Guardia took the floor to label Cord "low, dishonest, a liar and a gangster." Prolabor congressmen, who were increasing in number by 1932 owing to the Depression, rushed to attack Cord. "There is not a meaner employer of scab labor than this man," La Guardia intoned. When he sat down to applause from his fellow lawmakers, Cord's chances for an airmail contract were dead.

Because Cord's offer to carry the mail more cheaply than the established operators threatened vested interests, labor and capital had good reason to make common cause against him. But it was the pilots who did him the most damage. In short, there was much more to the "pilot mystique" than Cord reckoned.

Badly stung by the "Century Strike" (although in truth it was a lockout, not a strike), Cord opted to remove himself from public view. He was by no means through with commercial airline service—the profit potential was enormous and his position in the industry was strong. But in order to defuse congressional criticism, Cord necessarily had to operate behind the scenes, manipulating things through subordinates such as C. R. Smith. For several years he lived in the Waldorf-Astoria Hotel in New York, while he rode the stock market and oversaw his airline investments. When Aviation Corporation, the parent of American Airlines, bought out Cord for 140,000 shares of stock, he became chairman of its board of directors. Ultimately Cord parlayed this position into effective control of American, but deferred to C. R. Smith, who assumed the chief executive officer's position. In 1936, fearful that his notoriety might jeopardize American's airmail contracts, Cord effectively severed all relations with the airline in exchange for $4 million.

For a time Cord became a recluse on the model of Howard Hughes. He returned to California, invested heavily in real estate, and compiled a considerable fortune. In 1939 he moved to Nevada and settled on an isolated 3,340-acre ranch. He invested in radio and television properties, had interests in shipbuilding during World War II, and stayed out of public view. In the 1950s he ran and won election to Nevada's senate and went on to become a political power in the state.

Cord died on January 2, 1974, at the age of seventy-nine, a multimillionaire. He was remembered chiefly as an automotive innovator and secondarily as a rapacious exploiter of labor.

References:

R. E. G. Davies, *Airlines of the United States since 1914*, revised edition (Washington, D.C.: Smithsonian Institution, 1982);

George E. Hopkins, *The Airline Pilots: A Study in Elite Unionization* (Cambridge, Mass.: Harvard University Press, 1971);

Hopkins, "The Century Strike—1932," *Airline Pilot*, 44 (March 1975): 30-33, 51;

Hopkins, *Flying the Line: The First Half Century of the Air Line Pilots Association* (Washington, D.C.: Air Line Pilots Association, 1982).

Robert L. Crandall

(December 6, 1935 -)

by Lloyd H. Cornett, Jr.

Montgomery, Alabama

CAREER: Regional credit supervisor, Eastman Kodak Company (1960-1962); chief, computer programming division, Hallmark Cards (1962-1966); assistant treasurer (1966-1970), vice-president of systems and data services (1970-1971), vice-president and controller, Trans World Airlines (1971-1972); senior vice-president and treasurer, Bloomingdale Brothers (1972-1973); senior vice-president for finance (1973-1974), senior vice-president for marketing (1974-1980), president and chief executive officer (1980-1985), chairman, American Airlines (1985-).

Robert Lloyd Crandall first became noted in the airline industry for his computer skills. Given credit for modernizing American Airlines' computer system, he rose to the presidency of the airline at a time when deregulation was taking a heavy economic toll on the nation's major air carriers. An innovative manager, Crandall developed a variety of programs to compete in the new environment, including a two-tier wage system and a frequent-flier program. Under his driving leadership, American Airlines prospered in the midst of chaos. Many industry observers consider him the most successful of the post-deregulation generation of airline executives.

Crandall was born on December 6, 1935, in the small town of Westerly, Rhode Island, the son of Lloyd Evans and Virginia Beard Crandall. His father held a succession of jobs during a time of economic depression and war before settling on a career in insurance. Crandall led a nomadic life as a boy, attending 14 schools in 12 years. He finally graduated from Barrington (R.I.) High School in 1953. He attended William and Mary College from 1953 to 1955, then transferred to the University of Rhode Island at Kingston, from which he graduated with a bachelor of science degree (with majors in insurance and finance) in 1957. After serving a

Robert L. Crandall (courtesy of American Airlines)

brief tour in the U.S. Army Reserve as a second lieutenant of infantry, he married Margaret Jan Schmults, his high school sweetheart. The couple had three children: Mark William, Martha Conway, and Stephen Michael.

Crandall entered the prestigious Wharton School of the University of Pennsylvania following his marriage. He graduated in 1960 with a master's degree in business administration. He then embarked on a varied business career that included four employers over the next 13 years.

Crandall's first position after leaving Wharton was with the Eastman Kodak Company of Rochester, New York. After serving two years as a regional credit supervisor, he left Kodak and moved to Kansas City, Missouri, where he established an automated receivables system for Hallmark Cards. He remained with that company for four years, becoming chief of the computer programming division. In 1966 Crandall shifted from greeting cards to aviation, accepting the post of assistant treasurer with Trans World Airlines (TWA). During his seven years with TWA he climbed the corporate ladder, first becoming vice-president of systems and data services, then vice-president and controller. Apparently a larger salary lured him to New York City in 1972 as senior vice-president and treasurer with Bloomingdale Brothers. His stint with the trendy department store chain lasted but a year. Crandall again shifted his allegiance to aviation—this time as senior vice-president for finance with American Airlines. This move ended his firm-hopping but not his ascension up the corporate ladder.

When Crandall moved to American in 1973, he joined an air carrier that was beset by problems, including a nationwide recession, rising fuel costs, overexpansion, labor difficulties, and sinking employee morale. The airline lost $48 million during the year. American's new president, Albert V. Casey, who had just come from his role as Times Mirror chairman, needed all the help he could find to make the company profitable once again.

As senior financial officer at American, Crandall was in charge of data processing, a task he relished and one which brought him to the attention of the entire industry. He soon discovered that the airline's data processing system—labeled SABRE for Semi-Automated Business Research Environment—had stagnated since its introduction in the early 1960s. SABRE had been a leader in the field, reducing the time involved in making reservations from around 45 minutes to 3 seconds. By the 1970s, however, the system still used typewriter displays when the preferred displays had become cathode ray tubes (CRT). Ironically, American had more than 2,000 CRTs stored in a basement in Tulsa, Oklahoma, where they collected dust while the company's managers debated what should be done with them.

Crandall immediately set about modernizing the SABRE system. It took three years, but by 1976 he had in place a system that not only could be used to keep track of passengers, car rentals, hotel reservations, seat preferences, and other items, but could also be employed as a marketing device. Crandall persuaded travel agencies to become part of the SABRE network. American then collected a rental for use of the necessary machines, plus a fee from every reservation booked through them. Eventually American cornered over 40 percent of the travel agency market.

Crandall soon gained a reputation as being a man in a hurry. A workaholic, he was the first to arrive in the morning and the last to leave. Budget meetings began early—an employee once arrived in pajamas to make his point—and continued until Crandall was satisfied that he knew every detail of the subjects under discussion. Amazed employees watched in awe as Crandall had his coffee cup filled incessantly, yet refused to adjourn for even a short time. An associate was heard to remark that Crandall had to have "mankind's biggest bladder." Crandall demanded a great deal of his employees—and of himself. He believed that "the airline business is the closest thing there is to legalized warfare—and we regard winning as essential." Bearing the nickname "Fang" with pride, Crandall did not like to lose.

Crandall's attention to detail became legendary. Nothing proved too minor for cost reduction. For example, he found that by omitting olives from American's on-board salads, he could save $40,000 a year. The olives disappeared. A suggestion from a flight attendant to reuse the plastic lids on coffee pots was adopted, leading to savings of $60,000 a year. In another case Crandall ordered a reduction in security guards at American's station on St. Thomas in the Virgin Islands. Although this led to lower costs, he remained unsatisfied. Crandall next had the remaining security personnel replaced by guard dogs. Still unhappy, he got rid of the animals in favor of a tape of their growls.

These small savings helped, but they really were more symbolic than anything else. Moving up to senior vice-president for marketing in 1974, Crandall had to deal with the more urgent problem of filling American's empty seats. He developed several innovative marketing strategies, most notably the Super Saver fares. Introduced in 1977, these fares provided deep discounts for nonrefundable round trip tickets that were purchased well in advance and included a minimum stay. Sales rose appreciably, leading charter operators to sue the airline—unsuccessfully.

The astute Casey and the hardworking Crandall managed to turn around the airline's financial picture. American posted a profit of $20.4 mil-

American Airlines Boeing 727 (courtesy of the National Air and Space Museum)

lion in 1974. After a disappointing year in 1975, which saw losses of $20 million, the airline went on to record profits of $76.3 million in 1976, $81 million in 1977, and $134.4 million in 1978.

The Airline Deregulation Act of 1978, which Crandall fought and considered a curse on the airlines, changed all the rules, propelling the industry into a precarious new environment that was marked by the appearance of low-cost airlines and nearly ruinous fare wars. American went from a profit of $87.4 million in 1979 to a loss of $76 million in 1980. Casey, who had suffered four heart attacks and a stroke, moved up to chairman of the board. On July 16, 1980, the forty-four-year-old Crandall replaced him as president and chief executive officer of the airline.

Crandall faced a major economic challenge in his new job. Rising fuel prices once again ate into profits. Labor costs were enormous, especially compared to those of the new nonunion, no-frills air carriers. Faced with mounting debts and an aging fleet (many of the aircraft were over ten years old),

Crandall had to reduce operating costs while simultaneously rebuilding and modernizing.

Crandall sold the company's gas-guzzling fleet of Boeing 707s, purchased fuel efficient aircraft, reconfigured existing transports to secure more seats, and dropped unprofitable routes. He fought off Delta Airlines' attempt to establish a "megahub" at Dallas-Ft. Worth, then set up one of his own at Chicago. He reduced American's staff of 41,000 by 7,000. Instead of seeking wage- and work-rule concessions from his remaining employees, he adopted the novel approach of a two-tier wage system. He told the unions that American would not furlough any more workers if they allowed the company to hire new employees at reduced wage scales. While this proposal aroused great suspicion among the unions, it finally was approved in 1983 after considerable negotiation. Over the next five years Crandall managed to pare labor costs to 6 percent of operating costs (still high when compared to Continental Airlines' 22 percent). This enabled American to grow from within and avoid mergers, although the airline did acquire AirCal, Inc., in July 1987 in order to gain a foothold in the western part of the United States.

Another Crandall innovation that spread throughout the entire industry was the idea of "airline brand loyalty." Thus was born the frequent-flier program which encouraged passengers to fly American and accumulate mileage that they could trade in for free tickets. American labeled the scheme "AAdvantage." All other air carriers in the country quickly adopted similar programs.

Crandall also kept his pledge to modernize American's fleet. Between 1983 and 1987 he added 150 new aircraft, some by purchase and others by a new strategy called rent-a-plane leaseback. By 1988, a year that saw American's operating profits soar to $801 million, the airline had 156 aircraft on order, with options for 100 more.

Time has not mellowed the chain-smoking executive. As late as 1987, films shown in a sales meeting at American portrayed Crandall dressed in a camouflage suit, face painted as if for a Green Beret raid, holding a rifle, and carrying the simple message that American took no prisoners. Relentless, untiring, and aloof, he still played to win.

Crandall's draconian measures to keep American in the black during a turbulent era of deregulation succeeded. While such former industry giants as Eastern, Continental, Braniff, and Pan American fell on hard times, some never to recover, American not only survived, it prospered. Few industry observers doubted that the key to the airline's success was the managerial skill of Robert Crandall.

References:

L. J. Davis, "Bob Crandall Wants It All," *New York Times Magazine*, September 23, 1990, part 2, pp. 24-25, 42, 44, 46;

Scott Hamilton, "Chairman of American Airlines Seeks Regulations on Employee Benefits," *Airline Executive*, 11 (June 1987): 34-36;

Kenneth Labich, "Bob Crandall Soars by Flying Solo," *Fortune*, 114 (September 29, 1986): 118-121, 124;

Colin Leinster, "How American Airlines Mastered Deregulation," *Fortune*, 109 (July 11, 1984): 38-40, 43, 45, 47, 49, 51;

Peter Nalty, "America's Toughest Bosses," *Fortune*, 119 (February 27, 1989): 40-43, 46, 50, 54;

Eric Pace, "Airline President," *New York Times*, November 23, 1980, section 3, p. 6;

Robert J. Serling, *Eagle: The Story of American Airlines* (New York: St. Martin's Press/Marek, 1985);

Richard Woodbury, "How the New No. 1 Got There," *Time*, 134 (May 15, 1989): 57.

Edward J. Crane

(February 7, 1928 -   )

by Dina M. Young

Washington University

CAREER: Accounting department comptroller (1951-1960), vice-president, comptroller (1960-1965), vice-president, treasurer (1965-1968), executive vice-president, treasurer (1968-1971); president and chief executive officer, Ozark Air Lines (1971-1987); president and chief executive officer, Ozark Holdings (1984-1987); vice-chairman, Trans World Airlines (1986-1990).

Edward J. Crane, airline executive, was born in St. Louis, Missouri, on February 7, 1928, the son of Joseph and Blanche Newmann Crane. His parents were of Irish and English descent and provided him and his sister with a stable living during the De-

pression through Joseph Crane's job as a clerk with the Wabash Railway Company. Edward Crane attended McBride High School, a parochial school in St. Louis, where he excelled in athletics. Following graduation in 1946, he joined the Marine Corps, serving in the ground crew of the service's aerial component.

After his military duties Crane enrolled at St. Louis University, where he graduated with a bachelor's degree in marketing and finance. A friend had told Crane that Ozark Air Lines was short of help in the finance department. Looking for a temporary job, Crane applied at Ozark, and in February 1951, just ten days after his graduation from college, he

Edward J. Crane (courtesy of Trans World Airlines)

was hired by the airline as an accounting comptroller. Although the company had been organized several years previously, it was only shortly before Crane began at Ozark that the airline initiated interstate service.

Ozark Air Lines was founded September 1, 1943, by a group of aviation-oriented businessmen led by H. D. "Laddie" Hamilton, himself a pilot. The airline's first route followed a triangular course from Springfield to Kansas City to St. Louis, all within the Missouri border owing to the lack of a federal certificate permitting interstate service. In 1946 the Civil Aeronautics Board (CAB) recommended Ozark for subsidized routes in Missouri, Oklahoma, and Kansas. The CAB later decided to give the routes to Parks Air Transport of East St. Louis, Illinois. This loss plunged Ozark into a period of dormancy, and for a time the corporation existed only on paper. But Parks experienced severe financial trouble and failed to meet the CAB deadline for servicing the new routes. The CAB then rescinded Parks's certificate and awarded a large portion of the Parks routes to Ozark. Parks's stockholders

agreed to sell out to Ozark and on September 26, 1950, the day Ozark's CAB certificate became effective, and the revitalized airline inaugurated service to Chicago from its base in St. Louis.

Crane began at Ozark four months after the first interstate flight, when the fledgling airline had four DC-3 aircraft and perhaps 40 employees. During his first year he married Margaret Struif of St. Louis; the couple had four children. Crane's rise through the ranks at Ozark began in 1956 when he was made chief accountant. Promotions followed regularly thereafter, and Crane was elected treasurer in 1965. Methodical and ambitious, Crane expected quite a lot from the people who worked for him. "I suppose, coming up through the accounting department as I did," he once said, "that I became somewhat of a perfectionist. In accounting, you know, you can't tolerate too many mistakes."

The 1960s were years of growth for Ozark. By 1964 the airline had achieved an annual passenger total of nearly one million, a fivefold increase over a ten-year period. Under Thomas L. Grace, company president from 1963 until 1971, Ozark entered the jet age. In 1965 the airline embarked on a plan to trade its entire fleet of prop planes for a modernized all-jet fleet of Fairchild Hiller FH-227B turboprops and Douglas DC-9 pure jets. The transition was completed by 1968, the year that Crane, who some say provided the financial wizardry to make Grace's plan work, became executive vice-president.

In 1971, following Grace's death, the forty-three-year-old Crane was unanimously elected Ozark's president and chief executive officer. Crane's philosophy of "steady but controlled expansion" led Ozark to become one of the fastest growing airlines in the three-year period prior to deregulation in 1978, with a growth rate averaging about 20 percent.

Ozark raised some of the strongest objections against airline deregulation before it became law in 1978. However, once the landmark legislation was enacted Crane's company proved that it had the ability to survive and indeed thrive in an altered marketplace. Taking advantage of the new freedoms airlines were given, Ozark entered new markets, such as that for Florida vacation travelers, while halting service to weaker lower-volume markets. In mid 1978, its pre-deregulation growth cycle continuing, the airline launched an $82.5 million reequipment program, ordering ten new aircraft, including two

Boeing 727 trijets. Flight engineers were hired and their training began in preparation for the delivery of the jets in the fall of 1979. Unfortunately, Ozark's promising growth spurt coincided with an all-time low in its labor relations.

In May 1978 seven of Ozark's 400 flight attendants were suspended when they failed to meet specified height-to-weight requirements. Coming at a time when many other airlines had either done away with or stopped enforcing their weight policies, the incident at Ozark received embarrassing national attention. The Association of Flight Attendants (AFA) affiliate at Ozark filed a federal lawsuit and took its case to the U.S. Equal Employment Opportunity Commission, charging that the company's weight guidelines were both unfair and sexist. Crane contended that the policy was reasonable because flight attendants had more contact with the public than other airline employees. A year after the flight attendants' suspension, a U.S. District Court held that the actions of the airline constituted sex discrimination in violation of Title VII of the Civil Rights Act of 1964.

This episode strained relations between the AFA and Ozark management. When the union's contract expired in August 1978, efforts to negotiate an extension failed, and a seven-week strike ensued in September 1979, shutting down operations in every city Ozark served in its 21-state region. Then, in May 1980, a strike by 693 Aircraft Mechanics Fraternal Association members over pay, fringe benefits, and pension issues idled 4,200 Ozark noncontractual employees for 25 days.

The airline was left reeling by the effects of the strikes; losses amounted to $5.7 million in 1979, and financial analysts predicted that it was only a matter of time before Ozark would be taken over by another airline. At one point the company had less than $3 million in the bank, hardly enough to pay a week's worth of bills. Crane recollected those dark days: "There were times when I thought we would observe the 30th anniversary of our founding by going out of business."

Fast and decisive action was needed to save the airline, and it came partly in the form of aircraft sales. Twenty minutes after taking delivery of the two 727s it had ordered, Ozark sold them for a profit of $3.5 million. "We really wanted those planes," Crane remarked. "Selling them set back our plans by three to five years."

Financial priorities demanded a shift from the policy of systematic and well-planned growth that had characterized Crane's management style. A stock issue of 1.7 million shares raised $18.5 million, which for the most part was used to retire debts.

Crane, a physically robust though taciturn man, proved to be a dynamic leader as Ozark struggled to survive. "When we were wrapped up in hard times we did a lot of thinking," he said. "The result, I would say, has been a complete restructuring of the operation." Ozark historically financed most of its capital expenditures with long-term debt, much of it carrying fluctuating interest rates tied to the prime rate. By retiring those debts with the profits from the stock issue, Ozark saved a sizable $10,000 a day in interest losses.

In labor-management relations a complete turnaround took place after the two crippling strikes. In August 1980 leaders of the Air Line Pilots Association at Ozark met with Crane and a company attorney to devise a plan to forestall a strike after the existing pilots' contract expired the following February. The result of the meeting was a letter of agreement that called for 30 days of direct negotiations followed, if necessary, by 30 days of mediation and as a last resort 30 days of binding arbitration. The pilots and the company reached agreement within the period of direct negotiations, and the contract was signed and in the hands of the pilots before the expiration date. Encouraged by the pilots' success, the flight attendants, dispatchers, agents, and mechanics all agreed to expedited negotiation agreements. "I think it became apparent to both management and our employees that we were going to have to work together or we were in real trouble," Crane said of the new atmosphere in labor relations. Management also instituted a voluntary employee stock purchase plan, in which 20 percent of the company's workers participated.

Under Crane's leadership, Ozark was nicknamed "the little airline that could," as improved labor-management relations and upgrades in service brought the company back from the brink of disaster in 1980 to a year of tremendous success in 1981. Service was opened to San Antonio as well as additional cities in Florida, making Ozark the leading carrier into that state from St. Louis. In 1981 Ozark had a net operating income of $17.1 million and took record profits in a year when fewer than ten other carriers in the country made money.

The future looked bright for the nation's 16th-largest airline. The next few years saw cautious expansion for Ozark as flights were added to new cities and planes were added to the fleet. Growth continued in the deregulated environment at a pace which Crane characterized as "modest success." Ozark also formed a holding company, Ozark Holdings, which Crane felt would provide more flexibility in organization, operation, and administration. In 1985 Ozark Holdings bought Midcoast Aviation, an airport-services company at St. Louis's Lambert Field that was thought would provide a complement to the airline.

Ozark's competitive environment changed in 1985 when low-cost carriers such as Southwest Airlines and People Express entered the St. Louis market. As these and other discount carriers began to knock down fares nationwide, Ozark's profits rapidly evaporated. Although it weathered deregulation quite successfully for several years, Crane's company was in a grim situation when Carl C. Icahn bought Trans World Airlines (TWA), which accounted for 55 percent of passenger traffic at Lambert Field, in the summer of 1985. Icahn succeeded in obtaining significant pay concessions from two of TWA's three main unions—the Air Line Pilots Association and the International Association of Machinists—and TWA became an even lower-cost carrier than Ozark.

Ozark asked for concessions from its major unions in December of 1985, but the unions resisted. As losses continued to mount, speculation increased that a merger was inevitable. Crane acknowledged that there had been several suitors during the prosperous years, but the success of the airline gave management the luxury of discouraging them. That success, however, also made it difficult to convince the company's unions that concessions really were needed.

Conditions reached a crisis state in the second half of 1985. After earning almost $8 million in the first half of the year, Ozark lost almost all of it back in the second half, finishing the year with a profit of only $636,000. In February 1986, Ozark accepted TWA's $224 million takeover bid.

Crane dubbed the combination of the two airlines "a natural" and said that "by agreeing to be sold to TWA, Ozark has made a decision that is good for its shareholders, its employees and the St. Louis area." Icahn called Crane "a driving force in the building of Ozark." In September 1986, after the U.S. Transportation Department approved TWA's acquisition, Crane became vice-chairman of the TWA board. In January 1987 he retired from Ozark Airlines and Ozark Holdings, and in January 1990 he retired from his positions at TWA.

References:

Eric Bramley, "Traffic, Profits Grow at Ozark," *American Aviation,* 28 (March 1965): 53-55;

Virginia Hick, "Ozark's Edward J. Crane Retires," *St. Louis Post-Dispatch*, February 4, 1987, section B, p. 1;

Anne Kelleher, "Ozark: The Down-to-Earth Airline That's Flying High," *Air Line Pilot,* 51 (June 1982): 12-16, 44;

Glennon Kidd, "Wings Over the Ozarks," *American Aviation History Society Journal,* 22 (Fall 1977): 181-187;

Henry Lefer, "Ozark is Better Than You Think," *Air Transport World,* 19 (June 1982): 40-44;

Robert Sanford, "Ozark Airlines Hits an Updraft," *St. Louis Post-Dispatch*, March 1, 1982, section B, p. 1;

Ted Schafers, "Ozark Taking Steps to Improve Profits," *St. Louis Post-Dispatch*, February 20, 1984, section A, p. 17;

Paul Wagman, "Airline Merger 'Natural,'" *St. Louis Post-Dispatch*, March 1, 1986, section A, p. 1;

Dina M. Young, telephone interview with Edward J. Crane, June 22, 1990.

Archives:

The TWA Public Affairs Department in St. Louis, Missouri, holds files on Crane and the history of Ozark Airlines.

Edward J. Daly

(November 20, 1922 - January 21, 1984)

by Roger D. Launius

National Aeronautics and Space Administration

CAREER: Semiprofessional boxer (1938-1939); U.S. Army (1941-1946); vice-president, Midway Aviation (1947-1948); president and chief executive officer (1950-1982), chairman World Airways (1950-1984).

Chicago native Edward J. Daly was a born maverick. He cultivated the image throughout his life and relished it as his epitaph. For more than 30 years he guided World Airways' growth from an obscure "supplemental carrier" to a hugely profitable charter service in the 1960s and 1970s. Unlike so many of the one-horse airline operators of the immediate post-World War II era, Daly was able to make the transition from propeller- to jet-driven planes, in 1962 purchasing some of the first Boeing 707s and, later, 747s and DC-10 wide-bodies. By the late 1960s World Airways was the largest and most profitable of the supplementals, a position it continued to hold through the early 1980s. That is one of the most important legacies left by the feisty, irascible Irishman.

Daly was born the son of a fireman in Chicago on November 20, 1922. When he was fifteen, his father died and left him on his own. He tried semi-pro boxing for a time, and was successful, winning a Golden Gloves award, but Daly knew that his future lay in other directions. For a short time he attended the University of Illinois, working toward a degree in chemical engineering, but finances and interest did not hold out. In December 1941, with the United States thrust into World War II, Daly was drafted into the army. He spent the war in Hawaii, Saipan, Tinian, and other parts of the western Pacific. Attaining the rank of sergeant, he was wounded and received the Purple Heart.

Mustered out of the service at the end of the war, Daly went to work for Scotty O'Carroll's Midway Aviation company in Chicago. Officially given

Edward J. Daly (courtesy of World Airways)

the title of vice-president, Daly spent most of his time handling bookings and other administrative chores associated with keeping small, nonscheduled air carriers operating at Midway Airport. It was at this time that Daly first perceived the potential of mass air transportation. Determined to enter the field, he borrowed $50,000 from a trucking company to purchase World Airways, a small, down-at-the-heels airline that had been incorporated in Delaware on March 29, 1948. The company amounted to little more than a Letter of Registration from the Civil Aeronautics Board (CAB) granting permission to operate certain air transportation services, a handful of aging airplanes, and a few marginally profitable routes. In later years Daly liked to let others believe the apocryphal story that he had won World Airways in a poker game, a tale that went along with the devil-may-care persona he cultivated.

When Daly took over World in July 1950 it owned three Boeing 314 seaplanes that were being used for a shuttle service between San Juan, Puerto Rico, and New York City. World was also flying a war-surplus C-46 in support of the Distant Early Warning (DEW) Line that had been established in the Arctic during the early years of the cold war. Daly continued both of these operations, which paid the bills for the little company but not much else. Looking for ways to expand, he acquired additional aircraft by any means possible. A notable episode involved the purchase for $35,000 of a fire-damaged military DC-4 at Northolt Airport, near London. The plane had to be rebuilt and recertified. To avoid a stiff British tax due a certain time after the sale, Daly brought in a team of workers, rented a limousine in which to sleep and work, and made repairs to the aircraft around the clock. He flew the aircraft out of England on the day before the tax was due.

The purchase of the DC-4, as well as another which he leased, allowed Daly to expand World's activities during the next several years. He was an aggressive and imaginative salesman, but his efforts were usually most successful when tied to the larger concerns of national defense. Daly supported resupply of DEW Line sites in the Arctic under government contract and obtained contracts with the Military Air Transport Service (MATS) to airlift troops overseas. Daly's most important early decision involved the movement of World Airways into transpacific airlift services. He moved the company's headquarters from Teterboro, New Jersey, to Oakland, California, in March 1956 to place it closer to the new market.

Daly did not abandon Atlantic operations after the move to Oakland, however. World was heavily involved in the airlift of 35,000 Hungarian refugees to the United States following the uprising against Communist rule in October 1956. Daly's two DC-4s made 14 transatlantic trips carrying refugees. Indicative of the way he operated in future missions, Daly flew to Vienna to meet the refugees

personally and to help them aboard his aircraft for the flight to the United States.

During the years after the Hungarian episode, World built a solid reputation as a contractor, moving personnel and cargo for the U.S. Department of Defense. On December 16, 1956, Daly received a contract from MATS for scheduled airlifts between Tokyo, Okinawa, Taiwan, and Manila. Since the contract went into effect on the first of the year, he moved quickly to transfer his two DC-4s and almost 100 employees from Oakland to Tokyo to begin the service. Another major step forward came on January 29, 1959, when the CAB gave World a Supplemental Air Carrier certificate, allowing nonscheduled operations in the United States. This action made possible the favorable June 15, 1960, decision by the Department of Defense to award World a Logistics Air Lift transcontinental contract to deliver parts and supplies between American military installations. To fulfill the terms of the contract Daly leased from another bidder (Resort Airways) seven pressurized DC-7s, which had a much greater capability than his DC-4s. This enormously important victory laid the groundwork for World's future expansion. During the next two years, the airline made a profit of $5.5 million.

Daly could then have relaxed like so many supplemental airline leaders who raked in the profits from defense contracts, but he was never interested in the status quo. He used the profits from the 1959 and 1960 contracts to expand his business. In 1961 he brought into operation eight DC-6s and four Lockheed Super Constellations. A year later he added three Lockheed L-1649s. All were efficient, modern aircraft. In fact, his fleet of 15 aircraft were among the finest owned by any of the supplemental carriers.

On June 7, 1962, Daly demonstrated most clearly his expansive philosophy by placing an order for three of the new Boeing 707-320Cs, the long-range version of the revolutionary jetliner. This was the first jet aircraft order from any of the supplemental carriers, and their delivery made World Airways instantly the strongest supplemental. When Daly placed the first World 707s on their Pacific run the next summer, it signaled a radical transformation in the charter airline business and served notice to other supplementals that they had to follow or be left in the dust. No longer would contractors willingly suffer gruelingly long island-hopping flights across the Pacific, when World's

707s could make the 6,000-mile trip between California and Japan in under ten hours.

Daly was willing to take this important step into the jet transportation arena in part because of the July 10, 1962, passage of the Supplemental Air Carrier Act, which was designed to weed out weaker and less safe carriers. He knew that World Airways would prosper under the act if its equipment and service were efficient and modern. One of the important provisions of the act came under section 401, which allowed the supplemental airlines to apply for certification for regular operations within certain geographic regions. Daly immediately turned the act to his advantage and gained for World Airways a solid position in the Pacific Basin.

Daly continued to hustle and expand during the next few years. Several successes in 1966 solidified World's preeminent position among the supplementals. On March 14 Daly secured for World—nine other supplementals were also successful in this—permission both for permanent domestic charter and inclusive air tour operations and for worldwide charter operations. On April 18, Daly took World public and sold 19.5 percent of his stock in the company for $22.9 million, in the process netting about $17 million in profit. On September 30, the CAB granted World Airways international authority for charters and inclusive air tours in the Caribbean, South America, and the Pacific; later in the year it added semipermanent authority for transatlantic operations. Finally, on December 22, Daly placed an order for three Boeing 747 wide-bodied jets and two more 707-320Cs. Although the acquisition of these aircraft had to be postponed until 1972, because of World's failure to obtain permission to enter the transcontinental scheduled market, the 747 order signified the airline's coming of age. More than ever before, Daly was a force to be reckoned with in the aviation industry.

The industry took notice of the ambitious Irishman when on April 26, 1967, he applied to the CAB to move into the scheduled airlines' ranks by proposing to operate a $75 transcontinental thrift fare service. Daly had every reason to believe that World's efficient management team and its up-to-date fleet could have fulfilled any customer's expectations, but he was not allowed even to try. In the era before the deregulation of the airline industry, the proposal had to pass through a series of difficult gates before the CAB would approve it. Every

competitor threw up whatever opposition it could to Daly's plan, and it was not approved. Daly had to begin a modest retrenchment to ensure that World would not show a loss for the year, and he began to diversify his assets by forming the Worldamerica Investors Corporation and buying the First Western Bank and Trust Company of California. These efforts proved exceptionally lucrative; he sold the bank in 1974 for $115 million in cash.

During all this time, Daly's public image as a hard-drinking, hard-working, hard-playing aviation entrepreneur grew. It may have been a generally accurate portrait, for Daly was a jolly, volatile, brilliant businessman who could fire an employee in one breath and tell him to get back to work with a bonus in the next. He was also loud and boisterous, with a flair for the dramatic. On first appearance Daly impressed many as a rude, uncultured buffoon, but that image masked a sharp and persevering business sense. His decisions on World's management were usually correct, and his lieutenants and stockholders quickly learned to trust his judgment. He surrounded himself with exceptionally capable officials, and he drove them as hard as he did himself. He kept strange hours, working as the manner suited him, and if he thought he needed to discuss an issue with one of his senior executives he would call or in some cases demand that they come into the office in the middle of the night. But success tends to breed greater devotion to duty, and Daly's employees were generally loyal and dedicated, and well rewarded for both.

Daly also wanted to make the world a better place. Over the years several of his projects drew attention to this area of his personality. He would brook no racism in his company. In 1955 he hired August Martin, who was probably the first African-American airline pilot. Daly was adamant in his instructions to his staff: "If he can fly, you put him to work." When one of World's pilots refused to fly with Martin, Daly happily accepted his resignation. Daly also had several pet philanthropic projects. In the 1960s he began sending 5,000 needy children to the circus each year and taking 1,000 children to the Oakland Symphony at Christmas to hear the *Nutcracker* Suite. He also built a swimming pool for the wards of the Alameda County Juvenile Hall.

As the United States slipped into the quagmire that became the Vietnam War, Daly became heavily involved in providing airlift services for the Depart-

World Airways Boeing 707 (courtesy of MAP Photos)

ment of Defense. On July 1, 1968, World Airways began to provide rest and rehabilitation flights from Vietnam to Japan and Australia for American servicemen. The airline also undertook to deliver the *Stars and Stripes*, the armed forces newspaper, from its place of publication in Japan to Vietnam. During Christmas 1971, Daly developed a program in concert with the USO to provide low-cost round-trip air service between Vietnam and Oakland, California. More than 23,000 soldiers took advantage of this opportunity, and, in typical fashion, Daly was present to help the troops board flights from Saigon and to deliver hams, turkeys, and Christmas trees by the thousand for those who could not leave.

World also became dramatically involved in the final events of the Vietnam War. In February 1975 Daly executed a contract to transport supplies, mostly ammunition and other war matériel, into Phnom Penh, Cambodia, threatened by the Communist Khmer Rouge. Using two DC-8s, World averaged six round trips a day and delivered 3,493 tons of cargo from Tan Son Nhut Air Base, South Vietnam, to Pochentong airport near Phnom Penh. Daly thought, and events proved him right,

that the military equipment included in airlift would be useless—the war in Cambodia was nearly lost—and he thought the best form of assistance would be food and other staples to assist the starving and injured residents of Phnom Penh. In a continuation of this airlift, between February 27 and April 16 World hauled in 292 missions about 10,000 tons of rice into the city, enough for some 60 million meals. Daly ended the effort only when the Khmer Rouge finally occupied the airport.

Meanwhile, World became active in transporting many desperate refugees who were trying to flee South Vietnam. In December 1974 the North Vietnamese army had attacked South Vietnamese forces, operating since March 1973 without the assistance of U.S. combat troops, in Phouc Long Province. Saigon's demoralized forces crumbled easily, and during the first part of 1975 victorious North Vietnamese armies swept southward. By late March 1975 an estimated 100,000 refugees had moved into the port of Da Nang and were awaiting transportation further south. On March 27, the day after the North Vietnamese captured the key city of Hue, a World Airways Boeing 727 carried 200 refugees from Da Nang to Nha Trang. The airline completed three more flights before South Vietnamese officials closed the Da Nang airport. On March 29, after failing to obtain American or Vietnamese permission to continue the rescue missions because of unsafe conditions at the airport, Daly met with chief pilot Kenneth W. Healy and asked him if he would be willing to fly into Da Nang despite the restrictions. Healy quickly agreed. Daly later told reporters, "People who should have been doing something about it sat on their asses and refused to move." Just after noon, two World Airways 727-100s left Tan Son Nhut Air Base, without clearance or permission.

When the 727s reached Da Nang, the first plane, with Healy at the controls and Daly aboard, made a pass over the runway at about 200 feet. As it appeared clear, they decided to land. The second aircraft continued in a holding pattern nearby. Healy slowed down but never stopped on the wide taxiway that paralleled the runway. Suddenly, thousands of people rushed the plane. As flight attendant Jan Wollett recalled, "They were running, they were on motorcycles, they were in vans, they were in jeeps and cars and personnel carriers, they were on bicycles—they were coming in anything they could find to get into the aircraft."

Healy warned the second plane not to land as soldiers and civilians, men, women, and children fought to climb aboard. Daly, who had gone back to the airstair to assist refugees, was mauled as able-bodied men threw off those less capable of defending themselves. He even used the butt of a pistol to ward off desperate boarders. Soon someone yelled, "We're full," and Healy increased the speed of the aircraft to prevent the mob from swamping the plane. The 727 accelerated down the taxiway as people climbed onto the wings, and then fell off as the jet became airborne. A distraught soldier hurled a hand grenade and badly damaged the flaps on the right side. Healy could not retract his landing gear because several people had crawled into the wheel wells. Shortly after the 727 became airborne, the pilot of the second plane reported seeing someone lose his grip on the landing gear and fall to his death. Sadly, there were only ten women and one baby among the 268 people who jammed themselves into the plane and into the wheel wells. This was the last flight out of Da Nang. The next day it fell to the North Vietnamese without resistance.

This did not end Daly's efforts to evacuate refugees from danger, however. On April 2, 1975, an un-authorized World Airways DC-8 flight evacuated 58 orphans between eight months and 11 years of age and 27 adult escorts (including six Vietnamese adults without passports and visas) from Saigon to Oakland. When the United States embassy refused to supply him with milk and the other basic items the children would need, the undaunted Daly loaded the aircraft with milk, baby food, and diapers at his own expense. Once again, Healy was pilot and Daly was aboard. As the aircraft began to taxi toward the runway at Tan Son Nhut Air Base, the control tower turned off the runway lights and ordered the DC-8 crew, "Don't take off! Don't take off! You have no clearance!" The air controllers later stated that authorities had closed the runway in anticipation of a Viet Cong attack. At Daly's direction, Healy continued to taxi, and as soon as he reached the runway he gave the DC-8 full power and took off into the darkness. "I just didn't get the message in time," he later explained.

Daly's maverick approach toward these evacuation flights was implicitly sanctioned the next day when President Gerald R. Ford announced that the U.S. government would provide airlift service for over 2,000 other Vietnamese orphans in a program called Operation BABYLIFT. Daly and World were heavily involved in this effort as well. Of the 2,894 orphans that reached the United States by May 9, the date that the State Department officially ended the evacuation of the children, privately contracted airlines had carried 1,090 of them.

Throughout the evacuation of Vietnam, Daly played by his own rules. It made him a hero to the American people. He epitomized his maverick image at a formal press conference following the first flight from Da Nang. When the debate got too heated, Daly drew the pistol he reportedly always carried and laid it on the table beside him. A reporter quoted him as saying, "I'll shoot the next God-damned man who talks while I'm talking." Later, Daly presumably told officials at Clark Air Base, the Philippines, that the president's military adviser had given permission for World Airways to land at Clark. Military officials checked and found that statement inaccurate. Gen. P. K. Carlton, head of Military Airlift Command, warned the Pacific Air Forces that Daly was out of control and operating as a law unto himself. He punctuated the conversation with a description of Daly: "He is a drunken SOB." Regardless of what American officials might have thought, for a short time in 1975 the pistol-packing Daly was more like Errol Flynn than a millionaire airline owner. The caption for a *Newsweek* magazine photograph of Daly sporting an Army Green Beret hat perhaps described him best: "Swashbuckler Daly of World Airways: The Hero was 'obnoxious' but brave."

The fall of South Vietnam was the high point in a career laced with action and not a little adventure. Daly savored the limelight that his refugee flights brought him. He probably also savored the complaints from certain government quarters regarding his disdain for regulations, especially since the rulemakers could do nothing about it. But it also seems that Daly was genuinely concerned for the welfare of those he tried to help. He was not primarily involved in the evacuation of Vietnamese refugees because he wanted glory, even though he might have enjoyed that part of it as well.

The years that immediately followed the Vietnam episode were relatively calm. World continued to rake in record profits, in the process steadily expanding its private charter business. Daly also continued World's role as a contract carrier for the Department of Defense. World's jet capability was among the best of any commercial carrier, and Daly improved it even further with the acquisition of DC-10s in 1978.

When Congress passed the Airline Deregulation Act it signaled the realization of one of Daly's longstanding wishes. Finally World could break into the scheduled ranks with limited routes. Daly quickly purchased another Boeing 747 and ordered six more DC-10s.

The very law that Daly thought would help World enter the elite among air carriers nearly destroyed the company. After deregulation Daly overextended the airline; the payments on the new aircraft and other infrastructure were too great to manage. In addition, competition among the carriers grew fierce. Although World inaugurated several routes between California and the East Coast on April 11, 1979, the airline did not compete as well for passengers as Daly had anticipated. Also, the DC-10s, on which Daly had placed much hope for the future, were grounded for structural inspections and repair following a spectacular and tragic crash of a United Air Lines DC-10 at Chicago's O'Hare International Airport on May 25, 1979. Finally, a strike by World employees between August and December 1979 completely shut down flight operations.

World lost a reported $28 million in 1980 and more than $20 million in 1981, and matters slid downhill from there. Daly's airline was not alone in recording losses: the five biggest American lines lost a combined $790 million in 1981. But by the first part of 1982 Daly's company was in serious trouble. He remarked on March 1: "I'm not running scared, but if I don't get relief, I will be out of business. It might be a week or a month. The labor force and the bankers will make the decision." A week later Daly journeyed to Washington to petition the CAB for a moderate amount of regulation to end the cutthroat competition between the carriers. He told the media that fares "were too high in the transcontinental markets, and World did something about it to the public's advantage and our own; now they are too low, and I will not remain silent, even though our proposal may offend deregulation purists." Daly's proposal met with a general derision. Alan M. Pollock, a representative of the CAB, commented: "This is really like having New York Air petition us and call for some kind of controls on Eastern Airlines because New York Air hasn't yet been able to win the shuttle wars." Daly got nowhere.

Daly began serious retrenchment efforts in mid 1982, a year in which World lost a record $58 million. He laid off more than 1,000 employees; requested that the Commerce Department defer payments on a $4 million loan on a hangar for the company in Oakland; pledged more than $5 million in personal assets to rescue the company; energized the company to compete more effectively for fares in the market; and worked with banks and other companies to obtain additional funding, forestall other loans coming due, and build a solid financial structure. This was not a successful effort. During the first quarter of 1982 Daly's company lost $13.3 million. He obtained a series of debt extensions from his creditors during the first half of 1982, enabling him to restructure the more than $17 million owed by World and stave off bankruptcy. But Daly was unable to remain at the head of World during this process. Amid the crisis the board and stockholders called for Daly's resignation. On November 15, 1982, he stepped down as president and chief executive officer of World Airways, although he remained chairman of the board, and appointed as president Brian C. Cooke, a longtime vice-president at World. An editorial in the *New York Times* in September 1982 perhaps expressed the fate of Daly and World best: "It's sad when any enterprise fails, especially so when the enterprise made a difference in people's lives."

World was never the same after Daly stepped down. It went through four presidents in five years and only began to recover in 1987 after a drastic retrenchment and reorientation back to contract work. In the meantime Ed Daly died on January 21, 1984, not long after his sixty-first birthday. He had been a unique individual, one who spent a lifetime building a great corporation which not only was extremely successful for most of his career, but also remarkably beneficent. World Airways bore the impression of Daly at every turn. It was his legacy and his epitaph.

References:

Coy F. Cross II, *MAC and Operation BABYLIFT: Air Transport in Support of Noncombatant Evacuation Operations* (Scott Air Force Base, Ill.: Office of History, Military Airlift Command, 1989);

R. E. G. Davies, *Airlines of the United States since 1914*, revised edition (Washington, D.C.: Smithsonian Institution, 1982);

Davies, *Rebels and Reformers of the Airways* (Washington, D.C.: Smithsonian Institution, 1987);

Alan Dawson, *55 Days: The Fall of South Vietnam* (Englewood Cliffs, N.J.: Prentice-Hall, 1977);

World Airways, *The History of World Airways in Southeast Asia, 1956-1975* (Oakland, Cal.: World Airways, 1975).

Archives:

The Office of History, Military Airlift Command, Scott Air Force Base, Illinois, houses the Civil Reserve Air Fleet Records, which contain information on the work of World Airways as a contract carrier for the U.S. Department of Defense, and the Vietnam Airlift Records, 1965-1975, which detail the role World and other air carriers played in supporting the U.S. military effort in Vietnam. The Scott Air Force Base Office of History also holds an unpublished report entitled "Operation BABYLIFT 3 April-13 May 1975." The Office of History, Pacific Air Forces, Hickam Air Force Base, Hawaii, holds an unpublished report entitled "The Fall and Evacuation of South Vietnam."

Ralph S. Damon

(July 6, 1897 - January 4, 1956)

by Joseph F. Ross

Prachuap Khiri Khan, Thailand

CAREER: Pilot, U.S. Army Air Service (1918); vice-president and general manager (1931-1932), president, Curtiss Aeroplane and Motor Company (1932-1936); vice-president, American Airlines (1936-1941); president, Republic Aviation Corporation (1941-1943); vice-president to president, American Airlines (1943-1948); president, Transcontinental and Western Air/Trans World Airlines (1949-1956).

Ralph Shepard Damon began a lifelong career in aviation as an army pilot during World War I. From 1931 until his death in 1956 Damon held a series of executive positions that, among other accomplishments, enabled him to play a leading role in bringing the cost of air travel within the reach of the general public. During World War II he organized the mass production of the P-47 Thunderbolt, a fighter plane that proved decisive in the tactical air war against Germany. At the time of his death, Damon was president of Trans World Airlines, then owned by Howard Hughes.

Born on July 6, 1897, in Franklin, New Hampshire, the son of William Cotton Damon and Effie Ives, Ralph Damon received his B.A. cum laude from Harvard University in mid 1918. There being no sign then of war's end, he abandoned long-held plans to become an astronomer and instead joined the U.S. Army Air Service where, through pilot training, his fascination for aviation began. Following the war, with the infant aviation industry offering little opportunity for a relatively inexperienced pilot, Damon worked for a time as a millwright and as leader of a construction crew. In 1922 he married

Ralph S. Damon (courtesy of the National Air and Space Museum)

Harriet Dudley Holcombe; the couple had four children.

In that same year, with airmail pilots pushing aviation to its limits and beyond, Damon joined the Curtiss Aeroplane and Motor Company, then a struggling enterprise but destined to produce several well-known airmail and passenger aircraft. In a hectic decade of historical events such as Charles A. Lindbergh's solo flight across the Atlantic Ocean and the stock market crash of 1929, Damon contributed to the development and production of several significant Curtiss aircraft, including the Robin, the Thrush, and the Condor, the first airliner to provide sleeping accommodations. Damon personally tested the bunks of the Condor, lurching as though airborne in turbulence and flinging himself at the berth from every possible angle. An affable, wiry man who exuded energy, Damon rose quickly with Curtiss, from factory superintendent to vice-president and general manager, and in 1932 at the age of thirty-five, to president of the company.

By 1936 the Douglas DC-2 had captured the passenger aircraft market from Curtiss. At the same time, the plunge of airmail subsidies from $1.09 to 54 cents a mile had doomed the production of planes used solely to carry mail. With aviation turning to passengers (the fabled DC-3 was already on the drawing boards) Damon accepted an offer to join the rapidly growing American Airlines as vice-president for operations. His talents for organizing and motivating employees helped to build American into a leading coast-to-coast airline.

Shortly before Pearl Harbor, Gen. H. H. Arnold of the Army Air Corps and Under Secretary of War Robert Patterson persuaded Damon to take charge of the Republic Aviation Corporation with the specific task of putting the desperately needed P-47 fighter plane—the Thunderbolt—into mass production. Two years later, with production of the nearly indestructible P-47 (grateful airmen called it "The Jug") up from zero to 450 a month, Damon returned to American Airlines, then fully engaged in the war effort. As executive vice-president he successfully negotiated the purchase of American Export Airlines, a strategy designed to gain postwar access to overseas markets. In 1945 Damon was named president of American, replacing C. R. Smith who, on returning from military service, had been elevated to chairman of the board.

Damon soon found himself at odds with Juan Trippe, aviation pioneer and president of Pan American Airways. As early as 1944 Trippe was petitioning Congress to adopt as the nation's international air policy the device of a "chosen instrument" to compete against subsidized foreign air carriers. First advancing the idea of a single U.S. flag carrier, Trippe later proposed a cooperative venture in which several U.S. airlines would hold stock. Damon, whose overseas subsidiary was struggling to establish a foothold in the North Atlantic market, saw what Trippe had in mind: a monopoly which wealthy Pan American would control and which Trippe would run.

Shortly before the German surrender in May 1945, Damon appeared before the Senate Commerce Committee's subcommittee on aviation and argued that wartime duty with the army's Air Transport Command and the navy's Air Transport Service had fully prepared domestic airlines for international operations. Damon called for regulated competition—the allocation of international routes in the same manner as domestic routes. Congress and the Civil Aeronautics Board agreed with Damon, and awarded route certificates not only to Pan American but also to American Airlines and Transcontinental and Western Air (TWA).

For good or ill, regulated competition would continue for more than three decades. In the short term, it left American and TWA struggling to catch up with an airline that had far greater international experience as well as name recognition. Pan American would remain the dominant international carrier in the postwar period, carrying the bulk of the small volume of premium overseas traffic.

Meanwhile, without consulting Damon, board chairman C. R. Smith had entered into secret negotiations with Pan American to sell American's money-losing subsidiary, now called American Overseas Airlines (AOA). To Damon, who had labored long and hard to secure access to overseas markets during Smith's wartime absence, the sale of AOA to Pan American was tantamount to giving aid and comfort to the enemy. Saying, "There comes a time when a man has to stand up and be counted," Damon resigned shortly after the merger agreement was announced in December 1948. Ignoring several other offers, Damon accepted Howard Hughes's blandishments and became TWA's third postwar president, a position that had been vacant for the previous eight months, and one which Damon would use to put his stamp on commercial aviation.

Although many industry observers expected a clash between owner and president, it did not come about. Hughes, whose eccentricities and interference with the management of his airline were legendary, and Damon, whom author Robert J. Serling once likened to "a somewhat baggy-looking British civil servant," managed to find a modus operandi—as indeed they had to if TWA was to survive. Not only was eight months of leaderless operation being felt at ticket counters from San Francisco to Bombay, but also TWA's three-year accumulated losses stood at $18.6 million, its aircraft fleet was outdated, and employee morale mirrored the record drop of their number from 17,000 to 12,000.

The postwar years had placed enormous strains on most U.S. airlines. Huge investments in aircraft, equipment, property and personnel combined with rising costs, increased competition, and a virtually flat passenger load curve to cause economic misery for the entire industry. TWA had had the additional financial and operational burden of establishing its overseas routes and melding them into a cohesive network. Crippled for part of 1946 by both a pilot strike and the temporary grounding of its long-range Lockheed Constellations, TWA's rush to expand had gone on unabated, a situation made

no better by the running feud between then-president Jack Frye and owner Hughes. The airline that Damon inherited in early 1949 was overextended, underfinanced, ill-equipped, and nearing bankruptcy.

Overlooking a first-quarter loss of $3.5 million, Damon would later comment, "I've always had the good fortune to join a winning team just as it is starting to win." Fortune did play a part, as increasing traffic made 1949 a turnaround year for the industry, but Damon made the difference at TWA. Unprepossessing in a battered hat and rumpled suit, Damon spent much of his first year riding TWA's far-flung network, surveying operations and boosting employee morale by assuring them that he carried no axe but that he would let the deadwood fall. Of TWA's aircraft problems, Damon said, "We fly too many miles with money-losing equipment and not enough miles with money-making equipment." In the domestic market, TWA's aging DC-3s were competing against modern and more efficient Convairs and Martins, while its early model Constellations were losing international traffic to the new and superior Douglas DC-6s.

Lacking cash for new aircraft, and with lenders frightened off by the free-fall of TWA stock from $74 to $16, Damon moved quickly to make TWA's balance sheet more attractive. To retroactive airmail payments of $2.5 million he added $4 million through the sale of common stock (most of it to current stockholders), and a further $2 million by centralizing aircraft maintenance. Better utilization of Constellations and the leasing of 12 Martin 2-0-2s brought a systemwide profit by late spring. By mid year, having opened flying to the mass market with the introduction of low-fare *Sky Coach* flights, Damon could forecast black ink by year's end. In a test of strength, he overcame Hughes's preference for the DC-6, convincing him to use the established relationship with Lockheed and over 20 Super Constellations instead.

Damon spent much time and effort trying to defeat the merger of Pan American and American Overseas, then awaiting President Harry S. Truman's signature. Damon knew that two years earlier, Trippe had approached Hughes with an offer to buy TWA's international routes, so he saw the merger battle as part of a larger effort to defeat Trippe's dream of a "chosen instrument." In the end, Damon lost the battle but won the war. Truman approved the merger, but at the same time he turned Trippe's dream into a nightmare by giving TWA authority to compete against Pan American in its major markets of London and Frankfurt.

Decisions taken by Damon in his early years as president ensured that TWA would realize a steadily growing profit throughout his tenure. The boom in air traffic made 1951 the most profitable year in airline history to date; TWA alone carried 2.25 million domestic and international passengers. Passenger miles flown by major domestic carriers doubled in 1952, while Damon's introduction of first- and tourist-class fares on the same flight was doing the same for international traffic. By then, TWA had $100 million invested in a modern fleet of 61 short-range Martins and 78 medium- and long-range Constellations, with all but $6 million of that debt retired by income from revenues.

Still fascinated by the cosmos, and proud of being named an honorary fellow of the Harvard Observatory, Damon made time for his hobby as an amateur astronomer. However, he looked forward far more than he did upward. Speaking to the Newcomen Society in North America in late 1952,

Damon said, "Air transportation is a dynamic business. . . . The jet age is on the horizon and [quoting Kipling] 'We are at the opening verse of the opening chapter of endless possibilities.'" But, ailing and overworked, Damon did not live to see the jet age. A slender man who unaccountably took to severe dieting, he entered the hospital in late 1955 and on January 4, 1956, died of pneumonia. Ralph Damon's passing was mourned by virtually all who knew him during three decades of working his will on aviation.

Publication:

"TWA": Nearly Three Decades in the Air (New York: Newcomen Society in North America, 1952).

References:

"Mr. Damon Begins to Move," *Fortune*, 40 (July 1949): 65-67;

Robert W. Rummel, *Howard Hughes and TWA* (Washington, D.C.: Smithsonian Institution, 1991);

Robert J. Serling, *Eagle: The Story of American Airlines* (New York: St. Martin's Press/Marek, 1985);

Serling, *Howard Hughes' Airline: An Informal History of TWA* (New York: St. Martin's Press/Marek, 1983).

Thomas H. Davis

(March 15, 1918 -   )

by William M. Leary

University of Georgia

CAREER: Aircraft salesman (1939-1940); vice-president (1941-1943), president (1943-1981), chairman (1981-1983), chairman of the executive committee (1983-1988), Piedmont Aviation.

Thomas Henry Davis was born on March 15, 1918, in Winston-Salem, North Carolina, the son of Egbert L. and Annie Shore Davis. His father was an executive with the R. J. Reynolds Tobacco Company who later founded and became president of Security Life and Trust Company. Raised in Winston-Salem, Davis graduated from Reynolds High School. While in high school, he learned to fly, soloing on January 29, 1935, at the age of sixteen. He attended the University of Arizona between 1935 and 1939, taking the premed program, but he left prior to graduation because of asthma.

In the summer of 1939 L. S. McGinnis of

Winston-Salem's Camel Flying Service, which held the North Carolina franchise for Piper Cubs and Stinson Reliants, offered Davis a sales position. "I jumped at the chance to get paid to fly," Davis later recalled, "rather than having to rent an airplane to build up my flight time." The following year Davis paid off McGinnis's note to the Wachovia Bank and became the company's principal stockholder. On July 2, 1940, he dissolved Camel and formed Piedmont Aviation, Inc.

Piedmont prospered under Davis's leadership. A typical fixed-base operation, the company sold and serviced aircraft, offered flight training, and flew charters. By the time of American entry into World War II in December 1941, it had become one of the largest wholesale aircraft dealers in the country. During the war Piedmont devoted the

Thomas H. Davis (courtesy of USAir)

major portion of its activities to training pilots for the Air Transport Command and turning out instructors for army flying schools. In the process it compiled an outstanding safety record, with no serious injuries or fatalities.

Two important events in Davis's life took place in 1944. On October 28 he married Nancy Carolyn Teague; the couple had five children. Also, looking ahead to the postwar period, Davis filed an application with the Civil Aeronautics Board (CAB) to provide scheduled local air service in the mid-Atlantic region.

On April 4, 1947, the CAB authorized Piedmont Aviation to serve local communities in North Carolina, Tennessee, Kentucky, Ohio, West Virginia, and Virginia. On January 1, 1948, Davis divided the company into the Piedmont Airlines Division and the General Aviation Division, each to operate autonomously under the corporate structure of Piedmont Aviation. At the same time he conducted a successful public stock offering to raise money for the airline.

Preparation for flight operations was a hectic but satisfying time for Davis. Personnel had to be

hired, a traffic department organized, equipment purchased, and myriad details attended to. In characteristic fashion, Davis decided to buy DC-3s from air carriers that were upgrading their equipment rather than purchase cheaper Douglas transports on the war surplus market. In the long run, he explained, this would save money. Piedmont would obtain a more complete history with the air carrier DC-3s, making modifications "simpler and eventually cheaper."

Service began on February 20, 1948. In its first year Piedmont carried 80,000 passengers. Over the next five years the airline became the leading local service carrier in the southeastern United States.

In the early 1950s Davis began to search for a replacement for the DC-3s. Piedmont drew up a set of specifications that led to the production of the Fokker F-27 turboprop. Piedmont took delivery on the first eight F-27s in 1958. Three years later Davis obtained—on highly favorable terms—TWA's remaining fleet of Martin 404s, making Piedmont the first local service carrier to be completely equipped with pressurized aircraft.

As the airline was acquiring more modern equipment, its route system was expanding. Piedmont reached Washington, D.C., in 1955, Atlanta in 1962, and New York in 1966. As traffic increased, Davis took the airline into the turbojet era. In 1967 Piedmont purchased two Boeing 727s. The following year it acquired 12 Boeing 737s, an airplane that proved especially suitable for the airline's short-haul routes. Also, at the end of the decade, Piedmont placed into service 21 60-passenger Nihon YS-11s, becoming the leading U.S. operator of the Japanese-built turboprop transport.

The 1970s were years of growth and profitability under Davis's careful management. The airline was oriented toward the business traveler. Davis emphasized on-time performance and courteous service, and Piedmont became an industry leader in both categories. Employee morale tended to be high, as the company avoided layoffs and promoted from within. Davis's gentle paternalism gave employees the feeling that they belonged to a family, and that the person in charge of the company genuinely cared for their welfare—which he did.

Even before deregulation, Piedmont had become an important regional carrier with routes to Boston, Philadelphia, Pittsburgh, and Denver. Although Davis initially opposed deregulation, he

Piedmont Nihon YS-11 (courtesy of the National Air and Space Museum)

quickly accepted the inevitable. The airline's post-deregulation strategy, he commented, was "not vastly different from the growth program we had been working on for many years. Deregulation simply made it all possible at a much faster pace."

Avoiding direct competition with major carriers, Piedmont emphasized hub-and-spoke routes, centered on Charlotte and (later) Dayton and Baltimore. In 1979 the airline had the highest growth rate of all local service carriers. Expanding into Florida and Texas, it recorded a net profit of $11.6 million.

In 1983, having successfully navigated the treacherous currents of deregulation, Davis gave up his responsibilities as chief executive officer of the airline. He remained with Piedmont as chairman of the executive committee on the board of directors. From its modest beginnings, Piedmont had become the nation's ninth largest airline (in 1984), with 14.1 million passenger boardings, revenues of nearly $1 billion, and net earnings of over $58 million.

In 1987 USAir purchased Piedmont, by then with 22,000 employees and 205 aircraft, for $1.6 billion in the largest merger in airline history. "Under all the circumstances," Davis has observed, "and considering the alternatives, merger was the best course of action." Still, it is not difficult to imagine the feeling of sorrow that he likely experienced when the Piedmont logo passed into history at the end of the decade. Certainly, many air travelers in the southeastern United States shared the sense of loss.

Publications:

"How to Start an Airline," *Air Transport*, 5 (October 1947): 47-50;

The History of Piedmont: Setting a Special Pace (New York: Newcomen Society in North America, 1982).

References:

R. E. G. Davies, *Airlines of the United States since 1914*, revised edition (Washington, D.C.: Smithsonian Institution, 1982);

George C. Eads, *The Local Service Airline Experiment* (Washington, D.C.: Brookings Institution, 1972);

Henry Lefler, "Piedmont Played the Game and Won," *Air Transport World*, 22 (January 1985): 32-35, 38;

Kay Pinckney, "Why Piedmont Succeeds Where Others Fail," *Airline Executive*, 7 (January 1983): 22-26;

Paul Seidenman and David J. Spanovich, "Piedmont: A Shining Star of Deregulation," *Airline Executive*, 8 (October 1985): 20-22.

Personal Correspondence:

Letter, Thomas H. Davis to William M. Leary, May 16, 1990.

Delta Air Lines

by W. David Lewis

Auburn University

and

Wesley Phillips Newton

Auburn University

Delta Air Lines began when Louisiana agricultural extension agent Collett Everman "C. E." Woolman, U.S. Department of Agriculture entomologist Dr. Bert R. Coad of the Delta Laboratory at Tallulah, George B. Post of New York-based Huff Daland aircraft manufacturers, and an army pilot on leave, Harold R. Harris, combined their expertise to produce a crop-dusting technique, a dusting plane, a commercial organization to utilize both, and a sales strategy to win acceptance of the dusting services. Harris managed the operations and Woolman, on leave from his extension job, marketed the services of Huff Daland's dusting division stemming from Post's innovation. Based in Monroe, Louisiana, Huff Daland Dusters concentrated on the cotton-rich Mississippi Delta region but ranged as far away as Peru, where Woolman and Harris also sought airline concessions for the financial interests that stood behind Huff Daland.

In 1928 the controlling northern interests decided to sell the assets of the dusting division. Woolman induced some planters, businessmen, and bankers in the Monroe area to join in the purchase of the assets. Late in 1928 they chartered Delta Air Service, Inc., based in Monroe, with Woolman as general manager. In 1929, with dusting still the main activity, Delta's commercial operations began. Woolman had become infected with the airline virus and purchased for the company two small, six-passenger Travel Air planes. On June 17, 1929, one of the Travel Airs, piloted by John Howe, made the first Delta airline flight in inaugurating passenger service from Dallas to Monroe. The fledgling line extended to Atlanta via Meridian and Birmingham by June 1930. But Delta's airline business was awash

in red ink and the company's only chance to recoup was to win an airmail contract for the route. The prospect at first seemed good, with the passage of the Air Mail (Watres) Act of 1930 giving Postmaster General Walter Folger Brown broad authority to parcel out airmail contracts. To achieve stability, Brown decided to award contracts to the better-financed lines if they followed his dictates, and called a secret conference in Washington to establish guidelines with the beneficiaries. Tipped off, Woolman crashed the meeting. Although he was able to negotiate with Eastern and then American, his efforts came to naught and Delta sold its airline rights to the latter, reverting almost exclusively to crop dusting. From late 1930 to 1934 the Depression kept Delta mired in doldrums while it eked out an existence by dusting and conducting fixed-base operations at Monroe.

In 1933 a Senate committee chaired by Alabama Democrat Hugo Black began to probe the awarding of ocean mail and, later, airmail contracts under Brown. As a result of its findings, all domestic airmail contracts were canceled and the Army Air Corps took over airmail delivery for a brief, disastrous time. Among the reforms that flowed from the Black committee's work was rebidding on airmail routes by all legitimate aspirants. Delta bid on its old route and received the contract.

Delta's route 24 stretched from Dallas to Charleston, South Carolina. The first planes of the reinvigorated airline division were secondhand, high-wing, single-engine Stinson-Ts with a capacity of seven, including pilot, copilot, and five passengers. They were soon joined by new low-wing Stinson-A trimotors with a capacity of ten, including eight pas-

Delta Air Service Travel Air 6000, 1929 (courtesy of the National Air and Space Museum)

sengers. These aircraft were few in comparison to the rather large fleet of dusting planes under Bert Coad's direction; until the end of the decade, crop spraying and mail carriage were Delta's main revenue sources. The Stinsons were relics of a passing era with their cloth skin and fixed landing gear, for aircraft design was undergoing a great technological leap. They were all the company could afford, however, until wealthy Delta president C. E. Faulk loaned the enterprise money in 1936 to purchase its first modern aircraft—three Lockheed L10B Electras with all-metal skin, retractable landing gear, and a capacity of 12, including 10 passengers. These Electras, and a publicity campaign that gave Delta the image of an airline for the Southern Gentleman and Southern Belle, combined to coax more and more passengers aboard. Within the company itself Woolman successfully promoted the idea that Delta was an extended family and he the prudent, firm, but benevolent patriarch.

Delta's crews were a composite of former dusting pilots and airline veterans. They suffered only one fatal accident in the 1930s, the crash of a Stinson-A in Texas with the loss of all four persons aboard. Although corporate headquarters remained

in Monroe, Atlanta became the maintenance and main crew base in 1936. Over the next few years momentous changes took place. Delta procured a larger airliner, the Douglas DC-2, and hired its first female flight attendants. Beginning in 1940 a series of even more significant steps were taken. First, the board went public with Delta's stock; next, it approved the purchase of the 21-passenger Douglas DC-3, the first super airliner; and, last, it followed Woolman's lead in agreeing to move the company's headquarters to Atlanta. This was accomplished in March 1941, perhaps accentuated by Delta's acquisition of a new route, Atlanta to Cincinnati via Knoxville and Lexington, in January. But the main reason for the shift was that Atlanta was a major transportation hub and had financial institutions with ample capital to support the company's growth.

When Japanese planes attacked Pearl Harbor, life changed for all American airlines. Delta, as did the others, saw most of its planes sequestered by the military, and many crews and support personnel were taken into the armed services. But the company made the most of what it had left and took on various defense chores, such as refitting military

Delta Stinson Model A

planes and flying military cargo on special flights. Statistically, it was the most efficient of the airlines in wartime. Many servicemen and their dependents made their first flights aboard a Delta plane, adding to the potential for expanded postwar interest in air travel. Meanwhile, Woolman was planning for the return of peace. Toward the close of the war the armed services began to return Delta aircraft, and at the end the Civil Aeronautics Board (CAB) rewarded Delta with the longest and most lucrative prize it had yet bestowed—the 1,028-mile Miami-Chicago route.

Delta, like other airlines, took advantage of the war's end and rushed to add new facilities and four-engined aircraft such as the Douglas DC-4, the civilian version of a military transport. But all the airlines were overly optimistic about the public's postwar rush to embrace air travel. As a result, they all went through bumpy times and had to retrench. At the beginning of the 1950s, however, the skies began to clear.

Its acquisition of the Miami-Chicago route made Delta, which changed its name to Delta Air Lines, Inc., in 1945, a competitor with Eastern. Under Edward V. Rickenbacker, the latter was the nation's number-one airline, while Woolman's line was only regional. But it was a feisty regional, and

in the choice of planes it held its own over the Miami-Chicago route. In the postwar decade Woolman made several decisions that contrasted with those made by Rickenbacker; in the long run these contributed to Delta's eventual achievement of major status and to Eastern's decline. Delta chose to avoid purchasing the Lockheed Electra L-188 propjet—the intermediate stage between piston engine planes and pure jets. Eastern and some of the other lines adopted this plane, which was a disaster. Woolman also chose to make the "third man" in the cockpit, mandated by the CAB for larger airliners, another pilot instead of a less expensive flight engineer, sparing the company costly jurisdictional disputes in the future. In the tradition of southern conservatism, Woolman kept down unionism in Delta, with only the pilots maintaining a union over the long haul. In the place of unions he substituted an extended-family mystique and general benefits to match those that accrued from unionism.

The next step toward major-airline status came in 1953 when Delta was the surviving corporation in a merger with another regional, Chicago and Southern. As a result, Woolman's company acquired routes connecting Chicago with New Orleans, Houston with Detroit, and New Orleans with several places in and around the Caribbean,

Delta Lockheed L-049 Constellation (courtesy of the National Air and Space Museum)

making Delta an international line.

With the jet age looming, Woolman and his colleagues had to make a crucial decision—which of the two available jets to choose, the Boeing 707 or the Douglas DC-8. They chose the latter, advanced versions of which would be flying for Delta and other airlines long after the 707 was finished. Woolman was aboard the DC-8 that began that airliner's commercial life in 1959. The flight also highlighted a prized route Delta had acquired in 1955—from Atlanta to New York via Washington and other stops, an acquisition that had broken Eastern's previous monopoly. Later, in 1965, Delta pioneered the short-ranged DC-9, whose design the company's engineers and pilots had influenced.

The late 1950s and early 1960s brought some rather serious problems in the form of a severe recession in 1957 and difficulties with noise restrictions on jet engines that forced a delicate balance between abatement procedures and safety margins. Delta managed to placate the newly created Federal Aviation Administration (FAA) on the latter, and good times returned in the early 1960s. These would last for a decade.

In 1962, Delta finally reached the West Coast by securing a route that connected Los Angeles, San Francisco, and other western cities with Dallas-Ft. Worth, making the airline continental as well as intercontinental. To complement this expansion, Delta was instrumental in blocking a merger between Eastern and American. Such welcome developments, however, were matched by one traumatic event, the death in 1966 of the man who had personified Delta: C. E. Woolman.

Though Woolman had been the patriarch with the final say, he had not run the airline alone. His style was quickly superseded by a group approach to management that had been subtly forming even before his death. Vice-presidents, such as Richard S. Maurer of the legal department, and a web of assistant vice-presidents functioned in a finely meshed system, at the top of which were the president and chairman of the board, functioning like orchestral conductors. W. T. Beebe, from personnel, succeeded Woolman as chairman of the board, and Charles Dolson, a veteran pilot from the early Delta airmail days, continued as president until he retired in 1972, when he was succeeded by David C.

Lockheed L-1011 (courtesy of the National Air and Space Museum)

Garrett from operations. In 1978, as Beebe prepared to retire, Garrett was named chief executive officer. Once a week, all of the senior executives and some of the junior ones met to plan and coordinate policy. Key strategies that Woolman had initiated—the extended-family mystique, frugality in everything but operations and equipment, and a balanced fleet—continued to be emphasized.

It was fortunate that the transition from one-man rule to the group approach had been smooth, for the 1970s brought "stagflation" that affected all areas of American business. The Arab oil boycott and the "Sporty Game" that led to competition between wide-bodied superjets hit airlines especially hard. Delta would make it through this flak, not unscathed but still flying high.

The decade started out well, with Delta absorbing Northeast Airlines, giving it entry into Boston and other New England markets. But then came the economic crunch, with rising jet fuel costs. An economic downturn in 1975 was particularly difficult to weather, but Delta came out of it and prospered again by the end of the decade. Fleet

standardization was one reason for its success. After trying small numbers of Boeing 747s and stretched DC-8s, Delta settled on the Lockheed L-1011 as its widebody, deciding that it was more cost efficient. For Delta, it proved a good decision. More advanced versions of the DC-9 and the Boeing 727, the industry's mid-range workhorse, replaced older aircraft. An increase in airline passenger travel was another reason for returning prosperity. Also helpful was Delta's strategy of "hub and spoke" operations, developed by marketing executive Thomas Miller, in which traffic from small- and medium-sized cities was funneled through gateway cities such as Atlanta, leading to the saying that in order to get to heaven or hell one had first to "change planes at Atlanta." In tense battles with Eastern before the CAB, Delta gained access to Tulsa and Denver, and then won perhaps its most prestigious prizes up to that time, the right to fly to England and Germany as the CAB opened up transatlantic sky lanes. Although it moved somewhat more slowly than some other airlines, Delta gradually gave women and blacks more access to mid- and lower-range managerial positions and to copilot status.

Delta entered the 1980s with a proud record overall and high expectations. It finished the decade with a mixed bag of accomplishments. Ironically, Delta had opposed deregulation when it was under consideration in the 1970s, but at the end of the 1980s it opposed any move to reregulate. It was one of the increasingly small number of big winners in the deregulation scramble for new routes and non-stop service. Delta planes soon flew into such places as Paris, Tokyo, Seoul, and Honolulu. In 1986 Delta also added substantially to its route system by acquiring Western Airlines.

In fleet selection, the company began to phase out its old standbys, the DC-9, Boeing 727, and DC-8. The replacements were the short-range Boeing 737, medium-range Boeing 767, and long-range Boeing 757. The L-1011s were improved, and Delta began to receive new aircraft from a company that the "Sporty Game" had temporarily eliminated from commercial airliner competition, McDonnell-Douglas, which began to produce its MB series.

Delta continued to receive awards and accolades as the best and least complained-about airline. After a severe slump in 1982-1983 that abruptly reversed its long-standing position as the most consistently profitable air carrier, it began to earn money again. But a dark side appeared in the form of an image problem that would have caused C. E. Woolman enormous grief. This negative publicity grew out of a series of bizarre incidents, including one in which a Delta airliner landed at the wrong airport; unfortunately, the incident did not result from an emergency. More serious, however, were two fatal accidents. Delta had suffered others since the first in 1935; in 1947, in one of the most singular accidents in airline history, it lost several important members of its management team. Other fatal crashes had taken place in 1953, 1960, 1967, and 1973, but the company had then gone 12 years without one, to the envy of the industry. This flawless string ended in August 1985 with the crash of an L-1011 at the Dallas-Fort Worth airport. The heavy loss of life was at first blamed on a windshear, but the National Transportation Safety Board later concluded that it was due to pilot error. Delta disputed the findings. Another fatal crash took place in 1988, but with far less loss of life.

Veteran personnel head Ronald W. Allen became Delta's president in 1983 and its chief executive officer in 1987. Under his leadership Delta launched new international routes to such places as Denmark, Japan, and Taiwan and entered into a formal partnership with blue-ribbon carriers Singapore Airlines and Swissair. With the demise of its once bitter rival, Eastern, Delta added to its resources by acquiring such important assets as Eastern's gate positions at Hartsfield International Airport in Atlanta, where it controlled 80 percent of the market by 1991. During the summer of 1991 Delta became even more powerful by purchasing rapidly sinking Pan American's shuttle service between Boston, New York, and Washington, D.C., taking over its routes to 23 European cities, acquiring a substantial stake in the reorganized airline, adding 21 Airbus A-310s and 24 other aircraft to its fleet, and absorbing approximately 6,600 former Pan Am employees. The value of the deal to creditors was reported as up to $1.776 billion, but actual up-front cost to Delta was $621 million at maximum, which the firm hoped to reduce to $526 million through sale of spare parts and other fiscal measures. C. E. Woolman's heritage of thrifty management was still alive. Even though Delta reported the worst loss in its history in 1990, this was only its second annual deficit since 1947, and it appeared in late 1991 to be poised for renewed growth as one of the nation's three largest commercial air carriers.

References:

"Airline Soars with Its Feet on the Ground," *USA Today*, July 17, 1991, pp. B1-2;

R. E. G. Davis, *Delta: An Airline and Its Aircraft* (Miami, Fla.: Paladwr Press, 1990);

W. David Lewis and Wesley Phillips Newton, *Delta: The History of An Airline* (Athens: University of Georgia Press, 1979);

John Newhouse, *The Sporty Game* (New York: Knopf, 1982).

Archives:

C. E. Woolman's business correspondence and other Delta Air Lines papers are to be found at Delta General Offices, Hartsfield International Airport, Atlanta, Georgia.

Terrell C. Drinkwater

(July 15, 1908 - January 7, 1985)

by Earl H. Tilford, Jr.

Air Force Air Command and Staff College

CAREER: Attorney, Denver, Colorado (1932-1942); executive vice-president, director, general manager, Continental Air Lines (1942-1944); vice-president, American Airlines (1944-1947); president, Western Airlines (1947-1969).

Terrell Croft Drinkwater was born in Denver, Colorado, on July 15, 1908, the son of Ray L. and Geraldine Croft Drinkwater. Raised in Colorado, he attended the University of Colorado at Boulder where he earned his A.B. degree in 1930 and a law degree two years later. Drinkwater passed the Colorado bar examination and hung out his shingle as an attorney in Denver. In September 1933 he married Helen Louise Kiddoo, who bore him two children, Dorsey Ann and Terrell Thomas Drinkwater. Their son, Terrell, pursued a career in journalism, becoming well known in his own right as West Coast correspondent for CBS television news in the 1970s.

After earning an advanced law degree in 1937, Drinkwater continued to practice law in Denver. His specialty was aeronautical law, and that made him a potentially valuable asset to the civil aviation industry of the 1940s. In 1942 he left private practice to take a position with Continental Airlines. Rising rapidly, he became in two years executive vice-president, director, and then general manager. After his successful, albeit short, stint with Continental, Drinkwater accepted in 1944 a vice-presidency with American Airlines. He worked for American for three years while simultaneously serving as vice-president and director of American Overseas Airlines. During this period he established a reputation as an efficient airline executive.

At the end of World War II, surplus military aircraft were abundant and inexpensive. Many air carriers took advantage of this opportunity to expand their inventories. The Los Angeles-based Western

Airlines was no exception, ordering war surplus DC-3s and DC-4s as the company's executives sought to enlarge the airline's fleet in anticipation of route expansion and a booming passenger business. In 1946, however, Western suffered three of the nine fatal crashes among domestic U.S. carriers. This unfortunate turn of events worsened an already shaky financial situation. By the end of the year, Western's financial losses totaled $9 million. After Western's president and principal stockholder, Charles Coulter, resigned, the board of directors offered the job to Drinkwater. Leaving an established and profitable American Airlines to take on the challenge of turning around a faltering regional carrier constituted a considerable risk. Nevertheless, as 1947 began, the thirty-nine-year-old Drinkwater became Western's fourth president.

Described by aviation writer Robert J. Serling as "a tall husky man with a pixielike smile, a brilliant mind, an iron will, and a proclivity for bow ties, pipes, and good whiskey," Drinkwater became nearly synonymous with Western Airlines. Over the next two decades, TCD (as he was known) built Western into a major regional carrier which, at its zenith, was on the verge of becoming one of the nation's major airlines. As controversial as the Drinkwater era was at Western, during his presidency the airline enjoyed a period of sustained growth. After he was forced out of the executive suite 22 years later, Western was never again the same.

Drinkwater hoped to make Western one of the top large American international carriers. But his first task in the late 1940s was to find a way to avoid financial disaster. The new president began by selling Western's Los Angeles-Denver route and four newly acquired DC-4s, along with their supporting ground equipment, to United Air Lines for $4.75 million. Additionally, United agreed to as-

Terrell C. Drinkwater

sume responsibility for paying for five DC-6s ordered in 1946 by Drinkwater's predecessor. To reduce costs further, Drinkwater shifted other airplanes to hangars in Nevada where taxes and rents were lower than they were in California. He also pruned the work force to 1,600 by eliminating 1,000 jobs. While some around the corporate board room objected to Drinkwater's sale of the Los Angeles-Denver route—one considered by many to be a "jewel" in the Western crown—Drinkwater was convinced that his strategy of "constructive contraction" would slim Western down to the point that it would be healthier and more competitive.

Slowly the ledger turned from red to black. The first step on the way back to corporate health was to make Western profitable as a regional carrier. Drinkwater's management philosophy was dictatorial in that he centralized the decision making on himself. To make sure decisions flowed smoothly from his office to the flight ramp, he hired what Serling described as one of the best batches of middle managers in the industry. Drinkwater was convinced that if each facet of the company worked well—accounting, ticketing, maintenance, etc.—then the decisions he made at the cor-

porate level would be translated into effective operations.

Drinkwater was an enigmatic man. Superficially, he was a "hail fellow well met" with the attendant backslapping and joviality of manner. His large grin and friendly demeanor belied an incisive mind; he was a shrewd businessman and a scholarly and tenacious lawyer. Yet he had his failings. He could be stubborn, petty, unforgiving, and vindictive. He disdained political propriety. As a conservative Republican, he hated dealing with unions. Ironically, Western became one of the most unionized airlines in the country during his presidency. Worse than unions, Drinkwater resented what he perceived to be interference by the federal government in his endeavors. Reportedly, in the early 1960s, he let it be known to presidential advisers that should President John F. Kennedy ask him to make concessions during a flight engineer's strike, he would refuse.

After Western Airlines regained some of its financial strength in the early 1950s, Drinkwater's strategy of constructive contraction gave way to controlled expansion. That decade turned out to be the best in Western's long and tumultuous history. In 1956, after five years of increasing profits, Western posted a record $3 million on the positive side of

Western Airlines Boeing 737 (courtesy of the National Air and Space Museum)

the ledger. The next year, the airline broke into the international market by opening a Los Angeles-Mexico City route.

Drinkwater approached expansion cautiously. His conservatism was not always appreciated by other executives at Western. Some argued for a more rapid expansion of aircraft inventory, along with a quick conversion to jet airliners. But Drinkwater guided Western slowly from piston aircraft to jets via an intermediate transition through Lockheed L-188 Electra turboprops, ordered in 1957. By the end of the 1950s, Western had six Electras in its inventory, the last of the DC-3s had been retired, and Drinkwater had signed a contract to purchase three Boeing 720 jetliners and arranged to lease a pair of Boeing 707s.

Drinkwater's political conservatism might have contributed to the thwarting of what he believed was a potentially profitable move for Western, the acquisition of a mainland-to-Hawaii route. At the end of the Dwight D. Eisenhower administration, Drinkwater filed application with the Civil Aeronautics Board (CAB) to acquire a piece of the

Pacific market. On the last full day of the Eisenhower presidency, January 19, 1961, the CAB voted to allow Western to acquire its Hawaii route. However, President Kennedy overturned the award, touching off a legal battle that lasted throughout the 1960s. The delay in obtaining final approval to move into the potentially lucrative Hawaii market bedeviled Drinkwater to the end of his tenure as Western's president.

During Drinkwater's 22 years as Western's president, he instituted several new concepts, of which some worked and some did not. One that failed—but was ahead of its time—was the introduction in 1949 of cut-rate, no-frills flights. By eliminating in-flight meals, Drinkwater shaved an average of 5 percent from the price of many West Coast fares. The public, however, was not ready for that kind of economy, and Western's share of that particular market plummeted despite the marginally lower rates. After six months, Drinkwater reestablished food service and business picked up.

Characteristically, having tried one extreme of austerity, Drinkwater seemed to bounce to the other. After he and his wife were served champagne on an overseas airline, Drinkwater introduced champagne flights on Western. This innovation was so popular that he ordered in-flight meals improved to the point that on some flights Western passengers were served steak and champagne meals. The public's positive reaction to fine in-flight dining so encouraged Drinkwater that he expanded his gourmet marketing approach by introducing a "Hunt Breakfast" for early morning travelers to dine on omelets, sausage, ham, or bacon—a first for the passenger airline industry.

Drinkwater brought Western Airlines a long way. By the end of the 1960s it was firmly placed among the nation's financially healthy carriers. It seemed ready to move into the overseas market with the final approval of the Hawaii route when President Lyndon B. Johnson, in early January 1969, confirmed a CAB decision granting Western routes between mainland cities and Hawaii, to include one between Anchorage and Honolulu. By this time, Drinkwater's dominance at Western made him synonymous with the airline. Perhaps this overbearing management style eclipsed the abilities of other talented executives who might have helped him stave off the takeover bid by one of America's most talented entrepreneurs and financiers, Las Vegas entertainment industry mogul Kirk Kerkorian.

Western's descent from economic viability to financial disaster began when Kerkorian purchased nearly one-third of Western's stock in 1969. After he gained a controlling interest in the airline, Kerkorian placed a block of supporters on the board of directors to displace Drinkwater from the presidency into a powerless position as chairman of the board. After a year as the ceremonial board chairman, a broken Drinkwater retired. Within six years Kerkorian had turned his full attention to the motion picture industry and had sold his stock in Western.

After the bitter corporate infighting surrounding Kerkorian's purchase of controlling interest and Drinkwater's subsequent resignation as president, Western struggled through 15 years of mostly bad times. A series of successive executives strode through what can only be described as a "revolving door" to the president's office. Finally, almost mercifully, on April 1, 1987, Delta Air Lines purchased Western for $860 million.

In retirement Drinkwater stayed in Los Angeles. He served as president of the Union Bank of Los Angeles and was a member of the board of directors of the Hollywood Turf Club. On January 7, 1985, at the age of seventy-six, he died of pancreatic cancer.

References:

R. E. G. Davies, *Airlines of the United States since 1914*, revised edition (Washington, D.C.: Smithsonian Institution, 1982);

Robert J. Serling, *The Only Way to Fly* (Garden City, N.Y.: Doubleday, 1976).

Henry A. Duffy

(September 27, 1934 -   )

by George E. Hopkins

Western Illinois University

CAREER: Pilot, U.S. Army (1956-1962); pilot, Delta Air Lines (1962-1983); president, Air Line Pilots Association (1983-1990).

Henry A. "Hank" Duffy was the fifth president of the Air Line Pilots Association (ALPA), International (AFL-CIO), a union of professional airline pilots who fly for U.S. commercial carriers. As of 1990 the ALPA represented some 40,000 pilots, about 32,000 of whom were actively flying the line. The remaining 8,000 pilots were either furloughed, on strike, or on probation and hence had no representational status other than apprentice membership. Duffy became president of ALPA in 1983, and his term of office expired on December 31, 1990. He was not a candidate for reelection and retired from flying after leaving ALPA's presidency.

Born on September 27, 1934, in Norfolk, Virginia, Duffy began flying in the U.S. Army after graduating from the University of Miami, Florida, in 1956. An accomplished horn player who attended college on a music scholarship, Duffy majored in business and earned an army commission through the ROTC program at Miami. While in the army, Duffy became a qualified aviator on several aircraft, including helicopters. Upon leaving military service in 1962, Duffy obtained employment with Delta Air Lines, where he advanced rapidly to his captaincy owing to that airline's phenomenal expansion. By 1970 Duffy was a fully qualified jet captain, flying McDonnell-Douglas DC-9 aircraft. He subsequently commanded DC-8 jet aircraft.

Duffy's election to the presidency of ALPA in 1982 at the age of forty-eight was in some respects a tribute to the corporate culture of Delta Air Lines. Like the companies for which they fly, the various pilot groups which make up ALPA tend to exhibit a character which reflects the corporate culture in which they live. Eastern Air Lines pilots,

Henry A. Duffy (courtesy of the Archives of Labor and Urban Affairs, Wayne State University)

for example, during the era of Capt. Edward V. Rickenbacker tended to be close-lipped "company men." Years later, as Eastern's corporate culture changed, the airline's pilots became equally close-lipped advocates of union solidarity. Some airline pilot groups have traditionally been more militant in their unionism than others. Northwest Airways, for example, has had more than its share of pilots' strikes. United's pilots occupy a kind of traditional middle ground, willing to fight management when pushed, but on the whole rather amenable to company policies.

Delta's pilots have traditionally been the least militant and most company-oriented pilot group in ALPA. Delta's pilots have never had a strike, have never suffered from seasonal layoffs, and have benefited from what is generally regarded (historically) as the most enlightened and efficient management in the industry, which makes understandable their almost apologetic approach to unionism. Delta's pilots have the only significant union on Delta's property. (The dispatchers, who direct company flight operations on a daily basis, are also unionized, but they are a very small group.)

Hank Duffy, unlike most Delta employees, was an active unionist almost from his first days with the airline. During his 20 years as a line pilot, Duffy held several significant ALPA jobs, including the important Retirement and Insurance Committee chairmanship. His performance in these technical "nuts and bolts" ALPA offices (as opposed to the purely "political" side of ALPA activities) brought him favorable notice from the pilots of several airlines. The fact that he was active in Republican party politics in Georgia (where Delta is based), as a county chairman, indicated that he fit the image that most pilots had of themselves as reluctant unionists with conservative sympathies.

The election of Ronald Reagan as president in 1980 accelerated the pattern of ominous change which airline pilots had begun experiencing after the passage of the Airline Deregulation Act of 1978. While the conservative Republican revival of the Reagan years won support from most airline pilots owing to their economic status and social attitudes, nevertheless Reagan's antiunion tendencies were worrisome. Despite their ideological Republicanism, most pilots realized that they benefited from government regulation. Airline deregulation, although a product of the Jimmy Carter administration, was strongly supported by Republicans. ALPA president John J. O'Donnell had aligned the union solidly against deregulation—with minimal results. Hence, when O'Donnell's term expired in 1982, it was logical for the pilots to seek a leader like Duffy, whose Republican credentials and background in Delta's successful corporate culture promised compatibility with the Reagan "revolution."

Duffy's qualification for ALPA's presidency was thus based upon long years of work in the union's technical infrastructure, and the widely shared perception among airline pilots that he was likely to be effective in dealing with the Republican administration. O'Donnell's announcement that he would not stand for reelection prompted Duffy to announce his candidacy. Shortly after Duffy launched his campaign, however, O'Donnell changed his mind and entered the race, seeking a fourth four-year term. Duffy's strategy was based upon an open campaign with no incumbent, and later he readily admitted that if O'Donnell had not hesitated in announcing for reelection, Duffy would not have run. "A lot of people wanted to support me," Duffy declared in a 1990 interview, "but we couldn't convince them that anybody had a chance against a twelve year incumbent."

But O'Donnell's temporary noncandidacy opened the door to Duffy, whose support snowballed. By the time O'Donnell entered the race, another candidate, John Gratz, the leader of Trans World Airlines' pilots, also announced for the presidency. Gratz, a Boeing 747 captain flying international routes out of New York, spearheaded the attack against O'Donnell, allowing Duffy to occupy the middle ground. In a close and bitterly contested election at the 1982 meeting of the board of directors (ALPA's principal governing body), Duffy outpolled his two opponents and became the first president in ALPA's history to accede to the office by ousting an incumbent.

Despite Duffy's Republicanism, the Reagan years were difficult for ALPA. Duffy admits that his party affiliation was of minimal help in dealing with an administration overwhelmingly hostile to labor unions—even conservative ones like ALPA. Accordingly, Duffy moved ALPA further along toward an open identification with unionism and the major institutions of organized labor (a policy begun by his predecessor). To the surprise of many of his pilots, Duffy began playing an active role in the labor movement, building alliances with other union leaders for the battles which he realized would be inevitable—his personal party affiliation notwithstanding.

"In retrospect," Duffy declared in 1990, "I would distrust most of the Reagan administration's objectives. The people they brought in were so right-wing that it was not the Republican Party I had known. I didn't recognize that (hostility) as so deep philosophically, but it pervaded the whole administration."

In a series of battles during Duffy's presidency, ALPA received no help from the Republican administration. Beginning with the Continental Airlines strike of 1983, during which Frank Lorenzo, the chief executive officer of the airline, used bankruptcy laws to invalidate ALPA's contract, and ending with President George Bush's veto of a congressional bill requiring a special emergency investigation of the Eastern Airlines strike of 1989, ALPA has sustained a series of defeats at the hands of the Republican administrations. Further adding to ALPA's difficulties under Duffy, a series of mergers among troubled carriers generated internal battles between pilot groups, which led many observers to question the union's viability. The most significant victory ALPA scored during the Duffy years was the monthlong 1985 United Air Lines pilots' strike, which proved that with careful organization and planning ALPA could still prevail.

Counterbalancing the internal schisms and external woes which hampered Duffy during his tenure as ALPA's president, the union showed a marked ability to gain congressional support. ALPA's Political Action Committee was generally regarded as one of the best-financed in Washington, D.C., and its impact belied the union's relatively small membership. Furthermore, Duffy's campaign to bring "third level," or regional commuter airlines, within the ALPA fold was markedly successful. In fact, the membership losses incurred by ALPA at such famous old airlines as Continental and Braniff (owing to employer hostility and bankruptcy) during the 1980s actually were made up by new members from these smaller airlines. Owing to the fact that these new ALPA recruits earned less than the pilots ALPA lost, and the union's income is derived from a dues system based upon a percentage of income, ALPA's financial situation (aggravated by strikes and other crises) became precarious during Duffy's tenure.

Special assessments levied upon the membership to support strikes by Eastern and Continental pilots imposed a heavy burden on ALPA, with many members choosing to leave the union rather than pay the mandatory assessments. Still, as proof that a spirit of solidarity and brotherhood still prevailed among airmen, despite the stresses of deregulation, 90 percent of all working airline pilots voluntarily paid the special assessments. Observers credit much of ALPA's continued viability during the troubled 1980s to Duffy's leadership.

References:

Henry A. Duffy Biographical Data Sheet, Air Line Pilots Association, Washington, D.C.;
George E. Hopkins, Interview with Henry A. Duffy, June 10-11, 1990.

Richard C. du Pont

(January 2, 1911 - September 11, 1943)

by W. David Lewis

Auburn University

and

William F. Trimble

Auburn University

CAREER: Gliding champion (1930s); vice-president (1938-1940), president, All American Aviation (1940-1943); special assistant to Gen. H. H. Arnold, head of U.S. Army Air Forces glider program (1943).

Richard Chichester du Pont, a pioneer in the commercial utilization of nonstop airmail pickup and delivery and a prophet of the feeder line concept, was born in Wilmington, Delaware, on January 2, 1911, into a family whose wealth derived from technologically oriented enterprise. A model airplane enthusiast at an early age, du Pont was taught to fly a powered aircraft by his brother, Alexis Felix du Pont, Jr., a pilot for the Ludington Line. Captivated at an early age by gliding, du Pont

Richard C. du Pont

left the University of Virginia in 1932 without graduating and soon went to California to study aeronautical engineering at the Curtiss-Wright Technical Institute in Glendale. There he met Hawley Bowlus, an expert in glider technology, under whose instruction he became adept in designing, building, and flying such aircraft.

Du Pont quickly mastered thermal soaring, where maximum advantage is taken of upward air currents to maintain altitude. Returning east in 1933, he took part in the annual National Gliding and Soaring Meets at Elmira, New York, and became one of the world's outstanding glider pilots, setting an American and international record for distance (158.3 miles) in 1934, establishing a national record for altitude (6,223 feet) the same year, and winning national soaring championships (the Edwin S. Evans Trophy) in 1934, 1935, and 1937. He married Helena Allaire Crozier, a fellow gliding enthusiast, in 1934.

In 1938 du Pont met Lytle S. Adams, who had developed a technology by means of which specially equipped aircraft picked up and discharged air-

mail without landing. This method used a delivery rope stretched between two vertical posts and special shock-absorbing equipment enabling a low-flying plane to engage the rope with a cable and grappling hook, carrying aloft an attached mailbag while simultaneously dropping an incoming bag to the ground. Lacking financial means to transform this concept from an invention into a full-fledged commercial innovation, Adams turned for help to du Pont, who backed him with a $45,000 loan and an $85,000 investment that permitted activation of a previously dormant corporation, All American Aviation, Inc., established by Adams in 1937. Du Pont became president of the firm, and Adams vice-president and technical consultant. Winning a contract for two experimental airmail routes from the U.S. Post Office Department, connecting 52 small communities scattered throughout Pennsylvania and West Virginia, the firm bought five Stinson SR-10C Reliants and recruited pilots. It began formal service on May 12, 1939, after conducting two months of experimental operations.

Believing that the techniques developed by Adams were undependable, du Pont alienated the inventor by hiring a team of engineers and technicians to modify the pickup system in a series of experiments conducted without Adams's participation at Granogue, Delaware, in early 1939. The modifications enabled the company to carry out successful scheduled operations in 1939 and 1940 and to apply for a permanent certificate from the Civil Aeronautics Authority. Worsening relations between du Pont and Adams, however, led to an attempt by the latter to block certification. When this failed, du Pont exercised provisions in their 1938 agreement permitting him to buy out Adams.

Assuming full control of All American, du Pont tried vigorously to expand its operations by seeking approval from the Civil Aeronautics Board (CAB) for a series of pickup routes scattered throughout the eastern United States. In the process, the firm further improved its technology and conducted experimental night operations with special lighting equipment. Well aware that profits would be limited so long as the company conducted only airmail service, du Pont also tried to secure federal approval of combining passenger and pickup operations, arguing that this would democratize air travel and facilitate connections between small communities and large nodal centers. Despite a determined lobbying and public relations campaign, however, the CAB refused to implement du Pont's ideas.

During World War II, the large volume of mail sent from the home front to members of the armed services enabled All American to earn modest but dependable profits. Meanwhile, du Pont spearheaded efforts to combine the company's pickup technology with gliding. Techniques were developed by means of which a glider was attached to the delivery rope and carried aloft by an engined aircraft. The glider was thus transformed into an aircraft that could be used over and over again in a variety of military operations. The same method was successfully applied to picking up human beings stranded in remote areas or trapped behind enemy lines. Du Pont believed that this technology could be adapted for peacetime use by engined planes that would fly from one large city to another, picking up and cutting loose small passenger-carrying gliders at points in between. Obviously inspired by the analogy of locomotives pulling passenger cars, this idea was taken seriously by some aviation enthusiasts but never came close to adoption.

In April 1943 du Pont's creative combination of pickup and glider technology won him appointment by Gen. H. H. ("Hap") Arnold as a special assistant in charge of the Army Air Forces glider program. Reporting for duty in June, du Pont observed Allied glider operations in North Africa and Sicily before proceeding in August to March Field in California, where the army was testing experimental gliders. On September 11, 1943, he and five companions were towed aloft in one of the new motorless aircraft. Shortly after the tow line was released at 3,000 feet, the glider fell into a spin from which recovery was apparently impossible. Du Pont bailed out with two others, but his parachute malfunctioned and he plunged to his death. He was post-

humously awarded the army's Distinguished Service Medal and the Franklin Institute's John Price Wetherill Medal for his contributions to the war effort and his pioneering work with the airmail pickup.

Du Pont's successful implementation of Adams's pickup technology to provide airmail service to small towns in remote locations captured the spirit of the New Deal by conveying an image of aerial democracy. Strange as some of his ideas may seem today, du Pont was also a pioneer of the feeder line concept that was implemented by the CAB after the war to connect smaller communities with trunk line carriers operating out of large metropolitan airports. Fittingly, after being forced to abandon the airmail pickup technique in 1949 because improved ground delivery systems had made it uneconomical, All American became a successful feeder line serving the Mid-Atlantic region and later blossomed, first as Allegheny Airlines and then as USAir, into a major commercial carrier.

References:

W. David Lewis and William F. Trimble, *The Airway to Everywhere: A History of All American Aviation, 1937-1953* (Pittsburgh: University of Pittsburgh Press, 1988);

Paul A. Schweizer, *Wings Like Eagles: The Story of Soaring in the United States* (Washington, D.C. & London: Smithsonian Institution, 1988);

Page Shamburger, "All American Aviation," *American Aviation Historical Society Journal*, 9 (Fall 1964): 198-206;

Harry R. Stringer, ed., *A Headline History of the Air Pickup, 1939-1942, As Told in Selected Press and Magazine Articles and Photographs, Newspaper Captions and Public Documents* (Wilmington, Del. & Pittsburgh: All American Aviation, n.d.);

William F. Trimble, *High Frontier: A History of Aeronautics in Pennsylvania* (Pittsburgh: University of Pittsburgh Press, 1982).

Eastern Air Lines

by W. David Lewis

Auburn University

Eastern Air Lines, which was once the most profitable of all American trunk carriers but fell into bankruptcy in 1989, began as Pitcairn Aviation, Inc., organized in September 1927 by Harold Pitcairn, a member of a Pittsburgh family that had made a fortune in the plate glass industry. Together with airplane designer Agnew Larsen, Pitcairn had developed a racing plane known as the Fleetwing. Acquiring other aircraft, he established airfields, a flying school, and an aerial excursion service at Bryn Athyn and Willow Grove, Pennsylvania, near Philadelphia, beginning in 1924. By September 1927 his planes had carried more than 30,000 passengers, mostly in short flights.

Modifying his Fleetwings for airmail operations, Pitcairn developed a successful plane known as the Mailwing and won a contract from the Post Office Department in February 1928 to operate Contract Air Mail (CAM) route 19, from New York to Atlanta via Philadelphia, Baltimore, Washington, D.C., Richmond, and the Carolinas. Later that year Pitcairn consolidated this artery with CAM-10, running from Atlanta to Miami and previously operated by Florida Airways. The two formerly separate routes were now combined as CAM-25. Establishing fixed-base operations in connection with this mail route, Pitcairn also began scheduling passenger flights, starting with a shuttle between New York and Philadelphia in September 1928 and adding service to Baltimore and Washington in May 1929.

Fascinated by the prospects of rotary-wing aircraft, Pitcairn began manufacturing autogiros in 1929 under contract with the Spanish inventor Juan de la Cierva. In June of that year, he sold his mail, passenger, and fixed-base operations to Clement M. Keys, a Canadian-born entrepreneur. Keys had earlier secured control of the Curtiss Aeroplane and Motor Company and consolidated it with the Wright Aeronautical Corporation. Developing North American Aviation Corporation (NAAC) as

the operational arm of the resulting Curtiss-Wright Corporation, he had played an important role in forming two giants of the early commercial aviation industry, National Air Transport (NAT) and Transcontinental Air Transport (TAT). Administered by Thomas A. Doe, one of Keys's lieutenants, Pitcairn Aviation became a wholly owned subsidiary of NAAC and was renamed Eastern Air Transport (EAT) in January 1930.

Because of its big-business connections, EAT was one of the companies favored by Postmaster General Walter Folger Brown when he reshaped the nation's commercial air map in 1930 following passage of the Air Mail (Watres) Act in April of that year. Doe represented the firm at the so-called spoils conferences that were conducted in Washington by Brown to divide the nation's commercial air map among firms he favored. By the time these controversial meetings took place, however, Keys was already starting to lose power in the growing industry; not long before, William E. Boeing and Frederick B. Rentschler had wrested control of NAT from him in a Wall Street battle marking the emergence of United Air Lines as a transcontinental carrier.

Keys still controlled TAT and EAT, but was obliged to bend to various pressures from federal administrators during the spoils conferences. By forcing a merger between TAT, Western Air Express, and Pittsburgh Aviation Industries Corporation, which claimed important operating rights across Pennsylvania and had powerful connections with the Mellon family, Brown created Transcontinental and Western Air, Inc., to connect New York City and Los Angeles by way of a central route through Pittsburgh and St. Louis. EAT tried to gain a comparable southern artery through Atlanta and Dallas but failed because of a ruling by Comptroller General John McCarl that forbade granting a company an extension longer than its existing route. As a result, the passenger operations of Delta Air Serv-

Eastern Air Transport Curtiss T-32 Condor

ice, a small firm from which Eastern had hoped to acquire operating rights between Atlanta and Dallas-Ft. Worth, were instead secured by Southern Air Fast Express, a subsidiary of American Airways. The episode cast a long shadow upon the future, for Delta would later emerge once more as a passenger carrier and ultimately survive EAT's successor, Eastern Air Lines, in one of the classic wars in the entire history of American commercial aviation.

Despite failing to become a transcontinental line, EAT emerged from the spoils conferences as a highly favored enterprise. In 1931 Brown awarded it permanent certification for CAM-25, even though this involved rejection of a much lower bid by an airline headed by Charles T. Ludington, a Philadelphia aviation enthusiast, for the right to carry mail between New York City and Washington. Thanks to Brown's action, EAT continued to command a potentially lucrative vacation route from the heavily populated northeastern region to Florida. It consolidated this role in July 1931 by acquiring a former Pan American subsidiary, New York Airways, thereby gaining access to Atlantic City. In 1933 it also bought Ludington's airline, which was nearing bankruptcy after trying unsuccessfully to compete with Eastern on the New York-to-Washington route without a mail contract. EAT thus gained a virtual monopoly of air traffic along the eastern seaboard.

Having lost heavily in stock transactions resulting from the onset of the Great Depression, Keys was no longer in control of either NAAC or EAT by the time of the Ludington purchase. After he was forced to sell out in 1932, United Aircraft Corporation, the parent firm of United Air Lines, attempted to gain control of his former assets, but the move was successfully opposed by Brown because of the damaging effect it would have had upon competition within the airline industry. Instead, General Motors (GM) bought a controlling interest in NAAC in February 1933, thereby taking command of EAT. Ernest R. Breech, a GM executive, was placed in charge of NAAC while Doe remained president of EAT, which was operated as a division of the larger holding company.

In 1933 and 1934 a congressional committee headed by Alabama senator Hugo Black conducted a sensational investigation of alleged criminal misconduct by Brown in awarding airmail contracts. Brown's action in turning down Ludington's earlier bid in favor of EAT was an important factor leading to the probe. Hoping to embarrass the previous Hoover administration, President Franklin D. Roosevelt canceled existing airmail contracts, leading to an uproar when inexperienced army pilots suffered a series of fatal crashes flying the mail. Although no criminal acts on the part of Brown were proven, Black's inquest led to passage of an act forbidding the awarding of new airmail contracts to firms that

Eastern Air Lines Douglas DC-7B (courtesy of the National Air and Space Museum)

had participated in the 1930 spoils conferences, proscribing executives who had participated in the meetings from holding further positions in companies receiving such contracts, and prohibiting aircraft manufacturing firms from operating commercial airlines.

By cosmetically reorganizing under a slightly new name, Eastern Air Lines, EAT remained an airmail contractor, but Doe had to be jettisoned because he had attended Brown's conferences. Under a legal technicality, GM kept control of Eastern, and Breech temporarily assumed Doe's place. Discouraged by the line's failure to earn profits, he yielded operational control to World War I fighter ace Edward V. "Eddie" Rickenbacker in December 1934.

Under Rickenbacker's leadership, Eastern modernized its fleet, acquiring Douglas DC-2s and Lockheed Electras. Overcoming losses that had reached $1.5 million in 1934, the firm became modestly profitable. It expanded in 1936 by purchasing the Wedell-Williams Transport Corporation, gaining a route from New Orleans to Houston. In 1938 GM decided to detach Eastern from NAAC and sell

it. Initially, rental car magnate John Hertz was granted an option to acquire the airline, but Rickenbacker succeeded in organizing a syndicate of backers that submitted a higher bid and took control of the now independent enterprise. In the process, Rickenbacker moved from general manager to president.

As the airline industry prepared for the new regulatory order that was to come into effect under the recently enacted Civil Aeronautics Act of 1938, Eastern scored a coup by winning an airmail route from Houston to Brownsville, Texas, in a bitter battle with Braniff Airways, outbidding Braniff by offering to carry mail gratis. Under the "grandfather" provisions of the 1938 legislation, Eastern was confirmed in its possession of routes from New York-Newark to Miami and New Orleans and from Chicago to Florida. Additional route acquisitions to such places as Tampa, San Antonio, and St. Louis further swelled Eastern's system, which covered approximately 5,400 miles by 1940, making it the dominant carrier east of the Mississippi. Like most other trunk lines, the company adopted the Douglas DC-3 as the flagship of its "Great Silver Fleet." As passenger traffic multiplied, the firm's profits grew, exceeding $1.5 million in 1940.

During World War II, Eastern established a noteworthy Military Transport Division that carried cargo and armed services personnel from Miami to Puerto Rico, Trinidad, British Guiana, Brazil, and Accra in western Africa via Ascension Island. As planes and personnel were absorbed by the war effort, domestic operations shrank and service to such places as St. Louis was temporarily suspended. Late in the war years, however, the company won important new route awards from New York to Boston and St. Louis, gaining access to markets previously restricted to American Airlines. During much of the war, Rickenbacker himself surrendered day-to-day supervision to subordinates while conducting fact-finding tours for the War Department in such places as Great Britain, the South Pacific, China, and the Soviet Union. Having already narrowly escaped death in the crash of an Eastern DC-3 near Atlanta in 1941, he survived a harrowing 24 days with several companions on a raft in the Pacific Ocean late in 1942 after an aircraft in which he was flying to New Guinea became lost en route to Canton Island.

During the immediate postwar years, with Rickenbacker again in active command, Eastern was at the peak of its power and prosperity. While other carriers wallowed in red ink during a period of readjustment that bottomed out in 1947-1948, the line earned consistent profits. Nevertheless, the seeds of its later decline were already being sown. Even before the war ended, the Civil Aeronautics Board (CAB) broke Eastern's monopoly of vacation service on the East Coast by awarding National Airlines a route from Jacksonville to New York in February 1944. Early in 1946 this carrier began head-to-head competition with Eastern in nonstop Miami-New York operations. More significant for the future, however, was the emergence of Delta as a significant factor in markets previously controlled by Eastern. Having reentered passenger operations in 1934 by receiving a route from Dallas-Ft. Worth to Charleston, South Carolina, Delta had previously complemented Eastern's system by feeding passengers into such places as Birmingham and Atlanta. In 1945, however, the CAB awarded Delta a major vacation route from Chicago to Miami, breaking a former Eastern monopoly and making the two firms bitter rivals.

The dynamics of competition with Delta had much to do with Eastern's choice of aircraft in the postwar era. After Delta gained an initial advantage by introducing Douglas DC-4s on the Chicago-to-Miami route, Eastern countered with the same plane and subsequently raised the ante in 1947 by deploying pressurized Lockheed L-749 Constellations. When Delta in turn adopted the Douglas DC-6B, Eastern responded with stretched L-1049 Super Constellations, after which Delta acquired Douglas DC-7s. Meanwhile, Eastern narrowly averted a debacle by supporting the Glenn L. Martin Company in the development of a new twin-engined airliner for short-haul markets. After the initial plane in this series, the Martin 2-0-2, established a poor safety record when introduced by Northwest, Rickenbacker helped engineer a financial bailout that enabled Martin to develop a much better plane, the 4-0-4, which was used extensively by Eastern.

Although Eastern held its own with Delta and other competitors in the adoption of new equipment, it began to lose ground with Delta in a key aspect of utilization when the two lines differed in their response to new federal regulations mandating the use of three crew members in the cockpits of four-engined planes. While Eastern, along with many other carriers, employed flight engineers to occupy the third seat, Delta opted to use pilots who were trained as flight engineers but could be promoted to copilot and captain in due course. By taking this course, Delta avoided having members of two different unions in the cockpits of its planes and escaped labor disputes that later plagued Eastern.

After 1945 the CAB was much less generous to Eastern in new route awards, while continuing to strengthen its competitors. In 1948 the CAB admitted National to point-to-point service between Miami and New York. Late in 1955 Delta, which had recently grown much larger by acquiring Chicago and Southern in a merger, also won operating rights from Atlanta to New York via Charlotte, Washington, D.C., Baltimore, and Philadelphia. Although Eastern managed to secure such new destinations as San Juan from the CAB, and also commenced service to Mexico City in 1957 under a long-delayed bilateral agreement between the United States and Mexico, it was forced to turn to merger as its principal means of expansion. After a long battle with National, it finally succeeded in absorbing Colonial Airlines in 1956, giving it access to cities in the Middle Atlantic region and to such important foreign destinations as Bermuda and Montreal.

Eastern Lockheed L-188 Electra (courtesy of the National Air and Space Museum)

During the late 1950s and early 1960s, Eastern's competitive position deteriorated further. A series of strikes, connected in part to dissension in the cockpits of its planes between pilots and flight engineers, led to interruptions of service from which other carriers, especially Delta, profited. Poor passenger service resulted in the formation by disgruntled patrons of an organization known as WHEAL, an acronym for "We Hate Eastern Air Lines." Rickenbacker also erred in adopting a highly conservative position regarding the adoption of jet aircraft, opting for the turboprop Lockheed L-188 Electra and losing precious time in acquiring Douglas DC-8s by holding out for larger Pratt and Whitney JT-4 engines while Delta secured earlier deliveries by settling for smaller JT-3s. Although Eastern had the distinction of being the first airline to put the Electras into service in 1959 a series of crashes due to structural defects led federal authorities to impose speed restrictions pending extensive modifications. As a result, Delta gained significant speed advantages over Eastern by successfully introducing DC-8s and Convair 880s on routes shared by the two companies. Eastern also failed to secure long-haul transcontinental routes while both Delta and National won operating rights to the Pacific

Coast in 1961. As a result, Delta was able to optimize the cost benefits of jet transportation while Eastern, with a route system dominated by short hauls, could not.

Increasingly dissatisfied with Rickenbacker's performance, board chairman Laurance Rockefeller and other directors of the company began to force changes. In 1959 Malcolm A. MacIntyre, formerly a lawyer for American Airlines and undersecretary of the U.S. Air Force, became president and chief executive officer while Rickenbacker moved up to chairman of the board. MacIntyre made an outstanding contribution not only to Eastern but to American commercial aviation in general by spearheading the company's Air Shuttle service between New York City and Washington, providing cut-rate guaranteed service every two hours without requiring reservations. Thanks to this pioneering innovation, Eastern established a virtual monopoly of a highly strategic market.

Despite spearheading the shuttle and accelerating moves to acquire such jet aircraft as the Boeing 720 and 727, the latter of which was introduced into service by Eastern in 1964, MacIntyre could not overcome Eastern's chronic problems. He also suffered interference from Rickenbacker, who was temperamentally unable to relinquish control after heading the enterprise for so many years. Various difficulties, including Eastern's failure to win a transcontinental route from the CAB in 1961, an abortive attempt to merge with American, renewed labor difficulties, and an unsuccessful effort to extend the shuttle concept into the market between New York and Miami, further undermined confidence among Eastern's directors. Late in 1963 they sacked MacIntyre and forced Rickenbacker into retirement. Floyd Hall, who had been a senior vice-president at TWA, now took over as chief executive.

Inheriting five years of red ink, Hall swept out executives, installed new leadership, and instituted an ambitious program, "Operation Bootstrap," to improve revenues and passenger service by enhancing employee morale, optimizing on-time performance, providing enhanced in-flight amenities, and greatly accelerating the acquisition of new equipment, including Douglas DC-9 aircraft. Thanks to his efforts, WHEAL was disbanded in 1965. Eastern's image was also boosted by a $10 million investment through which the company became the "official airline" of Disney World, which was being built near Orlando.

Three years of improved financial performance ended in 1967 when Eastern began once more to lose money in the wake of renewed labor problems and the increasingly massive expenditures required to implement Hall's multifaceted programs. Hope for the future, however, was buoyed by important new route acquisitions that, for the first time, made the company a transcontinental carrier. In 1967 it won a route to Portland and Seattle via St. Louis, and in 1969 it received the long-coveted right to fly from Atlanta to Los Angeles. Through mergers in 1967 and 1971, Eastern also acquired Mackey Airlines, giving it access to the Bahamas, and purchased Caribair, a small Puerto Rico-based enterprise with markets in such places as Trinidad and the Virgin Islands.

Nevertheless, Eastern's difficulties continued to mount. In part because of its extensive Caribbean operations, it was plagued by hijacking to a greater degree than many other carriers. In addition, Hall himself began to suffer from poor health. In 1968, while continuing as chief executive officer, he became chairman of the board and secured the ap-

pointment of Arthur Lewis, a senior vice-president who had earlier headed Hawaiian Airlines, as president. Disagreements between Hall and Lewis, however, led the latter to resign before the end of the year, after which Samuel Higginbottom, a former TWA administrator who had taken charge of maintenance at Eastern in 1964, became president and chief operating officer. Exacerbated by the existence within the company of two headquarters, a financial one in New York City and an operational one in Miami, tensions grew within the enterprise. In part, the infighting was connected with aircraft selection as wide-bodied jet aircraft came into use. After briefly considering the Boeing 747, Eastern chose the Lockheed L-1011 Tristar, with unfortunate results. Besides experiencing serious technical difficulties with its Rolls-Royce RB-211 engines, the company suffered further embarrassment when an Eastern L-1011 crashed in the Everglades in December 1972, killing 98 of the 176 persons aboard. Late the following year, Higginbottom, who had favored the L-1011 and subsequently took a position with Rolls-Royce, resigned amid increasing disagreements with Hall over marketing policies and other matters. Moving to Miami, Hall now assumed full charge of the company.

Not long before, as Eastern's condition continued to deteriorate, Rickenbacker had passed from the scene. He died in Switzerland on July 23, 1973, from pneumonia and cardiac complications following an emergency operation in New York for an aneurysm. Grateful to Hall for kindnesses the latter had shown him in the difficult circumstances attending his forced retirement, he willed a treasured hat that he had worn while marooned on the raft in 1942 to Eastern's current chief executive, apparently as a symbolic token of Hall's leadership of the airline Rickenbacker had loved so much.

Hall, however, could not reverse the company's continuing downward slide. As its financial condition worsened and morale sagged, he and the directors pondered how best to relieve him of responsibilities he was obviously unable to bear. Their choice fell upon Frank Borman, an ex-astronaut who had been hired by Hall as vice-president of maintenance in 1970 after serving as a technical consultant to the firm. Promoted to vice-president for operations after six months on the job, he had been loyal to Hall despite being dismayed by the way in which the company was run, and had attracted favorable attention from Walter

Boeing 727-100

Hitesman, a new director who had been assigned by Laurance Rockefeller to prepare a confidential report on the reasons underlying Eastern's persistent malaise. On May 25, 1975, Borman was named president and chief operating officer.

Borman moved swiftly to deal with Eastern's problems, imposing upon it a strict discipline derived from his years of military experience. Despite Hall's desire to continue as board chairman, Borman forced him to retire. Convincing union leaders that the company's plight was desperate, Borman negotiated a wage freeze with Eastern's workers by promising them profit-sharing in return under a "Variable Earnings Plan" (VEP). After commissioning an independent study by aviation consultant R. Dixon Speas, Borman ruthlessly trimmed the executive hierarchy he had inherited from Hall, recruited new managerial talent, and concentrated all aspects of the company's operations in Miami. Appearing personally in television commercials, he launched an aggressive advertising campaign to give Eastern a dynamic new image. Convinced that the company must phase out obsolete equipment as rapidly as possible, he negotiated the acquisition of 23 Airbus A-300 planes under highly advantageous terms. Not long thereafter, Eastern acquired a substantial number of Boeing 757s.

Under Borman's administration, Eastern experienced four profitable years from 1976 through 1979, achieving total net earnings of nearly $198 million. By contrast, the company had lost approximately $114 million during the 15 years before he

took charge. After passage of the Airline Deregulation Act of 1978, however, Eastern's fortunes began once more to decline. Heavy fixed expenses, related to the enormous debts Borman had created by purchasing so many new planes, were partly responsible, as were high labor costs. Fearing that the company's recovery was still too fragile for it to compete effectively in a free market situation, Borman fought against enactment of the new legislation. After it became law, his misgivings were quickly justified. In 1980 a new and highly aggressive president, Charles Bryan, was elected by Eastern's district of the International Association of Machinists and Aerospace Workers (IAM); he quickly commenced a drive against the VEP, the results of which had been disappointing to workers. Meanwhile, Eastern was forced to slash prices in order to compete with other operators in the deregulated marketplace. In 1980 it suffered its first net loss, $17.3 million, in five years; in 1981 much more red ink flowed, producing a $66 million deficit.

Believing that Eastern could develop highly profitable Latin-American markets because of its Miami gateway, Borman purchased Braniff's South American routes as that carrier skidded toward bankruptcy. In 1982, however, Eastern incurred a further deficit of nearly $75 million. Meanwhile, the VEP was replaced, under pressure from the IAM, by an "Employee Investment Program," requiring the company to guarantee repayment with interest of employee withholdings that had been subject to fluctuating returns under the previous plan. In

1983, bowing to further IAM demands because of his conviction that the company could not survive a strike, Borman agreed to a 32.2 percent pay raise, but subsequently negotiated a substantial cut in labor costs for 1984 in exchange for an agreement putting four representatives from Eastern's various unions on the company's board of directors. Securing a last-minute extension of this contract through 1985 and inaugurating an overnight cargo operation known as the "Moonlight Special" in the spring of that year, Eastern began once more earning modest profits, only to be rocked by renewed fare wars that reduced the net gain to $6.3 million by the end of the year.

By early 1986 Eastern was locked in another round of contract discussions with union leaders. Partly because of Borman's tendency to predict bankruptcy to labor while issuing optimistic forecasts to lending institutions, he had lost credibility with workers by this time. Pointing out that the company was once again in the black, Bryan refused to accept a 20 percent cut in labor costs demanded by Borman. When last-minute negotiations collapsed, Borman and a majority of the directors decided on the morning of February 24, 1986, to sell the airline to Frank Lorenzo, who, after acquiring Continental Airlines in 1981, had dealt with similar labor problems by taking that carrier into Chapter 11 bankruptcy.

Adding Eastern to the transportation empire controlled by his Texas Air holding company, Lorenzo began a policy of calculated harassment of the company's labor unions, and also began mobilizing funds with which to survive a strike into which he hoped to force Bryan's machinists when their contract expired in 1987. While refusing Lorenzo's terms, Bryan refrained from calling a strike, and federal administrator Walter C. Wallace of the National Mediation Board (NMB) declined to certify the existence of an impasse that would have forced a walkout to take place within 30 days. As the stalemate continued and Eastern's financial situation deteriorated, Lorenzo was forced to liquidate assets in order to keep the company solvent. Selling aircraft and reducing the company's work force by an estimated 25 percent, he also tried to dispose of its shuttle service, but was temporarily blocked when union leaders took him to court. Meanwhile, deficits continued to mount; in 1988 Eastern lost a record $335 million.

As the airline's plight became more and more desperate, its unions tried to orchestrate a buyout, offering to trade future wage cuts and other concessions for Lorenzo's departure. Although several potential bidders were courted, including Carl Icahn of TWA, nothing came of these moves. Frustrated, the unions launched a media campaign against Lorenzo that succeeded in weakening his public image. After renewed efforts to find a buyer for the firm had fallen through, Wallace formally intervened as a federal mediator in the deadlocked situation between Eastern and the IAM. When talks to resolve the issues failed, Wallace set the NMB's 30-day clock in motion, and the strike that Lorenzo had been seeking for so long finally materialized early in March 1989. Hoping to crush it by staying in operation with substitute mechanics, Lorenzo was foiled when most of the company's pilots and flight attendants refused to cross IAM picket lines. As a result, operations were drastically cut. On March 9 Lorenzo took the company into Chapter 11 bankruptcy.

Well before the walkout, investors had been trying to organize a buyout of Eastern under which former baseball commissioner Peter V. Ueberroth would assume leadership of the company. These efforts were now intensified, and a widely publicized deal was worked out under the prodding of Washington attorney David I. Shapiro, who had been appointed to supervise the process by federal bankruptcy judge Burton R. Lifland. Although Eastern's unions agreed to the plan, Lorenzo stymied it by refusing to appoint a trustee to administer the company until the takeover was finalized, and remained in charge of the bankrupt enterprise under receivership. Continuing to strip Eastern of its assets in order to maintain severely shrunken levels of service, Lorenzo sold the firm's northeastern corridor shuttle—its only really profitable remaining operation—to New York financier Donald Trump for an estimated $350 million, and raised another $450 million by selling off an assortment of planes, gates, and routes.

Meanwhile, Lorenzo and his associates set forth a survival plan that involved liquidating yet more properties, such as its South American routes, in order to satisfy its creditors and stay in operation as a much smaller airline with Atlanta as its hub. Eastern's boardings in that city, however, fell from 8.3 million in 1986 to 4.3 million in 1989, while Delta's blossomed from 11.5 million to 14.3

million in the same period. Despite desperately slashing fares to attract customers, Eastern incurred further huge deficits, losing more than $800 million in 1989. As creditors became convinced that they would not receive more than a minor fraction of their claims, Lifland finally removed Lorenzo from power in April 1990 and appointed Martin R. Shugrue, Jr., whom Lorenzo had earlier fired as president of Continental Airlines, to take charge as trustee. Shortly afterward, the company sold its South American routes, reducing it to little more than the small, regional enterprise it had been half a century before.

Pledging to make Eastern "a little better every day," Shugrue launched a "100 day campaign" to improve service, win back passengers, and avoid liquidation. By September, however, the company was still losing more than $1 million per day and was projecting a loss of more than $500 million for the year. Having disposed of approximately $1.5 billion in assets since entering bankruptcy in 1989, it had little more to sell to keep it in the air, and faced mounting fuel costs in the wake of the diplomatic and military crisis that had broken out in the Persian Gulf. Owing $672 million to secured creditors and another $1.2 billion in unsecured obligations, its future was bleak. On January 18, 1991, Eastern issued a public statement that it would stop flying at midnight and announced plans to "sell off its planes and other assets," terminating the tragic life of what had once been America's most profitable air carrier. The *New York Times* called it "by far the largest casualty of the pressures brought by the deregulation of the industry 13 years ago."

References:

Aaron Bernstein, *Grounded: Frank Lorenzo and the Destruction of Eastern Airlines* (New York: Simon & Schuster, 1990);

Frank Borman, with Robert J. Serling, *Countdown: An Autobiography* (New York: Morrow, 1988);

R. E. G. Davies, *Airlines of the United States since 1914*, revised edition (Washington, D.C.: Smithsonian Institution, 1982);

"Eastern Airlines Is Shutting Down and Plans to Liquidate Its Assets," *New York Times*, January 19, 1991, pp. 1, 48;

"Eastern Airlines: 100 Days and Still Flying," *USA Today*, September 12, 1990, p. 7B;

Michael Ennis, "Sky King," *Business Month*, 131 (September 1988): 26-29, 32-34;

Mark Ivey and Gail De George, "Lorenzo May Land A Little Short of the Runway," *Business Week* (February 5, 1990): 46-48;

Edward V. Rickenbacker, *Rickenbacker: An Autobiography* (Greenwich, Conn.: Fawcett, 1969);

Robert J. Serling, *From the Captain to the Colonel: An Informal History of Eastern Air Lines* (New York: Dial, 1980);

Stratford P. Sherman, "Eastern Air Lines on the Brink," *Fortune*, 108 (October 17, 1983): 102-109;

Alfred P. Sloan, Jr., *My Years with General Motors* (Garden City, N.Y.: Doubleday Anchor, 1963);

William F. Trimble, *High Frontier: A History of Aeronautics in Pennsylvania* (Pittsburgh: University of Pittsburgh Press, 1982).

Robert E. Ellis

(January 2, 1903 -   )

by Claus-M. Naske

University of Alaska Fairbanks

CAREER: Pilot, southeast Alaska (1929-1935); president, Ellis Air Transport/Ellis Air Lines (1936-1962); vice-president for sales, Alaska Coastal-Ellis Air Lines (1962-1968); director, Alaska Airlines (1968-1981).

Robert Edmund Ellis was born on January 2, 1903, in St. Albans, Vermont, the son of Charles H. and Mathilde E. Deschenes Ellis. He attended local schools in St. Albans. In 1919 Ellis entered the U.S. Naval Academy, but he resigned after two years and moved to Seattle, Washington, where he worked in the lumber export business. He joined the naval reserves in 1926, learned to fly the next year, and was commissioned an ensign in 1928.

In April 1929 Ellis served as navigator on an Alaska Washington Airways Lockheed Vega, flown by Anscel Eckmann, that made the first nonstop flight from Seattle to Juneau (in 7 hours and 33 minutes). He remained in Alaska, flying for several small airlines and charter companies. In 1930 he married Margaret E. Roehr; the couple had three children.

Ellis decided to go into business for himself in 1936 and established Ellis Air Transport at Ketchikan in southeast Alaska. Using a single-engine Waco cabin monoplane, he began service with a fisheries charter to Bristol Bay. Later in the year he inaugurated a regular schedule to Prince of Wales Island.

Operating a combination of scheduled and charter services, Ellis Air Transport soon became a vital part of the region's life. Whether flying a doctor to a remote wilderness community for a medical emergency or carrying band members to a concert, Ellis Air Transport provided a reliable means of reaching areas in hours that otherwise would take days. Unfortunately, profits failed to

Robert E. Ellis (portrait by Harvey Goodale; courtesy of the Robert C. Reeve Collection)

match the level of gratitude that was expressed by the people of southeast Alaska.

In 1941 Ellis was recalled to active duty. He served with the navy in Alaska during World War II, keeping an eye on the progress of his company. Released from military service, in November 1945 he purchased a Navy Grumman Goose in Georgia, which he flew to Ketchikan. Following modifications, the aircraft entered service in 1946 with a renamed Ellis Air Lines.

Ellis Air Lines made noteworthy progress over the next decade. In 1955 the airline had 100 employees, 13 airplanes including 9 Grummans, and flew 56,000 passengers. It operated routes from Ketchikan to Juneau via Wrangell and Petersburg, and Ketchikan to Sitka via Edna Bay and other island communities. Ellis Air Lines also flew a shuttle service to Annette, and it operated an international route to Prince Rupert, British Columbia.

In addition to his airline duties, Ellis became active in politics. He served as mayor of Ketchikan from 1947 to 1949 and as territorial senator from 1955 to 1959.

In 1962 Ellis Air Lines merged with Alaska Coastal Airlines, a larger company that operated similar routes from Juneau. Alaska Coastal brought 16 aircraft and 150 employees to the new Alaska Coastal-Ellis Air Lines, while Ellis contributed 9 air-

craft and 100 employees. Shell Simmons of Alaska Coastal became president of the company, and Ellis took over as vice-president for sales.

Six years later the company merged with Alaska Airlines. Ellis served on the board of directors of Alaska Airlines until 1981, when he retired to Ellis Island in Ward Cove, Alaska.

Publication:
What ... No Landing Field? (Haines, Alaska: Lynn Canal Publishing Co., 1969).

References:
Archie Satterfield, *The Alaska Airlines Story* (Anchorage: Alaska Northwest Publishing Co., 1981);

Satterfield and Lloyd Jarman, *Alaska Bush Pilots in the Float Country* (New York: Bonanza Books, 1969);

Faith Sherman, *Goodbye Goose: The Story of Ellis Air Lines* (Tygh Valley, Oreg.: Privately published, 1981).

Federal Aviation Administration

by Edmund Preston

Washington, D.C.

The mission of the Federal Aviation Administration (FAA) is to ensure the safety of civil aviation and to promote aeronautics and air commerce. In pursuit of these interrelated goals, the agency engages in a broad range of programs. It operates a national system of air traffic control and air navigation used by both civil and military aviators. The FAA makes and enforces safety rules and issues certificates required for airmen, aircraft, and air carriers. Among its other activities are aviation security regulation, international assistance, and the promotion of a national airport system.

The FAA has had several predecessors since the federal government first began to regulate civil aeronautics in 1926. In the period immediately preceding the agency's creation, most aviation responsibilities were divided between two organizations. The Civil Aeronautics Board handled economic regulation and safety-rule making, while the Civil Aviation Administration enforced the safety rules and operated the air traffic control system. During the 1950s, however, an increase in air traffic

and the expected introduction of jet transports created a demand for a single powerful organization uniting all the principal safety-related functions. The result was the Federal Aviation Act of 1958, which established a Federal Aviation Agency to be headed by an administrator reporting directly to the president. The new FAA assumed the responsibilities of the Civil Aeronautics Administration, as well as the safety-rule-making function of the Civil Aeronautics Board (which remained an economic regulator until phased out of existence during the five years following 1978).

The first administrator of the FAA was Elwood R. Quesada, a former air force general who conducted a vigorous safety campaign and presided over a great expansion of personnel and facilities. Quesada's policy of concentrating program authority within Washington headquarters was reversed under his successor, Najeeb E. Halaby, who adopted the decentralized pattern of operation that the agency was to retain for over a quarter century. The last administrator to head an independent FAA was William F. McKee, another air force general, during whose tenure the last word of the agency's name was changed to "Administration." This change occurred on April 1, 1967, when the agency became one of several model organizations within the newly created Department of Transportation.

Events since the passage of the Federal Aviation Act have added to the scope of the FAA's activities. In the 1960s, for example, the rise of air piracy as a significant threat to U.S. aviation involved the agency in combating this crime. Since December 1972 the FAA has regulated an airport security program under which airline personnel screen boarding passengers to detect concealed weapons, and the agency has subsequently required other procedures to deter hijacking and sabotage. In 1968 the FAA was empowered to set noise standards for aircraft, an authority subsequently used to require the phaseout of first-generation jet airliners that were not modified for quieter operations. Under legislation enacted in 1970, the FAA began setting minimum safety standards for air carrier airports. At the same time, Congress set up a trust fund, supported by user taxes, from which the agency makes grants for airport improvements. In 1987, however, the FAA lost one of its longstanding functions when two major airports serving the national capital area were transferred from its control to that of a regional authority.

In terms of personnel and resources, the most demanding of the FAA's responsibilities is the national airspace system. Besides maintaining equipment to assist navigation and landing, the agency operates three main types of facilities to assure the separation of aircraft in flight. En route flights are controlled from Air Route Traffic Control Centers, of which there are 20 in the contiguous United States. Aircraft approaching a major airport come into contact with Terminal Radar Approach Control Facilities, known as TRACONs. In the immediate terminal area, they become the responsibility of the Air Traffic Control Tower. In addition, Flight Service Stations provide weather briefings and other services, primarily to nonairline pilots.

When federal air traffic control began in 1936, controllers estimated the positions of aircraft with the aid of blackboards, maps, and movable markers. By the time of FAA's creation, they were using a second-generation system based upon radar. In the 1960s the FAA began introducing a third generation of equipment that employed computer tech-

nology to automate some of the controllers' tasks and to provide important information about the aircraft appearing as targets on their radarscopes. Increasing traffic made further improvements necessary, and additional features that predict hazards and provide warnings were subsequently introduced. In 1988 the FAA completed the deployment of Host Computer Systems, designed to increase the capacity of the existing system while laying the foundation for even higher levels of automation. In addition to air traffic control improvements, the FAA's research and development program has pursued such varied goals as new systems for the detection of hazardous weather, better understanding of human factors in aviation safety, and the perfection of an airborne collision warning device.

Perhaps the most fundamental aspect of the FAA's work is to ensure that safety standards are met through the process of certification. Persons wishing to become pilots must pass written and flight examinations appropriate to the type of certificate and rating they desire. To maintain their status, they must remain able to pass flight checks, as well as physical examinations conducted by FAA-designated private physicians. The FAA also certificates airline dispatchers, aircraft mechanics, and flight instructors. In addition, airlines and flight schools must demonstrate their ability to meet safety standards before receiving an operating certificate, and are subject to a continuing program of inspection.

In the case of aircraft certification, FAA engineers work with factory engineers to ensure that a new design meets safety standards. The award of a Type Certificate is followed by issuance of a Production Certificate once the manufacturer demonstrates the ability to maintain quality control. Each individual aircraft must then receive an Airworthiness Certificate before entering service, and operators must obtain FAA approval before making modifications that might affect safety. The agency issues Airworthiness Directives and/or regulations whenever new information indicates that the interests of safety demand changes in equipment, aircraft structure, or flight procedures. (Such insights are often derived from accident analyses conducted by the FAA or by the independent National Transportation Safety Board, which has primary responsibility for investigating accidents.) FAA inspectors examine both private and commercial aircraft to check their ongoing compliance with airworthiness standards.

At the close of fiscal 1989, the FAA had 49,000 full-time, permanent employees, approximately 2,500 of whom worked at the Washington headquarters. About 3,200 employees worked at the Mike Monroney Aeronautical Center, a depot and training facility at Oklahoma City, and over 1,100 more were employed at the FAA Technical Center, a research and testing installation near Atlantic City, New Jersey. Nearly all of the other personnel were assigned to offices and facilities grouped within six regions. Under a reorganization begun in 1988, the directors of these regions were retitled regional administrators and deprived of some of their former authority. The agency began the "straightlining" of program control from Washington headquarters to the field, with the objective of achieving more efficient and uniform operations.

More than 16,000 of the FAA's employees at the end of fiscal 1989 were air traffic controllers. In the 1960s discontent within this key element of the agency's work force led to its organization by the Professional Air Traffic Controllers Organization and to a widespread "sickout" in 1970. After a period of relative harmony, labor friction began again and culminated in 1981 with President Ronald Reagan's dismissal of over 12,000 controllers for participating in an illegal strike. The agency continued to operate the airspace system but for a time was obliged to impose severe restrictions on air traffic. The FAA subsequently rebuilt the system, then expanded its capacity to handle the great increase in air travel encouraged by the phasing out of airline economic regulation.

References:

Arnold E. Briddon and others, *FAA Historical Fact Book* (Washington, D.C.: U.S. Department of Transportation, 1974);

Federal Aviation Administration, "Federal Aviation Administration," undated pamphlet;

Federal Aviation Administration, "This Is the FAA," draft pamphlet, 1990;

Richard J. Kent, Jr., *Safe, Separated, and Soaring: A History of Federal Civil Aviation Policy, 1961-1972* (Washington, D.C.: U.S. Department of Transportation, 1974);

Nick A. Komons and others, "Aviation's Indispensable Partner Turns 50," Federal Aviation Administration pamphlet, 1986;

Edmund Preston, *Troubled Passage: The Federal Aviation Administration During the Nixon-Ford Term, 1973-1977* (Washington, D.C.: U.S. Department of Transportation, 1987);

Stuart I. Rochester, *Takeoff at Mid-Century: Federal Civil Aviation Policy in the Eisenhower Years, 1953-1961* (Washington, D.C.: U.S. Department of Transportation, 1976).

Federal Express

by Dominick A. Pisano

National Air and Space Museum

Although the idea of air express was introduced in November 1910, when Philip O. Parmalee transported ten bolts of silk from Dayton to Columbus for the Morehouse-Martens Company, it took until 1973 for the concept to mature into a major business enterprise. It was then that Frederick W. Smith demonstrated the advantages of an air express door-to-door package service operating from a geographically central hub. The company was called Federal Express, and it was so successful that it quickly spawned several imitators and competitors.

Incorporated on June 1, 1971, Federal Express originally was based in Little Rock, Arkansas, the home of Arkansas Aviation, a firm owned by Smith that bought and sold used jet aircraft. He later moved the company to his home town of Memphis, Tennessee. Using the Memphis facility as the core of the Federal Express system of sorting and distribution, Smith began flying to 22 cities in April 1973, using Dassault Falcon business jets.

Following the deregulation of the air cargo industry in 1977, Federal Express grew rapidly. Deregulation enabled the company to expand both domestically and internationally, using such larger aircraft as Boeing 727s and McDonnell Douglas DC-10s. Today it claims to provide direct service to nearly the entire population of the United States, flying to 303 airports throughout the country.

The concept behind the Federal Express system is simple. Mail and packages are sorted at night at the Memphis facility during a critical two-hour period, then placed on aircraft for delivery the next day. Every working day, the company delivers more than one and a half million items in 126 countries around the world. The company also makes worldwide use of some 29,000 vehicles, each equipped with a radio and a computer, and has more than 1,550 staffed offices and 25,000 drop-off points.

Using a sophisticated network of computers and telecommunications, Federal Express is capable of tracking each package it ships. Company personnel use small hand-held computers called "Supertrackers" to monitor the movement of shipments through the system. The information is relayed to computers which are connected with "Powership" terminals located in the offices of the company's customers. This network allows the customers to know the whereabouts of a shipment anywhere in the world 24 hours a day.

Federal Express, which reached $1 billion in revenues in 1983, became the world's leading small-package carrier. In 1988 it grew even larger with the acquisition of the giant Flying Tigers air freight line. Following the merger of the two companies in 1989, Federal Express recorded a total operating revenue of $6.4 billion for the year, ranking it below only American, United, and Delta.

References:

R. E. G. Davies, "The History of Air Express in the United States," SAE Technical Paper Series no. 840706, 1984;

Robert A. Sigafoos and Roger R. Easson, *Absolutely Positively Overnight: The Unofficial Corporate History of Federal Express* (Memphis, Tenn.: St. Luke's Press, 1988);

Robert Sobel and David B. Sicilia, *The Entrepreneurs: An American Adventure* (Boston: Houghton Mifflin, 1986).

Flight Attendant Labor Organizations

by Georgia Panter Nielsen

San Jose, California

Well into the mid 20th century, only attractive, slender, unmarried and childless women could be employed or remain employed as stewardesses on most airlines in the United States. Some carriers permitted a pregnant, unwed stewardess to keep her job if she had an illegal abortion or gave her baby up for adoption. Despite the existence of rigidly enforced—often unwritten—rules that governed the personal lives of stewardesses, the industry could rely on waiting lists of hundreds of young women who were eager to fill vacancies.

Called sky girls, the stewardess group was taken seriously as a work force by practically no one. "The stewardess was an important part of our culture," recalled John Hill, a lawyer retired from United Air Lines. "This was not a working woman; this was a glamour job." A male passenger, traveling from Boston to San Francisco on United Air Lines in the mid 1960s, went further, commenting that "stewardesses are America's vestal virgins."

The nation's first commercial airlines were men's territory. Pilots were expected to take care of the mail, not look after the needs of the few intrepid air travelers who might be crammed into the mail compartment. With the appearance of larger aircraft that could accommodate passengers in the cabin, a few fledgling airlines experimented with male flight attendants or stewards to help the busy pilots. Stewards often loaded baggage, ticketed passengers, and provided in-flight services that might include dispensing chewing gum for ear discomfort and serving sandwiches and beverages. In one instance, the New England & Western Air Transportation Company, which operated in Massachusetts and New York during the summer of 1930, hired black men to work as "Pullman porters" on their planes.

The position of flight attendant remained largely undefined until Ellen Church entered the aviation industry in 1930. A registered nurse who had learned to fly, Church approached Steve Stimpson

Ada Brown and Frances Hall during negotiations that led to the establishment of the Air Line Stewardesses Association in 1945 (courtesy of the Association of Flight Attendants)

of Boeing Air Transport and asked for a job as a pilot. Instead, Stimpson and Church created a stewardessing occupation for registered nurses. Stimpson tried to sell his idea of a nurse-stewardess to his superiors, citing the national publicity that would result. William A. Patterson, assistant to the president of Boeing Air Transport, decided to embark on what others in the airline industry considered a daring experiment. He gave his approval to hire eight nurses to work as stewardesses on a three-month trial basis. On May 15, 1930, at 8 A.M., a Boeing trimotor left Oakland for Chicago with Ellen Church on board as the first female crew member in a commercial airline.

Although some pilots complained that they were too busy to look after a helpless—and useless—female, passengers applauded the experiment. The industry soon realized the marketing potential of having females on the nation's airliners. In an era when most people were apprehensive about the safety of flying, the fact that young women routinely took to the skies served to encourage otherwise reluctant air travelers.

The airlines quickly promoted a glamorous image of stewardessing. For William Patterson, who became the president of United Air Lines, the successor company to Boeing Air Transport, stewardesses had a special aura. As his associate John Hill recalled: "My God, it was an honor to be a stewardess. United had started the profession of stewardessing and they were proud of it."

The reality of the job belied the emerging public perception of the sky girl. From the beginning there were complaints about working conditions and salaries. Jesse Carter, one of the original eight stewardesses hired by Boeing, quit after two months of flying. The job was unexciting, she pointed out, and the unpressurized airplanes caused her ears to ache. Above all, she was flying about 100 hours a month and making only $125. Inez Keller, also hired as one of the original stewardesses, left after four months, complaining that the flight from Oakland to Cheyenne, which was supposed to take 18 hours, usually took 24 exhausting hours to complete.

Although the well-designed DC-3, which made its debut in 1936, could fly coast-to-coast with only four or five stops, the flight attendant's work load increased enormously. The situation grew worse during World War II. In 1942, for example, United Air Lines carried more passengers more miles with half as many planes as it used in 1941. The military's wartime need for nurses also forced the airlines to abandon the requirement that stewardesses have medical expertise.

As World War II began to wind down, many stewardesses felt that they were forgotten workers. While pilots began to negotiate for higher wages and improved working conditions, flight attendants with United Air Lines made the same base pay of $125 a month that they had earned in 1930. Furthermore, there was no provision for maximum monthly hours of flying.

Despite the many problems, a union for stewardesses seemed out of the question. Coming from white, middle-class families, stewardesses generally were unsympathetic toward unions. They considered themselves to be elite temporary workers, viewing their job as something to enjoy before getting married and raising a family. At the same time, established unions did not consider flight attendants an attractive target for organization. Their low wages would not generate much income for dues. Also, prevailing ideas suggested that female labor was short-term and undependable. Finally, government reg-ulations did not require airlines to carry cabin atten-dants. In the event of a strike, airlines could either train personnel to replace stewardesses within a few days or do what Eastern Air Lines had done in 1934 and dispatch planes without them.

Ada Brown, a nurse-stewardess for United Air Lines, began the arduous task of forming the first flight attendant union in 1944. Hired in 1940, Brown had flown as a stewardess, then accepted a su-pervisory position. She attempted to improve the sta-tus of flight attendants, but met only frustration. "I tried to get improvements for the girls with salary, flight regulations, and protection from unjust firing," she recalled. "We were always promised things, but nothing was ever done." On December 16, 1944, she left her management position and re-turned to flying the line for the specific purpose of or-ganizing a union.

Brown appointed herself as the organizer at United's San Francisco base, then recruited Sally Thometz at Denver, Frances Hall at Chicago, and Sally Watt at Portland and Seattle to "sign them up for a union." Operating openly, Brown knew that she "had to be quick" due to the high turnover of stewardesses, who averaged a nine-month tenure. Edith Lauterbach, who worked in the organizing ef-fort, remembered that many stewardesses balked at the idea of joining a labor organization that they as-sociated with blue-collar workers. In an effort to neu-tralize this bias, Brown quickly dropped the word "union" and substituted "association." Thus was born the new Air Line Stewardesses Association (ALSA).

Within two months Brown and her inexperi-enced volunteers had signed up 75 percent of United's 300 stewardesses, written a constitution and bylaws for the association, and elected five offi-cers (all of whom had been organizers). Concur-rently, the women drew up a proposed contract to present to United and initiated organizing efforts on other airlines, including Braniff, Continental, and Western.

The women of ALSA soon began negotiations with United for a union contract. Although skepti-cal at first about sitting down at the bargaining table with females, United's management quickly re-alized that the union leaders were serious, espe-cially over the issue of limiting monthly flight hours. Finally, after some tough negotiating, United and ALSA signed a contract on April 25, 1946

(backdated to be effective on January 1, 1946). Every word of this landmark agreement broke new ground. The union secured the first increase in base wage since 1930, a limit of 85 flight hours a month (which became the industry standard), and a griev-ance procedure. Nothing was done to mitigate the airline's—and the industry's—unyielding practices of firing women for becoming married, pregnant, older, or overweight. These matters seemed beyond the scope of collective bargaining.

The founders of the first flight attendant associ-ation envisioned an affiliated union, governed and administered by flight attendants from all the na-tion's air carriers. Ada Brown, who fell victim to the no-marriage rule at age thirty in 1947, cau-tioned in her farewell address that it would be "un-wise to remain independent" and "essential to have the power that a national union could offer." Accord-ingly, on December 2, 1949, the United flight atten-dants merged their independent ALSA with the larger Air Line Stewards and Stewardesses Associa-tion (ALSSA), which had been formed in 1946 by the Air Line Pilots Association (ALPA).

By the time ALSSA held its first convention in June 1951, an impressive organizational drive by the pilots' union had signed up approximately 3,300 flight attendants on 13 trunk airlines and 11 feeder lines. ALSSA had negotiated more than 55 contractual agreements and other related docu-ments between 18 airlines and their flight atten-dants.

Meanwhile other events contributed to im-prove the position of flight attendants. In 1951 an amendment to the Railway Labor Act enabled unions to negotiate terms for collection of dues from workers represented by the union. This gave ALSSA the ability to collect dues from a work force composed primarily of women with a high attrition rate caused by no-marriage rules. The following year a new civil air regulation required airlines to carry flight attendants aboard their aircraft for rea-sons of safety.

ALSSA's delegates at their first convention called upon the union's officers to obtain certifica-tion or government licensing of flight attendants, negotiate union shops, and petition for an indepen-dent charter from the American Federation of Labor. All three demands conflicted with the priori-ties of the Air Line Pilots Association. The result was a decade of bitter fighting. The problems grew worse with the advent of the jet age at the end of

Steve Stimpson, who originated the idea of employing registered nurses as flight attendants in 1930, with United Air Lines stewardesses in uniforms illustrating the history of flight-attendant fashion (courtesy of the National Air and Space Museum)

the 1950s. For flight attendants the new airplanes signaled a deterioration in work rules; they wanted a reduction in flight hours. The pilots, already in a dispute with flight engineers over the coveted cockpit jobs, pressured the flight attendants to abandon their demand for reduced hours. The always fragile affiliation between pilots and flight attendants threatened to disintegrate.

Pressured by the parent American Federation of Labor, ALPA tried to maintain ALSSA as an umbrella organization. At the same time, the Transport Workers of America (which had affiliated Pan American's flight attendants in 1946) challenged ALPA for the right to represent the cabin crews. In 1961 and 1962, voters in 29 elections involving over 8,700 flight attendants tried to settle the matter of representation. Flight attendants with the large regional carriers decided to remain with ALSSA, but as locals of the Transport Workers Union. The stew-

ardesses (and a few Hawaiian stewards) of United Air Lines, the largest U.S. air carrier, along with cabin attendants from 19 other airlines voted to go with ALPA's newly created Steward and Stewardess (S & S) Division.

A "separate but equal" structure within ALPA housed the S & S Division during the 1960s. Although certainly separate, the division hardly was equal. As long as the pilots outnumbered the stewards and stewardesses, which they did at the time, there seemed little threat that the flight attendants ever would gain much power in the union. At their conventions the pilots paid little attention to the women who represented the S & S Division, segregating them in a manner reminiscent of the treatment of women in medieval churches.

Meanwhile the changing social mores of society during the 1960s forecast a change in status for women in the United States. The enactment of Title

VII of the Civil Rights Act of 1964 gave flight attendants a weapon to attack the discriminatory restrictions which airlines imposed upon women. No-marriage rules, weight restrictions, pregnancy taboos, and age limitations for female flight attendants could be attacked through Title VII. Indeed, the anticipation of class-action suits based on Title VII prompted most airlines to relax their discriminatory practices through collective bargaining. United Air Lines was a notable exception; it remained committed to its no-marriage policy. This led to one of the largest class-action suits ever brought in the United States. Over 1,500 claimants sought reinstatement with the airline, while thousands of subsequently hired flight attendants fought to retain their seniority. Litigation over job entitlements, remedies, and seniority dragged on for more than ten years.

In the early 1960s ALPA's pilots had referred to the "stewardess problem." Ten years later it had become simply "the problem," as the introduction of jumbo jets caused flight attendant ranks to reach unprecedented levels. Under the structure of the union, the S & S Division could influence the election of ALPA's president. Now that flight attendants had the numbers to exert real power, the pilots wanted them out. Even those who wished to maintain a close relationship with the S & S Division advocated a change in ALPA's constitution to insure continued control by the pilots.

Many flight attendants also argued for autonomy. Kelley Rueck, leader of the S & S Division in 1972, had to deal with a variety of views. While some leaders wanted a complete break with the pilots, others were content with the status quo. A sizable number wanted an independent status that would be acceptable both to pilots and flight attendants. Many of the same emotional elements that had deeply split the rank and file during the early 1960s debate on reaffiliation were again present. Sentiment ranged from the militancy of the Continental Airlines flight attendants, who wanted "a showdown with the pilots," to the more moderate views of the representatives of United, the union's largest carrier.

Rueck knew that the financially weak S & S Division needed access to an effective and efficient bureaucratic organization such as that which the pilots' union had developed. Possibilities for other union affiliations were explored, but the timing and circumstances did not favor a reunification of the S & S Division's 14,000 members with the 15,000

Continental Airlines flight attendant Cindy Benton conducting water evacuation practice (courtesy of the National Air and Space Museum)

members of the Air Line Steward and Stewardesses Association. (The ALSSA group would undergo an enormous upheaval in the late 1970s with the majority of members taking radical steps for independence.)

Painstaking discussions over the next three years between ALPA and the S & S Division eventually led to the formation of the Association of Flight Attendants (AFA). The organizational structure of the new group was officially approved on December 27, 1973. The affiliation agreement provided for a gradual progression toward independence. Under its provisions, the flight attendants would continue to use ALPA's essential administrative services and office space. ALPA would lend its help in securing a line of credit and assist in training programs. The flight attendants also asked for and received representation to the AFL-CIO conventions.

Most aspects of this administrative agreement would last for five years; either party could withdraw from it by a two-thirds vote. Most important to both parties, bargaining rights would be transferred from ALPA to the Association of Flight Attendants in a ratification procedure designed by the National Mediation Board. The ratification process from AFA's carrier members took six years and was completed on March 30, 1979.

During its first years of existence the AFA grew rapidly. In 1969 the S & S Division had represented 10,000 members; by 1974 the AFA had 20,000. When Kelly Rueck, AFA's first president, relinquished her office to Pat Robertson at the end of 1975, she observed: "No organization provided a finer system of representation for its members than AFA. The democracy and member participation is not found in most labor organizations because it is considered too cumbersome and costly."

Despite the healthy status of the AFA, the union had been unable to retain all of the 20 carriers that had been part of the S & S Division. Flight attendants at National, Northwest, and Wien Air Alaska all voted to leave AFA for other union affiliations. In 1976 Continental took an even more radical course and formed an independent and unaffiliated union. This option also appealed to the 16,000 members of the Transport Workers Union, who voted to disaffiliate and formed companywide independent unions at American, TWA, and Pan American. AFA president Pat Robertson was not impressed. "Eventually they'll all come back," she predicted. "It's tough out there by yourself."

Riding a crest of feminism during the mid 1970s, the AFA gained contractual improvements for its members, including union security and retirement plans. However, the impact of the Airline Deregulation Act of 1978 placed the union—and the industry—under severe stress. To counter the effects of increased competition and a sagging economy, employers demanded concessionary agreements from the flight attendants and other workers. The AFA quickly acquired expertise in such matters as corporate takeovers, leveraged buyouts, and employee ownership plans, seeking to develop and apply responsible strategies to the collective bargaining process. In several instances, AFA attempted to assist carriers facing bankruptcy by contributing to cost savings and job security through novel proposals. Nonetheless, strife and conflict filled the nation's airways during the early 1980s, as over 20,000 of the nation's 60,000 flight attendants walked picket lines, out on strike or supporting strikes by other labor groups.

It was in a chaotic environment of mergers, job losses, acquisitions, two-tier wage scales, company failures, speculative buyouts, and growing concern over safety issues that the AFA finally received its long sought after charter from the AFL-CIO. On February 23, 1984, as Secretary of Transportation Elizabeth Dole pointed out, the AFA became "the first American union with all women leaders to be chartered by the AFL-CIO."

As the airline industry entered the last decade of the 20th century, the AFA remained the strongest force in the flight attendants' labor movement, representing over 28,000 of the industry's approximately 70,000 cabin crew members (projected to rise to over 100,000 by the end of the 1990s). Other flight attendants belonged to affiliates of the Transport Workers Union and International Brotherhood of Teamsters, and to four independent unions. The AFA continued to advocate a single union as the best way to cope with the continuing shocks of deregulation. As the 1990s began, whether or not it would be successful remained to be seen.

References:

William H. Chafe, *The American Woman: Her Changing Social, Economic, and Political Roles, 1920-1970* (London: Oxford University Press, 1972);

George E. Hopkins, *The Airline Pilots: A Study in Elite Unionization* (Cambridge, Mass.: Harvard University Press, 1971);

Georgia Panter Nielsen, *From Sky Girl to Flight Attendant: Women and the Making of a Union* (Ithaca, N.Y.: ILR Press, 1982).

Archives:

Information on flight attendant labor organization can be found in the files of the Association of Flight Attendants, Washington, D.C., and in the Walter P. Reuther Library of Labor and Urban Affairs, Wayne State University, Detroit, Michigan.

Flight Engineers International Association

by Nick A. Komons

Washington, D.C.

The Flight Engineers International Association (FEIA), a labor union affiliated with the AFL-CIO, was organized in December 1948 to represent airline cockpit crew members belonging to the flight engineers' craft.

The founding of FEIA coincided with the rapid growth of the flight-engineer profession on the commercial airways in the immediate post-World War II period. The standard cockpit crew in domestic air passenger carriage prior to 1947 was made up of pilot and copilot. Two related developments led to a sudden demand for flight engineers: (1) the appearance of such piston-driven, four-engine airliners as the Lockheed L-049 Constellation, which came equipped with a flight engineer's station; and (2) a rule promulgated by the Civil Aeronautics Board (CAB) in 1948 that required the presence of a flight engineer on all aircraft certificated for a maximum takeoff weight of more than 80,000 pounds. The CAB had concluded that the cockpit work load of these airliners was so high that it demanded the services of an extra crew member. Virtually all four-engine air transports that appeared on the airways after the war exceeded the 80,000-pound takeoff weight.

Federal regulations permitted flight engineers to come from either a mechanic's or a pilot's background. U.S. flag carriers had traditionally put mechanics in the flight engineer's seat; the majority of domestic carriers followed this pattern. Braniff, Delta, Capital, Panagra, and Northeast, however, chose to employ pilots. United used both pilots and mechanics.

Flight engineers, in casting about for a labor union to represent their interests, sought to join the Air Line Pilots Association (ALPA); but ALPA refused to admit flight engineers who came from the mechanics' ranks. Under its bylaws, only males who were "legally qualified to serve as pilot or copilot on aircraft in interstate or foreign commerce"

were eligible for membership. Rather than change its bylaws, ALPA subchartered a flight engineers union. Preferring direct membership, flight engineers formed their own union. The American Federation of Labor, ALPA's parent, seeing trouble brewing and believing that airborne personnel properly belonged to a single class or craft, urged pilots to accept flight engineers and flight attendants directly into their union. The pilots again refused. In December 1948 the AFL countered by chartering the Flight Engineers International Association. The overwhelming majority of active flight engineers joined FEIA.

The presence of two collective bargaining units in the same cockpit proved disruptive. On three airlines the right to represent flight engineers changed hands seven times in ten years. Nevertheless, FEIA managed to hold its own. In the mid 1950s it represented the flight engineers on all but four certificated route air carriers. FEIA's dominance proved short-lived, however.

In 1956 ALPA changed its discriminatory membership policy; it thereafter allowed any person who served as a flight crew member to join the union. At the same time, with turboprop and turbojet airliners nearing their inauguration on the civil airways, ALPA adopted a resolution declaring that no turboprop or turbine-powered aircraft "will be operated unless and until it is manned at all flight stations by a qualified pilot." ALPA justified its attack on FEIA members by arguing that jets had operational problems that required a degree of crew coordination not possible with a nonpilot present in the cockpit. ALPA also argued that a third pilot would provide an extra margin of safety in the event that pilot or copilot was incapacitated. The union had obviously decided to preempt the third seat on jetliners.

FEIA, however, stood its ground, and those airlines that had traditionally used mechanics as flight engineers succumbed to the threat of a pilots' strike by putting a fourth man—i.e., a third pilot—in the cockpit of their jets. Taking on an extra crew member, even if he had no useful duties, these lines reasoned, was preferable to allowing their expensive new airplanes to sit idle during a strike. Capitulating to ALPA's demands cost these lines dearly in inflated payrolls and put them at a competitive disadvantage. Understandably, Pan Am, American, Western, Eastern, and TWA were anxious to reduce their jet crew complement to three.

In August 1959 ALPA filed a petition with the National Mediation Board alleging that a representative dispute existed among the employees of United Air Lines. In January 1961 the board found that all flight deck personnel of United constituted one craft for purposes of representation and ordered an election. Outnumbered by ALPA members by a ratio of 3 to 1, FEIA stood no chance of winning the election. In May 1961 ALPA was certified as the representative of all flight deck crew members at United. Except for FEIA, organized labor welcomed the Mediation Board's decision. In 1958 the AFL-CIO Executive Council had asked the two unions to merge, asserting that the close relationship required on the flight deck made it "imperative" that all cockpit crew members belong to the same labor organization. FEIA had rejected the labor federation's recommendation.

Although the Mediation Board made it clear that its decision applied only to United, FEIA knew that ALPA could use the decision as a precedent and, with its numerical superiority, drive FEIA from the field. The flight engineers' position was made still weaker by ALPA's success in placing an unneeded fourth man in the cockpit of seven major lines. In February 1961, 3,500 flight engineers at Pan Am, American, TWA, Eastern, National, Flying Tiger, and Western staged a wildcat strike in protest of the Mediation Board's decision. President John F. Kennedy established a presidential commission headed by Wisconsin University law professor Nathan Feinsinger to study the problem and make recommendations. FEIA was persuaded to call in its members while the commission's investigation was in progress.

The commission urged the two unions to merge. As for the fourth man, the commission declared the position useless and called for its gradual elimination. Finally, it concluded that flight engineers should thereafter come from the ranks of pi-

lots and recommended that mechanic-trained engineers be given pilot training at company expense.

By 1964 all airlines that had been using a four-person crew had obtained the right to eliminate the fourth man. In most cases this was achieved in one of two ways: by ALPA's willingness to cross the picket lines of FEIA and help management break strikes; or through arbitration agreements or collective bargaining that provided for flight engineers to take pilot training. In nearly every case labor peace was bought at the expense of FEIA. In 1960 the union represented flight engineers at eight major airlines and had a total U.S. membership of 3,215; by 1966 it had representation rights only at American, National, and Pan Am, and its U.S. membership had been cut to 1,300.

FEIA suffered another setback in 1964 when the Federal Aviation Agency replaced the 80,000-pound rule in favor of work load as the criterion for determining crew complement. The rule change was followed by the type certification of such models as the DC-9, the BAC One-Eleven, and the Boeing 737 with a two-man flight deck. Avionics had replaced the flight engineer. The trend toward a two-person crew continued. Every air transport of note developed since the late 1970s appeared with a two-person cockpit. Even new series of 1960s vintage air transports that had originally been introduced with a three-person crew were produced in the late 1980s with highly automated cockpits configured for only two crew members. Unless this trend is reversed, the future of the flight engineer on the airways—and hence of FEIA—will become as dim as that of the navigator and the radio operator.

References:

John M. Baitsell, *Airline Industrial Relations: Pilots and Flight Engineers* (Cambridge, Mass.: Harvard University Press, 1966);

Mark L. Kahn, "Collective Bargaining on the Airline Flight Deck," in Harold M. Levinson and others, *Collective Bargaining and Technological Change in American Transportation* (Evanston, Ill.: Transportation Center at Northwestern University, 1971);

Nick A. Komons, *The Third Man: A History of the Airline Crew Complement Controversy, 1947-1981* (Washington, D.C.: U.S. Department of Transportation, 1987);

United States Presidential Commission [Feinsinger Commission], *Report to the President, May 24, 1961* (Washington, D.C.: U.S. Government Printing Office, 1961).

Flying Tiger Line

by John C. Bishop

Auburn University

The Flying Tiger Line, destined to become the world's premier air freight carrier, began as one of the many fledgling airlines that appeared at the end of World War II. Embodying the hopes and dreams of former military pilots, the overwhelming majority of these nonscheduled passenger and freight lines lasted for only a short time. Robert W. Prescott, however, was more persistent and more fortunate than his fellow pilots.

On June 25, 1945, Prescott and several other former members of Gen. Claire L. Chennault's American Volunteer Group, popularly known as the "Flying Tigers," incorporated the National Skyway Freight Corporation. With the help of Samuel Mosher of the Signal Oil and Gas Company, they raised enough money to put a down payment on 12 Budd RB-1 Conestogas. In August, Prescott began coast-to-coast air freight service with the easily loaded and poorly performing aircraft. By the end of the year, the company managed to raise $2.5 million from Wall Street investors, providing short-term security for the new airline.

In 1946 National Skyway began what would turn out to be a lengthy association with the U.S. military when it secured a lucrative contract from the Air Transport Command. The military supplied 32 C-54s, which the airline operated on transpacific routes, making 28 flights a week to military bases in Asia.

Early in 1947 Prescott moved the prospering air freight line to Burbank, renamed it the Flying Tiger Line, and acquired C-47s to replace the troublesome Budds. By the end of the following year, the company was one of only six all-cargo lines that remained in operation following the cutthroat competition of the postwar period. On April 24, 1949, the survivors attained a measure of permanence when the Civil Aeronautics Board awarded them five-year experimental scheduled operating certificates.

Prescott's good luck continued into the 1950s. Shortly before the outbreak of the Korean War, he leased 25 C-46s from the military. This placed him in an excellent position to take advantage of the wartime boom that soon followed. As the war wound down in 1953, the Flying Tiger Line ordered two DC-6As, which it later used to inaugurate overnight transcontinental cargo service on February 13, 1955. In that same year it ordered ten Lockheed L-1049H Super Constellations, and it entered the passenger charter business.

The airline prospered during the 1960s. Early in the decade the Flying Tiger Line acquired ten Canadair CL-44Ds, a swingtail turboprop freighter with a payload of 65,000 pounds. The new airplane failed to last out the decade, being replaced by turbojet DC-8-63Fs capable of carrying 50 tons of cargo. Both the CL-44Ds and DC-8-63Fs made numerous flights across the Pacific in support of the American war effort in Vietnam.

Following continued growth during the 1970s, the Flying Tiger Line took over rival Seaboard World Airlines on October 1, 1980, becoming the undisputed leader of the air freight industry. It served five continents across three oceans with its fleet of 26 DC-8-63Fs, 13 giant Boeing 747 freighters (with a payload of 125 tons), and three Boeing 747 passenger transports.

The 1980s, however, brought economic disaster to the carrier. In the wake of deregulation, the Flying Tiger Line lost many of its traditional customers who either started their own airlines (such as the United Parcel Service) or used the services of new companies (such as the aggressive Federal Express). Also, the company's military business fell off. Plagued with high labor costs, Flying Tiger Line suffered a series of crippling losses. On January 31, 1989, Federal Express purchased the nation's pioneering air freight line for $880 million.

Flying Tiger Budd RB-1 Conestoga (courtesy of the National Air and Space Museum)

References:

John C. Bishop, "Delivery of Goods by Air: The United States Air-Cargo Industry, 1945-1955," in *Essays in Economic and Business History*, volume 7, edited by Edwin J. Perkins (Los Angeles: Economic and Business Historical Society, 1989);

David L. Brown, "Can Wolf Save the Tigers?," *Airline Executive*, 11 (March 1987): 19-21, 49;

Frank J. Cameron, *Hungry Tiger: The Story of the Flying Tiger Line* (New York: McGraw-Hill, 1964);

R. E. G. Davies, *Airlines of the United States since 1914*, revised edition (Washington, D.C.: Smithsonian Institution, 1982);

J. Philip Geddes, "The Flying Tiger Line: A Profile of the World's Largest All-Cargo Carrier," *Interavia*, 25 (September 1970): 1099-1102;

Kenneth G. Friedkin

(September 1, 1915 - March 17, 1962)

by Joseph E. Libby

University of California, Riverside

CAREER: Director of training, British Flight School (1940-1941); director of training, U.S. Air Force Training School (1942-1944); president, Friedkin Aeronautics (1945-1949); president, Pacific Southwest Airlines (1949-1962).

Kenneth Friedkin founded Pacific Southwest Airlines (PSA) in San Diego, California, and built it into one of the most successful intrastate air carriers in the United States. He put together an efficient organization combining low fares with a familylike atmosphere, creating a model other airlines sought to emulate. Born into a period of cutthroat competition, PSA, along with North American Airlines and other low-fare carriers, played a significant role in the introduction of lower-cost coach fares.

Kenneth Giles Friedkin was born in Utica, New York, on September 1, 1915. His formal education beyond high school consisted of one year at a community college. His interest in aviation developed early. At the age of seventeen he learned to fly, and by the late 1930s he had become a flight instructor at Plosser Air College in Glendale, California. By 1940 he had moved north to Bakersfield, California, where for two years he trained American volunteer pilots for the British Royal Air Force's Eagle squadron. When the United States entered World War II, Friedkin moved to Sweetwater, Texas, where he operated the nation's first flight school to train Women's Auxiliary Service Pilots. In 1944 he worked as test pilot for Convair Aircraft Company, and also became a pilot for a Consolidated-Vultee contract carrier called Con Airways. This company contracted with the military to fly supplies and personnel across the North Atlantic to England and Europe.

After the war, Friedkin settled in San Diego, California. Hoping to cash in on the large numbers of returning U.S. servicemen anxious to learn to fly,

Friedkin joined with Joe Plosser, Jr., and opened the Friedkin School of Aeronautics at Lindbergh Field. Using a Ryan PT-19 rebuilt by Friedkin, the school offered flight and instrument instruction in programs leading to basic pilot's licenses and Flight Instructor and Air Transport Pilot ratings.

By the end of 1947, as the number of students applying to the school began to drop off, Plosser sold out his share of the enterprise to San Diego mortgage broker Victor Lundy. With the new partner, Friedkin decided to compensate for the loss of students by opening a freight service. The business proved to be anything but lucrative. At one point, Friedkin contracted to carry live bait from Mexico to the Colorado River. During the flight, the pilot was required constantly to splash salt water on the fish to keep them alive. The experience convinced Friedkin and his flight instructors, who had to make the flights, to switch to a charter passenger service. In 1948 Friedkin changed the name of his company to Friedkin Aeronautics and began his charter service using a war surplus Cessna UC-78 Crane. As the five-seat capacity of the airplane limited the company's abilities to attract business, Friedkin decided to establish an intrastate commercial airline.

Pacific Southwest Airlines, as the new carrier was called, began operations with a single DC-3 on May 6, 1949. Initially the airline flew weekly from San Diego to Oakland, with a stop at Burbank. The original fare for the three-city route was $15.60. The airline caught on quickly. By the end of 1949, Friedkin had leased a second DC-3, and, using his former flight instructors as airline pilots, Pacific Southwest carried 15,011 passengers over 321,000 miles. After its first eight months of operation, PSA showed a net profit of $11,984. The following year the number of passengers carried over the same three-city route tripled. Confident of the airline's potential, Friedkin began to expand. On July

4, 1951, PSA inaugurated service from San Diego and Burbank to San Francisco. In 1952 Friedkin added two more DC-3s to PSA's fleet, and in 1953 he began service between San Diego, Burbank, and Long Beach.

Despite showing losses between 1952 and 1954, PSA's popularity continued to grow. Its only competition in the low-fare market in the state was California Central Airlines, which had inaugurated its Burbank-to-Oakland service in January 1949, five months before Friedkin opened PSA. When California Central went bankrupt in February 1954, the result of financial mismanagement, Friedkin and PSA were left alone in California's low-fare market.

PSA's popularity rested largely upon its fares. Friedkin consistently set the airline's fares at 20 percent below his nearest competitor. He succeeded where other low-fare carriers such as North American Airlines failed because PSA flew entirely within the state of California. Consequently, it fell under the jurisdiction of the California Public Utilities Commission rather than the Civil Aeronautics Board (CAB) in Washington, D.C., which governed all interstate carriers. The California Public Utilities Commission placed fewer fare and route regulations on PSA than the CAB would have, which allowed Friedkin the advantage of matching his service to demand. By increasing the number of flights available during holidays and decreasing flights during slack periods, PSA was able to fly with more full seats than other airlines.

Friedkin believed that flying should be fun, and that good passenger relations began with good employee relations. He saw PSA and its employees as an extended family. By its tenth anniversary the airline had nearly 300 employees, most of whom knew each other on a first-name basis. In the airline's company newsletter, articles submitted by employees often ran under their first names, accompanied by their photographs. Friedkin and his wife, who was vice-president of the airline, were known simply as "Ken and Jean." Until the mid 1970s the company even provided a Christmas turkey to each employee. This family atmosphere carried over into passenger relations, compensating for PSA's "no frills" service and enhancing the airline's image as "The World's Friendliest Airline."

By the end of 1958 Friedkin had dropped PSA's unprofitable routes to Oakland and Long Beach and opened service to Los Angeles Interna-

tional Airport. He had replaced all of the airline's DC-3s with larger DC-4s, allowing the airline to carry 295,818 passengers nearly two million miles. The airline's progress convinced Friedkin that the time had arrived for PSA to enter the jet age. In June 1957 he stunned the aviation community by announcing plans to purchase two new Sud Caravelle jets. The $5 million cost of the two French-built jets, however, proved to be too much for PSA to handle. Unable to finance the purchase of the jets, Friedkin canceled the order.

When the Caravelle purchase fell through, Lockheed Aircraft Corporation stepped in and offered PSA its new L-188 turboprop Electra. With a cruising speed twice that of the DC-4, and its quiet, vibration-free, pressurized cabin, the Lockheed Electra was an ideal airplane for the intrastate carrier. In September 1957 Friedkin ordered three of the turboprop airplanes at a cost of $8 million. Financing for the purchase came through a lease arrangement with Barron Hilton, son of hotel tycoon Conrad Hilton. The first Electra entered service for PSA in November 1959, cutting the time of the airline's Los Angeles-San Francisco flight by 40 minutes.

The Electra proved so successful that by the end of 1960 Friedkin had dropped the four DC-4s from PSA's fleet. As a consequence of the Electra purchase, profits for that year totaled only $499, yet Friedkin went ahead with the acquisition of a fourth Electra in 1961. In that year PSA carried 713,064 passengers over 3.3 million miles, yielding the airline a profit of $310,483. Financially, 1962 proved to be an even better year. A fifth Electra was added in April, and profits for the year passed the $1 million mark. Sadly, though, Friedkin did not live to see it. He died of a cerebral hemorrhage at the age of forty-six on March 17, 1962. The presidency of PSA passed on to J. Floyd Andrews, who had been with Friedkin since 1947, when he joined Friedkin Aeronautics as a flight instructor.

During his 12 years as president of PSA, Kenneth Friedkin forged what was perhaps the most successful low-fare airline in the United States. In the beginning, he had hoped that PSA would eventually fly a plane out of San Francisco every 30 minutes. He envisioned a time when catching a plane would be like catching a bus. Although these dreams were not satisfied, Friedkin did succeed in helping to make the San Diego-Los Angeles-San Francisco air corridor the most heavily traveled route in the world.

References:
Jackson S. Elliott, "The Grimace on the Grinning Bird," *Business Forum*, 5 (July 1975): 6-12;
William A. Jordan, *Airline Regulation in America* (Baltimore: Johns Hopkins University Press, 1970);
Mary Brandt Kerr, "The P.S.A. Story," *PSA Magazine* (December 1987): 27-55, 60-85;
William S. Reed, "Hilton Leases Electras to Intra-State Line," *Aviation Week*, 71 (November 30, 1959): 39-40;
William A. Schoneberger, with Paul Sonnenburg, *California Wings: A History of Aviation in the Golden State* (Woodland Hills, Cal.: Windsor Publications, 1984);
John Wegg, "PSA—The Smile is Gone," *Airliners*, 1 (Spring 1988): 4-21.

Frontier Airlines

by Myron J. Smith, Jr.

Tusculum College

Frontier Airlines began operations on June 1, 1950, with 400 employees and a fleet of 12 Douglas DC-3s. The new company grew out of the expansion of Monarch Airlines, which had acquired Challenger Air Lines of Salt Lake City in December 1949, and Arizona Airways of Phoenix four months later. By 1951 Frontier's routes stretched to 40 cities in seven states from Montana to the Mexican border. By 1959, after the acquisition of additional markets, expanding high-altitude operations and traffic growth led to the introduction of pressurized Convair CV-340s.

In March 1962 the Goldfield Corporation of San Francisco acquired Frontier. Under the dynamic leadership of a new president, Lew Dymond, the airline continued to expand throughout the Rocky Mountain area. In 1966 Frontier became the first local service carrier to introduce the Boeing 727 trijet. On October 1, 1967, it acquired Central Airlines of Fort Worth (founded in 1949), allowing the carrier to operate in a total of 14 states. The enlarged airline retired the last of its DC-3s in 1968; the following year it began to phase Boeing 737s into its fleet.

Frontier broke the 21 million mark in accumulated passenger boardings in 1971. With inauguration of service to Winnipeg, Canada, on July 1, 1974, the company became an international carrier. Frontier had its most successful year to date in 1978. In addition to a 26.2 percent rise in traffic and a record profit of $13.7 million, it added eight Boeing 737s to its fleet and became a three-nation carrier by launching service to two Mexican cities on November 3.

Despite skyrocketing fuel prices and an 11.3 percent traffic decline from the level in 1979, service over the new routes allowed a cushion sufficient to grant Frontier a record $23.2 million net profit in 1980. By the end of 1981 the airline had 5,800 employees, 45 Boeing 737s, 15 Convair CV-580s, and a route network which included 86 cities in 27 states, Mexico, and Canada.

Frontier Airlines became the prime subsidiary of newly created Frontier Holdings, Inc., on May 6, 1982. Two weeks later the carrier introduced the McDonnell-Douglas MD-80, and on June 1 Frontier went "all jet" with the retirement of its 15 remaining CV-580s. At the same time, intense competition, a Christmas blizzard which closed the Denver airport, and the termination of service to 11 smaller cities drove traffic downward by 7 percent. As a result, net earnings of $15.9 million were less than half of 1981's profits, suggesting that all was not well with the carrier.

In 1983 Frontier posted a net loss of $13.8 million, the first deficit in more than a decade. The year 1984 saw the downward spiral continue. Despite a cost-saving labor agreement, an 11.2 percent increase in passenger boardings, and a rise in revenues, the net loss of $31.3 million meant that a drastic change would have to be made if the airline were to survive.

Early in 1985 the airline's board of directors approved a plan that would have allowed Frontier's employees to purchase the airline for $17 a share, totaling $211 million. In early October, however, Frank Lorenzo made an offer to Frontier's stockholders which was substantially above that which the carrier's employees could muster. The employees, fearful of Lorenzo's reputation, threatened court action on the grounds that such an acquisition would result in a monopoly of the Denver market by Lorenzo's Continental Airlines. People Express Airlines then entered the picture and offered stockholders $24 per share. The offer was accepted, much to the delight of the airline's employees.

References:

Roger J. Bentley, "The Frontiersman," *American Aviation Historical Society Journal*, 13 (Fall 1968): 189-192;

R. E. G. Davies, *Airlines of the United States since 1914*, revised edition (Washington, D.C.: Smithsonian Institution, 1982);

Frontier Airlines, *Frontier Airlines: Historical Highlights* (Denver: Frontier Airlines, 1985).

Jack Frye

(March 18, 1904 - February 3, 1959)

by Patricia A. Michaelis

Kansas State Historical Society

CAREER: Partner, Burdett Flying School (1923-1926); vice-president to president, Aero Corporation of California (1926-1930); vice-president, Western Air Express (1930); vice-president for operations (1930-1934), president, Transcontinental and Western Air (1934-1947); president, General Aniline and Film Corporation (1947-1955); president, The Frye Corporation (1955-1959).

William John Frye, known commonly as Jack Frye, had a major impact on the growth of commercial aviation in the United States during his 36 years in the industry. Not only did he preside over an airline that grew from a company with 600 employees to a $70 million corporation with 17,000 employees and a worldwide route network, but he also made vital contributions to the industry's technological progress. Under Frye, Transcontinental and Western Air (TWA) became a leader in high-altitude research and fostered the development of a series of advanced transport aircraft, including the DC-1, DC-2, Boeing 307, and Lockheed Constellation.

Frye was born on March 18, 1904, near Sweetwater, Oklahoma, the son of William Henry and Nellie Cooley Frye. His mother died when he was eight years old, and he was raised by his father and grandparents on the family's 15,000-acre ranch in the Texas Panhandle near Wheeler. Frye dropped out of high school at age seventeen and spent a year in the Army Engineer Corps. In 1923 he moved to the Los Angeles area, where he worked

Jack Frye (courtesy of Trans World Airlines)

as a dishwasher and soda jerk. Interested in flying, he used his earnings to take lessons at a local airfield. Before the end of the year, he had borrowed money from his brother to buy a half interest in the Burdett Flying School, whose major asset was a single Curtiss Jenny.

TWA Boeing 307 Stratoliner

Burdett developed slowly over the next two years, adding a second Jenny and expanding into movie stunt flying. In February 1926 Frye and two associates bought out the original owner of the company and renamed it the Aero Corporation of California. Aero prospered as regional distributor for Eaglerock and Fokker airplanes. It also operated one of the finest flying schools in the country, operated charters, and developed a profitable maintenance business. On November 28, 1927, Aero capitalized on the "Lindbergh boom" by using a subsidiary named Standard Air Lines to begin a scheduled passenger and express service between Los Angeles and Tucson via Phoenix with a six-passenger Fokker F-VII.

Frye, who often flew trips for the airline, extended service to El Paso in 1928. The following year Standard became the western link in an air-rail transcontinental schedule. Beginning on August 4, 1929, passengers could travel from New York to St. Louis by rail, connect with a Southwest Air Fast Express Ford Trimotor for a flight to Sweetwater, then take the overnight train to El Paso. Standard took over at that point, carrying passengers to Los Angeles in Fokker F-X Trimotors along what its advertisement brochures described as "the Fair Weather Route." If all went on schedule, the coast-to-

coast trip could be made in 43 hours and 40 minutes.

In May 1930, with Standard feeling the effects of the early stages of the Great Depression, Frye and his associates sold the airline to Harris M. Hanshue of Western Air Express. Frye went with the merged companies as vice-president for operations. Before the year ended, Postmaster General Walter Folger Brown forced the merger of Western and Transcontinental Air Transport. Frye remained in charge of operations for the new Transcontinental and Western Air.

Under Frye's direction, TWA inaugurated the first all-air transcontinental service on October 25, 1930. The trip took 36 hours and required an overnight stop in Kansas City. Two years later, on November 5, 1932, TWA began flying through the night on the route, reducing coast-to-coast travel time to 24 hours.

Frye played a key role in the search for a replacement for TWA's Fokker transports, which had been removed from passenger service following an accident on March 31, 1931, that resulted in the death of Notre Dame football coach Knute Rockne. In August 1932 Frye wrote to the nation's leading aircraft manufacturers, setting out the specifications for an all-metal, three-engined transport that could carry 12 passengers at a cruising speed of 146 miles per hour over a distance of 1,060 miles. "This plane fully loaded," Frye stressed, "must make satisfactory take-offs under good control at any TWA airport on any combination of two engines."

Only Donald Douglas responded to Frye's demanding requirements. The twin-engine DC-1, able to take off with a single engine in the event of an engine failure, first flew on July 1, 1933. The production model, the 14-passenger DC-2, went into service with TWA the following year. The new Douglas transport reduced transcontinental travel time to 16 hours.

On February 18-19, 1934, Frye made a dramatic demonstration of the capabilities of the impressive Douglas airliner. Responding to President Franklin D. Roosevelt's decision to cancel all airmail contracts, Frye and Edward V. Rickenbacker, vice-president of Eastern Air Transport, set out from Los Angeles in TWA's DC-1 on a record-breaking transcontinental flight. One of the few airline executives to hold a transport pilot's license, Frye flew the last load of airmail to Newark (with two refueling stops) in 13 hours and 4 minutes.

A year that began badly ended well for Frye. Following a series of reorganizations caused by the Air Mail Act of 1934, which returned the airmail to private contractors, Frye was named president of TWA on December 27. In the short space of 11 years Frye had risen from a high school dropout and soda jerk to the youngest airline president in the country. And, as TWA chronicler Robert J. Serling has emphasized, "Brash, energetic and fiercely competitive, he was the quintessential airline leader at the crossroads in aviation history."

TWA became known as a "pilot's airline" under Frye. Despite limited financial resources, TWA took the lead in exploring high-speed, high-altitude, all-weather flying. This work led to the development of the Boeing 307, the first pressurized passenger transport. Introduced by TWA in July 1940, the airplanes gave Frye a competitive edge on the transcontinental route before American entry into World War II in December 1941 resulted in their transfer to the army for use in the foreign courier service.

By the time the 307s appeared, TWA's ownership had changed hands. John D. Hertz, who held 11 percent of the airline's stock and controlled its board of directors, had opposed Frye's plans to acquire the new—and expensive—transports. Convinced that Hertz, who lacked a background in

aviation, was standing in the way of the airline's technological progress, Frye persuaded Howard Hughes, an old friend, to acquire a controlling interest in the company.

With Hughes's sympathetic support, TWA continued its technological leadership of the industry. The results of the Hughes-Frye partnership could be seen in 1944 when TWA took delivery on the first Lockheed-049 Constellation. In April, Frye and Hughes flew the triple-tail airliner from Burbank to Washington, D.C., in a record 6 hours and 58 minutes.

TWA, which became the nation's third largest air carrier (after United and American) before U.S. entry into World War II, gained considerable experience on international routes during the war years. Frye used the airline's wartime work to challenge Pan American's monopoly of overseas markets. In July 1945 the Civil Aeronautics Board granted TWA the authority to fly to Europe, with onward rights to India. In August 1946 the airline received permission to fly across southern Asia to Shanghai.

Frye's own tenure with TWA came to an end in February 1947. Ever since Hughes had taken control of the airline in 1939-1940, Frye had been engaged in a constant struggle for power with Noah Dietrich, the new owner's chief assistant. In 1946 the temporary grounding of TWA's Lockheed Constellations to correct a design flaw, a pilots' strike, and the postwar recession had combined to give Dietrich the ammunition that he needed to get rid of his hated rival. Frye resigned to avoid being fired.

Frye landed on his feet. He became president of the General Aniline and Film Corporation at a salary that was four times what he had earned with TWA. On July 21, 1950, he married Nevada Smith, a former Las Vegas show girl. According to author Robert J. Serling, this was Frye's fourth marriage. Details of the first two marriages are not known. His third marriage was to Helen (Varner) Vanderbilt, former wife of Cornelius Vanderbilt, Jr. They were wed on January 1, 1941, and divorced in 1950. Only the union with Nevada Smith produced a child, a daughter.

In 1955 Frye resigned from General Aniline and formed his own company, The Frye Corporation, to develop a rugged trimotored airplane for use in underdeveloped countries. The Northrop company built a prototype, called the Pioneer, which Frye used to interest potential investors and customers. He raised $2 million for the project, to which he added his own savings. He moved to Tucson, Arizona, and was planning a site for his factory when he was struck and killed by a drunk driver on February 3, 1959.

References:

"Chest Expansion of an Airline," *Fortune*, 31 (April 1945): 132-138, 192, 195-196, 199;

Robert J. Serling, *Howard Hughes' Airline: An Informal History of TWA* (New York: St. Martin's Press/ Marek, 1983);
TWA Pilots' Master Executive Council, *TWA: A Pictorial History* (N.p.: Privately published, 1981).

Archives:

Information on Jack Frye's tenure at Transcontinental and Western Air can be found at the Trans World Airlines Archives, Kansas City, Missouri.

Edgar S. Gorrell

(February 3, 1891 - March 5, 1945)

by Dominick A. Pisano

National Air and Space Museum

CAREER: Officer, U.S. Air Service (1912-1920); executive, Marmon Motor Company (1920-1925); vice-president and general manager to president, Stutz Motor Car Company (1925-1935); president and chairman, Edgar S. Gorrell Investment Company (1935-1945); president, Air Transport Association of America (1936-1945).

Edgar Staley Gorrell, though little remembered after his career was over, was one of the most prominent figures in the early history of aviation in the United States. As a bright, young staff officer, he served as a member of the important Bolling Mission that helped to shape the role of American aviation in World War I. He later compiled an exhaustive official history of the wartime activities of the U.S. Air Service. In 1936 he became the first president of the Air Transport Association, the newly established trade organization of the airline industry. A tireless spokesman for the airlines, he drafted the plan that resulted in the smooth mobilization of the airlines during World War II.

Gorrell was born in Baltimore, Maryland, on February 3, 1891, the son of Charles Edgar and Pamelia Stevenson (Smith) Gorrell. His father was a carpenter and construction superintendent. Educated in public schools, Gorrell went on to the U.S. Military Academy. He graduated from West Point in 1912 with a B.S. degree in engineering and a commission as second lieutenant of infantry. In 1915 Gorrell transferred to aviation and learned to fly at the Signal Corps flying school at Coronado, California. Assigned to the 1st Aero Squadron, he took

Edgar S. Gorrell

part in the punitive expedition against Mexico in 1916. It was during this episode that Gorrell won a reputation for being feisty and outspoken when he criticized the army for the "horrible shape" of the squadron. "The airplanes," he later wrote, "were not fit for military service, especially along the border." With engines that produced "only four horsepower over the amount necessary to fly at sea level," the Curtiss JN3s "were not stable, and . . . were liable to get into a spin or do a number of other highly undesirable things." Returning from Mexico, Gorrell entered the Massachusetts Institute of Technology, where he received an M.S. degree in aeronautical engineering in the spring of 1917.

In May 1917, the month after the United States entered World War I, Gorrell was sent to Europe as part of the Aircraft Production Board aeronautical mission headed by Col. Raynal C. Bolling. This important mission, made up of army and navy officers, industrial specialists, and mechanics, was charged with evaluating aircraft production in Europe so that the resulting information could be used in manufacturing warplanes in the United States. In November of that year, Gorrell submitted to the air staff an American plan for strategic bombing. In the words of a prominent air strategist in World War II, Gen. Laurence S. Kuter, Gorrell's report was "the earliest, clearest, and least known statement of the American conception of air power." In October 1918 Gorrell, at age twenty-seven, became one of the youngest colonels since the Civil War. On December 4, 1918, shortly after the Armistice, Gorrell was appointed assistant chief of air staff. Later designated chief historian, he was given the responsibility of compiling an account of American air activities during the war.

In 1940, some 20 years after he had left the Air Service, Gorrell looked back on this chapter of his life in a lecture given at Norwich University in Vermont titled *The Measure of America's World War Aeronautical Effort*. He reflected that he once believed "his" history, which runs to 280 volumes, with thousands of photographs, charts, and tabulations, "would later be made available to the air officers under the American flag everywhere so they could take it home to their quarters and study it, perhaps pipe in mouth and carpet-slippered feet on the desk, learning now of one event and later of another, and calmly and gradually profiting by the lessons learned and the mistakes made by those who had pioneered."

But this did not happen. After Gorrell's history had been completed in 1919, it was placed "in the vaults of the War Department in Washington, some of the pages torn, some yellowing, many hard to read. But small use has been made of it . . . because of its inaccessibility." (Gorrell's history is now in the collection of the National Archives and is available on 58 rolls of microfilm.)

Gorrell's historical work led him to the conclusion that aircraft alone could not prevail against a hostile army. This view placed him out of step with many fellow airmen who became air power enthusiasts and argued—often with great passion—for the establishment of a separate air force. This may have been a factor in his decision to resign his commission on March 19, 1920, although the bleak postwar prospects for the military services were reasons enough to seek a career in business. He promptly secured a position as an industrial engineer with the Nordyke & Marmon automobile company of Indianapolis. The following year, on December 21, he married Ruth Maurice. The couple had two children.

The hardworking, hard-driving Gorrell quickly made his mark in the automobile industry. In February 1924 he was elected vice-president of the Marmon Motor Company. The next year he resigned to become vice-president and general manager of the Stutz Motor Car Company. Responsible for introducing the Blackhawk, a companion to the famous Bearcat, and for designing the braking system of the Stutz Super Bearcat, he was appointed president of the company in 1929. When Stutz fell victim to the Great Depression, Gorrell left it in 1935 and formed his own firm, the Edgar S. Gorrell Investment Company.

During his association with Stutz, Gorrell had been asked by Secretary of War George H. Dern to become a civilian member of the Special Committee on the Army Air Corps, otherwise known as the "Baker Board," named after its head, Newton D. Baker. The board, which included such other figures in aviation as James H. "Jimmy" Doolittle, George W. Lewis, Carl Compton, and Clarence Chamberlin, investigated the Army Air Corps in the wake of President Franklin D. Roosevelt's cancellation of the airmail contracts in 1934. Maj. Gen. Benjamin D. Foulois, chief of the air corps, hailed the board's report as "the first comprehensive outline of War Department policy with respect to aviation that the Army has ever had."

In January 1936, Gorrell became the first president of the Air Transport Association (ATA), a trade group made up of scheduled air carriers in the United States. It was to this position that he devoted the next major part of his life. The ATA was formed by leading members of the airline industry, including William A. Patterson, Thomas E. Braniff, Edward V. Rickenbacker, C. R. Smith, and Jack

Frye, "to promote and develop the business of transporting persons, goods and mail by aircraft between fixed termini, on regular schedules and through special service, to the end that the best interests of the public and the members of the Association be served."

Gorrell was not always popular with the membership of the ATA, but he was indefatigable in getting the organization's message to the right people, especially members of Congress. Taking office in the midst of a controversy over airline safety, Gorrell found himself under fire almost immediately. To counter criticism of the airlines, he issued a press release that praised the overall safety record of the industry. Next, he protested to Will H. Hays, head of the Motion Picture Producers and Distributors of America, an organization designed to regulate the business and morals of the film industry, about the film melodrama *Ceiling Zero*. This film, Gorrell claimed, portrayed aviation in a negative way, and he managed to have included in the film a prologue asserting that it was not a true depiction of the state of aviation in the United States.

As head of the ATA, Gorrell pursued a bold program that both promoted the industry and helped prepare it for an eventual war. Testifying before Senator Royal S. Copeland's Commerce Committee, Gorrell emphasized that the salary limit of $17,500 for airline executives had to be removed, that the United States needed aeronautical research to keep ahead of Germany and Italy, which were perceived to be advancing dangerously in that area, and that the airways were in need of safety improvements, including communication and weather aids. As Fowler Barker commented in a 1944 article in *Air Transport*, the perception that as head of ATA Gorrell represented all the airlines was especially significant. It gave him, Barker wrote, an edge "over an airline president, the assistant postmaster general or civil aeronautics administrator" in providing congressional testimony.

In his various appearances before Congress, Gorrell was noted for dramatically illustrating his testimony with charts and statistics. To underscore the need for more aviation weather stations, Gorrell produced a huge map of the United States with black crosses marking the site of recent airline crashes and red symbols nearby to point up the lack of weather facilities. Another of Gorrell's visual aids was a black fiber case, weighing more than 100 pounds, which contained a thousand or more color-coded index cards, each noting a weather station (blue), radio range (buff), landing field (yellow), and teletype station (pink) throughout the United States. The cards were arranged by state, type of facility, and airline route, and tabbed to indicate where improvements were needed.

When war came in December 1941, Gorrell and the airlines were prepared sufficiently to prevent President Roosevelt from putting into action a December 14, 1941, executive order that would have placed commercial aviation in the hands of the War Department. Largely because of the efforts of Gorrell, who had drafted wartime mobilization plans for the airlines during his tenure at ATA, special troops were flown on a secret mission to South America shortly after the Japanese attack on Pearl Harbor. During this time, commercial airliners were ordered to land at the closest airport, passengers were taken off, the aircraft refueled and equipped with spare parts, maps, and mechanics. They were then flown to military bases, where troops and supplies were placed on board and rushed to their secret destination.

Gorrell remarried on February 22, 1945, to Mrs. Mary Frances (O'Dowd) Weidman. Shortly thereafter, on March 5, he died of a heart ailment. At his request, an air force plane scattered his ashes over the U.S. Military Academy at West Point.

In *Air Transport at War*, published in 1946, Reginald M. Cleveland paid handsome tribute to Gorrell. Noting that Gorrell's "persistence and his activities . . . did not always run parallel with those of his major associates," his death nonetheless represented "a sacrifice to the cause which he had so ardently furthered and as a result of immense hours of work, unflagging energy and a constant devotion to the promotion of transportation by air."

Publication:

The Measure of America's World War Aeronautical Effort (Northfield, Vt.: Norwich University, 1940).

References:

Fowler Barker, "Airline Association President," *Air Transport* (April 1944): 53, 55; (May 1944): 73-74, 77-78; (June 1944): 73, 75-76, 79; (July 1944): 63-64, 67;

Reginald M. Cleveland, *Air Transport at War* (New York: Harper, 1946);

William B. Courtney, "Don't Call Me Napoleon," *Collier's* (August 7, 1937): 25-26, 58.

Vern C. Gorst

(August 18, 1876 - October 18, 1953)

by Patricia A. Michaelis

Kansas State Historical Society

CAREER: Partner, Gorst and King (1912-1953); president, Pacific Air Transport (1926-1928); partner, Barnes and Gorst (1928-1935); president, Gorst Air Transport (1929-1933).

A colorful figure in the early history of commercial aviation in the United States, Vern Centennial Gorst established the contract airmail route between Seattle and Los Angeles during the 1920s. His company, Pacific Air Transport, later became part of United Air Lines. Gorst also operated a highly successful seaplane shuttle service on Puget Sound. Most historians would agree with veteran aircraft manufacturer and aviation chronicler Grover Loening that Gorst ranks as "one of the most advanced and farsighted of U.S. airline pioneers."

Gorst was born in Belle Prairie, Minnesota, on August 18 in the centennial year of 1876. He was one of eight children of John Phillip and Lorinda Moore Coe Gorst. In 1881 the family moved to Fort Ripley, Minnesota, where Gorst's father logged and ran a sawmill. When Gorst was twelve years old, the family relocated to a 60-acre plot on the shores of Puget Sound, near what is now Port Orchard, Washington. His father continued in the logging and sawmill business on the West Coast.

Gorst took his first job at age seventeen, working as a water boy for the Navy Department during the construction of the Bremerton Navy Yard. He also for a time attended the Acme Business College in Seattle. In February 1896, Gorst went to Alaska in search of gold. After eight months of prospecting in the field around Cook's Inlet, he and a partner sold their claim for $21,000.

The affluent young miner returned to Washington, where he attended the University of Washington for several months. After losing most of his money in real estate, he went back to Alaska in the spring of 1897. He remained in the Klondike region for six years. "It was the happiest time of my life," he later said. In addition to prospecting, he operated a dogsled freight business, his first transportation venture. On August 8, 1901, he married Julia Johnson in Dawson, Yukon Territory, British Columbia.

In 1903 Gorst built a house in Port Orchard, Washington. For the next seven years, he operated a motor launch service on Puget Sound, between Port Orchard and Mannett. In 1910 he moved to Jacksonville, Oregon, where he began the first motor stage line in the state, running between Jacksonville and Medford. Two years later he formed a partnership with Charles O. King and started a second line in the Coos Bay area. Over the next two decades the firm of Gorst and King opened eight additional stage lines in Oregon and California.

Gorst first became attracted to aviation in 1913. Gorst and King formed the Coos Bay Aircraft Company and purchased a Martin hydroplane. Gorst taught himself to fly, with the idea of starting an airline. He soon discovered, however, the air transport had not yet reached a point where it could return a profit.

Gorst never lost interest in aeronautics. In 1925, when the Post Office decided to contract with private operators to carry airmail, he persuaded fellow bus company owners to fund an aerial survey for a possible West Coast airmail line. In November 1925 he accompanied R. B. Patterson in a Laird Swallow on a 19-day exploration of the terrain between San Francisco and Seattle. Apparently satisfied with the result, Gorst submitted a bid for Contract Air Mail Route 8 (CAM-8), which extended from Los Angeles to Seattle via San Francisco.

On January 1, 1926, Gorst learned that the Post Office had accepted his bid. The following

Vern C. Gorst (front) on the deck of his Boeing B-1-D Flying Boat

week he formed Pacific Air Transport (PAT) to operate the route. But raising funds to get started proved a major challenge. Bus company owners put up another $14,000; however, this fell far short of the projected $500,000 he would need. Gorst then took to the road, peddling stock through the Pacific Northwest. While Portland department store owner Julius Meier invested $25,000, most sales were in the hundred-dollar range. Eventually, he collected $135,000, to which he added a personal investment of $40,000.

In March San Diego aircraft manufacturer F. Claude Ryan flew Gorst from San Francisco to Seattle in the new Ryan M-1 cabin monoplane. Similar to the airplane that Charles A. Lindbergh later would use to cross the Atlantic, the M-1 featured the new air-cooled Wright Whirlwind engine. Impressed with the aircraft's performance, Gorst ordered ten Ryans.

Expenses quickly mounted. The Post Office, which set the schedule on mail routes, required PAT to depart from Los Angeles at midnight and from Seattle before daybreak. As the government had not yet assumed responsibility for lighting the airway, Gorst had to pay for the equipment that pilots

needed for nighttime navigation. Although Gorst bought searchlights as cheaply as possible, it still cost the company $20,000.

Short of funds, Gorst hired pilots who were willing to take part of their pay in shares of stock. He also traded stock for gasoline from Standard Oil and for other services. Later the Wells Fargo Bank of San Francisco provided a loan of $5,000. Bank officer William A. Patterson, who recommended the loan, took an interest in the airline and served as Gorst's unofficial financial adviser. Later, Patterson would become head of United Air Lines.

Service on CAM-8 began on September 15, 1926. At first all went well. By the end of the year, PAT had carried over 19,000 pounds of mail, together with 102 hardy souls who rode along with the mail sacks. During the winter, however, the airline suffered three fatal accidents as pilots struggled to maintain schedules during harsh weather conditions.

Traffic increased with improving weather. During 1927 PAT carried over 76,000 pounds of mail and 10,252 passengers. But Gorst remained chronically short of operating funds. Also, PAT faced new competition for passengers in California, especially from Maddux Air Lines and its Ford Trimotor transports. Aware that his struggling company lacked the money to purchase larger airplanes, Gorst eventually agreed to sell PAT to William E. Boeing on January 1, 1928. He received $94,000 for his stock in the airline, which was absorbed into Boeing Air Transport on December 17, 1928.

Gorst remained active in aviation for the next decade. He purchased a Boeing B-1-D Flying Boat, hired pilot Percy Barnes, and obtained a contract from the Post Office for the international airmail route between Seattle and Victoria, British Columbia. Barnes and Gorst, a company based on an equal share of profits, operated the route from July 1, 1928, to December 31, 1935. Gorst also formed the Seattle Flying Service on June 15, 1928, which flew charters, offered flying lessons, and performed maintenance work.

Gorst's most ambitious venture came in 1929. Hoping to exploit air transport opportunities in Alaska, he purchased a Loening Cabin Amphibian. In April, he set out from Seattle with pilot Clayton Scott, bound for Cordova. The two men made several flights in Alaska, including the first trip across the Gulf of Alaska from Cordova to Juneau, but Gorst decided not to start an Alaskan airline. Instead, he returned to the United States and in June opened a seaplane shuttle service between Seattle and Bremerton.

Using two Loenings, Gorst operated hourly flights, 11 times a day, on the 12-mile run across Puget Sound. The service proved popular. During its first four months of operation, Gorst Air Transport carried some 17,500 people, an impressive total for this formative stage of passenger-carrying airlines. With the onset of the Great Depression, however, business slowly fell off. In 1930 the shuttle service carried 15,000 passengers during 12 months of operation. The next year, 12,000 people made the ten-minute trip. Gorst, who had become

a licensed transport pilot in 1930 and often flew the shuttles, discontinued service in October 1932. The airline resumed flying the following year and carried 4,235 passengers and over 4,000 pounds of express during several months of operation before shutting down for good. Given the nature of the economy, the collapse of the enterprise did not come as a surprise.

Gorst also served as West Coast distributor for Loening. In 1930 he sold three amphibians to Joseph J. Tynan, Jr., who wanted to start a shuttle service between San Francisco and Oakland. As part of the sales agreement, Gorst operated Air Ferries, Ltd., for its first 45 days and insured that it was running smoothly before turning it over to Tynan.

Gorst, who flew many charter flights to Alaska during the 1930s and at one point came close to starting a Washington-Alaska airline, went into semiretirement before the end of the decade. He piloted a light plane for the Civil Air Patrol during World War II, operated a successful fish hatchery, and resumed one of his bus routes. At the time of his death from Hodgkin's disease on October 18, 1953, he was running a stage line between North Bend and Marshfield, Oregon.

References:

Wilbur H. Gorst, *Vern C. Gorst, Pioneer and Grandad of United Airlines* (Coos Bay, Ore.: Gorst Publications, 1979);

Robert E. Johnson, *Airway One: A Narrative of United Air Lines and Its Leaders* (Chicago: United Air Lines, 1974);

Grover Loening, *Amphibian: The Story of the Loening Biplane* (Greenwich, Conn.: New York Graphic Society, 1973);

Frank J. Taylor, *High Horizons: Daredevil Flying Postmen to Modern Magic Carpet—the United Air Lines Story* (New York: McGraw-Hill, 1964).

Archives:

United Air Lines Archives, Chicago, Illinois.

Daniel Guggenheim

(July 9, 1856 - September 28, 1930)

by Richard P. Hallion

Office of Air Force History

CAREER: Partner, M. Guggenheim's Sons (1882-1916); partner, Guggenheim Exploration Company (1899-1916); partner, Guggenheim Brothers (1916-1923); founder, Daniel and Florence Guggenheim Foundation (1924); founder, Daniel Guggenheim School of Aeronautics, New York University (1925); founder, Daniel Guggenheim Fund for the Promotion of Aeronautics (1926).

Harry F. Guggenheim

(August 23, 1890 - January 22, 1971)

CAREER: U.S. Navy (1917-1921, 1942-1945); adviser to the chancellor, New York University (1925); president, Daniel Guggenheim Fund for the Promotion of Aeronautics (1926-1930); member, Commission of Experts to the League of Nations for Limitations on Air Armaments (1927); delegate, Third Pan American Conference (1927); delegate, International Conference on Civil Aeronautics (1928); U.S. ambassador to Cuba (1929-1933); president and director, Daniel and Florence Guggenheim Foundation (1930-1971); member, Main Committee, National Advisory Committee for Aeronautics (1931-1938); chairman, New York City Airport Authority (1946).

The father-and-son team of Daniel and Harry F. Guggenheim dramatically transformed the face of world aviation through a series of philanthropic grants that established research and educational programs in the aerospace sciences. Daniel Guggenheim, one of seven brothers and three sisters (an eighth brother died in childhood), was born in Philadelphia on July 9, 1856, the son of Swiss Jewish parents who had immigrated to the United States to escape a religious war and Swiss anti-Semitism.

Left to right: Robert Goddard, Harry Guggenheim, and Charles A. Lindbergh, 1930 (courtesy of the National Air and Space Museum)

Guggenheim's father, Meyer, a shrewd businessman, expanded the family's business interests from lace, housewares, and stove polish to silver mining; son Daniel spearheaded the expansion of that mining business into a worldwide mining and smelting empire that ranged from Chile to Alaska. Guggenheim saw the airplane as a natural extension of the transportation revolution begun by the railroads; when his son Harry became a naval pilot in World War I, he encouraged him to think about what the airplane could accomplish for business and commerce once the war was over. After the war he looked for various ventures to endow before establishing the Daniel and Florence Guggenheim Foundation in 1924. The next year Harry, then serving as an adviser to the chancellor of New York University, mentioned that the school wanted to establish a laboratory and endow a program in aeronautical engineering. His father saw this as the opportunity to influence the future of aeronautics and undertook, on his own, to give a $500,000 grant creating the Guggenheim School of Aeronautics at NYU.

The resulting outpouring of support led Daniel and Harry to establish a general fund, the Daniel Guggenheim Fund for the Promotion of Aeronautics, that lasted from 1926 to 1930. In that time, it endowed major schools of aeronautical engineering at the California Institute of Technology, the Massachusetts Institute of Technology, the Georgia School (later Institute) of Technology, the University of Washington, the University of Michigan, Stanford University, and the University of Akron. In addition, it supported major research in the areas of instrument flying technology and techniques, airline and airway development and operation, and short-takeoff-and-landing aircraft design and development. Other grants supported publicity campaigns to make the American public "air minded" (including tours by aviators Richard Byrd and Charles Lindbergh), town marking to assist navigation, and the use of airmail.

In the view of professional aeronautical engineers, researchers, and airmen, the accomplishments of the Guggenheim fund were remarkable. The National Advisory Committee for Aeronautics (the forerunner of the National Aeronautics and Space Administration) noted that the fund was one of the most important factors in the advance of aviation between 1926 and 1930 and judged its educational work "outstanding." Charles Lindbergh considered it "timely, well directed, and of extraordinary benefit to aeronautical progress," further remarking that "aviation will always owe a debt of gratitude to Daniel Guggenheim."

Harry Guggenheim made significant contributions of his own to aviation following the death of his father in 1930. Like his father, he believed in the potential of the airplane to influence world commerce and world peace. Guggenheim served on a variety of boards and directorates in the 1930s and retained close ties to the aviation community, particularly with Charles Lindbergh. During this time, the two men were instrumental in supporting the work of rocket pioneer Robert Goddard. On the basis of Guggenheim funding, Goddard was able to

conduct significant flight test experimentation and development of liquid-fueled rockets. So extensive was his insight and work that, by the time of his death in 1945, a liquid-fueled rocket could not be built without infringing on one or more of Goddard's patents.

Guggenheim also served as a member of the prestigious Main Committee of the National Advisory Committee for Aeronautics from 1931 to 1938. During World War II he returned to naval service, attaining the rank of captain, and eventually flying as a combat observer on carrier air strikes against Japan in 1945. In the post-World War II years Guggenheim held a series of civic and public service positions that kept him busy; he is perhaps best-known for his establishment of the Long Island newspaper *Newsday*, which he ran jointly with his wife, Alicia Patterson Guggenheim. He argued against the Truman Doctrine and its policy of containment, believing that the vital interests of the United States lay in the Western Hemisphere, and not in Asia or Europe.

In the post-1945 years Guggenheim resumed his friendship with Lindbergh (which had been strained by Lindbergh's isolationist stance in the years before Pearl Harbor), worked to secure Goddard's position in history, and attempted to duplicate his father's success in setting up a major series of grants to aviation. The amount of money needed in the post-1945 world to affect the future of flight was, of course, well beyond what even the Guggenheims could provide, and the overall impact of these grants, which set up a series of specialized laboratories and research programs nationwide in a variety of technical areas, must be judged not nearly as successful as the earlier grants were from 1926 to 1930. Nevertheless, the grants that were made greatly benefited particular areas of aerospace interest, especially aviation medicine, propulsion, aviation safety, and the design of flight structures. Ironically, when Guggenheim died quietly on January 22, 1971, the man who had devoted so much of his life to the cause of aeronautics was remembered primarily for his founding of *Newsday*.

Publications of Harry F. Guggenheim:

The Seven Skies (New York: Putnam's, 1930);
The United States and Cuba (New York: Macmillan, 1934);
Hemispheric Integration Now: An Address (Gainesville: University of Florida Press, 1951).

References:

Reginald M. Cleveland, *America Fledges Wings: The History of The Daniel Guggenheim Fund for the Promotion of Aeronautics* (New York: Pitman, 1942);

John H. Davis, *The Guggenheims: An American Epic* (New York: Morrow, 1978);

Richard P. Hallion, *Legacy of Flight: The Guggenheim Contribution to American Aviation* (Seattle: University of Washington Press, 1977);

Milton Lomask, *Seed Money: The Guggenheim Story* (New York: Farrar, Straus & Giroux, 1964);

Harvey O'Connor, *The Guggenheims: The Making of An American Dynasty* (New York: Covici, 1937).

Archives:

The papers of the Daniel Guggenheim Fund for the Promotion of Aeronautics are in the collections of the Manuscript Division, Library of Congress, Washington, D. C. Relevant materials may also be found in the archives of the California Institute of Technology, Pasadena, California, particularly the papers of Robert A. Millikan, a fund trustee. The Robert H. Goddard papers are at Clark University, Worcester, Massachusetts.

Najeeb E. Halaby

(November 19, 1915 -   )

by W. Alfred Dahler

Kemper Military School

CAREER: Lawyer, O'Melveny and Myers, Los Angeles (1940-1942); test pilot, Lockheed Aircraft Corporation (1942-1943); naval aviator and test pilot (1943-1946); Research and Intelligence Branch, U.S. Department of State (1946-1948); foreign affairs adviser, U.S. Department of Defense (1948-1953); deputy assistant secretary of defense (1952-1953); administrator, Federal Aviation Agency (1961-1965); senior vice-president (1965-1968), president (1968-1971), chief executive officer, Pan American World Airways (1970-1972).

Najeeb E. Halaby, aviator, lawyer, government administrator, corporate executive, and entrepreneur, was born on November 19, 1915, in Dallas, Texas, the only child of Najeeb and Laura Wilkins Halaby. Halaby's father came from what was then Greater Syria, which later became Lebanon. Around 1900 the father, about twelve years old and accompanied by one of his brothers, immigrated to the United States, sold off a few of the family goods, and brought the rest of the family to their new homeland. The father became an unusually gifted entrepreneur, establishing an excellent reputation as an importer of fine fabrics, rugs, and works of art. Eventually settling in Dallas, Texas, he met Laura Wilkins, an interior decorator and designer. Their mutual cultural interests blended into a business partnership as well as a matrimonial one.

During the 1920s, the financially secure Halaby family enjoyed the good life America had to

Najeeb E. Halaby (courtesy of the National Air and Space Museum)

offer. However, in 1927 the parents were divorced and Najeeb was sent to a private boarding school in New York. His father died about eight months later, and Najeeb and his mother moved to California. Shortly thereafter, his mother decided to send him to a do-everything-for-yourself boys' school in northern Michigan, called Leelanau, in Glen Arbor. Williams Beals, the headmaster, had a tremendous impact in molding Halaby's character, instilling in him a desire to perfect and serve society and to care about fellow human beings and the underprivileged.

Halaby went on to attend Stanford University, from which he graduated in 1937 with a degree in political science. He attended the University of Michigan Law School for two years, then transferred to Yale Law School, where he received his LL.B. degree in 1940. Returning to California, Halaby joined the law firm of O'Melveny and Myers in Los Angeles. In addition to his corporate practice, he also worked with the Legal Aid Society, assisting indigent blacks, poor whites, and Mexicans with legal problems.

In 1932 Halaby had learned how to fly in an OX-5 Travel Air two-seat biplane, soloing after only six hours of dual instruction. (He dubbed himself a "natural born" pilot, having the natural coordination essential for above-average cockpit performance.) When American involvement in World War II became a distinct possibility, the government started a Civilian Pilot Training Program. Halaby promptly enlisted to train as an instructor. He got up at dawn to take flying lessons, worked at his law firm during the day, and returned in the evening to continue flying lessons. Aware that the Lockheed Aircraft Corporation needed pilots, he left his law firm and the flight academy to take on a full-time job in aviation. While working at Lockheed, he enrolled in aeronautical engineering courses at the University of California, where he developed an interest in scientific aircraft testing techniques.

After delivering a Lockheed Lodestar to the Navy Flight Test Section at Anacostia in the nation's capital, Halaby expressed his desire to join the navy and serve his country. Three days later he was commissioned a lieutenant, junior grade, in the Naval Reserve. Assigned to the Carrier Fighter Test Section, Flight Test, Naval Air Test Center, Patuxent River, Maryland, he became a sort of a barnyard aeronautical engineer, specializing in strange and exotic fighter aircraft. Later he was named project pilot for the first American-built jet, the YP-59, in which he established an altitude record of 46,900 feet. Halaby also completed the first

transcontinental jet flight in American aviation history. His one regret, he later wrote, was that he never saw combat (the navy obviously felt that he was too valuable as a test pilot to be released for combat duty). While in the navy, Halaby met Doris Carlquist; they were married in 1946 in the Washington Cathedral.

Halaby left the navy as a full lieutenant in 1946 to join the Research and Intelligence Branch of the State Department. In this capacity he served as a civil aviation adviser to the government of Saudi Arabia, King Ibn Sa'ud 'Ab al-'Aziz, and SAUDIA, the royal family airline. In 1948 Halaby was hired by the Department of Defense as an assistant to John H. Ohly. Ohly's responsibilities included international affairs, foreign intelligence, and liaison with the Joint Chiefs of Staff. Halaby worked as part of a group that developed NSC-68, which became the cornerstone of America's foreign and defense policy during the cold war. He survived the transition from the Democratic administration to a Republican one, serving as deputy assistant secretary of defense for international affairs.

In 1953 Halaby decided to leave federal service when Laurance Rockefeller, chairman and director of the Rockefeller Center, Inc., offered him a position as a personal troubleshooter. Halaby's duties for Rockefeller included working on a company called Reaction Motors (an early manufacturer of rocket engines), doing a survey of Eastern Airlines, and taking an intensive training course in investment banking at Smith, Barney and Company.

When the Dwight D. Eisenhower administration in 1955 formed the Aviation Facilities Study Group to examine the long-range needs for aviation facilities and aids, Halaby was named vice-chairman of the body, on loan from the Rockefeller office. One of the group's more far-reaching recommendations called for the creation of a special assistant to the president, with offices in the White House. This individual, among other tasks, would draw up a plan for organizing a new civil aviation agency. The group recommended Edward P. Curtis, vice-president of Eastman Kodak, for the job. After Curtis accepted the post, he recommended that Halaby be named Civil Aeronautics Administration administrator. Halaby demurred, saying that he needed to make more money after his many years in government service.

In 1956 Halaby decided that the time had come to leave the Rockefellers and look for challenging employment elsewhere. He returned to California and accepted the executive vice-presidency of Servo-Mechanisms, Inc., a $20 million-a-year electronics subsystem manufacturer with plants in Los Angeles and Long Island, New York. While on the West Coast, Halaby served as a lecturer at the University of California at Los Angeles. He also established an individual law practice.

Shortly after the election of John F. Kennedy as president in 1960, Halaby received intimations that he was being considered for the position of administrator of the Federal Aviation Agency (FAA). An expert aviation specialist with outstanding government credentials, Halaby appealed to Kennedy because he was bright, sophisticated, and blessed with the dry wit that the president cherished in his appointees. Theodore Sorensen, recalling Kennedy's selection process, wrote:

> The men he picked were for the most part men who thought his thoughts, spoke his language and put their country and Kennedy ahead of any other concern.... They were, like him, dedicated but unemotional, young but experienced, articulate but soft-spoken. There were no crusaders, fanatics or extremists from any camp; all were nearer the center than either left or right. All spoke with the same low-keyed restraint that marked their chief, yet all shared his deep conviction that they would change America's drift.

Halaby, who fit this description almost perfectly, informed Kennedy that he was only interested in the position if it were clearly understood that he would report directly to the president and that he be named presidential aviation adviser as well as FAA administrator. Kennedy consented on both counts. Halaby skillfully handled the delicate political process of confirmation by the Senate, and on March 3, 1961, he was confirmed as the second administrator of the FAA.

While waiting for confirmation, Halaby served as a consultant to the FAA. It was during this time that serious safety questions were being raised about the Lockheed Electra. After personally test-flying the Electra, Halaby expressed his firm conviction that the aircraft was not only safe but also was an extremely fine machine. Halaby was criticized from several quarters for his personal involvement in test-flying the aircraft and was accused of

"headline hunting." His hands-on style of leadership often would be criticized by unfriendly politicians during his term as FAA administrator, but it worked for most FAA employees and for the client organizations served by the agency.

Although controversy and crises often became a way of life for Halaby after he assumed his duties as FAA administrator, he started out on a conciliatory note. In the beginning, the Air Transport Association, Airline Pilots Association, and Aircraft Owners and Pilots Association were all favorably impressed with the new administrator. Halaby made it clear that he wanted to maintain the FAA's reputation for strict enforcement of the rules of the air while at the same time making his agency more responsive to the aviation community's views.

Halaby also reversed his predecessor Elwood R. Quesada's quest toward management centralization of the FAA in Washington, taking the position that the agency had to concentrate its effort in the field. He established seven regions, each directed and managed by a regional administrator, and curtailed the authority and responsibility of the functional staff groups within the FAA. Halaby established Project Horizon to define the technical, economic, and military objectives of the federal government throughout the spectrum of aviation and to facilitate long-range planning. In addition, he initiated Project Beacon to prepare a practicable long-range plan to insure efficient and safe control of all air traffic within the United States. He had hoped that both projects would provide focus for the government's aeronautical policies and eliminate controversy, but this was not to be. Instead, he faced numerous bureaucratic battles, as various agencies fought for control over the formulation of transportation policy. Halaby had to use all his powers of persuasion and his position as aviation adviser to the president to break the logjam.

Halaby then turned his fence-mending activities toward general aviation. He sent a letter to every licensed pilot in the United States and invited their comments, criticisms, and suggestions on all aviation matters. He followed this up by going out into the field and holding "Hangar Flying Sessions" or "Air Share Meetings," personally meeting with the aviation public.

Halaby's attitude toward air traffic controllers was one of tremendous respect for the vast majority of them, sympathy toward their problems, and an intense awareness of their dedication and devotion to their duties. He was shocked at the dingy, overcrowded, and almost primitive working conditions that existed in the air traffic control centers. Controllers were using World War II radar equipment to handle 600-mile-an-hour jet traffic and were keeping track of flights with the old "shrimp boat" method dating back to the DC-3 days. Halaby did much to alleviate the technical as well as the human problems in the air traffic control system. He launched an intensive retraining program at the FAA's Oklahoma City training center and managed to get three pay raises for the controllers. When President Kennedy signed the order authorizing the creation of federal employee unions, Halaby felt that an exemption should be made for air traffic controllers, placing them into the same category as members of the armed forces, the CIA, and other agencies dealing in national defense or security matters. He suggested the formation of a Federal Aviation Service for controllers within the FAA. His efforts were not supported by Kennedy, however. This eventually led to the formation of the Professional Air Traffic Controller Organization (PATCO)—and the confrontation between President Ronald Reagan and PATCO in the early 1980s.

In the 1960s spokesmen for the aviation industry predicted that other countries would launch Supersonic Transport (SST) programs even if the United States did not. Halaby quickly decided that the SST was an important goal for the country and one that would fit well with the Kennedy administration's vision of America's future. Although he found strong interest in the project on Capitol Hill, he had a much more difficult time selling the program to the American air carriers. The airlines questioned the economic viability of the SST, seeing it as a venture that might be undertaken more for reasons of national prestige than for a commercial success. Halaby remained a strong advocate of the SST program throughout the Kennedy years and into the Lyndon B. Johnson administration. He later wrote that, at the time he got involved in the project, the SST looked like the airplane of the future; however, he later admitted that he was not sorry that the project never got off the ground. An American SST, he finally concluded, would have been a financial disaster for all concerned: manufacturer, government, and airlines.

Halaby knew that his ultimate effectiveness as FAA administrator would be measured by his impact on aviation safety. He worked tirelessly during

his five years as administrator to improve the safety of the airways, especially in the area of government-industry cooperation. His formation of a joint civil-military program doubled radar coverage of en route traffic. He upgraded the proficiency of flight inspectors, introduced new tools to help controllers, renewed the Aid to Airports Act, improved air to ground communications, set up a system of inspection for airport operators, clamped down on falsification of aviation records, and rolled back the first wave of skyjacking. He joined with the Civil Aeronautics Board in setting up a new accident-investigation school, improved regulations governing emergency evacuations, stepped up medical investigation of general aviation accidents, and ended turbulence upset as a major safety hazard. He enlarged the area of positive air traffic control to cover virtually the entire country, developed better approach and runway lighting, began experiments on the use of parallel runways, increased radio range coverage by 17 percent, and added 58 new instrument landing systems to airports served by air carriers.

Faithfully serving President Kennedy, Halaby established an impressive record as FAA administrator. Because of his efforts, much of the early controversy surrounding the agency subsided. He opened avenues of communication within the FAA and with the aviation community, disarming much of the animosity against the agency that had grown up under Quesada. He amply demonstrated his management skills and managed to survive intragovernmental struggles over control of aviation policy while at the same time strengthening the FAA's position as an independent agency. Halaby came to understand politics as the art of the possible.

After President Kennedy's assassination in November 1963, it quickly became clear that Halaby, who had had a close personal working relationship with Kennedy, would not enjoy the same access to Lyndon Johnson. Increasingly frustrated in his attempts to incorporate aviation programs into Johnson's vision of the Great Society, he valiantly struggled against the new tide. Fearing a return to the neglect of the early 1950s, he fought the Bureau of the Budget's proposed cuts in FAA's fiscal 1966 budget.

Unhappy with his lack of access to the White House and disillusioned by the administration's relative disinterest in aviation, Halaby was ready to return to private life. He had served longer than any previous FAA or CAA administrator, and the rigors of the 24-hour-a-day job and the many political battles he had fought had taken their toll. He also had made a considerable financial sacrifice to serve in the government.

Halaby resigned on his own accord, but apparently under unfriendly circumstances. President Johnson never acknowledged his resignation with a traditional "personal regret" letter. However, during his successor's swearing-in ceremony, Johnson did have some kind words of gratitude for Halaby, praise that he certainly had earned by his exemplary performance as FAA administrator. A greater tribute came from FAA professionals. On Halaby's last flight (from Los Angeles to Washington) as FAA administrator, the personnel of the various control centers relayed messages of regret of his leaving and thanked him for his concerns and the exceptional support he had provided to the FAA and its personnel.

Before leaving the FAA, Halaby prepared a memo for the president, suggesting the creation of a department of transportation even though such a department would end the FAA's coveted independent status. Halaby further suggested that the chief officer of the department be given cabinet status. Eventually, these changes would be made.

Early in 1965 Halaby had organized a conference at the FAA called the "Annual Shareholders Meeting of the Aviation Community," an informal exchange of ideas about mutual aviation problems. Harold Gray, newly elected president of Pan American World Airways, had been so impressed with the meeting that he had suggested to Juan Trippe, founder and chief executive officer of the airline, that Halaby be considered for an executive position. Trippe had shown interest in the suggestion. Although no job offer had been forthcoming, there seems to have been an understanding that something would be available for Halaby should he decide to leave the government.

Negotiations for Halaby to join Pan Am started soon after he left the FAA. Halaby had reservations about joining the airline for several reasons. First, he believed that his deteriorating relationship with President Johnson might make him less valuable to the company than Trippe assumed. Second, he was concerned about Pan Am's labor relations. Third, he was troubled by the airline's lack of service competitiveness, and the poor communications between marketing and operation personnel. Fi-

nally, having enjoyed a virtual monopoly in the international markets, Pan Am might have great difficulties in facing fresh, aggressive competition.

Trippe finally convinced Halaby to join Pan Am as a senior vice-president by promising to retire within a year or 18 months and revitalizing the executive management functions at Pan Am. Halaby accepted Trippe's offer, expecting an equal chance at the chief executive officer job with Gray when Trippe retired. Unfortunately for Halaby, a newspaper story stating that Halaby was going to be Trippe's heir caused him serious relationship problems with the other Pan Am executives and their staffs.

Halaby received some unpleasant surprises upon joining Pan Am. Rather than being given a top priority airline assignment, he found himself shuffled into miscellaneous nonairline activities away from the operating line of command. Also, Trippe began to pressure Halaby to visit Washington on behalf of Pan Am and act as a lobbyist. Despite these drawbacks and frustrations, Halaby found working for Pan Am to be an exciting challenge.

Officially, Halaby became senior vice-president of Pan Am's Guided Missile Range Division. Also under his jurisdiction were the Business Jet Division, a partnership with the French Avions Marcel Dassault Company to manufacture a business jet; New York Airways, a scheduled helicopter service; project STOL (Short Takeoff and Landing) operations in the busy northeastern corridor; and the operation of Teterboro Airport and East Side Metroport for helicopters. As Halaby later put it, he became vice-president in charge of diversification without the hotel organization (a subsidiary of Pan Am). Later, he also became involved in this area.

Starting in 1966, Trippe and Pan Am made several financial decisions which later proved detrimental to Pan Am in general and Halaby specifically. Trippe ordered 25 Boeing 747s for $525 million—the largest single purchase of one type of aircraft in the history of commercial aviation. Later, Gray made a commitment for eight additional 747s. Also, Gray purchased a new $98 million maintenance center at JFK Airport and spent $126 million on the Worldport, Pan Am's terminal facilities at JFK.

In May 1968 Trippe decided to retire. Gray was selected as Pan Am's chief executive officer, and Halaby was promoted to president. Upon

Gray's retirement in 1970, Halaby assumed full command of Pan Am, being elevated to chief executive officer while retaining the presidency. The biggest challenge Halaby faced was to change Pan Am's archaic personnel policies. He had to convince employees that the company was in a competitive struggle to survive and that there had to be communication and collaboration between the unions and management. Under Halaby's direction, Pan Am instituted a program of decentralized management, delegating authority to the field functions. He tried to get across the fact that the company really cared about its employees, that Pan Am had serious problems that could only be solved if management and labor pulled together, and that everyone had to realize that the passengers came first—not the executives or the employees.

Problems of increased competition started to plague Pan Am during the Johnson and Richard M. Nixon administrations. Overseas routes were opened to numerous American air carriers in addition to the already heavy competition from foreign airlines. For Pan Am, which had no domestic routes to subsidize its overseas network, the situation approached economic disaster. Previously profitable routes turned into ribbons of red ink. Facilities and personnel were wastefully duplicated. Attempts to increase efficiency collided with government-promoted competitive waste—more aircraft and more airlines flying fewer people for more fuel and higher prices. To ease Pan Am's financial problems, Halaby explored merger possibilities with TWA, Eastern, American, United, and Delta. He was convinced that the best solution to Pan Am's problems would be a merger with an airline that had an existing domestic-route structure.

Then, just as Pan Am acquired its new Boeing 747s, the 1969-1971 economic recession depressed air traffic, adding to Pan Am's problem of overcapacity. In addition, the 747s developed costly powerplant difficulties that caused interrupted trips, canceled flights, and added $2.5 million a month in additional operating costs. Finally, hanging over Pan Am's head was $1 billion in debt plus huge interest and rental charges.

Because of all the airline's woes, it became clear to Halaby that he could no longer carry the multiheaded role that had been thrust upon him—keeping the directors and shareholders happy, holding bankers at bay, negotiating mergers, lobbying in Washington, and running the day-to-day opera-

tion of an international airline. With the approval of the board of directors, he brought in William Seawell as president in charge of Pan Am's daily operations.

Looking back at the time in 1970 when he assumed both the presidency and the chief executive officership of Pan Am, Halaby later wrote in his autobiography: "I now see it would have taken a man with much greater airline-operating experience and a successful student of Machiavelli to run a company as big as Pan Am, one so involved in self-satisfaction, prior arrogance toward the public and the government, and one internally full of divided loyalties and prejudices."

Hiring Seawell, however, did not alleviate Halaby's problems; instead, it compounded them. Charges soon were levied against Halaby that he was interfering with Seawell's operation of the company. A special board committee, unfriendly to Halaby, examined the complaint and recommended to the board that Halaby resign. During a special board meeting in March 1972, Halaby offered, if given the board's confidence, to continue for another two years; lacking such confidence, he would stay on until a new chief executive officer could be named, or resign immediately. The board chose to accept his immediate resignation. Seawell then was named president and chief executive officer.

Leaving Pan Am, Halaby felt that he had suffered a defeat and a disappointment, but that he had not failed. He went on to form an international venture-capital group, Halaby International, with operations in the Middle East and Southeast Asia. Admitted to the New York bar in 1973, Halaby functioned as an international negotiator and problem solver. He also became a civil aviation adviser to the government of Jordan, where he was instrumental in developing the Arab Air Service Corporation, Ltd., to train pilots, mechanics, controllers, and other civil airmen for all the Arab world.

Halaby and the former Doris Carlquist were divorced in 1977; they had three children: Christian (a professional musician), Alexa (a lawyer), and Lisa (who married King Hussein in 1978 and became Queen Noor of Jordan). After his divorce Halaby married Jan Allison Coates.

Publication:

Crosswinds: An Airman's Memoir (Garden City, N.Y.: Doubleday, 1978).

References:

Richard J. Kent, Jr., *Safe, Separated and Soaring: A His-*

tory of Federal Civil Aviation Policy 1961-1972 (Washington, D.C.: U.S. Government Printing Office, 1980);

Theodore Sorenson, *Kennedy* (New York: Harper & Row, 1965).

George R. Hann

(November 7, 1891 - June 5, 1979)

by William F. Trimble

Auburn University

CAREER: Lawyer and financier (1920s-1970s); president, Pittsburgh Aviation Industries Corporation (1928-1934); chairman, Capital Airlines (1948-1960).

In May 1928 George Rice Hann, a prominent Pittsburgh lawyer and trust company executive, determined to do "something to make the business men of the City ... air minded." With C. Bedell Monro, Frederick R. Crawford, and Norman Allderdice, Hann raised nearly $1.2 million from a door-to-door solicitation of the Pittsburgh business community. The money capitalized Pittsburgh Aviation Industries Corporation (PAIC), formed in December 1928 as a holding company with subsidiaries in passenger air transport, aerial photography, flight training, airports, and aircraft manufacturing. As president, director, and the major stockholder in PAIC, Hann worked tirelessly to secure favorable treatment for the new company during the restructuring of the nation's airmail system in 1930. That year, Postmaster General Walter Folger Brown forced the acquisition by PAIC of Clifford Ball's Pennsylvania Air Lines, thereby giving Hann's company the lucrative Cleveland-Pittsburgh-Washington airmail route and embarking Hann on a long and successful career as an airline financier.

Born in Birmingham, Alabama, on November 7, 1891, Hann was the son of Charles and Annie Sykes Hann. From Birmingham, Hann and his family moved to Brookline, Massachusetts. He attended Phillips-Andover Academy in Massachusetts and received his bachelor's degree from Yale in 1913. A year later he joined the Union Trust Company in Pittsburgh, working his way into the legal branch of the trust department. After serving two years as

a naval officer during World War I, Hann received a law degree from the University of Pittsburgh in 1919. Given responsibility for handling the estate of iron-ore magnate Henry W. Oliver in 1920, Hann quickly learned the intricacies of high finance and established important business contacts in Pittsburgh and New York.

Hann's involvement in aviation stemmed from the reorganization and expansion of the Fairchild Aviation Corporation in 1926. Hann became a close friend of Sherman Fairchild, spent considerable time at the company's headquarters in Farmingdale, New York, and took seats on Fairchild's board of directors and executive committee. The Fairchild connection was Hann's link to the New York financial world. By 1928 he had met and forged friendships with key people in the Barnsdall Oil Company, IBM, Otis Elevator, and, most significant, the Lehman Brothers investment house. Hann's experience and his contacts in business and financial circles helped convince Postmaster General Brown in 1930 that PAIC was a viable enterprise with the resources necessary to foster the growth of commercial aviation.

PAIC's corporate strength played a major part in Brown's strategy of establishing three coast-to-coast air routes. Transcontinental Air Transport (TAT), established in 1928, used rail connections on the mountainous eastern and western segments of its route. When Brown negotiated a merger of TAT and Western Air Express in 1930, the resulting company, Transcontinental and Western Air (TWA), bid on and received the midcontinent route. Hann insisted, however, that PAIC, holding what he called a "pioneering equity" in TWA's air route across Pennsylvania, receive a 5 percent interest in the new company. One of PAIC's executives, Richard W. Robbins, became president of TWA in 1931.

PAIC's success was a model for Hann in putting together a second and much larger aviation holding company. Through Lehman Brothers and W. A. Harriman and Company in New York, Hann devised a scheme to underwrite the financing of the Aviation Corporation (AVCO) in 1929. With Hann as vice-chairman of both the board of directors and the executive committee, AVCO went on a buying spree that resulted in the acquisition of Colonial Airways, Universal Aviation, Interstate Airlines, Braniff, Embry-Riddle, and Fairchild. From the consolidation of AVCO's smaller holdings emerged American Airways, which won the coveted southern transcontinental airmail route.

When the special investigating committee of Senator Hugo Black uncovered collusion among the airlines and Postmaster General Brown in letting airmail contracts in 1930, Hann and other airline executives were caught in a storm of criticism. President Franklin D. Roosevelt responded by canceling all airmail contracts in February 1934. After a brief and tragic interlude when the Army Air Corps attempted to fly the mail, Congress enacted new legislation that prevented holding companies from owning both aviation manufacturing firms and airlines and forced the reorganization of all airlines holding contracts under the previous airmail law. The measure prohibited the new companies from receiving airmail contracts if they retained executives who had been involved with Brown in the 1930 negotiations. Accordingly, Pennsylvania Air Lines emerged as Pennsylvania Air Lines and Transport Company, and AVCO shed American Airways, which became American Airlines. Hann relinquished his seats on the boards of both companies while still wielding considerable influence through his substantial stock holdings.

Hann's continued financial interest was most evident in the subsequent development of Pennsylvania Air Lines. Largely through Hann's intervention, PAL in 1936 bought Central Air Lines, a Pittsburgh company that had received the Cleveland-Washington airmail route in the shakeup of 1934. The merged company, named Pennsylvania-Central Airlines Corporation (PCA), was in a relatively better position to expand service in the Northeast.

With improved equipment, chiefly the fabled DC-3, PCA turned the corner to profitability by 1939. After the war, PCA challenged the Big Four on longer and more competitive routes; it was renamed Capital Airlines in 1948, reflecting its less regional orientation. Although Hann remained at arm's length on most management decisions, he used his position as chairman of the board to engineer the purchase of Vickers Viscount turboprops in 1955. Capital employed the sleek British aircraft on many of its nonstop routes, including New York to Chicago and connections to Florida. Falling revenues, labor troubles, and the increased debt load imposed by the Viscount acquisition eventually proved more than the company could bear. In 1960 Hann stepped down as chairman of the board as the company slid toward bankruptcy. The end came only a few months later when United Air Lines announced the purchase of Capital. The acquisition of Capital, formalized in 1961, made United the nation's largest air carrier.

Following the buyout, Hann retained major stock holdings in United, although he refrained from any management decisions. He died at his estate, "Treetops," in Sewickley Heights, Pennsylvania, on June 5, 1979, leaving behind one of the world's most extensive collections of Russian icons. A tough-minded financier, Hann represented the second generation of airline leaders, who in the 1920s and 1930s consolidated the gains of the aviation pioneers to create a modern air transport system.

Publications:
"1928—Pittsburgh and Aviation—1933," *Greater Pittsburgh*, 15 (January 1934): 44-45.

References:
"Air Merger," *Bulletin Index* (Pittsburgh), 109 (October 29, 1936): 21-22;

"George R. Hann on the Early Aviation Industry in Pittsburgh," *Western Pennsylvania Historical Magazine*, 61 (July 1978): 233-245;

Frank C. Harper, *Pittsburgh of Today: Its Resources and People*, volume 3 (New York: American Historical Society, 1931), pp. 81-82;

"Pittsburgh Aviation Industries Corporation," *Aero Digest*, 24 (March 1934): 23-28, 64;

William F. Trimble, *High Frontier: A History of Aeronautics in Pennsylvania* (Pittsburgh: University of Pittsburgh Press, 1982).

Harris M. Hanshue

(July 7, 1881 - January 8, 1937)

by Patricia A. Michaelis

Kansas State Historical Society

CAREER: Pacific Coast agent, Apperson Brothers Automobile Company (1914-1924); founder, president, and general manager, Western Air Express (1925-1934); president, Fokker Aircraft Company (1930-1932); president, Transcontinental & Western Air (1930-1931).

Airline pioneer Harris Mathewson "Pop" Hanshue was the founder and president of Western Air Express, the most successful of the early commercial air transport companies in the United States. He also served as first president of Transcontinental & Western Air (TWA), which became one of the dominant airlines in the passenger aviation industry.

Hanshue was born in Mendon, Michigan, on July 7, 1881, the son of John Jay and Mary Mathewson Hanshue. He attended public schools in Lansing and Kalamazoo, then went on to the University of Michigan, where he studied civil engineering. His early business experience was in the automobile industry. He worked for the Olds Motor Works in Lansing, then moved to California as a mechanic for the company in 1903. He soon left his original employer and was associated with several companies in the automobile business. For a time, he raced automobiles with some success. In 1914 he became the Pacific Coast agent for Apperson Brothers Automobile Company of Kokomo, Indiana. With headquarters in Los Angeles, he operated a successful automobile dealership for the next ten years. On October 7, 1914, he married Irene Victoria McMillen; they had two children.

The enactment of the Air Mail Act of 1925 attracted Hanshue and a group of prominent Angeles businessmen to commercial aviation. On July 15, 1925, they organized Western Air Express (WAE), with Hanshue as president. Four months later, on November 7, WAE secured a contract

Harris M. Hanshue (courtesy of the National Air and Space Museum)

from the Post Office to operate the new airmail route (CAM-4) between Los Angeles and Salt Lake City.

WAE opened service on CAM-4 with six Douglas M-2s on April 17, 1926. Two weeks later, it began carrying passengers in the M-2s, which had space for two people in the cargo area. By the end of the year, WAE had transported 66,000 pounds of mail and 209 intrepid passengers, recording a profit of $28,674.

WAE continued to operate in the black during 1927. Passenger traffic doubled. Also, thanks to airmail payments, WAE became the first airline to pay a dividend to its stockholders. Even more important was the signing on September 15 of a $180,000 loan agreement with the Daniel Guggenheim Fund for the Promotion of Aeronautics for development of a "Model Airway" between Los Angeles and San Francisco. The Guggenheims wanted to encourage popular support of air travel by demonstrating its reliability and safety. Hanshue, who firmly supported passenger operation, used the money to purchase three Fokker F-10 trimotored transports.

Service on the "Model Airway" began on May 26, 1928. It was soon supported by another Guggenheim Fund-supported project—a model weather reporting network. A group of weather reporting stations collected data for daily forecasts that warned of poor flying conditions. This helped to account for WAE's 99 percent on-schedule reliability during the first seven months of accident-free operation on the route. The service proved popular, and some 3,000 people flew between Los Angeles and San Francisco during 1927 in the spacious 12-passenger Fokkers.

Taking advantage of the boom in aviation securities that followed Charles A. Lindbergh's dramatic transatlantic flight, Hanshue and Frank A. Talbot, president of the Richfield Oil Company and one of WAE's principal investors, formed Western Air Express, Inc., on October 1, 1928. Capitalized at $5 million, the new company acquired control of the Fokker Aircraft Corporation of America, which had manufacturing plants in New Jersey and West Virginia. The airline promptly ordered five giant four-engine Fokker F-32s for its growing passenger service.

WAE's continued expansion in 1929 included a new route from Los Angeles to Kansas City, opened in June. Hanshue also acquired West Coast Air Transport, which operated a passenger service between San Francisco and Seattle. During the year, WAE carried nearly 22,000 passengers and made a profit of $1.87 million (thanks to airmail revenues from CAM-4).

In May 1930 Hanshue added Standard Airlines, a passenger line with routes from California to Texas, to his rapidly growing company. By this time, WAE had become the nation's largest airline, using its fleet of 40 airplanes to fly more route miles and carry more passengers than any competitor.

Also in May, Hanshue was called to Washington for a series of meetings with Postmaster General Walter Folger Brown and other major airline operators. Intent on rationalizing the nation's air transport system, Brown had decided on a route network that featured three transcontinental lines. Brown had earmarked the central route for a new company that would result from the merger of WAE and Transcontinental Air Transport, which had pioneered an air-rail service between New York and Los Angeles and competed with WAE on the Kansas City-Los Angeles segment of the route. Hanshue bitterly opposed the proposed merger, and did his best to prevent it. Brown, however, used his power to award airmail contracts to force the issue. The "shotgun wedding" took place on October 1, 1930, with the formation of Transcontinental & Western Air.

Hanshue became president of the new TWA for a time, but he resigned in July 1931 and returned to WAE, which had not completely disappeared following the merger agreement. Financially crippled, the airline continued to operate several of its old routes. In 1934 Hanshue fell victim to the recriminations that followed the Black committee's investigation of Postmaster Brown's award of airmail contracts. A new Air Mail Act forced out of the airline business individuals who had participated in what became labeled "spoils conferences" with Brown in 1930. Ironically, this included Hanshue, who had opposed Brown. As airline chronicler Robert J. Serling has observed: "His 'crime' had been to attend an infamous meeting at which he had been mugged. He was not only blameless for what had happened but had tried to stop at least some of it."

Hanshue later was allowed to join Eastern Air Lines. In ill health, with high blood pressure and cardiac problems, he had few duties and soon resigned. He also served as a director of the National Aviation Corporation, Pacific Zeppelin Transport Company, and Hollywood National Bank. He founded the Waterman Arrowplane Company in 1936 and, at the time of his death, he was involved in organizing the Stewart Gravel Mine Company in Gold Run, California. Hanshue died of a cerebral hemorrhage on January 8, 1937.

Publications:
"Western Business Takes *the* Air," *Western Flying* (Janu-

ary 1926): 9-10;

"The Economics of Air Transport," *Western Flying* (June 1927): 11-12, 70;

"Financing Air Transport Lines," *Popular Aviation* (May 1929): 16, 90, 92.

References:

R. E. G. Davies, *Airlines of the United States since 1914* (Washington, D.C.: Smithsonian Institution, 1982);

Richard P. Hallion, *Legacy of Flight: The Guggenheim Contribution to American Aviation* (Seattle: University of Washington Press, 1977);

Patricia A. Michaelis, "The Development of Passenger Service on Commercial Airlines, 1926-1930," dissertation, University of Kansas, 1980;

Robert J. Serling, *The Only Way to Fly: The Story of West-*
ern Airlines, America's Senior Air Carrier (Garden City, N.Y.: Doubleday, 1976);

United States Senate, Special Committee on Investigation of Air Mail and Ocean Mail Contracts, 73rd Congress, 2nd Session, *Hearings,* 9 volumes (Washington, D.C.: U.S. Government Printing Office, 1934).

Archives:

Information on Harris M. Hanshue can be found in the papers of the Daniel Guggenheim Fund for the Promotion of Aeronautics at the Library of Congress; the Commerce Papers at the Herbert Hoover Presidential Library, West Branch, Iowa; the Department of Commerce Papers, Record Group 237, National Archives; and the Trans World Airlines Archives, Kansas City, Missouri.

Hawaiian Airlines

by William M. Leary

University of Georgia

Hawaiian Airlines Douglas DC-3 (courtesy of the National Air and Space Museum)

Hawaiian Airlines was organized on January 30, 1929, as Inter-Island Airways. It took its name from the enterprise's major investor, the Inter-Island Steam Navigation Company. On November 11, 1929, the airline began operations from Oahu to Hawaii's other major islands, using two eight-passenger Sikorsky amphibians.

Inter-Island Airways suffered losses during its first five years of operation, as it slowly built up air traffic among the islands. In 1934 it obtained an air-mail contract from the U.S. Post Office. Although the payments did not provide a subsidy, the additional revenue marked the beginning of profitability. Between 1929 and 1949, the company returned an average earning on investment of 8.5 percent.

In 1941 the airline inaugurated DC-3 service on its interisland routes. On October 1 of that year it changed its name to Hawaiian Airlines. When interisland steamship service was suspended following the Japanese attack on Pearl Harbor in December, the airline became a vital link in the region's transportation system. In addition to passengers, it began to carry large amounts of cargo. This led in 1942 to the granting of an air cargo certificate by the Civil Aeronautics Board.

The postwar years brought competitive challenges to the airline, especially with the appearance in 1949 of Trans-Pacific Airlines (renamed Aloha Airlines in 1959). The struggle for traffic between Hawaiian and Trans-Pacific/Aloha continued for the next 20 years, with each company struggling for advantage. During this period, Hawaiian introduced Convair 580 prop-jet equipment in 1958 and DC-9 service in 1966. The two competitors discussed a merger in 1970-1971, but they were unable to agree on terms.

The 1970s brought mixed success for Hawaiian, with the airline carrying more than three million passengers a year by the end of the decade; but the 1980s saw financial problems that threatened the existence of the company. Deciding that in an era of deregulation, it had to expand outside Hawaii in order to grow, the airline in 1983 used three DC-8s to start a worldwide charter service and a new scheduled service to American Samoa and Tonga. Two years later, it purchased five Lockheed L-1011s and began a scheduled and char-

ter service to the mainland of the United States. In 1987 and 1988, however, Hawaiian lost $17.6 million. Mounting economic difficulties forced it in 1988 to sell for $20 million a 20 percent share of the company to a subsidiary of Japan Air Lines. Late in 1989, a year that saw Hawaiian post a net loss of $42.7 million, an investment group headed by Thomas Talbot and former baseball commissioner Peter Ueberroth acquired control of this financially troubled airline. The new management, however, proved unable to stem the airline's losses, which reached $98 million in 1990. The only bright spot in Hawaiian's generally dismal picture came late in the year with the sale of 25 percent of the carrier to Northwest Airlines for $20 million.

References:

Stan Cohen, *Hawaiian Airlines: A Pictorial History of the Pioneer Carrier in the Pacific* (Missoula, Mont.: Pictorial Histories Publishing Co., 1986);

Arthur D. Lewis, *Hawaiian Airlines: America's Pioneer Carrier in the Pacific* (New York: Newcomen Society in North America, 1960);

J. R. Williams, "Hawaiian 5-0," *Air Line Pilot*, 48 (November 1979): 12-15, 57.

Helicopter Airlines

by William M. Leary

University of Georgia

Helicopters came into widespread use during World War II. By 1945 the military services were operating more than 4,000 of the rotary wing aircraft, all designed by Igor Sikorsky. Following the war, the air force conducted experiments for the Post Office that looked into the possibility of employing helicopters to transport the mail in the Los Angeles and Chicago metropolitan areas. Receiving a favorable recommendation, postal officials decided to try a full-scale test of helicopter mail service. Accordingly, on May 22, 1947, the Civil Aeronautics Board (CAB) awarded Los Angeles Airways a three-year temporary certificate for local mail service.

Los Angeles Airways (LAA) owed its existence to the vision of Clarence M. Belinn. A Pennsylvania hard-coal miner as a youth, Belinn had served in

the Army Air Corps from 1925 to 1929. He went on to work in the maintenance departments of several air carriers, ending up between 1940 and 1944 with Hawaiian Airlines. Having met Igor Sikorsky, Belinn became a "true believer" in the future of helicopters. In 1944 he brought together a group of local businessmen and formed Los Angeles Airways. When the Post Office was looking for a company to carry the first helicopter mail, LAA was ready to undertake the task.

Equipped with five Sikorsky S-51s, the designer's first postwar helicopter, LAA began operations on October 1, 1947. By the end of the year, it had flown 210,000 pounds of mail between Los Angeles International Airport and the roof of the downtown Post Office Annex, and on a circular route that in-

Chicago Helicopter Sikorsky S-55 (courtesy of the National Air and Space Museum)

cluded the San Fernando Valley, San Bernardino, and Newport Beach. In 1948 the airline carried 2.5 million pounds of mail, a figure that rose to 6.1 million pounds in 1954.

In the early 1950s, LAA added air express and passenger service to its highly successful airmail operations. The first helicopter air express service began in December 1953, followed by scheduled passenger service in November 1954. By 1956 LAA was operating 72 daily flights to 16 cities, using seven-passenger Sikorsky S-55s.

The second scheduled helicopter airline to start up was Helicopter Air Service of Chicago. Certified by the CAB in 1949, the company first flew the mail on August 20. Initially its schedule called for 18 trips a day between Midway Airport and the downtown Post Office, plus three daily round trips to 34 suburban heliports. Using six tiny Bell 47s, distinguished by their bug-eyed canopies and skeletal tails, the airline compiled an impressive performance record, carrying 14 million pounds of mail during its first five years of operation.

In 1956 the company changed its name to Chicago Helicopter Airways (CHA) and began scheduled passenger service between Midway and O'Hare airports with three S-55s. The new passenger business proved an immediate success. In 1957 CHA carried 55,000 customers. The next year it added 12-passenger S-58s to its fleet and became the first helicopter airline to carry more than 100,000 people (108,911). This number rose to 204,000 in 1959 and 309,000 in 1960.

New York Airways (NYA), the third and destined to become the largest of the helicopter airlines, got off the ground on October 15, 1952. At first it flew mail only between the three major airports in the Greater New York area—La Guardia, Idlewild, and Newark. But it quickly expanded its schedule to include various suburban communities and began to carry freight. On July 8, 1953, 16 months before Los Angeles Airways, NYA inaugurated the first-ever scheduled helicopter passenger service. By 1959 the airline was carrying 10,000 pas-

Sikorsky S-61N (courtesy of the National Air and Space Museum)

sengers a month, using 15-passenger, twin-rotor, Vertol 44-Bs.

Although the three scheduled helicopter airlines registered impressive increases in traffic during the 1950s, high operating costs led to ever greater federal subsidies. In 1954 the government paid the helicopter airlines $2.6 million. This rose to $4.8 million in 1959. Unhappy with this trend, the CAB planned to phase out subsidy payments by 1970. However, political action caused a more abrupt end to federal largess.

Many congressmen had been unhappy with governmental support for a service that seemed to benefit only a few individuals. Also, critics had become suspicious of the continued high costs of operating the helicopter airlines. This suspicion seemed confirmed when a new helicopter company applied for CAB certification—without a subsidy.

San Francisco-Oakland Helicopter Airlines (SFO) had been incorporated in 1961 by five former executives of Los Angeles Airways. On June 1 it had begun operations between the downtown areas and airports of the two bayside cities, using an Air Taxi Certificate. During 1962 SFO flew 100 flights daily and carried 104,000 passengers.

When they applied to the CAB for permanent certification, SFO executives cited Los Angeles Airways and New York Airways as examples of ineffi-

ciency, claiming that a properly run company could make a profit without subsidy. Congressional opponents of subsidy, well aware that helicopter airlines had received $42.4 million in federal support between 1954 and 1963, had the ammunition that they needed to terminate funding. In 1964 the legislature voted to end all subsidies, effective April 1, 1965.

Chicago Helicopter Airways was the first to go under. By 1962 all major airlines had completed their move from Midway to O'Hare, causing CHA's passenger traffic to plummet. Without a subsidy, it could survive only if a trunk airline would be willing to underwrite its operations. Unable to find such a benefactor, CHA ceased scheduled operations on January 1, 1966.

Los Angeles Airways came next, although its future looked promising for a time. Following the end of subsidy, LAA reached an agreement with United and American Airlines for loan guarantees. It abandoned all nonpassenger service and concentrated on building up traffic with its 28-passenger, twin turbine S-61Ls. Business was encouraging. In 1967, its peak year, LAA carried 396,000 passengers. By early 1968 it was making over 60 daily flights to Anaheim and lifting some 1,000 passengers a day. Two fatal accidents during the year, however, brought a sharp decline in traffic. Competition from air taxi operators also caused revenue problems. LAA purchased two twin-Otter turboprops in 1970 in an effort to compete with the air taxi companies, but a six-month pilots' strike crippled the airline. It went out of business in October 1970.

New York Airways survived the longest. Pan American Airways became NYA's major financial backer after the end of subsidy, eventually acquiring 44 percent of the company. In 1965 Pan American purchased and leased to NYA three Vertol-107 helicopters, adding to the airline's fleet of 25-passenger, twin rotor, gas turbine machines. At the same time, NYA began to land on the top of the Pan Am Building in downtown Manhattan. The service between airports and midtown proved popular, carrying 300,000 passengers during its first year of operation. NYA's peak year came in 1972, when it airlifted 360,000 passengers and posted the first—and only—profit in its history. In 1977, however, the airline came under fire following a spectacular accident that occurred on the top of the Pan Am Building. On May 17 the landing gear of a Sikorsky S-61L collapsed on landing. The helicopter rolled over on its side, causing the main rotor blades to snap off. Four people on the roof were killed, as was one pedestrian on the street below the building. The airline struggled on for two more years, until a crash at Newark Airport in April 1979 put the company into bankruptcy.

San Francisco-Oakland Helicopter Airlines, the only nonsubsidized helicopter airline, also failed to survive. After a promising beginning in the early 1960s, SFO was forced to turn to the trunk carriers for assistance, signing loan agreements with TWA and American in 1965. Its best year was 1969, when it carried 320,000 passengers. A general decline in airline business in 1970, however, reversed this trend and forced SFO to seek protection under the bankruptcy laws. Reorganized, it conducted limited operations until a strike by mechanics in 1976 caused it to shut down. The company was liquidated in August 1977.

The bright postwar promise of helicopter air service never materialized. The major problem, as historians A. Gerald Peters and Donald F. Wood have pointed out, was "the extremely high cost of operating helicopters and helicopter airlines." Helicopters were expensive to buy and to operate. They required a good deal of maintenance, leading to low utilization. All the helicopter airlines ended up in the red. Los Angeles Airways lost $6.5 million between 1964 and 1970, while San Francisco-Oakland lost $4.7 million between 1969 and 1976. New York Airways suffered the greatest loss: $8 million between 1969 and 1978. "Like supersonic transport," Peters and Wood have concluded, "the airline helicopter represents an exciting technological development whose commercial market has not yet come."

References:

Robert L. Cummings, Jr., "Vertical Transport Business," *Journal of the Royal Aeronautical Society*, 64 (April 1960): 199-210;

Richard G. Hubler, *Straight Up: The Story of Vertical Flight* (New York: Duell, Sloan & Pearce, 1961);

"Los Angeles Airways: 18 Years of Ups and Downs," *American Aviation*, 29 (December 1965): 52-54ff;

Frank G. McGuire, "Helicopters—Have the Promises Been Fulfilled for Scheduled Service?," *Air Transport World*, 18 (March 1981): 70-74;

A. Gerald Peters and Donald F. Wood, "Helicopter Airlines in the United States 1945-75," *Journal of Transport History*, 4 (February 1977): 1-16.

Paul Henderson

(March 13, 1884 - December 19, 1951)

by W. David Lewis

Auburn University

and

Wesley Phillips Newton

Auburn University

CAREER: Executive, building supply and contracting industry (1910-1917, 1919-1922); officer, U.S. Army Ordnance Department (1917-1918); second assistant U.S. postmaster general (1922-1925); general manager, National Air Transport (1925-1928); vice-president, United Air Transport (1928-1934); real estate developer and investor (1934-1946).

Paul Henderson, pioneer in the early development of American airmail and airline executive, was born on March 13, 1884, in Lyndon, Kansas, the only child of Clark Ebenezer Henderson and Flora Anne Waddell Henderson. When he was very young the family moved to Chicago. While he was in high school his father died, precluding any opportunity he had of attending college. In high school, he met his future wife, Mabel Madden, daughter of a veteran Republican congressman, Martin B. Madden. They were married on June 11, 1910, and had five children.

Instead of going to college, Henderson went to work for one of Martin Madden's businesses, the Western Stone Company, a building supply and contracting firm operating in the Chicago area. In 1916 Henderson was made president of the firm. When the United States entered World War I he was inducted into the army, attaining the rank of major in the ordnance branch. While in France, he observed the military use of airmail.

Returning to Chicago after the war, Henderson held executive posts in several different quarry-related industries. His rank of lieutenant colonel in the Army Reserve led people to refer to him as "Colonel Henderson" throughout his career. He was one of the first post-World War I figures to advocate

Paul Henderson (courtesy of the National Air and Space Museum)

the establishment of municipal airports. Along with his contacts in Republican politics through his father-in-law, this advocacy was a factor in his being named second assistant postmaster general in the Warren G. Harding administration in 1922.

Henderson's principal responsibility as second assistant postmaster general was airmail, which the Post Office Department had carried exclusively within the United States since 1918 when it inherited that responsibility from the army. Airmail was in an experimental phase in the immediate postwar world. That it should succeed in the United States was especially crucial, for, unlike the situation in the leading European countries, which directly subsidized their major airlines, airmail subsidy offered the sole possibility for government aid to commercial aviation in the otherwise laissez-faire American environment.

Henderson took over a service that seemed barely worthwhile. It employed for the most part obsolete military surplus planes; had no bona fide airways system and hence could not engage in night flying; relied on transfer of mail to and from trains, which were much more reliable and economical and almost as fast; and produced a steady flow of red ink. In terms of percentage, its pilot casualty rate was far below that of nongovernmental flying in general, but the death of airmail pilots in operational accidents received much media attention.

Although Henderson had initial doubts about the worth of the service, he was determined to improve it. He knew that its routes had to be extended and that it must be in continuous operation over those routes. In order to accomplish the first objective, there had to be an airways system; to achieve the second, night flying was essential. In addition to men and planes, he relied on the fact that all landing fields from which departmental planes flew in and out on a regular basis were equipped with radio stations, primitive but nonetheless useful for relaying weather reports and other information. There had also been some night flying experimentation by the department. Henderson wrangled some funds to continue it, and also tapped the army air service's experience and expertise in night flying. Over a strip of terrain between Dayton and Columbus, Ohio, two military pilots flew back and forth, guided by a series of beacons, floodlights, and illuminated markers. When they successfully completed 25 of 29 flights, Henderson knew that his lighted airways system could do the job. He had learned that an airways system is basically a ground system.

To commence scheduled night service, Henderson selected the relatively flat terrain between Chicago and Cheyenne, Wyoming. Lights and emergency landing fields could be conveniently placed along this route segment, and its easternmost and westernmost terminals could be reached in a day from the east and west coasts respectively. The Chicago-Cheyenne strip, which was opened for overnight service in July 1924, became the midsection of the central continental airway. During the next year it was extended eastward to New York City. Under Henderson's direction, experiments with lighting and other related technology and improvements in airmail planes took place in cooperation with private industry. He was also a capable and energetic public relations man, arguing the case for airmail and airways before various civic and business organizations. One of his primary themes was that his department was demonstrating the practicality of aviation in commercial development. This message was based on something concrete—an excellent skyways system that in a few years would crisscross much of the country.

Henderson worked closely with Representative M. Clyde Kelly in preparing a bill that, when it became law in 1925, authorized the transfer of airmail delivery from the Post Office Department into private hands. While the transition was under way, Henderson, who came to be called the "Father of Night Airmail Service," praised his department for its key role in the development of commercial aviation up to that point. He also lobbied before a congressional committee for federal legislation to regulate flying, arguing that no substantial private investment in aviation would be forthcoming until such regulation was in force. In 1926 the Air Commerce Act, following the lines advocated by Henderson and other supporters, passed Congress.

In August 1925 Henderson left government service to enter the airline industry. He became general manager of the newly created National Air Transport (NAT), which successfully bid on the New York-Cleveland-Chicago airmail contract. After NAT became part of United Air Transport in 1928, he was named vice-president of the latter company. He also played a role in the founding of Transcontinental and Western Air, predecessor of Trans World Airlines. As president of the aviation industry's chief booster organization, the Aeronautical Chamber of Commerce, he threw himself into the cause of advancing the industry and promoting aviation securities. One of Henderson's chief problems in his postgovernmental career was that he spread himself too thinly. For a while, however, he enjoyed his work and received substantial financial rewards for the first time. For these reasons, he declined President Herbert Hoover's offer to become assistant secretary of commerce for aeronautics. An honorable person, he saw nothing wrong in helping an official of the aviation regulatory branch of the Commerce Department obtain a loan to acquire stock in aviation in that boom period for such securities. He himself managed to survive the onslaught of the Great Depression. Then, in 1930, he encountered the beginning of his Waterloo, which came from another direction.

With the advent of the Hoover administration, Henderson had become United's main representative in Washington, D.C. As such, he was invited to Postmaster General Walter Folger Brown's "spoils conferences" in 1930. Henderson had helped Brown draft the McNary-Watres bill, but came to dislike his high-handed ways. When Senator Hugo Black's special investigating committee began in 1933 to look into circumstances surrounding Brown's contract awards, Henderson approached Black and agreed to send the committee a memorandum detailing some of these circumstances, and was a key witness before the committee in describing the events of the "spoils conferences." None of this, however, spared him from

the fate of the airline executives who had attended these meetings—banishment from the airline industry.

This experience broke Henderson's spirit. Although he engaged in a variety of non-aviation-related business endeavors, including real estate development in the Maryland suburbs of Washington, D.C., and various investment activities, he was never able to regain the success and prominence he had once enjoyed. During World War II, however, he was consulted by Gen. Henry H. ("Hap") Arnold on aviation-related matters. Henderson's health broke in 1946 following the death of a son in an air crash. After five declining years, he died in Washington in 1951.

References:
Nick A. Komons, *Bonfires to Beacons: Federal Civil Aviation Policy Under the Air Commerce Act, 1926-1938* (Washington, D.C.: U.S. Department of Transportation, 1978);

William M. Leary, *Aerial Pioneers: The U.S. Air Mail Service, 1918-1927* (Washington, D.C.: Smithsonian Institution, 1985);

Frank J. Taylor, *High Horizons* (New York: McGraw-Hill, 1951).

Eddie Hubbard

(1889 - December 18, 1928)

by F. Robert van der Linden

National Air and Space Museum

CAREER: Pilot and flight instructor, U.S. Army Signal Corps (1916-1917); test pilot, Boeing Airplane Company (1917-1920); owner, Hubbard Air Transport (1920-1927); vice-president of operations, Boeing Air Transport (1928-1928).

Edward "Eddie" Hubbard was an early aviator whose uncommon vision for the future paved the way for the expansion of the commercial air transportation industry and was largely responsible for inspiring the creation of one of that industry's giants, United Air Lines. Although little information exists about this aviation pioneer, his contributions were instrumental in inspiring the vast network of

American air routes. Were it not for his untimely death in 1928 at the age of thirty-nine, Hubbard would certainly have left an even greater mark on the face of American air transportation.

Hubbard first came to public attention in 1916. He had been flying with the army since 1912 and was a flight instructor at Rockwell Field in San Diego, California. On July 4, 1916, he was in Seattle as part of the military's Independence Day celebrations to demonstrate the speed and potential of the airplane to the gathered throng of spectators. Together with Lt. E. T. Condon, Hubbard flew a bag of letters from the 13th Naval District in Seattle to Fort Lewis in nearby Tacoma. The return flight ran

Eddie Hubbard (courtesy of the Boeing Company Archives)

into a stiff headwind, forcing the pair to average an unimpressive 35 miles per hour. Hubbard was undaunted and immediately realized the viability of regularly scheduled airmail service.

In 1917 his flying skills caught the attention of William Boeing, who hired him as a test pilot for Boeing's new aircraft manufacturing firm. Hubbard's professionalism and cautious approach to his flying were instrumental in the successful development of Boeing's earliest aircraft and also prepared him well for an approaching opportunity.

In early 1919, as part of a business exposition across the border in Vancouver, British Columbia, businessman E. S. Knowlton inquired of the local postmaster if he could arrange to have a load of mail carried between Canada and the United States. Postmaster R. G. MacPherson readily assented, and immediately Knowlton contacted Boeing to see if he could make the flight. An eager Boeing agreed. Boeing selected Hubbard to pilot his delicate C-700 floatplane, and together they flew the 125 miles to Vancouver through a blinding snowstorm that forced them to alight in nearby Anacortes for the night until they could proceed the next day. On March 3 they arrived at the Royal Vancouver Yacht

club where they loaded a pouch of 60 letters and flew the first international airmail back to Lake Washington in Seattle. Hubbard again was deeply impressed with the possibilities of a regular service and mentioned it to Boeing, who took note of the suggestion.

The next year, fired by the notion of starting an airmail service, Hubbard resigned from the Boeing firm and began a series of survey flights beginning in July 1, 1920, between Seattle and Victoria, British Columbia. His efforts reaped dividends when, on October 15, armed with a foreign airmail contract from the U.S. government which paid $200 for each round trip, the newly created Hubbard Air Transport opened the first regularly scheduled international airmail service. On that blustery afternoon, before a small group of 50 people gathered at the shore of Lake Union, Hubbard and Seattle postmaster Edward McGrath loaded five sacks of mail into Hubbard's floatplane and took off for Victoria, 84 miles away, where steamships from the Orient made their first stop on the American continent. His objective that day was the Japanese vessel *Africa Maru*, which was set to sail that evening. The trip took 50 uneventful minutes, and Hubbard was welcomed by a crowd of thousands who wished to witness the historic flight.

Despite the primitive state of aircraft and engines and often daunting weather conditions, Hubbard fulfilled the terms of the contract, completing ten round trips each month. He turned a healthy profit from the start, which he wisely invested in Boeing stock and in real estate. Soon he acquired a larger Boeing B-1 flying boat and, based on his initial success, was able to win further contracts with ease. He carried from 25,000 to 50,000 pounds of mail each year from 1920 until 1927, when Hubbard Air Transport was acquired by Percy Barnes and Vern Gorst, and renamed the Seattle-Victoria Air Mail Line. It was superseded in 1937 by United, when that airline opened a new route from Seattle to Vancouver.

The fate of Hubbard's business is ironic as he played a crucial part in the creation of United. Hubbard did not leave the airline business when he sold his company in 1927. Instead, he rejoined Boeing in the fall of 1926 and brought with him a new idea for a much greater enterprise. Through his connections Hubbard had learned of the Post Office's plan to turn over its routes to private contractors. He was particularly interested in the route from Chicago to San Francisco.

Hubbard approached Claire Egtvedt, Boeing's chief designer, with his proposal, since Boeing president Philip Johnson was out of town. Intrigued, Egtvedt sat down with Hubbard and calculated that they could place a competitive bid using Boeing's new Model 40 biplane. The Model 40 was one of the first mail planes equipped with the more efficient Pratt & Whitney Wasp air-cooled radial installed in place of the bulky and troublesome watercooled Libertys that powered its competitors. Egtvedt was convinced, and the two approached William Boeing for approval, with Hubbard emphasizing the great success of his air transport company, which Boeing had helped create. Initially they were turned down, but Boeing, after a long conversation with his wife that evening, saw the possibility for profit in the contract despite the gamble. In addition, Hubbard's scheme created a ready-made market for his aircraft at a time when the company needed more orders.

Boeing supported Hubbard's plan and backed his bid to the Post Office. On January 15, 1927, the bids were opened, and the Chicago-to-San Francisco route awarded to Hubbard and Boeing despite the fact that they appeared to underbid severely. To the astonishment of the airline community, the newly formed Boeing Air Transport not only survived its beginning on July 1, 1927, but prospered because of the efficiency of its fleet of 25 Boeing 40s and the management of Boeing's team led by Hubbard as vice-president of operations.

Hubbard would not enjoy the success of his vision for long. On December 18, 1928, while shoveling snow outside his Salt Lake City home, he suffered a fatal heart attack. He was replaced at Boeing Air Transport by a recently hired young man who would quickly prove a worthy successor: William A. Patterson.

Boeing Air Transport soon became the core of the expanding air transport enterprise of Boeing and his partner Frederick Rentschler, who expanded their relationship from the time of the development of the Model 40 and built the giant United Aircraft and Transport Corporation holding company. From the management of Boeing Air Transport came the leaders who would form United Air Lines and build it into one of the largest airlines in the world, begun through the inspiration of one quiet, enterprising airmail pilot, Eddie Hubbard.

References:

R. E. G. Davies, "Eddie Hubbard's Airline," *Air Pictorial*, 28 (November 1966): 412-413;

Frank Macomber, "Pioneer Flying Mailman Made a Million at It," *Tacoma News Tribune and Sunday Ledger*, October 11, 1970, p. A-16;

Frank J. Taylor, *High Horizons: Daredevil Flying Postmen to Modern Magic Carpet—The United Air Lines Story* (New York: McGraw-Hill, 1951).

Howard Hughes

(December 24, 1905 - April 5, 1976)

by R. E. G. Davies

National Air and Space Museum

CAREER: Owner, Hughes Tool Company (1924-1976) and, at various times, pilot, motion picture producer and studio owner, aircraft designer and manufacturer, airline owner and operator, hotel and casino owner, and entrepreneur.

The biography of a great personality in aviation normally revolves around his or her achievements: in manufacturing, such as the career of Donald Douglas; in airline promotion, such as with Juan Trippe; or as a pilot, such as Charles Lindbergh. One of the problems in dealing with the complex character and accomplishments of Howard Hughes is not only that he was supremely successful in each of these three categories of aeronautical prowess, but also that he was able to maintain his authority in all three fields simultaneously. At the zenith of his career, during the post-World War II period of airline expansion, he owned almost all the stock in Trans World Airlines, one of the biggest in the world; he had created its flagship, the Constellation, the best airliner in the world; and he was able to fly it as well as any four-ringed captain.

Even more astonishing is to reflect that this tri-faceted period of his life had been preceded by another. During the 1930s he had achieved fame as one of Hollywood's leading film producers, had beaten several speed records in specially modified racing airplanes, and had received international acclaim for a round-the-world flight that was remarkable in that it was flown by a production airliner that was modified only by elaborate high-technology equipment, not in its basic design or performance. Just as Howard Hughes had contributed to U.S. leadership in airliner design by being the driving force behind the Lockheed Constellation, he had also awakened the world to the importance of advanced instrumentation and ground installations of navigational aids.

Howard Hughes

Such prowess in a multiplicity of disciplines, each requiring stringent standards of performance as a condition of active participation, would have been sufficient for most overachievers. But Hughes combined his many talents as a participant with those of a visionary who could foresee the full potential of the many assets under his control or influence. And just as Charles Lindbergh applied his energies to the furtherance of airline operating techniques, through his role as technical adviser to Pan American and Transcontinental Air Transport during the air industry's adolescent years, Howard

Hughes did so during a later era, carrying on, as it were, where Lindbergh left off, in an environment of challenging technology and powerful competitive forces. Hughes has been described as a phenomenon, and such a description needs no reservation or qualification.

Sadly, much of this illustrious career has been forgotten during the past 20 years or so, the result of a wave of adverse media publicity conducted with considerable cynicism, amounting at times to contempt. For in his later years, Hughes began to shun the public acclaim that he had previously tolerated, and indeed enjoyed, first to become a privileged recluse, and then, as his health deteriorated, to decline into a state of eccentricity that was at once pathetic and sordid. Recalling Shakespeare's Seven Ages of Man, he ended his life sans respect, sans fame, sans everything. If he was conscious of such attributes at the time of his death—appropriately on board an airplane—it was a bitter end to the life of a great man.

What were the formative influences, and what were the genealogical factors, family relationships, and educational avenues by which this man was able to attain such a multitude of achievements well before the age when most ordinary folk, not to mention acknowledged heroes and leaders, have even decided upon a single vocation. Howard Hughes would have been welcomed on the couch of any psychiatrist, and would have been eagerly sought after by any psychologist seeking an eminent case study in human behavior—although chances are Hughes would have ended up writing books about his interviewers, or at least sponsoring such works. For all his achievements, he seldom put anything down on paper. He was the supreme chairman of the board, ordaining matters of policy, but leaving the minutiae of organization and management to others.

A comparison with Lindbergh even reaches into Hughes's ancestry. Lindbergh's father was a prominent lawyer and politician. Hughes's father was an engineer whose patented rotary drill revolutionized the scope of oil prospecting. Both men's lives were overshadowed in the halls of fame by those of their sons, both of whom in their time became national heroes and household words.

Hughes's paternal grandfather, Felix, was from Scottish pioneer stock. A veteran of the Union army in the Civil War, he became a lawyer in Lancaster, Missouri, and married Jean Summerlin, a devout and cultured Southerner. They were married

for 61 years and had four children, of whom Howard, Senior, was the second, born in 1869. He was more of a mechanical bent than of an academic disposition, but he did go to law school as a filial duty. He passed the Iowa bar examination and joined his father for a short time, but soon went to seek his fortune in the mining industry. In his words, he "turned greaser and sank into the thick of it. Roughneck, owner, disowner, promoter, capitalist, and 'mark'—with each I can claim kin, for I have stood in the steps of each."

Such qualities were apparently attractive to a young lady of a respectable family from Beaumont, who was prepared to overlook Howard Hughes, Senior's, tendency to lose small fortunes as quickly as he made them. From French Huguenot stock, Allene Gano, born in 1883, was the daughter of William Beriah Gano, who was also a lawyer, and a very successful one, having graduated from the Harvard Law School and become a judge. Her mother, "Nettie" Grissim, had graduated from the prestigious Wellesley College, had a degree in music, and was a cultured lady in every respect. Allene would thus have appeared to have been an unlikely partner in life for the adventurous Howard Hughes, Senior, but a romantic alliance ensued, and they were married on May 24, 1904. Howard Hughes, Junior, middle name Robard, was born on Christmas Eve, 1905, at 1404 Crawford Street, Houston. On the doctor's advice, after a difficult delivery, Howard and Allene made Howard Robard their only child.

During the younger Hughes's infancy, Howard Hughes, Senior, made one of those discoveries that, in any field of mechanics or engineering, could be termed to be revolutionary, almost to the level of epoch-making, comparable with the invention of the cotton gin or the development of the Bessemer steel-making process. He had teamed up with Walter Bedford Sharp, an experienced oil-field specialist who had patented a process of injecting compressed air into the wells to increase the rate of flow. Working together, they were just as frustrated as hundreds of other prospectors because many promising oil strike locations had to be abandoned because the standard "fishtail" drilling bits could not penetrate solid rock strata. Then, in 1908, a young millwright, Granville Humason, reputedly meeting Hughes in a Shreveport bar and showing him a model of a unique drill bit design based on two conical cutters, sold his idea to Hughes for $150.

Hughes promptly worked on the idea to develop it into a working prototype, sold a half-interest to Sharp for $1,500, and took a trip to Washington, D.C., to patent the Hughes Rotary Drill Bit. It was to be the foundation of a billion-dollar fortune.

When Howard, Senior, astonished the oil world in June 1909 by drilling through 14 feet of rock at Goose Creek, Texas, in only 11 hours, Howard, Junior, aged four, was the apple of his mother's eye and, like many an only child, was given a privileged and sheltered childhood, made even more privileged by the growing wealth that his father's invention brought into the family and even more sheltered by a loving mother's overprotectiveness. But the resultant child, somewhat introspective, was to grow into a man whose self-created fame and fortune was anything but self-effacing.

Like his father, young Hughes tended to devote his educational opportunities more to practical mechanical interests than to his formal lessons. His father encouraged him by giving him a bench in the tool company's plant, and Hughes responded by making a motorized bicycle, remarkably similar to those that were to become popular in Europe after World War II. He built himself a radio transmitter, partly from an old doorbell, became a ham radio operator, call sign RCY, and formed the local group of amateurs. He learned to play the saxophone and, while attending Fessenden School in Massachusetts in 1920-1921, took up the game of golf, which he continued to play during his adult life. His father, by then active in California, transferred the young Hughes to Thacher School in Ojai, to be closer to him. The boy was still somewhat shy, with no ambition to become a team player, and spent much of his spare time horseback riding in the adjacent hills north of Los Angeles.

On March 29, 1922, tragedy struck. Hughes's mother, Allene, went into the hospital in Houston for minor surgery, but never recovered from the anesthetic. She was only thirty-nine, and Hughes, Senior, was grief-stricken, to the extent that he asked Allene's younger sister, Annette, to come to Pasadena to help guide his son through his adolescence, and arranged for him to attend the California Institute of Technology in that city. But although young Hughes attended some classes, he spent far more time with his uncle Rupert Hughes, a successful author and screenwriter for the Goldwyn Studios. The hitherto solitary and shy boy suddenly encountered the frenzied life-style of those who were famous as

well as rich. If he mourned his mother's death, he did so in the glamorous environment of movie sets where, no doubt, he first acquired an interest in movie-making.

Then, just as suddenly as with his mother's death, Hughes, Junior, lost his father, who, on January 14, 1924, died from a massive heart attack while attending a routine company meeting. At the age of eighteen the younger Hughes was abruptly orphaned, and the inheritor of a large fortune. It was not as large as some would believe, amounting to about $650,000; but it was large enough, equivalent to about $10 million in 1990 dollars. Showing a quite astonishing grasp of the financial and legal aspects of the situation, he systematically set about the task of putting his inheritance under his exclusive control, acting with a business acumen that would have gotten him straight A's in short time at any business school, but which did not rate highly with his relatives.

His father's partner, Walter Sharp, had died in 1917, and Hughes, Senior, had bought out Sharp's widow. He had left half of his estate to Allene and a quarter to his only son, so that young Hughes immediately had three-quarters of the Hughes Tool business. The remaining shares were allocated to the grandparents and to Rupert Hughes. Although, as a minor under Texas law, he was supposed to be unfit to manage his own affairs, Hughes found a loophole. Under the Texas Civil Code he could be declared a legal adult if he could prove his competency. He studied the affairs of the Hughes Tool Company so assiduously that, when he filed the formal petition on his nineteenth birthday, the judge, who was one of Hughes's regular golfing partners, signed the order within two days. Hughes, Junior, promptly instructed the company's lawyers to buy out his relatives' minority shareholding, so that at the age of nineteen Howard Hughes, Junior, was in control of the entire Hughes Tool Company, still expanding phenomenally and providing its sole owner with all the capital he needed to indulge in any whim that took his fancy.

Such an unattractive act in the pursuit of absolute wealth, and particularly at the age of nineteen, would make the notoriously acquisitive television soap opera families look like charitable institutions. Certainly Hughes had been what is popularly described as a loner, but there is little evidence that he actually disliked his family, especially Uncle Rupert, who had introduced him to the marvels of Hollywood. His attitude then, so callously displayed, was to characterize his behavior throughout his life. Was this almost obsessive self-centered concentration on himself the result of his upbringing? Had he been nurtured in the atmosphere of the nuclear family, with a father at home, brothers or sisters, and a less indulgent mother, would he have acted differently then and afterward? Such speculation is debatable, but possibly irrelevant. The fact is that, for the rest of his life, he continued to treat friends, casual acquaintances, and girlfriends alike with the same casual indifference as when, as an impetuous youth, he took over his father's wealth.

At least in one respect, at first, he played by the conventional rules. On June 1, 1925, he married Ella Rice, a sophisticated Houston debutante from the same family that had founded Rice University. It was an important social event in Houston, and he and his bride moved to Los Angeles so that he could be near his business outlets, his movie industry hobby, and—his home overlooked the course of the Wilshire Country Club—his favorite sport, golf.

Hughes had already demonstrated a penchant for business while at Fessenden School. His mother used to send him a steady supply of grapefruit, presumably to encourage him to eat healthful food, but he sold most of the fruit to his classmates. Now he undertook a housecleaning of the Hughes Tool Company, replaced those he considered to be incompetent, and hired, among others, an accountant named Noah Dietrich, who was to manage the Hughes fortunes for the next 30 years. Hughes was able to leave the day-to-day operations of his business, which was to expand mightily and become a complex conglomerate, to Dietrich, while he was left to ordain policy, direct lines of research, and spend most of his time on his hobbies.

Holding a virtual monopoly in the supply of "rock-eater" drilling bits for the oil industry, and protected by ironclad patents, the Hughes Tool Company effectively ran itself under Dietrich's supervision. Left to follow his own flights of fancy, Hughes became involved with the promotion of a steam car, developed during the late 1920s. He abandoned the idea with alacrity when he discovered that, without proper supervision, his engineers had lost sight of the main objective of the project and had constructed a vehicle in which the driver had a fairly good chance of scalding himself to death. Hughes never again delegated policy control of a project. Indeed, his involvement in any major enter-

prise from then on was so intense that he gained a reputation for intolerable interference in his constant search for perfection.

During his twenties, Hughes's main preoccupation was in making movies. He used his natural innovative talent, a sharp intellect, and his unlimited financial resources to pursue his ambition not only to produce motion pictures but later to direct them as well. The activity culminated in the production of a film that was to take its place as one of the landmarks in motion picture production and rated as a classic for all time. Such an attainment reflected Hughes's determination not simply to be good at anything he attempted, but to be the best. He may have been one of the millions of people who, rightly or wrongly feeling that in one way or another they have been deprived of an opportunity to prove their real worth, make special efforts to "show the world." In the case of Hughes, the essential ingredient of an open-ended bank account almost guaranteed success in anything on which he set his heart.

Even in a biography aimed to emphasize aviation accomplishment, Hughes's motion picture career cannot be ignored, for his greatest success was *Hell's Angels*, which opened at Grauman's Chinese Theater on Hollywood Boulevard on June 20, 1930, and is still acknowledged as one of the finest motion pictures about aviation ever made. Half a century later it is screened now and again, and in spite of the stilted dialogue and other shortcomings that were typical of an art form still feeling its way, some of the sequences have never been surpassed in technique and realism. The ominous foreboding of the nose of a German Zeppelin emerging from the cloud formation during a night bombing raid is unforgettable to any who have seen the film, as are the realistic dogfights that only a dedicated producer with immense wealth could have contrived.

Hell's Angels was a manifestation of Hughes's intense interest in aviation that he seems to have acquired at the time. He began the film on October 21, 1927, and it took nearly three years to make. It cost almost $4 million, employed 20,000 people, and its final cut of 15,000 feet of film was selected from 2.5 million. During its production, talking films had unceremoniously made silent films obsolete, and accelerated the retirement of film stars whose voices did not match their good looks. Ever the perfectionist, and certainly not one to be defeated by events, Hughes reshot the film and created the first of many stars that he discovered, Jean Harlow. For the realistic air scenes, he purchased 87 vintage World War I aircraft and hired 137 top aviation stuntmen, including the famous Roscoe Turner, who also supplied the twin-engined Sikorsky transport airplane that appeared in the film as a Gotha bomber.

Hughes himself learned to fly when he launched the picture in 1927, obtained his transport rating in 1928, and earned a commercial multi-engine and instrument rating shortly afterward. As in every field of endeavor, he had been a quick learner, and in the making of *Hell's Angels* he received a harsh lesson as a supplement to his theoretical and practical flying schoolwork. Impatient with a pilot who claimed that a certain maneuver was impossible, Hughes tried to demonstrate that he was wrong. For once in his life, he had to admit defeat. The pilot was right: Hughes crashed the aircraft exactly in the manner predicted by the pilot, was pulled out of the wreckage unconscious, and sustained a crushed cheekbone.

While *Hell's Angels* represented the zenith of Hughes's filmmaking career, it was by no means the only production of which he had every right to be proud. And there were others that are best forgotten and rightly condemned to permanent obscurity. Indeed, his first film, *Swell Hogan*, was so bad that it was never released, and, typically, Hughes had all copies of it destroyed. He could not bear imperfection, and was certainly not prepared to reveal his own failures to the public. But two of the five pictures that preceded *Hell's Angels* were not bad. *Everybody's Acting* had good reviews, and *Two Arabian Knights*, which introduced William Boyd to the screen, won the Academy Award for Lewis Milestone as best director of 1927.

At first the Hughes films were produced by the Caddo Rock Drill Company of Louisiana, a subsidiary of the Hughes Tool Company, and were released through various distributors such as Paramount and United Artists. These included another notable film, *Scarface*, directed by Howard Hawks and starring Paul Muni and George Raft. Other famous names under the Hughes banner included Billie Dove, Pat O'Brien, and even Spencer Tracy, together with Adolphe Menjou, Edward Everett Horton, and Walter Catlett. Much later, during World War II, Hughes resumed his filmmaking and produced *The Outlaw*. The film itself was not outstanding, but the so-called vital statistics of its

leading actress, Jane Russell, were, and Russell brought a different kind of fame to Howard Hughes that had nothing to do with aviation.

From 1949 to 1955 Hughes also acquired control of RKO Radio Pictures, Inc., and oversaw the production of more than 50 feature films, of which he was personally involved in ten. But by this time moviemaking was for Hughes a rich man's hobby, as his main preoccupation was still aviation, with which he had a lifelong affair that had begun with *Hell's Angels* and when he had learned to fly in 1927.

With Noah Dietrich and others looking after the Hughes Tool Company, Hughes was free to indulge himself in the lavish life of what came to be known as that of a playboy. Not only that, as a millionaire and, after 1928, once more eligible as a prospective husband, he became one of the participants in the glittering parade of star-studded parties, receptions, and other gatherings that epitomized the artificial life of Hollywood during its greatest and most notorious years. Ella Rice had left him because she seldom saw him; he seemed to have time for her only when there was nothing else to do. Unlike so many of the film stars and associated hangers-on who represented a superficial existence and had little other interest beyond the immediate confines of Hollywood, Hughes was different. His diamond-sharp mind was constantly seeking outlets for his fertile imagination, and, in spite of his cloistered upbringing, he was supremely fit as well as attractively debonair. All these talents were channeled into an almost fanatical romance with aviation, and, like so many who have been exposed to the aeronautical virus, he became an addict.

Hughes's first direct contact with flying occurred when, at the age of fourteen, while at Fessenden School, he was allowed to take a ride in an old Curtiss OX-5-engined flying boat. He was given this as a present from his father, who had told him that he could have anything he wanted if Harvard won its annual boat race against Yale. History will never know what might have happened to young Howard's aviation career had Yale won the boat race.

During the first year of filming *Hell's Angels* Hughes took flight training at Clovis Field, Santa Monica. Always interested in mechanical things, he had already acquainted himself with the basic elements of aeronautics, so that his interest in obtaining a pilot's license was more than a passing fancy.

Hughes and his H-1 racer (courtesy of the National Air and Space Museum)

He received his Transport Pilot's License, Number 4223, on November 16, 1928.

After basking in the reflected glory, much deserved, of *Hell's Angels* and making a few more pictures, including *Scarface* and *The Front Page*, Hughes's life-style took a sudden change of direction in 1932. Abandoning Hollywood's glamour, he disappeared from public—and even private—view for a couple of months during the summer of that year, and under the name of Charles Howard flew as a copilot for American Airways between Fort Worth and Cleveland, part of American's transcontinental air route. In those days, part of the copilot's job was to unload the baggage. Hughes probably holds the record as the world's most affluent baggage handler in the business.

He later flew TWA Douglas DC-2s, but his aviation passion at the time—he was only twenty-seven when he worked for American—was air racing. He acquired the taste for speed that befell, and sometimes consumed, so many aviation enthusiasts who followed in the footsteps of the Wright brothers. He had obtained his pilot's license in a

Waco biplane, but, predictably, he wanted something better. Casting aside any aspirations to become a part-time airline pilot, he bought a civil variant of the Boeing P-12 two-seat, open-cockpit biplane, the fastest pursuit airplane of its day and operated by both the army and navy air forces. He paid $45,000 for the airplane and spent a further $75,000 in modifying it to his own specifications. Displaying an impressive grasp of the essentials for high-speed flight, he contracted with the Douglas company to reduce the wing and tail areas, remove one of the seating compartments, and fit a more powerful 450-horsepower Pratt & Whitney Wasp engine, complete with the latest NACA cowling to cut drag to a minimum.

With this aircraft, and after an interlude during which he purchased a British luxury yacht, the fifth largest in the world, he entered his Boeing 100A Special in the All-American Air Meet. On January 14, 1934, at this air meeting, he won the Sportsman Pilot Free-For-All race, almost lapping the second-place entrant. Arguably, nobody else stood a chance. Some sportsmen may have had the ability, and some may have had the money; but none had both, and none possessed the intuitive skill to devise a demonstrably practical way to extract the best advantage from the essential ingredients for success.

This achievement drew the attention of the press and public to the fact that Hughes was more than a rich industrialist, more even than a successful moviemaker; he was a prize-winning racing pilot, the stuff of which heroes are made. And he did not disappoint his growing army of fans and admirers. Whether because he sought secrecy for its own sake or as an instinctive protective shield against the possibility of revealed failure; or whether he simply enjoyed the satisfying element of surprise when the secret is finally revealed: whatever the reason, Hughes's next project was conducted behind closed doors. Not satisfied with the Boeing 100A, he decided to go into the aircraft manufacturing business himself, and the Hughes Aircraft Company was founded in Culver City, California, in 1934.

Hughes's ambition was quite simple: to build an aircraft that would capture the world's landplane speed record. The press loved the idea and kept a vigil at Culver City, in the hope of obtaining a glimpse of what they dubbed the Hughes Mystery Ship. Accustomed to many millionaire pipe dreams that never materialized, the skeptics were soon silenced. Personally supervising every stage and every detail of construction (with bitter memories of the steam car fiasco, no doubt), Hughes assembled a team of engineers and mechanicians, and a good designer, Dick Palmer, from Caltech and possibly one of the least known or recognized of some of the great designers of the 1930s. Within eighteen months, on August 18, 1935, the Hughes H-1 was revealed. It was clearly in a class of its own. Its clean, flush-riveted fuselage was matched by an equally clean single cantilevered monoplane wing, with not a single strut or brace or wire. The engine was a Pratt & Whitney Wasp radial, with horsepower augmented to 1,000, and neatly cowled. The retractable gear was mechanically operated.

Such an airplane was built for sheer speed. Within a month, on September 13, 1935, Hughes flew it over a three-kilometer course at Santa Ana's Martin Field. Watched overhead by aviator compatriots Paul Mantz and Amelia Earhart, he made six officially timed runs, and was confirmed as having beaten the existing world land-plane speed record

of 314 mph, held by the Frenchman Raymond Delmotte, with a speed of 352.39 mph. On the seventh run, a clogged fuel line forced him to make a wheels-up landing in a nearby beet field, but the H-1 was relatively undamaged, and it resides today as a prized exhibit at the National Air and Space Museum in Washington, D.C.

Hughes was not content even with this claim to fame, during an age when the whole world was captivated by aviation record breaking, in speed, distance, altitude, endurance—almost any conceivable measure and enough to fill a Guinness Book, had one existed at the time. One such challenge was the U.S. transcontinental speed record, and he did not even wait to repair his proven H-1. He bought a Northrop Gamma from Jackie Cochran, fitted it with a Wright Cyclone 925 horsepower engine, and on January 13, 1936, took off from Burbank, California, on what he alleged was a test run. When he landed at Newark, New Jersey, he had beaten the transcontinental speed record with a time of 9 hours 27 minutes.

During the next few months, he flew the Gamma all around the country, breaking various point-to-point records as he did so. But for Hughes this was almost incidental. He was, at the same time, systematically carrying out his own personal program of flight testing. He was intensely concerned with accurate instrumentation, carefully testing and calibrating parameters of speed, altitude, and fuel consumption. Most important, he demonstrated that instruments calibrated at sea level have to be adjusted for high-altitude flying.

The charismatic Hughes was awarded the Harmon Trophy for his record-breaking transcontinental flight in the Gamma. When the time came, on January 19, 1937, to go to New York to receive the prestigious award, he did so with an élan that could not be matched. The Hughes H-1 was now repaired and furthermore modified for long-distance flying with an increased engine power rating and a set of longer wings. He arrived at Newark, having flown the H-1 from Los Angeles in 7 hours 28 minutes at an average speed of 332 mph over the 2,490 miles. He had beaten his own speed record by two hours, and it was not to be beaten again for seven years, appropriately enough by himself. Hughes owned the transcontinental record for more than a decade, a measure of sustained excellence in achievement that was truly astonishing.

The new transcontinental time could have been a few minutes shorter, had Newark's runways not been so congested when Hughes arrived. Perhaps they were not expecting him quite so soon. But even more noteworthy was that Hughes had flown the H-1 at an altitude of 14,000 feet, using oxygen equipment, and the engine was supercharged to cope with the more rarefied air at that height. Perhaps Hughes had yet another aviation goal in mind.

At this stage in the succession of famous flights that were to go into the record books, the temptation to compare Hughes, as has been suggested above, with Charles Lindbergh is a strong one. Following Lindy's epic transatlantic solo flight in 1927, the Lone Wolf—as he became known—had concentrated on contributing his skills and experience for the furtherance of commercial aviation, through survey flights for Pan American Airways, and in planning the transcontinental air route for Transcontinental Air Transport. Now Hughes echoed this approach by seeking to combine an epic flight with a demonstration of how the contemporary technology of those elements of airline operations not directly related to the airframe or engine construction could be properly utilized to serve the pilots and the airplanes. Much of Lindbergh's later work had revolved around surveying transocean air routes to identify and to analyze weather patterns, preferred staging points and emergency fields, and navigational aids. For a variety of reasons, Lindbergh's involvement in aviation receded in the mid 1930s, and Hughes stepped into his shoes as the standard-bearer for the advancement of airline procedures and practices.

The manner in which he achieved it was admirable. He set out to fly around the world, along the route flown by Wiley Post in 1933, and to do it in a modern passenger-carrying airliner. This time he was in no hurry. He spent two years in meticulous planning. First he made a careful evaluation of all the available airliners. No doubt he looked very carefully at the two American airliners that had come in second and third in the great England-Australia Air Race of 1934, the Douglas DC-2 and the Boeing 247 respectively. He eventually chose the Lockheed 14, the Super-Electra, the twin-engined 12-seat airliner that went into service as the *Sky Zephyr* with Northwest Airlines in September 1937. The aircraft was big enough to carry a crew of four besides himself and a substantial payload

not only of fuel but also of the latest communications and navigational equipment, automatic and blind-flying instruments, and a new Sperry Gyro Pilot to maintain level flight. And, for a transport airplane, it was fast.

The aircraft was nicknamed the Flying Laboratory; and so it was. Nothing was left to chance. Indeed, such was the thoroughness of the preparation that the completion of the flight was almost a foregone conclusion and of secondary importance to the testing of the operation as a proving flight for more regularly scheduled long-distance flying in the future. His crew comprised a first-class team, each one with a specialized role to play. Harry Conner was the copilot and, as was the custom at the time, also a backup navigator; Tom Thurlow was the ship's navigator; Dick Stoddard was the radio operator and Ed Lund the flight engineer. To support them on the ground, a global communications network was established to provide accurate weather information, a service that only the financial resources of a man such as Hughes could provide, for at the time neither the airlines nor the nations of the world had yet addressed themselves to the problem, at least with global and international perspectives, as opposed to limited and self-serving national objectives. Special fuel stations were set up at the scheduled landing fields at Paris, Moscow, Omsk, Yakutsk, Fairbanks, and Minneapolis. Only two countries, the Soviet Union and the United States, were involved. Major General Baidukov, copilot to Valery Chkalov, the famous flyer who first flew across the Polar regions in 1937 nonstop from Moscow to the United States, remembers with respect that when refueling in Moscow, Hughes himself watched every stage of the refueling process with an eagle eye.

And so, leaving Floyd Bennett Field, New York, on July 10, 1938, Hughes and his crew, almost as a matter of routine, flew around the world, albeit on a route that was 16,000 miles or so, rather than the 25,000-mile great circle distance that is the earth's circumference, in less than four days at an average speed of 202 mph. This was only half of Wiley Post's time and fully justified Hughes's choice of equipment. The DC-2 or the Boeing 247 would have been at least 50 mph slower. Before he took off, Hughes made a rare speech for the reporters and the crowd that assembled to see him off, and it was a memorable one. He said, "We hope that our flight may prove to be a contribution to the cause of friendship between nations and that through their outstanding flyers, for whom the common bond of aviation transcends national boundaries, this cause may be furthered." After the flight, he said, "If credit is due to anyone, it is due to the men who designed and perfected to its present remarkable state of efficiency the modern American flying machine and equipment. If we made a fast flight, it is because so many young men in this country went to engineering schools, worked hard at drafting tables, and designed a fast airplane and navigation and radio equipment which would keep the plane upon its course. All we did was operate this equipment and plane according to the instruction book accompanying the article."

In the celebration of the event, the fact that his nonstop first segment from New York to Paris had cut Lindbergh's time by half, and that a damaged strut in the landing gear delayed the flight in Paris for eight hours—these items went almost unnoticed. But the full importance of the fulfillment of a carefully planned exercise, carried out with precision and accuracy, under complete control for every mile of the journey, thanks to the superb communications system established by Hughes, was not lost on the airlines. Neither was the drama of the occasion lost on an American public that adores heroes and makes sure they know it. Hughes and his crew received the traditional ticker-tape welcome both in New York and in Chicago. He received his second Harmon Trophy, the Collier Trophy, the Octave Chanute Award, a Congressional Medal, a Diploma of Honor from the Ligue Internationale des Aviateurs, and hundreds of other citations.

Almost as though Fate had taken a hand, events moved as though an unseen autopilot was guiding Hughes toward his destiny. By the end of the year he was in control of Transcontinental and Western Air, one of the largest airlines in the United States—and, curiously, one that had, until Lindy fell out of favor, been called *The Lindbergh Line.* Here was an opportunity to put into effect all his ideas for systematically controlled scheduled flying, to sponsor an airliner that could meet his exacting standards of excellence, and to be in control of the entire process. The manner in which this transpired was interesting, if only because, in the first place, the initiative came from someone else.

Transcontinental and Western Air (TWA) had been the product of an enforced merger—the notorious Shotgun Marriage—in 1930, when Postmaster

General Walter Folger Brown had refused to award an airmail contract to two airlines competing on the same transcontinental route: Western Air Express and Transcontinental Air Transport. They were at first reluctant bedfellows but developed not only into one of the largest airlines, but also into one of the industry's technical leaders. Jack Frye, TWA's first president, had, in fact, been the inspiration behind the development of the first Douglas commercial twin-engined airliner, the DC-1, which begat the DC-2, which in turn begat the world-famous DC-3. TWA had led the way in conducting experiments with high-altitude flying, to rise "above the weather" as it was popularly described, and had placed an order for the Boeing 307 Stratoliner, a four-engined long-range airplane that, but for the outbreak of World War II, might have carved an even more important niche for itself in airline history, other than being the world's first pressurized airliner, able to cruise at 20,000 feet, where the turbulence was comparatively slight and free of the cloud-induced "air-pockets" that caused so much airsickness among passengers.

Originally in the hands of the Pennsylvania Railroad, control of TWA had passed to an uneasy partnership of John Hertz, owner of Yellow Cabs, and Lehman Brothers, the financiers, following the divestiture of railroad stock after the revelations of the airmail scandal of 1934. Jack Frye and his chief lieutenant, Paul Richter, decided that they were unable to work with Hertz, thought about starting another airline, and approached Hughes for financing. Hughes came up with a better idea: that he should buy enough stock of TWA to outvote Hertz in a proxy fight for control, if necessary. In any event, Hertz was ready to sell, and Hughes became, at the end of 1938, the largest single shareholder in TWA, with 25 percent of the stock, worth $1.6 million—almost small change for Hughes at that time. By 1940 he controlled TWA, and by the mid 1950s built up his holdings to 78 percent.

Jack Frye had ordered the Stratoliner in 1936, but there had been problems. TWA had experienced financial setbacks as its technical lead with the DC-2 had been overtaken by American's introduction of the DC-3. Hertz had procrastinated in the progress payments. And the Stratoliner itself had undergone the teething troubles that any innovative product has to suffer as new technology is digested by the engineers and designers who have to make the ideas work. One of the aircraft had crashed, un-

TWA Lockheed L-1049 (courtesy of the National Air and Space Museum)

fortunately with an inspection team from the Dutch airline, KLM, on board. Hughes bought one himself, and he may have had ideas about another dramatic record-breaking flight. But on this occasion, with memories of the outstanding success of the round-the-world flight still satisfactorily fresh, and with war clouds gathering, he turned his attention to a more ambitious project.

In an inspired partnership, Hughes and Frye crystallized their ideas to visualize the Constellation airliner, to be built by Lockheed, under the design leadership of Kelly Johnson, who had produced the Lockheed 14 that Hughes had selected for his global flight. At a historic meeting in June 1939, Hughes, Frye, and a TWA team met Lockheed president Robert Gross, and designers Hall Hibbard and Kelly Johnson, to establish the broad specifications. These were a tremendous challenge. The new airliner had to be pressurized—Hughes was convinced of that necessity from his flying, and so were Frye and TWA from their own experiments under the

guidance of Tommy Tomlinson. The size was set at 60 seats, the range at 3,500 miles, and the speed at 300 mph. These three performance criteria were not only about double that of anything flying at the time, even the Stratoliner; they were 50 percent better than the nearest rival project, the Douglas DC-4, a 40-seat unpressurized airliner already on the drawing boards at Santa Monica.

Hughes insisted on secrecy, a condition that was readily accepted by all parties, and strictly observed until the exigencies of war demanded that the armed forces could benefit from what promised to be a revolutionary advance in the construction of large transport aircraft, commercial or military. The price tag set by Lockheed was $450,000 for each aircraft, and this presented a problem for a cash-starved TWA. Hughes had the answer, with a plan that was bold and simple. The Hughes Tool Company would purchase the aircraft, and then pass them on to TWA at terms that could be worked out later. For Hughes, who owned the tool company and at the time about 70 percent of TWA, such terms were academic, little more than a bookkeeping transaction. In practice, it was the enabling act that gave the green light to Kelly Johnson to go ahead with all speed and without budgetary constraints. One cross that they all had to bear was Hughes's constant interference, prying into every aspect of the design and construction in his quest for perfection. Such forbearance was not in vain, for together Lockheed and Hughes produced one of the greatest airliners in air transport history.

In December 1941 the cloak of secrecy had to be lifted, as all aircraft production had to be geared to the war effort. The Lockheed Model 049—to give the Constellation its official designation—became the U.S. Army's C-69 transport, and the U.S. Navy's R70/R7V. While the secret was out, and TWA's competitors now became aware of a new threat, Hughes persuaded Gross not to sell Constellations to any direct transcontinental competitor. Thus Eastern Air Lines and Chicago and Southern, for example, operating north-south routes, as well as Pan American, at that time not encroaching on TWA's territorial sphere of influence, put their names down on the order book, but transcontinental airlines such as United or American were tied to the slower, unpressurized, and smaller Douglas DC-4. For TWA, revenge was sweet. For in 1933 a Boeing-United combination had refused to sell the Boeing 247, the world's first "modern" airliner, to any other airline.

On April 17, 1944, Hughes and Frye broke another record in spectacular, almost storybook fashion. Even a world war could not keep Hughes out of the limelight. The gossip in Washington had been that the armed forces were distinctly lukewarm about the new Lockheed aircraft and that many of the top-ranking men in the corridors of power were skeptical about the prospects for success of an airliner whose specification seemed to go beyond the threshold of practicability. The doubters were put to shame when Hughes and Frye flew into Washington only 6 hours 58 minutes after leaving Burbank. This was not even an aircraft built to set speed records. It was a commercial airliner. As a pacesetter, it was clearly in a class of its own.

Provocatively, Hughes painted the aircraft in TWA's colors, although it was legally a U.S. Army aircraft. But for generals to protest on such a technicality in the face of such clearly demonstrated technical superiority would have made them the object of ridicule. Hughes undoubtedly enjoyed his moral victory, and there must have been some red faces in the Pentagon. In swashbuckling fashion, he also made some demonstration flights for government officials, and on one occasion he took the entire Civil Aeronautics Board (CAB) for a ride, even cutting two engines in flight to emphasize the superb performance of the Constellation. The reactions of the CAB to this procedure are not recorded.

The Lockheed Constellation has been assessed for its place in history by many aviation historians and detailed comparisons have been made of its superiority over its U.S. rivals and its effect on the postwar development of civil airliners as a whole. The facts and the statistics are absolute and set down in hundreds of books for the technical record. Less credit has been given, however, to the inspired vision of the man who set the demanding specification, placed the launching order for the production, and devised the necessary financing scheme to convert what so easily could have been just another stillborn idea into a reality. Lockheed's Robert Gross and Kelly Johnson rightly deserve the fullest praise for having produced a masterpiece, and the folk at TWA, especially Jack Frye, for having crystallized into shape the specification details. But without Howard Hughes, there would never have been a Lockheed Constellation.

And without the Constellation, the introduction of pressurized 300 mph airliners may have been delayed until the late 1940s, or even the early 1950s. For there would have been no challenger for the Douglas DC-4, also produced at first as the U.S. Army's C-54 transport in large numbers and released for the commercial market before the end of 1945. The 250 mph unpressurized 40-seater would have been the standard specification for perhaps half a postwar decade, and the Boeing Stratocruiser, developed from the army's KC-135 tanker and riding on the wings of the B-52 bomber, may have had a very different future. So too might have some of the overseas challengers, notably the British, who had been forced to abandon three promising projects at the outbreak of World War II in 1939, but whose national airline, BOAC, had been forced to become one of the Constellation's early customers in 1946. Without the "Connie," which author Peter W. Brooks shrewdly described as America's Secret Weapon in the battle for postwar airline supremacy, U.S. airlines would not have enjoyed their position of dominance, and the United States itself would not have commanded the authority in international commercial aviation that it quickly assumed as soon as the war was over.

Charles Lindbergh's 1927 transatlantic flight has correctly been credited as one of the main incentives for the surge in interest and support for the airline industry in the late 1920s, a surge that brought the United States to a convincing and overwhelming pinnacle of leadership in civil aviation affairs worldwide. Equally, Hughes's sponsorship of the Lockheed Constellation could be judged to have been a major factor in preserving that leadership in the post–World War II era.

Such a claim for respect and reverence in the annals of aviation history have unfortunately—and somewhat unfairly—been overshadowed by Hughes's more direct involvement with another ambitious project, and one that carried his name, which was doubly unfortunate, because it was not a success. For in spite of his achievements in breaking speed records, flying around the world, or being the driving force behind a major advance in the construction of transport aircraft, Howard Hughes is remembered for his accomplishments in aviation mostly for the "Spruce Goose."

This was the name given by the press to the HK-1 Hercules flying boat. This was the huge aircraft that a headline-hungry world welcomed as an excuse for the use of superlatives, and for once, the term *giant* was not misplaced. But the popular name given to the Hercules was not popular at Culver City, and any employee who might have had the temerity to use it in Hughes's presence is said to have risked instant dismissal. For the term seemed to be a disparaging one, and although it was ultimately to become a flying white elephant, it was nevertheless a supreme technical achievement, built with precision and superb craftsmanship and designed to an exacting specification laid down by defense authorities in Washington.

The construction of the Hercules was not, as is too widely imagined, the result of a whim on the part of an impetuous and foolhardy millionaire. The motivation was a praiseworthy effort to find a solution to the formidable logistics problem of sending supplies, either to besieged Britain, in the front line of the Nazi threat to complete its occupation of the whole of Europe, or to the armed forces of the United States in a faraway foreign theater of war. In both cases, there was the everpresent threat of the German U-Boat submarines which, in the sum-

mer of 1942, came very close to cutting the shipping convoys' transatlantic route by the mere threat of their presence.

Henry Kaiser, the man who had revolutionized shipbuilding techniques by introducing assembly-line production for his Liberty Ships, and who had watched them being sunk as quickly as he could build them, had the inspiration of building giant flying boats that could deliver the goods without fear of torpedoes. His grandiose vision was for a fleet of 5,000 of these huge aircraft, each one large enough to carry 60 tons of cargo (for example a Sherman tank) or a company of troops. The whole idea at first seemed preposterous, especially at a time when strategic materials such as steel and aluminum were in short supply. Kaiser had the inspiration to approach the one man who combined the necessary aeronautical knowledge with the resources needed to build such an enormous airplane: Howard Hughes.

The millionaire flyer and aircraft constructor was fascinated by the challenge to do something that seemed to be beyond any other manufacturer's comprehension. Kaiser persuaded him to undertake the task, and they formed the Kaiser-Hughes Corporation on November 16, 1942. The government placed an order for three prototype flying boats, including one static test model, broadly according to Kaiser's ambitious specification and on a nonprofit basis. It was to be built of wood, and Kaiser-Hughes leased from the Fairchild Corporation a bonding process involving the use of special glues to laminate wood veneers, and improved upon it. Anyone who inspects the Hercules can testify to the superb craftsmanship and obvious strength achieved by the materials used.

The work proceeded during the peak years of World War II, 1943 and 1944. A special hangar had to be built to house the construction, which was built in secret, both by government insistence and by Hughes's natural bent. The statistics surrounding the HK-1 were themselves impressive: the hangar was 750 feet long, 250 feet wide, and 100 feet high; the graving dock in Long Beach Harbor was 290 feet long; and the distance between hangar and dock was 28 miles. The move alone took two days, needed extraordinary precautions and partial demolition work, and taxed the patience of ten police forces. By the time this event took place, in 1946, the Hughes Hercules was already in trouble. The war had ended, so who needed it? The original

$18 million contract had been spent, but Hughes had put $7 million of his own money into it as well, and was not about to abandon the project. He persuaded the authorities to allow him to finish one big flying boat of the three ordered.

As the aircraft neared completion and the huge wings were joined to the huge fuselage, still under the Hughes eagle eye and controlled by his often irritating insistence on perfection, he was under attack politically as a Senate subcommittee sought to prove that he had undertaken the project for ulterior motives, including profit at the expense of the government, that is, the taxpayer. For a man who was worth many times more than the Hercules project, and one who had furthermore put a substantial sum of money into it himself, the whole idea was ludicrous. The senators met their match. As they cross-examined him, Hughes countered with cold facts and a stout defense of his motives and won public sympathy, even admiration. When, in desperation, one senator demanded yet more documentary evidence and asked if Hughes would produce the necessary papers, Hughes's succinct reply (after a well-timed theatrical pause), "No Sir, I don't think I will," was acclaimed as a victory for free enterprise against bureaucracy, and the ulterior motives were perceived to be on the other side. Howard Hughes was still a public hero.

This was in August 1947. Just over two months later, on November 2, Hughes piloted the HK-1 Hercules on its first flight. It was also the only flight and was not exactly world-shattering, as had been most of his previous efforts. It was little more than a test hop, reaching perhaps about 70 feet in altitude over a distance of about a mile. There has been much speculation as to whether Hughes intended the great aircraft to fly or not. He may have been making a fast taxi test, and the clean aerodynamics provided enough lift to break it clear of the wave tops; or it may have been a mischievous demonstration that Hughes was still master of his fate. For, intended or not, there was never a second when this enormous machine, the biggest aircraft in the world until the Boeing 747 of the late 1960s, was not under complete control. The Senate hearings came mercifully to a close on November 22, 1947.

Subsequently, the Hughes Hercules was preserved in a specially built hangar, under constant climate control, so that when it was finally purchased by funds generated by the Committee to Save the Fly-

ing Boat and acquired eventually by the Wrather Corporation, the good citizens of Long Beach claimed it as their very own. It was first moved from its hangar on October 29, 1980. Even that required a massive effort, as the land had settled and the water in the dock was therefore much higher so that some of the hangar structure had to be removed. Then a great domed stadiumlike building was erected to house it, and the "Spruce Goose"—the media had condemned this beautiful aircraft to the ignominy of this nickname—was opened to public view on May 14, 1983, appropriately within a stone's throw of that other elegant giant of another transport era, the *Queen Mary* luxury liner.

While all the postwar controversy about the justification of the Hercules was going on, Hughes was actually more interested, and certainly more involved, in another aeronautical project, a high-altitude photo-reconnaissance aircraft for the army, the Hughes XF-11. This was started in 1943 but, like the great flying boat, was not completed before the end of World War II. It too suffered an ignominious fate, of a far different kind.

When the time came for its maiden test flight, on July 7, 1946, Hughes, as usual, claimed the right to test-fly his own airplane. Like all his productions, there was something unusual about the equipment, in this case a twin-boomed fuselage design, and contra-rotating propellers, powered by two Pratt & Whitney R-4360 3,000 horsepower engines, the same as the eight on the Hercules, and among the most powerful piston engines ever built. After a 45-minute routine flight, without incident, and just before returning to land at Culver City, one of the contra-rotating propellers went into full reverse pitch. Out of control, and already flying low, Hughes could not bail out. He tried to reach some open ground at the Los Angeles Country Club, but never got there. He crashed into some houses on Wilshire Boulevard, in a spectacular ball of fire and smoke. Unbelievably, he was pulled to safety, with severe injuries. His chest was crushed; his ribs were cracked or broken; he had wounds and minor cracks in the face and scalp, extensive burns, cuts, and abrasions. One lung had collapsed and the other was damaged. The doctors gave him little chance of survival.

This was a different kind of challenge. Hughes was made of what, in later, more sensational character descriptions, became known as "the right stuff." He walked out of the hospital after five weeks. He must have driven the hospital authorities and staff to desperation, as his insatiable urge for innovation, improvement, and perfection took him into the field of hospital equipment, including a remote-controlled, retractable bedpan. The hospital must have been as pleased to see him go as he was to get back to the business of overseeing the completion of the Hercules and the redesigning of the XF-11. Rather like a fallen horseman who tries to return to the saddle as quickly as possible to wipe out the psychological effect, Hughes test-flew the XF-11 again on April 5, 1947; but this was an academic exercise, as the requirement for such an advanced photo-reconnaissance aircraft had receded, at least until the cold war grew warmer and Lockheed came up with the U-2.

At the time of the dreadful crash and the miraculous recovery there were those who said that Hughes would never be the same again, because of the effect of his injuries. And there is much circumstantial evidence to suggest that he did undergo a mental as well as a physical change during the 1950s. He became more reclusive, avoiding publicity and public appearances, becoming something of a mystery man because of his self-banishment from all but a few of his more immediate contacts. There are very few known photographs of Hughes after the Senate investigation; and the Hercules and the XF-11 became museum pieces. His personal contacts with his staff diminished in frequency, although he maintained his masterly grip on all his affairs by telephone, habitually in the middle of the night. He kept the oddest kind of waking hours and seemed completely unaffected by the thought that the people who were running his various companies might prefer more orthodox cyclic patterns. He was known to have conducted long conversations from telephone booths and was believed to have arranged meetings in public lavatories, so intense was his obsession for privacy. The word spread that Hughes had become an eccentric.

Eccentric or not, he made a success of the next objective of his concentrated genius for doing things in a big way. There was little to challenge his competitive spirit in the aircraft manufacturing field, although there were notable successes in the helicopter division of the Hughes Aircraft Company, which also became prominent in the field of electronics, especially for space applications; and in air navigation, as a distant legacy of the original pioneering work performed in his 1938 round-the-world flight. Seeking an outlet for his insatiable ambition in all fields of aviation, he set out to make Transcontinental and Western Air one of the largest, if not the largest, airlines in the world. Evidence of this goal was the change of TWA's name, on May 17, 1950, to Trans World Airlines.

There were indications that, already, Hughes had been casting his eyes toward the idea of a globe-encircling airline network, to complement or to compete with the chosen instrument, Pan American Airways. Because of his secretive approach, and because decisions were typically made by Hughes himself, without advice or consultation, there is no documented evidence that he systematically set out to turn TWA into an intercontinental airline with round-the-world capability. But there is considerable circumstantial evidence to suggest that he had this ambition in mind. In 1943 TWA had invested in TACA, the Central American airline that was a thorn in Pan American's side, and which had set up subsidiaries in all the countries from Mexico to Panama. Early in 1944 the capital was increased, and at the end of 1945 TWA acquired the balance of the stock, by which time other South American countries had TACA affiliations. As TACA had interests in British West Indian Airways and in Aerovias Brasil, an optimistic cartographer could have made—and did, on timetables published at the time—the new TACA look like another Pan American airline empire. But there was little substance to the disjointed collection of uncoordinated members of the TACA family; and any ambitions that Hughes and TWA might have had toward challenging Juan Trippe in this chosen sphere of influence came to naught.

Other indications of global aspirations came as World War II drew to its close. TWA purchased 20 percent of Hawaiian Airlines stock in May 1944, and a minor shareholding in Philippine Airlines in August 1945. It then proceeded to help form several airlines in Europe and the Middle East, with both financial and management involvement: Ethiopian Airlines in December 1945, TAE (Greece) in April 1946, and Saudi Arabian Airlines, Linee Aeree Italiane, and Iranian Airways in September-October 1946. A glance at a world map shows an interesting pattern that comes close to putting a girdle around the earth, by a system of interlocking relationships, both at the airline and the governmental level, with TWA as the common thread linking them all.

As the international airline policy unfolded after World War II, and the United States itself broke the Pan American monopoly on overseas air routes, it became clear that many different airlines would be allocated continental areas in which they would be permitted, even encouraged, to supplement Pan American's presence. Braniff Airways was given South America, Northwest Airways the northern Pacific, and there were other awards. But the plum went to TWA, on a group of routes and destinations to Europe and onward to the Indian subcontinent. By this time Frye had left, in 1947, and his place had been taken by Ralph Damon, one of the most respected airline industry leaders of his time. Concentrating on the North Atlantic, the Hughes-Damon team built TWA into a great airline whose name became as well known in London, Paris, Rome, Athens, and Cairo as Pan American's. In due course it even overtook Pan American to become the leading passenger carrier on the North Atlantic air route, the most important and lucrative in the world.

Damon's death, in 1956, came as a great blow to Hughes, who seemed to be like a captain of a ship in dangerous tidal waters but who has suddenly lost his pilot overboard. The relationship between TWA's owner and the succession of presidents who followed Damon was never the same. Carter Burgess was president for a year and never met Hughes. Certainly the tendency toward unorthodox modes of business behavior seemed to increase after Damon's death, and the passion for solitude and secrecy was ever present in Hughes's behavior.

One good example of this was the discussion with the Bristol Aeroplane Company in 1957. Hughes's attention had been drawn to the four-engined turboprop airliner, the Bristol Britannia, whose performance across the Atlantic was excellent, and even better than that of the succession of Constellation airliner variants that Hughes and TWA had helped to sponsor during the lifetime of that great piston-engined airplane. Arrangements were made for the Britannia to be brought to Toronto, whereupon Peter Masefield, then head of Bristol Aeroplane, conducted lengthy discussions with Hughes at a California telephone number. Eventually satisfied with what he heard, Hughes said he would come to inspect the Britannia, and Masefield inquired as to when he would arrive. "In about five minutes," came the reply. Hughes had been installed in the room above, and the telephone calls had been relayed.

The Bristol aircrew who had flown the Britannia to Toronto had been waiting for the great man to arrive and had been understandably skeptical about his abilities, as he had become more inaccessible and withdrawn from public contact. After Hughes had made his presence felt, he armed himself with the weighty manuals, climbed on board the Britannia, and demanded privacy while he studied them. He was there all night and in the morning said he was ready to fly. Courteously invited to take the right-hand seat, he declined, insisting—above mild protests about the inherent problems of flying a new aircraft with different propulsion than he had been used to—that he take the left seat. He took the Britannia on a series of "circuits and bumps" and according to one witness did so perfectly. Flying to Toronto as skeptics, the crew returned to Bristol almost in awe of a man who was clearly in complete charge of what he was doing and, eccentric or not, was a pilot of great prowess.

Hughes had an interest in the Whispering Giant, as the Britannia was known, because he was seeking a solution to the problem of keeping up with the Pan American competition. On October 13, 1955, Juan Trippe had announced his epoch-making order for what were then called the Big Jets. The order was for 25 Douglas DC-8s and 20 Boeing 707s, and such a quantity was not only unprecedented, it sent shudders of alarm throughout the intercontinental airline world, which beat a pathway to Long Beach for the DC-8s and particularly to Seattle for the 707s. But the lines did not, at first, have TWA as one of the more aggressive standard-bearers of progress because, for the first time in his life, Hughes did not have a bottomless pit of financial resources on which to draw.

At the very time when Hughes and TWA needed cash as they had never needed it before, the Hughes private bank, his own Hughes Tool Company, suffered a sharp decline in earnings. Under arrangements first instigated back in the days when the Constellation was launched, TWA aircraft were financed by Hughes Tool, not from traditional capital sources such as banks and insurance companies. And he could not fall back on an alternative source, the Hughes Aircraft Company, because Hughes himself had transferred ownership to the Howard Hughes Medical Institute, which was a nonprofit research foundation, unable to put any of its assets at risk. Ironically, an ostensibly charitable act was now working against its instigator.

Desperate to obtain quick delivery of a big fleet of jet aircraft, TWA lacked the means to buy them. It could not make progress payments to Boeing for the 33 Boeing 707s it had ordered, and neither could it honor its commitments to Convair for 30 Convair 880s that Hughes had also ordered. Years previously Hughes Tool had put $10 million cash into TWA when, in 1946, the airline had suffered setbacks from a pilots' strike, crashes, and the grounding of the Constellation. The Hughes Tool Company had taken back convertible notes and the power to name the majority of TWA's directors, and the Equitable Life Insurance Company, holding $40 million in loan debentures, agreed on the condition that if TWA defaulted, the tool company's stock could be put into an Equitable-controlled voting trust. This clause had lain dormant for 12 years but now resurfaced as a weapon with which Equitable, now regarded by the financial world as a champion of their interests against mavericks such as Hughes, could go into the attack.

In 1958 TWA was living precariously, and Hughes had to raise a $12 million short-term loan from Equitable, on a 90-day guarantee by the Hughes Tool Company. The insurance company insisted that long-term financing must be arranged quickly, or it would invoke the voting-trust clause of the 1946 agreement. During the next two years Hughes manipulated TWA's money in a desperate rearguard action, while a fine management team and disciplined staff not only kept the airline going, but did so with a touch of élan, as the long-range Lockheed L-1649A Starliner, last of a fine line, and with New York-Frankfurt nonstop capability, entered service.

In May 1960, as a condition of a $300 million long-term financing plan from Irving Trust—and nothing less would be sufficient for TWA to remain competitive as the Jet Age got under way—Hughes was forced into a corner. He had to agree that Equitable's old long-term loan should be converted to a short-term loan. One clause of the agreement was critical, and it became a Damocles sword. If any change of management was considered to be adverse, Equitable could demand that the 77 percent of stock held by Hughes be put under the control of a voting trust. On July 27, 1960, president Charles Thomas resigned, and on December 31, 1960, Hughes had to surrender. In this battle of ti-

tanic financial forces, no quarter was asked or given, and magnanimity for a fallen idol was not on Equitable's agenda. It placed Hughes's stock in the hands of a voting trust and appointed a new board and a new management. It also filed an antitrust suit against the Hughes Tool Company on the grounds that, as both supplier and financier of TWA's aircraft, it had excluded other suppliers.

Hughes fought on, countering suits with countersuits. Yet for all the concealment of his daily affairs and of his real personality, there must also have been a large element of equanimity in his makeup, allowing his mind to function simultaneously on different wavelengths without interference. For most people, the battle for control for TWA would have been all-consuming. But Hughes continued to wheel and deal in other directions. The Civil Aeronautics Board even allowed him to obtain control of Northeast Airlines and, in apparent sympathy for his cause, declared in July 1964 that he could resume control of TWA if he disposed of his interest in Northeast. But in that direction he had finally met his match at the hands of Equitable's lawyers. In September 1968 the Hughes Tool Company had to pay $138 million in treble damages. After a tremendous tactical defense, he was forced to retire, defeated. He had lost a decisive battle that had swung the tide of the boardroom war, but Hughes's surrender was not total, and it was not without compensations.

An airline, as a dynamic public utility, whatever its ownership and whatever the slings and arrows of outrageous financial fortune, carries on with its work of carrying passengers and freight even in the face of adversity. In TWA's case, it shared in the fantastic airline boom of the 1960s that the Jet Age had launched. The stock had held its own, and in May 1966 Howard Hughes had sold his trustee-held percentage through a secondary offering to the general public. At $86 each, 6,584,937 shares changed hands in 20 minutes, making for Hughes $566,304,582—more than enough to cover the triple damages.

A common reflection by the public at the news, and knowing the image of eccentricity that had been fed to it by the sensation-hungry press and media, was "If this is eccentricity, then I'd like a piece of it." But more serious issues were at stake, involving the fate of courageous individual innovators who dare to challenge the orthodox, entrenched financial establishment. *Fortune*, a publication of great repute in the world of business, commerce, and finance, observed that "this is the largest sum to come into the hands of one man at one time." It also published a penetrating analysis of the whole episode that did little to enhance the reputation of the financial community. Why, *Fortune* respectfully asked, should the owner of 77 percent of the stock of a company, however unorthodox he may be, be prevented from voting the stock? How much power should large-scale lenders be allowed to protect their loans? And what is the public interest (a phrase familiar to the Civil Aeronautics Board) in the case of an airline, which is a quasi-public utility?

But this was armchair quarterbacking after the game was won and lost. *Fortune* seemed to have come down on Hughes's side, an outcome from which Hughes may have derived some cynical comfort. But more likely, he accepted the defeat phlegmatically, much in the way that a grand master will accept defeat in the intellectual marathon of a world chess championship. He had himself been a master manipulator and a ruthless one if necessary to achieve his own ends. Now he had been outmaneuvered and he accepted it. But those who knew him, and even those who were merely distant observers of the scene, predicted that one underlying characteristic of Hughes's personality and character would not be snuffed out by a major catastrophe. This characteristic was his love of aviation and his love of commercial air transport. If he had liked to build airplanes, and had been thrilled to fly them and break records, it was the airline business that consumed his intellect, because its influence was so vast, its challenges so diverse, and its technical intricacies of such compelling interest. And sure enough, Hughes could not bear to be parted from the airline scene.

He had aviation in his bloodstream. At the age of sixty-three, he was too old to make record-breaking flights in the supersonic era; and he was rumored to be in delicate health, with a hearing problem, though not yet to be classified as infirm. But, not yet ready for a quiet retirement, he was one of the richest men in the world. His mind was still razor sharp, and to maintain his addiction with the airline business, and knowing that the doors of TWA were closed, he looked elsewhere.

After the protracted litigation that led to the adverse verdict in September 1968, Hughes moved quickly and, as ever, secretively. A series of events occurred in the western United States that ostensibly had nothing to do with Hughes. Indeed, airline industry observers and even aviation journalists who prided themselves on keeping their ears to the ground had not the slightest idea that another Howard Hughes coup was in the making. The whole affair was vintage Hughes.

Even before the triple-damages decision, moves were afoot to produce a merger between three of the local service airlines in the West: West Coast, Pacific, and Bonanza. The driving force behind the merger was Nick Bez, head of West Coast Airlines in Seattle, who emerged as the chairman of the new airline, Air West. Combined operations began on July 1, 1968. Six weeks later—and even before the litigation over the Hughes Tool Company damages was drawn to a conclusion—on August 12, Bez (who died not long afterward) announced that the Hughes Tool Company had agreed to buy the airline for $90 million. The directors of Air West, some of whom had been controllers of their own fates, and who first heard the news on the radio, were said to have been unhappy at this sale. Bez, they perceived, had been the front man for Howard Hughes.

There followed a series of events that would provide ample material for a comic opera libretto, a soap opera, or even a farce. On December 27, 1968, the Bez group carried the shareholders' vote by a narrow margin. The next day the directors reversed the decision because of a last-minute counteroffer from another airline. On December 31, 13 of the directors, previously voting against the Hughes faction, recanted and voted for it. There was much speculation as to the reasons for the change of minds, and to the manipulative measures that may have been taken to change those minds. Eventually, in July 1969, the Civil Aeronautics Board and President Richard M. Nixon approved the acquisition of Air West by the Hughes Tool Company. On March 31, 1970, a new corporation, the Hughes Air Corporation, was formed, and in July of that year Air West was renamed Hughes Air West. As before, Hughes injected fresh capital into the new airline, through the Hughes Air Corporation, 78 percent of which was owned by Hughes Tool and 22 percent by Hughes.

The comic opera moved into the second act. In December 1972 a Federal Grand Jury indicted Hughes for conspiracy, and half the lawyers west of the Rocky Mountains went to work again. Federal

Judge Bruce Thompson quite blatantly sided with Hughes, and the case dragged on with witnesses for both sides alternately giving evidence, or declining to do so, or retracting it. Some of them took prolonged vacations, destinations unknown, and one of the witnesses was Jimmy the Greek, of Las Vegas gambling notoriety. Ultimately, in January 1979, the Summa Corporation, yet another Hughes-inspired entity and the legal body responsible for liabilities in the case, agreed to pay $37 million in damages to the plaintiffs, the former shareholders of Air West, who had been deprived of their birthrights back in 1968.

The last act in this slice of airline history, which had all the elements of a theatrical production, belonged purely and simply to Howard Hughes. After a period of obsessive isolation from the public, during which his few confidants were drawn mainly from members of the Mormon church and his places of residence included whole floors of hotels that he owned in Las Vegas or which he rented in Bermuda, the Bahamas, or in London, Howard Hughes died on board his private airplane en route to Mexico, where it was believed he may have been seeking special medical treatment. The date was April 5, 1976. He was seventy years old.

If ever a man had lived his three score years and ten to the fullest, Howard Hughes was that man. The last of those years were conducted in a cloistered environment with few human contacts, to such an extent that he might have been a Trappist monk for all the communication that emanated from him. He was known to hold a deep mistrust for almost everyone, even his doctors. He would insist on a standard of hygiene for his dietary needs that would have been far too high for any hospital; yet at the same time, some of his habits were rumored to be squalid, even disgusting. Those who claimed to have seen him alleged that he was untidily bearded, unkempt and completely careless about his appearance, and unwashed, even incontinent, to the extent that he could have made good use of the retractable bedpan that he had once designed. The full and true account and description of his eccentricity toward the end may never be known, as only a few people set eyes on him during the last five years of his life, and those that did are not telling.

But old age and the ailments that accompany advancing years are no respecters of persons. Hospi-

tals, nursing homes, and our own homes are frequently the last refuges of those who have become senile. In Hughes's case, he had the money to be able to deteriorate and to die in complete privacy, if not with complete dignity. But what a life had gone before!

He is remembered by the general public as being—long before eccentricity took hold—an unashamed philanderer, taking or paying for women as they took his fancy, rewarding them with money or fame. In this respect, he was not alone. The list of presidents, prime ministers, kings, emperors, literary and musical geniuses, and other notabilities whose indiscretions matched Howard Hughes's would fill a book. Nobody knows whether or not he was kind to animals. He was certainly unkind to some people. Yet, paradoxically, he could often be kind, although such examples are usually quoted defensively as exceptions to the rule. His known record shows that he simply used his immense wealth in a self-centered way, indulging himself in whatever activity took his fancy: to build an airplane, to beat a world record, to buy an airline, to sleep with any woman he chose, without giving a thought to anyone else's feelings or sensibilities.

To compare Howard Hughes with Charles Lindbergh is tempting to any biographer. Both were tall, attractive youths when they started their aviation careers. Both were excellent pilots, and both achieved fame by making some great flights that went into the record books. Both made great contributions to the science and the operational procedures of airline practice, through their admirable survey flights. Both were solitary people, becoming more so with advancing age. Both had notoriety forced upon them by events and circumstances of their own making. Both enjoyed the zenith of popular acclaim with ticker-tape parades, and both were condemned to public contempt in later life. In their advancing years, both were interested in, and became deeply involved with, medical science; both became reclusive in their dotage; and both died in seclusion.

While neither had ever been poor, Hughes was so rich that in that category there was no comparison. Both became richer the longer they lived, but Hughes was a magnate, compared with whom Lindbergh was merely comfortably off with a few million dollars. Both had fame and fortune, admiration and acclaim thrust upon them for their deeds and accomplishments. Hughes's haul was prodigious. He was acclaimed as a filmmaker and even won prizes as an amateur golfer.

The level of his talents at the peak of his career during the 1950s was astonishing. He owned TWA, one of the largest airlines in the world, which operated one of the best airliners in the world (and one of the greatest in air transport history), which he had financed and helped to develop and was able to fly as a pilot as well as any of TWA's captains. Leaving aside his prowess as a filmmaker, a sportsman, and a lover, any single element of his varied talents in the aviation world would have been worth a lifetime of endeavor for lesser mortals. Nobody has ever possessed such a wealth of aeronautical talent in all its aspects as Howard Hughes. He was phenomenal.

References:

Charles Barton, *Howard Hughes and His Flying Boat*
(Fallbrook, Cal.: Aero, 1982);

R. E. G. Davies, *Airlines of the United States since 1914*, revised edition (Washington, D.C.: Smithsonian Institution, 1982);

Davies, *Rebels and Reformers of the Airways* (Washington, D.C.: Smithsonian Institution, 1987);

Noah Dietrich, *Howard: The Amazing Mr. Hughes* (Greenwich, Conn.: Fawcett, 1972);

John J. McDonald, *Howard Hughes and His Hercules* (Shrewsbury, Eng.: Airlife, 1981);

Charles J. V. Murphy and Thomas A. Wise, "The Problem of Howard Hughes," *Fortune*, 59 (January 1959): 79-82;

James B. Phelan, "Howard Hughes," *Saturday Evening Post*, 236 (February 9, 1963): 15-23;

Robert W. Rummel, *Howard Hughes and TWA* (Washington, D.C.: Smithsonian Institution, 1991);

Robert J. Serling, *Howard Hughes' Airline: An Informal History of TWA* (New York: St. Martin's/Marek, 1983).

Hughes Air West

by Joseph E. Libby

University of California, Riverside

A regional airline serving the western United States during the 1970s, Hughes Air West grew out of a plan by millionaire Howard Hughes to transform McCarran Field in Las Vegas, Nevada, into a major international airport. Hughes hoped to link overseas carriers with regional, domestic airlines, creating a transportation hub for the entire southwestern section of the country. Air West, the regional airline Hughes acquired for the domestic side of his operation, became Hughes Air West.

Late in 1968 Hughes began searching for a domestic carrier, focusing his attention upon Air West, a Seattle-based airline. Air West had been created in April 1968, when the Civil Aeronautics Board authorized the merger of West Coast Airlines of Seattle, Pacific Airlines of San Francisco, and Bonanza Airlines of Las Vegas into a single operation. Nick Bez, who put the deal together, hoped to create an airline to serve the entire West Coast. Air West began operations on July 1, 1968. However, the independent nature of the three component companies quickly led to conflict as each airline resisted the merger. Further troubles occurred when the company's new computer reservation system failed, generalizing seemingly endless problems for passengers.

Within six weeks of beginning operation, Bez announced Hughes's offer to purchase the troubled airline. Despite opposition, Bez managed to convince a majority of the shareholders to accept the Hughes offer. When last minute attempts to locate other potential purchasers failed, stockholders accepted the Hughes buyout. The agreement was signed on December 31, 1968. The Civil Aeronautics Board officially approved the sale in July 1969. Over the next 12 months, Hughes reorganized the company, streamlining its management structure, and developing a new image for the airline. In July 1970 the airline was officially renamed Hughes Air West, and began operations from its new headquarters in San Mateo, halfway between San Francisco and San Jose. The reorganization brought about a strong financial recovery. By 1972 the airline showed a net profit of $2 million, after having lost $21 million in 1969. Throughout the 1970s the company's bright yellow airplanes, popularly known as "flying bananas," became a common sight over the western United States.

Almost immediately, however, legal problems arose. In December 1972 a federal grand jury, examining the 1968 buyout of Air West, indicted Hughes for conspiring to force the shareholders to sell. Despite Hughes's death in April 1976, the case continued. Finally, in January 1979, the chief beneficiary of the Hughes estate, the Summa Corpora-

tion, agreed to pay $37 million to the former shareholders of Air West. In October 1980, one and a half years after the conclusion of the conspiracy case, the Summa Corporation sold the airline to Republic Airlines of Minneapolis, Minnesota, for $38 million.

References:

R. E. G. Davies, *Airlines of the United States since 1914* (London: Putnam's, 1972);

William A. Schoneberger, with Paul Sonnenburg, *California Wings: A History of Aviation in the Golden State* (Woodland Hills, Calif.: Windsor Publications, 1984).

Croil Hunter

(February 18, 1893 - July 21, 1970)

by W. David Lewis

Auburn University

CAREER: Credit agent (1914-1917), treasurer, Fargo Mercantile Company (1919-1928); artillery officer, U.S. Army (1917-1919); eastern regional manager, First Bancredit Corporation (1928-1932); traffic manager (1932), vice-president and general manager (1933-1937), president and general manager (1937-1953), chairman (1953-1965), chairman emeritus, Northwest Airlines [Northwest Airways to 1934] (1965-1970).

Croil Hunter, who built Northwest Airlines into a large transcontinental and international carrier and played a key role in developing the "Great Circle Route" between the United States and the Far East, was born on February 18, 1893, in Casselton, North Dakota, the son of John Croil Hunter and Emma Schulze Hunter. His father was a wholesale grocer of Scottish ancestry who had immigrated to the United States from Canada and built a thriving business, the Fargo Mercantile Company, in Fargo, North Dakota. After attending public schools in Fargo, Hunter matriculated at the Sheffield Scientific School of Yale University in 1912 but left without graduating in 1914 to become a credit agent in the family firm after the death of his father. Entering military service in 1917, he was sent overseas and rose to the rank of captain in the 338th Field Artillery by the time of

Croil Hunter (courtesy of Northwest Airlines)

his honorable discharge in 1919. Returning home, he became treasurer of the Fargo Mercantile Company for nine years. He married Helen Floan, daughter of a merchant from St. Paul, Minnesota, on February 24, 1923. They had two children: a daughter, Andrea, and a son, John Croil.

In 1928 Hunter moved to New York City to become eastern representative and regional office manager of the First Bancredit Corporation, an installment loan subsidiary of the First Bank Stock Corporation of Minneapolis. Returning to Minnesota in 1932, he became traffic manager of Northwest Airways, which, with backing from such persons as Henry Ford, had won airmail route CAM-9, between Chicago and the Twin Cities, in 1926. Initially headed by an aviation-minded seed dealer, Charles Dickinson, the enterprise grew under the leadership of Col. L. H. Brittin, an engineer who had developed a friendship with Ford and persuaded the latter to include the Twin Cities on one of his aerial reliability tours. Aided by Detroit capital, Northwest had established passenger service to a growing network of destinations in Illinois, Iowa, Minnesota, Nebraska, North Dakota, and Wisconsin, and also developed an international route to Winnipeg, Manitoba, in cooperation with Western Canada Airways. By the time Hunter joined the corporation, local businessmen from the Twin Cities had bought out most of the Michigan shareholders.

Although he had no previous experience in airline operations, Hunter's business acumen and familiarity with the region in which Northwest conducted its operations served the company well as it expanded its route system westward through Montana and reached Spokane, Washington, in October 1933. In early December of that year, after Brittin and Hunter had fought a bitter struggle with United to win approval from the Commerce and Post Office Departments, Northwest established service to Seattle and Tacoma and started billing itself as the "Northern Transcontinental Line," even though Chicago remained its eastern terminus. Meanwhile, Hunter won promotion to vice-president and general manager of the enterprise.

The following year, American commercial aviation entered a period of turmoil as a U.S. Senate committee chaired by Hugo Black investigated alleged illegalities in the awarding of airmail routes under the Herbert Hoover administration. During the hearings, Brittin tore up some allegedly personal papers in the files of former federal aviation administrator William P. MacCracken that were under subpoena by the Black committee. When these were pasted together by postal officials and found to pertain to air-

mail matters, Brittin was cited for contempt of Congress, served a brief jail term, and resigned his post at Northwest. Meanwhile, President Franklin D. Roosevelt canceled existing airmail contracts, and new regulations went into effect under the Airmail Act of 1934 after a brief but disastrous experiment of using army pilots to fly the mail. In the process of reorganization that followed, Northwest temporarily lost its original routes to such places as Chicago and Fargo and was forced to reacquire them from Hanford Tri-State Airlines. In reestablishing itself, the company followed the example of several other trunk lines by adopting a slightly modified new name, and became known as Northwest Airlines.

Having already begun to replace Northwest's motley assortment of earlier aircraft with more up-to-date planes, Hunter pursued a vigorous program of technological modernization to improve service on the sparsely populated routes connecting the relatively few major cities served by the company. In 1934 Northwest became the first carrier to operate the ten-passenger Lockheed L-10A Electra, based upon specifications developed by the airline's engineering department. It set a speed record on the Chicago-Twin Cities artery and became a mainstay on the Chicago-to-Seattle route. In 1937, the year in which he became president of Northwest while retaining his post of general manager, Hunter deployed the first of 12 new Lockheed 14-H Sky Zephyrs, which carried 14 passengers and had an even faster cruising speed than the L-10A. When these proved accident-prone and were temporarily grounded by federal officials, Hunter secured a loan from the Reconstruction Finance Corporation in 1939 and began acquiring 21-passenger Douglas DC-3s, which cruised at 185 miles per hour and were rapidly becoming standard on America's domestic airways. At this time, the company also began employing stewardesses. As Hunter's modernization program progressed, the number of passengers enplaned by Northwest rose from 12,097 in 1934 to 136,797 in 1940. By the end of the fiscal year ending June 30, 1941, income from passenger traffic exceeded airmail earnings for the first time since Northwest's founding.

Hunter, however, had even larger goals in mind, laying plans to connect the region served by Northwest with Asian destinations by following the "Great Circle Route" via Alaska. In addition to furnishing the shortest way to get from North America to the Far East, such a route also had the advantage of staying close to islands and landmasses where refueling bases and emergency landing facilities could be maintained. In 1939 Northwest applied to the Civil Aeronautics Board (CAB) for a route from Chicago to Calcutta via Seattle, Fairbanks, and points on the Siberian and Chinese mainland. Shortly thereafter, having personally taken part in a survey flight to the Far East via the Great Circle, Hunter filed an amended application with the CAB for a route from Seattle to Tokyo, with stops at Anchorage and the Aleutian Islands. At the same time, he tried to elevate Northwest to the status of a truly transcontinental carrier by seeking CAB approval for flights from Minneapolis-St. Paul to New York City via Milwaukee and Detroit.

Partly because of diplomatic and military developments that were steadily increasing the likelihood of American involvement in a Pacific war, Hunter's ambitious schemes to establish commercial air routes to Asia did not materialize at this time. Nor did his transcontinental project win support from the CAB. After the Japanese bombing of Pearl Harbor, however, visions that had not been fulfilled in peacetime began to reach fruition in a period of global conflict. Impressed by the record Northwest had established in conducting passenger operations over rugged terrain in bitterly cold weather, the Air Ferrying Command utilized its personnel in building airfields and other facilities in Alaska and the Aleutians. Under a contract signed in February 1942, Northwest started moving troops and cargo to these areas over what became known as the "Flying Boxcar Line." Having already pioneered in 1938 the use of oxygen masks for flying at high altitudes, Northwest also participated in a project at Minnesota's Mayo Clinic to test the limits of human endurance under such conditions, and took part in evaluating different types of deicing methods. It established centers at St. Paul and Vandalia, Ohio, to modify bombers for use in extreme temperatures and test aircraft for defects, and also participated in an important research program for the U.S. Navy to prevent precipitation and other natural causes from interfering with radio signals.

During the war, operating three supply routes from Minneapolis-St. Paul to Nome via Anchorage, Fairbanks, and Ft. Yukon, Northwest pilots flew approximately 21 million miles transporting armed forces personnel and cargo, gaining valuable experience coping with adverse weather and difficult ter-

rain. Deliveries of personnel and supplies over the "Flying Boxcar Line" played an important role in enabling the United States to drive the Japanese out of the Aleutians. Because of its excellent wartime record, the company won a coveted army-navy "E" and solidified its claim to preferment whenever opportunities for regular commercial service in the northern Pacific might return.

On December 16, 1944, one of Hunter's most important goals was achieved when Northwest was granted a route from Milwaukee to New York City, enabling it to join American, TWA, and United as one of the nation's four transcontinental air carriers. Coast-to-coast operations from Seattle to New York were begun in June 1945. Securing authorization to fly to the Far East, however, was more difficult, for efforts by Northwest and other airlines to conduct international operations were bitterly opposed by Pan American's powerful chief executive, Juan Trippe. In 1943, however, Northwest applied to the CAB for a postwar commercial route following its existing military airways to Nome and proceeding from that point to Markova and Yakutsk in Siberia, Manchouli in Manchuria, and Peking in China before branching in two directions—to Manila via Shanghai and to Calcutta via Chungking. This was still pending when the war ended in 1945.

After the war, Northwest's repeated proposals finally bore fruit. On June 20, 1946, the CAB issued a decision permitting it to join Pan American as one of the nation's two transpacific air carriers. On September 1, 1946, Hunter's projected Great Circle Route began to materialize when Northwest inaugurated commercial service from Seattle to Anchorage. This was followed by flights from Chicago to the same city via Edmonton in January 1947. A last-ditch effort was made by an important ally of Trippe, Senator Patrick McCarran of Nevada, to block implementation of transpacific service by Northwest, but this ended in failure after congressional hearings in which Hunter testified against Trippe's monopolistic efforts. In July 1947 Northwest began service from the Twin Cities and Seattle to Tokyo, Seoul, Shanghai, and Manila, with stops at Edmonton, Anchorage, and Shemya, a desolate outpost on the westernmost fringe of the Aleutians. Within the next few years, service began to Honolulu, Okinawa, and Hong Kong; during the same period, Taipei on the island of Formosa (Taiwan) was substituted for Shanghai after Communist forces es-

Northwest Boeing 377 Stratocruiser (courtesy of the National Air and Space Museum)

tablished control on the Chinese mainland. Meanwhile, Northwest continued to expand its domestic system, winning new routes to Cleveland, Pittsburgh, and Washington, D.C.

While this expansion took place, Hunter continued to enlarge and modernize Northwest's fleet, adding four-engine Douglas DC-4s in 1946. When these unpressurized planes were soon outperformed by newer airliners in the postwar era, Hunter acquired Boeing 377 Stratocruisers, putting them into service in 1949. Equipped with 3,500-horsepower Pratt & Whitney Wasp Major engines and having a range of 4,600 miles, these double-deck aircraft were thought to be particularly well suited to Northwest's transcontinental and Great Circle airways, and were introduced with a massive advertising campaign that included airborne fashion shows featuring University of Minnesota coeds. The Stratocruisers' extremely fuel-intensive engines, however, resulted in high operating costs, adversely affecting the company's profits.

Hunter also made an unfortunate choice in deciding to adopt a new twin-engine plane, the 2-0-2, built by the Glenn L. Martin Company as a potential replacement for the DC-3. The design of this craft proved deficient when cracks developed in the wing structure under stress, leading to a 1948 crash near Winona, Minnesota, in which 37 passengers were killed. After this, federal officials temporarily grounded Northwest's entire fleet of 2-0-2s pending modifications. More fatal crashes in the early 1950s led to further groundings, forcing the company to sell its existing planes after absorbing heavy losses.

Northwest's experience in flying the Great Circle proved highly valuable after the outbreak of the Korean War in June 1950. During that conflict, the company's DC-4s flew approximately 13 million miles of airlift operations for the Military Air Transport Service, transporting 40,000 armed forces personnel and 12 million pounds of cargo while maintaining its regularly scheduled commercial activities. One of its DC-3s was purchased by the United Nations and gained fame as "UN-99," shuttling wounded servicemen and military cargo between Japan and Korea.

Substantial operating losses, related in large part to the difficulties experienced with the Martin 2-0-2 and the high cost of flying the Stratocruisers, put Northwest in a steadily worsening financial position. In 1951, the firm's 25th anniversary year, Hunter effected a merger agreement with Capital Airlines. Strongly entrenched in the Northeast and Midwest and possessing important southeastern routes, Capital might have provided a logical complement to the system Hunter had developed, but the deal ultimately fell through when it failed to win ratification by two-thirds of Northwest's stockholders, many of whom feared, with good cause, that their company's headquarters would be shifted from the Twin Cities to the East Coast if it were approved. As dissension spread among the directors, Northwest searched for a new president, and a veteran aviation administrator, Harold R. Harris, was selected. He took charge in January 1953, and Hunter became chairman of the board. Conditions continued to deteriorate, however, and Harris left after only a year in office. In September 1954 former CAB chairman Donald R. Nyrop, who had been Hunter's original first choice, assumed the post Harris had vacated.

Despite the problems that marked his final years as president, Hunter made an outstanding contribution to the development of Northwest Airlines. In 1938, his first full year after assuming command of the enterprise, Northwest's total operating revenues aggregated slightly in excess of $2 million, more than half of which came from mail receipts. In 1953, by the time he moved up to board chairman, the corresponding figure exceeded $66 million, most of which was earned from passenger operations, cargo, and military airlift. Stockholder equity in the firm grew from approximately $1.3 million to almost $25 million during the same 15-year period. The scope of the company's operations was indicated by the fact that approximately 1.1 million passengers flew more than 850 million revenue miles in 1953. In 1938 the firm had flown only 21 million passenger miles.

Under Nyrop's leadership, Northwest returned to the status of a profitable airline. Hunter's legacy of service to the Orient via the Great Circle was further developed, highlighted by such achievements as the inauguration of "Polar Imperial Ser-

vice" from New York City to Tokyo via Anchorage in 1959. Nyrop also won CAB approval for Northwest to inaugurate service to Miami, fulfilling yet another vision nurtured by Hunter, who had earlier established an interchange operation from the Twin Cities to Florida in cooperation with Eastern. Beginning with deployment of Douglas DC-8-31s in September 1960, Northwest entered the jet age, adding such turbine-driven planes as the Boeing 707-320, 720B, 727-100, and 727-200 within the next several years.

As these developments took place, Hunter remained as chairman of the Northwest board. He retired from that position in 1965, but continued his association with the company as chairman emeritus until his death in St. Paul on July 21, 1970. Funeral ceremonies took place in St. Paul at St. John's Episcopal Church, to which he had belonged for many years.

Hunter's career brought him various awards. In 1947 the International League of Aviators conferred upon him its Diploma of Honor, and he also served on the executive committee of the International Air Transport Association. Off the job, Hunter was devoted to duck shooting and fishing, enjoyed golf and tennis, was an enthusiastic bridge player, and maintained a keen interest in music and the study of history. Impressive in bearing, he was described in his prime as "wiry, energetic, as friendly as the dogs he slightly pampers, as casual as the snap-brim hat he wears."

From a global point of view, Hunter's outstanding achievement was the role he played in the development of the Great Circle Route, which substantially reduced flying time from the United States and Canada to the Far East. It was due to his tireless efforts in this connection that the airline he led became familiarly known by the name that was for many years emblazoned on its distinctively red-tailed planes: Northwest Orient.

References:

R. E. G. Davies, *Airlines of the United States since 1914*, revised edition (Washington, D.C.: Smithsonian Institution, 1982);

Davies, *A History of the World's Airlines* (London: Oxford University Press, 1964);

Davies, "Northwest by East: The Story of Northwest Orient Airlines," *Exxon Air World*, 23 (1970);

Stephen E. Mills, *More than Meets the Sky: A Pictorial History of the Founding and Growth of Northwest Airlines* (Seattle: Superior Publishing Co., 1972);

Stanley N. Murray, "Commercial Air Transportation in North Dakota, 1928-1945," *Aerospace Historian*, 33 (June 1987): 74-89;

Kenneth D. Ruble, *Flight to the Top* (New York: Viking, 1986);

Bill Yenne, *Northwest Orient* (London: Bison, 1986).

Carl C. Icahn

(February 16, 1936 -   )

by William M. Leary

University of Georgia

CAREER: Apprentice broker, Dreyfus Corporation (1960-1963); options manager, Tessel Patrick & Company (1963-1964), Gruntal & Company (1964-1968); president and chairman, Icahn & Company (1968-   ); chairman, Trans World Airlines (1986-   ).

Carl C. Icahn became one of the most successful of a new breed of Wall Street stockbrokers who specialized in corporate takeovers during the 1970s and 1980s. Usually, Icahn and his fellow entrepreneurs were interested only in the substantial profits that resulted from their activities. And the financial rewards were impressive. As Andrew Singler, chairman of Champion Paper, remarked in 1985: "The robber barons look like corner muggers in comparison to the amounts that are now being made." Rarely did the takeover experts remain long enough to become involved in managing their new acquisitions, preferring to take a quick profit from a rise in stock prices or from the sale of the corporation or its assets. In 1986, however, a combination of circumstances led Icahn to assume control of Trans World Airlines (TWA). To the surprise of many observers, he proved an adept manager, rescuing the company from financial disaster.

Icahn was born in the Bayswater section of Queens, New York, on February 16, 1936, the only son of Michael and Bella S. Icahn. His father was a lawyer and a cantor at the local synagogue, while his mother taught school. Icahn graduated from Far Rockaway High School in 1953, then attended Princeton University, where he majored in philosophy, indulged his passion for chess, and won the prestigious John Guthrie McCosh Award for his senior thesis, "An Explication of the Empiricist Criterion of Meaning." A student of modest financial means who had to work during the summer to help pay his way through school, Icahn wanted to pursue a ca-

Carl C. Icahn (courtesy of Icahn Enterprises)

reer in business; his mother wanted him to become a doctor. Bowing to her wishes, he entered New York University's School of Medicine following his graduation from Princeton in 1957. After three unhappy years, he abandoned his medical studies and secured a position as an apprentice broker with the Wall Street firm of Dreyfus Corporation.

Icahn soon was caught up in the excitement of the market. He made $50,000 his first year, then lost it in one week the next year. During this apprenticeship, he decided that he needed to specialize in order to succeed on Wall Street. Concentrating on options trading, Icahn joined Tessel Patrick & Company in 1963, then went with Gruntal & Company the following year. In 1968 he used his personal savings of $100,000, plus $400,000 that he borrowed from his uncle, M. Elliot Schnall, who owned a company that manufactured loose-leaf binders, to buy a seat on the stock exchange and open his own brokerage firm.

Icahn & Company initially traded in stocks and bonds. It soon turned to options, then entered the new field of risk arbitrage, trading in bills of exchange on stocks in order to take advantage of slight differences in price on various markets. In 1978 Icahn first became involved with corporate takeovers. Noticing that the stock of the Tappan Company, an appliance manufacturer, was selling far below its stated book value, he purchased some 292,000 shares of Tappan stock for $3 million. Winning election to the company's board of directors, Icahn persuaded his fellow members to accept an attractive $18-per-share tender offer from AB Electrolux of Sweden. This brought Icahn a profit of $2.8 million on his stock.

Icahn had found his niche. He became extraordinarily skilled at identifying companies with undervalued stock, then securing the necessary financing (often through the use of "junk" bonds) to acquire a substantial block of the stock. Often, the stock would increase in value as the company's directors tried to fight off a takeover effort. Icahn could then sell his holdings for a handsome profit. Sometimes he would gain control of a company, then sell it (or its assets) for a substantial gain. Between 1978 and 1985, Icahn & Company took over 15 major companies and recorded an estimated gross profit of $100 million.

Icahn, with his graying black, wavy hair and dark brown eyes, was known as an intensely private man who rarely socialized. While never denying that personal profit was a primary motive for his activities, Icahn bridled at the notion that corporate takeovers were bad for the nation's economic or social structure. "The assets of our country," he once argued, "are mired in the quicksand of waste." Many corporations, he believed, supported huge, expensive, inefficient, and unnecessary bureaucracies. Icahn saw himself as fighting for the rights of shareholders who were not receiving their proper reward.

Beyond the purpose and profit, however, lay the sense of challenge and excitement. "What really turns me on is the excitement of it all," he admitted. "The game gets in your blood, though, because when you're in it, it's like being in the middle of a tiger hunt, and the tigers are coming at you and you've got a spear." Not surprisingly, Icahn's trophies hang on the wall of his office: framed covers of annual reports of corporations that have succumbed to his spear.

In 1984 Icahn identified Trans World Airlines as the next target for takeover. Early in 1985 he put together a group of investors and purchased 6.7 million shares of TWA stock for $95 million. Having acquired a 20.5 percent interest in the company, Icahn then offered to buy TWA's remaining stock for $18 a share, or $600 million. TWA's management tried to fight off the takeover by arranging a friendly merger with Frank A. Lorenzo's Texas Air Corporation. Frightened that Lorenzo, who had a strong antiunion reputation, might secure control of the airline, TWA's pilots and mechanics voted to accept substantial wage cuts *only* if Icahn won the bidding war. After Icahn raised his offer to $24 a share, the airline's board of directors voted on August 20 to accept it. Although TWA's dramatic losses during the fourth quarter of 1985 led to a substantial downward revision of Icahn's offer, one of the largest corporate takeovers in history was accomplished by the end of the year.

Icahn had acquired an airline on the verge of financial disaster. TWA lost $193 million in 1985, two-thirds of the loss coming during the last three months of the year. Icahn's stock, for which he had paid $300 million, was not worth $227 million—and going down. In order to avert a substantial personal loss, and to honor agreements with the pilots and mechanics, Icahn had no choice but to step in and attempt to restore the airline to financial health.

Problems abounded. There had been a sharp decline in transatlantic traffic due to the falling value of the dollar and to terrorist threats against U.S. aircraft; TWA had an aging fleet of transports that were not fuel efficient; and the airline had some of the highest labor costs in the industry. Although Icahn's agreement with the pilots and mechanics promised to reduce labor costs, the flight attendants refused to agree on wage concessions and threatened to strike.

Icahn embarked on a bold course of action. On March 1, 1986, he spent $225 million to purchase Ozark Airlines, TWA's chief rival in the Midwest. The next month 4,000 TWA flight attendants went out on strike. Icahn hired replacements. Without support from the pilots, the strike collapsed at the end of 90 days. In April a bomb blew a hole in the side of a TWA Boeing 727 on approach to Rome. As transatlantic traffic already was declining, Icahn cut the airline's European operations by 20 percent. Later he abandoned TWA's money-losing Pacific routes. All the while, Icahn and his associate D. Joseph Corr worked to dismantle TWA's bloated bureaucracy and bring about more cost efficient operations.

Losses during the first half of 1986 amounted to a staggering $276 million. But the airline turned a profit of $70 million during the third quarter and ended the year with losses cut to $106 million. On a positive note, operating expenses during the year stood at $3.26 billion, down from $3.86 billion in 1985. The black ink returned the next year, with an operating profit of $233.9 million. In 1988 this figure increased to $259.4 million. The airline, however, took a nosedive in 1989, recording a net loss of $298.5 million, including $193.9 million in interest payments on the heavily leveraged company.

Icahn seemed to enjoy the challenge of managing a major airline, and there even were suggestions that he was not immune to the romantic allure of aviation. He once compared the airline business to a chess game, where one develops a winning strategy by a complex manipulation of routes, prices, and schedules. Also, in the office of the man whose favorite poem is Rudyard Kipling's "If," models of

TWA's airplanes came to compete for attention with the framed covers of takeover corporations' annual reports.

Nonetheless, TWA's prospects remained bleak. The airline lost $237.6 million in 1990, and it appeared fated to join the growing ranks of once great air carriers in Chapter 11. In a last ditch effort to avoid bankruptcy, in September 1991 Icahn reached an agreement with the airline's creditors on a reorganization plan that would reduce his control from 90 percent to somewhere between 45 and 20 percent. In return the creditors agreed to accept a combination of cash, stock, and new debt securities. The plan would eliminate approximately $1 billion of TWA's debt. Whether it would save the airline remained to be seen.

Publications:

"When You're in It . . . ," *Institutional Investor*, 21 (June 1987): 328-330;
"The Case for Takeovers," *New York Times Magazine*, January 29, 1989, p. 34.

References:

David L. Brown, "TWA Looks for Best Year," *Airline Executive*, 11 (June 1987): 24-26;
Colin Leinster, "Carl Icahn's Calculated Bets," *Fortune*, 111 (March 18, 1985): 142-144, 148;
Carol J. Loomis, "The Comeuppance of Carl Icahn," *Fortune*, 113 (February 17, 1986): 18-25.

International Air Transport Association

by Robin Higham

Kansas State University

The International Air Transport Association (IATA) is an international trade organization that had 153 member airlines in 1990. Based in Montreal, Canada, it conducts its business in French and Spanish and will correspond in English. While it cooperates with the International Civil Aviation Organization (ICAO), its standing committees—airmail advisory, airport financing and charges policy, the charges working group, facilitation advisory, the fuels trade group, legal, medical advisory, public relations advisory, security advisory, technical, and traffic—reflect

its participants' interests. A staff of 463 handles the work load of these committees as well as all the other business taken up in annual general meetings called to set international fares.

IATA developed in 1945 out of a standoff between the older European International Air Traffic Association, a clearinghouse established in 1919, and a more internationalist rival, the Conference of International Air Transport Operators favored by U.S. airlines. The Europeans opposed free-floating fares and free entry into the market since almost all

European airlines were the "chosen instruments" of their governments. Pan American Airways led the internationalists, who wished to lower the 1939 one way transatlantic fare from $375 to $275. At the end of World War II the Europeans could not see themselves able to meet either the price or the capacity threat from U.S. carriers. However, as a consequence of the globe-girdling air transport network established during World War II and of the 1944 founding of ICAO, in 1945 the modern IATA came into being.

The most disputed and obviously critical area of IATA jurisdiction for many years would be the North Atlantic; by the 1970s the major airlines would declare that they could not make money there. North Atlantic flights were first limited to two a week, until the Anglo-American Bermuda Agreement of 1946, which remained in force until modified in 1986. At Bermuda the United States and the United Kingdom agreed to accept IATA as the faresetting body. At the same time, subsidies made the question of competitive pricing moot.

In the IATA there were three regional conferences, in which a carrier had only one vote regardless of size, and where unanimity was the rule. As all meetings have been held in secret, the press has sometimes played up disputes into much more than they really have been. There have, it is true, been disagreements. But in fact these are usually discussed in advance of the meetings and frequently have been solved by small gatherings of affected parties who either fashion a uniform position or work out a compromise. Rarely have crises led to stalemates.

In the 1945-1969 period two major crises were caused by the U.S. Civil Aeronautics Board's insistence on looking after the "public welfare." The first crisis developed at the annual meeting at Miami, Florida, in 1955 over reducing tourist fares. At Cannes in 1956 a compromise was reached which continued the Miami fare arrangement until March 1958, when tourist fares dropped 20 percent and high-density seating was installed. In effect the Miami agreement became the basis for the formation of economy class flights, which started in 1958. In 1962 came the Chandler, Arizona, crisis over reducing the round-trip discount from ten percent to five. The United States and Canada balked, but the Europeans stood their ground, and the U.S. State Department forced the CAB to back off. But three airlines, all national carriers—El Al of Israel,

Air Canada, and Aer Linte of Ireland—held out. In order to avoid the rule of unanimity, it was decided merely to bypass them and maintain the cartel instead. Government approvals were sought and when these were achieved in spring 1964 unanimity was a de facto process.

During these formative years there were other notable disputes, because then as now most carriers flew the same equipment on the same routes. In the late 1950s the great open-faced sandwich battle was fought at the annual meetings over Scandinavian Air Services' gourmet sandwiches, which the airline served in economy class. Then came TWA's introduction of in-flight movies, which were opposed by most other airlines on cost grounds. A series of disagreements occurred over how much baggage to allow passengers, how much to encourage carry-on luggage, and how to get passengers to check their luggage so that it could be inspected.

Unlike U.S. carriers, non-American members of IATA have no problem belonging to pooling arrangements as a means of controlling excess capacity. In the wake of deregulation in the United States, IATA faced the challenge of Laker Sky-Train and of Super Apex (advance purchase excursion) air fares. It also wrestled from 1973 on with air fares linked to the costs of fuel, which quadrupled in price, and set freight as well as passenger rates. By the early 1980s airlines worldwide were beginning once again to lose money, and that placed a strain on fares and on IATA itself. Noise also reared its ugly head as another costly item restricting night operations and ultimately requiring the retrofitting of silenced engines, and that too added to the pressure on fares and rates.

By the 1990s the IATA faced shrinking membership not only as a result of the fallout from U.S. airline deregulation in 1978, but also because of the mergers and cross-ownership moves among European carriers preparing to face a united European market in 1993.

References:

K. G. J. Pillai, *The Air Net: The Case Against the World Aviation Cartel* (New York: Grossman, 1969);

Anthony Sampson, *Empires of the Sky* (New York: Random House, 1984);

Mahlon R. Straszheim, *The International Airline Industry* (Washington, D.C.: Brookings Institution Transportation Research Program, 1969).

International Civil Aviation Congress

by Roger E. Bilstein

University of Houston—Clear Lake

During World War II it became clear that air transportation would play a major role in the postwar world. Planning for the orderly progress of international air transport stirred conflicting issues of national interest and became the subject of considerable study and speculation.

American air carriers faced the postwar era of international air routes with several issues hotly debated. Pan American lobbied intensively to enhance its preeminent status as America's international airline, a position just as intensively contested by TWA and other carriers with an appetite for overseas routes. American aviation leaders clashed with the British in determining which international routes would be served by their respective countries, while dozens of nations stood on the sidelines. There was talk of an all-encompassing international aviation organization, but the scope of its activity and regulatory powers remained unsettled.

This was the background of the International Civil Aviation Congress, a convention of delegates from 52 countries held in Chicago late in 1944. There had been considerable debate in the United States as to the relative degree of control of international air routes. Adolph A. Berle, Jr., an assistant secretary of state, adhered to what was called the "open-sky concept," an approach subject to numerous interpretations but one that generally favored a minimum of nationalistic regulations. At the other end of the American spectrum was a handful of U.S. senators who worried that either unrestrained competition or strict regulations would favor weaker airways in the short run and inevitably result in the erosion of American international routes, since they would face stiff competition from heavily subsidized foreign flag lines. They wanted a strong, single, American international airline to compete against the foreign carriers—the position favored by Pan Am. L. Welch Pogue, chairman of the Civil

Aeronautics Board (CAB), occupied the middle ground. While opposing monopolistic domination of American overseas routes by one airline, he was unwilling to see American expertise and leadership in international transport flying, developed in World War II, dissipated by blind adherence to open-skies arrangements. Pogue accepted the concept of open skies in principle but felt that specifics should be negotiated on a bilateral basis.

The British, lacking a fleet of advanced, long-range transports, pursued their own goals. During the war, the British aircraft industry had concentrated on fighters and bombers, with the result that the large-scale production of air transports and the operation of Allied air transport networks generally went to the Americans. When the war was over, the British expected an opportunity to reestablish aeronautical preeminence in their traditional spheres of influence. This hopeful assumption ran headlong into American aeronautical expansionism articulated by the congresswoman from Connecticut, Claire Boothe Luce. She proclaimed that "American postwar aviation policy is simple: We want to fly everywhere. Period!!!" The British hoped to counter this kind of aerial imperialism through a complicated quota system for the distribution of traffic, regulation of fares, frequency of flights, and amounts of subsidies.

The British and the Europeans had good reason for arguing in favor of procedures that would have, in effect, "internationalized" world air routes. Most European air traffic was international. In America, the opposite was true; U.S. domestic lines carried eight or nine times the traffic of international routes. When the United States demanded equal access to European world routes but refused to let the Europeans tap into the American market, the British and their European allies saw the United States as excessively greedy.

Against this background of conflicting proposals and national self-interest, the International Civil Aviation Conference gathered in Chicago on November 1, 1944. For 37 days the delegates alternately plunged into rancorous debate or sat around in bored frustration as Americans, British, and Canadians locked horns in clandestine bargaining sessions. Many delegates talked of quitting Chicago and heading home. To keep the conference going, Fiorello La Guardia, the mayor of New York City and a member of the American delegation, challenged the delegates to roll up their sleeves and keep the conference alive. CAB member Edward Pearson Warner apparently played a useful role too; Pogue recalled that Warner became an effective facilitator in negotiations with the British and Canadians.

The problem of fares and flight schedules was left hanging, but other key issues were resolved. The right to navigate the skies of foreign countries, along with certain landing rights at foreign airports, were accepted as the Transit Agreement. The adoption of the International Convention on Civil Aviation, one of the most significant agreements to come out of the Chicago conference, provided for the formation of the International Civil Aviation Or-

ganization (ICAO), composed of an assembly of all members and an elected council of 21 seats. The operational functions of the ICAO were included in a dozen technical annexes, which were eventually worked into the original convention. The annexes spelled out uniform international rules and procedures on communications, traffic control, licensing, aerology, and navigation. After affiliating with the United Nations as a specialized agency in 1947, ICAO became an outstanding factor in the creation of a safe, regularized international aviation system.

References:

Eric Bramley, "Five Documents Emerge from Conference," *American Aviation* (December 15, 1944): 17, 20;

J. A. Miller, "Air Diplomacy: The Chicago Civil Aviation Conference of 1944," dissertation, Yale University, 1971;

Henry Ladd Smith, *Airways Abroad: The Story of American World Air Routes* (Madison: University of Wisconsin Press, 1950);

Eugene Sochor, *The Politics of International Aviation* (Iowa City: University of Iowa Press, 1991);

John Parker Van Zandt, "Quiz on Crucial Conference," *American Aviation* (January 1, 1945): 28-31.

International Civil Aviation Organization

by Roger E. Bilstein

University of Houston—Clear Lake

With headquarters in Montreal, Canada, the International Civil Aviation Organization (ICAO) is a permanent organization of independent countries with responsibilities for the safe and orderly development of international civil aviation. In 1989 there was a total membership of 162 states.

During World War II, it became evident that progress in aviation was going to revolutionize postwar civil aviation, especially the international airline industry. Some bilateral and multilateral agreements had been worked out during the 1920s and 1930s, relating to navigational rights over foreign airspace, customs procedures, accident liability involving third parties on the ground, and other issues. But the expected proliferation of postwar air-

lines underscored the need for comprehensive and uniform international standards. This led to the Chicago Conference of November 1944, at which delegates from 52 countries hammered out 96 articles of the Convention on International Civil Aviation. This document set the stage for uniform procedures relating to crossing national frontiers, customs and immigration, communications, navigational systems, and uniform rules for traffic control. After 26 countries had ratified the Convention, the International Civil Aviation Organization (ICAO), formed on April 4, 1947, assumed responsibility for implementing and modifying international standards as needed. Although ICAO became a specialized agency of the United Nations in the same year, UN membership was not a requirement for ICAO members. The expenses of ICAO are apportioned among its own member states.

ICAO has a sovereign body, the assembly, and a governing body, the council. The assembly normally meets every three years, convened by the council. During assembly sessions, each state has one vote, and decisions are based on a majority vote unless otherwise indicated by the original Convention. Assembly sessions, lasting three weeks, consider the total work of the ICAO in its technical, economic, and legal responsibilities.

The council is a permanent body responsible to the assembly and comprises 33 states which the assembly elects for a three-year term. In choosing council members, three basic criteria are followed in order to provide approximate representation. The first criterion concerns elections of countries of chief importance to air transport, normally 10 in number, and normally reelected. The second criterion includes states that make the largest contributions for facilities supporting air transport, normally 10 or 11 in number. The third criterion concerns election of states so as to ensure geographic representation on the council.

One of the major duties of the council is to establish international standards and to issue a class of documents known as Recommended Standards, all of which become annexes to the original Convention. Further, the council can serve as arbiter on conflicts between members or on issues involving the implementation of Convention statutes.

In addition to the council, the Montreal headquarters is also home to several standing committees that provide continuity and carry out day-to-day operations. These include the Air Navigation Commission, the Air Transport Committee, and the Committee on Joint Support of Air Navigation Services.

The Air Navigation Commission is principally concerned with operational issues, including airworthiness of planes, communications, weather forecasting, navigational aids, ground support, aeronautical charts, and so on. In these areas, the ICAO concentrates on achieving necessary levels of standardization, so that reliable, safe, and efficient operations will be consistent among all member countries. During the 1980s, ICAO paid special attention to data interchange systems, automation of air traffic, and improved meteorological services. There have been

special projects devoted to the adaptation of satellites for air navigation.

During the late 1980s, international concern about the environment prompted the ICAO to take an in-depth look at the problem of aircraft noise. For new aircraft, tougher standards were instituted, and older planes were required to replace noisy engines or to be reequipped with noise-suppression kits. Similarly, airlines were required to meet new standards for aircraft engine emissions, including smoke and fuel vented into the atmosphere. More recently, the ICAO has been issuing recommendations to combat terrorism aboard aircraft throughout airport complexes. New clauses regarding techniques for screening luggage and for maintaining security control of transit passengers were added to ICAO's technical annexes to the original Convention.

While many issues are indeed global, considerable regional planning is required, and such issues are normally handled through seven regional offices located in Bangkok, Cairo, Dakar, Lima, Mexico City, Nairobi, and Paris.

Within the Air Transport Committee, various bureaus cooperate to standardize regulations and paperwork relating to a myriad of documentary factors. These involve visas and passports, mail, cargo clearances, and related matters. Much thought has been given to the reduction of procedural formalities while retaining essential forms for individual countries. This ICAO committee has also been successful in coping with the problem of multiple taxation by exempting fuel, lubricants, and other consumables taken on by a plane that makes stops in several different countries. In addition, income taxes, property taxes, and other levies have been reciprocally exempted. The Air Transport Committee is responsible for gathering statistics, for preparing various forecasts, and cooperation with the Universal Postal Union in setting up equitable mail conveyance rates on a global basis. The Transport Committee also conducts numerous workshops and planning sessions on a regional basis to keep ICAO standards reasonable and consistent.

Since a high proportion of international air traffic moves between Europe and North America via the Great Circle Route, the location of Iceland and Greenland is important. Aircraft in this transatlantic corridor require high levels of air traffic control and meteorological services, which is the role of the Committee on Joint Support of Air Navigational Services. Iceland and Greenland host six meteorological stations, various telecommunications networks, and transatlantic cable links between North America and Europe; Iceland is home to a major area control center. Costs for these are allocated in proportion to aerial crossings of the various carriers, and the Joint Support Committee is not only busy in managing these facilities but also in handling the finances.

Although much of ICAO's role is advisory, there is a growing tendency to provide operational assistance as well. At the request of various foreign administrative groups, the ICAO has provided assistance to airline managers on matters relating to route structure, fares, and maintenance. In addition to preparation of comprehensive development plans

in cooperation with international development banks, ICAO has also assisted in establishment of the technical infrastructure, such as site selection for airports, runway design and construction, and specifications of air traffic control systems.

As a result, the ICAO has become a major force in global air transportation.

References:

"ICAO: Co-operation for Orderly Development of Air Transport," *Impact of Science on Society*, 32 (Fall 1984): 271-276;

Memorandum on ICAO: The Story of the International Civil Aviation Organization (Montreal: Public Information Office of the ICAO, 1987);

Eugene Sochor, *The Politics of International Aviation* (Iowa City: University of Iowa Press, 1991).

Alfred E. Kahn

(October 17, 1917 -   )

by Robin Higham

Kansas State University

CAREER: Professor of Economics, Cornell University (1947-1989); chairman of the Public Service Commission, State of New York (1974-1977); chairman of the Civil Aeronautics Board (1977-1978); chairman, Council on Wage and Price Stability (1978-1980).

Alfred E. Kahn, a tenured economics professor at Cornell University and a lifelong advocate of free-market competition, was born on October 17, 1917, in Paterson, New Jersey. He was one of three children of Jacob Kahn and Bertha Orlean, Russian-Jewish immigrants to the United States. Kahn's father was employed in one of the local silk mills, but his son went to Evander Childs High School in New York City, from which he graduated at the beginning of the New Deal in 1933. Three years later, at age nineteen, he received his bachelor's degree in economics summa cum laude from New York University and was elected to Phi Beta Kappa. He stayed on for another year to obtain a master's degree and then went west to the University of Missouri for further study, but he soon returned to the East Coast. He finished his Ph.D. at Yale University

in 1942. His doctoral dissertation, *Great Britain and the World Economy*, was published in 1946.

While writing his dissertation Kahn worked at the Brookings Institution in Washington, D.C., as a research economist; at the Justice Department in the antitrust division; and at the Department of Commerce in the international economics unit—at that time all were rather small organizations. Kahn then spent a brief three months in the U.S. Army as a private from June to September 1943 before leaving Washington to serve on the Commission on Palestine Surveys in New York City and then, briefly, for the Twentieth Century Fund. In the fall of 1945 he moved to Ripon College in Wisconsin as an assistant professor and chairman of the economics department. It soon became evident that Kahn was a man of experience and talent. In 1947 he was called to Cornell University in Ithaca, New York, where he rose to be chairman of the economics department in 1958, dean of the College of Arts and Sciences in 1969, and a member of the board of trustees from 1964 to 1969.

At Cornell, Kahn did what good professors were supposed to do and had the time to do in the

Alfred E. Kahn

1950s and 1960s—he wrote articles and books. His first book, coauthored with Joel B. Dirlam and published in 1954, focused on competition and the fairness of antitrust policy; his second, coauthored with Melvin Gardner de Chazeau and published in 1959, dealt with integration and competition in the oil industry. In 1970 he published *The Economics of Regulation: Principles and Institutions*, which became a standard economics text. In these works Kahn argued that market forces should be allowed to control economic enterprise and that government regulation was counterproductive. He made his case both from historic British experience and from his intimate knowledge and observance of U.S. affairs in his own time. By the 1970s Kahn was a well-known economist, respected both in academic and practical circles.

On April 29, 1974, Governor Malcolm Wilson of New York appointed Kahn chairman of the State Public Service Commission. Kahn saw the appointment as an opportunity to cut consumer costs by revising the utilities' rate structures, replacing inefficient management, and spurring competition. Innovations introduced during his time as chairman included lower electricity rates for off-peak usage, allowing customers to hook up their own equipment to the New York Telephone Company's system, and charging customers for directory assistance and crediting those who did not use it. Word of what was happening in New York reached President Jimmy Carter, who appointed Kahn to succeed John Robson as chairman of the Civil Aeronautics Board (CAB).

The CAB had come into being in 1938 to regulate the airlines and was chiefly noted for setting airline fares and delineating routes and services. It was a natural place for a man who had spent many years not only advocating the removal of regulation and the unfettering of free enterprise, but one who knew the legal sides of antitrust activities as well. Those few new carriers who had entered the market since 1938 had generally been forced to merge or were squeezed into bankruptcy.

By the time Kahn reached Washington in June 1977, the winds of deregulation had been blowing for some time. The CAB itself had begun a study of regulatory reform in 1974 under urging of the Ford administration. Senator Edward M. Kennedy of Massachusetts had held hearings on the subject of airline deregulation. But these were not the only breezes blowing. Moves were afoot in other areas, notably trucking, to deregulate and avoid the transfer of wealth through governmental rules. Increasingly the argument was for flexible pricing, yet the CAB was locked into the price making rules which had come out of the 1974 Domestic Passenger Fare Investigation. The board had begun to make use of the discount fare idea when Kahn was appointed by President Carter, himself a believer in deregulation, and it was Kahn who did a great deal in his short tenure as chairman of the CAB to expand upon the examples of Texas International's "Peanuts Fare" and American Airlines' "SuperSaver" program. The latter was some 30 percent below the economy-class fare on the New York-San Francisco and New York-Los Angeles runs. By March 1978 it had been shown that these new low fares, by then widely used, were not driving supplemental carriers out of business, in part because they had picked up the charter seats from the regular airlines. By March 1978 most cities served by the trunk carriers had access to the new low fares.

The CAB had restricted new entry into the market as it was required to do by the act of 1938 and the supplemental legislation of 1958. But by the end of 1977 the CAB was working to make incremental adjustments in this area. At the same time, the arrival of new technology had outdated many of the CAB's route requirements, and thus the board was also in the process of removing these restrictions. To speed its work the CAB started calling for written submissions of direct and rebuttal exhibits, skipping time-consuming oral arguments, before Kahn took office. The Kahn board built on this precedent and added a show-cause procedure even where an incumbent carrier objected that considerable revenues might be diverted by another carrier being allowed onto a route. The Kahn board sought throughout 1978 to find cases in which it could clearly separate "need for service" from "carrier selection" issues.

These policies were only partly developed when Congress began work on aviation reform legislation early in 1978. The legislators liked what the Kahn board and its predecessors had been doing because consumers were gaining from declining prices while airline profits rose. But while this resulted in the rapid passage of airline deregulation legislation later in that year, it was deceptive because the improved results owed much to the economic recovery from the depression of the early 1970s and the crisis of the oil embargo of 1973. Load factors rose an average of five points from 1977 to 1978, and revenues for the certificated carriers rose by 82 percent.

Besides dealing with the lowering of fares, Kahn as CAB chairman presided over the opening of U.S. domestic routes to passengers on foreign international flights which made two stops in the United States. He also encouraged Freddie Laker's London-New York low-fare shuttle and the entry of the new American companies into the transatlantic market. On the other hand, when Jimmy Carter, after the Bermuda II bilateral agreement with Britain, exercised his right to overrule the CAB recommendation and gave the Dallas-London nonstop service to Braniff rather than Pan American, Kahn openly disagreed with the president. The chairman of the CAB saw his job as "to protect competition, not companies." He argued that competition made companies careful and efficient.

Kahn left the CAB in the fall of 1978 when Carter appointed him as adviser on inflation and chairman of the Council on Wage and Price Stability. This was not an appointment that was likely to win plaudits, since his mandate, at least in his own eyes, was to cut down the masses of federal regulations which hampered business. He soon made a plethora of bureaucratic enemies, who saw him as a harbinger of unemployment. Moreover, after his victory at the CAB he had a national reputation as a leading regulatory economist and a pragmatic bureaucrat.

Kahn found it much more difficult in his new job to find areas in which competition could be as easily and openly encouraged as in the airline industry. He was a broadminded, visionary analyst, not a manager. Moreover, he was so in demand as a speaker that he claimed that he could get nothing done. As the Carter administration drew to a close, Kahn returned to his post at Cornell, from which he retired in 1989. After his government service he also served as a special consultant to National Economic Research Associates, Inc. In the 1980s he continued to serve on various New York State advisory committees in the utility field and as a member of the State Council on Fiscal and Economic Priorities.

Kahn had an academic interest in the regulatory process and some experience with control of utilities before he was selected to head the CAB. He arrived there in June 1977 when the deregulation momentum was already in significant flow. His job was aided by the fact that both the CAB and Congress were already working to change the old price, route, and entry structure into a freer system. While the 1978 deregulation act was significant, it was not revolutionary. In those markets where there was competition between city pairs, ticket prices declined sharply, but in those where there was little or none, they rose dramatically. New airlines entered the market, but by 1990 about half of them had folded or been absorbed into other companies, and even among the major players there had been a rash of mergers. Passenger rates declined in 1978 and 1979, but the amount of money lost by the airlines decreased significantly. Above all, it appeared that the basic laws of the "dismal science" worked once there was free competition. The big got bigger while the smaller lines disappeared. Consumers who lived in highly competitive markets benefited, but others paid higher prices.

Publications:

Great Britain and the World Economy (New York: Columbia University Press, 1946);

Fair Competition: The Law and Economics of Antitrust Policy, by Kahn and Joel B. Dirlam (Ithaca, N.Y.: Cornell University Press, 1954);

Integration and Competition in the Petroleum Industry,
  by Kahn and Melvin Gardner de Chazeau (New
  Haven, Conn.: Yale University Press, 1959);
The Economics of Regulation: Principles and Institutions,
  2 volumes (New York: Wiley, 1970-1971);
"Deregulation and Vested Interests: the Case of the Air-
  lines," in *The Political Economy of Deregulation: in-
  terest groups in the regulatory process*, edited by
  Roger G. Noll and Bruce M. Owen (Washington,
  D.C. & London: American Enterprise Institute for
  Public Policy Research, 1983), pp. 132-151.

References:
Elizabeth E. Bailey, "Deregulation and Regulatory Reform of U.S. Air-Transportation Policy," in *Regulated Industries and Public Enterprise*, edited by
  Bridger M. Mitchell and Paul R. Kleindorfer (Lexington, Mass.: Lexington Books, 1980);
Anthony E. Brown, *The Politics of Airline Deregulation*
  (Knoxville: University of Tennessee Press, 1987);
Emmette S. Redford, *The Regulatory Process, with Illustrations from Commercial Aviation* (Austin: University
  of Texas Press, 1969).

Stanley C. Kennedy

(July 7, 1890 - April 19, 1968)

by William M. Leary

University of Georgia

CAREER: Accounting clerk to president, Inter-
Island Steam Navigation Company (1912-1948);
pilot, U.S. Navy (1917-1919); vice-president
(1929-1932), president (1932-1955), chairman,
Inter-Island Airways/Hawaiian Airlines (1955-
1968).

Stanley Carmichael Kennedy brought scheduled air transportation to Hawaii. He saw the potential of aviation for Hawaii while serving as a naval
flier during World War I. Later he pioneered air
routes throughout the island chain. "It required
great tenacity and strength of purpose," his successor as president of Hawaiian Airlines, Arthur D.
Lewis, has emphasized, "together with a very real
type of courage, to establish scheduled airline service back in 1929." Following World War II, his
airline became the sole means of intercity transportation in Hawaii, connecting Honolulu with cities on
Maui, Kauai, Molokai, Lanai, and the Big Island of
Hawaii.

Kennedy was born in Honolulu on July 7,
1890, the son of James Alexander and Minnie Catherine Kirkland Kennedy. His father, a native of Scotland, had come to the United States in the early
1870s, first settling in San Francisco, then moving
to Hawaii in 1878. Young Kennedy attended the
prestigious Punahou School in Honolulu. He went
on to Stanford University, receiving his B.A. degree
in 1912. Returning to Hawaii, Kennedy joined the
Inter-Island Steam Navigation Company, of which

*Stanley C. Kennedy (courtesy of Stanley C.
Kennedy, Jr.)*

his father was president, as a clerk in the accounting department. He subsequently held several minor
positions with the company, including purser on
one of the firm's steamships.

Following American entry into World War I, Kennedy enlisted in the U.S. Navy as a seaman, second class. He volunteered for flight training and was sent to the Massachusetts Institute of Technology for six weeks of ground school. Transferred to Pensacola for flight training, he received his wings and commission as ensign in January 1918. After three months with the office of naval operations in Washington, he returned to Pensacola and received instruction in the piloting of large flying boats. Posted to Killingholme Naval Air Station in England in August 1918, Kennedy flew two-engine Curtiss H-16 flying boats on long antisubmarine patrols over the North Sea. It was during this time that he began to think about the advantages of air transportation for his home islands.

Kennedy returned to his post with the Inter-Island Steam Navigation Company in March 1919. Three years later he was promoted to secretary and treasurer of the firm, the primary transporter of passengers and cargo in the territory. In 1926, the year his father died, he became assistant general manager. Meanwhile, on December 3, 1919, he had married Martha Gordon Davenport. The couple had two children.

In 1928, with enthusiasm for aviation running high in the wake of Charles A. Lindbergh's dramatic transatlantic flight the previous year, Kennedy persuaded his board of directors that the time was right to look into the possibility of an air service to connect the main islands of the territory. They agreed. On January 30, 1929, Inter-Island Airways was formed as a separate company in order to qualify for a five-year tax exemption that was being offered by the Hawaiian legislature as a way to encourage aviation enterprises. Although the Steam Navigation Company hoped to sell stock in the airline to the public, a tepid response forced the parent company to acquire 76 percent of its subsidiary's stock. Inter-Island Airways started out with paid-in capital of $313,880.

Kennedy retained his position with the parent company (becoming president and general manager in 1933), but he devoted most of his time to the airline, serving as vice-president and general manager. His main initial concern was identifying an appropriate airplane for Inter-Island Airways. He knew that the people of the territory had to be persuaded that flying was safe, especially after the adverse publicity that had followed in the wake of the Dole Derby of 1927, an ill-fated air race from Oakland

to Honolulu that had cost the lives of 11 fliers. Although he planned to use airfields on the islands of Oahu (John Rodgers Field), Kauai (Port Allen), Lanai (Lanai City), Maui (Maalaea), and Hawaii (Hilo), he selected an amphibian aircraft for the airline, the twin-engine Sikorsky S-38, to provide an added measure of safety. "Our pilots will have always before them the ideals of safety and regularity of performance," he stressed, "but primarily safety, and to that everything else will be subordinated."

While awaiting delivery of two S-38s, Inter-Island Airways used a single-engine Bellanca monoplane to give interested customers ten-minute hops over the city, a move designed more for publicity than for the $5 charged for a ride. Scheduled service began on November 11, 1929, when Captain Charles Irving Elliott set out with 11 passengers from Honolulu to Hilo via Maui. The advantages of air travel were apparent from the outset. The trip to Hilo would require 14 hours by steamship; the S-38 could cover the 216 miles in three hours, including the stop at Maui.

Despite the savings in time afforded by air travel, the volume of passenger traffic disappointed Kennedy and his backers. In its first full year of operation, the airline carried 10,367 passengers. The impact of the Great Depression, however, caused these numbers to decline, reaching a low of 6,868 passengers carried in 1933. Not surprisingly, the airline had suffered steady financial losses since its inception. The situation did not improve until 1934, when Inter-Island managed to secure a mail contract from the U.S. Post Office. Although the agreement provided for only a service payment and not a subsidy, the additional revenue was welcome. Late in the year an optimistic Kennedy, since 1932 president of the airline, placed orders for two 16-passenger Sikorsky S-43s.

Inter-Island posted its first profit in 1935, carrying more than 13,000 passengers. Traffic grew steadily until 1938. In the summer of that year a strike by employees of the parent Steam Navigation Company left the airline as the sole means of interisland passenger transportation. This called attention to the air carrier in dramatic fashion. It transported more than 28,000 passengers in 1938, many of whom flew for the first time.

Progress took place rapidly thereafter. In 1941 Kennedy ordered three DC-3s, at a price of $483,000, for his growing company. He used the delivery of the new airplanes in August to generate

Inter-Island Sikorsky S-38 (courtesy of the National Air and Space Museum)

enormous publicity for the airline. The three sleek transports flew in formation from Oakland to Honolulu, covering the distance in 14 hours and 58 minutes, the longest overwater flight ever made by a DC-3 to that time. During 1941 Hawaiian Airlines (as it became on October 1) carried 23 percent of the 211,520 interisland passengers, with the Steam Navigation Company transporting the balance.

Although its aircraft and ground facilities suffered major damage during the Japanese attack of December 7, 1941, the airline was able to resume operations within two weeks. With steamship service suspended, Hawaiian Airlines (HAL) became the only means of interisland transportation. Under the direct supervision of military authorities, its three DC-3s carried passengers under a strict system of government priorities. The airline's normally high load factor increased to 100 percent on most flights. Thanks to greater utilization, the three airplanes were able to carry 82,000 passengers in 1942, 108,000 in 1943, and more than 110,000 in 1944. At the same time, HAL used its two S-43s to airlift freight among the islands, having received the

first air cargo certificate from the Civil Aeronautics Board (CAB) on March 20, 1942.

The end of the war brought the return of tourists to Hawaii, and in greater numbers than ever before. During 1948, a year in which the Steam Navigation Company discontinued passenger service, HAL carried more than 350,000 passengers in its fleet of 12 DC-3s. When an antitrust action forced the Steam Navigation Company to give up control of the airline, Kennedy (who was president of both companies) decided to remain with HAL.

Kennedy soon faced strong competition to HAL's monopoly of scheduled air service in Hawaii. Trans-Pacific Airlines (TPA) had begun operations on a nonscheduled basis in 1946. Kennedy had managed to obtain an injunction—on the grounds that TPA was flying *scheduled* service without the CAB's permission—in 1947 that forced the rival company to suspend its activities. In 1950, however, the CAB granted Trans-Pacific a temporary certificate to conduct scheduled passenger service in competition with HAL.

Kennedy fought the decision, pointing out that HAL not only provided adequate service for the islands but also had recorded average earnings during the period 1929 to 1949 that equaled an 8.5 percent return on invested capital. Competition, he warned, would result in a need for federal subsidy. But the CAB remained unmoved, citing "the imperative need for competitive air service in the Hawaiian Islands."

Kennedy's prediction about the necessity for subsidy soon proved accurate. After Trans-Pacific lost money in 1949-1950, the CAB granted it a subsidy of $127,000 in 1951. At the same time, HAL received a subsidy of $272,000. By 1955 subsidy payments to both carriers amounted to more than $1 million—and this was only the beginning. During this same period, HAL's share of interisland passenger traffic dropped each year, reaching 68.8 percent in 1955. Competition, however, was not the only factor in HAL's need for subsidy. In April 1951 Kennedy had ordered six Convair 340s, costing $3.6 million (with spares). The first of these pressurized aircraft went into service on January 19, 1953.

In 1955 the sixty-five-year-old Kennedy decided to give up active management of the company. As he had pointed out on the 25th anniversary of the airline, "air transportation has evolved from a thrilling event for the venturesome few to its present status as a practical, economic and efficient means of transportation for the Territory's half-million residents." Kennedy was especially proud of the airline's safety record. Throughout its existence, Inter-Island/HAL had never suffered a passenger or crew fatality in scheduled operations. He had made good on his pledge in 1929 to make safety the foremost goal of the company.

Kennedy went on to serve as chairman of the board of HAL. Under the management of Arthur D. Lewis (to 1963) and John H. Magoon, Jr., who became president and chief stockholder in 1964, the airline continued to prosper. In 1966 HAL introduced pure jet DC-9s on its interisland routes. The following year the CAB ended subsidy payments for the airline. In 1968 HAL flew 1.4 million passengers and had $25 million in assets. And its safety record was still intact when Kennedy died of a heart attack on April 19, 1968.

References:

Stan Cohen, *Hawaiian Airlines: A Pictorial History of the Pioneer Carrier in the Pacific* (Missoula, Mont.: Pictorial Histories Publishing Co., 1986);

William J. Horvat, *Above the Pacific* (Fallbrook, Cal.: Aero, 1966);

Arthur D. Lewis, *Hawaiian Airlines: America's Pioneer Carrier in the Pacific* (New York: Newcomen Society in North America, 1960);

Vernon A. Mund, *Competition and Regulation in Air Transportation in Hawaii* (Honolulu: University of Hawaii Press, 1965).

Archives:

"Statement of Stanley Kennedy of the Inter-Island Airways of Hawaii before the Federal Aviation Commission," dated October 5, 1934, is in the library of the National Air and Space Museum, Washington, D.C.

Kirk Kerkorian

(June 6, 1917 -   )

by Earl H. Tilford, Jr.

Air Force and Air Command Staff College

CAREER: Pilot, Royal Air Force Transport Command (1942-1944); president, Los Angeles Air Service/Trans International Airlines (1947-1962, 1964-1968); president, International Leisure Corporation (1968-   ); major stockholder, Western Airlines (1970-1976); owner, MGM Corporation (1974-   ).

Kirk Kerkorian's grandfather, Kaspar Kerkorian, the first of his family to come to the United States, emigrated from Armenia in 1890, settling in the San Joaquin Valley of southern California. By the turn of the century, he had saved enough money to send for his son Ahron. The new arrival worked hard as a farmer, earned his own nest egg, then sent for his sweetheart, Lily. At first the Kerkorians prospered, and Ahron and Lily had four children. Kerkor "Kirk" Kerkorian, their youngest, was born on June 6, 1917, in Fresno, California.

The family's comfortable life disintegrated in the sharp depression that followed the end of World War I. Try as he might, Ahron never recovered his prosperity. Young Kirk knew poverty, as his father moved from job to job, vainly trying to re-establish himself. Kerkorian grew up tough, and after many scrapes he ended up in a youth reformatory. Following his release he returned to junior high school where he learned auto mechanics before dropping out to help support the family. As a result, the man who was destined to become one of the wealthiest entrepreneurs in the country had only an eighth-grade education.

After serving a stint in the Civilian Conservation Corps during the Great Depression, Kerkorian began buying old jalopies for $100 each, refurbishing them, and selling them to hot rodders for a $5 to $10 profit. At the same time, he built a modest career as an amateur boxer. Kirk "Rifle Right"

Kirk Kerkorian (Wide World Photos)

Kerkorian won many more bouts than he lost and considered turning professional.

In 1939 the twenty-two-year-old Kerkorian discovered flying. He worked at extra jobs to earn enough for lessons and secured his commercial pilot's license in 1941, just in time to get a job with the Royal Air Force's Transport Command as a contract pilot. During World War II Kerkorian ferried RAF planes from Canada to England, Africa, and India. Along the way he met and married Hilda Schmidt in January 1942. Earning $1,000 a month, Kerkorian saved $12,000 by war's end. He used the money to start a company that purchased bargain-priced C-47s and C-54s, which he converted to DC-3s and DC-4s, then sold to airlines and other purchasers. In 1947 he formed his own airline, the Los Angeles Air Service.

The single DC-3 Los Angeles Air Service, which he formally incorporated in 1948, was the first step along the road to a financial empire based on leisure and entertainment. At first, he bought and sold airplanes; later, he traded in real estate and hotels; finally, he bought and sold airlines and corporations. While developing Los Angeles Air Service, Kerkorian continued rebuilding and selling airplanes. He once bought a wrecked British Overseas Airways Lockheed Constellation for $150,000 and an undamaged wing from a crashed French-owned Constellation, then put the two together into a refurbished, flyable airplane at a total cost of $480,000. Kerkorian leased the transport for several years, earning $350,000 before selling it to Israel's El Al Airlines for $750,000. In all, he cleared over a half million dollars on the deal.

While flying honeymoon couples to Las Vegas in the late 1940s, Kerkorian became convinced that the Nevada town would be the place to make a fortune. As his Los Angeles Air Service evolved into a contract airline, hauling men and supplies to the Far East during the Korean War, Kerkorian began moving into the hotel business in Las Vegas. His first effort, like his first marriage, failed in the early 1950s. In 1952 Kerkorian divorced Hilda Schmidt. In 1955 a hotel he bought for $50,000 went broke within six months. But Las Vegas was going to be good to Kirk Kerkorian. In 1954 he met his second wife, Jean Maree Hardy, an English-born Las Vegas dancer, and married her in December. Meanwhile, his Los Angeles Air Service, which had been shut down for a short while, reopened in May 1954. In 1960, he renamed the company Trans International Airlines (TIA).

In the early 1960s aviation, real estate, and entertainment began to come together for Kerkorian. In 1962 he borrowed money to purchase a Douglas DC-8, making TIA the first supplemental airline to operate a jet. His military contract business doubled, and earnings soared from a little over $230,000 in 1961 to $1.1 million the following year. That same year he paid $90,000 for a 70-acre lot in Las Vegas. Shortly thereafter Ceasar's Palace hotel and casino went up on the property. Kerkorian collected $2 million in rent before selling the land to the hotel in 1968 for $5 million. By the end of the decade, some were comparing Kerkorian to another Las Vegas aviation and real estate entrepreneur: Howard Hughes.

Meanwhile TIA was growing with new jets and, as the Vietnam War heated up, new military contracts. In 1968 Kerkorian sold his 58 percent interest in TIA to the Transamerica Corporation for a personal profit of $104 million.

By then Kerkorian was well into the hotel business. In August 1967 he bought the Flamingo Hotel for $12.5 million. He also owned the Bonanza Hotel. Kerkorian wanted to go beyond these nice, but rather ordinary, Las Vegas hotels. In 1968 he established the International Leisure Corporation with money he made from selling land to Caesar's Palace and TIA to Transamerica. Kerkorian went public with 17 percent of the International Leisure stock to raise the additional money he needed to build the International Hotel, billed at its opening in 1969 as the world's largest resort hotel. The International housed many exclusive shops, five gourmet restaurants, and over 1,500 rooms for guests who could busy themselves in the world's largest casino or swim in the International's pool, the second largest man-made body of water in Nevada, second only to Lake Mead. Within a month of its opening, the International was bringing Kerkorian more than a million dollars a month in profit.

At the same time, Kerkorian shifted the focus of his evolving financial empire from Las Vegas to the West Coast. He also expanded from the hotel and real estate industries by reentering the aviation industry and moving into motion pictures. In December 1968 he offered to purchase 1.5 million shares of stock in Western Airlines (WAL). Western was a Los Angeles-based regional carrier which had prospered under two decades of leadership from its often domineering president, Terrell C. Drinkwater. By then Western was ready to make the transition from regional carrier to a major transcontinental airline with substantial international and overseas routes to Mexico, Canada, and Hawaii. It was on the brink of joining the ranks of the nation's largest airlines. By early 1970 Kerkorian had gained control of WAL by purchasing 30.5 percent of its stock. He also took charge of the board of directors and forced Drinkwater out of the presidency by booting him upstairs to become chairman of the board—a ceremonial and relatively powerless position. After a year of corporate impotence Drinkwater retired, leaving Western to Kerkorian and his hand-picked executives.

Kerkorian streamlined operations at WAL by cutting staff and by canceling plans to purchase Boeing 747 wide-body transport aircraft. His uncanny ability to do the right thing at the right time paid off in this case because Western was not stuck with the gas guzzling 747s during the price hikes that followed in the wake of the 1973 and 1974 Arab oil embargoes.

While Kerkorian was moving back into the airline industry, he also expanded his leisure-entertainment empire by taking over Metro Goldwyn Mayer (MGM). Since 1924 MGM had been in the motion picture industry. After Kerkorian managed to purchase 50.1 percent of its stock, he began diversifying its interests. Under the guidance of a Kerkorian-appointed president, MGM announced in 1971 that it would invest money in luxury cruise liners and in a new Las Vegas resort hotel. The 2,000-room MGM Grand Hotel, which opened in December 1973, supplanted the International as the world's largest resort hotel. As was typical of the Kerkorian style, MGM slimmed its corporate staff while manifesting innovative approaches to entertainment. While he was chairman of the board of MGM from 1974 to 1979, it moved into the video and made-for-television entertainment markets. MGM also picked up the production company United Artists (UA) to become MGM/UA.

Fighting the Vietnam War without putting the nation's economy on a war footing fostered inflation that got underway at about the same time Kerkorian shifted his financial empire west and diversified it. Since Kerkorian's shift was financed largely with loans, he was caught with dwindling revenues and rising interest rates. At one point he was forced to sell his own private and luxuriously appointed DC-9, a symbol of great personal pride to him. In late 1972 Kerkorian offered 500,000 shares of WAL stock at $15.62 per share. By piecemeal selling off of Western stock and by some imaginative stock maneuvering with MGM, he managed to survive the uncertain economic times of the mid 1970s.

The airline industry was among the most hard-pressed by the doubts and malaise that plagued the American social, economic and political scene in the post-Vietnam era. High fuel prices and airline

deregulation also worked their woes on WAL. Kerkorian was always seen as the outsider at Western, which had a curious, familylike quality to its executive corps. And Kerkorian, used to strong Armenian family ties, understood the difference between family and business; Western Airlines was the latter. Accordingly, he reduced his holdings until by 1976 his stock interests at WAL totaled only about 17 percent. In January 1976, as Western Airlines prepared to celebrate its 50th anniversary as the nation's oldest air carrier, Kerkorian offered to sell the 2.5 million shares he still held in the company. Western purchased all of them for $30.5 million.

Kerkorian then focused his attention on remodeling the MGM/UA entertainment empire as part of his vision of a leisure-minded America. More than anything else, Kerkorian was a master of synergies throughout his business dealings. He worked airlines, real estate, and entertainment companies around the central idea that Americans had more money and time on their hands than they knew what to do with.

As the 1990s dawned Kerkorian remained in Beverly Hills, California, where he continued to buy and sell real estate, hotels, and airlines. His next airline venture involved the funding of MGM Grand Air. Launched in September 1987, MGM flew two round trips daily between Los Angeles and New York in 34-passenger Boeing 727-100s. Featuring luxurious service, the airline charged $2,034 for the round trip and operated with a load factor of 75 percent. Kerkorian remained one of the country's great wheeler-dealers, a thoroughly unique individual who maintained a deserved reputation for forthright honesty and integrity.

References:

Irwin Ross, "Kirk Kerkorian Doesn't Want All the Meat Off the Bone," *Fortune,* 80 (November 1969): 144-148, 184-186;

Robert J. Serling, *The Only Way to Fly* (Garden City, N.Y.: Doubleday, 1976);

Dial Torgenson, *Kerkorian: An American Success Story* (New York: Dial Press, 1974).

Clement M. Keys

(April 7, 1876 - January 12, 1952)

by Edward M. Young

Moody's Investors Service

CAREER: Reporter and editor, *Wall Street Journal* (1901-1906); financial editor, *World's Work* (1906-1911); investment banker, C. M. Keys & Co. (1911-1916); vice-president to president, Curtiss Aeroplane and Motor Corporation (1916-1923); president, Curtiss Aeroplane and Motor Company (1923-1932); president, Curtiss-Wright Corporation (1929-1932); director, National Air Transport (1925-1930); chairman, Transcontinental Air Transport/Transcontinental & Western Air (1928-1931); chairman, North American Aviation (1929-1931).

Clement Melville Keys, journalist, financier, and a leader in the development of commercial aviation in the United States, was born on April 7, 1876, in Chatsworth, Ontario, Canada. He was one of nine children of George Keys, a country minister, and Jessie Margaret Evans Keys. Keys attended the University of Toronto and graduated in 1897 with a B.A. in Liberal Arts. Unable to enter the business world as he had hoped because of the severe economic depression in North America, he accepted a job at Ridley College in St. Catherine's, Ontario, where he spent three years teaching classics.

In 1901 Keys moved to New York City to build a career in business. He worked first as a freelance journalist, then obtained a position with the *Wall Street Journal.* He was later to say that he became a financial reporter in order to train for his future, believing that as a journalist he would learn to evaluate companies and financial issues clearly and without bias. His entry into the financial world coincided with a period of consolidation within American industry. Keys witnessed these changes and reported on the men who built the great business and financial empires. He grew especially knowledgeable about the transformation of the American railroads, becoming railroad editor of the

Clement M. Keys (courtesy of the National Air and Space Museum)

Journal in 1903. While working for the newspaper, Keys married Florence E. Hayes, the daughter of a New York insurance broker. They had two daughters.

In 1905 Keys began contributing articles to the monthly magazine *World's Work.* This led to a permanent position as financial editor for the magazine in 1906. For the next several years Keys reported on the American business scene, covering developments in industry and finance. In writing about the leading businessmen of his day, he often examined their managerial philosophy. He came to appreciate how the details of organization could contribute to a successful enterprise; this insight later would characterize his own approach to the aviation industry.

Among the leaders in industry and finance, Keys most admired individuals like James J. Hill and Edward H. Harriman. These men—"the builders"—acted as agents of development and progress, transforming their dreams into reality and contributing to the betterment of the nation. Harriman, for example, was the apostle of better railroads; his principal aim was to improve his roads rather than simply build more of them. In transforming the Union Pacific from a wreck into a giant in the railroad industry, Harriman had displayed a genius for detail, carefully scrutinizing the most minute aspects of the railroad's operations. Writing in 1906, Keys commented that Harriman's accomplishments represented "triumphs of method, of science applied to transportation."

Keys was offered the position of editor in chief of *World's Work* in 1911, but he declined, feeling that the time had come to give up his passive reportorial role and become directly involved in finance. He left the magazine and set up an investment advisory firm, C. M. Keys & Company. Using to advantage the reputation and contacts that he had made as a journalist, he built up a group of clients among the larger industrial corporations. As his advisory business prospered, he became more active in a broad range of corporate financial activities. Finally in 1916 he moved directly into investment banking, selling and underwriting bonds and other types of securities.

Keys first became involved in aviation at the invitation of Glenn Curtiss, who early in 1916 consulted Keys for investment advice. Keys joined the Curtiss company later that year as a nonsalaried vice-president, advising on financial matters. This association lasted until July 1917, when Keys left the company following a reorganization. He soon rejoined it, however. When the flood of orders that Curtiss received following the entry of the United States into World War I proved beyond the company's capacity to manage, Glenn Curtiss persuaded John N. Willys, president of the Willys-Overland Automobile Company and an executive familiar with the techniques of mass production, to acquire a controlling interest in the company and oversee its wartime expansion. In turn, Willys who knew Keys from previous business dealings, asked him in November to rejoin the company as vice-president and chairman of the finance committee.

Over the next year Keys arranged the financing to support Curtiss's rapid growth. At its peak the company operated nine plants with a work force of over 18,000, supported by an extensive experimental research department in Garden City, Long Island. Between July 1917 and March 1919, Curtiss delivered 5,221 aircraft under government contracts; this represented one-third of total U.S. wartime aircraft production.

The government poured hundreds of millions of dollars into the aviation industry during the war, but soon after the armistice it abruptly canceled orders for thousands of aircraft, giving little thought to the impact on the industry. With no significant source of demand for aircraft apart from the military, the industry underwent a rapid and severe contraction. The management of Curtiss Corporation, however, expecting that the end of the war would bring about a boom in civil aviation and private flying, developed several small commercial aircraft types, built up a sales organization in the United States, Latin America, and the Orient, and then turned to its remaining plants to build an inventory of aircraft.

While Curtiss was developing its strategies for the postwar market, Keys was involved in an effort to formulate a government policy on aviation. The United States had emerged from the war with no coherent plan of how to utilize aviation for either national defense or commerce. To stimulate government thinking, Secretary of War Newton Baker organized a mission to study military and commercial aviation in Europe, then recommend ways that Washington might promote aviation in the United States. Keys joined the group as a representative of the aviation industry and was chosen to head the mission's technical committee.

The American Aviation Mission, as it was called, left for Europe in May 1919. It spent two months in England, France, and Italy, visiting government aviation ministries, military air services, and the leading aeronautical manufacturers. Keys saw the best aircraft and engine technology that Europe had to offer, and he came away believing that in certain areas, particularly engine development, Curtiss had the potential to surpass the world's leaders.

In its report to Secretary Baker, the mission urged Washington to formulate a comprehensive policy for the development of aviation, stressing that a healthy aeronautical industry could only be maintained by a continuing program of military production until commercial demand developed. Despite their report, no government policy was forthcoming. Instead Washington initiated a system of competitive bidding for the few military contracts available. Under this procedure, the government would buy the rights to a design, then call for bids for production. At the same time, Washington compounded the problems of the struggling industry by dumping surplus aircraft and engines on the civilian market at prices well below cost.

Curtiss came under increasing financial pressure in 1920. With no demand for new commercial aircraft and with government orders unpredictable under the new competitive bidding system, the Willys-Overland interests decided to reconsider their commitment to the aviation industry. On a Friday in August a representative of Willys-Overland told Keys that the Curtiss Aeroplane and Motor Corporation would go into receivership on the following Tuesday. The company had $650,000 in bank debts coming due, which the Willys-Overland people were not prepared to meet. Over the weekend Keys thought about all the effort that had gone into building up the company's research department and engineering staff. Convinced that the Curtiss engineering technique was every bit as good as the ones he had seen in Europe, he believed that the company had a promising future.

On Monday night Keys met with the board of directors and offered to buy all the common stock of Curtiss for the cash equivalent of the bank debts that were coming due. The directors readily agreed. The next day he raised the $650,000 on his own credit and paid off the banks. Keys then became president of the Curtiss Aeroplane and Motor Company, an enterprise with little market for its products and apparently on its way to posting a substantial loss. However, it had the largest group of aeronautical engineers in the industry. And it had a resourceful leader.

Although Keys believed in the future of aviation, he recognized that it had to become a business, subject to the same disciplines of profitability and sound finances as other industries. Here was a

challenge and an opportunity to become a "builder." He could emulate the achievements of Harriman in an emerging industry. But it was a field fraught with risks. Aviation was different from other industries because the airplane—its design, production, and operation—was exceptionally demanding. To a greater extent than other industries, aviation had to be based on highly skilled personnel and careful planning. Mirroring Harriman's approach to the railroads, Keys emphasized attention to detail, so much so that he is credited with the phrase "90 percent of aviation is on the ground and 10 percent is in the air." Applying the basic lessons that he had learned from studying other industries, Keys adopted a strategy that the General Electric Company had used with great success. He decided to let the laboratory run the business, believing that a company should put out products of such obvious engineering excellence that "domination of the market is assured."

Despite the company's precarious financial position, Keys immediately began concentrating all available resources on research and development. Curtiss needed a product that could sustain it until demand improved, and Keys believed that it had one. Since 1917 Curtiss had been working on an engine that had showed great promise; it combined small frontal area with high power. Having seen the best European aero engines, Keys was certain that the Curtiss product was superior. The Willys-Overland interests had been unwilling to support its development, but after he became president, Keys ordered work on the engine resumed.

Keys planned to use the new engine to win back aviation speed records that were held by European aircraft. He realized that the speed contests provided a grueling test for both airframe and engine; racing planes were in effect prototypes for new fighter planes. The U.S. Army and Navy, which were interested in setting records as a way to draw attention to aviation, turned to Curtiss to design racing planes that were to be built around the powerful new Curtiss D-12 engine. In 1922 Curtiss racers won the Pulitzer Trophy Race and four days later set a new world speed record. The crowning achievement for the Curtiss engine came at the Schneider Trophy races of 1923, held in England. To the astonishment of European participants, Americans swept the field, setting new course records. The D-12 engine was recognized as a magnificent technical achievement and did much to restore confidence in American aviation. Keys's faith in devoting scarce resources to this effort was rewarded late in 1923, when the army placed orders for 25 Curtiss pursuits powered by D-12s, the first in a long line of Curtiss fighters.

Orders from the army and navy for engines, racing planes, and small numbers of new aircraft helped Curtiss eke out a profit during a period when most aviation manufacturers were struggling to survive. Curtiss was both a beneficiary and a victim of the competitive bidding system, winning some contracts by underbidding other manufacturers and losing contracts for its own designs to others. While continuing to invest in development projects, Keys also was working to improve the financial position of the firm. He had taken over a company heavily in debt. In 1923 he reorganized it into the Curtiss Aeroplane and Motor Company, which took over all manufacturing operations, and the Curtiss Assets Company, which acquired all inventories of surplus airplanes and engines. By removing these inventories, he reduced the debt of the Curtiss Aeroplane and Motor Company to a more appropriate level and began building the financial reputation it would need to attract capital in the future.

In 1924 Keys gave up his Canadian citizenship and became a naturalized U.S. citizen. During the same year, he married for a second time, to Indiola Arnold Reilly. They had no children.

The aviation industry's hand-to-mouth existence during the early 1920s meant that even the strongest companies could not generate the profits necessary to fund future growth or to attract new investment. Keys corresponded frequently with the heads of the Army Air Service and the Naval Air Service to protest against the damage that government practices were inflicting on the industry. When called before the numerous congressional committees examining the aviation industry, Keys constantly pointed to the destructive effects of the government's lack of a coherent aviation policy. He was sharply critical of the competitive bidding system, and he complained about competition from military factories and design bureaus. No manufacturer could afford to develop a design without a guarantee of proprietary design rights, he argued, nor could the industry support the engineering and skilled workers it needed without a sustained level of profit. Keys did not want government subsidies for aviation, but he did call upon the government to support aviation through a sustained procurement program and by building the infrastructure—airways and landing fields—necessary for the development of commercial aviation.

Based on the recommendations of the Morrow Board, in early 1926 Congress passed the Air Commerce Act for the promotion of commercial aviation; it also authorized five-year procurement programs for the army and navy. The competitive bidding system was abolished. Curtiss was a direct beneficiary of the new program, receiving large orders for pursuit and observation planes. The company's profits doubled in 1926 and again in 1927, enabling Keys to complete his strengthening of Curtiss's financial position. By the end of 1927 he had eliminated the company's debt. Having helped Curtiss survive the lean years, he now was in a position to expand into new areas of aviation.

While aware that military sales would continue to constitute the bulk of the company's business, Keys had a broader vision of the opportunities now available. He looked upon Curtiss primarily as a preeminent engineering company with an unparalleled ability to design aircraft for either the civil or military market. This would be the foundation. From this base, however, Keys wanted to expand into other profitable products and markets. Because aviation was such a highly specialized endeavor, he set out to create separate, specialized business units to be responsible for different tasks. He envisioned a vertically integrated business combination that would cover all aspects of aviation. There would be a company to manufacture airplanes, one to train pilots, another to operate airlines, and so forth. All this would be financed by businessmen who were willing to invest capital and take risks. Keys was determined that all the companies have sound financing, and this meant equity, not debt. Given all the risks involved, he once commented, aviation investments were not for "widows and orphans."

The opportunity to realize this vision came with the boom that followed Charles A. Lindbergh's dramatic transatlantic flight of May 1927. Money for aviation ventures poured into the stock market, giving rise to a surge of activity in all aspects of aeronautical development.

Keys promptly positioned Curtiss to benefit from the new circumstances, beginning two years of prodigious activity during which he built Curtiss into the second-largest manufacturing and transportation group in the country. To capitalize on the growing commercial aviation field, Keys initiated several measures. With Maj. William Robertson of the Robertson Aircraft Company in St. Louis, he organized the Curtiss-Robertson Manufacturing Company early in 1928 as the commercial aircraft arm of the Curtiss group; this company would manufacture and sell commercial aircraft designed by the Curtiss engineering team. At the same time, Keys completely reorganized and expanded the Curtiss Flying Service to provide not only flying training but also to serve as a sales and distribution network for commercial aircraft. To expand Curtiss's list of aircraft, he purchased a substantial interest in the Reid Aircraft Company, a Canadian manufacturer of light airplanes, and established the Curtiss-Caproni Company to build larger aircraft designed by Giovanni Caproni. To finance this expansion, Keys took advantage of the positive investment climate to raise money through the sale of new common stock. In the course of 1928 the Curtiss Aeroplane and Motor Company doubled in size.

While expanding the manufacturing side of the company, Keys was also involved in developing commercial air transport. Believing that the airplane would become a major means of transportation, he saw the development of commercial aviation as the industry's greatest challenge. If successful, airline companies not only would become significant businesses in their own right, but they also would create a steady demand for aircraft. Keys decided to set up airlines that were linked to a manufacturing group, thereby creating a captive market for the group's products.

Approaching the problem of air transport with his usual cautious realism, Keys aimed at the creation of a viable commercial business, one that would earn a business profit. While convinced that the carriage of airmail would produce this profit, he was skeptical about the outlook for passenger service, given the aircraft then available. He recognized that carrying passengers was a vastly different and more complicated endeavor than flying the mail. Passenger airlines would have to prove themselves to the public through an unblemished safety record and provide competitive fares before they would be accepted as a general means of transportation.

His first venture into air transportation, not surprisingly, involved the airmail. In 1925, when the Kelly Act opened the door for the transfer of air-

mail from the Post Office to private operators, Keys organized National Air Transport (NAT), with the backing of business interests in Chicago, to fly the mail from Chicago to New York. NAT was incorporated on May 21, 1925, with an initial capital of $2 million, substantially higher than most of the other new companies. NAT first won the airmail route from Chicago to Dallas, which it began flying in 1926 with ten Curtiss-built mail planes; it was awarded the coveted New York-Chicago route in 1927. Within a relatively short time, NAT built up a profitable airmail and express package business.

Despite his earlier misgivings, by early 1928 Keys gave serious thought to starting a passenger airline. Growing public acceptance of aviation meant that a potential market existed. Larger aircraft, featuring powerful and reliable engines, were coming into production, opening up the possibility of safe air travel. Although Keys was reluctant to convert NAT into a passenger line because of the difficult terrain between New York and Chicago (the route crossed the Allegheny mountains) and because he felt that passengers might interfere with the profitable airmail operation, he proved receptive when approached by Charles Lindbergh. Keys supported Lindbergh's idea for a transcontinental airline and arranged for a group of businessmen as well as his own companies to provide the necessary financial backing for the venture. In May 1928 Transcontinental Air Transport (TAT) was organized, with Keys as president and Lindbergh as chairman of the technical committee. The new company bore the Keys hallmark of a large initial capital of $5 million, plus sound organization. Intending to carry passengers between New York and Los Angeles without a postal subsidy, TAT represented an important step in the development of American commercial aviation.

With only rudimentary instruments and no navigational aids, nighttime flying was considered too hazardous for passengers. Keys therefore brought in the Pennsylvania Railroad as a backer, arranging for an innovative combined air-rail service. The airline would fly passengers during the day while the railroad carried them at night. Following a year of careful route planning by Lindbergh and the building of a supporting ground network of radio and weather stations, TAT launched scheduled service in July 1929 with Ford trimotors. Shortly thereafter, Keys arranged for TAT to acquire Maddux Air Lines, which provided a Los Angeles-San Francisco connection for the transcontinental route. He later

Pilot Bert Acosta with the Curtiss Navy racer that won the Pulitzer Trophy in 1921, the year after Keys assumed ownership of Curtiss Aeroplane and Motor Corporation (courtesy of the National Air and Space Museum)

invested in Varney Air Lines, a pioneer operator of mail routes in the Pacific Northwest.

Keys's interests in aviation were not constrained by product, type of service, or national boundaries. His desire was always to capitalize on opportunities where there was a potential for earning a good return. As a journalist Keys had developed an interest in international markets, and, to a greater extent than most of his peers in the industry, he sought out opportunities for aviation abroad. In 1921 he had set up the Curtiss Aeroplane Export Company to act as the foreign sales representative for Curtiss products. When more funds became available in 1928, he reorganized and recapitalized the company, enabling it to expand its sales efforts. Curtiss Export went on to generate substantial and highly profitable sales in Asia and Latin America for the parent company's aircraft and motors.

Keys also extended his overseas activities to cover commercial air transport. In 1928 he organized Intercontinental Aviation to develop airlines

in foreign countries. Despite the press of his other activities, Keys actively negotiated with governments in Europe, Asia, and Latin America, seeking opportunities for new ventures. Through Intercontinental Aviation, Keys became a founder of Compañía Nacional Cubana de Aviacíon Curtiss, SA, a Cuban airline, and owned a controlling interest in Cía de Aviacíon Faucett, SA, an airline in Peru. Perhaps his most ambitious project was a joint venture with the Chinese government to set up the China National Aviation Corporation, the first successful commercial airline in that country.

As investment capital continued to pour into the aviation industry, Keys raised substantial funds in the stock market to create new vehicles to expand what was rapidly becoming an aviation empire. To broaden the financial scope of the Curtiss group, Keys set up the National Aviation Corporation as an investment holding company to underwrite, sell, and invest in aviation securities. At the end of 1928 Keys organized North American Aviation as a centralized financial entity, separate from the Curtiss group, to make permanent investments in existing aviation firms and to support promising new developments.

Keys had intended that this new holding company would have substantially greater financial resources than Curtiss itself. North American was established with an initial capital of $25 million, twice that of the Curtiss Aeroplane and Motor Company. With Keys as president, North American soon began to invest in a variety of aviation ventures, acquiring the Sperry Instrument Company, Pitcairn Aviation (which held the airmail contract between New York and Miami), and buying large shares of Curtiss-related companies such as TAT and Intercontinental Aviation. By 1929 Keys had built the Curtiss Aeroplane and Motor Company into a group of over 20 interrelated companies involved in aircraft and engine manufacturing, transportation, service, and financing, with a market capitalization—thanks to the stock market boom—of over $175 million.

Following the pattern of other industries, many of the manufacturing and transportation companies that had started up as the aviation industry expanded began to be consolidated into ever larger groupings. By early 1929 three large and powerful groups were forming. That spring, Keys began discussing with Richard F. Hoyt, an investment banker and chairman of the Wright Aeronautical Corporation, a possible merger that would link the Curtiss and Wright interests. The two groups were in many ways complementary: Wright was a major manufacturer of air-cooled engines, which Curtiss lacked, and Hoyt had interests in several aircraft manufacturers that would enhance Curtiss's range of products. On August 6, 1929, the merger of the two groups took place when the Curtiss-Wright Corporation was formed with Hoyt as chairman and Keys as president. This combined grouping, which linked the two most prominent names in American aviation history, was the second largest in the industry.

The Curtiss-Wright merger saw Keys at his peak. He was now chairman or director of over 26 companies that covered the entire spectrum of the aeronautical industry. His airline interests spanned the continent and were growing abroad. No other individual in the industry could match the breadth of his interests and activities. He was the industry's acknowledged leader, acclaimed as an "empire builder of the air." The press eagerly sought the views of a man they began to refer to as the "Harriman of Aviation." Despite his growing fame, Keys remained a quiet, soft-spoken man who preferred to remain in the background, directing the web of the companies he had created rather than seeking publicity.

Within a few months of the Curtiss-Wright merger, the aviation boom ended. The October 1929 crash of the stock market ended the rush to invest in the industry, while the economic decline that followed brought about a sharp reduction in the demand for aircraft. Keys initially was optimistic that the growth in demand would resume and was confident that 1930 would show a substantial volume of new business. As the year progressed, however, it became clear that the civil aircraft market was in a steep decline. Military sales helped the Curtiss Aeroplane and Motor Company achieve a profit, but the Curtiss-Wright Corporation ended 1930 with a substantial loss in its civil aircraft and service divisions.

While coping with a declining volume of business on the manufacturing side, Keys continued to devote considerable energy to building his airline interests, although not without setbacks. Early in 1930 he became chairman of TAT-Maddux Air Lines. At the time, TAT was losing significant amounts of money, as its air-rail service was proving expensive to operate and offered no real advantage in time or price over all-rail transportation. The TAT experiment was demonstrating that no airline could survive without a government airmail contract. Under pressure from Postmaster General Walter Folger Brown, Western Air Express agreed to merge with TAT-Maddux in order to win a key transcontinental airmail contract. TAT and Western each took a 47.5 percent share in the new company which became Transcontinental & Western Air (TWA). Keys became chairman of the board of the new company. In August it began the first all-air, coast-to-coast service. The air-rail service, which Keys had thought would be a permanent form of transportation, ended in October.

While TWA struggled to turn a profit, Keys was transforming Pitcairn Aviation from a pure airmail carrier to a passenger airline. In January 1930 the company's name was changed to Eastern Air Transport (which became Eastern Air Lines in 1934), with Keys as chairman of the board. The company first expanded capacity on its existing mail routes between New York and Miami, offering a double service on some sections, then added a new route linking New York and Boston. Keys was not unmindful of the potential for passenger business along the densely populated East Coast, and he sought to exploit it. Eastern Air Transport began passenger service in August with a route from New York to Richmond; this was extended to Atlanta later in the year. A further extension to Miami enabled passengers to fly from New York to South America. As passenger volume grew, Eastern bought Condor and Kingfisher aircraft from Curtiss, providing the captive market that Keys had intended. This was especially important for Curtiss, as the Condor had not proved competitive with the Ford trimotor.

Not all Keys's airline ventures were successful. In early 1930 Keys faced a challenge for control of National Air Transport (NAT). Frederick Rentschler, chairman of the United Aircraft Corporation, saw NAT as a natural addition to his company's Chicago-San Francisco airline. In March 1930 Rentschler persuaded NAT's Chicago backers to sell their NAT stock to him, giving United control of more than one-third of the company. He then began buying additional shares on the open market. In early April Keys rejected Rentschler's offer to exchange one share of United for three and one-half shares of NAT, leading to a battle for control of NAT that was reminiscent of the Hill-Harriman struggles of an earlier era. Keys and his allies on NAT's board attempted to amend the company's bylaws to prevent a takeover and to give time to arrange an exchange of shares with North American Aviation. Rentschler, however, was able to circumvent this in the courts. With Rentschler in control of 57 percent of NAT's stock, Keys had to admit defeat. NAT's directors accepted an exchange offer of three NAT shares for one United share. NAT later would form part of the new United Air Lines.

As the Depression deepened, Keys came under increasing financial and personal pressure. The stress of managing his diverse group intensified as the performance of the individual units worsened. Orders for commercial aircraft continued to decline, while military orders dropped as the army and navy came to the end of their procurement programs. Foreign sales evaporated as the Depression spread around the world. The airlines were struggling as well: despite the mail contract, TWA continued to record losses. With Curtiss-Wright unable to

pay dividends, its stock plummeted in value. From a peak of $30 a share at the time of the merger, Curtiss-Wright shares fell to $1.25 by early 1932. Having invested heavily in his aviation ventures, as well as in other stocks, Keys suffered massive personal losses.

For Keys, never in robust health, the strain became too great to bear. He resigned his position as chairman of North American Aviation on December 31, 1931. On January 7, 1932, he announced that he was resigning all his other offices and severing all connection with the aviation industry. He cited reasons of health and a desire to devote more time to his personal affairs. Although at the time he expressed a desire to resume his activities at some point in the future, he never again held a position of influence within the aviation industry.

For the next ten years Keys lived quietly in semi-retirement, serving on the board of several small industrial companies. He was chairman of the McKenzie Muffler Company and the Buffalo Pressed Steel Corporation, and a director of the Montauk Beach Company. In 1942 he reentered the aviation industry in a small way when he founded C. M. Keys Aircraft Services to provide financial services to companies involved in military contracts. His last aviation venture was to help in 1947 to establish Peruvian International Airways, an airline linking New York and Lima via Cuba and Panama. Keys had been intrigued with the possibilities of this route in the later 1920s, but had been unable to develop it at the time. He resurrected the idea toward the end of World War II and won backing for the venture, but the airline was not a success and went bankrupt after 15 months of operation.

Keys took no further part in aviation. He died at his home in New York City on January 12, 1952, following a stroke, at the age of seventy-five.

Publications:

"Value of Racing Planes," *Aero Digest,* 7 (October 1925): 535-536, 568-570;

"The Outlook for Commercial Aviation," *Machinery* (February 1929): 419-421;

"Aviation and Its Future," *U.S. Air Services* (March 1929): 43, 46-48.

References:

Thomas G. Foxworth, *The Speed Seekers* (Garden City, N.Y.: Doubleday, 1974);

Elsbeth E. Freudenthal, *The Aviation Business, From Kitty Hawk to Wall Street* (New York: Vanguard, 1940);

William M. Leary, *The Dragon's Wings: The China National Aviation Corporation and the Development of Commercial Aviation in China* (Athens: University of Georgia Press, 1976);

Harold Mingos, "The Harriman of Aviation," *New York Herald Tribune*, June 2, 1929;

Earl Reeves, *Aviation's Place in Tomorrow's Business* (New York: Forbes, 1930);

Henry Ladd Smith, *Airways: A History of Commercial Aviation in the United States* (New York: Knopf, 1942).

Archives:

The papers of Clement M. Keys are at the National Air and Space Museum, Smithsonian Institution, Washington, D.C.

Harding Luther Lawrence

(July 15, 1920 -   )

by Roger E. Bilstein

University of Houston—Clear Lake

CAREER: General sales manager, vice-president for traffic and sales, Pioneer (formerly Essair) Air Lines (1947-1955); vice-president for traffic and sales (1955-1957), vice-president for executive administration (1957-1958), executive vice-president, director (1958-1965), president, director, Braniff Airways (1965-1968); chairman and president (1968-1970), chairman and chief executive officer, Braniff International (1970-1980).

After meeting Harding Luther Lawrence, more than one person remarked that he looked like the sort of tall, square-jawed, silver-haired, deep-voiced swashbuckler that Hollywood would cast as an airline president. In an industry noted for larger-than-life personalities, Lawrence's career had the sweep and brilliance of a shooting star. Considering the man's hubris, it was also a career whose finish would have suited the most traditional of Greek tragedians.

Born in Perkins, Oklahoma, on July 15, 1920, Lawrence was eleven years old when his parents moved to Gladewater, in East Texas. That might have been a dead-end move from one small town to another, but East Texas sprouted with oil gushers during the 1930s, and the laborer's hotel run by the Lawrences prospered as a result of the oil boom. Lawrence and his two older brothers worked at odd jobs to help support the family during the Depression; there was enough money for Lawrence to enroll at the University of Texas in 1939. With the advent of World War II, Lawrence became a ground-school instructor for a flight program run by a civilian contractor and wound up as

Harding L. Lawrence (courtesy of the History of Aviation Collection, University of Texas at Dallas)

one of its managers. Meanwhile, he earned his B.B.A. degree in 1942, the year he married Jimmie Bland. After the war, in 1947, he joined a small commuter airline, Pioneer, based in Houston, as general sales manager.

Pioneer, then known as Essair, had gone into business in January 1939 but had to suspend operations seven months later because Braniff Airways convinced the Civil Aeronautics Board (CAB) of redundant competition due to the limited market. In 1943 the CAB reversed itself and Essair began Houston-Abilene service at the end of World War II. In 1946 the company changed its name and for the next decade became a pugnacious competitor throughout Texas and into New Mexico. Lawrence was promoted to vice-president of traffic and sales, and his aggressive style had impressed far bigger airlines, including Continental, which negotiated a merger with Pioneer in 1955. Robert Six, Continental's own charismatic chieftain, later claimed that one of the reasons he went after Pioneer was to bring in the thirty-five-year-old Lawrence. Installed as vice-president for traffic and sales at Continental, Lawrence soon emerged as Six's principal confidant and heir apparent.

While Lawrence had his own distinct personality, he and Six shared many traits, including a volatile temper. At Continental, Lawrence's secretary often shut his office door to cut off his voluble profanity during budget reviews. After kicking a steam radiator one day, Lawrence had to spend several weeks hobbling around the office. Lawrence also shared Six's penchant for razzle-dazzle publicity schemes. Continental's "Gold Carpet Service" had ground support crews doing a parade-ground drill when greeting incoming planes; gold paint embellished the prosaic helmets of mechanics. In the early 1960s, Lawrence became one of the principals in a promotional campaign that gave Continental's planes a highly distinctive paint scheme and the catchy slogan, "Proud Bird with the Golden Tail." The agency that devised the campaign included an attractive divorcée—Mary Wells—who made an indelible impression on Lawrence.

By 1964 Lawrence had received queries from other airlines that wanted him as senior officer. But he continued at Continental, where Six relinquished more and more authority, to the point that Lawrence was president of the airline in everything but name. Nonetheless, at the age of forty-five, Lawrence felt he deserved that title as well; after Continental relocated from Denver to new corporate headquarters in Los Angeles, and Six continued to retain the presidency, Lawrence accepted an offer to join Braniff Airways in 1965 as president and director.

Using techniques learned from his stint at Continental, Lawrence took Braniff by storm, transforming it from a staid, midsized operation into a jazzy,

expansionist upstart. Twelve months after his arrival, Braniff's net profit shot from $5 million to $18 million; profits over the next five years surpassed the combined total of the previous 38 years. Braniff and Harding Lawrence became the talk of the industry.

Rumors were also circulating about Lawrence's floundering marriage. Two months after his divorce from Jimmie in 1967, he wed Mary Wells, who by then headed her own advertising agency in New York. The ceremony took place in the town hall in Paris, France, reflecting the sense of international flair and style that unquestionably marked the development of Braniff over the next decade and a half.

Braniff had expanded from its midwest-midsouth axis toward the East Coast and south across Latin America as far as Buenos Aires, Argentina. Notwithstanding its reputation as a conservative airline, Braniff had done some impressive pioneering on its South American network. Its Latin American presence surged after Lawrence negotiated a merger with Pan American-Grace Airways, giving roughly half of U.S. international routes in Latin America to Braniff. From there, Braniff stretched across the Pacific: European markets came in the late 1970s. Following airline deregulation in 1978, Lawrence launched dozens of new routes in the United States.

All this was accompanied by one of the most flamboyant marketing offensives the industry had seen. With style-conscious Mary Wells as consultant, Lawrence approved a total reworking of the paint designs of Braniff's planes, which emerged in a spectrum of stunning hues: orange, emerald green, royal blue, and more. High-style fashion went into cabins, waiting rooms, ticket counters, and uniforms, the last of which were given a special gloss of haute couture by Italian designer Emilio Pucci. Lawrence delighted in modern art, so it was no accident that Alexander Calder accepted his invitation to paint two planes in eye-popping abstract patterns. In 1979 Braniff leased a Concorde supersonic transport for special Dallas-to-London and Paris service. In that year, revenues topped $1.3 billion, but expenses were greater, and the company lost $38 million. In 1980 Braniff lost $128 million.

Fuel costs (which had risen by over 50 percent) were only part of the problem. Lawrence's legendary temper spilled out of the boardroom into public tirades at ticket agents and stewardesses in flight. No executive meeting seemed complete without a severe dressing-down of at least one vice-president. A few corporate officers learned to shrug off these blistering sessions; most simply preferred to keep quiet and never report any negative information. C. Edward Acker, Braniff Airways' astute president and chief operating officer after Lawrence assumed the chairmanship and presidency of Braniff International in 1968, had given wise counsel and valiantly served as devil's advocate, but he resigned in 1975 after an investigation concerning Braniff's campaign contributions to Richard M. Nixon's presidential reelection campaign in 1972. Due to rapid expansion, there were extremely serious deficiencies in Braniff's mushrooming middle and lower management ranks and no formal system for employee evaluation. Communication eroded, morale eroded, service eroded, passengers went elsewhere, and no corrective action was taken. Facing mounting losses, Lawrence resigned in 1980 and went into retirement at the age of sixty. Despite a corporate rescue effort over the next two years, Braniff failed to recover its losses and filed for Chapter 11 bankruptcy protection in 1982.

References:
Byron Harris, "The Man Who Killed Braniff," *Texas Monthly*, 10 (July 1982): 116-120, 183-189;

John J. Nance, *Splash of Colors: The Self-Destruction of Braniff International* (New York: Morrow, 1984);

Robert J. Serling, *Maverick: The Story of Robert Six and Continental Airlines* (Garden City, N.Y.: Doubleday, 1974).

Charles A. Lindbergh

(February 4, 1902 - August 26, 1974)

by Richard P. Hallion

Office of Air Force History

CAREER: Pilot, U.S. Army Air Service (1925); airmail pilot, Robertson Aircraft Corporation (1926-1927); trustee, Daniel Guggenheim Fund for the Promotion of Aeronautics (1927-1930); technical adviser, Transcontinental Air Transport/Transcontinental and Western Air (1929-1941); adviser to the Daniel and Florence Guggenheim Foundation (1930-1940); technical adviser and director, Pan American Airways (1930-1974); member, National Advisory Committee for Aeronautics (1931-1939); technical adviser, Ford Motor Company (1942); technical adviser, United Aircraft Corporation (1942-1945); special adviser on research and development, U.S. Air Force (1948-1956).

Charles Augustus Lindbergh, the most distinguished aviator of his generation, was born at his grandmother's home in Detroit, Michigan, on February 4, 1902, and died on Maui, Hawaii, on August 26, 1974. A superlative pilot, Lindbergh greatly influenced the technical and commercial development of aviation both in the United States and abroad. His solo flight across the North Atlantic in May 1927 triggered an enthusiastic outburst of interest in aviation and aviation services; thereafter, though he continued to fly, he became best known as a spokesman for a variety of causes, most involving the development of commercial air transport and aviation safety.

Lindbergh served as an adviser to the aircraft industry, particularly to two major airlines: Transcontinental Air Transport (TAT, predecessor to Transcontinental and Western Air, which evolved into Trans World Airlines), and Pan American Airways. His contribution to the establishment of TAT's route network was so great, in fact, that the line was referred to as "The Lindbergh Line." In addition, acting on Lindbergh's advice, aviation philanthropists Daniel and Harry Guggenheim granted financial assistance to rocketry expert Robert Goddard.

Before World War II Lindbergh toured European aeronautical establishments, including those of Nazi Germany. A staunch proponent of American defense preparedness, he was nevertheless labeled an isolationist in foreign policy matters, although he believed he merely favored an "independent" American foreign policy, free—as much as pos-

Charles A. Lindbergh in front of the Spirit of St. Louis, *the Ryan monoplane he flew across the Atlantic Ocean on May 20-21, 1927*

sible—from foreign entanglements. His position against American intervention in World War II drew much criticism, including the displeasure of President Franklin D. Roosevelt, who compared him to the Copperheads of the American Civil War era and who privately (and unjustly) considered him pro-Nazi. In April 1941, responding to Roosevelt's criticisms, Lindbergh resigned his commission as a reserve officer in the U.S. Army Air Corps. Once the United States entered the war, he attempted to rejoin the military, but was told that he would first have to recant his previous stance. He refused to do so, and chose instead to serve energetically as a technical air adviser to the Ford Motor Company and United Aircraft Corporation. Lindbergh also flew as a combat observer in the Southwest Pacific theater; on one occasion he shot down an attacking Japanese fighter. At the end of the war he toured Europe as a member of an Allied technical intelligence team examining the Nazi aeronautical research and development establishment.

Shocked by his exposure to the slave labor of Camp Dora, a camp that furnished inmates who were subsequently worked to death in the Nordhausen production facility building V-2 terror rockets, Lindbergh returned to the United States deeply troubled by the linkage between science, technology, and modern war. Already a prolific author, he addressed the moral dimension of science and technology with increasing frequency and fervor. His continued association with the American defense establishment led him to consider further the role of ethics in military affairs.

Though not religious in the commonly accepted sense of the word, Lindbergh had a strong sense of divine creation and existence, with feelings that came close to embracing the doctrine of pantheism. In the 1970s he embarked on a new career as a spokesman for the environment and for primitive cultures and societies. He championed a return to a simpler, more naturalistic life. While these new positions did not represent a total rejection of technology, it can be said that in later life Lindbergh embraced a suspicious view of technology: he came to believe that the most appropriate technological solutions to the problems of nations and peoples were not always the most complex, intrusive, and costly—in spiritual, as well as material terms. For these reasons, Lindbergh opposed the construction of an American supersonic transport (SST) to rival the French Concorde. While he was not the only critic of SST development, his stature gave him much influence, and American airline design firms eventually rejected the SST.

Lindbergh was the son of Charles Augustus Lindbergh, Sr., for several terms a representative in the Minnesota state legislature, and Evangeline Land Lodge Lindbergh. He was raised on a small farm in Minnesota to reflect his Populist father's suspicion of big business, banking interests, and foreign powers, particularly Great Britain. Like many early aviators from farm environments, Lindbergh, an innate tinkerer, acquired good mechanical skills. His interest in aviation developed casually, and overtook his interest in his own education. Though he remained an avid reader and observer of the public scene his entire life, his formal education ended after two unimpressive years at the University of Wisconsin as an engineering student. He literally taught himself to fly a Curtiss Jenny biplane, and, as with many young air-minded men of his generation, flew as a barnstormer and parachute jumper, notably with Bud Gurney; his lanky appearance earned him the nickname "Slim."

Eager to become a professional pilot, Lindbergh joined the U.S. Army Air Service (predecessor to the Army Air Corps) in 1925 and received military pilot training culminating in the award of his wings and a commission as a second lieutenant. While in flight training, he survived a midair collision by parachuting safely to earth—it was one of the first uses of a parachute by an American military pilot for lifesaving purposes. Because there were few opportunities in the military for full-time service pilots, Lindbergh remained in the air reserve and looked for work in the aviation field. He briefly flew as a free-lance test pilot, again having to parachute to safety; an experimental biplane refused to come out of a spin, and he had to jump for his life at low altitude, having just enough height for the chute to open.

The Air Mail Act of 1925 greatly accelerated the growth of commercial aviation in the United States by encouraging private firms to bid for airmail contracts. Lindbergh joined the Robertson Aircraft Corporation of St. Louis in 1926 and began a career as an airmail pilot. Flying the mail in the 1920s was only marginally safer than flying as a barnstormer or test pilot, and he had to make no less than two emergency parachute jumps at night; during one, he was nearly hit by his errant plane as it circled to earth.

While working as an airmail pilot Lindbergh heard of the $25,000 Raymond Orteig Prize, offered for the first successful airplane flight from New York to Paris. This fascinated him; as a pilot he appreciated the challenge, and as a technologist he had the necessary insight to realize that the approach most competitors were taking would not work. They intended to fly large multiengine biplanes with several crew members across the Atlantic. Lindbergh placed his faith in a smaller, more streamlined single-engine machine that would take fullest advantage of advances in the development of powerful lightweight radial piston engines and in single-wing designs. He broached the idea of a transatlantic flight to a group of St. Louis businessmen, and secured their backing. Then he journeyed to New York, intending to purchase a Bellanca cabin monoplane to make the trip. He had been misled by his discussions with the Bellanca firm, however, and discovered that Bellanca was willing to sell him an airplane only on the condition that they choose

the pilot. Lindbergh, angry, returned to St. Louis, and, with the continuing support of his colleagues, approached a relatively new aircraft company, Ryan Airlines of San Diego, California, to commission an airplane based upon a successful airmail aircraft design they had placed in service.

The resulting pilot-designer partnership was one of the most successful in aviation history. Ryan chief engineer Donald A. Hall had responsibility for the overall design of the craft, but Lindbergh participated actively in all phases, offering many practical suggestions. Nothing was compromised in the quest for endurance and range. The resulting airplane, the Ryan NYP, named the *Spirit of St. Louis*, became, aside from the Wright brothers' Kitty Hawk biplane, the best-known airplane in history. In May 1927, it took to the air. Satisfied with its basic handling and performance characteristics, Lindbergh immediately flew it across the United States, setting a new transcontinental speed record from San Diego to New York (with a brief stop in St. Louis) of 21 hours and 20 minutes. It was good preparation for the flight to follow. His arrival in New York attracted a great deal of publicity, for, unlike such aviation luminaries as Richard Byrd, Rene Fonck, and Charles Nungesser—all at some state of preparation for the transatlantic attempt—Lindbergh was an unknown. The boyish, somewhat shy, and good-looking young pilot immediately became the target of intense press scrutiny. Before the press had a chance to learn much, however, he departed for Paris.

Lindbergh's journey across the Atlantic on May 20-21, 1927, ranks as one of the great adventures of all time. A feat of rare human endurance, the flight covered 3,614 miles in 33 1/2 hours, and Lindbergh had actually gone without sleep for 57 1/2 hours by the time he touched down at Le Bourget Field in Paris. Though he was dubbed "Lucky Lindy" by the press, Lindbergh actually prepared meticulously for the trip, taking a genuine "leave nothing to chance" approach that greatly enhanced his prospects for success. But, perhaps because he and his little airplane seemed so modest in comparison to the high-tech efforts of his fellow transatlantic contestants, people in Europe and the United States responded with an explosion of enthusiasm with the news of his safe landing. After visits to several European capitals, the new hero arrived in America to a tumultuous reception, including a ticker-tape parade in New York City.

Lindbergh (left) with Pan American Airways president Juan T. Trippe (courtesy of the National Air and Space Museum)

Lindbergh had numerous opportunities to cash in on his fame had that been his intention. But he was, in fact, a proponent of the new gospel of aviation, and his concern was with advancing the art and science of aeronautics. Accordingly, he limited his subsequent business activities to those that would directly benefit the cause of flight. This characteristic greatly increased the admiration that Americans, especially representatives of the aviation community, had for him. He joined the Daniel Guggenheim Fund for the Promotion of Aeronautics as a fund trustee, and flew the *Spirit of St. Louis* around the United States on behalf of the fund to encourage the use of the airmail, promote "airmindedness," and urge the marking of towns with large signs and symbols as an aid to aerial navigation. In 1930 he worked closely with philanthropists Daniel and Harry Guggenheim to award research grants to Massachusetts physicist Robert Hutchings Goddard, the father of the liquid-fuel rocket. Lindbergh and the Guggenheims were more inclined to examine the potential of the rocket as

an emergency power unit for an ailing airplane, but were willing to support him in any case. The meetings between Lindbergh, Goddard, and the Guggenheims established friendships that lasted until Goddard's death in 1945.

Lindbergh devoted an increasing amount of time to the study of air transport and the development of long-range flying techniques and air routes. In this activity, he collaborated actively with airline pioneer Juan T. Trippe, a close friend and founder of Pan American Airways, and with Transcontinental Air Transport. Lindbergh and his wife, Anne Morrow Lindbergh, who took an active interest in aviation, mapped air routes for both airlines throughout the Americas and in Asia. The Lindberghs were best known for pioneering in 1931 the so-called "Great Circle Route" that ran "North to the Orient" from Maine across Canada, Alaska, the Bering Strait, and down the western coast of Siberia to Japan and China. It was Lindbergh who recommended that TWA purchase the Douglas DC-1 airliner, stipulating that it be able to take off on only

Lindbergh paying a visit to his restored boyhood home, Little Falls, Minnesota, 1971 (Minnesota Historical Society)

one engine from any field on TWA's route system and that it be able to maintain level flight on one engine over the highest mountain range on the airline's routes. This demanded extraordinary design efforts to achieve, but the resulting airplane—which did not itself enter service but which served as a prototype for a larger and more powerful model, the DC-2—had a profound impact upon international air transport design. The production DC-2 fully met the expectations of its designers and led to the DC-3, which must be considered the most successful propeller-driven piston-engine airliner ever developed.

Lindbergh was by nature an experimentalist, and he avidly followed all the various technical advances made in aviation in the 1920s and 1930s, such as short-takeoff-and-landing (STOL) designs and concepts, the introduction of such devices as the wing slat and wing flap (to improve the lifting characteristics of wings at low speeds and high angles of attack), autogiros (rotary-wing predecessors to the helicopter), and the debate between whether or not the land plane or the seaplane should dominate international air commerce. Although he was

open minded on the last question, he was primarily a proponent of the long-range land plane. His interest in this matter led to his assisting the Irish government in 1936 when Irish president Eamon de Valera worked to establish a major airport in that country. Lindbergh was responsible for locating the facility at Shannon, near Limerick, which has since become a major international air terminus.

Lindbergh's role in these activities is all the more remarkable when one realizes that he was then a man only in his mid thirties. His perspective and interests were those of a renaissance man. Although imperfect in his knowledge and appreciation of the subtlety of contemporary events, he always had a strong desire to master a diverse range of subjects ranging from international affairs to bioethics, anthropology, and aviation. His own maturation of views and interests as a young man in the 1920s and 1930s led him to seek the advice and counsel of a wide range of prominent individuals, including Teilhard de Chardin, the French Christian mystic, and Alexis Carrel, a controversial French physician and medical researcher. These widening interests eventually had an impact on

Lindbergh's work in aviation. For example, in 1939 Lindbergh was offered the chairmanship of the prestigious National Advisory Committee of Aeronautics (NACA), a governing body composed of the most eminent authorities in commercial and military aviation, aeronautical engineering, and meteorology. He had already served for eight years as a member of the NACA Main Committee, but declined the invitation, stating—with complete sincerity—that his greatest interests lay in other fields and that he did not wish to devote his entire attention to aviation.

Until his death, Lindbergh observers would be at times astonished at his forays into other fields. His acquaintance with Carrel blossomed into a full-fledged research partnership, and, after the Lindberghs moved to Europe, Lindbergh was a frequent visitor to the Carrels' summer home on the island of St. Gildas, France. Together with Carrel, he developed the organ perfusion pump to keep organs bathed in fluid prior to transplant. This contribution was a major step in medical technology in the interwar years and would have been sufficient to secure his place in history even if he never had a career in aviation. In a similar manner, his commitment to the environment and the protection of primitive peoples was so overwhelming that, shortly before his own death, he ventured deep into the rain forest of the Philippine Islands with groups of like-minded people, heavily armed to defend—by force, if necessary—the rights and lives of the people against encroaching civilization.

Following his move to Europe in 1935 after the kidnapping and murder of his first son, Lindbergh became increasingly active in foreign affairs. While he retained his interest in aviation, those interests were more and more replaced by concern over the course of American foreign policy. Lindbergh always feared communism more than facism or nazism, though he could by no means be considered an ally or admirer of Adolf Hitler. Lindbergh had a Eurocentric view of the world; in this view, the European peoples, particularly the Northern European peoples (as exemplified by Americans), were the carriers and advancers of civilization. Others, notably the Slavic and Asian peoples, threatened European hegemony. For these reasons—at once the products of his midwestern Scandinavian heritage and nineteenth-century Populist background—he saw "Asiatic" Russia as an increasing threat to Europe. The activities of the Comintern and the overt assis-

tance offered by Joseph Stalin to the leftist government of Loyalist Spain confirmed in his mind what he perceived to be the expansionist, intrusive, and uncivilized nature of the Soviet state.

To Lindbergh, the tragedy was that the European nations could not unite to confront the Soviet threat. America's great virtue, he believed, was its belief in democracy, and its great security was the distance that separated it from foreign shores. He recognized that America could be threatened only by air or sea attack, and, consequently he championed a strong national defense in case the country was ever attacked. In addition, he believed that America should steer its own foreign policy course, unswayed by the appeal or needs of nations that, in an almost Social Darwinist view of the world, were unable to take care of themselves. This argument was not a popular one in the late 1930s, particularly as the threat of German and Japanese expansionism overtook that of Stalinism.

Lindbergh had journeyed to Germany to inspect its aircraft industry, and, while there, had received a minor Nazi medal, awarded—much to his surprise—at a cocktail party. The furor that erupted over this seriously damaged his credibility. Critics mistook his warnings of German aeronautical excellence as endorsements of the German system, which they were not, and pointed to the medal as evidence of the reward for services he was providing the Nazi state. Once war broke out in September 1939, Lindbergh's activities drew more and more attention, including covert government surveillance ordered by President Franklin Roosevelt. Lindbergh's criticism of Jewish activists working to influence American foreign policy drew charges of anti-Semitism. The relationship between Lindbergh and Harry F. Guggenheim (Daniel, Guggenheim's father, had died in 1930) grew very strained, and it was not until after the war that the men resumed their friendship. The increasing bitterness of the political debate in the United States eventually tarnished Lindbergh's popular reputation; no longer was he the boyish hero, the reclusive grief-stricken father, or the dabbler in medicine. Rather, he was seen by the popular press as a divisive force in American politics and, increasingly, as a sympathizer of the Nazi government. The Japanese attack upon Pearl Harbor destroyed Lindbergh's political influence, for it left (as he recollected) "no practical alternative" but war.

Lindbergh's wartime service nonetheless was most distinguished. Rebuffed in his efforts to rejoin the air service, he went to work for the aircraft industry as a technical consultant. Not content to remain in the United States, he went to the Southwest Pacific and flew numerous combat sorties in P-38 and F4U fighters with army and marine squadrons. On one of these he shot down a Japanese fighter. On another he confronted the essential violence of war and rejected it, refusing an opportunity to strafe an unidentified individual walking across a beach. As shocked as he was by the rapid stripping away of civilized behavior that accompanied frontline combat, his touring, after the war, of the institutionalized brutality of the Nazi slave labor system stunned him. Never again would he consider aviation divorced from ethical, social, and cultural values. To him, science, technology, and ethics became inexorably intertwined. Writing three years after the war, and after the atomic bomb had forever changed the nature of warfare, he stated that future society had to be based upon "simplicity, humility, contemplation, [and] prayer."

Lindbergh did not have the influence in the postwar years that he had had in the years before. Aviation had grown too big for one man, no matter how knowledgeable, to have such a profound impact. He continued to consult with the government on defense and aviation matters, but his writings turned more and more contemplative. The publication of his book *The Spirit of St. Louis* in 1953 resulted in a resurgence of interest in him. This definitive account of the flight—replacing an earlier, hastily written account prepared just after his return from Europe in 1927—must be ranked the finest pilot memoir ever written. The publication of two further memoirs, *Wartime Journals* (1970) and *Autobiography of Values* (published posthumously in 1978), rekindled much of the controversy that surrounded him in the isolationist debates of the late 1930s and early 1940s, even as they added greatly to an understanding and perspective of him. Reviewers seemed unsure of how to regard his writings, and some tried to evaluate his beliefs on such matters as marriage and the role of women from the perspectives of 1970s social philosophy and values. Always a popular subject for biographers, he proved elusive, triggering simplistic treatments. Biographers have shown less interest in Lindbergh overall than they have in Lindbergh the spokesman for the America First movement. In the final analysis,

however, Lindbergh remains America's greatest aviator, a charismatic, supremely gifted, and multitalented individual.

Publications:

"Going over the Side in a Parachute," *U.S. Air Services* (February 1927): 42-43;

We: The Famous Flier's Own Story of His Life and Transatlantic Flight, Together with His Views on the Future of Aviation (New York: Putnam's, 1927);

The Culture of Organs, with Alexis Carrel (New York: P. B. Hoeber, 1938);

"Appeal for Peace," *Vital Speeches of the Day* (August 15, 1940): 644-646;

"Who are the War Agitators?," *Des Moines Register*, September 12, 1941, section 6, p. 1;

Of Flight and Life (New York: Scribners, 1948);

The Spirit of St. Louis (New York: Scribners, 1953);

The Wartime Journals (New York: Harcourt Brace Jovanovich, 1970);

Boyhood on the Upper Mississippi (St. Paul: Minnesota Historical Society, 1972);

Autobiography of Values (New York: Harcourt Brace Jovanovich, 1978).

References:

Wayne S. Cole, *Charles A. Lindbergh and the Battle against American Intervention in World War II* (New York: Harcourt Brace Jovanovich, 1974);

Tom D. Crouch, ed., *Charles A. Lindbergh: An American Life* (Washington, D.C.: Smithsonian Institution, 1977);

Kenneth S. Davis, *The Hero: Charles A. Lindbergh and the American Dream* (Garden City, N.Y.: Doubleday, 1959);

Susan M. Gray, *Charles A. Lindbergh and the American Dilemma: The Conflict of Technology and Human Values* (Bowling Green, Ohio: Bowling Green State University Popular Press, 1988);

Brendan Gill, *Lindbergh Alone* (New York: Harcourt Brace Jovanovich, 1977);

Richard P. Hallion, *Legacy of Flight: The Guggenheim Contribution to American Aviation* (Seattle: University of Washington Press, 1977);

Anne Morrow Lindbergh, *Hour of Gold, Hour of Lead: Diaries and Letters of Anne Morrow Lindbergh, 1929-1932* (New York: Harcourt Brace Jovanovich, 1973);

Leonard Mosley, *Lindbergh: A Biography* (Garden City, N.Y.: Doubleday, 1976);

Walter S. Ross, *The Last Hero: Charles A. Lindbergh* (New York: Harper & Row, 1976).

Archives:

Charles A. Lindbergh's papers are in the manuscript collection of the Sterling Memorial Library, Yale University.

Frank Lorenzo

(May 19, 1940 -)

by Edmund Preston

Washington, D.C.

CAREER: Financial analyst, Trans World Airlines (1963-1965); financial analysis manager, Eastern Air Lines (1965-1966); chairman, Lorenzo, Carney & Company (1966-); chairman, Jet Capital Corporation (1969-); president (1972-1980), chairman, Texas International Airlines (1980-1990); president (1980-1985), chairman and chief executive officer, Texas Air Corporation/Continental Airlines Holding (1986-1990).

Many of the changes that transformed American air transportation in the era of deregulation were pioneered by Frank Lorenzo, a self-made entrepreneur who assembled the nation's largest complex of airlines under the control of his Texas Air Corporation. Even before the end of federal economic controls, Lorenzo had introduced the cost-cutting practices and discounted fares that were to become typical. He adopted a tough stance toward organized labor in an industry whose managers had frequently submitted to union demands. Lorenzo also led the way in practicing leveraged takeovers of his rivals, and his success in this contributed to the growing consolidation that followed deregulation's earliest phase. This innovative career made Lorenzo a controversial figure, often praised for financial brilliance yet condemned by many as a ruthless manipulator.

A native of New York City, Francisco Anthony Lorenzo was born on May 19, 1940. He was the youngest of the three sons of Olegario and Ana Lorenzo, who as children had emigrated from Spain. His father was a hairdresser and beauty shop proprietor who took an interest in the stock market. Frank Lorenzo spent his youth in the Rego Park neighborhood of Queens, and attended Forest Hills High School. He studied economics as a Columbia University undergraduate, helping to pay his way by jobs that included driving a Coca-Cola truck. Vice-president of his fraternity, Sigma Chi, Lo-

Frank Lorenzo (courtesy of the National Air and Space Museum)

renzo was widely known on campus. He is reported to have been nicknamed "Frankie Smooth Talk" and to have gained notoriety for his role in a plot to rig a student election. His record was nevertheless good enough to permit him to enter Harvard Business School after graduating from Columbia in 1961. He ran a profitable campus newsstand at Harvard and was chosen vice-president of the Finance Club. Earning his M.B.A. degree in 1963, he served in the army briefly before beginning his business career that same year.

Lorenzo had been fascinated by airlines since boyhood, and at fifteen had bought shares in Trans World Airlines (TWA) after a trip to Europe on that carrier. TWA gave him his first professional job, as a financial analyst. In 1965 he and other staff members accompanied TWA's president Floyd Hall in a move to Eastern Air Lines. Lorenzo did well as a financial analysis manager at Eastern, but resigned the following year to become an entrepreneur. His partner was Robert J. Carney, a Harvard Business School classmate who had been working for the investment concern of S. G. Warburg. Each put up $1,000 to found Lorenzo, Carney & Co., a financial consulting firm specializing in aviation. In 1969 the two contributed $35,000 each to form a new company, Jet Capital Corporation. They raised over $1 million for Jet Capital in a 1971 stock offering, while maintaining majority control, and planned to use these funds to enter the aircraft leasing business. An economic downturn soon made leasing seem a poor prospect, however, and the partners began to consider applying their capital and expertise directly to an airline. Their chance came that same year when Chase Manhattan Bank asked them to assist one of its faltering clients.

The airline that claimed the attention of Lorenzo and Carney was a Houston-based regional carrier over three decades old and known for most of its existence as Trans-Texas Airways. A victim of overexpansion, it had begun losing money in 1967. The following year it became Texas International (TI) Airlines, a name justified only by weekly service to two Mexican airports. The grander title did not spell success, however, and TI had accumulated a staggering debt by 1971. Yet Lorenzo and Carney judged the company to be sound in terms of its personnel and equipment. Acting as consultants for $15,000 per month, they saved the airline from bankruptcy with a plan that included refinancing and $1.5 million in fresh capital. Most of the new funds came from Jet Capital, which received 24 percent of TI's equity and a controlling share of its voting rights. The Civil Aeronautics Board (CAB) gave final approval to the plan on August 10, 1972. That same month, Lorenzo was named the airline's president and chief executive officer, while Carney became executive vice-president.

The carrier that Lorenzo now controlled was hardly a giant of the industry, but its assets were not inconsiderable. TI had about 2,000 employees and operated a fleet of 15 McDonnell-Douglas DC-9 jets and 15 Convair 600 turboprop aircraft. The thirty-two-year-old Lorenzo was hailed as perhaps the youngest airline president on record, and his success was soon followed by marriage on October 14, 1972. His bride, Sharon Neill Murray, was the daughter of a Florida real estate investor. A graduate of Mount Holyoke, she had worked in a New York law firm. The couple were to become the parents of a son and three daughters.

Lorenzo set to work to return Texas International to health, trimming the payroll, eliminating service to about 20 unproductive destinations, and seeking more profitable routes. TI quickly broke into the black, showing a profit of $320,000 for 1973. Its progress was interrupted late in the following year, however, when a strike of ground workers stopped operations for over four months. Lorenzo's decision to face a walkout rather than accept the union's demands was a harbinger of his future policies toward labor. The settlement in April 1975 balanced pay raises against concessions that management said would increase productivity. Lorenzo reportedly criticized the union for selfishness in a poststrike interview said to have increased resentment among the employees.

Heavy losses during 1975 forced Lorenzo to obtain new terms from TI's creditors, but in 1976 the airline could claim the largest profit in its history, $3.2 million. During the following year, Lorenzo introduced an important innovation: "peanut fares" discounted deeply enough to lure standby passengers into otherwise empty seats on certain flights. Federal regulators previously would have denied such a tactic to an interstate carrier, but the Civil Aeronautics Board was beginning to adopt a more flexible stance toward competition. The CAB permitted a one-year trial, starting in January 1977, and peanut fares quickly became a widely emulated success. Higher load factors helped TI double its profits in 1977, and by the end of the year its modernized fleet included 26 DC-9 jets. In 1978 the company paid its first cash dividends in over a decade.

The game in which Lorenzo scored these achievements was about to experience a drastic change of rules. The growing movement for airline deregulation would soon bring the phaseout of the Civil Aeronautics Board and free the industry's managers for the kind of direct competition that very few of them welcomed. Lorenzo believed that the new situation would make rapid growth imperative. "We were a small Texas airline without a name franchise, with no public identity, without any large aircraft," Lorenzo explained later to writer Kenneth Labich. "It looked like we were going to be the ham in someone else's sandwich." This judgment doubtless reinforced a personal drive to enter air transportation's major league.

Even before the enactment of the Airline Deregulation Act in August 1978, Lorenzo was preparing the first of a series of seemingly reckless takeover attempts. Texas International began buying stock in National Airlines and made headlines by announcing its intention to acquire the far-larger carrier. National's chairman responded by negotiating a sale to Pan American. While the still-powerful Civil Aeronautics Board considered the issue, *Forbes'* James Cook journeyed to Houston to interview the man whom he styled "Lorenzo the Presumptuous." Cook pointed out that TI was already shouldering a formidable debt and would have to raise at least $200 million more to make the acquisition a reality. In reply, Lorenzo calmly cited his organization's past record for generating capital. Although a settlement in July 1979 placed Pan Am in control of the disputed airline, TI emerged from the affair with a handsome reward. The sale of its shares in National garnered a pretax profit of about $46 million.

Trans World Airlines, which was experiencing financial difficulties but possessed assets several times larger than those of TI, became Lorenzo's next quarry. In September 1979 he invited TWA president L. Edwin Smart, Jr., to breakfast at New York's Carlyle Hotel. Lorenzo reportedly broached a purchase proposal that caused the incensed Smart to walk out of the meeting. Although TI continued to buy stock in the beleaguered international carrier, acquiring as much as 4 percent, Lorenzo decided to sell the shares a few months later.

During most of 1980, Lorenzo interrupted his takeover attempts to restructure his operations and create a new airline. His first step was the formation on June 11 of Texas Air Corporation, a holding company that acquired Texas International. In September, Texas Air in turn formed a regional carrier to operate under the name of New York Air. The new subsidiary's freedom from labor contracts was expected to give it an advantage against the existing airlines of the Northeast. It began flying on December 19, competing against Eastern Air Lines for the lucrative shuttle trade between New York and Washington. New York Air's low fares forced Eastern to cut some prices and offer discount coupons, developments that deregulation advocates quickly cited as evidence that their policy was helping the consumer.

The year 1980 also saw the departure of Donald C. Burr from Lorenzo's organization. A fellow M.B.A. from Harvard, Burr had joined Texas International in 1973 and became its president five years later. He was best man at Lorenzo's wedding and became the godfather of one of his children. Despite this apparent closeness to TI's president, Burr became discontented. "It was grind, grind, grind, with no better purpose than to grind out some profits," he later explained to writer Sara Rimer. "It had no vision, no excitement." Soon after his resignation, Burr organized an egalitarian new airline named People Express.

By the end of 1980, Lorenzo was laying the groundwork for a new takeover campaign, one whose ultimate success would make him a national figure. The objective this time was Continental Air Lines, a carrier with headquarters in Los Angeles and routes that spanned the country and touched points across the Pacific. The airline had been damaged by a strike in 1976, and lost money heavily as the decade waned. Continental's stock was modestly priced, and its assets included a fleet of DC-10 wide-body jets that made it a tempting prize. In February 1980 the carrier came under the chairmanship of Alvin L. Feldman, whose previous leadership at Frontier Airlines had gained him a reputation as an effective manager. Feldman was on the verge of achieving a promising merger with Western Airlines when Lorenzo's challenge placed him on the defensive.

In February 1981 the public learned that Texas International had gained a stock interest in Continental of over 9 percent. Lorenzo made a tender offer for a large additional bloc as a step toward takeover. Feldman appealed to the courts and to the Civil Aeronautics Board for protection, but could not prevent TI from sewing up 48.5 percent of his company's stock. Fearing that Lorenzo's victory would result in personnel reductions and equipment sales, a group of Continental employees devised an imaginative defense based on an Employee Stock Ownership Plan (ESOP). They proposed that Continental issue enough new stock to dilute TI's 48.5 percent interest and permit the ESOP to buy control. The plan won Feldman's support and $185 million in promised loans from a group of banks led by Security Pacific International. Continental had difficulty in winning approval to issue the new shares without a stockholders' vote, however, and its financial position continued to deteriorate. Another setback came on August 6, when the Civil Aeronautics Board made public its decision not to block TI's takeover drive.

On August 9, 1981, Feldman approved an announcement that the ESOP plan had lost the support of its bankers and no longer seemed a likely possibility. That evening he killed himself in his office at Los Angeles International Airport. Feldman's suicide seemed triggered by the looming TI takeover, but the death of his wife one year earlier was evidently an underlying cause. The ESOP organizers vowed to fight on, but they had little prospect of success. On October 13 President Ronald Reagan's decision to uphold the Civil Aeronautics Board's ruling ended hope of federal intervention, and Texas International acquired Continental the following month. Control of both airlines placed Lorenzo at the head of the nation's seventh-largest air carrier organization.

For some time, the triumph appeared to be a dangerous one. Continental experienced an operating loss of $100 million in 1981, a year in which a strike by air traffic controllers created a restricted and uncertain environment. Lorenzo merged Texas International into Continental in October 1982, and raised money through aircraft sales, stock offerings, and loans. He received some wage concessions from labor, but considered them too little to offset the carrier's continuing difficulties. In March 1983 he laid off 15 percent of Continental's employees. A mechanics' strike in August failed to ground the airline, but losses mounted sharply as Lorenzo pressed employees for the kind of agreements he deemed satisfactory.

On September 24, 1983, Lorenzo began implementing a drastic scheme. Continental shut down its operations and filed to reorganize under Chapter 11 of the bankruptcy code, claiming that excessive labor costs made the step necessary. At a news conference the following Monday, Lorenzo announced the airline's rebirth as a discount carrier that would fly to 25 of the 76 destinations previously served. He offered to employ 4,200 of the 12,000 former personnel, but with revised work rules and reduced benefits. Wages would be slashed sharply—to about half their previous level, in many cases—with top pay for pilots and executives dropping to $43,000. Lorenzo included himself in this salary cut (although his income from other sources made hardship unlikely).

Considering its large cash reserves, Continental could not have attempted to use Chapter 11 in

this way before the Bankruptcy Reform Act of 1978 ended the requirement that a debtor be insolvent before seeking protection. It was nevertheless far from certain that Lorenzo would succeed in voiding the union contracts, and months of legal wrangling on the issue lay ahead. Meanwhile, many of the airline's employees were determined to challenge management's unilateral action.

Four days after the "new Continental" began operations on September 27, 1983, the company's unionized pilots and flight attendants walked off the job. The strikers claimed that they had offered to make reasonable sacrifices, and denounced the bankruptcy as a cynical ploy. Lorenzo was labeled the "number one union buster in the United States" by William L. Sheri, an aviation industry representative whose congressional testimony was quoted in the *Journal of Commerce*. Many of those walking the picket lines wore black armbands displaying the Continental logo crossed out, but management insisted that the carrier was far from dead. Posting bargain fares to attract passengers, the airline was able to keep most scheduled flights operating.

Although the Air Line Pilots Association (ALPA) did not follow through on a threatened national walkout, the union gave the strikers vocal backing. "If Continental gets away with this obvious ploy to destroy its unions," wrote ALPA president Henry A. Duffy, "every other unionized enterprise in the country can do the same." ALPA members maintained an intensive watch for evidence to support their charge that the airline was unsafe, and made sure that lapses were highly publicized. One such incident involved Lorenzo himself, who was a passenger aboard a Continental flight that mistakenly landed on a taxiway at Denver's Stapleton International Airport. Federal Aviation Administration inspectors found that Continental had infringed on certain regulations, but the agency's leaders defended the airline's basic safety and refused to ground it. Meanwhile, nonstriking pilots reported instances of radio interference and other forms of harassment.

In January 1984 Lorenzo won a key victory when a court endorsed the legitimacy of the bankruptcy filing. Continental managed to rebuild much of its strength in the following months. By year's end the airline was employing about 10,000 people, serving 70 destinations, and able to report an annual profit of $50.3 million. The strike dragged on until October 1985, when a court-ordered settle-

Lorenzo (right) with outgoing Eastern Air Lines chairman Frank Borman following Lorenzo's purchase of Eastern for Texas Air Corporation, February 1986

ment allowed pilots to return to work with their previous seniority, as vacancies arose, or accept a severance payment. Both sides agreed to drop a tangle of claims and suits, including the union's appeal of a ruling in favor of Lorenzo's use of Chapter 11 to overturn labor contracts. (Under new legislation, however, it became difficult for other managers to follow his example.)

Lorenzo's reputation as a fierce opponent of labor hampered him in a new round of attempts to acquire other airlines. In June 1985 he once again made an effort to get control of Trans World Airlines, then the object of a hostile raid by real estate tycoon Carl Icahn. TWA's management was willing to accept Lorenzo as a rescuer, and a merger agreement seemed certain. The airline's unions, however, did not wish to place their members under the man who created the "new Continental." Their promise of major wage concessions to Icahn spurred him to outbid Texas Air. As in his earlier campaign to acquire National Airlines, however, Lorenzo emerged with a substantial profit on the stock purchased during the battle. Union opposition was also a factor in blocking Texas Air's acquisition of Frontier Air-

lines, which was instead bought by People Express in the fall of 1985.

These abortive ventures were followed by Lorenzo's dramatic takeover of Eastern Air Lines. Rated the third largest among the nation's air carriers, Eastern had long been financially shaky and prey to trouble with its strong labor organizations. Former astronaut Frank Borman seemed to be making headway for a time after becoming president of the airline in 1975, but he was unable to achieve a sustained improvement. Borman's problems included the enmity of firebrand Charles Bryan, who represented the airline's mechanics and certain other ground workers as an official of the International Association of Machinists (IAM). In 1983 Eastern's three major unions accepted a profit-sharing scheme and seats on the board of directors in exchange for a wage freeze. The arrangement failed to produce a lasting upswing, however, and by early 1986 the airline's creditors were demanding that it achieve broad savings in labor costs by February 28. One week before that date, Lorenzo proposed to buy control of Eastern for about $600 million. He demanded $20 million simply for making the offer, and required an answer before February 24.

As Lorenzo's deadline approached, Borman pressed the unions for broad concessions, including a 20 percent pay cut, which he presented as the only alternative to the airline's sale or bankruptcy. During hectic negotiations on the night of February 23, the pilots' union accepted the company's terms, but Bryan remained adamant. Lorenzo withdrew his offer at midnight, then agreed to allow Eastern's board of directors to consider it for a few more hours. Bryan indicated that the mechanics would accept a 15 percent pay reduction, but only if Borman resigned. Spurning this proposal, the board voted to accept Lorenzo's offer.

This decision placed Texas Air on the brink of becoming the nation's largest airline complex, and its stock soared. Despite the added load of debt that Eastern would bring into his already leveraged operation, Lorenzo seemed to be riding high. Financial analyst Mike Derchin predicted that within three to five years Eastern would be transformed into a "fairly major low cost carrier" able to put "a tremendous amount of pressure on the other airlines." But Derchin noted that this promising future depended on the conclusion of more favorable labor agreements than Borman had been able to achieve.

Lorenzo attempted to convince Eastern's employees that his antiunion image was a false one, and Bryan was at first optimistic about his ability to deal with the incoming management. Very soon, however, the IAM boss was leading an effort to find an alternative purchaser before the Texas Air takeover could become final. Another obstacle for Lorenzo was the Department of Transportation, which rejected the merger in August on the grounds that it would stifle competition. The Department reversed this decision on October 1, however, after Texas Air took steps to allow Pan American's new shuttle to compete more effectively with Eastern's in serving Washington, New York, and Boston. Lorenzo was named chairman of Eastern's board in mid-October, and the airline's stockholders approved the merger with Texas Air on November 25, 1986. The final price was about $676 million.

While establishing his control of Eastern, Lorenzo also acquired People Express, the most spectacular of the post-deregulation upstarts. The airline had proved more successful at rapid growth than sustained profits, and founder Donald Burr began seek-

ing a buyer in June 1986. Texas Air's agreement to purchase People and nearly all of the assets of its bankrupt subsidiary, Frontier Airlines, was announced in September. Lorenzo's offer of less than $300 million was reduced still further by the time the agreement became final at the end of the year. In January 1987 Texas Air announced that the operations of both People and New York Air would merge into those of Continental at the beginning of February. In contrast to these nonunion subsidiaries, Eastern continued to be run as a separate enterprise.

By the spring of 1987, Lorenzo headed one of five major air carrier operations that controlled well over 70 percent of the nation's domestic airline traffic (the other four were American, Delta, United, and Northwest). In some ways, his organization seemed the strongest of the group, with the most revenue passenger miles, the largest share of the market, and the lowest labor costs in comparison to income. Yet Texas Air was standing on a mountain of debt and posting heavy operating losses. Lorenzo's strategy included new "Maxsaver" fares designed to give his carriers leadership in the discount field. He tried to win heavy concessions in contract negotiations with the unions at Eastern, including 47 percent pay cuts for machinists and baggage handlers, and began to trim the workforce. IAM leader Bryan lost his seat on the board of the airline, which came under the presidency of Phillip J. Bakes.

Lorenzo also began to dispose of some of Eastern's assets. In April 1987 a Texas Air subsidiary called System One acquired the airline's computerized reservation system. Instead of collecting fees from other carriers wishing to share the efficient system, Eastern was now obliged to pay for its use. Critics attacked the deal as an example of a tendency to shift valuable holdings to more favored portions of the Texas Air complex. Eastern's unions turned to the courts in an effort to limit management's powers to sell assets and cut back on operations deemed marginal. They gained some success early in 1988, only to lose in an appellate decision during the summer. In October Eastern announced an agreement to sell its shuttle operation to New York financier Donald Trump for some $365 million.

In April 1988, meanwhile, doubts about safety standards at Eastern triggered a special inspection by the Federal Aviation Administration (FAA), which had already slapped the airline with penalties made final in 1987 at a stiff $9.5 million. The agency subsequently broadened the inspection to include Continental. The FAA's parent Department of Transportation also conducted an investigation of Texas Air's fitness to run its subsidiary air carriers. On June 3 federal authorities announced their decision to allow operations to continue, but warned that the unusually bitter labor-management friction at Eastern was a potential threat to the airline's safety.

This same conflict escalated toward a disruptive strike as negotiators failed to agree on terms for new union contracts. The National Mediation Board was unable to break the deadlock, and the legally required "cooling off" period of 30 days began on February 1, 1989. As the month waned, the Mediation Board urged President George Bush to appoint an emergency panel to help resolve the issue. As March began, Eastern tried to isolate the militant mechanics union by offering the pilots a contract featuring modest raises and a five-year guarantee of job security. Lorenzo backed this move with a videotape, delivered to each pilot's home, in which he appealed for support and warned that the crisis threatened Eastern's survival.

On March 3 a *Washington Post* editorial summed up the issues at stake: the mechanics union wanted annual raises totaling $50 million, Lorenzo wanted cuts of three times that amount, and neither side was entitled to much sympathy. The *Post* believed that it was not the responsibility of the federal government to rescue the disputants from the "accumulated results of their own misjudgments and bad temper." President Bush evidently agreed, and his refusal to intervene was announced that same day. The employees represented by the IAM walked off the job just after midnight, supported by both pilots and flight attendants. The action grounded most of Eastern's flights and stranded travelers over a wide area.

While some observers likened the strike to a suicide pact, others saw it as a chance to reverse the unfavorable tide that organized labor had faced during the Reagan era. Lorenzo quickly applied for Chapter 11 protection from Eastern's creditors, and for a time the bankruptcy court allowed him much latitude in reorganizing the airline as a smaller carrier. In April 1989 former baseball commissioner Peter V. Ueberroth offered to buy the airline for about $464 million. The deal collapsed, however, when Lorenzo rejected a union demand that a trustee take control until the sale became final. Eastern sold off assets to raise cash, and rebuilt much of its operation with nonstrikers and newly hired employees. Unions representing the pilots and flight attendants decided on a return to work in November 1989, leaving only the diehard IAM on strike.

During that same month, however, Eastern began to experience sharp difficulties in filling the seats on its expanding flights. Fare cuts failed to remedy the situation, and the promising recovery stalled. The confidence of Eastern's creditors drained away, and in the spring of 1990 a group of them requested the bankruptcy court to appoint a trustee. The court complied on April 17, placing control of the airline in the hands of Martin R. Shugrue. Since he had reportedly forced Shugrue to resign as president of Continental, Lorenzo may have found the appointment doubly galling. He nevertheless declined to appeal the decision, and promised to give the trustee his assistance. The *New York Times* quoted the judge as saying that Lorenzo's management of Eastern was "suggestive of parental neglect" and that he was "not competent to reorganize this estate." While the Texas Air chief defended his record at Eastern, he had clearly suffered a humiliating reverse.

In August 1990 Lorenzo stunned the industry when he announced that he was selling his interest in Continental Airlines Holding (the new name of Texas Air Corporation as of June 1989) to Scandinavian Air Service (SAS). "I have been a lightning rod for much of the attacks that the company has taken," he commented. "I have seen that it is a reasonable time to step down." SAS paid a total of $52.5 million to increase its share of Continental Holding from 9.9 to 16.8 percent. Lorenzo received $30.5 million. He agreed to remain out of the airline business for seven years.

Accounts of Frank Lorenzo's personality have depicted him as taciturn, reserved, and even shy. His intensity is reflected in his long-standing dedication to jogging, and he has participated in more than one marathon. This exercise helped him shed extra pounds and become the "trim, rather boyish-looking man" that interviewer James Cook described in 1978. Since then, Lorenzo's fitness has no doubt helped him to ward off the burnout that some believed would result from the pressures of his turbulent career. He lives in a Georgian-style house in Houston, and is regarded as a devoted husband and father who carefully guards the privacy of his family. Lorenzo's relations with business associates, however, have often been less than harmonious. His portrait appeared on the cover of a February 1989 issue of *Fortune* containing a report on America's seven "toughest bosses" as selected by a poll. The article cited complaints that Lorenzo demanded 14-hour workdays from his executives, relied too much on an established cadre within his organization, and tended to undermine managers by dealing directly with their subordinates. Other sources described him as preferring fast results to careful organization or planning, but also emphasized his grasp of financial issues.

More than once, Lorenzo has been called the exemplar of a new breed of airline executives, immune to the romance of flying and dedicated to an unswerving quest for profits. In Lorenzo's case, this pursuit included a keen interest in personal enrichment through such means as stock options, according to a detailed biographical article by William P. Barrett. While Lorenzo's admirers have praised his persuasiveness, Barrett and other critics have characterized him as a glib talker ready to make promises later discarded. Another writer, Henry Fairlie, has described Lorenzo as gaining influence from the recruitment of former federal officials into his organization, and from the appointment of his ex-associates to government posts. Fairlie noted that T. Glover Roberts, the judge who ruled in the Continental bankruptcy case, soon joined a law firm representing that airline.

The charge most frequently leveled against Lorenzo is unfairness toward his enterprises' employees. His defenders have replied that labor's enmity toward him is based on an unrealistic rejection of the economic facts of the deregulated age. "We are not union busters," Lorenzo was quoted by *Barron's* as saying on the eve of the Eastern takeover, "we are airline builders." With the exception of New York Air, however, his building has usually consisted of combining existing carriers that were sometimes downsized in the process. In a June 1988 editorial, *Aviation Week and Space Technol-*

ogy stated that Lorenzo's hard-nosed attitude had amplified the problems accompanying his takeovers and mergers. The journal commented that his "apparent insensitivity to the human element" was "appalling" in an industry based upon service. While acknowledging his contribution to the success of deregulation, *Aviation Week* called upon him to make a similar contribution "to the human relations aspects" of his operations. By the time of his withdrawal from the air transport business in 1990, Lorenzo's impact on the industry seemed far from constructive.

References:

Russell Bailey, "Management by Bankruptcy," *Air Line Pilot* (February 1984): 20-23;

William P. Barrett, "Top Gun," *Texas Monthly* (March 1987);

Aaron Bernstein, *Grounded: Frank Lorenzo and the Destruction of Eastern Air Lines* (New York: Simon & Schuster, 1990);

James Cook, "Lorenzo the Presumptuous," *Forbes* (October 30, 1978): 115-117;

R. E. G. Davies, *Rebels and Reformers of the Airways* (Washington, D.C.: Smithsonian Institution, 1987);

Thomas G. Donlan, "Preparing for Takeoff," *Barron's* (March 3, 1986): 8-9, 20, 22;

Pete Endagario and others, "Frank Lorenzo, High Flier," *Business Week*, March 10, 1986, pp. 104-107;

Henry Fairlie, "Air Sickness," *New Republic* (June 5, 1989): 14-18;

Kenneth Labich, "Winners in the Air Wars," *Fortune* (May 11, 1987): 68-79;

"Lorenzo: The Empire Builder," *Aviation Week and Space Technology*, June 20, 1988, p. 9;

Michael Murphy, *The Airline That Pride Almost Bought* (New York: Watts, 1986);

Peter Nulty and Karen Nikel, "America's Toughest Bosses," *Fortune* (February 27, 1989);

Sara Rimer, "The Airline That Shook Up the Industry," *New York Times Magazine*, December 23, 1984;

"The Troubled Path to Eastern's Strike," *New York Times*, March 8, 1989;

Eric Weiner, "Lorenzo to Leave Airline Industry—Deal Selling Continental Stock," *New York Times*, August 10, 1990, pp. 1, C20.

C. Townsend Ludington

(January 16, 1896 - January 18, 1968)

by William M. Leary

University of Georgia

CAREER: Pilot, U.S. Navy (1917-1919); president, B.B.T. Corporation of America (1923-?); member, board of directors, various aviation enterprises (1925-1947); chairman, Ludington Line (1930-1933); president, Aircraft Owners and Pilots Association (1939-1952).

A wealthy Philadelphian, Charles Townsend Ludington learned to fly during World War I. Thereafter he devoted his life to a variety of aeronautical enterprises. His most historically significant activity came during the early 1930s, when he provided the capital for a pioneering air-shuttle service between Newark and Washington, D.C., via Philadelphia (Camden Airport) and Baltimore. Denied an airmail contract, the marginally profitable Ludington Line was sold to Eastern Air Transport in 1933. Twenty-eight years later, Eastern Air Lines would revive the air-shuttle concept, and with great success.

Ludington was born in New York City on January 16, 1896, the son of Henry and Ethel Mildred (Saltus) Ludington. His father was a lawyer and publisher. Ludington grew up in Philadelphia as a member of an affluent and socially prominent family. Graduating from the Haverford School in 1915, he entered Yale University. Two years later, following American entry into World War I, he left school and joined the U.S. Navy. Ludington learned to fly during the war. He also acted as supervisor of the Aviation Quartermaster Division, Mechanics School, San Diego Naval Air Station.

After studying at the Massachusetts Institute of Technology for two years after the war, Ludington returned to Yale in 1922 and completed his graduation requirement, receiving his B.A. degree as a member of the class of 1919. On June 27, 1922, he married Constance Guyot Cameron. The couple had three daughters and a son.

C. T. Ludington

An aviation enthusiast, Ludington formed several organizations during the early 1920s, including the Ludington Exhibition Company (1922) and the Ludington Flying Service (1923) that conducted a variety of flying activities from the Philadelphia Municipal Airport. In 1923 he organized and became president of the B.B.T. Corporation of America, which designed and manufactured beacons and lenses for the lighted airways of the period, along with airport floodlights. In 1925 he served as a member of the Joint Committee on Civil Aviation, a prestigious group that had been formed by Secretary of Commerce Herbert Hoover to make a comprehensive survey of all aspects of commercial aviation.

Ludington came to devote a good deal of attention to the developing airline industry. He became a director of National Air Transport in 1925, remaining on the board of this major airline until 1930. Between July and September 1929, the Ludington Flying Service operated Cape Cod Airway between Camden Airport (which Ludington and his brother Nicholas had founded in 1927) and Woods Hole, Massachusetts.

In the spring of 1930, Ludington decided to support a proposal for an air-shuttle service that had been developed by Paul F. Collins and Eugene L. Vidal. Fired during a retrenchment by Transcontinental Air Transport, a pioneering passenger-carrying airline, Collins and Vidal had become convinced that an air shuttle could attract a substantial number of the 175,000 individuals who traveled every week between New York, Philadelphia, and Washington. They persuaded Ludington to put up $250,000, which was used to purchase six Stinson trimotors (for $22,500 each) and to provide initial operating funds. Collins believed that the ten-passenger Stinsons would show a profit if operating costs could be kept below 40 cents an hour. He had his work cut out: at the time, operating costs for single-engine aircraft commonly ran three times higher.

The New York, Philadelphia & Washington Airway Corporation, commonly known as the Ludington Line, began service on September 1, 1930. Offering hourly flights from 8 A.M. to 7 P.M. between Newark, Camden, Baltimore, and Washington, the airline attracted more than 15,000 passengers during its first three months in business. Collins and Vidal believed that high frequency, low cost service was the key to success. "Every Hour on the Hour—Your Watch is Your Timetable" was the airline's advertising slogan—and philosophy. Charging little more than train fare, and with an emphasis on economy, the Ludington Line operated at a 60 percent load factor and registered a profit of $8,073 at the end of the year. While this was a modest sum, it marked the first time that an American airline had made a profit without government assistance.

Collins, in charge of operations, managed to reach his target of 40 cents an hour by a variety of devices, including the use of regular automobile gasoline in place of the expensive high-test fuel once the airplanes reached cruising altitude. He even sold advertising space inside the airplanes. Meanwhile, Vidal waged a highly successful campaign to promote the airline. His most effective technique was a series of 24 billboards that he placed along the New York-Washington route of the Pennsylvania Railroad. Each billboard showed a picture of an airplane, together with the words: "If you'd flown Ludington, you'd have been there."

Although the passenger business returned modest profits, Ludington realized that the key to financial success lay in an airmail contract. In July 1931, however, Postmaster General Walter Folger Brown awarded the prized contract to Eastern Air Transport (Eastern Air Lines after 1934)—and this despite the fact that Ludington had bid 25 cents a mile to Eastern's 89 cents. It took 18 months for Eastern's subsidized transports to force the Ludington Line out of business. In February 1933 Ludington sold the airline to Eastern, receiving the cost of his original investment.

Despite his disappointment over Postmaster General Brown's policy of favoring a few, large air carriers, Ludington's interest in aviation continued. He was a cofounder and director of both the Jacobs Aircraft Engine Company (1927-1937) and the Kellett Aircraft Company (1928-1943), an innovative manufacturer of rotary wing aircraft; he also served as board chairman and vice-president of Ludington-Griswold, Inc., a company concerned with aerodynamic research, aircraft design, and tooling. He was one of the five founders of the Aircraft Owners and Pilots Association in 1939, and he served as the organization's president until 1952.

Ludington retired from business in 1947, although he remained active in several aeronautical organizations. He also loved the water, and he designed several sailboats and motorboats for his own use. He died in Miami, Florida, on January 18, 1968.

References:

R. E. G. Davies, *Airlines of the United States since 1914*, revised edition (Washington, D.C.: Smithsonian Institution, 1982);

Paul F. Collins, *Tales of an Old Air-Faring Man* (Stevens Point, Wis.: UWSP Foundation Press, 1983).

William P. MacCracken, Jr.

(September 17, 1888 - September 19, 1969)

by David D. Lee

Western Kentucky University

CAREER: U.S. Army Signal Corps Aviation Section (1917-1919); Assistant Secretary of Commerce for Aeronautics (1926-1929); aviation attorney and lobbyist (1919-1934).

A pioneer in the federal regulation of commercial aviation, William P. MacCracken, Jr., was born on September 17, 1888, in Chicago, Illinois. His parents were homeopaths and hoped he would pursue a medical career, but MacCracken earned a law degree from the University of Chicago and started a legal practice. America's entry into World War I sharply altered his career. Although MacCracken initially planned to seek a naval commission, a friend urged him to consider the Army Signal Corps Aviation Section. With no experience in aeronautics, MacCracken, who had never even driven a car, entered pilot training at Rich Field in Waco, Texas. The Armistice found MacCracken still in Texas, flying the night bombardment course at Ellington Field. Discharged in January 1919, he returned to his Chicago law practice.

Increasingly intrigued by the legal implications of flight, MacCracken attended an American Bar Association (ABA) session on air law, but he came away disappointed because the principal paper focused on sea law while saying virtually nothing about the legal issues raised by aviation. At a time when only two states and five cities had laws regulating flying, MacCracken and New York attorney Charles Boston persuaded the ABA to appoint a Special Committee on the Law of Aviation. With Boston as chair and MacCracken as a member, the committee found that the progress of commercial aviation required creditable procedures for licensing pilots and certifying aircraft. The industry would not attract significant investment until such safety-related issues were resolved. The committee unanimously concluded that only the federal government could assume these responsibilities. However, the

William P. MacCracken, Jr. (courtesy of the MacCracken family)

committee also concluded that the government could not assume such responsibilities without a constitutional amendment to provide a basis for its authority in this area, an assertion MacCracken did not accept. When the report attracted a barrage of criticism, Boston resigned in disgust and MacCracken assumed the chairmanship.

His efforts to secure a federal air law launched MacCracken's career as an aviation lobbyist. Rejecting the states' rights view that the federal government could not regulate intrastate flying, MacCracken insisted that the safety of the system required that a single agency be responsible for all civilian flying. Indeed, the Supreme Court ruled in a 1922 case, *Railroad Commission of Wisconsin* v. *Chicago, B.&O. R. Co.*, that if interstate and intrastate commerce were so intermingled that Congress could not exercise effective control over interstate commerce without incidental regulation of intrastate commerce, "such incidental regulation is not an invasion of State authority." The ruling gave valuable legal support to MacCracken's point of view, and he set to work drafting a bill for consideration by the House Committee on Interstate and Foreign Commerce. Although committee chair Samuel Winslow supported the concept, the zealous MacCracken drafted a measure which was far too detailed and comprehensive to win passage. Simultaneously, he opposed a bill introduced by Senator James Wadsworth which avoided the pitfall of excessive detail but limited the government's authority to enforce its regulations. With the industry's support divided between the two proposals, neither could win passage.

Recognizing the need to establish an industry consensus on such issues, MacCracken took an active role in building a new trade association. With the oldest and largest civil aviation organization, the Aero Club of America, splintered by internal disputes, MacCracken and others founded the National Aeronautic Association (NAA), an umbrella group for aviation's diverse interests. MacCracken helped to draw up the papers of incorporation for the NAA and presided over its organizational meeting. Its creation boosted aviation's stock with the government, especially Secretary of Commerce Herbert Hoover, who considered constructive industrywide organizations crucial to economic progress. The NAA thus was an important step toward winning Hoover's support for a federal air law.

The drive for an air law was further complicated by a disagreement about the best way for the government to assume its regulatory responsibilities. Air power enthusiast Gen. Billy Mitchell championed the establishment of an aeronautics department patterned on the British model which would oversee both civilian and military flying, but MacCracken and most civilian government officials opposed such a department. Like many early advocates of aviation regulation, MacCracken saw useful parallels in government regulation of shipping. "Water transportation for commercial purposes is not under the Navy Department," MacCracken de-

clared, "and I have never known of anyone wanting it put there." Instead MacCracken wanted the Department of Commerce to regulate civilian flying.

The push for an air law climaxed when a special congressional investigating committee headed by Representative Florian Lampert and the President's Aircraft Board chaired by Dwight Morrow returned similar findings about government regulation of civilian flying. They rejected the idea of a unified department of aeronautics and recommended the Department of Commerce assume responsibility for assuring the safety of commercial aviation and for promoting the industry. MacCracken played a crucial role in guaranteeing that the pending legislation concentrated authority in the hands of the central government, despite critics who insisted regulatory responsibility be decentralized. After Senator Hiram Bingham introduced a bill largely shaped by states' rights concerns, MacCracken persuaded Representative Schuyler Merritt and Representative James Parker to work for legislation giving principal authority to the federal government. To Bingham's chagrin, MacCracken's ploy succeeded, and the Air Commerce Act of 1926 vested most authority for commercial aviation in the federal government. The new act also created the post of assistant secretary of commerce for aeronautics. Secretary Hoover offered the post to Paul Henderson and Hollingshead Taylor but turned to MacCracken when both men refused the job. The new assistant secretary took office on August 11, 1926.

During his three years as assistant secretary, MacCracken left an enduring imprint on aviation regulation in the United States. "The first thing we needed," he later recalled, "was a system of Air Commerce regulations." Aeronautics Branch staff members and attorneys from the department solicitor's office developed a system of rules which MacCracken then submitted to industry representatives for their criticism. This collaborative approach characterized MacCracken's approach to regulation and became an enduring precedent for regulating the aviation industry. Moreover, MacCracken enforced the newly developed rules with a measure of leniency. He often approved waivers of the rules and usually punished violators with a reprimand or a small fine. Only gradually did he move toward tougher enforcement.

The Air Commerce Act did not create any new agencies within the Department of Commerce and provided only $550,000 for aeronautical activities, so the new assistant secretary created the Aeronautics Branch from the resources of existing agencies. In developing the nation's airways, for example, MacCracken and his associates built on the work of the U.S. Air Mail Service. The Air Mail Service had lighted a 2,041-mile route from New York to Salt Lake City, a route which the Air Commerce Act transferred to the Department of Commerce. The Aviation Branch completed the airway to San Francisco, and by 1929 the nation had lighted 10,183 miles spread over 27 airways. The lighted airways system made night flying common in the United States at a time when Europe still approached the idea with caution. In 1928 the branch received the Collier Trophy for its work in this area.

The act charged the Commerce Department with licensing pilots. The requirements stipulated a minimum age of eighteen and U.S. citizenship for industrial, commercial, and transport licenses, and age sixteen and any citizenship for private licenses. Applicants for transport licenses needed 100 hours of solo flight while those in the other classifications needed only 50. The flight test consisted of maneuvering around two pylons 1,500 feet apart, execution of five figure-eights, and three landings. Transport pilots had to demonstrate their ability to handle special emergencies. Secretary Hoover believed the honor of receiving the first license should go to MacCracken, but MacCracken proposed to waive the medical requirements and issue the first license to the world's first pilot, Orville Wright. Only after Wright declined the honor did MacCracken take the license.

The medical examination requirement for pilots gave rise to another enduring feature of government regulation, the designee system. While the military could draw on its own doctors to conduct such exams, the Department of Commerce did not have a staff of physicians. Consequently the branch began to designate private physicians as aviation medical examiners. (MacCracken's father was one such early designee.) Because the regulation of aviation often required the professional skills of people who were not on the staff of the Department of Commerce, the branch quickly applied the designee system to other professionals such as pilots, engineers, and mechanics whose skills were essential to the successful regulation of aviation.

MacCracken also pioneered the use of the type certificate. With only eight people in the Engineering Section of the Aeronautics Branch, the government clearly could not inspect every single plane to determine its airworthiness, so MacCracken focused on the manufacturing process. Instead of inspecting every airplane built, the branch issued certificates covering all aircraft of identical design and construction. Once branch inspectors ascertained the airworthiness of a new aircraft type, they issued a certificate that authorized the manufacturer to produce aircraft of "an exact similarity of type, structure, materials, assembly, and workmanship." This important innovation remains at the heart of federal procedures for certifying aeronautical products.

MacCracken also faced the related problem of determining the airworthiness of aging equipment already in service. World War I surplus equipment posed a special problem. Over one ten-month period reviewed by the Aviation Branch, war-surplus equipment experienced structural failures at twice the rate of newer aircraft. Already suspicious of the airworthiness of those decade-old planes, MacCracken contemplated banning them altogether, but many air transport operators used this equipment extensively, simultaneously creating a lucrative market for suppliers of spare parts needed to keep the planes flying. Industry officials persuaded MacCracken that operators could compete successfully only by updating their equipment. MacCracken decided to determine airworthiness of such planes on a case-by-case basis, and the operators did indeed move toward newer, faster, and more sophisticated aircraft.

Such government regulations rooted in pragmatism and dialogue with the industry fostered dramatic improvements in aviation technology. Aviation Branch engineers did not intervene directly in the design process, but they gave manufacturers wide latitude in developing new equipment. Within three years, the branch issued 390 type certificates for airplanes and 65 for engines. Generally speaking, these increasingly powerful aircraft carried more load with less structure. The changes included closed cockpits, single wings, metal props, and stressed metal skins.

MacCracken also demonstrated a certain flair for promoting the industry. When Charles A. Lindbergh returned from his celebrated flight to Paris, MacCracken and Harry Guggenheim persuaded him to undertake a 48-state tour in the *Spirit of St. Louis*, a tour cosponsored by the Daniel Guggenheim Foundation and the Department of Commerce. Lindbergh traveled 20,000 miles in three months, stumping for airport construction and urging the use of airmail. In March 1928 MacCracken involved Lindbergh in yet another promotional project, namely giving short airplane rides to members of Congress, the Supreme Court, and foreign ambassadors and their families. MacCracken greeted the passengers personally, many of whom would be voting on future appropriations for the Aviation Branch.

Like many federal regulators, MacCracken eventually left government service to return to the industry he had been charged with regulating. On October 1, 1929, he resigned from the Department of Commerce and resumed his lucrative career as an aviation attorney and lobbyist. However, MacCracken soon found himself involved in a controversial effort by the Hoover administration to reshape the commercial aviation industry. Postmaster General Walter Folger Brown wanted transport companies to carry people and goods as well as mail. He saw airmail contracts as a kind of subsidy which would support companies until the public developed the "habit and practice . . . of using aviation in the ordinary affairs of life." Because the existing airmail laws actually discouraged passenger transportation, Brown sought new legislation which would give him the authority to set rates designed to encourage passenger service. In the process Brown would bypass competitive bidding and award contracts based on negotiations with the stronger firms. MacCracken assisted in drafting such a bill, but the measure encountered fierce resistance from Representative M. Clyde Kelly, who strongly opposed the elimination of competitive bidding. MacCracken ultimately negotiated a compromise with Kelly which maintained competitive bidding but gave the postmaster general the authority to extend existing routes. The Air Mail Act of 1930, also known as the Watres Act, became law in April 1930.

Still preferring negotiation over competitive bidding, Brown convened a conference of airmail carriers and a few favored carriers who did not have contracts. The participants elected MacCracken to chair the meeting and met for two weeks in a futile effort to apportion the airmail contracts among themselves. When MacCracken reported to Brown that the meeting was hopelessly deadlocked and invited

him to referee the differences, Brown seized the invitation aggressively, and built routes, assigned contracts, and compelled mergers to shape commercial aviation in accord with his plans. MacCracken's clients generally flourished under the Brown system.

While representing his clients in the tumultuous domestic airmail controversies, MacCracken also worked extensively with the awarding of overseas airmail contracts. Shortly after leaving government service, he accepted the post of chairman of the board of the New York, Rio, and Buenos Aires Line (NYRBA). The company believed that MacCracken's political connections would help it to secure a contract to fly the U.S. airmail along the east coast of South America. Within a year, however, MacCracken helped to engineer a hostile takeover of NYRBA by Pan American Airways, its chief competitor and a particular favorite of Walter Folger Brown. Pan Am obtained the contract NYRBA had sought, and Pan Am head Juan Trippe paid MacCracken $4,000 in legal fees.

The change of presidential administrations in 1933 brought an abrupt shift in MacCracken's fortunes. Air transport operators disgruntled by Brown's policies helped to spark a Senate investigation of his actions. As part of its inquiry the investigating committee, chaired by Hugo Black of Alabama, subpoenaed MacCracken and his papers relating to airmail contracts. Reluctant to comply, MacCracken asked the committee to allow him to contact each of his clients requesting permission to release their files. Black countered that MacCracken's work as a lobbyist was not the sort of lawyer-client relationship which merited confidentiality, but he reluctantly permitted MacCracken to delay complying with the subpoena. With the files still under subpoena, MacCracken and two associates removed material later revealed to pertain to airmail issues. An outraged Hugo Black called on his Senate colleagues to try MacCracken and the others on contempt charges.

MacCracken compounded the gaffe with a bizarre ritual based on his contention that while the Senate could cite him for contempt, only a court could try him. With the other defendants appearing before the Senate as ordered, MacCracken went into hiding. His attorney announced that the accused would surrender himself only in the presence of a judge. Clearly MacCracken would then ask immediately for a writ of habeas corpus. When the Senate adjourned on Friday, however, MacCracken abruptly reappeared, eager to be arrested before the Senate reconvened on Monday. To avoid MacCracken, Senate sergeant-at-arms Chesley Jurney hid until Monday morning, when he arrested MacCracken and delivered him to the Senate. After brief deliberation, the body sentenced MacCracken to ten days in the District of Columbia jail. He continued to resist the Senate's authority, but ultimately the U.S. Supreme Court unanimously rejected MacCracken's appeal and forced him to serve his sentence.

MacCracken emerged from jail with his aviation career at an end. The Air Mail Act of 1934 prohibited companies holding airmail contracts from employing any participants in the 1930 "Spoils Conference" which MacCracken had chaired. The blacklisted MacCracken never worked in aviation again. Deeply hurt by the events of 1934, he nevertheless showed amazing resilience in building a new career as a successful lobbyist for the American Optometric Association. Only in MacCracken's last years did aviation acknowledge the importance of his early contributions. His most notable honor came in 1959, when the organization he had helped

to found, the National Aeronautic Association, awarded him its prestigious Wright Brothers Memorial Trophy in recognition of his role in establishing commercial aviation.

References:
Nick A. Komons, *Bonfires to Beacons: Federal Civil Aviation Policy Under the Air Commerce Act, 1926-1938* (Washington, D.C.: U.S. Department of Transportation, 1978);

Komons, "William P. MacCracken and the Regulation of Civil Aviation," in *Aviation's Golden Age: Portraits from the 1920s and 1930s*, edited by William M. Leary (Iowa City: University of Iowa Press, 1989);

Michael Osborn and Joseph Riggs, eds., *"Mr. Mac:" William P. MacCracken on Aviation, Law, Optometry* (Memphis, Tenn.: Southern College of Optometry, 1970).

Archives:
A substantial body of William P. MacCracken's papers is held by the Herbert Hoover Presidential Library in West Branch, Iowa. Family members hold additional papers. The National Aeronautic Association holds valuable material pertaining to MacCracken as does the National Archives, Record Group 237 (Aeronautics Branch records) and Record Group 28 (Air Mail Service records).

Patrick A. McCarran

(August 8, 1876 - September 28, 1954)

by Donald R. Whitnah

University of Northern Iowa

CAREER: Attorney (1901-1954); representative, Nevada state legislature (1903); district attorney, Nye County, Nevada (1907-1913); associate justice (1913-1916), chief justice, Nevada Supreme Court (1916-1918); U.S. senator (1933-1954).

Patrick Anthony McCarran was born on August 8, 1876, near Reno, Nevada, the son of Irish immigrants. He was valedictorian of his Reno High School class in 1897 and then attended the University of Nevada, dropping out before finishing his senior year but later awarded honorary M.A. and L.L.D. degrees from the university. He married Martha Harriet Weeks, and they had five children. After engaging for several years in farming and sheep raising, he began the study of law. In 1902 he won a seat in the Nevada legislature. But law

was his major interest, and he gained admission to the Nevada bar and practiced for several years in mining boom towns. He served on the Nevada Supreme Court from 1913 to 1918, the last two years as chief justice. He reached his ultimate goal, the U.S. Senate, in 1932 after two unsuccessful attempts in 1916 and 1926. Listed as a Democrat, he really was a fiercely independent conservative who joined Republican conservatives in a bipartisan coalition, opposing many New Deal-Fair Deal domestic programs. In 1933 he attacked the Roosevelt administration's move to reduce veterans' benefits. He also opposed Roosevelt's Supreme Court packing plan of 1937, for which he was never forgiven.

McCarran's prowess increased in the 1940s with chairmanships of the Judiciary Committee and the Appropriations Subcommittee. He boasted of

Patrick A. McCarran

being feared rather than loved on the American political scene. Better known for his zealous anticommunism after World War II and his antics to restrict immigration to the United States, McCarran also contributed heavily to the development of aviation. He sponsored the initial legislation to establish an independent agency that led to the Civil Aeronautics Authority in 1938. Ironically, when running for reelection to the Senate in 1938, he did not emphasize his role in this boon to aviation.

McCarran had for several years understood the battle lines in Washington over control of aviation, particularly the efforts of the Post Office Department, the Interstate Commerce Commission (ICC), and the Department of Commerce to thwart the notion of an independent bureau. He held the support of the Air Line Pilots Association (ALPA) and was quite disgruntled over several air accidents in the winter of 1936-1937. Earlier he joined several colleagues in investigating the Post Office's granting of airmail contracts in 1934.

McCarran long favored the independent control of aviation as a public utility. Roosevelt and Senators Hugo Black and Kenneth McKeller, among others, favored Post Office control. Aviation inter-

ests, particularly United Air Lines, approved McCarran's stance.

In 1938, though Roosevelt ignored McCarran at every turn, the latter's idea became part of the law. In introducing his bill to create the Civil Aeronautics Authority, McCarran stressed repeatedly the role of safety as the key to an improved aviation system. He demanded technical regulation by a strictly monopolistic governmental authority. Aviation was so vital that McCarran even proposed a standing committee in the Senate for it as well as future cabinet status. In answering the opposition favoring ICC control, McCarran characterized that bureau as too overburdened and held that aviation needed a distinct, specialized governing body.

Off the Senate floor McCarran continued to promote aviation regulation, attempting to clarify public confusion over the industry. He claimed there had been too much political interference with aviation, bemoaned the reluctance of investors to plunge into the industry, warned that the United States must act soon to prevent a marked rise in accidents to levels worse than other forms of transportation, cried for states' cooperation with the federal aviation control organization, and urged greater heed to maintenance and airport improvements. Public confidence in aviation could be attained only through thorough regulation. The mystery of aviation finance also had to be clarified. There was no room for the spoils system among regulators. Other legislation was needed to assure federal control over foreign carriers. To his critics, McCarran asserted that he wanted to include private aviation under his proposed controls. He denounced competitive bidding for leading to monopoly and the elimination of smaller operators.

McCarran was annoyed during the 1938 Senate haggling over the fact that government bureaucrats had spent many hours attempting to block his legislation. He particularly resented the Treasury Department. He criticized Senator Harry S. Truman and others for watering down his provision on conflict of interest. He also chafed under the elimination of provisions for annual airline industry audits.

Meanwhile, Senators Truman and Royal Copeland moved against McCarran in the Senate, fearing he would never compromise with competing versions of air-regulation legislation. Particularly upsetting to McCarran was the diminishment of the authority of the president to remove aviation officials. Despite McCarran's vehement opposition to segments of the revised bill, it passed. Truman and Bennett Clark controlled McCarran in the maneuvering to final passage and assured that the new administrator would report to the president.

During World War II McCarran criticized the army's arrogance toward airline regulation. He lamented that the Civil Aeronautics Authority (CAA) did a better job of pilot training than either the navy or the army. He fought to retain for five years after the war the War Training Service but had to settle for a two-year extension, which never really gained funding from the Budget Bureau. In August 1944 McCarran protested the firing of CAA administrator Charles Stanton by holding up for a month the appointment of Theodore P. Wright.

In late 1944 McCarran entered the fray in support of massive airport funding, a campaign that foresaw the explosion of aviation following the war. It resulted in the Federal Airport Act of 1946, a five-year plan for at least $500 million covering both small and large airports. The law originally was set to expire in 1953; McCarran's bill extended it for another five years.

McCarran did not always win funds in Congress for aviation. Also, in his last few years in the Senate he worried over the need of increased funds for CAA testing programs and the threat of foreign lines to American companies. He bemoaned the lack of a national development program for the coming jet age.

McCarran's many contributions to the development of federal aeronautical policy were overshadowed by his strident support of Pan American Airways's efforts to dominate postwar international air routes. In May 1944 McCarran introduced a bill to create "The All-American Flag Line." He envisioned a private company with $1 billion in capital, raised largely through the sale of government bonds, with Pan American owning all of the voting stock. "As Britannia has ruled the waves in the past," McCarran stated in 1945 during hearings on the bill, "it is my ambition that Columbia should rule the air in the future." With critics charging that McCarran confused Columbia with Pan American, the bill went down to defeat.

On September 28, 1954, McCarran went to Hawthorne, Nevada, to give a speech. After finishing his remarks, he stepped down from the platform, collapsed, and died instantly from a massive heart attack.

References:

Jerome E. Edwards, *Pat McCarran: Political Boss of Nevada* (Reno: University of Nevada Press, 1982);

Nick A. Komons, *Bonfires to Beacons: Federal Civil Aviation under the Air Commerce Act, 1926-1938* (Washington, D.C.: U.S. Department of Transportation, 1978);

Stuart A. Rochester, *Takeoff at Mid-Century: Federal Civil Aviation Policy in the Eisenhower Years, 1953-1961* (Washington, D.C.: U.S. Department of Transportation, 1976);

Donald R. Whitnah, *Safer Skyways: Federal Control of Aviation, 1926-1966* (Ames: Iowa State University Press, 1967);

John R. M. Wilson, *Turbulence Aloft: The Civil Aeronautics Administration Amid Wars and Rumors of Wars, 1938-1953* (Washington, D.C.: U.S. Department of Transportation, 1979).

Midway Airlines

by Myron J. Smith, Jr.

Tusculum College

Midway Airlines holds a special place in U.S. commercial airline history. Organized in 1979, it was the first all-jet airline ("new entrant") to be created as a direct result of the Airline Deregulation Act of 1978. It launched low-fare service on November 1 from Chicago's Midway Airport to Cleveland, Detroit, and Kansas City, using three McDonnell-Douglas DC-9-10s. By year's end, the company had boarded 60,000 passengers.

In 1980 Midway flew 461,945 travelers and added five DC-9s to its fleet. As expected in a time of fierce competition, operating expenses exceeded revenues, and the carrier suffered a $4.9 million loss. The financial picture brightened considerably in 1981 despite the Professional Air Traffic Controllers strike. Traffic rose to 748,000, and the route network was stretched to a total of 14 markets. The airline recorded a net profit of $7.5 million on revenues of $73.8 million. In 1982 the three-year-old airline passed the million-passenger mark for the first time; it acquired eight more DC-9s to feed its thriving Midway hub. Recession and toughening competition, however, caused a change in management. After auditors noted the year's meager profit of $346,000, a new team headed by former Federal Express president Arthur C. Bass was brought in to enhance the airline's shrinking profitability.

With the large carriers, led by American Airlines, matching Midway's discount fares, management decided to shift tactics. In an effort to attract business travelers, the airline began a new service, called Midway Metrolink, which featured fine food and extra-wide seating at prices up to 20 percent below the full-coach fare of the major carriers. This new marketing tactic failed to reverse the airline's declining fortunes. Midway recorded record losses of $15 million in 1983 and $22 million in 1984.

Early in 1985, with the airline losing $4 million a month and headed for bankruptcy, Midway's top management changed again. This time, David R. Hinson, one of the company's original investors, was invited to act as both president and board chairman. In an effort to curb losses, Hinson cut both routes and frequencies in the airline's nine-state service region. At the same time, he returned to Midway's no-frills roots. The results were gratifying. After cutting losses in 1985, the airline turned a profit of $6.9 million in 1986, marking its best economic performance in five years.

Following a two-year policy of cautious expansion from its Midway Airport hub, the airline in 1989 was ready to embark on a more ambitious course. Early in the year, it ordered 74 new jets from McDonnell-Douglas at a cost of $2 billion. In September it purchased for $210 million a package of assets from financially troubled Eastern Air Lines that included gates and facilities at Philadelphia, routes from Philadelphia to Toronto and Montreal, and 16 DC-9-30s. Shortly thereafter, it began nonstop service from Philadelphia to seven Florida cities. At decade's end Midway and American West stood as the only surviving airlines of any size that were started following the Airline Deregulation Act of 1978. However, the pressures of expansion combined with the effects of recession in 1991 caused losses to mount, and Midway ceased operations on November 13, 1991.

References:

R. E. G. Davies, *Airlines of the United States since 1914*, revised edition (Washington, D.C.: Smithsonian Institution, 1982);

J. A. Donoghue, "Midway Airlines Goes for the Business Market," *Air Transport World*, 20 (June 1983): 40-44;

Don Knoles, "Midway's Bold Effort to Set Aviation History," *Airline Executive*, 3 (October 1979): 28-31;

Agis Salpukas, "Midway Finds a Niche by Trial and Error," *New York Times*, November 23, 1987, pp. D1, D10;

Jan W. Steenblik, "The 'Darling of Deregulation' Grows Up," *Air Line Pilot*, 57 (May 1988): 10-15, 49.

Mohawk Airlines

by William M. Leary

University of Georgia

Mohawk Airlines started out as an air taxi service in upstate New York. C. S. Robinson, an inventor, businessman, and owner of Robinson Aviation, decided toward the end of World War II that there was a need for air service between Ithaca and New York City. On April 6, 1945, he established the Airline Division of Robinson Aviation and began to fly occasional trips between the two cities with three-passenger Fairchild F-24s. Encouraged by the traffic, in February 1948 he obtained a temporary certificate from the Civil Aeronautics Board (CAB) as a local service carrier to conduct scheduled operations over the route.

Robinson Airlines, as it was renamed, began scheduled service on September 18, 1948. Acquiring four DC-3s, it quickly expanded its Ithaca-based routes throughout the state. In 1950 it added a major north-south route between Watertown and New York City, together with an important east-west line between Buffalo and Albany. By 1955, when it received permanent certification, Mohawk Airlines (as it had become on January 1, 1953) served 28 cities, carried nearly a quarter-million passengers, and had operating revenues in excess of $3 million. That same year it introduced Convair 240s on its routes, becoming the first local service carrier to fly pressurized aircraft.

Mohawk's growth continued over the next ten years. Under the aggressive leadership of Robert E. Peach, it secured routes to Detroit and Erie in 1956, then obtained nonstop authority between New York City and Syracuse in 1957, placing it in di-rect competition with American Airlines on this important short-haul route. In 1961 Mohawk took over routes in eastern Vermont and New York, including a major line from New York City to Albany, that had been operated by Colonial Airlines.

Mohawk led the local service airlines into the jet age when it placed four BAC One-Elevens into service on its main routes in July 1965. The following year, it introduced turboprop Fairchild-Hiller FH-227s on its secondary routes. In 1969 Mohawk carried 2.6 million passengers in its fleet of 23 BAC One-Elevens and 17 FH-227s. Unfortunately, it also lost $4.7 million as it competed with trunk carriers while struggling to pay for its new equipment.

The airline's losses continued into 1970. In 1971 it approached economic collapse as a result of a 154-day strike by its pilots. On April 12, 1972, following CAB approval, Allegheny Airlines, the nation's largest local service carrier, acquired through merger the weakened Mohawk.

References:

R. E. G. Davies, *Airlines of the United States since 1914,* revised edition (Washington, D.C.: Smithsonian Institution, 1982);

George C. Eads, *The Local Service Airline Experiment* (Washington, D.C.: Brookings Institution, 1972);

Robert E. Peach, *Four-Seaters to Fan Jets: The Story of Mohawk Airlines* (New York: Newcomen Society in North America, 1964).

C. Bedell Monro

(February 26, 1901 - June 30, 1972)

by William F. Trimble

Auburn University

CAREER: Airline executive (1920s-1940s); president, Pennsylvania Air Lines (1934-1936); president, Pennsylvania-Central Airlines (1936-1947).

Few events sparked more controversy in the early airline business than the cancellation of airmail contracts by President Franklin D. Roosevelt in 1934. Coming on the heels of the special investigating committee chaired by Senator Hugo Black, the airmail cancellation led to a shakeup in the executive leadership positions of the nation's airlines. In 1930 Postmaster General Walter Folger Brown initiated his notorious "spoils conferences," which had divided up airmail contracts among a handful of select companies. The Black-McKellar Act, passed in the wake of the 1934 airmail cancellations, stipulated that all those who had attended the spoils conferences would have to relinquish their positions before their companies could bid on new contracts. Consequently, George R. Hann turned over his position as president of Pittsburgh Aviation Industries Corporation (PAIC), a holding company and owner of Pennsylvania Air Lines, to C. Bedell Monro, secretary and director of the company.

Charles Bedell Monro was born in Pittsburgh on February 26, 1901, to William L. Monro and Violet K. Bedell Monro. W. L. Monro, president of the American Window Glass Company, was one of the wealthiest and most prominent men in the city. C. Bedell Monro went to the right schools—Shady Side Academy in Pittsburgh, Phillips-Exeter Academy in New Hampshire, and Harvard, where he received his bachelor's degree in 1923. He received a master's degree in English from the University of Pittsburgh in 1926, and for a time taught at the university. During this time he coauthored a boys' adventure book, *The Quest of the Moonfish*.

Monro became interested in aviation in 1928 when he and Frederick R. Crawford attempted to raise $150,000 to establish a passenger airline be-

C. Bedell Monro

tween Pittsburgh and New York. The preliminary work of Monro and Crawford impressed George Hann, who invited them to join with him in the stock subscription that resulted in the creation of PAIC later in the year. Until the airmail cancellation crisis of 1934, Monro worked closely with Hann as PAIC acquired Pennsylvania Air Lines and the lucrative airmail contract between Washington and Cleveland via Pittsburgh. In accordance with the Black-McKellar legislation, PAIC divested itself of the airline operation, which reorganized into Pennsylvania Air Lines and Transport Company (PAL).

As PAL's president, Monro shepherded the company through the difficult 1930s. An early major disappointment was the loss of the airmail contract on the Washington-Cleveland route to Central Air Lines, formed in Pittsburgh by Theodore

Taney and James G. Condon with important financial backing from John D. and Richard W. Coulter. Fortunately, PAL acquired the airmail contract on the route between Detroit and Milwaukee, which guaranteed a modicum of federal subsidy over the next two years. In the meantime Monro did all he could to bolster PAL's precarious financial position by emphasizing passenger operations. Cut-rate fares and bigger, faster Boeing 247Ds helped attract customers on the crucial Washington-Cleveland corridor. Substantial increases in passenger volume and revenue failed to keep the company from losing money in 1935 and 1936.

Merger with Central Air Lines was the only logical solution to PAL's financial problems. Competing over parallel routes with PAL, Central, too, was bathed in red ink. But Central's leaders resisted Monro's suggestions for a buyout until they lost financial control of the airline to Sigmund Janas of American Airways. In the meantime PAL quietly bought Janas's Central stock for what Monro said was "a nice sum" until it was in a position to force the merger. The result of the merger was Pennsylvania-Central Airlines Corporation (PCA), organized in 1936.

It was some time before PCA realized the full benefits of the acquisition of its chief competitor. Despite the consolidation of its headquarters and maintenance and operations facilities at Pittsburgh's Allegheny County Airport and the inauguration of new routes in 1937 and 1938, the company continued to lose money. Not until 1940, following the acquisition of DC-3s, did PCA start to show modest profits, and these quickly turned into losses the following year. Compounding the company's woes were fatal accidents in 1940 and 1941. As did all airlines, PCA fared much better during the war years. With lucrative military air cargo contracts and, in 1945, receipt of a route between New York and Chicago, PCA consistently made profits, which in turn allowed the order of new Douglas four-engine DC-4s. In 1946 PCA became the first airline to inaugurate domestic DC-4 service.

World War II brought other changes to PCA. Because of increasingly cramped conditions at Allegheny County Airport, the airline in 1942 moved its headquarters and operations and maintenance base to Washington, D.C.'s National Airport. Not only did National have more room, but Washing-

ton was more conveniently located as PCA expanded its routes southward. PCA also changed its name, becoming PCA-The Capital Airline in 1944. (In 1948 PCA was dropped altogether, and the company became Capital Airlines.)

Monro's grip on PCA's management began to loosen as the airline vied with the "Big Four" trunk carriers in the immediate postwar period. New equipment and longer routes did little to change PCA's essentially regional orientation or its short-haul route structure. Monro made repeated entreaties before the Civil Aeronautics Board for more lucrative connections to offset losses on PCA's marginal feeder routes but received no satisfaction. The results were inevitable, as the airline piled up huge deficits in 1946 and 1947. Although the public record is not clear, it seems PCA's board split into two camps on the question of retaining Monro in the top position. Rather than deepen the internal crisis and further jeopardize the airline, Monro in October 1947 announced his resignation, turning the presidency over to James H. Carmichael, formerly executive vice-president. Monro retained his seat on the board of directors and continued as a minority stockholder until the 1961 merger of Capital and United.

After leaving PCA, Monro founded United Services Associates, a management consulting firm in Washington. He died of a heart attack on June 30, 1972. Neither flier nor financier, Monro entered the airline industry through family connections and considerable personal wealth. Once in, however, he was instrumental in the decision making that transformed Pennsylvania-Central from a small regional carrier into an airline that narrowly missed becoming a major competitor on the national scene.

References:
"Air Merger." *Bulletin Index* (Pittsburgh) 109 (October 29, 1936): 21-22;
Frank C. Harper, *Pittsburgh of Today: Its Resources and People*, volume 4 (New York: American Historical Society, 1931); p. 401;
William F. Trimble, *High Frontier: A History of Aeronautics in Pennsylvania* (Pittsburgh: University of Pittsburgh Press, 1982);

Unpublished Document:
A scrapbook of C. Bedell Monro is in the possession of Mrs. C. Bedell Monro, Sumner, Maryland.

Morrow Board

by David D. Lee

Western Kentucky University

In 1925, responding to strong criticism of government aviation policy expressed by Gen. Billy Mitchell and to growing demands from the industry for effective federal regulation, President Calvin Coolidge appointed the President's Aircraft Board to "study the best means of developing and applying aircraft in national defense." Although a House Select Committee chaired by Representative Florian Lampert had been studying aviation for several months, Coolidge feared the committee would support Mitchell and other "air power" advocates in recommending that a British-style department of aeronautics take responsibility for both military and civilian aviation, an approach the president opposed. Coolidge hoped to preempt the Lampert committee with a report from his own blue ribbon panel.

The board's nine members included industry representative Howard Coffin of the Hudson Motor Company and the National Aeronautic Association; legislators Hiram Bingham (the only flier on the board), James S. Parker, and Carl Vinson; engineer William Durand of the American Society of Mechanical Engineers and the National Advisory Committee for Aeronautics; military officers Rear Adm. Frank Fletcher and Maj. Gen. James G. Harbord; and Judge Arthur C. Denison of the Sixth Circuit Court of Appeals. All but Vinson were Republicans. Coolidge named his longtime friend Dwight W. Morrow of the House of Morgan to chair the group despite Morrow's protests that he knew nothing of flying. Morrow had received a note about such an assignment from Coolidge in March 1925, but he heard nothing further about the appointment until he read of it in a newspaper on September 13. Official notification from Coolidge arrived the next day. The energetic secretary of commerce, Herbert Hoover, believed he had persuaded Coolidge to appoint the board, a dubious assertion, but he did play an important part in persuading his reluctant fellow cabinet members, Secretary of War Dwight Davis and Secretary of the Navy Curtis Wilbur, to accept an investigation of military aviation by the independent engineers of the Aircraft Board.

The "Morrow Board" conducted a thorough inquiry into all facets of aviation. Although charged specifically with considering the role of aviation in national defense, the board concluded, as Morrow put it, that because commercial aviation was "one of the backgrounds of national defense that subject is properly one that it wants to include within its studies." Between September 21 and October 16, 1925, it heard 99 witnesses including the outspoken Billy Mitchell, recently demoted to colonel for publicly criticizing his superiors. Morrow shrewdly permitted Mitchell to talk at such great length that the officer's points vanished in some five droning hours of testimony spread over two days.

Much more effective was the blunt, concise Hoover who came "primed with facts," according to the *New York Times,* to state his views on government establishment of airways, federal licensing of pilots and aircraft, and local sponsorship of airports. "Without such services. . . ," Hoover stated, "aviation can only develop in a primitive way." Regarding Mitchell's charges of inadequate air defense, he expressed his conviction that strong commercial aviation would bolster national security while keeping the cost to the government low. "With this minimum extension of government activity," he concluded, "we can secure a commercial aviation in the United States without subsidy."

As Coolidge had anticipated, the Morrow Board rejected the idea of a single aeronautics department. In its report to Coolidge on November 30, 1925, the panel recommended that civilian aviation be supervised by the Department of Commerce through a new bureau of air navigation administered by an assistant secretary for aeronautics.

Members of the Morrow Board with military escorts at Mitchell Field, Long Island, October 1925 (left to right): Lt. John F. Whiteley, James S. Parker, Arthur C. Dennison, Dwight W. Morrow, Hiram Bingham, Frank F. Fletcher, James G. Harbord, Lt. Col. Benjamin D. Foulois (courtesy of the National Air and Space Museum, Air Force Collection)

Also, the government should continue to expand the airmail service. On the military side, the board acknowledged the growing importance of the airplane in warfare but rejected Billy Mitchell's contention that the United States was in danger of air attack. It suggested that the Air Service be rechristened as the Air Corps, a name change weakly implying a status in the defense hierarchy parallel to that of the Marine Corps. The board also recommended that the Air Corps be represented on the General Staff and that the War Department and the Navy Department each establish an assistant secretary for aeronautics. Endorsing Hoover's contention that a strong aircraft manufacturing industry would bolster national defense, the board emphasized domestic and international aircraft sales as a crucial ingredient in maintaining military preparedness without relying on large government expenditures for air defense.

Almost simultaneous reports from the Lampert committee and a Hoover-established joint committee of the Commerce Department and the American Engineering Council reinforced the Morrow Board report. Both agreed with the board that the Department of Commerce should regulate civilian flying, although the Lampert committee recommended that military aviation be included with other service branches under a department of defense. Collectively, these reports represented a hard-won consensus about federal regulation of civilian flying, a vital step toward a federal air law.

Accordingly, Coolidge endorsed the Morrow report in his annual message to Congress on December 8. Working with Commerce Department solicitor Stephen B. Davis, two board members, Senator Hiram Bingham and Representative James Parker, plus Representative Schuyler Merritt prepared a bill rooted in the Morrow Board recommendations. Hailed as the "legislative cornerstone of the industry," the Air Commerce Act of 1926 became the legal basis for federal regulation of commercial aviation. The Morrow Board report also influenced the Air Corps Act of 1926 which upgraded the Air Service to the Air Corps, created assistant secretaries for air in the War and Navy Departments, and authorized a five-year expansion program.

References:
R. E. G. Davies, *Airlines of the United States since 1914,* revised edition (Washington, D.C.: Smithsonian Institution, 1978);
Nick A. Komons, *Bonfires to Beacons: Federal Civil Aviation Policy Under the Air Commerce Act, 1926-1938*

(Washington, D.C.: U.S. Department of Transportation, 1978);
President's Aircraft Board, *Hearings* and *Report of the President's Aircraft Board* (Washington, D.C.: U. S. Government Printing Office, 1925).

Marion Lamar Muse

(June 4, 1920-   )

by Larry D. Sall

University of Texas at Dallas

CAREER: Accountant, Price, Waterhouse & Company (1942-1943, 1945-1948); U.S. Army Corps of Engineers (1943-1945); secretary-treasurer and chief financial officer, Trans-Texas Airways (1948-1960); assistant vice-president for corporate planning, American Airlines (1960-1962); vice-president for finance, Southern Airways (1962-1965); president, Central Airlines (1965-1967); president and chief executive officer, Universal Airlines (1967-1969); chief executive officer, Southwest Airlines (1971-1978); chairman (1981-1986), chief executive officer, Muse Air (1984-1986).

Airline executive Marion Lamar Muse, better known as Lamar Muse, was born on June 4, 1920, in Houston, Texas. In 1926 his parents, Hiram Marion Muse and Nan Urquhart Muse, moved the family to Palestine, Texas. Besides Lamar, his parents had another son, Kindred, and a daughter, Marian. Hiram Muse was the chief engineer on the Sunshine Special, a passenger train which ran between Palestine and Houston.

Lamar Muse began his education shortly after moving to Palestine, attending Lamar Elementary School and graduating from Palestine High School in 1937. He enjoyed school, and once recalled his father saying that someone would have to burn the school down to get him out. Music was his top priority during his teen years. He played the saxophone, clarinet, and flute so well that he and some friends were able to form a swing band, known as the Leland Adams Dance Band, which attracted a large following in East Texas. In 1937 the band played for John William Bergin, president of Southwestern University of Georgetown, Texas. Bergin wanted a band for his school and offered scholarships to Muse and his fellow musicians. For the next two

Marion Lamar Muse

years Muse played music for Southwestern and in the process discovered his life's professional passion, accounting. In 1939 he transferred to Texas Christian University in Fort Worth for his last year of college.

The following year Muse returned to Palestine and took a truck-driving job with the Pessoney Candy Company, one of the companies he had worked for as a high school student. A few months of truck driving were sufficient to inspire him to seek employment utilizing his accounting skills. In January 1941 he became a cashier with the Fehr Baking Company in Houston.

At the beginning of 1942 Muse joined the accounting firm of Price, Waterhouse & Company in Houston at the urging of influential friends. In 1943 he enlisted in the U.S. Army Corps of Engineers and saw duty in France and Germany. With the end of the war, he returned to Price, Waterhouse, became a senior accountant, and passed the CPA exams. Although the work was enjoyable, he realized that his career would not flourish at Price, Waterhouse, so in 1948 he left that firm and began a career in aviation that would see him revolutionize that industry before he finished.

Trans-Texas Airways (TTA) was one of 13 local service carriers created by the Civil Aeronautics Board (CAB) after World War II. Anywhere from 50 to 80 percent of revenues for these local service carriers came from mail pay, so when Muse joined Trans-Texas Airways as its first secretary-treasurer and chief financial officer, mail pay was his paramount interest.

For the next 12 years Muse made TTA the most profitable carrier in the local service industry. Actually, only TTA and Pacific Air Lines in California made any profit at all; the other 11 local service carriers had net losses. Muse went against prevailing wisdom in the local service industry by opting to receive permanent rates for mail pay based on historic costs. He would renegotiate these rates periodically for future terms of the contract. With a fixed rate for a fixed term, Muse had to keep a sharp eye on company costs and thereby maintained an efficient, cost-effective operation. The other carriers opted for temporary rates determined after the fact. Those rates consisted of net costs minus disallowance, plus a return allowance. Such a system did not promote efficiency.

Muse's success at TTA attracted attention, and in 1960 he was recruited by American Airlines as its first assistant vice-president for corporate planning. Securing appropriate aircraft was one of the issues Muse investigated for American, which was then looking for a replacement for its Convair fleet. Boeing was then developing the 727 and 737. Muse felt the 737 offered the best potential for American, but the flight department preferred the 727-100, a plane which, Muse said, "never made a buck for any-

body." Eventually, the Convairs were replaced by BAC One-Elevens, which Muse felt to be a mistake.

Another matter was the new competition from Eastern Air Lines in the Boston, New York, and Washington, D.C., market. American dominated that market before Eastern introduced a shuttle service which guaranteed the customer a seat without the need of a reservation. Muse wanted to counter Eastern's ploy with a program to fly the customer free if American could not provide a seat within 30 minutes of his desired flight. That would allow American to decide whether to provide extra lifts or to utilize otherwise unsold seats on the next-scheduled flight. American's marketing department proposed instead to upgrade the service on these 45- to 55-minute shuttle flights with a full meal, complete with china, linen napkins, and crystal. Besides exhausting the flight attendants, this program, which was adopted in place of Muse's plan, saw American's market share drop to the point that the routes were conceded to Eastern for several years.

Having lost two battles at American, and not really enjoying life in New York, Muse moved on to Atlanta where he became vice-president for finance for Southern Airways in 1962. As with Trans-Texas, Southern Airways was part of the local service industry, but by 1962 local service carriers were no longer receiving individual temporary or permanent mail rates; instead, the industry negotiated class subsidy rates directly with the CAB. Muse managed for profit, and because he understood the intricacies of the rate formula, he could adjust the costs and scheduling toward that end. Southern Airways was the most profitable carrier in the industry during Muse's tenure from 1962 to 1965.

In 1965, for the first time, Muse assumed managerial control of an airline, Central Airlines of Fort Worth, Texas, and stated that, as a result, his ulcers disappeared. As Central's president, Muse began experimenting with promotions to attract and maintain a good customer base. He realized that an unoccupied airline seat was worthless after the flight took off. So he offered "buy one, get one free" promotions and other incentives, which would be taken up by other carriers in time. However, in October 1967 Central was merged with Frontier Airlines, and Muse went to Detroit to become president, chief executive officer, and a 5 percent owner of Universal Airlines. Universal operated passenger charter flights and negotiated service contracts with the military. Neither area was very stable, and Muse did not regard either with enthusiasm. However, the airline's semi-scheduled cargo operation for the automobile industry did appeal to Muse's organizational talents.

Operating out of Willow Run Airport, Universal developed a "hubbing" operation for the movement of auto parts. This was the first practical application of the soon common practice of bringing cargo or passengers in from various points to a central hub to send them on to their destination. Every night Universal passed an average of 2.5 million pounds of cargo through the Willow Run terminal. Because auto parts vary greatly in weight and size, Muse developed an "either/or" freight rate. Freight was hauled either based on its weight or the space it occupied, whichever was higher. With these innovations in rates and hubbing, Muse turned Universal around from near financial collapse to a $2.8 million profit after one year on the job. The airline made $4.5 million the next year in 1968. Universal's fleet grew to 80 planes, and it became the nation's largest cargo carrier. With the auto industry as its prime customer, Universal's future seemed secure; however, the company's majority owners decided greater success could be had through the use of Boeing's new 747 aircraft. Muse disagreed, feeling the 747 was not cost-effective in Universal's market, and being a man of outspoken conviction, he made his convictions abundantly clear to the other owners. Consequently, Muse was fired; the remaining three years of his contract and his share of the company were settled for cash, leaving him both wealthy and unemployed. Universal went ahead with the 747 plan and filed for bankruptcy within a year. In 1969, at less than fifty years of age, Muse retired to Conroe, Texas, to enjoy his fortune.

While Muse was turning Universal around, back in his home state Rollin King and Herbert Kelleher began laying the foundation of what would become Southwest Airlines. Using Pacific Southwest Airlines in California as a model, they envisioned an airline with a large market solely within the boundaries of Texas and, therefore, outside the jurisdiction of the CAB. Besides the advantage of operating under the Texas Aeronautics Commission instead of the CAB, Kelleher and King hoped to fly out of Love Field in Dallas and Hobby Airport in Houston. Those facilities were closer and more convenient to their respective business districts than the new larger facilities being planned or in operation.

Dallas-Fort Worth (DFW) Airport was the result of a shotgun marriage of the two cities arranged by the CAB, which also obtained agreements from all the CAB-regulated airlines operating out of Love Field and Fort Worth's Greater Southwest Airport to move to DFW as soon as it was open. However, Kelleher and King believed that their company was not bound by this deal since it was not under CAB jurisdiction and not party to an agreement concluded before the creation of their company in March 1967. Texas International and Braniff Airlines disagreed, and for several years Kelleher spent most of his time in court battling these companies as well as the cities of Dallas and Fort Worth. In December 1970 the U.S. Supreme Court refused to review a unanimous decision of the Texas Supreme Court upholding the certification of Southwest Airlines by the Texas Aeronautics Commission. Though lawsuits disputing Southwest Airlines' use of Love Field would continue for several more years, principally pursued by Braniff and Texas International, the Supreme Court's refusal to interfere in the intrastate dispute cleared the way for Southwest to begin operations.

Muse was tiring of early retirement just as King and Kelleher were seeking someone to get Southwest into the air. The three got together, and in January 1971 Muse was made chief executive officer of Southwest Airlines. For the next five-and-a-half months, he worked out the details of getting Southwest into the air. Financing, facilities, equipment, personnel selection, advertising, pricing, and legal matters all had to be arranged before a passenger could be boarded. On June 18, 1971, with these things under control, Southwest Airlines took to the air with three Boeing 737s and revolutionized air travel in Texas. Muse offered air service between Dallas, Houston, and San Antonio at prices that competed with the cost of driving. He kept costs down with a simple ticketing procedure, using cash-register tapes. Meals on flights consisted of peanuts, called Love Bites, for Muse used Love Field's name in every way he could to encourage an informal, festive aura in the operation. There were no assigned seats, which greatly simplified the reservation system. Ground operations concentrated on getting the planes back in the air as quickly as possible, where they produced revenue. Lower weekend and evening fares brought out passengers who had never flown before, traveling for pleasure or family business. The low fares and the festive atmosphere demystified flying, creating an entirely new market. Grandparents flew on weekend visits, as did children from divorced families, weekend vacationers, college students, and others for whom flying had never been a cost-effective alternative to driving or staying at home. Muse trained his personnel to put passengers at ease and dressed the flight attendants in outfits that did not remind them of the boardroom.

These innovations did not go unchallenged by Southwest's two main competitors, Braniff and Texas International (TI). In addition to court challenges, Braniff and TI cut their fares on competing routes. In 1973 Braniff slashed its fare on competing routes to $13, about half the daytime fare on Southwest. Muse's reaction was volcanic, but after editing his remarks, Southwest countered with the slogan: "Nobody's going to shoot Southwest Airlines out of the sky for a lousy $13.00." Braniff's ploy backfired, and it came out looking like a bully, and Southwest's business went to new highs. In addition, passengers willing to pay full fare received a complimentary fifth of premium-quality liquor. For a short time in 1973, Southwest Airlines was the largest distributor of Chivas Regal in Texas. Business travelers charged the flights to their expense accounts and kept the liquor.

The battle with TI culminated over routes to the Rio Grande valley. South Padre Island near Harlingen, Texas, was developing into one of the state's greatest beach attractions, and between Harlingen, Brownsville, and McAllen there was a large enough population to make a profitable market. TI had been cultivating the area for some time before Southwest decided to expand into it. Labor costs were higher for TI than Southwest because TI's pilots belonged to the Air Line Pilots Association and Southwest's pilots did not. Another problem for TI was that all its routes were under CAB jurisdiction, unlike Southwest. This put TI at a great disadvantage in the Rio Grande valley. It felt it had either to expel Southwest or convince the CAB to let it abandon the area. Ultimately, as Southwest expanded to Austin, Midland-Odessa, El Paso, and other Texas markets, TI was forced to reorganize and surrender those markets to Southwest.

By 1978 Southwest Airlines was extremely profitable, a Texas institution thoroughly identified with its flamboyant chief, Muse. The airline was growing rapidly, but Muse, seeking even more opportunities for expansion, put together a plan for an airline to operate out of Chicago's Midway Airport, the Chicago equivalent of Love Field in Dallas. This new venture would be called Midway Air, and Muse would go to Chicago to get it started. After a few years the plan called for Muse's son, Michael, to take over Midway Air, former Dallas city manager George Schrader to become chief executive officer of Southwest Airlines, and, finally, for Muse to become chairman of the board of the holding company that would own both airlines. In the meantime, Muse put a deposit on six new Boeing planes. These actions, Muse's high-profile management style, and his aggressive approach alienated King to the point that the two men regarded each other with considerable hostility. The fight over the expansion plans to Midway and the deposit on the Boeing planes as well as their personal animosity led Muse to attempt to remove King from the board of directors. King lobbied the board prior to a meeting on March 28, 1978, so that instead of ousting King, it accepted Muse's resignation.

After his abrupt termination at Southwest Airlines, Muse took some time to reflect on his future and decided he did not want to solve other people's problems again. Instead he decided to start his own company. In 1981 that company began doing business as Muse Air. Muse raised capital and became chairman of the board while his son, Michael, became chief executive officer. Muse's reputation as an airline mastermind was so widespread that the company's name seemed natural, and there was great optimism among investors that Muse would be able to create another miracle.

Muse Air was to be a nonsmokers' airline which, while offering low fares, would provide assigned, comfortable seating and generally good service. It was one of the most admired airlines of its time by those who flew it, but not enough people did. Competing head-to-head with Southwest Airlines, it became known as "Revenge Air." That struggle took more capital than Muse Air could generate. In 1984 Muse turned to Texas investor Harold Simmons for a cash infusion, but as a condition, Simmons insisted that Muse take over operation of the airline from his son. The next year Southwest bought Muse Air for about $72 million. In 1986 Muse Air became TransStar and finally was liquidated altogether.

One of the problems which beset Muse Air was the cost and built-in bias of the automated reservation services owned by American Airlines and United Air Lines. These services, used by travel agents to book flights, tended to favor the flight availability of the companies which owned them. In addition, they were very expensive to use; Muse felt the costs were arbitrary and excessive.

When asked to summarize his business principles, Muse wrote:

> "Tell the truth, and sell cheap." Somebody more famous than I said that, but I picked it up early in my career as my credo. It incorporates several important principles.
> 1. Practice absolute unimpeachable integrity with every person you come in contact with including investors, suppliers, employees, customers, media, and family.
> 2. Invent, create, manufacture, provide, or market a product or service which a broad market can consume and as a result, be better off for having done so—i.e., a needed product or service which is unusual and not easily duplicated.
> 3. Instill in your associates the same pride and determination you have to produce the very best product, the most efficiently, and at the lowest practical cost.
> 4. Sell that product at a price that produces such a benefit to the user that markets expand exponentially; permitting unit cost improvement that no competitor can match.

Muse married Juanice Gunn of Palestine, Texas, on June 21, 1941. The couple had three children: Diane Quigley, Michael, and Deborah. In 1974 Muse's wife died of cancer. He later married Barbara Deese of Houston and in the process enlarged his family to include Lisa Muse, an adopted daughter, and Cullene Vaughn and Connie Jordan, stepdaughters. As of 1990, Muse had four grandchildren.

References:
James Fallows, "'The Great Airline War,'" *Texas Monthly*, 3 (December 1975): 76-81, 121-145;

"Fasten Your Seat Belts," *Texas Monthly*, 10 (November 1982): 140-142;

Greg Jones, "Is Big Daddy Really Back?" *D Magazine*, 8 (November 1981): 132-135, 197-203;

John Kirkpatrick, "Lamar and Michael Muse," *Dallas Morning News*, June 19, 1983, High Profile section, p. 4;

"Musing on What Might Have Been," *Texas Monthly*, 14 (April 1986): 108-110;

Helen Parmley, "Lamar Muse Ponders Life with Southwest," *Dallas Morning News*, May 4, 1978, p. A6;

Larry D. Sall, Interview with Marion Lamar Muse, Richardson, Texas, May 17, 1990.

Archives:
A file on M. Lamar Muse is in the History of Aviation Collection, University of Texas at Dallas Library, Richardson, Texas.

National Airlines

by George E. Hopkins

Western Illinois University

National Airlines was the creation of George T. Baker, a Chicago-based entrepreneur who bought a local charter operation called the National Airlines Air Taxi System, moved it to Florida, and transformed it into a scheduled airline. The key to this metamorphosis was President Franklin D. Roosevelt's abrupt cancellation of all existing airmail contracts in February 1934. This draconian action came as a result of hearings conducted by Senator (later Supreme Court Justice) Hugo A. Black into the letting of awards in 1930 by Walter Folger

Brown, postmaster general in Herbert Hoover's administration. Alleging fraud, malfeasance, and corruption, Roosevelt nullified the existing airmail contracts and reopened the bidding.

Although the major carriers regained most of their routes, the situation did prove beneficial to local service operators, like Baker, who had neither the equipment nor experience to challenge the established airlines on long-haul operations. But the small aviation entrepreneurs could compete on shorter routes. Airmail subsidy was the key to profitability for all airlines. By underbidding the "ma-

National Airlines Lockheed L-18 Lodestar (courtesy of the National Air and Space Museum)

jors" on a few selected short-haul routes, airlines such as National secured a toehold in the industry.

On October 15, 1934, National began serving the St. Petersburg-Daytona Beach route, using three Ryan monoplanes. The fledgling airline gradually expanded its service to other Florida cities, but it remained essentially an intrastate carrier during the first decade of its existence.

National began to emerge as a trunk airline in February 1944, when it won permission from the Civil Aeronautics Board (CAB) to fly the lucrative New York-Miami route. National was poorly equipped to serve this winter vacation market, since it operated only 17-seat Lockheed Lodestars. Although not as elegant or economic as the DC-3s of Eastern Air Lines, National's main rival on the route, the Lockheeds were used to inaugurate a "show the flag" service while Baker waited for the end of the war and the opportunity to purchase new airplanes.

In February 1946 National began direct, over-water service on the New York-Miami route, using four-engine DC-4s. When Eastern introduced Lock-

heed Constellations in 1947, the aggressive Baker countered with the new pressurized DC-6. The technological battle, part of a larger and bitter rivalry with Eastern, would continue for more than 30 years.

It is ironic that National's breakthrough from a local service to a trunk carrier had come about as an inadvertent gift from Edward V. Rickenbacker, Eastern's president. Always an unlovable curmudgeon, Rickenbacker was known as a fierce Republican partisan and outspoken critic of President Roosevelt and all his works. In a business that depended entirely upon the decisions of government regulators who had been appointed through political processes, overt partisanship of the kind that Rickenbacker displayed could be suicidal. Although there is no direct proof that the Roosevelt administration had influenced the CAB to grant National a share of Eastern's most lucrative market because of Rickenbacker's political views, that possibility cannot be discounted. Certainly, Rickenbacker believed that his airline had been punished, and his bitter feud with Baker, which was both personal and professional, made National a logical instrument of retaliation. And there was a further irony in the affair: Baker was as hostile to Roosevelt and his New Deal as was Rickenbacker.

By 1948, Baker's feisty little airline had won considerable acceptance by the traveling public. Adroit publicity focusing on celebrity patrons had transformed National into "The Airline of the Stars," and its state-of-the-art cabin service contrasted favorably with Eastern's stodginess. Then disaster struck National in the form of a pilots' strike.

The root cause of the strike, many observers believed, was Baker's inveterate antiunionism. He recently had broken the mechanics' union, and the pilots were convinced that they were next. The proximate cause of their walkout was Baker's highhanded firing of a pilot following a minor accident. The lengthy dispute, the longest in the history of the pilots' union, the Air Line Pilots Association (AFL-CIO), lasted from February 3 to November 24, 1948. It damaged National's stature and eroded the gains it had achieved against Eastern. In the end, the pilots won. But the chief cause of victory was not the pilots' mass picketing and boycotts, but pro-labor president Harry S. Truman's surprise reelection in November. Faced with a postelection order from the CAB that threatened to withdraw National's certification and put it out of business (ostensibly because of its poor economic condition), Baker settled with his pilots. Both sides believed that politics had played a crucial role in ending the dispute.

Increased competition from Delta and Northeast Airlines cut into National's profits during the 1950s; however, the company continued to expand, adding important routes to Havana and to the West Coast of the United States in 1961. In 1962 Baker, whose managerial limitations had become increasingly apparent, sold National to Lewis B. Maytag, Jr., former owner of Frontier Airlines.

National's performance remained spotty during the 1960s, largely owing to weaknesses in its route structure and management. Despite several impressive firsts, such as being the first airline to operate jets in domestic passenger service (through an interchange agreement with Pan American World Airways) and the first to fly from Miami to London (in May 1970), the airline's financial position left much to be desired. At various times National had tried to strengthen its route structure by acquiring smaller carriers, but without success.

Inevitably, National became a merger target. Rumored and actual suitors included Northwest Airlines and Frank Lorenzo's Texas Air Corporation. In the end, Pan American won the bidding war. National and Pan Am were logical merger partners, as each brought strengths which tended to cancel the other's weaknesses. On October 26, 1980, National formally ceased to exist, disappearing into the Pan American system.

References:

R. E. G. Davies, *Airlines of the United States since 1914*, revised edition (Washington, D.C.: Smithsonian Institution, 1982);

George E. Hopkins, *The Airline Pilots: A Study in Elite Unionization* (Cambridge, Mass.: Harvard University Press, 1971);

Hopkins, *Flying the Line: The First Half Century of the Air Line Pilots Association* (Washington, D.C.: Air Line Pilots Association, 1982);

Hopkins, "Maybe We Should Help Pan Am," *Washington Monthly*, 8 (September 1976): 53-61;

Robert J. Serling, *From the Captain to the Colonel: An Informal History of Eastern Airlines* (New York: Dial Press, 1980);

Brad Williams, *The Anatomy of an Airline* (Garden City, N.Y.: Doubleday, 1970).

National Air Transport

by William M. Leary

University of Georgia

Organized in response to passage of the Air Mail (Kelly) Act of 1925, National Air Transport (NAT) represented a significant vote of confidence by an important segment of the business community in the future of commercial aviation in the United States. Clement M. Keys, president of the Curtiss Aeroplane & Motor Company, took the lead in raising $2 million from prominent businessmen in New York, Detroit, and Chicago to form an airline that would take advantage of the opportunities presented by the government's new policy to encourage private operation of air transport routes.

Keys and his associates—which included names such as Wrigley, Armour, and Rockefeller—incorporated National Air Transport on May 21, 1925. With an authorized capital of $10 million, the new company was hailed by the press as the "most ambitious attempt to promote air transportation in this country." Howard E. Coffin, a Detroit industrialist who had headed the Aircraft Production Board during World War I, became chairman of NAT; Paul Henderson, known as "father of the night airmail," left his position with the Post Office to take day-to-day charge of the new line as general manager.

When the Post Office awarded the first airmail contracts under the Kelly Act on October 7, 1925, NAT secured CAM-3, which linked Chicago and Dallas. Service along the route, which included five intermediate stops, began on May 12, 1926. The following year, NAT won a heated battle against a company formed by a group of Post Office Air Mail Service pilots and took over the eastern portion of the prized transcontinental route. Using a number of the Post Office's airmen and aircraft, NAT began flying between New York and Chicago on September 1, 1927.

Throughout its existence, NAT emphasized its role as a mail carrier, although it did operate daily passenger service between Chicago and Kansas City between February 1 and September 30, 1928. Mail traffic increased steadily. In 1927, NAT flew 15,125 miles and carried 282,884 pounds of mail; in 1929, the airline flew over 2.6 million miles and carried more than 2 million pounds of mail. Also, under Paul Henderson's leadership, NAT continued in the tradition of technological pioneering that had been established by the Air Mail Service and did important work in the areas of instrument flying, development of radio aids to navigation, and testing of anti-icing equipment.

The year 1930 saw the climax of a bitter proxy battle for control of the airline that was waged between Clement Keys and Frederick B. Rentschler of United Aircraft. Rentschler, whose Boeing Air Transport operated the Chicago-San Francisco portion of the transcontinental route, wanted NAT in order to complete the link between the two coasts. On March 31, Rentschler scored a major victory when he acquired a one-third interest in NAT from the airline's Chicago backers. On May 7, he completed the purchase of the company. NAT flew as a separate division of the United Air Lines system until July 1, 1931, at which time United's component airlines lost their individual identities.

References:

Paul T. David, *The Economics of Air Mail Transportation* (Washington, D.C.: Brookings Institution, 1934);

R. E. G. Davies, *Airlines of the United States since 1914*, revised edition (Washington, D.C.: Smithsonian Institution, 1982);

Henry Ladd Smith, *Airways: The History of Commercial Aviation in the United States* (New York: Knopf, 1942).

National Transportation Safety Board

by Robert Burkhardt

Lewes, Delaware

The first federal law dealing with air accidents was the Air Commerce Act of 1926. As part of his duties under this law, the secretary of commerce was authorized to "investigate, record and make public the causes of accidents in civil air navigation." Several years passed before the secretary decided to formalize his agency's investigations. This inactivity did not go unnoticed by Congress. When crashes were investigated, congressmen were quick to criticize both the poor quality of the investigators and the less-than-objective reports that they issued.

In the case of one accident—that of a DC-2 in Missouri on May 6, 1935—Congress became directly involved in the investigation, not only because it had lost one of its own, Republican senator Bronson M. Cutting of New Mexico, but also because there was strong anti-New Deal sentiment in the legislature and many senators and representatives were dissatisfied with the Franklin D. Roosevelt administration's regulation of the infant air transport industry under the Air Commerce Act.

Earlier air crashes involving prominent persons, such as the accident in 1931 that killed Notre Dame football coach Knute Rockne and the one that claimed the life of humorist Will Rogers, added fuel to the congressional fires. Amendments to the Air Commerce Act in 1934 and 1937 considerably strengthened the authority of Commerce Department investigators, who were given the power to issue subpoenas and to examine witnesses under oath. An important amendment that helped bring out the facts about air crashes was a prohibition against the use of government accident reports in civil suits.

In the late 1930s air crashes continued to make headlines and spur congressional and administration tinkering. The spectacular explosion of the dirigible *Hindenburg* in 1937, for example, led to the 1938 passage of the Civil Aeronautics Act, which established a semi-independent Civil Aero-

nautics Authority (CAA) and placed within it an independent Air Safety Board. Although nominally part of the CAA, the board members were all to be presidential appointees, one of whom by law had to be an active pilot. However, having an independent agency operating within the CAA—with no clear division of responsibilities for safety-rule making—led quickly to internal conflicts and to further congressional action.

In 1940 Congress separated rule making from accident investigation responsibilities by establishing two independent agencies: the Civil Aeronautics Board (CAB) for economic rule making and accident investigation, and the Civil Aeronautics Authority for safety regulation. Then, with war clouds gathering, President Roosevelt by executive order reorganized the two agencies, abolishing the CAA's Air Safety Board and replacing it with a Bureau of Safety within the CAB.

The National Transportation Safety Board as it was constituted at the start of the 1990s was created by the Transportation Act of 1966. It began operating in April 1967 with a nucleus staff drawn almost entirely from the CAB's Bureau of Safety, transferred—along with the necessary funding—by the 1966 act to the NTSB. The first five members of the NTSB, all promptly confirmed by the Senate, were former CAB chairman Joseph J. O'Connell, Jr., Oscar M. Laurel, Louis M. Thayer, John M. Reed, and Francis H. McAdams. O'Connell, a former chairman of Lake Central Airlines as well as the CAB's chairman when it was responsible for air safety investigations, was particularly well qualified.

The Senate also strongly supported Francis H. McAdams, a former navy pilot and CAB member as well as an attorney who had specialized in aircraft accident claims. Thayer, too, was well qualified, bringing to the board long years of experience in the U.S. Coast Guard, where he had worked on maritime accident investigations, retiring as rear admiral. By approving members like O'Connell and McAdams, and in transferring the CAB's air accident investigations unit intact to the new NTSB, Congress was also endorsing the investigative methods and procedures developed by the CAB's highly skilled accident investigation unit. These techniques, said Congress, were to be expanded and applied to rail, highway, marine, and pipeline accidents. But where the CAB's Bureau of Safety made its recommendations and presented its conclusions directly to the CAB, which then had the authority to decide whether or not to make these findings public, all of the NTSB's findings were to be placed on record for public inspection and comment.

The 1966 act placed the NTSB within the Department of Transportation (DOT) for housekeeping purposes. But the DOT was also responsible for administering the Federal Aviation Administration (FAA), and the FAA was all too frequently—at least for the DOT's taste—found by the NTSB to be responsible, to greater or lesser degrees, for air accidents. Soon a conflict of interest developed. The Richard M. Nixon White House did not want one of its DOT agencies criticizing another in public. The belief that the NTSB was somehow not a "team player" also reflected in appropriations requests, which had to clear both the DOT and the White House Office of Management and Budget. The result was that, while the NTSB's workload expanded, its annual working funds remained constant, or were even cut back. Efforts by the Nixon White House to pack the board with members who could be depended on to be more responsive to the party line resulted in long confirmation delays and outright congressional rejection of nominees.

Reports of undue White House influence over the NTSB compelled Congress to pass the Independent Safety Board (ISB) Act of 1974. This law severed all NTSB ties to the DOT. While the president still had the authority to make nominations to fill NTSB vacancies, the new law took away from him the unilateral right to designate the board's chairman, who thereafter had to be confirmed by the Senate. The law also attempted to correct a loophole in the old law that had allowed federal agencies to ignore NTSB safety recommendations. Under the ISB Act, non-DOT federal agencies could still disregard the NTSB, but DOT agencies were required to respond to NTSB safety recommendations in writing within 90 days.

To keep the Office of Management and Budget (OMB) from intimidating the NTSB budget process, Congress also decreed that all NTSB budget requests should also be sent to the appropriate congressional committee for its information. Low funding levels continued, however, making it necessary for the NTSB to continue to delegate to the FAA the job of investigating most private-plane accidents. Although Congress often tried to help by appropriating more money than the OMB would allow the board, the NTSB continued into the 1990s to be understaffed, with only about 325 full-time employees. In contrast, the budget and staff of the DOT's National Highway Traffic Safety Administration—which does not arouse the kind of executive branch resentment the NTSB does—is about ten times as large.

One reason the NTSB can get pushed around by the White House is that the board has no constituency in the way the Department of Agriculture has the farmers behind it or the Department of Transportation can count on the support of the airlines and the railroads. Since the NTSB's findings often identify problems in the safety programs of transportation organizations, it not only has few supporters, but it also frequently makes enemies. The airlines seldom appreciate the adverse publicity they get from NTSB hearings and recommendations. The FAA almost always resents NTSB criticisms of its controllers, maintenance inspectors, and its air traffic control procedures. Of course, no airline pilot likes it when the board finds "pilot error" to be a factor in an accident. And the Air Line Pilots Association objects to the public release of the transcripts of cockpit voice recorders.

In its own publications, the NTSB makes no apologies for its role as a transportation safety advocate. Nor does the board make anything of the fact that it is a politically oriented agency, operating under a law that says no more than three of its five members may be of the same political party. Administrations after Nixon's continued to try to pack the board with "independents" who were active, long-term supporters of the president's party.

Congress, particularly if it is controlled by the Democrats when a Republican is in the White House, does not take that kind of political base stealing quietly. In 1985 the Senate rejected two of President Ronald Reagan's three nominees to the board. The third nominee, John K. Lauber, had as strong a set of credentials for the job as anyone who had previously served. Lauber had a doctorate in psychology, was a recognized expert on human factors contributing to air accidents, and, at the time he was nominated, was serving as chief of the Aeronautical Human Factors Research Office at the NASA Ames Research Center. He was enthusiastically supported for NTSB membership by several aviation organizations, including the politically powerful Aircraft Owners and Pilots Association.

In addition to the periodical battle between the president and the Senate over the qualifications of nominees to the NTSB, every two years the president is called upon to designate one of its members to be chairman, subject to Senate confirmation. This might seem a routine matter, but it has often given rise to a great deal of lobbying on the part of both NTSB members and congressmen who have been induced to back one or another member for those key posts. The chairman is in effect the chief operating officer of the board. He is the decision maker regarding personnel changes, budgets, reorganizations, and work assignments.

While air accidents dominate the board's workload, accidents involving surface modes—maritime, highway, railroad, and pipeline—are equally important. A third function of the board is to act on appeals from FAA license revocation actions. These appeals are heard by the NTSB's administrative law judges—a procedure taken over from the CAB. The general counsel's office also has authority to represent the board in the U.S. courts on appeals of board rulings on airman license actions and also on appeals of decisions made by the commandant of the U.S. Coast Guard. While the general counsel and his staff are seldom involved in these court appeals, they do prepare most of the board's final comments on legislation pending in Congress.

With a staff of about 200, the Office of Aviation Safety makes up the largest part of the NTSB. As part of its aviation accident investigation work, the office operates technical laboratories to prepare readouts from flight data recorders and cockpit voice recorders, which are required by the FAA to be aboard all large transport aircraft, and, since October 1991, all commuter aircraft. The office also operates its own metallurgical laboratory to study the effect of metal fatigue and other mechanical failure in transport accidents.

The NTSB also deals with "intermodal" safety problems, such as the transport of hazardous materials by surface or air. The board has investigated everything from natural gas pipeline leaks to military bomb explosions. It is also an active participant in investigations of overseas air accidents, almost always when U.S.-manufactured aircraft are involved but often also at the invitation of non-U.S. investigators who want the benefit of the board's knowledge and experience. The NTSB also produces special studies that involve more than one mode. And, while it usually takes a collegial approach to its work, members frequently publish papers and deliver speeches.

The NTSB has a remarkably high rate of turnover in both members and staff. A small part of this results from the fact that the board has had its share of members and staff who have been less than wise in their actions or their public statements. One member, for example, was not confirmed for a second term when it was disclosed that she had owned stock in an airline that was the subject of an accident investigation. And one board chairman was not reappointed after he publicly took issue with the DOT on the advisability of making the NTSB wholly independent of the DOT. This conflict between the board and the DOT and the White House received a public airing by the Senate during the debate over separating the NTSB from the DOT in 1974.

As part of its 1974 investigation into allegations that the Nixon White House had threatened to "discipline" the Republican members of the board if they continued to support independence from the DOT, a formal letter of inquiry was sent to each member by the chairman of the Senate Committee on Commerce, Science and Transportation. All the members denied that they were subjected to such discipline but, acting on the political maxim that where there was so much smoke there must be at least a small fire, Congress passed the ISB Act. Congress did not want to free the board completely from the president's fiscal controls, however, so the NTSB's annual budget requests continued to be processed by the OMB, although they also required concurrent approval by Congress.

Some of the NTSB's difficulties can be attributed to the absence of an enforcement capacity. Since it is powerless to enforce its recommendations, it must rely on "jawboning" if it wants to have any effect on the real world of transport safety. This means that dealing with the media—particularly television—is an important part of the board's job. Since the media prefers to deal with a single individual in authority, the NTSB chairman and—particularly—the head of the accident investigations "go-team" (the job rotates among the members) are forced to operate in the glare of the television lights.

Appearing on the evening news program discussing the great air crash of the day can be heady stuff to any politician. It can also arouse concern, if not hostility, from officials in the White House as well as on Capitol Hill. In a June 1988 article in *Air Transport World*, Joan M. Feldman was critical of two NTSB chairmen, James King and James Burnett, for deviating from what she called the NTSB's traditional "low-profile, studied, technical approach" to adopt a "high-profile, shoot-from-the-hip public stance."

When, after the delay of a year and a half, NTSB member James L. Kolstad was named to replace James Burnett as chairman in 1990, a staff reorganization was ordered and a new head of the office of Aviation Safety was appointed from outside the agency. This new air safety chief was recruited from the FAA, which drew a succinct critical comment from ex-chairman Burnett: "Put-

ting all of our resources into one aviation czar and bringing in someone from the Department of Transportation to head it is not a good idea."

References:
Joan M. Feldman, "Safety by Grandstanding," *Air Transport World* (June 1988);
Richard J. Kent, Jr., *Safe, Separated, and Soaring: A History of Federal Civil Aviation Policy, 1961-1972* (Washington, D.C.: U.S. Department of Transportation, 1980);
Nick A. Komons, *Bonfires to Beacons: Federal Civil Aviation Policy under the Air Commerce Act, 1926-1938* (Washington, D.C.: U.S. Department of Transportation, 1978);
Komons, *The Cutting Air Crash: A Case Study in Early Federal Aviation Policy* (Washington, D.C.: U.S. Department of Transportation, 1973);
Edmund Preston, *Troubled Passage: The Federal Aviation Administration During the Nixon-Ford Term, 1973-1977* (Washington, D.C.: U.S. Department of Transportation, 1987);
John R. M. Wilson, *Turbulence Aloft: The Civil Aeronautics Administration Amid Wars and Rumors of Wars, 1938-1953* (Washington, D.C.: U.S. Department of Transportation, 1979).

Orvis M. Nelson

(March 18, 1907 - December 2, 1976)

by Roger D. Launius

National Aeronautics and Space Administration

CAREER: Technician (1927-1929), pilot, U.S. Army Air Corps (1932-1935); pilot, United Air Lines (1935-1946); president and general manager, Transocean Air Lines (1946-1960); contract pilot (1960-1966); aviation promoter (1966-1976).

Orvis M. Nelson founded one of the most significant and unusual airlines of the immediate post-World War II era. Transocean Air Lines emerged as Nelson's brainchild while he was flying during World War II as a pilot for United Air Lines, under contract with the War Department's Air Transport Command. While crossing over the vast expanses of the Pacific Ocean, Nelson realized that the future development of the region was tied to the expansion of commercial aviation. He achieved his goal of starting an airline in 1946, and for the next 14

years Transocean Air Lines plied the world's airways, conducting charter flights and operating as a subcontractor for other carriers. Nelson battled bias and business rivalry during the course of his company's operation, and eventually succumbed in 1960 to the federal regulations imposed on supplemental carriers. He did not live to see the deregulation of the airlines in 1978, although he surely would have been pleased with the decision—even though it came too late for Transocean.

Orvis Marcus Nelson was born in Tamarack, Minnesota, on March 18, 1907. Growing up in the lumbering business of the upper Midwest, he attended school only irregularly. Inspired by Charles Lindbergh's epic transatlantic flight in 1927, Nelson joined the U.S. Army Air Corps, serving as a technician during the aerial survey of the Philippine

Orvis M. Nelson (courtesy of Arue Szura)

Islands. But he soon grew unhappy with this job, disappointed because he was not able to fly as much as he wanted. In 1929 he purchased his remaining time (a common practice), left the military, and enrolled in tiny Franklin College in Indiana, where he received a degree in mathematics in 1932. Still wanting to fly, he reenlisted in the Army Air Corps and entered flight training, graduating from Kelly Field in October 1933.

Nelson served as a military pilot for two years, assigned much of that time to the 11th Bombardment Squadron at March Field, California. After flying the mail with the Army Air Corps, Nelson resigned his commission on July 1, 1935, and went to work for United Air Lines. Flying in DC-2s and DC-3s during the latter part of the 1930s, Nelson built a reputation as a reliable, capable, and conscientious pilot. After the United States entered World War II, he was sent by United to fly defense-related missions in Alaska under contract to the Air Transport Command. Later, he transferred to the California-Hawaii route, in the process seeing for the first time the vast potential of air transportation in the Pacific Basin.

Even before this realization, his fellow pilots acknowledged Nelson's leadership by choosing him in 1942 as first vice-president of the Air Line Pilots Association. Not long thereafter, he became ALPA's chief representative in discussions with management and government officials. One of the issues he negotiated was the question of whether airline pilots should continue to fly as civilians under contract to the military or be commissioned in the Army Air Forces. The outcome was decided in favor of maintaining them as airline employees, and Nelson and his fellow pilots flew throughout the war in airline rather than Army Air Forces uniforms.

In August 1945, while stranded on Okinawa during a typhoon, Nelson and some other United pilots began to talk about the future. Holed up in a tent as torrential rains and high winds swirled around them, they concluded that it would be years before the Japanese would be able to run their own airline and that it would be lucrative for United to extend its operations to the Orient. If United was unwilling to take this chance, some enterprising men should step in and take advantage of the opportunity. The United pilots at this session—Sid Nelson, Harry Huking, Sherwood Nichols, and Nelson—agreed that they would do the job if United declined. They even came up with a name for the proposed airline: ONAT, for Orvis Nelson Air Transport Company.

Although the idea might have been dreamed up over a few drinks during a Pacific typhoon, Nelson and the others were serious about pursuing it. Nelson later met with United leaders and argued that the airline should open a Far Eastern division. When he could not persuade them, he returned to the line and flew domestic routes for United during the winter of 1945-1946. His attempt to convince United of the Pacific's potential, however, had not fallen on completely deaf ears. On March 9, 1946, Jack Herlihy, United's vice-president for operations, asked Nelson if he would be interested in acting as a subcontractor for United to operate a military airlift route between San Francisco and Hickham Field, Hawaii. There was one big catch: flying had to begin within ten days. Nelson jumped at the opportunity. On March 18, 1946, ONAT got its start as an unincorporated firm, flying the contract missions with surplus C-54s. The financial arrangements assured solvency for Nelson's first airline venture, resulting in initial profits that ran as high as $2,000 a day. Later, on June 1, 1946, ONAT was incorporated as Transocean Air Lines (TOA), with headquarters at Oakland, California. Nelson owned 27 percent of the company's stock.

Nelson soon proved to be an air transport entrepreneur with considerable imagination and flair. He quickly developed a special relationship with Philippine Air Lines that allowed TOA to subcontract for regular charter flights between San Francisco and Manila. On July 23, 1946, a TOA DC-4 named *Taloa-Manila Bay* inaugurated the contract with Nelson at the controls and his wife, Edith, serving as stewardess. Aboard were 35 passengers and a small amount of cargo. Island-hopping across the Pacific, Nelson encountered difficulties at every turn. He later recalled: "Whether the difficulties could be laid to obstructionism by some of our competitors in the Pacific or just the usual official red tape, I can't say, but I do know that when the *Taloa-Manila Bay* showed up on its return trip in Honolulu we still had no permission to use the islands." These roadblocks turned out to be only the first of many that would be thrown at Nelson's upstart airline by business competitors and government officials.

A major change to Nelson's company came near the end of 1946 when United decided to give up its military contract for the San Francisco-Hawaii route. As the subcontractor operating this service, TOA decided to bid on it. However, for a variety of reasons, some of them political, it lost the bid to The Flying Tiger Line. Loss of the lucrative contract, which had assured operating capital for TOA, forced Nelson to search desperately for other business. He began by taking over TWA's contract to run Philippine Air Lines' East Asian operations. He also aggressively sought charter flights throughout the world. For instance, his company flew several missions between Great Britain and Canada, hauling about 7,000 English immigrants to Toronto in 1947. Of this operation, Nelson recalled: "This Canadian job was our first contract for what you might call the mass movement of people by air and the lessons we learned from this project served us well on later jobs of similar nature—such as the transportation of the workers to the Pacific islands and the movement of refugees from China and the carriage of religious groups in the Middle East."

Other contracts followed for worldwide airlift missions. During the Berlin Airlift of 1948-1949, Nelson's company operated several routes of the Military Air Transport Service, which was devoting virtually all of its resources to the emergency. In 1951, two years after the Department of the Interior took over responsibility for administering the American trust territories of Micronesia, TOA secured a contract to provide air services in the Central Pacific. It began scheduled flights from Guam on July 1, 1951, using a fleet of four PBY-5A flying boats that had been supplied by the navy. During the Korean War of 1950 to 1953, TOA dedicated seven DC-4s to the military airlift, and during the first two years of the war carried 7,112 litter patients, 20,000 military passengers, and 9.96 million pounds of cargo on 673 flights. This same period saw the great expansion of oil production in the Middle East, leading Nelson to branch out into contract work in that region as well. TOA also made numerous refugee airlifts. In 1956 and 1957, for example, the airline transported several groups of Hungarian refugees, displaced during the Russian invasion of their country, from West Germany to the United States.

Nelson was open to anything that would turn a profit. At one point, he courted filmmakers in California and managed to secure more than his share of contract work for movies. In 1953 he leased aircraft and crews to Hollywood to make two John Wayne movies, *Island in the Sky*, about a World War II transport aircraft downed in Labrador, and *The High and the Mighty*, a classic airplane film about an inflight disaster during a passenger flight from Hawaii. In addition, Nelson operated seven DC-4s carrying $6.2 million worth of gold bars from Japan to New York City in the early 1950s. Finally, in a 1954 operation called "Noah's Ark," Nelson's company flew a DC-4 containing 550 rabbits, 30 goats, and 2 million bees from California to Pusan, South Korea, on a church-supported project to rebuild the war-torn nation.

By 1953 Nelson had built Transocean into the largest of the supplemental carriers, with a fleet of 114 aircraft, more than 3,000 employees, and 28 offices scattered throughout the world. It also had branched out into support operations. Richard Thruelson, who published a history of TOA in 1953, noted that Nelson's company

> . . . owns and operates one of the country's
> largest aircraft and engine plants in Oakland.
> . . . staffs a string of its own bases which
> stretch around the world.
> . . . operates two airport restaurants.
> . . . runs a hotel—on Wake Island.
> . . . owns and operates a printing plant in Oakland.

Transocean Air Lines Grumman SA-16A (courtesy of the William T. Larkins Collection)

... has a heavy construction company engaged in road- and bridge-building on the West Coast.

... operates a barber shop.

... owns and operates a chemical plant.

... has a crop dusting operation working at home and abroad.

... runs an automotive sales and service company on Okinawa.

... has a world-wide trading division which deals in such diverse items as Afghanistan fishmeal and Swiss watches.

... has an industrial development division which manufactures aircraft components for Navy fighters.

... is busy supervising the reactivation of Japanese domestic airlines.

... owns and operates the Taloa Academy of Aeronautics.

... runs the 3,000,000-square-mile interisland air transport system for the Department of the Interior in the Trust Territory of the Pacific Islands.

... flies approximately 10 percent of the U.S.-to-Korea airlift.

... owns an interest in the Philippine Air Lines, which it reactivated on a worldwide basis after the war.

... flies a "vittles" airlift from Africa to the desert oil outposts of the Middle East.

While Nelson expanded and diversified opera-

tions, Transocean ran into all manner of opposition from competitors and government officials. As a nonscheduled carrier, TOA lacked a clear sanction to operate from the Civil Aeronautics Board (CAB), which was under political pressure from the established carriers to safeguard their prerogatives. This made it almost impossible to raise money. As aviation historian R. E. G. Davies has appropriately suggested, Nelson was caught in a classic catch-22 situation: "Without the blessing of the C.A.B. an airline lacked respectability in the eyes of the financiers, but the C.A.B. would not provide the respectability unless the airline was well financed."

Constantly strapped for cash to operate, and unable to borrow funds to update the airline's equipment, by 1957 Nelson was in serious financial trouble. As a last-ditch effort to save Transocean, he agreed to sell 40 percent of the company to the Atlas Corporation, a New York investment consortium. Thereafter, Nelson was forced to watch as Atlas stripped Transocean of most of its diversified operations. By January 1960, his business empire had crumbled beneath him. On July 11, 1960, Transocean's last remaining business, the contract with the Department of the Interior for airlift in Micronesia, expired, and the company declared bankruptcy. The obituary for Transocean appeared in the *New York Times* on September 3, 1960:

> Fourteen double-deck stratocruisers once valued at $14,000,000 were sold as scrap yesterday for $105,000. The airliners, once the pride of Transocean Airlines, were bought at auction by the Airline Equipment Company of Newark.

Nelson had not given up without a fight. He had struggled throughout the latter half of the 1950s to overcome what he considered needless governmental restrictions on supplemental carriers, rules designed to buttress the position of the established airlines. For him, Public Law 87-528, passed on July 10, 1962, partially vindicated his position by establishing the permanent role of the supplemental carriers as a legitimate part of the nation's air transport system. But it was a case of too little, too late. Nelson spent the rest of his life lobbying for a deregulation of the airline industry. On October 6, 1976, he asked Congress to "take the necessary steps to force deregulation by the [Civil Aeronautics] Board to the greatest extent possible. Start with cancelling control over air fares, give unlimited right of entry into the airline business domestically and right of entry and departure from points served." Always optimistic, he concluded: "We have people standing by, many of the Transocean originals, eager to get Transocean back in the air." Unfortunately he died before the passage of the Airline Deregulation Act of October 1978.

After the collapse of Transocean, Nelson worked for a time as a pilot with other companies, but in 1966 he gave up flying and moved back to Minnesota. A few years later, he returned to California and worked as an air transport consultant for several firms. He died of a heart attack on December 2, 1976.

References:

R. E. G. Davies, *Rebels and Reformers of the Airways* (Washington, D.C.: Smithsonian Institution, 1987);

Roger D. Launius, "Operation SAFE HAVEN: MATS and the Hungarian Airlift," *Airlift: The Journal of the Airlift Operations School*, 11 (Winter 1989): 17-21;

Stuart I. Rochester, *Takeoff at Mid-Century: Federal Civil Aviation Policy in the Eisenhower Years* (Washington, D.C.: Federal Aviation Administration, 1976);

Arue Szura, *Folded Wings: A History of Transocean Air Lines* (Missoula, Mont.: Pictorial Histories Publishing Co., 1989);

Frederick C. Thayer, Jr., *Air Transport Policy and National Security: A Political, Economic, and Military Analysis* (Chapel Hill: University of North Carolina Press, 1965);

Richard Thruelson, *Transocean: The Story of an Unusual Airline* (New York: Holt, 1953).

Archives:

Information on Orvis M. Nelson and Transocean Air Lines is in the Civil Reserve Air Fleet Records, 1948-1989, Office of History, Military Airlift Command, Scott Air Force Base, Illinois. Anne M. Bazzell discusses Transocean's role in the Korean War in an unpublished manuscript, "The Korean Airlift: What the Conflict of 1950-1953 Taught Us," in the Office of History, 834th Airlift Division, Hickham Air Force Base, Hawaii.

New York, Rio, and Buenos Aires Line

by Roger D. Launius

National Aeronautics and Space Administration

The New York, Rio, and Buenos Aires Line, commonly known as the NYRBA Line, was the brainchild of Ralph A. O'Neill, a World War I flier and aviation promoter. While serving as an adviser to the Mexican Air Force between 1920 and 1925, O'Neill recognized the tremendous potential for commercial aviation along South America's eastern coast. He understood that the movement of people and goods by air would greatly aid the development of modern commerce in a vast region that

was starved for rail and road transportation. In order to survey the area more thoroughly, O'Neill in 1928 contracted to sell Boeing aircraft in South America. Although the sales effort failed miserably, he succeeded in laying the groundwork for an airline that would operate from New York, down the eastern coasts of North and South America, to the Argentinian capital of Buenos Aires.

After securing the firm support of Robert Wood Bliss, American ambassador to Argentina, who looked upon the air route as a means of building cordial relations between the United States and Latin America, O'Neill returned to New York during the winter of 1928-1929 to recruit investment capital for the proposed NYRBA Line. At a time when aviation was the darling of Wall Street, he quickly secured the necessary financial support. James H. Rand, Jr., chief executive officer of the Remington-Rand Corporation, was the primary investor, along with Reuben Fleet of Consolidated Aircraft Corporation, who would provide aircraft for the airline.

The NYRBA Line was formally incorporated on March 17, 1929. In July, O'Neill and several companions made a trailblazing flight along the proposed route, establishing formal contacts, exciting public interest, and developing governmental support. Since the new line planned to use 14 of Consolidated Aircraft's huge Commodore flying boats, O'Neill took special care to obtain the necessary landing and dock space at each stopping point along the coast.

The company began scheduled operations on August 21, 1929, using Ford Trimotors for an overland route between Buenos Aires and Montevideo, Uruguay. On September 1 NYRBA added a Buenos Aires-Santiago service, the first transcontinental route in South American history. On February 19, 1930, O'Neill made good on his promise to begin scheduled service between New York and Buenos Aires within a year of incorporation. The inaugural flight reached the United States six days after departing Buenos Aires.

From the beginning, Juan Trippe of Pan American Airways had wanted to forestall competition from NYRBA in Latin America. Every step forward by O'Neill had produced increased efforts by Trippe to force the line out of business. While attempts to harass NYRBA's flight operations proved futile, Trippe's influence with the U.S. Post Office was another matter. NYRBA needed a postal subsidy from Washington in order to survive. When Postmaster General Walter Folger Brown made it clear he would not award airmail contracts in the region to any company other than Pan American, NYRBA's days were numbered.

On August 19, 1930, James Rand agreed to sell out to Pan American for $2 million, about $3 million less than the initial capitalization of the company a year and a half earlier. On September 15 Trippe formally acquired NYRBA's assets, and what had been the airline with the world's longest route ceased to exist. Pan American promptly took over NYRBA's schedule, using its Commodores to fly the route between Buenos Aires and Miami.

References:

R. E. G. Davies, *Airlines of the United States since 1914*, revised edition (Washington, D.C.: Smithsonian Institution, 1982);

Davies, *Rebels and Reformers of the Airways* (Washington, D.C.: Smithsonian Institution, 1987);

Elsbeth E. Freudenthal, *The Aviation Business: From Kitty Hawk to Wall Street* (New York: Vanguard, 1940);

Ralph A. O'Neill, with Joseph F. Hood, *A Dream of Eagles* (Boston: Houghton Mifflin, 1973).

North American Airlines

by Joseph E. Libby

University of California, Riverside

North American Airlines was the first carrier to offer cheap, "no frills" air travel to the American public. The brainchild of Stanley Weiss, the airline began service in November 1945, as Fireball Air Express. Taking advantage of the availability of war surplus Douglas C-47s, Weiss and his partner, Charles Sherman, began flying freight on a nonscheduled basis from Long Beach, California, to New York City. Within one year, Fireball Air Express began to offer passenger service, prompting Weiss to change the company's name to Standard Air Lines. Shortly thereafter the Civil Aeronautics Board (CAB) granted the airline a certificate to operate as a "Large Irregular Carrier."

In 1948 the CAB limited the number of round-trip flights by irregular carriers to eight per month. The following year, as a result of these restrictions, Weiss merged Standard Air Lines with its chief competitor, Viking Air Lines of Burbank, California. The two companies formed a ticketing organization offering transcontinental service to the public on one of the member airlines. Called the North American Airlines Agency, the merger doubled the number of planes available to the group. It also doubled the number of flights allowed by the CAB certificates, still held in the names of the original companies. In 1950 Weiss and his associates acquired four other irregular carriers: Twentieth Century Airlines, Trans-National Airlines, Trans-American Airlines, and Hemisphere Air Transport. The addition of these carriers increased the size of North American's fleet to 14 DC-3s and one DC-4. By combining the CAB certificates of all of the member companies, North American Airlines Agency could offer a coordinated schedule of transcontinental flights for $99 one way, and $160 round trip.

North American Airlines became increasingly popular with the public over the next few years. By 1954 the airline carried 194,000 passengers, surpassing the total number carried by the three smallest regular domestic airlines combined. Cost cutting came through efficient operation. By eliminating the luxury service offered by the regular carriers, Weiss and his associates kept their fares low. They also cut costs by flying at 85 percent capacity or better. Passengers occasionally had to wait a day or two for their airplane to fill up, but they seemed ready to accept the inconvenience in return for the cheaper fare. At no time was the airline criticized for violating maintenance procedures or safety standards.

Opposition from the established regular carriers grew during the early 1950s. Working through the CAB, the regular airlines fought to have North American's certificates revoked for violating the flight restrictions placed on irregular carriers. Finally, in July 1955, the CAB revoked North American's certificates. While appeals kept the airline in operation, another lawsuit, brought by North American Aircraft Company, forced Weiss to change his airline's name to Trans-American Airlines. In January 1957 the CAB rejected Weiss's final appeal. Four months later, the U.S. Supreme Court upheld the CAB rulings, closing the airline, and ending the first major experiment in no frills, low-cost air transportation.

References:

R. E. G. Davies, *Airlines of the United States since 1914* (London: Putnam's, 1972);

Davies, *Rebels and Reformers of the Airways* (Washington, D.C.: Smithsonian Institution, 1987);

William A. Schoneberger, with Paul Sonnenberg, *California Wings: A History of Aviation in the Golden State* (Woodland Hills, Cal.: Windsor, 1984).

North Central Airlines

by William M. Leary

University of Georgia

The history of North Central Airlines began in 1940, when executives of the Four Wheel Drive Auto Company of Clintonville, Wisconsin, purchased two four-passenger Waco biplanes to fly company personnel to Chicago. Also used by nearby firms, the service became so popular that Four Wheel Drive formed Wisconsin Central Airlines on May 15, 1944, and applied to the Civil Aeronautics Board (CAB) for authority to operate scheduled air services in the area. In line with its policy of encouraging feeder airlines, the CAB approved a three-year temporary certificate in 1947. At the same time, it required Four Wheel Drive to divest itself of ownership of the company. The airline's officers responded by launching what proved to be a successful campaign to sell stock to local citizens. Arthur E. A. Mueller, a foundry owner, was a leading supporter and eventually majority owner of the airline.

Operations got underway on February 24, 1948, with three nine-passenger Lockheed 10A Electras. The first year proved difficult for the fledgling airline. Without government assistance, Wisconsin Central had to establish its own system of navigational aids at a cost of $100,000. Also, the severe winter of 1948-1949 created difficult operating conditions. However, traffic slowly increased. In 1950 the airline purchased six 26-passenger DC-3s from Trans World Airlines. Shortly thereafter, the CAB renewed the company's operating certificate and granted it 900 miles of new routes extending from Chicago to Minneapolis.

Reflecting its growing area of operation, the company changed in name in December 1952 to North Central Airlines. At the same time, it moved its headquarters to Minneapolis. Under the leadership of President Hal N. Carr, the airline continued to expand its route system and increase its revenues. Beginning in 1954 it began to turn a profit.

North Central was one of the first local service airlines to utilize a loan guarantee program, ap-

proved by Congress in 1958, to modernize its fleet of 32 DC-3s. In 1959 North Central purchased five pressurized Convair 340s from Continental Air Lines, marking the beginning of a program to replace its entire inventory of DC-3s. With new equipment, North Central was able to compete successfully with the trunk carriers on several routes. For example, in 1961 the airline held a 60 percent share of the Chicago-Milwaukee market against Northwest, United, Eastern, and American.

Expansion continued during the prosperous 1960s, especially after the CAB decided to allow local service carriers to grow larger as a way to reduce subsidies (which reached $8 million for North Central in 1961). In 1967 North Central began to convert its entire fleet of 28 Convair 340/440s to turboprop Convair 580s. In the same year, it took delivery on three new 100-passenger Douglas DC-9-30s, at a cost of $4 million each.

During the 1970s, North Central became what the *New York Times* termed "a textbook case of what freedom from Government regulations can do for a business." In 1977, as the CAB relaxed its control of the airline industry, North Central added flights and entered new markets, eventually reaching the resort areas of Florida and Arizona. At the same time, it continued to serve its network of small communities, as long as the cities provided enough passengers to reach a break-even point. In 1978 North Central recorded a 38 percent gain in passenger-miles to 9.1 billion. It also posted a profit of $22.2 million on revenues of $299.1 million. By the beginning of 1979, the airline had over 4,000 employees and operated a fleet of 56 aircraft, including 33 DC-9s.

In May 1979 the CAB approved the merger of North Central and Southern Airways, creating the nation's 13th largest airline. North Central clearly was the dominant partner in the merger. The holder of each share of Southern stock received 2.1

North Central shares, an exchange valued at $25 million. On July 1, 1979, a new entity, Republic Airlines, took over the assets and routes of both carriers, its corporate structure dominated by former North Central executives. Thus passed out of existence one of the more successful local service airlines, a longtime industry leader in operating performance despite the severe winters that it so frequently encountered.

References:

George C. Eads, *The Local Service Airline Experiment* (Washington, D.C.: Brookings Institution, 1972);

Terry M. Love, "The Aircraft of North Central Airlines," *American Aviation Historical Society Journal*, 22 (Winter 1977); 276-289;

Arthur E. A. Mueller, *Air Service for Main Street, U.S.A.* (New York: Newcomen Society of North America, 1961);

"Southern and North Central Air Seeking Strength in Merger," *New York Times*, March 19, 1979, pp. D1, D3.

Northeast Airlines

by Lloyd H. Cornett, Jr.

Montgomery, Alabama

By 1933, airmail service covered most of the United States with the exception of six states, including Maine, Vermont, and New Hampshire. Despite a severe depression and the failure of an earlier attempt to operate an air service in New England, the Boston & Maine and Maine Central Railroads joined forces to form an airline to serve the area. Boston-Maine Airways began service from Boston to Bangor and Burlington on August 11, 1933, with two 10-passenger Stinson Trimotors. Two months later, on October 27, an agreement with Central Vermont Airways added a feeder service through Vermont that connected with the original line. Finally, on March 20, 1934, the airline extended the Burlington route to Montreal.

Operating conditions on the airline's routes could only be described as primitive. Airports often consisted of converted hay pastures, and navigational aids were rudimentary or nonexistent. Still, Boston-Maine Airways carried 1,904 passengers during its first 17 months in business. Passengers alone, however, did not produce enough revenue to support the operation, and the railroads had to subsidize losses. It was in this setting that the so-called airmail scandal erupted.

In February 1934 President Franklin D. Roosevelt canceled all commercial airmail contracts after a special congressional committee charged that collusion had taken place between the airlines and the postmaster general during the administration of Herbert Hoover. Army Air Corps pilots took over flying the mail, but inexperience and inadequate equipment combined with terrible weather to force cancellation of military operations within a few weeks. Having no other choice, the Post Office again called for commercial bids. On June 5, 1934, Boston-Maine Airways secured a contract for the 401-mile route from Boston to Burlington via Bangor.

Revenue of 29.5 cents a mile to carry the mail helped the finances of the struggling airline, but profits still proved elusive. Nonetheless, the railroads continued to support the airline, authorizing funds to purchase Lockheed Electras in 1936-1938 and DC-3s in 1941. The owners, hoping to raise additional capital, decided on a public stock offering. To make the proposal more palatable, they changed the name of the company to Northeast Airlines, effective November 19, 1940. At the time of the stock offering in January 1941, Northeast ranked 11th in passengers carried among domestic airlines.

Following American entry into World War II, Northeast was called upon to devote four-fifths of its resources to military operations across the North Atlantic. Although the airline had never before flown beyond Montreal, it quickly responded to the new challenge. Within a year Northeast was operating a regular schedule for Air Transport Command to Labrador, Greenland, Iceland, and Scotland. As historian R. E. G. Davies has emphasized, Northeast routinely crossed over the "most inhospitable, barren, and frigid land ever known to witness operation of a civil airliner."

Northeast wanted new routes as the war drew to a close, but first government regulators forced the railroads to divest themselves of the airline's stock. They did so, reluctantly, selling 90 percent of their holdings to the Atlas Corporation on January 15, 1944. Five months later, the Civil Aeronautics Board (CAB) awarded Northeast the coveted New York-Boston route. While only 185 miles long, this route carried a high volume of passengers. To compete with American Airlines, Northeast introduced DC-4s into service on May 15, 1946. Unfortunately, the new equipment did not help; American retained its virtual monopoly on the New York-Boston run.

With losses mounting, Northeast searched in vain for a merger partner. The airline then sought relief through route expansion, but this had only limited success because the CAB either delayed or outrightly rejected Northeast's applications. Not until 1956 did the company secure a major route award, when the CAB allowed it to enter the highly profitable run from New York to Miami. For a short time, Northeast made money, but intense competitive pressure from Eastern Airlines soon dashed hopes of major revenue gains. By 1960 Northeast's debts had reached $10 million.

The 1960s saw important managerial changes. In 1961 the CAB pressured Atlas to relinquish control of the airline on the grounds that its part ownership of Consolidated Vultee, an aircraft manufacturer, constituted a conflict of interest. In response, Atlas transferred its stock to the Hughes Tool Company. For a time, this move proved advantageous for the airline, as Howard Hughes kept it afloat with loans of money and aircraft. Eventually, however, economic pressures led to Northeast's sale to the Storer Broadcasting Company in July 1965. The new owner authorized badly needed equipment

purchases: F-227s replaced DC-3s on the shorter routes, and DC-9s took over from the DC-6s and Boeing 727s on the longer ones. The airline also introduced a new paint scheme: subdued colors gave way to yellow, black, and white markings. Northeast's new airplanes became known as "Yellowbirds."

The airline expanded in the late 1960s, adding new service between Montreal and Miami, Boston and Bermuda, New York and the Bahamas, Burlington and Chicago, and, best of all, Miami and Los Angeles. Still, Northeast continued to lose money. Unable to stave off what appeared to be an inevitable disaster, Storer began negotiations for a merger—a not unfamiliar activity for Northeast. Finally, in 1969 an agreement was reached with Northwest Airlines. The CAB, however, would not allow Northwest to inherit the Miami-Los Angeles route, which killed the deal. Delta Airlines then stepped into the picture. Delta's stockholders approved a merger in October 1971. Despite opposition from Eastern and National Airlines, the CAB gave its blessing in April 1972. On August 1, following approval by Northeast's shareholders, "the Yankee fleet" of "New England's own airline" passed from the scene.

References:

R. E. G. Davies, *Airlines of the United States since 1914*, revised edition (Washington, D.C.: Smithsonian Institution, 1982);

George E. Gardner, *First in New England Skies! 20th Anniversary Northeast Airlines (1933-1953)* (New York: Newcomen Society in North America, 1953);

W. David Lewis and Wesley P. Newton, *Delta: The History of an Airline* (Athens: University of Georgia Press, 1979);

Alvin Moscow, *Tiger on a Leash* (New York: Putnam's, 1961);

Robert W. Mudge, *Adventures of a Yellowbird: The Biography of an Airline* (Boston: Brandon, 1969).

Northwest Airlines

by William M. Leary

University of Georgia

Northwest Airlines grew out of the efforts of Detroit and Minneapolis-St. Paul businessmen to operate Contract Airmail Route 9 (CAM-9) between Chicago and the Twin Cities. The Post Office originally awarded the route to Charles Dickinson, who began service on June 7, 1926. A series of accidents and inadequate financing brought flight operations to an end in July. Col. L. H. Brittin of St. Paul found financial backing to organize Northwest Airways on August 1 1926, and take over Dickinson's contract. Northwest inaugurated service on CAM-9 on October 1, 1926.

Using three Stinson Detroiter monoplanes, Northwest managed to continue mail flights over the winter, an impressive accomplishment given the harsh weather conditions and primitive facilities of the region. In July 1927 it began to carry passengers on the route. Over 100 brave souls flew between Chicago and the Twin Cities before the onset of inclement weather forced the airline to suspend service in October. The following June, however, Northwest again took passengers along with the mail; this time passenger service proved permanent. In 1928 Northwest carried more than 6,000 passengers.

Between 1928 and 1933 Northwest Airways expanded westward, eventually reaching Seattle. On April 16, 1934, the company changed its name to Northwest Airlines. Later in the year it introduced into service 12-passenger Lockheed L-10 Electras. It did not acquire DC-3s until March 1939.

World War II brought about major changes in Northwest's fortunes. On February 26, 1942, it signed a contract with the Air Transport Command for a scheduled service between Minneapolis and Fairbanks. Northwest not only operated this inland route to Alaska but also (for a time) flew between Seattle and Anchorage. In addition, the airline extended its Alaskan service to Attu in the Aleutian Islands. Equally important to the airline's future

was the award by the Civil Aeronautics Board (CAB) of a Milwaukee-New York route. On June 1, 1945, Northwest opened service on the new route, becoming the nation's fourth transcontinental air carrier (with United, American, and TWA).

Although delighted with the eastward extension across the continent, Northwest had even more dramatic news in 1946. On August 1, President Harry S. Truman approved the CAB's recommendation for a "Great Circle Route" to the Orient for Northwest. Two months later it began service to Anchorage. On July 15, 1947, Northwest used DC-4s to extend the Great Circle Route to Tokyo, Seoul, Shanghai (later replaced by Taipei), and Manila. Also, thanks to another CAB award, on December 2, 1948, the airline inaugurated the Pacific Northwest's first service to Hawaii, flying to Honolulu from Seattle and Portland.

Northwest Airlines made an important contribution to the war efforts in Korea, making 1,380 round trips to the Far East between 1950 and 1953 with DC-4s under military charter. The airline's economic situation, however, deteriorated during the early 1950s. In 1949 Northwest had introduced pressurized Boeing 377 Stratocruisers on its international routes. Although providing luxurious accommodations for passengers, the airplane had such high operating costs that it consistently lost money for the airline. Also, the Martin 2-0-2s that Northwest used on its domestic routes were plagued by a series of fatal accidents. In 1954 Donald W. Nyrop became president of what industry analysts considered "a shaky airline."

Nyrop, who controlled Northwest's destiny for the next 24 years, quickly restored the company to financial health. Under his direction the airline became legendary for its parsimonious approach to the air transport business. The airline's corporate headquarters at the Minneapolis-St. Paul Airport stood as the symbol of Nyrop's business philoso-

*Inauguration of Northwest's Boeing Stratocruiser transcontinental service, Idlewild Airport, New York, 1949
(courtesy of the National Air and Space Museum)*

phy. The building, which could easily be mistaken for a hangar, had no windows and few amenities for its occupants. However, as Nyrop pointed out, it only cost $1.75 a square foot, compared to the much higher prices paid by competitors. And, he observed, "There is no way they are five or six times more productive than we [are]."

Nyrop embarked on a cautious policy of expansion. In 1955 the CAB granted Northwest a share of the competitive Chicago–New York market. Later in the decade, the airline expanded into Florida. New equipment replaced the unproductive Boeings and accident-plagued Martins. In September 1960 Northwest began pure-jet service with DC-8s. Ten years later, on July 1, 1970, it inaugurated Boeing 747 service between Chicago and Tokyo.

By the time Nyrop retired in 1978, Northwest had the industry's highest profit margin (averaging 7.8 percent over ten years) and lowest debt-to-equity ratio (14:86). The airline owned its entire fleet of 105 airplanes and had a long-term debt of $104 million. Its 11,445 employees produced $91,000 per capita, the best record in the business, while its airplanes needed a load factor of only 42 percent to break even. Characteristically, in 1978 Northwest also experienced a strike by its pilots, their third job action in six years.

Northwest responded slowly to the demands of deregulation. The airline increased transatlantic service, begun in 1977, to Great Britain and Scandinavia, and it opened new routes to the southwestern United States and California. Not until the mid 1980s did the airline emphasize domestic hubs and purchase a share of a computer reservations system. In 1986 Northwest took part in another industry trend when it purchased (for $884 million) rival Republic Airlines. Three years later, Northwest itself became the target of various takeover efforts. In June 1989 a group headed by Alfred Checchi and Gary

Northwest Douglas DC-8 (courtesy of the National Air and Space Museum)

Wilson raised $900 million in equity capital (with one quarter coming from KLM Royal Dutch Airlines) and made a successful bid of $3.65 billion for the company. By the end of the year, the airline, which had *no* long-term debt in 1982, was $2.9 billion in the red.

Fortunately for the new owners, Northwest recorded a record net profit of $355.2 million in 1989. Although 1990 started well, the airline suffered major losses in the fourth quarter and ended the year with a net loss of $10.4 million (and an operating loss of $141.7 million). Still, Northwest's owners remained optimistic about the future and continued to expand, acquiring Eastern's gates and slots at Washington National Airport and purchas-

ing a 25 percent interest in Hawaiian Airlines for $20 million. However, it remained clear that profits would have to be high during the remainder of the 1990s for debt-ridden Northwest to survive.

References:

"Dealmakers in the Cockpit," *Business Week*, March 5, 1990, pp. 54-57, 60, 62;

J. A. Donoghue, "Northwest: Rough Ride to a Competitive Fortress," *Air Transport World*, 25 (October 1988): 28-32, 34, 36-37;

Hugh D. Menzies, "Don Nyrop Keeps a Tight Rein on Northwest," *Fortune*, 98 (August 14, 1978): 142-144, 146;

Kenneth D. Ruble, *Flight to the Top* (New York: Viking, 1986).

Donald W. Nyrop

(April 1, 1912 -   )

by Donna M. Corbett

Smithsonian Institution

CAREER: Attorney, General Counsel's Office, Civil Aeronautics Authority (1939-1941); executive officer to chairman, Civil Aeronautics Board (1942); Air Transport Command, U.S. Army Air Forces (1942-1946); member, U.S. delegations, International Civil Aviation Organization assemblies (1946, 1947); deputy administrator for operations (1948-1950), administrator, Civil Aeronautics Administration (1950-1951); chairman, Civil Aeronautics Board (1951-1952); private law practice (1953-1954); president and chief executive officer (1954-1976), chairman and chief executive officer, Northwest Airlines (1976-1978).

Best known for his quarter-century at the helm of Northwest Airlines, Donald William Nyrop's career also included important contributions to the federal regulation of commercial aviation. During the 1950s, Nyrop held the highest civilian aviation posts in the U.S. government, as Civil Aeronautics administrator and Civil Aeronautics Board chairman. Later in the decade, and for the ensuing 24 years, he headed Northwest Airlines, transforming a problem-plagued carrier into one of the world's leading airlines. Nyrop's career, in both government and the airline industry, was characterized by dedication to economy, efficiency, and operational safety.

Nyrop was born to a family of Danish heritage in Elgin, Nebraska, on April 1, 1912; his father was a banker in the small community. He attended Doane College in Crete, Nebraska, receiving an A.B. degree in history in 1934. During the following year, he moved to Washington, D.C., and spent his days working as an auditor in the U.S. General Accounting Office while attending George Washington University law school at night. He was admitted to the District of Columbia bar in 1938, and completed his LL.B. degree the following year.

Donald W. Nyrop (courtesy of Northwest Airlines)

In the spring of 1939, Nyrop approached his fellow midwesterner L. Welch Pogue, general counsel of the Civil Aeronautics Authority (CAA), to discuss employment prospects at the nine-month-old agency. Impressed with the young attorney's agile mind, Pogue hired Nyrop as a staff attorney in the new route proceedings section of the CAA General Counsel's Office.

After several months Nyrop was transferred, within the General Counsel's Office, to the section which handled legal matters relating to aircraft accident investigation. There he met Frank Caldwell, a former Boeing Air Transport and United Air Lines operations manager, who was one of the agency's leading accident investigators. Though many years Nyrop's senior, Caldwell befriended the young attorney, taking him along on accident investigations and sharing his insight into (in Nyrop's words) "what would cause things to go right and what would cause things to go wrong." From this experience Nyrop developed a lifelong interest in aviation safety.

In January 1942 L. Welch Pogue, newly appointed chairman of the Civil Aeronautics Board, invited Nyrop to become his executive assistant. Later that year, however, Nyrop left this civilian position to join the U.S. Army Air Forces, where he served as executive operations officer in the Air Transport Command. He achieved the rank of lieutenant colonel and was awarded the Legion of Merit upon his return to civilian life in January 1946.

After World War II, Nyrop spent two years with the Air Transport Association, handling operational matters related to the establishment of peacetime overseas routes for U.S. airlines. In 1946 and 1947 he was a member of the official U.S. delegations to the International Civil Aviation Organization assemblies.

Nyrop returned to government service in August 1948 as executive assistant to civil aeronautics administrator Delos W. Rentzel. In June 1949, following Rentzel's reorganization of the CAA, he was appointed deputy administrator for operations. Administrator Rentzel, as Nyrop later recalled, "painted with a broad brush and needed someone to fill in the details," and Nyrop, responsible for budget, personnel, and management, was clearly second in command at the agency. Thus the aviation community was not surprised when he succeeded Rentzel as administrator of civil aeronautics on October 4, 1950.

As head of the Civil Aeronautics Administration, Nyrop was responsible for a federal agency with more than 18,000 employees and an annual budget of over $187 million. The thirty-eight-year-old administrator faced decisions on technical aviation matters, such as the initial installation of high-intensity runway approach lighting, as well as administrative issues regarding the relative priorities of civilian and military aviation during the Korean War. For the first time, during this "period of limited mobilization," as Nyrop described it, aircraft en-

tering coastal Air Defense Zones were required to file flight plans, and all licensed pilots were required to obtain CAA identification cards. The CAA worked with the National Production Authority to allocate manufacturing resources for aircraft, spare parts, and equipment and to enable airlines to obtain replacement parts and avionics devices. Despite some discussion of placing the CAA, like the Coast Guard, under military control for the duration of hostilities, the agency remained firmly in civilian hands, a development attributed to Nyrop's opposition to militarization.

After less than six months as civil aeronautics administrator, Nyrop was called to the White House where President Harry S. Truman asked him to assume chairmanship of the Civil Aeronautics Board (CAB). Although initially reluctant to leave the CAA, where he felt great progress was being made on several issues, such as safety regulation of nonscheduled airlines, he acceded to Truman's wishes. His nomination as CAB chairman was sent to the Senate on March 19 and confirmed on April 17, 1951.

As CAB chairman, Nyrop continued to play an active role in the promotion of aviation safety. The CAB was responsible for investigating accidents and for making recommendations for corrective action to the CAA. While heading the CAA, Nyrop had tightened the agency's scrutiny of nonscheduled airlines, correcting inadequate operating and pilot training procedures. A year later, during his CAB chairmanship, an unprecedented series of five New York-area airliner accidents, which began in December 1951 and continued through the following spring, shook public confidence in the safety of air transportation. As a result, Newark Airport was temporarily closed, and flights to La Guardia Airport were drastically curtailed. Evincing his own interest in air safety, which dated from his early days at the old Civil Aeronautics Authority, Nyrop became, in January 1952, the first chairman of the Civil Aeronautics Board to visit an accident investigation site.

International routes were of special concern to Nyrop's Civil Aeronautics Board. The initial postwar international route certificates were due for renewal, and hearings on North Atlantic route cases were held in the autumn of 1951. The award of a permanent North Atlantic route certificate to Trans World Airlines effectively ended Pan American Airways's vision of a "chosen instrument" monopoly of that route, completing the work begun in 1944 with the CAB's initial proposal of international routes for multiple U.S. carriers.

In Nyrop's view, the Civil Aeronautics Board had "a dual responsibility of developing air transportation while at the same time reducing the dependency of the airlines on federal subsidy." The growth of air coach services served both aims. Through the relatively simple device of increasing seating density on aircraft, airlines could, according to the CAB, reduce operating costs per seat mile by as much as one-third. Nyrop predicted in a 1952 speech before the Conference on Airport Management and Operations, "In time, coach travel may well be the predominant form of air travel within the U.S.," and he credited the CAB with encouraging coach travel's growth. At the board's urging, and "despite considerable opposition" by some airlines, coach fares were reduced by 11 percent between 1951 and 1952, with coach services increasing to 16 percent of all domestic traffic.

Prior to Nyrop's tenure as chairman of the Civil Aeronautics Board, airmail payments to airlines were combined with direct subsidy payments, and both were paid by the Post Office Department. Under a new program, originally recommended by the Hoover Commission, airmail and subsidy payments were separated, with subsidy, appropriated by Congress from tax funds, clearly distinguishable from mail payments. Subsidy was reduced, with the "big four" airlines (American, Eastern, TWA, United) and several smaller carriers removed from subsidy altogether. Under Nyrop's leadership, the CAB even managed to recover excess subsidy payments; between September 1951 and October 1952, the federal treasury netted $11,311,000 in refund payments from airlines.

Nyrop, said a CAA official, was "the only executive in Washington who made a crusade out of saving money for the taxpayer." In a city where any budget increase is considered a victory, Nyrop had reduced the CAA's budget by $13 million and considered it a triumph. At the CAB he had similar control of budget and cost containment. In this, as in other administrative matters, Nyrop was clearly in charge. A 1950 reorganization of the CAB had transferred administrative functions from the entire board to the chairman's office, and he took full advantage of the opportunities presented. He maintained direct control over the CAB staff, with power to hire and fire personnel and to plan their

caseload. Despite rumors that the CAB might be placed under the secretary of commerce, Nyrop guarded the board's, and his own, independence. Aviation writer Wayne W. Parrish noted that Nyrop as CAB chairman was "fair-minded to an extreme . . . an excellent administrator and organizer," but "his devotion to getting things done rubbed several of his colleagues the wrong way." After Nyrop resigned the chairmanship in October 1952, the board's four remaining members conducted their own reorganization, curbing some of the chairman's control by regaining a share of supervisory authority over the CAB staff.

Nyrop's resignation from the Civil Aeronautics Board during the final months of President Truman's last term enabled Truman's successor to select his own CAB chairman. Nyrop entered private law practice, joining the Washington, D.C., firm of Klagsbrunn, Hanes & Irwin. His legal work included representation of cities seeking direct or additional air service in government route proceedings. He also became director of the newly formed Conference of Local Airlines in March 1953, and participated in the local carriers' bid for legislation authorizing permanent local service route certificates.

In the summer of 1954, three members of the Board of Directors of Northwest Airlines visited Nyrop in his Washington law office and asked him to consider accepting the airline's presidency. Nyrop requested 60 days in which to examine the airline and weigh his decision. There was much to consider.

Northwest Orient (as the carrier was known) was an airline in trouble. Its board of directors, characterized more by dissension than unity, was divided between local Minneapolis-St. Paul investors and New York financial interests. The airline's last president, Harold Harris, left after little more than a year, citing "basic and irreconcilable differences of opinion" between himself and a majority of the board. The company's financial situation could hardly have been worse: a special committee met weekly to count the cash on hand and rarely found enough to meet the payroll for more than 35 or 40 days. Metal plaques proclaiming "Mortgaged to Banker's Trust Co." were mounted on the cockpit doors of 20 aircraft, and banks were uninterested in advancing credit for additional aircraft purchases needed to modernize the fleet.

Northwest Airlines's problems arose, in large part, from its dismal safety record of the early 1950s. The darkest days of 1950 and early 1951, when one of the company's Martin 2-0-2 aircraft crashed, on average, every 45 days, were over; but confidence in the airline was shaken, and a few residual safety problems still remained. Perhaps no one in aviation understood Northwest's safety problems better than Nyrop. In February 1951, as civil aeronautics administrator, Nyrop led a team of CAA investigators, including safety authorities Ernest Hensley and Harold Hoekstra, on a special safety inspection of the Minnesota-based airline. As a result of their investigation, which followed two weeks of Washington conferences with the airline's top officials, the CAA ordered Northwest to establish higher minimum allowable weather conditions for operations, to change its pilot training methods (including retraining many of its pilots), and to upgrade its maintenance procedures.

Throughout this troubled period, George Gardner, former Northwest Airlines operations manager and president of Northeast Airlines, under whom Nyrop had served in the Air Transport Command, urged Northwest's board to offer the presidency to Nyrop. Northwest clearly needed an executive of sufficient stature to revive confidence in the weakened carrier. The airline had first approached Nyrop in 1952, after he had announced his resignation from the Civil Aeronautics Board. But at the time Nyrop was uninterested; he had already decided to enter private law practice, and he was also mindful of the inappropriate appearance of a sudden move from government to regulated industry.

Nyrop announced his acceptance of the Northwest presidency at a St. Paul press conference in September 1954. He accepted the position "because," he said, "I believe in the future of this carrier." Personal reasons also played a part in his decision; he and his wife, Grace, had decided that the Midwest would be a good place to raise their young family. At the age of forty-two, Nyrop became the youngest chief executive of any major U.S. airline.

Nyrop's first task was to restore the financial community's faith in Northwest Airlines. During his first year, he negotiated $18 million in bank credit agreements, then $29.5 million in 1955, and ever-increasing totals in subsequent years. The airline began to pay off its debts; within months of Nyrop's arrival, he and board chairman Croil Hunter were able to hold a ceremonial "burning of

the mortgage," using acid to dissolve the offending metal aircraft plaques. In May 1955 Northwest further reassured the investment community by issuing the airline's first common stock dividend since 1946. Before the end of his first year at the company, Nyrop was able to boast: "Northwest Airlines is the only airline in the United States that doesn't owe a dime."

Creating order from the chaos of Northwest's aircraft fleet was also among Nyrop's first priorities. The airline suffered from a chronic equipment shortage which dated back to its voluntary grounding of the Martin 2-0-2 fleet in March 1951. Upon his arrival at Northwest, Nyrop inherited a motley collection of airplanes which included Boeing Stratocruisers and Douglas DC-6s, DC-4s, and DC-3s. Four Lockheed Super Constellations ordered by his predecessor, Harris, had yet to arrive. Even aircraft of the same type were from different sources (some DC-4s, for example, were converted military C-54s), and they contained varying equipment which required dissimilar spare parts. Instrumentation also varied from cockpit to cockpit, making pilot training difficult to standardize.

Nyrop adopted a program to rationalize the fleet. He began by ordering new Douglas DC-6B airplanes. (Aircraft manufacturer Donald Douglas demonstrated his faith in Nyrop's ability to enhance the airline's fortunes by earmarking 14 DC-6Bs on the manufacturing line for Northwest, even though the airline had made down payments for only ten aircraft.) In subsequent years Nyrop followed with additional purchases of DC-6B and DC-7C aircraft, the latter especially suited to the airline's long transpacific routes. He also began to sell the airline's smaller, nonpressurized aircraft, retaining the enormous (and enormously popular) Boeing Stratocruisers for first-class domestic service.

Fleet standardization became a familiar theme throughout Nyrop's years at Northwest. By eliminating all but a few aircraft types, the airline was able to reduce its stocks of spare engines and parts and lower its capital outlay on maintenance equipment and personnel training. Further slashing costs, Nyrop consolidated Northwest's maintenance operations in the Twin Cities, eliminating additional maintenance bases in Seattle and New York. Within a year of his arrival, he announced the airline's intention to build a 75-acre centralized facility at the Minneapolis-St. Paul International Airport, which would include engine and airframe overhaul facili-

Nyrop (right) with Northwest chairman Croil Hunter (courtesy of Northwest Airlines)

ties, line maintenance hangars, and a new headquarters office building.

In addition to cutting costs, Nyrop began to reduce Northwest's dependence on government subsidy. Subsidy, he said, "is like a cost-plus contract. It undermines efficiency." Northwest's domestic system had already been weaned from subsidy, under the program established by CAB chairman Nyrop, but the airline's international routes still required subsidy payments. Northwest's new policy, "to stand on our own two feet," sent a clear and confident message to the financial community. It was also designed to have an effect on Northwest's international route certifications.

Throughout the 1950s, Northwest fought repeated battles over certification of its Great Circle Route across the North Pacific. The route, first awarded on a temporary basis in 1946, came up for CAB proceedings in 1954. In the Transpacific Renewal Case, the CAB recommended that Northwest's authority be made permanent and that Pan

American Airways's application to compete on the route be denied. President Dwight D. Eisenhower, however, ordered the CAB to award Northwest only a temporary, seven-year certificate, under the mistaken belief that Northwest, like Pan American, still required heavy subsidy payments. After many years of seesawing legal battles (including four instances in which the Eisenhower administration reversed CAB decisions favoring Northwest over Pan American), Northwest finally received its permanent route authority to Tokyo in 1957, a decade after initiating service. But the airline still faced years of wrangling over Pan American's efforts to duplicate Northwest's route.

The airline, in billing itself as "Northwest Orient," expressed its enormous pride in the hard-fought transpacific routes. Nyrop's arrival at Northwest ushered in a new era of heightened passenger service which, even on domestic flights, featured an Oriental flair. First-class passengers were offered hot, scented *oshibori* towels. On the double-decked

326

Boeing Stratocruiser, travelers could descend a spiral staircase to the "Fujiyama Room" lounge, where a cabin attendant, sometimes of Asian descent, would serve drinks and Oriental-style delicacies. Northwest operated its own in-flight kitchens, with chefs who excelled at teriyaki dishes. As its radio and television commercials, which ended with the exotic sound of a gong, suggested, the Minnesota-based airline's "Imperial" service brought something of a cross-cultural experience to its mid-America passengers.

But despite the new cosmopolitan emphasis, Northwest Orient remained very much a product of the upper Midwest. Most of its employees were progeny of the region, and, upon taking charge of the airline, Nyrop decided that he would not impose newly hired outsiders on the homegrown personnel group. Instead he enlisted University of Minnesota industrial psychologists to gauge the talent already present in upper- and middle-management ranks. Under longtime president Croil Hunter's casual administrative approach, the airline had hired indiscriminately and fired no one. But Northwest's new president, fresh from the reorganization of two government agencies, demonstrated a willingness to apply new, scientific management techniques to the hidebound company.

A great believer in centralization, Nyrop applied himself to every detail of Northwest's management. Analyzing budgets down to the smallest figures, peering into equipment lockers, paying early morning visits to the airport ("if there was a stuck baggage conveyor, he knew about it," said one employee), he created a new atmosphere of precision at Northwest. He demonstrated a unique talent for quantifying every detail. One day, walking past a company executive changing a burned-out light bulb, Nyrop asked the executive if he knew the bulb's price. Nyrop knew, and further commented that it was equivalent to the profit earned on one passenger flying between Chicago and the Twin Cities. At his insistence, invoices remained attached to packages containing spare parts and equipment so that every mechanic could know exactly how much each item cost. The contagion of cost consciousness spread; years later, echoing Nyrop, the most common question heard at Northwest's maintenance base remained: "Do you know how much that part cost us?"

Nyrop's Northwest Orient Airlines never had more than 17 vice-presidents, at a time when other airlines had as many as 60. Each vice-president reported directly to Nyrop, and under them were the supervisors and foremen. The lean organizational structure suggested Nyrop's abhorrence of committees; when Northwest executives attended industry meetings, they traveled alone. On one occasion, when another airline sent a team of ten engine specialists to inspect a JT9D jet engine that Northwest had operated without failure for a record 8,300 hours, an employee noted, "Northwest would have sent one good man."

Nyrop left a discernible imprint on Northwest's facility at the Minneapolis-St. Paul Airport. Completed in 1961, it combined general offices, maintenance, and ground services under one roof, which enabled Nyrop, with his eye for detail, to keep constant watch over every aspect of the airline's operations. The hangarlike headquarters building became, over the years, the subject of much comment for its lack of typical office amenities, such as carpeting and wall hangings. Located a few hundred yards from a major airport's active runway, the windowless structure insulated executive staff from distractions, noise, and pollution. While the headquarters building was not palatial, it was eminently practical. In the late 1970s, while other airlines paid $10 or more per square foot for office space, Northwest continued to lease its building for $1.75 per square foot. Designed with flexible partitions instead of permanent office walls, the building was intended for ultimate use as a maintenance support area. The airline finally outgrew its airport headquarters in 1986, after Nyrop's retirement. During the Nyrop years, however, it served as the airline's nerve center, and strategically placed at its core was Nyrop's office.

To outsiders, Nyrop and Northwest's concentrated attention to thrift sometimes seemed an odd eccentricity. But, as *Fortune* magazine noted, "Don Nyrop's tightfisted approach to business is hardly unusual among successful executives who came of age during the Depression." As in a family enterprise, Northwest employees were encouraged to think of every corporate dollar spent as equivalent to one of their own; simple, direct solutions merited highest praise. After receiving a McDonnell Douglas service directive to repair faulty DC-10 lavatory door locks (at an estimated cost of $5,030 per aircraft), Northwest's maintenance vice-president devised a simpler repair using a 70-cent chicken coop latch purchased at his neighborhood hardware store. Nyrop, accompanied by Northwest treasurer Donald Hardesty, once explained to a New York securities analysts' meeting: "We're just a couple of country boys from the middle west trying to apply the basic philosophy of running a good farm to running an airline."

Nyrop's commonsense approach to cost containment became apparent in the late 1950s, as Northwest prepared for the introduction of jet airliners. Ignoring the publicity garnered by its competitors, Northwest was one of the last major airlines to order jet aircraft. But it reaped other benefits from the delay. As Nyrop intended, the airline saved money on deposit and interest payments while obtaining more advanced, longer-range aircraft. He also deliberately kept Northwest's initial jet order small, so that fleet standardization decisions could be made later, after the various new aircraft had proven themselves. Northwest's first jets, Lockheed Electra propjets and Douglas DC-8s, flew in 1959 and 1960; within a few years the airline acquired Boeing 720Bs and long-range Boeing 707-320s. Nyrop then standardized on Boeing equipment, and the DC-8s were sold. By 1963 Northwest was "The Fanjet Airline," the first airline to discard its original "straight" jets for newer, more efficient turbofan models.

Selling and buying airplanes became a consistently profitable sideline for Nyrop's Northwest. In the late 1960s and the 1970s, Nyrop sold or bought an airplane, on average, every 26 days. Taking advantage of inflation and the strong market for used aircraft, he ultimately streamlined Northwest's fleet to include only three aircraft types: Boeing 727s and 747s, and McDonnell Douglas DC-10s. In the process, Northwest earned a tidy profit ($51 million, for example, in 1977). The airline paid cash for its airplanes, and routinely sold them for little less than original price. The DC-10s, in keeping with the standardization theme, were equipped, like the 747s, with Pratt & Whitney JT9D engines, reducing the need for spares. ("Spare parts," Nyrop noted, "don't make money.") They were also outfitted for greater range and extra cargo capacity.

Nearly every U.S. airline attempted cargo operations in the years following World War II, but most had curtailed or suspended their freight business by the 1960s. Nyrop remained a firm believer in cargo operations long after other airlines had abandoned the field. A Northwest freight manager, Thomas Nolan, convinced Nyrop in the 1950s that

cargo operations could be of growing importance to the airline's profitability. Northwest invested in large cargo doors in its Boeing 707s, launched the cargo version of the Boeing 727, and converted large piston-engined airliners to freighters in the last years before their retirement. It became the only U.S. airline to operate the freighter version of the Boeing 747; executives of other airlines were stunned when Nyrop announced the purchase of three of these aircraft in 1975 at a price of over $90 million. But as the economies of Pacific Rim nations boomed in the 1970s and 1980s, freight operations became an increasingly profitable enterprise for Northwest Airlines.

With aircraft holds full of cargo, and operating costs carefully controlled, Northwest could afford to deploy large airplanes on lightly populated routes. Small cities on Northwest's domestic route map received Boeing 727 service; larger cities were likely to be visited by wide-bodied DC-10s. Northwest's low break-even load factors became legendary throughout the airline industry. In 1977, when United Air Lines had to fill 59 percent of its seats to recover its costs, Northwest required a break-even load factor of only 42 percent.

Despite his well-known economies, Nyrop was willing to invest corporate resources "where," in his words, "it really counted": in safety-related activities. Northwest pilot Paul Soderlind, working with airline chief meteorologist Daniel Sowa, conducted pioneering analyses of clear air turbulence, windshear, and mountain wave turbulence. Their work, which garnered numerous air safety awards, led to new techniques for avoiding the turbulence "upset" accidents which plagued the early jetliners, and led Northwest to become the only airline providing real-time weather information to all aircraft in flight. Northwest also introduced the concept of Line Oriented Flight Training, which used advanced aircraft simulators to train pilots in principles of crew coordination and realistic problem solving. Nyrop's devotion to fleet commonality also provided significant safety enhancements, with each Northwest aircraft, even of different types, sharing nearly identical cockpit instrumentation. For many years, under Nyrop's leadership, Northwest enjoyed the best safety record among major air carriers; when British aviation writer J. M. Ramsden published his book *The Safe Airline* in 1976, the airline he chose as his example was Northwest.

Nyrop once noted, "People like to work if you set an example," and his long hours on the job revived the midwestern work ethic that Northwest had partially lost in the years prior to his arrival. Nyrop and his lieutenants could often be found at their desks on weekends. Despite the long hours, and although they were paid less than some senior pilots, his executives tended to spend their entire careers at Northwest. Their loyalty to Nyrop was legendary. They were aware that, despite tales of idiosyncratic frugality, he could also be extraordinarily generous, maintaining his own fund for employees facing unexpected hardships, such as a child's extended medical expenses. Pilots and mechanics, many of whom Nyrop knew by name, felt they could always obtain an appointment to see him, and distant station managers telephoned him with their dilemmas.

As the airline industry grew, however, the Northwest employees' sense of shared enterprise began to fray at the edges. In the 1970s, an era of troubled airline labor relations, Northwest's were among the most troubled of all. A series of bitter strikes, by the Brotherhood of Railway and Airline Clerks and the Air Line Pilots Association (ALPA), focused national attention on Nyrop's strict management style and on the industry's Mutual Aid Pact.

The Mutual Aid Pact (MAP), established in 1958, enabled a strikebound airline to share the windfall profits earned by its fully operating competitors. In the 20 years between 1958 and 1978, two airlines, Northwest and National, garnered more in MAP payments than all other airlines combined. Critics accused Northwest's management of relying upon Mutual Aid funds to sustain profits while maintaining a tough negotiating stance. Neither management nor labor appeared to have great economic incentive to end their disputes quickly. During the 109-day 1978 pilots' strike, for example, ALPA members received from $450 to $750 in monthly assessments drawn on the paychecks of other airlines' members, and the airline received $104.8 million from the MAP fund. Northwest's uninterrupted profitability in the face of prolonged strikes helped to galvanize public and congressional opinion against the airlines' Mutual Aid Pact.

Nyrop, however, attributed Northwest's persistent (although drastically reduced) profits to its firm policy of continued operations throughout the course of a strike. Management employees kept a reduced schedule of flights in the air; at the same time, Nyrop hoped, they regained valuable frontline operating experience.

Strikes at Northwest were often bitterly fought. During the 1978 ALPA strike, both sides contended for public sympathy in full-page newspaper advertisements. But the striking pilots' anger focused more upon union members who crossed picket lines than upon the airline chief executive who sometimes joined them outside the airport terminal for a cup of coffee. Pilots who fought Nyrop across the bargaining table expressed great respect for him as an individual; in later years Nyrop would be an honored guest at gatherings of the Retired Northwest Airlines Pilots Association.

Despite accusations that Northwest ignored the traveling public in the company's hard-nosed willingness to take strikes, Nyrop belonged to a generation of airline executives who perceived their industry as providing a "quasi-public" service. Many of his days in airline management were spent visiting smaller communities on Northwest's route map, meeting with civic and business leaders who desired expanded schedules or more convenient service. Northwest was proud of its long tradition of serving the smaller cities of its home region, such as Billings and Fargo, and, with its low cost structure, it could afford to provide service in the newest jet aircraft.

But despite his belief in the public service nature of the airline industry, Nyrop was not a great champion of government regulation. In 1976 he suggested that Northwest's development of new aircraft noise abatement techniques illustrated "that airline managements can take effective action in an environmental area without direct involvement—or control—by the federal government." The following year he told the Senate Commerce Committee: "Simply stated Northwest Airlines is in favor of 'real deregulation.'" With his experience among both the regulators and the regulated, Nyrop could speak with some authority on the subject, and he became one of the first airline executives to support the principle of regulatory reform. He foresaw a reduction in CAB filings and their costs to taxpayers; greater airline pricing flexibility, resulting in lower passenger fares and cargo rates; and route awards based on an airline's efficiency rather than its weakness. Recalling a theme of his earlier career, Nyrop also hoped that deregulation would initiate a reduction in local service airline subsidies. But airline deregulation would prove a disappointment, as government subsidies for "essential air service" only increased in deregulation's wake.

Donald W. Nyrop retired from active management of Northwest Airlines on December 31, 1978. He was succeeded by M. Joseph Lapensky, a 33-year veteran of the airline, who had been named Northwest president in October 1976. Nyrop remained a member of Northwest's board of directors until 1984.

Shunning personal publicity, Nyrop consistently attributed Northwest's success to the dedicated employees he found in all departments. Nevertheless, it is difficult to imagine that Northwest could have been as much of a success without Nyrop's influence. His insistence on economy, safety, and efficiency made Northwest, generally ranked the seventh largest U.S. airline, regularly first in profits. From a weak, struggling carrier, he crafted a strong and admired corporation, "an airline," noted *Flight International*, "known worldwide not only for its belt-tightening and profits but also for its technical and operational wizardry." *American Aviation* called it "one of the truly remarkable success stories of world air transportation." But in a paradox of contemporary business practices, Nyrop's achievement, in constructing the enormously profitable Northwest Airlines of the 1960s and 1970s, unwittingly helped to create an attractive target for the corporate raiders of the 1980s.

Nyrop has been described as "taciturn to a fine point, never wasting time on irrelevancies, very self-sufficient as an individual . . . a close-mouthed straight-shooter." Keenly interested in every aspect of the airline business, he was equally at home in boardroom or hangar, and he could be gruff or

charming, as the occasion demanded. Nyrop married Grace Cary, a former American Airlines stewardess, in 1941; they had four children and several grandchildren. After he retired, Nyrop pursued interests in art collecting, travel, and sports (his son became a professional hockey player), and he remained an attentive observer of the airline industry in which he served for so many years.

Publication:

"Civil Air and National Defense," *Skyways*, 10 (March 1951): 10-11, 48-49, 54.

References:

Hugh D. Menzies, "Don Nyrop Keeps a Tight Rein on Northwest," *Fortune*, 98 (August 14, 1978): 142-146;

Stephen E. Mills, *More Than Meets the Sky: The Founding and Growth of Northwest Airlines* (Seattle: Superior Publishing Co., 1972);

Wayne W. Parrish, "Nyrop Makes His Mark In One Decade at Northwest," *American Aviation*, 28 (December 1964): 48-50;

Kenneth D. Ruble, *Flight to the Top* (New York: Viking, 1986);

Ruble, "Northwest's Nyrop, Master of Control," *Corporate Report*, 6 (September 1975): 17-19, 74-79;

John R. M. Wilson, *Turbulence Aloft: The Civil Aeronautics Administration Amid Wars and Rumors of Wars, 1938-1953* (Washington, D.C.: U.S. Department of Transportation, Federal Aviation Administration, 1979).

Archives:

A small group of Northwest Airlines records, including some items from the Nyrop years, is housed at the Minnesota Historical Society in St. Paul. The author's personal interviews with Donald W. Nyrop and other former Northwest Airlines executives, staff, and crew members were invaluable in the preparation of this essay.

J. J. O'Donnell

(January 14, 1925 -   )

by Nick A. Komons

Potomac, Maryland

CAREER: U.S. Air Force (1949-1951); Air Force Cambridge Research Center (1952-1956); pilot, Eastern Air Lines (1956-1970); president, Air Line Pilots Association (1971-1983); U.S. assistant secretary of labor (1983-1984); chairman of the board, TSI, Inc. (1984-1985).

John Joseph O'Donnell, 20th-century labor union official, was born on January 14, 1925, in Lowell, Massachusetts, to John William and Gladys Shaw O'Donnell. He enlisted in the navy at age seventeen following U.S. entry into World War II and served two years in the Pacific theater. Discharged in 1946, he started a small business with the help of the GI Bill. Three years later, however, he was back in uniform, taking flight training with the U.S. Air Force. His air force tour of duty over in 1951, he returned to Massachusetts, where he joined a unit of the Air Force Cambridge Research Center that was doing experimental work in radar siting. Then, in 1956, he left the Cambridge-based laboratory for Eastern Air Lines.

No sooner did O'Donnell join the ranks of Eastern's pilots than he became involved in the affairs of the Air Line Pilots Association (ALPA), the largest airline pilots union in the United States. His interests were in insurance and pension programs. His work in these areas was impressive and quickly caught the attention of his colleagues at Eastern and ALPA. They soon elevated him to Eastern Air Lines's Pilots Negotiating Committee and to the ALPA Retirement and Insurance Committee. He held these posts until his election to ALPA's presidency in 1970.

The 1970 election was the longest in ALPA's history. With ten candidates in the field and no issues of overriding concern, the convention took four days and 15 ballots to make a choice. In the end the matter was decided as much by the personalities of the candidates as anything else—and

J. J. O'Donnell (courtesy of the Air Line Pilots Association)

O'Donnell certainly had the most charismatic personality of the lot. He eventually was elected to two additional four-year terms, winning the 1978 election by acclamation.

If any issue came close to dominating O'Donnell's first term as ALPA president it was hijacking. Beginning in the early 1960s as a phenomenon principally characterized by members of the American Cuban community diverting airliners to Cuba, air piracy had become by 1970 an instrument of the political terrorist. Labor Day weekend 1970 was a nightmare. Arab terrorists, calling themselves the Popular Front for the Liberation of Palestine, hijacked one Swiss and three American airliners over Europe, blew them up, and held their passengers and crews for ransom. Fourteen months later hijacking assumed a new aspect when one D. B. Cooper successfully demanded $200,000 and four parachutes by threatening to blow up a Northwest airliner en route from Portland to Seattle. Over the next seven months U.S. air carriers experienced 17 extortion attempts.

O'Donnell reacted to the hijacking threat by pursuing two policy objectives, one domestic, one international. The role of the Federal Bureau of Investigation (FBI) during hijackings, largely undefined by the president or the Congress, gave O'Donnell pause. On more than one occasion FBI agents appeared to O'Donnell to have been more concerned with foiling hijackers than safeguarding the lives of passengers and crew. An Eastern copilot had already been shot and killed by a hijacker, and O'Donnell wanted no repeat of that incident. He wanted the airline captain, in consultation with the Federal Aviation Administration (FAA), to have exclusive authority to deal with hijackings in progress. On the international front, O'Donnell's chief concern was that many governments, particularly Middle Eastern states, provided safe havens to hijackers. He wanted the members of the International Civil Aviation Organization (ICAO), an instrumentality of the United Nations, to impose economic sanctions against any nation refusing to extradite hijackers.

In 1971 some ALPA locals toyed with the idea of staging a 24- or 48-hour walkout to protest the seeming powerlessness of governments to deal with the menace. O'Donnell did not discourage such talk. He felt, in fact, that staging such a protest would test the union's solidarity. But ALPA talked while the International Federation of Air Line Pilots Associations (IFALPA) acted. On June 19 IFALPA staged a 24-hour worldwide strike that brought to a standstill operations in more than 30 countries. Traffic in the United States, however, was not disrupted to any significant degree. When the call came from IFALPA, the U.S. union was by no means united on the question. Pilots on airlines that had suffered most at the hands of hijackers were eager to support the strike, while pilots on other lines preferred to ignore the call. This division among locals, coupled with a federal restraining order secured by the Air Transport Association, kept 90 percent of ALPA's members on the job. O'Donnell was disappointed, but an international

agreement denying safe haven to hijackers could be pursued in other ways.

Meanwhile, relations between ALPA, the FBI, and the FAA became strained to the breaking point. In November 1972, during a marathon three-day hijacking of a Southern Airways DC-9, FBI agents attempted to keep the aircraft on the ground at Orlando, Florida, by shooting out its tires. In response, the hijackers shot and seriously wounded the copilot and ordered the pilot to take off. The crippled airliner barely cleared the Orlando runway and made a flat-tire landing on a bed of foam in Havana.

It was a near thing. Only the extraordinary skill and iron nerve of the pilot had avoided disaster. ALPA and the Air Transport Association were furious at the FBI, and said so publicly and most emphatically during congressional hearings. Congress eventually responded with the Antihijacking Act of 1974, which, among other things, gave the FAA exclusive jurisdiction over an airplane "from the moment when all external doors are closed following embarkation until the moment when one such door is opened for disembarkation." In early 1975, following the guidelines of this legislation, the FBI and the FAA signed a memorandum of understanding governing the responsibilities of each agency during a hijacking. One of O'Donnell's goals had been achieved.

The other was more elusive, mainly because it was tied so intimately to the political quagmire that was the Middle East. To O'Donnell's regret, a 17-nation hijacking conference sponsored by ICAO in September 1972 failed to reach agreement on the imposition of sanctions against nations providing havens to hijackers and terrorists. A ray of hope did shine through in February 1973 when Cuba and the United States signed an agreement calling for the extradition of hijackers; however, in 1976 Cuba abrogated the agreement. O'Donnell had to settle for small victories, and one came in 1978 during the economic summit conference in Bonn of the seven largest industrial democracies, the United States, West Germany, France, Great Britain, Japan, Canada, and Italy. The leaders of these states resolved to cut off air traffic to and from any country that harbored or refused to extradite or prosecute hijackers. The Bonn Resolution fell short of being a worldwide agreement, but it did demonstrate the resolve of the world's leading economic powers.

O'Donnell faced another issue that was not nearly as intractable as hijacking, the Age-60 Rule. Promulgated by the FAA in 1960, the rule prohibited anyone who had attained age sixty from serving as pilot or copilot on certificated route air carriers in domestic or international scheduled passenger service. Understandably, with the rule forcing some of its members into earlier than expected retirement, ALPA fought it in and out of court from the day FAA proposed it, charging that it was arbitrary and that it had been arrived at without evidentiary hearings. For its part, FAA argued that the rule was reasonable and that medical evidence supported its contention that individuals who had reached that age were at a greater risk, on average, of suffering sudden death or acute incapacitation than the rest of the population. The courts agreed with the FAA.

By the time O'Donnell assumed office, ALPA's membership was by no means solidly opposed to retiring at the age of sixty. ALPA's younger members—men and women who had learned to fly after World War II—now dominated the union. These people did not want to wait an additional five to ten years before becoming captain; they wanted sixty-year-olds to vacate the left seat. O'Donnell stood with this younger group. He even advocated ALPA's adopting a policy making age sixty a mandatory retirement age. In effect, he wanted ALPA formally to sanction the Age-60 Rule.

Strong pockets of opposition to Age-60 still existed within the union. In 1979 a group of 300-odd ALPA members led by Captain Jack Young, an Eastern Air Lines pilot, launched a campaign to kill the rule. Young and his followers were all nearing sixty, and they wanted to keep their jobs. Allied with them was Representative Claude Pepper, a crusty New Deal relic from Florida who had become the guru of the aged. Pepper introduced a bill that would have raised the mandatory retirement age of airline pilots to seventy. Other, but less radical, bills went into the legislative hopper.

O'Donnell equated Young's behavior to someone who did not understand that "you can't have your cake and eat it too." Pilots had used the Age-60 Rule as a lever to negotiate generous pay and retirement benefits. O'Donnell himself, when he served on negotiating committees, had been instrumental in obtaining these agreements. He had argued that the rule forced pilots to lose what would have normally been "five of our highest years of earn-

ing power." So he demanded—and got—pay and pension plans that took account of those lost years. "Now," O'Donnell explained, "a lot of guys got their pensions up there—$40,000, $50,000, or $60,000—and all of a sudden they're at age 60 [and] they want to go beyond." If Young succeeded, pension plans would not build up so rapidly as before; nor would pilot pay rise so fast. It was clear to O'Donnell that ALPA had a vested interest in the Age-60 Rule.

O'Donnell found strong allies in a group of 508 furloughed Pan American pilots who had organized themselves into an association called Janus. Pan American had not hired a single pilot since 1968. If Congress forced the airline to retain its pilots beyond age sixty, it would seriously jeopardize the return to flight status of the furloughed airmen.

With ALPA, Janus, and the FAA joining forces, the Pepper bill was beaten back. Congress satisfied itself by passing legislation in 1979 calling for the National Institutes of Health (NIH) to determine whether the rule was warranted. The NIH-sponsored study concluded that while there was nothing special about age sixty, pilot skills did deteriorate with age; however, the rate of deterioration varied from individual to individual, and no measurement existed that could accurately assess the deterioration of such skills. The threat to the rule had ended for the time being. Meanwhile, in November 1980 ALPA's board of directors had come around to O'Donnell's position by formally endorsing the mandatory retirement of airline pilots at age sixty.

O'Donnell's 12 years in office were perhaps the most fateful in the history of the Air Line Pilots Association since the 1930s, the union's seminal years. His last two terms in office in particular saw the airline industry undergo great change, not all of which was welcomed by the pilots' union. It was O'Donnell's unhappy lot to find himself in a position of trying to hold back change while alternately attempting to drag his union kicking and screaming into the modern age.

The issues that overshadowed all others during O'Donnell's tenure were airline deregulation and crew complement. The two issues were interrelated. American commercial air transportation had been a regulated industry since 1938. A Federal agency—the Civil Aeronautics Board (CAB)—awarded routes and set fares. The CAB was highly protective of the existing industry. In the 40 years that the industry was regulated, no new trunk and few new regional lines were allowed to enter the field. At the same time, the CAB was extremely generous in its fare-setting practices as well as in dispensing subsidies to lines serving unprofitable routes. In short, the CAB had fostered the development of an airline cartel—albeit a cartel that provided good service, but at a hefty price.

By the time Gerald R. Ford became U.S. president, the sentiment began to take hold with influential political circles that competition would work like a breath of fresh air on the airline industry. Ford himself adopted this view, as had Senator Edward M. Kennedy. Ford, with Kennedy's backing, proposed legislation deregulating the industry.

ALPA and the majority of the airlines fought the Ford proposal to a standstill. Pilots had prospered under regulation, and they were not eager to embark on an unknown course. The decade of the 1970s had been particularly good to ALPA's members, with salaries and fringe benefits rising steadily, until $100,000 salaries for senior cockpit personnel became commonplace. With little or no competition to worry about and with the CAB ready to raise fares virtually on request, the airlines preferred to indulge in this generosity rather than risk costly strikes.

Deregulation's fortunes took a turn for the better when Jimmy Carter entered the White House and appointed Alfred Kahn to the CAB chairmanship. A skilled salesman and accomplished economist, Kahn played a decisive role in the passage of the Airline Deregulation Act of 1978. This legislation had a profound effect on the way the airlines, as well as ALPA, conducted their business. In the new competitive environment, efficiency and productivity became a means to survival. The easy ways of the past were over for ALPA. It could no longer get what it wanted merely for the asking. O'Donnell blamed Carter. "In the twenty-seven years that I was involved in the airline industry," O'Donnell said in 1986, "nobody shafted us more than Carter. . . . He was the one who signed the air deregulation bill."

Deregulation not only had an impact on salaries and benefits, it also helped promote a change in the standard size of the cockpit crew. Beginning with 1948, the standard crew on the majority of airlines consisted of pilot, copilot, and flight engineer. In the mid 1960s, because of the simplicity of the jet engine and advances in avionics, manufacturers began making airliners that did not require a flight

engineer. These aircraft—Douglas DC-9s and Boeing 737s—were designed for the short-haul market only, and ALPA accepted them at first with little or no opposition. As their number grew, however, and as larger models were introduced, ALPA adopted a mandatory policy demanding that all new jetliner models be manned by three pilots. It justified this policy by insisting that safety required the third man, even though no evidence, statistical or otherwise, supported that contention. ALPA, in the eyes of many, was engaging in featherbedding. The policy succeeded on some lines, particularly at United; but it also cost the union a great deal in prolonged strikes and goodwill. It also meant unnecessary labor costs for the airlines that accepted a third man in cockpits designed for two. These losses could be sustained before 1978; with deregulation and the appearance of new airlines with a nonunionized labor force they were unacceptable. Understandably, airlines began ordering in large numbers new fuel-efficient airliners with two-person cockpits.

Perhaps more than any of his colleagues, O'Donnell understood that the realities of deregulation demanded that the flight engineer had to be jettisoned from aircraft designed for two-person crews. "There is no way in which we can refuse to take account of these new productivity pressures in the deregulated environment and the meaning of two or three crew members in our new technology aircraft," he told his membership. With his union divided on the issue, however, it would be no easy task. In the end, O'Donnell persuaded President Ronald Reagan's secretary of transportation, Drew Lewis, to ask the president to convene a presidential board to examine the question. O'Donnell agreed to abide by the findings of the board if ALPA could pick two of the board's three members, including its chairman. On July 2, 1981, a task force headed by former FAA administrator John L. McLucas concluded that crew complement was a design specification. Two pilots were adequate for airplanes designed for two, three for airplanes designed for three. Moreover, neither design had a safety advantage over the other.

ALPA's executive board ratified the McLucas task force verdict. So, in that sense, O'Donnell had won; he had brought his union into the world of deregulation. But he won at great personal cost. The experience had been wrenching, and O'Donnell had made enemies. Not unexpectedly, he lost his bid for a fourth term as ALPA president.

O'Donnell left ALPA on January 1, 1983, and later that winter joined the Reagan administration as assistant secretary of labor for legislative affairs. The following year he was persuaded to head a small manufacturing concern in Rockville, Maryland, and soon found himself working as hard as he had at ALPA. When his wife demanded a reason for this renewed headlong plunge into work, O'Donnell retired. He had by this time reached age sixty.

References:
Elizabeth E. Bailey, David R. Graham, and Daniel P. Kaplan, *Deregulating the Airlines* (Cambridge, Mass.: MIT Press, 1985);

George E. Hopkins, *Flying the Line: The First Half Century of the Air Line Pilots Association* (Washington, D.C.: Air Line Pilots Association, 1982);

Nick A. Komons, *The Third Man: A History of the Airline Crew Complement Controversy, 1947-1981* (Washington, D.C.: U.S. Department of Transportation, 1987);

Thomas K. McCraw, *Prophets of Regulation* (Cambridge, Mass.: Harvard University Press, 1984);

Stuart Nixon, "ALPA's 50 Years: A Capsule History," *Air Line Pilot*, 50 (July 1981): 7-31;

Edmund Preston, *Troubled Passage: The Federal Aviation Administration During the Nixon-Ford Term, 1973-1977* (Washington, D.C.: U.S. Department of Transportation, 1987).

Archives:
A transcript of an interview with J. J. O'Donnell by Nick A. Komons and Edmund Preston is in the Federal Aviation Administration's History Files at FAA Headquarters, Washington, D.C.

Ralph A. O'Neill

(December 7, 1896 - October 23, 1980)

by Roger D. Launius

*National Aeronautics and
Space Administration*

CAREER: Junior partner, Kempton & O'Neill Customs Assayers (1915-1917); pilot, U.S. Army Air Service (1917-1918); engineer, Hercules Power Company (1919-1920); adviser, Mexican Air Force (1920-1925); salesman, Boeing Airplane Company (1927-1928); president, New York, Rio, and Buenos Aires Line (1929-1930); president, Bol-Inca Mining Corporation (1933-1980).

Ralph A. O'Neill made the first serious effort to link the North and South American continents by air. Responsible for the creation of the New York, Rio, and Buenos Aires Line (NYRBA) in 1929, he proved the viability of long distance airline operations. In less than two years, O'Neill's NYRBA—the airline with the longest route in the world at the time—became the first air transport company to provide passenger, mail, and express services between North and South America. NYRBA also was the first airline to carry passengers and mail on a regular basis over the Andes Mountains.

Operating a fleet of luxurious flying boats, it set standards for service and safety that were emulated by the entire airline industry.

Ralph O'Neill was born on December 7, 1896, in Cananea, Sonora Province, Mexico, to Ralph Lawrence and Dolores Avila y Landa O'-Neill. His father, an American citizen, left Mexico after his bank failed in the panic of 1907 to establish another in Nogales, Arizona. O'Neill grew up in the mining towns of the American Southwest. In 1913, after graduating from El Paso High School, he took a job in the testing department of the International Smelting and Refining Company of Utah. Two years later, he borrowed $5,000 from his father's bank and became a junior partner in Kempton & O'Neill Customs Assayers, a firm that specialized in assaying gold. Clearing $25,000 during his first six months with the company, O'Neill used the money to finance a stay at Lehigh University, where he enrolled as a special student to study mining engineering.

Ralph A. O'Neill (courtesy of Mrs. Ralph A. O'Neill)

When the United States entered World War I in 1917, O'Neill enlisted in the U.S. Army Air Service. In part, he selected the aviation branch as a way to avoid the infantry. More important was the memory of a visit to the Panama Pacific Exposition, held in San Francisco in 1915. While there, he became entranced at the spectacle of a night flying demonstration that was put on by Art Smith, a famous barnstorming pilot. He retained a vivid impression of how Smith flew over the darkness of San Francisco Bay "with bright, streaming phosphorous flares attached to his fragile plane. As I watched him wheel, loop, and cavort above a fascinated crowd, the great shimmering flares trailing filaments between the stars, I felt a strange quickening inside."

Graduating with honors from the ground school at Princeton, New Jersey, O'Neill was transferred to the Royal Flying Corps of Canada for flight training. He received his wings and commission as a second lieutenant in January 1918. Sent to France, O'Neill was assigned to the 147th Aero Squadron of the 1st Pursuit Group. He went on to compile an exceptional war record, flying 99 combat missions, shooting down six German planes,

and receiving three Distinguished Service Crosses and the Croix de Guerre with Palm.

When O'Neill returned from France in 1919, he sold his mining interests and joined the Hercules Power Company of Magna, Utah, as a field engineer. While traveling in Arizona, he met Adolfo de la Huerta, a leading Mexican revolutionary. Huerta asked O'Neill to assist him in establishing a rebel air arm to help overthrow the Mexican government. Although O'Neill turned him down, Huerta went away with a high opinion of the young American war hero. When the revolution succeeded, President Huerta hired O'Neill as a technical adviser to develop an air force for the country.

O'Neill arrived in Mexico City in August 1920. Over the next five years, he organized, equipped, and trained six pursuit squadrons for the Mexican Air Force. In 1924 he directed the efforts of the fledgling air arm in helping to put down a rebellion against the government. O'Neill resigned his post in 1925 and returned to the United States. During his stay in Mexico, he had gained a tremendous appreciation for Latin America, its language, its problems, and, most important, its potential. He also saw more clearly than most the role of air transportation in tapping the resources of the area.

In the fall of 1927, following a reserve tour with the Army Air Service, O'Neill began work for the Boeing Airplane Company as a sales agent for Latin America. By this time, his plans for an airline to connect the North and South American continents had matured, and he planned to use his sales position as a means of scouting the area and making business contacts for an airline that would run the entire east coast of the Americas from New York to Buenos Aires.

O'Neill arrived in Rio de Janeiro on March 18, 1928. During the next two months, he made the social rounds in Brazil, drumming up interest in aviation, demonstrating his Boeing F2B fighter, and generally creating a media event everywhere he went. In late May, while on a trip between southern Brazil and Buenos Aires, O'Neill flew into a *surazo,* a vicious storm originating in the Antarctic, and crashed into a mountain near Montevideo, Uruguay. He demolished his demonstrator and nearly himself. This accident ended his work for Boeing, whose leaders already had become impatient with his lack of sales.

After recovering from his injuries, O'Neill returned to the United States to search for investors to finance his planned airline that would operate along the east coasts of both North and South America. The line would be some 7,800 miles long, extending from New York to Buenos Aires, operating from dawn to dusk, and making stops every 250 miles to refuel and pick up and drop off passengers. Each day, a through passenger would be able to travel about 1,000 miles. The entire trip would take a week. Flying seaplanes, O'Neill planned to use the harbors of the great South American cities as the landing areas, each with its own support facilities to service the aircraft and care for the passengers and cargo. Since about 60 percent of the mail traffic between the United States and Latin America was with Argentina, O'Neill believed that such an airline would be profitable within a short period.

At first, however, he had little success in attracting investors. Juan T. Trippe and Richard F. Hoyt of Pan American Airways, who had visions of creating a vast airline system of their own in Latin America, tried to undercut his efforts. In spite of their activities, O'Neill finally managed to spark the interest of James H. Rand, Jr., chief executive officer of the Remington-Rand Corporation. Rand played a key role in lining up other backers. These included Frank C. Munson of the Munson Steamship Line, William B. Mayo of the Ford Motor Company, Reuben Fleet of Consolidated Aircraft Corporation, James E. Reynolds of International Founders, and Lewis Pierson of the Irving Trust Company. At Pierson's request, his son-in-law Richard B. Bevier was named a vice president of the planned company.

With adequate funding assured, O'Neill formally incorporated the New York, Rio, and Buenos Aires Line in Delaware on March 17, 1929. With offices at the Graybar Building in New York City, the company secured some $8.5 million from its sponsors during the next 13 months. The line also contracted with Reuben Fleet's Consolidated Aircraft Corporation for 14 of its new Commodore flying boats. Accommodating 24 passengers in four compartments, the Commodores far surpassed the equipment of competitor Pan American Airways. Furthermore, an angry Juan Trippe could not purchase the aircraft as long as manufacturer Fleet backed NYRBA. This fact only added fuel to the growing rivalry between Pan American and NYRBA.

Following a survey flight to Buenos Aires in June and July, NYRBA opened service between the

NYRBA routes (courtesy of Mrs. Ralph A. O'Neill)

Argentine capital and Montevideo on August 21, 1929. The following month, O'Neill inaugurated a Buenos Aires-Santiago route, using Ford trimotors to cross the hazardous Andes; by the end of the year, O'Neill's line was operating twice a week over the route. In November the Brazilian government permitted the incorporation of a subsidiary, NYRBA do Brazil, which allowed operation within the country. By the end of the month, O'Neill started another route from Buenos Aires to Asunción, and by the end of the year, the airline connected Buenos Aires and Rio de Janeiro.

While O'Neill personally supervised operations in South America, a split was developing in New York over the organization and leadership of the airline. O'Neill wanted an east coast seaplane route, where 80 percent of the population of South America and virtually all of the capital and industry were located. Other senior leaders in NYRBA favored the use of land planes on a west coast route. Led by Richard Bevier, this rival faction struggled for power with O'Neill over the direction of the company. In June 1929, against O'Neill's wishes, Bevier sent John Montgomery on a survey trip from Panama through Peru to Chile to test the potential of a west coast route. Later, the Bevier faction made preparations to buy several land planes and hired pilots to fly them. When O'Neill encountered several of the pilots in Miami, he summarily fired them all. He then went to James Rand and demanded that Bevier and his supporters be dismissed. Recognizing that this was impossible because of investment dollars controlled by Bevier, Rand counseled patience—a quality that O'Neill did not possess in abundance.

Juan Trippe watched the activity at NYRBA with great interest during the winter of 1929-1930. The stock market crash had created an especially difficult business climate for NYRBA and its investors, a situation only made worse by the squabbles between the line's leaders. Meanwhile, O'Neill's assertive personality alienated many of the people he needed on his side to help NYRBA. Still, Trippe recognized O'Neill's efforts as a genuine challenge to his company, and he worked hard behind the scenes to ensure that NYRBA did not receive the one item that would guarantee its success: a U.S. airmail contract.

While Trippe tried to persuade government officials in Washington that Pan American should be the country's "chosen instrument" to conduct international airmail service, O'Neill struggled in Latin America to meet his commitment to fly the mail from Buenos Aires to the United States within a year of incorporation. He also had promised to make the trip within seven days. Accordingly, he personally flew the inaugural mission of Argentine government mail from Buenos Aires on February 19, 1930. The flight proved chaotic, with several accidents en route that forced frequent changes of aircraft. Although the mail reached Miami on schedule on February 25, it had been a close call.

The early months of 1930 saw a full-scale war in Latin America between Pan American and NYRBA. Publicly, both O'Neill and Trippe directed their employees to extend the other line every courtesy, but this was mostly for show. Trippe's employees whispered in the ears of South American government officials that NYRBA was inefficient and suggested that O'Neill be held strictly to his contracts. Both sides engaged in "dirty tricks" that represented a potential hazard to air safety. All the while, NYRBA was losing approximately $400,000

a month. Without an airmail contract from the Post Office, the future of the enterprise seemed doubtful.

In December 1929 NYRBA's directors hired William A. MacCracken, former assistant secretary of commerce for aeronautics, as chairman. This choice had been made because it was believed that MacCracken might be able to use his contacts in Washington to secure an airmail contract. However, in April 1930 MacCracken secretly began discussions with Trippe about the possibility of a merger. The talks continued without O'Neill's knowledge, although it seems that Rand and a few of NYRBA's other principal owners knew about them. O'Neill tried to stave off a sale, but the other investors, most of whom had been hurt in the stock market crash, could no longer tolerate NYRBA's losses. Trippe offered to trade one share of Pan American's stock for 5.2 shares of NYRBA's. This represented about $2 million, a payment of approximately 33 cents on the dollar on the total NYRBA investment. It amounted to a demand for unconditional surrender.

Despite a last ditch effort by O'Neill to continue independently, the NYRBA board of directors voted on August 19, 1930, to capitulate to Pan American. O'Neill was distraught. Hours following the decision to sell out, he later recalled, "I sat in my office alone, gazing moodily at New York's leaden, darkening sky. To my very depths I felt the tragedy of broken dreams and lost years of superhuman efforts; it was almost unbearable."

NYRBA went under not because it had failed to compete successfully in an open marketplace but because the federal government supported Pan American. Postmaster General Walter Folger Brown refused to award NYRBA a mail contract, preferring to use Pan American as the "chosen instrument" of national policy. O'Neill was justifiably angry.

On September 15, 1930, NYRBA was formally merged into Pan American by a stock transfer between the two companies. Nine days later, Postmaster General Brown awarded Pan American the east coast airmail route for South America. Trippe offered most of NYRBA's employees a job with Pan American. He even asked O'Neill to stay on and manage the airline's east coast division. According to O'Neill's version of events, he replied: "Listen, Juan, there's nothing more to say except that you[']re the last man on earth I would work for. I put too much of myself into NYRBA to ever think of running it for you."

Still in his thirties, O'Neill returned to his former profession of mining. Within two years, he had gone to South America and set up the Bol-Inca Mining Corporation to extract gold from a 290,000-acre claim in the Bolivian jungle. He remained for many years with this prosperous company, which was nationalized by the Bolivian government in 1969. O'Neill retired to Atherton, California. There, he wrote his autobiography (with Joseph F. Hood), *A Dream of Eagles,* which told his side of the story of the dispute between NYRBA and Pan American. He died on October 23, 1980, after heart surgery at the age of eighty-three.

Publication:

Ralph A. O'Neill, with Joseph F. Hood, *A Dream of Eagles* (Boston: Houghton Mifflin, 1973).

References:

William A. M. Burden, *The Struggle for Airways in Latin America* (New York: Council on Foreign Relations, 1943);

Robert Daley, *An American Saga: Juan Trippe and His Pan Am Empire* (New York: Random House, 1980);

R. E. G. Davies, *Airlines of the United States since 1914,* revised edition (Washington, D.C.: Smithsonian Institution, 1982);

Davies, *Rebels and Reformers of the Airways* (Washington, D.C.: Smithsonian Institution, 1987);

Alexander de Conde, *Herbert Hoover's Latin-American Policy* (Stanford: Stanford University Press, 1951);

Elsbeth E. Freudenthal, *The Aviation Business: From Kitty Hawk to Wall Street* (New York: Vanguard Press, 1940);

Matthew Josephson, *Empire of the Air: Juan Trippe and the Struggle for World Airways* (New York: Harcourt, Brace, 1943);

Wesley Phillips Newton, *The Perilous Sky: U.S. Aviation Diplomacy and Latin America, 1919-1931* (Coral Gables, Fla.: University of Miami Press, 1978).

Archives:

Information on Ralph A. O'Neill and the New York, Rio and Buenos Aires Line can be found at the National Archives in Washington, D.C., in Record Group 59, Diplomatic Branch, American International Airways; Record Group 151, Records of the Commerce Department, Bureau of Foreign and Domestic Commerce, General Latin America; the Francis White Papers in the Diplomatic Branch of Record Group 59; and the papers on Pan American Airways in the Diplomatic Branch of Record Group 59. The National Archives also houses an unpublished manuscript produced by Pan American Airways, "Outline History of the Latin American Services," Exhibit 83 to the Civil Aeronautics Board, Docket 535. Additional information can be found at Pan American World Airways Foundation Archives (especially PAF 40.04.00) in New York City.

Ozark Air Lines

by Myron J. Smith, Jr.

Tusculum College

Although it was organized on September 1, 1943, Ozark Air Lines did not receive its Civil Aeronautics Board (CAB) certificate to begin intrastate operations from Springfield, Missouri, until July 1950. When the certificate of Parks Air Transport of St. Louis was canceled that summer, Parks's routes were awarded to Ozark, which inaugurated DC-3 flights between St. Louis and Chicago on September 26. In its first full year, the carrier transported a total of 49,000 passengers. By the 1960s, Ozark had CAB authority to serve a route network stretching through the central Midwest, including cities in Kentucky, Missouri, Illinois, Nebraska, and Minne-

sota. In October 1964 it traded several Convair carriers to Mohawk Airlines in exchange for Martin 404s; two years later, on July 8, 1966, it entered the jet era when it commenced DC-9 service.

As was the case with many local service operators, Ozark began a dramatic expansion following passage of the Airline Deregulation Act in 1978. The company added six cities (Philadelphia, Atlanta, Miami, Ft. Lauderdale, Orlando, and Tampa) to its route network and committed $85 million to the purchase of two Boeing 727s and eight DC-9s. Traffic rose 13 percent in that year and revenues went up 20 percent to $230 million, leaving a record net profit of $8.2 million. Ozark entered the Houston and New Orleans markets in 1979; however, a six-week strike lowered overall passenger boardings by 11.6 percent for the year. Although revenues increased 1.6 percent to $233.4 million, expenses jumped 12.9 percent to $236.6 million. The airline's net loss of $883,000 in 1979 was its first financial reversal in three years.

In 1980 a labor dispute combined with declining traffic and rising costs to produce another net loss, this time of $289,000. However, Ozark rebounded the next year. With the addition of three new markets, the St. Louis-based company became the major carrier between St. Louis and Florida. The new Sunshine State business, harvested with the aid of three new DC-9-80s, helped boost traffic by 6.8 percent. Revenues climbed 29 percent to $383 million with only a 17.2 percent rise in expenses. As a result of these shifts and various economies, a record $16.3 million net profit was posted—much to the relief of company officials and stockholders.

Ozark became a transcontinental carrier in 1982 when it began flights to six new cities, including San Diego. As additional DC-9s were acquired, enplanements rose a modest 2.2 percent from 1981, while profits dipped slightly to $7.5 million. In 1983 the company inaugurated service to three more Sunbelt cities, and, partially as a result, traffic jumped 12.3 percent to $429 million, leaving a net profit of $1.95 million. Expansion in 1984 included additional routes to Florida and North Carolina, giving Ozark a route network that included 66 cities in 25 states across the country. As two new McDonnell Douglas MD-80s joined the fleet, passenger boardings topped the five million mark for the first time, this despite competitive pressure at the carrier's St. Louis hub from both TWA and Southwest

Airlines. On the year, operating revenues shot skyward 8.6 percent to $465.7 million while expenses rose only 4.5 percent over 1983. As a result, a net profit of $12.7 million was earned, the second-largest in the carrier's history.

Ozark's economic fortunes began to decline in 1984. Although passenger traffic increased by 11.6 percent, the airline earned only $636,000 on revenues of $480 million. After recording an unprofitable summer quarter in 1985 (usually the airline's peak season), Ozark became receptive to a merger overture by TWA. On March 1, 1986, TWA purchased Ozark's stock for $250 million. Although the Justice Department's Antitrust Division recommended that the merger be disapproved on the grounds that TWA competed with Ozark on 80 percent of its domestic routes, the Department of Transportation agreed to the acquisition, arguing that other competitors would "prevent the merged carriers from exercising market power." In 1988 a study by the Government Accounting Office concluded that TWA's fares at St. Louis rose at more than twice the national average following its merger with Ozark, giving rise to calls for Congress to re-regulate air fares.

References:

R. E. G. Davies, *Airlines of the United States since 1914,* revised edition (Washington, D.C.: Smithsonian Institution, 1982);

Howard Gold, "The Visible Airline," *Forbes,* 135 (May 20, 1985);

Anne Kelleher, "Ozark: The Down-to-Earth Airline That's Flying High," *Air Line Pilot,* 51 (June 1982): 6-12;

Glennon Kidd, "Wings Over the Ozarks: A History of Ozark Air Lines," *American Aviation Historical Society Journal,* 22 (Fall 1977): 181-187;

William F. Mellberg, "Three Swallows Would Get You There: The Story of Ozark Air Lines," *Airliners,* 3 (Summer 1990): 28-38.

Pacific Northern Airlines

by William M. Leary

University of Georgia

A pioneering Alaskan air carrier, Pacific Northern Airlines started as a charter service that began operations from Anchorage in 1932. Arthur G. Woodley, who had learned to fly in the Army Air Corps, recognized the many advantages of air transportation in a sprawling territory that lacked railroads and highways. At a time when it took a dog team a month to travel from Anchorage to Nome at a cost of $750, Woodley could make the trip in under six hours and charge $150. Of course, few people *wanted* to go from Anchorage to Nome. During his first year of charter flying, mainly in southern Alaska, Woodley carried only 53 passengers.

Business built up slowly. Woodley soon added weekly trips to Kuskokwim, a mining and trapping area in the interior, and to the fishing center of Bristol Bay. Woodley Airways, as it officially became in January 1945, led the way in developing commercial air transport in the isolated and, until World War II, largely neglected territory of Alaska. The first Alaska airline to operate multiengined equipment (Stinson trimotors), it also was the first to use instrument flight procedures.

In 1940 Woodley applied to the Civil Aeronautics Board (CAB) for a route certificate to fly scheduled service between Anchorage and Juneau; however, the CAB turned down the request on the grounds that such service was not required. With Alaska's rapid growth during World War II, the board had cause to change its mind. On June 20, 1946, it authorized Woodley Airways—renamed Pacific Northern Airlines (PNA) on August 1, 1947—to fly from Anchorage to Juneau via Cordova and Jakutat.

On September 29, 1950, PNA attained the prestigious status of a trunk airline when the CAB awarded it the important route from Anchorage to Seattle. Eight months later, the CAB expanded PNA's authority to cover a Seattle-Fairbanks route. The airline inaugurated service on both routes in October with newly acquired DC-4s. By 1959 PNA was using six Lockheed Constellations to carry twice as many passengers to and from Alaska as Pan American World Airways, the next leading airline.

In 1961 Woodley borrowed $11 million, which equaled a year's gross revenue, to order two Boeing 720As. The new jet transports went into service on the Anchorage-Seattle run on April 27, 1962. PNA recorded its best year in history in 1965, with a record gross revenue of $30 million and a net profit of $2 million. Nonetheless, Woodley found it difficult to borrow money to finance the purchase of four Boeing 727s. In October 1966 merger talks began with Western Airlines. An agreement was reached that provided for an exchange of one share of Western stock for two shares of PNA stock. The merger became effective on October 1, 1967, at which time PNA lost its identity.

References:
Robert E. Bedingfield, "Personality: Pioneer on Top of the World," *New York Times,* June 28, 1959, section 3, p. 3;

R. E. G. Davies, *Airlines of the United States since 1914,* revised edition (Washington, D.C.: Smithsonian Institution, 1982);

Robert J. Serling, *The Only Way to Fly* (Garden City, N.Y.: Doubleday, 1976).

Pacific Southwest Airlines

by Myron J. Smith, Jr.

Tusculum College

Founded by Kenneth G. Friedkin as a fixed-base and charter operation at San Diego in 1945, Pacific Southwest Airlines (PSA) began cut-rate intrastate flights to San Francisco with a single DC-3 on May 6, 1949. By the end of its first year of low-fare service, the infant airline had transported 15,000 passengers. By 1952, with continued growth, three more DC-3s had been acquired.

Buoyed by success, PSA launched Los Angeles-Oakland operations in January 1955. Traffic increased so quickly that by December it had become necessary to replace the 31-seat DC-3s with 70-seat DC-4s. Patronized by large segments of the commuting public and virtually ignored by larger competitors, the airline boldly sought to handle its mounting loads by leasing three 98-seat Lockheed L-188 Electras in November 1959. As the 1960s progressed, PSA's frequency, reliability, and low fares on its California routes threatened the larger Pacific Air Lines, forcing it into merger in 1968. By this time, PSA was offering 73 different operations in the Los Angeles-San Francisco corridor and had extended to Sacramento. The low-fare, high-frequency strategy led this California carrier to the enviable position of being among the world's leaders in the number of passengers boarded.

In 1978—the year of the Airline Deregulation Act—the Civil Aeronautics Board allowed PSA to become an interstate airline by awarding it authority to serve Reno and Las Vegas. During the year, traffic increased 7.8 percent, revenues rose 19.8 percent to $230 million, and net income zoomed upward 452 percent to $11.6 million. Simultaneously, PSA became the first airline to order the McDonnell Douglas DC-9-80. It also leased two Lockheed L-1011s. Unfortunately, one of the company's Boeing 727s collided with a Cessna 172 over San Diego, resulting in the first fatal mishap in the carrier's history.

PSA's route system increased to 15 cities in early 1979 with the addition of Phoenix and Salt Lake City. During that year, passenger boardings rose 11 percent, revenues increased by 27.5 percent to $299 million, and another record profit ($23.3 million) was posted.

The 1980s saw continued expansion as new aircraft came into service. In December 1981 the airline added Seattle and Tucson to its route system. With gate slots and assets acquired from Braniff International Airways, PSA attempted to open a Texas division in 1982, but a federal court decision killed the plan. On its existing routes, the company generated a net profit of $18.6 million.

In 1983, despite increases in traffic and revenues, the airline suffered a net loss of $12.6 million, its first financial reversal in years. The company managed to negotiate cost-savings agreements with its employees in 1984, but a fare war with AirCal contributed to another deficit of $4.8 million.

In 1985 PSA continued to compete with AirCal for the lucrative California market, committing $1 billion for a new fleet of British-made BAC-146 transports. By now, PSA was the 13th-largest airline in the country, serving 30 cities in the western United States and Mexico.

On December 8, 1986, USAir announced that it was acquiring PSA for $397 million. Following approval of the merger in January 1987 by the Department of Transportation, PSA continued to operate as a subsidiary of USAir. On December 7, 1987, a PSA BAC-146 crashed while en route from San Francisco to Los Angeles, shortly after the pilot had reported gunfire in the cabin. All 44 people on board the aircraft were killed. An investigation pointed to the actions of a disgruntled airline employee.

In April 1988 the merger was completed and PSA disappeared. Many people on the West Coast bemoaned the loss of the freewheeling, wisecracking style of this California pioneer of low-fare shuttle service, contrasting it favorably to the conservative, corporate image of the East Coast-based USAir.

References:

R. E. G. Davies, *Airlines of the United States since 1914*, revised edition (Washington, D.C.: Smithsonian Institution, 1982);

Scott Hamilton, "USAir's Western Thrust: PSA Was an Obvious Choice," *Airline Executive*, 11 (February 1987): 24-25;

William A. Jordan, *Airline Regulation in America: Effects and Imperfections* (Baltimore: Johns Hopkins University Press, 1970);

Edward Robert Shenton, "David Against Goliaths," *Aeroplane*, 111 (February 3, 1966): 4-7;

Harold D. Watkins, "Pacific Southwest Airlines: Special Report," *Aviation Week and Space Technology*, 79 (July 1, 1963): 48-49; (July 8, 1963): 37-38;

John Wegg, "PSA: The Smile Has Gone," *Airliners*, 1 (Spring 1988): 4-21.

Pan American Airways

by Wesley Phillips Newton

Auburn University

Pan American Airways was born amidst international intrigue and domestic rivalry, in which three groups of entrepreneurs vied for the coveted U.S. airmail contract to be awarded in 1927 for the route from Key West, Florida, to Havana, Cuba. The first group, led by Wall Street speculator Richard F. Hoyt, emerged from the recent failure of Florida Airways. The second, calling itself Pan American Airways, stemmed from the plans of some ex-military and active-duty flyers to promote a U.S. airline in Latin America. The third, consisting mainly of young scions of wealth with names such as Vanderbilt and Rockefeller, but led by Juan T. Trippe, had formed the Aviation Corporation of America after having failed to push New England-based Colonial Airways toward expansion. The Post Office Department, concerned about German and French airline activities in Latin America, forced the three groups to cooperate. Trippe emerged as president of the designated operating company, Pan American Airways, holder of the Key West-Havana airmail contract, while Hoyt was named chairman of a renamed holding company, Aviation Corporation of the Americas.

Pan American raced to meet the Post Office's deadline of October 19, 1927, to begin the mail service, using a borrowed Fairchild seaplane for the first run. A week later the airline received the first of several Fokker trimotors to fly the mail and, beginning early in 1928, the first passengers from Key West to Havana.

In the fall of 1927 the U.S. government formulated an aviation policy to help protect its commercial and strategic interests in Latin America, especially regarding the Panama Canal. Pan American Airways was a chief beneficiary of that policy, and became the government's unofficial "chosen instrument" for overseas aviation operations. One of the keys to the government's ability to select one "instrument" was the passage of legislation in March 1928, amended in 1929, that permitted the postmaster general to choose the recipient or recipients of foreign airmail contracts according to whom he thought could best do the job. Another key in Pan American's selection as the government's "chosen instrument" was the lobbying energy and debating skill of Juan Trippe. He was the driving force behind Pan Am, which received contract after contract from 1928 through 1931. In 1928 the airline was awarded foreign airmail (FAM) route 5 from Florida to Cuba, Mexico, Central America, and the Canal Zone and FAM-6, from Cuba to the Dominican Republic, Haiti, and Puerto Rico. The former contract carried an option to extend the route westward along the South American coast and the latter an option to extend the route through the Leewards and Windwards to South America. Also in 1928 the airline received FAM-7, from Miami to Nassau, and in 1929 it was awarded FAM-8, from the Mexican border to Mexico City, with options to extend to Central America.

Pan American Martin M-130 "China Clipper" (courtesy of the National Air and Space Museum)

The problems associated with starting the foreign routes were numerous. Negotiations for landing rights were arduous and often protracted, particularly in Mexico, Guatemala, Venezuela, Colombia, Chile, Ecuador, and most of the French colonies. These were places where the United States was seen in an especially bad light, where nationalistic forces favored boosting native airlines. The company frequently used former U.S. diplomats and powerful Latin American insiders to win concessions.

In the end Pan American absorbed all its U.S. rivals save W. R. Grace, a conglomerate of transportation, mining, and agricultural interests on the western side of South America, long influential in that area. Trippe was forced to enter into a 50-50 partnership with Grace to implement FAM-9, awarded in 1929 for service down the western side of Central and South America across the Andes to Argentina.

Otherwise, the most stubborn American competitor was a cluster of U.S. interests organized as the New York, Rio, and Buenos Aires Line (NYRBA) and led by former World War I fighter ace Ralph O'Neill. Backed by Remington Rand's

money and a fleet of Consolidated Commodore flying boats, NYRBA concentrated on gaining concessions and constructing facilities on the South American east coast before Pan American began to bargain there. During 1929 and 1930 O'Neill got his service functioning and made a trial flight to the United States. The Post Office decided to support Pan Am in its rivalry with NYRBA and withheld advertising for bids on FAM-10 for the South American east coast until the Depression whittled down NYRBA and forced its sale to Pan Am.

Trippe and Pan American encountered their worst problems in highly nationalistic countries. This was particularly true in Mexico, where Compañía Mexicana de Aviación began operating in various parts of the country in 1928, the year Pan Am began to seek concessions. Mexican law prohibited foreign airlines from operating under their own names, so Pan Am bought a controlling interest in Compañía Mexicana in 1929. It retained its Mexican facade and thus was able to carry Pan American mail. Mexicana had American personnel from its birth. This was not the case with the foreign airline considered the most threatening to the Panama Canal, the German-controlled SCADTA in

Colombia. In a secret arrangement in 1931 Pan Am bought financial control of SCADTA, but Germans were allowed to retain operational control. In some countries, such as the Dominican Republic, Pan American was able to create its own subsidiary feeder line.

By 1930, even with its assured Post Office subsidy, Pan Am's holding company, whose name was changed that year to Pan American Airways Corporation, had a cash flow problem. During the Depression banks refused to make loans. Trippe and wealthy Pan Am director C. V. Whitney had to endorse notes amounting to almost a million dollars to obtain funds. Most of the company's capital was obtained through the backing of Trippe's wealthy friends until 1945.

Pan American's aircraft were a mixture of land planes such as the Fokker and Ford trimotors and, later, the incomparable DC-3. As far as Trippe was concerned, however, the most important aircraft were seaplanes. Beginning on October 19, 1927, with the borrowed Fairchild seaplane, Pan American employed amphibians—the small Sikorsky S-38 and the larger S-40—and flying boats such as Commodores gained from the NYRBA takeover. Both Charles A. Lindbergh and chief engineer-operations manager André Priester, sometimes disputing one another, contributed to the design of the S-40. These seaplanes were used for operations in the Gulf-Caribbean region and in certain waters off South America. At the same time they were being used experimentally to prepare Pan American for the realization of Trippe's ambition to conquer the oceans.

Since 1928 Trippe had been negotiating with officials of Imperial Airways, Aeropostale (later part of Air France), and Deutsche Luft Hansa (DLH) to arrange some sort of joint transatlantic venture. One of the essential problems in the discussions was that profit was the bottom line for entrepreneur Trippe, whereas the representatives of the European state airlines had to appease official dictates. Along with the great distances involved, weather variables, landing rights, technological limitations, and financing all hampered negotiations.

Charles Lindbergh and his wife Anne made two extended survey flights in behalf of Pan American—one in 1931 to navigate a "Great Circle Route" to the Orient, and another in 1933 to investigate both the northernmost route to Europe, via Greenland and Iceland, and the southern route that used the Azores as a stepping stone. Lindbergh was not enthusiastic about the frigid Alaskan route, but he felt that the northernmost transatlantic route could be utilized in warm weather. The southern transatlantic route, though it involved extensive overwater flying, was the most feasible in terms of weather. In 1934 the transatlantic priority took a back seat as negotiations with the European lines stalled.

It was the route across the Pacific via Hawaii and Wake Island to the Philippines and ultimately to the Chinese mainland that was first exploited. Once again Pan American became a "chosen instrument," this time primarily of the U.S. Navy, which was anxious to construct air facilities on Guam, Wake, and Midway as a counterweight to the rumored fortification by the Japanese of its mandated islands across the central Pacific. With the naval leases of these three islands, Pan American set to work blasting coral, erecting shacks and, on Wake—the main base after Hawaii—building a fancy hotel for commercial travelers. Lindbergh and Priester designed a flying boat specifically for travelers as well as mail and cargo—the S-42. Trippe wanted an even swifter "clipper," mainly equipped to carry mail and crew at first, and the Martin company responded by designing the M-130.

Pan American test pilot Edward Musick flew the S-42 in the Caribbean and off California before the crucial test flight to Hawaii in the spring of 1935. On the return flight the fuel load barely sufficed. Besides technological problems, two potential barriers loomed in the way of a clear and uncontested Pacific service. One was the Senate committee investigation of the Hoover administration's award of airmail contracts, and the other was the presence of several potential rivals that had been encouraged by the work of the investigating committee. Trippe was able to hurdle both barriers by a combination of luck, Pan Am's lingering reputation of "chosen instrument," and his skill for absorbing competitors. Service across the Pacific began in November 1935 with an M-130 flying boat, "The China Clipper," taking the lap to Honolulu in stride. Only three M-130s were produced. They were supplemented on shorter runs by the S-42s. Eventually a few Boeing 314s, superclippers that Trippe had ordered, saw service in the Pacific. But most of the 14 Boeings flew regularly across the Atlantic.

Pan American Boeing 314 (courtesy of the National Air and Space Museum)

Trippe and G. E. Woods-Humphrey, his opposite number with Imperial Airways, worked out a joint venture to monopolize most of the air routes of the Atlantic. But when the Boeing 314 "Yankee Clipper" with the first scheduled Pan American mail took off for Britain in May 1939, Juan Trippe was no longer the head of Pan American. He had been downgraded to general manager in a coup led by his old comrade C. V. Whitney. The Pan Am board had tired of Trippe's secretive ways and the fact that the transpacific service was a losing proposition.

The board soon became aware, however, that the airline could not be run as efficiently or aggressively without Trippe as both coach and quarterback. In 1940 it reinstated him, just in time to counter the greatest challenge to Pan American's overseas monopoly since NYRBA—an airline subsidiary of the American Export shipping line. Despite the opposition of Trippe, American Overseas Airlines began service to Europe later in the year.

Pan American's operations in World War II consisted mainly of the construction of a network of military air bases; the establishment of an airway system connecting South America with Africa over which troops and supplies flowed; special cargo and VIP-carrying missions; and limited commercial airline flights, principally in mostly neutral Latin America. Much of Trippe's wartime energy was

spent soliciting military business for his "Community Company," but during the war much of the executive branch turned against Trippe's monopolistic tendencies.

To finance the purchase of the Boeing 314s, Pan American had issued equipment trust notes at four percent per annum. To gain needed capital in 1940, Pan American issued stock in the amount of $6.3 million. This was insignificant in contrast to the amount needed for postwar aircraft, since the heyday of the flying boat as the primary transoceanic airliner had ended. In addition, because postwar foreign routes had been parceled out to several domestic airlines, Trippe sought domestic routes for his company, hoping to link his international gateways, and not be at a disadvantage vis-à-vis domestic lines with foreign routes. In 1945 he secured $43 million in equity capital with Lehmann Brothers as underwriters. Thereafter Trippe had little difficulty obtaining large blocks of standby capital. The airmail subsidy, however, was still Pan Am's principal means of reducing debts.

Immediately after World War II, however, Pan American failed to win a domestic route, and its monopoly on overseas routes was forever shattered. But the company still retained the largest slice of the overseas pie. After weathering with rival airlines a financially bleak period in the late 1940s, due mainly to overexpansion, Pan American enjoyed a

Boeing Stratocruiser (courtesy of the National Air and Space Museum)

boom in prosperity in the 1950s that extended into the 1960s. Americans wanted to travel abroad as tourists, and international business travel steadily increased.

In the mid 1950s Trippe also decided to invest in American versions of the pure jet airliners that the British had pioneered and then failed with because of several disastrous crashes. He began to pressure American aircraft and engine manufacturers to design and produce jets. They responded, and the result was the first generation of American civil jets. In the early 1960s jets such as the Boeing 707, the Douglas DC-8, and the shorter-range DC-9 began replacing slower piston-engine airliners.

Pan American did not continue to rely exclusively on its airline business after the war. Beginning in the 1950s the company began to diversify: it won an air force contract to create a missile tracking range down the South Atlantic; it also operated a nuclear engine testing laboratory in Nevada. Trippe pushed the company into marketing a corporate jet called the Falcon, manufactured in conjunction with the Dassault company of France. He involved Pan American in the construction of the largest office building in New York and took perma-

nent lease on it. The company also operated one of the largest chains of hotels in the world.

In the mid 1960s Trippe once again put the pressure on American manufacturers to produce a wider-bodied transport with at least three engines. But in 1968, several years before the resulting Boeing 747 and Douglas DC-10 were ready to operate, Trippe retired as chairman and chief executive of Pan Am. He selected Harold Gray, a former Pan American pilot, as chairman, and Najeeb Halaby, former head of the Federal Aviation Administration, as president and chief operating officer. Gray and Halaby inherited a whirlwind of financial chaos. The year 1969 brought the first in a series of multimillion dollar losses, caused seemingly by a sudden dropoff of air travelers, expenses associated with the purchase of the Boeing 747s, the dawn of a decade of "stagflation," and, beginning in 1973, the Arab oil embargo. As its problems multiplied, Pan American became the target of intense consumer criticism for its poor service.

Gray, a practical man but not good at public relations, was ill with cancer during his 18 months at the helm. In November 1969 he was succeeded by Halaby, a man who was relatively inexperienced in

Boeing 747 (courtesy of MAP photos)

the running of an airline. By 1972 he had alienated powerful members of the Pan Am board. In March he resigned. His successor was a retired brigadier general, William Seawell, who had been a vice-president with American Airlines. Seawell began a program of retrenchment, cutting personnel by almost half. He gave up some of Pan Am's unprofitable routes, including those in the pioneer area of the Caribbean. At the depth of its fortunes it was felt by outsiders, and even Seawell himself, that the company might have to go into receivership. But in 1977, with the losses since 1969 having reached almost $400 million, the situation improved. Encouraged, Seawell decided to take advantage of the Airline Deregulation Act of 1978 by applying for a merger with National Airlines. In 1980 Pan American took over National and at long last linked its international gateways. But long-range jet aircraft had eliminated any advantage to be gained from possessing domestic routes. Moreover, there were problems of matching up National's fleet of DC-10s with Pan American's recently ordered Lockheed L-1011s.

In 1980 the red ink resumed. Seawell sold the lease on the Pan Am office building and got rid of the hotel chain and the corporate jet division. In September 1981 C. Edward Acker of Air Florida succeeded Seawell. As deficits grew Acker decided on radical surgery. In 1985 he sold 23 percent of Pan American's routes, including the entire Pacific network, to United Air Lines. This sale of assets kept the cash flowing and the planes in the air. Acker imitated the daring of the older Pan American by opening in 1986 a Pan Am shuttle service in the corridor linking Washington, New York, and Boston.

Although Acker experienced some short term successes, his efforts to return Pan American to profitability failed. After the airline suffered a net operating loss of $170.3 million in 1987, the company's directors obtained Acker's resignation in January 1988. But it seemed to make little difference who was running the airline. In 1989 the company suffered a staggering loss of $437.1 million. Shortly thereafter it placed the shuttle service up for sale in an effort to raise cash. Most industry analysts were pessimistic about the future of the nation's pioneering international air carrier.

Their pessimism was warranted. Mounting debts soon forced Pan Am to declare bankruptcy under Chapter 11. In the scramble among major competitors to gain parts of the beleaguered airline, Delta Air Lines emerged a big winner. On August 12, 1991, the Bankruptcy Court of the South District of New York approved an agreement between Pan American and Delta whereby the latter purchased Pan Am's Washington-New York-Boston shuttle; transatlantic authority from New York's JFK International Airport; routes to various European cities; Pan Am's Frankfurt, Germany, hub; and 21 Airbus A-310 and 24 Boeing 727-200 aircraft. For these assets Pan Am's creditors received $1.776 billion. Delta absorbed over 6,000 Pan Am employees and promised investments in the reorganized company designed to save the jobs of some 13,000 Pan Am employees. But as Pan Am continued to generate red ink, Delta withdrew its promise of investment, and Pan Am went under in December 1991.

References:

Marylin Bender and Selig Altschul, *The Chosen Instrument* (New York: Simon & Schuster, 1982);

Robert Daley, *An American Saga: Juan Trippe and His American Empire* (New York: Random House, 1980);

R. E. G. Davies, *Pan Am: An Airline and Its Aircraft* (New York: Orion Books, 1987);

Kenneth Labich, "How Airlines Will Look in the 1990s," *Fortune* 121 (January 1, 1990): 50-51, 54-56.

Pan American-Grace Airways

by Wesley Phillips Newton

Auburn University

Pan American-Grace Airways, (Panagra), a pioneering airline on the west coast of South America, was the result of a marriage of convenience between the Pan American Airways' holding company, the Aviation Corporation of the Americas, and W. R. Grace & Company, a giant New York-based transportation, mining, and agricultural corporation operating in South America. The roots of Panagra lay in the crop-dusting business—true also of another American airline, Delta. The latter's founder, C. E. Woolman, was originally a field representative on the west coast of South America for U. S. financial interests that stood behind Pan American Airways. He and Harold R. Harris, a former army pilot, headed a Louisiana-based crop-dusting subsidiary of an aircraft manufacturing company controlled by the interests that backed Pan American. While directing crop-dusting activities in Peru, Woolman and Harris also negotiated for airline concessions in Peru and Ecuador, concessions intended to be assigned later to some organizational form of Pan American.

In Peru fiesty American aviation pioneer Elmer J. Faucett contested Woolman for an international concession. Aided by another American, Harold B. Grow, a reserve U.S. Navy captain in charge of developing Peruvian aviation on contract with the Peruvian government, Woolman received the international concession. Harris eventually won a concession in Ecuador. Pan American expected to cash in on these concessions and establish the sole American airline service from Panama to Chile. But a seemingly insurmountable barrier, W. R. Grace, stood in the way.

Talks between Pan American head Juan T. Trippe and Grace officials took place over the last six months of 1928. Each side discovered the other had a strength that had to be taken into account: Pan American, backed by the U.S. government, had a de facto monopoly on airline service between Panama and the U.S. mainland; but Grace, long entrenched in South America, would not be bought out and, furthermore, had a communications network that would take much time and money to duplicate. Talks culminated in the formation of a 50-50 partnership to work the concession Woolman had won in Peru. The resulting airline had taken the corporate name Peruvian Airways. The arrangement became more formal on January 25, 1929, with the creation of a new company, Pan American-Grace Airways. Each partner controlled half the initial $1 million in capital. In October 1929 a Panagra Ford Trimotor flew over the Andes from Santiago, Chile, to Buenos Aires, Argentina, to inaugurate the last link of foreign airmail (FAM) route 9, the postal route awarded Panagra by Postmaster General Walter Folger Brown in March. On the return flight

John D. MacGregor, vice-president and general manager of Panagra, rode as a passenger.

MacGregor, a former Pan American field negotiator, was Trippe's choice to lead Panagra from his base in New York. The field head of Panagra was Harold Harris, based in Lima. C. E. Woolman had returned to Louisiana late in 1928, where he founded Delta from the core of the old crop-dusting company's assets he and others purchased. Grace's representative on the Panagra board was Robert H. Patchin, whose zest for aviation had helped motivate Grace to take the air transport plunge. Trippe insisted that there be no president of Panagra, to give the impression that he was its leader. From the outset the board often disagreed on operations policy. In Chile, for example, nationalistic sentiment over a Chilean army airline service combined with traditional anti-American feeling to make bargaining difficult. Pan American representatives wanted to be hardnosed, especially concerning a Chilean demand for what amounted to a bribe, which Grace representatives saw as a financial commitment to Chilean aviation development. The issue was finally compromised by making the payment through a separate and secret contract.

For the first few years of its life Panagra experienced stout competition from the French Aeropostale company and the German-controlled SCADTA line based in Colombia. Problems at home undermined Aeropostale, but the leader of SCADTA, Peter Paul von Bauer, tried to organize a coalition of anti-Panagra elements to weaken the American line. In the end Grow influenced Peru to remain aloof from the coalition, and the von Bauer initiative failed. (Kept secret from Grace was an arrangement Trippe made with von Bauer in 1931 whereby Pan American's holding company secured financial control of SCADTA: Trippe did not want to share this accord with Grace.) After von Bauer's failure the American airline New York, Rio, and Buenos Aires (NYRBA) sought to reach across the Andes from the east to the west coast, but the U.S. post office department defeated NYRBA by refusing to grant it an airmail contract, and Pan American absorbed it. After that Panagra's main competition came from disparate and relatively weak sources such as the army line in Chile (which became the state line, LAN); Faucett's service in Peru; and the German-controlled line, Lloyd Aéreo Boliviano (LAB). LAB was strong enough to keep Panagra out of Bolivia until 1941. In 1935 an American line

employing Curtiss Condors began to operate in Peru but suspended operations in 1941.

Trippe lacked interest in Panagra because he had only a 50 percent stake in it. Panagra's fleet lagged from 1929, when it operated mainly Ford Trimotors, until 1934, when it purchased one of the first fruits of the technological revolution in aviation, the Douglas DC-2. In 1937 Panagra began to purchase Douglas DC-3s.

World War II gave Panagra the chance to stretch its wings when a U.S. embargo on aviation fuels to Axis companies drove lines such as LAB out of business, allowing Panagra to penetrate Bolivia for the first time. Panagra wanted to stretch its wings to the United States, asserting its independence to a degree, but Trippe had enough clout to block that move.

In 1946 a company financed with U.S., Peruvian, and Canadian capital, Peruvian International Airways, was organized to give Panagra its only dangerous international competition since 1930. Flying DC-4s, it accomplished something Panagra could not—it made its first scheduled flight to New York in 1948. It was, though, unable to match Panagra on the South American west coast and soon thereafter failed. In the 1960s Panagra began to encounter the kind of competition that it could not beat—local airlines that thrived on a lowfare clientele. This market had not existed before; only the affluent could afford Panagra's fares.

Meantime relations between Pan American and Grace executives grew worse, especially with the advent to the headship of Grace of J. Peter Grace in 1946. He made it plain he would not be bullied by Trippe. In 1961 an antitrust suit against both companies resulted in a not guilty verdict for Grace and a guilty verdict for Pan American on the grounds of its obstructionist tactics on the Panagra board. Pan American was ordered to sell its interest in Panagra. Trippe tried to purchase Grace's interest, and J. Peter Grace was willing to sell, but the Civil Aeronautics Board (CAB) disapproved, feeling Pan American had had its day of expansion in Latin America. On December 28, 1966, the CAB approved the sale of Panagra to Braniff Airways.

References:

Marylin Bender and Selig Altschul, *The Chosen Instrument* (New York: Simon & Schuster, 1982);

Lawrence A. Clayton, *Grace: W. R. Grace & Co.: The Formative Years, 1850-1930* (Ottawa, Ill.: Jameson Books, 1985);

R. E. G. Davies, *Airlines of Latin America since 1919* (Washington, D.C.: Smithsonian Institution, 1984);

Wesley Phillips Newton, *The Perilous Sky: U.S. Aviation Diplomacy and Latin America, 1919-1931* (Coral Gables, Fla.: University of Miami Press, 1978);

Andrew B. Shea, *Panagra: Linking the Americas during 25 Years* (New York: Newcomen Society in North America, 1954).

William Allan Patterson

(October 1, 1899 - June 13, 1980)

by F. Robert van der Linden

National Air and Space Museum

CAREER: Messenger to loan officer, Wells Fargo Bank & Trust Company (1914-1929); assistant to the president, Boeing Airplane Company and Boeing Air Transport (1929-1931); president, Boeing Air Transport, Pacific Air Transport, National Air Transport, and Varney Air Lines (1931-1934); vice-president, (1933-1934), president (1934-1963), chairman and chief executive officer, United Air Lines (1963-1966).

On April 28, 1966, after over three decades of service, William Allan Patterson stepped down from his post of chief executive officer of the largest air carrier in the United States, United Air Lines. Under his stewardship, United grew from a small company operating open cockpit biplanes to an industry leader flying the latest jet transports. Patterson was among the original airline greats, including C. R. Smith, Jack Frye, Juan Trippe, and Edward V. Rickenbacker, whose personalities left lasting imprints on the companies they were largely responsible for creating. For almost 40 years, United Air Lines reflected the forceful determination of Patterson to build it into one of the world's leading airlines, a pioneer and industry leader in numerous crucial aspects of American air transportation.

Personable, outgoing, and often controversial, "Pat" Patterson was noted for his conservative business sense, which often contrasted with his more flamboyant contemporaries. Unlike Rickenbacker and others, Patterson was a banker not a pilot by trade, and he applied his practical knowledge of American business with a buff's enthusiasm for aviation at a time when flight captured the imagination of a generation. Farsighted individuals such as Patter-

William A. Patterson (courtesy of the National Air and Space Museum)

son combined their talents and enthusiasms to mold aviation into a practical and profitable system of mass transportation.

Patterson's early life left an indelible imprint on the future airline executive. His childhood was turbulent though on the surface it should have been ideal. He was born on October 1, 1899, in Honolulu, Hawaii, to William and Mary Castro Patterson. His early years were spent in the idyllic setting of territorial Hawaii in the town of Waipahu where his father worked as the manager of a large sugar plantation.

Despite the comfortable setting, plantation life was punctuated by labor strife. One of Patterson's earliest memories was of his father on a horse with whip in hand riding down a crowd of striking Japanese workers. This ugly scene was typical of the management practices on the plantation and resulted in the senior Patterson's transfer to Puerto Rico, once the strike was settled, although the family remained in Hawaii.

The enforced separation was painful and turned worse after Patterson's father contracted malaria. The family was reunited in San Francisco but their joy was brief. Patterson's father passed away soon afterward, leaving his wife and seven-year-old son alone. Their grief was compounded when the attending priest refused to perform last rites on Patterson's Scots-Irish Protestant father. Comforted instead by a Methodist minister, Mary, a Catholic of Portuguese descent, renounced her faith and raised her son in the tolerant atmosphere of Methodism and later, Christian Science.

Mother and son returned to Hawaii, where life grew increasingly difficult for them. No longer could they live the comfortable existence of the family of a plantation manager. Forced by circumstances and supported by her father, Mary enrolled her thirteen-year-old son in a Honolulu military academy and left for San Francisco to attend business school. The young Patterson was miserable under the strict discipline of the school and ran away to join his mother, only to be caught and punished. Undaunted, he succeeded in his second escape attempt and made his way to the Honolulu waterfront where he persuaded the captain of the four-masted *Annie Johnson* to hire him as a cabin boy.

Loaded with raw sugar, the sickly sweet smell of which permeated the ship, the *Annie Johnson* slowly made its way to San Francisco with a very seasick cabin boy on board. Twenty-three miserable days later, Patterson was reunited with his mother. He enrolled at the John Swett Grammar School, attending classes by day and working odd jobs in the evening, including time as a grocery clerk, walking a newspaper route, and hawking programs at the local baseball park. At the age of fourteen, he graduated and, despite his excellent grades, he immediately sought full-time employment rather than attend high school as his mother wished. After searching the want ads, young Patterson responded to a request placed by the Wells Fargo Bank. Impressed with the adolescent's scholarship medal which Patterson wisely remembered to bring, Assistant Cashier Arthur Oliver hired Patterson as a $25 a month messenger.

Patterson had deliberately chosen employment over education, but this shortsighted decision did not last for long. At the end of his first day at the bank, he was befriended by Assistant Cashier F. I. Raymond, who talked him into attending night school at Humbolt High. Taken under Raymond's wing, Patterson took classes recommended by his mentor that would further his career in banking. Over the course of the next 13 years, Patterson earned his high school diploma and the equivalent of three years of college credit at the American Institute of Banking. Recalling these difficult years, Patterson remarked, "I was often hungry. I could spend only 25 cents for a meal. At a Boos Brothers cafeteria on Powell Street I always ordered the same things, for fear that any variation might cost a nickel or more."

Patterson's ability and enthusiasm won him many friends at Wells Fargo who helped him fill the emotional void of his early childhood. As a result, young Patterson matured rapidly and advanced quickly. Soon promoted to teller, he earned the respect and admiration of his superiors by spotting a forged check on his first day at his new post. His employers were impressed, but he still remained somewhat introverted.

This too changed when Patterson's widowed mother remarried. After this major event, Patterson left home and joined 15 of his colleagues in a large boarding house. The atmosphere resembled a college fraternity, filled as it was with young bankers, shippers, and other businessmen. His character blossomed into that of a personable, confident extrovert, despite his inherent conservativeness. A bottle of ink Patterson poured into the bathtub while a compatriot was bathing before his wedding earned him the acceptance of his fellow roomers.

Following America's entry into World War I Patterson enlisted in the army, but the Armistice was signed before he was shipped to camp, so he returned to Wells Fargo. It was at this time that he was first introduced to aviation. In 1919 on a clear summer's day, Patterson ventured down to San Francisco's Crissy Field, intrigued by the presence of barnstormers. For the princely sum of $5 Patterson received his first flight, a quick 20-minute tour of the Bay in a rickety biplane, which left him with a deep impression of the great potential of aviation as well as its hazards.

Not long thereafter, in 1923, Patterson met Vera Anita Witt, a University of California coed working as an adding machine operator at the bank. On June 20, 1924, they were married, and the happy union produced two children, a son, William, and a daughter, Patricia.

During the 1920s Patterson gradually moved up the Wells Fargo ladder to a $350-a-month position as assistant to the vice-president in charge of new business, Clare W. Banta. One noontime on a March 1927 business day, Patterson's career took a fateful turn. Most of the bank's officers were at lunch, leaving the twenty-seven-year-old Patterson to mind the store. While they were gone a potential new client walked through the door.

Vern C. Gorst was an enterprising bus-line operator who had been operating a contract air mail route between Seattle and Los Angeles since September 15, 1926. Gorst's airline, Pacific Air Transport (PAT), was in financial trouble. An excellent promoter and idea man, Gorst unfortunately lacked financial resources and skills. By March 1927, PAT was in a serious crisis, forcing Gorst to search for additional funds.

Pacific Air Transport was headquartered at Crissy Field from where Patterson had taken his first flight. Gorst lived frugally in a seedy Mission Street hotel to save money and was constantly searching for inexpensive engines and aircraft parts wherever they could be found. Gorst turned to Wells Fargo with a scheme to fund the raising of an engine from the remains of an aircraft that had plunged into the bay. Patterson was intrigued with the man and his ideas but was skeptical of the scheme. Gorst thought he could raise the virtually new engine for a few hundred dollars.

Patterson listened intently but questioned the condition of an engine that had been submerged in saltwater. Daunted, Gorst withdrew his request but managed in the process to capture Patterson's attention. The young banker went with Gorst back to Crissy Field to examine PAT's operation more closely in the hope of helping the struggling airline in some other manner. Patterson examined PAT's books and facilities and interviewed its pilots and mechanics. This lunchtime trip convinced Patterson of

the practicality of commercial aviation despite its high risk.

The normally conservative Patterson approved a $5,000 loan to PAT even though he did not have the authority. Patterson's superiors were understandably concerned when they discovered this development. Banta, in whose name the loan was made, trusted Patterson's judgment, but the bank's president, Frederick Lipman, was worried that the loan would probably go bad and ruin Patterson's confidence. Instead of rebuking the young vice-president, Lipman encouraged Patterson to monitor PAT's operations closely until the loan was repaid. He did more than that. Patterson reorganized the airline's bookkeeping system and became the company's de facto financial adviser, arranging subsequent loans and creative ways for PAT to purchase fuel and supplies. This attention turned PAT into a profitable business and banker Patterson into an aviation enthusiast.

In the meantime, other interests were expanding into the lucrative air transport field. In Seattle, Boeing Airplane Company test pilot Eddie Hubbard approached William Boeing, with whom he had earlier worked in creating an airmail line between Seattle and Victoria, Canada, with a novel idea. Working through designer-in-charge Claire L. Egtvedt and manager and chief salesman Philip G. Johnson, Hubbard proposed that Boeing bid on the U.S. Post Office contract airmail route between San Francisco and Chicago. The bid would be based on the far greater efficiency of Boeing's new Pratt & Whitney Wasp-powered Model 40 mailplane. The operation of the route would garner much needed revenue and also open a new market for this remarkable aircraft. William Boeing agreed, and the newly formed Boeing Air Transport (BAT) won the contract in 1927.

Gorst was also impressed with the efficiency of the Boeing Model 40 and attempted to acquire several for his still struggling enterprise, which was facing stiff competition. Harris Hanshue, owner of Western Air Express, offered to purchase PAT. Acting on Patterson's advice, Gorst rejected this plan, which would have hurt PAT's nonvoting stockholders, and instead offered the airline to Boeing Air Transport. Patterson suggested to William Boeing that BAT buy all of PAT's stock at a fair price and merge the company, provided that all of PAT's employees were kept. This was the first but not the last time that Patterson took special interest in the

*Patterson (left) and aircraft manufacturer Glen L. Martin with a model of the Martin 2-0-2, January 1946
(courtesy of the National Air and Space Museum)*

personal welfare of the airline's employees. Boeing readily agreed, and Patterson was entrusted with the necessary financial arrangements.

After Gorst accepted BAT's bid, which to his credit was actually less than Western's offer, Patterson returned to his job at Wells Fargo, but not for long. Philip Johnson, president of the Boeing Airplane Company, had been greatly impressed with Patterson's professionalism and concern for PAT's employees and stockholders, and asked him to return to Seattle for a weekend of general conversation about business and a proposed Mexican airmail deal.

After a pleasant discussion with Boeing, Johnson took Patterson on a tour of the Boeing factory. In the company office Johnson revealed his hand, showing Patterson into a newly furnished but unoccupied office. Johnson needed an assistant and offered twenty-nine-year-old Patterson the job. Stunned, Patterson called home and after a discus-

sion with his wife, accepted the promising offer. Aviation was far more challenging than banking, though Lipman promised to keep Patterson's job open for three years in case the opportunity soured. It never did.

When Patterson moved into his new office on April 15, 1929, the aviation industry was undergoing a dramatic metamorphosis. By the late 1920s, Wall Street had discovered the profitable potential of aviation and sought to exploit its opportunities to the fullest. Great fortunes were to be made in this nascent industry, and aviators and businessmen alike combined their forces to build vast aviation empires almost overnight. William Boeing was in the forefront of this movement.

Following the success of the Boeing Model 40, Frederick Rentschler, president and founder of Pratt & Whitney Aircraft, builders of the revolutionary air-cooled Wasp radial engine that powered the Model 40, proposed to his friend Boeing that their companies join forces to create a large holding company that would allow them to call upon much greater financial resources than individually possible. The February 1929 merger created one of the first, and by far the largest, aviation holding companies, United Aircraft and Transport Corporation (UATC). The new UATC quickly expanded, absorbing not only Boeing and Pratt & Whitney but also Hamilton and Standard propeller manufacturers, Jack Northrop's Avion Corporation, Stearman, Chance Vought, Sikorsky, and Boeing Air Transport.

Philip Johnson was ostensibly president of BAT but was increasingly preoccupied in running the new holding company. This left the actual operation of the airline in the hands of his capable new assistant. Patterson's first task was to clean up the details of the earlier acquisition of PAT. This meant acquiring all of the outstanding PAT stock regardless of cost. Patterson quickly accomplished the stock purchase despite the efforts of a Portland attorney to form a syndicate to drive up the price of the once worthless paper. The last two certificates were acquired from an Oregon madame at an exorbitant price of $666 a share.

While Patterson was attending to business, Rentschler and Johnson were striving to create a national air transportation operation to exploit further the rewards of the lucrative airmail contracts offered by Postmaster General Walter Folger Brown. BAT and PAT already controlled important west coast routes, but UATC wanted more. On June 30, 1929, Stout Air Lines was acquired along with its fleet of Ford Trimotors, which operated from Detroit to Cleveland and Chicago. Soon Rentschler seized National Air Transport, in a brilliant proxy battle, from Clement Keys, founder of North American Aviation, another holding company, who built NAT to fly the mail between New York and Chicago. By gaining control of NAT, Rentschler created the first transcontinental air route and linked Seattle with the corporation's headquarters in New York. Two months later UATC acquired the last link in its chain, purchasing Varney Air Lines on June 30 to forestall potential competition in the Pacific Northwest.

For a year these individual air transport companies operated independently, making the coordination of routes, schedules, and equipment difficult. In order to rationalize this collection of airlines, a new management company—United Air Lines—was formed on July 1, 1931, to streamline opera-

tions. Headquarters for this new company were moved from Seattle to the center of United's route system in Chicago, along the main line from San Francisco to New York.

As vice-president of United Air Lines, Patterson led the move eastward. As Philip Johnson's additional duties increasingly took him away from airline operations, Patterson's responsibilities grew. He had learned the airline business while on the job and quickly demonstrated his acumen, based firmly on his years of banking experience, by straightening out Pacific Air Transport and the factory operations of Boeing Airplane. Soon Patterson was running BAT. After the formation of United Air Lines, Patterson was promoted to president of the individual companies in the summer of 1931 and given the task of bringing order out of chaos to the nation's newest and largest airline system. This task he accomplished while allowing the member companies to maintain their organizational independence.

During this time, Patterson made countless routine decisions in running the daily affairs of United Air Lines. Earlier, in 1930, one decision was to have an industrywide effect. Stewards had served passengers for some time, especially on the state-run airlines of Europe. The thought of female stewards was at first received with great skepticism. The novel idea was the creation of Steve Stimpson, the San Francisco traffic manager for Boeing Air Transport. Stimpson had spent a bumpy flight on a Boeing Model 80-A serving coffee and soothing the nerves of ruffled passengers, a job normally performed by the copilot. After this experience, he suggested that BAT hire stewards to perform these duties. Before his idea could be approved, Ellen Church met with Stimpson and suggested that nurses be employed for these duties. A nurse herself, Church offered to recruit other nurses as flight attendants. Stimpson was intrigued and contacted "Big Pat" Patterson (not William), who hired the flight crews. He promptly rejected the scheme. Stimpson appealed to his boss, "Little Pat." Patterson realized the potential advantage and favorable publicity of stewardesses in reassuring a nervous public as to the safety of flying and in providing more personal service to passengers than could the copilot. After a discussion with his wife, Patterson approved the idea, creating a new vocation in air transportation.

Patterson began to assert his personal style of leadership by demonstrating his commitment to his airline and, more important from a long-term management perspective, his dedication to his employees. Early on he won his well-deserved reputation for beneficent paternalism, although he disliked the label.

In 1933 Patterson was entrusted with the task of merging the remnants of Varney completely into Boeing Air Transport. When he was informed that the merger would force the layoff of many loyal employees during the depths of the Great Depression, Patterson personally visited every employee on the Seattle-to-Salt Lake City route and was able to find most of them positions elsewhere in the company. The decision to retain valued employees demonstrated Patterson's belief that people were a company's most important assets. His loyalty to his staff reaped great dividends in worker morale and company loyalty, which in turn produced greater efficiency and productivity.

Patterson continued this practice well into the 1940s, consulting on a first-name basis with virtually his entire staff each year until the burden of travel overtook his health. After that he communicated through the company newsletter and correspondence. Still, every employee received personal notes from Patterson during times of personal tragedy or joy. For instance, each new United baby received a pink or blue blanket from the president.

A major turning point in Patterson's career coincided with a watershed year in the history of American air transportation. In January 1934, Senator Hugo Black opened the investigation into the awarding of the airmail contracts by Postmaster Brown. For over a month a steady stream of witnesses appeared before Black's committee detailing the inner workings of the huge aviation holding companies, especially UATC, which profited greatly, though quite legally, from the contracts.

After sufficient circumstantial evidence of wrongdoing was unearthed, new Postmaster General James A. Farley approached President Franklin D. Roosevelt, who promptly canceled the airmail contracts. The subsequent tribulations of the army's efforts to fly the mail in abominable weather with inadequate aircraft led to the death of ten aviators and a public outcry. Roosevelt returned the contracts to the commercial airlines, but with significant restrictions mandated by the Air Mail Act of 1934.

First, the great holding companies were broken up. No longer could an aircraft manufacturer also own an airline. This meant that UATC was split, and United Air Lines given its independence. The new law forbade any airline officer who participated in the so-called Brown "spoils conferences" in 1930 from working with any airline that received a government airmail contract. This meant that United Air Lines president Philip Johnson was banned from U.S. aviation, although he was never charged, tried, or convicted of any wrongdoing. In addition, no airline that received a contract was allowed to bid on any of the new contracts. Realistically this was not possible, so the major airlines simply altered their corporate names in small ways. With Johnson forced out by the government, the control of United was firmly placed in the hands of Patterson.

Patterson's managerial skills proved invaluable during this trying time. After his promotion to the post of president of United Air Lines on April 13, 1934, he was again faced with the task of supervising a merger, this time coordinating the assimilation of United's four component firms. Again he traveled the length and breadth of United routes, meeting each of his 1,400 employees in order to learn their concerns and problems. His efforts proved successful and the reorganization proceeded efficiently. The merger was officially completed on May 1, 1934.

At this time United was the largest airline in the United States and a pacesetter in the industry. With no government mail subsidy, Patterson sought other sources of revenue, which would give United a solid position once the crisis passed. He called on his traffic managers to increase ridership and cargoes to offset staggering winter losses. The effort paid off by 1937 when passenger mileage increased by 50 percent and cargo traffic rose from virtually nothing to 4.5 percent of total revenue.

One of Patterson's first decisions as United president was crucial to the airline's future. When the airmail was returned to the airlines in the spring of 1934, many of the former carriers feared that many of the new but small and undercapitalized entrants would underbid them and capture their former routes. A good banker and businessman, Patterson saw the folly in attempting to compete by bidding at unprofitably low levels. The tactic paid off as United won back all but one of its former routes; its solid financial backing and stable management ensured the reliable service at a fair rate that the government demanded.

Patterson chose to handle the airmail episode in a professional manner, bidding fairly against his competition, but he felt that the government had not behaved appropriately. Unlike other airline executives who chose diplomacy in dealing with the government, Patterson was outraged by the treatment meted out to Johnson and sought to clear his friend's name through legal means. Risking government animosity and retaliation, Patterson pursued his suit against the advice of others, asking $2.8 million in damages. Despite increasingly strained relations with the Roosevelt administration, Patterson pressed the case for nine years until the courts ruled that while the cancellation was legal, United was entitled to compensation for lost revenue and was awarded $364,000.

Once the dust had finally settled from the airmail episode, Patterson could finally turn his attention back to business and found United in an immediate predicament. Separated from its parent company and hurt by the three month absence of airmail revenue, United was also handicapped by obsolescent equipment.

The Boeing 247, the first modern all-metal airliner, which combined a cantilevered wing with a semi-monocoque fuselage with two cowled radial engines, variable-pitch propellers, and retractable landing gear, dominated air travel when it appeared with United in 1933. Unfortunately, by 1934 it was completely outclassed by the introduction of the Douglas DC-2 by Transcontinental and Western Air. When the even better DC-3 appeared in 1935, United, freed from its corporate ties with Boeing, purchased ten. Patterson realized that United had paid a high price for pioneering a new type of aircraft that was not exactly what the airline needed and vowed never to make that mistake again.

After the first DC-3s entered service with United in 1937, Patterson wisely did not sell off his entire fleet of 247s. Instead, he leased or sold most of them at generous terms to smaller airlines whose routes fed into United's. As a result, Western, Pennsylvania (later Pennsylvania Central); Wyoming Air Service; and National Parks received virtually new 247s along with material support. With updated 247-Ds, United continued service on lesser routes and experimented with the industry's first air coach service briefly in 1940. Between Los Angeles and San Francisco, United flew passengers in fully depreciated 247s for the remarkably low fare of $13.90. The route, with several intermediate stops, was

flown successfully until 1942, when the war curtailed much civil aviation.

To entice passengers back to United and into its new DC-3s, Patterson initiated "Sky Lounge" service, which featured deluxe accommodations and only 14 seats rather than the normal 21. The $2 fare increase unfortunately kept customers away, and the idea was abandoned. Soon the "Sky Lounges" were converted to sleepers for transcontinental service, which also was unpopular. Eventually Patterson relented and allowed the DC-3s to fly with their original complement of seats.

On the advice of Steve Stimpson, the inspiration behind the stewardess program, Patterson instituted a promotional campaign to entice women to fly by permitting husbands to take their spouses with them on business trips at no charge. This plan resulted in an increase in traffic, but then it was discovered that many of the traveling companions were not wives. Patterson quickly canceled the scheme.

One idea that did work was the establishment of the first airline flight kitchen, at Oakland, California, in 1937. The kitchen allowed meals to be prepared immediately before flights, without the need for caterers. The idea was a success, and flight kitchens complete with Swiss chefs were established throughout the United system.

Cut off by the government from acquiring new routes, in part because of the continuing lawsuit over the airmail cancellations, Patterson watched the competition grow at United's expense. He attempted to bolster United's flagging position in the industry by acquiring Pennsylvania Airlines and later Western, with which a close working relationship had arisen from the 247 deals.

In 1936 Patterson attempted to acquire Pennsylvania Airlines, which was then in financial straits. The merger was blocked by the Interstate Commerce Commission, and Pennsylvania then merged with Central to form PCA. In 1937, United had better luck purchasing the well-traveled Denver-to-Cheyenne route from Wyoming Air Service, connecting the Colorado state capital and regional financial center with United's mainline.

Patterson appeared on the brink of success in negotiations with the newly formed Civil Aeronautics Board (CAB) in acquiring Western Air Express. Western was close to bankruptcy in 1939 and was offered to United by Western's stockholders. Despite opposition from American and TWA, the CAB's examiner, jurist Roscoe Pound, recommended the merger. Unfortunately, the CAB overturned the decision and denied the merger.

Patterson was not one to let such setbacks hurt his company. Foremost in his mind was safety. He thought safe flying made good sense from a business perspective as well as from a humanitarian point of view. Stated Patterson in 1947, "If we take a chance and send a plane from Chicago to New York and it gets through, we gain $3,000 in revenue. If it cracks up, it costs us $1 million. All humanitarian principles aside, who'd gamble with the odds a million to three thousand against you?"

Under Patterson United established a research and communications laboratory to solve flight safety problems. Using a modified Boeing 247-D christened the "Flying Lab," United developed a static suppressor and a terrain clearance indicator, a device Patterson called "one of the most important technological advancements in the history of air transportation." Other breakthroughs included an instrument landing system, terrain-viewing television, and new meteorological equipment and reporting services. United was also a pioneer in radar-equipped aircraft, two-way air-to-ground radio, and radio range facilities.

Patterson's desire to maintain good lines of communication to promote cooperation among United's employees continued throughout his tenure with the airline. When United grew too large for Patterson to visit every employee each year, he became one of the first airline executives to establish a personnel department. After 1935 the Personnel Department had the task of keeping the president informed of important events and to promote the "human touch" through training and providing opportunities for advancement. When Patterson could no longer travel the line, the Personnel Department established a question-and-answer column in the company magazine through which he could communicate directly. Under Patterson's direction United became the first airline to argue for minimum wages for pilots, and it created a system of benefits including health and retirement funds before most of the industry did likewise. Patterson also began an employee credit union and a company medical center.

As with most executives, Patterson had no special love for unions, feeling that they exercised too much power. He did, however, form a practical working relationship with United's unions from the

start. Earlier in 1933, when he visited Newark to avert a pilots' strike, he listened to the pilots' grievances, agreed that they were "90 percent right," and set out along the line for two months to ask for suggestions. When the introduction of the Boeing 247 threatened pilot layoffs, Patterson worked with the Air Line Pilots Association (ALPA) to forge a practical working solution that preserved the jobs and United's business needs. In 1951, when Patterson defeated an ALPA strike for a new pay formula, he ordered all other United employees not to voice any animosity toward the pilots, as he was concerned with preserving their dignity as well as United's pay formula and labor peace. One dividend of this attitude came when United was the only major airline to avoid a strike when jet airliners were introduced.

In order to rationalize traffic forecasting and help plan for future growth, Patterson created an economics planning division to coordinate these activities. One of its first projects was the development of the huge Douglas DC-4E four-engined pressurized airliner. While his economics division saw the need for this aircraft, Patterson realized the wisdom of sharing development expenses and persuaded American, Eastern, Pan American and TWA to contribute. The aircraft would have revolutionized air travel, but its complex systems made it too expensive to fly. Nevertheless, though only United operated the sole DC-4E on experimental service, the concept later bore fruit with the simpler DC-4, which began the series of classic four-engined Douglas airliners culminating in the graceful DC-7.

By the beginning of World War II, Patterson had restored prosperity to United and had placed the airline on a firm financial and organizational footing. As with the other carriers, United drastically cut back its civil operations during the war. Thirty-seven of United's fleet of 70 aircraft were sold or transferred to the government and flown with United crews. Together with the military's global Air Transport Command, United flew 37 million contract miles across the Pacific, 10 million miles domestically, and 4.5 million miles between the continental United States and Alaska. United's maintenance center in Cheyenne, Wyoming, modified 5,736 aircraft and trained hundreds of ground and flight crews.

Despite the greatly increased wartime business, Patterson was not swayed by the vociferous prophets who saw the airplane replacing the automobile and the freight train. United ran a huge cargo operation during the war, but Patterson, his conservatism readily apparent, rejected the siren songs, emphasizing in lectures and articles that only because military necessity outweighed costs was air freight practical on a large scale. When market forces returned, so would reality. Stated Patterson, "If all the hot air on the subject circulating today were stored, it would create enough energy to fly all the planes in the U.S. without gasoline." He realized then that the industry was still new and its equipment too inefficient to produce the new era in mass air transportation envisioned by many.

During World War II Patterson made a controversial decision that gained him the lasting animosity of many of his peers. United's economic and traffic department compared statistics and prepared forecasts for the North Atlantic route, which was to be reopened for commercial use after the war. Pan American Airways, under the dominant leadership of Juan T. Trippe, pioneered the route in 1939 and expected reinstatement. Other airlines, especially American and TWA, wanted a share in the market and were willing to fight to get it. Trippe argued that only one airline operating with State Department approval as the sole U.S. representative—the "chosen instrument"—could compete with the state airlines of Europe.

To Trippe's delight and the others' dismay, Patterson agreed. United's forecasters concluded that there would be insufficient traffic to permit open competition. Patterson felt that the industry and the nation would be better served if America's aviation resources were pooled behind one U.S. international carrier. According to Patterson, "Our studies have shown that, great as the prospects are ahead, the transocean field will present a relatively narrow market for some time to come.... We have pointed out that a multiplicity of airlines in the transocean field might well produce dangerous, even disastrous operating results.... We believe that, in attempting to meet such competition and also to compete with one another, our present domestic airline operators might well face ruin unless heavily subsidized."

Patterson's domestic rivals vehemently disagreed and thought him a stooge for Trippe, which he was not. Patterson, always the practical banker, had made a rational, unemotional decision based on the evidence. Nevertheless, the decision led to many uncomplimentary characterizations. His curt ways with his peers did little to alter their opinions.

Patterson's support for the chosen instrument idea also reflected his unhappy experience in foreign business affairs. In 1943 he approved United's purchase of Líneas Aéreas Mineras, South America (LAMSA) of Mexico. He hoped to expand United's operations southward but was constantly stymied by CAB politics and an unstable Mexican economy. After injecting money, equipment, and expertise into reviving the airline, Patterson admitted defeat and sold LAMSA in 1952. Asked in a 1961 interview to list his biggest mistake, Patterson cited this episode: "It cost $3 million. Ultimately we got $2.6 million back—not counting the time and effort we put into it. Whatever air transport knowledge I have is based on 32 years of making mistakes and learning how not to repeat them." After LAMSA, he made a conscious effort to concentrate solely on domestic operations.

Despite the failure of the postwar boom, crowded conditions on the ground, and a rash of accidents after the war, Patterson remained optimistic about the future. He was determined that United was to keep abreast of the competition while making rational decisions on future aircraft acquisitions. His first move involved reequipping United's entire fleet with the new Douglas DC-6 and Martin 3-0-3, accepting immediate delivery of unpressurized, war surplus DC-4s in the meantime.

The entry of the DC-6 into United in the spring of 1947 went smoothly after much preparation. Patterson wished to avoid problems and the grounding that TWA experienced with its Lockheed Constellation and had this new four-engined pressurized long-range airliner thoroughly tested in service conditions for four months before it flew a paying passenger. With the DC-6, Patterson hoped to attract frustrated passengers back to United, but unfortunately that did not happen without the teething problems he had wished to avoid. Later in 1947 one of his new DC-6s exploded over Bryce Canyon National Park. Working with American, with which United had shared development, the Douglas Company grounded the aircraft until the faulty fuel transfer and vent system was corrected. After service was resumed, the DC-6 proved itself one of the most successful and profitable piston-engined airliners ever built.

Development problems also led to the cancellation of the Martin 3-0-3; United eventually acquired Convair 340s for its shorter routes. In addition, Patterson purchased seven of the luxurious double-decked Boeing 377 Stratocruisers for United's premier routes to Hawaii from San Francisco and Los Angeles. Popular with travelers, the 377 proved unpopular with United because of its high operating and maintenance costs.

As well as the DC-6 performed, it lacked sufficient range for transcontinental flight. Patterson had hoped to continue operating it until jet airliners arrived. Unfortunately, the pressures of competition did not give him the luxury of time, so he turned again to Douglas in 1952 for the DC-7. This aircraft had the necessary range but was cursed with unreliable engines, which greatly increased its operating costs. Despite the added speed and comfort of the new Douglas, Patterson admitted "the industry would have been better off without the DC-7."

The jet airliner was the coming revolution in the air transport industry, and Patterson was determined that United would make the correct decision from the outset and not waste millions on the wrong aircraft. He was willing to let the competition secure a temporary advantage by introducing jets first, letting them sort out the bugs, while United prepared. Initially Patterson favored the turboprop because of its promised efficiency. "For domestic operations," he stated in 1953, "it shows greater potential for the airline than the pure jet because it can be used for more intermediate business." He maintained important reservations nonetheless, since turboprops were as yet unproven. "They are very promising," he stated, "but you must face the fact that you are dealing with a paper engine." By 1955 Patterson turned solely to pure jets, skipping the intermediate stage. Commenting on the T34 engine for the proposed Lockheed design, Patterson remarked, "It takes six years to develop properly an engine suitable for commercial operation. The T34 is so young that no one knows exactly what it can do. Personally, I don't think it's worth the risk we would have to take. On the other hand, it does appear that we can operate a jet transport as cheaply as we can one of our DC-6Bs."

Patterson had his facts straight. Since 1945 United had been examining the jet airliner, operating a "paper" jet airline in 1952 to explore the difficulties. Flying simulated coast-to-coast round trips daily for two years, United gained invaluable experience, with meteorologists and dispatchers preparing the same forecasts and computations they would for actual flights.

Both the turboprop and the first-generation jets were rejected because of unanswered questions about cost, reliability, and the relative advantages of new versus proven technology. Countering TWA's threat to introduce turboprop Constellations, Patterson calmly replied that while TWA would have a temporary advantage, "let's look at it another way. This speed advantage will last for two, possibly three, years. But when we get our jets, we'll cruise . . . 125 miles per hour faster than any turboprop. On long, cross-country hauls, the turboprop will be an obsolete airplane, and before it's half depreciated at that. We've got to look further ahead. We can't take the risk of obsolescence before we get started." United took a similar gamble 20 years earlier by pioneering the revolutionary 247 and lost. Patterson was not going to repeat the same mistake twice. He would let others take the risk.

Patterson waited patiently for the right jet to appear. In 1950, he sent two of his staff to Britain to examine the world's first jet airliner, the de Havilland DH-106 Comet. While impressed with the Comet's engineering, Patterson fully understood its poor economics. "When we buy an airplane, we must satisfy ourselves that along with technological progress and advancement, the end economic result will be better than with equipment presently in use or that the cost per ton-mile will be lower. Under no economic circumstances could we justify purchase of the British Comet."

Instead, he turned to Boeing and Douglas, as did his primary competitor, American Airlines. Still, Patterson showed his cautious nature. "We are definitely going into jets," he stated clearly in 1955, "but first we've got to have a plane that has been conceived with a commercial objective in mind. A plane that will have all of the necessary economics in it, all the consideration for the comfort of passengers." Much to the industry's surprise, this meant purchasing the planned Douglas DC-8 and not the Boeing 707, actually in production. Patterson was willing to wait for the right aircraft rather than settle for an earlier delivery of an aircraft that did not meet his requirements exactly. The 707 started life as a military tanker, and in its original configuration was one seat too narrow for United's needs.

In the long run, the decision was proved correct, but Patterson took much criticism from share-

United Air Lines Douglas DC-6 in front of the newly opened terminal at Seattle-Tacoma Airport, August 1949 (courtesy of the National Air and Space Museum)

holders and others when American introduced its 707s in early 1959, nine months before United could inaugurate its DC-8s. He defended himself well: "When we made our decision in 1955, we decided that this race was going to be a long one, and that the company leading at the quarter-mile post may not be the one leading at the end of the race." By the spring of 1961 the results were clear. After over 25 years in second place, United took first place from American in operating revenue, revenue passengers, and revenue passenger mileage, despite flying less route mileage, after its jets were fully integrated and the merger with Capital Airlines completed.

The DC-8 was but one of the three types of jets Patterson felt were necessary to complete United's master plan to cover its 14,000-mile route network with jets by 1965. The DC-8 satisfied the long-range requirement ably. The Boeing 720, a derivative of the 707, filled the medium-range routes.

Eighteen 720s were ordered in 1957. For the shorter routes Patterson made a radical departure for a U.S. aviation executive not befitting his conservative nature—he purchased from abroad. In France, Sud Aviation had produced the Caravelle, the first twin jet, with engines mounted on the rear of the fuselage, not on the wing. The Caravelle, the world's first short-range jet airliner, entered service with Air France in 1959, receiving immediate passenger acceptance.

Word of the glowing reports reached Patterson who sent a delegation, including pilots, to France to test this new aircraft. They, too, were impressed with the Caravelle's quietness, refinement, and performance, and reported back favorably to Patterson. Won over, Patterson ordered 20 Caravelles in 1960 to complete his drive to make United the first all-jet airline. In service the Caravelles were popular with travelers, but not profitable, and they were eventually replaced by the largcr and very successful three-engined Boeing 727, for which United was a launch customer. United also assisted in the development of the smaller 737 short-haul airliner. Patterson's last equipment order came in 1965 when he authorized the purchase of 35 727s, 70 737s, and seven additional DC-8s for $375 million—at that time the largest commercial aircraft order in history.

Patterson's last major decision as United's president was potentially his most hazardous. In 1938 he had attempted to acquire the lucrative eastern routes of Pennsylvania Central Airlines but had failed. Renamed Capital Airlines after World War II, the airline struggled for years, expanding too rapidly and overextending its resources. By the late 1950s it was near bankruptcy after its unwise purchase of the British four-engined turboprop, the Vickers Viscount. With Capital on the brink of collapse, Patterson stepped in in 1960 with an offer to purchase the failing airline, provided that none of the routes were given away to United's competitors. The CAB reluctantly complied, and on June 1, 1961, the merger was completed—at least on paper.

The integration of Capital into United proved quite difficult, causing much temporary damage to United's reputation for on time performance and quality service. Eventually the problems were solved, and United emerged as the nation's largest airline, but not before suffering huge financial losses. Patterson anticipated short-term difficulties and strove to increase United's productivity. Speaking to United stockholders he declared, "While there will be non-recurring costs in connection with the merger, we expect them to be more than offset through savings achieved by the most determined cost control in your company's history." In fact revenues increased 35 percent, and earnings 104 percent, until an industrywide slump at the end of 1961 wiped out these gains, and plunged United into the red. "We didn't think the traffic slump would be as bad as it was," stated Patterson. Eventually he straightened out the difficult merger, but not without many sleepless nights for the sixty-two-year-old president.

In 1963, once the crisis had passed, Patterson spoke at length about the merger to *American Aviation*. "I'm satisfied that the merger was good for United. Last year was the first full year that we had anywhere near a normal operation, without all the growing pains, creaks, and little dissensions that

you get when you move 7,000 people into a new organization, but it contributed $4.5 million to our improved result last year. The mistakes—I thought we had made a very serious mistake when we decided for months in advance to prepare every detail for immediate integration at 12:01 A.M. the night the merger was approved. And we did, we moved right in. Well, I thought at United Air Lines that the world had fallen on us. I never saw a standard of service lower, the integration of people, moving of people. On one side, we had a group of people that never had a dime spent on them in training, people were suspicious of their company because of threats of bankruptcy, lack of security—and for six months I thought that this was a hell of a mistake to drive this through so quickly. And then it started to blossom. Then I looked back and said to myself, thank God we got it over in a hurry."

In 1963, Patterson realized that it was time he relinquished some of his duties and began searching for his replacement. After a search within United, Patterson selected Edward Keck as president, moving himself to the post of chief executive officer and chairman of the board. Keck, a quiet, remote individual, stood in stark contrast to the personable Patterson. His selection reflected a criticism hurled at Patterson concerning his propensity to promote from within. Patterson's United was seen as a loyal but complacent company, which reacted to competition rather than taking a leadership position despite its financial strength. When confronted with these complaints, Patterson retorted, "I'm not going to start firing people just to meet that criticism. . . . Also, a major executive shake-up would reflect on me. Why should it take me 18 years to learn that they were bad?" Indeed, this approach reflected perfectly Patterson's character and underscored the degree to which Pat Patterson and United Air Lines were one and the same.

In 1965, realizing that aviation "is a young man's business," Patterson asked to be named chairman of the board "with only advisory powers," retiring from the airline that was his life. On April 28, 1966, Patterson turned over the reins of power to his successor and withdrew into retirement at the age of sixty-six.

Despite a game leg he suffered in 1950, which required a radical artery transplant, Patterson enjoyed his retirement until a prolonged illness and pneumonia took his life on June 13, 1980. Thus ended the career of one of the great names in American commercial aviation, who led and built a small, struggling company into one of the largest and most successful in the airline industry.

References:

Lawrence M. Hughes, "The Tortoise That Won the Race," *Sales Management*, 87 (August 4, 1961): 36-38, 64-66;

Wayne W. Parrish, "A Dynamo Named Pat Speaks His Mind," *American Aviation*, 27 (December 1963): 46-52;

William A. Patterson, "A 'Chosen Instrument'—Yes," *Flying*, 35 (September 1944): 26-27;

"Patterson Speaks His Mind," *American Aviation*, 16 (February 16, 1953): 16-20;

"Raven Among Nightingales," *Time* (April 21, 1947): 89-93;

Frank J. Taylor, *High Horizons: Daredevil Flying Postmen to Modern Magic Carpet—The United Air Lines Story* (New York: McGraw-Hill, 1951);

Taylor, *"Pat" Patterson* (Menlo Park, Cal.: Lane Magazine & Book Co., 1967);

"Unfulfilled Promise?," *Forbes*, 89 (March 1, 1962): 16-17;

"United Bets on Slow Start to Win Jet Race," *Business Week* (June 13, 1959): 82-83;

"United Charts a New Flight Plan," *Business Week* (August 14, 1965): 128-131;

"Unromantic Argonaut," *Forbes*, 75 (February 15, 1955): 19-23.

Robert E. Peach

(March 9, 1920 - April 20, 1971)

by William M. Leary

University of Georgia

CAREER: Pilot, U.S. Navy (1942-1945); pilot and traffic manager (1946-1947), general manager and executive vice-president (1948-1954), president (1954-1968), chairman, Robinson Airlines/Mohawk Airlines (1968-1971).

Robert English Peach, who began as a part time pilot, presided over the growth of Mohawk Airlines, one of the most innovative of the local service carriers that emerged after World War II. Under Peach's aggressive leadership, Mohawk by 1965 carried more passengers than any other feeder airline in the country. In 1955 the airline became the first local service carrier to fly pressurized aircraft; ten years later, it was the first to operate pure jet equipment. Mohawk led the way in many areas, including the use of a computerized reservations system. Peach also earned the praise of civil rights leaders by hiring in 1957 the first black stewardess to fly on regularly scheduled commercial flights in the United States.

Peach was born in Syracuse, New York, on March 9, 1920, the son of John Clayton and Alexandra Emily (Kelley) Peach. His father sold insurance. Educated in Syracuse public schools, he attended Hamilton College in upstate New York, where he worked in a fraternity house for his room and

Robert E. Peach

board. After receiving an A.B. degree in June 1941, he entered the University of Chicago Law School on a scholarship. Following the American entry into World War II in December 1941, he left school and joined the U.S. Navy.

Peach became a naval aviator and initially was assigned to fly four-engine patrol planes with Fleet Air Wing II at San Diego. Transferred to Hawaii in 1943, he piloted patrol planes from Kaneohe Bay, then Kwajalein and Eniwetok as the war moved west. He undertook hazardous long-range missions, participated in the aerial mining of Truk harbor, and shot down two Japanese planes. In 1944 he returned to the United States to form and take command of a new patrol squadron. During this time, he married Martha Minge Clarke on August 8, 1944. The couple had five children.

Peach went back to the Pacific later in 1944, leading his squadron on numerous missions from its base on Saipan. Later, he commanded a unit of nine planes and 200 men that was attached to the seaplane tender *Casco*. On one flight off the coast of Korea, Peach was shot down and rescued. A lieutenant commander at the end of the war, he received two Distinguished Flying Crosses and other decorations for valor.

Peach resumed the study of law at Cornell University in the fall of 1945. At the same time, he flew out of the nearby airport as a part-time pilot for Robinson Aviation, Inc. C. S. Robinson, a local entrepreneur and inventor, had been using a four-seat Fairchild F-24 and a three-seat Cessna to fly between his home in Ithaca and his business in New Jersey. So many people had been hitching rides that he decided to begin an air taxi service to handle the traffic. Acquiring a second F-24, he established the Airline Division of Robinson Aviation on April 6, 1945. Peach became the third pilot hired by Robinson.

Traffic was so encouraging that by the end of the year Robinson had added two four-passenger twin-engine Cessna T-50s to his small fleet of single-engine airplanes. During its first partial year of operation, the company carried 900 passengers. Convinced that there was a future in air transportation, Robinson in 1946 replaced the Fairchilds and Cessnas with four seven-passenger Beechcraft D-18s. By this time, Peach had decided that aviation was more interesting than the law and joined full time what had become Robinson Airlines as pilot and traffic manager.

Settling into his new position, Peach's first task was to reorganize the growing airline's traffic and sales department. At the same time, he shared responsibility for the operational management of the line. Peach also took charge of processing the airline's route application. He had cause to celebrate when the Civil Aeronautics Board (CAB) on February 20, 1948, certified Robinson Airlines as a local service carrier.

The airline's new status led to a decision to replace the D-18s with DC-3s. Edwin A. Link, inventor of the popular Link trainer and a member of the airline's board of directors, lent the company $75,000 to help finance the purchase. Later in the year, the airline launched a private financing program, selling $456,000 in convertible debentures to prominent businessmen along the route from Ithaca to New York. The company began scheduled operations on September 18, 1948. In 1949, its first full year of certification, the airline carried 43,000 passengers in its fleet of five DC-3s.

During this time of growth, Peach's responsibilities had increased. In 1947 he became acting general manager of the airline. The following year, he rose to general manager and executive vice-president. Under his direction, the airline continued to expand its route system. In 1950, with ten DC-3s in service, it added a major north-south route between Watertown and New York City, and an important east-west route between Buffalo and Albany. On January 1, 1953, the company's name was changed to Mohawk Airlines. The next year Peach became president of the airline.

By 1955 Mohawk had come a long way from its modest beginnings. It now served 28 cities, carried 223,000 passengers during the year, had an operating revenue of almost $3 million, and posted a profit of $160,000. The airline's tenth anniversary year also saw two important milestones in the company's history: (1) it received permanent certification from the CAB, and (2) it placed into service three Convair 240s, becoming the first feeder airline to operate pressurized equipment.

To Peach's great annoyance, the CAB took a dim view of his effort to modernize Mohawk's fleet. Over the next three years, the board disallowed expenses for the pressurized transports, severely cutting the airline's subsidy. "Under less enthusiastic public response and less determined and aggressive ownership and management," Peach later recalled, "the company would have necessarily been liquidated."

The CAB proved ambivalent about the status of local service carriers. On the one hand, it did

Mohawk BAC One-Eleven (courtesy of the National Air and Space Museum)

not want them to compete directly with the trunk carriers. On the other, the board came under increasing political pressure to reduce the subsidies that were required if the "feeders" were to fly only unprofitable routes. While objecting to Mohawk's acquisition of new airplanes, the board in 1957 authorized the airline to fly nonstop between Syracuse and New York, placing it in direct competition with American Airlines on a major short-haul route. Peach realized that Mohawk could not make money by flying DC-3s on this route in competition with American's superior equipment. He believed that he had no choice except to continue the program of replacing the older airplanes with Convairs.

The year 1957 saw Mohawk move its headquarters from Ithaca to a new complex at Oneida County Airport, near Utica, New York. During that same year, and long before the civil rights movement gained national attention, Peach hired the first black stewardess to fly for a scheduled airline in the United States. At the time, this represented a bold departure from traditional practice and won Peach the plaudits of civil rights leaders.

Peach placed Mohawk in the forefront of

local service carriers. In 1962 Mohawk became the first scheduled airline to adopt a systemwide Telpak telephone communications and reservations system in combination with a Univac computer reservations center. This enabled Mohawk's personnel to make a reservation or obtain flight information in four seconds. Nor was this all. He took an even bolder step during 1962 when Mohawk stunned the industry by announcing an order of $17 million for four 79-passenger British-built BAC One-Elevens.

Having led the way with pressurized equipment, Mohawk now took the leadership in bringing pure jet transports to the local service carriers. Again, the reason had to do with competition. With American Airlines inaugurating jet service from Syracuse, Rochester, and Buffalo in January 1965, Peach noted, "I think it would be somewhat naive to assume this had no relation to the scheduled delivery of Mohawk's first BAC One-Eleven fan jet the following month."

Peach was a "hands-on" type of manager. Early every morning, he presided over a briefing that was held in an amphitheater at Mohawk's headquarters. With the airline's outlying management offices linked by telephone, there followed a detailed discussion of the previous day's operations and the prospects for the current day. Disliking office routine, Peach often went out and flew to the stations along Mohawk's routes, observing operations and listening to complaints. Typically, in January 1966, when a blizzard blocked roads and prevented many of the airline's personnel from reaching the airport, Peach pitched in and helped load baggage on the airplanes.

Six feet tall and athletically trim from tennis, Peach was described in 1966 as a man with "gray eyes, brown hair, a ruddy complexion and a high brow that gives an impression of tremendous power and drive." Recalled by an associate as "marvelously arrogant" and "very independent," Peach took great pride in being president of an airline that in 1965 carried more passengers than any local service carrier in the country.

Mohawk continued to expand during the remainder of the 1960s, attaining the status (if not the name) of a major regional carrier by the end of the decade. In 1969, Peach's last full year as chief executive officer, Mohawk flew to 87 cities in an area bounded by Minneapolis, Toronto, and Washington, D.C. With a fleet of 23 BAC One-Elevens and 17 Fairchild-Hiller F-227 turboprops, it carried 2.6 million passengers. During Peach's 15 years as head of the airline, Mohawk grew from 354 to 2,490 employees, while its operating revenue increased from $3.6 million to $64.1 million. Marring this rosy picture, however, was an overall loss of $4.7 million, caused largely by the purchase of new equipment.

In 1970 Peach announced that he was retiring from active management of the company "for medical reasons." That same year, he obtained a divorce and married Ann Carol Tarbanic. Peach remained as chairman of the airline's board of directors and watched as Mohawk suffered a bitter 154-day pilots' strike that began during the winter of 1970-1971 and shut down operations. In serious financial difficulties, Mohawk announced on April 14, 1971, that it would merge with Allegheny Airlines. Peach resigned from the board that same day, citing "business reasons." Six days later, he died of self-inflicted gunshot wounds to the head.

Publication:
"Four-Seaters to Fan Jets": The Story of Mohawk Airlines, Inc. (New York: Newcomen Society in North America, 1964).

References:
George C. Eads, *The Local Service Airline Experiment* (Washington, D.C.: Brookings Institution, 1972);
Tania Long, "Mohawk President Pilots Airline Toward Unsubsidized Operation," *New York Times*, August 28, 1966.

Archives:
A copy of a speech delivered by Robert E. Peach, "Free Enterprise in a Regulated Economy," the 1965 Salzberg Lecture, Syracuse University, November 8, 1965, is at George Arents Research Library, Syracuse University.

People Express

by Edmund Preston

Washington, D.C.

The swift rise and fall of People Express typified the opportunities and dangers of the early years of airline deregulation, yet the company itself was highly individual. The enterprise was directed throughout its brief career as an independent carrier by Donald C. Burr, a Stanford graduate who received his M.B.A. degree from Harvard in 1965. After eight years with the National Aviation Corporation, a securities firm, Burr joined Frank Lorenzo's Texas International Airlines in 1973. He became the chief operating officer in 1978, but left within two years to found his own airline.

Several factors favored an upstart, "no-frills" airline in 1980. The legislation enacted two years previously had removed barriers to entry into an industry in which federal economic regulation had long sheltered the dominant companies. Employees laid off by other airlines offered a source of nonunion labor, and Germany's Lufthansa Airlines was willing to sell Boeing 737s on reasonable terms. To finance the new enterprise, Burr was able to enlist the help of the venture capital firm of Hambrecht & Quist. An initial stock offering raised about $25 million.

People Express began scheduled service at Newark Airport on April 30, 1981, offering flights to Buffalo, Columbus, and Norfolk. The airline had at that time about 250 employees and three aircraft, with eleven more on order. Burr's plan was to price fares low enough to lure passengers who might otherwise travel by automobile. To make these deep discounts possible, he controlled costs through such tactics as low wages, the use of contractors instead of employees for many tasks, and a stark absence of customer amenities. The strategy worked, and People Express quickly expanded its routes. The airline's operating revenues hit $10 million in 1983, and its stock peaked at 25.5 in July of that year.

Burr ran his airline according to an egalitarian philosophy that mandated only three levels of man-

agement. Top executives were paid modest salaries and obliged to work without the help of personal secretaries. Employees were encouraged to participate in decision making, and were "cross-utilized" in more than one job specialty. Everyone was given a managerial title, including pilots (flight managers) and flight attendants (customer service managers). The airline required all personnel to own at least 100 shares of its stock, and attempted to foster a strong sense of belonging and loyalty.

Growth was another of Burr's management precepts. He continued to add new destinations even as competition stiffened and the value of his company's stock declined. In the autumn of 1985, People Express acquired Frontier Airlines for $300 million. The subsidiary gained Burr a new hub at Denver, but his position was now precarious. A unionized carrier serving business travelers, Frontier proved difficult to remold into a no-frills operation. By the end of August 1986, it had ceased flying and was under Chapter 11 protection.

Meanwhile, Burr had been seeking a buyer for the airline he had founded. In September 1986, the public learned that Lorenzo's Texas Air holding company would acquire People Express and nearly all the assets of bankrupt Frontier. The price of the package was announced at $297 million, less than People had so recently paid for Frontier alone, and was reduced to an even lower level by the time the sale became final late in 1986. Burr stayed on briefly, but left in mid April 1987. By that time, Lorenzo had merged People's flight operations into those of Continental Airlines.

Overexpansion was clearly a key factor in the People Express debacle. Some have also blamed Burr's policy of promoting from within the organization, which denied his company the experienced executives and specialists that might have made large-scale success possible. Once it challenged established airlines on their most profitable routes, Peo-

People Express Boeing 747 (courtesy of the John Wegg Collection)

ple Express was unable to match such advantages as their efficient reservation system and ability to deliver more reliable service.

References:

William P. Barrett, "Top Gun," *Texas Monthly* (March 1987);

John A. Byrne, "Donald Burr May Be Ready to Take to the Skies Again," *Business Week,* January 16, 1989, pp. 74-75;

O. Friedrich, "Donald Burr," *Time* (January 7, 1985): 40-41;

James Ott, "Texas Air Agrees to Acquire People Express for $297 Million," *Aviation Week & Space Technology* (September 22, 1986): 30-32;

Bill Powell, "Donald Burr: A Fallen Hero," *Newsweek* (July 7, 1986): 36-37;

Sara Rimer, "The Airline That Shook the Industry," *New York Times Magazine,* December 23, 1984.

Piedmont Airlines

by William M. Leary

University of Georgia

Piedmont Airlines grew out of an aircraft sales, service, flight training, and charter operation that was founded in Wilmington, N.C., on July 2, 1940, under the name of Piedmont Aviation. In 1944 the company applied to the Civil Aeronautics Board for permission to fly local service routes in the area. In April 1947, the board granted Piedmont a three-year certificate to provide air service to 37 cities in North Carolina, Tennessee, Kentucky, Ohio, West Virginia, and Virginia.

Piedmont Airlines, an autonomous division of Piedmont Aviation, began operations from its new headquarters in Winston-Salem on February 20, 1948. During the first year, the airline used its DC-3s to carry more than 80,000 passengers. By 1950, it had become the leading local service carrier in the Southeast. Under the prudent leadership of Thomas H. Davis, Piedmont continued a policy of careful expansion for the next quarter century, reaching Washington in 1955, Atlanta in 1962, New York City in 1966, and Nashville, Memphis, and Chicago by 1968.

As Piedmont's route structure grew, its equipment improved. In November 1958, the airline introduced into service Fokker F-27 turboprops. Four years later, President Davis purchased 17 Martin 404s from TWA for a bargain price, and used them to retire the airline's DC-3s. In 1967 Piedmont began pure jet operations with two Boeing 727s. These were followed in 1968 by a fleet of 12 Boeing 737s, which became the airline's mainstay aircraft for longer routes. Beginning in 1969, Piedmont used 60-passenger Nihon YS-11s on its shorter routes, becoming the leading U.S. operator of the Japanese-built turboprop.

Piedmont prospered under deregulation. In 1978 it extended service to Boston, Philadelphia, Pittsburgh, and Denver, carrying 4.6 million passengers and flying 1.4 billion revenue passenger miles

(RPM). The following year it expanded into Florida and Texas, registering a 34 percent increase in RPM and doubling its net profits to $11.6 million.

Both traffic and profits continued to increase in the 1980s, as Piedmont concentrated on operations from its hubs at Charlotte, Dayton, and Baltimore, while successfully avoiding destructive competition with major carriers. In 1985 Piedmont served 100 cities in 24 states with a fleet of 64 Boeing 737s, 34 Boeing 727s, and 20 Fokker F-28s. It carried more than 18 million passengers, had revenues of over $1 billion, and posted a record net profit of $66.7 million.

In April 1987, during a wave of airline mergers, USAir purchased Piedmont for $1.6 billion. The largest merger in airline history took nearly three years to complete. Although August 5, 1989, was the formal merger date, marking the integration of Piedmont's 205 aircraft and 22,000 employees into USAir's 226 aircraft and 27,000 employees, negotiations with Piedmont's pilots delayed the full implementation of the process until February 1, 1990.

References:

Thomas H. Davis, *The History of Piedmont: Setting a Special Pace* (New York: Newcomen Society in North America, 1982);

George C. Eads, *The Local Service Airline Experiment* (Washington, D.C.: Brookings Institution, 1972);

Joan M. Feldman, "Blending the Elements of a Major Empire," *Air Transport World,* 25 (June 1988): 28-32, 41;

Henry Lefer, "Piedmont Played the Game and Won," *Air Transport World,* 22 (January 1985): 32-35, 38;

Paul Seidenman and David J. Spanovich, "Piedmont: A Shining Star of Deregulation," *Airline Executive,* 8 (October 1985): 32-35, 38.

Pioneer Air Lines

by William M. Leary

University of Georgia

Pioneer Air Lines began as a Houston-based company named Essair, an acronym for *Efficiency, Safety,* and *Speed* by *Air*. In January 1939 Essair obtained authorization to fly an experimental local passenger service between Houston and Amarillo via Abilene and other small communities. However, Braniff Airways appealed the award, causing Essair to postpone inauguration of service on the route. The Civil Aeronautics Board (CAB) eventually ruled in Essair's favor but not until November 5, 1943; by this time, military demands caused additional delays. On July 14, 1944, the CAB created a new category of local service (or feeder) airline, with Essair the first such carrier to be certified.

Essair finally got off the ground on August 1, 1945, using three Lockheed 10A Electras to fly one daily round trip between Houston and Amarillo via Austin, San Angelo, Abilene, and Lubbock. By the end of the year, the airline had carried 4,452 passengers.

Essair underwent significant changes in 1946. Maj. William Long, a World War I flier and noted barnstormer who had been the company's major source of funding, was joined by Gen. Robert T. Smith, a prominent lawyer and former executive vice-president of Braniff Airways, who purchased a half interest in the airline for $200,000. Shortly thereafter, Essair changed its name to Pioneer Air Lines and adopted the bison as its trademark. In August, Pioneer became the first local service airline to move up to DC-3s. Despite an average load factor of 54 percent with its nine-passenger Lockheeds during the first 13 months of operation, the airline purchased nine C-47s (for $160,000) from the War Assets Administration and converted them to 24-passenger DC-3s. Finally, Pioneer secured the first authorization by a local service carrier to fly at night and under instrument conditions.

In 1947-1948, as the DC-3s came into service, Pioneer obtained new routes from the CAB that extended its area of operation northward to Dallas and westward to Albuquerque. Competing with trunk carriers on half its routes, Pioneer managed to turn a profit of $250,000 in 1949 and 1950. In order to keep pace with the larger airlines, Pioneer in June 1952 replaced its entire fleet of 11 DC-3s with nine 36-seat Martin 202s, bought from Northwest Airlines for $300,000 each. It also announced plans to purchase five pressurized Convair 340s, at a cost of over $4 million, to be delivered in 1954. At the same time, it asked the CAB for an increase in mail pay to cover the operating costs of the new equipment.

In March 1953 the CAB refused to grant the additional funds, stating that "we do not recognize competitive considerations as a significant justification for subsidizing new equipment." Although the board later would reverse this position and display a more sympathetic attitude toward local service carriers that sought to upgrade their equipment, the change came too late for Pioneer. The airline was forced to sell its Martins and reacquire DC-3s. By the summer of 1953, Pioneer was losing $3,000 a day. Faced with financial disaster, the airline's owners signed a merger agreement with Continental Airlines at the end of the year. After the CAB approved the merger in December 1954, Pioneer passed out of existence on April 1, 1955.

References:

R. E. G. Davies, *Continental Airlines: The First Fifty Years, 1934-1983* (The Woodlands, Tex.: Pioneer Publications, 1985);

George C. Eads, *The Local Service Airline Experiment* (Washington, D.C.: Brookings Institution, 1972);

Brian Lusk, "Flying the Range," *Airliners,* 3 (Spring 1990): 28-35, 46-48.

L. Welch Pogue

(October 21, 1899 -   )

by Paul A. Cleveland

Birmingham-Southern College

CAREER: Lawyer, Ropes, Gray, Boyden & Perkins (1927-1933); partner, Searle, James & Crawford (1933-1938); assistant general counsel (1938), general counsel, Civil Aeronautics Authority/Civil Aeronautics Board (1938-1942); member (1942), chairman, Civil Aeronautics Board (1943-1946); managing partner, Pogue & Neal (1946-1967); managing partner, Jones, Day, Reavis & Pogue (1967-1981).

Lloyd Welch Pogue was instrumental in shaping U.S. commercial aviation policy during and after World War II. His initial interest in the airline industry developed in the late 1930s when he was practicing law in New York City. Recognizing the potential of this budding industry, he secured a legal position in 1938 with the Civil Aeronautics Authority. He went on to serve as chairman of the Civil Aeronautics Board.

Born on October 21, 1899, to Leander and Myrtle (Casey) Pogue, Pogue grew up on his parents' farm, located 20 miles northeast of Red Oak in southwestern Iowa. His mother taught him at home through the seventh grade. He went on to graduate from Red Oak High School.

With limited funds, Pogue had to struggle for his higher education. He entered Grinnell College in 1918, where he enlisted in the Student Army Training Corps. The money from this position, coupled with the aid of a small scholarship, provided the necessary financing to attend school. The end of World War I, however, brought an honorable discharge from the training corps and a national economic crisis. Pogue had to return to the family farm in 1919 to earn money to continue his education. In 1920 he transferred to the University of Nebraska after locating steady work in the Lincoln area. He finally received his A.B. degree in 1924, having studied the liberal arts and law.

L. Welch Pogue

Pogue once again returned to the family farm, where his father wanted his two sons to remain and one day take over the operation. But Pogue wanted to become a lawyer. In spite of the advice of family and friends, he left the farm and entered law school at the University of Michigan, from which he graduated in 1926.

Pogue went back to Nebraska only long enough to marry Mary Ellen Edgerton on September 8, 1926. He later would write of his wife: "[She] encouraged and inspired me in all of my undertakings and deserves great credit in my major undertakings where vision and courage were required." This supportive relationship would produce three sons: Richard Welch, William Lloyd, and John Marshall.

The newlyweds moved to Cambridge, Massachusetts, where Welch enrolled in Harvard Law School. After graduating in 1927 with a doctorate of judicial science, he joined the Boston firm of Ropes, Gray, Boyden & Perkins, the second largest legal firm in the country. Pogue specialized in corporate financial law. In 1930 he gained his first international experience when he spent a year in Europe, helping to open a branch office in Paris. Three years later, he became a partner in the New York firm of Searle, James & Crawford, continuing to work in corporate financial law.

While in New York, Pogue first became attracted to the developing field of aviation. Convinced that air travel would grow rapidly in the years ahead, he decided to learn more about the industry. This eventually led, in the fall of 1938, to a position as assistant general counsel of the newly created Civil Aeronautics Authority. Within six months Pogue was promoted to general counsel of the agency, which was reorganized as the Civil Aeronautics Board (CAB) in 1940.

In January 1942 President Franklin D. Roosevelt appointed Pogue to a six-year term on the five-member CAB. The next year, Roosevelt selected him as chairman of the CAB, a position Pogue would hold until 1946.

During his first two years on the CAB, Pogue concentrated on policy decisions that were designed to assist America's war effort. Air routes had to be altered to suit wartime needs, and a system of travel priorities had to be developed. The CAB eliminated certain routes, suspended the route certification process, authorized special new air carrier service where necessary, and placed restrictions on nonessential traffic. Although more than half of the airlines' equipment was employed exclusively for military purposes, civilian air traffic decreased only by 27 percent in 1943. At the same time, international airlines increased their plane-miles by 21 percent.

As World War II drew to a close, questions about the shape of postwar air travel began to come to the fore. Adolf A. Berle, Jr., a State Department official and confidant of President Roosevelt, advocated an open-skies policy that would give the United States a dominant position in the postwar pe-

riod. Pogue took a more moderate position, arguing for bilateral negotiations. Berle's view initially prevailed. In 1944 representatives of 54 nations assembled in Chicago in an effort to reach a multilateral agreement outlining international air rights and operations. Although a sharp clash between the United States and Great Britain made it impossible to conclude a multidimensional accord, the Chicago Conference managed to lay the technical foundations for international air travel. Pogue took a prominent role at Chicago, chairing the subcommittee that drafted a charter for what became the International Civil Aviation Organization.

In 1946 the administration of Harry S. Truman accepted Pogue's position on international aviation agreements. Pogue helped shape the bilateral Bermuda Agreement between the United States and Great Britain. This document, which defined routes, landing rights, frequency of service, and other matters of mutual concern, became the model for similar agreements between the United States and other nations. As historian Henry Ladd Smith has observed, the Bermuda Agreement stands as "one of the most important documents in the history of international air transportation."

Meanwhile, the CAB was deciding which U.S. airlines should fly the postwar international routes. Pan American Airways and its political allies argued for a single national flag carrier that would be dominated by Pan American. Pogue supported a more competitive system. In July 1945 the CAB decided the important North Atlantic Case, which gave important routes to Europe not only to Pan American but also to American Export Airlines (owned by American Airlines) and TWA. This competitive arrangement spelled the end of Pan American's hope for a continuation of its prewar monopoly and set the tone for the development of the nation's international air policy.

Among the more important decisions taken by the CAB with respect to domestic airlines, the establishment of a new classification of air carrier stands out. Even before the war ended, Pogue recognized the need for smaller airlines to serve communities that the trunk carriers were ignoring. On July 11, 1944, the CAB authorized a new classification, feeder airlines (later known as local service airlines), designed to link the smaller communities to large cities where trunk connections could be obtained. This decision opened the way for an entirely new level of air service, marking the growing maturity of the domestic air transport industry.

Under Pogue's direction the CAB also took the lead in seeking to reduce air fares. On February 27, 1943, it ordered 11 of the 16 certified trunk carriers to show reason why passenger fares should not be lowered. Within five months, five of the carriers had responded with rate reductions of from 6 to 7.6 percent. Most of the remaining airlines fell in line by the end of the year. This marked the first significant action that the CAB had ever taken with respect to passenger air fares.

On June 1, 1946, Pogue stepped down as chairman of the CAB and returned to private law practice. By this time he was recognized as a leading authority on domestic and international air transportation law. There was general agreement that he had been instrumental in defining the nature of the postwar airline industry.

In partnership with George Neal, who also had been associated with the CAB, Pogue quickly developed a prosperous legal practice, signing up many of the nation's leading airlines as clients. His firm, known as Jones, Day, Reavis & Pogue after a merger in 1967, frequently represented these airlines in cases before the CAB, often functioning as a lobbyist. Even when the efforts of the law firm failed, the rewards would be generous. In 1967-1968, for example, Eastern Air Lines' unsuccessful effort to secure transpacific routes brought the firm more than a million dollars in legal fees.

In January 1981 Pogue retired from the active practice of law. He remained occupied with a variety of activities, taping law books for the blind, serving as a volunteer tour guide at the National Air and Space Museum, and rebinding valuable old books. Recognized by the Society of Senior Aerospace Executives as a "living legend," he received their prestigious Golden Eagle Award in 1988. In making the presentation, the society called attention to a "lifelong dedication to aviation [that] has left an enduring mark on the air transportation industry."

References:

Robert Burkhardt, *CAB—The Civil Aeronautics Board* (Dulles International Airport, Va.: Green Hills Publishing Co., 1974);

Alan P. Dobson, *Peaceful Air Warfare: The United States, Britain, and the Politics of International Aviation* (New York: Oxford University Press, 1991);

John Marshall Pogue, *Pogue/Pollock/Polk Genealogy* (Baltimore: Gateway Press, 1990);

Samuel B. Richmond, *Regulation and Competition in Air Transportation* (New York: Columbia University Press, 1961);

Henry Ladd Smith, *Airways Abroad* (Madison: University of Wisconsin Press, 1950);

U.S. Civil Aeronautics Board, *Civil Aeronautics Board Reports to Congress: Fiscal Year 1968* (Washington, D.C.: U.S. Government Printing Office, 1968).

Otto Praeger

(February 27, 1871 - February 4, 1948)

by William M. Leary

University of Georgia

CAREER: Journalist, Texas and Washington, D.C. (1887-1914); postmaster of Washington, D.C. (1914-1915); second assistant postmaster general (1915-1921); adviser to the Post and Telegraph Department, government of Siam (1928-1933).

Often called the "father of Air Mail," Otto Praeger was born in Victoria, Texas, on February 27, 1871, the son of Herman Praeger and Louisa Schultze. Herman had emigrated from Dresden in 1851. In 1879 the family moved to San Antonio, where Herman opened a hardware store. Educated in local schools, Otto Praeger left San Pedro High School prior to graduation to take a job as a reporter on the *San Antonio Express*. Six years later, he entered the University of Texas as a nondegree student and took courses in political economy, psychology, history, and literature. Praeger enjoyed his three years at Austin, which, he later wrote in an unpublished autobiography, provided a necessary foun-

Otto Praeger (courtesy of the Praeger family)

dation for "solid journalistic work." Not only did he gain a greater knowledge of the arts and sciences, but he also learned even more valuable lessons: "To observe, to analyze and to weigh are the priceless gifts that I carried back into my profession from my alma mater."

Praeger rejoined the *Express* in 1897, eventually rising to the position of city editor. Seeking a new challenge, he resigned in 1904 and went to Washington, D.C., as political correspondent for three Texas newspapers, including the influential *Dallas News.* He spent ten fulfilling years in the nation's capital, reporting "the stirring events that marked the rise, sweep and eclipse of the Progressive movement in our national politics."

In 1914 Praeger's friendship with Postmaster General Albert S. Burleson, a fellow Texan, led to his appointment as postmaster of Washington, D.C. The former newspaperman proved an extremely adept civil servant, working to reform and modernize the city's antiquated postal system. Searching for ways to reduce cost and improve service, Praeger replaced the privately contracted horse-drawn postal truck system with a highly successful government-owned automotive service. Impressed with Praeger's energy and determination,

Burleson appointed him second assistant postmaster general on September 1, 1915, with responsibility for the delivery of all mails in the United States and its territories.

Many schemes to expedite mail delivery crossed Praeger's desk. Among the most promising were plans to use airplanes to deliver mail in remote areas of the country. When Praeger failed to interest private companies in such a technologically challenging enterprise, he decided that the Post Office would have to undertake experiments to prove the practicality of airmail service. After consulting with the National Advisory Committee for Aeronautics, the government's expert body on all things aeronautical, Praeger drew up plans to operate a trial route between Washington, D.C., and New York. Before the Post Office could purchase aircraft, however, the Army Air Service volunteered to fly the route using its existing planes, preempting the Post Office's effort to achieve independent operation of the service.

The nation's first regularly scheduled airmail service began on May 15, 1918, when Lt. George L. Boyle took off from Washington's Polo Field in a Curtiss JN-4H ("Jenny") bound for Philadelphia, the intermediate stop on the route to New York. Unfortunately, Boyle became lost shortly after takeoff and had to make a forced landing that damaged his aircraft. Although the other segments of the route operated without incident, Boyle's misfortune came to typify the strained relationship between the military and the Post Office. Convinced that army pilots lacked the necessary skill and motivation to make the experiment a success, Praeger convinced Postmaster Burleson to terminate the arrangement. The Air Service flew for the last time on August 10. Two days later the Post Office began operations on the route with its own planes and pilots.

Praeger was determined to make the U.S. Air Mail Service a success. Having promised Burleson that airplanes could deliver mail on schedule regardless of weather, he pushed pilots to the limits of existing technology. He also realized that the true potential of the airplane could be demonstrated only over longer distances. While maintaining the Washington–New York route, Praeger embarked on ambitious plans for coast-to-coast airmail service. On July 1, 1919, after several false starts, regular service began between New York and Chicago. Over the next 14 months Praeger secured airfields, installed communications, and sought new air-

Left to right: Praeger, Washington postmaster Merritt O. Chance, Postmaster General Albert S. Burleson, and President Woodrow Wilson at the inauguration of the Washington-New York airmail route, May 15, 1918 (courtesy of the National Archives)

planes for the route from Chicago to San Francisco. Finally, on September 8, 1920, the Post Office inaugurated transcontinental airmail service.

As the Democratic administration of Woodrow Wilson prepared to leave office, and with Republicans showing signs that they might be reluctant to continue with the government-operated Air Mail Service, Praeger decided to stage a dramatic demonstration of the progress and potential of airmail. On February 22-23, 1921, the Post Office flew a one-time day-and-night route between San Francisco and New York in 33 hours and 20 minutes, setting a new transcontinental mail record. As the *New York Times* noted, "The United States has distanced all countries in transportation of mails through the air."

Praeger, whose driving leadership was crucial to the success of the airmail, was a "hands-on" manager who savored the details of the Post Office's pioneering aerial mail service. "He knew the name of every pilot, mechanic and other employee down to watchman," a subordinate observed. "He knew the

location and condition of every ship in the service." Sitting in his office, legs tucked underneath him, cigar in hand, Praeger would listen to advice, but he did not hesitate to make operational decisions—despite his lack of background in aviation. Energetic, stubborn, and impatient with minor obstacles, he never wavered in his determination to prove the value of commercial aviation. The airplane, he believed, would one day become more effective than the railroad as an agent of communications and transportation in the nation's economy. As aviation commentator Gill Robb Wilson later wrote: "His vision during the formative days of national air policy was one of the truly opportune assets of United States air history."

The Air Mail Service compiled an impressive record under Praeger's leadership. Between May 15, 1918, and March 15, 1921, it flew 1,683,589 miles and carried 1,559,269 pounds of mail. The Post Office had proved that airplanes could fly over long distances on regular schedules. But the human cost had been high—far too high, according to

De Havilland DH-4B (courtesy of the National Air and Space Museum)

Praeger's critics: 18 pilots had died while flying for the U.S. Air Mail Service.

Out of a job after Republican Warren Harding assumed the presidency, Praeger moved to St. Louis and worked as the manager of sales and promotion for a pharmaceutical company. After the death of his wife, Ella Krueger, on August 7, 1924 (they had been married on October 24, 1906, and had three sons), Praeger opened a postal information service in New York City. In 1928 he accepted a position as adviser to the Post and Telegraph Department of the government of Siam (later Thailand). Shortly before departing for Asia, he married Carrie Will Coffman, 28 years his junior, on April 20, 1928. This union, by all accounts an extraordinarily happy one, produced three daughters over the next five years.

Praeger played a key role in establishing civil aviation in Siam. Until his arrival, the Siamese army had been operating mail and passenger service in the country. Having decided to relieve the military of these duties, the government appointed Praeger managing director of the newly formed Aerial Transport of Siam Company. By the time he left South-

east Asia in 1933, Praeger had successfully launched Siam's first civil airline.

With the election of a Democratic administration, Praeger returned to government service in 1933 as assistant to the president of the Merchant Fleet Corporation and member of the financial committee of the United Shipping Board. He retired to southern California in 1936 and purchased a lemon grove in Escondido. In less than a year, however, a severe freeze ruined his crop and damaged the trees, causing financial disaster. In his late sixties, bankrupt, bothered by arthritis, and with three young daughters to raise, Praeger had to seek employment.

Between 1940 and 1946, Praeger held a series of minor positions with the Post Office, the National Youth Administration, and the Office of Defense Transportation. He died of a heart attack on February 4, 1948.

References:

William M. Leary, *Aerial Pioneers: The U.S. Air Mail Service, 1918-1927* (Washington, D.C.: Smithsonian Institution, 1985);

Niels Lumholdt and William Warren, *The History of Aviation in Thailand* (Hong Kong: Travel Publishing Asia Limited, 1987);

Henry Ladd Smith, *Airways: The History of Commercial Aviation in the United States* (New York: Knopf, 1942);

Gill Robb Wilson, "Praeger, 'Father of Air Mail,'" *New York Herald Tribune*, February 13, 1948.

Unpublished Document:

Otto Praeger, "Moss from a Rolling Stone," typescript autobiography in the possession of the Praeger family, Rye, New York.

Archives:

The extensive archives of the U.S. Air Mail Service can be found in the Records of the United States Post Office, Record Group 28, National Archives, Washington, D.C.

Robert W. Prescott

(May 5, 1913 - March 3, 1978)

by John C. Bishop

Auburn University

CAREER: Pilot, American Volunteer Group (1941-1942), Transcontinental & Western Air (1942-1943), China National Aviation Corporation (1943-1944); president, National Skyway Freight Company (1945-1947); president, Flying Tiger Line (1947-1978).

Robert William Prescott, the seventh of George Washington and Una Stewart Prescott's eight children, was born in Fort Worth, Texas, on May 5, 1913. In 1934, after completing an uninspired academic career at Fort Worth's Central High School, he entered Compton Junior College in Los Angeles, California. Prescott supported himself by working for the Goodyear Tire and Rubber Company. Awarded an associate of arts degree in 1936, he entered Loyola Law School. Again, he had to work his way through school, this time as a delivery truck driver for the Challenge Cream and Butter Company. While at Loyola, Prescott became interested in flying. Returning to California, he completed his preflight training at Long Beach in 1939. This led to an appointment to the navy's air training center at Pensacola, Florida. Following his graduation, he remained at Pensacola as an instructor, with the rank of ensign, for nine months.

In September 1941 Prescott left the navy and joined Claire L. Chennault's quasi-official American Volunteer Group. Stationed at Toungoo, Burma, Prescott flew Curtiss P-40 Tomahawk pursuit planes for what became known as the "Flying Ti-

Robert W. Prescott (courtesy of the National Air and Space Museum)

gers." During the early months of 1942, he was credited with shooting down six Japanese aircraft.

Following disbandment of the "Flying Tigers," in mid 1942, Prescott returned to the United

States and joined the Intercontinental Division of Transcontinental & Western Air (TWA, later Trans World Airlines). At one point he carried Ambassador Joseph E. Davies to his post in Moscow. In 1943 he left TWA to fly for the China National Aviation Corporation, a subsidiary of Pan American Airways that operated on the famous "Hump" route between India and China. Prescott flew 300 trips over the Himalayas, growing familiar with Curtiss C-46s and the potential of transporting cargo by air.

Prescott came back to the United States in 1944, and married Helen Ruth Verheyden in November. While honeymooning in Acapulco he met two men, Allen Chase and James E. Davidson, who were interested in forming a cargo airline (Aerovias Azteca) to transport goods between the southwestern United States and northern Mexico. This led to a meeting with the group's third partner, Samuel Mosher of the Signal Oil and Gas Company of Los Angeles, who hired Prescott to locate airplanes for the airline. This was no easy task, as most aircraft were committed to the military in early 1945. Eventually he found 14 Budd RB-1 Conestogas. Carrying two thoroughbred horses, two leased Budds made Aerovias Azteca's first and only flight to Mexico City, where the Mexican government seized the airplanes on legal grounds.

Following the failure of Aerovias Azteca, Prescott wanted to buy the remaining Budds and sell them for a profit. When Mosher turned down this proposal, Prescott countered with a plan to use the transports to start a cargo airline. This idea appealed to Mosher. Also a commercial flower grower, he was eager to enter eastern markets. He offered matching funds, which enabled Prescott and a small group of friends to make a down payment of $90,000 on the Budds. On June 25, 1945, the National Skyway Freight Corporation came into existence with Prescott as president and Mosher as chairman of the board. The new company located its headquarters at the Long Beach Municipal Airport.

National Skyway flew its first load of commercial cargo, a consignment of grapes from Bakersfield to Atlanta, in August 1945. Later in the year the company sought more permanent funding. Thanks in large part to the growing reputation of the airline, Prescott and Mosher were able to raise $2.5 million through the sale of stock. By this time Prescott was gaining a reputation as an aggressive

and competent businessman. He was a hands-on manager, who did everything from flying planes to loading and unloading cargo and handling administrative tasks. Highly safety conscious, he made safe operations a prominent feature of the company throughout its 44-year history.

In 1946 Prescott successfully bid for Air Transport Command's transpacific contract. This award, which was won by a margin of one-tenth of a cent a ton-mile, enabled the airline to gain substantial income and experience in the air freight business. National Skyway had only to supply administrative, flight, and maintenance personnel; ATC furnished 32 C-54s. This contract not only allowed the firm to survive the vicious competition of the postwar years, but it also opened the door to the Asian air routes which were to become the company's most important commercial operation.

In January 1947 Prescott sought to capitalize on the popularity and recognition of the "Flying Tigers" by changing the name of the company to the Flying Tiger Line. Also, because of inadequate facilities at Long Beach, he was forced to relocate to the Lockheed Air Terminal in Burbank.

After the ATC contract expired in late 1947, Prescott turned once more to the domestic market, replacing the troublesome Budds with C-54s and C-47s. In 1949 the Tiger Line achieved a measure of permanence when it received an experimental five-year scheduled operating certificate from the Civil Aeronautics Board. Encouraged by this development, Prescott leased 25 C-46s from the U.S. Air Force. The timing of the move could not have been better, because the outbreak of the Korean War in June 1950 led to a booming air cargo business. Flying Tiger Line took full advantage of the situation and operated frequent military contract flights to the Far East.

On February 13, 1955, Flying Tiger Line began overnight transcontinental cargo service with new DC-6As, the cargo version of the popular, and economical, Douglas transport. Prescott also won a small victory on the issue of carrying mail. He had complained that the passenger airlines were able to carry freight at rates below cost because this part of their business was being subsidized with profits from high passenger and airmail rates. Also, despite the substantial income they received from carrying mail, they were not able to respond in an emergency when the military needed their equipment, leaving the unsubsidized cargo lines to take up the

Flying Tiger Line Douglas DC-8-63 (courtesy of MAP Photos)

slack. In May 1955 the Civil Aeronautics Board granted Flying Tiger Line a special exemption to carry mail. However, this did not settle the issue, which would not be resolved while Prescott remained president of the airline.

During the 1960s Prescott saw his firm become the world's undisputed leader of the air cargo business. In 1966 a major change took place when the Civil Aeronautics Board granted cargo airlines the exclusive privilege of selling "blocked space," that is, space that would be paid for by a shipper whether it was used or not. Prescott realized that, in order for the company to continue to grow, it would need airplanes with substantially increased capacity. The line already had made great strides since the days of the Budds, with their 10,000-pound capacity. In turn, Prescott had acquired C-46s (14,000 pounds), DC-6As (32,000 pounds), Lockheed 1049Hs (46,000 pounds), and finally in 1961 turboprop swingtail Canadair CL-44s (65,000 pounds). In 1966 he committed the company to the largest order in the history of the air freight industry, signing an agreement with the Douglas Aircraft Company for 17 DC-8-63F turbojet freighters at a cost of $206 million.

Again, Prescott's sense of timing was impeccable. The growing demands of the Vietnam War filled the new airplanes, as well as the coffers of Flying Tiger Line. Also, on September 4, 1969, the Civil Aeronautics Board granted the airline the first scheduled all-cargo Pacific Ocean route, route 100.

Prescott died at his home in Palm Springs, California, on March 3, 1978. He left behind his wife, Dr. Anne-Marie Bennstrom, whom he had married on July 16, 1962, and two daughters by his first marriage. At the time of his death, the outspoken air-cargo entrepreneur had built his struggling postwar company into what historian R. E. G. Davies has termed "the world's greatest freight airline." His passing was not only a deep personal loss to his friends and family, but also it deprived the airline of his leadership during the difficult days that followed deregulation. His pioneering company failed to cope with the new environment and was sold to Federal Express in 1989.

References:

Robert Bedingfield, "Personality: Tiger Flying Where It Pays," *New York Times*, November 13, 1960, section 3, p. 3;

Frank Camerson, *Hungry Tiger: The Story of the Flying Tiger Line* (New York: McGraw-Hill, 1964);

Gerald Fraser, "Robert Prescott, Ex-Fighter Pilot and Founder of Airline for Cargo," *New York Times,* March 5, 1978, p. 36;

"Purring Again," *Forbes,* 99 (January 1967): 34-35;

"Robert W. Prescott of the Flying Tiger Line," *Nation's Business* (October 1970): 65-72.

André A. Priester

(September 29, 1891 - November 28, 1955)

by Wesley Phillips Newton

Auburn University

CAREER: Managerial assistant, KLM, Amsterdam Airport (1919-1925); general manager, Philadelphia Rapid Transit Air Service (1926); chief engineer, Pan American Airways (1927-1939); vice-president, Pan American World Airways (1939-1953, 1954-1955).

André A. Priester, chief engineer and later vice-president of Pan American Airways, the first great American international airline, was born in Java on September 29, 1891, and died in Paris on November 28, 1955. Priester was born into the family of a minor Dutch colonial bureaucrat. This family environment contributed to two traits Priester would display as an airline executive—authoritarianism and a feel for underdeveloped cultures and territory. As a teenager he went to Holland to study at a technical high school, capping this with pursuit of an engineering degree at Munich Institute for Technology and then at the famed Zurich Polytechnicum. He was caught up in the slowly maturing age of manned flight and took flying lessons, but never soloed.

In 1919 Priester became assistant to the manager of the Dutch air firm KLM at the Amsterdam airport, but postwar advancement was slow. At age thirty-four he decided to seek better opportunities in what seemed the mecca of aviation, the United States. With little money and a halting command of English, he and his wife crossed the Atlantic in second class to avoid the stigma of disembarking at Ellis Island. They proceeded to Detroit, which Priester mistook for the aviation capital of the United States. He could not find work there, and his wife's employment in a hotel as a domestic kept them afloat.

Priester contacted fellow Dutch émigré Anthony Fokker, who had recently opened up an aircraft factory in New Jersey. Fokker arranged for Priester to secure a job managing a small airline sponsored by the Philadelphia Rapid Transit (PRT) by touting him as an expert on aviation. The Philadelphia Exposition was in progress in 1926, and during the five months of its existence the PRT airline flew tourists between Philadelphia and Washington, D.C. During his employment Priester began to develop his managerial style, stressing orderliness and safety through strict discipline and collegiality. Priester's English remained of the comic strip Dutch variety, and at first the pilots and ground crew were amused and, behind his back, mimicked him. He had a small, thin physique for which his bald head seemed outsized. In his stern application of discipline he evoked the image of a comic opera Prussian drill sergeant. But his charges soon discovered he was serious and persistent.

During his stay in Philadelphia, Priester met various people associated in one way or the other with the aviation business, including the young general manager of New England-based Colonial Airlines, Juan T. Trippe. This contact helped to rescue him from another spell of oblivion after the PRT airline folded when the exposition ended. Priester had returned to Detroit to take a job on a Ford assembly line when, early in 1927, Trippe wrote him about the possibility of establishing an international airline and wanted Priester's ideas on it. Obviously Priester's recommendations impressed Trippe, for when the latter left Colonial and formed the new organization, Pan American, he sent for Priester.

Priester's disciplined and orderly approach to business exemplified the newly mature status of aviation. The public, which the airlines wanted to attract, and the Commerce and Post Office departments, toward which the airlines looked for regulation and airmail subsidies, expected orderliness and an atmosphere of security. Priester, for all his unintentionally comic mannerisms, was a leader of the new age, a hands-on manager who insisted that his pilots fly safely using procedures he carefully set down, that mechanics wear clean overalls and tend to their aircraft with precision, and that flight stewards clean up the aircraft when a flight was over. He, not Juan Trippe, who did not like to travel around inspecting aircraft and personnel and facilities, was the executive most likely to enforce the rules. Priester was the man who came asking questions about slack on-time records or rumors that the pilots were drinking too much off duty. He was a fanatic about drinking, and for a long time no alcohol was permitted, even for passengers, on board Pan American aircraft. Although Trippe was a former naval officer who thought of Pan American somewhat in naval terms, it was Priester who dressed the crews in naval officer-style uniforms to give an impression of discipline and stability.

Priester's style took hold at Pan American and through Pan American at other airlines. He cared for his subordinates, even though he had difficulty demonstrating it. Pan American employees came to sense it, and over time Priester became a revered figure throughout the airline industry.

Priester was a key participant in Pan American's rise to airline dominance in Latin America, a rise that saw few accidents and fatalities despite the widely varying terrain and weather. As chief engineer he also contributed to the planning and design of a series of seaplanes to which Trippe gave the name "clipper" to equate them with the great American sailing ships that plied the seas in the 19th century. These clipper aircraft would enable Pan American to conquer the Pacific and Atlantic. Priester and Charles A. Lindbergh, consultant to Pan American, disagreed over the design of the Sikor-

sky S-40, a large amphibian, and again over the S-42, a flying boat, which originated as Lindbergh's design. Lindbergh, however, favored land planes for transoceanic commercial flight, while Priester pushed the concept of the seaplane. Trippe set the general specifications for the next in the series of clippers, the Martin 130; but Priester contributed much in the way of design ideas for the greatest and last of the clippers, the Boeing 314.

Priester enjoyed Trippe's confidence and esteem until a new breed of pilots, products of recent military service or conditioned by the technological revolution in aviation of the 1930s, began to join Pan Am in the late 1930s. They chafed under Priester's rules and regulations. Trippe began to grow impatient. Then came the traumatic crisis of 1939, in which Trippe was replaced as Pan Am's chief by C. V. Whitney. Priester accepted the change and was promoted to the rank of vice-president. When Trippe returned to power, he took reprisals against those he considered disloyal in the crisis. However, because of Priester's service and reputation in the industry, Trippe proceeded slowly in his case. In a reorganization of Pan American at the end of World War II Priester's status as head of all technical aspects of the company was downgraded. His importance declined thereafter. This hurt Priester deeply, but there was nothing he could do.

In 1953 Trippe took away Priester's title of vice-president. A distraught Priester confronted Trippe when he was finally able to wrangle a one-on-one conference. Trippe feigned not to have realized the importance of his demotion and promised to restore the title. But the restoration was without substance. One of Priester's remaining badges of status was his position as chairman of the technical committee of the International Air Transport Association. He died of a heart attack on November 28, 1955, while attending an association meeting in Paris.

References:
Marylin Bender and Selig Altschul, *The Chosen Instrument* (New York: Simon & Schuster, 1982);
Robert Daley, *An American Saga: Juan Trippe and His Pan Am Empire* (New York: Random House, 1981).

Professional Air Traffic Controllers Organization

by Nick A. Komons

Potomac, Maryland

The Professional Air Traffic Controllers Organization (PATCO) was a labor union that enjoyed a brief and largely turbulent 14-year existence representing air traffic controllers at air route traffic control centers and air traffic control towers. All of its members were employees of the Federal Aviation Administration (FAA), the government agency charged with operating a common civil-military system of air traffic control and air navigation.

PATCO was founded as a professional society—not a labor union—on January 3, 1968, by a small group of air traffic controllers in the New York City area. Within six months, the organization's membership had soared to 5,000; at its peak, in 1981, PATCO had some 15,000 members.

It was the policies of two presidents, John F. Kennedy and Lyndon B. Johnson, that helped pave the way to PATCO's founding. Kennedy energized the union movement in the federal government when, on January 17, 1962, he issued an executive order that guaranteed the right of federal employees to join "employee organizations" and engage in limited collective bargaining. Salaries and hours remained the province of Congress; moreover, federal employees were never given the right to strike. Johnson's fiscal policies created the conditions that bred discontent among controllers' ranks. In order to finance Great Society programs and the Vietnam War, Johnson kept FAA budgets—and those of other traditional federal agencies—at no-growth levels. The result was that a badly needed airways modernization program languished in Congress for lack of administration support. Federal appropriations for expanding the nation's woefully inadequate airport capacity were pared to the bone by the people running Johnson's budgetary apparatus. More important, controller staffing levels did not come close to keeping up with traffic growth. In the five years preceding the founding of PATCO, FAA's con-

troller work force increased by only 8.5 percent, while air traffic jumped by more than 50 percent.

FAA kept traffic flowing by working controllers harder. Overtime became a way of life at major air transportation hubs. Not surprisingly, PATCO's early years were characterized by extreme militancy. Its policies during the first 28 months of its existence were largely influenced and formulated by Michael J. Rock, a New York-based air traffic controller who became the organization's chairman of the board, and F. Lee Bailey, the famed trial attorney, who held the post of executive director.

PATCO's first job action occurred on July 3, 1968, when Rock announced "Operation Air Safety." Rock maintained that air traffic supervisors were violating FAA-prescribed aircraft separation standards in order to accommodate the high levels of traffic. Thereafter, Rock said, PATCO-affiliated controllers would "work by the book" in order to ensure safety. The controller "slowdown" came at the height of the summer tourist season and helped precipitate an air traffic jam of monumental proportions. On July 19 a total of 1,927 aircraft in the vicinity of New York City were delayed in taking off or landing, some for as long as three hours. One transcontinental flight was actually delayed on the ground in Los Angeles because of traffic congestion in New York.

FAA management knew that PATCO-affiliated controllers were taking part in an illegal job action. Left unchallenged, this defiance of authority could lead to graver acts of defiance. But management also knew that controllers' nerves were already frayed, and a heavy-handed approach might make matters worse. Moreover, FAA managers recognized that the controllers' plight had attracted public sympathy. FAA decided that it would not admit publicly that a slowdown had taken place. PATCO now knew that it possessed leverage.

PATCO picket line in front of the New York Air Traffic Control Center, August 1981 (AP/Wide World Photos)

Before 1968 was out, FAA agreed to permit a voluntary payroll deduction plan for the payment of PATCO dues, with the understanding that PATCO would remain a professional society. In January 1969, however, the Civil Service Commission (CSC) ruled that by entering into the dues withholding agreement PATCO had forfeited its status as a professional society and had now become an employee organization—that is, a union. That made PATCO subject to the Standards of Conduct and the Code of Fair Labor Practices; it also made the organization eligible for formal recognition as a labor bargaining organization.

Although the newly installed Richard M. Nixon administration increased controller staffing and sought new airport and airway legislation that would expand system capacity and give controllers modern tools with which to work, the period between June 1969 and April 1970 was marked by turmoil. Inciting discontent was Rock's and Bailey's way of amassing support among the rank and file. PATCO called a strike—referred to euphemistically by the union as a "sickout"—over a seemingly

minor matter in the spring of 1970, and 3,000 controllers failed to show up for work. The strike ended when the courts issued contempt citations against the union. FAA suspended nearly 1,000 controllers and fired 52 for their role in the strike. Smarting from this humiliating defeat, PATCO forced Bailey and Rock to step down. The punishment meted out by the FAA, however, did not stick. Shortly after the strike, the Marine Engineers Beneficial Association (MEBA) took in the beleaguered controller union as an affiliate; it also helped get it back on its feet with generous loans. Then, in 1972, MEBA president Jesse Calhoun, as part of the price for handling U.S. wheat shipments to the Soviet Union, extracted a promise from the Nixon administration to allow fired controllers to apply for reinstatement. Of the 52 fired, 46 applied and were rehired.

Rock's successor, John F. Leyden, was a moderate. On April 23, 1970, on assuming PATCO's presidency, Leyden promised to put an end to the "showboat-gunboat" approach of his predecessor and replace it with "firm and reasonable persuasion." Owing in great measure to his skilled leadership, the rest of the 1970s were prosperous years for PATCO that saw it grow in wealth, power, and influence. These years also saw controllers' working conditions improve profoundly. Congress helped, as did the Nixon administration. In 1970 Congress enacted the Airport and Airway Development and Revenue Acts, which gave the FAA the wherewithal to expand airport capacity and put in place a modern, semi-automated air traffic control system. At the same time, staffing increased. Then, in May 1972, it passed the Air Traffic Controllers Career Program Act, which established a more liberal retirement system for controllers than the rest of the federal civilian work force and a second career training program. Later that year, the Department of Labor certified PATCO as the exclusive representative for FAA's air traffic controllers. The union was now on its way.

Despite his soft talk, Leyden was not one to eschew action. He used different tactics than his predecessors. Strikes and sickouts were dropped from the union's repertoire of job actions. Instead, Leyden relied on the slowdown as his major coercive weapon. By his own reckoning he ordered no fewer than nine traffic slowdowns in his decade-long tenure. The slowdown was a successful device because it was extremely difficult for the FAA to document that controllers were deliberately slowing down their pace. It was also effective because—unless quickly ended—it could cost the airlines millions in extra fuel during a period of rising petroleum prices. The tendency therefore was to give the union what it wanted. The most successful slowdown engineered by Leyden occurred in July 1976 when the Civil Service Commission dragged its feet in completing a controller pay-reclassification study. On the third day of the slowdown, the CSC agreed to expedite its review. Then, in November, when all signs pointed to a CSC decision unfavorable to the union, PATCO let it be known through the grapevine that a slowdown was a distinct possibility during the Thanksgiving weekend—invariably the weekend with the heaviest traffic of the year. Two weeks before the holiday, the CSC announced that controllers in certain high activity facilities would be upgraded from GS-13s to GS-14s.

The next time Leyden used this tactic it blew up in his face. In March 1978 FAA and PATCO concluded a labor-management agreement that included a provision whereby FAA would pay con-

trollers' salaries while they were on foreign or domestic familiarization flights (FAMs). In theory such flights were beneficial, because they helped acquaint controllers with pilots' duties. In the past airlines had cooperated with this program and given free seats to controllers on FAM duty. The 1978 contract, however, was the first to specify overseas familiarization flights. Some airlines refused to give controllers free transportation abroad, particularly to popular vacation spots—spots where most FAM participants suddenly wanted to go. PATCO staged intermittent slowdowns to protest the refusal of these carriers to cooperate. That brought the federal courts and the Justice Department down on the union. When it was all over, PATCO had been (1) fined $100,000 for violating a 1970 permanent injunction against illegal job actions, and (2) warned by Justice that future job actions could lead to criminal prosecutions. In the bargain, an angry Congress refused to fund the second career training program for medically disabled controllers.

Leyden now became vulnerable and, in January 1980, he fell victim to a palace coup engineered by Robert Poli, who succeeded him to the union's presidency. Poli adopted the aggressive tactics of Bailey and Rock in the vain hope that he could achieve for controllers financial parity with airline pilots. So confident was Poli of success that he openly tipped his hand. He pumped money into a "strike fund" that had been created by Leyden. He put together and widely distributed a strike plan that easily fell into the government's hands. When negotiations on a new contract began, he took a tough stand, rejecting nearly everything Drew Lewis, the new secretary of transportation, put on the table. Instead, he held out for the provisions in a bill drafted by PATCO's legal staff and introduced by Representative William L. Clay that would have provided higher salaries for some controllers than for members of the president's cabinet.

On June 22, 1981, however, after a marathon bargaining session between PATCO and government officials, it appeared that an acceptable compromise had been reached, with a seemingly satisfied Poli putting his signature on an agreement. Ten days later, Poli voted along with every other member of the PATCO executive board to recommend to the membership that it reject the contract. On July 29 PATCO announced that its rank and file had turned down the proposal by a vote of 13,495 to 616. Shortly thereafter, at a press conference in Washington, Poli announced that his union would go on a nationwide strike unless the government met PATCO's demands. Eleventh-hour negotiations failed to bring an agreement.

Beginning at 7 A.M. EST, on August 3, nearly 12,300 PATCO members went on strike. Shortly before 11 A.M. President Ronald Reagan issued the strikers an ultimatum to return to work within 48 hours or face dismissal. At the same time, the government moved swiftly on three fronts—civil, criminal, and administrative—to bring the full force of the law to bear on the strikers. These actions would eventually destroy the union.

Poli, the PATCO board, and the great majority of the PATCO membership had firmly believed that a strike would bring air traffic in the United States to its knees. FAA, however, had been preparing for this moment for months. With its controller work force cut to a mere 4,199, the aviation agency kept the airways open by pressing approximately 3,000 of its air traffic control supervisory personnel into controlling traffic. This combined force of nonstriking controllers and supervisory personnel was sufficiently large to implement a plan dubbed "Flow Control 50," whereby air carriers were required to cancel approximately 50 percent of their scheduled peak-hour flights at 22 major airports. Stringent flow control restrictions were imposed on flights going into and out of other than the selected 22 terminals. The plan was centrally directed by a flow control facility at the FAA's headquarters in Washington, D.C. Flow Control 50 worked. That meant the strike had no chance of succeeding.

It also meant that PATCO would no longer be a force to reckon with. In October, the Federal Labor Relations Authority decertified the organization, thus denying it the right to represent federal workers and collect dues. With its financial assets tied up by federal courts, on November 26, 1981, PATCO filed for protection under Chapter 11 of the federal bankruptcy law. On the last day of 1981, Robert Poli resigned. Gary Eads stepped into the union's presidency to oversee the organization's dismantlement. PATCO owed $40 million, including $33.4 million in court-imposed penalties for violating an antistrike injunction, while its assets came to a mere $5 million. On July 2, 1982, the union's lawyers filed a motion in a U.S. bankruptcy court for liquidation under Chapter 7 of the Federal Bankruptcy Act. The controllers who took part in the strike were never reinstated. However, while blocking their reemployment by the FAA, President Reagan did eventually permit the dismissed controllers to apply for employment elsewhere in the federal government.

References:

"Air Wars: The FAA and PATCO," *FAA World* (August 1980): 28-32;

Richard J. Kent, Jr., *Safe, Separated, and Soaring: A History of Federal Civil Aviation Policy, 1961-1972* (Washington, D.C.: U.S. Department of Transportation, 1980);

Edmund Preston, *Troubled Passage: The Federal Aviation Administration During the Nixon-Ford Term, 1973-1977* (Washington, D.C.: U.S. Department of Transportation, 1987).

Archives:

The Federal Aviation Administration History Files at FAA headquarters in Washington, D.C., holds transcripts of interviews of Langhorne Bond by Nick A. Komons, Washington, D.C., January 13 and February 9, 1981; of Edward V. Curran by Nick A. Komons and Edmund R. Preston, Washington, D.C., April 12, 1984; of J. Lynn Helms by Nick A. Komons and Edmund Preston, Washington, D.C., January 23, 25, and 26, 1984; and of John F. Leyden by Nick A. Komons and Edmund R. Preston, Washington, D.C., May 11, 1984.

Provincetown-Boston Airline

by William M. Leary

University of Georgia

The origins of Provincetown-Boston Airline go back to February 1946, when John Van Arsdale founded the Cape Cod Flying School at Hyannis, Massachusetts. A former wartime weatherman who had learned to fly after washing out of military flight training, Van Arsdale moved his school to Provincetown in 1948, where he also offered air taxi service. On November 30, 1949, he changed the name of this service to Provincetown-Boston Airline (PBA) and began summertime shuttle flights between the two points, cutting a five-hour road trip to 30 minutes. PBA was a real "mom-and-pop" operation. Van Arsdale flew the planes, his wife sold tickets, and his children did odd jobs around the small airport.

In 1957, in an effort to overcome the seasonal nature of PBA's operations, Van Arsdale made an agreement with Naples Airlines, a company that flew a shuttle service between Naples and Miami and had similar seasonal problems, to lease planes and trade personnel. Three years later, after the city of Naples refused to renew the owner's airport lease, Van Arsdale purchased the airline and operated it under PBA colors.

Van Arsdale was a cautious man. "Dad's philosophy was to entrench yourself and avoid competition," his son John, Jr., once observed. "When someone would threaten to come in on top of Dad he would run to the state public service commissioners, the Civil Aeronautics Board, and the FAA to complain." Under the senior Van Arsdale's careful management, the small commuter airline recorded a modest profit every year from 1949 to 1980.

In April 1980 Van Arsdale turned over management of the airline and its fleet of aging but carefully maintained piston-engine transports (six Martin 404s and twelve DC-3s) to his sons John, Jr., and Peter. The younger generation had ambitious plans for PBA in the unregulated environment of the 1980s. Within two years the airline rapidly expanded its routes, adding service to 21 markets. New equipment also appeared, including six turboprop Embraer EMB-110 Bandeirantes. PBA boarded 479,802 passengers in 1981, up 50 percent from 1980.

The years 1982 and 1983 saw continued growth, with passenger boardings of 727,716 and 931,751. In 1983, with additional airplanes, including Nihon YS-11s, and new routes, PBA posted a record net profit of $2.3 million on revenues of $41.4 million.

PBA's world came apart in 1984. The first nine months of the year saw the airline heading for its best year in history, with 1.1 million passengers boarded and a net profit of $3.4 million. On November 10, however, the Federal Aviation Agency withdrew PBA's operating certificate, citing numerous safety violations. Later in the month the FAA permitted the airline to resume operations with its smaller aircraft while working toward full restoration of its certificate. But the airline's efforts to regain public confidence suffered an irreparable blow on December 6, when a PBA Bandeirante crashed on takeoff from Jacksonville, killing 13 people. Suffering from a severe cash-flow problem, PBA entered Chapter 11 bankruptcy in March 1985. Although the FAA in May restored the company's authority to operate larger aircraft, the fate of this pioneering commuter airline had been sealed. PBA struggled along into 1986, at which time it was acquired by People Express.

References:

Lou Davis and Dave Higdon, "PBA's Grounding: Its Causes and Effects," *Air Transport World*, 22 (January 1985): 72-77, 79, 81;

Curtis Hartman, "PBA: A Tale of Two Airlines," *Inc.*, 5 (February 1983): 51-53, 55, 58, 60-61;

Hartman, "Tail Spin," *Inc.*, 7 (March 1985): 88-92, 94, 96, 98, 100.

Elwood R. Quesada

(April 13, 1904 -   )

by Michael H. Gorn

Environmental Protection Agency

CAREER: U.S. Army Air Corps (1927-1941); commander, First Air Defense Wing and Twelfth Fighter Command, North Africa (1942-1943); commander, Ninth Fighter Command and Ninth Tactical Air Command, U.K. and Germany (1943-1945); commander, Third Air Force and Tactical Air Command (1946-1948); chairman, Joint Chiefs of Staff Technical Planning Committee (1949-1950); commander, Joint Task Force 3 (1950-1951); vice-president, Olin Industries (1951-1953); vice-president, Lockheed Aircraft (1953-1955); private investor (1955-1957); presidential assistant for aviation and chairman of the Airways Modernization Board (1957-1959); first administrator, Federal Aviation Agency (1959-1961); part owner, Washington Senators baseball team (1961-1962).

Among the countless Americans who made important contributions to the success of military and civilian aviation, few exerted more influence in war and peace than Elwood Richard "Pete" Quesada. His activities spanned five decades, from the days of barnstorming aerial cowboys to the era of transatlantic jet travel. In between, his ideas shaped the course of air combat and laid the basis for safe, regular commercial air service.

Born in Washington, D.C., on April 13, 1904, to a Spanish father and an Irish-American mother, Quesada grew up in a self-described immigrant household. His boyhood, nonetheless, seemed unremarkably middle class. His father descended from a line of Spanish bankers and achieved modest prosperity as a consultant on currency engraving to the U.S. Treasury Department.

Bright and hardworking, Quesada attended Technical High School in Washington and won honors as an all-district football quarterback. He also excelled in tennis, earned summer income as a lifeguard in the Tidal Basin Pond, and sold Crackerjacks to baseball fans at Griffith Stadium. After grad-

Elwood R. Quesada (courtesy of the Federal Aviation Administration)

uation he attended briefly the Wyoming Methodist Seminary in Wilkes-Barre, Pennsylvania, but transferred to the University of Maryland on a football scholarship. He finally received his A.B. degree from Georgetown University.

Sports not only preoccupied Quesada in his school days but also led to military service. Asked to quarterback the Army Flying School's football team, Quesada went to Brooks Field, Texas, in 1924 and enrolled as a primary cadet in order to compete on the gridiron. Although a broken leg soon ended his football career, he turned out to have talent in the air. Winning a position in the select advanced flight training school, he graduated in

1925 with a reserve commission as second lieutenant.

Athletics, however, continued to lure Quesada, and he left the military to sign a $1,000 baseball contract with the St. Louis Cardinals. His sporting career proved to be short-lived; he failed to hit major league pitching. Quesada left baseball to do criminal investigations for the Detroit office of the Treasury Department. Though steady, the job lacked the thrill he had known in the huddle and the cockpit. When the Army Air Corps (as it became in 1926) announced its intention to bring on active duty a few reserve officers, Quesada leapt at the chance, and in January 1927 he received a regular Air Corps commission.

Lieutenant Quesada's first assignment, as engineering officer at Bolling Field, Washington, D.C., initiated an unusual career in which the roles of military aide and high profile flyer would coexist throughout the years. Socially clever, he succeeded in linking his fortunes to men of prominence, but, as a highly skilled pilot, he was never far from the joystick.

At Bolling, Quesada first came to the attention of the commanding general of the Air Corps, Maj. Gen. James E. Fechet, during an emergency flight to Labrador. His skill in ferrying the general to the site of the *Bremen*, a downed German aircraft, won him the job of Fechet's flying aide. When the Air Corps decided late in the 1920s to launch a campaign to stimulate public support for aviation, Fechet picked Quesada to copilot a historic endurance flight and capture headlines for the corps. During a span of continuous flying in January 1929, he and Majs. Carl A. Spaatz and Ira Eaker logged 11,000 hours aboard a three-engined Fokker named *Question Mark*. Roving back and forth between San Diego and Los Angeles, *Question Mark* underwent 43 aerial refuelings, proving the procedure's efficacy and setting a world record for hours aloft.

Quesada then undertook a quieter assignment as assistant to the U.S. military attaché in Cuba. He returned to Bolling Field in 1932 to serve as executive officer and flying aide to F. Trubee Davison, assistant secretary of war for air. The next year, after leaving government for the presidency of the New York Museum of Natural History, Davison persuaded Quesada to fly him the length of Africa in search of wild animals.

Another notable patron of the first lieutenant—commanding general of the Army Air Corps Maj. Gen. Benjamin Foulois—arranged his next assignment. After government mail contracts with several commercial airlines had been canceled due to fraud, Foulois chose Quesada to be a mainstay in the Air Corps drive to make the necessary deliveries. Between February and June 1934 he transported letters and parcels as chief pilot between Newark, New Jersey, and Cleveland, Ohio. But the 18 other routes did less well: 66 Air Corps planes crashed and 12 pilots died. In midyear, new contracts were signed with the air carriers and Quesada's career returned to previous form. Again a flying aide, this time he also undertook research assignments for Gen. Hugh Johnson, President Franklin D. Roosevelt's director of the National Recovery Administration (NRA).

When the NRA discontinued operations, Quesada worked briefly as Secretary of War George Dern's assistant and, at Fort Benning, Georgia, acted as aide to Brig. Gen. George C. Marshall. This phase of his service (1934-1936) ended with a tour as assistant to Brig. Gen. Frank M. Andrews. Andrews organized the new General Headquarters Air Corps at Langley Field, Virginia, and put Quesada in charge as commander of the headquarters squadron. It was an important assignment because it marked the army's first step towards granting its air arm some degree of autonomy.

Between the end of Quesada's service with Andrews in 1936 and the fateful year of 1941, he rounded out his education and honed his already significant administrative and diplomatic talents. He attended the Air Corps Tactical School at Maxwell Field, Alabama, and the Army Command and Staff College at Fort Leavenworth, Kansas. In mid 1937 he put this knowledge to work at Mitchel Field, New York, where he briefly saw his first operational duty as flight commander of the First Bomb Squadron. A year later he went to Buenos Aires, where he served as technical adviser to the Argentinian Air Force. Here he spent over two pleasant years teaching his hosts American methods of flight instruction, maintenance, and supply. In September 1940 Quesada reasserted his love of the cockpit by flying from the Argentine capital to Norfolk, Virginia, marking the first solo completion of that route. He reported for duty the next month as an intelligence analyst in the Office of the Chief of the Air Corps, with promotion to the rank of major. Finally, in July 1941, he returned to Mitchel Field as a lieutenant colonel in command of the Thirty-third Pursuit Group.

Following American entry into World War II, Quesada was promoted to colonel and given command of the First Air Force, whose mission was to defend the eastern United States against German air attack. In 1943, now with the first star on his shoulder, Quesada took command of the Twelfth Fighter Command in North Africa. Both Quesada and his superior, Air Vice Marshall Sir Arthur Coningham, head of the Northwest Africa Coastal Defense Force, became strong advocates of an independent role for tactical air power. Their doctrine of air superiority and offensive air operations, rather than serving as air artillery for the ground forces, won many converts among leaders of the U.S. Army Air Forces.

After eight months and many operational flights in the Tunisian, Sicilian, Corsican, and Italian campaigns, Quesada went to England in October 1943 to prepare for the invasion of Europe. In charge of the Ninth Fighter Command, he moved quickly to bring together an effective force of 36,000 men and more than 1,500 P-38s, P-47s, and P-51s. He conducted rigorous combat drills based on the interdiction techniques that he had employed in North Africa.

Quesada landed his own P-38 on Normandy Beach on June 7, 1944—D day plus 1. Working in tandem with Gen. Omar Bradley's First Army, Quesada's airmen harassed German tank columns and radioed back information on German positions. The "pilots' general," as he was now known, again learned the value of full-fledged cooperation between air and land forces. The Battle of the Bulge proved an impressive demonstration of these lessons, as Quesada's Ninth Fighter Command helped stall German tank columns by blasting shut narrow passes and rendering vital roads impassable.

Returning home with a distinguished combat record on March 1, 1946, Quesada assumed command of the Third Air Force, soon to become the Tactical Air Command (combining the Third, Ninth, and Twelfth Air Forces). He threw himself into his duties, becoming an outspoken advocate of both an independent air force and a continuation of close cooperation between ground and air combat elements. Although Quesada introduced the P-80 and P-84 jets into service, added other equipment to Tactical Air Command's inventory, and conducted

highly successful joint army-air force exercises, his efforts soon ran into the economic realities of postwar America. In 1948, at a time of tight military budgets, Air Force Chief of Staff General Hoyt S. Vandenberg decided to use his limited resources to strengthen the Strategic Air Command at the expense of other elements of the air force. Frustrated with the neglect of close air support, Quesada resigned from active duty in October 1951.

Personal reasons also governed Quesada's decision to leave the air force. Married during the war to Kate Davis Pulitzer, daughter of St. Louis publisher Joseph Pulitzer, he decided that civilian life offered better financial rewards for his wife and young son. After two years as vice-president of Olin Industries, Quesada moved to California to become vice-president of Lockheed Aircraft's new Missile Systems Division. He resigned in 1955 after becoming embroiled in a policy dispute and then embarked on several successful investment ventures, not least of which involved support for promising inventors.

While Quesada might have satisfied his desire for financial comfort, his love of flight and sense of public duty had not diminished. When Kodak vice-president Edward P. Curtis declined President Dwight D. Eisenhower's invitation to be his special assistant for aviation and chairman of the Airways Modernization Board (AMB), the president turned to his old comrade-in-arms. On August 16, 1957, the Senate confirmed Quesada as presidential assistant and chairman of the AMB.

Curtis had laid the foundation for civil aviation reform in 1956 and 1957 while leading a White House panel on commercial air transport. He had proposed that the AMB act as a unifying force, integrating research and development for civil and military air traffic, regulating all necessary funding, and forging these advances into a coherent air control and navigation system. Looking to the future, Curtis's group wanted an independent Federal Aviation Agency (FAA), with direct executive authority, to carry on the work of the Commerce Department's Civil Aviation Administration (CAA). Until the FAA became a reality, however, the interim AMB (composed equally of civilian and military representatives) would have to suffice. A chairman of unusual strength and diplomacy would be needed to lay the groundwork for the new agency.

Quesada had his work cut out for him. With ever increasing private and commercial air traffic, and with orders for jet airliners racing ahead of the capacity of manufacturers to fulfill them, he established a special task force to explore the technical possibilities of a modern air traffic control system. At the same time, he sought to ease the problem by persuading the air force to allow civilian traffic to use portions of its designated air space and by integrating civil and military radar systems.

Quesada also struggled to prepare the way for a new FAA. Resistance to the agency came from several quarters, especially the Civil Aeronautics Board (CAB) and Department of Defense. Quesada wanted the FAA to acquire all functions related to safety and flight rules, as well as exercising operational control over all airspace in the country. But the CAB would not relinquish its regulatory role without a fight, while Defense raised objections about access to the skies in wartime.

At this point Quesada received invaluable help, although he would have preferred a different source. In April 1958 an Air Force F-100F fighter plane struck a United Air Lines DC-7 over Las Vegas, Nevada, killing 49 people. The following month an Air National Guard jet trainer collided with a Capital Airlines Viscount over Brunswick, Maryland, resulting in the death of 12 passengers. The ensuing furor quieted Quesada's CAB and Defense adversaries. More important, the crashes inspired Senator Mike Monroney, Oklahoma Democrat and chairman of the Senate's Aviation Subcommittee, to press for an FAA bill.

During the ensuing debate over the exact nature of the new agency, Quesada and Monroney became friends and collaborators rather than opponents. Day after day and long into the night, the master of tactical air power and the clever Oklahoma politician struggled to find institutional remedies for the crisis in commercial aviation. The principal issue in dispute involved the relationship between civilians and the military in the agency. Quesada won the point that the FAA's deputy administrator should come from the military services. But Monroney exacted two concessions: the administrator must be a civilian, and officers assigned to the agency must be subject to its directives, not to those of the Pentagon. Another vexing problem concerned FAA authority in wartime. The White House group wanted military control of airspace during national crises, but in light of recognized emergency presidential powers, conceded the civilian control argument to Monroney with the expectation that the

FAA would be militarized by executive order. Goodwill between Quesada and Monroney failed to break one final impasse—the status of air traffic controllers during war. They agreed to postpone the debate and let the FAA administrator and Defense officials resolve it. In fact, legislative solutions to this complex question would likewise elude future aviation leaders.

The problems of accident review and safety regulations lent themselves to easy resolution. Quesada agreed to Monroney's scheme of continuing to vest the CAB with full responsibility for accident investigations. This would prevent conflicts of interest with the industries the FAA sought to regulate. On the other hand, the senator granted the wisdom of placing safety rule-making powers in Quesada's office since such rules ultimately bore directly on the economic well-being of airline manufacturers and air carriers.

On July 1, 1958, Quesada and Monroney released the bill to Congress. With minor amendments, the Federal Aviation Act became law on August 23 with President Eisenhower's signature. In just three months, Elwood Quesada had orchestrated a workable administrative solution to the nation's most intractable transportation problem.

On November 1, 1958, Quesada became the first administrator of the Federal Aviation Agency. He plunged into the job with his customary zeal, bringing to the task well-practiced administrative skills. Possessed of considerable charm and good humor, Quesada also was an individual of high principle, with a keen sense of public duty. These latter qualities could make him prickly and unyielding at times, as strong-willed airline executives and even stronger-willed pilots, forced to accept tough regulations and uncompromising enforcement, would soon find out.

One of Quesada's first problems concerned the continuation of federal aid to airports. Powerful administration forces opposed the program, due to expire in mid 1959, arguing that airports were local institutions and should be funded locally. Nonetheless, Senator Monroney drafted a bill to extend federal assistance four more years and increase allocations to $100 million per year. He saw airports as part of the national transportation system and deserving of federal support. But when budget-conscious President Eisenhower vetoed the legislation, he brought down on himself and Quesada howls of disapproval. Monroney vowed to

Quesada being sworn in as the first Federal Aviation Administrator as President Dwight D. Eisenhower looks on (courtesy of the U.S. Department of Transportation)

reintroduce the measure in the Senate. To avoid further embarrassment, the administration countered with a proposal to reduce federal aid over a four-year period, starting with a generous first-year subsidy of $200 million. Eisenhower's advocate was Quesada, who not only had to appear before Congress to refuse funds for his own agency but also had to oppose his loyal friend, Mike Monroney. Yet the former air ace did so successfully, telling the senators that the bill under discussion would fatten the billfolds of local constituents, not improve safety in the skies. His testimony succeeded in whittling down the program to two years duration at a cost of $63 million annually.

Quesada meant every word he said about the greater importance of safe skies over impressive terminal buildings. Safety became the crusade of his administration. Under his determined leadership, the highest possible safety standards for flight operations, maintenance, and pilot proficiency remained

in full force in the face of advancing technology and ever-crowded airways. Despite intense pressure from airlines and aircraft manufacturers, Quesada tolerated no infractions of regulations. In this area his soldierly qualities served him well. Important rules would not be disregarded, and new guidelines would receive expeditious action.

Quesada started his war on regulatory laxity with a full assault on the Airline Pilots Association (ALPA), the powerful pilots' union with which the CAA had often avoided confrontation. Quesada first took on the organization when he insisted on enforcing an old rule that required flight crew members to remain at their stations at all times. The near fatal crash of a Pan American jet flying on unattended autopilot triggered the action. ALPA strenuously objected to the measure as punitive and dictatorial, but Quesada's inspectors continued to write up violators. Throughout the summer of 1959, ALPA waged a publicity war against the FAA and its leader. Quesada responded with even keener adherence to the regulations. Not only did he rescind a no-culpability clause for pilots reporting hit-or-miss incidents but he also directed that the men in the cockpits take electrocardiogram tests every year.

The FAA's most unpopular safety code required pilots to retire at age sixty, and restricted jet training to those under fifty-five. ALPA's leadership denounced these practices, demanding proof that older men were less safe than younger ones, and suggesting that all airliners carry not only copilots but also flight engineers with flying certification. This issue eventually reached the Supreme Court, which upheld Quesada's hard line on safety. Shortly after this legal victory, a series of aircraft accidents early in December 1959 prompted the FAA chief to order his inspection staff on a month-long regimen of 24-hour-a-day shifts, which increased surveillance eightfold over normal checks. Despite charges by ALPA of harassment by incompetent inspectors, Quesada persisted in his policy of forcing the pilots (and their union) to accept vigorous oversight of cockpit procedures.

Quesada showed much the same face to the airline industry and to owners of small aircraft. He required all airliners to carry airborne weather radar, although he agreed to extend compliance deadlines. Maintenance infractions yielded fines of $1,000 to $1,500, and he led efforts to tighten standards on the shop floors. Private pilots also felt the pull of Quesada's regulatory levers. The Aircraft Owners and Pilots Association (AOPA) bridled at Strategic Air Command exercises which swallowed up large corridors of formerly open airspace. Even more provocative to AOPA, Quesada insisted that all pilots receive physical exams only from FAA-designated doctors. Furious editorials written by AOPA members spread across the nation's newspapers, and in January 1960 ALPA joined them in blasting FAA policies.

Despite these measures air crash fatality rates rose during 1959, raising questions about the FAA's effectiveness. The fact that commercial carriers flew more people far greater distances than ever before counted less than the exaggerated testimony of professional pilots, private flyers, and the airline industry. An infuriated Quesada appeared before Senator Monroney's Aviation Subcommittee to refute charges of tyranny and incompetence. Under questioning, he took credit for the absence of midair colli-

sions during 1959 and leveled his guns at flight crews and faulty maintenance, to which he attributed 75 percent of the accidents that year. Stung by ALPA and AOPA denunciations, Quesada blistered the "special interest groups" who resorted to "pure invective and intemperate attack." His counteroffensive won some important backers, and he stepped up the pace. Quesada was featured on radio and television, in newspapers, and even on the cover of *Time* magazine, spreading his message of airline safety above all other considerations.

One last, white-hot controversy burned through Quesada's final months in office. On October 4, 1960, 62 people died when a Lockheed Electra passenger aircraft plunged into Boston Harbor, the fifth time in two years that one of these new and much-heralded airliners had fallen out of the sky. Two of the most frightening episodes occurred earlier that year when one wing ripped from the fuselage of an Electra flying over Buffalo, Texas, and another tore off of a sister aircraft over Tell City, Indiana. Ninety-seven passengers perished in the two disasters. Nonetheless, on March 23, 1960, Quesada told a tense meeting at FAA headquarters that, despite the urgings of the CAB to ground the plane, all Electras would continue to fly. However, he did order all 96 airplanes in service to be flown at greatly reduced speed, from a maximum of 315 down to 259 mph. Quesada also put NASA's experimental wind tunnel at Langley, Virginia, at Lockheed's disposal and directed FAA investigators to subject the entire Electra fleet to thorough structural examinations.

The decision to keep the airliners in service in spite of their dubious record whipped up bitter exchanges between Senator Vance Hartke of Indiana and Quesada. Hartke demanded that the Electras be withdrawn from commercial use immediately. When he met with an emphatic refusal, the senator raised serious but unsubstantiated charges about Quesada's relationship with Lockheed, his former employer. Meanwhile, as ugly jokes about Electras made the night club circuit, bookings on their flights plunged. But the general's tenacity paid off. The slower speeds stemmed the problem, at least temporarily. At the same time, punishing and exhaustive flight tests by Lockheed's engineers led to the conclusion that the Electras, the pride of commercial aviation, would require extensive modifications to correct serious structural defects.

Quesada seemed to be borne out until the October 1960 crash in Boston. But here, too, fortune smiled on him. He scoured the accident scene himself and noticed bird carcasses everywhere. A local ornithologist declared they had been ingested in the Electra's engines, an interpretation accepted by Quesada. The finding subjected the FAA chief and his staff to more public denunciation; many suspected a cover-up of yet another example of structural failure. To the disgust of Quesada's enemies, laboratory tests proved a flock of starlings had indeed caused the mishap. Thus, as each Electra was brought to the Lockheed hangars for modification, the rest of the fleet remained in service.

As the election of 1960 approached, Quesada made clear his plans to retire from the FAA. Despite harsh opposition during his last months in office, he succeeded in establishing the lasting principle of safety first in the skies. Unpopular as he may have been in some quarters, the first FAA administrator imbued his staff with a determination to make tough regulations and enforce them with zeal. Failure to act with decision would not only threaten the survival of the infant agency which he led but also would risk more fatalities. At the founding of the FAA, Quesada left upon it an indelible mark of integrity and devotion to public service.

His double career—as chief inventor of American tactical air power and as a champion of the ground rules of modern jet travel—ended when he closed the door of his FAA office on January 20, 1961. The general said he wanted to have some fun. He presided over the firm which developed L'Enfant Plaza in Washington, D.C., and, even better, returned to baseball as co-owner of the Washington Senators. More important, he continued to comment on military and civil aviation, lived to see a renewed interest in tactical air power during and after the Vietnam War, and watched with pleasure as a vigorous FAA took root among the other agencies of government.

References:

"The Bird Watcher," *Time* (February 22, 1960): 16-19;

Richard H. Kohn and Joseph P. Harahan, eds., *Air Superiority in World War II and Korea: An Interview with Gen. James Ferguson, Gen. Robert M. Lee, Gen. William Momyer, and Lt. Gen. Elwood R. Quesada* (Washington, D.C.: Office of Air Force History, 1983);

Stuart I. Rochester, *Takeoff at Mid-Century: Federal Civil Aviation Policy in the Eisenhower Years, 1953-1961* (Washington, D.C.: U.S. Government Printing Office, 1976);

John Schlight, "Elwood R. Quesada: Tac Air Comes of Age," in *Makers of the United States Air Force*, edited by John Frisbee (Washington, D.C.: Office of Air Force History, 1987), pp. 177-204.

Archives:

Papers relating to the career of Elwood R. Quesada can be found in the Manuscripts Division of the Library of Congress, Washington, D.C.; the Dwight David Eisenhower Library, Abilene, Kansas; and the Archives of the Federal Aviation Administration, Washington, D.C.

Robert C. Reeve

(March 27, 1902 - August 25, 1980)

by Claus-M. Naske

University of Alaska Fairbanks

CAREER: Pilot, Pan American-Grace Airways (1929-1932); bush pilot and charter operator, Valdez and Fairbanks (1932-1947); president, Reeve Aleutian Airways (1947-1978).

Robert Campbell Reeve was a pioneer bush pilot who was responsible for developing air service in Alaska from Anchorage to the Aleutian Islands. Through careful management, he nurtured the growth of Reeve Aleutian Airways from postwar DC-3s to Lockheed and Nihon turboprops. Flying in difficult operating conditions, Reeve Aleutian compiled one of the best safety records in the industry. Reeve never became wealthy, but he had the satisfaction of overcoming severe challenges that would have defeated a less determined individual.

Reeve and his twin brother, Richard Dodge, were born in Waunakee, Wisconsin, on March 27, 1902, the sons of Hubert L. and Mae (Davenport) Reeve. Their mother died in 1904. Although their father remarried, the boys grew up without close parental supervision. At age fifteen, following American entry into World War I, Reeve persuaded an army recruiter that he was old enough to enlist. Rising to the rank of sergeant, he spent most of the war guarding an explosives factory in West Virginia.

Reeve went back to high school after the war. A few weeks later, however, the restless young man left for San Francisco, where he shipped out as an ordinary seaman on a steamer bound for the Orient. Reeve jumped ship in Shanghai and took a job with the British-run Chinese Maritime Customs Service. He returned to the United States in 1921, finally finished high school, then enrolled in the University of Wisconsin. He enjoyed college life, so much so that he was asked to leave school prior to graduation.

Having developed an interest in airplanes during his wartime service, Reeve decided to make a career in aviation. He went to Texas in 1926, where

Robert C. Reeve (portrait by Harvey Goodale; courtesy of the Robert C. Reeve Collection)

he traded work on an airfield for flying lessons. Eventually he secured both pilot and engine mechanic licenses. He sought to further his flying career by joining the Army Air Corps, but high blood pressure resulted in a medical discharge.

In 1929 Reeve began flying for Pan American-Grace Airways (Panagra), which opened an airmail route between Miami and Lima, Peru, in May. He remained with the company until 1932, gaining a good deal of experience in dealing with the primitive and often hazardous flying conditions that ex-

Reeve in front of a Reeve Aleutian Airways route map, 1953 (courtesy of the Robert C. Reeve Collection)

isted in South America. At one point, he established a new speed record between Santiago and Lima, covering the 1,900 miles in 20 hours.

Reeve's interest in Alaska came about through a series of unrelated incidents. He had met a famous Klondike gold rush character, "Swiftwater Bill" Gates, in Chile, and the old prospector had filled his ears with stories from the fabled rush. Also, he had talked to Eddie Craig, general manager at the famous Kennecott copper mine in Alaska's Wrangell Mountains. The tales of gold, and a new country to explore, intrigued Reeve. When he crashed a Lockheed Vega in January 1932 on the runway at Santiago, he decided that the time had come to explore opportunities in the far North.

Reeve stopped in Wisconsin en route to Alaska, where he contracted a mild case of polio that weakened one of his legs. He recovered sufficiently to take passage on a ship bound for Seward, Alaska. From there, he took the Alaska Railroad to Anchorage, arriving with 20 cents in his pocket. Un-

able to find work, he borrowed $25 from a local pilot and stowed away on a ship going to Valdez. Reeve managed to talk businessman Owen Meals into allowing him to repair, then lease, a wrecked Eaglerock biplane.

Reeve began charter flying in the summer of 1932. His first major contract involved carrying supplies to the isolated mining community of Chisana. By the spring of 1933, he had cleared $2,000, paid in gold dust. He promptly went to Fairbanks and bought a Fairchild 51, a high-wing, six-passenger cabin monoplane. He put down $1,500 for the airplane, similar to one he had flown in South America, with $2,000 payable over the next two years.

When Reeve returned to Valdez, he became involved with the famous Big Four mine. Located 30 miles outside Valdez, on the Brevier Glacier, 6,000 feet above sea level, the mine was owned by Jack Cook. However, Cook lacked the capital to operate it. Mining engineer Clarence Poy agreed to buy the mine, to be operated by Cook, after Reeve agreed to fly in mining supplies at 4 to 5 cents a pound. In one month, Reeve hauled some 30 tons of supplies to the mine, quickly gaining a reputation as a skilled glacier pilot.

Two events made 1936 a memorable year for the hardworking bush pilot. He purchased a second airplane, a Fairchild 71, and he married Janice Morisette. The union, a happy one by all accounts, produced three sons and two daughters.

Reeve continued to fly out of Valdez until 1940, logging more than 2,000 glacier landings and carrying over one million pounds of freight. He had a turn of bad luck in 1939, however. In the spring, a violent windstorm wrecked his Fairchild 71. After spending the summer working on the airplane, his hangar burned down—with the newly repaired Fairchild inside. Also, because he had done only limited flying in the four months prior to passage of the Civil Aeronautics Act of 1938, he qualified for only a small area under the "grandfather rights" that were granted to charter pilots in 1939.

In January 1941 a discouraged Reeve moved to Fairbanks. There, his prospects brightened as the federal government initiated several construction projects. Hired by the Morrison-Knudsen Company, he flew supplies to an airfield construction site 100 miles east of Fairbanks. The flying business grew rapidly following American entry into World War II in December. In November 1942 Reeve signed a contract with the Alaska Communications System to transport personnel throughout the territory.

Having done a good deal of flying in the Aleutian Islands during the war, Reeve became convinced that the area could support a scheduled air service. On March 24, 1947, he incorporated Reeve Aleutian Airways and began to fly charter service between Anchorage and Attu, using four war surplus DC-3s to cover the 1,780 miles. The following year, he secured a temporary certificate to operate a scheduled mail and passenger service to the Aleutian chain. Reeve now became a full-time executive, allowing his pilot's license to lapse.

Reeve worked hard to make the venture a success. However, the strain led to a heart attack in March 1951. Later in the year, he suffered a second attack, followed by a bout with pneumonia. He was forced to take a year off the demanding job. He spent most of the time hunting and hiking, a regimen that restored his health.

The 1950s brought a steady increase in business for the fledgling carrier. By the end of the decade, the airline had acquired three long-range DC-4s. It also obtained three Curtiss C-46s, which were used primarily to carry freight in support of the DEW Line construction project that began in 1957.

In the early 1960s, three pressurized DC-6s replaced the DC-4s as business continued to grow. Later in the decade, the first of three Lockheed Electras went into service. In 1972-1973 the airline purchased two Nihon YS-11 turboprops, its first new aircraft.

In 1978 Reeve gave up the presidency of the airline in favor of his son Richard. He no doubt watched with pleasure as the airline secured a long-sought route between Cold Bay and Seattle. Reeve died in his sleep on August 25, 1980, a year that saw his airline carry 82,000 passengers and record a net profit of $1.58 million.

References:
Stan Cohen, *Flying Beats Work: The Story of Reeve Aleutian Airways* (Missoula, Mont.: Pictorial Histories Publishing, 1988);

Beth Day, *Glacier Pilot: The Story of Bob Reeve and the Flyers Who Pioneered Alaska's Skies in Single-Engine Planes* (Sausalito, Cal.: Comstock Editions, 1981);

Claus-M. Naske, *Edward Lewis Bob Barrett . . . A Life in Politics* (Fairbanks: University of Alaska Press, 1979).

Republic Airlines

by Myron J. Smith, Jr.

Tusculum College

Republic Airlines was born as a national carrier on July 1, 1979, with the merger of North Central Airlines and Southern Airways. During the remainder of that year, operating over old routes and new, Republic transported more than 12 million passengers and recorded an operating profit of $28 million. Its future appeared bright.

During 1980, the airline added 31 nonstop services on its U.S.-Canadian route network and experienced an 8.8 percent traffic boost to 13.2 million. On October 1, it acquired the routes, assets, and debts of Hughes Air West; however, the costs of the merger led to a $38.3 million loss on the year on revenues of $917 million. Nonetheless, Republic joined the ranks of the major air carriers under the Civil Aeronautics Board's newly introduced classification scheme.

The year 1981 was not a good one for Republic. The PATCO air traffic controllers strike that summer forced suspension of service to 27 cities. Despite revenues of $1.45 billion, expenses brought a net loss of $46.3 million. Although traffic increased in 1982, excessive expenses (mainly interest on a huge debt) produced another net loss of $39.9 million. As a result of fare wars and higher labor costs, Republic posted its fourth straight net loss in 1983, a record $111 million (for a total of $235.5 million since 1980). As passenger boardings dipped 1.3 percent to 17.7 million and cumulative debt climbed to $797 million, investors and others wondered if the carrier might soon go under.

Daniel F. May became Republic's chief executive officer in April 1984, and Stephen Wolf, former president of Continental Airlines, took over as the carrier's president. The new management launched aggressive measures to prevent the company from sinking into a sea of red ink. They negotiated new union contracts with Republic's employees, and, in the largest route realignment since the company was formed, suspended service to 23 cit-

ies and added eight new destinations. Emphasizing more effective scheduling, they increased flights at the three major hubs of Detroit, Minneapolis, and Memphis. Innovative marketing programs were undertaken, and the airline's frequent flyer plan was expanded in a partnership with Pan American Airways. In an effort to improve its feeder system, Republic purchased 9 percent of the Michigan-based commuter Simmons Airlines. Despite a drop in traffic for 1984, these measures not only averted bankruptcy but also produced record earnings of $29.5 million. Even the debt was reduced.

By 1985 Republic had become the nation's seventh-largest airline. Its 100,000-mile transcontinental route network served 110 cities and extended from Canada to the Cayman Islands. In late April 1985 it inaugurated flights to nine new markets. By summer, the carrier's fleet of 160 McDonnell Douglas DC-9s, Boeing 727s, and Convair CV-580s were making 1,040 departures daily.

On January 23, 1986, Northwest Airlines announced that it would purchase Republic for $884 million. This largest merger since deregulation in 1978 would make Northwest the nation's fifth-largest airline, moving up from tenth place. Despite objections from the Justice Department on antitrust grounds, the Department of Transportation approved the agreement on July 31, 1986.

References:

David L. Brown, "Republic's Stephen Wolf: The Right Man at the Right Time," *Airline Executive*, 9 (January 1985): 20-22;

Dennis Carlton, William Landes, and Richard Posner, "Benefits and Costs of Airline Mergers: A Case Study," *Bell Journal of Economics*, 11 (Spring 1980): 65-83;

R. E. G. Davies, *Airlines of the United States since 1914*, revised edition (Washington, D.C.: Smithsonian Institution, 1982);

Joseph S. Murphy, "Meet Republic Airlines: Giant New Regional," *Airline Executive*, 3 (September 1979): 39-50;

Jan W. Steenblik, "Republic Airlines Flying Out of the Woods," *Air Line Pilot*, 52 (May 1983): 6-12.

Edward V. Rickenbacker

(October 8, 1890 - July 23, 1973)

by W. David Lewis

Auburn University

CAREER: Mechanic, salesman, and automobile racing driver (1906-1917); fighter pilot and commander, 94th Aero Pursuit Squadron (1918); vice-president and sales director, Rickenbacker Motor Company (1919-1926); president, Indianapolis Motor Speedway (1927-1945); sales representative, Cadillac Division, General Motors Corporation (1927-1929); vice-president for sales, Fokker Division, General Motors Corporation (1929-1932); vice-president, American Airways (1932-1933); vice-president, North American Aviation Corporation (1933-1934); general manager (1934-1938), president (1938-1953), chairman, Eastern Air Lines (1953-1964).

Edward V. Rickenbacker (courtesy of Eastern Air Lines)

Edward Vernon "Eddie" Rickenbacker, the central figure in the development of Eastern Air Lines and one of the most important executives in the history of American commercial aviation, was born in Columbus, Ohio, the son of William Rickenbacher, a construction worker and builder, and Elizabeth Basler Rickenbacher. Both his father, who was of German ancestry, and his mother, who was of French descent, had immigrated to the United States from Switzerland. They were deeply imbued with what their son later described as "a sense of duty and a tireless willingness to work," and gave him stern but loving parental discipline. The highly traditional values that pervaded their tiny home, which his father built with his own hands, remained with him throughout his entire life. So, also, did the emotional impact of the taunts that he endured from schoolmates because of his shabby clothing—particularly the ribbing he endured from being forced to wear a pair of mismatched shoes that his father had cobbled together for him.

Given such nicknames as "Dutchy" and "Kraut" because of the thick European accent with which he spoke in his early years, Rickenbacker retained the Germanic spelling of his surname until after he became an internationally famous fighter pilot in World War I; writing to a friend at some point in 1918, he acted on impulse in signing the letter "Eddie Rickenbacker," drawing attention to the second "k" by bracketing it. This led to newspaper stories that he had "taken the Hun out of his name," and the change became permanent. Having been given no middle name at birth, he had chosen the initial "V" during his prewar career as a racing driver, selecting "Vernon" to go with it because he liked the way it sounded. Considering the degree to which his life epitomized the concept of the "self-made man" that was so deeply ingrained in the midwestern American culture into which he had been born, it was only fitting that, to a large degree, he had invented his own name as he forged his own distinctive identity.

One of eight children, Rickenbacker was orphaned at an early age when his father was killed by an assailant in 1904. He quickly learned to be self-reliant, and began earning money by selling junk to a neighborhood dealer even before he started for school. Thanks in part to early lessons in thrift and the work ethic, he formed a lifelong hatred of anything that even vaguely smacked of socialism or the welfare state. Another persistent trait from childhood was a penchant for flirting with danger that involved him in numerous brushes with serious injury or death. Surviving countless accidents and escapades, one of which stemmed from a youthful attempt to fly by attaching an umbrella to a bicycle and swooping down a steep roof into a sandpile that he had built "to provide a soft place to land just in case," engendered a conviction that he had been spared for extraordinary accomplishments. It also produced a simple but deeply felt religious faith to which he frequently referred in his later speeches and writings.

A tough, rebellious youth who started smoking when he was five years old and was constantly embroiled in fights, Rickenbacker quit school in the seventh grade, at age thirteen, to help support his widowed mother. After working at a variety of jobs—lining molds in a glass factory, making cores in a foundry, sealing bottles at a brewery, polishing headstones for a monument maker, and operating a lathe at a machine shop, among others—he became consumed by a passion for automobiles, deriving deep enjoyment and aesthetic satisfaction from driving and repairing the primitive and unreliable vehicles that were just beginning to emerge from the "horseless carriage" age. Securing employment with Lee Frayer, a designer and maker of racing cars, he took correspondence courses in automotive technology, combined the knowledge he gained with on-the-job experience, and followed Frayer when the latter became chief engineer for the Columbus Buggy Company. Attracting the attention of its president, Clinton D. Firestone, Rickenbacker was soon demonstrating its products in such places as Atlantic City and Chicago and solving mechanical problems for dealers in Texas, Nebraska, and Arizona. By

1910, at the age of nineteen, he was a branch manager, with six salesmen working under him. The following year, he suffered a permanent visual impairment when a surgical procedure to remove a red-hot cinder that had lodged in one of his eyes left him with a blank spot in his vision. With characteristic determination, he learned to adjust and did not let his partial blindness interfere with his subsequent careers as an automobile racer and a combat pilot.

Rickenbacker had already assisted Frayer as a riding mechanic when the latter took part in the Vanderbilt Cup auto race on Long Island in 1906. Demonstrating and promoting his employer's Firestone-Columbus cars soon led him to become a racing driver himself. Establishing a reputation as a frequent winner at relatively small events in Iowa and Nebraska, he signed on as a relief driver with Frayer in major races against established competitors at such places as the Indianapolis Speedway. Leaving the Columbus firm in 1912, he was attracted to the Mason Automobile Company by the opportunity to work with its chief engineer, Fred Duesenberg, and made a significant breakthrough by driving a Duesenberg racer to victory in a major 300-mile race at Sioux City in 1913. Joining renowned racers Barney Oldfield and Bill Carlson as a driver for the Maxwell Automobile Company, he won national recognition with a series of dramatic wins against the best competition in the country, surviving numerous brushes with disaster and becoming famous as the "Speedy Swiss," the "Big Teuton," and the "Dutch Demon." Taking part three times in the Indianapolis 500, he also set a world speed record of 134 miles per hour in a Blitzen-Benz racer in an event at Daytona Beach, Florida. A spectacular duel with rival Johnny Aiken at the Indianapolis Speedway in 1916, in which Rickenbacker crossed the finish line on his brake drums after losing his wheels, brought him particular acclaim even though he did not win the race. Meanwhile, he sharpened his managerial skills by imposing tight discipline on the pit crews that serviced his racing cars. Winning $60,000 in 1916 alone, he finished his driving career late that year with a victory at Ascot Park in Los Angeles.

In the closing months of the 1916 racing season, Rickenbacker was invited by British racing promoter Louis Coatalen to go to England to help design cars for the Sunbeam Motor Company, which was still participating in American auto races despite the ongoing European war. Not realizing that a series of unanticipated events was about to shift his career in a radical new direction, he accepted.

Just before Rickenbacker left for England, airplane designer and builder Glenn Martin took him on a brief but exciting flight that renewed his boyhood interest in aviation. He also assisted an officer of the Army Air Service, T. F. Dodd, by helping him restart the engine of his plane after Dodd had experienced ignition problems. Rickenbacker's trip to England was complicated by two British intelligence agents who, after talking to him on shipboard, concluded that he was a German spy and arrested him upon his arrival in Liverpool. After being temporarily held incommunicado, he was rescued by Coatalen. While assisting the latter in redesigning racing cars, his imagination was stirred by encounters with young recruits of the Royal Flying Corps at the Brooklands Speedway, which had been converted into an airfield and training station, and by conversations with their instructors, who were veterans of aerial combat in France. As intervention by the United States in the war became increasingly imminent, Rickenbacker conceived the idea of organizing a volunteer group of American racing drivers to become fighter pilots on the Western Front. He tried to implement this plan after returning home, but could not interest the Army Signal Corps.

After American entry into the war, Rickenbacker was offered a chance to join the U.S. Army as a driver on the staff of Gen. John J. Pershing. Enlisting as a sergeant, he took ship for France. Dodd, who was now Pershing's aviation adviser, was aboard the vessel. Becoming a driver for Dodd in France, and displaying his mechanical ability by quickly repairing the latter's Mercedes when Col. William "Billy" Mitchell happened to be a passenger, led to his reassignment to Mitchell, commencing a fateful relationship that Rickenbacker exploited to the utmost. Through Mitchell's influence, he won admission to pilot training, falsely certifying his age as twenty-five; his real age of twenty-seven, two years over the limit, would have disqualified him. Becoming an engineering officer at the Issoudun airfield after completing his primary flight instruction, he persuaded his superior, Maj. Carl "Tooey" Spaatz, to assign him to aerial gunnery school and joined the 94th Aero Pursuit Squadron in March 1918 as a combat pilot.

Under the tutelage of such veteran flyers as Raoul Lufbery, Rickenbacker became highly adept at aerial warfare. "An amazing judge of speed and distance," as aviation writer Arch Whitehouse later characterized him, he possessed "the racing driver's inherent trick of timing," and bagged his first kill on April 29. By the end of May, he had scored the five victories required to become an ace, and won the French Croix de Guerre. His success, coupled with his previous fame as a racing driver, won him growing attention on the home front. From this time on he would be a national hero, usually referred to as "Eddie Rickenbacker." Actually, he disliked the nickname "Eddie" because he thought it conveyed the image of a "little fellow," but it stuck with him all his life.

After being hospitalized for much of the summer of 1918 because of an ear abscess, Rickenbacker returned to his unit, which had become famous as the "Hat-in-the-Ring Squadron," in September. Soon he became its commanding officer, wearing a specially designed uniform because he considered the regular one insufficiently dashing. While being trained as a fighter pilot, he had declared that "aerial warfare is nothing more than scientific murder," and he proceeded to develop it into an art form while escaping without injury from a succession of death-defying incidents that he later described in vivid detail in his published recollections of the war. By the time the armistice was declared on November 11, 1918, he had fought in 134 missions and scored 25 official victories, making him America's "Ace of Aces." His record, all the more remarkable for having been achieved in such a short time, won him the Congressional Medal of Honor in 1930.

Rickenbacker came home a hero whose fame rivaled that of his celebrated contemporary, Sgt. Alvin York. The society to which he returned had become increasingly intolerant of radicalism, and such events as the "Red Scare" of 1919 may have intensified his already well-developed tendencies toward ultraconservatism. With the aid of publicist Laurence La Tourelle Driggs, he published a book, *Fighting the Flying Circus*, on his combat experiences. In it, he celebrated "that intimate friendship that . . . cemented together brothers-in-arms into a closer fraternity than is known to any other friendship in the whole world." He also counseled political and military leaders on the implications of the war regarding future aviation policy, took lessons in public

Rickenbacker during World War I. The arrows marked on the photograph indicate bullet holes in Rickenbacker's plane (courtesy of Eastern Air Lines).

speaking, and promoted the sale of Liberty Bonds. Falling in love with Adelaide Frost Durant, a Californian he had met before the war, he married on September 16, 1922. She had previously been married to Clifford Durant, son of General Motors executive William C. Durant. Unable to have children of their own, the Rickenbackers adopted two sons, David Edward and William Frost.

After considering various peacetime career alternatives, Rickenbacker organized a group of business supporters to develop a medium-priced, six-cylinder automobile, the Rickenbacker, advertised as "A Car Worthy of Its Name." The venture did well for a time, but its promoters blundered by prematurely introducing four-wheel brakes before the rest of the industry was prepared for the innovation, leading to bitter attacks by competitors who claimed that it would cause skidding and accidents. Due to the adverse publicity, sales plummeted. After going deeply into debt in an effort to help his

dealers, Rickenbacker resigned as vice-president and sales director of the firm, which went out of business in 1927. Leaving deep scars, the episode cast a long shadow on his future. Many years later, when his slowness in switching from piston-driven to jet aircraft seriously injured Eastern Air Lines in competing with other carriers, he explained that the results of introducing four-wheel brakes had made him leery of taking the lead in adopting technological innovations.

Refusing to declare bankruptcy after his automotive debacle, Rickenbacker spent the next few years recouping his fortunes and paying off his debts. In 1927, with the aid of a syndicate of Detroit bankers, he took control of the Indianapolis Speedway, which he modernized and administered until after World War II. During 1927 he also joined General Motors Corporation (GM) as a sales representative for its Cadillac Division. In 1928 he was assigned to promote the LaSalle, a new luxury car that Cadillac had recently introduced. Despite the energy with which he pursued his duties, however, he did not find his work fulfilling. Flying had become more important to him, but, with commercial aviation still in its infancy, opportunities for establishing a business career in the field were hard to find.

Throughout the postwar era Rickenbacker devoted much of his spare time to changing this situation by stimulating public interest in aviation. In 1920 he took part in a cross-country aerial tour utilizing Junkers F-13 aircraft to demonstrate the advantages of duralumin construction. In May of the following year, flying most of the way in de Havilland DH-4 planes modified for extra fuel capacity, he set a new transcontinental speed record from San Francisco to Washington, D.C. Characteristic of many of his exploits in this era, the trip was punctuated by a crash at Cheyenne, Wyoming, and a forced landing near Hagerstown, Maryland. Whenever possible, he also flew while promoting the Rickenbacker automobile.

Rickenbacker's first foray into commercial aviation came in 1926. Together with a former comrade in the Hat-in-the-Ring Squadron, Reed Chambers, he became involved in Florida Airways, which won an airmail contract for the route from Miami to Jacksonville via Tampa. Later that year, the firm expanded its operations into Atlanta. The venture did not prosper, however, and was soon sold to Harold Pitcairn, who combined it with his existing airmail route from New York City to Atlanta.

By the late 1920s, thanks in part to the large procurement program recommended by the Morrow Board and the sensational publicity attending Charles A. Lindbergh's solo flight from New York to Paris, the prospects of making money in military and commercial aviation had become sufficiently bright to attract large-scale investment by important business corporations. This quickly opened up the career opportunities for which Rickenbacker had been waiting. In 1929, under Rickenbacker's prodding, GM became involved in aviation by acquiring control of the Allison Engineering Company, the Bendix Aviation Corporation, and the Fokker Aircraft Corporation of America. Quickly resigning his post with Cadillac, Rickenbacker moved to New York and joined GM's newly acquired Fokker Division as vice-president for sales.

After the onset of the Great Depression, GM consolidated Fokker with other assets in a new entity, the General Aviation Manufacturing Corporation, and shifted production to the Baltimore area. Despite desiring to stay with GM, Rickenbacker did not want to leave New York and resigned in March 1932 to become a vice-president of American Airways. Among other duties, he traveled frequently to Washington to optimize relations with government officials in the steadily growing web of regulatory activities affecting commercial aviation.

American's backers, who included such powerful Wall Street financiers as W. Averell Harriman and Robert Lehman, had developed a massive but poorly coordinated network of airmail and passenger routes under the umbrella of a large holding firm, the Aviation Corporation (AVCO). Soon after Rickenbacker joined the organization, Harriman and Lehman became embroiled in a bitter proxy fight with automobile manufacturer Errett L. Cord, who had become a director in AVCO after developing two air transport enterprises of his own but failing to secure an airmail contract. When Cord won the battle and moved American's headquarters from New York to Chicago, Rickenbacker's ties with Harriman and Lehman led him to leave the company in February 1933.

Temporarily unemployed, Rickenbacker capitalized upon his previous involvement at GM to remain in the airline industry by interesting that firm's assistant treasurer, Ernest R. Breech, in gaining control of the North American Aviation Corporation (NAAC), a large holding company that had gone into receivership as the result of the financial reverses suffered during the Great Depression by its founder, Clement M. Keys. After the idea won support from GM's chief executive, Alfred P. Sloan, and a competing move by United Aircraft to acquire NAAC fell through due to objections by the outgoing Herbert Hoover administration, the merger was effected. Among the assets secured by GM in this highly important transaction was Eastern Air Transport, a totally owned subsidiary of NAAC that Keys had purchased from Pitcairn in 1929. In addition, NAAC also had significant holdings in Transcontinental and Western Air (TWA) that now came under GM control. In April 1933 most of the assets of General Aviation Corporation were sold to NAAC, making it one of the nation's three largest aeronautical enterprises. Returning to GM as a result of these developments, Rickenbacker, who played a strong advisory role in the GM-NAAC merger negotiations, became vice-president of NAAC, while Breech became president.

Within a year, the world of American commercial aviation was thrown into turmoil by public exposure of alleged improprieties in the awarding of lucrative airmail contracts by President Hoover's postmaster general, Walter Folger Brown, who had forced a major reorganization upon the industry in 1930 following passage of the Air Mail (Watres) Act. Animated by a desire to embarrass the Hoover administration, a senatorial committee headed by Hugo L. Black of Alabama conducted a sensational investigation. In the process, existing airmail contracts were canceled and President Franklin D. Roosevelt ordered army pilots to fly the mail routes.

Although Rickenbacker had supported Roosevelt's election in 1932, he had already become alienated because of his strong dislike of the ways in which the New Deal was departing from traditional governmental approaches to business and the economy. The crisis of 1934 completed his estrangement. Enraged by the cancellation of existing airmail contracts, Rickenbacker charged that placing the responsibility of flying the mail in the hands of military pilots who had been inadequately trained for it and who lacked proper equipment with which to negotiate the nation's network of airmail routes constituted "legalized murder," and he made a vehement radio address criticizing Roosevelt's action. Just before the cancellation of the contracts went into effect, Rickenbacker added a further defiant gesture. Joining TWA's vice-president for operations, William J. "Jack" Frye, at the controls of a highly advanced new airliner, the Douglas DC-1, he flew the last regular airmail shipment from Los Angeles to Newark, New Jersey. Racing against a severe storm that was closing in on the East Coast, the plane arrived at the Newark airport in the record time of slightly more than 13 hours, dramatizing the performance standards that had been attained by the commercial aviation industry under private management.

Always quick to lose his temper, Rickenbacker was prone to exaggeration. His characterization of Roosevelt as a murderer was intemperate and ill considered, widening a breach between the two men that never healed. Nevertheless, Rickenbacker's criticism of the president was to some extent vindicated when a series of crashes, some fatal, followed the commencement of airmail flights by army pilots in what turned out to be an abnormally severe winter. As the toll continued to mount and public outrage intensified, fresh airmail legislation was hastily introduced and Postmaster General James A. Farley reopened bidding for new contracts pending its passage.

At Farley's insistence, no airlines that had participated in the infamous "spoils conferences" that Brown had held in 1930 could receive new route awards, and executives who had attended these meetings were proscribed from holding office in firms carrying airmail. After going through the charade of making minor name changes to comply with Farley's demands—Eastern Air Transport, for example, now became Eastern Air Lines—the former contractors won back most of their old routes, albeit with lower rates. In the reorganization that ensued under the Air Mail (Black-McKellar) Act of 1934, air transport was separated from aircraft manufacturing, and airmail contractors were forbidden to hold conflicting interests in other firms.

These changes had important consequences, both for Rickenbacker and for General Motors. Disposing of its holdings in several aviation enterprises, NAAC divested itself of its stock in TWA, and GM in turn sold its stake in that line to Lehman Brothers and the Atlas Corporation in 1935. Under a technicality in the Black-McKellar Act, relating to the fact that NAAC produced only military aircraft, GM retained control of Eastern Air Lines. That company, however, was an increasingly unprofitable and demoralized enterprise. In a move to rectify the situation, Breech put Rickenbacker in charge of the carrier as general manager in December 1934.

At the time Rickenbacker took command, Eastern was still relatively small, employing less than 500 persons. It had lost approximately $1.5 million in 1934 and had an antiquated fleet. Other than the experience and loyalty of its employees, its most valuable assets, particularly important because of their vacation appeal, were routes connecting New York and Chicago to Florida via the Atlanta gateway.

Plunging vigorously into his new duties, Rickenbacker replaced Eastern's obsolete Curtiss Condors and Pitcairn Mailwings with Lockheed L-10 Electras and Douglas DC-2s. Firing old and jaded executives, he recruited fresh managerial talent, reorganized the company's traffic department, instituted a stock-option plan to enhance employee performance and morale, and inaugurated pioneering medical and meteorological departments. By spearheading acquisition of the Wedell-Williams Transport Corporation late in 1936, he added Houston to a growing list of destinations. Fiercely conservative, he successfully put down a strike among Eastern's mechanics that began late in 1937, but soon thereafter invited the International Association of Machinists (IAM) to organize the company's maintenance workers and cooperated with them in establishing a 40-hour week, increased wages, and vacation benefits. Meanwhile, group insurance and pension benefits were provided to all employees. This multifaceted program quickly paid off. Achieving a modest profit of $38,000 in 1935, Eastern was soon firmly in the black.

Proud of his accomplishment, Rickenbacker was infuriated to discover, early in 1938, that GM had given rental car magnate John Hertz an option to buy Eastern for $3 million. Prior to the time Rickenbacker had taken over, the company had been valued at only $1 million, and he credited himself with making the difference. Protesting to GM president Sloan, he received a commitment from the latter to give him control of Eastern if he could raise $3.5 million in cash within 30 days. Aided by William Barclay Harding of Smith, Barney & Co., who was instrumental in securing funding from the Kuhn, Loeb banking interests, Rickenbacker managed to raise the money. With Sloan's continuing support, he won approval of his bid from the directors of NAAC over the opposition of Breech, with whom he had quarreled over new route acquisitions and who favored selling the enterprise to Hertz. Still anxious about whether his supporters could actually produce the cash required to implement his victory at the NAAC board meeting, which occurred on a Friday, in time to meet the expiration of the 30-day deadline late Sunday afternoon, Rickenbacker impetuously roused Sloan from bed in the middle of Saturday night to make sure that the money would be forthcoming by the stipulated time. It was, and Rickenbacker took over as president of Eastern Air Lines in April 1938.

As Rickenbacker assumed his new role, the airline industry was awaiting passage of the Civil Aeronautics Act, which was signed into law by Roosevelt at the end of June 1938 and went into effect at the beginning of August. The impending implementation of this key statute, which removed the power of the Post Office Department to determine new routes, lent urgency to a bitter proceeding in which Eastern was contending with Braniff for a vital artery from Houston to Brownsville, Texas, which both lines intended to use as a future springboard for penetration of Mexican markets. Here again Rickenbacker demonstrated the brashness that was so basic to his nature. After staging a series of bold maneuvers to force a decision by postal authorities before the new law went into effect, he climaxed one of the most dramatic bidding wars in the history of American commercial aviation with a winning but highly controversial offer to carry airmail over the route for absolutely nothing in order to secure the potentially lucrative passenger revenue.

Passage of the Civil Aeronautics Act placed Eastern and other U.S. airlines under the most stringent government regulation they had experienced to date. In 1940 Roosevelt tightened the web by streamlining the system and putting both safety and economic regulation in the hands of a powerful Civil Aeronautics Board (CAB). The airlines, however, benefited from receiving permanent certification for the so-called grandfather routes they had developed; in Eastern's case, such rights were granted for the company's lucrative routes from New York and Chicago to Florida. During the next few years, Rickenbacker won entry to important new destinations, including St. Louis. By the end of the decade, Eastern's sprawling system encompassed nearly 5,400 miles, connecting 40 cities in 17 states east of the Mississippi River. Persuading his directors to issue $3 million in new stock, he purchased a fleet of Douglas DC-3s and moved the company's headquarters into the top floors of a swanky new skyscraper, known as the Eastern Air Lines Building, in Rockefeller Center. Beginning in 1938, the company became the first U.S. airline to carry mail without subsidy, an accomplishment of which Rickenbacker was extremely proud. By relentlessly driving down costs, he augmented Eastern's net earnings to $1.5 million in 1940, making it the most profitable enterprise in the entire industry. During 1941 its 39 DC-3s, collectively known as "The Great Silver Fleet," carried more than 300,000 passengers, solidifying the company's status as one of the nation's three largest airlines.

On the night of February 26, 1941, Rickenbacker experienced one of the most dramatic of the periodic brushes with death that punctuated his career. After accepting a speaking invitation from civic leaders in Birmingham, Alabama, he took a Douglas DST, the "sleeper" version of the DC-3, from New York to Atlanta on the first leg of his trip. Making an instrument approach to the Atlanta airport under cloudy conditions, the pilot failed to realize that he was flying too low, and the plane crashed into some trees near the field. Pinned in the wreckage until dawn, Rickenbacker suffered multiple injuries including severe cranial and eye damage, several broken ribs, a smashed pelvis, a crushed hip socket, a fractured knee, and a severed nerve resulting in prolonged paralysis covering the left side of his body. Somehow retaining the presence of mind to warn some nearby survivors not to start a fire to warm themselves while waiting for help to arrive, he shouted commands to a group of able-bodied passengers who improvised a chain of communications that brought ambulances to the scene. After being freed from the twisted metal and enduring an agonizing ride to Atlanta's Piedmont Hospital, he was gradually nursed through an excruciating process of recovery in which he repeatedly summoned his will to live despite having a succession of eerie near-death experiences. Finally, after more than four months, he was released. For the rest of his life he walked with a limp and suffered other permanent effects of the accident, which, however, only increased his "conviction that surely I was being permitted to continue living for some good purpose."

While Rickenbacker convalesced from his ordeal, the Japanese attack on Pearl Harbor brought the United States into World War II. Despite his battered physical condition, Rickenbacker was eager to become involved. Throughout the interwar years he had been a persistent advocate of military preparedness, supporting Gen. Billy Mitchell's campaign for the development of an independent air force and calling Mitchell's 1925 court-martial conviction "a crime against posterity." He became increasingly shrill after a visit to Europe in 1935 during which he witnessed at first hand the buildup of the German air arm and was dismayed by key British leaders who lacked the will to face up to the growing threat posed by Hitler's ambitions. For a time during the late 1930s, Rickenbacker espoused isolationism. After the outbreak of World War II, however, he became convinced that the United States would be dragged into the conflict without being ready to meet its demands. When war came, therefore, he was impatient to do his part.

Despite the bitter animosity that existed between him and Roosevelt, Rickenbacker had powerful friends in Washington, among them the commanding officer of the Army Air Forces, Gen. H. H. "Hap" Arnold, and Secretary of War Henry L. Stimson. Thanks to their support, he became deeply involved in a succession of wartime assignments. To Roosevelt's credit, the president made no apparent effort to block these missions, as he did in the case of another hero he did not like, Col. Charles A. Lindbergh.

Rickenbacker's wartime activities began in March and April 1942 when, at Arnold's request, he visited a large number of air bases in an effort to identify problems that were impeding training and morale. Discovering serious shortages of equipment, which he traced to poorly coordinated transportation, he presented his findings to military officials in Washington and subsequently helped develop a plan under which commercial airlines turned planes and personnel over to the armed forces. Shortly thereafter, again at Arnold's request, he made a series of speeches and broadcasts aimed at dispelling public criticism of alleged defects and inadequacies in various types of aircraft being deployed by the United States in the rapidly escalating war effort.

In September 1942 Rickenbacker went to England at Stimson's request to visit Army Air Forces installations and report on preparations for expanded operations against the Axis. After conversing with such leaders as Churchill, Dowding, Harris, and Trenchard, he toured airfields, witnessed mock combat between Allied planes and captured German aircraft, interviewed pilots, and returned to the United States with specific criticism of American equipment and recommendations for future development. On his way home he had the heady experience of carrying a set of plans from Gen. Dwight D. Eisenhower relating to the latter's impending invasion of North Africa, adding to his already deep sense of self-importance. He presented these to Stimson along with his own report.

Rickenbacker's next mission led to one of the most dramatic episodes in his entire career and produced another of his periodic brushes with death. Asked by Stimson to conduct a fact-finding tour in the South Pacific similar to the one he had just completed in Europe, and to carry a special secret message to General Douglas MacArthur, he flew to Honolulu and departed from Hickam Field shortly

Rickenbacker (center on steps) greets Eastern Air Lines captains M. A. C. Johnson (to his right) and H. T. Merrill (to his left) and passengers after the group set a Miami-to-New York speed record of 3:29.45 in a Lockheed Constellation, La Guardia Airport, May 17, 1947 (courtesy of the National Air and Space Museum)

after midnight on October 21, 1942, aboard a B-17 on the first leg of his trip. Following a circuitous route in order to avoid Japanese-held territory, the plane was first bound for Canton Island, after which it was to proceed to the Fiji Islands, New Caledonia, and Brisbane en route to a rendezvous with MacArthur in New Guinea. Upon descending in the morning for a planned landing at Canton, however, Rickenbacker and the crew failed to sight the island and soon ran short of fuel. After radio contact with Canton and Palmyra failed to clarify their position, they jettisoned as much equipment and personal belongings as possible, did their best to secure adequate provisions, donned life preservers, positioned themselves near the three life rafts with which the aircraft had been supplied, and crash-landed in the waves as the engines died. Dazed from the impact, the members of the party managed to board the

rafts, although some of them were painfully injured from being thrown against metal objects as the plane hit the water.

Thus began an epic struggle for survival against the odds. In the confusion of scrambling out of the stricken B-17, the water and rations assembled during the final stages of the flight had been left behind, leaving only a few oranges. Lashing the rafts together, the eight men drifted aimlessly while sharks, attracted by blood from the injured crew members, circled around and bumped against the undersides of the tiny vessels during the interminable nights. Like the others, Rickenbacker and the two men with whom he shared one of the rafts were scorched and blistered by the sun by day and suffered intensely from cold by night. Cramped for space, their bodies ached and the slightest contact resulted in sores that itched unmercifully from the salt that they could not prevent from accumulating on their skin. Strange apparitions assailed their disordered imaginations, and they talked crazily about food as they ate their few oranges and unappeasable hunger set in. Trying to maintain some degree of morale, Rickenbacker organized prayer sessions at which the helpless men sang hymns and read passages from a Bible that one of them had put in his pocket.

On the eighth day of this waking nightmare, as if in answer to a prayer, a bird landed on Rickenbacker's raft. Catching it, he wrung its neck, stripped off its feathers, and shared it with his seven companions. Using its intestines for bait, they improvised a fishing line and caught a mackerel and a sea bass. Rain came, washing away encrusted salt and providing drinking water that was collected in a bucket and painstakingly rationed. Despite such occasional relief, one of the men, Sgt. Alex Kaczmarczyk, died and was buried at sea. As the ordeal continued, Rickenbacker, drawing on what he later called "the wisdom that comes to older men," alternately cajoled and hectored his remaining companions to brace their waning spirits. His abrasive tongue produced what Robert J. Serling has characterized as "a kind of sullen hatred" on their part. "Several of the boys confessed that they once swore an oath to live for the sheer pleasure of burying me at sea," Rickenbacker later recalled.

On the afternoon of the 19th day a plane appeared in the sky but flew away without sighting the rafts despite frenzied efforts by Rickenbacker and the others to attract attention. Ignoring Rickenbacker's disapproval, pilot William T. Cherry detached the smallest of the three rafts and paddled away; soon, two others, navigator John J. de Angelis and copilot James C. Whittaker, also departed, taking an unconscious crew member, Sgt. James W. Reynolds, with them. Together with his aide, Col. Hans C. Adamson, and Sgt. John F. Bartek, both of whom were unconscious, Rickenbacker floated on toward apparent doom. Suddenly, however, their raft was spotted on the 24th day by a navy plane, and they were taken to a base in the Ellice Islands. The four crew members who had departed earlier were also rescued. The nightmare was over.

Back home, the ordeal suffered by the group, whose members had been almost universally given up for dead despite continuing search and rescue ef-

forts, produced one of the year's most sensational news stories. The dramatic episode brought even greater fame to Rickenbacker, who was characterized as "Iron-Man Eddie" and "The Man Who Always Comes Back." Continuing his mission after his recovery, Rickenbacker delivered Stimson's secret message to MacArthur, visited bases in New Guinea and Guadalcanal, and returned home via Samoa and Hawaii, arriving in Washington on December 19, 1942. Receiving a hero's welcome, he held press conferences and recounted his experiences in a national radio broadcast. Later, he published a book about the ordeal, *Seven Came Through*, which was also serialized in *Life* magazine.

Witnessing the privations endured by American servicemen in the Pacific theater embittered Rickenbacker toward workers on the home front who, he believed, were not supporting the war effort with maximum vigor. Somehow finding the resilience to conduct a transcontinental speaking tour of defense factories, he alienated many of his listeners with his rhetoric. After recovering sufficiently from his experiences on the raft, he accepted yet another mission from Secretary Stimson, this time to North Africa, the Middle East, and Asia. With help from Lend-Lease director Edward R. Stettinius, Jr., and Russian ambassador Maxim Litvinov, the Soviet Union was also added to the itinerary despite a notable lack of enthusiasm on the part of the State Department and President Roosevelt himself. Apparently the Russians believed that Rickenbacker's advice to pilots and technicians who used and serviced American equipment provided through Lend-Lease would be helpful to the Soviet war effort, while Stettinius was interested in what Rickenbacker could discover about the utilization and disposition of American supplies. Much to Rickenbacker's satisfaction, the State Department was kept uninformed about the Russian part of his mission.

Flying to the North African front via Natal and Dakar, Rickenbacker inspected bases in Morocco and Algeria, visited Eisenhower and James H. "Jimmy" Doolittle in Algiers, flew across Tunisia and Libya to Cairo, and proceeded to Iran, where he watched pursuit planes being assembled in scorching heat at a factory in Abadan for subsequent delivery to the Soviet Union. Continuing to India, which depressed him because of its squalor, he flew over the Hump to China, where he had tea with Madame Sun Yat-sen and was filled with contempt by the corruption prevailing in Chiang Kai-shek's government. Returning via the Hump to India, he met Gen. Joseph "Vinegar Joe" Stilwell and proceeded to Tehran.

At last came the part of the trip that Rickenbacker had most anticipated. Throughout his journey he had repeatedly enjoyed surreptitious encounters with Soviet officials who knew about his plans to visit Russia. Flying through a pass in the Elburz Mountains to an initial stop at Kuibyshev, he followed a twisting route to Moscow, carefully plotted to avoid proximity to the front lines. State Department representatives in the Soviet capital, who had been kept in the dark about his plans by Russian authorities until just before his arrival, were understandably curious about his presence, and he amazed them by telling them that he had received permission to visit defense-related facilities and interview military personnel. Litvinov, whom he had met once in Cairo, was now in the Soviet capital, and facilitated tours of air bases at which Rickenbacker passed along practical information to pilots who were flying American planes received under Lend-Lease. At the front he was escorted to a heavily camouflaged aerodrome where he lectured to pilots and engineering officers on the idiosyncracies of Douglas A-20 light bombers. He was taken to another facility where he provided similar instruction about the Bell P-39 Airacobra. Back in Moscow, he toured the Stormovik factory and was permitted to study the construction and operation of this superb antitank weapon at first hand. After viewing the bombed-out ruins of Stalingrad, he started his homeward journey via Tehran and Cairo. Before returning to America, he visited Great Britain and briefed Churchill on his Russian tour, after which he flew to New York via Greenland and Newfoundland.

Stimson had been receiving a steady flow of reports from Rickenbacker as the latter's mission proceeded. Along with other civilian and military officials, he was more thoroughly briefed following the captain's return. After a reunion with his wife, Rickenbacker, resentful that Roosevelt had shown no apparent interest in talking to him about his Russian trip, went on his final wartime mission for Stimson, visiting bases in the American Northwest from which Lend-Lease supplies were ferried to Siberia, and then proceeding to inspect airfields and other facilities in the Aleutian Islands.

Rickenbacker placed a high estimate on the value of the information he had gathered for government leaders and the advice he had given to military personnel in the various places he had visited. In his autobiography he took credit for such postwar developments as the appointment of Walter Bedell Smith as ambassador to Moscow, and indicated that Roosevelt might have understood Stalin and the Russians better if he had only solicited his opinions. Obviously, both Arnold and Stimson held his expertise in high esteem, but an informed estimate of his contributions to the war effort must await detailed study. Certainly his wartime experiences, particularly his harrowing ordeal in the South Pacific, contributed further to his heroic public image, and their publicity value was fully exploited by Eastern Air Lines in the postwar years.

While Rickenbacker was gone, such subordinates as traffic manager Paul Brattain and operations chief Sidney Shannon administered Eastern Air Lines, which made noteworthy contributions of its own to the war effort. Its Military Transport Division, whose olive-drab planes were jokingly called "The Great Chocolate Fleet," transported approximately 130,000 passengers and 45 million pounds of supplies, logging more than 33 million miles in the process. Flying over virtually impenetrable jungles in such places as Brazil and long stretches of uninterrupted water in the South Atlantic while transporting cargo and military personnel between such outposts as Trinidad, Natal, Ascension Island, and Accra, its pilots never canceled an assignment and lost only one plane during the entire war. Meanwhile, on the home front, the few aircraft that had not been pressed into military service were heavily utilized by a shrunken staff.

Returning to more normal duties after his wartime adventures, Rickenbacker presided over the most profitable carrier in the nation. During the late 1940s, Eastern's earnings exceeded those of the rest of the industry put together. But the causes of its ultimate decline were already present, and for these Rickenbacker himself was at least partly responsible. It is difficult not to conclude that his wartime experiences, including his ordeal in the South Pacific and the impact on his already inflated ego of his interactions with powerful leaders, intensified potentially self-destructive traits that were already present prior to the conflict, increasingly impairing his judgment and producing costly mistakes that gradually undermined the future of the firm he headed. As Robert J. Serling has aptly stated, "Eastern entered the postwar era ... with a time bomb buried in the inflexible personality of the man who ruled the Great Silver Fleet."

The time bomb was already ticking at an airline meeting in Havana in April 1945 at which Rickenbacker's penchant for reckless pronouncements involving Roosevelt surfaced once again. Upon being informed about FDR's sudden death, he began a luncheon presentation by telling his listeners he was glad it had happened. This caused such a furor that he was forced to return to the United States, leaving his embarrassed company to be represented by Brattain. Such indiscretions could not help but adversely prejudice Eastern's chances in key route deliberations conducted by the CAB, whose members were appointed by Democratic administrations during this critical period.

At this time CAB policy was already turning against some of Eastern's vested interests, making Rickenbacker's poor judgment doubly risky. Anticipating an upward surge in air traffic, the CAB entered the postwar era committed to encouraging competition on routes that had previously been operated by only one carrier. In 1944 it had already taken away Eastern's stranglehold on service between New York and Florida by admitting National Airlines to this key market. In August 1945, four months after Rickenbacker's Havana outburst, it broke Eastern's monopoly of the nonstop Chicago-to-Miami vacation trade by awarding Delta authority to operate between those cities.

Of the two rivalries that were thus launched, National versus Eastern and Delta versus Eastern, the latter was easily the more significant. Beginning in the mid 1920s as a crop-dusting enterprise led by a Louisiana agricultural agent, C. E. Woolman, Delta had attempted to develop a passenger route between Dallas-Fort Worth and Atlanta, only to be forced in Brown's "spoils conferences" to sell its operation to American Airways. In 1934, however, Delta took advantage of Roosevelt's cancellation of existing airmail contracts to win a mail route between Dallas-Fort Worth and Charleston, South Carolina. Until 1945 it fed east-west traffic into the Eastern system at Birmingham and Atlanta, and the interests of the two lines, one huge and the other tiny, were complementary. Woolman later made a jesting reference to this when a group of airline executives scrambled for taxi space after a meeting in Washington, and Rickenbacker asked if he could sit

on his lap. "Well, Eddie," Woolman quipped, "I've been helping support you for years, so I might as well do it some more."

This was a barbed comment; by the time it was made, Delta and Eastern had become bitter enemies. In Woolman, whose genial, homespun manner masked one of the shrewdest minds in commercial aviation, Rickenbacker had found a worthy adversary, no matter how disdainful he might be toward the upstart airline and its unassuming leader. In time, Delta would not only far surpass Eastern, indeed it would survive it, after Eastern went bankrupt and passed out of existence in 1991. Such things would have seemed preposterous in 1945.

National's chief executive George T. Baker was also a determined foe. Early in 1946 he beat Eastern to the punch by deploying Douglas DC-4s in nonstop traffic between Miami and New York. Soon, however, National became embroiled in labor disputes that for a time threatened its very life and seriously impaired its capacity to compete. With Delta it was different. Woolman also got the jump on Rickenbacker by introducing DC-4s in nonstop service between Chicago and Miami in November 1946, temporarily taking away much of Eastern's patronage. When Rickenbacker countered with Lockheed L-649 and L-749 Constellations, Delta renewed the battle by adopting the Douglas DC-6B and met Eastern's subsequent switch to L-1049 Super Constellations by acquiring a fleet of Douglas DC-7s. National pursued a similar course, but lacked Delta's financial resources.

Rickenbacker underestimated both Delta and National, allowing them to place DC-4s in competition with Eastern on long nonstop routes while he could offer nothing better than DC-3s that lacked the range to fly the same distance without refueling. He displayed similar myopia by doggedly persisting with plans to acquire a postwar fleet of impossibly slow Curtiss C-46 airliners out of friendship for the president of Curtiss-Wright, Guy Vaughn, even though his closest advisers tried vainly to deter him. Only when Curtiss-Wright failed repeatedly to deliver the planes as scheduled because it continually shifted its manufacturing facilities from one city to another did Rickenbacker finally cancel the order. As in the case of his ill-considered remarks in Havana, he was putting emotion before clearheaded business thinking.

At about the same time, Rickenbacker nearly led Eastern into another debacle by deciding to acquire a new plane, the 2-0-2, that Martin was developing as a successor to the DC-3. Luckily for Eastern, Northwest introduced the plane into service and suffered enormous financial damage when its lack of airworthiness led to a series of fatal crashes that produced temporary grounding by federal authorities and caused pilots and passengers alike to refuse to fly in it. By arranging emergency financing that enabled Martin to retool and develop a much better aircraft, the 4-0-4, Rickenbacker salvaged a bad situation that might otherwise have strained Eastern's resources to the utmost, but his tendency to make hasty decisions without heeding knowledgeable subordinates was clearly in evidence long before he made far more disastrous choices in the future. Significantly, Woolman listened to advisers within the Delta organization, and avoided adopting the Martin 2-0-2 because of their warnings.

Woolman bested Rickenbacker decisively in another key decision made in response to changing federal regulations, one of which required three persons in the cockpits of such four-engine aircraft as the Lockheed Constellation and the Douglas DC-6. Like several other airlines, Eastern opted to put a mechanic trained as a flight engineer in the third seat. According to Serling, Rickenbacker adopted this policy not only because he accepted Lockheed's judgment that it was advisable but also because "he had a soft spot for mechanics." Once again he was letting emotional considerations get in the way of clear thinking. In Serling's words, "His vulnerability in this area would cost the airline dearly because it wasn't the first time he was to let sentimentality override the advice of his officers."

Counseled by key advisers that following the same policy would engender conflict between members of two unions in the same cockpit and create a situation in which the flight engineer would become frustrated with a dead-end job, Woolman decided to fill the third seat with a pilot who had been trained as a flight mechanic and who could, in time, advance to copilot and pilot. He stuck to this decision in 1953 when Delta acquired Chicago and Southern in a merger, inheriting in the process a group of mechanics who had been trained as flight engineers. Despite the severance costs involved, he let them go in a financially expensive settlement. Thanks to his wisdom—"We must never put a board on a man's head," he once stated—Delta escaped a series of jurisdictional strikes from which Eastern suffered enormous damage in the future.

Proud of his employees, Rickenbacker had not hesitated in the prewar period to be highly abrasive in confronting passengers who were rude to Eastern's flight attendants. According to his autobiography, this usually resulted in a change of heart among the offending parties. However praiseworthy such loyalty to the company's employees may have been, it coexisted with a lack of concern about passenger comfort and courteous service that contrasted sharply with Woolman's insistence upon unfailing deference to the needs of those who flew aboard Delta's planes. During the postwar era, Rickenbacker's attitude that Eastern owed the traveling public nothing except moving them from place to place won the company the unenviable distinction of being the only carrier in the entire industry whose patrons actually formed an organization to vent their collective displeasure about the way they were treated. Known as WHEAL—an acronym for "We Hate Eastern Air Lines"—it was started by two Pittsburgh businessmen. It bought advertising space in newspapers to vent its outrage, and had a membership estimated by one of Eastern's own officers at "several thousand." It did not disband until 1965, after Eastern's directors had forced Rickenbacker into retirement.

Rickenbacker also displayed another attitude that did not win universal approval from his own employees. Prior to the war he had for a time refused to hire female cabin attendants, who, he reasoned, would soon get married and leave the company anyway. During and after the war Eastern had to abandon this policy, but Rickenbacker's patronizing attitude toward women—clearly revealed by his use of the term *girlie* in references to stewardesses—was never far under the surface. In at least one case, the fact that a managerial employee of the company was actually a woman had to be hidden from him by using her initials instead of her given name.

Such attitudes were widespread throughout the industry, as they were in American society at large; Rickenbacker was merely showing his customary forthrightness by being open about them, and in any case his male chauvinism did little or nothing to hurt Eastern at the time. In other ways that were much more important to good corporate public relations, however, Rickenbacker was just as maladroit. One of these involved the type of savvy that

Eastern Lockheed Super Constellation (courtesy of the National Air and Space Museum)

was instrumental in winning new routes. Here, as in other respects, Delta was much more adept.

Skillfully taking advantage of sectional pride and the overrepresentation of committee chairmen from the South at a time when the South was still solidly Democratic, Woolman and his legal department lobbied effectively in Washington for important route extensions. Those efforts culminated in a significant victory in 1955 when, after a massive public relations campaign, Delta won authorization from the CAB to operate in the crucial Atlanta-Washington-Baltimore-Philadelphia-New York corridor. Because Delta was far better able than National to offer Eastern effective competition in this extremely lucrative market, the outcome of the long, drawn-out proceeding was a major defeat for Eastern, which fared poorly in CAB route cases during the first postwar decade.

To what degree this and other setbacks were due to Rickenbacker's propensity for making offensive remarks about politicians and other public servants with whose views he disagreed, particularly if they happened to be Democrats, is impossible to say. In fairness to him, the CAB often tried deliberately to strengthen smaller carriers vis-à-vis larger

ones in order to promote competition within the industry, boding ill for Eastern in key route proceedings. Certainly, however, the impression that Rickenbacker's penchant for alienating influential people was not an asset in such matters was widespread throughout the industry. His most important director, Laurance Rockefeller, was convinced that this was the case.

Throughout the postwar years, Eastern did succeed in adding new destinations to its system, but these were usually smaller cities requiring more and more uneconomical short hops. In most such cases, it would have been better for the company not to have gone to the trouble of serving these small cities. Really lucrative new markets, such as Mexico City and San Juan, were secured much more slowly through the complex regulatory maze. Ultimately, Eastern was more successful in obtaining such prizes through merger, as in 1956 when, after a bruising battle with National, it took over Colonial Airlines and won access to such places as Montreal, Ottawa, and Bermuda in the bargain.

During the mid 1950s, mistakes in aircraft selection also became a significant factor in Eastern's competitive decline. Having proved itself in military aircraft, the jet engine was about to enter American commercial aviation. For executives who were used to the economics of piston-driven power plants, this was a worrisome matter, but Pan American Airways and American Airlines forced the issue in 1955 by placing orders for Boeing 707s. Despite the fact that Eastern was in a good position to acquire a jet fleet, because Rickenbacker's dogged insistence on low costs had kept it relatively free of debt, its leader—to the dismay of many of his subordinates—decided to invest approximately $100 million in purchasing a large number of Lockheed L-188 Electras, a turboprop plane. Although the move made some sense in view of the relatively short flights that continued to characterize Eastern's route structure, the purchase fell into a pattern on Rickenbacker's part, probably rooted in emotional considerations having partly to do with the ill-fated motorcar he had produced in the 1920s, to leave technological pioneering to other carriers and go slow on the acquisition of jet aircraft. This was to have disastrous consequences for Eastern.

Partly because his advisers counseled against the L-188 and partly because American and Eastern had tied up most of Lockheed's available production, Woolman chose to order six Douglas DC-8s for Delta. Soon thereafter, he took advantage of Howard Hughes's growing financial difficulties by acquiring three Convair 880s, exceptionally swift planes that were being developed largely for use by TWA. In September 1959 and May 1960 Delta introduced both of these aircraft into scheduled commercial service. They quickly won passenger favor because of their speed and ability to fly at comfortably high altitudes. Meanwhile, the Electra, which Eastern introduced in January 1959, became temporarily a pariah of the airways when American, Braniff, and Northwest all suffered crashes in utilizing it, due to structural problems in the design of its wings and engine nacelles. Though refraining from grounding the craft, federal authorities imposed severe speed limitations upon it. While flying their company's jets, Delta's pilots made a sport of looking for L-188s bearing Eastern's markings, pointing them out to passengers on the intercom, and triumphantly zooming past them. Even after the L-188 became a highly airworthy craft, it was no match for jet competition on most major routes unless these involved relatively short flights.

Besides having erred by investing so heavily in the L-188, Rickenbacker made an even worse mis-

take by passing up an opportunity to acquire DC-8s before either Delta or National ordered them. He did so because he was unimpressed with the JT-3 engines with which available models were equipped, and therefore decided to hold out for ones with more powerful JT-4s. Despite the fact that a majority of his executives wanted to play it safe by ordering six DC-8s with JT-3 engines and pointed to the potentially disastrous results if Delta or National got them first, Rickenbacker had his way and suffered the consequences when Woolman acquired his Douglas ships and Baker managed to lease two Boeing 707s from Pan American. Further difficulties resulted when Rickenbacker dropped an option for some additional DC-8s because he doubted that Eastern could fill their seats.

At about the same time, Rickenbacker compounded his problems by spending a considerable amount of money on the acquisition of propeller-driven Convair 440s to replace even more outmoded aircraft he had inherited from Colonial in the 1956 merger. Having invested so heavily in these already obsolete planes and in the L-188s, he was too strapped for funds to make the decisive entry into the jet age that the situation demanded. Rationalizing in his autobiography he complained about having to "replace perfectly good piston-powered and turboprop airliners with expensive new jets," but this was a poor effort to explain away his succession of failures in the crucial business of new aircraft selection.

This was not Rickenbacker's only attempt to make a virtue of policies that harmed Eastern's best interests. In his autobiography, he also wrote with pride about extended staff meetings, involving hundreds of managerial employees occupying various levels of responsibility, who were required to present brief oral reports on the operations they performed while he presided, ready to pounce upon them at any moment to justify a particular statement. Rickenbacker believed that such conclaves would help his subordinates learn how better to "think on their feet," but actually they terrified those who underwent the ordeal, some of whom received "a good hard rap on the leg" from the boss if they shook too noticeably from their anxiety as they cowered at the microphone. Najeeb Halaby, a young naval intelligence expert who had won the confidence of Laurance Rockefeller and who later headed both Pan American and the Federal Aviation Administration, attended such a meeting at

Miami Beach as a fact finder for Rockefeller and was appalled. "I had never seen a more dictatorial example of centralized management nor such public humiliation of employees," he later wrote.

Beginning in the late 1950s, unhappiness among Eastern's employees became rampant as jurisdictional conflicts between the Air Line Pilots Association and the Flight Engineers International Association contributed to an outbreak of strikes from which the company suffered badly. One such walkout, in 1958, took place at the peak of the normally profitable winter tourist season, lasted 39 days, and provided a temporary bonanza to Delta, which was unaffected by the strike and picked up the slack. Although the stoppage clearly indicated the extent to which Rickenbacker had miscalculated by choosing to mix pilots and mechanics in the first place, he ended it by agreeing to put not merely three, but four, persons in the cockpits of the jet planes that Eastern was just beginning to acquire, resulting in serious cost increases.

As Halaby's mission indicated, Rockefeller and other directors were becoming increasingly worried about Rickenbacker's conduct of Eastern's operations by the late 1950s. In 1958, as a result of this concern, Malcolm MacIntyre, who had been an extremely able lawyer for American Airlines and undersecretary of the Air Force, was appointed president and chief executive officer of Eastern, and Rickenbacker moved up to chairman of the board. Because the latter could not give up the authority he had wielded so long, however, it was an impossible situation from the start. By constantly interfering with MacIntyre's decisions, Rickenbacker undermined his ability to deal effectively with such problems as a renewal of labor strife in the early 1960s, the need to bring the company abreast of the technological changes demanded by the industrywide switch to jet planes, and the resentment of veteran Eastern executives who had wanted to succeed Rickenbacker themselves. Without proper backing from the directors, MacIntyre's intended status as chief executive became little more than a hollow title.

Rickenbacker's continuing active involvement in Eastern contributed to further disaster in 1961 when intemperate remarks that he made at an Atlanta luncheon about John F. Kennedy, who had been recently elected to the presidency, helped sabotage the company's chances of winning a transcontinental route to the Pacific Coast, which it desperately needed to balance the relatively short

flights that dominated its schedules. Instead, Delta and National were the chief winners. Increasingly frustrated by their inability to solve the company's problems, the directors instigated a merger with American that neither MacIntyre or Rickenbacker really wanted, but this met almost unanimous resistance from the rest of the industry and was abandoned after a determined attack led by Delta in a bitter CAB proceeding. During the battle, Delta's lawyers repeatedly received anonymous tips and other information leaked to them by disgruntled Eastern employees, indicating how badly Rickenbacker's policies had undermined morale. Ironically, the defeat of the merger attempt worsened morale even further by convincing many of the company's rank and file that its plight was hopeless.

Despite the quick success of a key innovation for which MacIntyre was largely responsible, a New York-to-Washington shuttle service that was launched in April 1961, the directors eventually concluded that the only way to salvage Eastern was to force both MacIntyre and Rickenbacker to leave. On January 1, 1964, Rickenbacker's long association with the enterprise he had alternately built into the industry's most successful carrier and led down the path toward its ultimate downfall came to an end. Showing magnanimity despite his bitterness and disillusionment, he issued a statement asking the company's employees to support Floyd Hall, a senior vice-president with TWA who had been appointed by the directors to replace both himself and MacIntyre.

While Hall launched an extremely expensive program to rescue Eastern that ultimately led to his own replacement by Frank Borman, Rickenbacker went into retirement. Aided by his longtime secretary, Margaret "Sheppy" Shepherd, and by freelance writer Booten Herndon, he spent much of his time preparing an autobiography that was published by Prentice-Hall in October 1967 and quickly went through many reprintings. In an effort to communicate his increasingly anachronistic attitudes to young people at a time when campuses were beginning to seethe with protest stemming from ideologies with which he was totally at odds, he arranged to have copies placed in the libraries of as many secondary schools, colleges, and universities as possible. In addition, he carried on an active correspondence from his office at Rockefeller Plaza, gave periodic public speeches in which he inveighed against the evils of left-wing doctrines, and dreamed of a future in which the United States would impose its will on the rest of the planet with the aid of space technology and nuclear weapons, destroying any nation that dared to "threaten world peace."

Partly motivated by his strident anticommunism, Rickenbacker continued to maintain an active interest in world affairs. Not long after being forced into retirement, he traveled to Africa, then a focal point of world concern in the wake of the power struggles set in motion by Belgium's granting of independence to the Democratic Republic of the Congo, "to get firsthand knowledge of the many political changes taking place there." On his return to the United States, he went to Germany, saw the Berlin Wall, and had lunch with two surviving veterans of Richthofen's "Flying Circus," against which he had fought so many years before. With the consent of Soviet officials, he visited the Hero Veteran Graveyard in East Berlin and paid homage at the graves of three of Germany's greatest World War I aces: Boelcke, Richthofen, and Udet. He was denied permission, however, to have his picture taken at the monument honoring Germany's "Ace of Aces," Richthofen.

Despite such episodes life became increasingly barren for Rickenbacker during his retirement. Traveling occasionally to New York to dine with old friends at his favorite restaurant, the Louis XIV, he spent most of his time at his home in Miami, reliving the past and explaining to visitors what had gone wrong at Eastern, leveling much of the blame at MacIntyre. Just before his eighty-second birthday he suffered a stroke and underwent emergency surgery for a life-threatening aneurysm. Meanwhile, the health of his wife, Adelaide, also deteriorated. Attempting to help her gain relief from acute glaucoma, which was threatening her eyesight, and also wanting to revisit the graves of his ancestors, he took her to Zurich for treatment by an ophthalmological specialist in July 1973. Not long after their arrival, Margaret Shepherd, who had also made the trip, noticed that he was breathing with difficulty and summoned a physician. Taken to a hospital, he was diagnosed as having pneumonia. After experiencing intense pain, he died in his sleep on July 23.

Rickenbacker's ashes, enclosed in a metal container, were brought back to the United States in one of Eastern's DC-8-61s, which had been dispatched by Hall with a full crew of pilots and cabin attendants. A memorial observance was held at the Key Biscayne Presbyterian Church on July 27, with "Jimmy" Doolittle as the main speaker, and the ashes were interred not long thereafter in the city of Rickenbacker's birth, Columbus, Ohio, while a group of jet interceptors from the 94th Fighter Squadron roared overhead in tribute to the role he had played in that famous unit's early history. A memorial fountain commemorating his services to Eastern and to aviation as a whole was later built outside the company headquarters at Miami.

Rickenbacker's failings are obvious. Autocratic, egotistical, heedless of advice to which he should have listened, and incapable of admitting a mistake, he left behind him a legacy of unfortunate decisions that continued to haunt the shrunken remains of Eastern Air Lines as it approached corporate death in the early 1990s mired in receivership. Nevertheless, he should be remembered not only for his shortcomings but also for his many achievements. Both as one of the greatest fighter pilots in the history of aerial warfare and as one of a small cadre of pioneers who dominated the formative years of American commercial aviation, rightfully described by R. E. G. Davies as "giants among a band of intuitive executives who counted few pygmies in their numbers," he merits an honored place in the evolution of aeronautics. A person of enormous physical and moral courage, warm in his friendships and capable of great kindness to valued associates, he was deeply loved by an army of admirers, many of them Eastern employees and executives who remained steadfastly devoted to him even when they disagreed with his policies and feared for their impact upon the future of the company.

Above all else, Rickenbacker should be seen as an exaggerated mirror image of certain traits that were deeply imbedded in the American society into which he was born. Passionately individualistic, he personalized everything with which he came into contact, was guided by his emotions, and clung to simple explanations of complex phenomena that were too difficult for him to grasp. Consequently, he was increasingly incapable of understanding the changes that were taking place around him. His failures of judgment in business and technological matters must be seen in this light. One of his closest associates once described him to Serling as "an outstanding leader of a small to medium-sized company" who was "mentally unequipped to move into an era when air transportation was on the verge of becoming mass transportation." Serling himself characterized Rickenbacker as a "nineteenth-century American trying hard to cope with the twentieth century—a task in which he achieved both magnificent success and dismal failure." Both statements are apt.

Publications:
Fighting the Flying Circus (New York: Stokes, 1919);
Seven Came Through (Garden City, N.Y.: Doubleday, 1954);
Rickenbacker: An Autobiography (Englewood Cliffs, N.J.: Prentice-Hall, 1967).

References:
Hans Christian Adamson, *Eddie Rickenbacker* (New York: Macmillan, 1946);

R. E. G. Davies, *Airlines of the United States since 1914*, revised edition (Washington, D.C.: Smithsonian Institution, 1982);
Finis Farr, *Rickenbacker's Luck: An American Life* (Boston: Houghton Mifflin, 1979);
Najeeb E. Halaby, *Crosswinds: An Airman's Memoir* (Garden City, N.Y.: Doubleday, 1978);
W. David Lewis and Wesley Phillips Newton, *Delta: The History of An Airline* (Athens: University of Georgia Press, 1979);
Arthur Pound, *The Turning Wheel: The Story of General Motors Through Twenty-five Years, 1908-1933* (Garden City, N.Y.: Doubleday, Doran, 1934);
Robert J. Serling, *From the Captain to the Colonel: An Informal History of Eastern Air Lines* (New York: Dial Press, 1980);
Alfred P. Sloan, Jr., *My Years with General Motors* (Garden City, N.Y.: Doubleday, 1972);
Henry Ladd Smith, *Airways: The History of Commercial Aviation in the United States* (New York: Knopf, 1942).

William B. Robertson

(October 8, 1893 - August 1, 1943)

by William M. Leary

University of Georgia

CAREER: Pilot, U.S. Air Service (1917-1918); president, Robertson Aircraft Corporation (1919-1928); president, Curtiss-Robertson Airplane Manufacturing Company (1928-1930); vice-president, Curtiss Wright Airplane Company (1930-1933); president, Robertson Aircraft Corporation (1933-1943).

A pioneering airline operator and aircraft manufacturer, William Bryan Robertson was one of the few aeronautical entrepreneurs to prosper during the 1920s. Starting out as a barnstormer after World War I, he built in St. Louis the nation's largest private aircraft repair, rebuilding, and supply facility. In 1927 he began service on the contract airmail route between St. Louis and Chicago. Two years later, he became president of a manufacturing company that built Curtiss airplanes. Although Robertson fell on hard times during the Great Depression, his prospects brightened in 1942 when he obtained a contract to manufacture gliders. A tragic accident in 1943, however, ended the career of this prominent figure in the early history of the industry.

Robertson was born in Nashville, Tennessee, on October 8, 1893, the son of John Joseph, a grain merchant, and Myrtle (Harmon) Robertson. Educated in public and private schools in Nashville and, after 1903, St. Louis, Robertson found employment in the grain and milling business. Following American entry into World War I in April 1917, he joined the army as a private. He went on to take flight training and received his wings and commission in 1918. The Armistice in November 1918 caused the army to cancel his orders for overseas service. He was discharged in February 1919.

Like so many young men who learned to fly during the war years, Robertson decided to make a career in aviation. He was one of the few who succeeded. Together with his younger brother Frank (1898-1934), who also had been a wartime pilot, Robertson borrowed $1,800 from his father and purchased a surplus Curtiss JN-4 ("Jenny"). The brothers barnstormed throughout the Midwest, selling rides and appearing in air shows. In February 1921 they formed the Robertson Aircraft Corporation, capitalized (on paper) at an optimistic $15,000.

William B. Robertson (left) with his brother, Frank. The pair cofounded the original Robertson Aircraft Corporation in 1921 (courtesy of the Missouri Historical Society).

Robertson expanded the activities of the company during the mid 1920s to include a flying school, renovation and repair shop, and sales. During 1925, the flying school graduated 49 students, while the sales organization sold 76 airplanes. The company, its capitalization increased to $500,000, had become the nation's largest aeronautical rebuilding, overhaul, repair, and supply organization.

Two other important events in Robertson's life took place at this time. In 1923 the army organized the 110th Observation Squadron of the Missouri National Guard. Robertson, who had taken a leading role in sponsoring and promoting the organization, became its first commanding officer. This carried a promotion to the rank of major, a title that Robertson often used. The following year, on May 3, he married Marjorie Livingston. The couple had one son.

In 1925 the U.S. Post Office began the process of contracting with private companies to carry airmail. Robertson made the winning bid for Contract Air Mail Route Number 2, which stretched

from St. Louis to Chicago. Investing $30,000 in the operation, Robertson's airline began flying the mail on April 15, 1926. The company started out with five de Havilland DH-4s, four Curtiss Orioles, and three pilots, including the youthful chief pilot, Charles A. Lindbergh.

During its first year, the airline received $71,644 from the post office, which failed to cover expenses. Business improved during the summer of 1927, thanks in large part to the new public enthusiasm for aviation that followed Lindbergh's epic transatlantic flight in June (which Robertson had backed).

During the fall of 1927, Robertson and other local business leaders persuaded Clement M. Keys, president of the Curtiss Aeroplane & Motor Company, to locate a manufacturing facility in St. Louis. On January 28, 1928, Robertson became president of the Curtiss-Robertson Airplane Manufacturing Company, formed to build the Curtiss Robin, a three-passenger cabin monoplane. The Curtiss-Keys interests held 50 percent of the stock in the business, which was capitalized at $500,000. Shortly thereafter, Robertson sold his interest in the airline to Arnold Stifel, a local stockbroker, for $300,000, or ten times his original investment. Two years later, after several corporate changes, the pioneering airline venture became part of American Airways (American Airlines after 1934).

In addition to his responsibilities for overseeing the manufacture of the Robins, Robertson undertook a variety of other assignments for the Keys organization, including projects to develop commercial aviation in Turkey and China. In 1929, for example, Robertson led a survey party to Shanghai. On April 20, he signed an agreement with the Chinese government that marked the beginning of the China National Aviation Corporation, the country's most important air carrier during the next two decades.

In 1930 the newly formed Curtiss-Wright Corporation combined the Curtiss-Robertson and Travel-Air companies under the name of the Curtiss-Wright Airplane Company. The reorganization brought in Walter Beech of Travel-Air as president, with Robertson and Ralph Damon as vice-presidents. While Robertson remained with Curtiss-Wright until 1933, his employment did not prevent him from returning to the airline business.

In April 1930 Robertson joined with his brother to form Robertson Airplane Service, which started daily scheduled passenger flights from St.

Louis to New Orleans in Ryan monoplanes that were similar to the one that Lindbergh had used to cross the Atlantic. The Robertsons applied for an airmail contract, but Postmaster General Walter Folger Brown turned them down and awarded the route to American Airways. In 1934, after President Franklin D. Roosevelt canceled all airmail contracts, they reapplied for the route. This time, they lost the bid by one cent.

After his brother died of tuberculosis in 1934, Robertson retired from the airline business and went back to operating a small flying school at the St. Louis Municipal Airport. He later submitted bids for airmail routes in the Midwest, but without success. In 1942 he returned to manufacturing, obtaining subcontracts to build Waco CG-4A gliders. On August 1, 1943, Robertson and seven promi-

nent business and civic leaders, including Mayor William Dee Becker, took part in the first public demonstration of a St. Louis-built glider. Released over the Municipal Airport from its tow plane at 1,500 feet, the glider lost a wing (later blamed on a defective fitting) and spun into the ground, killing all on board.

References:

James J. Horgan, *City of Flight: The History of Aviation in St. Louis* (Gerald, Mo.: Patrice Press, 1984);

William M. Leary, *The Dragon's Wings: The China National Aviation Corporation and the Development of Commercial Aviation in China* (Athens: University of Georgia Press, 1976);

Henry Ladd Smith, *Airways: The History of Commercial Aviation in the United States* (New York: Knopf, 1942).

Charles H. Ruby

(June 26, 1909 - December 1, 1990)

by George E. Hopkins

Western Illinois University

CAREER: Aviation mechanic and corporate pilot (1927-1935); pilot, National Airlines (1935-1962); president, Air Line Pilots Association (1962-1971).

Charles H. Ruby became a local leader of the airline pilots' union, the Air Line Pilots Association (ALPA), International (AFL-CIO), while flying for National Airlines. As Master Executive Council chairman in 1948, he led National's pilots during the longest strike in the history of the union to that date. In 1962 Ruby won election as president of the national union, becoming the third person to hold the office. He served until 1971, providing leadership during a turbulent era that saw the existence of the union threatened by the defection of American Airlines' pilots. He also spoke for airline pilots at a time of mounting concern over airport and in-flight security that followed in the wake of a series of "skyjackings."

Ruby was born on June 26, 1909, in Mt. Vernon, Illinois. His father was an itinerant musician, and his mother was a hatmaker. The family traveled a great deal before moving to St. Petersburg, Florida, where they owned and operated a small gro-

cery store. Ruby received an indifferent education. In an interview in 1980, he was vague about his early schooling, although he apparently graduated from high school in St. Petersburg. In any event, he learned to fly at the Robertson Aircraft Corporation in St. Louis, benefitting from the instruction of pioneer aviators Joseph Hammer and Waldo Roby. He went on to earn a mechanic's license for airframes and engines, plus a commercial transport pilot's license. Unable to find a job as an airline pilot during the worst years of the Great Depression, Ruby worked as a corporate pilot and mechanic until 1935, when he finally obtained a pilot's position with National Airlines in Miami, Florida.

Ruby joined the Air Line Pilots Association (ALPA) in 1937 and soon became active in the union. He earned national recognition as a labor leader during a bitter strike at National that lasted from February 3 to November 24, 1948. During the dispute, Ruby led the pilots in a nationwide campaign to persuade air travelers to boycott the airline, which had hired replacement pilots and resumed scheduled operations. In September the Civil Aeronautics Board ordered an investigation into the possible dismemberment of National, citing the airline's precarious financial situation. Following Harry S. Truman's surprise victory in the presidential election in November, National's management settled the strike on terms favorable to the pilots. Both sides believed that political factors had led to the resolution of the dispute.

Ruby won further acclaim among professional airline pilots for his resolute stand during the "war of the blues and grays" (so called because the replacement pilots wore uniforms of a different color from the striking pilots'), which followed settlement of the strike. Few of the replacements, who wound up at the bottom of the company's seniority list, survived at National.

Ruby joined management in 1954 and served as chief pilot until July 1961. He managed to walk a difficult tightrope during these years, establishing himself as a competent administrator without damaging his standing among the line pilots. When he left office, Ruby declared—with pride and relief—that he was departing "of my own volition and in good standing with the management and pilots."

Proof of this assertion came in 1962, when he was elected president of the national union. He took office just in time to face ALPA's greatest crisis since its organization in 1932. In 1963 pilots of American Airlines, comprising ALPA's second largest group (after United Air Lines), left the union to form their own independent company union. Although Ruby failed to prevent the defection of the American pilots, he succeeded in limiting the loss of membership to a single pilot group. Many observers credited his firm, moderate leadership with preserving the union, which easily could have fallen apart in the early 1960s. ALPA's difficulties included bitter internal rivalries which had plagued the union since the 1950s, and the increasing affluence and consequent antiunion attitude of many pilots who preferred to think of themselves as "professionals" rather than labor union members. "I assure you," Ruby warned his fellow pilots, "that personal experience has taught me that the fruits of serious dissension among us are plucked by management and do not yield gains to any of us."

After limiting the damage caused by the American pilots' defection, Ruby spent the balance of his presidency dealing with other serious issues. Following the union's move from Chicago to Washington,

D.C., the center of its legislative lobbying activities, Ruby guided the organization through the difficult early days of "skyjacking," ensuring that the pilots' voices were heard during the debate over airport and in-flight security. He brought to this and other problems an extensive background of technical expertise, especially in the demanding areas of aircraft certification and air safety.

Ruby's association with the technical activities of the union proved a mixed blessing. While respected by the professional aviation community, critics inside the union contended that he was neglecting the "political" side of his duties. Certainly, there was a coolness to Ruby's relations with the barons of organized labor, particularly George Meany, president of the AFL-CIO. Also, Ruby's personality was characterized by a certain "roughness," stemming from his lack of a college education. Indeed, many pilots saw him as a "country boy" who did not fit the sophisticated image of the modern jet captain.

Ruby had sufficient popularity with the membership to win a second term as president in 1966, but the election was close. Opposition continued thereafter, and he faced several recall attempts, including one that failed by a single vote. Many union activists saw Ruby as a transitional figure who lacked the sophistication to deal effectively with the rapidly changing nature of the airline industry. But Ruby, with his roots deeply planted in the origins of commercial aviation, survived two full terms as the spokesman for the nation's airline pilots. Declining to run for a third term, he retired to his home in Jacksonville, Florida. Ruby died in Jacksonville on December 1, 1990.

References:

George E. Hopkins, *Flying the Line: The First Half Century of the Air Line Pilots Association* (Washington, D.C.: Air Line Pilots Association, 1982);
Hopkins, Interview with Charles H. Ruby, December 19, 1979;
"Meet Your Officers," *Air Line Pilot*, 31 (July-August 1962): 16-17;
Brad Williams, *The Anatomy of an Airline* (Garden City, N.Y.: Doubleday, 1970).

Archives:

Records of the Air Line Pilots Association are housed at the Walter P. Reuther Library, Wayne State University, Detroit, Michigan.

St. Petersburg-Tampa Airboat Line

by Edmund Preston

Washington, D.C.

The first use of the airplane for regular passenger service resulted from a contract signed on December 17, 1913, between the Benoist Aircraft Company and the city of St. Petersburg, Florida. The company was headed by Thomas W. Benoist, operator of an aircraft factory and flying school in St. Louis, Missouri. Hampered by a city tax of $15 per flight, he had responded favorably to Percival E. Fansler's proposal for a venture in Florida.

An electrical engineer turned promoter, Fansler had read of the success of Benoist's flying boats and conceived the idea of commercial passenger service between St. Petersburg and Tampa. The two cities were separated by Tampa Bay, and the journey between them required two hours by steamer, six by automobile, and up to twelve by rail. Fansler's plan roused enthusiasm among St. Petersburg citizens eager to "boost" their community.

Benoist agreed that the St. Petersburg-Tampa Airboat Line would operate according to a fixed schedule, making two round-trips across Tampa Bay daily except Sundays. The city guaranteed that the line would receive at least $50 for each day the flights were made during the first month of service, and $25 for each such day during the succeeding two months. Local businessmen contributed to the subsidy fund, and also helped to pay for the rail shipment of Benoist's equipment.

The airboat readied for initial service was designated Model 14, No. 43, denoting that it was Benoist's 43d flying machine and was intended for sale in 1914. Its single hull was designed to carry the pilot and one passenger, although two small passengers sometimes squeezed aboard. The craft was 26 feet long and had double wings spanning 44.5 feet. Power was provided by a 75 horsepower Roberts two-cycle engine that turned a propeller mounted aft of the wings. Benoist later shipped two more airboats to St. Petersburg, one larger than the original craft and the other a small model used for instruction.

Heralded by a parade, band music, and speeches, the line began service on the first day of 1914. The first few rides were auctioned off to benefit a civic project, and former mayor Abe C. Pheil paid $400 for the initial passage. A crowd of some 3,000 persons watched Pheil and the line's chief pilot, Tony Jannus, take off for Tampa at 10:00 A.M. Although forced down midway by engine trouble, the pair reached their destination in 23 minutes, and returned on schedule at 11:30 A.M.

After the first few trips, the one-way fare for the St. Petersburg-Tampa flight was $5, an amount considered very low compared to the usual fees of exhibition fliers. The line charged higher prices for the special flights that brought in much of its revenue. Counting all operations, the line carried about 1,200 passengers, as well as cargo that included fresh flowers, ham, and bacon. Poor weather and engine trouble apparently caused cancellation of the scheduled flights on about seven days, although one source states that 18 days were lost for these reasons. No injuries occurred, although at least two minor accidents damaged the aircraft.

The Benoist company's contract with St. Petersburg expired with the waning of the tourist season at the end of March 1914. Fansler, who handled the bookkeeping, was unable to persuade city officials to renew the agreement. The line's achievements were nevertheless sufficient to secure its claim to represent the world's earliest regularly scheduled passenger service by airplane. While some credit Germany's Deutsche Luftschiffahrts Aktien Gesellschaft (DELAG) with conducting earlier regular passenger flights, that enterprise had involved only lighter-than-air craft.

References:

R. E. G. Davies, *Airlines of the United States since 1914* (London: Putnam's, 1972);

Davies, *A History of the World's Airlines* (London: Oxford University Press, 1964);

Gay Blair White, *The World's First Airline: The St.* Petersburg-Tampa Airboat Line (Largo, Fla.: Aeromedical Consultants, 1984).

Clarence N. Sayen

(February 11, 1919 - August 16, 1965)

by George E. Hopkins

Western Illinois University

CAREER: Flight instructor, U.S. Army (1942-1944); pilot, Braniff Airways (1944-1951); executive vice-president (1949-1951), president (1951-1962), Air Line Pilots Association; entrepreneur and consultant (1962-1965).

Clarence N. "Clancy" Sayen was the second president of the Air Line Pilots Association (ALPA). He succeeded to the office in 1951 as the result of a revolution within the union which overthrew the founder, David L. Behncke. Sayen's initial tenure as ALPA's president was temporary, but in 1952 he was elected in his own right and served until 1962, when he resigned in midterm.

The contrast between Behncke and Sayen could not have been more extreme. Behncke was self-educated; Sayen held university degrees through the graduate level. Behncke was a pioneer aviator who was present at the creation of commercial aviation as a pilot for Northwest Airways in 1926; Sayen was a reluctant pilot who much preferred academic pursuits and sought to find more intellectually challenging work than flying. Behncke was rough-edged and bore a class-based grudge against "the establishment"; Sayen was urbane, self-confident, and at home in any setting. Although Sayen was completely loyal to Behncke and played no role in his overthrow, many pilots always considered him an interloper who was unqualified for the job because he had never been anything more than a copilot during his flying career. Behncke had never been anybody's copilot.

Born on February 11, 1919, Sayen grew up in northern Michigan, the son of a lumberjack. Despite a childhood accident which cost him two segments of his right index finger, he became a

Clarence N. Sayen (courtesy of Louis N. Braun)

standout athlete in high school. He worked intermittently as a lumberjack and crewman aboard a Great Lakes steamer until graduating from college in 1942. As an undergraduate student at Northern Michigan University in Marquette, Sayen set a high standard of academic achievement. Dark, intense, and articulate, he wrote for the campus newspaper and was a multiple-sport athlete.

After learning to fly in the Civilian Pilot Training Program, Sayen served as a U.S. Army flight instructor training military pilots. His undergraduate degree was in education, and Sayen relished teaching. After gaining employment as a pilot with Braniff in 1944, Sayen earned a Master of Arts degree at Southern Methodist University in Dallas. His field was geography, and he impressed his professors with his diligence, wit, and energy. Sayen seriously considered giving up flying for doctoral work and an academic career during the late 1940s, and he flirted repeatedly with the idea for the remainder of his life.

In 1946, when Sayen was twenty-seven years old, he won election as the Braniff copilots' representative in ALPA. During the 1947 convention, Sayen attracted attention with his articulate, knowledgeable work on the complicated retirement issue. Behncke had avoided dealing with longevity issues such as pensions, because he believed aviation was so dangerous that pilots should not expect to live to retirement. Sayen impressed Behncke so much that when the membership forced him to create an executive vice-president's position to handle ALPA's administrative chores, he chose the young Braniff copilot for the job.

Sayen rapidly made himself indispensable. He won high praise from both Behncke and the many pilots who dealt with him. In 1951, Sayen cast his lot totally with ALPA, resigning from Braniff in order to become a career employee. When the revolution against Behncke broke out, Sayen became the anti-Behncke candidate by default. He is generally credited with holding ALPA together during the Behncke ouster.

In 1952, American Airlines captain Bart Cox challenged Sayen for the ALPA presidency. Sayen's performance during the Behncke ouster convinced the majority of pilots that he should be given a full term. But recurrent difficulty with the American Airlines pilot group marred Sayen's tenure. He performed brilliantly in contract negotiations, supplying just the right mixture of reasonableness and toughness. During the late 1950s, ALPA contracts became the marvel of organized labor, as pilots moved well into the upper reaches of the comfortable middle class. Sayen negotiated the first jet contracts, which brought airline captain pay to more than $35,000—pilot wages unheard of only a few years previously.

In addition, Sayen sought ruthlessly to democ-

ratize the constitution and bylaws of ALPA, so that no recurrence of Behncke's autocratic rule would be possible. Sayen succeeded to the point that ALPA came to rank as one of the most democratic of American unions. "The only thing that cuts off debate in an ALPA meeting," one observer said, "is exhaustion."

By the early 1960s, Sayen was growing weary of the job. He had achieved all that he could reasonably hope for, and the friction with the American Airlines pilot group over such issues as crew complement and the role of professional flight engineers (as opposed to pilots) in the cockpit, showed no signs of abating.

In 1962, as part of what seemed to be to the culmination of a classic mid-life crisis, Sayen resigned from ALPA to seek new fields to conquer. He confessed to friends that he had grown tired of negotiating raises for pilots who in his opinion already had enough money.

The last phase of Sayen's career was curious. Shortly after leaving ALPA, he turned down repeated offers to join the John F. Kennedy administration. He entered the trucking business with a friend, former United Air Lines pilot H. B. Anders. But he remained interested in politics and cultivated connections with the liberal wing of the Democratic party. In 1964, Sayen campaigned actively for Lyndon B. Johnson. His goal seemed to be to amass a comfortable nest egg through business, and then enter politics full time. His close friend Lane Kirkland of the AFL-CIO believed that Sayen would have made an attractive candidate for important office.

But it was not to be. On August 16, 1965, while returning to Chicago from negotiations with Eastern Air Lines, which would have made him vice-president for West Coast operations, Sayen died in an airline accident. The Boeing 727 on which he was a passenger disappeared into Lake Michigan during a night approach to Chicago. The cause of the crash was never determined.

Reference:

George E. Hopkins, *Flying the Line: The First Half Century of the Air Line Pilots Association* (Washington, D.C.: Air Line Pilots Association, 1982).

Seaboard World Airlines

by John C. Bishop

Auburn University

Arthur and Raymond Norden joined fellow veteran Air Transport Command pilots Carl D. Brell, Warren H. Renninger, and Wallace P. Neth to found Seaboard & Western Airlines (later Seaboard World Airlines) on September 16, 1946. The all-cargo airline began service to Europe on May 10, 1947, using a military surplus C-54 to carry commodities between the United States and Luxembourg. On July 8, 1947, the Civil Aeronautics Board (CAB) designated Seaboard a "Large Irregular Carrier." Later, with President Dwight D. Eisenhower's support, the CAB certified Seaboard as a scheduled overseas carrier on August 16, 1955.

Seaboard introduced scheduled cargo service on April 10, 1956. It pioneered the use of Super Constellation freighters (Lockheed L-1049D and later L-1049H), providing a payload of 37,000 pounds. These aircraft eventually replaced Seaboard's 17,000-pound capacity C-54s. Improved business led to daily flights after September 1, 1957. Difficulties with the Super Constellation's engines, however, combined with the U.S. military's increasing dependence on its own Military Air Transport Service to turn profits into losses. Despite a deficit of over $12 million between 1959 and 1961, airline president Raymond Norden went ahead with plans to acquire Canadair's new 62,000-pound payload swing-tail CL-44s. By 1964 all Super Constellations were taken out of service.

A corporate reorganization, prompted by the airline's losses, led to Norden's replacement by Richard M. Jackson on November 1, 1960. The following April, the company changed its name to Seaboard World Airlines. Jackson returned Seaboard to profitability in 1962, in part because of the introduction of fixed-cost "Blocked Space" agreements, which required contracting shippers to pay for fixed cargo space whether used or not. Seaboard sold these Blocked Space agreements to Lufthansa and other European airlines.

Success led to expansion, and in 1964 the company leased its first 90,000-pound payload-capable Douglas DC-8F. Variations of the DC-8F series, in concert with a few Boeing 707-320Cs, dominated Seaboard's fleet until the giant Boeing 747 came into service in 1974. The 747's 254,000-pound payload capacity changed the complexion of the air freight industry. Seaboard responded by pioneering the use of intermodal containers for cargo. These door-to-door 8x8x20-foot containers reduced handling and increased security.

Seaboard's undiversified structure proved a long-term weakness, with profits often depending upon irregular improvements in technology. Losses caused by inflation and higher fuel costs in the early 1970s turned to profits in 1977 after Seaboard adapted its operations to the revolutionary 747. These profits, in turn, attracted the attention of Tiger International, Inc., parent company of the Flying Tiger Line, which purchased 9.9 percent of Seaboard's stock in February 1978. Thirty-two months later, and at a cost of $450 million, Seaboard merged with Flying Tiger Line to form one of the world's largest cargo airlines.

References:

R. E. G. Davies, *Airlines of the United States since 1914*, revised edition (Washington, D.C.: Smithsonian Institution, 1982);

Joan Feldman, "Flying Tiger Line and Seaboard: After 32 Months, Finally a Merger," *Air Transport World*, 18 (January 1981): 40-43;

"Seaboard Makes Air Cargo Pay," *Interavia*, 22 (April 1967): 486-488;

Nawal K. Taneja, *The U.S. Air Freight Industry* (Lexington, Mass.: Lexington Books, 1979);

Arthur Wallis, "It's Tough at the Top But That's the Way Seaboard's Richard Jackson Likes It: An Interview," *Interavia*, 31 (June 1976): 529-530.

Sheldon B. Simmons

(October 8, 1908 -   )

by Don Dawson

Ketchikan, Alaska

CAREER: Electrician and powerhouse operator, Alaska-Juneau Gold Mine and Lomen Commercial Reindeer Company (1928-1935); pilot, Panhandle Air Transport Company (1935); pilot, part-owner, president, Alaska Air Transport (1935-1939); pilot, part-owner, president, Alaska Coastal Airlines (1939-1962); president, Alaska Coastal-Ellis Airlines/Alaska Coastal Airlines (1962-1968); vice-president, Alaska Airlines (1968-1981).

Sheldon Bruce Simmons, pioneer bush pilot of the Alaskan Panhandle and airline founder, was born October 8, 1908, in a log cabin just outside the small town of Weippe, Clearwater County, Idaho, located about 50 miles east of Lewiston. Shell was the youngest of three sons born to Benjamin Thomas Simmons and Edith Grant Simmons; his older brothers, Russell and Harold, were ten and twelve years his senior, respectively. The family was of mixed Irish, English and German extraction, and the elder Simmons was a farmer and sharecropper by trade.

When young Shell was about eight years old, the family made a brief move to Richland, Washington, before resettling in the town of Grandview, Washington—part of a agricultural region located along the Yakima River. There Simmons spent his formative years, and his sturdy farmboy physique and determined nature made him a natural athlete on the Grandview High football team.

By the age of sixteen his spirit grew restless, driving him to quit school to make his way to the port of Bellingham, where he shipped out on a freighter bound for the Orient that summer. As a deckboy aboard the Admiral Line's SS *Admiral Crosskeys*, Simmons sailed to Tokyo for a month before cruising south to Shanghai. He celebrated his seventeenth birthday in the Yellow Sea. When his ship landed at Seattle carrying a large cargo of pea-

Shell Simmons (courtesy of Lloyd Jarman)

nuts, Simmons decided he had had enough and returned home.

Short of funds, Simmons made his way up to Ketchikan, Alaska, to find work. Arriving there by steamer on Christmas Eve of 1926, he worked for the New England Fish Company, driving a Dodge panel delivery truck for its grocery division, which serviced the local halibut fleet. He also performed some electrical work, learning on the job. In the fall of 1927 he returned home again to Grandview, this time entertaining thoughts of starting a career.

Simmons and his hometown friend Paul Bittner, who followed him up to Ketchikan to work for the summer, joined forces to drive a Model T from Grandview to Los Angeles to enroll in an electrician course. Bittner changed his mind after arriving and drove back home, but Simmons studied electrical engineering and power transmission at National Electric for nine months.

Simmons had been impressed by Alaska. After a brief visit home, he headed for the capital city of Juneau, where he found employment as an electrician at the Alaska-Juneau Gold Mine. The work was hard, at wages of about $3.50 per day, and he worked seven days a week with only two days off a year—the Fourth of July and Christmas. He kept busy at the mine's powerhouse and fixed hundreds of motors that were prone to burning out because of the incessant dampness.

After a short time in his new job, Simmons and a Russian coworker named Frank Zimniskey quit the mine and headed north to explore Alaska's interior. They took passage on a boat to Skagway, and from there they rode the narrow-gauge railway to the Canadian town of Whitehorse. There they purchased a 14-foot rowboat fitted with a small gas outboard and alternately drifted and motored 2,100 miles on a 28-day excursion down the Yukon River.

At Nome, Simmons landed a job as an electrician with the Lomen Commercial Reindeer Company, wiring their reindeer slaughter plant at Elephant Point northeast of Candle on the Seward Peninsula and also repairing the telephone line to Shelton, located on the Kuzitrin River northeast of Nome. After various jobs in several other small towns in the region, Simmons found work driving a Model T tractor during the construction of a new runway for the town of Candle, located on the southeast shore of Kotzebue Sound. One workday he watched the famous pioneer bush pilot Noel Wien approach the field in his Hamilton Metalplane. With the runway still unfinished, Wien overflew the riverbank on which he intended to land, just barely at flying speed, to estimate its length by eye. Simmons figured it stretched less than a thousand feet. Without a hitch, Wien landed, unloaded, and

took off again. At that moment Simmons realized that he was destined to become involved in aviation.

Simmons met a fur trader in Candle named Hilkie Robinson, who operated several trading posts in Candle and Deering and a small movie house in Candle. Robinson needed electrical power for the movie house, and Simmons provided it by patching his tractor's power-belt takeoff to the belt-driven generator of the theater's electrical system. His simple solution impressed the fur buyer. Robinson wanted to use an airplane to conduct his business throughout the interior, but the going rate of the local commercial flying operators was too steep for his budget. The two men made a deal whereby Simmons would return to the States to take flying lessons at his own expense, and Robinson would purchase a Travelair and hire Simmons as his pilot.

That winter Simmons headed back home to Grandview and started his flying lessons in nearby Yakima under the tutelage of a former World War I pilot instructor named John L. Seawell. The aircraft Simmons trained in was an Aerosport biplane, powered by a 65-horsepower LeBlond engine and featuring side-by-side seating in its open cockpit. On the day of his first solo—November 21, 1929—Simmons made a five-minute flight around the field. Back at the office he was handed a telegram from Robinson in Alaska stating their agreement was null and void: the 1929 stock market crash had ruined Robinson's fur business.

Undaunted, Simmons in the spring of 1930 returned to Juneau, where he took back his old job at the A-J Mine. But foremost on his mind was finding an opportunity to get into the aviation business. He persuaded two Juneau friends, Fred Soberg and Wallace Bergstrand, to invest $1,000 to purchase a crated, open-cockpit Curtiss JN4D Jenny biplane owned by two local doctors—H. C. DeVighne and Howe Vance. Through Vance a deal was negotiated whereby Simmons contributed his limited piloting experience to train his two partners to fly.

Stored inside a dockside warehouse for over a decade, the Jenny had been flown only briefly one summer as a land plane. The partners enlisted the aid of a local pilot named Richardson, with 16 hours of solo time to his credit, to try out the Jenny with Simmons aboard, using the tide-flats adjacent to Juneau's Kendler Dairies as their airfield. Richardson overshot his landing and ran into some stumps, damaging the plane's center section and wings.

Watching from the ground was Simmons's new bride, Shirley (the couple's four-year marriage produced no children and ended in divorce).

Undiscouraged by the setback, Simmons and his partners took on the task of mending the damage to the Jenny. Among its spare parts was a navy-surplus center-fuselage float. Simmons decided to rebuild the Jenny as a seaplane, a more feasible configuration for local operations because it compensated for the lack of an airfield. Without any aeronautical engineering background, Simmons and his partners repaired and modified the hybrid Jenny seaplane and fashioned outboard wing floats to complement the center pontoon. The reworking and repairs took over a year.

After final rigging of the Jenny was completed on June 16, 1931, Simmons took the seaplane up for an early test flight to avoid attention in case of a mishap. He brought along Soberg, whose duty would be to act as a movable ballast to correct the airplane's questionable balance. Their 45-minute proving flight around the Gastineau Channel waterfront was somewhat harrowing, as their makeshift engineering, and Soberg's reluctance to move at all, made the hybrid Jenny only marginally airworthy. After two more test hops, Simmons remounted the upper wing slightly aft, moved the center pontoon almost one foot forward, and modified the wing and float struts. He and his associates flew the revamped plane for over 40 hours before it became too waterlogged to fly safely and was dismantled. It was the only seaplane Jenny ever flown in Alaska.

During this period Simmons took additional flight training and obtained his private pilot's license. Soon the partners enlisted a fourth member, Casey Rolfe, and purchased an Aeromarine Klemm monoplane from Seattle's Northwest Air Service. Though it was too small to fly paying customers, the Klemm was a vast improvement over the Jenny, and Simmons used it to obtain his commercial pilot's license in Juneau in May 1933. Though Simmons once tried unsuccessfully to employ the Klemm in a prospecting venture, the plane was used primarily as a pleasure craft and trainer. The Klemm even made three and a half trips between Alaska and Seattle before being written off after a rough-water takeoff attempt by Juneau doctor L. P. Dawes.

Commercial aviation enterprises in southeast Alaska were mostly seasonal ventures financed by outside interests during Simmons's early flying days. Alaska-Washington Airways (AWA) of Seattle had begun operations in the spring of 1929 using six Lockheed Vega floatplanes stationed at major Panhandle communities. AWA changed hands in 1932 and became Alaska Southern Airways, which folded in 1934. Gorst Air Transport and Pioneer Airways were the competition; the latter company became Ketchikan Airways in 1932 and went out of business in 1934.

Simmons became acquainted with Ketchikan Airways' pilot Chet McLean, who gave him some instruction in Seattle in 1932. Two years later McLean joined forces with two Juneau businessmen, C. V. Kay and Karl Kyle, to promote a Juneau-based airline, Panhandle Air Transport Company (PATCO), which purchased a modern Stinson on floats. McLean ferried the Stinson from New York on wheels that winter, shipping the floats by freighter. After starting business, McLean exhibited a cavalier attitude and lost his job. Simmons was hired as his replacement on a part-time basis and soon gave up his mining job when PATCO asked him to work full time or quit.

Simmons's new job was short-lived, however. PATCO's lone Stinson was badly damaged during a winter storm in March 1935, and PATCO's two owners could not afford to rebuild it. They sold the wreck to Simmons for a dollar. Simmons decided to lobby Juneau's business community to acquire the necessary capital to rebuild the Stinson and form his own airline. His initial investors were Tom Morgan, a lumber company owner; Dan Moller, a U.S. Forest Service employee; Dr. W. W. "Bull" Council; Tom McCall, an automobile dealer; Joe Meherin, a Hills Bros. Coffee salesman; and Grover Graham, chief engineer for the Northland Transportation steamship line. In April 1935 Simmons was able to inaugurate his first airline company—Alaska Air Transport (AAT).

Simmons transported the PATCO Stinson down to Seattle's Northwest Air Service for repairs, repainting it in fleet colors of blue and gold. After two months the Stinson was finished and AAT began operations. The timing was perfect, as Pan American's subsidiary—Pacific Alaska Airways (PAA), Simmons's only serious competition at the time—had just suspended its Panhandle seaplane operations after briefly servicing the area.

Simmons augmented his fleet with the addition of a Bellanca Skyrocket and one of PAA's Fairchild 71s and hired additional pilots. Simmons became the first commercial pilot to fly year-round in southeast Alaska, dedicating all his energies and profits toward the success of his airline. He grew proficient as a pilot, flying in all types of weather, often logging up to 18 hours a day during peak summer months. In the initial decade of his own operations, he frequently opted to accept company stock shares from his backers in lieu of cash when profits were insufficient to pay his salary. Simmons's biographer Archie Satterfield described him during this early stage as "a picture of poverty in flight. He wore old clothes with his shirt tail hanging out and a jacket caked with oil and mud. He never had the time to take a vacation nor the money to support one. His whole life was wrapped around his airline."

Simmons's tireless drive gave his young airline the momentum it needed to insure its success, and his reputation as a skilled flyer attracted new business. During his career as a pilot Simmons accomplished many daring rescue and relief flights at great personal risk. He shrugged off accolades, considering the challenges merely part of the job. Simmons took a hands-on approach in running his business. A skilled aircraft mechanic as well, his engineering background enabled him to devise many practical innovations to improve seaplane operations. As the airline grew, Simmons began hiring talented individuals for the various departments of his company. One of the first was maintenance expert Gordon Graham, a veteran of most of the pioneer Alaskan airlines.

In July 1936 Simmons faced a new competitor: Marine Airways, founded by Juneau charter-boat businessman James V. Davis and veteran Alaska pilot Alex Holden. They purchased a Bellanca Pacemaker on floats and soon added a Fairchild 71. The Fairchild was alternately operated both on floats and on wheels to utilize the new Juneau landing field built by Pan American in 1935, enabling Marine to fly between Juneau and nearby mining strips and across the Canadian border by 1937.

Simmons responded by acquiring a Bellanca Skyrocket in the summer of 1936, followed by the first of two Lockheed Vegas and an ex-PAA Fairchild 71—all fitted with floats. His fleet was pared down in June 1938 when the Bellanca was lost in a hangar fire in Juneau. Simmons also lost the Fairchild that same year in a water crash off Chichagof Island following a fuel stoppage. Despite severe facial

lacerations and the partial loss of his nose, Simmons dove under water to extricate a female passenger, then helped all five of his passengers to shore before securing help. The only person aboard who was injured, Simmons was hospitalized for several days in Juneau and then traveled to the Mayo Clinic to undergo plastic surgery. As soon as his doctors would allow it he returned home to resume management of his airline.

On May 27, 1939, Simmons and Holden merged their operations. Operating under the new title of Alaska Coastal Airlines (ACA), the new organization continued to base itself in Juneau. By this time other regional airlines had established themselves as formidable competitors. At Ketchikan, Herb Munter's Aircraft Charter Service and pioneer Alaska flyer Bob Ellis's Ellis Air Transport had started up in 1935 and 1936, respectively; and Petersburg hosted the formation of Tony Schwamm's Petersburg Air Service in 1937. The Alaska Coastal merger resulted from Simmons and Holden's need to strengthen their footing amid the threat presented by these newer competitors. In the summer of 1940 the business was further threatened when Pan American reentered the scene by introducing Sikorsky S-42 flying boats carrying mail and passengers on a biweekly shuttle service between Seattle-Ketchikan and Juneau.

The regional companies unanimously protested Pan Am's move and responded in collaboration by initiating biweekly schedules of their own between Ketchikan and Juneau, alternating flights between the companies that competed with Pan Am. That move, combined with the predominantly inclement and fickle panhandle weather, convinced Pan Am to suspend its service later in the year in favor of a landplane route to Juneau and points north. Such struggles were refereed by the Civil Aeronautics Authority (CAA), which was still in the early stages of implementing regulation for Alaska.

On December 23, 1940, Simmons married Bernice "Bea" Readle, in a ceremony in Ketchikan. Shell and his new bride lived in Juneau, where their only child, Shelby Lloyd Simmons, was born on June 29, 1943.

By the start of World War II, Ellis Air Transport had merged with Munter's operation, and Alaska Coastal had grown appreciably through the addition of more aircraft and personnel. Wartime demands forced both Ellis and Alaska Coastal to scale back their operations.

After V-J Day, Simmons capitalized on the sudden availability of cheap, war-surplus Grumman Goose amphibians and began converting them into nine-seat commercial airliners. Soon the Goose became the mainstay of both Ellis's and Alaska Coastal's fleets. The sturdy twin-engined amphibians proved to be ideal for panhandle operations because they operated on water and on land with equal facility. In late 1949 Simmons and Holden acquired the first of three navy-surplus Consolidated PBY Catalina twin-engined patrol bombers for conversion into 24-passenger airliners. In 1959 Ellis followed suit with a single PBY. In the late 1950s Alaska Coastal and Ellis had up to nine Gooses apiece in service, and routes were shared on a friendly basis. An eventual merger between the two airlines became the logical next step.

Negotiations toward that end were discussed, and on April 1, 1962, the Civil Aeronautics Board (CAB) approved the formation of Alaska Coastal-Ellis Airlines, then the world's largest scheduled commuter airline to operate amphibian aircraft exclusively. With Simmons as president, the new company represented a $2.5 million investment in facilities, equipment, and airplanes and a $2 million payroll for 264 employees. Coastal-Ellis became an international carrier, permanently certificated for scheduled service to more than 60 communities in southeast Alaska and between Ketchikan and Prince Rupert, British Columbia. The company also flew irregular service and charter service throughout all of Alaska. In 1962 Coastal-Ellis logged 8,078,000 revenue passenger miles. The process of merging the companies had been a monumental accomplishment. Simmons stated, "Plaudits of praise are due our hardworking, capable, and skilled personnel. The degree of success achieved by the consolidation is largely due to their assistance, cooperation and earnest desire to make it work. Continuation of this attitude will enable the company to glide over any rough spots it may encounter."

In 1966 the company name was shortened to Alaska Coastal Airlines, and it began upgrading its Goose fleet with more powerful and reliable turbine-jet prop power plants. The company also purchased a twin-engined Convair 240 land plane for scheduled route service between Juneau, the new airport at Sitka, and Annette Airport, which since 1947 had been Ketchikan's official air terminal for large airliner service. The final air link to and from Ketchi-

kan was connected by Goose and PBY Catalina shuttles to the town waterfront.

Through grandfather rights established in the 1930s, Coastal enjoyed a veritable monopoly of commercial air service within the southeastern Alaska region. There was some consideration of eventually initiating large piston or jet airliner service between southeast Alaska and Seattle, but strict government regulation in effect prevented the move at that time. As a result, the airline's growth was limited and Simmons, along with fellow executives Bob Ellis and O. F. Benecke, began to consider the idea of a merger with another large Alaskan carrier.

The airlines that came courting were Wien Consolidated and Alaska Airlines. Simmons and his board decided to go with Alaska, which had CAB authority to operate to the U.S. mainland. Discussions commenced in March 1967, and the CAB recommended approval that September. In March 1968 President Lyndon B. Johnson approved the merger, which was completed by an exchange of stocks on April 1, 1968. Simmons, Ellis, and Benecke were given board positions and a large number of Coastal employees took jobs with the new company. As part of the agreement, Alaska continued flying the Goose, Catalina, and Convair regional schedule and charter service established by Coastal-Ellis until the fall of 1973. Alaska sold the Grummans and Catalinas and discontinued the service to concentrate on running airport-to-airport schedules in southeast Alaska, using jet and propjet wheelplanes.

That marked the end of an era in Alaskan commercial aviation in which Shell Simmons had been a key player. An objective and expert assessment of Simmons's significance to Alaskan commercial aviation was given by Burleigh Putnam, chief Civil Aeronautics Authority inspector for the Alaska region during World War II. Putnam, who had worked with most of Alaska's great aviation figures, including Noel Wien, Bob Reeve, and Art Woodley, once remarked, "I think that Shell Simmons is the man most responsible for what took place. The things he did to improve reliability and performance of his airplanes is a story in itself; and Bob Ellis was not far behind him. I have long felt that these two men did more than anyone else to develop aviation in Alaska. Very few people have any idea how much they contributed. Operators in the Interior did their part too, but not in the same way. Some will argue the point, but I think the performance of Alaska Airlines today is attributable to a very large degree to Simmons. He had the unusual ability to hire good men—outstanding of which, is O. F. Benecke. He doesn't take any stock in heroism or that sort of stuff. To him, it was just a routine aspect of being in the business. I think most, if not all the oldtimers felt the same way."

On October 29, 1981, both Shell Simmons and Bob Ellis were bestowed with the lifetime honorary title of directors emeritus on the board of Alaska Airlines at a banquet given in their honor. For many years Simmons continued flying as a private pilot in Alaska with his Coastal-Ellis fleet veteran Cessna 185 floatplane, often flying shuttles down to the Seattle area. In retirement Shell and Bea Simmons purchased a winter home in Desert Hot Springs, California, spending the rest of the

year in Juneau. On February 11, 1983, Bea Simmons passed away in Desert Hot Springs. Completely retired from both business and active flying, Simmons moved permanently back to Juneau.

Unpublished Document:
Letter from Burleigh Putnam, Fallbrook, Cal., to Don Dawson, April 22, 1982.

References:
Lloyd R. Jarman, "My Favorite Bush Pilot," *Seattle Post-Intelligencer*, August 29, 1976, pp. 10-11;
Archie Satterfield, *The Alaska Airlines Story* (Anchorage: Alaska Northwest Publishing Co., 1981);
Satterfield and Lloyd Jarman, *Alaska Bush Pilots In The Float Country* (Seattle: Superior Publishing Co., 1969);
Shirwood Wirt, "Sheldon Simmons, Alaska Pilot," *Alaska Sportsman* (December 1939): 10-11, 25-27.

Robert F. Six

(June 25, 1907 - October 6, 1986)

by William M. Leary

University of Georgia

CAREER: Partner, Mouton & Six (1935-1936); operations manager (1936-1938), president (1938-1980), chairman, Continental Airlines (1980-1982).

Few airline executives have dominated their companies the way that Robert Forman Six dominated Continental Airlines for more than four decades. Labeled a "maverick" and a "rebel," he transformed what he once described as "a $2 airline" with 530 miles of routes in the desert Southwest into a global carrier that recorded consistent and often handsome profits before succumbing to the perils of deregulation. A charismatic leader, he put together a masterful combination of quality service, economical operations, and flamboyant promotion in his uphill battle against the giants of the industry. Along the way, the blunt, outspoken, and hot-tempered Six frequently challenged the conventional wisdom of his peers, and he was more often right than wrong.

Six was born on June 25, 1907, in Stockton, California, the son of Clarence Logan and Genevieve Peters Six. His father, a prominent plastic sur-

geon, wanted Six to become a doctor. Six, however, had plans to attend the U.S. Naval Academy. As it happened, he did so poorly in mathematics at St. Mary's High School in Oakland that he dropped out at the end of his sophomore year. For a time, he worked as a factory hand, then he shipped out as a merchant seaman. He ended up as a bill collector in Stockton for the Pacific Gas and Electric Company. Each morning, he later recalled, he would leave with a stack of bills and a set of tools. If the delinquent farmer could not pay his bill, Six would climb the nearby pole and disconnect his power.

Inspired, as were so many young men, by Charles A. Lindbergh's dramatic flight from New York to Paris in May 1927, Six began taking flying lessons. In 1929 he received his pilot's license. By that time both his parents had died, and he felt "at loose ends, cast adrift." He used part of his inheritance to purchase a three-passenger Travelair biplane. With it he formed Valley Flying Service, gave scenic rides, flew charters, and raced on weekends. Interested in a career as an airline pilot, he enrolled in the Boeing Air Transport School. However, when school authorities discovered that he had been re-

Robert F. Six (courtesy of the National Air and Space Museum)

cruiting students to work on his Travelair, they expelled him.

In 1930 Six left for China in hopes of landing a job with the China National Aviation Corporation (CNAC). Although he flew a few test flights on CNAC aircraft with a friend who worked for the company, he was not hired. He spent 18 months in China, returned briefly to the United States, then traveled in France and Spain for another year. Later in life, Six declined to elaborate on his years abroad, commenting only that they had afforded a valuable educational experience.

Six came back to the United States in 1934. After a brief stint as a day laborer in a cement plant, he got a job driving a delivery truck for the *San Francisco Chronicle*. During this time, he met Henriette Erhart Ruggles, a divorcée with two children and daughter of William H. Erhart, chairman of the board of Charles Pfizer & Company, a large pharmaceutical concern. Shortly after they began seeing one another, Mrs. Ruggles's children died in a house fire. Six provided needed emotional support following the tragedy. The couple was married in August 1934.

In 1935 Six returned to the aviation business. Forming a partnership with Monty Mouton, he acquired the distribution rights for Beechcraft in northern California, Oregon, and Washington. The two men did well, considering the depressed state of the economy, but Six was not satisfied. In July 1936 he persuaded his father-in-law to invest $90,000 in Varney Air Transport, giving him a 40 percent interest in the company. Six, who had authority to vote the stock, joined Varney as operations manager in El Paso, Texas.

Begun in July 1934 by Walter T. Varney and Louis H. Mueller as the Southwest Division of Varney Speed Lines, the airline held the airmail contract for the 530-mile route between Pueblo, Colorado, and El Paso (CAM-29). Varney had left the company after a few months for other ventures, and it had been operated after December 1934 by Mueller as Varney Air Transport. Although at first glance the airline seemed to have limited potential, flying a north-south route through sparsely populated country, Six was determined to make it a success. "He was very aggressive and ambitious," Mueller recalled, "with a great desire to learn."

In May 1937, at Six's urging, Varney Air Transport joined with United Air Lines in purchasing the airmail contracts held by Wyoming Air Service. United acquired the Denver-Cheyenne portion, while Varney obtained the crucial Denver-Pueblo segment. In order to comply with new government regulations that required radio equipped, multiengine aircraft on airmail routes, Six and Mueller mortgaged their homes as security for a $5,000 down payment on each of three Lockheed 12s. With radio equipment borrowed from United, the eight-passenger transports went into service on July 1, 1937. At the same time, Six changed the name of the company to Continental Air Lines (later Continental Airlines). Before the year ended, he moved the company's headquarters—and its 15 employees—from El Paso to Denver.

On February 3, 1938, Six was elected president of the airline that he had been running for the past year. One of his first moves was to hire Robert "Ted" Haueter from TWA as vice-president for operations. Continental, Haueter remembered, was "in awful shape." He proceeded to bring the airline up to prevailing operational standards, and the hot-tempered Six had the good sense to listen to him—most of the time.

Also in 1938 Six took the company public in an effort to raise money for new aircraft. Working with Lehman Brothers, he obtained $280,000 through the sale of stock. He used the funds to purchase two Lockheed 14 Electras. The aircraft were needed. Not only was passenger traffic developing nicely between Denver and El Paso, but also in July 1939 Continental obtained a new route from Pueblo to Wichita. In 1940 Six bought three 16-passenger Lockheed Lodestars for his growing company. During the fiscal year that ended on June 30, 1941, Continental carried 17, 232 passengers, bringing in $218,000 in revenue. Airmail added $491,000 to the airline's coffers. By the end of 1941 Continental had acquired three more Lodestars and had extended its Pueblo-Wichita route to Tulsa.

Following American entry into World War II in December 1941, Continental surrendered three of its six Lodestars to the War Department. In August 1942 Six joined the Air Transport Command as a captain, turning over control of Continental to Denver lawyer Terrell C. Drinkwater. Six ferried a B-24 to Australia, then spent two months on New Caledonia. He returned to the United States and served for a time as operations officer at Hamilton Field, California. Later, he was transferred to Morrison Field, Florida. Rising to the rank of lieutenant colonel, he became deputy commander of the base.

While Six was away, Continental continued to operate its mail and passenger services on a restricted basis, using a system of wartime priorities. In February 1942 the airline obtained a contract from the War Department to modify B-17s at its Denver maintenance base. In October 1943 Continental opened the Denver Modification Center, an impressive complex that included two 600-foot-by-400-foot hangars, which it used to modify both B-17s and B-29s.

By 1944 reports had begun to reach Six that all was not well in the executive ranks at Continental. Drinkwater, who had been doing a fine job of running the company, showed increasing signs of wanting to remain as its chief executive. Following a minor cerebral hemorrhage that resulted in his grounding, Six arranged a discharge from the service. While awaiting release, he returned to Continental and quelled Drinkwater's "palace revolt." As biographer Robert J. Serling has emphasized, "Six had his airline back, and it was for keeps this time."

Six reminiscing with Varney Air Transport president Louis H. Mueller, 1952 (courtesy of the National Air and Space Museum)

Continental remained essentially a regional carrier for the next decade, as the Civil Aeronautics Board (CAB) granted only modest route improvements. In 1944 Continental began flying between Denver and Kansas City. In July 1946 it added Oklahoma City to its route network. Five years later, it reached Houston. Meanwhile, Six purchased new equipment for the line. The Lodestars gave way to DC-3s in 1945, and in 1948 he bought five pressurized Convair 240s. In the early 1950s Continental began operating four-engine DC-6Bs on interchange routes with American Airlines (Houston-Los Angeles) and Mid-Continent (Denver-St. Louis).

Impatient with the glacial pace of CAB decision making, Six sought to expand through merger. In December 1953 he reached an agreement to acquire Pioneer Airlines, the nation's oldest local service carrier, for $768, 815 in cash and 65,000 shares of Continental stock with a book value of $390,000. Approved by the CAB in December 1954, the merger gave Continental access to every city in Texas with a population of over 100,000. It also brought to Continental's executive ranks the talented Harding Lawrence, Pioneer's vice-president for traffic and sales. Lawrence soon became Six's top assistant.

These years also saw important developments in Six's personal life. In 1952 his marriage to Henriette Ruggles ended in divorce. The following year, he wed Ethel Merman, the dynamic star of Broadway and Hollywood musicals.

On November 14, 1955, Continental's fortunes changed forever. At long last the CAB reached a decision in the important Denver Service Case. Continental received permission to operate the route from Chicago to Los Angeles via Kansas City and Denver, with nonstop authority between all city pairs. In an instant, Continental became a truly national air carrier for the first time. But there was a catch: Continental would have to compete for traffic on the route with three of the industry's giants—United, American, and TWA.

Six acted with stunning boldness. One month after the award, he ordered five DC-7Bs, fifteen turboprop Vickers Viscount 810-Ds, and four Boeing 707 jet transports. The new equipment cost $64.3 million at a time when Continental had a net worth of $5.5 million. As Six later admitted, "We could easily have gone broke."

Having bet the company on his ability to compete in the major leagues, Six realized that the tight federal regulation of the industry allowed him to gain an advantage over his rivals in only two ways: he could offer better service, and he could run a more efficient airline.

In April 1957 Six began operations on the new route with DC-7Bs. He configured the airplanes for all-coach, pitting the 365 mph transports against the 300 mph DC-6s that his competitors used for coach-class passengers. Furthermore, he offered an enhanced coach service, with hot meals instead of box lunches, seat selection, and other amenities normally associated with first-class travel. As coach passengers were attracted to Continental, the other airlines on the route were forced to match the new standard.

In May 1958 Six introduced the Viscount II on the route. With its competitors operating piston engine equipment, Continental soon captured nearly half the first-class passengers on the route. This was only the beginning. On June 8, 1959, Six began Golden Jet Boeing 707 service between Chicago and Los Angeles, placing on board an extra crew member called "Director-Passenger Service" to assist travelers. The public responded with enthu-

siasm. It took only three months for Continental to carry its 50,000th jet passenger. During this first year of jet service, the airline recorded gross revenues in excess of $40 million (up from $5.7 million in 1959) and an all-time net profit of $1.7 million.

As superior equipment and outstanding service attracted passengers to Continental, Six gave equal attention to promoting efficient operations. His most important contribution in his area came with the adoption of a progressive maintenance program for Continental's jet fleet. Instead of taking airplanes out of service for several days to perform major maintenance requirements, Continental developed a system of continuous maintenance whereby the needed work was broken down into small segments that could be done during short, frequent visits to the airline's maintenance base. This system, which later was adopted by the entire industry, enabled Continental to fly its jets an average of fifteen hours a day when industry utilization averaged about 9 hours.

The test of Six's ability to lower costs was the airline's break-even load factor—that is, the number of seats on an airplane that had to be filled in order for a flight to break even on operating expenses. In 1961 Continental had to sell only 37 percent of the seats on its Boeing 707s to break even. The industry average at this time was 52 percent.

Continental's efficient operations led Six to take a controversial position during the economic hard times that hit the airline industry in the early 1960s. Between 1950 and 1958 revenue passenger-miles (RPM) had grown by an average of 18 percent a year, giving the industry a comfortable profit margin. During the period from 1959 to 1961, however, RPM slowed to an average of 6 percent a year. This came at a time when the airlines had made heavy financial commitments for jet transports. The industry's answer to the problem was to ask the Civil Aeronautics Board for an increase in fares.

Six took a contrary position. Continental, he pointed out, had posted the highest operating profit in domestic trunk service in 1960 because it was run efficiently. The industry's losses were being generated by the large carriers. Rather than undertaking the difficult task of cutting costs, the big airlines preferred to seek fare increases. For his part, Six asked the CAB in 1960 to cut fares, arguing that cheaper fares would attract additional passengers and solve the industry's financial problems.

Unwilling to adopt such a radical solution, the board turned down Six's request. In the summer of 1962, however, they approved an "experimental" decrease in fares for Continental's new three-class service.

By the early 1960s Six's personal and professional life were attracting considerable attention from the media. His marriage to Ethel Merman ended in divorce in 1960. On August 24, 1961, he married Audrey Meadows, who had become known to millions of television viewers as the long-suffering wife of bus driver Ralph Kramden (played with gusto by Jackie Gleason) on "The Honeymooners."

He also was the subject of a profile in *Fortune* in 1963. This article described the fifty-five-year-old Six as "a tall hulking man with rough hewn features and heavy-lidded eyes that sometimes make him look sleepy when he is most alert." A voluble talker, Six was known for his hot temper and earthy language. *Fortune* found him "something of a cowboy *manqué*," who had organized a group of executives into a fast-draw team ("The Six Guns") and enjoyed life on his Lazy 6 ranch in Colorado. Six, however, also kept an apartment in New York City, where he led an active social life, enjoyed fine food and wine, and collected modern French art.

As head of Continental, Six had a reputation as a penny-pincher. At the same time, he paid his employees generously. Also, he supported an aggressive advertising policy that stressed Continental's service, spending more than twice the industry average. Although he had no trouble delegating authority to such talented subordinates as Harding Lawrence and financial vice-president Alexander Damm, he kept in close touch with all aspects of the airline's operations through an elaborate reporting system.

Six stressed employee productivity as the key to profit. He had no elaborate theory of how to motivate employees; instead, he offered a "simple idea." According to Six, "People work harder and work smarter if they find their work satisfying and know that it is appreciated."

In July 1963 Six moved the airline's headquarters from Denver to Los Angeles, a relocation that emphasized his plans for Continental's future expansion. Ever since his youthful visit to China, he had been attracted to the Pacific. The time had now come, he believed, for the airline to implement a strategy of growth that would emphasize transpacific operations.

In May 1964 Six signed a contract with the Military Airlift Command to transport troops and cargo to military bases throughout Asia. Charter flights began on September 4 with two Boeing 707-320s. As U.S. involvement in the Vietnam War increased, Continental was called upon to play an ever larger role in moving men and materials across the Pacific. During 1967, the contract's high point, the airline used ten Boeing 707-320s to fly 1,323 round trips to Asia. The contract, which lasted until April 1973, enabled Continental to make a tidy profit while gaining valuable experience on Pacific routes.

The 1960s also saw Continental active in two other Pacific ventures. On September 1, 1965, Six purchased Bird & Son, a Laotian-based company that operated charter flights for a variety of American governmental agencies in Southeast Asia. Renamed Continental Air Services, the airline continued to perform quasi-military work relating to the "secret" war in Laos.

Another Pacific operation began in 1968 when Six signed a five-year contract with the Interior Department to provide air service for the scattered trust territory of Micronesia. Based on Saipan, Air Micronesia initially used a Boeing 707-100, a DC-6B, and two Grumman SA-16s on routes to nine islands. Although Air Micronesia suffered a net loss of $3 million during its first four years, it provided compelling testimony of Six's commitment to the Pacific region.

On December 19, 1968, outgoing president Lyndon B. Johnson ruled in favor of Continental's route applications to Australia and New Zealand. However, Johnson's successor, Richard M. Nixon, withdrew the awards. Continental did receive access to Hawaii from a variety of mainland cities, along with other airlines. The airline opened service to Hawaii on September 9, 1969. On June 26, 1970, it began flying Boeing 747s on the Chicago-Los Angeles-Honolulu route. Again, superior service attracted passengers to what advertisements called "the proud bird with the golden tail."

Continental finally became a transcontinental carrier in 1974, when the CAB awarded it a Houston-Miami route. But Six still had his eyes on the Pacific. In July 1977 he finally achieved his long desired route to Australia and New Zealand, thanks to President Jimmy Carter. This opened wide the door to the Pacific. The following year, Continental expanded its operations, starting a route between Los Angeles and Taipei.

Continental had its best year ever in 1978, posting a net profit of $49.1 million. The airline, however, began to feel the effects of deregulation in 1979. As historian R. E. G. Davies has explained, "Its problem was simply that it seemed to have lost control of its cost structure at the very time when its revenues were put beyond its control by deregulation." Forced to suspend passenger service to Taipei, Continental lost $13.1 million during the year.

The situation only grew worse. Seeking help to survive in the new, deregulated environment, Six brought in A. L. Feldman as president in February 1980 and moved up to chairman of the board. The change failed to reverse the airline's declining fortunes. During 1980 Continental suffered a net loss of $20.7 million. Without the sale of three aircraft, hotels on Guam and Saipan, and tax credits, it would have been $78 million. In August 1981, with the red ink becoming a torrent, the heavily pressured Feldman committed suicide. Continental lost a staggering $60.3 million for the year. On July 13, 1982, the airline's stockholders approved a merger with Frank A. Lorenzo's Texas Air Corporation.

Six, an ardent opponent of deregulation, seemed powerless to affect events as Continental headed for disaster. He retired in 1982, deeply unhappy with the fate of the company that he had led for 44 years. Six died in his sleep at his home in Los Angeles on October 6, 1986.

Publication:

Continental Airlines: A Story of Growth (New York: Newcomen Society in North America, 1959).

References:

R. E. G. Davies, *Continental Airlines: The First Fifty Years, 1934-1984* (The Woodlands, Tex.: Pioneer, 1984);

Davies, *Rebels and Reformers of the Airways* (Washington, D.C.: Smithsonian Institution, 1987);

Michael Murphy, *The Airline That Pride Almost Bought* (New York: Watts, 1986);

Irwin Ross, "Bob Six's Bag of Tricks," *Fortune*, 67 (February 1963): 130-132, 194, 196, 198;

Robert J. Serling, *Maverick: The Story of Robert Six and Continental Airlines* (Garden City, N.Y.: Doubleday, 1974);

Robert L. Whearley, "The Highflying Robert Six," *Saturday Evening Post*, 236 (February 23, 1963): 82, 94.

Earl F. Slick

(November 20, 1920 -   )

by John C. Bishop

Auburn University

CAREER: Pilot, Air Transport Command (1942-1945); president, Slick Airways (1946-1962); chairman, Slick Corporation (1962-1972); director, United States Filter Corporation (1972-1981).

Earl Frates Slick, the second son of Tom B. Slick, Sr., and Berenice Frates Slick, was born on November 20, 1920, in Baltimore, Maryland. His father discovered the Cushing Oil Field in Oklahoma and other major fields, earning the title of "King of the Wildcatters." This sense of risk-taking led Earl Slick into several business ventures, principally Slick Airways and Slick Corporation. After his father's death in August 1930, Earl and brother Tom, Jr., inherited 44 percent of their father's fortunes. The sons received their inheritance in thirds, distributed

when they reached the ages of thirty, forty-five, and fifty-five.

Slick graduated from Phillips Exeter Academy in 1939 and entered Yale University in 1940. He joined the Army Air Corps in 1941, earned his wings, and was assigned to the Air Transport Command. One of his most memorable trips as a military pilot came with the unintentional nonstop flight of the first B-24 across the Atlantic Ocean from South America to Dakar. During his military service, Slick married Jane Pierce on March 22, 1943.

While serving with Air Transport Command, Slick met Col. Sam Dunlap III, who convinced him that the future of the airline industry lay in air cargo. In August 1945 Slick purchased nine Curtiss

Earl F. Slick

C-46s from the War Assets Administration. They had cost the government $1.8 million; he paid $247,500. With Dunlap's help Slick arranged to have the transports flown to San Antonio's Alamo Airport, which he leased after the military left. Separated from the service in December 1945, he incorporated Slick Airways the following January. The company inaugurated transcontinental air freight service on March 4, 1946.

Slick Airways managed to survive the intensely competitive postwar years thanks in large part to Slick's innovative management and a $3 million investment on the part of the Slick family. By 1951 the company had become the largest all-cargo airline in the United States. Befitting its status, in April of that year it had the distinction of being the launch customer for the DC-6A Liftmaster, the cargo version of the pressurized Douglas transport (DC-6B) that went into passenger service at the same time.

During the early 1950s, a bitter competitive struggle with the certified airlines put substantial financial pressure on the company. In 1950 Slick filed a $30 million lawsuit against American, United, TWA, Air Cargo Inc. (a freight forwarder),

and the Air Transport Association, charging all with antitrust violations. One of the principal goals of his lobbying efforts was the separation of mail pay from subsidy. He argued that the passenger lines received a double subsidy from airmail transport; first, they were paid too much to carry it, and, second, they incurred no costs from sales, billing, bad accounts, or losses. Although not opposed to the concept of subsidy, Slick was opposed to subsidies that were hidden in mail payments. Since cargo airlines initially did not receive airmail business and they never received a direct subsidy, he believed that the passenger carriers, who were also in the air freight business, had an unfair competitive advantage.

Slick concluded that the best hope for his airline lay in a merger with the Flying Tiger Line, another leading cargo carrier that had prospered during the Korean War due to military contracts. On March 26, 1953, Slick and Flying Tiger Line president Robert E. Prescott reached an agreement on terms. Although the Civil Aeronautics Board initially approved the merger, opposition from the scheduled passenger carriers and labor difficulties caused the plan to collapse.

As Slick had expected, the airline ran into increasing difficulties as the subsidized passenger carriers competed for the air freight market. Early in 1958, Slick Airways abandoned scheduled freight service and concentrated on contract operations. The airline slowly recovered as a contract carrier. In October 1959 it ordered six Canadair CL-44 swingtail turboprop freighters. Three years later, it resumed scheduled transcontinental service. However, this renewal lasted only until August 1965, when the airline again suspended scheduled operations.

In 1960 Slick attempted to diversify his interests by purchasing the Illinois Shade Company for $6.3 million. Two years later, he formed a holding company, named the Slick Corporation, for his growing operations. In 1966, Slick Corporation left the air cargo business when it transferred most of the assets of Slick Airways to Airlift International.

Slick Corporation, which purchased the Drew Chemical Company in 1968, prospered as a producer of chemical processing systems, industrial air pollution control equipment, and home furnishings. Slick, who served as chairman of the corporation's board, directly held 10 percent of its common stock. In 1972 Slick Corporation was absorbed by United States Filter Corporation. Slick remained on the board of directors of United States Filter until it merged with Ashland Oil in 1981. After that he became involved in the financing of real estate projects, especially shopping centers, such as Sun Belt Historic Properties, Ltd., and in environmental matters.

References:

Loren Coleman, *Tom Slick and the Search for the Yeti* (Boston: Faber & Faber, 1989);

George Groh, "Earl Slick and His Cargo Line," *Flying*, 45 (August 1949): 21-22;

"Slick Airways: Sparking the Air Freight Industry," *Fortune*, 42 (July 1950): 72-74, 132, 134;

"The Slicks: What Rich Men's Sons Can Do," *Business Week*, November 17, 1951, pp. 66-68, 70, 73-74.

C. R. Smith

(September 9, 1899 - April 4, 1990)

by Roger E. Bilstein

University of Houston—Clear Lake

CAREER: Bookkeeper (1915-1924); accountant, Peat, Marwick & Mitchell (1924-1926); assistant treasurer, Texas-Louisiana Power (1926-1928); vice-president, Southern Air Transport (1928-1930); vice-president (1930-1934), president (1934-1942), chairman and chief executive officer, American Airways/American Airlines (1946-1968, 1973-1974); Air Transport Command (1942-1945); U.S. secretary of commerce (1968); partner, Lazard Frères (1968-1973).

From 1928 until 1967 C. R. Smith played a key role in the evolution of air transport in the United States. He began as the accountant for a company known as Southern Air Transport and ended as chief executive officer of American Airlines, the company he led through most of his active career. During the four decades that Smith spent with the airline industry, strong personalities who closely identified with their companies dominated the field:

William A. "Pat" Patterson of United, Juan Trippe of Pan Am, Eddie Rickenbacker of Eastern, Howard Hughes of Trans World Airlines, C. E. Woolman of Delta, and C. R. Smith of American. Smith ran his airline with a mixture of laissez-faire and a firm hand. Employees generally had considerable opportunity to institute improvements and suggest new ideas, but if C. R. said no, even though logic might indicate otherwise, his was the last word.

Smith's airline was one of the leaders in an industry that went from 150 mph trimotors to 600 mph trijets in less than a lifetime. If opposed to painted airliners (bare-metal planes became an American "signature" over the years), Smith was nonetheless adaptable to major changes such as pressurization of aircraft, the introduction of jets, and various electronic innovations. His airline absorbed his attention seven days a week. Few contemporaries gave as much energy to the airline industry as a whole, and in later years Smith spent nearly as

C. R. Smith (courtesy of the National Air and Space Museum)

much time on industrywide issues as he did on his own company.

Cyrus Rowlett Smith was born on September 9, 1899, in Minerva, Texas. The impoverished Smith family moved frequently, as C. R.'s father won and lost jobs all over Texas and Louisiana. After settling in Amarillo, the elder Smith left the house one day and vanished, leaving his wife, nine-year-old C. R., and six younger brothers and sisters to fend for themselves. Fortunately, Mrs. Smith had some education; she took in boarders, found a teaching job, became politically active, and held several appointive posts, including supervisor of the state census. Meanwhile, C. R. added to the meager family funds by working as an office boy for a wealthy cattle baron. He developed a deep appreciation for western legends and lore, a characteristic he maintained all his life.

Smith's entry into the business world came at the age of sixteen, when he got a job as bookkeeper at a small bank. Then he took a similar job at a cotton mill. Eventually he won special permission to enroll in business studies at the University of Texas, where he graduated in 1924. In Dallas he took a position as accountant for Peat, Marwick

and Mitchell and Company, which quickly put him to work on complex assignments, including audits for public utilities. In 1926 an executive for the Texas-Louisiana Power Company hired Smith as assistant treasurer. When the firm's president bought several small airlines that merged to form Southern Air Transport in 1928, he convinced Smith to keep its books and keep a general eye on operations. Smith agreed to take the airline job on a temporary basis, and he also spent extra time learning to fly. Within two years he was Southern's vice-president and general manager. In 1930 Southern Air Transport was absorbed by a group known as AVCO, one of the largest aerial conglomerates of the era. One of the principals of AVCO was Lamotte Cohn, who made Smith his adviser and vice-president of the AVCO subsidiary American Airways.

As vice-president Smith quickly pushed for the acquisition of an improved version of the Curtiss Condor twin-engine biplane. The first Condors had been introduced by Eastern, and Smith became intrigued by a subsequent prototype equipped with Pullman-style berths, which he considered a strong selling point for passengers on American's transcontinental routes. He convinced E. L. Cord, AVCO's chief, to invest in this unusual arrangement. Moreover, the American version of the Condor featured soundproofing and three-bladed, variable-pitch propellers that reduced vibration in the cabin. Passengers loved the plane and Smith scored points with airline management, but pilots distrusted the plane in icing conditions and also thought it was prone to catch fire.

In late 1933 and early 1934 a Senate committee chaired by Hugo Black of Alabama conducted a review of alleged monopolistic practices in the airline industry, and a thorough reorganization followed. American suffered less than most, although AVCO was forced to divest its manufacturing units, which in any case had been performing poorly. Because Smith seemed so committed to developing American's passenger business rather than rely on government airmail subsidies, Cord made him president of the reorganized and renamed American Airlines in 1934. Later the same year Smith married Elizabeth L. Manget; the couple had one son, but the marriage soon ended, and Smith never remarried.

With Smith at the helm and increasingly in charge, Cord withdrew from the scene. As American Airlines evolved, it developed a personality shaped by its dynamic president. Smith was determined to keep American not only the biggest airline in the United States but also to make it a worldwide leader. Moreover, he was committed to the restoration of the industry's credibility after the airmail scandal hearings and to the increase of public confidence in air travel. During the Depression, when there was intense competition with railroads for a shrunken travel market, it was imperative to improve the airlines' image on probity and safety.

In 1934 American had about 1,000 employees, most of whom Smith knew by name. Even though the company grew, he did his best to keep in personal touch with all personnel. He disliked lengthy executive meetings and long correspondence. All his life he typed out much of his own correspondence and memos—invariably brief and to the point. Personnel who received Smith's terse communiqués quickly realized that safety was the central goal of airline operations. Following that were marketing, service, and equipment.

As soon as Smith became president of American, safety and equipment came to the fore in the form of a series of crash landings involving the Condor. Although Smith had been personally responsible for the Condor's acquisition, he was disappointed with its increasingly depressing safety record. Fortunately, a newer plane had been ordered before Smith became president of American, and he pressed it into service as a Condor replacement. It was the Douglas DC-2, stronger and faster than the Condor or anything else in the American fleet. American began DC-2 service toward the end of 1934, but Smith soon decided that it, too, needed replacement. With 14 seats, the DC-2 actually carried four less passengers than a Condor in its daytime configuration. It also proved balky to handle in the air and on the ground, and its range turned out to be limited; westbound flights on the New York-Chicago run, if they encountered strong headwinds, often had to land en route for fuel.

There are many stories about the origins of the redoubtable DC-3 airliner, one of the classics of air transport history. In the corporate lore of American Airlines the company itself played a large role, starting with the discussions of Smith and Bill Littlewood, American's chief engineer, for a DC-2 replacement. Following these talks, so the American version goes, Smith called Donald Douglas in Santa Monica, California, demanding a modified DC-2 to carry 21 passengers during the day and sleep 14 dur-

ing night segments. Douglas demurred, pointing out that his company could barely keep pace with the current volume of DC-2 orders. Smith kept pressing his argument, to the point of committing his airline to 20 of the new planes with an option for 20 more, even though a complete design did not exist on paper. Douglas finally agreed to mount a thorough design study. At an estimated $100,000 per plane, Smith needed $4 million, which he did not have. He hopped a plane to Washington, D.C., for a conference with an old acquaintance from Texas, Jesse Jones. As head of the Reconstruction Finance Corporation, Jones had the sort of money Smith needed. Such a loan would not only keep American in the air but would also boost the aircraft industry and the suppliers of radio equipment, upholstery, electrical equipment, and so on. Smith got a total loan of $4.5 million to launch the Douglas Sleeper Transport, which was eventually labeled the DC-3.

Although the DC-3 became standard equipment on every major airline in the United States and amassed an enviable safety record, the public still harbored strong fears about airline safety. Smith faced the issue head on in 1937, composing the first draft of a letter that eventually appeared in the most widely read periodicals of the era. The full-page advertisement asked, "Why dodge this question: afraid to fly?" The ad went on to state that every form of transportation carried an element of risk, but emphasized that airline travel was certainly not unsafe. Air travel was gaining in popularity, and if your competitors flew, then you needed to consider the benefits of flying—it was not only good business, but enjoyable and safe. For an industry that had been reluctant to address the safety issue, the ad was a bombshell. The campaign, while making it clear American was doing a good job, was also an effort to boost the industry as a whole.

American Airlines had barely grown accustomed to its up-to-date DC-3 transports when Smith uncorked another surprise. He intended to move corporate headquarters from Chicago to New York City. The move coincided with the opening of La Guardia Field, the nation's newest airport.

Fiorella La Guardia, mayor of New York City, for years had tried to bring a major airfield to New York City, since he felt Newark, New Jersey, was too far away and located in an alien state as well. As a former pilot in World War I, La Guardia was a strong supporter of aviation, and he was determined to get scheduled service into his city. More than any other airline figure whose planes carried New York passengers, Smith sensed the possibilities of an early alliance with La Guardia. By getting in on the ground floor, American could garner the best hangar and terminal facilities and negotiate favorable rental fees. Smith proceeded to back La Guardia's airport plans. At about the same time, in 1938, Smith had hired a new president, Orval McKinley Mosier, otherwise known as "Red."

In contrast to Smith's sedate apprenticeship as an accountant, Red Mosier's aviation career had been as colorful as his name. Mosier was born in Pawnee, Oklahoma, in 1897, when Oklahoma was still Indian territory. He seems to have gotten through the eighth grade and then turned to other pursuits: brawler, bronc buster, and crack shot. He entered the air service in World War I and met La Guardia. After the war he trained polo ponies, played semipro baseball, and made a considerable reputation as a professional pilot for corporations. He became city manager of Oklahoma City, joined Braniff Airways as vice-president and general manager in 1937, and jumped to American as vice-president the next year. He seemed the ideal choice to palaver with the mercurial La Guardia about American's place in the new airport complex under construction.

American's New York quarters offered a superior venue for a unique marketing gambit that Smith had introduced some time earlier. To recognize special customers, celebrities, and politicians who flew American, Smith came up with the idea of an "Admirals Club" certificate to complement the "Flagship" theme of the company's airliners. Among the early members of the Admirals Club was a large contingent of hotel porters, since they might guide potential passengers to American. During press conferences for the opening of La Guardia Field, the mayor offhandedly remarked that he would even rent his sumptuous VIP suite at the airport to raise money. Mosier quickly seized the opportunity, and the suite became the first Admirals Club facility. American gradually expanded the idea to its major hubs around the country, and other airlines eventually followed suit.

In New York City Smith settled into a comfortable duplex near the Queensborough Bridge. His fascination with western memorabilia made visiting his home a somewhat disconcerting experience for sophisticated guests. The walls of the duplex were decorated with western oil paintings by Remington

and Russell—along with bleached cattle skulls, Texas longhorns, and buffalo heads. Curtains hung from rods fashioned from branding irons, and silver dollars studded the top of his old-fashioned western bar. The motif carried into the bedroom, where window drapes were cut to the shape of cowboy chaps and the lamp on the nightstand was made from an antique Colt six-shooter.

As much as Smith enjoyed his bit of western Americana, the advent of World War II meant that he spent little time there. The civil airline fleet of the United States already had an operational blueprint to use in case of a national emergency. Edgar Gorrell, a veteran of the U.S. Army Air Service in World War I, had become president of the Air Transport Association (ATA). He recognized the potential military value of the growing airline fleet of cargo planes and began planning for an aerial mobilization in 1936 with the cooperation of the "Big Four" of the airline industry (American, TWA, United, and Eastern). The plans had been updated over the years and included options for the disposition of planes, flight crews, and ground personnel on 24 hours' notice. When Pearl Harbor was bombed on December 7, 1941, Gorrell had a program ready for implementation. The ATA proposal was championed by Gen. H. H. "Hap" Arnold of the Army Air Corps and helped form the nucleus of the Air Transport Command (ATC).

The ATC itself grew out of the Ferrying Command, established earlier in 1941 to fly Lend-Lease aircraft to shipment and dispersal points overseas. When the Ferrying Command came to be seen to be the basis for a worldwide air transport system, Arnold and other air corps officers decided to bring in someone with more experience to manage the large flotilla of aircraft that was bound to grow even larger. In 1942 Smith became a colonel in the air corps and deputy commander to the ATC's chief, Brig. Gen. Harold Lee George. It was a credit to Smith's management style that American Airlines was able to keep running effectively (albeit with a smaller fleet of planes) in his absence. American's Flagship Fleet dropped from 79 to 41 airplanes; the total number of U.S. civil airliners dropped to 176 from a total of 359. The airline industry did its best to meet civilian demands during the war by squeezing more air time out of each plane. In the case of American Airlines, Smith's management team managed to wring out 30 percent more flying hours per year.

American Airlines Douglas DC-3 (courtesy of the National Air and Space Museum)

As a wartime successor, Smith might have chosen Ralph Damon, director of operations, but Damon took a leave of absence to take over Republic Aviation, manufacturer of the P-47 Thunderbolt fighter. Red Mosier, American's director of public affairs, had been a Smith confidant for several years; many expected him to get the nod. Charles Rheinstrom from marketing was also a possibility. But none of Smith's management group received the coveted spot. It has been speculated that Smith wanted to avoid naming a strong individual to direct the airline. By the time Smith returned, such a person might have taken over. Such a coup was in fact attempted at Continental while Bob Six was in the service during the war. Smith's choice as successor, approved by the airline's board of directors, was a junior member of the board itself, Alexander Kemp.

Kemp was president of Pacific Mutual Life Insurance when he joined the American board in 1941. Thus, he had experience from a corporate president's point of view. Kemp did not have to worry about selling air travel during the war, since the demand for air travel overwhelmed the few dozen remaining planes. During the war he turned in a creditable performance and expanded American in

important ways by initiating international routes through the acquisition of American Export Lines and by starting service to Mexico.

In the meantime Smith settled into his job as the operations chief for the ATC. At the beginning of the war the preferred route to the European Theater was across the South Atlantic from Natal, Brazil, to Dakar, Senegal. Smith listened carefully to those who argued for a North Atlantic crossing, flying the Great Circle Route from Newfoundland to Greenland, Iceland, and Great Britain. Smith authorized a technical staff and a survey flight in a former American DC-3 manned by American personnel. Having proved the feasibility of a North Atlantic service, the ATC soon launched dozens of similar ferry and cargo flights. By the summer of 1945 the ATC had concluded some 7,000 transatlantic missions, averaging nearly 500 flights per month. While American Airlines crews and others honed their skills over Atlantic waters, Pacific Coast routes north to Alaska proved particularly challenging, and Northwest Airlines crews picked up the task of initiating pilots unaccustomed to the rigors of Arctic flying.

During the war contract work led to the expansion of American's personnel. Workers repaired weary C-47 and C-54 transports, converted B-24 bombers into C-87 transports, modified C-54 cargo planes into hospitals, and reworked balky C-46 transports. By war's end American's work force had soared from 4,000 in 1940 to 11,450 in August 1945. As the war wound down, American had begun converting C-47s into DC-3 airliners, so that it entered the postwar era with 93 operational planes of this type.

There were also some C-54 (DC-4) transports, a legacy of the acquisition of American Export Airlines, which had been flying the C-54 across the South Atlantic to Lisbon under contract to the ATC. American Export's arrival on the scene had been particularly turbulent, since it won its certificate against the strenuous opposition of Pan American. But American Export came under American's control as a subsidiary in the summer of 1945, just before the return of Smith, who left the service with the rank of major general.

After an absence of several years, perhaps there was bound to be some reshuffling of people and power. Damon had already returned from his sojourn at Republic Aircraft; Smith convinced the board of directors to install Damon as president of American Airlines. Smith became chairman of the board and president of American Overseas Airlines, the new name for American Export. When he instituted personnel changes in advertising, an angry Charles Rheinstrom resigned his marketing post to join a New York investment firm—Dillon, Read—as a consultant on airline affairs. The new marketing head at American was Richard Deichler, who had worked for Smith in the ATC. Eventually another ATC cohort, Harold Harris, came on board to run American Overseas. Larry Fritz, a third ATC carryover, became vice-president for operations.

Smith himself spent more and more time in travel to Washington, as a wave of regulatory decisions came out of the postwar CAB, which was inundated with new route applications after the war. Smith was particularly interested in acquiring Mid-Continent Airlines, a carrier whose routes included many cities not served by American flights. But not even Smith could win every battle, and the carrier was eventually taken over by Braniff.

Smith also shared Bill Littlewood's anxiety in acquiring a postwar replacement for the DC-3 and in finding a good design for transcontinental routes; the DC-4 was unpressurized and was obviously a stopgap airplane. The most promising successor to the DC-3 appeared to be a Consolidated-Vultee design, the CV-110. Negotiations were complicated by Consolidated-Vultee's impending sale to General Dynamics as its Convair division. Littlewood's proposals resulted in several significant design changes, such as the first foldable stairway built into an airliner as part of the fuselage. He also influenced the plane's final designation, CV-240, with the "40" representing the number of seats. The CV-240 won an $18 million contract with American in 1946, largely because it offered important operational advantages by being pressurized, permitting it to fly above bad weather to keep its schedules intact.

For the major carriers pressurized transports became a basic requirement. American also needed larger, four-engined aircraft and joined with rival United to order the DC-6 from Douglas. Both needed a plane to compete with the fast, pressurized Constellations operated by TWA on transcontinental routes. The DC-6 not only would be faster, it also would be air-conditioned. The latter feature had a curious history. Just before Rheinstrom resigned he had become aware that painting the top of a plane's fuselage white would reflect solar rays and could cool the interior by as much as 15 degrees. But Smith heard that United had pioneered that idea and refused to copy his strongest rival. The American fleet would hew to shiny (and bare) metal fuselages with distinctive paint trim only. And so air conditioning was built into the DC-6 at American's behest.

A somewhat similar pattern occurred in the case of American's short-lived experiment with the air freight division, begun in 1946. The airline had made a step in this direction in 1943, developing a New York-to-Los Angeles run toward the end of the war. St. Joseph, Missouri, was picked as the site for the new air cargo division. An important criterion was the city's central location as a refueling stop for DC-4s on transcontinental flights. There were six of the transports assigned to the new cargo operation, three on each coast. At the end of each business day they all headed to St. Joseph, which served as a hub. Freight was sorted out, then flown to various destinations: Los Angeles, St. Louis, Atlanta, Chicago, and other cities. The system anticipated the sort of operation later conducted by Federal Express, but the market was not there. American Airlines lost a quarter of a million dollars in 1946, and the introduction of the DC-6 and CV-240 threatened to increase the deficit. Trimming was necessary, and cargo flights were only marginally profitable. Despite opposition from associates who wanted more time for marketing, Smith was adamant. The DC-4s were reconverted to passenger planes, and the cargo division was shut down.

The transition to new equipment in the postwar years was not always a smooth process. After the DC-6 began flight operations, a rash of in-flight fires grounded the entire fleet for four months in 1947 until the cause, a fuel transfer vent, was pinpointed and fixed. American lost $7 million in revenues, a staggering sum in those years. More deficits piled up when American Overseas pilots went on strike in the fall of that same year. For all his concern about employees, Smith did not get on well with unions, and he intensely disliked the president of the Air Line Pilots Association, David Behncke. The strike was not long—about two weeks—and turned on tentative phrasing of an agreement, but Smith remained angry about the additional red ink caused by the sudden walkout. The DC-6 problems, strike actions, nagging equipment problems throughout the industry, and slumping passenger traffic all contributed to a glum postwar adjustment.

Controlling costs became a major issue, especially with American's plans for additional expenditures to achieve a completely new postwar fleet by 1950. Finance represented a weak spot in the entire airline industry, still comparatively young and inexperienced, especially in view of soaring equipment costs for bigger, more complex postwar airliners. Smith realized that finance was not his strong point, and he took corrective action.

Smith went outside the industry to find someone with long years of experience in large and multifaceted corporate operations, especially corporations selling direct to the consumer. He picked William J. Hogan, who became a vice-president and treasurer. After 15 years on the controller's staff at Firestone Tire and Rubber, Hogan had gone on to H. J. Heinz, where he had been treasurer, comptroller, director, and a member of the executive board. He had the breadth and depth of experience Smith wanted, and he was known for his brilliant financial mind. He was also known as imperious and single-minded. During his two decades at American, Hogan clashed with many, including some senior executives who went to Smith's office with a

"Hogan-or-me" ultimatum only to find that Hogan's position was the one that counted.

Slowly the airlines began to develop more sophistication in finance and marketing. Although there had been some collaboration in collocation of ticket offices before the war, the American facility at 42nd Street and Park Avenue soon became outmoded after 1945. Traffic-choked streets were upsetting limousine service and airline departures. American Airlines handled some 40 percent of New York's metropolitan air traffic and desperately needed an alternate location. Acting on their own, Smith and Hogan bought several parcels of real estate near the Queens Midtown Tunnel, the main link to La Guardia Field and the proposed Idlewild airport. With some subtle arm-twisting by Smith, other airlines joined American to set up the East Side Airlines Terminal. American, Eastern, TWA, United, and Pan Am each held 15 percent of the stock; smaller shares were taken by Allegheny, Braniff, Capital, Colonial, Mohawk, National, Northeast, and Northwest. The terminal opened in 1953, and its success prompted a similar West Side Airlines Terminal only two years later.

Domestic operations began to improve, boosting American's balance sheets and building a reputation as one of the best-run systems in the industry. The international routes to Europe fared less well, and Smith began thinking about selling American Overseas, 62 percent of whose stock was held by American. The problem was that he did not tell Damon about it, nor did he inform the American Overseas board. It was one of those baronial decisions that Smith took it upon himself alone to make.

In the first place, the American Overseas acquisition had been made in Smith's absence. More to the point, there were problems in making it work. American Overseas had unusually keen competition over the North Atlantic from a pair of much larger and experienced rivals—TWA and Pan Am. Moreover, increasing competition came from foreign carriers such as BOAC, Air France, SAS, and Swissair, often with crucial support from their respective governments. American Overseas had been able to hold its own and had a good reputation, but American's analysis revealed that a disproportionate amount of corporate management time was going to run the transatlantic operation. Smith concluded that American was far better off in cultivating its traditional domestic routes.

Douglas DC-7 (courtesy of the National Air and Space Museum)

Late in 1948, Smith began confidential discussions with Juan Trippe, intending to sell American Overseas to Pan Am. Only a couple of corporate lawyers were let in on the negotiations. When the agreement was signed in December, American Overseas' board, which included the president of American, Damon, was faced with a fait accompli. Damon resigned and went to TWA as its new president; Smith again became president of American.

Controversy continued to swirl around Smith's move. American Overseas personnel were unhappy, a mood matched by the CAB, where Damon of TWA was strenuously opposing Pan Am's coup, arguing that TWA would be overwhelmed on Atlantic routes. The CAB rejected the agreement, and it went to the White House for President Truman's signature. Debate over Truman's actions still continued, to the effect that he first upheld the CAB vote (TWA was strong in Missouri) then reversed himself under pressure from Smith's Democratic friends in Texas. Carlene Roberts, American's expert on regulatory matters, may have helped solve the imbroglio by brokering a clause allowing TWA to compete with Pan Am on certain routes. The case went all the way to the Supreme Court; TWA eventually got access to London and

Rome, Trippe reluctantly agreed, and the sale was consummated. Smith's reputation wilted during the affair, and he later hinted that maybe he should have kept American Overseas. In the meantime, his attention to purely domestic issues enhanced American's business in that area.

The airline industry had given only passing attention to reduced fares or similar promotions to increase patronage. The number of seats on a DC-3 simply did not lend itself to fare-cutting, and early postwar profit margins were too slim to justify radical manipulation of passenger-load factors. But Smith kept asking his traffic managers if some sort of incentive might attract enough extra traffic to offset reduced prices. In 1948 a study group decided to make a thorough analysis and began by monitoring daily load factors over a six-month period. They uncovered a distinctive travel pattern. Favorite travel days were Friday and Sunday afternoons. Sales began to fall on Mondays and remained at their lowest from Tuesday through Thursday. The lowest load factors of all showed up on flights between Saturday noon and Sunday noon.

After juggling the figures, the study group came up with a scheme that satisfied Smith. For wives who flew with husbands paying full fare,

American offered a 50 percent discount during the lowest passenger-load periods—Saturday noon to Sunday noon and Tuesday through Thursday. American became the first airline to offer such an attractive travel option, and the plan was not only a success with travelers but also made money. Within a couple of months, United and other competitors were advertising similar plans.

Innovations in fare structures, purchase of new aircraft, expense accounts, and virtually everything financial had to receive the imprimatur of Smith's financial mandarin, Bill Hogan. Generally officers at American simply gritted their teeth and put up with Hogan's acerbic style. As one veteran remarked, Hogan was one of the most disagreeable but one of the most competent men he had ever known. Executives who challenged Hogan, even those close to Smith—no matter how long they had been with the airline—either left the company or accepted the inevitable. Hogan played a major role in making American's operating costs the lowest in the industry. Realizing this, Smith supported his chief financial officer against all comers, even old favorites like the free-wheeling Red Mosier, whose star began to fade. Hogan's financial acumen became a significant factor in decisions to order newer aircraft like the DC6-B, an acquisition in which Hogan's advice to Smith was equal to that of American's legendary chief engineer, Bill Littlewood.

However, neither Smith nor Bill Hogan had foreseen the impact of nonscheduled airlines—but then, the whole industry was caught off guard by this bumptious group. The upstart nonscheduled operations bought war-surplus transports, hired ex-military pilots, and became aggressive competitors. Their biggest impact occurred on long-haul routes, where the established scheduled airlines had reigned supreme. The "nonskeds" came up with the idea of group travel, offered bargain-basement fares to popular vacation spots, and attracted many travelers who had never flown before. In addition, they developed a strong air cargo business, cutting into military contract operations that had traditionally gone to the major airlines.

The major airlines tried to rein in the new competition by relying on regulatory strictures applied through the CAB. In Washington, Carlene Roberts, head of American's office there, stood out as a leader in the offensive. In 1951 Smith promoted her to vice-president, making her the first woman

among the major carriers to attain that status. Eventually, the major airlines realized that the nonscheduled operations could only be contained by offering similar travel packages. During the late 1940s and early 1950s the scheduled airlines (whose one-class service up to this point was basically first-class service) began offering coach fares.

The drive to expand coach class was one of the reasons that Smith began badgering Douglas to develop a bigger and faster airliner, the DC-7. He planned for the new plane to enter service on American's premier coast-to-coast routes, releasing older equipment to take over the coach-class markets. In addition, he wanted the plane to be able to beat the high-powered Lockheed Constellations of TWA, which were faster than current American Airlines airliners on transcontinental routes and which could fly nonstop on eastbound runs. The Douglas hierarchy wavered; they felt jet transports were only a few years away and did not see the need for a new piston-engine transport. But Smith was determined, hinting he might go elsewhere for the plane he wanted and end the close business relationship with Douglas. Finally, Douglas agreed.

The DC-7 began service in 1953. American launched it with elaborate publicity, and the plane was, indeed, a ribbon-winner on nonstop transcontinental routes. But Smith had ignored concerns that the huge, complex, turbo-compound engines built by Curtiss-Wright would be troublesome. Unscheduled stops due to engine problems became a way of life until the plane was finally retired. The plane also sparked a feud with the pilot's union, the Air Line Pilots Association, because nonstop westbound flights often encountered headwinds that raised flight time to over eight hours—a violation of union rules. The dispute was being worked out when technicalities aroused Smith's ire again, and the union struck American. Both sides finally reached a settlement, including a waiver of the eight-hour rule for DC-7 crews, although Smith and the unions still viewed each other with jaundiced eyes.

The DC-7 affair reflected Smith's determination to keep a close rein on company affairs. There was always room for other points of view, but if Smith disliked something, it became a dead issue. In the late 1950s a management consultant firm recommended a major reorganization. Smith put it into effect, including a "senior council" of himself and four senior vice-presidents. Dutifully, the senior council convened once a week, but it seems to have made few major collective decisions. As one of the members later recalled, "C. R. wasn't a very good government-by-committee man. He liked to decide things for himself." When the issue of painting airplanes came up again in the late 1950s, some maintenance personnel spent nearly a year experimenting with various coatings and recording temperatures. There was no doubt—white paint could keep planes warmer in winter and cooler in the summer. A presentation to Smith included several binders of conclusive data. Smith said no. The planes stayed unpainted.

In marketing Smith always seemed to be more adventurous. During the brief DC-7 era he took a great interest in promoting "Royal Coachman" flights, publicized by a British actor in authentic British coachman's outfit and tooting an original eighteenth-century coach horn. It was a theme easily adapted to airline service, although the name is said to have been suggested by Smith, based on his favorite fishing fly. Old hands at American also credited Smith himself for the original idea leading to the "Music 'til Dawn" radio shows, which began in 1953, ran coast-to-coast for over a decade, and won a Peabody Award for excellence. The show itself was substantial in length, running from 11:30 P.M. to 6 A.M.. The opening theme music, "That's All," became indelibly linked to American, and the format of high-quality "easy-listening" musical selections with infrequent ads garnered an extensive audience. American aired the program until 1969, when television had absorbed much of the late-night audience, but the familiar strains of "That's All" stirred many fond memories for loyal listeners.

The 1950s were years of swift transition in the airline industry. In June 1955 American ordered Lockheed Electra turboprops; in November the airline ordered its first jet transport, the Boeing 707. That same year Smith took the initiative in setting up a major new instructional facility, the stewardess college in Dallas. The instructional complex eventually became the Learning Center, dedicated to training flight attendants as well as a cross-section of other personnel. Dedicated in 1957, the college always benefited from Smith's personal attention, since he believed that cabin attendants played a crucial role in the highly competitive airline industry.

As gas turbine equipment began entering service in the late 1950s and early 1960s, the industry went through a series of strikes by various unions jockeying for position in the new jet age. The pilot's union wanted flight engineers to be qualified pilots; flight engineers (characteristically ex-mechanics, not pilots) were not happy to leave their own union; airline management wrung its hands over escalating costs. Smith got major airlines to sign a mutual aid pact, a complicated formula whereby a struck carrier got some revenues from competitors who benefited from additional business. The unions objected, but Smith's plan stuck until deregulation arrived in the late 1970s.

The transition to gas turbines brought additional problems. The Lockheed Electra experienced some disastrous crashes due to wing failures. Investigators eventually traced the problem to severe harmonic vibration characteristics in the wing and nacelle structures. With Smith's support, American engineers contributed to the solution of this industrywide problem, and American also helped restore passenger confidence with a candid publicity campaign to explain both the reason for the crashes as well as the steps taken to end the danger. The problem with the Convair 990 jet transport was not safety but performance. Smith had ordered the plane based on its high speed—as usual, he was out to beat the competition. No amount of modification seemed to help, and American soon sold its Convair jets.

The early 1960s included modernization in the business of passenger reservations. All airlines had some sort of automated system in operation by this time, but early equipment required many manual operations, and the data storage remained woefully inadequate. Smith and IBM's Tom Watson discussed the issues one day during a chance meeting (or so the story goes), and IBM eventually got a contract that resulted in the Semi-Automated Business Reservations Environment, otherwise known as SABRE. When SABRE went operational in 1962, it cut American's reservation process time from 45 minutes to three seconds. The system became a key marketing weapon in American's continuous jousting with its competitors.

While he maintained a vigorous schedule during these years, Smith also began the moves that prepared the way for his inevitable retirement, naming George Marion Sadler as American's president. Sadler had been with American since 1941, except for wartime duty. He rose through the ranks in customer service to become vice-president and general manager of the airline in 1959. His promotion in 1959 coincided with a rejuvenation of the board of

Convair 990 (courtesy of the National Air and Space Museum)

directors with several men who shared Smith's general outlook but who were valued for their independent judgments. For all his reputation as a decisive executive, Smith also recognized the need for vigorously argued alternatives. But when Smith announced his retirement in 1967, Sadler's health was failing due to cancer. Thus, American's general counsel, George Spater, not Sadler, became the airline's leader. Spater had been in the air transport business since 1934, working with TWA, among others.

The Spater regime, which lasted to 1973, was turbulent. American's experiments with diversification, including hotels and recreation complexes, floundered. There were other troubles, including financial kickback scandals in the marketing department. Meanwhile, Smith spent part of this time as secretary of commerce, serving for nine months in 1968. Smith then joined the investment firm of Lazard Frères, where he was at work when he received a call to direct American Airlines once more.

Although an executive committee of American's board of directors had been vigorously searching for Spater's successor, some candidates refused

and others did not seem to measure up. As the weeks passed, the airline's deficits continued to mount and morale plummeted. In desperation, the search committee turned to Smith, who grudgingly agreed to return for six months but refused to take any compensation.

During Smith's reprise at American during 1973 and 1974, no dramatic, overnight recovery from the company's financial woes occurred. Smith trimmed expenses by laying off some 1,300 personnel and cutting back some operations. Smith's most important contributions related to improving company morale. It would be easier to find and install a successor. The nominee was Albert Vincent Casey, a man with no airline experience but someone with a strong background in finance and transportation. Casey joined American in 1974; he helped bring the company into the black and implemented the decision to move American's headquarters from New York to Dallas in 1979. As airline deregulation brought total restructuring of the industry, he stepped aside in 1980 for a new president, Robert Crandall.

When he left in 1974, Smith said he intended to stay out of the airline business for good. He had a DC-6 mind, he explained, implying that the jet-age industry had changed far too much. Smith had certainly been one of the principal figures in that change. Moreover, many American Airline personnel had gone on to leadership positions throughout the industry. This notable influence reflected one of Smith's outstanding traits—his interest in the overall air transport business and a career in which he generously allocated his own time as well as that of his company in resolving industry issues. While Smith received a variety of awards over his lifetime, they were exclusively related to his aviation career. Service in World War II brought a Distinguished Service Medal, Legion of Merit, and others, including designation as Commander, Order of the British Empire. Later in his career he was named to the Aviation Hall of Fame, Travel Hall of Fame, and Business Hall of Fame. He received no awards from civic or humanitarian agencies. The citations underscore the single-mindedness with which he pursued

his chosen profession of air travel. Within the scope of that profession, his influence was fundamental. He was a builder.

Publications:
"A.A." *American Airlines—Since 1926.* (New York: Newcomen Society in North America, 1954);
"Airline Outlook," *Air Affairs*, 1 (Summer 1947): 493-501.

References:
"Airline in the Black," *Fortune*, 19 (February 1939): 60-65;
Jack Alexander, "Just Call Me C. R.," *Saturday Evening Post*, 213 (February 1, 1941): 9-11;
"The Big Money Airline," *Fortune*, 49 (December 1951): 87-92;
R. E. G. Davies, *Airlines of the United States since 1914* (Washington, D.C.: Smithsonian Institution, 1982);
Robert J. Serling, *Eagle: The History of American Airlines* (New York: St. Martin's Press / Marek, 1985);
Henry Ladd Smith, *Airways: The History of Commercial Aviation in the United States* (New York: Knopf, 1942).

Frederick W. Smith

(August 11, 1944 -   )

by Dominick A. Pisano

National Air and Space Museum

CAREER: U.S. Marine Corps (1966-1969); president, Arkansas Aviation (1969-1971); president, Federal Express Corporation (1971-   ).

Frederick Wallace Smith, the founder of Federal Express Corporation, has become known in the air cargo business as an entrepreneur without a peer, a man who took an idea, developed in an undergraduate term paper, and parlayed it into a multibillion-dollar business venture. As so often happens in the history of American business enterprise, Smith's extraordinary success can be explained in terms of the right man, in the right place, at the right time.

Smith took advantage of the consequences of the high-technology revolution that began in the 1950s. By the 1960s, as Robert Sobel and David Sicilia have pointed out in their book *The Entrepreneurs*, "the American economy was increasingly becoming based more upon services and lightweight

high technology products than bulk manufacturing. . . . Now, highly trained scientists and technicians were developing services and products based upon electronic devices rather than tons of steel. From 1972 to 1982, electronic components production grew by an average of 9.9 percent per annum; in the same period, steel production declined by 4.3 percent per annum."

Unlike the old factory system, which depended on a manufacturing company's closeness to raw materials, the high-tech companies were situated in major cities such as Boston, New York, and San Francisco to attract the scientists, engineers, and technicians needed to make the firms successful. This high-technology revolution made it imperative that a company be able to transmit information and small goods across the country, or even around the world, in a matter of hours rather than days. The only way for a company to do this would be to ship by air instead of using surface transporta-

Frederick W. Smith (courtesy of Federal Express)

tion. Smith not only understood this, but he also was prepared to take the risks necessary to capitalize on it.

Smith was born on August 11, 1944, in Marks, Mississippi, the son of Frederick and Sally Wallace Smith. He grew up in Memphis, Tennessee. As a boy, he suffered from a disease called Calve-Perthes, which affected his hipbone. He developed an interest in the history of the Civil War, had a collection of toy soldiers, and often visited Shiloh battlefield in the company of his mother. After he had completed grammar school, he entered Memphis University School, a private preparatory school, where he did well in academics and athletics (basketball and football) and was a student leader. At the age of fifteen, he and two classmates started the Ardent Record Company, which continued to exist in Memphis through the early 1990s.

Smith's interest in business enterprise is not surprising; his family background was entrepreneurial. His father founded and was chairman of Dixie Greyhound Bus Lines, one of the largest bus companies in the South. He even built the first bus from a truck body and served as a driver when the company was in its infancy. In 1934 the elder Smith opened Toddle House, a successful quick-service national restaurant chain. The company was sold in 1961 for a reported $22 million. When he died in 1948 at the age of fifty-three, the elder Smith left his son a considerable fortune.

About the time Smith founded the Ardent Record Company, he also learned to fly, an interest that was to have a significant effect on his life. In 1962 he entered Yale University, majoring in economics and political science. Smith was an average student, preferring the fraternity life of Yale to the classroom. He worked as a campus disc jockey, entered the Marine Corps ROTC, and, with the help of two professors, revived the Yale Flying Club.

Deciding to combine his love of flying with his academic pursuits, Smith wrote a junior term paper analyzing freight service. He concluded that a market existed for a company that could ship "high-priority, time-sensitive goods." He pointed out that instead of being expedited to their destinations, packages were "hippety-hopping around the country from city to city and from airline to airline before reaching their destination." He also observed that "there was no control over the packages by the originating air carrier if the packages had to be carried by additional airlines before reaching their ultimate destination."

Smith's professor disagreed, pointing out that federal regulation would hinder an express service such as Smith described from ever becoming a reality. Besides, competition from other, better-established air carriers would prevent the company from succeeding. He gave Smith a "C" on the paper.

After receiving his commission in the Marine Corps in 1966, Smith went to Vietnam as a platoon leader (later, company commander) with the First Marine Division. Upon returning to the United States, he won his wings, then went back to Vietnam for a second tour of duty, flying A4D Skyhawks and OV-10 Broncos. He was discharged as a captain in July 1969, having been awarded the Silver Star, Bronze Star, two Purple Hearts, and other decorations.

After Smith left the service, he purchased a controlling interest in Arkansas Aviation Sales, a company located in Little Rock that serviced corporate turboprop and jet aircraft. Although the company had sales of $1 million, it was losing money. Smith reversed this. He increased revenues to $9 million and eventually made a profit of $250,000.

Smith had never lost sight of his air express idea. He was convinced that there was indeed a market for a company to transport time-sensitive, important packages and papers. His definition of "time-sensitive" was "one for which the consequences of failure to deliver within a specified period of time would far outweigh any consideration of reasonable rate comparability." "If you offer two services," Smith said, "and one of them is 15, 20, 30, 40, percent higher on one hand and it gets the documents or items there on time, and a cheaper service whose reliability is not nearly so great, the shipper will always take, if it is time-sensitive, the more reliable method, rather than the cheaper method."

In May 1971 Smith asked the members of the board of Frederick Smith Enterprise Company, Inc., a family trust of which he was chairman, to approve funding for a company to transport cash letters from district banks overnight for the Federal Reserve System. The board agreed to invest $250,000 in the scheme: Smith matched this amount with his own funds. On June 18, 1971, Smith incorporated the company, which he called Federal Express Corporation, based on the expectation that it would soon have a contract with the Federal Reserve System. This did not happen, however, because all the Federal Reserve Banks in various districts throughout the country were highly competitive, and each wanted to transport its own cash letters.

Although disappointed, Smith pushed ahead with his idea for a small-package airline. Late in 1972 he decided to move his operation from Little Rock, the site of Arkansas Aviation, to his hometown. Memphis was more conducive to his plans for several reasons. First, it was close to the targeted market cities for small package distribution, and thus fulfilled the conditions for Federal's "hub-and-spokes" concept of distribution. Borrowed from United Parcel Service's system of package distribution, interstate trucking companies, and the switching system used by the telephone company, the "hub-and-spokes" idea was simple. Packages would be flown into Memphis, the hub of the system, sorted at night, and then transshipped to their ultimate destination around the country.

More important, Memphis provided a more favorable climate for Federal to do business than Lit-

tle Rock. As Robert A. Sigafoos and Roger R. Easson have pointed out in their history of Federal Express, "Little Rock could not justify a huge capital outlay on airport improvements for a company which at that time in late 1972, had not inaugurated its priority package airline operation.... The favorable lease terms provided by the [Memphis] Airport Authority to an unproven company with very limited capital was a stroke of good fortune for Smith and his associates. It is doubtful that any other major metropolitan airport would have made such a similar generous deal to an unproven company run by a twenty-eight year-old with limited business experience."

While trying to get the company on its feet, Smith commissioned two consulting firms to study the potential market for an express service. Their reports indicated that customers were dissatisfied with the freight services that were then operating, among them Emery Air Freight and Flying Tiger, despite the fact that each of these companies was taking in revenues of more than $100 million a year. Also, they pointed out that the majority of the commercial airliners in the United States were not flying from 10 P.M. to 8 A.M. Thus, Smith was presented with the opportunity to take advantage of the downturn in commercial aviation at night and early morning to provide overnight delivery.

Despite all of the hopeful indications, Federal Express had to go through some noticeable birth pangs. "Early internal policy and administrative decisions," Sigafoos and Easson have noted, "were often hammered out in 'knock down-drag out' meetings extending late into the night. Sixteen-hour days were common. Bitter disputes would sometimes occur, and Smith would lose his temper." They quote Irby Tedder, the company's original financial officer, as saying: "Smith and his key people didn't know how to manage anything. They all came in with a lot of wild ideas of how to put Federal Express together, and only a few of them made any sense. They were an impetuous bunch."

Yet a persistent Smith soon began to acquire aircraft for the company's fleet. He had decided on the twin-engine Dassault Falcon 20 after being impressed with the business jet's size, capacity, and range. The Falcon could carry eight to ten passengers or three tons of freight. He wanted to modify the passenger door of the Falcon, which was 59 inches wide and 31 and a half inches high, to enable it to carry large cargo loads. Other than that,

Federal Express Dassault Falcon 20 (courtesy of the National Air and Space Museum)

he had only to paint the aircraft in the distinctive Federal Express purple, orange, and white colors.

Unfortunately, Smith was so cash poor that he could not meet his commitments to Pan American Airways' Business Jet Division, from whom Smith had an option to purchase 23 Falcons. He eventually struck a deal with Pan Am in January 1973, offering payment in the form of warrants to buy common stock in the company. Thus, Smith gained a fleet of aircraft for Federal Express without a heavy expenditure of cash.

An even more serious problem was that the Falcon 20 exceeded the Civil Aeronautics Board's weight limit for air taxis, making it technically impossible for Federal to use it. Smith wanted the CAB to change the rules or grant him a waiver. Thanks in part to the efforts of Washington attorney Ramsey D. Potts, the CAB agreed to amend the rule on July 18, 1972. However, due to objections from the Airline Pilots Association, North Central Airlines, and Hughes Air Corporation, it was not until December 5, 1973, that a U.S. Circuit Court

of Appeals in the District of Columbia ruled favorably on the change.

Conscious that the company had passed another important milestone, Smith ordered test operations to begin on the night of March 12, 1973, targeting 11 cities, including Dallas, Jacksonville, Atlanta, Kansas City, St. Louis, and Cincinnati, as part of the distribution network. But that night only six packages arrived in Memphis. (This was such an embarrassment to the company that its public relations office does not mention it in any of its press releases.) On April 17, Federal tried again, this time with 25 cities in its network, but the volume was again disappointing, a mere 186 packages. On hand that night were Charles Lea and Richard H. Stowe of New Court Securities Corporation, an investment banking/venture capital concern based in New York that was interested in financing the company. Lea was not impressed and reportedly said, "We didn't think Federal Express was living up to its plan, and we lost interest."

To make matters worse, the company was steadily losing money. At the end of April 1973, Federal's deficit was $4.4 million. After three and one half months of operation, volume was disappointing, with a combined daily package count of 296 for New York, Chicago, Philadelphia, St. Louis, Detroit, and Denver. By the end of September 1973 the deficit had risen to $7.8 million.

Realizing that he would have to begin scrambling for additional financing, Smith sought the assistance of White, Weld, & Company, a New York-Chicago investment banking establishment that earlier had showed an interest in the company. By September 1972 White, Weld had outlined a financial package that included $3,250,000 from Smith's family trust. Five months later, with the company on the verge of bankruptcy, White, Weld asked Smith to put up an additional $1.5 million in equity.

Desperate to save Federal Express, Smith forged the signature of Robert L. Cox, a Memphis attorney who was Enterprise Company's board secretary, to a loan note he had secured from the Union Bank in Little Rock. This led to Smith's indictment in federal court for using false documents to defraud Union Bank. His defense was that he and the Enterprise Company were one and the same and that the loan officer at Union Bank was aware that he had signed Cox's name to the agreement. He was eventually cleared of the charges.

Finally, on November 13, 1973, a credit agreement was signed which provided Federal with $52 million. Even so, for the next three years the company still was in danger of going broke. Two more rounds of financing in March and September 1974 took place before the company had sufficient cash to pay its bills. Shortly before the March agreement was signed, Federal's investors and lenders held a meeting in Chicago to decide whether to oust Smith from his position as head of the company. Smith survived but only by a slender thread.

After years of operating on the margins, Federal eventually made a dramatic turnaround. In July 1975 the company began to show a profit, with a net income of $55,000. By May 31, 1976, the company had a net annual income of $3.6 million, and three years later it had achieved a position of leadership in the small package shipping business in terms of both volume and profit, with 19 percent of the market in total priority air shipments of under 100 pounds.

During this period, Federal's growth was aided by several factors. As Sobel and Sicilia have

pointed out, "Federal came into being at a time when airline traffic was expanding rapidly. Total industry revenues, which came to $7.2 billion in 1970 and $11.2 billion in 1972, rose to $19.9 billion by 1977. Finding themselves in the unusual position of being short on carriers, the major delivery services dropped service to many smaller cities. As a result, they were unable to service their small-freight customers as well as they had earlier, opening the way for Federal Express to fill the gap. In addition, there was a long United Parcel strike in 1974, followed by the collapse of rival REA Express, which provided Federal with new opportunities."

Another important factor was federal deregulation of the air cargo industry, which allowed Smith to operate aircraft larger than the Falcon 20. In December 1977 he bought 11 Boeing 727-100s, enabling the company to expand capacity. (By 1983, Federal Express operated 38 Boeing 727-100s.) These developments, as well as Federal's subsequent maturation, induced Smith to sell the company's stock on the open market. In 1978 Federal Express went public, selling 783,000 shares at $24 a share, and raising some $17.5 million in additional equity.

Federal Express's success has also been credited to imaginative advertising and marketing techniques that were largely the idea of J. Vincent Fagan, a senior vice-president in charge of market planning and research. Fagan believed that Federal was wasting money on its sales force and that more attention should be given to advertising. From 1974 to 1983, Fagan's staff worked with the firm of Ally & Gargano of New York on five advertising campaigns. The first of these, "America You Have a New Airline" began in 1975; the second, "Twice as Good as the Best in the Business," was launched shortly afterward; the third, "Take Away Our Planes and We'd Be Just Like Everybody Else," in 1976, was directed toward a competitor, Emery.

The fourth campaign, introduced in 1977, was the most important because it made use of wacky and provocative humor to get Federal's message across to a mass audience. In one ad, which drew the wrath of the postmaster general and the American Postal Workers Union, two postal clerks ignore patrons waiting for service while they discuss retirement. The most memorable Federal Express advertisements, however, emphasized Federal's speed in delivering packages to their destination. They featured actor John Moschitta, posing as a no-

nonsense executive who talks very fast, while in the background his assistant hurries frantically to complete a duplicating job. The message, of course, was that in a highly competitive, business environment, where profits are measured by how quickly a company can respond to the demands placed on it, Federal Express delivered on time.

Success has not come without some criticism, especially about the rigidity of Federal's corporate culture and its resistance to the unions. Unlike other express companies where unionization is a way of life, Federal has managed to withstand attempts to organize its employees, maintaining that the unions would dictate work rules. This, Smith maintains, would be destructive: "Drivers at 10:20 A.M. probably would not have the incentive to get those last packages delivered before the 10:30 A.M. deadline as the company had committed to do. Any strike would be a disaster to us." Instead, employees are given incentives in the form of promotions from within, profit-sharing, and an open-door-to-management policy.

Failures, too, have accompanied Federal's success. Hotel-Pak, an exclusive service contract with the major hotel chains, lasted little more than a year. Federal also managed to survive the failure of ZapMail, an electronic transmission facsimile network introduced in the mid 1980s, about which Smith was very optimistic. Federal steadily lost money on this undertaking: $128.9 million in losses against $14.7 million in revenue in fiscal 1985, and $140.9 million in losses against $33 million in revenues in fiscal 1986. Among the reasons cited for the debacle were the high expense to the customer and competition from telecommunications companies.

Nevertheless, Federal Express became the world's largest small-package carrier during the 1980s, operating a fleet of 8 DC-10-10s, 11 DC-10-30s, 21 Boeing 727-200s, 39 Boeing 727-100s, and 66 Cessna 208s by 1987. It grew even larger in January 1989 when it acquired Flying Tiger, the biggest cargo carrier in the industry. Flying Tiger merged into Federal Express in August 1989, putting Frederick Smith atop a multibillion dollar operation with a promising future. He had come a long way since the "C" on his Yale term paper.

References:
Robert A. Sigafoos and Roger R. Easson, *Absolutely Positively Overnight: The Unofficial Corporate History of Federal Express* (Memphis: St. Luke's Press, 1988);
Robert Sobel and David Sicilia, *The Entrepreneurs: An American Adventure* (Boston: Houghton Mifflin, 1986).

Southwest Airlines

by George E. Hopkins

Western Illinois University

Southwest Airlines began operations on June 18, 1971, as an intrastate carrier serving the Dallas-Houston market. It was the creation of Rollin W. King, an Ohio aviation entrepreneur who had moved to Texas in the 1960s. While working as a corporate pilot, King gained the support of influential members of the Texas business and political establishment, among them Herbert D. Kelleher (an associate of Governor John C. Connally), Robert Strauss, and John Murchison of the Dallas-based Murchison Brothers. This kind of backing caused one editorial observer to comment during the company's formative stage: "Southwest Airlines won't use aviation fuel—just political power."

Southwest modeled itself on the highly successful California intrastate carrier, Pacific Southwest Airlines (PSA). The courts earlier had permitted intrastate airlines freedom from economic regulation by the Civil Aeronautics Board (CAB), so long as they did not cross state lines. PSA, by initially serving only the San Francisco-Los Angeles market, had proved that a "no frills" airline that offered service between two large cities could be profitable. Texas, which had three of the nation's ten largest cities (Dallas, Houston, and San Antonio), was ripe for this kind of airline operation.

The crucial event in the formation of Southwest Airlines came with the opening of Dallas-Fort Worth Airport in 1970. Because the new airport was a considerable distance from downtown Dallas, the CAB arranged a "shotgun wedding" among the airlines which served the greater Dallas area (including Braniff and Texas International), forcing them to abandon close-in Love Field, which was preferred by most commuters. But the dictates of the CAB did not extend to intrastate carriers, and this gave Southwest a golden opportunity.

King and his backers quickly took advantage of the situation and created Southwest for the purpose of using the convenient Love Field. Despite massive legal challenges from everyone involved, the airline won permission from the Texas Aeronautical Commission to serve the Dallas-Houston market via Love Field. Using Boeing 737s and featuring streamlined "no reservation" ticketing, attractive young stewardesses in "hot pants" outfits, and a variety of marketing gimmicks (such as a free bottle of Chivas Regal liquor for passengers who paid the full one-way ticket price of $26 in lieu of a discounted fare), Southwest's business boomed.

Much of Southwest's success was due to Marion Lamar Muse, an experienced American Airlines executive who assumed operational control of the airline, relegating King to a vice-presidency. Following airline deregulation in 1978, Howard Putnam replaced Muse, who left to form his own airline, MuseAir. Southwest rapidly expanded outside Texas under Putnam's leadership, setting the industry standard for low cost, no-frills service, and prospering while copycat operations like People Express failed. After Putnam left in 1981 to become head of Braniff Airways, Southwest continued to thrive in the deregulated environment under the presidency of charismatic Herbert Kelleher, one of the airline's original supporters. By 1990 Southwest had attained major airline status, flying 9.9 billion revenue passenger miles and recording an operating profit of $81.6 million on operating revenues of $1.18 billion. At a time when the airline industry was reporting record losses, feisty Southwest remained profitable.

References:

Danna K. Henderson, "Consistent Profit Growth Is Basically Southwest," *Air Transport World*, 19 (September 1982): 16-17;

George E. Hopkins, "The Texas Airline War," *Washington Monthly*, 8 (March 1976): 12-19;

Joseph S. Murphy, "Southwest Builds Ten-Year Success on Productivity, High Morale," *Airline Executive*, 24 (June 1981): 10-15.

Texas International Airlines

by William M. Leary

University of Georgia

Texas International Airlines first appeared following World War II as one of the new Local Service carriers that had been authorized by the Civil Aeronautics Board to serve smaller communities throughout the country. R. Earl McKaughan, owner of Aviation Enterprises, a Houston-based aircraft sales and service business, obtained a three-year certificate in 1946 for five routes within the state of Texas. Under the name of Trans-Texas Airways, McKaughan's company inaugurated DC-3 service out of Houston on October 11, 1947.

The next two decades saw a process of slow expansion. By 1949 the Trans-Texas route system in-

cluded service to San Antonio, El Paso, Dallas, Galveston, and Brownsville. In 1953 the airline reached beyond the borders of the state to Shreveport and Memphis. By the end of the 1950s, it had added Little Rock and New Orleans to its regional network. Trans-Texas introduced the first of 25 pressurized Convair 240s in April 1961. At the same time, it expanded into New Mexico.

A major turning point for the airline came in 1966. In an unusual move, the Civil Aeronautics Board allowed the Local Service carrier to operate international routes, flying from Texas border towns to the Mexican cities of Monterrey, Tampico, and

Veracruz. In keeping with its new status, Trans-Texas entered the jet age. The airline earlier had decided to convert its entire fleet of Convair 240s to turboprop transports by replacing their piston engines with Rolls-Royce Darts. The first modified Convair 600 went into service on March 1. Only eight months later, Trans-Texas began flying the first of seven Douglas DC-9s, purchased at a cost of $51 million.

The expense of the new equipment proved too much for Trans-Texas's owners. In 1968 they sold the airline to Minnesota Enterprises, Inc., and the new management renamed it Texas International. Service quickly expanded to Denver and Salt Lake City, and in 1970 the Civil Aeronautics Board granted Texas International nonstop authority for the important route from Albuquerque to Los Angeles. Despite these moves, the airline's financial woes continued. Between 1968 and 1971, Texas International lost over $20 million.

On the verge of bankruptcy, the airline changed owners again on August 10, 1972, when Jet Capital Corporation, the creation of Frank A. Lorenzo and Robert J. Carney, acquired a controlling interest in the carrier. Under Lorenzo's management, the economic health of the company slowly improved. Lorenzo cut wages, giving the airline one of the lowest operating costs among regional carriers. He added new routes while eliminating unprofitable ones, and he replaced the airline's Convairs with DC-9s. In 1976 Texas International recorded a profit of $3.2 million, its first black ink in years.

With deregulation approaching, Texas International in 1977 became the first airline to offer deeply discounted fares. Known as "Peanut Fares," the tariffs rivaled bus fares on certain routes during off-peak hours. Lorenzo believed that discounting not only was inevitable under deregulation but also was desirable. Indeed, he considered discounting as the key to profitable growth. In the short term, at least, the strategy worked. In 1977 Texas International's revenue passenger miles increased by 23 percent, while profits soared to $8 million.

The airline embarked upon a policy of selective expansion following passage of the Airline Deregulation Act of 1978. In 1979 it flew to Baltimore, St. Louis, Kansas City, and Las Vegas; added nonstop service from Dallas to Los Angeles; and posted a record net profit of $40.5 million. The following year, Texas International became part of Texas Air Corporation, Lorenzo's new holding company. After an unprofitable year in 1981, Lorenzo merged the airline with his recently acquired Continental Airlines on July 13, 1982. It took until October 31 to integrate the two airlines, at which time the colors of Texas International disappeared from the skies.

References:

John Cook, "Lorenzo the Presumptuous," *Forbes*, 122 (October 30, 1978): 115-117;

R. E. G. Davies, *Continental Airlines: The First Fifty Years, 1934-1984* (The Woodlands, Tex.: Pioneer, 1985);

Davies, *Rebels and Reformers of the Airways* (Washington, D.C.: Smithsonian Institution, 1987);

George C. Eads, *The Local Service Airline Experiment* (Washington, D.C.: Brookings Institution, 1972).

Stuart G. Tipton

(December 26, 1910 - August 14, 1981)

by William M. Leary

University of Georgia

CAREER: Attorney, Resettlement Administration (1935); attorney, Treasury Department (1935-1938); attorney, Civil Aeronautics Authority (1938-1940); assistant general counsel, Civil Aeronautics Board (1940-1944); general counsel (1944-1955), president (1955-1972), chairman, Air Transport Association of America (1972-1974); senior vice-president, Pan American World Airways (1974-1977).

As president of the Air Transport Association of America, the trade organization of the nation's scheduled airlines, Stuart Guy Tipton acted as the leading spokesman for the industry during two decades of tremendous economic growth and technological change. He was especially effective in presenting the industry's position on such matters as air safety and the financing of new jet aircraft to the five-member Civil Aeronautics Board (CAB). In fact, according to CAB historian Robert Burkhardt, his relationship with the airline industry's regulatory agency was so close that he was sometimes referred to as its sixth member.

Tipton was born on December 26, 1910, in Knightstown, Indiana, the son of Guy Stuart and Bessie Walter Tipton. After graduating from Knightstown High School in 1928, he attended Wabash College in Crawfordsville, Indiana, earning his B.A. degree in 1932. Tipton spent the summer in Switzerland following graduation, then entered Northwestern University Law School, where he obtained his J.D. in 1935. Learning that $15 a week was the best salary he could expect as an attorney in his hometown during the Great Depression, he secured a job in Washington with the Resettlement Administration for $40 a week. The philosophy of the New Deal, however, did not appeal to the young conservative from Indiana. "After six weeks," he later recalled, "I was convinced that the Government was

Stuart G. Tipton (courtesy of the Air Transport Association of America)

wild and I started looking around for something else."

Tipton soon joined the Treasury Department. While there, he worked on the interagency committee that drafted the Civil Aeronautics Act of 1938, a landmark piece of legislation that would define the government's relationship with the airline industry for the next 20 years. Tipton also saw a personal relationship come to fruition during this period. In 1937 he married Lorraine Arnold, whom he had met at Northwestern University. The couple had four daughters.

In 1938 Tipton left the Treasury Department and went with the newly created Civil Aeronautics Authority. When this agency divided in 1940 into the Civil Aeronautics Administration and the Civil Aeronautics Board, which would exercise economic and safety oversight over the airline industry, Tipton decided to go with the CAB as assistant general counsel. Four years later, he accepted an attractive offer from the Air Transport Association of America. "By that time," Tipton explained, "the job [at the CAB] wasn't creating any great stimulus. It was paying only $7,500 a year and the A.T.A. offered me twice that. Naturally, I took it."

Founded in January 1936 as the trade organization for the nation's scheduled airlines, the Air Transport Association (ATA) served the industry in three broad areas. First, it was concerned with operations and safety, facilitating the exchange of information among member airlines. Second, it promoted passenger and cargo services through such means as operating an Airlines Clearing House for the settlement of interairline accounts. Finally, the ATA represented the airline industry to the government, frequently appearing before Congress to testify on behalf of the airlines.

Tipton served as the ATA's general counsel until 1955, then became president of the organization. Unlike the strong personalities of his predecessors, especially Earle L. Johnson, Tipton (known as "Tip") was a more mild-mannered individual. Soft-spoken, with an ever-present corncob pipe in hand, he quickly gained the respect of Congress for his honesty, integrity, and understanding. He worked especially well with the CAB. "His observations have led to a calm and usually philosophical point of view that seldom generates any heat," CAB historian Burkhardt has written, "though Tipton always stands willing to shed what light he can on the airline industry's problems of the moment."

Tipton faced two major problems when he became president of the ATA. The first involved air safety. Testifying before a Senate committee in 1956, he stated: "After careful study, we have come to the conclusion that the major problem facing the Civil Aeronautics Administration—and one of the most critical problems confronting all American aviation—is the problem of our air navigation

traffic control system." He came to favor the creation of a new, independent body to control aviation, and he supported legislation to create the Federal Aviation Agency in 1958.

The other significant problem that occupied much of Tipton's time and attention concerned the need to finance the airlines' new jet equipment. The industry, he pointed out in frequent speeches, proposed to invest $3 billion during the period from 1958 to 1963 to secure aircraft that would shrink the world by 40 percent and have an enormous impact on the American economy. When the CAB proved reluctant to approve fare increases to help fund this huge investment, Tipton initiated a general passenger fare investigation that led to the needed increases. This action, he believed, was in the public interest because the public would benefit from the new jet transports.

Tipton, in fact, saw the airline industry as an agent of the public interest. "It is," he once said, "the innovator and initiator of every expanding, safer, better, more efficient and more economical service." He called for "a creative relationship" between the industry and the government, arguing that American economic success had been fostered by a "pragmatic blending of private initiative and government power." One of the most articulate spokesmen for the regulated philosophy that had governed the airline industry since 1938, Tipton believed that the system had created a strong and vigorous industry that provided the American people with the finest air transport system in the world.

Tipton continued to voice the concerns of the industry in his quiet and effective manner until he retired in 1974. Hired by Pan American World Airways as senior vice-president for federal affairs, he remained in Washington and served as the airline's lobbyist to the federal government. He held this position for three years, then acted as a consultant to Pan American until his death on August 14, 1981.

Reference:
Robert Burkhardt, *CAB—The Civil Aeronautics Board* (Dulles International Airport, Va.: Green Hills Publishing Co., 1974).

Archives:
A small amount of material relating to Stuart G. Tipton's career, mainly copies of speeches, can be found in the library of the Air Transport Association of America, Washington, D.C.

Transamerica Airlines

by William M. Leary

University of Georgia

Transamerica Airlines, the most successful supplemental carrier during the 1970s, had a modest beginning as one of the many nonscheduled airlines that appeared after World War II. Kerkor "Kirk" Kerkorian, an ambitious pilot and budding entrepreneur who sold used airplanes, founded Los Angeles Air Service in 1947 (incorporated in 1948) and began flying a DC-3 on charters between Los Angeles and Las Vegas. Certified by the Civil Aeronautics Board (CAB) in 1949, the company added a DC-4 early in 1950, just in time to take advantage of military contract work at the outbreak of the Korean War.

Los Angeles Air Service recorded only modest profits during the 1950s, and at several points it ceased operations. When the CAB announced in 1951 that it might restrict the operations of nonscheduled air carriers, Kerkorian shut down the airline and sold its planes. In May 1954 he started up again, remaining in business until January 1957. Los Angeles Air Service began flying again in December 1958. Two years later, to avoid confusion with Los Angeles Airways, a helicopter operator, Kerkorian changed the name of the company to Trans International Airlines (TIA).

The turning point in the airline's history came in 1962. Kerkorian borrowed money to purchase a Douglas DC-8, becoming the first supplemental carrier to operate jet equipment. As a result, TIA's military contract business doubled. Earnings, which had stood at $236,604 in 1961, shot up to $1.1 million. "That was the real breakthrough," Kerkorian later commented.

In October 1964 the Studebaker Corporation, looking to diversify, purchased the airline for $2.7 million in stock. Kerkorian remained in operational control of the rapidly growing company. TIA acquired additional jet equipment, won new military contracts, gained both transatlantic and transpacific authority, and became the first supplemental airline

to provide jet charter service for affinity groups. In 1966, however, Studebaker changed its mind about diversification and resold the much larger airline back to Kerkorian for a bargain price of $2.5 million. Two years later, Kerkorian sold his 58 percent interest in the company to the giant Transamerica Corporation at a personal profit of $104 million.

TIA during the 1970s became the largest and most profitable of the supplemental air carriers, operating a wide variety of military and civilian, passenger and cargo flights. It specialized in the carriage of livestock, dating this expertise to 1968, when it transported 7,000 head of cattle from Texas to Chile. In 1976 TIA further enhanced its cargo operations when it merged with the prosperous Saturn Airways, acquiring a fleet of Lockheed Hercules transports. Three years later, in May 1979, the airline began scheduled transatlantic passenger service to Amsterdam, supplementing its booming charter business. In October, the company's corporate parent renamed it Transamerica Airlines.

Transamerica Airlines had a banner year in 1980. Ranked as the number one charter operator on both the Atlantic and Pacific, it posted a profit for the 20th time in 21 years (suffering a loss only during the fuel crisis of 1974). The airline had an impressive fleet of airplanes, including 2 Boeing 747s (with 6 more on order), 12 DC-8s, and 3 DC-10-30s, all fully convertible for either passenger or cargo use. In addition, it flew 8 Lockheed Electra turboprops and 12 Lockheed L-100-30s (the civilian version of the military C-130) in domestic cargo operations. Passenger traffic accounted for approximately half of the airline's total sales, with transportation of cargo accounting for the remainder. Military passengers and cargo provided some 40 percent of the airline's business.

The airline continued to make money during the early 1980s, recording a profit of $38.1 million in 1984. However, that year saw a decline in the company's market share that was caused by new competitors who used leased equipment and non-union employees to lower prices. The airline asked its pilots to accept a 10 percent cut in wages, but talks broke down in November. The company had a less successful year in 1985. The North Atlantic charter business fell off, while competition from low-cost airlines forced it to abandon scheduled passenger service. Despite a profit of $20.8 million, there were abundant signs that the airline's corporate parent was growing increasingly unhappy about a component which accounted for some 6 percent of the conglomerate's total revenues.

In January 1986 the Transamerica Corporation announced that it intended to sell its airline, car rental, and manufacturing businesses in order to concentrate on insurance and financial services. Unable to locate a buyer for the airline, the parent company closed it down at the end of September and sold off its airplanes and other assets.

References:

J. A. Donoghue, "Transamerica Quietly Makes a Profit Year after Year as a General Store," *Air Transport World*, 18 (February 1981): 54-56, 58-59;

Joan M. Feldman, "TIA Stirs Up Emotions at Transamerica," *Air Transport World*, 21 (December 1984): 30-32;

Irwin Ross, "Kirk Kerkorian Doesn't Want All the Meat Off the Bone," *Fortune*, 80 (November 1969): 144-148, 184, 186;

"TransAmerica Head Spurs Divestitures," *New York Times*, February 3, 1986, IV: 2.

Trans Caribbean Airways

by William M. Leary

University of Georgia

Trans Caribbean Airways (TCA) was organized in May 1945 by O. Roy Chalk, a London-born entrepreneur whose parents had emigrated from Russia to England, then moved to New York. Chalk grew up on Manhattan's Upper West Side, worked his way through New York University's night school, earned a law degree, then directed his considerable energies to real estate and construction. Noting the rapid growth of New York City's Puerto Rican population, Chalk decided that a good deal of money could be made by providing low-cost air transportation between New York and San Juan. Pan American Airways, which had a monopoly on the route, catered to business traffic and charged premium prices.

TCA began operations as a nonscheduled carrier in December 1945, using two war-surplus C-47s that Chalk had purchased for $6,000 and converted to civilian airliners. Heavy traffic encouraged Chalk to raise $250,000 and purchase DC-4s, which began flying to the Caribbean in August 1946. Chalk applied to the Civil Aeronautics Board (CAB) for permission to operate scheduled service to San Juan from New York and Miami; however,

the CAB turned him down and awarded the routes to Eastern Air Lines. Undeterred, he acquired three DC-6As, which TCA operated in a high-density seating configuration on charter flights to the Caribbean. The airplanes also enabled TCA to take advantage of military contracts following the outbreak of the Korean War in June 1950.

Chalk continued to seek certification from the CAB but with disappointing results. On June 15, 1956, however, TCA inaugurated biweekly low-fare flights to Puerto Rico under the new Supplemental Air Carrier classification of 1955. Finally, on November 15, 1957, the CAB certified TCA as a regularly scheduled airline, the first time in its history that the board had permitted a supplemental carrier to attain such status. TCA at long last inaugurated scheduled service between New York and San Juan on March 8, 1958.

Certification, however, did not guarantee success. TCA encountered increased competition from Eastern and Pan American, which matched the airline's low fares and flew superior equipment. In 1964, TCA finally entered the jet age when it leased a DC-8F from Seaboard World Airlines for weekend passenger flights to San Juan and Aruba. But TCA continued to fall into debt, even defaulting on payment to its pilots' pension fund.

In January 1970, TCA and American Airlines agreed to merge. Under terms of the arrangement, Chalk netted a reported $18 million in American stock, plus a long-term consultant's contract. American advanced TCA $5 million to keep it operating until the CAB ruled on the merger; it also guaranteed a loan of $7 million to Chalk so that he could meet his payroll. In return, American secured eight unneeded airplanes, plus attractive routes from Washington and New York to Puerto Rico, the Vir-

gin Islands, Haiti, and the Netherlands Antilles. In March 1971, the necessary approvals secured, American absorbed TCA. Over the next six months, American took over first place on the New York-San Juan route.

References:

R. E. G. Davies, *Airlines of the United States since 1914*, revised edition (Washington, D.C.: Smithsonian Institution, 1982);

Robert J. Serling, *Eagle: The Story of American Airlines* (New York: St. Martin's/Marek, 1985).

Transcontinental Air Transport

by George E. Hopkins

Western Illinois University

Transcontinental Air Transport (TAT), which started service in 1929, was a pioneering coast-to-coast passenger airline that combined air and rail transport. Passengers boarded the Pennsylvania Railroad's "Airway Limited" in New York City for an overnight ride to Port Columbus, Ohio, where they enplaned on Ford trimotor aircraft for a daylong flight to Waynoka, Oklahoma. At Waynoka, passengers boarded the Atchison, Topeka, & Santa Fe Railroad for another overnight ride, this time to Clovis, New Mexico. The final leg was again by air, terminating at Los Angeles. Eastbound passengers reversed the process, leaving Los Angeles by air and completing the trip by rail in New York City. Elapsed time for the transcontinental air-rail trip was 48 hours, with a fare of $337 to $403, one way, depending upon the passenger's choice of railroad accommodations. The air segment was single class.

TAT's originator was Clement M. Keys, former editor of the *Wall Street Journal*, protégé of railroad baron James J. Hill, and president of the Curtiss Aeroplane & Motor Company. The airlines of the late 1920s concentrated on mail service, flown by single-engine aircraft. Passengers were not a priority, although the early airlines sometimes offered rudimentary accommodations for intrepid air travelers. Keys believed that new, large, multiengine transports, such as the Ford trimotor and Fokker

F-X, meant that an airline devoted exclusively to carrying passengers might succeed, even without a postal subsidy. In order to make the service as safe as possible, TAT flew only during daylight and over relatively flat terrain.

Organized in May 1928 and capitalized at $5 million, TAT began operations in July 1929. Keys employed Paul Henderson, a former postal official and head of the U.S. Air Mail Service, as vice-president of the line, with veteran airmail pilot Paul F. Collins as general superintendent. The celebrated Charles A. Lindbergh served as technical consultant, allowing the company to use the motto "The Lindbergh Line." Publicity was a corporate priority. Lindbergh symbolically launched the first trip by pressing a button in Los Angeles to start the westbound New York train on July 7, 1929, and he flew the inaugural flight eastbound from Los Angeles the next day, as 100,000 spectators looked on.

TAT set new standards for comfort, speed, and safety. It was deliberately elitist, catering to the most affluent class of business and celebrity travelers. Each aircraft had a kitchen and a uniformed male flight attendant to serve meals. But for all its pioneering efforts to create a luxury passenger service, TAT did not long survive as a separate airline. It fell victim to declining revenues after the stock market crash of 1929, and to the determination of Postmaster General Walter Folger Brown to rationalize the nation's air transportation system. By offering the powerful inducement of a mail contract, Brown forced Keys to accept a merger with Western Air Express (WAE). In July 1930, TAT and WAE became Transcontinental and Western Air, the progenitor of Trans World Airlines. (TWA).

References:
Paul F. Collins, *Tales of an Old Air-Faring Man* (Stevens

Point, Wis.: UWSP Foundation Press, 1983);

R. E. G. Davies, *Airlines of the United States since 1914*, revised edition (Washington, D.C.: Smithsonian Institution, 1982);

George E. Hopkins, "Transcontinental Air Transport," *American Heritage*, 27 (December 1975): 22-28;

TWA Pilots' Master Executive Council, *The Making of an Airline* (N.p.: Privately printed, 1981).

Transocean Air Lines

by Roger D. Launius

*National Aeronautics and
Space Administration*

Transocean Air Lines emerged after World War II as one of the nation's leading supplemental air carriers. Launched on March 18, 1946, by Orvis M. Nelson, a United Air Lines pilot who had seen the possibility of intercontinental commercial air operations while flying during the war under contract with the Air Transport Command, Transocean started up with a profitable subcontract from United Air Lines to make periodic flights from San Francisco to Honolulu for the military services. Assured of initial survival in the highly competitive postwar market, the fledgling carrier quickly developed other clients and diversified its business holdings.

Nelson's forceful efforts led to far-flung operations. Forming a partnership with the nationalized Philippines Air Lines (PAL), he established a shuttle service between the West Coast of the United States and the Philippine Islands that proved both lucrative to Transocean and efficient to PAL. Extensive charter work followed, with numerous flights between Great Britain and Canada in the late 1940s. In November 1948, Transocean opened a twice-daily scheduled service between Rome, Italy, and Caracas, Venezuela.

By 1953 Transocean was the largest of the supplemental carriers, with a fleet of 114 aircraft, more than 3,000 employees, and 28 offices scattered throughout the world. It also performed contract maintenance work for other carriers at 16 locations in Europe and the Pacific as well as at its

headquarters maintenance complex in Oakland, operated a heavy construction company which specialized in building airports, and had begun modest efforts at manufacturing aircraft components.

Despite the diversification, Transocean's primary interest remained air transport, and its biggest customer was the Department of Defense. During the Berlin Airlift of 1948-1959, Transocean operated several routes for the Military Air Transport Service, which was devoting nearly all its resources to Berlin. Later, during the Korean War, it accounted for approximately 10 percent of the military's transpacific airlift.

In 1951 Transocean won a contract to provide air transport for the American trust territories of Micronesia. Using a fleet of four PBY-5A flying boats supplied by the navy, it began scheduled operations on July 1, 1951, flying throughout Micronesia from its base on Guam. This service continued until 1960.

Throughout the latter half of the 1950s, Transocean struggled to overcome governmental restrictions on supplemental carriers, mounting an expensive but ultimately unsuccessful campaign to challenge Pan American's dominance of the transpacific route from the West Coast to Hawaii and Guam. Forced to sell off many of its assets to meet losses, by 1958 it had a fleet of only 12 aircraft. On July 11, 1960, United States Overseas Airlines took over the route network of the bankrupt carrier.

Transocean Curtiss C-46F (courtesy of the William T. Larkins Collection)

References:
R. E. G. Davies, *Airlines of the United States since 1914*, revised edition (Washington, D.C.: Smithsonian Institution, 1982);
Davies, *Rebels and Reformers of the Airways* (Washington, D.C.: Smithsonian Institution, 1987);
"Flying Handyman," *Time*, 52 (November 22, 1948): 92, 94, 96;

Arue Szura, *Folded Wings: A History of Transocean Air Lines* (Missoula, Mont.: Pictorial Histories Publishing Co., 1989);
Richard Thruelsen, *Transocean: The Story of an Unusual Airline* (New York: Holt, 1953).

Trans World Airlines

by Patricia A. Michaelis

Kansas State Historical Society

Trans World Airlines traces its origins to Postmaster General Walter Folger Brown's efforts to rationalize the nation's air transport network. In 1930 Brown made it clear that he wanted only three coast-to-coast air routes. As postal mail contracts were needed for the airlines to survive, operators had no choice but to bow to Brown's wishes. On July 19 a reluctant Western Air Express merged with Transcontinental Air Transport and Pittsburgh Aviation Industries Corporation to form Transcontinental and Western Air, Inc. (TWA). Brown awarded the new company a prized airmail contract on August 25.

TWA inaugurated transcontinental mail service from New York (Newark) to Los Angeles (Glendale) on October 25, 1930. The trip took 36 hours, including a 12-hour overnight stop at Kansas City. Not until November 5, 1932, did TWA begin round-the-clock service on the route, carrying both mail and passengers.

Under the leadership of Jack Frye, TWA contributed significantly to the airline industry's technological development during the 1930s. Known as a "pilots' airline," TWA did pioneering work in radio navigation and high-altitude flying. It also provided the impetus for a new generation of transports, including the Douglas DC-1/DC-2 and the Boeing 307 Stratocruiser. On July 8, 1940, the pressurized Boeing 307 began flying across the country in 13 hours and 40 minutes.

Although a technological success, the airline produced meager profits for its owners during the 1930s. Concerned about plans to cancel developmental work on the Boeing Stratocruiser, Frye persuaded aviation enthusiast and multimillionaire Howard Hughes to invest in the company. By April 1939 Hughes had become TWA's principal stockholder. He not only encouraged Frye to continue the Boeing program, but he also became an enthusiastic supporter of—and contributor to—plans that led to the Lockheed L-049 Constellation. On April 17, 1944, Hughes and Frye flew the first Constellation nonstop from Burbank to Washington, D.C., in 6 hours and 58 minutes.

TWA made a major contribution to military air transport during World War II. Shortly after the Japanese attack on Pearl Harbor in December 1941 the airline formed an Intercontinental Division to operate routes across the North and South Atlantic and to fly high government officials, including President Franklin D. Roosevelt, to destinations around the world. By August 1945 the Intercontinental Division had 1,943 employees and 27 Douglas C-54 transports. It flew 9,528 transocean flights under military contract.

TWA's wartime service was rewarded in July 1945 with authorization to begin scheduled transatlantic passenger service. Despite the protests of Pan American Airways, which wanted to retain its monopoly of international routes, TWA inaugurated a New York-Paris schedule on February 5, 1946. The following month the airline reached Cairo via Rome and Athens. In 1947 it extended service to Bombay. By the time the company changed its corporate name to Trans World Airlines on May 17, 1950, it had indeed achieved a far-flung route system. (However, the title was not exact: TWA did not begin round-the-world service until August 1969.)

The 1950s saw the introduction of faster, longer-range transports on TWA's domestic and international routes. On October 19, 1953, the airline inaugurated the first scheduled nonstop Los Angeles-New York service (eastbound only) with Lockheed Super Constellations, flying from coast to coast in 8 hours. Three years later, on October 2, TWA used the long-range Lockheed 1649A, final version of the triple-tailed airliner, to fly nonstop from New York to Rome. The new Connie also began a polar route from Los Angeles and San Francisco to

Transcontinental and Western Northrup Alpha, 1930 (courtesy of the National Air and Space Museum)

Rome. The age of the piston-engine transport, however, was drawing to a close. On March 20, 1959, TWA began Boeing 707 jet service with a route between New York and San Francisco. Eight months later Boeing 707s started flying from New York to London and Frankfurt.

Purchase of the new jet equipment strained Howard Hughes's considerable financial assets, and he was forced to seek assistance from a group of Wall Street investment bankers. As a condition for their support, the bankers had forced Hughes to place his majority voting interest in TWA into a trust that they could control. In June 1961 the new president of TWA, Charles Tillinghast, sued Hughes under the antitrust laws, charging him with monopolizing the purchase of aircraft for his personal benefit. A lengthy legal battled ensued. After nearly 13 years of adjudication, the U.S. Supreme Court ruled in favor of Hughes, and he eventually received a judgment for over $1 million in legal costs. By that time, however, he had sold his TWA stock for a handsome profit, receiving $546.5 million in 1966.

While the legal battles were being fought, Tillinghast was attempting to diversify TWA as a way to offset the cyclical nature of the airline business. In 1967 TWA acquired Hilton International;

it operated the worldwide hotel chain as a wholly owned subsidiary. Later purchases included the Canteen Corporation (a vending machine company) and Century 21 (a real estate firm). Eventually, on January 1, 1979, TWA formed a holding company called the Trans World Corporation which assumed ownership of the airline and its various subsidiaries.

The airline went through difficult economic times during the 1970s. Desperately short of cash in 1975, TWA was forced to sell six Boeing 747s for a fraction of their value. Attempts to reduce costs produced only marginal improvements. The Airline Deregulation Act of 1978 further weakened TWA, already troubled by high labor costs and unproductive routes.

In 1985, corporate raider Carl Icahn purchased a controlling interest in TWA, which lost $193 million during the year. Intent on reviving a failing enterprise, Icahn reached an agreement with the airline's pilots and mechanics for wage concessions, abandoned unproductive Pacific routes, and purchased Ozark Airlines, TWA's chief rival in the Midwest. Although TWA recorded a profit in 1987 and 1988, the heavily leveraged company lost $298.5 million in 1989, including interest expenses of $193.9 million. The survival of the airline re-

Trans World Lockheed L-1011 (courtesy of the National Air and Space Museum)

mained an open question as the last decade of the 20th century began.

References:
"Chest Expansion of an Airline," *Fortune*, 31 (April 1945): 132-138, 192, 195-196, 199;

Ralph S. Damon, *TWA: Nearly Three Decades in the Air* (New York: Newcomen Society in North America, 1952);

R. E. G. Davies, *Airlines of the United States since 1914*, revised edition (Washington, D.C.: Smithsonian Institution, 1982);

Davies, *Rebels and Reformers of the Airways* (Washington, D.C.: Smithsonian Institution, 1987);

John McDonald, "Howard Hughes's Biggest Surprise," *Fortune*, 74 (July 1, 1966): 119-120, 169-171;

Charles J. V. Murphy and Thomas A. Wise, "The Problem of Howard Hughes," *Fortune*, 59 (January 1959): 79-83, 171-172, 174-175;

Robert J. Serling, *Howard Hughes' Airline: An Informal History of TWA* (New York: St. Martin's/Marek, 1983);

TWA Pilots' Master Executive Council, *TWA: A Pictorial History* (N.p.: Privately printed, 1981).

Archives:
The Trans World Airlines Archives are at company headquarters in Kansas City, Missouri.

Juan T. Trippe

(June 27, 1899 - April 3, 1981)

by Wesley Phillips Newton

Auburn University

CAREER: Bond salesman, Lee, Higginson & Company (1921-1923); president and general manager, Long Island Airways (1923-1925); managing director, Colonial Air Transport (1925-1927); managing director, Aviation Corporation of America (1927); president and general manager (1927-1968), chief executive officer (1927-1939, 1940-1968), chairman, Pan American Airways/Pan American World Airways (1940-1968).

Juan Terry Trippe, one of the founders of the U.S. aviation industry and a pioneer in international air commerce, was born in the resort town of Sea Bright, New Jersey, on June 27, 1899, the second son of Charles White and Lucy Adeline Trippe. After the death of his older brother in a train accident, two-month-old Juan became the focus of his parents' ambitions, even after the birth some 13 months later of another child, Katherine Louise. Lucy Trippe inherited from a half sister also killed in the accident property amounting to almost $200,000, a considerable sum in that day and the source of a rising tide of good fortune for the family. Charles White Trippe, formerly a railroad surveyor, adopted the more lucrative profession of investment banking and moved the family to New York City; he soon opened a bank and purchased a seat on the New York Stock Exchange. Besides managing her husband and children with great efficiency, Lucy Trippe invested in undeveloped properties, which later she sold as retreats for the wealthy and prominent. Trippe's parents did not neglect their son's education but stressed the practical aspect of learning and encouraged Trippe to participate in sports, which they felt promoted lasting social bonds.

By the time Trippe reached age ten in 1909 the sky had become his obsession. That summer the French aviators Latham and Blériot competed to become the first to fly across the English Channel—

Juan T. Trippe (courtesy of Pan American World Airways)

on his attempt Latham's engine gave out over the water, and a week later Blériot droned all the way from the French side to Dover. Around Central Park Trippe flew a large, rubber-band-powered model he built of Latham's "Antoinette." Later that same year Charles White Trippe took his son to see the fragile planes of the day demonstrate their speed and maneuverability over lower New York Bay. Trippe watched Wilbur Wright circle the Statue of Liberty and execute a figure eight that took him back to his starting point. He later dated his desire to learn to fly from the day of that barnstorming exhibition.

Educated in private schools, Trippe was not an exceptional student. At the age of fourteen he went to the Hill School, a private boarding academy near Philadelphia that was not quite as prestigious as Groton, to which his childhood friend Cornelius Vanderbilt "Sonny" Whitney had been sent. Called "Trippy" by classmates, the somewhat aloof Trippe became a debater and a lineman for the football team.

The United States entered World War I in the spring of the year Trippe graduated from the Hill School, but the war did not immediately affect his college plans. In the fall he went to Yale, which like other universities of the time was shedding its traditions and turning out increasing numbers of lawyers, financiers, and businessmen. The husky young man played for the freshman football team, which meant he was also required to serve in the campus ROTC unit. His lack of prep school achievement, however, condemned him to a lesser academic world at Yale. He studied in the university's Sheffield Scientific School, majoring in engineering. Not even the major applied science division of the university, the "Sheff" was for the "lesser breeds" ethnically as well as academically. There Trippe rubbed elbows with the majority of Yale's small number of Jews, Middle Easterners, and Asians in addition to most of the Anglo-Saxon lads of low economic status who attended Yale on scholarship. Trippe did manage to pledge to Delta Psi fraternity, where he gained a reputation for reticence among his brothers, who called him "Mummy." Despite his reserved manner, Trippe would occasionally enter into a debate over some issue or other and carry the argument through sheer persistence—a technique he was to use to advantage in his future career.

Trippe was at Yale only about a month when the developing war in Europe finally interrupted his education. On the day in November 1917 when Yale's freshmen football team defeated the squad from Harvard, Trippe and several teammates vowed to enlist in the U.S. Marine Corps to become aviation trainees. At the recruiting office Trippe failed the eye exam, but through connections his father secured him an appointment with Assistant Secretary of the Navy Franklin D. Roosevelt, who arranged a second try for Trippe. Since Trippe had memorized the smallest line of the chart in advance, he easily passed the exam and prepared to enter the Marine Corps. Somewhat belatedly he learned that the corps itself did not offer flight training. He managed to shift over to the navy and went to ground

school at the Massachusetts Institute of Technology and then to flight school, soloing over Long Island in the summer of 1918. In September he was commissioned an ensign in the Naval Reserve and assigned to Pensacola, Florida, for advanced training as a night bomber pilot. He was preparing for service in France when the Armistice intervened.

Early in 1919 Trippe returned to Yale, no longer a callow member of the class of 1920 but a veteran naval officer. Yale too had changed. The environment was more egalitarian. Entrance requirements had been standardized, all freshmen were required to take a common curriculum before specializing in their sophomore years, and Sheffield was slated to become Yale's sole professional school for the applied sciences beginning in the fall of 1921. Sports again took up much of Trippe's time. He played guard on the varsity football team and also rowed for the Yale crew, where he renewed his acquaintance with Sonny Whitney.

When a back injury forced Trippe from the football team and the crew, he took up golf and became a skilled player. Then a more cerebral activity caught his attention. To the fifth issue of the Yale magazine the *Graphic* he contributed an article on the coming prospects for transatlantic flight. Soon he became a member of the magazine's editorial board, and he went on to serve as its editor. Though the *Graphic* was not a leader among campus periodicals, it was a success as long as Trippe was associated with it. He became a meticulous and demanding editor and in the process learned a great deal about administrative organization.

What Trippe enjoyed doing most in college was flying. He was one of a group of 50 ex-military flyers who reconstituted the Yale Aero Club, which before the war had been the exclusive province of the Yale College elite. After the war bonds of military service and wartime flying took precedence over social and school ties. As secretary, Trippe was the only noncombat veteran to serve on the club's executive committee, which included navy ace David Ingalls. Trippe also served as secretary of an association of collegiate flying clubs and in 1920 copiloted a Curtiss Jenny to victory in a 25-mile race sponsored by the association.

After the death of his father during the summer before his senior year of 1920-1921, a sobered Trippe took over management of the family's bank, on its way to failure in the troubled postwar business climate, and spent his spare time flying and working for the *Graphic*. He took courses in business and engineering, but his grades still were not impressive. When he graduated from Yale, on the verge of twenty-two years of age, seemingly destined to follow in his father's footsteps, he accepted a position as a bond salesman with the Wall Street firm of Lee, Higginson & Company.

The major difference between Trippe and most of his fellows starting out on Wall Street was that they had more money. Trippe was not poverty stricken; however, his mother's real estate investments yielded a comfortable income. He lived in her apartment on East 76th Street, and joined the proper clubs and attended cocktail parties and other obligatory social events. After putting in a five- or six-hour day selling bonds he would head for the golf links, emulating his peers. But all this came to bore him during his two years on Wall Street. The one thing that sustained his interest was flying, a pastime he had in common with several of his stockbroker friends, including John A. Hambleton, from a family of Baltimore investment bankers who had once been in business with relatives of Trippe. On the weekends Trippe and Hambleton rented a secondhand flying boat and went stunting.

Hambleton was two years older than Trippe. He had attended Harvard and in 1917 had joined the U.S. Army, where he had done something Trippe had yearned to do—he had flown in combat on the Western Front as a pursuit pilot. He had been wounded and twice decorated with the Distinguished Service Cross. In many ways the two close friends were opposites. Hambleton was fair, lean, open, friendly, and modest. Trippe was dark, stocky, taciturn, aggressive to the point of arrogance, but careful around elders who could advance him. One of Trippe's most persuasive characteristics was his unexpected smile, which could both captivate and intimidate.

In the spring of 1923 Trippe entered the aviation business incorporating Long Island Airways with a capitalization of $5,000. He had carefully followed announcements in the papers about the sale of surplus military aircraft. Perhaps influencing his move was news of a promising airline service called Aeromarine Airways, which was flying surplus navy seaplanes on the Great Lakes in warm weather and between Key West and Havana in the winter. Trippe purchased seven single-engine amphibians equipped with pontoons for $500 each. Half the capital he put up himself and half he ac-

quired from wealthier young Wall Street friends: Sonny Whitney, William Rockefeller, and William Vanderbilt. Whitney and Rockefeller had flown in the war. Key to their support was Trippe's confidence that even though commercial aviation was experiencing the rough sledding of a pioneer endeavor, it was bound to succeed.

Long Island Airways operated in the summers of 1923 and 1924. Trippe rented an abandoned hangar at the former naval station at Rockaway Beach. He soon ceased to do much flying himself, hiring ex-military flyers. He had larger engines put on his planes in order to have the power to carry two passengers instead of one. From the outset he often tinkered with the design or configuration of planes that he owned or had on order from a manufacturer. Also, to learn the essentials of ground transportation and how these might be applied to air transport, he spent much time in the New York Public Library reading lengthy regulatory volumes. He secured letters of introduction from the influential fathers of friends so he could enter the otherwise closed inner chambers of great shippers such as the Pennsylvania Railroad. He lobbied for better terminal and landing facilities before a congressional subcommittee. In spite of his efforts, Long Island Airways failed to turn a profit. Late in 1924, as the equipment began to deteriorate, he sold his usable planes to his pilots. Trippe was ready to move on to larger possibilities.

These appeared in the form of a fundamental change in the nature of airmail delivery. With the passage of the Air Mail (Kelly) Act of 1925 the U.S. Post Office turned over its airmail service to private contractors, planning to award contracts for important feeder lines before any bidding was solicited for the main transcontinental route. Trippe incorporated several companies for the specific purpose of bidding on airmail contracts. Two of these, Alaska Air Transport and Buffalo Airlines, did not amount to much. Another, Eastern Air Transport, incorporated in Delaware to bid on the New York-Boston feeder contract, had more substance. Trippe went to Washington to engage in a tactic he often repeated in the future—lobbying for government largess and favors. Postal authorities suggested that he get together with a second group, Colonial Airlines, which was set to bid on the New York-Boston route.

Colonial Airlines was composed of a group of New England investors led by the governor of Connecticut, John Trumbull. Trippe changed the name of Eastern to Colonial Air Transport, and it was in this name that the bid was submitted for both groups, despite the fact that Trumbull's Colonial Airlines was considered the surviving corporation—perhaps as a face-saving gesture.

On October 7, 1925, Colonial Air Transport easily won the contract for the New York-to-Boston route, Contract Air Mail (CAM) 1. From that day until the inaugural flight nine months later, Trippe labored to create the physical part of the airline—leasing fields; hiring pilots, mechanics, and other personnel; and procuring aircraft. Also he promoted Colonial stock on Wall Street. Most investors who subscribed did so under the condition that Colonial seek the Key West-Havana mail route, vacant since Aeromarine Airways had failed. Trippe not only was amenable to this idea, he also had been giving it thought himself. The demise of Aeromarine offered some lessons: the mail contract had been only for southbound mail; after government support slackened, public interest did not remain high enough to sustain operations. Also, Aeromarine's equipment proved inadequate. On one of his Washington visits, Trippe discussed the Key West-Havana route with W. Irving Glover, second assistant postmaster general whose province was airmail. Glover seemed eager that a company such as Colonial be in line for the contract when it came up for bids.

In December 1925 Trippe persuaded famed aircraft designer Anthony Fokker, whose New Jersey factory was building two trimotors for Colonial, to make a demonstration flight to Havana, where Trippe had secured exclusive landing rights from the president of Cuba, Gerardo Machado. The rights were to give Trippe great future bargaining power.

The flight to Havana and back symbolized two things that the Trumbull faction had come to resent about Trippe. First, he had contracted not only for two Fokker trimotors but also two Ford trimotors as well. The construction of such large planes took time. Second, his ambitions for route expansion conflicted with their desire to concentrate on CAM-1 to make an immediate profit. In October 1926 Trippe persuaded the board to accept as president of Colonial retired army brigadier general John F. O'Ryan, a man with some experience in the field of land transportation. Trippe wanted a person the board would respect, but one who could ab-

sorb most of the heat and one he could control—in short, a figurehead.

Trippe's next goal was to win the contract for the New York-Chicago leg of the main transcontinental route, with bids due in January 1927. Again he ignored the New England directors' desire to concentrate on servicing CAM-1. He could not be a standpatter, because his wealthy friends and expectant backers wanted bigger things. This brought to a head a slowly simmering antipathy between Trippe and his supposed figurehead president. O'Ryan saw things the way the other directors did: Colonial needed to show a profit before expanding. From the beginning of operations the company had operated in the red. The expected revenue from airmail had not materialized. Nevertheless, Trippe went ahead and submitted a bid. Trumbull, however, placed the matter before Colonial's shareholders. Trippe lost by a four-vote margin out of 100 cast, and the bid was withdrawn. Trippe resigned from the board, his chance to become a prime mover on the domestic side of the American airline industry seriously, perhaps fatally, damaged. Colonial survived without the contract, eventually to become a component of American Airlines.

One of the most frustrating aspects of Trippe's defeat was personal. Since the summer of 1924 he had been courting a member of a wealthy and socially prestigious family, Elizabeth "Betty" Stettinius. They met through her brother, Edward R. Stettinius, Jr., the future secretary of state of the United States. Trippe was expected to succeed at business before they could be married. Although disappointed by Trippe's setback, in January 1927 Betty pledged her fidelity for as long as it took him to make his mark.

William Rockefeller, Sonny Whitney, and John Hambleton tried to salvage something from their group's investment in Colonial, but they had to accept losses. In the meantime, Trippe solicited funds for a new air corporation, one that he intended to become involved in various facets of aviation. Learning that a young ex-airmail pilot he had met a year or so before was planning to fly nonstop to Paris and win the $25,000 Orteig prize, Trippe went to Roosevelt Field, Long Island, on a rainy morning, May 20, 1927, and watched a silver monoplane struggle down the runway and barely clear the wires at the other end. When "the flying fool" returned as the "Lone Eagle," Trippe and his major partners in the contemplated new company agreed they would have to make contact with him. Although Charles A. Lindbergh declined a job offer, his flight to Paris had provided the spark for something that had been building but was yet to ignite—a boom in the aviation business and related frenzy of speculation on Wall Street. Trippe's friends and some other rich young men did not hold the Colonial fiasco against him. He still had the ability to convey a vision, aided by the excitement in the wake of Lindbergh's epic deed. Averell Harriman and William Beckers subscribed $50,000 each; Whitney, $49,000; Robert Thach, $30,000; William Vanderbilt, William Rockefeller, Hambleton, and Trippe himself, $25,000 each. Five other initial investors contributed smaller sums.

On June 2, 1927, Trippe, Whitney, Hambleton, Rockefeller, and Sherman Fairchild incorporated the Aviation Corporation of America. Whitney was elected chairman of the board. Trippe named managing director, gained permission from the board to submit bids for any airmail routes he felt worthwhile. He had surmised that a relatively new corporation named Pan American Airways seemed to have a favored position for the upcoming award of a Key West-Havana route, and he got permission to invest in it. He was soon aware that a third significant company interested in the contract was being chartered that June—Atlantic, Gulf, and Caribbean. The three rivals, with the encouragement of the Post Office Department, were forced to work out a merger over a period of several weeks.

During the negotiations a rival aviation entrepreneur, Richard Hoyt, after failing to absorb Pan American Airways, approached Trippe. Apparently Hoyt either knew in advance or learned in their face-to-face meeting that Trippe already held landing rights in Cuba. This knowledge and the youthful Trippe's firm stand led to a bargain in which the Aviation Corporation of America came out at least on equal terms. It depended, of course, on some kind of deal with Pan American Airways; if this took place the corporate name of the holder of the airmail contract was to be Atlantic, Gulf, and Caribbean, and Hoyt was to be chairman of the board of the merged companies. Trippe was to be general manager and his group was to hold the controlling shares.

The arrangement was put into effect in October 1927 and generally held up. The losers were John Montgomery and the Bevier brothers, who were pressured out. It continued to hold up when a

corporate reorganization took place in the summer of 1928 for the purpose of securing a vast increase in capitalization in the form of watered stock. The inflation of aviation stock on Wall Street was well underway. Hoyt remained chairman of the board of the restructured holding company, renamed the Aviation Corporation of the Americas, with Trippe general manager of the operating subsidiary, Pan American Airways, Inc. Corporate headquarters were in New York City.

After the original Aviation Corporation of America had been chartered in June 1927, Whitney, Hambleton, and Trippe received "management stock" in lieu of salaries. Trippe received over half the amount, which was based on time spent actually managing. His later wealth was based not on a salary but on the amount of stock he came to possess. The same was true for other patriarchs of the U.S. airline industry, such as C. E. Woolman of Delta. In the reorganization of 1928, Trippe secured the option to purchase the largest share of new stock allotted his group, just as Hoyt had the same privilege among his followers. Trippe gained the right to over 37,000 shares at the inflated price of $15 each. Even Lucy Trippe purchased 100 shares. Her son, on paper, was becoming a millionaire.

The U.S. mail contracts for Latin America all went to Pan American Airways. This constituted a profound change of policy on the part of the U.S. government, based largely on a fear of the threat posed by European-controlled commercial aviation in the vicinity of the Panama Canal. It was also due in part to the lobbying skill of J. T. Trippe, as he preferred to be known; he despised the name Juan and had no great affinity for Latin America, although he allowed letters to be sent out typed by a bilingual secretary and signed "Juan Trippe."

Postal officials were quickly swayed by Trippe. They worked to obtain legislation that would permit them to evade competitive bidding, and when they got it in 1928 the door was open for a "chosen instrument" of postal policy. The War and Navy Departments, with the impetus provided by Gen. H. H. "Hap" Arnold and several military "goodwill" flights to Latin America, were rarely hesitant to provide what aid they possibly could to the line that soon showed its effectiveness in competition with the Germans and French.

It was with the State Department that Trippe had his most difficult time. Some of its personnel,

Trippe (left) receiving the Collier Trophy from President Franklin D. Roosevelt for establishing Pan American's transpacific route, August 1937. Thomas H. Beck, president of Collier's Weekly, *looks on (courtesy of Pan American World Airways).*

both in Washington and in the field, seemed bound by the traditional policy of neutrality between competing American economic interests on foreign soil. Trippe worked hard to overcome this problem, particularly when he came up against the stubborn Ralph A. O'Neill, who, in partnership with Trippe's old enemies John Montgomery and Richard Bevier, began to establish an efficient, well-equipped line, New York, Rio & Buenos Aires (NYRBA), along the east coast of South America. In the end the Post Office Department dealt a fatal blow to NYRBA by withholding the airmail contract for service to the South American east coast until a weakening NYRBA sold out to Pan American.

Trippe early realized the vital need for good communications if Pan American was to expand throughout Latin America and ultimately across the oceans. Surface communications were functioning well in the 1920s but air-ground communications were still in the experimental stage. Perhaps his early radio training added to Trippe's incentive to have a system developed. He pursued and finally secured the services of New Yorker Hugo C. Leuteritz, an engineer with Radio Corporation of America (RCA) who had been trained by the navy.

Leuteritz had begun work on the problems of air-ground communications and radio navigation even before coming to Pan American. He devised a system using the loop antenna to be used as a direction finder. Pan American pilots at first scorned the device, but a crash at sea (in which Leuteritz himself was almost killed) coupled with Leuteritz's patient illustrations and explanations gradually won them over. Blunt with his superiors, he convinced Trippe that an RCA-developed system was inadequate and that he could do a better job.

By 1931 Trippe was more or less the master of Latin American commercial skies and was ready to take on the vaster skies that overlay the Pacific and the Atlantic. His was still the sole U.S. international airline and would remain so throughout the 1930s, when he undertook the spanning of the oceans. His competitors, and only then for the Atlantic routes, were European.

Trippe realized that the Fokker trimotors, Ford trimotors, and even the consolidated Commodore flying boats that were part of the NYRBA takeover were not fully adequate for Latin American operations. He sought something that would not only fly easily across the various stretches of the Gulf-

469

Caribbean and even across expanses of jungle and mountain but also could challenge the oceans—a passenger carrier rather than a cargo carrier. The designer he finally selected to build a "clipper," as he would call it and its successors, was a Russian émigré, Igor Sikorsky. Sikorsky had built the first four-engine bomber, during World War I in Russia; had experimented with helicopters; and in 1928 had a factory in Connecticut that produced a trim amphibian, the S-38. Sikorsky's idea for a clipper was a larger amphibian, which Lindbergh opposed but gradually gave in to and which became the S-40. In November 1931 Lindbergh flew an S-40 on its first commercial flight, from Pan American Operational Center Miami with ultimate destination Panama, with Sikorsky aboard to check things out. On the return trip, during the leg from Jamaica to Miami, night overtook them as a result of a rare Lindbergh miscalculation and they had to land at Miami in virtual darkness in a plane not equipped for night flying. The S-40 hit the water with a jarring impact that shook everybody up. Lindbergh was chagrined because of his error and Sikorsky because of his cumbersome design. The result was a collaboration that resulted in the first true ocean spanner, the S-42.

Trippe, who wanted to go in all directions across the oceans at the same time, sent out pathfinders to explore the possibilities. At his own initiative, Charles, with Anne, Lindbergh went north to the Orient in 1931 from Washington, D.C., touching Point Barrow, Alaska, before landing in Russian territory, Japan, and China. In 1933 the Lindberghs explored a northerly route across the Atlantic, going on to Scandinavia, Russia, England, France, Switzerland, Portugal, Azores, Cape Verde Islands, Brazil, the Caribbean, and Miami. Lindbergh had a mixed report about the northern route to the Orient, apparently more bad than good. Trippe, however, was encouraged enough to acquire two small airlines in Alaska and another in China.

Lindbergh felt that it was feasible to establish a service across the northernmost route of the Atlantic in the summer, with stops at Greenland and then a longer haul from Iceland to Scotland. On the second flight he had investigated part of a southerly route that Trippe was considering as an alternative, namely, Bermuda-Azores-Lisbon, perhaps flying from Newfoundland to the Azores and Portugal in warm weather and switching from Newfoundland to Bermuda in the cold.

Trippe earlier had negotiated a tripartite agreement with Britain's Imperial Airways and France's Aeropostale for service across one or more of the Atlantic routes. However, by 1934 the agreement had collapsed. Reluctantly, Trippe turned to the Pacific. As the weather in Alaska seemed forbidding, Trippe rejected the northern route in favor of one across the central Pacific. After poring over maps, he selected Wake Island as the next logical base beyond Hawaii, and then on to the Philippines and China. Meanwhile problems with the potential clipper developed. Tests by Lindbergh revealed that the S-42 could barely reach Hawaii under ideal conditions. It was back to the factory for range-stretching alterations. Trouble was also developing in the sea of politics during 1934. A special Senate committee chaired by Hugo L. Black was probing relentlessly into the award of airmail and ocean mail contracts by the previous Republican administrations. Pan American Airways was the only U.S. airline to escape cancellation of its contracts in the watershed changes in the American aviation industry that came in the wake of the Black committee findings. The hearings, however, did tarnish its reputation.

Trippe responded to these challenges with the tried-and-true methods of having powerful friends lobby on his and Pan American's behalf as well as on shrewd and persistent negotiations that resulted in the challengers selling out or being absorbed. A survey expedition went out to establish stepping-stones for crossing the Pacific. With pioneer Pan American pilot, the legendary Captain Edwin C. "Eddie" Musick at the controls, test flights of the improved S-42 took place in the Caribbean early in 1935. Further tests took place off the coast of San Francisco. The first survey flight left for Pearl Harbor in April with Musick in command. It landed safely to great acclaim. In October 1935 Postmaster General James Farley awarded the Pacific mail contract to Pan American. In November, with Musick at the controls, a new and much superior flying boat, the Martin M-130, dubbed by Trippe on acceptance "China Clipper," took off from San Francisco on the first scheduled service to Hawaii, amidst appropriate fanfare that included newsreel cameras, network radio coverage, and a speech by Trippe emphasizing Pan American's "chosen instrument" role without actually using the term.

Trippe did not allow his attention to be diverted from the Atlantic for long. He and Imperial Airways director general G. E. Woods-Humphrey got along, even though the former aimed for profit and the latter to please his imperial masters. In 1936 they signed an agreement for a joint transatlantic service, a "square deal," which in effect assured one another of monopoly. Trippe also signed an agreement in 1936 with the newest of the European state airlines, Air France, for a joint New York-Paris service. The first line actually to demonstrate a transatlantic service was the German DLH, which received permission from Washington to try something off New York City it had experimented with off South America, the launching of mail planes from a mother ship to the nearby shore. Washington, however, had no intention of allowing the Nazi government permanent extensive landing rights.

Despite French and German efforts to take part, transatlantic flying would be a British-American venture. Most of the essential bases and landing rights were controlled by the latter two. Still, implementation was fraught with problems. It was not until April 1937 that Great Britain granted Pan American, through Washington, monopolistic landing rights to the United Kingdom, Canada, Ireland, and Bermuda. In a separate agreement with Portugal, Pan American gained monopolistic landing rights in the Azores.

Another problem developed over the clipper. In 1936 Trippe had decided that transatlantic service required a bigger, more powerful, new flying boat. Glenn Martin was furious, for he had lost money on the M-130 and wanted at least a chance to recoup by building an expanded version of the seaplane. Sikorsky took the same position. Trippe, however, turned to Boeing.

Further troubles appeared on several fronts. The route across the Central American area lost money, draining profits from the Latin American service. At the same time Trippe's efforts to establish a route across the South Pacific were hindered by various difficulties and cost the life of Musick, whose S-42 exploded on a survey flight to Australia. In the United States serious opposition to Trippe arose both within the government and inside his own board of directors. Joseph P. Kennedy, chairman of the newly created Maritime Commission, attempted to bring Trippe's enterprise under maritime regulations and to encourage shipping lines to establish competitive airline subsidiaries. With the support of the revived interdepartmental aeronautical committee, Trippe kept Pan American clear of the

Maritime Commission. A potentially major rival, however, emerged with the creation by American Export Steamship Corporation of an aviation subsidiary, American Export Airlines.

One of the biggest threats to Pan American's monopoly came from the Civil Aeronautics Board Act of 1938. At the outset Trippe concentrated his lobbying efforts on having international airlines along with domestic lines included under the act rather than under the authority of some agency such as the Maritime Commission. He especially did not want domestic lines encouraged to intrude on the international scene. His representatives bombarded legislators and relevant members of the executive branch with unsigned memoranda and dramatic newsletters highlighting Pan American's deeds and contributions. Trippe appealed directly to President Roosevelt, urging him to place final authority for international routes in the hands of the chief executive. He was successful in this bit of lobbying, trusting in his ability to sway American chief executives in the future. In the final analysis, Trippe got half of what he wanted with the passage of the act: U.S. international airlines fell under the regulatory jurisdiction of the Civil Aeronautics Authority (CAA). Pan American was eligible for a "certificate of convenience and necessity" for its existing routes as long as it operated the service efficiently, and its passenger and cargo rates were to be set in the give-and-take of international competition (not by the CAA as originally proposed). Trippe promised not to conduct private diplomacy outside government channels. Most threatening, however, was that the act directed the CAA to give consideration to stimulating competition in both the domestic and international spheres in the future if it seemed to serve the commercial and security interests of the nation.

On March 14, 1939, Trippe was unexpectedly removed as chief executive officer of Pan American. Chairman of the Board Whitney led the coup and was elected the new chief executive officer. Prudently, Trippe chose not to engage in a stockholder fight. Whitney had him outvoted, Trippe having cashed in half his stock for such things as trust funds for his children. One of the factors that caused the board to take a dimmer view of Trippe was the matter of the Atlantic service. It had not begun because the new clipper was not ready until the beginning of 1939, a year after it had been promised by Boeing. It had not begun also because the British, having trouble procuring a suitable aircraft, stalled the inauguration of the joint service. Criticism in the United States about the monopolistic nature of the "square deal" was intensifying. But the situation improved when the Boeing 314 was ready and Trippe and the British agreed to eliminate the exclusivity feature of their agreement, in turn eliminating Pan American's obligation to wait on Imperial. On March 3, 1939, Eleanor Roosevelt christened the "Yankee Clipper" and Trippe spoke over network radio, comparing Pan American's deeds with those of the Yankee clipper ships of the 19th century. In May the first scheduled airmail to Europe was inaugurated; in June the first scheduled passenger service followed.

Trippe had managed to gain control of three airlines in three different foreign countries that gave Pan American Airways footholds in key places, although the nature of these footholds and of their operations was somewhat different. One of these airlines was in China (China National Aviation Corporation), another was in Mexico (Compañia Mexicana Aviación), and the third was SCADTA in Colombia. It was the circumstances of its control that brought one of two grave crises for Pan American in the early days of World War II, crises that summoned all of Trippe's shrewdness and manipulative talent. The other crisis involved the first bona fide American threat to Trippe's part of the transatlantic shuttle.

Colombians had joined SCADTA increasingly in the 1930s but Germans and a few Austrians, including the airline's president, Peter Paul von Bauer, still formed the administrative and operational core. The secret bargain, by which Pan American obtained a majority interest in the company in 1930, was still unknown to most Colombians. In the United States Trippe had at some point in the 1930s informed President Roosevelt and apparently reassured him about the arrangement. Some officials in the State Department who knew were uneasy about it the whole time. But the situation drifted and SCADTA deteriorated until war loomed. Trippe was then assailed on several sides. Von Bauer again wanted financial resuscitation, the U.S. military chiefs wanted the Germans out of SCADTA, and the State Department pressed Trippe for details of the arrangement. A persistent opponent of Trippe and other Pan American officials was the new U.S. ambassador to Colombia, Spruille Braden, a bull-like man who insisted that SCADTA was an immediate threat to the Panama Canal.

When Trippe finally confessed the details, Braden accused him of being pro-Nazi. Trippe felt obliged to send an emissary to the Colombian chief executive with the news that SCADTA was owned by Pan American. The president's most immediate reaction was to strip von Bauer of his recently acquired Colombian citizenship. The situation continued to drift for several months, for Trippe was no longer in charge at Pan American.

After war erupted in Europe, Washington pressured the various Latin American countries with Axis-connected airlines to nationalize them. The pressure was particularly heavy on Colombia, but with anti-U.S. sentiment to placate, sentiment dating from the loss of Panama at the turn of the century, the Colombia government resisted. With the return of Trippe to the status of chief executive officer at Pan American in January 1940, he was ready to see SCADTA nationalized but not immediately, as desired by the State, War, and Navy Departments. For one thing, he wanted to arrange for Pan American to recoup its investment; for another, Colombian public sentiment had to be prepared; and finally, Trippe had to convince his board. He seemed reluctant to hurt the Germans in SCADTA; also, they would be expensive to replace. Braden himself was ready for a phased nationalization. The Colombian government accepted the idea after the Nazi Blitzkrieg in Europe in the spring of 1940. By then Trippe was convinced of the necessity for swifter action, and he formulated a plan, which included readying a corps of American airline specialists to be hastily recruited, sneaking them into Colombia, and suddenly springing them on the SCADTA bases, backed by Colombian troops. This was accomplished in May 1940, and, as breathtakingly as Trippe had been removed from command at Pan American, the Germans and von Bauer were removed from SCADTA. Pan American was given majority stock in the nationalized company, renamed AVIANCA, with the Colombia government having the option to purchase these shares when it could afford to and convert AVIANCA into a fully Colombian state line. In time this was done.

Trippe then had to deal with the crisis that threatened Pan American's unofficial monopoly of Latin American and transatlantic routes. Pan American soon went head-to-head with American Export Steamship Lines and its subsidiary, American Export Airlines, in another classic duel bearing some resemblance to that fought against NYRBA. The big difference this time was that American Export had more official support, including the backing of the president and the State, Post Office, and War Departments. The struggle demonstrated that Trippe could still succeed even against great odds; but it was the zenith of his long drive to maintain a monopoly of American international airline business. In 1940, to enter the prosperous Latin American market, American Export attempted to acquire TACA, an airline located in Central America that had been built from scratch by New Zealand native Lowell Yerex. Trippe had his people in Central America move against TACA, while Yerex was in the United States to sell his airline to the Pan American foe. There were suddenly rival services, officials turned cold, contracts were canceled, and facilities were illegally sequestered. Overnight a once progressive TACA became a shell, nothing on which to base a request to the Civil Aeronautics Board (CAB) for certification to fly anywhere. The CAB did, however, grant American Export Airlines a certificate for transatlantic service. The State Department felt these acts hurt the United States' image in Central America and called Trippe to account. Trippe attempted to obscure the real issue by talking about threats to the Panama Canal against which Pan American Airways served as the main shield. The stroke that ended the interrogation came when the Pan American counsel inquired as to what authority the State Department had to challenge the business conduct abroad of a private American company in time of peace.

The contest was decided in Congress in 1941, after intense lobbying from both sides over whether an appropriation for an American Export transatlantic airmail service should be cut out or retained. When the debate in the Senate seemed to be going Pan American's way, Postmaster General George C. Walker tried to force Trippe and his associates out of the contest by threatening him with criminal antitrust prosecution. Trippe refused to bow. The final vote in the Senate was close, but the appropriation was eliminated.

Even while this controversy was in progress, President Roosevelt approached Trippe with a request that Pan American undertake, with government funding, to build 21 airports throughout Latin America to help counter the mounting Axis threat to the Western Hemisphere. At first Trippe refused and continued resisting official pressure while he weighed the pros and cons, at length deciding

the pros outweighed the cons. The airport construction program was underway when the Japanese bombed Pearl Harbor. This construction was but the first of several operations that were directly part of the defense and war effort. The company's commercial activities after Pearl Harbor were conducted mainly in Latin America.

Trippe did not wait long to give an answer to a similar request from Winston Churchill. The prime minister wanted Pan American to undertake construction of an airway system between South America and North Africa. Trippe ordered subordinates to do this as quickly as feasible. In addition to assisting the military effort against the Afrika Korps, such a system offered the prospect of widening Pan American's postwar air routes.

Trippe's uneven responses to situations and people were graphically illustrated by how he treated Charles A. Lindbergh and company executive Erwin Balluder. Lindbergh had thoroughly alienated the Roosevelt administration with his America First activities and was refused a chance to reenter the Army Air Forces, from which he had resigned before the war. He then turned to Trippe for an opportunity to play an important role in Pan American's military-related operations. Trippe stalled and finally told Lindbergh the White House objected, thus it was best to wait for the climate to improve. However, when the White House wanted Trippe to get rid of Balluder, an American citizen with German parentage, an anti-Semite, and an admirer of German culture, Trippe defended his subordinate and refused to dismiss him, although placing some restraints on him. Trippe's critics have pointed out that Lindbergh had remained neutral during the temporary replacement of Trippe by Whitney as chief executive officer; Balluder had been loyal.

In 1942 Hap Arnold, commanding the Army Air Forces, asked Trippe to take charge of the Air Transport Command with the rank of brigadier general. Trippe declined, saying he was too accustomed to being the final authority to fit into a military organization. This irked Arnold, who undoubtedly remembered that the name Pan American Airways had originated with him and that he had come close to leaving the service and taking the position that Trippe now held. These factors may not have had anything to do with the first break in Pan American's monopoly of U.S. international airline operations. However, with the strong encouragement of Arnold, 21 other American airlines began to carry

Trippe (center) after retiring in 1968, with Pan American chairman Harold E. Gray (left) and president Najeeb E. Halaby (courtesy of Pan American World Airways)

military cargo to various areas of the world. United, for example, invaded Pan American's Pacific preserve by flying to Australia; Eastern flew to Brazil; and even American Export Airlines revived and carried passengers and cargo to Britain. Arnold logically did not want to depend on one airline in time of war. But his irritation may well have played a role in a meeting he called in 1943 of U.S. airline representatives, including Pan American, at which he urged them (ordered, by some accounts) to expect worldwide competition in postwar skies for the health of future American air power.

Trippe quickly recognized the gravity of the challenge and immediately devised a scheme to meet it. He entitled it "The Community Company" plan. Behind it was the "chosen instrument" rationale but in a new and somewhat vague guise. In the spring of 1944 Trippe had one of his allies in the Senate, Patrick McCarran, who had been one of the principal authors of the Civil Aeronautics Act, introduce a bill that called for the creation of "The All-American Flag Line, Inc.," a private company, whose major capitalization was to be in the form of millions of dollars of government bonds.

Thus began a two-year battle in which Trippe took on most of the other large American airlines, some of the minor ones, the CAB, the White House again (this time under Harry Truman), various executive departments, and parts of Congress. To counter the effort to break the overseas monopoly, Trippe applied to the CAB for domestic routes. This time he suffered defeat.

Trippe's own performance as a witness before a Senate committee on behalf of the "All-American Flag Line" helped to doom the scheme. He rambled and was obscure and evasive. He refused to clarify the key point of whether or not his "community company" was in essence Pan American Airways in disguise. Trippe even ended up alienating the person who had originally favored his plan, the chairman of the Senate Commerce Committee that was holding the hearings. The day before the committee's negative vote on the bill, the CAB began parceling out overseas routes to various American airlines. Pan American's European awards were less than ideal.

Trippe continued to fight, and the bill was introduced again in 1945. Trippe put on a repeat performance, while President Truman threw his full weight against it. Knowledgeable on civil aviation affairs, Truman as a senator had voted in support of the earlier losing effort to give American Export Airlines an airmail appropriation. The vote in committee was firmly against reporting the bill to the Senate floor.

Trippe was not finished with the plan. He lobbied for a third try in 1947, this time with Republican lawmakers whose party now controlled Congress. When the bill was introduced in both houses, Trippe was more carefully coached. In answer to questions he insisted that should a "community company" be endorsed, Pan American as a separate entity would disappear. But he could not convince his opponents that such a company would still not be controlled by Pan American. This time he helped kill the bill by building into it various government subsidies that would enable the All-American Flagline to prosper in competition with the official flaglines of other nations. The bill failed to reach the floor of either house, and it died about the same time that Lucy Adeline Trippe did. With it died any further opportunity her son had of reviving the monopoly that was the obsession of his life. The only victory he achieved was to prevail upon C. R. Smith, the patriarch of American Airlines, to sell him American's overseas division called American Overseas Airlines (AOA), which had not been profitable. AOA had recently purchased American Export Airlines. The CAB had approved the American Airlines' purchase but voted against Pan American's acquisition of AOA. Trippe approached Secretary of State George C. Marshall, who persuaded President Truman to reverse the CAB decision against Pan American. It proved in the long run to be an important victory for Trippe because Pan American received some fine aircraft and, in a rearrangement by the CAB of cities to be served, Paris and Rome.

Ironically, it was C. R. Smith who dealt Trippe the final blow in the latter's move to acquire domestic routes. Both had taken options on a promising airliner for continental routes to be built by the Republic Aircraft Corporation. At the time Pan American and American were on opposite sides of the fence on the "community company" issue. Smith decided that he could weaken Pan American's case for domestic routes by undermining its chances for an airliner on which Trippe's application centered. Smith cancelled American's order for the Republic plane and the manufacturer, with only

Trippe's relatively small order, had to scuttle plans to put the new airliner into production.

One of Trippe's successful moves at the end of the war was to gain the financing needed for new planes and routes. In the process he outmaneuvered a crafty financial speculator named Floyd Odlum. With his traditional wealthy sources not able to provide the huge amount of capital Trippe projected for Pan American's postwar needs, he had turned to Odlum. The financier at first outsmarted Trippe and stood to make an excessive commission for his part in arranging the capital infusion. At the last minute, however, Trippe was able to back away because he had made another arrangement with the Kuhn Loeb bank on much better terms. It was partly luck but from that time on Wall Street viewed him as a financial genius. Trippe now had the funds to purchase new land planes in the abrupt transition from flying boats at the end of the war.

In spite of the fact that Pan American was no longer unchallenged by other American airlines in international skies and despite its failure to win a domestic route, the airline prospered after all the unsettling events of the 1940s were behind. Good times returned in the 1950s, and Pan American became more than just an airline as it began to diversify.

Trippe and Lindbergh became professionally close again after the war. Once more Lindbergh was a valued consultant and a top choice to be sent on technical missions. One of these missions was the investigation of jet aircraft developments in Europe, the German wartime breakthrough and the British postwar advances in the commercial field. Lindbergh recommended that Pan American work with American industry to develop a jet transport. Accepting that advice, Pan American became the U. S. leader in the introduction of the jet airliner.

Trippe played a singular role in this process, a role that was to prove of mixed benefit for both Pan American and the U. S. airline and aircraft manufacturing industries in general. His part in negotiating with, pushing, and demanding changes from Douglas, Boeing, and Pratt and Whitney (for jet engines) was characteristic of a long developed style. Out of Trippe's dealings with the aircraft manufacturers gradually emerged the first American jet airliners, the Boeing 707 and the DC-8. Trippe had avoided the intermediate step in the transition from the piston engine to the jet engine, the propjet, in the form of the Lockheed Electra, whose crashes and other problems had damaged the temporary lead of airlines such as Eastern. When the British lead in pure jets disappeared, Trippe had Pan American World Airways, as it was renamed, positioned by the late 1950s to take the United States into the pure jet era and to restore American leadership in airliner manufacture, a lead it had formerly gained and held with the DC-3. Trippe saw jets as a way to reduce cost and fares. A short time after signing contracts with both Douglas and Boeing for orders of their products-to-be, Trippe threw a party for delegates to the annual meeting of the International Air Transport Association held in New York City. To his guests he casually mentioned that he had just signed contracts to purchase forty-five new jet airliners. The shock waves were felt throughout the world. The jet age had truly arrived.

The great popularity of jets and postwar prosperity had created such a demand for air travel that the need arose for a larger and better aircraft than the Boeing 707 and DC-8. The search marked the beginning of the most grandiose and chancy of the "Sporty Games," in which an aircraft manufacturer literally bet the company over a new design. Trippe coaxed William Allen of Boeing to order the design of a "wide-bodied" jet airliner to be called the Boeing 747. By now the United States had become deeply involved in the Vietnam War, President John F. Kennedy was dead, and his successor Lyndon B. Johnson called for businessmen to cut back on their production so that inflation could be held down and more steel available for the war effort. Trippe had to persuade the president that the 747 program should go forward nonetheless. First he had to convince a skeptical Secretary of Defense Robert McNamara that to produce the 747 was a better buy than to convert the huge military transport, the Lockheed C-5A. After Trippe convinced him, the president gave the green light to Boeing.

For much of the 1960s it was the same Trippe technique—badgering and hectoring to change this and that about the 747 as it evolved. Remembering the grand style of the Boeing 314s, he won the addition of an upper story lounge reached by a spiral staircase. He also hounded Pratt and Whitney to come up with an engine that met his specifications. The plane as it took shape was not to be as spacious and fast as Trippe wanted but it cost more with each change. Also, a situation Trippe could not control began to take shape: other American

manufacturers decided to play this same "Sporty Game," as Lockheed and Douglas launched projects of their own. The competition was to prove one of the worst decisions ever made by American aircraft manufacturers.

At some point Trippe must have realized that the 747 adventure was not going to turn out the same as his earlier projects. Yet he seemed the same energetic, secretive, unfathomable, ruthless-when-he-felt-the-need, charming-when-necessary tycoon. He still did things in the largest way possible, including the construction, early in the 1960s, of the largest commercial building ever, on Park Avenue, to house his enterprise.

Trippe always had had an intuition about the future of the economy. Early in 1960 he sensed it was time to step aside. He arranged his succession in the person of veteran pilot Charles Gray. On May 7, 1968, he told his secretary of 18 years, Kathleen Clair, "I just want you to know that today I'm retiring as chairman." When tears appeared in her eyes, he failed to react.

Juan Trippe lived for almost 13 more years. If he suffered when the "Sporty Game" of the wide bodies almost broke the airlines and the manufacturers, when Pan American began to lose money, and when it was criticized for poor service, he did not show it. He lived to see the Boeing 747 become an accepted aircraft, beloved of pilots for its handling characteristics, and to see Pan American at long last acquire domestic routes. But these were small compensations. He was aware that he was widely blamed for Pan American's downward spiral. In the fall of 1980 Trippe suffered a cerebral hemorrhage; he died on April 3, 1981.

References:
Marylin Bender and Selig Altschul, *The Chosen Instrument* (New York: Simon & Schuster, 1982);

Robert Daley, *An American Saga: Juan Trippe and His American Empire* (New York: Random House, 1980);

Matthew Josephson, *Empire of the Air* (New York: Harcourt, Brace, 1944);

Wesley Phillips Newton, *The Perilous Sky: United States Aviation Diplomacy and Latin America, 1919-1931* (Coral Gables, Fla.: University of Miami Press, 1978).

Archives:
Trippe's papers are at the National Air and Space Museum, Washington, D.C. Other documents relating to Trippe are in the record groups of the Departments of Commerce, Defense, the Post Office, and State in the National Archives.

United Air Lines

by F. Robert van der Linden

National Air and Space Museum

One of the largest privately owned airlines in the world, United Air Lines played a major role in the development of air transportation in the United States and continued as an industry leader as it expanded across both the Atlantic and Pacific oceans after decades of domestic growth. United was formed on July 1, 1931, as a management company to coordinate the activities of its four component air carriers. Its immediate roots are traceable directly to Boeing Air Transport (BAT), which was created by the Boeing Airplane Company and began operations on July 1, 1927. Boeing Air Transport, the brainchild of Edward "Eddie" Hubbard, a Boeing test pilot and the founder of Hubbard Air Transport, bid on the U.S. Post Office contract for carrying mail between Chicago and San Francisco. Using Boeing 40 mail planes powered by efficient air-cooled Pratt & Whitney Wasp radial engines, BAT was able to bid substantially below its competitors and win the contract. The single-engine Model 40s could carry from two to four passengers and, to the amazement of the Post Office and the other carriers, made an immediate profit.

As the economy prospered and the stock market boomed in the late 1920s, investors turned their attention to aviation. Having developed an excellent working relationship in building the Model 40, William Boeing and Frederick Rentschler of Pratt & Whitney joined forces on February 1, 1929, to form what would become by far the largest aviation holding company, United Aircraft and Transport Corporation (UATC). Comprised of their respective companies, UATC could generate the necessary capital for additional expansion. Boeing Air Transport earlier purchased Pacific Air Transport in 1928 and, after the creation of UATC, began expanding eastward. On June 30, 1929, Stout Air Services was acquired, providing access to Detroit and Cleveland as well as a fleet of the latest Ford Trimotors. UATC's efforts to link BAT with the corporate head-quarters in New York were stymied by Clement M. Keys's National Air Transport (NAT), until Rentschler gained control of NAT in a brilliant proxy fight on May 7, 1930. The last link in the air transport chain of UATC was forged on June 30, when Varney Air Lines was purchased. Varney, which operated from Pasco, Washington, to Elko, Nevada, after opening one of the nation's first air-mail services by a private contractor on April 6, 1926, was the branch of the family tree through which United Air Lines claimed to be the nation's oldest airline.

In order to coordinate the activities of these companies, United Air Lines was officially formed as a management company for UATC's air transportation activities on July 1, 1931. Under the control of company president Philip Johnson, the four major component companies were formed into divisions of the new entity though they continued to operate under their original names. In 1933 Varney was absorbed into Boeing Air Transport, the details of which were completed by William A. Patterson, president of BAT and vice-president of United, who ran the daily operations of United Air Lines for Johnson.

For several years the various companies operated a diverse collection of aircraft including Boeing 40s, 80s, and Ford Trimotors. On March 30, 1933, United accepted delivery of the world's first modern airliner, the Boeing 247. Built exclusively for United, the 247 gave the airline a 50 percent speed advantage over its competition and, with its all-metal, twin-engined, cantilevered wing and retractable landing gear, revolutionized air travel, setting the standard for future airliner design. Carrying female flight attendants, an innovation begun on May 15, 1930, by BAT, United dominated the industry, but for only one more year.

Nineteen thirty-four was a watershed year for United Air Lines. Tied to UATC, the airline could

United McDonnell Douglas DC-10 (courtesy of the National Air and Space Museum)

only buy Boeing aircraft while the competition, especially Transcontinental and Western Air, introduced the superior Douglas DC-2, which combined the best features of the 247 with greater performance and passenger comfort, immediately rendering United's fleet obsolete. The temporary measures of introducing 15 improved 247-Ds and upgrading some of the 59 Boeing 247s allayed the situation until United could purchase more modern equipment.

That opportunity arose under unpleasant circumstances. Under the terms of the Air Mail Act of 1934, which resulted from President Franklin D. Roosevelt's cancellation of the airmail contracts, the airlines were divorced from the aircraft manufacturers, and the holding companies were dissolved. United president Johnson was forced to resign and was replaced by Patterson, whose first duty was to merge the separate divisions into one company. On July 20, 1934, United Air Lines Transport Corporation was formed; the name was later simplified to United Air Lines.

Faced with the growing obsolescence of his 247 fleet, Patterson sold or leased most of those aircraft to airlines that connected to United's routes and purchased Douglas DC-3s in 1936. United re-

gained its strength after the arrival of the DC-3s the following year. During this time United introduced several innovations to lure passengers, including the first flight kitchen in 1936. With a strong emphasis on safety, United opened a research and communications laboratory, pioneering many navigation and safety aids including static suppressors, terrain avoidance indicators, instrument landing systems, and two-way air-to-ground radio. In the late 1930s United led in a joint project between Douglas and five airlines in building the experimental DC-4E four-engined pressurized airliner. Though not a success, this project eventually led to the creation of the less complicated DC-4.

During World War II United turned over much of its fleet of 69 aircraft to the army and opened contract ferry routes for the Air Transport Command in Alaska and the Pacific, flying a total of 51.5 million miles in support of the war effort. United's maintenance base at Cheyenne, Wyoming, modified 5,736 aircraft, including installing the famous Cheyenne tail turret in numerous Boeing B-17 Flying Fortresses.

On March 1, 1946, United introduced Douglas DC-4s into service while awaiting the delivery of the faster, pressurized DC-6. At this time Patterson took a controversial stand in support of Pan American's concept of a "chosen instrument" international carrier. United's statisticians had determined that the international market was insufficient to support the operations of more than one U.S. airline against the state-owned European airlines. United concentrated strictly on domestic operations until 1985, with the unprofitable exception of its acquisition in 1943 of the Mexican airline LAMSA, which United sold nine years later.

Under Patterson's conservative leadership, United continued its growth and prosperity, introducing the DC-6 in 1947. In 1950 the luxurious double-decked Boeing 377 Stratocruiser was inaugurated on United's Hawaiian route, and in 1951 the world's first DC-6B was accepted into service. For shorter routes United selected the twin-engined Convair 340, which was delivered in late 1952.

The advent of the jet age held great promise for the future of air travel. As with the other major airlines, United began preparing for the arrival of the first practical jet airliner. As early as 1945 United initiated its investigation and in 1952 began operating a "paper" airline, simulating every contingency expected in the daily operation of jets. United's cautious approach delayed its transition to jet airliners until the airliner best suited to its needs could be found. United rejected the pioneering de Havilland Comet as too inefficient and turned down the Boeing 707 because of the restricted fuselage dimensions in the initial model. United watched as American Airlines introduced the 707 into service in early 1959, accepting the temporary losses that were incurred. Finally, on September 18, 1959, United introduced the Douglas DC-8 between San Francisco and New York and regained much of the lost ground.

United subsequently became the first U.S. airline to convert completely to jet aircraft. In 1960 the medium-range Boeing 720 was accepted to complement the long-range DC-8, and United took a bold step and became the first U.S. airline to purchase the Sud Aviation Caravelle, with its rear-fuselage-mounted twin-jet engines. Also in 1960 United ordered the distinctive Boeing 727 tri-jet for delivery in 1964.

Following these orders United took another bold move and acquired the ailing Capital Airlines on June 1, 1961. The merger moved United back into its leadership position ahead of American, for the first time since the air mail crisis of 1934, but

also proved a severe financial drain on the airline for several years. With this merger United also picked up a fleet of Vickers Viscount four-engined turboprop airliners.

Once the merger difficulties were solved and the operations of the two companies fully integrated, United continued its fleet modernization program. One of Patterson's last moves before his retirement came in 1965, when United placed the largest aircraft order in history up to that time, contracting for 70 737-200s, 35 727s, and 8 DC-8s, worth a total of $375 million.

On April 28, 1966, Patterson retired and was replaced by his hand-chosen successor, George E. Keck. The next several years were turbulent as United continued to grow. To assist in future diversification, in 1969 United became a wholly owned subsidiary of United Air Lines, Inc., a holding company, and subsequently purchased a major interest in the Western International hotel chain. The *Transpacific Route* case of 1969 gave United additional access to Hawaii from several additional cities in the East and Midwest at the cost of increased competition. United's position along its Hawaiian routes was strengthened on July 23, 1970, with the introduction of the wide-bodied Boeing 747. Between 1966 and 1969 United continued to garner steady profits.

In 1970, because of management problems, new equipment costs, increased competition on the Hawaiian route, and a general economic downturn, United sustained record losses of $46 million, resulting in Keck's removal. He was replaced by Edward E. Carlson from Western International, who immediately turned the company around through a major cost-cutting and decentralization program. By 1978 United turned a record $247 million profit and was flying 336 airliners, the largest private fleet in the world. Under Carlson, McDonnell Douglas DC-10s were introduced on transcontinental routes, greatly increasing capacity and profitability. United also became the launch customer for Boeing's latest widebody, the twin-jet 767, 30 of which were ordered on July 14, 1978, for delivery in 1982.

Carlson retired in 1978 and was succeeded by Richard J. Ferris. Because of the *Transpacific* case and other confrontations with the Civil Aeronautics Board, United felt stymied in its attempts to grow and looked forward to more open competition. Under Carlson and particularly Ferris, United was one of the first airlines to advocate industry deregulation, breaking with the other members of the Air Transport Association.

The great profits hoped for under deregulation failed to materialize in 1979 when a national fuel shortage, an economic recession, the grounding of all DC-10s by the Federal Aviation Administration, and a 58-day strike caused United to lose $99.6 million. Losses continued in 1980 and 1981 and were compounded by the air traffic controllers strike, which especially hurt United's operations at its Chicago hub. United rebounded into the black in 1982 as the economy recovered.

In 1984 United earned a record profit of $259 million, which set the stage for a bitter dispute in 1985 over the two-tiered wage scale, resulting in a prolonged strike that summer. Earlier, as part of United's diversification, it acquired the Hertz Corporation for $1.6 billion, adding this rental car company to United's hotel holdings. In a controversial move, Pan American's Pacific Division was purchased in October 1985 for $750 million, giving United additional routes in the central Pacific, Southeast Asia, Japan, Australia, and New Zealand. Following the purchase of 110 Boeing 737-300s and 6 additional 747s for $3.1 billion, and the acquisition of 25 737s from the defunct Frontier Airlines for $265 million, United continued its expansion by announcing in December the opening of a new north-south hub at Washington's Dulles International Airport.

Increasing discontent with the diversification program of United's parent corporation, renamed Allegis in 1986, prompted a move by United pilots to attempt to purchase control of the airline. Though this effort failed, continued pressure prompted Ferris's resignation in 1987 and the dissolution of Allegis as a full-service travel company. Under new chairman Stephen M. Wolf, United has continued to entertain proposals from its union for ownership.

After the turbulence of 1987 was settled, United renewed its efforts to modernize its fleet. In 1988 it placed a $2 billion order for 30 Boeing 757s to replace its DC-8s. The following year Wolf astonished the industry by ordering 370 new Boeing 737s and 757s valued at $15.75 billion to serve the airline well into the next century with a fleet of approximately 450 aircraft. This signaled a return by United to its primary interest in transportation with a renewed aggressive attitude to regain its lost initiative.

In May 1990 United also broke tradition by opening transatlantic service to Europe, overturning a company policy that was set by Patterson in the 1940s. By that time United felt that the market was sufficiently large to enable the company to open the new routes.

References:

"Mighty United—The Story of United Air Lines," *Esso Air World*, 22 (January-February 1970): 86-92;

Frank J. Taylor, *High Horizons: Daredevil Flying Postmen to Modern Magic Carpet—The United Air Lines Story* (New York: McGraw-Hill, 1951);

United Air Lines, *A Corporate and Legal History of United Air Lines and its Predecessors and Subsidiaries: 1925-1945* (Chicago: Twentieth Century Press, 1953);

United Air Lines, *A Corporate and Legal History of United Air Lines and its Predecessors and Subsidiaries: 1945-1955* (Elk Grove, Ill.: United Air Lines, Inc., n.d.);

"United: The Story of America's Oldest Domestic Airline," *Esso Air World*, 14 (May-June 1962): 142-148.

Archives:

Additional material may be found in the archives of the National Air and Space Museum, which houses a file and dossier on United Air Lines.

Inglis Moore Uppercu

(September 17, 1875 - April 7, 1944)

by William M. Leary

University of Georgia

CAREER: President, Uppercu Cadillac Motor Car Company (1908-1931); president, Aeromarine Plane & Motor Company (1914-1936).

A pioneer in the development of U.S. commercial aviation, Inglis Moore Uppercu was born in North Evanston, Illinois, on September 17, 1875, the son of Jesse Wheat and Laura Isabel Hildebrand Uppercu. In 1888 his father, a prominent Chicago lawyer, moved the family to New York City, where Uppercu attended public schools. After graduating from Brooklyn Polytechnic Institute, he entered Columbia Law School. A legal career, however, held little attraction for a young man who drove automobiles in competition for the Vanderbilt Cup. He left Columbia before graduation and joined the mechanical department of the Neostyle Company.

Uppercu worked for several of the early automobile companies before organizing the Motor Car Company of New Jersey, the sales agency for Packard and Cadillac, in 1902. Six years later he formed the Detroit Cadillac Motor Car Company (renamed the Uppercu Cadillac Motor Car Company in 1925) and became the exclusive agent for Cadillac and LaSalle cars in the greater New York City area. This company, which he sold to the General Motors Corporation in 1931, provided a secure financial base for Uppercu's aeronautical ventures.

Uppercu's first investment in aviation came in 1908, when he financed, for several hundred dollars, the Boland Aeroplane Company. Intended to produce a novel rear-engine, rudderless biplane, the company collapsed following the death of inventor Frank Boland, who was killed while demonstrating the airplane in 1913. The following year, Uppercu started the Aeromarine Plane & Motor Company and began to manufacture seaplanes. When the United States entered World War I in 1917, he received contracts from the navy to produce trainers.

Inglis Moore Uppercu (courtesy of the Uppercu family)

His factory at Keyport, New Jersey, built some 300 single-engine flying boats, becoming one of the navy's largest wartime suppliers of training aircraft.

Following the Armistice an optimistic Uppercu tried to exploit the commercial potential of seaplanes. One of his projects involved the purchase of several Curtiss F-5L twin-engine biplanes, which he converted to 11-passenger airliners. Although Uppercu produced what was widely acknowledged as the premier commercial airliner in the United States, he found no customers for his handsome flying boats. Undeterred, he decided to demonstrate the commercial potential of aviation by operating the aircraft himself.

In the summer of 1920, Uppercu used one of the F-5Ls for charter flights between New York City and the resorts of Atlantic City, Southampton, and Newport. A more ambitious venture came in October, when he purchased a controlling interest in Florida-West Indies Airways. One of the many postwar efforts to tap the potential of commercial aviation, this airline had been founded in 1919 by a group of former servicemen to fly between Key West and Havana. Although the owners had secured the first airmail contract in U.S. history in August 1920, they had been unable to raise enough capital to continue operations.

Uppercu's new Aeromarine-West Indies Airways (renamed Aeromarine Airways in 1921) began twice-daily flights over the 90-mile route from Key West to Havana in November 1920. The lure of gambling and drinking in Cuba for Prohibition-era Americans no doubt contributed significantly to a banner winter season for the airline. Over the next six months Aeromarine carried 1,100 passengers and 34,395 pounds of mail. The route, however, proved seasonal. In May, with traffic declining, Uppercu surrendered his far from lucrative mail contract and suspended service. Aeromarine's F-5Ls spent the summer flying charters out of New York City.

Uppercu reestablished the Key West-Havana route during the winter of 1921-1922. Although the one-year mail contract had not been renewed, business was good. The airline doubled its previous season's passenger traffic, carrying 2,399 customers without accident or injury. During the summer of 1922, Aeromarine not only flew the usual charters but also operated daily service between Cleveland and Detroit. In two months, that route carried 4,388 passengers.

The third winter season, 1922-1923, began with optimistic plans for expanded service throughout the Caribbean. On January 13, 1923, however, Aeromarine suffered its first fatalities, when four passengers drowned after an F-5L made a forced landing in the Straits of Florida. Shortly thereafter, the airline lost a second airplane in Havana's harbor when it broke loose from its moorings during a storm.

Those twin losses created a severe financial strain for the airline. Previously, money had been draining slowly out of Aeromarine. Intent on promoting commercial aviation, Uppercu had been prepared to use the profits from his Cadillac agency to underwrite the airline's losses. But the economic burden grew intolerable in 1923.

Aeromarine again migrated northward following the disastrous winter season in Florida; however, Uppercu suspended charter operations in July. While the popular Cleveland-Detroit route continued to operate throughout the summer, carrying more than 5,000 passengers between the two cities, future prospects for commercial air service remained bleak. Having suffered $500,000 in losses and without having located a customer for a single airplane, Uppercu sold Aeromarine to the Florida Railroad and Steamship Company. The new owner operated only a few charter flights before shutting down the airline at the beginning of 1924.

Uppercu had set out to demonstrate the economic viability of commercial aviation. Unfortunately, he had proved the opposite. As historian Henry Ladd Smith has noted, "The fact that such a well-managed line could not pay dividends without mail payments ... directed attention more than ever to the necessity of government help, preferably in the form of subsidy."

Government subsidy was just around the corner, but it came too late for Uppercu. No doubt disappointed, he never lost his interest in aviation. He supported the experiments of designer Vincent J. Burnelli, who was working on an innovative all-wing-fuselage airplane. Also, he toyed with idea of starting a commercial air service on the Great Lakes, but nothing came of it. He retired in 1938 and devoted most of his time to sailing his yacht *Seven Seas* in Caribbean waters. He died on April 7, 1944.

References:

William M. Leary, *Aerial Pioneers: The U.S. Air Mail Service, 1918-1927* (Washington, D.C.: Smithsonian Institution, 1985);

Leary, "At the Dawn of Commercial Aviation: Inglis M. Uppercu and Aeromarine Airways," *Business History Review*, 53 (1979): 180-193;

Henry Ladd Smith, *Airways: The History of Commercial Aviation in the United States* (New York: Knopf, 1942).

USAir

by William F. Trimble

Auburn University

When Allegheny Airlines became USAir on October 28, 1979, it assumed more than a new corporate identity. No longer a regional carrier, the new company now competed in the national market with the country's other major airlines. In the tumultuous early years of deregulation, USAir, under its president and chief executive officer, Edwin I. Colodny, cautiously expanded its route system to include connections in Florida, Texas, and Colorado. Not until 1983 did it offer nonstop flights from its major hub in Pittsburgh to the West Coast. USAir's policy in the early 1980s, known as "niching," concentrated on traditional market strengths while targeting specific geographic areas with carefully chosen equipment and services.

It is hard to imagine a more successful strategy. While other airlines were awash in red ink in the early part of the decade, USAir went from one record profit to another. In 1982 the company claimed the largest net earnings of any airline in the world; two years later it had a profit of more than $121 million. New equipment and facilities came on line during these years. USAir acquired Boeing 737-200s in 1982, and in 1984 placed in service the new Boeing 737-300. In 1981 USAir opened a new computer center in Virginia. The following year, the airline completed new aircraft overhaul and flight training facilities and expanded the number of passenger gates at Greater Pittsburgh International Airport. In 1983 USAir became the operating subsidiary of a holding company, USAir Group, Inc., which included four regional airlines, an aircraft leasing company, and aviation overhaul and maintenance firms.

Events largely beyond USAir's control forced it into mergers with other airlines in the latter part of the decade. As opportunistic companies such as Texas Air swallowed People Express, Eastern, and Continental in 1986 and 1987, USAir faced the uncomfortable choice of acquiring another airline or

facing the erosion of its competitive position. Niching was not enough. In late 1986 USAir acquired Pacific Southwest Airlines (PSA), a San Diego-based carrier with a strong route system on the West Coast. Shortly thereafter, USAir completed negotiations for the purchase of Piedmont Aviation, a profitable airline with a major hub in Charlotte, North Carolina. At the same time, the airline had to fend off an unfriendly takeover bid from Carl Icahn and rival TWA.

The mergers with PSA and Piedmont preserved USAir's position in the highly volatile airline market, but they came at considerable cost to the company. Although most analysts were optimistic about how well the acquisitions complemented USAir's fleet and route structure and the company took a conservative, step-by-step approach to the integration of PSA and Piedmont into the larger airline, the process did not go smoothly. Minor labor problems had to be resolved, equipment costs soared, and on-time performance fell off dramatically in 1989. As a consequence, the airline suffered its first losses in nearly a decade.

Although the full consequences of the mergers of the 1980s are hard to gauge, USAir is likely to remain one of the most successful companies in the airline industry through the end of the century. With a fleet of more than 400 aircraft, most of which are economical 737-300s, 737-400s, and new short-haul Fokker 100s, USAir is not faced with the need to replace large numbers of obsolescent aircraft. It will have up-to-date passenger facilities in Pittsburgh with the completion of the new midfield terminal in early 1993. Hubs and maintenance operations at Charlotte and San Diego provide room for growth, and more nonstop flights between midsize cities proved attractive to passengers. Rising fuel costs and an uncertain economic outlook may bring more trouble for USAir, but on the whole the firm came out of the turbulent era of deregulation with a more promising future than many of its competitors.

References:

Joan M. Feldman, "Blending the Elements of a Major Empire," *Air Transport World*, 25 (June 1988): 28-41;

W. David Lewis and William F. Trimble, *The Airway to Everywhere: A History of All American Aviation, 1937-1953* (Pittsburgh: University of Pittsburgh Press, 1988);

William F. Trimble, *High Frontier: A History of Aeronautics in Pennsylvania* (Pittsburgh: University of Pittsburgh Press, 1982);

"USAir Buy of PSA Would Create Sixth Largest U.S. Carrier," *Aviation Week and Space Technology*, 125 (December 15, 1986): 29-31;

"USAir: Fifty Years of Flying High," *USAir*, 11 (May 1989): 71-72.

U.S. Air Mail Service

by William M. Leary

University of Georgia

The U.S. Air Mail Service laid the foundations for commercial aviation in the United States. Between 1918 and 1927, this government-operated adjunct of the Post Office Department established the transcontinental air route from New York to San Francisco, inaugurated systematic night flying, and experimented with radio and instrument navigation. Operating coast to coast with remarkable regularity and safety, the Air Mail Service attracted the interest of commercial developers. Beyond question, the modern airline industry stems directly from the pioneering efforts of the Post Office.

The Air Mail Service grew out of the Post Office's interest in using the airplane to expedite the mails. Postal authorities began supporting aerial mail-carrying demonstrations as early as 1911. Later the Post Office tried to interest private contractors in flying the mail to remote areas in the United States and Alaska. Unable to attract responsible bidders due to the primitive state of aviation technology, Postmaster General Albert S. Burleson decided to establish a government-operated experimental service between Washington, D.C., and New York City in 1918. Before the Post Office could obtain airplanes and pilots, however, the U.S. Army Air Service volunteered to operate the route as part of its wartime training program.

Military pilots flew the mail from May 15 to August 10, 1918, making 270 flights and carrying 40,500 pounds of mail. Despite this accomplishment, relations between the army and the Post Office had not been amicable. Upset with flight cancellations, postal officials believed that, with few exceptions, the young Air Service fliers were not committed to solving the problems of daily scheduled flying. The Post Office preferred to do the job itself.

Determined to make the aerial experiment a success, Second Assistant Postmaster General Otto Praeger took charge of the Air Mail Service on August 12, 1918. Operating the Washington-New York route with its own planes and pilots, the Post Office demanded a standard of performance that produced impressive results. Praeger soon realized, however, that a longer route would be necessary to demonstrate the full potential of airmail. In October planning began for a New York-Chicago service as part of an eventual transcontinental route.

Establishing a coast-to-coast airway proved a tremendous challenge for Praeger and his associates. After several delays, regular service between New York and Chicago began on July 1, 1919. Finally, after securing airfields and establishing a ground communications system, transcontinental daytime operations got under way on September 8, 1920. On February 22-23, 1921, the Post Office demonstrated the full potential of the transcontinental route when it flew an experimental day-and-night flight between San Francisco and New York in 33 hours and 20 minutes. The fastest trains took more than four days to cover the same distance.

The Republican administration that took power in March 1921 did not look with favor on the U.S. Air Mail Service. Upset with the high human cost of airmail operations (18 pilots had died while flying for the Post Office) and philosophically opposed to government ownership, Republican postal

De Havilland DH-4Bs at Omaha, Nebraska, 1923 (courtesy of the National Air and Space Museum)

officials continued to fly the mail only because the government could not find anyone else to do the job. At the same time, the administration insisted that all flying be confined to the transcontinental route and that steps be taken to insure safer operations.

Despite the somewhat unpromising circumstances of being an unwanted example of "state socialism," the Air Mail Service went on to perfect the transcontinental service. Under the energetic and imaginative leadership of Second Assistant Postmaster General Paul Henderson, postal airmen continued to pioneer developments on the frontiers of aeronautics, especially in the areas of night and instrument flying. In February 1923 the Air Mail Service won the prestigious Collier Trophy, given for the year's most significant contribution to aviation, for flying between New York and San Francisco for one year without a fatal accident. It received the trophy the following year for establishing the lighted airway on the transcontinental route.

The Post Office began regular day-and-night transcontinental service on July 1, 1924. Demonstrating that long-distance flight operations could be conducted with regularity and safety, the Air Mail Service convinced private interests that flying the mail could be both feasible and profitable. The Republican administration of Calvin Coolidge further encouraged the formation of commercial airlines through federal regulation of aeronautics and postal subsidies. On June 30, 1927, the Post Office turned over the San Francisco-Chicago route to Boeing Air Transport. Three months later National Air Transport took over the Chicago-New York segment of the transcontinental route.

The U.S. Air Mail Service compiled an impressive record during its nine years of operation. Postal airmen flew over 13.7 million miles and carried over 300 million letters, setting a standard of excellence for bad weather and night flying that was unmatched in the world. The Post Office had demonstrated the practical value of air transportation and set the stage for the rapid development of the American airline industry.

References:

Paul T. David, *The Economics of Air Mail Transportation* (Washington, D.C.: Brookings Institution, 1934);

William M. Leary, *Aerial Pioneers: The U.S. Air Mail Service, 1918-1927* (Washington, D.C.: Smithsonian Institution, 1985);

Henry Ladd Smith, *Airways: The History of Commercial Aviation in the United States* (New York: Knopf, 1942).

Archives:

The extensive archives of the U.S. Air Mail Service are in the Records of the United States Post Office, Record Group 28, National Archives, Washington, D.C.

Walter T. Varney

(December 26, 1888 - January 25, 1967)

by William M. Leary

University of Georgia

CAREER: Pilot, U.S. Air Service (1917-1918); owner, aircraft sales and charter service (1919-1925); owner, Varney Air Transport (1926-1930); owner, Varney Speed Lines (1931-1933); partner, Varney Air Line (1934); owner, Líneas Aéreas Occidentales (1934-1935); employee, Lockheed Aircraft Company (1939-1954).

Walter Thomas Varney played a prominent role in the early development of air transportation in the Pacific Northwest and in California. The owner of a fixed-base service in the San Francisco Bay area, Varney became the first operator of two contract airmail routes in the Pacific Northwest. After selling his airline to the United Aircraft & Transport Company in 1930, he started a speedy and popular air service between the San Francisco and Los Angeles areas. Although he fell on hard times during the mid 1930s, he remained cheerful and optimistic, perhaps secure in the knowledge that his contributions to the developing airline industry would be long remembered.

Varney was born in San Francisco on December 26, 1888, the son of Thomas Humphrey Bennett and Ada (Hall) Varney. His father owned an outdoor advertising business. Educated in private schools, Varney went to work for his father in 1906. He later was employed by the Pacific Poster Advertising Company. These early experiences no doubt influenced his approach toward business. As biographer Barrett Tillman has observed, Varney was known as "a natural promoter and showman."

Varney joined the U.S. Air Service in December 1917, where he learned to fly. Discharged the following December, he opened a flying school in San Carlos, which he subsequently moved to San Mateo. In common with most fixed-base operators of the day, Varney did a little bit of everything. He taught students to fly, and he sold the popular Laird Swallow biplane. As the Varney Flying Circus, he performed at air shows. In 1922 he formed the Checker Air Service (in conjunction with the Checker Cab Company) to fly freight between San Francisco, Stockton, and Modesto.

In July 1925 Varney made the successful bid for Contract Air Mail Route Number 5 (CAM-5), which ran some 460 miles from Pasco, Washington, over the route of the northern transcontinental railroad, to Elko, Nevada, a stop on the Post Office's New York-Chicago airmail line. Varney began service on this route on April 6, 1926, with six Laird Swallows, piloted mostly by advanced students from his flying school. He had $30,000 in operating capital.

Varney Air Transport got off to a shaky start. The Swallows were powered by 150-horsepower Curtiss K-6 engines that quickly proved inadequate for the rugged mountainous terrain on the route. Three days after he inaugurated service, Varney had to shut down the line and order 200-horsepower Wright Whirlwind engines for the Swallows. Service resumed in early June. The new engines produced much better performance, and the airline went on to compile an impressive record for reliability.

Walter T. Varney (right) with United Air Lines employee C. T. Wrightson

In 1927 Varney Air Transport, by then equipped with Stearman C3Bs and using Salt Lake City in place of Elko as the line's southern terminus, flew 318,000 miles, carried nearly 60,000 pounds of mail, and received $180,000 from the Post Office. The next year was even better. The airline flew 370,000 miles, carried an impressive 133,000 pounds of mail, and received an even more impressive $400,000.

Varney expanded his operations in 1929. In January he acquired six larger Stearman M-2s to replace the C3Bs. He also bid successfully for CAM-32, connecting Portland with Seattle and Spokane. This route started on September 15. Finally, late in the year he placed into service the first of 13 Boeing 40Bs. Featuring an enclosed cabin for five intrepid travelers (the pilot sat outside), the new Boeings enabled Varney to begin passenger service in 1930.

Although the airline business in the Pacific Northwest showed promise of continued growth, Varney was ready for new challenges. In June 1930 he sold out to the United Aircraft & Transport Corporation (parent of the later United Air Lines) for $2 million. He used a good part of this money to pur-

chase six Lockheed Orions, a state-of-the-art six-passenger streamlined monoplane that could cruise at a breathtaking 175 mph. In April 1930 Charles Lindbergh had flown an Orion, the fastest transport of its day, from Glendale to New York in 14 hours and 45 minutes, setting a new transcontinental speed record.

On October 15, 1931, Varney began flying the Orions from Alameda Airport in Oakland to Sacramento and to Glendale, in the Los Angeles area. By 1932 Varney Speed Lines (or Varney Speed Lanes as it was sometimes called) offered six flights a day to Sacramento and four to Glendale. Covering the distance from the San Francisco area to the Los Angeles area in under two hours, the air service proved popular with California travelers, especially film stars and other public figures. In March 1932 Varney purchased Air Ferries, enabling him to offer connecting service from Oakland to downtown San Francisco.

Varney cut a flamboyant figure during these years. Drawn to speed, he owned two supercharged Dusenberg automobiles, one of which (a Bobtail Speedster) could reach 100 mph—in second gear! Leland S. Prior, an acquaintance, remembers Var-

Varney Air Transport Lockheed Vega (courtesy of the National and Space Museum)

ney as "a very friendly, gregarious extrovert who loved people, parties and having fun in general."

The good times ended on the night of March 25, 1933. Noel Evans, known as a careful pilot, was en route from San Leandro to Hayward with two passengers. It was a miserable night, with rain and poor visibility. Flying under a low ceiling, Evans hit a house in suburban Hayward. The Lockheed Orion exploded on impact, killing Evans, his passengers, and 12 people in the house. The accident received widespread publicity, causing travelers to avoid Varney Speed Lines. The company went out of business during the summer.

Varney may have been down but he was not out. On April 10, 1934, after obtaining a 20-year contract from the Mexican government, he began a mail service from Los Angeles to Tapachula, on the border of Guatemala, via Mexico City. By the end of the year, Líneas Aéreas Occidentales was flying to Mexico City three times a week, and once weekly to Tapachula. Also, in partnership with Louis Mueller, Varney started operating CAM-29, from Pueblo, Colorado, to El Paso, on July 15, 1934. This partnership, however, broke up before the end of the year, with Mueller remaining to run the line, which later evolved into Continental Airlines.

Varney's 20-year contract with the Mexican government came to a sudden end in January 1935. The authorities in Mexico City abruptly canceled the agreement and awarded the route to a subsidiary of Pan American Airways. Varney was not the first, and would not be the last person, to learn that Pan Am's Juan T. Trippe did not like competition.

Varney turned his attention to a silver mine in Sonora, Mexico, but this venture failed. In 1939, having gone through his millions, he found employment in the personnel department of the Lockheed Aircraft Company. This turn of the wheel of fate was not without irony. In 1932 Varney had bought a half-interest in the nearly bankrupt Lockheed for $20,000. He had sold his stock in 1933 and put the money in the failing Varney Speed Lines. He worked at various jobs at Lockheed, as a line inspector, copilot on the wartime Hudson bomber program, and head of the flight test instrument department. He retired in 1954. After a brief fling as an operator of sand and gravel trucks, he settled down to a more leisurely life of playing tennis (at which he excelled) and doting on his granddaughter. He was, according to one associate, "happy as a clam," content with his fate. He died on January 25, 1967. His career, biographer Tillman has emphasized, stands as "testimony to the tenacity, dedication, and exceptional resilience essential to success in any new field."

References:

R. E. G. Davies, *Rebels and Reformers of the Airways* (Washington, D.C.: Smithsonian Institution, 1987);

Barrett Tillman, "Six Million Miles: The Story of Varney Air Lines," *American Aviation Historical Society Journal*, 16 (Fall 1971): 175-183; (Winter 1971): 244-250;

Barbara Wood and Leland S. Prior, "Walter T. Varney," *American Aviation Historical Society Journal*, 31 (Winter 1986): 264-268.

Eugene L. Vidal

(April 13, 1895 - February 20, 1969)

by Dominick A. Pisano

National Air and Space Museum

CAREER: Officer, U.S. Army Air Service (1921-1926); assistant general manager, Transcontinental Air Transport (1929-1930); general manager, Ludington Airlines (1930-1932); director, Bureau of Air Commerce (1933-1937); consultant, Bendix Aviation Corporation (1937-1938); president, Aircraft Research Corporation and Vidal Research Corporation (1937-1969).

Eugene Luther Vidal, a star football player and Olympic athlete in his youth, was one of the founders of the Ludington Line, an innovative passenger air shuttle service that operated on the East Coast from 1929 to 1933. He went on to serve for four turbulent years as a director of the Bureau of Air Commerce in the administration of Franklin D. Roosevelt. An advocate of a "New Deal for Aeronautics," his plans to promote the light plane industry came to naught. At the same time, he came under heavy criticism for the administration's meager spending on air safety. As historian Nick A. Komons has commented, "The New Deal . . . spent huge sums on marginal aviation programs while economizing on such vital Department of Commerce activities as air regulation and airway development." In many ways, Vidal's governmental career was emblematic of Roosevelt's attitude toward aviation during his first term in office, a time noted for a lack of concentration on essentials.

Vidal was born on April 13, 1895, in Madison, South Dakota, the son of Felix Louis and Margaret (Rewalt) Vidal. He grew up in the small farming community and attended local schools, gaining a reputation as a talented athlete. Offered scholarships to several schools in the region, he selected the Uni-

Eugene L. Vidal (courtesy of the Federal Aviation Administration)

versity of South Dakota. Vidal went on to letter in football, baseball, basketball, and track. He graduated at the head of his class in 1916 with a degree in civil engineering. Vidal then entered the U.S. Military Academy, which was permitted under existing policy. He spent two years at West Point, coming to national attention as an All-American halfback on the football team.

Commissioned in 1918, Vidal served for two years in the Corps of Engineers, then transferred to the Air Service. In 1920 he represented the United States at the Antwerp Olympics, winning a silver medal in the pentathlon. On January 11, 1921, while serving as an instructor and part-time football coach at West Point, Vidal married Nina Gore, the daughter of Senator Thomas P. Gore of Oklahoma. The union, which ended in divorce in 1935, produced one child, novelist Gore Vidal.

Vidal left the army in 1926. He served as football coach at the University of Oregon for the 1926-1927 season. Then he sold real estate in Florida during the land boom in the state. In 1929 he became assistant general manager of Transcontinental Air Transport (TAT), one of the nation's leading airlines. Owned by financier Clement M. Keys, TAT opened air-rail service between New York and Los Angeles in July 1929. The onset of the Great Depression, however, caused the airline heavy financial losses. Early in 1930 Vidal and several other executives lost their jobs.

Vidal soon joined with ex-TAT general superintendent Paul F. Collins in developing a pioneering air shuttle service between New York, Philadelphia, and Washington, D.C. Commonly known as the Ludington Line, after financial backer C. T. Ludington, the company began hourly flights on the route on September 1, 1930. Operated with great efficiency, the airline returned a modest profit. Efforts to secure an airmail contract, however, did not gain the needed support of Postmaster General Walter Folger Brown. Despite Ludington's lower bid, Brown awarded the lucrative contract to Eastern Air Transport. In February 1933 Eastern acquired the Ludington Line.

Vidal was not long out of a job. In June 1933 the incoming Democratic administration of Franklin D. Roosevelt named Vidal chief of the Air Regulation Division in the Aeronautics Branch of the Department of Commerce. Three and a half months later, Vidal was appointed head of the organization. In commenting on his selection, newspapers acknowledged Vidal's airline experience while pointing out that he was a close personal friend of Elliott Roosevelt, the president's son, and had visited with the Roosevelt family at Warm Springs.

Vidal had a stormy tenure as director of the Aeronautics Branch, later renamed the Bureau of Air Commerce. He faced constant bureaucratic problems, as the chiefs of two strong divisions in the bu-

reau competed for power. Even more frustrating were the severe budgetary cuts that the administration imposed. As spokesman for the agency, Vidal had to assure Congress that the cuts could be made without impairing air safety.

On a more positive note, at least at first, was Vidal's crusade for a "New Deal for Aeronautics." In November 1933 he announced his intention to bolster the light plane industry, which had suffered more than its share of economic downturns, by promoting the manufacture of a cheap, easy-to-fly, private aircraft that would be sold to a mass market. This plan, which marked the New Deal's first attempt to shore up this long-neglected sector of the aviation industry, would be accomplished, Vidal believed, through a government-subsidized aviation industry program to produce an all-metal aircraft to exact specifications, with built-in safety devices, for $700.

Vidal was convinced that the potential market was made up of the "forgotten man of aviation," the private flyer, who, he said, "built model airplanes by the millions and trudge out to local airports each week-end to worship their idols from the ground and long for the day when they will have saved enough wherewith to buy a hop." In a speech to the Society of Automotive Engineers in April 1934, he explained his plan for the $700 airplane. "If there is such a thing as a New Deal for aviation," he said, "it is the recognition of the government's additional duty to aid in the development of a sound aviation industry, which means above all other things, the development of greater markets for products of that industry."

To oversee the "airplane for everyman" program, Vidal organized a development section within the Aeronautics Branch. Funding was to come from Harold Ickes's Public Works Administration (PWA), which had promised $998,000. This was later reduced to $500,000. In January 1934 a committee made up of prominent persons in aviation, among them J. Carroll Cone of the Aeronautics Branch, George Lewis of the National Advisory Committee for Aeronautics, Edward P. Warner, editor of *Aviation*, Amelia Earhart, and Maj. Alford Williams, was formed to explore ways in which the half-million-dollar grant could be distributed to the aviation industry.

The aviation press, regarded as a spokesman for the industry, was vehemently opposed to the idea. *Aviation*, the most prestigious journal in the aeronautical community, took a survey of the industry to determine the consensus on Vidal's idea. According to the magazine's findings, 64 percent of the airframe manufacturers and over 54 percent of the engine manufacturers opposed the $700 airplane project. Seventy percent of those polled by *Aviation* believed that their own business would suffer because prospective customers for light aircraft would delay purchasing until the $700 airplane appeared on the market.

Nevertheless, in view of the fact that a half-million dollars in PWA money was at stake, the industry was more than willing at least to put up a pretense of cooperation. In January 1934 representatives of the Aeronautical Chamber of Commerce, the trade association of the industry, met in New York to give their "wholehearted" endorsement to Vidal's project. Moreover, the chamber set up two industry committees to cooperate with the Bureau of Air Commerce. The first of these included representatives from the Taylor Aircraft Company, Curtiss-Wright, Waco Aircraft, Stinson, and Consolidated. Their task was to arrive at airframe and engine performance specifications and iron out the technical details of the $700 airplane. The other committee, composed of representatives from the Aeronautical Corporation of America, Curtiss-Wright, North American Aviation, Fairchild Aviation, and United Aircraft and Transport, was responsible for determining the legal and economic feasibility of establishing a corporation within the aircraft industry to develop and manufacture the airplane.

The industry's idea was to give the $500,000 PWA grant to a new corporation jointly owned by the other members of the industry and set up specifically to manufacture the $700 airplane. This company would in turn sell its stock to the other manufacturers. In this way, profits or losses could be evenly distributed throughout the industry and no one would suffer unduly.

When Roosevelt administration officials learned of the manufacturers' plans, they reacted negatively. Conferring with Roosevelt on January 24, 1934, Harold Ickes, chief of the Public Works Administration, told the president that he was concerned about rumors that indicated "collusion between men in the government and outside interests as a result of which this money will really be expended for the benefit of outside interests." On February 1, 1934, at a meeting of the Special Board for Public Works, Ickes informed Secretary of Commerce Daniel Roper, under whose jurisdiction the Aeronautics Branch came, that Roosevelt had decided not to approve the half-million-dollar grant.

Rather than give up the idea of the $700 airplane entirely, Vidal decided to have the Aeronautics Branch sponsor a design competition for a high-performance "safe" aircraft that would be used by Bureau of Air Commerce inspectors. Although the emphasis of the program had shifted from low cost to safety in design and thus ease of flying, Vidal hoped that the industry would be motivated by consumer pressure to produce an affordable aircraft for the private market. Such a plan would not only conform to Vidal's original goal of increased private aircraft sales but would also meet administration demands for competitive bidding for government contracts. When specifications for the safe aircraft were made public in July 1934, however, most of the established manufacturers, believing that the criteria were unrealistic and unacceptable, chose not to participate.

Vidal's troubles with the industry and its congressional supporters continued for the remainder of his term as director of the Bureau of Air Commerce, culminating in the furor over the bureau's supposed laxity in safety after Senator Bronson Cutting of New Mexico was killed in an aircraft accident in 1935. Looking for a scapegoat, Senators Hiram Johnson and Carl Hatch introduced a resolution on May 13, 1935, calling for an immediate investigation of the accident. New York Democrat Royal S. Copeland, chairman of the Senate Committee on Commerce, appointed a five-member subcommittee, which he would chair.

Although the evidence seemed unquestionably to point to negligence on the part of TWA, the Copeland committee, especially its chairman, Royal S. Copeland, appeared to be in sympathy with TWA and against the New Deal-era Bureau of Air Commerce. Copeland seemed to take delight in making the Bureau of Air Commerce the scapegoat in the Cutting crash investigation. The Copeland committee strongly condemned Roosevelt's Bureau of Air Commerce (and by inference the Roosevelt administration) for negligence in its duty to enforce air safety regulations. In a preliminary report, issued on June 30, 1936, the committee blamed the bureau for three defective navigational aids that it said were primarily responsible for causing the Cutting crash. The aviation press, always eager to condemn the Roosevelt administration for what it considered blatant mishandling of aviation matters, endorsed the committee's preliminary findings.

Although in 1935 Vidal could boast that there were only 4.78 passenger fatalities per 100 million passenger-miles flown, by 1936 the number of passenger fatalities had increased to 10.1 per 100 million passenger-miles, the largest it had been since 1932. The Cutting air crash was followed by five major air accidents, beginning in December 1936 and ending in January 1937. These disasters were responsible for the deaths of 32 persons, and, rightly or wrongly, Vidal bore the brunt of the blame.

On February 28, 1937, Vidal announced his resignation. The reaction from the aviation press was hardly unexpected. *Aero Digest*, for example, editorialized: "Eugene Vidal's belated note of resignation might well have been prefaced with the words the Duke of Windsor chose in announcing his abdication—'At long last.'" It concluded that "the President should recommend for this important post someone who knows at least what it is all about, and in whom the industry can place its confidence." Vidal's tormentor, Senator Copeland, was more generous. He was quoted by the *New York Times* as saying, "God couldn't run the Bureau as it is organized. I am firmly convinced that better air aids would have prevented recent air-line crashes and Vidal tried to get them, but he was helpless. I have the greatest respect for his ability and I am sorry that he has resigned."

Vidal remained active in aviation following his departure from government service. In 1933, before joining the Roosevelt administration, he had been one of the original stockholders (with Paul Collins, Amelia Earhart, and S. J. Solomon) of Boston-Maine Airways. In 1937 he joined the board of directors of the renamed Northeast Airlines and took an active interest in the company's affairs. Most of his time, however, was spent on a research laboratory that he founded in 1937. Vidal developed a process for manufacturing aircraft sections from molded plywood. Also, during the war years he built a radar target plane for the navy. In addition, Vidal served as a consultant to the Bendix Aviation Corporation and as a member of the Army Scientific Advisory Panel. From 1955 to 1965 he was aviation adviser to the army chief of staff.

In 1939 Vidal married Katharine Roberts. The couple had two children. Vidal died of cancer on February 20, 1969.

References:

Paul F. Collins, *Tales of an Old Air-Faring Man* (Stevens Point: University of Wisconsin/Stevens Point Foundation Press, 1983);

Tom D. Crouch, "An Airplane for Everyman: The Department of Commerce and the Light Plane Industry, 1933-1937," unpublished manuscript, National Air and Space Museum History Project Files, Washington, D.C.;

Nick A. Komons, *Bonfires to Beacons: Federal Civil Aviation Policy under the Air Commerce Act, 1926-1938* (Washington, D.C.: U.S. Department of Transportation, 1978);

Dominick A. Pisano, "The Civilian Pilot Training Program, 1939-1946: A Case Study of New Deal, War Preparedness-Mobilization Aviation Policy," dissertation, George Washington University, 1988.

Archives:

The Eugene Vidal Collection is at the University of Wyoming Transportation History Foundation, Laramie, Wyoming.

Edward P. Warner

(November 9, 1894 - July 12, 1958)

by Roger E. Bilstein

University of Houston—Clear Lake

CAREER: Engineering faculty, Massachusetts Institute of Technology (1919-1926); member, National Advisory Committee for Aeronautics (1919-1920, 1929-1945); U.S. assistant secretary of the navy for aeronautics (1926-1929); editor, *Aviation* (1929-1934); vice-chairman, Federal Aviation Commission (1934-1935); engineering consultant (1935-1938); member, Civil Aeronautics Authority/Civil Aeronautics Board (1939-1945); chairman of the interim council (1945-1947), president, International Civil Aviation Organization (1947-1957).

While aviation headlines of the 1920s, 1930s, and World War II fastened on speed and distance records, and colorful personalities, Edward P. Warner and others toiled behind the scenes at an equally important task—creating the environment for global air travel that emerged after 1945. Warner's aviation career embraced the roles of educator, engineer, consultant, author, and international civil servant. Between 1919 and 1957 he played a key role in shaping the course of U.S. and international aviation.

Warner was born on November 9, 1894, in Pittsburgh, Pennsylvania, the son of Robert Lyon and Ann Pearson Warner. Robert Warner, an electrical engineer, soon moved the family to Cambridge, Massachusetts, where Warner attended the Volkmann School in Boston and at an early age displayed the facility with numbers that impressed his contemporaries throughout his professional lifetime. Interested in flight while still a schoolboy, he and a friend built a glider and won a soaring meet at Boston in 1911. Warner produced the design and left his friend to do the actual piloting. Despite close family ties to Cornell University, his father's alma mater, Warner chose to attend Harvard. He received a B.A. with honors in 1916 and pursued additional work at the Massachusetts Institute of Technology, where he received a B.S. degree in

Edward P. Warner (courtesy of the National Archives)

1919. It was a measure of Warner's intellectual abilities that his MIT mentors put him in the classroom as an instructor in aeronautics during the first year of his graduate program.

There was a brief hiatus in Warner's teaching career during 1919 and 1920, when he worked for the fledgling National Advisory Committee for Aeronautics (NACA). NACA was completing work on research labs at its Langley center in Hampton, Virginia, and Warner joined the staff as NACA's first chief physicist, head of aerodynamic research, and head of flight research. Among other things he also designed the agency's first wind tunnel and managed the construction program for it. It was a promising start for a twenty-five-year-old engineer, but Warner, like many young NACA engineers, soon left, reportedly because of administrative turmoil at Langley. He returned to MIT after spending the summer of 1920 in Europe as a technical attaché for NACA. The European excursion was an early step toward the international activities that dominated Warner's later life. Moreover, it helped him maintain a NACA connection on several influential committees for the next 25 years.

An associate professor of aeronautical engineering, Warner remained at MIT for the next six years, reaching the rank of full professor. His former teacher Dr. Jerome C. Hunsaker had started one of America's first programs devoted to aeronautical engineering, and Warner became part of this pioneering curriculum. Among the students who passed through Warner's classes were future designers such as Leroy Grumman, James McDonnell, and Arthur Raymond as well as future officers such as Gen. James Doolittle and Adm. Felix Stump. As a teacher Warner was known as a rapid-fire lecturer, very professional and somewhat aloof in his relationships with students. But he was remembered with respect. Indeed, his ability to multiply four-digit figures in his head, among other feats, made him legendary.

The mid 1920s was a crucial period for American aviation. The U.S. Air Mail Service was beginning to establish itself, and several government committees were in the process of formulating legislation to shape the future of air transportation. Warner was in the middle of it all. Trained as an engineer, Warner nonetheless had a realistic understanding of the policy and institutional foundations needed for the future growth of aeronautics. During the early 1920s he helped draft the Massachusetts statutes for the regulation of aviation and became involved with the design and development of Boston's airport. The U.S. Mail Service hired him as consultant in 1924, and he made a thorough analysis of its equipment and navigational aids. These activities made Warner a nationally known aviation expert. He understood the realities of aircraft and flight operations, as well as the realities of regulation and balance sheets. For this reason he was named as a consultant to the President's Aircraft Board (the Morrow Board) in 1925, constituted to establish a coherent policy for both civil and military aeronautics.

In 1926, at age thirty-two, Warner left MIT to become assistant secretary of the navy for aeronautics, and for the next three years he played a leading role in the development of naval aviation. As editor of *Aviation* magazine (published by McGraw-Hill) from 1929 to 1934, his technical expertise and firsthand experience in the development of aeronautical policy helped make the publication into the leading American aviation journal of the day. He married Joan Potter in 1931; they had two children.

While continuing as editor of *Aviation*, Warner also became editorial assistant to the president of the McGraw-Hill Book Company and helped organize the Institute of the Aeronautical Sciences (which became the American Institute of Aeronautics and Astronautics in 1963). In 1929 he was appointed a member of the National Advisory Committee for Aeronautics, a position he held until 1945. Warner also was active in the Society of Automotive Engineers, serving as president in 1930.

During 1934 and 1935 Warner took a leave of absence from McGraw-Hill in order to serve as vice-chairman of the Federal Aviation Commission. He was appointed by President Franklin D. Roosevelt to analyze problems plaguing airmail service. At issue were reported irregularities in airmail contracts awarded during the Hoover administration. It was widely believed that Warner drafted much of the commission's final report, which eventually formed the basis for the Civil Aeronautics Act of 1938.

Between 1935 and 1938 Warner worked as a consulting engineer, becoming deeply involved in drawing up preliminary specifications for a four-engine airliner designed by the Douglas Aircraft Company, a concept that later evolved into the famous DC-4. In the course of this design work Warner developed a significant scientific technique of quantitative measurement and specification. Beginning with descriptions of desirable flying qualities for transport aircraft, as given by pilots, Warner converted these ideas into engineering language that could be incorporated into basic design specifications. The concept spurred further flying-quality research by NACA and was incorporated into airworthiness regulations for air transports.

In 1938 Warner became an economic and technical adviser to the Civil Aeronautics Authority, which became the Civil Aeronautics Board (CAB). He was appointed a member in 1939, serving as vice-chairman in 1941 and again from 1943 to 1945. His technical background and vast experience in aeronautical subjects eminently qualified him to do a great deal of work in the formulation of guidelines for the certification and regulation of airmen, aircraft, and flight operations.

During Warner's tenure on the CAB he became involved with international aspects of aviation operations, serving as a liaison between the CAB, the War Department, and the Department of the Navy, making trips to Alaska and the Caribbean. In 1941 Warner was a member of the W. Averell Harriman commission to England, where he assisted in working out details of the lend-lease program involving aircraft. Warner made other wartime trips, including another visit to England in 1944, when he accompanied Assistant Secretary of State Adolf A. Berle to discuss the nature of international air transport activities following the conclusion of World War II. This mission led directly to the calling of the International Civil Aviation Congress in November 1944, convened to discuss postwar international air transport operations.

From 1945 to 1947 Warner headed the interim council of the International Civil Aviation Organization (ICAO), which became an agency of the United Nations. In 1947, at age fifty-three, Warner was the popular choice as its first president. Under his presidency from 1947 to 1957, ICAO grew from 26 member nations to a total of 70. Writing for the journal *Air Affairs* in 1950, Warner summarized the goals of ICAO in terms encouraging the growth of civil aviation and promoting better international relations through civil aviation. In practical terms, this meant that ICAO took the lead in developing international standards for air transport licenses. Meteorological forecasts and en route information followed an ICAO format. For communications, international airports around the world adapted code signs and phraseology as specified by the agency. Charts, instrument approaches, and symbols were coordinated to uniform global standards. Taken collectively, this meant that airline pilots from France could negotiate American airspace just as routinely as the airspace of Venezuela, Sri Lanka, or Japan. Many of these developments grew out of the technical annexes which Warner had helped formulate during the International Civil Aviation Congress in 1944.

During his 12 years as head of ICAO (including the provisional body), Warner's position as pre-

siding officer of the council constituted but one element of a complex and demanding job. He regularly attended sessions of committees coping with administrative, legal, economic, and technical issues. Regional meetings took place in national capitals around the world, and Warner faithfully went to them all. His high ethical and moral standards never waned in these sojourns abroad. If hotels discriminated against people of any racial or ethnic backgrounds, Warner declined to stay there. In the process Warner also subordinated his American identity in the interest of international amity. Sir Frederick Tymms, the British delegate to ICAO and a friend of many years, emphasized that "he was, by nature, an 'internationalist.' " Another close associate remembered that Warner's absolute commitment to impartiality had its droll aspects. Warner's American passport expired, the friend explained, and Warner was "sincerely troubled over how he could swear the oath then required for a United States passport without prejudice to his over-riding responsibilities as a high international public servant."

Despite the multiplicity of ages, backgrounds, and careers of ICAO delegates, Warner unfailingly treated each person with respect. More often than not it was Warner who walked down the halls to visit a delegate's office in search of the unanimity which he so prized in ICAO decisions. Warner was repeatedly elected as ICAO president until he voluntarily retired in 1957. Warner's death on July 12, 1958, at Duxbury, Massachusetts, deprived the international aeronautical community of an elder statesman of the air age he helped so much to create.

Publication:
The Early History of Air Transportation (York, Pa., Maple Press, 1937).

References:
Roger E. Bilstein, "Edward Pearson Warner and the New Air Age," in *Aviation's Golden Age: Portraits from the 1920's and 1930's*, edited by William M. Leary (Iowa City: University of Iowa Press, 1989), pp. 113-126;

Theodore P. Wright, "Edward Pearson Warner: An Appreciation," *Journal of the Royal Aeronautical Society*, 62 (October 1958): 31-43.

Archives:
The Theodore P. Wright Papers, Olin Library, Cornell University, New York, include some correspondence with Warner; they primarily consist of numerous letters

from acquaintances. Miscellaneous files are scattered through the archives of institutions and agencies with which he worked, principally NACA, the Navy Department, the CAB, and ICAO.

Stanley D. Weiss

(June 8, 1910 -   )

by Joseph E. Libby

University of California, Riverside

CAREER: President, Standard Air Lines (1946-1950); president, North American Airlines (1949-1956); president, Trans-American Airlines (1956-1957); president, Twentieth Century Aircraft (1958-1962).

Stanley Dan Weiss revolutionized air travel in the United States by introducing coach fares to the airline industry. He created the first successful "no frills" service with his North American Airlines and from the late 1940s to the mid 1950s challenged the monopoly held by the major airlines over air travel. Although his airline survived only eight years, Weiss proved that an efficiently run carrier could charge low fares and still yield a profit.

Weiss was born June 8, 1910, in Gotebo, Oklahoma. The son of the town pharmacist, he initially planned to follow his father's trade. He attended Columbia University in New York City and in 1932 graduated with a degree in pharmacology. During the 1930s he developed an interest in aviation, and he learned to fly in 1937. Over the next few years he amassed several hundred hours of flight time, eventually receiving a transport pilot rating. In December 1941, as the United States entered World War II, Weiss joined the U.S. Army Air Corps. During his years in the military he served as a flight instructor and ferry pilot in both the Pacific and China-Burma-India theaters. With the rank of first lieutenant, he became one of the elite group of "hump" pilots, flying various transport and bomber aircraft over the rugged frontier of southwest China. His service during the war earned him an Air Service Medal and three Asiatic-Pacific Battle Stars.

Weiss's wartime experiences convinced him that his future lay in aviation, and like many other wartime pilots he dreamed of starting his own airline. Late in 1945, after settling with his family in

Stanley D. Weiss

Long Beach, California, he formed a partnership with Col. Charles Sherman, another army pilot seeking his fortune as an airline entrepreneur. Together they founded Fireball Air Express and purchased a war surplus Douglas C-47—the military version of the famed DC-3. Reliable and efficient to operate, these airplanes formed the backbone of hundreds of small air-transport companies created by ex-World War II pilots as they returned to civilian life.

Initially Weiss and Sherman planned to carry freight on coast-to-coast flights. But within one year Sherman had left the company, which had begun to carry passengers as well as freight. Changing the company's name to Standard Air Lines and charging a transcontinental fare of only $99 one way, Weiss began attracting large numbers of passengers. Weiss's airline and its low fares catered to families and vacation travelers, most of whom were first-time fliers. Sensing a tremendous opportunity to tap a new market of passengers, he orchestrated a series of mergers between 1949 and 1950, which resulted in the creation of North American Airlines. Through efficient operation Weiss and his associates were able to keep both costs and air fares down. The low fares increased the airline's popularity with the public and provided Weiss with opportunities to expand and upgrade the company's service.

An astute and honest businessman, Weiss established strong business relationships with many individuals in the airline industry. Despite open hostility from many of the large carriers, Weiss rejected opportunities to make a quick profit at the expense of his competitors. Seeking larger airplanes for North American Airlines, Weiss in 1955 purchased Eastern Air Lines's entire fleet of DC-4s, including $1 million worth of spare parts. When Eastern's replacement airplanes were not delivered on time, Weiss initiated the first sale-leaseback agreement in airline history when he leased the airplanes to the airline and returned the spare parts for the original purchase price. Eastern Air Lines president and former World War I flying ace Eddie Rickenbacker never forgot Weiss's honesty, and upon his retirement several years later he recommended Weiss as his replacement. Weiss refused the offer.

Earlier, in 1950, Weiss agreed to sell two DC-3s, worth $90,000 each, to Kenneth Friedkin, founder of Pacific Southwest Airlines. The deal had been verbal and closed with a handshake. Shortly afterward the outbreak of the Korean War boosted the value of the planes to $400,000. Despite the increased value of the DC-3s, Weiss made good on his word and sold the airplanes to Friedkin for the agreed-upon price.

Weiss's problems with the Civil Aeronautics Board (CAB) began in 1949, shortly after he established North American Airlines, and continued into the mid 1950s. Citing violation of federal regula-

tions concerning the number of flights allowed for irregular carriers such as North American, the CAB took actions to restrict Weiss's operations. Finally, in July 1955 the CAB revoked Weiss's operating certificates. For two years Weiss fought a series of legal battles with the CAB, charging that the board conspired with the major airlines to drive him out of business. Despite initial support from Congress his appeals failed. In April 1957 the U.S. Supreme Court upheld the CAB's actions, closing down the nation's first coach-fare airline.

Denied the right to operate an airline, Weiss turned to buying and leasing aircraft. He established a new company, Twentieth Century Aircraft, which both leased airplanes to other carriers and acted as a contract carrier by taking jobs which did not fall under CAB jurisdiction. During the late 1950s and early 1960s most of this contract work was with the military, ferrying troops to various destinations around the world. In 1962 the CAB denied Weiss's application to establish Twentieth Century as a certified airline. Locked out of airline operations, he continued to be active in buying and leasing aircraft into the mid 1970s.

Weiss's defeat in 1957 at the hands of the CAB seemed at the time to herald the end of coach fares. But his experiment had opened up flying to an entirely new market of individuals. For the first time, families and nonbusiness travelers could afford to fly. Weiss and his airline set the stage for the dozens of "no frills" airlines which followed, eventually forcing all of the major airlines to offer coach fares to remain competitive. Beyond the changes within the airline industry, the innovation of affordable air travel pioneered by Stanley Weiss revolutionized the travel habits of all Americans by providing an economical alternative to railroad and bus services.

References:

R. E. G. Davies, *Airlines of the United States since 1914* (London: Putnam's, 1972);

Davies, *Rebels and Reformers of the Airways* (Washington, D.C.: Smithsonian Institution, 1987).

Western Airlines

by Earl H. Tilford, Jr.

Air Force Air Command and Staff College

The Air Mail (Kelly) Act of February 1925 led to the birth of several air carriers, among which was Western Airlines (WAL), first incorporated as Western Air Express (WAE) on July 13, 1925. On April 17, 1926, its fleet of six Douglas M-2 mail planes flew from Vail Field, Los Angeles, to Salt Lake City by way of Las Vegas. The airline operated that route until WAL was absorbed by Delta Air Lines in 1987.

In May 1926 WAE started flying passengers perched on mail bags in the fuselage of the M-2s. Later that year, after losing a bid to fly mail east of the Rocky Mountains, WAE secured a $2.5 million grant from the Daniel Guggenheim Fund for the Promotion of Aeronautics to develop its passenger service. In 1927 it ordered three Fokker F-X 12-passenger trimotor planes, and in mid 1928 it initiated daily service between Los Angeles and San Francisco.

By 1930 WAE was flying passengers as far east as Kansas City and north to Seattle. To accommodate this expanding system, the airline purchased four four-engine Fokker F-32s. Unfortunately, these large but inefficient aircraft became profit drainers just when the Great Depression struck. Partly to head off financial disaster, but also to secure one of three coveted transcontinental air-mail contracts awarded by Postmaster General Walter Folger Brown, much of WAE joined with Transcontinental Air Transport (TAT) to form Transcontinental and Western Air, Inc. (TWA).

After the merger with TAT, what remained of WAE retained its original corporate identity along with a few routes. With the aid of loans from General Motors Corporation, which acquired a controlling interest in the airline in 1931, WAE limped back into action under the name of General Airlines. It soon reverted to its original name of Western Air Express and in 1937 bought National Park Airways to extend its service into Montana. On

March 11, 1941, WAE became Western Airlines. The airline was then flying seven DC-3s and two Boeing 247s, had a work force of 417, including 42 pilots, and operated a route structure concentrated west of the Rocky Mountains, along the Pacific Coast, north into Canada, and on to Alaska.

During World War II, WAL, like other American carriers, turned over part of its fleet to the War Department. At one point the airline had only three DC-3s flying reduced schedules over the San Diego-Los Angeles-Salt Lake City route as well as its traditional Los Angeles-San Francisco run.

Terrell C. Drinkwater, an airline executive and lawyer specializing in aeronautical law, became president of WAL early in January 1947. Under his direction the airline rebuilt its fleet and route structure. His first task, however, was to avert financial disaster by selling Western's Los Angeles-Denver route and four recently purchased war surplus DC-4s to United Air Lines for $4.75 million. He also cut the number of employees from 2,600 to 1,600—a strategy dubbed "constructive contraction."

Slowly WAL returned to profit-making status. By its 25th anniversary in 1951 the airline had a fleet of ten DC-3s, five DC-4s, and five DC-6Bs and a work force of 1,500. Annual profits exceeded $1 million over the next four years. By 1955 the WAL fleet numbered 31 planes, and 2,000 employees serviced a 5,525-mile system.

Drinkwater concentrated corporate decision-making at the top, while relying on what commercial aviation writer Robert J. Serling has called "the best middle management in the industry" for effective day-to-day operations. It worked as long as Drinkwater held the reins of power. By the late 1950s WAL had expanded its routes throughout the West, into Canada, and, with the inauguration of a Los Angeles-Mexico City route in 1957, south into Mexico. That same year fleet modernization began

Western Boeing 247 (courtesy of the National Air and Space Museum)

with the purchase of nine Lockheed Electra turboprops.

Despite its long corporate life WAL never became one of the nation's premier carriers. As the 1950s ended, the airline made a bid to get into the Pacific market with an application to the Civil Aeronautics Board for a portion of the West Coast-to-Hawaii routes. Difficulty in obtaining the Hawaii route, which was not finally secured until January 1969, typified the frustrations WAL experienced in the 1960s. Additionally, the transition to jets was under way, and Drinkwater, a conservative manager, was reluctant to pay several million dollars for a single aircraft. Consequently Western made the switch from propeller planes to an all-jet fleet more slowly than competing airlines. As the controversy over the Hawaii route continued, WAL gradually enlarged and upgraded its fleet while adding new routes. On July 1, 1967, it absorbed Pacific Northern Airlines to gain additional access into Canada and new routes in the Pacific Northwest. By the early 1970s WAL was contemplating a Los Angeles-Miami route as well as a Minneapolis-Hawaii run, and an order for four more DC-10s

was placed. Western seemed on the verge of taking its place among the nation's most prominent carriers.

The 1960s were not all good for WAL. There were strikes, and before the decade was over Western was among the most unionized of all American carriers, something the politically conservative Drinkwater resented. In December 1968 Las Vegas financier Kirk Kerkorian purchased 22 percent of WAL's stock. Within a year he controlled 30.5 percent and the board of directors. Kerkorian booted Drinkwater out of the presidency and into a ceremonial post as chairman of the board. On May 31, 1970, Drinkwater retired.

Kerkorian increased profits by reducing the number of employees and canceling an order for Boeing 747s, a wise move given the unexpected hikes in fuel costs of the mid 1970s. In 1972 Kerkorian began selling his WAL stock to finance other business ventures, and by 1976 he liquidated all of his WAL interests.

After Kerkorian sold his stock, WAL began stumbling toward financial oblivion. By the late 1970s there was talk of a merger with Continental.

When this did not develop, Air Florida voiced interest in acquiring WAL in the early 1980s but dropped the idea as Western's losses mounted. In September 1983 WAL offered its employees 27 percent of its stock in exchange for $40 million in pay cuts, averaging a 10 to 18 percent reduction per worker. All five of WAL's unions agreed to the plan, which took effect one month later. Unfortunately the financial situation continued to deteriorate as a string of ineffective chief executive officers shuffled through a revolving door to the president's office.

After a brief recovery in 1985 the red ink came flooding back in 1986. In September 1986 Delta and Western agreed to merge in an $860 mil-lion deal. Following months of court battles, the merger was completed on April 1, 1987, and Western Airlines ceased to exist.

References:

R. E. G. Davies, *Airlines of the United States since 1914*, revised edition (Washington, D.C.: Smithsonian Institution, 1982);

Irwin Ross, "Kirk Kerkorian Doesn't Want All the Meat off the Bone," *Fortune*, 80 (November 1969): 144-148, 184-186;

Robert J. Serling, *The Only Way to Fly* (Garden City, N.Y.: Doubleday, 1976);

Henry Ladd Smith, *Airways: The History of Commercial Aviation in the United States* (New York: Knopf, 1942).

Francis White

(March 4, 1892 - February 23, 1961)

by Wesley Phillips Newton

Auburn University

CAREER: U.S. diplomatic service (1915-1926); U.S. assistant secretary of state (1927-1934).

Francis White, career diplomat, skilled negotiator, and principal architect of the U.S. aviation diplomacy that produced a "chosen instrument" for international air service, was born in Baltimore, Maryland, on March 4, 1892, to Miles and Virginia Bonsal White. In 1913 he received his Ph.D. degree from Yale University's Sheffield School of Science, and he did postgraduate work in France and Spain. He entered the diplomatic service in 1915. After postings in China, Iran, Cuba, and Argentina he was put in charge of the Latin American desk in the State Department in 1922.

The Washington assignment began White's acquaintance with U.S. commercial aviation involvement in Latin America. He was mainly responsible for the formation of an interdepartmental committee on aviation that met periodically to consider ways to promote American commercial aviation in foreign areas, with a focus on Latin America, where European airlines were becoming entrenched. Not only did these ventures offer a challenge to the growing American economic position in Latin America, they also represented to White and the War and Navy Departments, particularly, an even more significant danger to the strategic position of the United States, especially the Panama Canal. The European presence was underscored in 1925 when Dr. Peter Paul von Bauer, managing director of SCADTA, a German-controlled airline in Colombia near the Panama Canal, came to Washington seeking an airmail contract for his proposed service between Colombia and the United States via the Canal, Central America, and Cuba. With White's and the military's opposition a key factor, von Bauer failed to get his contract, and service had to be held in abeyance. He did not give up, however, and a propaganda campaign he mounted put pressure on the U.S. government to seek an alternative. Early in 1927, with the U.S. Post Office Department advertising for bids on a Key West-to-Havana airmail contract, several American financial and entrepreneurial groups competed for the prize.

From this competition emerged a holding company, the Aviation Corporation of America, and its operating entity, Pan American Airways. Pan Am's president, Juan T. Trippe, was determined to dominate the skies of Latin America. In the fall of 1927, having learned of the rising wind of an American challenge to his ambitions, von Bauer returned to Washington to lobby for his airline. His presence, with the backing of the Colombian government, led to a meeting of the interdepartmental aviation committee chaired by White, who earlier in the year had been named U.S. assistant secretary of state. It was at this meeting on November 27 that a comprehensive aviation diplomacy was formulated. White and the Post Office Department representative described the recent activities of von Bauer and SCADTA as well as the growing envelopment of part of South America by a vigorous French airline, Aeropostale. The United States had a contestant, Pan American Airways, but it was just now getting underway and needed support. White felt it was the only viable American line currently in existence. The committee was unanimous in its recommendation that, to keep the American effort from being splintered, there should be legislation that would permit the postmaster general to award a contract for the carriage of mail to foreign areas to the company he felt could best do the job; in other words, a change that would render ineffective the then-current provision for the lowest bidder to win automatically.

The U.S. Congress enacted the change in March 1928. By that time White had concluded that Pan American Airways should receive all possible financial and diplomatic support, with the willing cooperation of the Post Office Department. All foreign airmail contracts went to Pan American for well over a decade.

Also, White sent directions to American diplomats in the field to bend every effort in support of Pan American's negotiations to win contracts from Latin American governments for their outgoing international mail and landing rights, for the use of those governments' communications networks, and for other assistance. Some field diplomats resisted these unusual directions but eventually complied.

White generally approved of Pan American attempts to gain a monopoly of airline service within a foreign country, even if those efforts sometimes provoked hostile reactions. After all, White and the postal authorities had combined to create a monopoly among competing American companies for Pan American Airways. In so doing they reversed a long-standing rule of American foreign policy which was never to discriminate in favor of one American commercial endeavor overseas against other Americans.

White's rationale for the creation of a "chosen instrument" was first and foremost strategic, but he did not neglect to stress the economic benefits he felt would accrue to U.S. firms doing business in Latin America from having one powerful and hence more efficient air carrier. He seems to have been sincere in his beliefs, even though the "chosen instrument" was a contradiction to the laissez-faire philosophy of the Republican administrations that fostered it.

White was one of the few officials in government informed by Trippe of a secret agreement with Peter Paul von Bauer by which Pan American gained financial control of a Depression-weakened SCADTA. A somewhat naive White approved because he was assured that SCADTA soon would be "Americanized." But this did not happen until World War II forced von Bauer and his German colleagues to give SCADTA over to Pan American after Colombia nationalized it.

Although the "chosen instrument" policy served U.S. interests during the 1930s, it would be replaced by competition in the postwar period. By that time, however, White had long since left government service.

References:

Marylin Bender and Selig Altschul, *The Chosen Instrument* (New York: Simon & Schuster, 1982);
Wesley Phillips Newton, *The Perilous Sky: U.S. Aviation Diplomacy and Latin America, 1919-1931* (Coral Gables, Fla.: University of Miami Press, 1978).

Noel Wien

(June 8, 1899 - July 18, 1977)

by Claus-M. Naske

University of Alaska Fairbanks

CAREER: Barnstormer (1921-1924); bush pilot (1924-1927); president, Wien Alaska Airways (1927-1929); president, Wien Airways of Alaska (1932-1935); vice-president, Northern Air Transport (1935); president (1936-1940), vice-president, Wien Alaska Airlines/Wien Air Alaska (1940-1977).

Noel Wien, a pioneering bush pilot who opened numerous air routes in the far north of Alaska, was born on June 8, 1899, at Lake Nebagamon, Wisconsin. He was one of five children of John Berndt Wien and his wife, both Scandinavian immigrants. When Wien was six years old the family moved to a farm in northern Minnesota, where he was raised. An indifferent student, he left school after completing eighth grade (which he had had to repeat). Wien then worked on the farm, drove a truck, and riveted buckles on harnesses in a Duluth factory. Excited by tales of World War I aviators, he went to Minneapolis in 1921 and used his small savings to learn to fly at the Curtiss Northwest Airplane Company, operated by Maj. Ray S. Miller. He became a barnstormer and spent several years touring the West with the Federated Flyers Flying Circus.

In 1924 Wien found work with the Alaska Aerial Transportation Company of Fairbanks. He arrived in Anchorage in June, together with a crated Standard biplane that had been purchased by his new employers. After assembling the plane, Wien gave sightseeing rides to more than 170 people, earning $1,700 for the company. On July 6 he flew from Anchorage to Fairbanks, making the first flight between the two points. He covered the 300 miles in three hours and 45 minutes.

Wien learned a great deal about bush flying during his first season in the Far North. Bush pilots, he came to understand, could open remote areas of the vast country that were almost impossi-

Noel Wien (portrait by Harvey Goodale; courtesy of the Robert C. Reeve Collection)

ble to reach by any other means. The isolated inhabitants of these tiny communities came to depend on air service for supplies and emergency medical assistance. Pilots had to be self-reliant, able to make repairs and replace equipment under difficult conditions.

Wien first flew to Brooks (later Livengood) on August 19. The round trip took two hours and 15 minutes, and Wien made it 30 times during the summer, carrying supplies to the 250 men who were working small gold claims. Other trips carried him to Circle Hot Springs, 90 miles northeast of Fairbanks, and to the community of Eagle, located on the Yukon River six miles west of the Alaska-Canada border. At one point he tried but failed to reach Wiseman, an isolated gold-mining settlement 185 miles northeast of Fairbanks. In the process he became the first pilot to cross the Arctic Circle. By the time operations came to an end in the late fall, he had logged over 139 hours. His success convinced many doubters that aviation was not only possible in the Far North but also uniquely suited to its empty spaces.

Wien spent part of the winter of 1924-1925 in the contiguous states. At the request of the newly organized Fairbanks Airplane Company, he bought a Fokker F-III for shipment to Alaska. He also hired his brother Ralph as a mechanic for the company.

Before the ice broke up in May and June 1925, Wien made 14 flights to various isolated communities north of Fairbanks, becoming the first man to land beyond the Arctic Circle. He also had the unwanted distinction of becoming the first bush pilot to be forced down in the Alaska wilderness. On May 5, while returning from the first flight ever made to Wiseman, he had to make an emergency landing due to bad weather in a remote area 40 miles southwest of Nenana. It took him four arduous days to walk to civilization.

Wien's escape from disaster taught him how ill-prepared he had been. Thereafter, he took with him a canvas bag filled with emergency items that included concentrated and lightweight food, a cup and small kettle, a waterproof case of matches, a small axe, and a long-barreled .30 caliber Mauser pistol with a stock that could be attached to convert it to a rifle. When there was room, he also carried a pair of trail snowshoes. Later, with the appearance of larger airplanes, Wien's assortment of emergency gear became larger and more sophisticated.

On June 5, 1925, Wien flew for the first time to Nome, some 570 miles from Fairbanks. This marked the beginning of his long association with the Bering Sea community, leading to the construction of an airport and the beginning of regular air service in 1927. While in Nome, Wien met and fell in love with Ada Bering Arthurs, an attractive seventeen-year-old. They were married four years later, on May 19, 1929. The couple had two sons and a daughter.

By 1927 Wien was ready to strike out on his own. Raising enough money to purchase a Stinson Detroiter, he opened for business in September as Wien Alaska Airways. He flew throughout the winter, the first pilot to do so. In the spring of 1928 he added a Waco biplane, which he taught his brother Ralph to fly. Following a successful summer, the company was formally incorporated in October with Wien as president and Ralph as vice-president.

In 1929 Wien sold his pioneering company to the giant Aviation Corporation for $25,000, signing a three-year non-competitive agreement. He flew for the renamed Alaska Airways until the summer of 1932. Then, freed from the restrictive terms of his sales agreement, he formed Wien Airways of Alaska, with bases at Fairbanks and Nome. In 1935 the company merged with Northern Air Transport, taking the name of the latter. A further reorganization took place the following year, with the name of the company again changing, this time to Wien Alaska Airlines. By 1938 the air carrier had eight airplanes and four pilots. It operated a variety of routes north, east, and west of Fairbanks, including eight airmail routes.

In 1940, with his wife ill and medical bills mounting, Wien sold his stock in the airline to his brother Sigurd (Sig) and moved south. Following his wife's recovery, Wien returned to Alaska and rejoined the family airline. He flew for the company until the mid 1950s, then worked in public relations. Named "Alaskan of the Year" in 1975 in recognition of his numerous contributions to the development of commercial aviation in the state, he died on July 18, 1977.

References:

Carol V. Glines, "The Wien Family Airline," *Air Line Pilot*, 49 (December 1980): 22-27;

Ira Harkey, *Pioneer Bush Pilot: The Story of Noel Wien* (Seattle: University of Washington Press, 1974);

Jean Potter, *The Flying North* (Sausalito, Cal.: Comstock Editions, 1977).

Wien Air Alaska

by Claus-M. Naske

University of Alaska Fairbanks

A family-owned airline for most of its history, what later became Wien Air Alaska began when pioneer bush pilot Noel Wien formed Wien Alaska Airways in September 1927. Using a four-seat Stinson Detroiter, Wien maintained service between Fairbanks and isolated interior settlements throughout the winter of 1927-1928, becoming the first pilot to continue operating throughout the year. In the spring of 1928 he purchased a second aircraft, a Waco biplane, which he taught his brother Ralph to fly. In 1929 the brothers sold the company to the Aviation Corporation.

In August 1932 Noel Wien started Wien Airways of Alaska, with major operating bases at Fairbanks and Nome. In 1935 the company merged with Northern Air Transport, taking the name of the latter. A further reorganization in 1936 resulted in a change of name to Wien Alaska Airlines. By 1938 the company was operating eight aircraft, including a Boeing 247D, on a variety of interior routes that radiated north, east, and west of Fairbanks.

In 1940 Noel Wien sold his stock in the company to his brother Sigurd. The airline prospered during the war years, flying military cargo and passengers throughout the territory. In 1946 it acquired Ferguson Airways; seven years later, Byers Airways joined the growing fold.

In February 1966 the company changed its name to Wien Air Alaska. Two years later, following a merger with rival Northern Consolidated Airlines, the company became Wien Consolidated Airlines. This designation lasted only until 1973, when the name was changed back to Wien Air Alaska. By then the airline had more than 800 employees. It flew nearly 10,000 route miles and served 190 airfields with its fleet of five Boeing 737s, five Fairchild-Hiller FH-227s, and assorted smaller aircraft.

The airline's demise began in June 1977 when its pilots went out on strike. They returned to work in March 1979 to a weakened airline. In the wake of the Airline Deregulation Act of 1978, Wien Air Alaska opened routes to Ketchikan, Juneau, and Seattle; however, the airline lost $1.7 million in 1979. Although the Wien family successfully fought off a takeover bid by Alaska Airlines, they lost control of the company in 1980 when the Household Finance Corporation of Chicago acquired a majority of the line's stock.

Under new management the airline turned a net profit of $1.6 million in 1981 and $4.8 million in 1982. The following year Household Finance sold the company to James J. Flood, who had been president of the airline since 1980. Although Wien Air Alaska flew over one million passengers between January and November 1984, mounting debts placed the company into Chapter 11 bankruptcy before the end of the year. It never reemerged.

References:

Judith Fuerst, "Ray I. Petersen," *Alaska Business Monthly* (January 1988): 32-33;

Carroll V. Glines, "The Wien Family Airline," *Air Line Pilot*, 49 (December 1980): 22-27;

Ira Harkey, *Pioneer Bush Pilot: The Story of Noel Wien* (Seattle: University of Washington Press, 1974);

Archie Satterfield, *The Alaska Airlines Story* (Anchorage: Alaska Northwest Publishing Co., 1981).

C. E. Woolman

(October 8, 1889 - September 11, 1966)

by W. David Lewis

Auburn University

and

Wesley Phillips Newton

Auburn University

CAREER: Plantation manager (1912); agricultural extension agent (1913-1916), district agricultural supervisor, state of Louisiana (1916-1925); sales representative, vice-president, Huff Daland Dusters (1925-1928); vice-president (1928-1934), general manager (1934-1945), president and general manager (1945-1965), chief executive officer and chairman, Delta Air Service/Delta Air Corporation/Delta Air Lines (1928-1966).

Collett Everman Woolman, better known throughout the aviation industry as "C. E.," built Delta Air Lines from a small, regional crop-dusting enterprise into one of the nation's largest airlines. Born on October 8, 1889, in Bloomington, Indiana, the son of Albert Jefferson Woolman and Daura Campbell Woolman, he grew up around Champaign-Urbana, Illinois, where his father taught physics at the University of Illinois. After graduating from high school there in 1908, he matriculated at the university the same year; among other activities, he sang in the glee club and, being tall and rawboned, went out for varsity football. His interest in flight appeared early; during his sophomore year in college, in 1909, he tended 800 traveling calves in order to get to the world's first aviation meet at Rheims, France. On his way back, he helped pioneer aviator Claude Grahame-White overhaul a rotary engine on shipboard in preparation for an air show in Boston.

Woolman graduated from the University of Illinois in 1912 with a degree in agriculture. Moving south, he became manager of a plantation in northeastern Louisiana. In 1913 he joined the extension department of Louisiana State University; the following year, after passage of the Smith-Lever Agricul-

C. E. Woolman (courtesy of Delta Air Lines)

tural Extension Act, he became one of the first county agents in the state, serving Ouachita Parish from an office in its chief city, Monroe, later to become the birthplace of Delta. In 1916, after becoming a district supervisor and moving to Baton Rouge, he returned briefly to Champaign to marry Helen Fairfield, a home economics teacher. A genial man who combined shrewdness with a folksy manner, he soon made numerous friends among influential planters and business leaders in northern Louisiana.

Traveling throughout Louisiana, Woolman became aware of the devastation inflicted upon cotton crops by the boll weevil. Not far from Monroe, at Tallulah, an entomologist, Dr. Bert Coad, was experimenting at the U.S. Department of Agriculture's Delta Laboratory with the aerial spraying of such insecticides as calcium arsenate upon infested cottonfields. Woolman worked closely with Coad, commencing a fateful lifetime relationship. Through a chance encounter with George B. Post, vice-president of the Huff Daland Company, an aircraft manufacturing firm headquartered in Ogdensburg, New York, Coad began utilizing modified biplane trainers in crop dusting. In 1924 the Ogdensburg firm established a separate division, Huff Daland Dusters, Inc., which was first headquartered at Macon, Georgia, but shifted its base to Monroe the following year. By this time, Woolman had become a sales representative for the company, working under Harold R. Harris, a former army pilot. A natural salesman, Woolman quickly became a major asset to his employers.

Extending its operations across the southern United States from North Carolina to California, Huff Daland Dusters also expanded into Latin America. In 1926 Woolman went to Peru to investigate sales possibilities on cotton-growing estates in that country. Early the next year, Huff Daland established operations there, disassembling dusting planes after the growing season had ended in the United States and shipping them to South America by way of the Panama Canal. Important diplomatic consequences resulted from this move as Huff Daland's parent firm, which had been renamed Keystone Aircraft Corporation after shifting its operating base to Bristol, Pennsylvania, came under the control of powerful Wall Street financiers including Richard F. Hoyt, who together with Juan Trippe played a leading role in the development of Pan American Airways. Desiring to establish operations in Peru, Pan American used the dusting firm as an entering wedge. Working closely with Harold B. Grow, a veteran American navy pilot who had become director of aviation in Peru, Woolman was instrumental in negotiating entry for Pan American into the Andean nation. This paved the way for the establishment in 1929 of a new international air carrier, Panagra, by Trippe and the Grace steamship interests.

Woolman's role in these developments whetted his interests in airline operations. As he prepared to return to the United States in 1928, an opportunity arose that ultimately led in this direction when Keystone officials decided to unload their Huff Daland subsidiary. Together with Harris and Irwin E. Auerbach, comptroller of the dusting firm, Woolman laid plans to raise the $40,000 necessary to purchase it. After foiling a plot by Auerbach to take over the enterprise by himself, Woolman and Harris secured sufficient backing from planters and businessmen in the Monroe area to acquire Huff Daland, which was renamed Delta Air Service, Inc. The new identity, suggested by their secretary, Catherine FitzGerald, was in honor of the flat, fertile Mississippi River delta in which the company had been born.

While Delta continued to spray crops, conduct the aerial inspection of levees, and run a flying school recently established by Huff Daland, Woolman pondered how to expand the firm into a passenger-carrying operation. In 1929 he joined forces with John S. Fox, a businessman and investor from Bastrop, Louisiana, who had established a flying service that included among its assets a single-engine, six-passenger Travel Air plane. By selling his enterprise to Delta, Fox became that company's largest stockholder, and Woolman was able to inaugurate passenger operations with a flight on June 17, 1929, from Dallas to Monroe. By the end of the summer, having added a second Travel Air on which Fox had secured an earlier option, the fledgling service extended from Fort Worth to Birmingham via Monroe and Meridian, Mississippi. Meanwhile, Harris became more and more deeply involved in Panagra and soon departed, leaving Woolman and Fox in command of Delta.

Although Delta had established service all the way from Fort Worth to Atlanta by June 1930, large losses were sustained in conducting passenger operations. The only way that the firm could maintain its passenger service was by securing a federal airmail subsidy, which was indispensable even to the largest airlines of the time. Hope for such a subsidy was kindled briefly when Congress passed the Air Mail (Watres) Act in the spring of 1930, encouraging the use of larger transport planes by prescribing payment to carriers based on the amount of space made available for mail, rather than on a pound rate. This expectation, however, proved naive, because Postmaster General Walter Folger Brown was determined to award contracts only to large carriers with powerful financial backers. Such contracts were doled out at a controversial "Spoils Conference" held at Brown's Washington office, to which Woolman was not invited. Woolman went anyway, but quickly saw that the situation was hopeless. Under the circumstances, the best he could do was to sell Delta's passenger operation to the Aviation Corporation (AVCO), a giant holding company that had recently consolidated an unwieldy conglomeration of airlines into American Airways. After AVCO secured an airmail contract from Atlanta to Fort Worth, Delta received a settlement that, at best, represented about 50 cents for each dollar that it had expended in developing the route.

Continuing to stay in business mainly as a crop-dusting enterprise, Delta managed to survive the badly depressed period of the early 1930s on a shoestring. Discouraged, Fox pulled out, a decision he was to regret for the rest of his life. Backed by a small but faithful cadre of planters and businessmen who lived in and around Monroe, Woolman kept Delta alive by combining his gift for salesmanship with a parsimonious managerial style that became his trademark. Finally, in 1934, an opportunity to reenter airline operations arose when President Franklin D. Roosevelt's recently established New Deal administration, seeking to embarrass the previous Republican leadership under Herbert Hoover, launched a sweeping investigation of the allegedly illegal way in which airmail routes had been dispensed by Brown in 1930. Existing contracts were annulled and the Army Air Corps temporarily flew the mail. A series of fatal crashes by inexperienced military pilots who lacked familiarity with the routes quickly discredited this ill-advised venture, and the investigation failed to produce conclusive proof that Brown had been guilty of criminal misconduct. Under the Air Mail Act of 1934, the same large carriers that had previously held airmail contracts, masquerading as new companies by adopting slightly altered names, regained most of their former routes. A few changes, however, did result. Using its influence with powerful southern Democrats in Washington, Delta won an airmail contract from Fort Worth and Dallas to Charleston, South Carolina, via such places as Shreveport, Monroe, Jackson, Meridian, Birmingham, Atlanta, and Columbia. Fresh capital was pumped into Delta by

Clarence E. Faulk, a wealthy Louisiana newspaper owner who became president while Woolman took the post of general manager. On July 4, 1934, the company conducted its inaugural passenger run as an airmail contractor from Monroe to Dallas, using a trimotor Stinson-T aircraft. Three days later service was commenced on the Atlanta-to-Charleston end of the system with pilot Charles Dolson at the controls; many years later, he would succeed Woolman as chief executive officer of Delta.

Although he continued to exercise general oversight of what now became the firm's dusting division, a part of Delta's operations that he would zealously preserve throughout the rest of his life, Woolman left day-to-day control of its activities to Coad and devoted himself from this point on to developing the airline. From 1934 until 1941 the firm's headquarters remained in Monroe, where Woolman administered operations through a small cadre of trusted associates including Laigh C. Parker, who left a position as district traffic manager for American to head Delta's traffic department; L. B. Judd, an entomologist with marked business abilities who became the firm's chief accountant; Pat Higgins, the former chief dusting pilot, who became operations manager until he died of cancer in 1940; and the ever-faithful secretary, Catherine Fitz-Gerald. Operationally, the line was broken into eastern and western divisions, with Atlanta as the dividing point. As traffic grew under Parker's constant promotional efforts, passenger earnings far outstripped dusting revenues by the end of the decade, and the firm as a whole became a modestly profitable enterprise, achieving a net return of $67,594 in 1939. Meanwhile, new equipment was added as the company progressed from Stinson-Ts to Lockheed Electras, acquired four secondhand Douglas DC-2s from American in early 1940, and took delivery of four new DC-3s beginning late that same year. After relying upon its copilots to provide cabin service throughout the decade, Delta started hiring female flight attendants at the time the DC-2s were added to its fleet; Laura Wizark, formerly with American, became the firm's pioneer stewardess.

In administering this growing operation, Woolman built the company in his own likeness, perfecting a managerial style that became legendary throughout the industry. Despite being a transplanted northerner, he had thoroughly assimilated southern ways, and skillfully created a corporate image based upon unfailing courtesy toward passengers, adherence to the "Golden Rule," maintaining a "personal touch," and manifesting an aggressive concern for safety and dependability. Traveling ceaselessly throughout the firm's network of stations, he prided himself on knowing each employee by name, did everything possible to inculcate a "family feeling" throughout the enterprise, and played a highly paternalistic role that harmonized well with the folkways of his adopted region. Though forced to accept unionization among the company's pilots and mechanics, he did his utmost to deal with employees on an individual basis, expressing his concern about whatever personal problems they might have, maintaining an "open door" policy in airing grievances, and keeping the firm's administrative hierarchy as simple as possible. Cultivating a homespun manner, he ceremoniously picked up rubber bands, paper clips, and pieces of safety wire to dramatize his hatred of waste, and presided in a fatherly way in awarding service pins at banquets and ceremonies throughout the system. Kind but nonetheless extremely firm whenever the situation demanded it, his style was perhaps best summed up by one discerning observer who called him a "gentle autocrat."

By 1941 Delta had clearly outgrown its northeastern Louisiana base. Its equipment needs, particularly after it became necessary to purchase a fleet of 21-passenger DC-3s, could not be met with capital available in and around Monroe. Due to a changing federal regulatory climate, the company also needed better legal advice than it could command in a provincial setting; in conducting a sale of stock in late 1939 and early 1940, for example, it unwittingly infringed upon procedures established by the Securities and Exchange Commission involving the difference between a private and a public issue, and had to be guided through a complicated remedial process by an experienced Atlanta underwriter, Richard W. Courts. Even more significant in its implications for the future was the passage of the Civil Aeronautics Act of 1938, which placed airlines under much stricter federal control, both with regard to safety and to economic development. In 1940, using powers granted to him under a controversial governmental reorganization act passed during the preceding year, President Roosevelt further tightened the growing regulatory web by placing economic control of commercial aviation in the hands of a Civil Aeronautics Board (CAB) that operated squarely under the executive branch. Relocation to

a major metropolitan base would enable Delta to participate more effectively in the increasingly rationalized and regulated industry that commercial aviation was becoming.

Responding to these developments, Woolman made the most crucial decision in Delta's history by deciding to move the firm's headquarters to Atlanta. Most of the stockholders, it appears, would have preferred Dallas, but Woolman believed that Atlanta would be a better base, not only because it was already the hinge of the system but also because the CAB had recently awarded Delta a new route from Atlanta to Cincinnati that made the Georgia capital even more of a central hub. The increasing role played in company affairs by Courts, who had recently persuaded tobacco magnate R. J. Reynolds to become a major investor in Delta, was also a factor; Courts later recalled having advised Faulk that the company would have to move to Atlanta if it wished to expand its system. Underscoring his message was a $500,000 loan from the Atlanta-based Trust Company of Georgia that enabled the company to go ahead with arrangements to buy DC-3s pending the successful outcome of a new stock issue. On March 1, 1941, Delta's board of directors bowed to Woolman's wishes and approved a resolution moving its headquarters to Atlanta.

Less than a year after this major shift, the country was plunged into World War II. All but four of Delta's planes were turned over to the armed services soon after the Japanese attack on Pearl Harbor, and by mid-1942 all senior pilots with military experience had been recalled to active duty. Early in the war the company also lost many clerical and maintenance workers whose services were hard to replace, and even such key executives as Laigh Parker, who contributed significantly to the operations of the Air Transport Command (ATC), were removed from their posts for the duration. Woolman's task, therefore, was to secure maximum utilization of remaining equipment and the greatest possible degree of efficiency in making use of the company's human resources in the face of mounting demands. These demands included modifying bombers, fighter planes, and trainers for use in various types of climates and conditions, depending upon the theaters of war in which they were to be deployed; conducting special instructional programs for both military and civilian personnel; and conducting emergency missions within the continental United States for the ATC. Predictably, Woolman's managerial skills were equal to the challenge. Late in the war a report issued by the CAB showed that Delta led all other American airlines in making use of available resources. Its planes, for example, flew an average of 14.02 hours a day, against an industry figure of 11.39, and covered 1,903 miles per day in contrast to an industry mean of 1,793. Partly because of high load factors and wartime price controls from which all airlines benefited, Delta emerged from the war in unprecedentedly good financial condition; the ratio between its assets and liabilities improved from 1.2 to 1 in June 1941 to 3.2 to 1 in mid 1945. To a considerable degree, however, the company's fiscal health also reflected Woolman's penchant for sound, conservative management.

Under the new federal regulatory system established in the late 1930s, all additions to the route structure of an airline required complex governmental hearings and CAB approval. In 1943 the CAB authorized Delta to add an extremely important city to its system: New Orleans. Well before the war ended, Woolman created a new planning and research department under the direction of Edward M. Johnson, who had previously been an assistant to Joseph B. Eastman, coordinator of transportation in the early days of the New Deal. Together Woolman and Johnson mapped out an ambitious program of postwar expansion involving applications for no less than ten prospective new routes, nearly every one of which would materialize in the future. The first major breakthrough in this effort occurred shortly after the end of the war, when, in August 1945, the CAB awarded Delta the longest single new route it had granted since its inception: a 1,028-mile run from Chicago to Miami. Because of its long-range implications, this was conceivably the most important of all the victories Delta won in CAB proceedings.

For the first time Delta had a major vacation route, inspiring it to advertise itself as "The Trunk Line to Sunshine." More importantly, however, the Chicago-to-Miami award transformed Delta's relationship with Eastern Air Lines, with profound consequences for the future. Both companies had commenced passenger operations in Atlanta during the same year, 1930, but Eastern, a major trunkline, had stayed to become the dominant air carrier serving the city while Delta reverted to being a mere crop-dusting company. After 1934, when Delta again started passenger operations in At-

lanta, one of the main functions of its east-west system was to feed traffic into Eastern's much larger north-south network, which included a lucrative route from New England and New York City to Miami. Prior to 1945, therefore, the relationship between the two carriers was complementary, as Woolman later indicated in his typically humorous way during an encounter with Eastern's chief executive, Edward V. ("Eddie") Rickenbacker, after a meeting of airline officials at Washington, D.C. In a scramble for taxis, Woolman had squeezed into the last seat in the last cab in sight, and Rickenbacker had asked if he might ride a short distance on Woolman's lap. "Well, Eddie," Woolman quipped, "I've been helping support you for years, so I might as well do it some more."

Although it was probably made in a good-natured way, Woolman's remark also had a cutting edge, because the CAB's 1945 route award to Delta had for the first time pitted it and Eastern against one another in a rivalry that became increasingly bitter over the years. At the beginning, it was an unlikely match, for Eastern, which already possessed operating rights between Chicago and Miami, was by far the most profitable firm in the industry and Delta was tiny by contrast. The outcome, however, was even more improbable. By 1990, long after both Rickenbacker and Woolman were in their graves, Delta, clearly the winner of the competitive war that was thus unleashed, was one of the nation's three largest airlines, while Eastern had gone bankrupt and passed out of existence. To a considerable degree, this dramatic outcome resulted from the dynamics of the relationship between the two airlines during the two decades following World War II, and from key decisions made by Rickenbacker and Woolman as they struggled against one another during this crucial period.

Throughout the postwar era, both Rickenbacker and Woolman wrestled with problems involving aircraft selection. Competing with Eastern forced Woolman to acquire progressively larger and faster planes to meet the demands of long-haul, non-stop runs between such destinations as Chicago and Miami. These ships were quite different from those required for previous short hops between the stations on Delta's prewar route system, most of which were relatively small. Acquiring bigger and speedier planes in turn forced Woolman to seek new routes between large nodal centers over which they could be effectively utilized when they were

Delta Air Lines Convair 340 (courtesy of the National Air and Space Museum)

not flying between Chicago, Atlanta, and Miami. Because such route awards usually required service to smaller cities, Delta had to schedule a mixture of long, nonstop flights with trips that included stops at intermediate destinations. This in turn made it necessary to select smaller but up-to-date aircraft that could serve such markets with optimum efficiency. As the process went on, continuous infusions of fresh capital had to be raised, the stakes constantly escalated, and penalties associated with making a bad decision became increasingly severe.

During the immediate postwar era, Woolman and his advisers managed to keep no worse than even with Eastern in this vital area of competition, and Rickenbacker only narrowly averted at least one major debacle. In February 1946 Delta got the jump on Eastern by putting a large new four-engine airliner, the Douglas DC-4, into service on nonstop flights between Chicago, Atlanta, and Miami. Stung by this development, Eastern fought back with the Lockheed L-649 Constellation, which was

not only faster than the DC-4 but also had the additional advantage of being pressurized. As Delta's sales curve plummeted, Woolman moved up to the Douglas DC-6B, a highly successful plane that won back customers and earned record profits. After Eastern again raised the ante by adopting the L-1049 Super-Constellation, a stretched model with turbocompound engines, Delta responded with the Douglas DC-7, which was comparable in size, similarly equipped, and slightly faster. For use on short runs Woolman was tempted by a new twin-engine craft, the Martin 2-0-2, but shied away from it when warned that it was structurally weak. Instead, he opted for thrift by having Delta's existing DC-3s modified to carry four additional passengers. Eastern also continued to use the DC-3, but Rickenbacker, seeking a replacement for this classic ship, invested heavily in the development of the 2-0-2. When its deficient wing structure led to a series of crashes, the CAB grounded it in 1948 and Martin nearly went bankrupt. Facing disaster, Rickenbacker orchestrated an emergency reorganization plan under which Martin stayed in business and produced a much better plane known as the 4-0-4. Eastern flew it successfully for years, but the entire episode foreshadowed future crises that would not turn out so well for Rickenbacker.

In addition to holding his own with Rickenbacker in aircraft selection during the immediate postwar era, Woolman gained a key advantage over his rival by making a shrewd decision that turned an apparent setback into a strategic advance. One of the reasons Woolman had selected the Douglas DC-6B to compete with Eastern's Constellations was that the "Connies" were required by new federal regulations to have a flight mechanic in the cockpit, in addition to the usual pilot and copilot. The cockpit of the DC-6 was designed for a traditional two-person crew. By 1948, however, the CAB was under increasing pressure from such unions as the Airline Flight Engineers Association (AFEA) to subject both the DC-6 and the Boeing 377 Stratocruiser to the new rule. Not wishing to see other manufacturers and carriers gain a competitive edge by introducing planes that were just as large and fast as the Constellations but required only two persons in the cockpit, Lockheed and the airlines that used its planes joined in the fight. Despite opposition from such major airlines as American and United, and from the Air Transport Association, which reflected the views of most airline managements, the CAB ultimately yielded to the pressure and stipulated that both the DC-6 and the Stratocruiser would be subject to the three-person rule after December 1, 1948.

Fortunately for Delta, there was some leeway in this ruling. Despite strong opposition from the AFEA, the CAB did not stipulate that the third crewman had to be a flight engineer, but could instead be a pilot who had been trained to play a flight engineer's role. Charles Dolson, Delta's vice-president of operations, and T. P. Ball, the company's chief pilot, urged Woolman to take advantage of this provision even though it would result in higher operating costs due to the fact that a pilot required more extensive training and received higher pay than a flight engineer. Putting members of two different unions in the cockpit, they argued, would create dissension, which would be only exacerbated by the fact that the flight engineer would hold a dead-end position and would never be able to aspire to the status and pay of a full-fledged airline captain.

Woolman accepted this reasoning. "We must never put a board on a man's head," he later stated, meaning that a third man in the cockpit would watch younger men rise above him while his own status was frozen, producing resentment and labor problems that Woolman was determined to avoid. It therefore became a settled Delta policy that the third crew member must be a fully qualified pilot who also possessed a flight engineer's certificate, and who would in due course advance to copilot and pilot. When Delta acquired another airline, Chicago and Southern (C&S), through a merger that took place in 1953, Woolman applied this policy to its flight engineers, most of whom resigned rather than accept ground-based jobs. They did so after being assured that if they took this course they would be treated under the merger's employee protective provisions as if they had been fired; as this entitled them to receive a severance pay of one year's salary free of tax, it carried with it a substantial benefit. The settlement cost approximately $250,000, but proved to be worth far more than that when, later in the decade, labor problems broke out on several airlines because of difficulties between pilots and flight engineers trained solely as mechanics, producing costly strikes while Delta remained unaffected. Eastern was among the carriers most badly hurt.

Reflecting its increased size and the predominance of passenger and airmail operations, Delta changed its name to Delta Air Lines, Inc., in October 1945. Plagued by poor health and failing eyesight, Faulk moved up to chairman of the board and Woolman became both president and general manager, clinging to the latter title because it emphasized his continuing hands-on role in running the organization. Due in part to the fact that postwar passenger demand did not live up to expectations, Delta and other airlines experienced financial rough going throughout most of the late 1940s. Labor problems exacerbated the situation, culminating in a wildcat strike against Delta by the International Association of Machinists in 1947. When this ended in failure for the union, the company declined to renew its previous contract. From now on, unionization at Delta would be limited chiefly to its pilots, whose essentially "maverick" chapter of the Air Line Pilots Association often sided with Woolman on important issues. Woolman was therefore able to continue imposing his own personal stamp on the enterprise with a minimum of internal interference.

Because of declining revenues throughout the industry, the CAB adopted an extremely conservative policy with regard to new route awards during this period. In order to achieve an expanded route structure that would optimize utilization of the larger aircraft he was acquiring in order to compete with Eastern, Woolman was therefore forced to look for a merger partner. After efforts to merge with National, Northeast, and Capital proved fruitless, Delta finally succeeded in 1953 in consummating a corporate marriage with Chicago and Southern, a slightly smaller line that had been developed by one of Woolman's closest friends, Carleton Putnam. Its domestic route structure connected Chicago with New Orleans by way of St. Louis and Memphis, included a route from Memphis to Kansas City, and also linked Houston and Detroit via Indianapolis and Toledo. In addition, C&S had recently been awarded international routes from New Orleans to such Caribbean destinations as Havana, San Juan, Montego Bay, Kingston, Aruba, Curaçao, and Caracas, and conducted interchange operations to Pittsburgh and New York City-Newark in cooperation with American and TWA. Through the merger, two distinctly regional airlines were transformed into an aspiring national carrier.

Although Putnam became for a time chairman of the board of the consolidated airline, temporarily known as Delta-C&S, he soon retired from active business life, leaving Woolman in effective charge. When his highly paternalistic managerial style conflicted with that of two former C&S executives, Sidney Stewart and Junius Cooper, who had come into the new organization as executive vice-president and vice-president for finance, these men quickly left the firm. Through the merger, however, Delta did gain two new executives, W. T. Beebe and Richard S. Maurer, who headed the company's personnel and legal departments, and proved more amenable to Woolman's idiosyncrasies. They became highly important in the future development of the firm. By 1955, "C&S" had been phased out of the corporate name and the enterprise had made a successful transition to cohesiveness under Woolman's undisputed leadership.

By this time the industry was enjoying much smoother financial sailing and the CAB was permitting increased competition on relatively long routes between major destinations. In contending for potentially lucrative route awards during this era, Delta did better than its major competitor, Eastern. This was in part because, under Woolman's leadership, Delta made maximum use of its contacts with key southern representatives and senators at a time when the South was still electing solidly Democratic delegations to Congress despite its developing infatuation at the national level with such Republican leaders as Dwight D. Eisenhower. Conversely, at the helm of Eastern, the politically archconservative Rickenbacker went out of his way to alienate influential Democrats and thus squandered some of his firm's potential influence in the regulatory arena.

In 1955 Delta mounted a highly effective public relations campaign that netted it one of the most important prizes in its history: a new 1,075-mile route from Atlanta to New York by way of Charlotte, Washington, Baltimore, and Philadelphia. Eastern, which had been contending for two separate routes between Dallas-Fort Worth and New York in the same case, merely received a new route between Atlanta and Pittsburgh and lost its previous monopoly on traffic between Atlanta and New York. The impressive victory at one stroke gave Delta access to four of the nation's largest metropolitan markets in the densely populated Northeast, located along what Woolman liked to call "America's Main Street." During this period, Delta also filled out its growing network of midwestern routes by gaining access to such cities as Dayton and Columbus.

In the wake of the merger with C&S, Woolman rapidly phased out the Lockheed Constellations that Putnam had previously acquired for long runs. Departing from its earlier "all Douglas" orientation, Delta gradually eliminated its remaining DC-3s from shorter routes and successfully substituted Convair CV-340s and CV-440s in their place. Throughout the early and mid 1950s, however, the major technological question facing Woolman and other airline executives was whether or not to switch from the highly complicated and extremely fuel-intensive turbocompound engines that powered the Douglas DC-7 and Lockheed L-1049 to the much simpler and more powerful jet engine, which had now proved itself in military service but was as yet untried by American carriers. Woolman's eventual response to this crucial question, resulting from a combination of pragmatism and pure luck, proved much more successful than that of Rickenbacker, further enhancing Delta's ability to compete with Eastern.

Like other American airline executives, Woolman was hesitant to depart from the reciprocating engines that had served airlines dependably for decades and embrace the unknown economics of the jet engine. His caution was reinforced by the spectacular and well-publicized crashes suffered by the world's first operational commercial jetliner, the De Havilland Comet, after the British began using it on international routes in 1952. When Pan American intensified the debate in 1955 by ordering the pioneer American jet transport, the Boeing 707, Woolman's first inclination was to compromise by adopting the Lockheed L-188 Electra, a turboprop design, which was also Rickenbacker's choice. Two things, however, changed Woolman's mind. One was opposition among Delta pilots and technicians to the complicated gearbox and propeller utilized by the hybrid L-188s; the second, and more important, was the fact that American and Eastern had virtually cornered the market on the Electras, producing a situation in which Lockheed could offer Delta only three of these new ships.

After considering the Boeing 707 and coming away skeptical about its potential economic performance on Delta's essentially medium-sized long hauls, Woolman opted for the Douglas DC-8. On September 18, 1959, when bad weather delayed an American Airlines flight from San Francisco to New York, Delta became the first carrier to put this highly successful model into operation, on a run from New York to Atlanta. Eastern had also ordered DC-8s, but Rickenbacker had decided to wait for models with more powerful JT-4 engines, opening the way for Delta to secure earlier deliveries by contenting itself with smaller JT-3 power plants and to get the jump on its rival. Meanwhile Woolman had also decided to acquire yet another jet transport, the Convair CV-880, when an opportunity arose to obtain three of these exceptionally swift planes as a result of the increasingly complicated finances of Howard Hughes, who had spearheaded its development for service on TWA. While a larger number of completed CV-880s were held up for delivery to TWA because of Hughes's troubles, Delta took possession of its first ship from Convair on February 10, 1960. Scarcely three months later, on May 15, it had the honor of introducing a major new jetliner into commercial service for the second

time in less than a year when a Delta CV-880 flew a passenger run from Houston to New York.

Although Eastern had the distinction of putting the first Lockheed L-188s into scheduled operation in December 1957, its adoption of the new turboprop soon proved disastrous. Deficiencies in the wing and engine installation resulted in a series of fatal crashes when the plane was put into service by American, Braniff, and Northwest, leading federal officials to impose severe speed restrictions on the ship. Unencumbered by such limitations, Delta's sleek new DC-8s and CV-880s easily outclassed Eastern's Electras; captains of the Delta planes delighted in calling the attention of their passengers to L-188s bearing Eastern's distinctive silver markings and triumphantly zooming past the lumbering craft. Meanwhile, before the end of 1958, Eastern was further hobbled by a strike conducted by its flight engineers and mechanics, resulting from issues caused by the "third crew member" controversy and the ways in which Rickenbacker had attempted to solve the pay differentials resulting from his use of flight engineers instead of pilots trained to act in this capacity. The walkout, which lasted for 39 days, grounded Eastern during the profitable Florida winter tourist season. Woolman's increasingly crowded planes picked up the slack, leading to substantially increased profits. Delta itself came under increased pressure during the same period from the Air Lines Stewards and Stewardesses Association and the International Brotherhood of Teamsters, but organizing drives by these unions failed, and temporary difficulties with the pilots in 1958 were resolved before they led to a strike.

Woolman's common-sense pragmatism guided him successfully through another thorny problem in the late 1950s when an increasing tendency among domestic airlines to serve alcoholic beverages put growing pressure on Delta to follow suit. True to its Bible-Belt origins, Delta had steadfastly refrained from serving such drinks, and such religious denominations as the Southern Baptists and Presbyterians sternly warned the company not to abandon this policy as the issue became heated in 1957. There is no doubt that Woolman himself would have preferred to keep Delta dry, but as evidence mounted that a growing number of the firm's passengers wanted the opportunity to drink cocktails and Eastern began gaining a competitive edge on key route segments by offering such service, Woolman yielded to the bottom line. On March 8, 1958, Delta reluc-

Douglas DC-7 (courtesy of the National Air and Space Museum)

tantly instituted liquor sales on flights between Houston and New York, being the last American domestic carrier to effect the change. Expansion of the service, with appropriate restrictions aimed at guarding against passenger intoxication, continued in the months that followed despite volleys of protest from fundamentalists and other critics, including some of the company's own employees. Throughout the tempest, Woolman was masterful in writing conciliatory letters to offended parties without backing down from a position that had become necessary because of Delta's expansion into more cosmopolitan markets outside the region and the imperatives of competition with Eastern and other trunk lines.

Pragmatic considerations also forced Woolman to compromise with increasingly strict standards involving noise pollution following the introduction of jet service, despite having to walk a tightrope between public clamor on the one hand and his rigid concern for safety in maneuvering in and out of airports on the other. In dealing with such issues, and with a tightening web of federal regulations and inspection procedures, he was fortunate in establishing a good working relationship with Gen. Elwood R. ("Pete") Quesada, who be-

came the first head of the Federal Aviation Agency (FAA; later Federal Aviation Administration) that was established with the passage of the Federal Aviation Act of 1958. Further headaches resulted from the onset in 1957 of the worst recession to hit the country since World War II, forcing the company to suspend dividends during the downswing until better times returned in the second quarter of 1959. Here again Woolman's common sense prevailed despite complaints from some of the stockholders affected.

During the 1960s such clouds lifted and the economics of jet transportation yielded a bonanza to Delta. Flying higher and faster than ever before, passengers enjoyed greatly increased comfort and arrived at their destinations unjaded after a few hours on trips that had previously required much more time and inconvenience. Consequently, demand grew rapidly. At the same time the dramatically lowered cost of jet fuel, essentially kerosene, as opposed to that of the high octane aviation gasoline formerly required by piston-driven power plants, and the markedly lessened maintenance schedules required by jet engines, resulted in greatly lowered costs per passenger-seat mile of air travel.

Such benefits were particularly pronounced on extremely long nonstop flights between major cities capable of producing large numbers of passengers. Delta won a critical victory in a bitterly contested new route proceeding, the Southern Transcontinental Service Case, just in time to capitalize on the new technology. No fewer than 11 carriers, including both Delta and Eastern, took part in the battle; appointing a distinguished law firm, Pogue and Neal, to supplement the efforts of its own legal department, Delta assembled mountains of evidence and pursued a vigorous public relations campaign. Heated debates before local constituencies took place between representatives of Delta and Eastern while lobbyists and lawyers pressed every potential advantage in Washington itself. Shortly after public hearings had been concluded, Rickenbacker made a major blunder by making extremely disparaging remarks about President-elect John F. Kennedy in an Atlanta speech; according to Malcolm MacIntyre, who had become president of Eastern in 1959 while Captain Eddie moved up to chairman of the board, this doomed Eastern's chances in the transcontinental case.

Whether or not Rickenbacker's indiscretion was a determining factor, the outcome of the proceeding was a triumph for Delta, which, in a CAB decision announced on March 13, 1961, gained 2,789 miles of new routes connecting its previous western terminus of Dallas-Fort Worth with such destinations as Los Angeles, San Francisco, San Diego, Oakland, and Las Vegas. Returning to the Atlanta Airport after a trip, Maurer, whose leadership had been highly instrumental throughout the fight, learned about the decision. Telephoning Woolman, he found him in an extremely jovial mood and later recalled the way the boss conveyed his elation. Over the years, when asked about how things were going, C. E. had developed the habit of striking a "poor boy" pose by answering, "I never felt better, and I never had less." This time, there was a different twist as Woolman exclaimed to Maurer, "I never felt better, and I never had more."

This key victory, to which only the Chicago-to-Miami and Atlanta-to-New York awards had been comparable in significance, came too late to be enjoyed by Delta's veteran traffic executive, Laigh Parker, who had died of cancer in December 1959. Fittingly, however, Parker's successor, Thomas M. Miller, capitalized upon it and other recent favorable trends by working out an innovation, known

as the "Early Bird-Owly Bird" plan, under which a large number of planes left their points of origin between 10 P.M. and 4 A.M., when lower night-coach fares were in force under CAB policy, in such a way as to converge upon Atlanta between 5 and 5:30 A.M., in time for other passengers to take off prior to 6:30 while the lower fares still applied. At first skeptical about the cost of the extra personnel required to staff and service the planes, Woolman subsequently saw the plan's merits and agreed to what turned into a highly successful marketing strategy. Later, prior to his retirement as an executive vice-president in 1973, Miller developed a "hub and spoke" concept by means of which Delta funnelled traffic from small and medium-sized cities to such nodal points as Atlanta, Memphis, Chicago, and Boston during specific time frames throughout the day, redistributing it to long-haul flights to major destinations. Besides facilitating an enormous variety of connections that would otherwise have been impossible, this strategy optimized load factors, conserved fuel, and encouraged Delta to hang onto smaller stations instead of turning them over to feeder lines.

Woolman's pragmatic willingness to consider new, untried ideas despite harboring initial doubts about them also influenced Delta's choice of new aircraft in the early 1960s. Though at first dubious, he agreed to arguments advanced by Delta engineer Arthur Ford about acquiring the Douglas DC-8-61, a stretched version of the basic DC-8 that could accommodate 195 passengers. Ford attracted the boss's attention by creating a model in which the 125 seats in a conventional DC-8 were painted gray; seven additional seats were painted red to signify the added cost of operating the new plane; and the remaining 63 were painted bright green and marked with large dollar signs. Woolman, convinced by this visual display, also supported Ford in helping design and develop the Douglas DC-9, the third jet aircraft Delta first introduced into service, in a flight from Atlanta to Kansas City on December 8, 1965. Both in its original form and in a stretched version known as the DC-9-32, this relatively small twin-engine commercial jet proved ideally suited for Delta's short-hop routes, again emphasizing Woolman's success in making decisions about new aircraft that balanced the varied requirements of the company's route system.

As Delta continued to prosper, Eastern suffered a succession of reverses. In order to settle the

1958 strike that had yielded such indirect benefit to Delta, Rickenbacker consented to having no less than four persons in the cockpit of each Eastern DC-8, including three pilots, one of whom had virtually no real duties, and a flight engineer. Besides further increasing costs that Eastern was ill-equipped to bear, this led to more conflict when an increase in inspection flights with FAA officials aboard resulted in the need to jam yet one more person into the cockpit. Objecting to the seating pattern devised by Eastern to accommodate the FAA, Eastern's pilots staged a brief but costly walkout in 1960 that led to the first annual deficit in the company's history. In 1961 the Flight Engineers International Association conducted a strike that affected several carriers, including Eastern, further damaging the firm's financial position. Forced to yield the presidency to MacIntyre, Rickenbacker continued to interfere in day-to-day operations, further complicating an already bad management situation. Despite phasing out its remaining Constellations and DC-7s, Eastern remained technologically backward compared to Delta, and its losses continued to mount even though MacIntyre introduced such successful innovations as the New York-Washington shuttle service for which the company became well known.

Hopes that Eastern might be able to effect significant cost reductions by winning long-haul east-west runs to balance the comparatively short-haul routes on its predominantly north-south system faded after the loss of the Southern Transcontinental Service Case in 1961. In a move similar to Delta's in the late 1940s, Eastern tried to solve the problem by effecting a merger with another carrier, and entered into serious talks for a consolidation with American that would have produced by far the largest airline yet to appear in United States. When the plan was submitted to the CAB in 1962, Delta led five other airlines in a successful fight to block it. Behind the scenes Woolman coached Maurer, who sometimes questioned witnesses so thoroughly as to create the impression that Delta was conducting the struggle alone. Warned by Woolman to permit lawyers from other carriers to participate more actively in cross-examinations, Maurer replied that they might not know the right questions to ask. "Just give 'em the questions," Woolman replied. The CAB rejected the merger.

Woolman's concern about Maurer's activities during the 1962 American-Eastern merger battle typ-

ified his desire to be involved in every aspect of Delta's operations. For decades he insisted on having the final word on every significant move; as board chairman R. W. Freeman once stated, Woolman was "of the old time management school," and did not believe in final delegation of authority. Another executive who was intimately familiar with the boss's style denied that Woolman was a complete autocrat; so long as it was understood that any significant departure from standard procedure had to be discussed with him in advance, Miller stated, Woolman allowed considerable autonomy within the company's operating decisions. Freeman concurred, stating that Woolman was not a tyrant, but simply regarded loyalty to himself as being synonymous with loyalty to Delta. Whatever the validity of such distinctions, Woolman kept a heavy paternal hand upon the firm he had guided for so many years.

So thoroughly had the identities of Delta and Woolman become interlocked that by the early 1960s it was difficult to mention one without thinking about the other. Throughout his career, Woolman, a compulsive workaholic, devoted himself so unstintingly to the company that he had little time for anything else. His two daughters, Barbara and Martha, undoubtedly suffered from lack of attention; Barbara later recalled that neither she nor her sister ever shared a picnic with their father, and could never count on awakening in the same room in which they had gone to bed because Woolman often brought home an "off-loaded" passenger to spend the night, necessitating a change in sleeping accommodations. Woolman may have been the only airline president in the industry who resolutely maintained a listed telephone number because he actually wanted to be available for any call, at any time of the day or night, that a disgruntled passenger might care to make.

One of Woolman's extremely few diversions from company affairs was his hobby of raising orchids in a greenhouse that he erected on his Northside Drive property in northwest Atlanta. He shared this with his wife, Helen, who kept records on the intricate process of breeding and crossbreeding. Orchids became part of his mystique: he presented them to company secretaries, to the sick, and to graduating stewardesses. A veteran flight attendant, Sue Myracle, recalled being thrilled when Woolman gave her an orchid when she graduated in the early 1960s.

Convair 880 (courtesy of the National Air and Space Museum)

Despite Woolman's deep desire to oversee everything that happened at Delta, his workaholic tendencies inevitably took their toll on even as rugged a constitution as his, and the grip of his paternal hand ultimately weakened. In 1958, in his words, "two severe cases of Flu started me on the downgrade and I wound up in the hospital for the first time in my life." Later that year, while visiting India, he suffered a heart attack, but was back at his desk in early 1959. As concern about his health began to spread, both within the company and among members of the business community, board chairman Freeman tried to persuade him to turn some of his day-to-day responsibilities over to an heir apparent. Still, however, he carried on the relentless pace of his work, refusing to face his own mortality and unable to conceive that anyone could take his place.

In April 1962 Woolman lost a personal and emotional mainstay when his wife of many years, Helen, died of cancer. Visiting the boss's house not long thereafter, Maurer accompanied Woolman on a visit to the greenhouse and remarked that many of the orchids were drooping and seemed neglected, whereupon Woolman replied that his heart was no longer in their cultivation. The daily routine of running Delta now became the only thing that continued to hold meaning for him. He did, however,

initiate a search for an executive vice-president, resulting in July 1963 in the appointment of Earl D. Johnson, whom he had come to know through Delta's acquisition of the Convair 880. Johnson's credentials were impressive; he had been president and vice-chairman of the board of General Dynamics, and under secretary of the army. His duties, however, were ill-defined, and Woolman was incapable of delegating any real authority to him. In addition, his presence aroused resentment among other Delta executives who were accustomed to the company's longstanding tradition of promoting from within and who pointed to his lack of experience in airline management. Personality clashes soon produced an impossible situation, and the company bought out Johnson's contract within a year.

In November 1965 the situation finally began to be resolved when Freeman stepped down as chairman of the board, as he had long desired to do, and Woolman moved into his place. Succeeding Woolman as president was Charles Dolson, whose service to the company as a captain, chief pilot, and operations head went all the way back to Delta's inauguration of airmail service in 1934; in his new capacity, he was to run the airline's day-to-day operations. At the same time, David C. Garrett, who had devised and executed an effective plan to prepare Delta's employees for jet operations in the

517

late 1950s, became vice-president of operations. These changes did much to assure important investors that a clear line of succession had been established and that continuity would be preserved in the event of Woolman's death.

Symbolic rites of passage began to take on special poignancy as Woolman's life slowly ebbed away. Late in 1964 Delta's pilots presented him with a large oil painting of himself. The following spring, not long after observing the 25th anniversary of the appointment of Delta's first female flight attendants, a group of the original stewardesses presented the boss with a model of a DC-2, the plane with which they had first flown for the company in 1940. The following year Catherine Fitz-Gerald celebrated her 40th anniversary with the firm and Woolman presented her with one of his now rare orchids. In February 1966 another link with the past snapped when Coad, who had run the crop-dusting division for many years at its base in Bryan, Texas, died. Although this had become little more than a tiny appendage to the company's business, Woolman had steadfastly refused to countenance cutting it loose, and now clung to the past by insisting that it continued to make "a considerable call on our time and energies."

Early in September 1966 company executives were told that Woolman would be out of town temporarily to attend a meeting of *Los Conquistadores del Cielo*, an organization of aviation personalities in which he had been active for many years. This was an elaborate ploy to hide the fact, known only to his daughters and a few highly trusted associates, that he was actually going to a Houston hospital to undergo surgery for a threatening aneurysm. The operation took place on September 7. For a few days he seemed to be recovering well, but suddenly, on September 11, he died.

Shock waves of grief spread throughout the Delta organization. Diane Stanford, a switchboard operator who had been summoned to company headquarters from entertaining guests shortly after news of Woolman's death reached Atlanta, recalled telling her friends that "Delta has died." As she sat at her post taking calls that poured in from all over the company's network of stations, she was inundated by waves of emotion as veteran employees, men as well as women, broke down and wept. On a rainy Tuesday morning, September 14, 1966, an estimated 1,500 to 2,000 mourners crowded into Atlanta's First Presbyterian Church to attend a

brief funeral service after which Woolman's body, which had been flown from Houston in one of the company's cargo planes, was laid to rest at Arlington Cemetery in the nearby suburb of Sandy Springs. In a tribute to him, James Montgomery, business editor of the *Atlanta Constitution*, called Delta "one of the last of a vanishing species—a large modern corporation stamped with the towering personality of a single individual," and characterized Woolman as "an exceptional human being, legendary in life for his integrity and wit as well as for his management skill." Nevertheless, as Montgomery pointed out, knowledgeable investors knew that the company was ready to carry on in his absence; indeed, on the first day of Wall Street trading after the announcement of his death, Delta stock advanced by almost six points. In Montgomery's perceptive words, Woolman's stubborn refusal to retire had provided "convincing evidence that he was in his later years sustained by the organization he fathered."

During the final years of Woolman's life, W. T. Beebe, in his capacity as head of personnel, had created a semisecret organization chart corresponding to the realities of the decision-making process that was gradually emerging at Delta underneath Woolman's ostensible one-man rule. After Woolman's death, this was implemented in a wave of promotions that produced a visible hierarchy of senior vice-presidents, vice-presidents, and assistant vice-presidents and a clearly articulated assignment of responsibilities. As had been already clearly indicated, Dolson took over as chief executive officer. When he retired in 1972, Beebe and Garrett followed him in this role in due succession.

Meanwhile the company continued to prosper; by the time of the 50th anniversary of passenger operations in 1979 it had absorbed Northeast Airlines in a merger that confirmed its status as one of the nation's largest trunk carriers, and added a major international route to London. Despite being initially opposed to the Airline Deregulation Act of 1978, it continued to thrive amid the intense competition that resulted from that crucial piece of legislation, and by 1991 was one of America's three largest carriers, serving a complex network of domestic and international destinations scattered across the face of the planet. Far different was the fate of Eastern, which staged a remarkable comeback under the leadership of ex-astronaut Frank Borman so long as the traditional regulatory system lasted but plummeted rapidly toward bankruptcy and oblivion after 1978.

Amid the company's constant growth and expansion, Delta executives did their utmost to keep Woolman's memory and legacy alive. They did so partly because of their realization that the "family feeling" so vigorously inculcated by Woolman was a major asset that must somehow be preserved through formal organizational effort as the firm grew ever larger. Unremitting attention to employee relations, dogged adherence to Woolman's emphasis upon promoting from within, and a rigid insistence on his policy of avoiding layoffs even in periods of economic stringency also helped preserve Delta's status as a dominantly nonunion employer, giving it flexibility in deploying personnel where they were most needed instead of having to abide by complex work rules, and also resulting in freedom from potentially costly strikes. In addition the company recognized the importance of keeping alive the tradition of courtesy and expertness in passenger relations that Woolman had done so much to develop; over the years, Delta preserved its status as one of the industry's leaders in generating the fewest complaints among ticket holders.

Delta also kept alive Woolman's tradition of combining conservative financial policies with constant modernization of its fleet. As a result it regularly led the industry in having the "youngest" assemblage of airliners, replacing once ultramodern Boeing 727s and Douglas DC-9s with up-to-date Boeing 757s and 767s and McDonnell-Douglas MD-80s. In these and other ways Delta continued to keep consistent forward momentum rather than lurch ahead in a pattern of "boom and bust" typifying other commercial carriers. To a large degree its corporate epic has been one long success story. In a statement made late in his own distinguished career, Maurer traced this record to the example set by its founding father: "Today, and in the days ahead, C. E.'s successors will be trying to maintain that lean, tough, service-oriented family-style group of loyal Delta personnel that Woolman struggled so long and against such severe odds to develop.... To the extent that they can achieve C. E.'s ideas and goals, so the Delta family of tomorrow should grow and prosper."

References:

John M. Baitsell, *Airline Industrial Relations: Pilots and Flight Engineers* (Cambridge, Mass.: Harvard University Press, 1966);

Eldon W. Downs and George F. Lemmer, "Origins of Aerial Crop Dusting," *Agricultural History*, 34 (July 1965): 123-135;

R. E. G. Davies, *Airlines of the United States since 1914* (Washington, D. C.: Smithsonian Institution, 1972);

Davies, *Delta: An Airline and Its Aircraft* (Miami: Paladwr Press, 1990);

W. David Lewis and Wesley Phillips Newton, *Delta: The History of An Airline* (Athens: University of Georgia Press, 1979);

Jim Montgomery, "Delta Bears the Stamp of Woolman's Hand," *Atlanta Constitution*, September 14, 1966;

Wesley Phillips Newton, *The Perilous Sky: U.S. Aviation Diplomacy and Latin America, 1919-1931* (Coral Gables, Fla.: University of Miami Press, 1978);

Carleton Putnam, *High Frontier: A Decade in the Pilgrimage of an Air Line Pioneer* (New York: Scribners, 1945);

Robert J. Serling, *From the Captain to the Colonel: An Informal History of Eastern Airlines* (New York: Dial Press, 1980);

Henry Ladd Smith, *Airways: The History of Commercial Aviation in the United States* (New York: Knopf, 1942);

John H. Van Deventer, Jr., "The Story of Keystone," *Air Transportation*, 6 (January 19, 1929): 54-55.

World Airways

by Roger D. Launius

*National Aeronautics and
Space Administration*

World Airways was incorporated on March 28, 1948, as a nonscheduled air carrier, but it remained basically an empty corporate shell until taken over by Edward J. Daly in 1950. Daly's management and leadership transformed the company, based in Oakland, California, into one of the most important supplemental air carriers in the United States.

Daly built an aggressive organization, based largely on contracts with the military services. In 1956 he used his two war-surplus C-46Es, the only aircraft World owned, to transport refugees fleeing Hungary to the United States during Operation SAFE HAVEN. An even more important step along the road to financial success came on June 15, 1960, when World obtained a major contract from the Department of Defense to deliver parts and supplies to military installations throughout the United States. This profitable agreement laid the foundations for subsequent expansion.

In May 1962 World Airways took a major step forward by ordering three new Boeing 707-320Cs. This move, the first jet order from any of the supplemental carriers, placed World in the forefront of the industry. The airline grew rapidly during the early 1960s. The Supplemental Air Carrier Act of 1962, designed to weed out weaker and less safe carriers, worked to World's advantage, as it eliminated competition. Although the company expanded its private charter business, military contracts remained its bread and butter. As the Vietnam War grew in intensity during the mid 1960s, World became one of the principal commercial carriers airlifting military personnel between the United States and Southeast Asia.

Ever anxious to expand, Daly applied to the Civil Aeronautics Board on April 26, 1967, to oper-

ate a scheduled $79 transcontinental thrift fare service. Although the proposal was not approved, World continued to branch out into new areas. By the end of the 1960s it was operating a fleet of nine Boeing 707s and four Boeing 727s, providing both intra- and intercontinental jet service on a charter basis.

The 1970s saw World add to its fleet with the acquisition of Boeing 747s in 1973 and DC-10s in 1978. The decade also saw World's dramatic participation in the final chapter of the Vietnam War. In 1975 the airline flew numerous missions into Da Nang and Saigon, often under extremely hazardous circumstances, as North Vietnamese forces drove to their final victory in the south.

World Airways finally broke into the ranks of the scheduled carriers following passage of the Airline Deregulation Act of 1978. Although it suffered severe financial difficulties during the early 1980s, in part due to overexpansion, the airline weathered the economic crisis. It continues to operate into the last decade of the 20th century as a primary supplemental carrier in the country.

References:
Coy F. Cross, II, *MAC and Operation BABYLIFT: Air Transport in Support of Noncombatant Evacuation Operations* (Scott Air Force Base, Ill.: Office of History, Military Airlift Command, 1989);
R. E. G. Davies, *Airlines of the United States since 1914*, revised edition (Washington, D.C.: Smithsonian Institution, 1982);
Davies, *Rebels and Reformers of the Airways* (Washington, D.C.: Smithsonian Institution, 1987).

Clarence M. Young

(July 23, 1889 - April 10, 1973)

by Tom D. Crouch

National Air and Space Museum

CAREER: Insurance claims specialist, Des Moines, Iowa (1910-1917); U.S. Army Signal Corps (1917-1919); Iowa state deputy insurance commissioner (1919); aviation business (1919-1922); executive secretary, Des Moines Municipal Research Bureau (1922-1925); director of aviation activities, Philadelphia Sesquicentennial Celebration (1926); director of air regulation (1926-1927), director of aeronautics, U.S. Department of Commerce (1927-1933); manager, Transpacific Division, Pan American Airways (1934-1945); member, Civil Aeronautics Board (1946-1947); vice-president, Pan American Airways (1950-1959).

Clarence Marshall Young was twenty-two years old when he saw an airplane for the first time. Rene Simon, Jack Frisbie, and Rene Barrier, representatives of the Moisant International Aviators, arrived in Des Moines, Iowa, on May 29, 1911. They were the survivors of a hard-luck outfit. The founder of the team, pioneer American aviator John Moisant, had died in a crash at New Orleans only five months before. Frisbie and Barrier had crashed their airplanes during an exhibition at Atlantic, Iowa, from May 15 to 19, 1911. Both planes and pilots were still under repair when the team arrived in Des Moines ten days later.

Rene Simon, dubbed "The Flying Fool," introduced local citizens to the wonders of the air age with a single flight on June 1. Other flights followed over the next three days, culminating in a spectacular performance on June 4, when all three pilots took to the air at once. Clarence Young, a fledgling lawyer, would never forget the sight.

Young was born in Colfax, Iowa, on July 23, 1889, the son of Theodore G. and Ella Foy Young. The family moved to Des Moines when Clarence was ten. He attended local schools, studying at nearby Drake University before moving east to earn an LL.B. from Yale. Young returned to Des Moines

Clarence M. Young (courtesy of Lois Moran Young)

and took a job as an insurance claims specialist with a local law firm in 1910.

The memory of those frail airplanes and their daring pilots lingered, however. With the American entry into World War I, Young traveled to Chicago to enlist in the Aviation Section of the Signal Corps. After minor surgery to correct a respiratory problem, he was accepted and ordered to ground school at Urbana, Illinois. One of three men in his class selected for immediate overseas duty, he was ordered to Paris, where he was offered a choice between an administrative job overseeing aerodrome construction or flight training followed by a posting as a bomber pilot serving with the Italian Corpo Aeronautica Militare. He reported to the flying school at Foggia, Italy, in September 1917.

Assigned to an Italian unit operating Caproni bombers against targets on the Austrian front in June 1918, Young suffered an engine failure on his first combat mission, and was forced to land behind enemy lines. He spent the five months prior to the Armistice as a prisoner of war. In recognition of his wartime service the Italian government named Young a Commander of the Order of the Crown.

Young was demobilized in February 1919, but enlisted in the U.S. Specialist Reserve Corps with the rank of captain soon thereafter. His long friendship with Charles A. Lindbergh began in 1925 when Lindbergh, then a young second lieutenant recently graduated from the Air Corps training facility at Kelly Field, Texas, was assigned to check the proficiency of Young's reserve unit during a summer encampment. Soon thereafter, Young was promoted to colonel and took command of the 313th Observation Squadron, Air Corps Reserve. He was proud of his military rank; it became his preferred title in civilian life as well. Nearly half a century later an obituary writer for the *Washington Post* noted the passing of Col. Clarence Young.

His wartime adventures behind him, Young returned to Des Moines and accepted an appointment as deputy insurance commissioner of Iowa in 1919. "That got a little too dry, and a little too prosaic," he recalled many years later. "So I talked a local automobile dealer into ... [entering] the aviation business." The pair bought and sold war-surplus aircraft, established a local airport, and offered the usual range of services, from weekend passenger hops to aerial photography of family farms. In 1922, after two years of struggle, Young and his partner, Clyde Erring, who was later elected governor of Iowa and a U.S. senator, sold out to another aspiring aviation entrepreneur.

Young spent the years from 1922 to 1925 as executive secretary of the Des Moines Municipal Research Bureau, returning to aeronautics in 1926 as director of aviation activities for the Philadelphia Sesquicentennial Celebration. The successful program of air races and exhibition flights drew considerable attention to the anniversary and to the promoter. As part of the celebration, Young was also involved in operating a passenger air service between Philadelphia and Washington, D.C.

Impressed by his combination of legal training, aeronautical experience, and administrative skill, William P. MacCracken, assistant secretary of commerce and chief of the newly created Aeronautics Branch, hired Young as chief of air regulation for the Department of Commerce in 1926. Congress had taken the first step toward the regulation of aviation in the United States with the passage of the Air Commerce Act of 1926. Based on a plan developed by Herbert Hoover, the act gave the Department of Commerce responsibility for air safety and the authority to establish regulations governing the operation of civil aircraft. As one knowledgeable commentator remarked, the Air Commerce Act was nothing less than "the legislative cornerstone of commercial aviation in America."

MacCracken and Young tackled the enormous task of regulating the emerging air industry together. Their joint achievements included the first licensing regulations for pilots and airplanes; establishment of the basic rules and procedures for the safe operation of commercial and private aircraft; creation of airway systems, complete with markings, lights, and radio beacons; and development of aircraft radios, instruments and other essential items of equipment. In addition, they encouraged airport planning, supported the creation of a weather forecasting system for aviators, and sponsored research in areas ranging from blind flying to the reduction of aircraft noise.

The division of labor between MacCracken and Young was clear. The assistant secretary spent a great deal of time touring the nation, explaining and building support for the Department of Commerce aviation program. Young remained at his desk in Washington, organizing and managing the effort.

Once the basic rules were established, Young faced the task of selecting the men who would enforce them. "When Clarence was hiring the inspectors," MacCracken recalled many years later, "I told him it was his job and he had to do it his way." Broad experience as a pilot and a thorough knowledge of aircraft technology were prerequisites for a good inspector, but Young recognized that judgment and skill in dealing with people were just as important. An inspector who wore "a big hat" and was inclined to exert his authority would do little to win respect and cooperation for the program.

*Young in a U.S. Commerce Department biplane during his tenure as director of aeronautics, 1927-1933
(courtesy of Lois Moran Young)*

Young's success as an administrator was a key element in the growth of American civil aeronautics in the years after 1926, and he was rewarded for his efforts. Promoted to the post of director of aeronautics in 1927, Young was named assistant secretary of commerce for aeronautics when Mac-Cracken left the agency in 1929. Young continued to guide the program he had helped to create until 1933, when he left office with the change of administrations.

Young made the transition from federal service to private enterprise in November 1934, when the legendary Juan T. Trippe hired him to manage the newly established Transpacific Division of Pan American Airways. He established the division headquarters at Alameda, California, with a staff of Pan Am veterans drawn from the original Latin American routes. Their task was to establish the world's first true transoceanic passenger air service across the world's largest ocean. The route was over 8,700 miles long—Alameda to Honolulu, then on to Mid-

way, Wake, Guam, Manila, and Hong Kong. Diplomatic problems would prevent the extension of the service to China for a time, however. Initially, Manila served as the final terminus.

The first task was to establish the way stations along the route. From the outset, U.S. naval officials, convinced that the Pan Am facilities would also serve their needs in an emergency, were virtual partners in the venture. They allowed Young to establish the first major overseas terminal at Pearl Harbor, and accepted jurisdiction over uninhabited Wake Island to assist the airline. Secretary of the Navy Claude Swanson signed contracts authorizing Pan Am to establish the additional bases on Midway and Guam. Together with the postmaster general, the attorney general, and the secretaries of state, war, and the Treasury, Swanson was also involved in the decision to award Pan Am a lucrative transpacific airmail contract that would help to subsidize the entire enterprise.

Late in March 1935 the SS *North Haven*

sailed from San Francisco. Aboard were 114 Pan American employees who would establish the island bases dotted across the vast Pacific. On October 9, 1935, the first of the large Martin M-130 flying boats that would operate over the route was ceremonially christened and turned over to the company. On November 22, 1935, Capt. Ed Musick lifted that airplane, the famous *China Clipper*, from the waters of San Francisco Bay, flew beneath the Golden Gate Bridge, and headed west for Hawaii on the first leg of the first scheduled transpacific passenger flight. Six days and 8,200 miles later, he landed safely in Manila Bay.

The Transpacific Division was in business, but the price of maintaining regularly scheduled service over such enormous distances was high. In 1937 Pan American's Pacific empire posted a loss of over half a million dollars. Nor could the losses be counted solely in dollars and cents. Ed Musick and his crew died in a midair explosion during a survey flight to New Zealand in January 1938. Six months later, the *Hawaiian Clipper*, carrying six passengers and a crew of nine, disappeared between Guam and Midway. Young and his coworkers had faced a constant struggle to maintain the schedule with a full complement of aircraft. In the wake of the tragic loss of two flying boats, they had little choice but to reduce operations drastically. By the middle of 1938 the division was suffering losses of up to $95,000 per month.

Appalled, the Pan American board of directors ousted Juan Trippe from the company in March 1939. He maneuvered himself back into control of the firm in less than a year. By the early months of 1940 corporate profits were clearly on the rise. Trippe's enormous gamble to bridge both the Pacific and the Atlantic by air was paying off at last.

Through it all, the men and women of the Pacific Division soldiered on. During its first five years of operation under Young's guidance, the Martin M-130 and Boeing 314 flying boats flown on the Pacific routes completed a grand total of 442 crossings, carrying an estimated 13,480,000 letters over 3,715,553 air miles. "As the Division has grown," remarked an editorial writer for the trade journal *U.S. Air Services*, "each step has been guided by Clarence Young."

After 11 years of service with Pan American, Young resigned his post in 1945. "I left . . . because of some differences of opinion during the war," he recalled many years later. "It was the expedient thing to do, both for the company and myself." He was not absent from Pan Am for long, however. After service as a member of the Civil Aeronautics Board from 1946 to 1947, Young returned to the airline as a vice-president in 1950, remaining until his final retirement at the age of seventy in 1959. Young died at Sedona, Arizona, on April 10, 1973. He was survived by his wife, former film star Lois Moran, and their only son, Timothy M. Young.

References:

Robert Daley, *An American Saga: Juan Trippe and His Pan Am Empire* (New York: Random House, 1980);

Nick A. Komons, *Bonfires to Beacons: Federal Civil Aviation Policy under the Air Commerce Act, 1926-1938* (Washington, D.C.: U.S. Government Printing Office, 1978);

Donald R. Whitnah, *Safer Skyways: Federal Control of Aviation, 1926-1966* (Ames: Iowa State University Press, 1967).

Archives:

A 1962 interview with Clarence M. Young by Charles E. Planck is in the files of the National Air and Space Museum, Washington, D.C.

Contributors

Linda Bilstein—*University of Houston—Clear Lake*
Roger E. Bilstein—*University of Houston—Clear Lake*
John C. Bishop—*Auburn University*
Robert Burkhardt—*Lewes, Delaware*
Paul A. Cleveland—*Birmingham-Southern College*
Donna M. Corbett—*Smithsonian Institution*
Lloyd H. Cornett, Jr.—*Montgomery, Alabama*
Tom D. Crouch—*National Air and Space Museum*
W. Alfred Dahler—*Kemper Military School*
R. E. G. Davies—*National Air and Space Museum*
Don Dawson—*Ketchikan, Alaska*
Michael H. Gorn—*Environmental Protection Agency*
Richard P. Hallion—*Office of Air Force History*
Robin Higham—*Kansas State University*
George E. Hopkins—*Western Illinois University*
Nick A. Komons—*Potomac, Maryland*
Roger D. Launius—*National Aeronautics and Space Administration*
William M. Leary—*University of Georgia*
David D. Lee—*Western Kentucky University*
W. David Lewis—*Auburn University*
Joseph E. Libby—*University of California, Riverside*
F. Robert van der Linden—*National Air and Space Museum*
Patricia A. Michaelis—*Kansas State Historical Society*
Claus-M. Naske—*University of Alaska Fairbanks*
Wesley Phillips Newton—*Auburn University*
Georgia Panter Nielsen—*San Jose, California*
Dominick A. Pisano—*National Air and Space Museum*
Edmund Preston—*Washington, D.C.*
I. E. Quastler—*San Diego State University*
Theodore W. Robinson—*Silver Springs, Maryland*
Joseph F. Ross—*Prachaup Khiri Khan, Thailand*
Larry D. Sall—*University of Texas at Dallas*
Myron J. Smith, Jr.—*Tusculum College*
Earl H. Tilford, Jr.—*Air Force Air Command and Staff College*
William F. Trimble—*Auburn University*
Donald R. Whitnah—*University of Northern Iowa*
Dina M. Young—*Washington University*
Edward M. Young—*Moody's Investors Service*

Index

The Airline
industry.

DATE			